Critical Values of t

ν	$t_{.100}$	$t_{.050}$	$t_{.025}$	$t_{.010}$	$t_{.005}$	$t_{.001}$	$t_{.0005}$
1	3.078	6.314	12.706	31.821	63.657	318.31	636.62
2	1.886	2.920	4.303	6.965	9.925	22.326	31.598
3	1.638	2.353	3.182	4.541	5.841	10.213	12.924
4	1.533	2.132	2.776	3.747	4.604	7.173	8.610
5	1.476	2.015	2.571	3.365	4.032	5.893	6.869
6	1.440	1.943	2.447	3.143	3.707	5.208	5.959
7	1.415	1.895	2.365	2.998	3.499	4.785	5.408
8	1.397	1.860	2.306	2.896	3.355	4.501	5.041
9	1.383	1.833	2.262	2.821	3.250	4.297	4.781
10	1.372	1.812	2.228	2.764	3.169	4.144	4.587
11	1.363	1.796	2.201	2.718	3.106	4.025	4.437
12	1.356	1.782	2.179	2.681	3.055	3.930	4.318
13	1.350	1.771	2.160	2.650	3.012	3.852	4.221
14	1.345	1.761	2.145	2.624	2.977	3.787	4.140
15	1.341	1.753	2.131	2.602	2.947	3.733	4.073
16	1.337	1.746	2.120	2.583	2.921	3.686	4.015
17	1.333	1.740	2.110	2.567	2.898	3.646	3.965
18	1.330	1.734	2.101	2.552	2.878	3.610	3.922
19	1.328	1.729	2.093	2.539	2.861	3.579	3.883
20	1.325	1.725	2.086	2.528	2.845	3.552	3.850
21	1.323	1.721	2.080	2.518	2.831	3.527	3.819
22	1.321	1.717	2.074	2.508	2.819	3.505	3.792
23	1.319	1.714	2.069	2.500	2.807	3.485	3.767
24	1.318	1.711	2.064	2.492	2.797	3.467	3.745
25	1.316	1.708	2.060	2.485	2.787	3.450	3.725
26	1.315	1.706	2.056	2.479	2.779	3.435	3.707
27	1.314	1.703	2.052	2.473	2.771	3.421	3.690
28	1.313	1.701	2.048	2.467	2.763	3.408	3.674
29	1.311	1.699	2.045	2.462	2.756	3.396	3.659
30	1.310	1.697	2.042	2.457	2.750	3.385	3.646
40	1.303	1.684	2.021	2.423	2.704	3.307	3.551
60	1.296	1.671	2.000	2.390	2.660	3.232	3.460
120	1.289	1.658	1.980	2.358	2.617	3.160	3.373
∞	1.282	1.645	1.960	2.326	2.576	3.090	3.291

Source: This table is reproduced with the kind permission of the Trustees of Biometrika from E. S. Pearson and H. O. Hartley (eds.), *The Biometrika Tables for Statisticians*, Vol. 1, 3d ed., Biometrika, 1966.

STATISTICS

FOR BUSINESS AND ECONOMICS

SEVENTH EDITION

JAMES T. MCCLAVE
INFO TECH, INC.
UNIVERSITY OF FLORIDA

P. GEORGE BENSON
GRADUATE SCHOOL OF MANAGEMENT
RUTGERS UNIVERSITY

TERRY SINCICH
UNIVERSITY OF SOUTH FLORIDA

Prentice Hall
Upper Saddle River, New Jersey 07458

Library of Congress Cataloging-in-Publication Data
McClave, James T.
  Statistics for business and economics / James T. McClave, P. George Benson,
Terry Sincich. — 7th ed.
      p.   cm.
  Includes bibliographical references and index.
  ISBN 0-13-840232-9
  ISBN 0-13-840265-5 (Annotated Instructor's Edition)
  1. Commercial statistics.   2. Economics—Statistical Methods.   3. Statistics.
I. Benson, P. George, 1946–   .   II. Sincich, Terry.   III. Title.
HF1017.M36   1998
519.5—dc21   97-13248
                                                                CIP

Executive Editor: Ann Heath
Editorial Director: Tim Bozik
Editor-in-Chief: Jerome Grant
Assistant Vice President of Production and Manufacturing: David W. Riccardi
Development Editor: Millicent Treloar
Cover and Text Design/Project Management/Composition: Elm Street Publishing Services, Inc.
Managing Editor: Linda Mihatov Behrens
Executive Managing Editor: Kathleen Schiaparelli
Marketing Manager: Melody Marcus
Creative Director: Paula Maylahn
Manufacturing Buyer: Alan Fischer
Manufacturing Manager: Trudy Pisciotti
Editorial Assistant: Mindy Ince
Assistant Editor: Audra Walsh
Cover and Interior Photos: David W. Hamilton/Image Bank

 © 1998 by Prentice-Hall, Inc.
Simon & Schuster / A Viacom Company
Upper Saddle River, NJ 07458

Printed in the United States of America
10   9   8   7   6   5   4   3   2   1

ISBN 0-13-840232-9

Prentice-Hall International (UK) Limited, *London*
Prentice-Hall of Australia Pty. Limited, *Sydney*
Prentice-Hall Canada, Inc., *Toronto*
Prentice-Hall Hispanoamericano, S.A., *Mexico*
Prentice-Hall of India Private Limited, *New Delhi*
Prentice-Hall of Japan, Inc., *Tokyo*
Simon & Schuster Asia Pte. Ltd., *Singapore*

CONTENTS

PREFACE

This seventh edition of *Statistics for Business and Economics* has been extensively revised to stress the development of statistical thinking, the assessment of credibility and value of the inferences made from data, both by those who consume and those who produce them. This is an introductory text emphasizing inference, with extensive coverage of data collection and analysis as needed to evaluate the reported results of statistical studies and make good business decisions. It assumes a mathematical background of basic algebra.

A briefer version of this book, *A First Course in Business Statistics*, is available for courses that include minimal coverage of regression analysis.

NEW IN THE SEVENTH EDITION

MAJOR CONTENT CHANGES

- Chapter 1 has been entirely rewritten to emphasize the science of statistics and its role in business decisions. Coverage of process and quality control is expanded (Section 1.4). Data collection from published sources, designed experiments, surveys, and observations are introduced in a new section (Section 1.6). Special attention is given to statistical thinking and issues of statistical ethics (Section 1.7).

- Chapter 2 now more thoroughly covers descriptive analytical tools that are useful in examining assumptions about data. A new introductory section (Section 2.1) presents both graphical and numerical methods for summarizing qualitative data. Time series plots and the graphing of bivariate data relationships are introduced in optional sections (Sections 2.3 and 2.10). There is a greater focus throughout on variability (Section 2.7). The discussion of statistical ethics is continued in Section 2.11.

- Chapter 7 has been extensively rewritten to emphasize confidence interval estimation procedures and their interpretation. The approach to small-sample confidence intervals is motivated by pharmaceutical testing requirements (Section 7.2). Two new optional sections cover the finite population correction (Section 7.5) and survey designs (Section 7.6).

- Chapter 8 features more balanced treatment of *p*-values and critical values in interpreting testing results (Example 8.6). New examples make greater use of computer solutions rather than formulas (Examples 8.4 and 8.6).

- Chapter 9 has been reorganized to present inference in the context of the experimental design used for data collection (Sections 9.1, 9.2, and 9.3).

- Chapter 10 includes an expanded coverage of correlation (Section 10.6), which continues the emphasis from Chapter 2 on bivariate linear relationships. Where appropriate, the emphasis has shifted from the discussion of formulas to the interpretation of computer output, including Excel spreadsheets.

- Chapter 11 has been revised to incorporate more extensive computer output, and inferences about the beta parameters include new material on confidence intervals (Section 11.4).

- Chapter 12 on model building includes a new introductory section that emphasizes the consequences of choosing the wrong model, i.e., errors in prediction. New material treats models with more than two quantitative variables.

- Chapter 15 contains a separate section on multiple comparisons with emphasis on computer output rather than formulas. Examples of both Bonferroni's and Tukey's methods are presented.

NEW PEDAGOGICAL FEATURES
- **Statistics in Action**—two or three features per chapter examine high-profile business, economic, government, and entertainment issues. Questions prompt the students to form their own conclusions and to think through the statistical issues involved.

- **Examples and Exercises**—More than 60% are new or revised, featuring real business data from 1990 to 1996.

- **Quick Review**—Each chapter ends with a list of key terms and formulas, with reference to the page number where they first appear.

- **Language Lab**—Following the Quick Review is a pronunciation guide to Greek letters and other special terms. Usage notes are also provided.

- **Showcases**—Six extensive business problem-solving cases, with real data and assignments, are now included in the text. Each case serves as a good capstone and review of the material that has preceded it.

- **Internet Labs**—This is a new feature to this edition. The Labs are designed to instruct the student in retrieving and analyzing raw data downloaded from the Internet.

TRADITIONAL STRENGTHS
We have maintained the features of *Statistics for Business and Economics* that we believe make it unique among business statistics texts. These features, which assist the student in achieving an overview of statistics and an understanding of its relevance in the business world and in everyday life, are as follows:

THE USE OF EXAMPLES AS A TEACHING DEVICE
Almost all new ideas are introduced and illustrated by real data-based applications and examples. We believe that students better understand definitions, generalizations, and abstractions *after* seeing an application.

MANY EXERCISES—LABELED BY TYPE
The text includes more than 1,400 exercises illustrated by applications in almost all areas of research. Because many students have trouble learning the mechanics of statistical techniques when problems are couched in terms of realistic applications, all exercise sections are divided into two parts:

Learning the Mechanics. Designed as straightforward applications of new concepts, these exercises allow students to test their ability to comprehend a concept or a definition.

Applying the Concepts. Based on applications taken from a wide variety of journals, newspapers, and other sources, these exercises develop the student's skills at comprehending real-world problems that describe situations to which the techniques may be applied.

A CHOICE IN LEVEL OF COVERAGE OF PROBABILITY
One of the most troublesome aspects of an introductory statistics course is the study of probability. Probability poses a challenge for instructors because they

must decide on the level of presentation, and students find it a difficult subject to comprehend. We believe that one cause for these problems is the mixture of probability and counting rules that occurs in most introductory texts. We have included the counting rules in a separate and optional section at the end of the chapter on probability. In addition, all exercises that require the use of counting rules are marked with an asterisk (*). Thus, the instructor can control the level of coverage of probability.

Extensive Coverage of Multiple Regression Analysis and Model Building

This topic represents one of the most useful statistical tools for the solution of applied problems. Although an entire text could be devoted to regression modeling, we believe we have presented coverage that is understandable, usable, and much more comprehensive than the presentations in other introductory statistics texts. We devote three chapters to discussing the major types of inferences that can be derived from a regression analysis, showing how these results appear in computer printouts and, most important, selecting multiple regression models to be used in an analysis. Thus, the instructor has the choice of a one-chapter coverage of simple regression, a two-chapter treatment of simple and multiple regression, or a complete three-chapter coverage of simple regression, multiple regression, and model building. This extensive coverage of such useful statistical tools will provide added evidence to the student of the relevance of statistics to the solution of applied problems.

Footnotes

Although the text is designed for students with a non-calculus background, footnotes explain the role of calculus in various derivations. Footnotes are also used to inform the student about some of the theory underlying certain results. The footnotes allow additional flexibility in the mathematical and theoretical level at which the material is presented.

Supplements for the Instructor

The supplements for the seventh edition have been completely revised to reflect the extensive revisions of the text. Each element in the package has been accuracy checked to ensure adherence to the approaches presented in the main text, clarity, and freedom from computational, typographical, and statistical errors.

NEW! Annotated Instructor's Edition (AIE) (ISBN 0-13-840265-5)

Marginal notes placed next to discussions of essential teaching concepts include:

- Teaching Tips—suggest alternative presentations or point out common student errors

- Exercises—reference specific section and chapter exercises that reinforce the concept

- 💾—identify data sets and file name of material found on the data disks.

- Short Answers—section and chapter exercise answers are provided next to the selected exercises.

Instructor's Notes by Mark Dummeldinger (ISBN 0-13-891243-2)

This new printed resource contains suggestions for using the questions at the end of the Statistics in Action boxes as the basis for class discussion on statistical ethics and other current issues, solutions to the Showcases, a complete short answer book with letter of permission to duplicate for student use, and many of the exercises and solutions that were removed from the sixth edition of this text.

INSTRUCTOR'S SOLUTIONS MANUAL BY NANCY S. BOUDREAU (ISBN 0-13-840307-4)
Solutions to all of the even-numbered exercises are given in this manual. Careful attention has been paid to ensure that all methods of solution and notation are consistent with those used in the core text. Solutions to the odd-numbered exercises are found in the *Student's Solution's Manual*.

TEST BANK BY MARK DUMMELDINGER (ISBN 0-13-840356-2)
Entirely rewritten, the *Test Bank* now includes more than 1,000 problems that correlate to problems presented in the text.

WINDOWS PH CUSTOM TEST (ISBN 0-13-621152-6)
MAC PH CUSTOM TEST (ISBN 0-13-621103-8)
Incorporates three levels of test creation: (1) selection of questions from a test bank; (2) addition of new questions with the ability to import test and graphics files from WordPerfect, Microsoft Word, and Wordstar; and (3) inclusion of algorithmic capabilities. PH Custom Test has a full-featured graphics editor supporting the complex formulas and graphics required by the statistics discipline.

POWERPOINT PRESENTATION DISK (ISBN 0-13-61116-2)
This versatile Windows-based tool may be used by professors in a number of different ways:

• Slide show in an electronic classroom

• Printed and used as transparency masters

• Printed copies may be distributed to students as a convenient note-taking device.

Included on the software disk are learning objectives, thinking challenges, concept presentation slides, and examples with worked-out solutions. The PowerPoint Presentation disk may be downloaded from the FTP site found at the McClave Web site.

DATA DISK (ISBN 0-13-840380-5)
The data sets described in Appendix B and the data for all exercises containing 20 or more observations are available on a 3½" diskette in ASCII format. When a given data set is referenced, a disk symbol and the file name will appear in the text near the exercise.

NEW YORK TIMES SUPPLEMENT (ISBN 0-13-261367-8)
Copies of this supplement may be requested from Prentice Hall by instructors for distribution in their classes. This supplement contains high interest articles published recently in *The New York Times* that relate to topics covered in the text.

MCCLAVE INTERNET SITE (http://www.prenhall.com/mcclave)
This site is a work in progress that will be updated throughout the year as new information, tools, and applications become available. The site will contain information about the book and its supplements as well as FTP sites for downloading the Powerpoint Presentation Disk and the Data Files. Teaching tips and student help will be provided as well as links to useful sources of data and information such as the Chance Database, the STEPS project (interactive tutorials developed by the University of Glasgow), and a site designed to help faculty establish and manage course home pages.

SUPPLEMENTS AVAILABLE FOR PURCHASE BY STUDENTS

STUDENT'S SOLUTIONS MANUAL BY NANCY S. BOUDREAU (ISBN 0-13-625260-5)

Fully worked-out solutions to all of the odd-numbered exercises are provided in this manual. Careful attention has been paid to ensure that all methods of solution and notation are consistent with those used in the core text.

STUDENT VERSIONS OF SPSS AND SYSTAT

Student versions of SPSS, the award-winning and market-leading commercial data analysis package, and SYSTAT are available for student purchase. Details on all current products are available from Prentice Hall or via the SPSS website at http://www.spss.com.

LEARNING BUSINESS STATISTICS WITH MICROSOFT ®EXCEL BY JOHN L. NEUFELD (ISBN 0-13-234097-6)

The use of Excel as a data analysis and computational package for statistics is explained in clear, easy-to-follow steps in this self-contained paperback text.

A MINITAB GUIDE TO STATISTICS BY RUTH MEYER AND DAVID KRUEGER (ISBN 0-13-784232-5)

This manual assumes no prior knowledge of MINITAB. Organized to correspond to the table of contents of most statistics texts, this manual provides step-by-step instruction to using MINITAB for statistical analysis.

CONSTATS BY TUFTS UNIVERSITY (ISBN 0-13-502600-8)

ConStatS is a set of Microsoft Windows based programs designed to help college students understand concepts taught in a first-semester course on probability and statistics. ConStatS helps improve students' conceptual understanding of statistics by engaging them in an active, experimental style of learning. A companion ConStatS workbook (ISBN 0-13-522848-4) that guides students through the labs and ensures they gain the maximum benefit is also available.

ACKNOWLEDGMENTS

This book reflects the efforts of a great many people over a number of years. First we would like to thank the following professors, whose reviews and feedback on organization and coverage, contributed to the seventh and previous editions of the book.

REVIEWERS INVOLVED WITH THE SEVENTH EDITION

Atul Agarwal, GMI Engineering and Management Institute; Mohamed Albohali, Indiana University of Pennsylvania; Lewis Coopersmith, Rider University; Bernard Dickman, Hofstra University; Jose Luis Guerrero-Cusumano, Georgetown University; Paul Guy, California State University-Chico; Judd Hammack, California State University-Los Angeles; P. Kasliwal, California State University-Los Angeles; Tim Krehbiel, Miami University of Ohio; David Krueger, St. Cloud State University; Mabel T. Kung, California State University-Fullerton; Jim Lackritz, San Diego State University; Leigh Lawton, University of St. Thomas; Peter Lenk, University of Michigan; Benjamin Lev, University of Michigan-Dearborn; Benny Lo; Brenda Masters, Oklahoma State University; William Q. Meeker, Iowa State University; Ruth Meyer, St. Cloud State University; Edward Minieka, University of Illinois at Chicago; Rebecca Moore, Oklahoma State University; June Morita, University of Washington; Behnam Nakhai, Millersville University; Rose Prave, University of Scranton; Beth Rose,

University of Southern California; Lawrence A. Sherr, University of Kansas; Toni M. Somers, Wayne State University; Kim Tamura, University of Washington; Bob VanCleave, University of Minnesota; Michael P. Wegmann, Keller Graduate School of Management; Gary Yoshimoto, St. Cloud State University; Doug Zahn, Florida State University

REVIEWERS OF PREVIOUS EDITIONS

Gordon J. Alexander, University of Minnesota; Richard W. Andrews, University of Michigan; Larry M. Austin, Texas Tech University; Golam Azam, North Carolina Agricultural & Technical University; Donald W. Bartlett, University of Minnesota; Clarence Bayne, Concordia University; Carl Bedell, Philadelphia College of Textiles and Science; David M. Bergman, University of Minnesota; William H. Beyer, University of Akron; Atul Bhatia, University of Minnesota; Jim Branscome, University of Texas at Arlington; Francis J. Brewerton, Middle Tennessee State University; Daniel G. Brick, University of St. Thomas; Robert W. Brobst, University of Texas of Arlington; Michael Broida, Miami University of Ohio; Glenn J. Browne, University of Maryland, Baltimore; Edward Carlstein, University of North Carolina at Chapel Hill; John M. Charnes, University of Miami; Chih-Hsu Cheng, Ohio State University; Larry Claypool, Oklahoma State University; Edward R. Clayton, Virginia Polytechnic Institute and State University; Ronald L. Coccari, Cleveland State University; Ken Constantine, University of New Hampshire; Robert Curley, University of Central Oklahoma; Joyce Curley-Daly, California Polytechnic State University; Jim Daly, California Polytechnic State University; Jim Davis, Golden Gate University; Dileep Dhavale, University of Northern Iowa; Mark Eakin, University of Texas at Arlington; Rick L. Edgeman, Colorado State University; Carol Eger, Stanford University; Robert Elrod, Georgia State University; Douglas A. Elvers, University of North Carolina at Chapel Hill; Iris Fetta, Clemson University; Susan Flach, General Mills, Inc.; Alan E. Gelfand, University of Connecticut; Joseph Glaz, University of Connecticut; Edit Gombay, University of Alberta; Paul W. Guy, California State University, Chico; Michael E. Hanna, University of Texas at Arlington; Don Holbert, East Carolina University; James Holstein, University of Missouri, Columbia; Warren M. Holt, Southeastern Massachusetts University; Steve Hora, University of Hawaii, Hilo; Petros Ioannatos, GMI Engineering & Management Institute; Marius Janson, University of Missouri, St. Louis; Ross H. Johnson, Madison College; Timothy J. Killeen, University of Connecticut; David D. Krueger, St. Cloud State University; Richard W. Kulp, Wright-Patterson AFB, Air Force Institute of Technology; Martin Labbe, State University of New York College at New Paltz; James Lackritz, California State University at San Diego; Philip Levine, William Patterson College; Eddie M. Lewis, University of Southern Mississippi; Fred Leysieffer, Florida State University; Pi-Erh Lin, Florida State University; Robert Ling, Clemson University; Karen Lundquist, University of Minnesota; G. E. Martin, Clarkson University; Brenda Masters, Oklahoma State University; Ruth K. Meyer, St. Cloud State University; Paul I. Nelson, Kansas State University; Paula M. Oas, General Office Products; Dilek Onkal, Bilkent University, Turkey; Vijay Pisharody, University of Minnesota; P.V. Rao, University of Florida; Don Robinson, Illinois State University; Jan Saraph, St. Cloud State University; Craig W. Slinkman, University of Texas at Arlington; Robert K. Smidt, California Polytechnic State University; Donald N. Steinnes, University of Minnesota at Duluth; Virgil F. Stone, Texas A & M University; Katheryn Szabet, La Salle University; Alireza Tahai, Mississippi State University; Chipei Tseng, Northern Illinois University; Pankaj Vaish, Arthur Andersen & Company; Robert

W. Van Cleave, University of Minnesota; Charles F. Warnock, Colorado State University; William J. Weida, United States Air Force Academy; T.J. Wharton, Oakland University; Kathleen M. Whitcomb, University of South Carolina; Edna White, Florida Atlantic University; Steve Wickstrom, University of Minnesota; James Willis, Louisiana State University; Douglas A. Wolfe, Ohio State University; Gary Yoshimoto, St. Cloud State University; Fike Zahroom, Moorhead State University; Christopher J. Zappe, Bucknell University

Special thanks are due to our ancillary authors, Nancy Shafer Boudreau and Mark Dummeldinger, and to typist Brenda Dobson, who have worked with us for many years; and to John McGill, who prepared the Powerpoint Presentation disk. Carl Richard Gumina has done an excellent job of accuracy checking the seventh edition and has helped us to ensure a highly accurate, clean text. The Prentice Hall staff of Ann Heath, Millicent Treloar, Mindy Ince, Melody Marcus, Jennifer Pan, Linda Behrens, and Alan Fischer, and Elm Street Publishing Services' Martha Beyerlein, Barb Lange, Sue Langguth, and Cathy Ferguson helped greatly with all phases of the text development, production, and marketing effort. We also thank Rutgers Ph.D. students Xuan Li and Zina Taran for helping us to identify new exercise material, and we particularly thank Professor Lei Lei of Rutgers for her assistance in exercise development. Our thanks to Jane Benson for managing the exercise development process. Finally, we owe special thanks to Faith Sincich, whose efforts in preparing the manuscript for production and proofreading all stages of the book deserve special recognition.

For additional information about texts and other materials available from Prentice Hall, visit us on-line at http://www.prenhall.com.

How to Use This Book

To the Student

The following four pages will demonstrate how to use this text in the most effective way—to make studying easier and to understand the connection between statistics and your world.

Chapter Openers Provide a Road Map

- **Where We've Been** quickly reviews how information learned previously applies to the chapter at hand.

- **Where We're Going** highlights how the chapter topics fit into your growing understanding of statistical inference.

CHAPTER 7

INFERENCES BASED ON A SINGLE SAMPLE
Estimation with Confidence Intervals

Where We've Been

We've learned that populations are characterized by numerical descriptive measures (called *parameters*) and that decisions about their values are based on sample statistics computed from sample data. Since statistics vary in a random manner from sample to sample, inferences based on them will be subject to uncertainty. This property is reflected in the sampling (probability) distribution of a statistic.

Where We're Going

In this chapter, we'll put all the preceding material into practice; that is, we'll estimate population means and proportions based on a single sample selected from the population of interest. Most importantly, we use the sampling distribution of a sample statistic to assess the reliability of an estimate.

269

SECTION 1.5   Types of Data   13

STATISTICS IN ACTION

1.1 QUALITY IMPROVEMENT: U.S. FIRMS RESPOND TO THE CHALLENGE FROM JAPAN

Over the last two decades, U.S. firms have been seriously challenged by products of superior quality from overseas. For example, from 1984 to 1991, imported cars and light trucks steadily increased their share of the U.S. market from 22% to 30%. As a second example, consider the television and VCR markets. Both products were invented in the United States, but as of 1995 not a single U.S. firm manufactures either. Both are produced exclusively by Pacific Rim countries, primarily Japan.

To meet this competitive challenge, more and more U.S. firms—both manufacturing and service firms—have begun quality-improvement initiatives of their own. Many of these firms now stress the management of quality in all phases and aspects of their business, from the design of their products to production, distribution, sales, and service.

Broadly speaking, quality-improvement programs are concerned with (1) finding out what the customer wants, (2) translating those wants into a product design, and (3) producing and delivering a product or service that meets or exceeds the specifications of the product design. In all these areas, but particularly in the third, *improvement of quality requires improvement of processes*—including production processes, distribution processes, and service processes.

But what does it mean to say that a process has been improved? Generally speaking, it means that the customer of the process (i.e., the user of the output) indicates a greater satisfaction with the output. Frequently, such increases in satisfaction require a reduction in the variation of one or more process variables. That is, a reduction in the variation of the output stream of the process is needed.

produced by a given machine are the same; no two transactions performed by a given bank teller are the same. He also recognized that variation could be understood, monitored, and controlled using statistical methods. He developed a simple graphical technique—called a **control chart**—for determining whether product variation is within acceptable limits. This method provides guidance for when to adjust or change a production process and when to leave it alone. It can be used at the end of the production process or, most significantly, at different points within the process. We discuss control charts and other tools for improving processes in Chapter 13.

In the last decade, largely as a result of the Japanese challenge to the supremacy of U.S. products, control charts and other statistical tools have gained widespread use in the United States. As evidence for the claim that U.S. firms are responding well to Japan's competitive challenge, consider this: The most prestigious quality-improvement prize in the world that a firm can win is the Deming Prize. It has been awarded by the Japanese since the 1950s. In 1989 it was won for the first time by an American company—Florida Power and Light Company. Other evidence of the resurgence of U.S. competitiveness includes a turnaround in market share for U.S. automakers: imports' share of the U.S. market decreased from a high of 30% in 1991 to 25% in 1995.

Focus

a. Identify two processes that are of interest to you.

b. For each process, part a, identify a variable that could be used to monitor the quality of the output

"Statistics in Action" Boxes Explore High-Interest Issues

- Highlight controversial, contemporary issues that involve statistics.

- Work through the **"Focus"** questions to help you evaluate the findings.

Shaded Boxes Highlight Important Information

- Definitions, Strategies, Key Formulas, and other important information are highlighted.

- Prepare for quizzes and tests by reviewing the highlighted information.

Interesting Examples with Solutions

- Examples, with complete solutions and explanations, illustrate every concept and are numbered for easy reference.

- Work through the solution carefully to prepare for the section exercise set.

- The end of the solution is clearly marked with a ⌐ symbol.

282 CHAPTER 7 Inferences Based on a Single Sample: Estimation with Confidence Intervals

Small-Sample Confidence Interval * for μ

$$\bar{x} \pm t_{\alpha/2}\left(\frac{s}{\sqrt{n}}\right)$$

where $t_{\alpha/2}$ is based on $(n-1)$ degrees of freedom

Assumptions: A random sample is selected from a population with a relative frequency distribution that is approximately normal.

EXAMPLE 7.2 Some quality control experiments require *destructive sampling* (i.e., the test to determine whether the item is defective destroys the item) in order to measure some particular characteristic of the product. The cost of destructive sampling often dictates small samples. For example, suppose a manufacturer of printers for personal computers wishes to estimate the mean number of characters printed before the printhead fails. Suppose the printer manufacturer tests $n = 15$ randomly selected printheads and records the number of characters printed until failure for each. These 15 measurements (in millions of characters) are listed in Table 7.4, followed by an EXCEL summary statistics printout in Figure 7.10.

a. Form a 99% confidence interval for the mean number of characters printed before the printhead fails. Interpret the result.

b. What assumption is required for the interval, part **a**, to be valid? Is it reasonably satisfied?

TABLE 7.4 **Number of Characters (in Millions) for $n = 15$ Printhead Tests**

1.13	1.55	1.43	.92	1.25
1.36	1.32	.85	1.07	1.48
1.20	1.33	1.18	1.22	1.29

FIGURE 7.10 EXCEL summary statistics printout for data in Table 7.4

Number	
Mean	1.238667
Standard Error	0.049875
Median	1.25
Mode	#N/A
Standard Deviation	0.193164
Sample Variance	0.037312
Kurtosis	0.063636
Skewness	-0.49126
Range	0.7
Minimum	0.85
Maximum	1.55
Sum	18.58
Count	15
Confidence Level(95.000%)	0.097753

*The procedure given in the box assumes that the population standard deviation σ is unknown, which is almost always the case. If σ is known, we can form the small-sample confidence interval just as we would a large-sample confidence interval using a standard normal z value instead of t. However, we must still assume that the underlying population is approximately normal.

Computer Output Integrated Throughout

- Statistical software packages such as SPSS, MINITAB, SAS, and the spreadsheet package, EXCEL, crunch data quickly so you can spend time analyzing the results. Learning how to interpret statistical output will prove helpful in future classes or on the job.

- When computer output appears in examples, the solution explains how to read and interpret the output.

Lots of Exercises for Practice

- Every section in the book is followed by an Exercise Set divided into two parts.

- **Learning the Mechanics** has straightforward applications of new concepts. Test your mastery of definitions, concepts, and basic computation. Make sure you can answer all of these questions before moving on.

- **Applying the Concepts** tests your understanding of concepts and requires you to apply statistical techniques in solving real-world problems.

---

88 CHAPTER 2 Methods for Describing Sets of Data

 2.87–2.96

Note: Exercises marked with 🖫 *contain data available for computer analysis on a 3.5" disk (file name in parentheses).*

Learning the Mechanics

2.87 Define the 25th, 50th, and 75th percentiles of a data set. Explain how they provide a description of the data.

2.88 Suppose a data set consisting of exam scores has a lower quartile $Q_L = 60$, a median $m = 75$, and an upper quartile $Q_U = 85$. The scores on the exam range from 18 to 100. Without having the actual scores available to you, construct as much of the box plot as possible.

2.89 MINITAB was used to generate the following horizontal box plot. (*Note:* The hinges are represented by the symbol "I".)

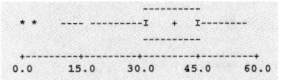

a. What is the median of the data set (approximately)?
b. What are the upper and lower quartiles of the data set (approximately)?
c. What is the interquartile range of the data set (approximately)?
d. Is the data set skewed to the left, skewed to the right, or symmetric?
e. What percentage of the measurements in the data set lie to the right of the median? To the left of the upper quartile?

2.90 MINITAB was used to generate the horizontal box plots below. Compare and contrast the frequency distributions of the two data sets. Your answer should include comparisons of the following characteristics: central tendency, variation, skewness, and outliers.

2.91 (X02.091) Consider the following two sample data 🖫 sets:

Sample A			Sample B		
121	171	158	171	152	170
173	184	163	168	169	171
157	85	145	190	183	185
165	172	196	140	173	206
170	159	172	172	174	169
161	187	100	199	151	180
142	166	171	167	170	188

a. Use a statistical software package to construct a box plot for each data set.
b. Using information reflected in your box plots, describe the similarities and differences in the two data sets.

Applying the Concepts

2.92 (X02.092) The table contains the top salary offer 🖫 (in thousands of dollars) received by each member of a sample of 50 MBA students who graduated from the Graduate School of Management at Rutgers, the state university of New Jersey, in 1996.

61.1	48.5	47.0	49.1	43.5
50.8	62.3	50.0	65.4	58.0
53.2	39.9	49.1	75.0	51.2
41.7	40.0	53.0	39.6	49.6
55.2	54.9	62.5	35.0	50.3
41.5	56.0	55.5	70.0	59.2
39.2	47.0	58.2	59.0	60.8
72.3	55.0	41.4	51.5	63.0
48.4	61.7	45.3	63.2	41.5
47.0	43.2	44.6	47.7	58.6

Source: Career Services Office, Graduate School of Management, Rutgers University.

a. The mean and standard deviation are 52.33 and 9.22, respectively. Find and interpret the z-score associated with the highest salary offer, the lowest salary offer, and the mean salary offer. Would you consider the highest offer to be unusually high? Why or why not?
b. Use a statistical software package to construct a box plot for this data set. Which salary offers (if any) are potentially faulty observations? Explain.

2.93 Refer to the *Financial Management* (Spring 1995) study of 49 firms filing for prepackaged bankruptcies, Exercise 2.22. Recall that three types of "prepack" firms exist: (1) those who hold no pre-filing vote; (2) those who vote their preference for a joint solution; and (3) those who vote their pref-

---

Real Data

- Most of the exercises contain data or information taken from newspaper articles, magazines, and journals published since 1990. Statistics are all around you.

Computer Output

- Computer output screens appear in the exercise sets to give you practice in interpretation.

End of Chapter Review

- Each chapter ends with information designed to help you check your understanding of the material, study for tests, and expand your knowledge of statistics.

- **Quick Review** provides a list of key terms and formulas with page number references.

- **Language Lab** helps you learn the language of statistics through pronunciation guides, descriptions of symbols, names, etc.

- **Supplementary Exercises** review all of the important topics covered in the chapter.

Exercises marked with 🖫 require a computer for solution.

Data sets for use with the 🖫 problems are available on disk.

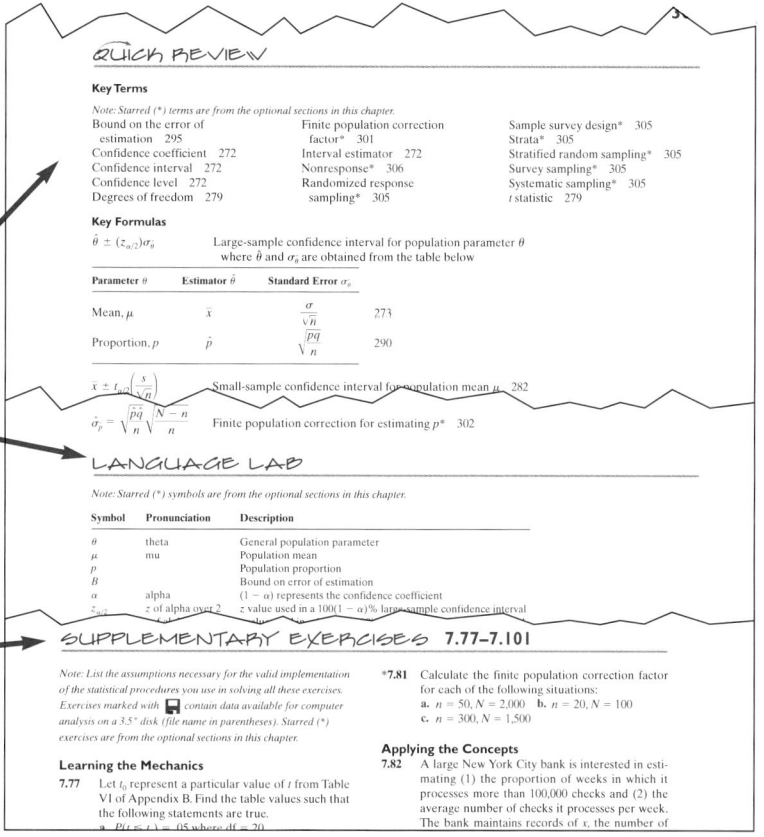

QUICK REVIEW

Key Terms

Note: Starred (*) terms are from the optional sections in this chapter.

Bound on the error of estimation 295
Confidence coefficient 272
Confidence interval 272
Confidence level 272
Degrees of freedom 279

Finite population correction factor* 301
Interval estimator 272
Nonresponse* 306
Randomized response sampling* 305

Sample survey design* 305
Strata* 305
Stratified random sampling* 305
Survey sampling* 305
Systematic sampling* 305
t statistic 279

Key Formulas

$\hat{\theta} \pm (z_{\alpha/2})\sigma_{\hat{\theta}}$ Large-sample confidence interval for population parameter θ where $\hat{\theta}$ and $\sigma_{\hat{\theta}}$ are obtained from the table below

Parameter θ	Estimator $\hat{\theta}$	Standard Error $\sigma_{\hat{\theta}}$	
Mean, μ	$\bar{x}$	$\dfrac{\sigma}{\sqrt{n}}$	273
Proportion, p	$\hat{p}$	$\sqrt{\dfrac{pq}{n}}$	290

$\bar{x} \pm t_{\alpha/2}\left(\dfrac{s}{\sqrt{n}}\right)$ Small-sample confidence interval for population mean μ 282

$\hat{\sigma}_{\hat{p}} = \sqrt{\dfrac{\hat{p}\hat{q}}{n}}\sqrt{\dfrac{N-n}{n}}$ Finite population correction for estimating p*   302

LANGUAGE LAB

Note: Starred (*) symbols are from the optional sections in this chapter.

Symbol	Pronunciation	Description
θ	theta	General population parameter
μ	mu	Population mean
p		Population proportion
B		Bound on error of estimation
α	alpha	$(1-\alpha)$ represents the confidence coefficient
$z_{\alpha/2}$	z of alpha over 2	z value used in a $100(1-\alpha)\%$ large-sample confidence interval

SUPPLEMENTARY EXERCISES   **7.77–7.101**

Note: List the assumptions necessary for the valid implementation of the statistical procedures you use in solving all these exercises. Exercises marked with 🖫 contain data available for computer analysis on a 3.5" disk (file name in parentheses). Starred (*) exercises are from the optional sections in this chapter.

Learning the Mechanics

7.77 Let t_0 represent a particular value of t from Table VI of Appendix B. Find the table values such that the following statements are true.
   a. $P(t \le t_0) = .05$ where df = 20.

*7.81 Calculate the finite population correction factor for each of the following situations:
   a. $n = 50, N = 2{,}000$ b. $n = 20, N = 100$
   c. $n = 300, N = 1{,}500$

Applying the Concepts

7.82 A large New York City bank is interested in estimating (1) the proportion of weeks in which it processes more than 100,000 checks and (2) the average number of checks it processes per week. The bank maintains records of x, the number of

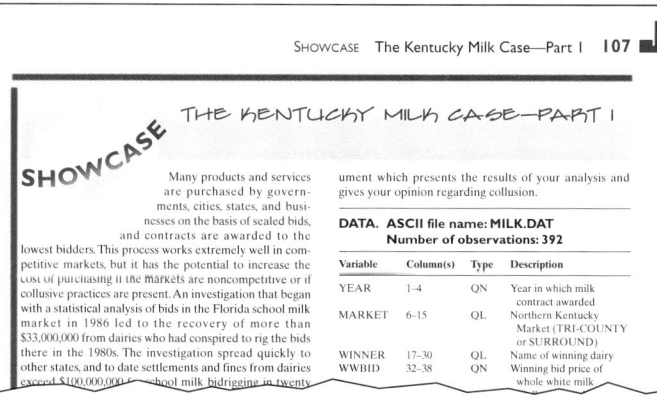

SHOWCASE   THE KENTUCKY MILK CASE—PART I

Many products and services are purchased by governments, cities, states, and businesses on the basis of sealed bids, and contracts are awarded to the lowest bidders. This process works extremely well in competitive markets, but it has the potential to increase the cost of purchasing if the markets are noncompetitive or if collusive practices are present. An investigation that began with a statistical analysis of bids in the Florida school milk market in 1986 led to the recovery of more than $33,000,000 from dairies who had conspired to rig the bids there in the 1980s. The investigation spread quickly to other states, and to date settlements and fines from dairies exceed $100,000,000 for school milk bidrigging in twenty

ument which presents the results of your analysis and gives your opinion regarding collusion.

DATA. ASCII file name: **MILK.DAT**
Number of observations: 392

Variable	Column(s)	Type	Description
YEAR	1–4	QN	Year in which milk contract awarded
MARKET	6–15	QL	Northern Kentucky Market (TRI-COUNTY or SURROUND)
WINNER	17–30	QL	Name of winning dairy
WWBID	32–38	QN	Winning bid price of whole white milk

- **Showcase** Six real-business cases put you in the position of the business decision maker or consultant. Use the data provided and the information you have learned in preceding chapters to reach a decision and support your arguments about the questions being asked.

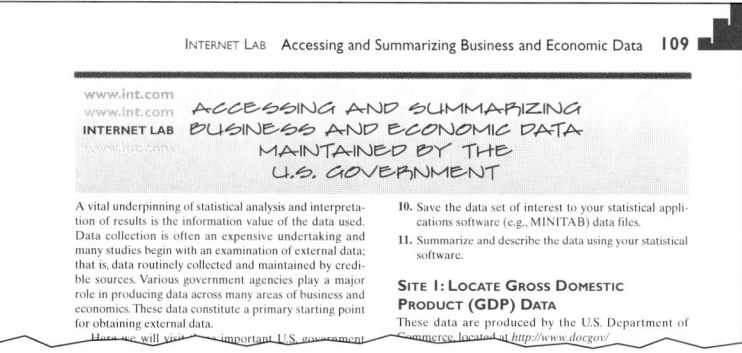

www.int.com
www.int.com
INTERNET LAB   ACCESSING AND SUMMARIZING BUSINESS AND ECONOMIC DATA MAINTAINED BY THE U.S. GOVERNMENT

A vital underpinning of statistical analysis and interpretation of results is the information value of the data used. Data collection is often an expensive undertaking and many studies begin with an examination of external data; that is, data routinely collected and maintained by credible sources. Various government agencies play a major role in producing data across many areas of business and economics. These data constitute a primary starting point for obtaining external data.
   Here we will visit two important U.S. government

10. Save the data set of interest to your statistical applications software (e.g., MINITAB) data files.
11. Summarize and describe the data using your statistical software.

SITE 1: LOCATE GROSS DOMESTIC PRODUCT (GDP) DATA
These data are produced by the U.S. Department of Commerce, located at *http://www.docgov/*

- **Internet Labs** follow the Showcase and are designed to help you retrieve and download raw data from the Internet for analysis. Knowing how to mine the Internet for reliable data, analyze it appropriately, and draw useful conclusions are important job skills for the 21st century.

CHAPTER 1

STATISTICS, DATA, AND STATISTICAL THINKING

Where We're Going

Statistics? Is it a field of study, a group of numbers that summarizes the state of our national economy, the performance of a stock, or the business conditions in a particular locale? Or, as one popular book (Tanur *et al.*, 1989) suggests, is it "a guide to the unknown"? We'll see in Chapter 1 that each of these descriptions is applicable in understanding what statistics is. We'll see that there are two areas of statistics: *descriptive statistics*, which focuses on developing graphical and numerical summaries that describe some business phenomenon, and *inferential statistics*, which uses these numerical summaries to assist in making business decisions. The primary theme of this text is inferential statistics. Thus, we'll concentrate on showing how you can use statistics to interpret data and use them to make decisions. Many jobs in industry, government, medicine, and other fields require you to make data-driven decisions, so understanding these methods offers you important practical benefits.

1.1   THE SCIENCE OF STATISTICS

What does statistics mean to you? Does it bring to mind batting averages, Gallup polls, unemployment figures, or numerical distortions of facts (lying with statistics!)? Or is it simply a college requirement you have to complete? We hope to persuade you that statistics is a meaningful, useful science whose broad scope of applications to business, government, and the physical and social sciences is almost limitless. We also want to show that statistics can lie only when they are misapplied. Finally, we wish to demonstrate the key role statistics play in critical thinking—whether in the classroom, on the job, or in everyday life. Our objective is to leave you with the impression that the time you spend studying this subject will repay you in many ways.

The *Random House College Dictionary* defines *statistics* as "the science that deals with the collection, classification, analysis, and interpretation of information or data." Thus, a statistician isn't just someone who calculates batting averages at baseball games or tabulates the results of a Gallup poll. Professional statisticians are trained in *statistical science*. That is, they are trained in collecting numerical information in the form of **data**, evaluating it, and drawing conclusions from it. Furthermore, statisticians determine what information is relevant in a given problem and whether the conclusions drawn from a study are to be trusted.

> **DEFINITION I.I**
> **Statistics** is the science of data. It involves collecting, classifying, summarizing, organizing, analyzing, and interpreting numerical information.

In the next section, you'll see several real-life examples of statistical applications in business and government that involve making decisions and drawing conclusions.

1.2   TYPES OF STATISTICAL APPLICATIONS IN BUSINESS

Statistics means "numerical descriptions" to most people. Monthly unemployment figures, the failure rate of a new business, and the proportion of female executives in a particular industry all represent statistical descriptions of large sets of data collected on some phenomenon. Often the data are selected from some larger set of data whose characteristics we wish to estimate. We call this selection process *sampling*. For example, you might collect the ages of a sample of customers at a video store to estimate the average age of *all* customers of the store. Then you could use your estimate to target the store's advertisements to the appropriate age group. Notice that statistics involves two different processes: (1) describing sets of data and (2) drawing conclusions (making estimates, decisions, predictions, etc.) about the sets of data based on sampling. So, the applications of statistics can be divided into two broad areas: *descriptive statistics* and *inferential statistics*.

> **DEFINITION I.2**
> **Descriptive statistics** utilizes numerical and graphical methods to look for patterns in a data set, to summarize the information revealed in a data set, and to present the information in a convenient form.

DEFINITION 1.3

Inferential statistics utilizes sample data to make estimates, decisions, predictions, or other generalizations about a larger set of data.

Although we'll discuss both descriptive and inferential statistics in the following chapters, the primary theme of the text is **inference**.

Let's begin by examining some business studies that illustrate applications of statistics.

Study 1   "Discrimination in the Workplace" (*USA Today*, Aug. 15, 1995).

According to *USA Today*, a record number of job discrimination cases—158,612—were filed with federal or state civil rights agencies in 1994. *USA Today* obtained information on each case from the Equal Employment Opportunity Center (EEOC). Then researchers at this national newspaper determined the basis of each of the 158,612 claims. They reported the results in the graph shown in Figure 1.1. The graph provides an effective summary of the 158,612 claims, clearly depicting that race and sex discrimination are the two most common bases for job discrimination complaints. Thus, Figure 1.1 is an example of *descriptive statistics.*

Study 2   "The Executive Compensation Scoreboard" (*Business Week*, Apr. 22, 1996).

How much are the top corporate executives in the United States being paid and are they worth it? To answer these questions, *Business Week* magazine compiles its "Executive Compensation Scoreboard" each year based on a survey of executives at the highest-ranking companies listed in the *Business Week 1000*. The average* total pay of chief executive officers (CEOs) at 362 companies sampled in the 1995 scoreboard was $3.75 million—an increase of 30% over the previous year.

To determine which executives are worth their pay, *Business Week* also records the ratio of total shareholder return (measured by the dollar value of a $100 investment in the company made 3 years earlier) to the total pay of the CEO (in thousand dollars) over the same 3-year period. For example, a $100 investment in Walt Disney Corporation in 1993 was worth $139 at the end of 1995. When this shareholder return ($139) is divided by CEO Michael Eisner's total 1993–1995 pay of $228.4 million, the result is a return-to-pay ratio of only .0006, one of the lowest among all other chief executives in the survey.

An analysis of the sample data set reveals that CEOs in the industrial high-technology industry have the highest average return-to-pay ratio (.048) while the

FIGURE 1.1

Basis of workplace discrimination claims filed in 1994

Source: *USA Today,* August 15, 1995, p. 10A. Copyright 1995 USA TODAY. Reprinted with permission.

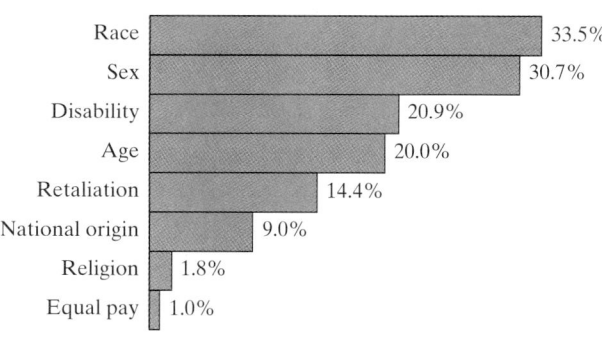

Race	33.5%
Sex	30.7%
Disability	20.9%
Age	20.0%
Retaliation	14.4%
National origin	9.0%
Religion	1.8%
Equal pay	1.0%

*Although we will not formally define the term *average* until Chapter 2, *typical* or *middle* can be substituted here without confusion.

TABLE 1.1 Average Return-to-Pay Ratios of CEOs, by Industry

Industry	Average Ratio
Industrial High-Tech	0.048
Utilities	0.046
Telecommunications	0.042
Services	0.036
Resources	0.028
Transportation	0.028
Financial	0.027
Industrial Low-Tech	0.025
Consumer Products	0.023

Source: Analysis of data in "Executive Compensation Scoreboard," *Business Week,* April 22, 1996, pp. 107–122.

CEOs in the consumer products industry have the lowest average ratio (.023). (See Table 1.1.) Armed with this sample information *Business Week* might *infer* that, from the shareholders' perspective, typical chief executives in consumer products are overpaid relative to industrial high-tech CEOs. Thus, this study is an example of *inferential statistics.*

Study 3 "The Consumer Price Index" (U.S. Department of Labor).

A data set of interest to virtually all Americans is the set of prices charged for goods and services in the U.S. economy. The general upward movement in this set of prices is referred to as *inflation;* the general downward movement is referred to as *deflation.* In order to *estimate* the change in prices over time, the Bureau of Labor Statistics (BLS) of the U.S. Department of Labor developed the Consumer Price Index (CPI). Each month, the BLS collects price data about a specific collection of goods and services (called a *market basket*) from 85 urban areas around the country. Statistical procedures are used to compute the CPI from this sample price data and other information about consumers' spending habits. By comparing the level of the CPI at different points in time, it is possible to *estimate* (make an inference about) the rate of inflation over particular time intervals and to compare the purchasing power of a dollar at different points in time.

One major use of the CPI as an index of inflation is as an indicator of the success or failure of government economic policies. A second use of the CPI is to escalate income payments. Millions of workers have *escalator clauses* in their collective bargaining contracts; these clauses call for increases in wage rates based on increases in the CPI. In addition, the incomes of Social Security beneficiaries and retired military and federal civil service employees are tied to the CPI. It has been estimated that a 1% increase in the CPI can trigger an increase of over $1 billion in income payments. Thus, it can be said that the very livelihoods of millions of Americans depend on the behavior of a statistical estimator, the CPI.

Like Study 2, this study is an example of *inferential statistics.* Market basket price data from a sample of urban areas (used to compute the CPI) is used to make inferences about the rate of inflation and wage rate increases.

These studies provide three real-life examples of the uses of statistics in business, economics, and government. Notice that each involves an analysis of data, either for the purpose of describing the data set (Study 1) or for making inferences about a data set (Studies 2 and 3).

1.3 FUNDAMENTAL ELEMENTS OF STATISTICS

Statistical methods are particularly useful for studying, analyzing, and learning about **populations**.

> **DEFINITION 1.4**
> A **population** is a set of units (usually people, objects, transactions, or events) that we are interested in studying.

For example, populations may include (1) *all* employed workers in the United States, (2) *all* registered voters in California, (3) *everyone* who has purchased a particular brand of cellular telephone, (4) *all* the cars produced last year by a particular assembly line, (5) the *entire* stock of spare parts at United Airlines' maintenance facility, (6) *all* sales made at the drive-through window of a

McDonald's restaurant during a given year, and (7) the set of *all* accidents occurring on a particular stretch of interstate highway during a holiday period. Notice that the first three population examples (1–3) are sets (groups) of people, the next two (4–5) are sets of objects, the next (6) is a set of transactions, and the last (7) is a set of events. Also notice that each set includes all the units in the population of interest.

In studying a population, we focus on one or more characteristics or properties of the units in the population. We call such characteristics *variables*. For example, we may be interested in the variables age, gender, income, and/or the number of years of education of the people currently unemployed in the United States.

DEFINITION 1.5

A **variable** is a characteristic or property of an individual population unit.

The name "variable" is derived from the fact that any particular characteristic may vary among the units in a population.

In studying a particular variable it is helpful to be able to obtain a numerical representation for it. Often, however, numerical representations are not readily available, so the process of measurement plays an important supporting role in statistical studies. **Measurement** is the process we use to assign numbers to variables of individual population units. We might, for instance, measure the preference for a food product by asking a consumer to rate the product's taste on a scale from 1 to 10. Or we might measure workforce age by simply asking each worker how old she is. In other cases, measurement involves the use of instruments such as stopwatches, scales, and calipers.

If the population we wish to study is small, it is possible to measure a variable for every unit in the population. For example, if you are measuring the starting salary for all University of Michigan MBA graduates last year, it is at least feasible to obtain every salary. When we measure a variable for every unit of a population, the result is called a **census** of the population. Typically, however, the populations of interest in most applications are much larger, involving perhaps many thousands or even an infinite number of units. Examples of large populations include those following Definition 1.4, as well as all invoices produced in the last year by a *Fortune* 500 company, all potential buyers of a new fax machine, and all stockholders of a firm listed on the New York Stock Exchange. For such populations, conducting a census would be prohibitively time-consuming and/or costly. A reasonable alternative would be to select and study a *subset* (or portion) of the units in the population.

DEFINITION 1.6

A **sample** is a subset of the units of a population.

For example, suppose a company is being audited for invoice errors. Instead of examining all 15,472 invoices produced by the company during a given year, an auditor may select and examine a sample of just 100 invoices (see Figure 1.2). If he is interested in the variable "invoice error status," he would record (measure) the status (error or no error) of each sampled invoice.

FIGURE 1.2
A sample of all
company invoices

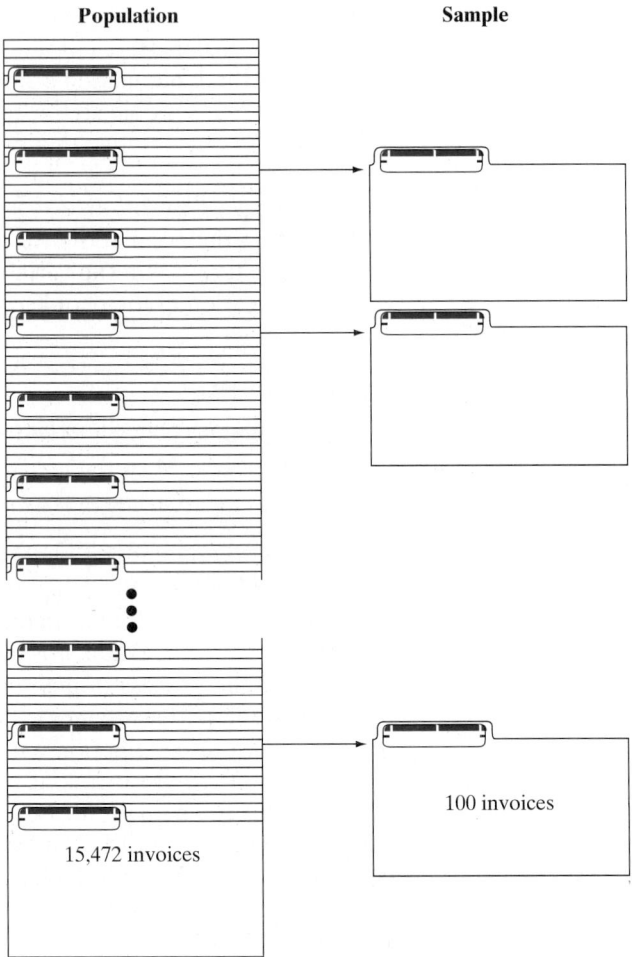

After the variable(s) of interest for every unit in the sample (or population) is measured, the data are analyzed, either by descriptive or inferential statistical methods. The auditor, for example, may be interested only in *describing* the error rate in the sample of 100 invoices. More likely, however, he will want to use the information in the sample to make *inferences* about the population of all 15,472 invoices.

DEFINITION 1.7
A **statistical inference** is an estimate or prediction or some other generalization about a population based on information contained in a sample.

That is, we use the information contained in the sample to learn about the larger population.* Thus, from the sample of 100 invoices, the auditor may estimate the total number of invoices containing errors in the population of 15,472 invoices. The auditor's inference about the quality of the firm's invoices can be used in deciding whether to modify the firm's billing operations.

*The terms *population* and *sample* are often used to refer to the sets of measurement themselves, as well as to the units on which the measurements are made. When a single variable of interest is being measured, this usage causes little confusion. But when the terminology is ambiguous, we'll refer to the measurements as *population data sets* and *sample data sets*, respectively.

EXAMPLE 1.1

A large paint retailer has had numerous complaints from customers about under-filled paint cans. As a result, the retailer has begun inspecting incoming shipments of paint from suppliers. Shipments with underfill problems will be returned to the supplier. A recent shipment contained 2,440 gallon-size cans. The retailer sampled 50 cans and weighed each on a scale capable of measuring weight to four decimal places. Properly filled cans weigh 10 pounds.

    a. Describe the population.

    b. Describe the variable of interest.

    c. Describe the sample.

    d. Describe the inference.

SOLUTION

    a. The population is the set of units of interest to the retailer, which is the shipment of 2,440 cans of paint.

    b. The weight of the paint cans is the variable the retailer wishes to evaluate.

    c. The sample is a subset of the population. In this case, it is the 50 cans of paint selected by the retailer.

    d. The inference of interest involves the *generalization* of the information contained in the weights of the sample of paint cans to the population of paint cans. In particular, the retailer wants to learn about the extent of the underfill problem (if any) in the population. This might be accomplished by finding the average weight of the cans in the sample and using it to estimate the average weight of the cans in the population. ∎

EXAMPLE 1.2

"Cola wars" is the popular term for the intense competition between Coca-Cola and Pepsi displayed in their marketing campaigns. Their campaigns have featured movie and television stars, rock videos, athletic endorsements, and claims of consumer preference based on taste tests. Suppose, as part of a Pepsi marketing campaign, 1,000 cola consumers are given a blind taste test (i.e., a taste test in which the two brand names are disguised). Each consumer is asked to state a preference for brand A or brand B.

    a. Describe the population.

    b. Describe the variable of interest.

    c. Describe the sample.

    d. Describe the inference.

SOLUTION

    a. The population of interest is the collection or set of all consumers.

    b. The characteristic that Pepsi wants to measure is the consumer's cola preference as revealed under the conditions of a blind taste test, so cola preference is the variable of interest.

    c. The sample is the 1,000 cola consumers selected from the population of all cola consumers.

    d. The inference of interest is the *generalization* of the cola preferences of the 1,000 sampled consumers to the population of all cola consumers. In particular, the preferences of the consumers in the sample can be used to *estimate* the percentage of all cola consumers who prefer each brand. ∎

The preceding definitions and examples identify four of the five elements of an inferential statistical problem: a population, one or more variables of interest, a sample, and an inference. But making the inference is only part of the story. We also need to know its **reliability**—that is, how good the inference is. The only way we can be certain that an inference about a population is correct is to include the entire population in our sample. However, because of *resource constraints* (i.e., insufficient time and/or money), we usually can't work with whole populations, so we base our inferences on just a portion of the population (a sample). Consequently, whenever possible, it is important to determine and report the reliability of each inference made. Reliability, then, is the fifth element of inferential statistical problems.

The measure of reliability that accompanies an inference separates the science of statistics from the art of fortune-telling. A palm reader, like a statistician, may examine a sample (your hand) and make inferences about the population (your life). However, unlike statistical inferences, the palm reader's inferences include no measure of reliability.

Suppose, as in Example 1.1, we are interested in estimating the average weight of a population of paint cans from the average weight of a sample of cans. Using statistical methods, we can determine a *bound on the estimation error*. This bound is simply a number that our estimation error (the difference between the average weight of the sample and the average weight of the population of cans) is not likely to exceed. We'll see in later chapters that this bound is a measure of the uncertainty of our inference. The reliability of statistical inferences is discussed throughout this text. For now, we simply want you to realize that an inference is incomplete without a measure of its reliability.

DEFINITION 1.8

A **measure of reliability** is a statement (usually quantified) about the degree of uncertainty associated with a statistical inference.

Let's conclude this section with a summary of the elements of both descriptive and inferential statistical problems and an example to illustrate a measure of reliability.

FOUR ELEMENTS OF DESCRIPTIVE STATISTICAL PROBLEMS

1. The population or sample of interest
2. One or more variables (characteristics of the population or sample units) that are to be investigated
3. Tables, graphs, or numerical summary tools
4. Conclusions about the data based on the patterns revealed

FIVE ELEMENTS OF INFERENTIAL STATISTICAL PROBLEMS

1. The population of interest
2. One or more variables (characteristics of the population units) that are to be investigated
3. The sample of population units
4. The inference about the population based on information contained in the sample
5. A measure of reliability for the inference

EXAMPLE 1.3

Refer to Example 1.2, in which the cola preferences of 1,000 consumers were indicated in a taste test. Describe how the reliability of an inference concerning the preferences of all cola consumers in the Pepsi bottler's marketing region could be measured.

SOLUTION

When the preferences of 1,000 consumers are used to estimate the preferences of all consumers in the region, the estimate will not exactly mirror the preferences of the population. For example, if the taste test shows that 56% of the 1,000 consumers chose Pepsi, it does not follow (nor is it likely) that exactly 56% of all cola drinkers in the region prefer Pepsi. Nevertheless, we can use sound statistical reasoning (which is presented later in the text) to ensure that our sampling procedure will generate estimates that are almost certainly within a specified limit of the true percentage of all consumers who prefer Pepsi. For example, such reasoning might assure us that the estimate of the preference for Pepsi from the sample is almost certainly within 5% of the actual population preference. The implication is that the actual preference for Pepsi is between 51% [i.e., (56 − 5)%] and 61% [i.e., (56 + 5)%]—that is, (56 ± 5)%. This interval represents a measure of reliability for the inference.

1.4   PROCESSES (OPTIONAL)

Sections 1.2 and 1.3 focused on the use of statistical methods to analyze and learn about populations, which are sets of *existing* units. Statistical methods are equally useful for analyzing and making inferences about **processes**.

DEFINITION 1.9

A **process** is a series of actions or operations that transforms inputs to outputs. A process produces or generates output over time.

The most obvious processes that are of interest to businesses are production or manufacturing processes. A manufacturing process uses a series of operations performed by people and machines to convert inputs, such as raw materials and parts, to finished products (the outputs). Examples include the process used to produce the paper on which these words are printed, automobile assembly lines, and oil refineries.

Figure 1.3 presents a general description of a process and its inputs and outputs. In the context of manufacturing, the process in the figure (i.e., the transformation process) could be a depiction of the overall production process or it could be a depiction of one of the many processes (sometimes called subprocesses) that exist within an overall production process. Thus, the output shown could be finished goods that will be shipped to an external customer or merely the output of one of

FIGURE 1.3
Graphical depiction of a manufacturing process

the steps or subprocesses of the overall process. In the latter case, the output becomes input for the next subprocess. For example, Figure 1.3 could represent the overall automobile assembly process, with its output being fully assembled cars ready for shipment to dealers. Or, it could depict the windshield assembly subprocess, with its output of partially assembled cars with windshields ready for "shipment" to the next subprocess in the assembly line.

Besides physical products and services, businesses and other organizations generate streams of numerical data over time that are used to evaluate the performance of the organization. Examples include weekly sales figures, quarterly earnings, and yearly profits. The U.S. economy (a complex organization) can be thought of as generating streams of data that include the Gross Domestic Product (GDP), stock prices, and the Consumer Price Index (see Section 1.2). Statisticians and other analysts conceptualize these data streams as being generated by processes. Typically, however, the series of operations or actions that cause particular data to be realized are either unknown or so complex (or both) that the processes are treated as **black boxes**.

DEFINITION 1.10
A process whose operations or actions are unknown or unspecified is called a **black box**.

Frequently, when a process is treated as a black box, its inputs are not specified either. The entire focus is on the output of the process. A black box process is illustrated in Figure 1.4.

In studying a process, we generally focus on one or more characteristics, or properties, of the output. For example, we may be interested in the weight or the length of the units produced or even the time it takes to produce each unit. As with characteristics of population units, we call these characteristics **variables**. In studying processes whose output is already in numerical form (i.e., a stream of numbers), the characteristic, or property, represented by the numbers (e.g., sales, GDP, or stock prices) is typically the variable of interest. If the output is not numeric, we use **measurement processes** to assign numerical values to variables.* For example, if in the automobile assembly process the weight of the fully assembled automobile is the variable of interest, a measurement process involving a large scale will be used to assign a numerical value to each automobile.

As with populations, we use sample data to analyze and make inferences (estimates, predictions, or other generalizations) about processes. But the concept of a sample is defined differently when dealing with processes. Recall that a population is a set of existing units and that a sample is a subset of those units. In the case

FIGURE 1.4
A black box process
with numerical output

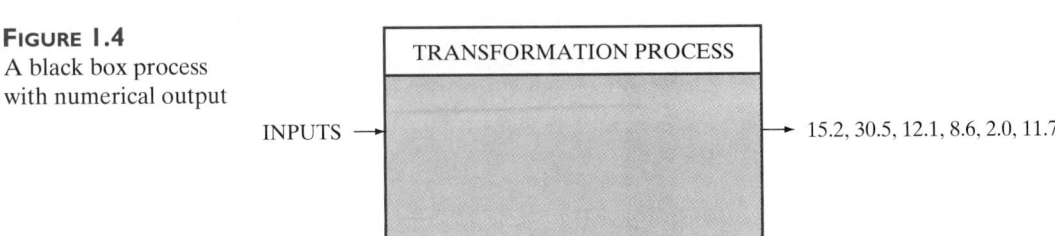

INPUTS →   TRANSFORMATION PROCESS   → 15.2, 30.5, 12.1, 8.6, 2.0, 11.7

---

*A process whose output is already in numerical form necessarily includes a measurement process as one of its subprocesses.

of processes, however, the concept of a set of existing units is not relevant or appropriate. Processes generate or create their output *over time*—one unit after another. For example, a particular automobile assembly line produces a completed vehicle every four minutes. We define a sample from a process in the box.

DEFINITION 1.11

Any set of output (objects or numbers) produced by a process is called a **sample**.

Thus, the next 10 cars turned out by the assembly line constitute a sample from the process, as do the next 100 cars or every fifth car produced today.

EXAMPLE 1.4

A particular fast-food restaurant chain has 6,289 outlets with drive-through windows. To attract more customers to its drive-through services, the company is considering offering a 50% discount to customers who wait more than a specified number of minutes to receive their order. To help determine what the time limit should be, the company decided to estimate the average waiting time at a particular drive-through window in Dallas, Texas. For 7 consecutive days, the worker taking customers' orders recorded the time that every order was placed. The worker who handed the order to the customer recorded the time of delivery. In both cases, workers used synchronized digital clocks that reported the time to the nearest second. At the end of the 7-day period, 2,109 orders had been timed.

a. Describe the process of interest at the Dallas restaurant.

b. Describe the variable of interest.

c. Describe the sample.

d. Describe the inference of interest.

e. Describe how the reliability of the inference could be measured.

SOLUTION

a. The process of interest is the drive-through window at a particular fast-food restaurant in Dallas, Texas. It is a process because it "produces," or "generates," meals over time. That is, it services customers over time.

b. The variable the company monitored is customer waiting time, the length of time a customer waits to receive a meal after placing an order. Since the study is focusing only on the output of the process (the time to produce the output) and not the internal operations of the process (the tasks required to produce a meal for a customer), the process is being treated as a black box.

c. The sampling plan was to monitor every order over a particular 7-day period. The sample is the 2,109 orders that were processed during the 7-day period.

d. The company's immediate interest is in learning about the drive-through window in Dallas. They plan to do this by using the waiting times from the sample to make a statistical inference about the drive-through process. In particular, they might use the average waiting time for the sample to estimate the average waiting time at the Dallas facility.

e. As for inferences about populations, measures of reliability can be developed for inferences about processes. The reliability of the estimate of the average waiting time for the Dallas restaurant could be measured by a bound on the error of estimation. That is, we might find that the average waiting time is 4.2 minutes, with a bound on the error of estimation of .5 minute. The implication would be that we could be reasonably certain that the true average waiting time for the Dallas process is between 3.7 and 4.7 minutes.

Notice that there is also a population described in this example: the company's 6,289 existing outlets with drive-through facilities. In the final analysis, the company will use what it learns about the process in Dallas and, perhaps, similar studies at other locations to make an inference about the waiting times in its populations of outlets.   ◼

Note that output already generated by a process can be viewed as a population. Suppose a soft-drink canning process produced 2,000 twelve-packs yesterday, all of which were stored in a warehouse. If we were interested in learning something about those 2,000 packages—such as the percentage with defective cardboard packaging—we could treat the 2,000 packages as a population. We might draw a sample from the population in the warehouse, measure the variable of interest, and use the sample data to make a statistical inference about the 2,000 packages, as described in Sections 1.2 and 1.3.

In this optional section we have presented a brief introduction to processes and the use of statistical methods to analyze and learn about processes. In Chapters 13 and 14 we present an in-depth treatment of these subjects.

1.5   TYPES OF DATA

You have learned that statistics is the science of data and that data are obtained by measuring the values of one or more variables on the units in the sample (or population). All data (and hence the variables we measure) can be classified as one of two general types: *quantitative data* and *qualitative data.*

Quantitative data are data that are measured on a naturally occurring numerical scale.* The following are examples of quantitative data:

1. The temperature (in degrees Celsius) at which each unit in a sample of 20 pieces of heat-resistant plastic begins to melt

2. The current unemployment rate (measured as a percentage) for each of the 50 states

3. The scores of a sample of 150 MBA applicants on the GMAT, a standardized business graduate school entrance exam administered nationwide

4. The number of female executives employed in each of a sample of 75 manufacturing companies

---

*Quantitative data can be subclassified as either *interval data* or *ratio data.* For ratio data, the origin (i.e., the value 0) is a meaningful number. But the origin has no meaning with interval data. Consequently, we can add and subtract interval data, but we can't multiply and divide them. Of the four quantitative data sets listed, (1) and (3) are interval data, while (2) and (4) are ratio data.

STATISTICS IN ACTION

1.1 QUALITY IMPROVEMENT: U.S. FIRMS RESPOND TO THE CHALLENGE FROM JAPAN

Over the last two decades, U.S. firms have been seriously challenged by products of superior quality from overseas. For example, from 1984 to 1991, imported cars and light trucks steadily increased their share of the U.S. market from 22% to 30%. As a second example, consider the television and VCR markets. Both products were invented in the United States, but as of 1995 not a single U.S. firm manufactures either. Both are produced exclusively by Pacific Rim countries, primarily Japan.

To meet this competitive challenge, more and more U.S. firms—both manufacturing and service firms—have begun quality-improvement initiatives of their own. Many of these firms now stress the management of quality in all phases and aspects of their business, from the design of their products to production, distribution, sales, and service.

Broadly speaking, quality-improvement programs are concerned with (1) finding out what the customer wants, (2) translating those wants into a product design, and (3) producing and delivering a product or service that meets or exceeds the specifications of the product design. In all these areas, but particularly in the third, *improvement of quality requires improvement of processes*—including production processes, distribution processes, and service processes.

But what does it mean to say that a process has been improved? Generally speaking, it means that the customer of the process (i.e., the user of the output) indicates a greater satisfaction with the output. Frequently, such increases in satisfaction require a reduction in the variation of one or more process variables. That is, a reduction in the variation of the output stream of the process is needed.

But how can process variation be monitored and reduced? In the mid-1920s, Walter Shewhart of the Bell Telephone Laboratories made perhaps the most significant breakthrough of this century for the improvement of processes. He recognized that variation in process output was inevitable. No two parts produced by a given machine are the same; no two transactions performed by a given bank teller are the same. He also recognized that variation could be understood, monitored, and controlled using statistical methods. He developed a simple graphical technique—called a **control chart**—for determining whether product variation is within acceptable limits. This method provides guidance for when to adjust or change a production process and when to leave it alone. It can be used at the end of the production process or, most significantly, at different points within the process. We discuss control charts and other tools for improving processes in Chapter 13.

In the last decade, largely as a result of the Japanese challenge to the supremacy of U.S. products, control charts and other statistical tools have gained widespread use in the United States. As evidence for the claim that U.S. firms are responding well to Japan's competitive challenge, consider this: The most prestigious quality-improvement prize in the world that a firm can win is the Deming Prize. It has been awarded by the Japanese since the 1950s. In 1989 it was won for the first time by an American company—Florida Power and Light Company. Other evidence of the resurgence of U.S. competitiveness includes a turnaround in market share for U.S. automakers: imports' share of the U.S. market decreased from a high of 30% in 1991 to 25% in 1995.

Focus

a. Identify two processes that are of interest to you.

b. For each process, part **a**, identify a variable that could be used to monitor the quality of the output of the process.

c. Walter Shewhart understood that variation is an inherent characteristic of the output of every process. Describe the possible variation over time in the output variables you identified in part **b**.

DEFINITION 1.12

Quantitative data are measurements that are recorded on a naturally occurring numerical scale.

In contrast, qualitative data cannot be measured on a natural numerical scale; they can only be classified into categories.* Examples of qualitative data are:

1. The political party affiliation (Democrat, Republican, or Independent) in a sample of 50 chief executive officers
2. The defective status (defective or not) of each of 100 computer chips manufactured by Intel
3. The size of a car (subcompact, compact, mid-size, or full-size) rented by each of a sample of 30 business travelers
4. A taste tester's ranking (best, worst, etc.) of four brands of barbecue sauce for a panel of 10 testers

Often, we assign arbitrary numerical values to qualitative data for ease of computer entry and analysis. But these assigned numerical values are simply codes: They cannot be meaningfully added, subtracted, multiplied, or divided. For example, we might code Democrat = 1, Republican = 2, and Independent = 3. Similarly, a taste tester might rank the barbecue sauces from 1 (best) to 4 (worst). These are simply arbitrarily selected numerical codes for the categories and have no utility beyond that.

DEFINITION 1.13
Qualitative data are measurements that cannot be measured on a natural numerical scale; they can only be classified into one of a group of categories.

EXAMPLE 1.5

Chemical and manufacturing plants sometimes discharge toxic-waste materials such as DDT into nearby rivers and streams. These toxins can adversely affect the plants and animals inhabiting the river and the river bank. The U.S. Army Corps of Engineers recently conducted a study of fish in the Tennessee River (in Alabama) and its three tributary creeks: Flint Creek, Limestone Creek, and Spring Creek. A total of 144 fish were captured and the following variables measured for each:

1. River/creek where fish was captured
2. Species (channel catfish, largemouth bass, or smallmouth buffalofish)
3. Length (centimeters)
4. Weight (grams)
5. DDT concentration (parts per million)

Classify each of the five variables measured as quantitative or qualitative.

SOLUTION
The variables length, weight, and DDT are quantitative because each is measured on a numerical scale: length in centimeters, weight in grams, and DDT in parts per million. In contrast, river/creek and species cannot be measured quantitatively: They can only be classified into categories (e.g., channel catfish, largemouth bass,

---

*Qualitative data can be subclassified as either *nominal data* or *ordinal data*. The categories of an ordinal data set can be ranked or meaningfully ordered, but the categories of a nominal data set can't be ordered. Of the four qualitative data sets listed above, (1) and (2) are nominal and (3) and (4) are ordinal.

and smallmouth buffalofish for species). Consequently, data on river/creek and species are qualitative. **L.**

As you would expect, the statistical methods for describing, reporting, and analyzing data depend on the type (quantitative or qualitative) of data measured. We demonstrate many useful methods in the remaining chapters of the text. But first we discuss some important ideas on data collection.

1.6 COLLECTING DATA

Once you decide on the type of data—quantitative or qualitative —appropriate for the problem at hand, you'll need to collect the data. Generally, you can obtain the data in four different ways:

1. Data from a *published source*
2. Data from a *designed experiment*
3. Data from a *survey*
4. Data collected *observationally*

Sometimes, the data set of interest has already been collected for you and is available in a **published source**, such as a book, journal, or newspaper. For example, you may want to examine and summarize the unemployment rates (i.e., percentages of eligible workers who are unemployed) in the 50 states of the United States. You can find this data set (as well as numerous other data sets) at your library in the *Statistical Abstract of the United States,* published annually by the U.S. Department of Commerce. Similarly, someone who is interested in monthly mortgage applications for new home construction would find this data set in the *Survey of Current Business,* another government publication. Other examples of published data sources include *The Wall Street Journal* (financial data), *The Sporting News* (sports information), and America Online (accessed over the Internet).*

A second method of collecting data involves conducting a **designed experiment**, in which the researcher exerts strict control over the units (people, objects, or events) in the study. For example, a recent medical study investigated the potential of aspirin in preventing heart attacks. Volunteer physicians were divided into two groups—the *treatment* group and the *control* group. In the treatment group, each physician took one aspirin tablet a day for one year, while each physician in the control group took an aspirin-free placebo (no drug) made to look like an aspirin tablet. The researchers, not the physicians under study, controlled who received the aspirin (the treatment) and who received the placebo. As you will learn in Chapter 15, a properly designed experiment allows you to extract more information from the data than is possible with an uncontrolled study.

Surveys are a third source of data. With a **survey**, the researcher samples a group of people, asks one or more questions, and records the responses. Probably the most familiar type of survey is the political polls conducted by any one of a number of organizations (e.g., Harris, Gallup, Roper, and CNN) and designed to

---

*With published data, we often make a distinction between the *primary source* and a *secondary source.* If the publisher is the original collector of the data, the source is primary. Otherwise, the data are secondary source data.

predict the outcome of a political election. Another familiar survey is the Nielsen survey, which provides the major television networks with information on the most watched TV programs. Surveys can be conducted through the mail, with telephone interviews, or with in-person interviews. Although in-person interviews are more expensive than mail or telephone surveys, they may be necessary when complex information must be collected.

Finally, observational studies can be employed to collect data. In an **observational study**, the researcher observes the experimental units in their natural setting and records the variable(s) of interest. For example, a company psychologist might observe and record the level of "Type A" behavior of a sample of assembly line workers. Similarly, a finance researcher may observe and record the closing stock prices of companies that are acquired by other firms on the day prior to the buyout and compare them to the closing prices on the day the acquisition is announced. Unlike a designed experiment, an observational study is one in which the researcher makes no attempt to control any aspect of the experimental units.

Regardless of the data collection method employed, it is likely that the data will be a sample from some population. And if we wish to apply inferential statistics, we must obtain a *representative sample*.

DEFINITION 1.14
A **representative sample** exhibits characteristics typical of those possessed by the target population.

For example, consider a political poll conducted during a presidential election year. Assume the pollster wants to estimate the percentage of all 120,000,000 registered voters in the United States who favor the incumbent president. The pollster would be unwise to base the estimate on survey data collected for a sample of voters from the incumbent's own state. Such an estimate would almost certainly be *biased* high.

The most common way to satisfy the representative sample requirement is to select a random sample. A **random sample** ensures that every subset of fixed size in the population has the same chance of being included in the sample. If the pollster samples 1,500 of the 120,000,000 voters in the population so that every subset of 1,500 voters has an equal chance of being selected, he has devised a random sample. The procedure for selecting a random sample is discussed in Chapter 3. Here, however, let's look at two examples involving actual sampling studies.

EXAMPLE 1.6

In the 1970s and early 1980s, state lotteries became commonplace in the United States. In 1985, the *Journal of the Institute for Socioeconomic Studies* (Sept. 1985) reported on a study designed to estimate the proportion of state lottery winners who quit their jobs within one year of striking it rich. Questionnaires were mailed to all 2,000 lottery winners who won at least $50,000 over the 10-year period 1976–1985. Of the 576 who responded, 11% indicated they had quit their jobs.

    a. Identify the data collection method.

    b. Are the sample data representative of the target population?

SOLUTION

a. The data collection method is a mail survey since questionnaires were mailed to lottery winners to elicit their job status (quit job within one year or not).

b. Because the data (576 responses to the job status question) clearly make up a subset of the target population (all 2,000 lottery winners), they do form a sample. But whether or not the sample is representative is unclear, since we are given no information on the 576 lottery winners who responded to the survey. However, mail surveys (and surveys in general) often suffer from *nonresponse bias*. The fact that only about one-fourth of the 2,000 lottery winners responded to the survey may indicate apathy on the part of lottery winners. A proportion much larger than 11% may have actually quit their jobs but were too busy enjoying their newfound fortune to bother responding to the survey.

EXAMPLE 1.7

Many business decisions are made because of offered incentives that are intended to make the decision-maker "feel good." Researchers at the Ohio State University conducted a study to determine how such a positive effect influences the risk preference of decision-makers (*Organizational Behavior and Human Decision Processes,* Vol. 39, 1987). Each in a random sample of 24 undergraduate business students at the university was assigned to one of two groups. Each student assigned to the "positive affect" group was given a bag of candies as a token of appreciation for participating in the study; students assigned to the "control" group did not receive the gift. All students were then given 10 gambling chips (worth $10) to bet in the casino game of roulette. The researchers measured the win probability (i.e., chance of winning) associated with the riskiest bet each student was willing to make. The win probabilities of the bets made by two groups of students were compared.

a. Identify the data collection method.

b. Are the sample data representative of the target population?

SOLUTION

a. The researchers controlled which group—"positive affect" or "control"—the students were assigned to. Consequently, a designed experiment was used to collect the data.

b. The sample of 24 students was randomly selected from all business students at the Ohio State University. If the target population is *all Ohio State University business students,* it is likely that the sample is representative. However, the researchers warn that the sample data should not be used to make inferences about other, more general, populations.

1.7 THE ROLE OF STATISTICS IN MANAGERIAL DECISION-MAKING

According to H. G. Wells, author of such science fiction classics as *The War of the Worlds* and *The Time Machine,* "*Statistical thinking* will one day be as necessary for efficient citizenship as the ability to read and write." Written more than a hundred years ago, Wells' prediction is proving true today.

STATISTICS IN ACTION

1.2 A 20/20 VIEW OF SURVEY RESULTS: FACT OR FICTION?

Did you ever notice that, no matter where you stand on popular issues of the day, you can always find statistics or surveys to back up your point of view—whether to take vitamins, whether day care harms kids, or what foods can hurt you or save you? There is an endless flow of information to help you make decisions, but is this information accurate, unbiased? John Stossel decided to check that out, and you may be surprised to learn if the picture you're getting doesn't seem quite right, maybe it isn't.

Barbara Walters gave this introduction to a March 31, 1995, segment of the popular prime-time ABC television program *20/20*. The story is titled "Facts or Fiction?—Exposés of So-Called Surveys." One of the surveys investigated by ABC correspondent John Stossel compared the discipline problems experienced by teachers in the 1940s and those experienced today. The results: In the 1940s, teachers worried most about students talking in class, chewing gum, and running in the halls. Today, they worry most about being assaulted! This information was highly publicized in the print media—in daily newspapers, weekly magazines, Ann Landers' column, the *Congressional Quarterly,* and *The Wall Street Journal,* among others—and referenced in speeches by a variety of public figures, including former first lady Barbara Bush and former Education secretary William Bennett.

"Hearing this made me yearn for the old days when life was so much simpler and gentler, but was life that simple then?" asks Stossel. "Wasn't there juvenile delinquency [in the 1940s]? Is the survey true?" With the help of a Yale School of Management professor, Stossel found the original source of the teacher survey—Texas oilman T. Colin Davis—and discovered it wasn't a survey at all! Davis had simply identified certain disciplinary problems encountered by teachers in a conservative newsletter—a list he admitted was not obtained from a statistical survey, but from Davis' personal knowledge of the problems in the 1940s ("I was in school then") and his understanding of the problems today ("I read the papers").

Stossel's critical thinking about the teacher "survey" led to the discovery of research that is misleading at best and unethical at worst. Several more misleading (and possibly unethical) surveys were presented on the ABC program. Listed here, most of these were conducted by businesses or special interest groups with specific objectives in mind.

The *20/20* segment ended with an interview of Cynthia Crossen, author of *Tainted Truth,* an exposé of misleading and biased surveys. Crossen warns: "If everybody is misusing numbers and scaring us with numbers to get us to do something, however good [that something] is, we've lost the power of numbers. Now, we know certain things from research. For example, we know that smoking cigarettes is hard on your lungs

---

The growth in data collection associated with scientific phenomena, business operations, and government activities (quality control, statistical auditing, forecasting, etc.) has been remarkable in the past several decades. Every day the media present us with the published results of political, economic, and social surveys. In the increasing government emphasis on drug and product testing, for example, we see vivid evidence of the need to be able to evaluate data sets intelligently. Consequently, each of us has to develop a discerning sense—an ability to use rational thought to interpret and understand the meaning of data. This ability is essential for making intelligent decisions, inferences, and generalizations.

DEFINITION 1.15

Statistical thinking involves applying rational thought and the science of statistics to critically assess data and inferences. Fundamental to the thought process is that variation exists in populations and process data.

and heart, and because we know that, many people's lives have been extended or saved. We don't want to lose the power of information to help us make decisions, and that's what I worry about."

Focus

a. Consider the false March of Dimes report on domestic violence and birth defects. Discuss the type of data required to investigate the impact of domestic violence on birth defects. What data collection method would you recommend?

b. Refer to the American Association of University Women (AAUW) study of self-esteem of high school girls. Explain why the results of the AAUW study are likely to be misleading. What data might be appropriate for assessing the self-esteem of high school girls?

c. Refer to the Food Research and Action Center study of hunger in America. Explain why the results of the study are likely to be misleading. What data would provide insight into the proportion of hungry American children?

Reported Information (Source)	Actual Study Information
Eating oat bran is a cheap and easy way to reduce your cholesterol count. (Quaker Oats)	Diet must consist of nothing but oat bran to achieve a slightly lower cholesterol count.
150,000 women a year die from anorexia. (Feminist group)	Approximately 1,000 women a year die from problems that were likely caused by anorexia.
Domestic violence causes more birth defects than all medical issues combined. (March of Dimes)	No study—false report.
Only 29% of high school girls are happy with themselves, compared to 66% of elementary school girls. (American Association of University Women)	Of 3,000 high school girls 29% responded "Always true" to the statement, "I am happy the way I am." Most answered, "Sort of true" and "Sometimes true."
One in four American children under age 12 is hungry or at risk of hunger. (Food Research and Action Center)	Based on responses to the questions: "Do you ever cut the size of meals?" "Do you ever eat less than you feel you should?" "Did you ever rely on limited numbers of foods to feed your children because you were running out of money to buy food for a meal?"

To gain some insight into the role statistics plays in **critical thinking**, let's look at a recent *AmStat News* article. This article describes how a group of 27 mathematics and statistics teachers, attending an American Statistical Association course called "Chance," used statistical thinking to evaluate the results of a study. Consider the following excerpt from the article.

There are few issues in the news that are not in some way statistical. Take one. Should motorcyclists be required by law to wear helmets?... In "The Case for No Helmets" (*New York Times*, June 17, 1995), Dick Teresi, editor of a magazine for Harley-Davidson bikers, argued that helmets may actually kill, since in collisions at speeds greater than 15 miles an hour the heavy helmet may protect the head but snap the spine. [Teresi] citing a "study," said "nine states without helmet laws had a lower fatality rate (3.05 deaths per 10,000 motorcycles) than those that mandated helmets (3.38)," and "in a survey of 2,500 [at a rally], 98% of the respondents opposed such laws."

[The course instructors] asked: After reading this [*New York Times*] piece, do you think it is safer to ride a motorcycle without a helmet? Do you think 98% might be a valid estimate of bikers who oppose helmet laws? What further statistical information would you like? [From Cohn, V. "Chance in college curriculum," *AmStat News,* Aug.–Sept. 1995, No. 223, p. 2.]

You can use several of the key ideas presented in this chapter to help you think statistically about the problem presented in this article. For example, before you can evaluate the validity of the 98% estimate, you would want to know how the data were collected for the study cited by the editor of the biker magazine. If a survey was conducted, it's possible that the 2,500 bikers in the sample were not selected at random from the target population of all bikers, but rather were "self-selected." (Remember, they were all attending a rally—a rally likely for bikers who oppose the law.) If the respondents were likely to have strong opinions regarding the helmet law (e.g., strongly oppose the law), the resulting estimate is probably biased high. Also, if the biased sample was intentional, with the sole purpose to mislead the public, the researchers would be guilty of **unethical statistical practice**.

You'd also want more information about the study comparing the motorcycle fatality rate of the nine states without a helmet law to those states that mandate helmets. Were the data obtained from a published source? Were all 50 states included in the study? That is, are you seeing sample data or population data? Furthermore, do the helmet laws vary among states? If so, can you really compare the fatality rates?

These questions led the Chance group to the discovery of two scientific and statistically sound studies on helmets. The first, a UCLA study of nonfatal injuries, disputed the charge that helmets shift injuries to the spine. The second study reported a dramatic *decline* in motorcycle crash deaths after California passed its helmet law.

Successful managers rely heavily on statistical thinking to help them make decisions. The role statistics can play in managerial decision-making is displayed in the flow diagram in Figure 1.5. Every managerial decision-making problem begins

FIGURE 1.5

Flow diagram showing the role of statistics in managerial decision-making

Source: Chervany, Benson, and Iyer (1980)

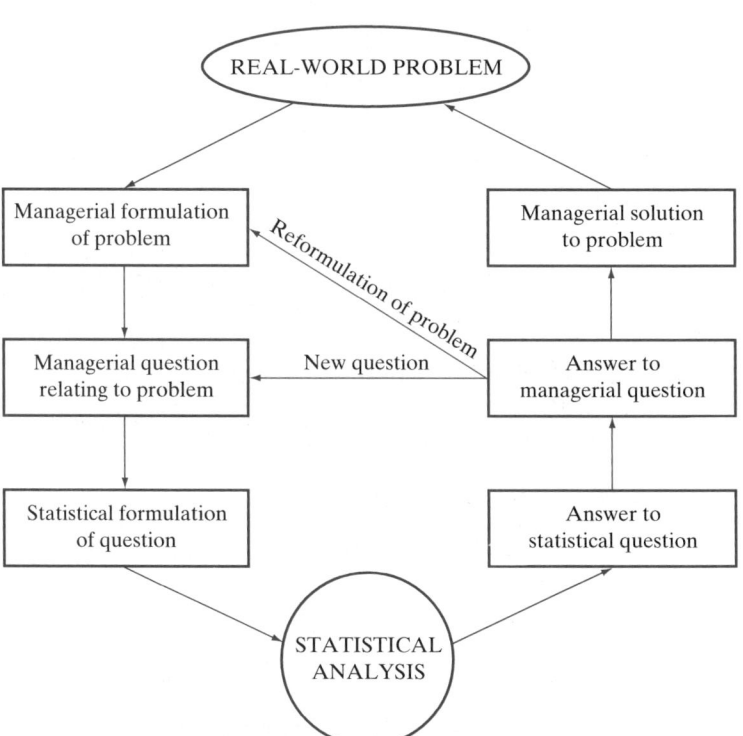

with a real-world problem. This problem is then formulated in managerial terms and framed as a managerial question. The next sequence of steps (proceeding counterclockwise around the flow diagram) identifies the role that statistics can play in this process. The managerial question is translated into a statistical question, the sample data are collected and analyzed, and the statistical question is answered. The next step in the process is using the answer to the statistical question to reach an answer to the managerial question. The answer to the managerial question may suggest a reformulation of the original managerial problem, suggest a new managerial question, or lead to the solution of the managerial problem.

One of the most difficult steps in the decision-making process—one that requires a cooperative effort among managers and statisticians—is the translation of the managerial question into statistical terms (for example, into a question about a population). This statistical question must be formulated so that, when answered, it will provide the key to the answer to the managerial question. Thus, as in the game of chess, you must formulate the statistical question with the end result, the solution to the managerial question, in mind.

In the remaining chapters of the text, you'll become familiar with the tools essential for building a firm foundation in statistics and statistical thinking.

QUICK REVIEW

Key Terms

Note: Starred (*) terms are from the optional section in this chapter.

Black box*   10
Census   5
Critical thinking   19
Data   2
Descriptive statistics   2
Designed experiment   15
Inference   3

Inferential statistics   3
Measure of reliability   8
Measurement   5
Observational study   16
Population   4
Process*   9
Published source   15

Qualitative data   14
Quantitative data   13
Random sample   16
Reliability   8
Representative sample   16
Sample   5
Statistical inference   6

Statistical thinking   18
Statistics   2
Survey   15
Unethical statistical
  practice   20
Variable   5

EXERCISES   1.1–1.30

Note: Starred (*) exercises are from the optional section in this chapter.

Learning the Mechanics

1.1 What is statistics?

1.2 Explain the difference between descriptive and inferential statistics.

1.3 List and define the four elements of a descriptive statistics problem.

1.4 List and define the five elements of an inferential statistical analysis.

1.5 List the four major methods of collecting data and explain their differences.

1.6 Explain the difference between quantitative and qualitative data.

1.7 Explain how populations and variables differ.

1.8 Explain how populations and samples differ.

1.9 What is a representative sample? What is its value?

1.10 Why would a statistician consider an inference incomplete without an accompanying measure of its reliability?

*1.11 Explain the difference between a population and a process.

1.12 Define statistical thinking.

1.13 Suppose you're given a data set that classifies each sample unit into one of four categories: A, B, C, or D. You plan to create a computer database consisting of these data, and you decide to code the data as A = 1, B = 2, C = 3, and D = 4. Are the data consisting of the classifications A, B, C, and D qualitative or quantitative? After the data are input as 1, 2, 3, or 4, are they qualitative or quantitative? Explain your answers.

Applying the Concepts

1.14 Consider the set of all students enrolled in your statistics course this term. Suppose you're interested in learning about the current grade point averages (GPAs) of this group.

a. Define the population and variable of interest.

b. Is the variable qualitative or quantitative?

c. Suppose you determine the GPA of every member of the class. Would this represent a census or a sample?

d. Suppose you determine the GPA of 10 members of the class. Would this represent a census or a sample?

e. If you determine the GPA of every member of the class and then calculate the average, how much reliability does this calculation have as an "estimate" of the class average GPA?

f. If you determine the GPA of 10 members of the class and then calculate the average, will the number you get necessarily be the same as the average GPA for the whole class? On what factors would you expect the reliability of the estimate to depend?

g. What must be true in order for the sample of 10 students you select from your class to be considered a random sample?

1.15 Pollsters regularly conduct opinion polls to determine the popularity rating of the current president. Suppose a poll is to be conducted tomorrow in which 2,000 individuals will be asked whether the president is doing a good or bad job. The 2,000 individuals will be selected by random-digit telephone dialing and asked the question over the phone.

a. What is the relevant population?

b. What is the variable of interest? Is it quantitative or qualitative?

c. What is the sample?

d. What is the inference of interest to the pollster?

e. What method of data collection is employed?

f. How likely is the sample to be representative?

1.16 Colleges and universities are requiring an increasing amount of information about applicants before making acceptance and financial aid decisions. Classify each of the following types of data required on a college application as quantitative or qualitative.

a. High school GPA

b. High school class rank

c. Applicant's score on the SAT or ACT

d. Gender of applicant

e. Parents' income

f. Age of applicant

1.17 Classify the following examples of data as either qualitative or quantitative:

a. The depth of tread remaining on each of 137 randomly selected automobile tires after 20,000 miles of wear

b. The occupation of each of 200 shoppers at a supermarket

c. The employment status of each adult living on a city block

d. The time (in months) between auto maintenance for each of 100 used cars

1.18 A food-products company is considering marketing a new snack food. To see how consumers react to the product, the company conducted a taste test using a sample of 100 randomly selected shoppers at a suburban shopping mall. The shoppers were asked to taste the snack food and then fill out a short questionnaire that requested the following information:

(1) What is your age?

(2) Are you the person who typically does the food shopping for your household?

(3) How many people are in your family?

(4) How would you rate the taste of the snack food on a scale of 1 to 10, where 1 is least tasty?

(5) Would you purchase this snack food if it were available on the market?

(6) If you answered yes to part (5), how often would you purchase the product?

a. Identify the data collection method.

b. Classify the data generated for each question as quantitative or qualitative. Justify your classifications.

1.19 All highway bridges in the United States are inspected periodically for structural deficiency by the Federal Highway Administration (FHWA). Data from the FHWA inspections are compiled into the National Bridge Inventory (NBI). Several of the nearly 100 variables maintained by the NBI are listed below. Classify each variable as quantitative or qualitative.

a. Length of maximum span (feet)

b. Number of vehicle lanes

c. Toll bridge (yes or no)

d. Average daily traffic

e. Condition of deck (good, fair, or poor)

f. Bypass or detour length (miles)

g. Route type (interstate, U.S., state, county, or city)

1.20 Refer to Exercise 1.19. The most recent NBI data were analyzed and the results published in the *Journal of Infrastructure Systems* (June 1995). Using the FHWA inspection ratings, each of the 470,515 highway bridges in the United States was categorized as structurally deficient, functionally obsolete, or safe. About 26% of the bridges were found to be structurally deficient, while 19% were functionally obsolete.

a. What is the variable of interest to the researchers?

b. Is the variable of part **a** quantitative or qualitative?

c. Is the data set analyzed a population or a sample? Explain.

d. How did the researchers obtain the data for their study?

1.21 The *Journal of Retailing* (Spring 1988) published a study of the relationship between job satisfaction and the degree of *Machiavellian orientation*. Briefly, the Machiavellian orientation is one in which the executive exerts very strong control, even to the point of deception and cruelty, over the employees he or she supervises. The authors administered a questionnaire to each in a sample of 218 department store executives and obtained both a job satisfaction score and a Machiavellian rating. They concluded that those with higher job satisfaction scores are likely to have a lower "Mach" rating.

a. What is the population from which the sample was selected?

b. What variables were measured by the authors?

c. Identify the sample.

d. Identify the data collection method used.

e. What inference was made by the authors?

1.22 Media reports suggest that disgruntled shareholders are becoming more willing to put pressure on corporate management. Is this an impression caused by a few recent high-profile cases involving a few large investors, or is shareholder activism widespread? To answer this question the Wirthlin Group, an opinion research organization in McLean, Virginia, sampled and questioned 240 large investors (money managers, mutual fund managers, institutional investors, etc.) in the United States. One question they asked was: Have you written or called a corporate director to express your views? They found that a surprisingly large 40% of the sample had (*New York Times*, Oct. 31, 1995).

a. Identify the population of interest to the Wirthlin Group.

b. Based on the question the Wirthlin Group asked, what is the variable of interest?

c. Describe the sample.

d. What inference can be made from the results of the survey?

1.23 *Corporate merger* is a means through which one firm (the bidder) acquires control of the assets of another firm (the target). During 1995 there was a frenzy of bank mergers in the United States, as the banking industry consolidated into more efficient and more competitive units. The number of banks in the United States has fallen from a high of 14,496 in 1984 to just under 10,000 at the end of 1995 (*Fortune*, Oct. 2, 1995).

a. Construct a brief questionnaire (two or three questions) that could be used to query a sample of bank presidents concerning their opinions of why the industry is consolidating and whether it will consolidate further.

b. Describe the population about which inferences could be made from the results of the survey.

c. Discuss the pros and cons of sending the questionnaire to all bank presidents versus a sample of 200.

*1.24 Coca-Cola and Schweppes Beverages Limited (CCSB), which was formed in 1987, is 49% owned by the Coca-Cola Company. According to *Industrial Management and Data Systems* (Vol. 92, 1992), CCSB's Wakefield plant can produce 4,000 cans of soft drink per minute. The automated process consists of measuring and dispensing the raw ingredients into storage vessels to create the syrup, and then injecting the syrup, along with carbon dioxide, into the beverage cans. In order to monitor the subprocess that adds carbon dioxide to the cans, five filled cans are pulled off the line every 15 minutes and the amount of carbon dioxide in each of these five is measured to determine whether the amounts are within prescribed limits.

a. Describe the process studied.

b. Describe the variable of interest.

c. Describe the sample.

d. Describe the inference of interest.

e. *Brix* is a unit for measuring sugar concentration. If a technician is assigned the task of estimating the average brix level of all 240,000 cans of beverage stored in a warehouse near Wakefield, will the technician be examining a process or a population? Explain.

1.25 *Job-sharing* is an innovative employment alternative that originated in Sweden and is becoming very popular in the United States. Firms that offer job-sharing plans allow two or more persons to work part-time, sharing one full-time job. For example, two job-sharers might alternate work weeks, with one working while the other is off. Job-sharers never work at the same time and may not even know each other. Job-sharing is particularly attractive to working mothers and to people who frequently lose their jobs due to fluctuations in the economy. In a survey of 1,035 major U.S. firms, approximately 22% offer job-sharing to their employees (*Entrepreneur*, Mar. 1995).

a. Identify the population from which the sample was selected.

b. Identify the variable measured.

c. Identify the sample selected.

d. What type of inference is of interest to the government agency?

1.26 The People's Republic of China with its 1.2 billion people is emerging as the world's biggest cigarette market. In fact, China's cigarette industry is the central government's largest source of tax revenue. To better understand Chinese smokers and the potential public health disaster they represent, door-to-door interviews of 3,423 men and 3,593 women were conducted in the Minhang District, a suburb of 500,000 people near Shanghai. The study concluded that "people in China, despite their modest incomes, are willing to spend an average of 60 percent of personal income and 17 percent of household income to buy cigarettes" (*Newark Star-Ledger,* Oct. 19, 1995).

a. Identify the population that was sampled.

b. How large was the sample size?

c. The study made inferences about what population?

d. Explain why different answers to parts **a** and **c** might affect the reliability of the study's conclusions.

1.27 Windows is a computer software product made by Microsoft Corporation. In designing Windows 95, Microsoft telephoned thousands of users of Windows 3.1 (an older version) and asked them how the product could be improved. Assume customers were asked the following questions:

    I. Are you the most frequent user of Windows 3.1 in your household?

    II. What is your age?

    III. How would you rate the helpfulness of the tutorial instructions that accompany Windows 3.1, on a scale of 1 to 10, where 1 is not helpful?

    IV. When using a printer with Windows 3.1, do you most frequently use a laser printer or another type of printer?

    V. If the speed of Windows 3.1 could be changed, which one of the following would you prefer: slower, unchanged, or faster?

    VI. How many people in your household have used Windows 3.1 at least once?

Each of these questions defines a variable of interest to the company. Classify the data generated for each variable as quantitative or qualitative. Justify your classification.

1.28 To assess how extensively accounting firms in New York State use sampling methods in auditing their clients, the New York Society of CPAs mailed a questionnaire to 800 New York accounting firms employing two or more professionals. They received responses from 179 firms of which four responses were unusable and 12 reported they had no audit practice. The questionnaire asked firms whether they use audit sampling methods and, if so, whether or not they use random sampling (*CPA Journal,* July 1995).

a. Identify the population, the variables, the sample, and the inferences of interest to the New York Society of CPAs.

b. Speculate as to what could have made four of the responses unusable.

c. In Chapters 6–9 you will learn that the reliability of an inference is related to the size of the sample used. In addition to sample size, what factors might affect the reliability of the inferences drawn in the mail survey described above?

*1.29 The Wallace Company of Houston is a distributor of pipes, valves, and fittings to the refining, chemical, and petrochemical industries. The company was a recent winner of the Malcolm Baldrige National Quality Award. According to *Small Business Reports* (May 1991), one of the steps the company takes to monitor the quality of its distribution process is to send out a survey twice a year to a subset of its current customers, asking the customers to rate the speed of deliveries, the accuracy of invoices, and the quality of the packaging of the products they have received from Wallace.

a. Describe the process studied.

b. Describe the variables of interest.

c. Describe the sample.

d. Describe the inferences of interest.

e. What are some of the factors that are likely to affect the reliability of the inferences?

1.30 The employment status (employed or unemployed) of each individual in the U.S. workforce is a set of data that is of interest to economists, businesspeople, and sociologists. These data provide information on the social and economic health of our society. To obtain information about the employment status of the workforce, the U.S. Bureau of the Census conducts what is known as the *Current Population Survey.* Each month approximately 1,500 interviewers visit about 59,000 of the 92 million households in the United States and question the occupants over 14 years of age about their employment status. Their responses enable the Bureau of the Census to *estimate* the percentage of people in the labor force who are unemployed (the *unemployment rate*).

a. Define the population of interest to the Census Bureau.

b. What variable is being measured? Is it quantitative or qualitative?

c. Is the problem of interest to the Census Bureau descriptive or inferential?

d. In order to monitor the rate of unemployment, it is essential to have a definition of "unemployed." Different economists and even different countries define it in various ways. Develop your own definition of an "unemployed person." Your definition should answer such questions as: Are students on summer vacation unemployed? Are college professors who do not teach summer school unemployed? At what age are people considered to be eligible for the workforce? Are people who are out of work but not actively seeking a job unemployed?

CHAPTER 2

METHODS FOR DESCRIBING SETS OF DATA

CONTENTS

STATISTICS IN ACTION

Where We've Been

In Chapter 1 we looked at some typical examples of the use of statistics and we discussed the role that statistical thinking plays in supporting managerial decision-making. We examined the difference between descriptive and inferential statistics and described the five elements of inferential statistics: a population, one or more variables, a sample, an inference, and a measure of reliability for the inference. We also learned that data can be of two types—quantitative and qualitative.

Where We're Going

Before we make an inference, we must be able to describe a data set. We can do this by using graphical and/or numerical methods, which we discuss in this chapter. As we'll see in Chapter 7, we use sample numerical descriptive measures to estimate the values of corresponding population descriptive measures. Therefore, our efforts in this chapter will ultimately lead us to statistical inference.

Suppose you wish to evaluate the managerial capabilities of a class of 400 MBA students based on their Graduate Management Aptitude Test (GMAT) scores. How would you describe these 400 measurements? Characteristics of the data set include the typical or most frequent GMAT score, the variability in the scores, the highest and lowest scores, the "shape" of the data, and whether or not the data set contains any unusual scores. Extracting this information by "eye" isn't easy. The 400 scores may provide too many bits of information for our minds to comprehend. Clearly we need some formal methods for summarizing and characterizing the information in such a data set. Methods for describing data sets are also essential for statistical inference. Most populations are large data sets. Consequently, we need methods for describing a sample data set that let us make descriptive statements (inferences) about the population from which the sample was drawn.

Two methods for describing data are presented in this chapter, one **graphical** and the other **numerical**. Both play an important role in statistics. Section 2.1 presents both graphical and numerical methods for describing qualitative data. Graphical methods for describing quantitative data are presented in Section 2.2 and optional Sections 2.3, 2.9, and 2.10; numerical descriptive methods for quantitative data are presented in Sections 2.4–2.8. We end this chapter with a section on the *misuse* of descriptive techniques.

2.1 DESCRIBING QUALITATIVE DATA

Recall the "Executive Compensation Scoreboard" tabulated annually by *Business Week* (see Study 2 in Section 1.2). *Forbes* magazine also conducts a salary survey of chief executive officers each year. In addition to salary information, *Forbes* collects and reports personal data on the CEOs, including level of education. Do most CEOs have advanced degrees, such as masters degrees or doctorates? To answer this question, Table 2.1 gives the highest college degree obtained (bachelors, masters, doctorate, or none) for each of the 25 best-paid CEOs over the 5-year period 1990–1994.

For this study, the variable of interest, highest college degree obtained, is qualitative in nature. Qualitative data are nonnumerical in nature; thus, the value of a qualitative variable can only be classified into categories called *classes*. The possible degree types—bachelors, masters, doctorate, and none—represent the classes for this qualitative variable. We can summarize such data numerically in two ways: (1) by computing the *class frequency*—the number of observations in the data set that fall into each class; or (2) by computing the *class relative frequency*—the proportion of the total number of observations falling into each class.

DEFINITION 2.1
A **class** is one of the categories into which qualitative data can be classified.

DEFINITION 2.2
The **class frequency** is the number of observations in the data set falling into a particular class.

DEFINITION 2.3
The **class relative frequency** is the class frequency divided by the total number of observations in the data set.

TABLE 2.1   Data on 25 Best-Paid Executives

CEO	Company	Highest College Degree Obtained
1. M. Eisner	Walt Disney	Bachelors
2. S. Weill	Travelers	Bachelors
3. A. O'Reilly	HJ Heintz	Doctorate
4. S. Hilbert	Consecto	None
5. B. Schwartz	Loral	Bachelors
6. H. Solomon	Forest Labs	Doctorate
7. L. Coss	Green Tree Financial	None
8. R. Goizueta	Coca-Cola	Bachelors
9. W. Sanders	Advanced Micro	Bachelors
10. S. Wynn	Mirage	Bachelors
11. J. Mellor	General Dynamics	Masters
12. R. Roberts	Comcast	Bachelors
13. P. Thomas	First Financial Mgmt.	Masters
14. R. Mark	Colgate-Palmolive	Masters
15. R. Manoogian	Masco	Bachelors
16. R. Richey	Torchmark	Doctorate
17. J. Donald	DSC Communications	Masters
18. J. Welch	General Electric	Doctorate
19. J. Hyde	Auto Zone	Bachelors
20. S. Walske	Parametric Tech	Masters
21. K. Lay	Enron	Doctorate
22. R. Araskog	ITT	Bachelors
23. D. Fuente	Office Depot	Masters
24. D. Tully	Merrill Lynch	Bachelors
25. C. Sanford	Bankers Trust NY	Masters

Source: Forbes, Vol. 155, No. 11, May 22, 1995.

Examining Table 2.1, we observe that 2 of the 25 best-paid CEOs did not obtain a college degree, 11 obtained bachelors degrees, 7 masters degrees, and 5 doctorates. These numbers—2, 11, 7, and 5—represent the class frequencies for the four classes and are shown in the summary table, Table 2.2.

Table 2.2 also gives the relative frequency of each of the four degree classes. From Definition 2.3, we know that we calculate the relative frequency by dividing the class frequency by the total number of observations in the data set. Thus, the relative frequencies for the four degree types are

$$\text{None:} \quad \frac{2}{25} = .08$$

$$\text{Bachelors:} \quad \frac{11}{25} = .44$$

TABLE 2.2   Summary Table for Data on 25 Best-Paid CEOs

CLASS	FREQUENCY	RELATIVE FREQUENCY
Highest Degree Obtained	Number of CEOs	Proportion
None	2	.08
Bachelors	11	.44
Masters	7	.28
Doctorate	5	.20
Totals	25	1.000

FIGURE 2.1
Bar graph for data on 25 CEOs

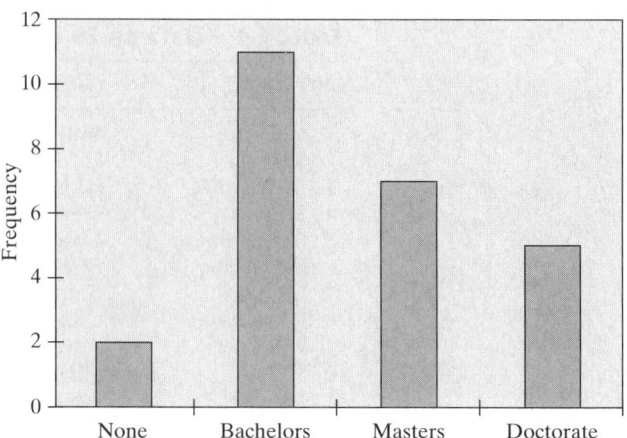

$$\text{Masters:} \quad \frac{7}{25} = .28$$

$$\text{Doctorate:} \quad \frac{5}{25} = .20$$

From these relative frequencies we observe that nearly half (44%) of the 25 best-paid CEOs obtained only their bachelors degree.

Although the summary table of Table 2.2 adequately describes the data of Table 2.1, we often want a graphical presentation as well. Figures 2.1 and 2.2 show two of the most widely used graphical methods for describing qualitative data— **bar graphs** and **pie charts**. Figure 2.1 shows the frequencies of "highest degree obtained" in a *bar graph* created using the EXCEL software package. Note that the height of the rectangle, or "bar," over each class is equal to the class frequency. (Optionally, the bar heights can be proportional to class relative frequencies.) In contrast, Figure 2.2 (also created using EXCEL) shows the relative frequencies of the four degree types in a *pie chart*. Note that the pie is a circle (spanning 360°) and the size (angle) of the "pie slice" assigned to each class is proportional to the class relative frequency. For example, the slice assigned to bachelors degree is 44% of 360°, or (.44)(360°) = 158.4°.

Let's look at a practical example that requires interpretation of the graphical results.

FIGURE 2.2
Pie chart for data on 25 CEOs

EXAMPLE 2.1

A group of cardiac physicians in southwest Florida have been studying a new drug designed to reduce blood loss in coronary artery bypass operations. Blood loss data for 114 coronary artery bypass patients (some who received a dosage of the drug and others who did not) were collected and are made available for analysis.* Although the drug shows promise in reducing blood loss, the physicians are concerned about possible side effects and complications. So their data set includes not only the qualitative variable, DRUG, which indicates whether or not the patient received the drug, but also the qualitative variable, COMP, which specifies the type (if any) of complication experienced by the patient. The four values of COMP recorded by the physicians are: (1) redo surgery, (2) post-op infection, (3) both, or (4) none.

    a. Figure 2.3, generated using SAS computer software, shows summary tables for the two qualitative variables, DRUG and COMP. Interpret the results.

    b. Interpret the SAS graph and summary tables shown in Figure 2.4.

SOLUTION

    a. The top table in Figure 2.3 is a summary frequency table for DRUG. Note that exactly half (57) of the 114 coronary artery bypass patients received the drug and half did not. The bottom table in Figure 2.3 is a summary frequency table for COMP. The class relative frequencies are given in the **Percent** column. We see that 75.5% of the 114 patients had no complications, leaving 24.5% who experienced either a redo surgery, a post-op infection, or both.

    b. At the top of Figure 2.4 is a side-by-side bar graph for the data. The first four bars represent the frequencies of COMP for the 57 patients who did not receive the drug; the next four bars represent the frequencies of COMP for the 57 patients who did receive a dosage of the drug. The graph clearly shows that patients who got the drug suffered more complications. The exact percentages are displayed in the summary tables of Figure 2.4. About 30% of the patients who got the drug had complications, compared to about 17% for the patients who got no drug.

    Although these results show that the drug may be effective in reducing blood loss, they also imply that patients on the drug may have a higher risk

FIGURE 2.3
SAS summary tables for DRUG and COMP

DRUG	Frequency	Percent	Cumulative Frequency	Cumulative Percent
NO	57	50.0	57	50.0
YES	57	50.0	114	100.0

COMP	Frequency	Percent	Cumulative Frequency	Cumulative Percent
1:REDO	12	10.5	12	10.5
2:INFECT	12	10.5	24	21.0
3:BOTH	4	3.5	28	24.5
4:NONE	86	75.5	114	100.0

*The data for this study are real. For confidentiality reasons, the drug name and physician group are omitted.

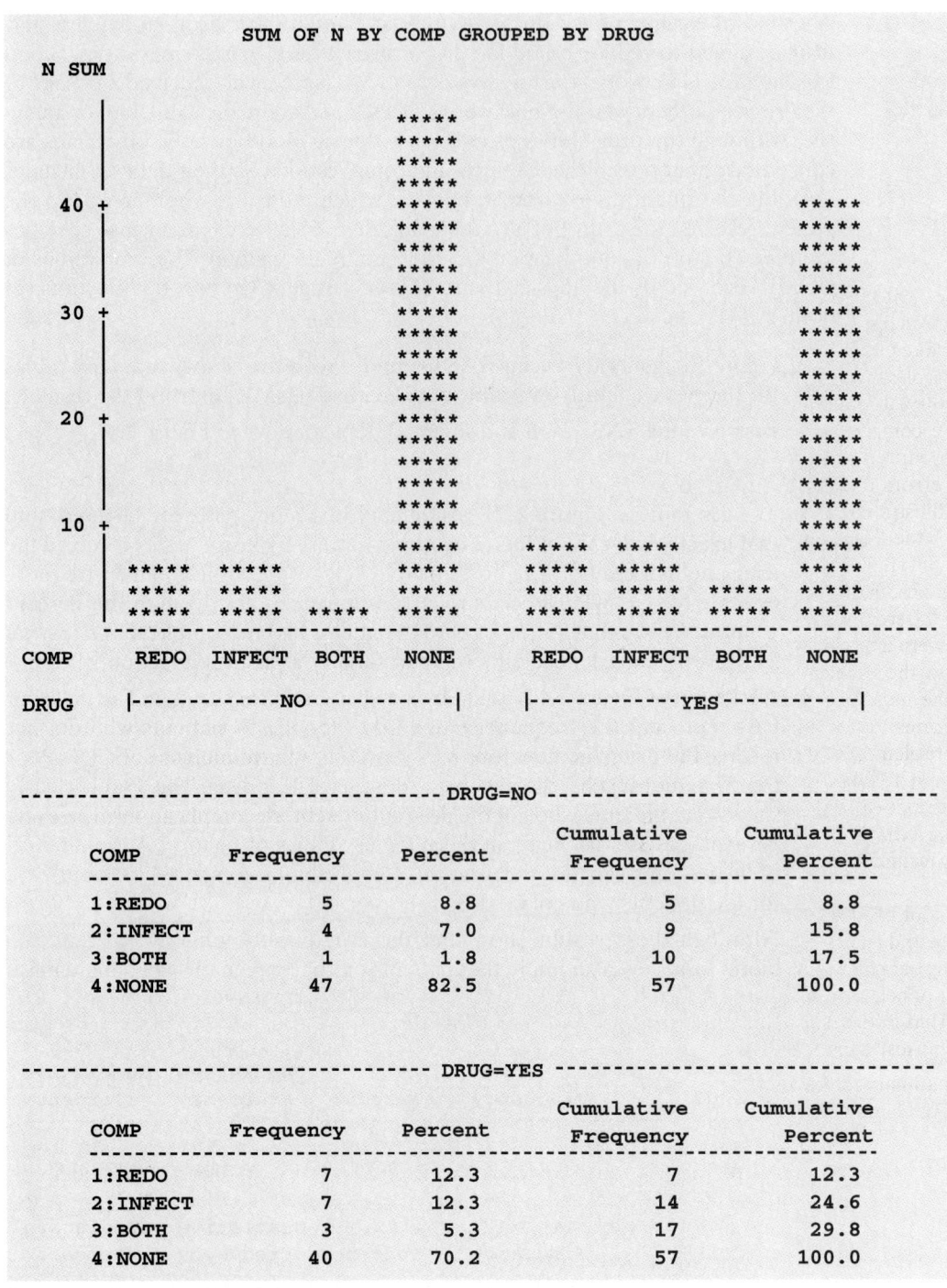

SUM OF N BY COMP GROUPED BY DRUG

---------------------------------- DRUG=NO ----------------------------------

COMP	Frequency	Percent	Cumulative Frequency	Cumulative Percent
1:REDO	5	8.8	5	8.8
2:INFECT	4	7.0	9	15.8
3:BOTH	1	1.8	10	17.5
4:NONE	47	82.5	57	100.0

---------------------------------- DRUG=YES ----------------------------------

COMP	Frequency	Percent	Cumulative Frequency	Cumulative Percent
1:REDO	7	12.3	7	12.3
2:INFECT	7	12.3	14	24.6
3:BOTH	3	5.3	17	29.8
4:NONE	40	70.2	57	100.0

FIGURE 2.4 SAS bar graph and summary tables for COMP by DRUG

STATISTICS IN ACTION

2.1 PARETO ANALYSIS

Vilfredo Pareto (1843–1923), an Italian economist, discovered that approximately 80% of the wealth of a country lies with approximately 20% of the people. V. E. Kane, in his book *Defect Prevention* (New York: Marcel Dekker, 1989), noted similar findings in other areas: 80% of sales are attributable to 20% of the customers; 80% of customer complaints result from 20% of the components of a product; 80% of defective items produced by a process result from 20% of the types of errors that are made in production. These examples illustrate the idea of "the vital few and the trivial many," the **Pareto principle**. As applied to the last example, a "vital few" errors account for most of the defectives produced. The remaining defectives are due to many different errors, the "trivial many."

In general, **Pareto analysis** involves the categorization of items and the determination of which categories contain the most observations. These are the "vital few" categories. Pareto analysis is used in industry today as a problem-identification tool. Managers and workers use it to identify the most important problems or causes of problems that plague them. Knowledge of the "vital few" problems permits management to set priorities and focus their problem-solving efforts.

The primary tool of Pareto analysis is the **Pareto diagram**. The Pareto diagram is simply a frequency or relative frequency bar chart, with the bars arranged in descending order of height from left to right across the horizontal axis. That is, the tallest bar is positioned at the left and the shortest is at the far right. This arrangement locates the most important categories—those with the largest frequencies—at the left of the chart. Since the data are qualitative, there is no inherent numerical order: They can be rearranged to make the display more useful.

Focus

a. Consider the following example from the automobile industry (adapted from Kane, 1989). All cars produced on a particular day were inspected for defects. The defects were categorized by type as follows: body, accessories, electrical, transmission, and engine. The resulting Pareto diagram for these qualitative data is shown in Figure 2.5(a) on page 32. Use the diagram to identify the most frequently observed type of defect.

b. Sufficient data were collected when the cars were inspected to take the Pareto analysis one step further. All 70 body defects were further classified as to whether they were paint defects, dents, upholstery defects, windshield defects, or chrome defects. All 50 accessory defects were further classified as to whether they were defects in the air conditioning (A/C) system, the radio, the power steering, the cruise control, or the windshield (W/S) wipers. Two more Pareto diagrams were constructed from these data. They are shown in panels (b) and (c) of Figure 2.5. This decomposition of the original Pareto diagram is called **exploding the Pareto diagram**. Interpret the exploded diagrams. What types of defects should be targeted for special attention by managers, engineers, and assembly-line workers?

of complications. But before using this information to make a decision about the drug, the physicians will need to provide a measure of reliability for the inference. That is, the physicians will want to know whether the difference between the percentages of patients with complications observed in this sample of 114 patients is generalizable to the population of all coronary artery bypass patients. Measures of reliability will be discussed in Chapters 7–9.

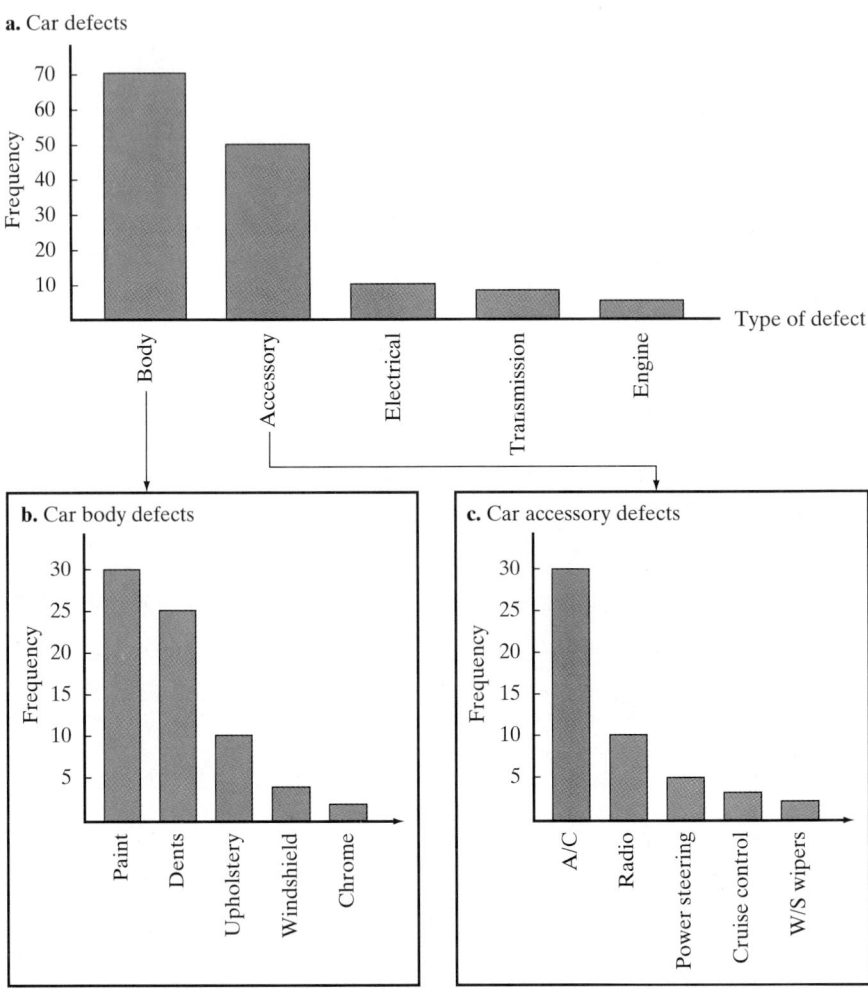

FIGURE 2.5
Pareto diagrams (Statistics in Action 2.1)

a. Car defects

b. Car body defects

c. Car accessory defects

EXERCISES 2.1–2.11

Note: Exercises marked with 💾 contain data available for computer analysis on a 3.5" disk (file name in parentheses).

Learning the Mechanics

2.1 Complete the following table.

Grade on Business Statistics Exam	Frequency	Relative Frequency
A: 90–100		.08
B: 80–89	36	
C: 65–79	90	
D: 50–64	30	
F: Below 50	28	
Total	200	1.00

2.2 A qualitative variable with three classes (X, Y, and Z) is measured for each of 20 units randomly sampled from a target population. The data (observed class for each unit) are listed below.

Y X X Z X Y Y Y X X Z X
Y Y X Z Y Y Y X

a. Compute the frequency for each of the three classes.
b. Compute the relative frequency for each of the three classes.
c. Display the results, part **a**, in a frequency bar graph.
d. Display the results, part **b**, in a pie chart.

Applying the Concepts

2.3 Disgruntled shareholders who put pressure on corporate management to make certain financial decisions are referred to as shareholder activists. In Exercise 1.22 we described a survey of 240 large investors designed to determine how widespread shareholder activism actually is. One of several questions asked was: If the chief executive officer and the board of directors differed on company strategy, what action would you, as a large investor of the firm, take? (*New York Times,* Oct. 31, 1995) The responses are summarized in the table.

Response	Number of Investors
Seek formal explanation	154
Seek CEO performance review	49
Dismiss CEO	20
Seek no action	17
Total	240

a. Construct a relative frequency table for the data.

b. Display the relative frequencies in a graph.

c. Discuss the findings.

2.4 According to Topaz Enterprises, a Portland, Oregon-based airfare accounting firm, "more than 80% of all tickets purchased for domestic flights are discounted" (*Travel Weekly,* May 15, 1995). The results of the accounting firm's survey of domestic airline tickets are summarized in the accompanying table.

Domestic Airline Ticket Type	Proportion
Full coach	.005
Discounted coach	.206
Negotiated coach	.425
First class	.009
Business class	.002
Business class negotiated	.001
Advance purchase	.029
Capacity controlled discount	.209
Nonrefundable	.114
Total	1.000

a. Give your opinion on whether the data described in the table are from a population or a sample. Explain your reasoning.

b. Display the data with a bar graph. Arrange the bars in order of height to form a Pareto diagram. Interpret the resulting graph.

c. Do the data support the conclusion reached by Topaz Enterprises regarding the percentage of tickets purchased that are discounted?

[*Note:* Advance purchase and negotiated tickets are considered discounted.]

2.5 "Reader-response cards" are used by marketers to advertise their product and obtain sales leads. These cards are placed in magazines and trade publications. Readers detach and mail in the cards to indicate their interest in the product, expecting literature or a phone call in return. How effective are these cards (called "bingo cards" in

the industry) as a marketing tool? Performark, a Minneapolis business that helps companies close on sales leads, attempted to answer this question by responding to 17,000 card-advertisements placed by industrial marketers in a wide variety of trade publications over a 6-year period. Performark kept track of how long it took for each advertiser to respond. A summary of the response times, reported in *Inc.* magazine (July 1995), is given in the table.

Advertiser's Response Time	Percentage
Never responded	21
13–59 days	33
60–120 days	34
More than 120 days	12
Total	100

a. Describe the variable measured by Performark.

b. *Inc.* displayed the results in the form of a pie chart. Reconstruct the pie chart from the information given in the table.

c. How many of the 17,000 advertisers never responded to the sales lead?

d. Advertisers typically spend at least a million dollars on a reader-response card marketing campaign. Many industrial marketers feel these "bingo cards" are not worth their expense. Does the information in the pie chart, part **b**, support this contention? Explain why or why not. If not, what information can be gleaned from the pie chart to help potential "bingo card" campaigns?

2.6 *Choice* magazine, a publication for the academic community, provides new-book reviews in each issue. Many librarians rely on these reviews to determine which new books to purchase for their library. A thorough study of the contents of the book reviews published in *Choice* was conducted (*Library Acquisitions: Practice and Theory,* Vol. 19, 1995). A random sample of 375 book reviews in American history, geography, and area studies was selected and the "overall opinion" of the book stated in each review was ascertained. Overall opinion was coded as follows: 1 = would not recommend, 2 = cautious or very little recommendation, 3 = little or no preference, 4 = favorable/recommended, 5 = outstanding/significant contribution. A summary of the data is provided in the bar graph on page 34.

a. Interpret the bar graph.

b. Comment on the following statement extracted from the study: "A majority (more than 75%) of books reviewed are evaluated favorably and recommended for purchase."

Source: Reprinted from *Library Acquisitions: Practice and Theory*, Vol. 19, No. 2, P. W. Carlo and A. Natowitx, "Choice Book Reviews in American History, Geography, and Area Studies: An Analysis for 1988–1993," p. 159. Copyright 1995, with kind permission from Elsevier Science Ltd, The Boulevard, Langford Lane, Kidlington OX5 1GB, UK.

2.7 The Internet and its World Wide Web provide computer users with a medium for both communication and entertainment. However, many businesses are recognizing the potential of using the Internet for advertising and selling their products. *Inc. Technology* (Sept. 12, 1995) conducted a survey of 2,016 small businesses (fewer than 100 employees) regarding their weekly Internet usage. The survey found 1,855 small businesses that do not use the Internet, 121 that use the Internet from one to five hours per week, and 40 that use the Internet six or more hours per week.
 a. Identify the variable measured in the survey.
 b. Summarize the survey results with a graph.
 c. What portion of the 2,016 small businesses use the Internet on a weekly basis?

2.8 Each week, *USA Today* reports on how much consumers like a major advertising campaign and how effective they think the ad is in helping the company sell its product. The topic of an August 1995 report was the "Obey your thirst" ad campaign for Sprite, a lemon-lime soft drink manufactured by Coca-Cola. A *USA Today*/Harris poll of 1,005 adults, selected nationwide, were asked, "Do you like the campaign?" and "How effective is the campaign?" The results are shown in the graphs below.

a. What type of graphical method is used to describe the data?
b. Interpret the results for the question: "Do you like the campaign?"
c. Interpret the results for the question: "How effective is the campaign?"

2.9 Transgenic plants are plants that have been genetically modified using current gene technology. For example, biologists have recently developed a transgenic tomato with improved storage properties. The *Journal of Experimental Botany* (May 1995) reported on the current level of experimentation with genetically modified plants. Each experiment was identified by its trait. The accompanying bar graph describes the number of approved trials of transgenic plants worldwide, by trait, from 1990–1992.
 a. Estimate the number of transgenic plant trials approved for herbicide tolerance over this period.
 b. Estimate the number of transgenic plant trials approved for developing virus-resistant crops over this period.
 c. Modify the bar graph to show relative frequencies rather than frequencies.

2.10 **(X02.010)** Owing to several major ocean oil spills by tank vessels, Congress passed the 1990 Oil Pollution Act, which requires all tankers to be designed with thicker hulls. Further improvements

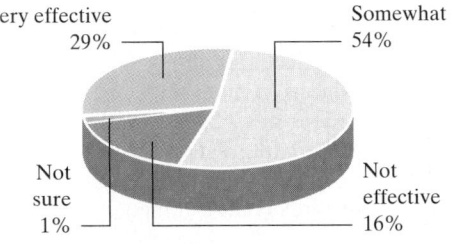

in the structural design of a tank vessel have been implemented since then, each with the objective of reducing the likelihood of an oil spill and decreasing the amount of outflow in the event of hull puncture. To aid in this development, J. C. Daidola reported on the spillage amount and cause of puncture for 50 recent major oil spills from tankers and carriers. The data are reproduced on page 36 (*Marine Technology,* Jan. 1995).

  a. Use a graphical method to describe the cause of oil spillage for the 50 tankers.

  b. Does the graph, part **a**, suggest that any one cause is more likely to occur than any other? How is this information of value to the design engineers?

2.11 Since opening its doors to Western investors in 1979, the People's Republic of China has been steadily moving toward a market economy. However, because of the considerable political and economic uncertainties in China, Western investors remain uneasy about their investments in China. In 1995 an agency of the Chinese government surveyed 402 foreign investors to assess their concerns with the investment environment.

Each was asked to indicate their most serious concern. The results appear below.

Investor's Concern	Frequency
Communication infrastructure	8
Environmental protection	13
Financial services	14
Government efficiency	30
Inflation rate	233
Labor supply	11
Personal safety	2
Real estate prices	82
Security of personal property	4
Water supply	5

Source: Adapted from *China Marketing News,* No. 26, November 1995.

  a. Construct a Pareto diagram for the 10 categories.

  b. According to your Pareto diagram, which environmental factors most concern investors?

  c. In this case, are 80% of the investors concerned with 20% of the environmental factors as the Pareto principle would suggest? Justify your answer.

2.2 GRAPHICAL METHODS FOR DESCRIBING QUANTITATIVE DATA

Recall from Section 1.5 that quantitative data sets consist of data that are recorded on a meaningful numerical scale. For describing, summarizing, and detecting patterns in such data, we can use three graphical methods: dot plots, stem-and-leaf displays, and histograms.

For example, suppose a financial analyst is interested in the amount of resources spent by computer hardware and software companies on research and development (R&D). She samples 50 of these high-technology firms and calculates the amount each spent last year on R&D as a percentage of their total revenues. The results are given in Table 2.3. As numerical measurements made on the

TABLE 2.3   Percentage of Revenues Spent on Research and Development

Company	Percentage	Company	Percentage	Company	Percentage	Company	Percentage
1	13.5	14	9.5	27	8.2	39	6.5
2	8.4	15	8.1	28	6.9	40	7.5
3	10.5	16	13.5	29	7.2	41	7.1
4	9.0	17	9.9	30	8.2	42	13.2
5	9.2	18	6.9	31	9.6	43	7.7
6	9.7	19	7.5	32	7.2	44	5.9
7	6.6	20	11.1	33	8.8	45	5.2
8	10.6	21	8.2	34	11.3	46	5.6
9	10.1	22	8.0	35	8.5	47	11.7
10	7.1	23	7.7	36	9.4	48	6.0
11	8.0	24	7.4	37	10.5	49	7.8
12	7.9	25	6.5	38	6.9	50	6.5
13	6.8	26	9.5				

		CAUSE OF SPILLAGE				
Tanker	Spillage (metric tons, thousands)	Collision	Grounding	Fire/ Explosion	Hull Failure	Unknown
Atlantic Empress	257	X				
Castillo De Bellver	239			X		
Amoco Cadiz	221				X	
Odyssey	132			X		
Torrey Canyon	124		X			
Sea Star	123	X				
Hawaiian Patriot	101				X	
Independento	95	X				
Urquiola	91		X			
Irenes Serenade	82			X		
Khark 5	76			X		
Nova	68	X				
Wafra	62		X			
Epic Colocotronis	58		X			
Sinclair Petrolore	57			X		
Yuyo Maru No 10	42	X				
Assimi	50			X		
Andros Patria	48			X		
World Glory	46				X	
British Ambassador	46				X	
Metula	45		X			
Pericles G.C.	44			X		
Mandoil II	41	X				
Jacob Maersk	41		X			
Burmah Agate	41	X				
J. Antonio Lavalleja	38		X			
Napier	37		X			
Exxon Valdez	36		X			
Corinthos	36	X				
Trader	36				X	
St. Peter	33			X		
Gino	32	X				
Golden Drake	32			X		
Ionnis Angelicoussis	32			X		
Chryssi	32				X	
Irenes Challenge	31				X	
Argo Merchant	28		X			
Heimvard	31	X				
Pegasus	25					X
Pacocean	31				X	
Texaco Oklahoma	29				X	
Scorpio	31		X			
Ellen Conway	31		X			
Caribbean Sea	30				X	
Cretan Star	27					X
Grand Zenith	26				X	
Athenian Venture	26			X		
Venoil	26	X				
Aragon	24				X	
Ocean Eagle	21		X			

Source: Daidola, J. C. "Tanker structure behavior during collision and grounding." *Marine Technology,* Vol. 32, No. 1, Jan. 1995, p. 22 (Table 1). Reprinted with permission of The Society of Naval Architects and Marine Engineers (SNAME), 601 Pavonia Ave., Jersey City, NJ 07306, USA, (201) 798-4800. Material appearing in The Society of Naval Architect and Marine Engineers (SNAME) publications cannot be reprinted without obtaining written permission.

FIGURE 2.6   A MINITAB dot plot for the 50 R&D percentages

sample of 50 units (the firms), these percentages represent quantitative data. The analyst's initial objective is to summarize and describe these data in order to extract relevant information.

A visual inspection of the data indicates some obvious facts. For example, the smallest R&D percentage is 5.2% and the largest is 13.5%. But it is difficult to provide much additional information on the 50 R&D percentages without resorting to some method of summarizing the data. One such method is a dot plot.

Dot Plots

A computer generated (MINITAB) **dot plot** for the 50 R&D percentages is shown in Figure 2.6. The horizontal axis of Figure 2.6 is a scale for the quantitative variable, percent. The numerical value of each measurement in the data set is located on the horizontal scale by a dot. When data values repeat, the dots are placed above one another, forming a pile at that particular numerical location. As you can see, this dot plot shows that almost all of the R&D percentages are between 6% and 12%, with most falling between 7% and 9%.

Stem-and-Leaf Display

Another graphical representation of these same data, a **stem-and-leaf display**, is shown in Figure 2.7. In this display the *stem* is the portion of the measurement (percentage) to the left of the decimal point, while the remaining portion to the right of the decimal point is the *leaf*.

The stems for the data set are listed in a column from the smallest (5) to the largest (13). Then the leaf for each observation is recorded in the row of the display corresponding to the observation's stem. For example, the leaf 5 of the first observation (13.5) in Table 2.3 is written in the row corresponding to the stem 13. Similarly, the leaf 4 for the second observation (8.4) in Table 2.3 is recorded in the row corresponding to the stem 8, while the leaf 5 for the third observation (10.5) is recorded in the row corresponding to the stem 10. (The leaves for these first

FIGURE 2.7
A stem-and-leaf display for the 50 R&D percentages

Stem	Leaf
5	2 6 9
6	0 5 5 5 6 8 9 9 9
7	1 1 2 2 4 5 5 7 7 8 9
8	0 0 1 2 2 2 4 5 8
9	0 2 4 5 5 6 7 9
10	1 5 5 6
11	1 3 7
12	
13	2 5 5

Key: Leaf units are tenths.

three observations are shaded in Figure 2.7.) Typically, the leaves in each row are ordered as shown in Figure 2.7.

The stem-and-leaf display presents another compact picture of the data set. You can see at a glance that most of the sampled computer companies (37 of 50) spent between 6.0% and 9.9% of their revenues on R&D, and 11 of them spent between 7.0% and 7.9%. Relative to the rest of the sampled companies, three spent a high percentage of revenues on R&D—in excess of 13%.

The definitions of the stem and leaf for a data set can be modified to alter the graphical description. For example, suppose we had defined the stem as the tens digit for the R&D percentage data, rather than the ones and tens digits. With this definition, the stems and leaves corresponding to the measurements 13.5 and 8.4 would be as follows:

Stem	Leaf		Stem	Leaf
1	3		0	8

Note that the decimal portion of the numbers has been dropped. Generally, only one digit is displayed in the leaf.

If you look at the data, you'll see why we didn't define the stem this way. All the R&D measurements fall below 13.5, so all the leaves would fall into just two stem rows—1 and 0—in this display. The resulting picture would not be nearly as informative as Figure 2.7.

HISTOGRAMS

A **relative frequency histogram** for these 50 R&D percentages is shown in Figure 2.8. The horizontal axis of Figure 2.8, which gives the percentage spent on R&D for each company, is divided into **intervals** commencing with the interval from (5.15–6.25) and proceeding in intervals of equal size to (12.85–13.95) percent. (The procedure for creating the class intervals will become clear in Example 2.2.) The vertical axis gives the proportion (or **relative frequency**) of the 50 percentages that fall in each interval. Thus, you can see that nearly a third of the companies spent between 7.35% and 8.45% of their revenues on research and development. This interval contains the highest relative frequency, and the intervals tend to contain a smaller fraction of the measurements as R&D percentage gets smaller or larger.

By summing the relative frequencies in the intervals 6.25–7.35, 7.35–8.45, 8.45–9.55, 9.55–10.65, you can see that 80% of the R&D percentages are between 6.25 and 10.65. Similarly, only 6% of the computer companies spent over 12.85

FIGURE 2.8

Histogram for the 50 computer companies' R&D percentages

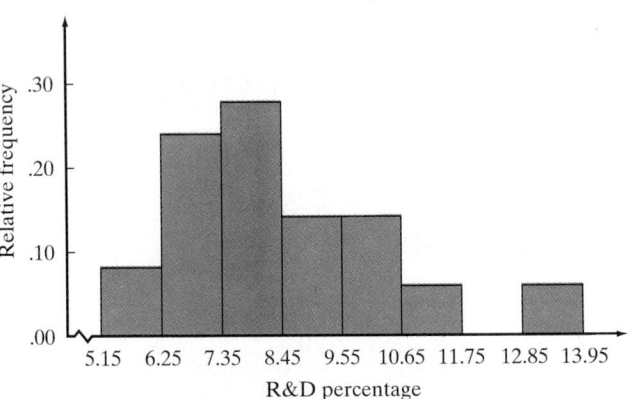

TABLE 2.4 Measurement Classes, Frequencies, and Relative Frequencies for the R&D Percentage Data

Class	Measurement Class	Class Frequency	Class Relative Frequency
1	5.15–6.25	4	$4/50 = .08$
2	6.25–7.35	12	$12/50 = .24$
3	7.35–8.45	14	$14/50 = .28$
4	8.45–9.55	7	$7/50 = .14$
5	9.55–10.65	7	$7/50 = .14$
6	10.65–11.75	3	$3/50 = .06$
7	11.75–12.85	0	$0/50 = .00$
8	12.85–13.95	3	$3/50 = .06$
Totals		50	1.00

percent of their revenues on R&D. Many other summary statements can be made by further study of the histogram.

Dot plots, stem-and-leaf displays, and histograms all provide useful graphic descriptions of quantitative data. Since most statistical software packages can be used to construct these displays, we will focus on their interpretation rather than their construction.

Histograms can be used to display either the frequency or relative frequency of the measurements falling into specified intervals known as **measurement classes**. The measurement classes, frequencies, and relative frequencies for the R&D percentage data are shown in Table 2.4.

By looking at a histogram (say, the relative frequency histogram in Figure 2.8), you can see two important facts. First, note the total area under the histogram and then note the proportion of the total area that falls over a particular interval of the horizontal axis. You'll see that the proportion of the total area above an interval is equal to the relative frequency of measurements falling in the interval. For example, the relative frequency for the class interval 7.35–8.45 is .28. Consequently, the rectangle above the interval contains .28 of the total area under the histogram.

Second, you can imagine the appearance of the relative frequency histogram for a very large set of data (say, a population). As the number of measurements in a data set is increased, you can obtain a better description of the data by decreasing the width of the class intervals. When the class intervals become small enough, a relative frequency histogram will (for all practical purposes) appear as a smooth curve (see Figure 2.9).

While histograms provide good visual descriptions of data sets—particularly very large data ones—they do not let us identify individual measurements. In contrast, each of the original measurements is visible to some extent in a dot plot and clearly visible in a stem-and-leaf display. The stem-and-leaf display arranges

FIGURE 2.9
Effect of the size of a data set on the outline of a histogram

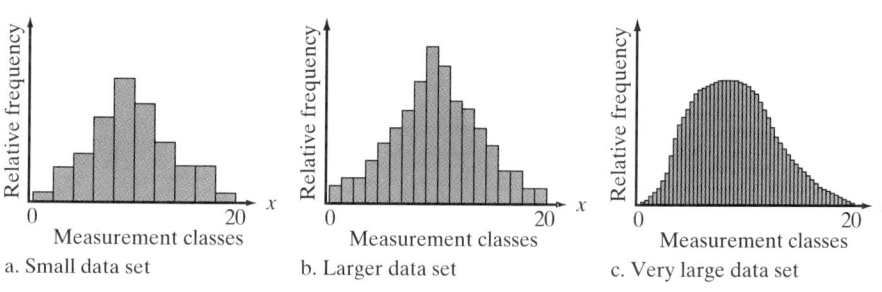

a. Small data set   b. Larger data set   c. Very large data set the data in ascending order, so it's easy to locate the individual measurements. For example, in Figure 2.7 we can easily see that three of the R&D measurements are equal to 8.2, but we can't see that fact by inspecting the histogram in Figure 2.8. However, stem-and-leaf displays can become unwieldy for very large data sets. A very large number of stems and leaves causes the vertical and horizontal dimensions of the display to become cumbersome, diminishing the usefulness of the visual display.

EXAMPLE 2.2

A manufacturer of industrial wheels suspects that profitable orders are being lost because of the long time the firm takes to develop price quotes for potential customers. To investigate this possibility, 50 requests for price quotes were randomly selected from the set of all quotes made last year, and the processing time was determined for each quote. The processing times are displayed in Table 2.5, and each quote was classified according to whether the order was "lost" or not (i.e., whether or not the customer placed an order after receiving a price quote).

a. Use a statistical software package to create a frequency histogram for these data. Then shade the area under the histogram that corresponds to lost orders.

b. Use a statistical software package to create a stem-and-leaf display for these data. Then shade each leaf of the display that corresponds to a lost order.

c. Compare and interpret the two graphical displays of these data.

SOLUTION

a. We used SAS to generate the frequency histogram in Figure 2.10. SAS, like most statistical software, offers the user the choice of accepting default class

TABLE 2.5 Price Quote Processing Time (Days)

Request Number	Processing Time	Lost?	Request Number	Processing Time	Lost?
1	2.36	No	26	3.34	No
2	5.73	No	27	6.00	No
3	6.60	No	28	5.92	No
4	10.05	Yes	29	7.28	Yes
5	5.13	No	30	1.25	No
6	1.88	No	31	4.01	No
7	2.52	No	32	7.59	No
8	2.00	No	33	13.42	Yes
9	4.69	No	34	3.24	No
10	1.91	No	35	3.37	No
11	6.75	Yes	36	14.06	Yes
12	3.92	No	37	5.10	No
13	3.46	No	38	6.44	No
14	2.64	No	39	7.76	No
15	3.63	No	40	4.40	No
16	3.44	No	41	5.48	No
17	9.49	Yes	42	7.51	No
18	4.90	No	43	6.18	No
19	7.45	No	44	8.22	Yes
20	20.23	Yes	45	4.37	No
21	3.91	No	46	2.93	No
22	1.70	No	47	9.95	Yes
23	16.29	Yes	48	4.46	No
24	5.52	No	49	14.32	Yes
25	1.44	No	50	9.01	No

FIGURE 2.10
SAS frequency histogram for the quote processing time data

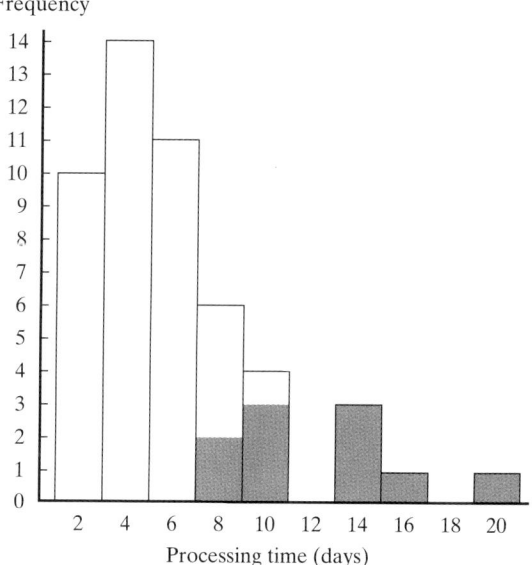

intervals and interval widths, or the user can make his or her own selections. After some experimenting with various numbers of class intervals and interval widths, we used 10 intervals. SAS then created intervals of width 2 days, beginning at 1 day, just below the smallest measurement of 1.25 days, and ending with 21 days, just above the largest measurement of 20.2 days. Note that SAS labels the midpoint of each bar, rather than its endpoints. Thus, the bar labeled "2" represents measurements from 1.00 to 2.99, the bar labeled "4" represents measurements from 3.00 to 4.99, etc. This histogram clearly shows the clustering of the measurements in the lower end of the distribution (between approximately 1 and 7 days), and the relatively few measurements in the upper end of the distribution (greater than 12 days). The shading of the area of the frequency histogram corresponding to lost orders clearly indicates that they lie in the upper tail of the distribution.

b. We used SPSS to generate the stem-and-leaf display in Figure 2.11. Note that the stem consists of the number of whole days (units and tens digits),

FIGURE 2.11
SPSS stem-and-leaf display for the quote processing time data

```
Frequency        Stem & Leaf
    5.00             1 .  24789
    5.00             2 .  03569
    8.00             3 .  23344699
    6.00             4 .  034469
    6.00             5 .  114579
    5.00             6 .  01467
    5.00             7 .  24557
    1.00             8 .  2
    3.00             9 .  049
    1.00            10 .  0
     .00            11 .
     .00            12 .
    1.00            13 .  4
    4.00  Extremes      (14.1), (14.3), (16.3), (20.2)
Stem width:      1.00
Each leaf:          1 case(s)
```

and the leaf is the tenths digit (first digit after the decimal) of each measurement.* The hundredths digit has been dropped to make the display more visually effective. SPSS also includes a column titled **Frequency** showing the number of measurements corresponding to each stem. Note, too, that instead of extending the stems all the way to 20 days to show the largest measurement, SPSS truncates the display after the stem corresponding to 13 days, labels the largest four measurements (shaded) as **Extremes**, and simply lists them horizontally in the last row of the display. Extreme observations that are detached from the remainder of the data are called **outliers**, and they usually receive special attention in statistical analyses. Although outliers may represent legitimate measurements, they are frequently mistakes: incorrectly recorded, miscoded during data entry, or taken from a population different from the one from which the rest of the sample was selected. Stem-and-leaf displays are useful for identifying outliers.

c. As is usually the case for data sets that are not too large (say, fewer than 100 measurements), the stem-and-leaf display provides more detail than the histogram without being unwieldy. For instance, the stem-and-leaf display in Figure 2.11 clearly indicates not only that the lost orders are associated with high processing times (as does the histogram in Figure 2.10), but also exactly which of the times correspond to lost orders. Histograms are most useful for displaying very large data sets, when the overall shape of the distribution of measurements is more important than the identification of individual measurements. Nevertheless, the message of both graphical displays is clear: establishing processing time limits may well result in fewer lost orders. ▙

*In the examples in this section, the stem was formed from the digits to the left of the decimal. This is not always the case. For example, in the following data set the stems could be the tenths digit and the leaves the hundredths digit: .12, .15, .22, .25, .28, .33.

EXERCISES **2.12–2.25**

Note: Exercises marked with 💾 contain data available for computer analysis on a 3.5" disk (file name in parentheses).

Learning the Mechanics

2.12 Graph the relative frequency histogram for the 500 measurements summarized in the accompanying relative frequency table.

Measurement Class	Relative Frequency
.5–2.5	.10
2.5–4.5	.15
4.5–6.5	.25
6.5–8.5	.20
8.5–10.5	.05
10.5–12.5	.10
12.5–14.5	.10
14.5–16.5	.05

2.13 Refer to Exercise 2.12. Calculate the number of the 500 measurements falling into each of the

measurement classes. Then graph a frequency histogram for these data.

2.14 SAS was used to generate the stem-and-leaf display shown here. Note that SAS arranges the stems in descending order.

Stem	Leaf
5	1
4	4 5 7
3	0 0 0 3 6
2	1 1 3 4 5 9 9
1	2 2 4 8
0	0 1 2

a. How many observations were in the original data set?

b. In the bottom row of the stem-and-leaf display, identify the stem, the leaves, and the numbers in the original data set represented by this stem and its leaves.

c. Re-create all the numbers in the data set and construct a dot plot.

2.15 MINITAB was used to generate the following histogram:

MIDDLE OF INTERVAL	NUMBER OF OBSERVATIONS	
20	1	*
22	3	***
24	2	**
26	3	***
28	4	****
30	7	******
32	11	***********
34	6	******
36	2	**
38	3	***
40	3	***
42	2	**
44	1	*
46	1	*

a. Is this a frequency histogram or a relative frequency histogram? Explain.

b. How many measurement classes were used in the construction of this histogram?

c. How many measurements are there in the data set described by this histogram?

2.16 The graph summarizes the scores obtained by 100 students on a questionnaire designed to measure managerial ability. (Scores are integer values that range from 0 to 20. A high score indicates a high level of ability.)

a. Which measurement class contains the highest proportion of test scores?

b. What proportion of the scores lie between 3.5 and 5.5?

c. What proportion of the scores are higher than 11.5?

d. How many students scored less than 5.5?

Applying the Concepts

2.17 Bonds can be issued by the federal government, state and local governments, and U.S. corporations. A *mortgage bond* is a promissory note in which the issuing company pledges certain real assets as security in exchange for a specified amount of money. A *debenture* is an unsecured promissory note, backed only by the general credit of the issuer. The bond price of either a mortgage bond or debenture is negotiated between the asked price (the lowest price anyone will accept) and the bid price (the highest price anyone wants to pay). (Alexander, Sharpe, and Bailey, *Fundamentals of Investments,* 1993.) The accompanying table contains the bid prices on May 31, 1996, for a sample of 30 publicly traded bonds issued by utility companies.

a. A frequency histogram was generated using SPSS and is shown on page 44. Note that SPSS labels the midpoint of each measurement class

Utility Company	Bid Price	Utility Company	Bid Price
Gulf States Utilities	$102\frac{3}{8}$	Indiana & Michigan Electric	$100\frac{1}{8}$
Northern States Power	$99\frac{1}{2}$	Toledo Edison Co.	$92\frac{7}{8}$
Indiana Gas	$102\frac{7}{8}$	Dayton Power and Light	$99\frac{1}{2}$
Appalachian Power	$97\frac{3}{8}$	Atlantic City Electric	$100\frac{3}{8}$
Empire Gas Corp.	70	Long Island Lighting	$91\frac{5}{8}$
Wisconsin Electric Power	$87\frac{1}{4}$	Portland General Electric	100
Pennsylvania Electric	$99\frac{7}{8}$	Boston Gas	$102\frac{7}{8}$
Commonwealth Edison	$89\frac{1}{8}$	Duquesne Light Co.	73
El Paso Natural Gas	$105\frac{1}{4}$	General Electric Co.	$93\frac{1}{8}$
Montana Power Co.	$100\frac{3}{8}$	Ohio Power Co.	$99\frac{7}{8}$
Elizabethtown Water	$103\frac{5}{8}$	Texas Utilities Electric	$100\frac{5}{8}$
Tennessee Gas Pipeline	$82\frac{1}{2}$	Central Power and Light	$100\frac{1}{8}$
Western Mass. Electric	$99\frac{5}{8}$	Boston Edison	$99\frac{3}{8}$
Carolina P&L	$99\frac{7}{8}$	Philadelphia Electric	99
Hartford Electric Lt.	$100\frac{1}{8}$	Colorado Interstate Gas	$114\frac{1}{4}$

Source: Bond Guide (a publication of the Standard & Poor Corporation), June 1996.

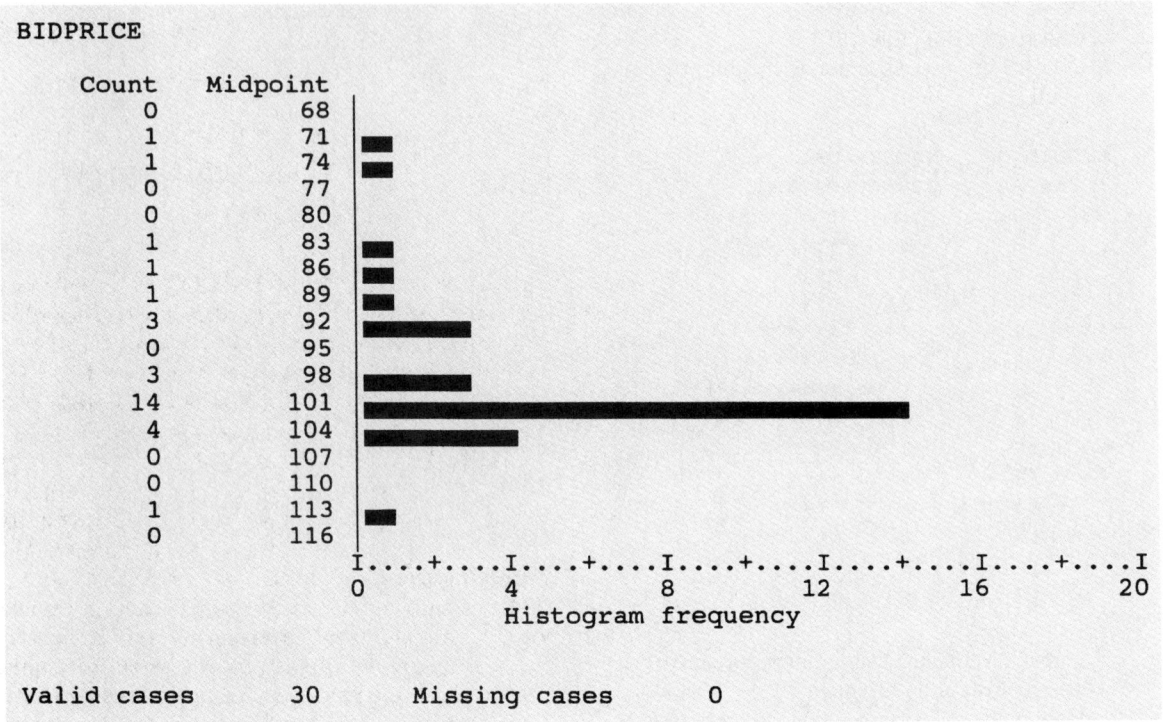

rather than the two endpoints, and plots the bars horizontally rather than vertically. Interpret the histogram.

b. Use the histogram to determine the number of bonds in the sample that had a bid price greater than $96.50. What proportion of the total number of bonds is this group?

c. Shade the area under the histogram that corresponds to the proportion in part **b**.

2.18 Production processes may be classified as *make-to-stock processes* or *make-to-order processes*. Make-to-stock processes are designed to produce a standardized product that can be sold to customers from the firm's inventory. Make-to-order processes are designed to produce products according to customer specifications. The McDonald's and Burger King fast-food chains are classic examples of these two types of processes. McDonald's produces and stocks standardized hamburgers; Burger King—whose slogan is "Your way, right away"—makes hamburgers according to the ingredients specified by the customer (Schroeder, *Operations Management*, 1993). In general, performance of make-to-order processes is measured by delivery time—the time from receipt of an order until the product is delivered to the customer. The following data set is a sample of delivery times (in days) for a particular make-to-order firm last year. The delivery times marked by an asterisk are associated with customers who subsequently placed additional orders with the firm.

50* 64* 56* 43* 64* 82* 65* 49* 32* 63* 44* 71
54* 51* 102 49* 73* 50* 39* 86 33* 95 59* 51*
68

The MINITAB stem-and-leaf display of these data is shown here.

```
Stem-and-leaf of Time      N = 25
Leaf Unit = 1.0

       3      3 239
       7      4 3499
      (7)     5 0011469
      11      6 34458
       6      7 13
       4      8 26
       2      9 5
       1     10 2
```

a. Circle the individual leaves that are associated with customers who did not place a subsequent order.

b. Concerned that they are losing potential repeat customers because of long delivery times, the management would like to establish a guideline for the maximum tolerable delivery time. Using the stem-and-leaf display, suggest a guideline. Explain your reasoning.

Company Identification Number	Penalty	Law*		Company Identification Number	Penalty	Law*
01	$ 930,000	CERCLA		16	90,000	RCRA
02	10,000	CWA		17	20,000	CWA
03	90,600	CAA		18	40,000	CWA
04	123,549	CWA		19	20,000	CWA
05	37,500	CWA		20	40,000	CWA
06	137,500	CWA		21	850,000	CWA
07	2,500	SDWA		22	35,000	CWA
08	1,000,000	CWA		23	4,000	CAA
09	25,000	CAA		24	25,000	CWA
09	25,000	CAA		25	40,000	CWA
10	25,000	CWA		26	30,000	CAA
10	25,000	RCRA		27	15,000	CWA
11	19,100	CAA		28	15,000	CAA
12	100,000	CWA		29	105,000	CAA
12	30,000	CWA		30	20,000	CWA
13	35,000	CAA		31	400,000	CWA
13	43,000	CWA		32	85,000	CWA
14	190,000	CWA		33	300,000	CWA/RCRA/CERCLA
15	15,000	CWA		34	30,000	CWA

*CAA: Clean Air Act; CERCLA: Comprehensive Environmental Response, Compensation, and Libility Act; CWA: Clean Water Act; RCRA: Resource Conservation and Recovery Act; SDWA: Safe Drinking Water Act.

Source: Tabor, R. H., and Stanwick, S. D. "Arkansas: An environmental perspective." *Arkansas Business and Economic Review,* Vol. 28, No. 2, Summer 1995, pp. 22–32 (Table 4).

2.19 **(X02.019)** Any corporation doing business in the United States must be aware of and obey both federal and state environmental regulations. Failure to do so may result in irreparable damage to the environment and costly financial penalties to guilty corporations. Of the 55 civil actions filed against corporations within the state of Arkansas by the U.S. Department of Justice on behalf of the Environmental Protection Agency, 38 resulted in financial penalties. These penalties along with the laws that were violated are listed in the table above. (*Note:* Some companies were involved in more than one civil action.)

a. Construct a stem-and-leaf display for all 38 penalties.

b. Circle the individual leaves that are associated with penalties imposed for violations of the Clean Air Act.

c. What does the pattern of circles in part **b** suggest about the severity of the penalties imposed for Clean Air Act violations relative to the other types of violations reported in the table? Explain.

2.20 **(X02.020)** In a manufacturing plant a *work center* is a specific production facility that consists of one or more people and/or machines and is treated as one unit for the purposes of capacity requirements planning and job scheduling. If jobs arrive at a particular work center at a faster rate than they depart, the work center impedes the overall production process and is referred to as a *bottleneck* (Fogarty, Blackstone, and Hoffmann, *Production and Inventory Management,* 1991). The data in the table below were collected by an operations manager for use in investigating a potential bottleneck work center.

MINITAB dot plots for the two sets of data are shown at the top of page 46. Do the dot plots suggest that the work center may be a bottleneck? Explain.

Number of Items Arriving at Work Center per Hour											
155	115	156	150	159	163	172	143	159	166	148	175
151	161	138	148	129	135	140	152	139			

Number of Items Departing at Work Center per Hour											
156	109	127	148	135	119	140	127	115	122	99	106
171	123	135	125	107	152	111	137	161			

2.21 (X02.021) The ability to fill a customer's order on time depends on being able to estimate how long it will take to produce the product in question. In most production processes, the time required to complete a particular task will be shorter each time the task is undertaken and, in most cases, the task time will decrease at a decreasing rate. Thus, in order to estimate how long it will take to produce a particular product, a manufacturer may want to study the relationship between production time per unit and the number of units that have been produced. The line or curve characterizing this relationship is called a *learning curve* (Adler and Clark, *Management Science*, Mar. 1991). Twenty-five employees, all of whom were performing the same production task for the tenth time, were observed. Each person's task completion time (in minutes) was recorded. The same 25 employees were observed again the 30th time they performed the same task and the 50th time they performed the task. The resulting completion times are shown in the table at right.

a. Use a statistical software package to construct a frequency histogram for each of the three data sets.

b. Compare the histograms. Does it appear that the relationship between task completion time and the number of times the task is performed is in agreement with the observations noted above about production processes in general? Explain.

2.22 Financially distressed firms can gain protection from their creditors while they restructure by filing for protection under U.S. Bankruptcy Codes. In a *prepackaged bankruptcy*, a firm negotiates a reorganization plan with its creditors prior to filing for bankruptcy. This can result in a much quicker exit from bankruptcy than traditional bankruptcy filings. Brian Betker conducted a study of 49 prepackaged bankruptcies that were filed between 1986 and 1993 and reported the results in *Financial Management* (Spring 1995). The table at the top of page 47 lists the time in bankruptcy (in months) for these 49 companies. The table also lists the results of a vote by each company's board of directors concerning their preferred reorgani-

Employee	PERFORMANCE		
	10th	30th	50th
1	15	16	10
2	21	10	5
3	30	12	7
4	17	9	9
5	18	7	8
6	22	11	11
7	33	8	12
8	41	9	9
9	10	5	7
10	14	15	6
11	18	10	8
12	25	11	14
13	23	9	9
14	19	11	8
15	20	10	10
16	22	13	8
17	20	12	7
18	19	8	8
19	18	20	6
20	17	7	5
21	16	6	6
22	20	9	4
23	22	10	15
24	19	10	7
25	24	11	20

zation plan. (*Note:* "Joint" = joint exchange offer with prepackaged bankruptcy solicitation; "Prepack" = prepackaged bankruptcy solicitation only; "None" = no pre-filing vote held.)

a. Construct a stem-and-leaf display for the length of time in bankruptcy for all 49 companies.

b. Summarize the information reflected in the stem-and-leaf display, part a. Make a general statement about the length of time in bankruptcy for firms using "prepacks."

c. Select a graphical technique that will permit a comparison of the time-in-bankruptcy distributions for the three types of "prepack" firms: those who held no pre-filing vote; those who voted their preference for a joint solution; and those who voted their preference for a prepack.

d. The companies that were reorganized through a leveraged buyout are identified by an aster-

Company	Pre-filing Votes	Time in Bankruptcy (months)
AM International	None	3.9
Anglo Energy	Prepack	1.5
Arizona Biltmore*	Prepack	1.0
Astrex	None	10.1
Barry's Jewelers	None	4.1
Calton	Prepack	1.9
Cencor	Joint	1.4
Charter Medical*	Prepack	1.3
Cherokee*	Joint	1.2
Circle Express	Prepack	4.1
Cook Inlet Comm.	Prepack	1.1
Crystal Oil	None	3.0
Divi Hotels	None	3.2
Edgell Comm.*	Prepack	1.0
Endevco	Prepack	3.8
Gaylord Container	Joint	1.2
Great Amer. Comm.*	Prepack	1.0
Hadson	Prepack	1.5
In-Store Advertising	Prepack	1.0
JPS Textiles*	Prepack	1.4
Kendall*	Prepack	1.2
Kinder-Care	None	4.2
Kroy*	Prepack	3.0
Ladish*	Joint	1.5
LaSalle Energy*	Prepack	1.6

Company	Pre-filing Votes	Time in Bankruptcy (months)
LIVE Entertainment	Joint	1.4
Mayflower Group*	Prepack	1.4
Memorex Telex*	Prepack	1.1
Munsingwear	None	2.9
Nat'l Environmental	Joint	5.2
Petrolane Gas	Prepack	1.2
Price Communications	None	2.4
Republic Health*	Joint	4.5
Resorts Int'l*	None	7.8
Restaurant Enterprises*	Prepack	1.5
Rymer Foods	Joint	2.1
SCI TV*	Prepack	2.1
Southland*	Joint	3.9
Specialty Equipment*	None	2.6
SPI Holdings*	Joint	1.4
Sprouse-Reitz	Prepack	1.4
Sunshine Metals	Joint	5.4
TIE/Communications	None	2.4
Trump Plaza	Prepack	1.7
Trump Taj Mahal	Prepack	1.4
Trump's Castle	Prepack	2.7
USG	Prepack	1.2
Vyquest	Prepack	4.1
West Point Acq.*	Prepack	2.9

*Leveraged buyout.

Source: Betker, B. L. "An empirical examination of prepackaged bankruptcy." *Financial Management*, Vol. 24, No. 1, Spring 1995, p. 6 (Table 2).

isk (*) in the table. Identify these firms on the stem-and-leaf display, part **a**, by circling their bankruptcy times. Do you observe any pattern in the graph? Explain.

2.23 **(X02.023)** While producing many economic benefits to the state of Florida, gypsum and phosphate mines also produce a harmful by-product: radiation. It has been known for a number of years that the mine tailings (waste) contain radioactive radon 222. In fact, new housing complexes built over the leveled piles of residue have shown disturbing radiation levels within the houses. The radiation levels in waste gypsum and phosphate mounds in Polk County, Florida, are regularly monitored by the Eastern Environmental Radiation Facility (EERF) and by the Polk County Health Department (PCHD), Winter Haven, Florida. The table below lists the measurements of the exhalation rate (a measure of radiation) of soil samples taken on waste piles in Polk County, Florida. They represent part of the data contained in a report by Thomas R. Horton of EERF.

SPSS was used to generate the first stem-and-leaf printout at the top of page 48. [*Note:* To save space, SPSS places the leaves for two consecutive stems into a single stem row.]

a. Interpret the display. Which digit(s) was used for the stem and which for the leaf? Find the largest measurement in the data set and locate it in the display.

b. Note that the presence of a measurement well removed from the main body of data somewhat distorts the display, since most of the data

Exhalation Rate of Soil Samples

1,709.79	4,132.28	2,996.49	2,796.42	3,750.83	961.40	1,096.43	1,774.77
357.17	1,489.86	2,367.40	11,968.23	178.99	5,402.35	2,315.52	2,617.57
1,150.94	3,017.48	599.84	2,758.84	3,764.96	1,888.22	2,055.20	205.84
1,572.69	393.55	538.37	1,830.78	878.56	6,815.69	752.89	1,977.97
558.33	880.84	2,770.23	1,426.57	1,322.76	1,480.04	9,139.21	1,698.39

Source: Horton, T. R. "A preliminary radiological assessment of radon exhalation from phosphate gypsum piles and inactive uranium mill tailings piles." EPA–520/5–79–004. Washington D.C.: Environmental Protection Agency, 1979.

```
Stem-and-leaf display for variable . . EXHLRATE
    0 . 22445668990123455677889
    2 . 013468880088
    4 . 14
    6 . 8
    8 . 1
   10 .
   12 . 0
```

```
Stem-and-leaf display for variable . . EXHLRATE
    0 . 2244566899
    1 . 0123455677889
    2 . 01346888
    3 . 0088
    4 . 1
    5 . 4
    6 . 8
    7 .
    8 .
    9 . 1
```

set is compressed into a small portion of it. The largest measurement was removed from the data set, and a new SPSS stem-and-leaf display was generated, the second printout shown above. Interpret this display, identifying the stem and leaf used. Using both displays, give a verbal description of the data.

2.24 It's not uncommon for hearing aids to malfunction and cancel the desired signal. *IEEE Transactions on Speech and Audio Processing* (May 1995) reported on a new audio processing system designed to limit the amount of signal can-

cellation that may occur. The system utilizes a mathematical equation that involves a variable, V, called a *sufficient norm constraint*. A histogram for realizations of V, produced using simulation, is shown below.

a. Estimate the percentage of realizations of V with values ranging from .425 to .675.

b. Cancellation of the desired signal is limited by selecting a norm constraint V. Find the value of V for a company that wants to market the new hearing aid so that only 10% of the realizations have values below the selected level.

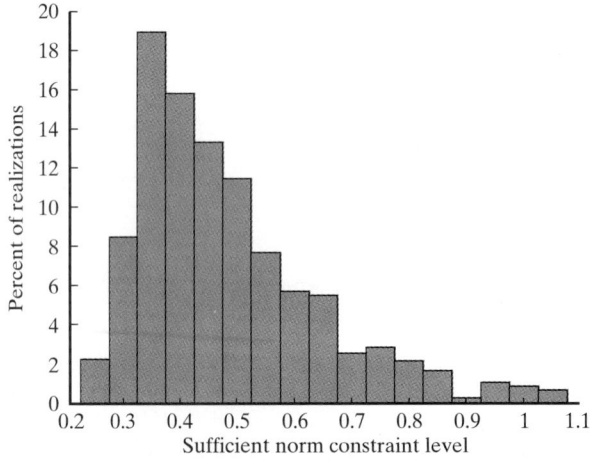

Source: Hoffman, M. W., and Buckley, K. M. "Robust time-domain processing of broadband microphone array data." *IEEE Transactions on Speech and Audio Processing*, Vol. 3, No. 3, May 1995, p. 199 (Figure 4). © 1995 IEEE.

2.25 **(X02.025)** Typically, the more attractive a corporate common stock is to an investor, the higher the stock's price-earnings (P/E) ratio. For example, if investors expect the stock's future earnings per share to increase, the price of the stock will be bid up and a high P/E ratio will result. Thus, the level of a stock's P/E ratio is a function of both the current financial performance of the firm and an investor's expectation of future performance. The table contains samples of P/E ratios from manufacturing firms and holding companies for the last day of March 1996

   a. Compare the P/E ratio distributions of manufacturing and holding firms using a graphical method.

   b. What do your graphs suggest about the level of the P/E ratios of firms in the manufacturing business as compared to firms in the holding business? Explain.

MANUFACTURING FIRMS		HOLDING COMPANIES	
Company	**P/E Ratio**	**Company**	**P/E Ratio**
Block Drug	9	EMC Ins. Group	8
Daig Corp.	38	First Essex Bancorp	9
Modtech Inc.	31	MLG Bancorp	14
Guest Supply	16	State Auto Financial	10
Astro Systems Inc.	36	Boston Bancorp	6
Fischer Imaging	33	Cellular Communications	48
Casino Data Systems	74	Anderson Group	5
Data Key Inc.	69	Provident Bancorp	12
Network Peripherals	23	Pubco Corp.	4
Brenco, Inc.	12	Condor Services	16
Day Runner	16	Eselco Inc.	16
Safeskin Corp.	16	Mesaba	2
Marisa Christina	14	Keystone Financial	13
Merix Corp.	17	JSB Financial	16
Cognex Corp.	39	Argonaut Group	14
FLIR Systems	17	ONBANCorp	12
Stant Corp	11	Great Amer. Mgmt. Invst.	3
Grief Bros. Corp.	13	CPB, Inc.	12
Computer Identics	37	GBC Bancorp	18
PRI Automation	14	California Bancshares	16

Source: Standard & Poor's NASDAQ and Regional Exchange Profiles, Mar. 1996.

2.3   THE TIME SERIES PLOT (OPTIONAL)

Each of the previous sections has been concerned with describing the information contained in a sample or population of data. Often these data are viewed as having been produced at essentially the same point in time. Thus, time has not been a factor in any of the graphical methods described so far.

Data of interest to managers are often produced and monitored over time. Examples include the daily closing price of their company's common stock, the company's weekly sales volume and quarterly profits, and characteristics—such as weight and length—of products produced by the company.

DEFINITION 2.4

Data that are produced and monitored over time are called **time series data**.

Recall from Section 1.4 that a process is a series of actions or operations that generates output over time. Accordingly, measurements taken of a sequence of units produced by a process—such as a production process—are time series data. In general, any sequence of numbers produced over time can be thought of as being generated by a process.

When measurements are made over time, it is important to record both the numerical value and the time or the time period associated with each measurement. With this information a **time series plot**—sometimes called a **run chart**—can be constructed to describe the time series data and to learn about the process that

FIGURE 2.12
Time series plot
of company sales

generated the data. A time series plot is a graph of the measurements (on the vertical axis) plotted against time or against the order in which the measurements were made (on the horizontal axis). The plotted points are usually connected by straight lines to make it easier to see the changes and movement in the measurements over time. For example, Figure 2.12 is a time series plot of a particular company's monthly sales (number of units sold per month). And Figure 2.13 is a time series plot of the weights of 30 one-gallon paint cans that were consecutively filled by the same filling head. Notice that the weights are plotted against the

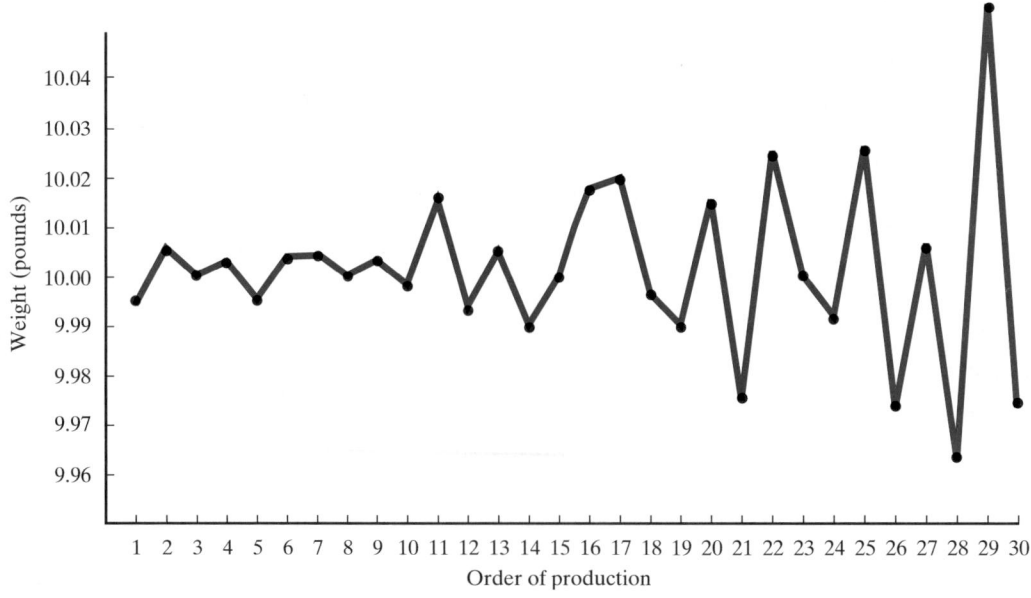

FIGURE 2.13   Time series plot of paint can weights

order in which the cans were filled rather than some unit of time. When monitoring production processes, it is often more convenient to record the order rather than the exact time at which each measurement was made.

Time series plots reveal the movement (trend) and changes (variation) in the variable being monitored. Notice how sales trend upward in the summer and how the variation in the weights of the paint cans increases over time. This kind of information would not be revealed by stem-and-leaf displays or histograms, as the following example illustrates.

EXAMPLE 2.3

W. Edwards Deming was one of America's most famous statisticians. He was best known for the role he played after World War II in teaching the Japanese how to improve the quality of their products by monitoring and continually improving their production processes. In his book *Out of the Crisis* (1986), Deming warned against the knee-jerk (i.e., automatic) use of histograms to display and extract information from data. As evidence he offered the following example.

Fifty camera springs were tested in the order in which they were produced. The elongation of each spring was measured under the pull of 20 grams. Both a time series plot and a histogram were constructed from the measurements. They are shown in Figure 2.14, which has been reproduced from Deming's book. If you had to predict the elongation measurement of the next spring to be produced (i.e., spring 51) and could use only one of the two plots to guide your prediction, which would you use? Why?

SOLUTION

Only the time series plot describes the behavior *over time* of the process that produces the springs. The fact that the elongation measurements are decreasing over time can only be gleaned from the time series plot. Because the histogram does not reflect the order in which the springs were produced, it in effect represents all observations as having been produced simultaneously. Using the histogram to predict the elongation of the 51st spring would very likely lead to an overestimate.

The lesson from Deming's example is this: For displaying and analyzing data that have been generated over time by a process, the primary graphical tool is the time series plot, not the histogram.

We cover many other aspects of the statistical analysis of time series data in Chapter 14.

FIGURE 2.14
Deming's time series plot and histogram

2.4 SUMMATION NOTATION

Now that we've examined some graphical techniques for summarizing and describing quantitative data sets, we turn to numerical methods for accomplishing this objective. Before giving the formulas for calculating numerical descriptive measures, let's look at some shorthand notation that will simplify our calculation instructions. Remember that such notation is used for one reason only—to avoid repeating the same verbal descriptions over and over. If you mentally substitute the verbal definition of a symbol each time you read it, you'll soon get used to it.

We denote the measurements of a quantitative data set as follows: $x_1, x_2, x_3, \ldots, x_n$ where x_1 is the first measurement in the data set, x_2 is the second measurement in the data set, x_3 is the third measurement in the data set, ..., and x_n is the nth (and last) measurement in the data set. Thus, if we have five measurements in a set of data, we will write x_1, x_2, x_3, x_4, x_5 to represent the measurements. If the actual numbers are 5, 3, 8, 5, and 4, we have $x_1 = 5, x_2 = 3, x_3 = 8, x_4 = 5$, and $x_5 = 4$.

Most of the formulas we use require a summation of numbers. For example, one sum we'll need to obtain is the sum of all the measurements in the data set, or $x_1 + x_2 + x_3 + \cdots + x_n$. To shorten the notation, we use the symbol Σ for the summation. That is, $x_1 + x_2 + x_3 + \cdots + x_n = \sum_{i=1}^{n} x_i$. Verbally translate $\sum_{i=1}^{5} x_i$ as follows: "The sum of the measurements, whose typical member is x_i, beginning with the member x_1 and ending with the member x_n."

Suppose, as in our earlier example, $x_1 = 5, x_2 = 3, x_3 = 8, x_4 = 5$, and $x_5 = 4$. Then the sum of the five measurements, denoted $\sum_{i=1}^{5} x_i$, is obtained as follows:

$$\sum_{i=1}^{5} x_i = x_1 + x_2 + x_3 + x_4 + x_5$$

$$= 5 + 3 + 8 + 5 + 4 = 25$$

Another important calculation requires that we square each measurement and then sum the squares. The notation for this sum is $\sum_{i=1}^{n} x_i^2$. For the five measurements above, we have

$$\sum_{i=1}^{5} x_i^2 = x_1^2 + x_2^2 + x_3^2 + x_4^2 + x_5^2$$

$$= 5^2 + 3^2 + 8^2 + 5^2 + 4^2$$

$$= 25 + 9 + 64 + 25 + 16 = 139$$

In general, the symbol following the summation sign Σ represents the variable (or function of the variable) that is to be summed.

The Meaning of Summation Notation $\sum_{i=1}^{n} x_i$

Sum the measurements on the variable that appears to the right of the summation symbol, beginning with the 1st measurement and ending with the nth measurement.

EXERCISES 2.26–2.29

Learning the Mechanics

Note: In all exercises, Σ represents $\sum_{i=1}^{n}$.

2.26 A data set contains the observations 5, 1, 3, 2, 1. Find:
a. Σx b. Σx^2 c. $\Sigma(x-1)$
d. $\Sigma(x-1)^2$ e. $(\Sigma x)^2$

2.27 Suppose a data set contains the observations 3, 8, 4, 5, 3, 4, 6. Find:

a. Σx b. Σx^2 c. $\Sigma(x-5)^2$
d. $\Sigma(x-2)^2$ e. $(\Sigma x)^2$

2.28 Refer to Exercise 2.26. Find:
a. $\Sigma x^2 - \dfrac{(\Sigma x)^2}{5}$ b. $\Sigma(x-2)^2$ c. $\Sigma x^2 - 10$

2.29 A data set contains the observations 6, 0, −2, −1, 3. Find:
a. Σx b. Σx^2 c. $\Sigma x^2 - \dfrac{(\Sigma x)^2}{5}$

2.5 NUMERICAL MEASURES OF CENTRAL TENDENCY

When we speak of a data set, we refer to either a sample or a population. If statistical inference is our goal, we'll wish ultimately to use sample numerical descriptive measures to make inferences about the corresponding measures for a population.

As you'll see, a large number of numerical methods are available to describe quantitative data sets. Most of these methods measure one of two data characteristics:

1. The **central tendency** of the set of measurements—that is, the tendency of the data to cluster, or center, about certain numerical values (see Figure 2.15a).

2. The **variability** of the set of measurements—that is, the spread of the data (see Figure 2.15b).

In this section we concentrate on measures of central tendency. In the next section, we discuss measures of variability.

The most popular and best-understood measure of central tendency for a quantitative data set is the **arithmetic mean** (or simply the **mean**) of a data set.

DEFINITION 2.5
The **mean** of a set of quantitative data is the sum of the measurements divided by the number of measurements contained in the data set.

In everyday terms, the mean is the average value of the data set and is often used to represent a "typical" value. We denote the **mean of a sample** of measurements by $\bar{x}$ (read "x-bar"), and represent the formula for its calculation as shown in the box.

FIGURE 2.15
Numerical descriptive measures

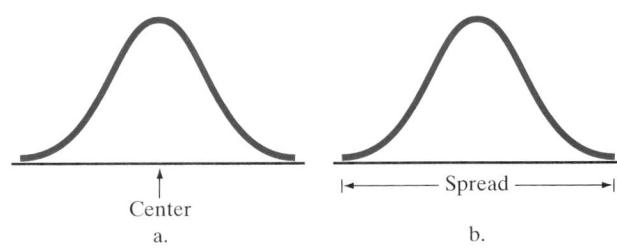

Center
a.

Spread
b.

Calculating a Sample Mean

$$\bar{x} = \frac{\displaystyle\sum_{i=1}^{n} x_i}{n}$$

EXAMPLE 2.4

Calculate the mean of the following five sample measurements: 5, 3, 8, 5, 6.

SOLUTION

Using the definition of sample mean and the summation notation, we find

$$\bar{x} = \frac{\displaystyle\sum_{i=1}^{5} x_i}{5} = \frac{5 + 3 + 8 + 5 + 6}{5} = \frac{27}{5} = 5.4$$

Thus, the mean of this sample is 5.4.*

EXAMPLE 2.5

Calculate the sample mean for the R&D expenditure percentages of the 50 companies given in Table 2.3.

SOLUTION

The mean R&D percentage for the 50 companies is denoted

$$\bar{x} = \frac{\displaystyle\sum_{i=1}^{50} x_i}{50}$$

Rather than compute $\bar{x}$ by hand (or calculator), we entered the data of Table 2.3 irto a computer and employed SPSS statistical software to compute the mean. The SPSS printout is shown in Figure 2.16. The sample mean, highlighted on the printout, is $\bar{x} = 8.492$.

Given this information, you can visualize a distribution of R&D percentages centered in the vicinity of $\bar{x} = 8.492$. An examination of the relative frequency histogram (Figure 2.8) confirms that $\bar{x}$ does in fact fall near the center of the distribution.

```
      RDEXP

Valid cases:        50.0   Missing cases:      .0    Percent missing:      .0

Mean        8.4920  Std Err      .2801  Min     5.2000  Skewness       .8546
Median      8.0500  Variance    3.9228  Max    13.5000  S E Skew       .3366
5% Trim     8.3833  Std Dev     1.9806  Range   8.3000  Kurtosis       .4193
                                        IQR     2.5750  S E Kurt       .6619
```

FIGURE 2.16   SPSS printout of numerical descriptive measures for 50 R&D percentages

---

*In the examples given here, $\bar{x}$ is sometimes rounded to the nearest tenth, sometimes the nearest hundredth, sometimes the nearest thousandth, and so on. There is no specific rule for rounding when calculating $\bar{x}$ because $\bar{x}$ is specifically defined to be the sum of all measurements divided by n; that is, it is a specific fraction. When $\bar{x}$ is used for descriptive purposes, it is often convenient to round the calculated value of $\bar{x}$ to the number of significant figures used for the original measurements. When $\bar{x}$ is to be used in other calculations, however, it may be necessary to retain more significant figures.

The sample mean $\bar{x}$ will play an important role in accomplishing our objective of making inferences about populations based on sample information. For this reason we need to use a different symbol for the **mean of a population**—the mean of the set of measurements on every unit in the population. We use the Greek letter μ (mu) for the population mean.

Symbols for the Sample and Population Mean

In this text, we adopt a general policy of using Greek letters to represent population numerical descriptive measures and Roman letters to represent corresponding descriptive measures for the sample. The symbols for the mean are:

$\bar{x}$ = Sample mean

μ = Population mean

We'll often use the sample mean, $\bar{x}$, to estimate (make an inference about) the population mean, μ. For example, the percentages of revenues spent on R&D by the population consisting of *all* U.S. companies has a mean equal to some value, μ. Our sample of 50 companies yielded percentages with a mean of $\bar{x} = 8.492$. If, as is usually the case, we don't have access to the measurements for the entire population, we could use $\bar{x}$ as an estimator or approximator for μ. Then we'd need to know something about the reliability of our inference. That is, we'd need to know how accurately we might expect $\bar{x}$ to estimate μ. In Chapter 7, we'll find that this accuracy depends on two factors:

1. The *size of the sample.* The larger the sample, the more accurate the estimate will tend to be.

2. The *variability,* or *spread, of the data.* All other factors remaining constant, the more variable the data, the less accurate the estimate.

Another important measure of central tendency is the **median**.

DEFINITION 2.6

The **median** of a quantitative data set is the middle number when the measurements are arranged in ascending (or descending) order.

The median is of most value in describing large data sets. If the data set is characterized by a relative frequency histogram (Figure 2.17), the median is the point on the x-axis such that half the area under the histogram lies above the median and half lies below. [*Note:* In Section 2.2 we observed that the relative frequency associated with a particular interval on the horizontal axis is proportional to the amount of area under the histogram that lies above the interval.] We denote the *median* of a *sample* by m.

FIGURE 2.17
Location of the median

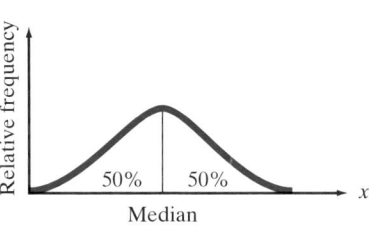

Median

> **Calculating a Sample Median, m**
> Arrange the n measurements from smallest to largest.
> 1. If n is odd, m is the middle number.
> 2. If n is even, m is the mean of the middle two numbers.

EXAMPLE 2.6

Consider the following sample of $n = 7$ measurements: 5, 7, 4, 5, 20, 6, 2.

    a. Calculate the median m of this sample.

    b. Eliminate the last measurement (the 2) and calculate the median of the remaining $n = 6$ measurements.

SOLUTION

    a. The seven measurements in the sample are ranked in ascending order: 2, 4, 5, 5, 6, 7, 20

       Because the number of measurements is odd, the median is the middle measurement. Thus, the median of this sample is $m = 5$.

    b. After removing the 2 from the set of measurements, we rank the sample measurements in ascending order as follows: 4, 5, 5, 6, 7, 20

       Now the number of measurements is even, so we average the middle two measurements. The median is $m = (5 + 6)/2 = 5.5$.

In certain situations, the median may be a better measure of central tendency than the mean. In particular, the median is less sensitive than the mean to extremely large or small measurements. Note, for instance, that all but one of the measurements in part **a** of Example 2.6 center about $x = 5$. The single relatively large measurement, $x = 20$, does not affect the value of the median, 5, but it causes the mean, $\bar{x} = 7$, to lie to the right of most of the measurements.

As another example of data from which the central tendency is better described by the median than the mean, consider the salaries of professional athletes (e.g., National Basketball Association players). The presence of just a few athletes (e.g., Michael Jordan, Shaquille O'Neal) with very high salaries will affect the mean more than the median. Thus, the median will provide a more accurate picture of the typical salary for the professional league. The mean could exceed the vast majority of the sample measurements (salaries), making it a misleading measure of central tendency.

EXAMPLE 2.7

Calculate the median for the 50 R&D percentages given in Table 2.3. Compare the median to the mean computed in Example 2.5.

SOLUTION

For this large data set, we again resort to a computer analysis. The SPSS printout is reproduced in Figure 2.18, with the median highlighted. You can see that the median is 8.05. This value implies that half of the 50 R&D percentages in the data set fall below 8.05 and half lie above 8.05.

Note that the mean (8.492) for these data is larger than the median. This fact indicates that the data are **skewed** to the right—that is, there are more extreme measurements in the right tail of the distribution than in the left tail (recall the histogram, Figure 2.8).

In general, extreme values (large or small) affect the mean more than the median since these values are used explicitly in the calculation of the mean. On the other hand, the median is not affected directly by extreme measurements,

```
        RDEXP
 Valid cases:           50.0   Missing cases:     .0   Percent missing:     .0

 Mean          8.4920   Std Err      .2801  Min     5.2000   Skewness        .8546
 Median        8.0500   Variance    3.9228  Max    13.5000   S E Skew        .3366
 5% Trim       8.3833   Std Dev     1.9806  Range   8.3000   Kurtosis        .4193
                                            IQR     2.5750   S E Kurt        .6619
```

FIGURE 2.18   SPSS printout of numerical descriptive measures for 50 R&D percentages

since only the middle measurement (or two middle measurements) is explicitly used to calculate the median. Consequently, if measurements are pulled toward one end of the distribution (as with the R&D percentages), the mean will shift toward that tail more than the median.

A comparison of the mean and median gives us a general method for detecting skewness in data sets, as shown in the next box.

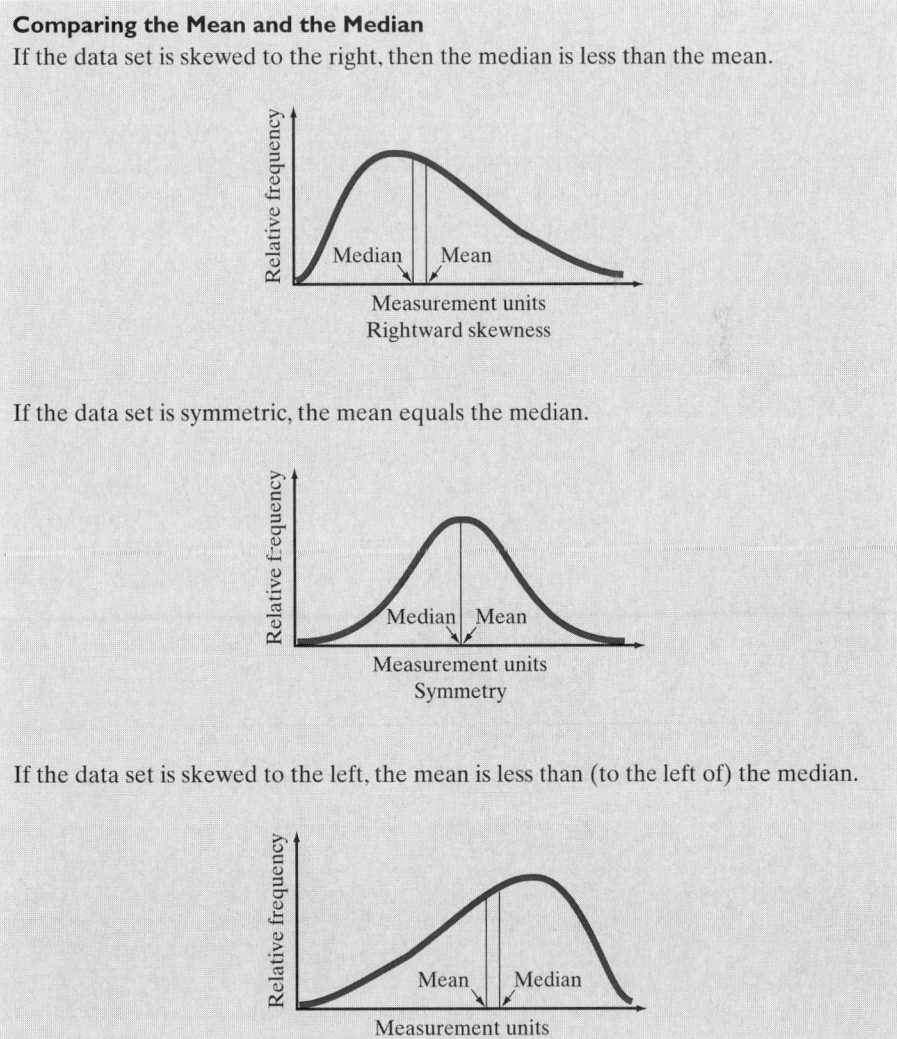

Comparing the Mean and the Median

If the data set is skewed to the right, then the median is less than the mean.

If the data set is symmetric, the mean equals the median.

If the data set is skewed to the left, the mean is less than (to the left of) the median.

A third measure of central tendency is the **mode** of a set of measurements.

DEFINITION 2.7
The **mode** is the measurement that occurs most frequently in the data set.

Therefore, the mode shows where the data tend to concentrate.

EXAMPLE 2.8 Each of 10 taste testers rated a new brand of barbecue sauce on a ten-point scale, where 1 = awful and 10 = excellent. Find the mode for the ten ratings shown below.

| 8 | 7 | 9 | 6 | 8 | 10 | 9 | 9 | 5 | 7 |

SOLUTION
Since 9 occurs most often, the mode of the ten taste ratings is 9.

Note that the data in Example 2.8 are actually qualitative in nature (e.g., "awful," "excellent"). The mode is particularly useful for describing qualitative data. The modal category is simply the category (or class) that occurs most often. Because it emphasizes data concentration, the mode is also used with quantitative data sets to locate the region in which much of the data is concentrated. A retailer of men's clothing would be interested in the modal neck size and sleeve length of potential customers. The modal income class of the laborers in the United States is of interest to the Labor Department.

For some quantitative data sets, the mode may not be very meaningful. For example, consider the pecentages of revenues spent on research and development (R&D) by 50 companies, Table 2.3. A reexamination of the data reveals that three of the measurements are repeated three times: 6.5%, 6.9%, and 8.2%. Thus, there are three modes in the sample and none is particularly useful as a measure of central tendency.

A more meaningful measure can be obtained from a relative frequency histogram for quantitative data. The measurement class containing the largest relative frequency is called the **modal class**. Several definitions exist for locating the position of the mode within a modal class, but the simplest is to define the mode as the midpoint of the modal class. For example, examine the relative frequency histogram for the R&D expenditure percentages, reproduced below in Figure 2.19. You can see that the modal class is the interval 7.35—8.45. The mode (the midpoint) is 7.90. This modal class (and the mode itself) identifies the area in

FIGURE 2.19
Relative frequency histogram for the computer companies' R&D percentages: The modal class

which the data are most concentrated, and in that sense it is a measure of central tendency. However, for most applications involving quantitative data, the mean and median provide more descriptive information than the mode.

EXERCISES   2.30–2.46

Note: Exercises marked with 💾 contain data available for computer analysis on a 3.5" disk (file name in parentheses).

Learning the Mechanics

2.30 Calculate the mode, mean, and median of the following data:

| 18 | 10 | 15 | 13 | 17 | 15 | 12 | 15 | 18 | 16 | 11 |

2.31 Calculate the mean and median of the following grade point averages:

| 3.2 | 2.5 | 2.1 | 3.7 | 2.8 | 2.0 |

2.32 Explain the difference between the calculation of the median for an odd and an even number of measurements. Construct one data set consisting of five measurements and another consisting of six measurements for which the medians are equal.

2.33 Explain how the relationship between the mean and median provides information about the symmetry or skewness of the data's distribution.

2.34 Calculate the mean for samples where
 a. $n = 10, \Sigma x = 85$ **b.** $n = 16, \Sigma x = 400$
 c. $n = 45, \Sigma x = 35$ **d.** $n = 18, \Sigma x = 242$

2.35 Calculate the mean, median, and mode for each of the following samples:
 a. $7, -2, 3, 3, 0, 4$ **b.** $2, 3, 5, 3, 2, 3, 4, 3, 5, 1, 2, 3, 4$
 c. $51, 50, 47, 50, 48, 41, 59, 68, 45, 37$

2.36 Describe how the mean compares to the median for a distribution as follows:
 a. Skewed to the left   **b.** Skewed to the right
 c. Symmetric

Applying the Concepts

2.37 The market value of a company varies from day to day depending on the price of the company's common stock and the number of shares of stock that are held by investors. The market value is determined by multiplying the share price by the number of shares outstanding. The table below lists the market value (in millions of dollars) for the ten most valuable health care firms and the ten most valuable banks.

a. Calculate the mean and median for each data set.

b. What do the mean and median indicate about the skewness of each data set?

c. In part **a**, neither median is equal to a value in its data set. Is this true for all data sets? Explain.

d. Based on your answer to part **a** and a visual inspection of the data sets, compare and contrast the market values of the ten most valuable health care firms and the ten most valuable banks.

2.38 💾 **(X02.038)** The Superfund Act was passed by Congress to encourage state participation in the implementation of laws relating to the release and cleanup of hazardous substances. Hazardous waste sites financed by the Superfund Act are called Superfund sites. A total of 395 Superfund sites are operated by waste management companies in Arkansas (Tabor and Stanwick, *Arkansas Business and Economic Review,* Summer 1995). The number of these Superfund sites in each of Arkansas' 75 counties is shown in the table at the top of page 60. Numerical descriptive measures for the data set are provided in the EXCEL printout below the table.

HEALTH CARE		BANKS	
Company	**Market Value**	**Company**	**Market Value**
Merck	$81,613	Citicorp	$33,329
Johnson & Johnson	60,564	Bankamerica	26,181
Bristol-Myers Squibb	43,008	Nationsbank	20,227
Pfizer	41,907	Chemical	17,942
Eli Lilly	33,437	First Union	16,810
Abbott Laboratories	33,072	J.P. Morgan	15,320
American Home Products	30,730	Banc One	15,235
Columbia/HCA	23,582	First Chicago	13,674
Pharmacia & Upjohn	21,215	Chase	13,216
Schering-Plough	20,441	Norwest	12,877

Source: "Business Week 1000." Business Week, March 25, 1996, p. 88.

3	3	2	1	2	0	5	3	5	2	1	8	2
12	3	5	3	1	3	0	8	0	9	6	8	6
2	16	0	6	0	5	5	0	1	25	0	0	0
6	2	10	12	3	10	3	17	2	4	2	1	21
4	2	1	11	5	2	2	7	2	3	1	8	2
0	0	0	2	3	10	2	3	48	21			

Source: Tabor, R. H., and Stanwick, S. D. "Arkansas: An environmental perspective." *Arkansas Business and Economic Review,* Vol. 28, No. 2, Summer 1995, pp. 22–32 (Table 1).

SITES	
Mean	5.24
Standard Error	0.836517879
Median	3
Mode	2
Standard Deviation	7.244457341
Sample Variance	52.48216216
Kurtosis	16.41176573
Skewness	3.468289878
Range	48
Minimum	0
Maximum	48
Sum	393
Count	75
Confidence Level(95.000%)	1.639542488

a. Locate the measures of central tendency on the printout and interpret their values.

b. Note that the data set contains at least one county with an unusually large number of Superfund sites. Find the largest of these measurements, called an **outlier**.

c. Delete the outlier, part **b**, from the data set and recalculate the measures of central tendency. Which measure is most affected by the elimination of the outlier?

2.39 Demographics play a key role in the recreation industry. According to D. A. Bergin (*Journal of Leisure Research,* Vol. 23, 1991), difficult times lay ahead for the industry. Bergin reports that the median age of the population in the United States was 30 in 1980, but will be about 36 by the year 2000.

a. Interpret the value of the median for both 1980 and 2000 and explain the trend.

b. If the recreation industry relies on the 18–30 age group for much of its business, what effect will this shift in the median age have? Explain.

2.40 (X02.040) Platelet-activating factor (PAF) is a potent chemical that occurs in patients suffering from shock, inflammation, hypotension, and allergic responses as well as respiratory and cardiovascular disorders. Consequently, drugs that effectively inhibit PAF, keeping it from binding to

human cells, may be successful in treating these disorders. A bioassay was undertaken to investigate the potential of 17 traditional Chinese herbal drugs in PAF inhibition (H. Guiqui, *Progress in Natural Science,* June 1995). The prevention of the PAF binding process, measured as a percentage, for each drug is provided in the accompanying table.

Drug	PAF Inhibition (%)
Hai-feng-teng (Fuji)	77
Hai-feng-teng (Japan)	33
Shan-ju	75
Zhang-yiz-hu-jiao	62
Shi-nan-teng	70
Huang-hua-hu-jiao	12
Hua-nan-hu-jiao	0
Xiao-yie-pa-ai-xiang	0
Mao-ju	0
Jia-ju	15
Xie-yie-ju	25
Da-yie-ju	0
Bian-yie-hu-jiao	9
Bi-bo	24
Duo-mai-hu-jiao	40
Yan-sen	0
Jiao-guo-hu-jiao	31

Source: Guiqui, H. "PAF receptor antagonistic principles from Chinese traditional drugs." *Progress in Natural Science,* Vol. 5, No. 3, June 1995, p. 301 (Table 1).

a. Construct a stem-and-leaf display for the data.

b. Compute the median inhibition percentage for the 17 herbal drugs. Interpret the result.

c. Compute the mean inhibition percentage for the 17 herbal drugs. Interpret the result.

d. Compute the mode of the 17 inhibition percentages. Interpret the result.

e. Locate the median, mean, and mode on the stem-and-leaf display, part **a**. Do these measures of central tendency appear to locate the center of the data?

2.41 Would you expect the data sets described below to possess relative frequency distributions that are symmetric, skewed to the right, or skewed to the left? Explain.

a. The salaries of all persons employed by a large university

b. The grades on an easy test

c. The grades on a difficult test

d. The amounts of time students in your class studied last week

e. The ages of automobiles on a used-car lot

f. The amounts of time spent by students on a difficult examination (maximum time is 50 minutes)

2.42 The salaries of superstar professional athletes receive much attention in the media. The multimillion-dollar long-term contract is now commonplace among this elite group. Nevertheless, rarely does a season pass without negotiations between one or more of the players' associations and team owners for additional salary and fringe benefits for *all* players in their particular sports.

a. If a players' association wanted to support its argument for higher "average" salaries, which measure of central tendency do you think it should use? Why?

b. To refute the argument, which measure of central tendency should the owners apply to the players' salaries? Why?

2.43 Refer to the *Financial Management* (Spring 1995) study of prepackaged bankruptcy filings, Exercise 2.22. Recall that each of 49 firms that negotiated a reorganization plan with its creditors prior to filing for bankruptcy was classified in one of three categories: joint exchange offer with prepack, prepack solicitation only, and no pre-filing vote held. An SPSS printout of descriptive statistics for the length of time in bankruptcy (months), by category, is shown below.

a. Locate the measures of central tendency on the printout and interpret their values.

b. Is it reasonable to use a single number (e.g., mean or median) to describe the center of the time-in-bankruptcy distributions? Or should

three "centers" be calculated, one for each of the three categories of prepack firms? Explain.

2.44 Major conventions and conferences attract thousands of people and pump millions of dollars into the local economy of the host city. The decision as to where to hold such conferences hinges to a large extent on the availability of hotel rooms. The table, extracted from *The Wall Street Journal* (Nov. 17, 1995), lists the top ten U.S. cities ranked by the number of hotel rooms.

City	No. of Rooms	No. of Hotels
Las Vegas	93,719	231
Orlando	84,982	311
Los Angeles–Long Beach	78,597	617
Chicago	68,793	378
Washington, D.C.	66,505	351
New York City	61,512	230
Atlanta	58,445	370
San Diego	44,655	352
Anaheim–Santa Ana	44,374	351
San Francisco	42,531	294

Source: Smith Travel Research, September 1995.

a. Find and interpret the median for each of the data sets.

b. For each city, calculate the ratio of the number of rooms to the number of hotels. Then find

```
       TIME
By  CATEGORY   Joint

Valid cases:          11.0   Missing cases:       .0   Percent missing:       .0

Mean         2.6545   Std Err       .5185   Min       1.2000   Skewness      .7600
Median       1.5000   Variance    2.9567   Max       5.4000   S E Skew      .6607
5% Trim      2.5828   Std Dev     1.7195   Range     4.2000   Kurtosis    -1.4183
                                            IQR       3.1000   S E Kurt     1.2794

---------------------------------------------------------------------------------

       TIME
By  CATEGORY   None

Valid cases:          11.0   Missing cases:       .0   Percent missing:       .0

Mean         4.2364   Std Err       .7448   Min       2.4000   Skewness     1.8215
Median       3.2000   Variance    6.1025   Max      10.1000   S E Skew      .6607
5% Trim      4.0126   Std Dev     2.4703   Range     7.7000   Kurtosis     2.6270
                                            IQR       1.6000   S E Kurt     1.2794

---------------------------------------------------------------------------------

       TIME
By  CATEGORY   Prepack

Valid cases:          27.0   Missing cases:       .0   Percent missing:       .0

Mean         1.8185   Std Err       .1847   Min       1.0000   Skewness     1.4539
Median       1.4000   Variance     .9216   Max       4.1000   S E Skew      .4479
5% Trim      1.7372   Std Dev      .9600   Range     3.1000   Kurtosis      .9867
                                            IQR        .9000   S E Kurt      .8721
```

the average number of rooms per hotel in each city.

c. Re-rank the cities based on your answer to part **b**.

2.45 **(X02.045)** According to the U.S. Energy Information Association, the average price of regular unleaded gasoline in the United States in 1993 was 89.6 cents including excise taxes. The table lists the average prices (in cents) in each of a sample of 20 states.

State	Price	State	Price
Arkansas	88.3	New Hampshire	93.2
Connecticut	104.3	New Jersey	88.1
Delaware	91.7	New York	78.5
Hawaii	119.0	North Dakota	91.0
Louisiana	89.8	Oklahoma	85.1
Maine	95.4	Oregon	102.9
Massachusetts	94.3	Pennsylvania	79.2
Michigan	83.2	Texas	90.0
Missouri	79.9	Wisconsin	94.4
Nevada	103.6	Wyoming	87.9

Source: Statistical Abstract of the ...ited States: 1995. U.S. Energy Information Association, *Petro... Marketing Monthly.*

a. Calculate the ...an, median, and mode of this data set.

b. Eliminate the highest price from the data set and repeat part **a**. What effect does dropping this measurement have on the measures of central tendency calculated in part **a**?

c. Arrange the 20 prices in order from lowest to highest. Next, eliminate the lowest two prices and the highest two prices from the data set and calculate the mean of the remaining prices. The result is called an 80% **trimmed mean**, since it is calculated using the central 80% of the values in the data set. An advantage of the trimmed mean is that it is not as sensitive as the arithmetic mean to extreme observations in the data set.

2.46 **(X02.046)** In recent years, the compensation of CEO's, entertainers, and professional athletes has been seriously questioned and often criticized by politicians, the media, and the general public. The table lists the total payroll (in millions of dollars) for active players for each major league baseball team in 1992 and 1995. Numerical descriptive measures for the two sets of data are shown in the MINITAB printouts at the bottom of the page.

Team	1995	1992
New York Yankees	$58.1	$34.9
Baltimore	48.7	24.0
Cincinnati	47.4	35.4
Atlanta	46.4	35.9
Toronto	42.1	49.2
Chicago White Sox	40.7	30.2
Cleveland	39.5	9.3
Boston	38.1	42.1
Colorado	38.0	*
Seattle	37.7	26.4
Chicago Cubs	36.8	32.4
Los Angeles	36.7	42.1
Texas	35.7	26.2
California	33.9	32.6
San Francisco	33.7	23.2
Houston	33.5	15.0
Oakland	33.4	48.0
Kansas City	31.2	32.0
Philadelphia	30.3	25.5
St. Louis	28.7	28.7
Detroit	28.7	28.2
San Diego	24.9	27.7
Florida	23.0	*
Pittsburgh	7.7	36.2
Milwaukee	17.1	30.0
Minnesota	15.4	27.3
Montreal	13.1	16.1
New York Mets	13.1	44.0

*Colorado and Florida joined the league in 1993.

Source: Newark Star-Ledger, December 4, 1995.

a. Find the mean team payroll in 1992 and interpret its value.

b. Find the median team payroll in 1992 and interpret its value.

```
Descriptive Statistics

Variable      N       N*      Mean    Median   Tr Mean    StDev    SE Mean
Sal92        26       2      30.87    30.10    31.00      9.59     1.88

Variable     Min     Max      Q1        Q3
Sal92        9.30    49.20   26.02     35.97


Descriptive Statistics

Variable      N      Mean    Median   Tr Mean    StDev   SE Mean
Sal95        28      32.63   33.80    32.61      11.80   2.23

Variable     Min     Max      Q1        Q3
Sal95        7.70    58.10   25.85     39.15
```

c. Repeat parts **a** and **b** for the 1995 team pay-rolls.

d. What do your answers to part **c** indicate about the skewness of the 1995 payroll data set?

e. Construct a relative frequency histogram for the 1995 team payrolls. Indicate the location of the mean, the median, and the modal class on your histogram.

2.6 NUMERICAL MEASURES OF VARIABILITY

Measures of central tendency provide only a partial description of a quantitative data set. The description is incomplete without a measure of the variability, or spread, of the data set. Knowledge of the data's variability along with its center can help us visualize the shape of a data set as well as its extreme values.

For example, suppose we are comparing the profit margin per construction job (as a percentage of the total bid price) for 100 construction jobs for each of two cost estimators working for a large construction company. The histograms for the two sets of 100 profit margin measurements are shown in Figure 2.20. If you examine the two histograms, you will notice that both data sets are symmetric with equal modes, medians, and means. However, cost estimator A (Figure 2.20a) has profit margins spread with almost equal relative frequency over the measurement classes, while cost estimator B (Figure 2.20b) has profit margins clustered about the center of the distribution. Thus, estimator B's profit margins are *less variable* than estimator A's. Consequently, you can see that we need a measure of variability as well as a measure of central tendency to describe a data set.

Perhaps the simplest measure of the variability of a quantitative data set is its *range*.

DEFINITION 2.8

The **range** of a quantitative data set is equal to the largest measurement minus the smallest measurement.

The range is easy to compute and easy to understand, but it is a rather insensitive measure of data variation when the data sets are large. This is because two data sets can have the same range and be vastly different with respect to data variation. This phenomenon is demonstrated in Figure 2.20. Although the ranges

FIGURE 2.20
Profit margin histograms for two cost estimators

a. Cost estimator A

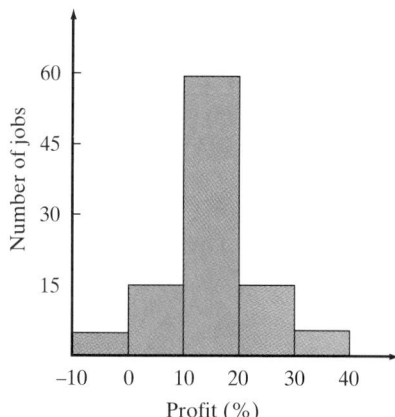

b. Cost estimator B

TABLE 2.6   Two Hypothetical Data Sets

	Sample 1	Sample 2
Measurements	$1, 2, 3, 4, 5$	$2, 3, 3, 3, 4$
Mean	$\bar{x} = \dfrac{1 + 2 + 3 + 4 + 5}{5} = \dfrac{15}{5} = 3$	$\bar{x} = \dfrac{2 + 3 + 3 + 3 + 4}{5} = \dfrac{15}{5} = 3$
Distances of measurement values from $\bar{x}$	$(1 - 3), (2 - 3), (3 - 3), (4 - 3),$ $(5 - 3)$ or $-2, -1, 0, 1, 2$	$(2 - 3), (3 - 3), (3 - 3), (3 - 3),$ $(4 - 3)$ or $-1, 0, 0, 0, 1$

are equal and all central tendency measures are the same for these two symmetric data sets, there is an obvious difference between the two sets of measurements. The difference is that estimator B's profit margins tend to be more stable—that is, to pile up or to cluster about the center of the data set. In contrast, estimator A's profit margins are more spread out over the range, indicating a higher incidence of some high profit margins, but also a greater risk of losses. Thus, even though the ranges are equal, the profit margin record of estimator A is more variable than that of estimator B, indicating a distinct difference in their cost estimating characteristics.

Let's see if we can find a measure of data variation that is more sensitive than the range. Consider the two samples in Table 2.6: Each has five measurements. (We have ordered the numbers for convenience.)

Note that both samples have a mean of 3 and that we have also calculated the distance, or **deviation**, between each measurement and the mean. What information do these distances contain? If they tend to be large in magnitude, as in sample 1, the data are spread out, or highly variable. If the distances are mostly small, as in sample 2, the data are clustered around the mean, $\bar{x}$, and therefore do not exhibit much variability. You can see that these distances, displayed graphically in Figure 2.21, provide information about the variability of the sample measurements.

The next step is to condense the information in these distances into a single numerical measure of variability. Averaging the distances from $\bar{x}$ won't help because the negative and positive distances cancel; that is, the sum of the deviations (and thus the average deviation) is always equal to zero.

Two methods come to mind for dealing with the fact that positive and negative distances from the mean cancel. The first is to treat all the distances as though they were positive, ignoring the sign of the negative distances. We won't pursue this line of thought because the resulting measure of variability (the mean of the absolute values of the distances) presents analytical difficulties beyond the scope of this text. A second method of eliminating the minus signs associated with the distances is to square them. The quantity we can calculate from the squared distances will provide a meaningful description of the variability of a data set and presents fewer analytical difficulties in inference-making.

To use the squared distances calculated from a data set, we first calculate the *sample variance.*

FIGURE 2.21
Dot plots for two data sets

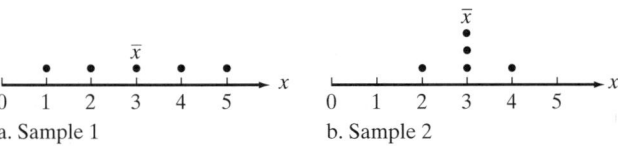

a. Sample 1   b. Sample 2

DEFINITION 2.9

The **sample variance** for a sample of n measurements is equal to the sum of the squared distances from the mean divided by $(n-1)$. In symbols, using s^2 to represent the sample variance,

$$s^2 = \frac{\sum_{i=1}^{n}(x_i - \bar{x})^2}{n-1}$$

Note: A shortcut formula for calculating s^2 is

$$s^2 = \frac{\sum_{i=1}^{n}x_i^2 - \frac{\left(\sum_{i=1}^{n}x_i\right)^2}{n}}{n-1}$$

Referring to the two samples in Table 2.6, you can calculate the variance for sample 1 as follows:

$$s^2 = \frac{(1-3)^2 + (2-3)^2 + (3-3)^2 + (4-3)^2 + (5-3)^2}{5-1}$$

$$= \frac{4+1+0+1+4}{4} = 2.5$$

The second step in finding a meaningful measure of data variability is to calculate the *standard deviation* of the data set.

DEFINITION 2.10

The **sample standard deviation**, s, is defined as the positive square root of the sample variance, s^2. Thus, $s = \sqrt{s^2}$.

The population variance, denoted by the symbol σ^2 (sigma squared), is the average of the squared distances of the measurements on *all* units in the population from the mean, μ, and σ (sigma) is the square root of this quantity. Since we never really compute σ^2 or σ from the population (the object of sampling is to avoid this costly procedure), we simply denote these two quantities by their respective symbols.

Symbols for Variance and Standard Deviation
s^2 = Sample variance
s = Sample standard deviation
σ^2 = Population variance
σ = Population standard deviation

Notice that, unlike the variance, the standard deviation is expressed in the original units of measurement. For example, if the original measurements are in dollars, the variance is expressed in the peculiar units "dollar squared," but the standard deviation is expressed in dollars.

You may wonder why we use the divisor $(n - 1)$ instead of n when calculating the sample variance. Wouldn't using n be more logical, so that the sample variance would be the average squared distance from the mean? The trouble is, using n tends to produce an underestimate of the population variance, σ^2. So we use $(n - 1)$ in the denominator to provide the appropriate correction for this tendency.* Since sample statistics like s^2 are primarily used to estimate population parameters like σ^2, $(n - 1)$ is preferred to n when defining the sample variance.

EXAMPLE 2.9   Calculate the variance and standard deviation of the following sample: 2, 3, 3, 3, 4.

SOLUTION

As the number of measurements increases, calculating s^2 and s becomes very tedious. Fortunately, as we show in Example 2.10, we can use a statistical software package (or calculator) to find these values. If you must calculate these quantities by hand, it is advantageous to use the shortcut formula provided in Definition 2.9. To do this, we need two summations: Σx and Σx^2. These can easily be obtained from the following type of tabulation:

x	x^2
2	4
3	9
3	9
3	9
4	16
$\Sigma x = 15$	$\Sigma x^2 = 47$

Then we use†

$$s^2 = \frac{\sum_{i=1}^{n} x_i^2 - \frac{\left(\sum_{i=1}^{n} x_i\right)^2}{n}}{n - 1} = \frac{47 - \frac{(15)^2}{5}}{5 - 1} = \frac{2}{4} = .5$$

$$s = \sqrt{.5} = .71$$

EXAMPLE 2.10   Use the computer to find the sample variance s^2 and the sample standard deviation s for the 50 companies' percentages of revenues spent on R&D.

SOLUTION

The SAS printout describing the R&D percentage data is displayed in Figure 2.22. The variance and standard deviation, highlighted on the printout, are: $s^2 = 3.922792$ and $s = 1.980604$.

You now know that the standard deviation measures the variability of a set of data and how to calculate it. But how can we interpret and use the standard deviation? This is the topic of Section 2.7.

---

*"Appropriate" here means that s^2 with the divisor of $(n - 1)$ is an **unbiased estimator** of σ^2. We define and discuss unbiasedness of estimators in Chapter 6.

†When calculating s^2, how many decimal places should you carry? Although there are no rules for the rounding procedure, it's reasonable to retain twice as many decimal places in s^2 as you ultimately wish to have in s. If you wish to calculate s to the nearest hundredth (two decimal places), for example, you should calculate s^2 to the nearest ten-thousandth (four decimal places).

FIGURE 2.22
SAS printout of
numerical descriptive
measures for 50 R&D
percentages

```
                         UNIVARIATE PROCEDURE
        Variable=RDPCT

                             Moments

            N                50   Sum Wgts          50
            Mean          8.492   Sum            424.6
            Std Dev    1.980604   Variance    3.922792
            Skewness   0.854601   Kurtosis    0.419288
            USS         3797.92   CSS         192.2168
            CV         23.32317   Std Mean      0.2801
            T:Mean=0   30.31778   Prob>|T|      0.0001
            Sgn Rank      637.5   Prob>|S|      0.0001
            Num ^= 0         50

                        Quantiles(Def=5)

            100% Max       13.5   99%            13.5
             75% Q3         9.6   95%            13.2
             50% Med       8.05   90%            11.2
             25% Q1         7.1   10%             6.5
              0% Min        5.2   5%              5.9
                                  1%              5.2

            Range           8.3
            Q3-Q1           2.5
            Mode            6.5
```

EXERCISES   2.47–2.58

Note: Exercises marked with 💾 contain data available for computer analysis on a 3.5" disk (file name in parentheses).

Learning the Mechanics

2.47 Answer the following questions about variability of data sets:
a. What is the primary disadvantage of using the range to compare the variability of data sets?
b. Describe the sample variance using words rather than a formula. Do the same with the population variance.
c. Can the variance of a data set ever be negative? Explain. Can the variance ever be smaller than the standard deviation? Explain.

2.48 Calculate the variance and standard deviation for samples where
a. $n = 10, \Sigma x^2 = 84, \Sigma x = 20$
b. $n = 40, \Sigma x^2 = 380, \Sigma x = 100$
c. $n = 20, \Sigma x^2 = 18, \Sigma x = 17$

2.49 Calculate the range, variance, and standard deviation for the following samples:
a. 4, 2, 1, 0, 1   b. 1, 6, 2, 2, 3, 0, 3
c. 8, −2, 1, 3, 5, 4, 4, 1, 3, 3
d. 0, 2, 0, 0, −1, 1, −2, 1, 0, −1, 1, −1, 0, −3, −2, −1, 0, 1

2.50 Calculate the range, variance, and standard deviation for the following samples:
a. 39, 42, 40, 37, 41   b. 100, 4, 7, 96, 80, 3, 1, 10, 2
c. 100, 4, 7, 30, 80, 30, 42, 2

2.51 Compute $\bar{x}, s^2$, and s for each of the following data sets. If appropriate, specify the units in which your answer is expressed.
a. 3, 1, 10, 10, 4   b. 8 feet, 10 feet, 32 feet, 5 feet
c. −1, −4, −3, 1, −4, −4
d. ⅕ ounce, ⅕ ounce, ⅕ ounce, ⅖ ounce, ⅕ ounce, ⅘ ounce

2.52 Using only integers between 0 and 10, construct two data sets with at least 10 observations each so that the two sets have the same mean but different variances. Construct dot plots for each of your data sets and mark the mean of each data set on its dot diagram.

2.53 Using only integers between 0 and 10, construct two data sets with at least 10 observations each that have the same range but different means. Construct a dot plot for each of your data sets, and mark the mean of each data set on its dot diagram.

2.54 Consider the following sample of five measurements: 2, 1, 1, 0, 3
a. Calculate the range, s^2, and s.
b. Add 3 to each measurement and repeat part **a**.
c. Subtract 4 from each measurement and repeat part **a**.
d. Considering your answers to parts **a**, **b**, and **c**, what seems to be the effect on the variability of a data set by adding the same number to or subtracting the same number from each measurement?

Applying the Concepts

2.55 (X02.055) The Consumer Price Index (CPI) measures the price change of a constant market basket of goods and services. The Bureau of Labor Statistics publishes a national CPI (called the U.S. City Average Index) as well as separate indexes for each of 32 different cities in the United States. The national index and some of the city indexes are published monthly; the remainder of the city indexes are published semiannually. The CPI is used in cost-of-living escalator clauses of many labor contracts to adjust wages for inflation (*Bureau of Labor Statistics Handbook of Methods,* 1992). For example, in the printing industry of Minneapolis–St. Paul, hourly wages are adjusted every six months (based on October and April values of the CPI) by 4¢ for every point change in the Minneapolis–St. Paul CPI. The table below lists the published values of the U.S. City Average Index and the Chicago Index during 1994 and 1995.

Month	U.S. City Average Index	Chicago
January 1994	146.2	146.5
February	146.7	146.8
March	147.2	147.6
April	147.4	147.9
May	147.5	147.6
June	148.0	148.1
July	148.4	148.3
August	149.0	149.8
September	149.4	150.2
October	149.5	149.4
November	149.7	150.4
December	149.7	150.5
January 1995	150.3	151.8
February	150.9	152.3
March	151.4	152.6
April	151.9	153.1
May	152.2	153.0
June	152.5	153.5
July	152.5	153.6
August	152.9	153.8
September	153.2	154.0
October	153.7	154.3
November	153.6	154.0
December	153.5	153.8

Source: CPI Detailed Report, Bureau of Labor Statistics, Jan. 1994–Dec. 1995.

a. Calculate the mean values for the U.S. City Average Index and the Chicago Index.
b. Find the ranges of the U.S. City Average Index and the Chicago Index.
c. Calculate the standard deviation for both the U.S. City Average Index and the Chicago Index over the time period described in the table.
d. Which index displays greater variation about its mean over the time period in question? Justify your response.

2.56 To set an appropriate price for a product, it's necessary to be able to estimate its cost of production. One element of the cost is based on the length of time it takes workers to produce the product. The most widely used technique for making such measurements is the **time study**. In a time study, the task to be studied is divided into measurable parts and each is timed with a stopwatch or filmed for later analysis. For each worker, this process is repeated many times for each subtask. Then the average and standard deviation of the time required to complete each subtask are computed for each worker. A worker's overall time to complete the task under study is then determined by adding his or her subtask-time averages (Gaither, *Production and Operations Management,* 1996). The data (in minutes) given in the table are the result of a time study of a production operation involving two subtasks.

	WORKER A		WORKER B	
Repetition	Subtask 1	Subtask 2	Subtask 1	Subtask 2
1	30	2	31	7
2	28	4	30	2
3	31	3	32	6
4	38	3	30	5
5	25	2	29	4
6	29	4	30	1
7	30	3	31	4

a. Find the overall time it took each worker to complete the manufacturing operation under study.
b. For each worker, find the standard deviation of the seven times for subtask 1.
c. In the context of this problem, what are the standard deviations you computed in part **b** measuring?
d. Repeat part **b** for subtask 2.
e. If you could choose workers similar to A or workers similar to B to perform subtasks 1 and 2, which type would you assign to each subtask? Explain your decisions on the basis of your answers to parts **a–d**.

2.57 The table lists the 1995 profits (in millions of dollars) for a sample of seven airlines.

Airline	Profit
Southwest	182.6
Continental	226.0
Northwest	342.1
Delta	510.0
U.S. Air	119.3
United	378.0
America West	54.8

Source: "*Business Week* 1000." *Business Week,* March 25, 1996, p. 90.

a. Calculate the range, variance, and standard deviation of the data set.

b. Specify the units in which each of your answers to part **a** is expressed.

c. Suppose America West had a loss of $50 instead of a profit of $54.8 million. Would the range of the data set increase or decrease? Why? Would the standard deviation of the data set increase or decrease? Why?

2.58   The U.S. Federal Trade Commission has recently begun assessing fines and other penalties against weight-loss clinics that make unsupported or misleading claims about the effectiveness of their programs. Suppose you have brochures from two weight-loss clinics that both advertise "statistical evidence" about the effectiveness of their programs. Clinic A advertises that the *mean* weight loss during the first month is 15 pounds, while clinic B advertises a *median* weight loss of 10 pounds.

a. Assuming the statistics are accurately calculated, which clinic would you recommend if you had no other information? Why?

b. Upon further research, the median and standard deviation for Clinic A are found to be 10 pounds and 20 pounds, respectively, while the mean and standard deviation for clinic B are found to be 10 and 5 pounds, respectively. Both are based on samples of more than 100 clients. Describe the two clinics' weight-loss distributions as completely as possible given this additional information. What would you recommend to a prospective client now? Why?

c. Note that nothing has been said about how the sample of clients upon which the statistics are based was selected. What additional information would be important regarding the sampling techniques employed by the clinics?

2.7   INTERPRETING THE STANDARD DEVIATION

We've seen that if we are comparing the variability of two samples selected from a population, the sample with the larger standard deviation is the more variable of the two. Thus, we know how to interpret the standard deviation on a relative or comparative basis, but we haven't explained how it provides a measure of variability for a single sample.

To understand how the standard deviation provides a measure of variability of a data set, consider a specific data set and answer the following questions: How many measurements are within 1 standard deviation of the mean? How many measurements are within 2 standard deviations? For a specific data set, we can answer these questions by counting the number of measurements in each of the intervals. However, if we are interested in obtaining a general answer to these questions, the problem is more difficult.

Tables 2.7 and 2.8 give two sets of answers to the questions of how many measurements fall within 1, 2, and 3 standard deviations of the mean. The first, which applies to *any* set of data, is derived from a theorem proved by the Russian mathematician P. L. Chebyshev (1821—1894). The second, which applies to mound-shaped, symmetric distributions of data (where the mean, median, and mode are all about the same), is based upon empirical evidence that has accumulated over the years. However, the percentages given for the intervals in Table 2.8 provide remarkably good approximations even when the distribution of the data is slightly skewed or asymmetric. Note that both rules apply to either population data sets or sample data sets.

TABLE 2.7   An Aid to Interpretation of a Standard Deviation: Chebyshev's Rule

Chebyshev's Rule applies to any data set, regardless of the shape of the frequency distribution of the data.

a. No useful information is provided on the fraction of measurements that fall within 1 standard deviation of the mean, i.e., within the interval $(\bar{x} - s, \bar{x} + s)$ for samples and $(\mu - \sigma, \mu + \sigma)$ for populations.

continued

b. At least $3/4$ will fall within 2 standard deviations of the mean, i.e., within the interval $(\bar{x} - 2s, \bar{x} + 2s)$ for samples and $(\mu - 2\sigma, \mu + 2\sigma)$ for populations.

c. At least $8/9$ of the measurements will fall within 3 standard deviations of the mean, i.e., within the interval $(\bar{x} - 3s, \bar{x} + 3s)$ for samples and $(\mu - 3\sigma, \mu + 3\sigma)$ for populations.

d. Generally, for any number k greater than 1, at least $1 - 1/k^2$ of the measurements will fall within k standard deviations of the mean, i.e., within the interval $(\bar{x} - ks, \bar{x} + ks)$ for samples and $(\mu - k\sigma, \mu + k\sigma)$ for populations.

TABLE 2.8 An Aid to Interpretation of a Standard Deviation: The Empirical Rule

---

The **Empirical Rule** is a rule of thumb that applies to data sets with frequency distributions that are mound-shaped and symmetric, as shown below.

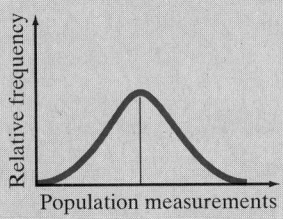

a. Approximately 68% of the measurements will fall within 1 standard deviation of the mean, i.e., within the interval $(\bar{x} - s, \bar{x} + s)$ for samples and $(\mu - \sigma, \mu + \sigma)$ for populations.

b. Approximately 95% of the measurements will fall within 2 standard deviations of the mean, i.e., within the interval $(\bar{x} - 2s, \bar{x} + 2s)$ for samples and $(\mu - 2\sigma, \mu + 2\sigma)$ for populations.

c. Approximately 99.7% (essentially all) of the measurements will fall within 3 standard deviations of the mean, i.e., within the interval $(\bar{x} - 3s, \bar{x} + 3s)$ for samples and $(\mu - 3\sigma, \mu + 3\sigma)$ for populations.

EXAMPLE 2.11 The 50 companies' percentages of revenues spent on R&D are repeated here:

13.5	9.5	8.2	6.5	8.4	8.1	6.9	7.5	10.5	13.5
7.2	7.1	9.0	9.9	8.2	13.2	9.2	6.9	9.6	7.7
9.7	7.5	7.2	5.9	6.6	11.1	8.8	5.2	10.6	8.2
11.3	5.6	10.1	8.0	8.5	11.7	7.1	7.7	9.4	6.0
8.0	7.4	10.5	7.8	7.9	6.5	6.9	6.5	6.8	9.5

We have previously shown that the mean and standard deviation of these data (rounded) are 8.49 and 1.98, respectively. Calculate the fraction of these measurements that lie within the intervals $\bar{x} \pm s$, $\bar{x} \pm 2s$, and $\bar{x} \pm 3s$, and compare the results with those predicted in Tables 2.7 and 2.8.

SOLUTION
We first form the interval

$$(\bar{x} - s, \bar{x} + s) = (8.49 - 1.98, 8.49 + 1.98) = (6.51, 10.47)$$

A check of the measurements reveals that 34 of the 50 measurements, or 68%, are within 1 standard deviation of the mean.

The next interval of interest

$$(\bar{x} - 2s, \bar{x} + 2s) = (8.49 - 3.96, 8.49 + 3.96) = (4.53, 12.45)$$

contains 47 of the 50 measurements, or 94%.

Finally, the 3-standard-deviation interval around $\bar{x}$,

$$(\bar{x} - 3s, \bar{x} + 3s) = (8.49 - 5.94, 8.49 + 5.94) = (2.55, 14.43)$$

contains all, or 100%, of the measurements.

In spite of the fact that the distribution of these data is skewed to the right (see Figure 2.8), the percentages within 1, 2, and 3 standard deviations (68%, 94%, and 100%) agree very well with the approximations of 68%, 95%, and 99.7% given by the Empirical Rule (Table 2.8). You will find that unless the distribution is extremely skewed, the mound-shaped approximations will be reasonably accurate. Of course, no matter what the shape of the distribution, Chebyshev's Rule (Table 2.7) assures that at least 75% and at least 89% ($\%$) of the measurements will lie within 2 and 3 standard deviations of the mean, respectively. **◣**

EXAMPLE 2.12

Chebyshev's Rule and the Empirical Rule are useful as a check on the calculation of the standard deviation. For example, suppose we calculated the standard deviation for the R&D percentages (Table 2.3) to be 3.92. Are there any "clues" in the data that enable us to judge whether this number is reasonable?

SOLUTION

The range of the R&D percentages in Table 2.3 is $13.5 - 5.2 = 8.3$. From Chebyshev's Rule and the Empirical Rule we know that most of the measurements (approximately 95% if the distribution is mound-shaped) will be within 2 standard deviations of the mean. And, regardless of the shape of the distribution and the number of measurements, almost all of them will fall within 3 standard deviations of the mean. Consequently, we would expect the range of the measurements to be between 4 (i.e., $\pm 2s$) and 6 (i.e., $\pm 3s$) standard deviations in length (see Figure 2.23).

For the R&D data, this means that s should fall between

$$\frac{Range}{6} = \frac{8.3}{6} = 1.38 \quad \text{and} \quad \frac{Range}{4} = \frac{8.3}{4} = 2.08$$

In particular, the standard deviation should not be much larger than $\frac{1}{4}$ of the range, particularly for the data set with 50 measurements. Thus, we have reason to believe that the calculation of 3.92 is too large. A check of our work reveals that 3.92 is the variance s^2, not the standard deviation s (see Example 2.10). We "forgot" to take the square root (a common error); the correct value is $s = 1.98$. Note that this value is between $\frac{1}{6}$ and $\frac{1}{4}$ of the range. **◣**

In examples and exercises we'll sometimes use $s \approx \text{range}/4$ to obtain a crude, and usually conservatively large, approximation for s. However, we stress that this is no substitute for calculating the exact value of s when possible.

Finally, and most importantly, we will use the concepts in Chebyshev's Rule and the Empirical Rule to build the foundation for statistical inference-making. The method is illustrated in Example 2.13.

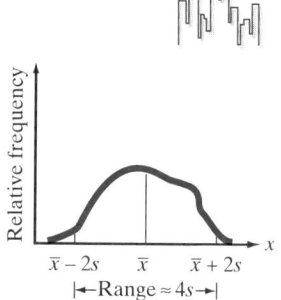

FIGURE 2.23
The relation between the range and the standard deviation

EXAMPLE 2.13

A manufacturer of automobile batteries claims that the average length of life for its grade A battery is 60 months. However, the guarantee on this brand is for just 36 months. Suppose the standard deviation of the life length is known to be 10 months, and the frequency distribution of the life-length data is known to be mound-shaped.

a. Approximately what percentage of the manufacturer's grade A batteries will last more than 50 months, assuming the manufacturer's claim is true?

b. Approximately what percentage of the manufacturer's batteries will last less than 40 months, assuming the manufacturer's claim is true?

c. Suppose your battery lasts 37 months. What could you infer about the manufacturer's claim?

SOLUTION

If the distribution of life length is assumed to be mound-shaped with a mean of 60 months and a standard deviation of 10 months, it would appear as shown in Figure 2.24. Note that we can take advantage of the fact that mound-shaped distributions are (approximately) symmetric about the mean, so that the percentages given by the Empirical Rule can be split equally between the halves of the distribution on each side of the mean. The approximations given in Figure 2.24 are more dependent on the assumption of a mound-shaped distribution than those given by the Empirical Rule (Table 2.8), because the approximations in Figure 2.24 depend on the (approximate) symmetry of the mound-shaped distribution. We saw in Example 2.11 that the Empirical Rule can yield good approximations even for skewed distributions. This will *not* be true of the approximations in Figure 2.24; the distribution *must* be mound-shaped and approximately symmetric.

For example, since approximately 68% of the measurements will fall within 1 standard deviation of the mean, the distribution's symmetry implies that approximately ½(68%) = 34% of the measurements will fall between the mean and 1 standard deviation on each side. This concept is illustrated in Figure 2.24. The figure also shows that 2.5% of the measurements lie beyond 2 standard deviations in each direction from the mean. This result follows from the fact that if approximately 95% of the measurements fall within 2 standard deviations of the mean, then about 5% fall outside 2 standard deviations; if the distribution is approximately symmetric, then about 2.5% of the measurements fall beyond 2 standard deviations on each side of the mean.

a. It is easy to see in Figure 2.24 that the percentage of batteries lasting more than 50 months is approximately 34% (between 50 and 60 months) plus 50% (greater than 60 months). Thus, approximately 84% of the batteries should have life length exceeding 50 months.

b. The percentage of batteries that last less than 40 months can also be easily determined from Figure 2.24. Approximately 2.5% of the batteries should fail prior to 40 months, assuming the manufacturer's claim is true.

c. If you are so unfortunate that your grade A battery fails at 37 months, you can make one of two inferences: either your battery was one of the approximately 2.5% that fail prior to 40 months, or something about the manufacturer's claim is not true. Because the chances are so small that a battery fails

FIGURE 2.24
Battery life-length distribution: Manufacturer's claim assumed true

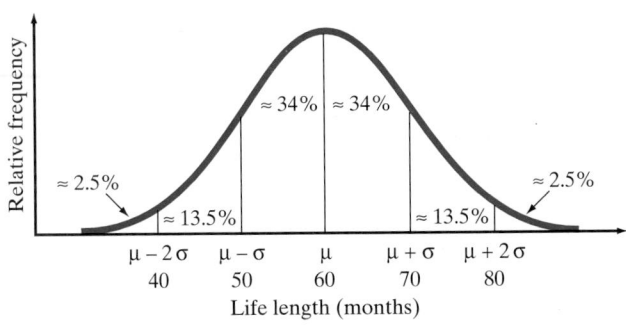

before 40 months, you would have good reason to have serious doubts about the manufacturer's claim. A mean smaller than 60 months and/or a standard deviation longer than 10 months would both increase the likelihood of failure prior to 40 months.*

Example 2.13 is our initial demonstration of the statistical inference-making process. At this point you should realize that we'll use sample information (in Example 2.13, your battery's failure at 37 months) to make inferences about the population (in Example 2.13, the manufacturer's claim about the life length for the population of all batteries). We'll build on this foundation as we proceed.

*The assumption that the distribution is mound-shaped and symmetric may also be incorrect. However, if the distribution were skewed to the right, as life-length distributions often tend to be, the percentage of measurements more than 2 standard deviations *below* the mean would be even less than 2.5%.

EXERCISES 2.59–2.74

Note: Exercises marked with 💾 *contain data available for computer analysis on a 3.5" disk (file name in parentheses).*

Learning the Mechanics

2.59 To what kind of data sets can Chebyshev's Rule be applied? The Empirical Rule?

2.60 The output from a statistical software package indicates that the mean and standard deviation of a data set consisting of 200 measurements are $1,500 and $300, respectively.
  a. What are the units of measurement of the variable of interest? Based on the units, what type of data is this: quantitative or qualitative?
  b. What can be said about the number of measurements between $900 and $2,100? Between $600 and $2,400? Between $1,200 and $1,800? Between $1,500 and $2,100?

2.61 For any set of data, what can be said about the percentage of the measurements contained in each of the following intervals?
  a. $\bar{x} - s$ to $\bar{x} + s$ **b.** $\bar{x} - 2s$ to $\bar{x} + 2s$
  c. $\bar{x} - 3s$ to $\bar{x} + 3s$

2.62 For a set of data with a mound-shaped relative frequency distribution, what can be said about the percentage of the measurements contained in each of the intervals specified in Exercise 2.61?

2.63 The following is a sample of 25 measurements:

7	6	6	11	8	9	11	9	10	8	7	7
5	9	10	7	7	7	7	9	12	10	10	8	6

  a. Compute $\bar{x}, s^2$, and s for this sample.
  b. Count the number of measurements in the intervals $\bar{x} \pm s$, $\bar{x} \pm 2s$, $\bar{x} \pm 3s$. Express each count as a percentage of the total number of measurements.
  c. Compare the percentages found in part **b** to the percentages given by the Empirical Rule and Chebyshev's Rule.
  d. Calculate the range and use it to obtain a rough approximation for s. Does the result

compare favorably with the actual value for s found in part **a**?

2.64 Given a data set with a largest value of 760 and a smallest value of 135, what would you estimate the standard deviation to be? Explain the logic behind the procedure you used to estimate the standard deviation. Suppose the standard deviation is reported to be 25. Is this feasible? Explain.

Applying the Concepts

2.65 Refer to the *Marine Technology* (Jan. 1995) data on spillage amounts (in thousands of metric tons) for 50 major oil spills, Exercise 2.10. An SPSS histogram for the 50 spillage amounts is shown at the top of page 74.
  a. Interpret the histogram.
  b. Descriptive statistics for the 50 spillage amounts are provided in the SPSS printout. Use this information to form an interval that can be used to predict the spillage amount for the next major oil spill.

2.66 (X02.066) As a result of government and consumer pressure, automobile manufacturers in the United States are deeply involved in research to improve their products' gasoline mileage. One manufacturer, hoping to achieve 40 miles per gallon on one of its compact models, measured the mileage obtained by 36 test versions of the model with the following results (rounded to the nearest mile for convenience):

43	35	41	42	42	38	40	41	41	40	40	41
42	36	43	40	38	40	38	45	39	41	42	37
40	40	44	39	40	37	39	41	39	41	37	40

The mean and standard deviation of these data are shown in the SAS printout at the bottom of page 74.
  a. Find the mean and standard deviation on the printout and give the units in which they are expressed.

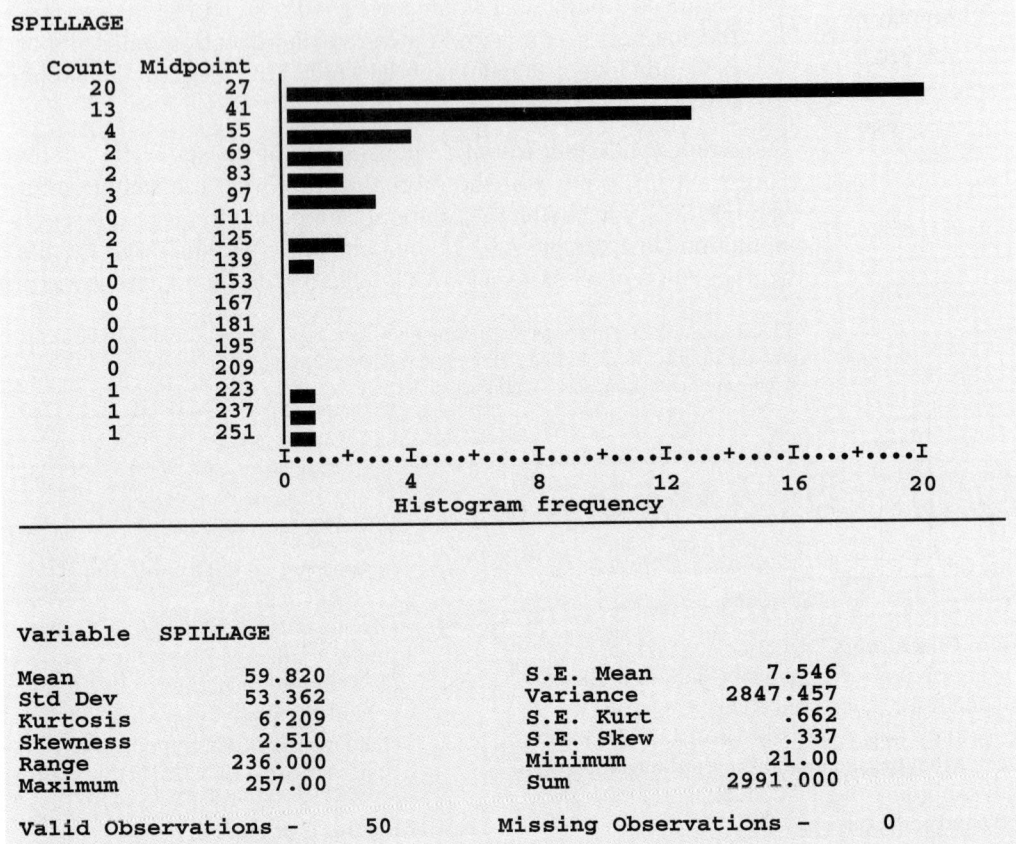

```
SPILLAGE

Count  Midpoint
   20       27  ████████████████████████████████████
   13       41  ██████████████████████
    4       55  ██████
    2       69  ███
    2       83  ███
    3       97  █████
    0      111
    2      125  ███
    1      139  ██
    0      153
    0      167
    0      181
    0      195
    0      209
    1      223  ██
    1      237  ██
    1      251  ██
                I....+....I....+....I....+....I....+....I....+....I
                0         4         8        12        16        20
                           Histogram frequency
```

```
Variable   SPILLAGE

Mean              59.820          S.E. Mean           7.546
Std Dev           53.362          Variance         2847.457
Kurtosis           6.209          S.E. Kurt            .662
Skewness           2.510          S.E. Skew            .337
Range            236.000          Minimum            21.00
Maximum          257.00           Sum              2991.000

Valid Observations -    50        Missing Observations -     0
```

b. If the manufacturer would be satisfied with a (population) mean of 40 miles per gallon, how would it react to the above test data?

c. Use the information in Tables 2.7–2.8 to check the reasonableness of the calculated standard deviation $s = 2.2$.

d. Construct a relative frequency histogram of the data set. Is the data set mound-shaped?

e. What percentage of the measurements would you expect to find within the intervals $\bar{x} \pm s$, $\bar{x} \pm 2s, \bar{x} \pm 3s$?

f. Count the number of measurements that actually fall within the intervals of part **e**. Express each interval count as a percentage of the total number of measurements. Compare these results with your answers to part **e**.

2.67 Refer to the *Financial Management* (Spring 1995) study of 49 firms filing for prepackaged bankruptcy, Exercise 2.22. Recall that the variable of interest was length of time (months) in bankruptcy for each firm.

a. A histogram (produced by MINITAB for Windows) for the 49 bankruptcy times is displayed on page 75. Comment on whether the Empirical Rule is applicable for describing the bankruptcy time distribution for firms filing for prepackaged bankruptcy.

b. Numerical descriptive statistics for the data set are shown in the MINITAB printout on page 75. Use this information to construct an interval that captures at least 75% of the bankruptcy times for "prepack" firms.

c. Refer to the data listed in Exercise 2.22. Count the number of the 49 bankruptcy times that fall within the interval, part **b**, and convert the result to a percentage. Does the result agree with Chebyshev's Rule? The Empirical Rule?

d. A firm is considering filing a prepackaged bankruptcy plan. Estimate the length of time the firm will be in bankruptcy.

2.68 Refer to the *Arkansas Business and Economic Review* (Summer 1995) study of the number of

```
Analysis Variable : MPG

N Obs   N      Minimum        Maximum           Mean        Std Dev
-----------------------------------------------------------------------
  36    36   35.0000000     45.0000000     40.0555556     2.1770812
-----------------------------------------------------------------------
```

```
Descriptive Statistics
Variable        N       Mean    Median   Tr Mean     StDev    SE Mean
Time           49      2.549    1.700     2.333      1.828     0.261

Variable      Min       Max      Q1        Q3
Time        1.000    10.100    1.350     3.500
```

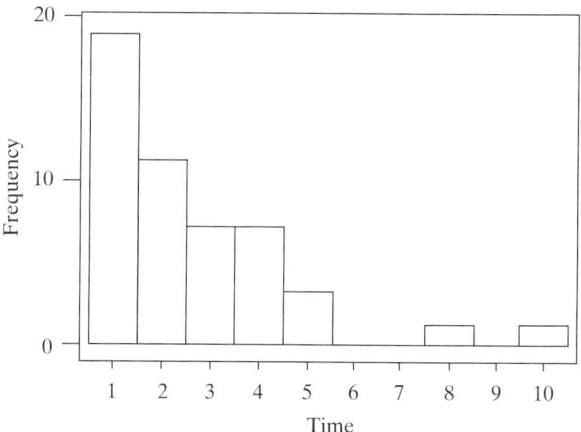

Superfund hazardous waste sites in Arkansas counties, Exercise 2.38. The data and EXCEL numerical descriptive statistics printout are reproduced below.

Calculate the percentage of measurements in the intervals $\bar{x} \pm s, \bar{x} \pm 2s$, and $\bar{x} \pm 3s$. Check the agreement of these percentages with both Chebyshev's Rule and the Empirical Rule.

SITES	
Mean	5.24
Standard Error	0.836517879
Median	3
Mode	2
Standard Deviation	7.244457341
Sample Variance	52.48216216
Kurtosis	16.41176573
Skewness	3.468289878
Range	48
Minimum	0
Maximum	48
Sum	393
Count	75
Confidence Level(95.000%)	1.639542488

2.69 The *American Rifleman* (June 1993) reported on the velocity of ammunition fired from the FEG P9R pistol, a new 9mm gun manufactured in Hungary. Field tests revealed that Winchester bullets fired from the pistol had a mean velocity (at 15 feet) of 936 feet per second and a standard deviation of 10 feet per second. Tests were also conducted with Uzi and Black Hills ammunition.

 a. Describe the velocity distribution of Winchester bullets fired from the FEG P9R pistol.

 b. A bullet, brand unknown, is fired from the FEG P9R pistol. Suppose the velocity (at 15 feet) of the bullet is 1,000 feet per second. Is the bullet likely to be manufactured by Winchester? Explain.

2.70 For each day of last year, the number of vehicles passing through a certain intersection was recorded by a city engineer. One objective of this study was to determine the percentage of days that more than 425 vehicles used the intersection. Suppose the mean for the data was 375 vehicles per day and the standard deviation was 25 vehicles.

 a. What can you say about the percentage of days that more than 425 vehicles used the intersection? Assume you know nothing about the shape of the relative frequency distribution for the data.

 b. What is your answer to part **a** if you know that the relative frequency distribution for the data is mound-shaped?

2.71 A buyer for a lumber company must decide whether to buy a piece of land containing 5,000 pine trees. If 1,000 of the trees are at least 40 feet tall, the buyer will purchase the land; otherwise, he won't. The owner of the land reports that the height of the trees has a mean of 30 feet and a standard deviation of 3 feet. Based on this information, what is the buyer's decision?

2.72 A chemical company produces a substance composed of 98% cracked corn particles and 2% zinc phosphide for use in controlling rat populations in sugarcane fields. Production must be carefully

3	3	2	1	2	0	5	3	5	2	1	8	2	12	3	5	3	1	3
0	8	0	9	6	8	6	2	16	0	6	0	5	5	0	1	25	0	0
0	6	2	10	12	3	10	3	17	2	4	2	1	21	4	2	1	11	5
2	2	7	2	3	1	8	2	0	0	0	2	3	10	2	3	48	21	

Source: Tabor, R. H., and Stanwick, S. D. "Arkansas: An environmental perspective." *Arkansas Business and Economic Review,* Vol. 28, No. 2, Summer 1995, pp. 22–32 (Table 1).

controlled to maintain the 2% zinc phosphide because too much zinc phosphide will cause damage to the sugarcane and too little will be ineffective in controlling the rat population. Records from past production indicate that the distribution of the actual percentage of zinc phosphide present in the substance is approximately mound-shaped, with a mean of 2.0% and a standard deviation of .08%.

a. If the production line is operating correctly, approximately what proportion of batches from a day's production will contain less than 1.84% of zinc phosphide?

b. Suppose one batch chosen randomly actually contains 1.80% zinc phosphide. Does this indicate that there is too little zinc phosphide in today's production? Explain your reasoning.

2.73 Many of the nation's largest newspapers have sharply raised prices to offset the increasing cost of newsprint, while others want to increase their circulation's share of revenue relative to advertising's share of revenue. Consequently, these newspapers have experienced a decline in daily circulation. The table lists the percentage change in daily circulation from 1994 to 1995 for 11 of the largest newspapers in the United States.

Newspaper	Percent Change
Wall Street Journal	−1.0
USA Today	+3.9
New York Times	−2.9
Los Angeles Times	−4.7
Washington Post	−2.1
New York Daily News	−2.0
Chicago Tribune	+0.9
Newsday	−8.5
Dallas Morning News	+1.8
Boston Globe	−1.5
San Francisco Chronicle	−4.0

Source: Audit Bureau of Circulations, *New York Times,* October 31, 1995.

a. Compute the mean and standard deviation of the percentage changes in daily circulation for the 11 newspapers.

b. Assume the data in the table are representative of changes in daily circulation of all large U.S. newspapers. Use the results, part **a**, to sketch the relative frequency distribution of the 1994 to 1995 percentage change in daily circulation.

c. One of the nations largest newspapers, the *Houston Chronicle,* increased daily circulation by 32.4% from 1994 to 1995. Based on the distribution, part **b**, would you expect to observe a +32.4% change in daily circulation? Explain. [*Note:* Between 1994 and 1995, the *Houston Post* closed, leaving the city with only one large newspaper, the *Chronicle.*]

2.74 (X02.074) When it is working properly, a machine that fills 25-pound bags of flour dispenses an average of 25 pounds per fill; the standard deviation of the amount of fill is .1 pound. To monitor the performance of the machine, an inspector weighs the contents of a bag coming off the machine's conveyor belt every half-hour during the day. If the contents of two consecutive bags fall more than 2 standard deviations from the mean (using the mean and standard deviation given above), the filling process is said to be out of control and the machine is shut down briefly for adjustments. The data given in the table are the weights measured by the inspector yesterday. Assume the machine is never shut down for more than 15 minutes at a time. At what times yesterday was the process shut down for adjustment? Justify your answer.

Time	Weight (pounds)	Time	Weight (pounds)
8:00 A.M.	25.10	12:30 P.M.	25.06
8:30	25.15	1:00	24.95
9:00	24.81	1:30	24.80
9:30	24.75	2:00	24.95
10:00	25.00	2:30	25.21
10:30	25.05	3:00	24.90
11:00	25.23	3:30	24.71
11:30	25.25	4:00	25.31
12:00	25.01	4:30	25.15
		5:00	25.20

2.8 NUMERICAL MEASURES OF RELATIVE STANDING

We've seen that numerical measures of central tendency and variability describe the general nature of a quantitative data set (either a sample or a population). In addition, we may be interested in describing the *relative* quantitative location of a particular measurement within a data set. Descriptive measures of the relation-

FIGURE 2.25
Location of 90th
percentile for yearly
sales of oil companies

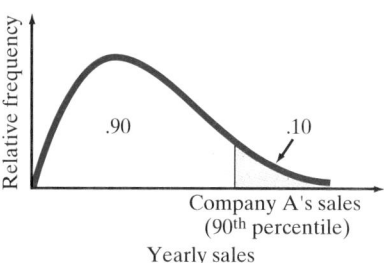

ship of a measurement to the rest of the data are called **measures of relative standing**.

One measure of the relative standing of a measurement is its **percentile ranking**. For example, if oil company A reports that its yearly sales are in the 90th percentile of all companies in the industry, the implication is that 90% of all oil companies have yearly sales *less* than company A's, and only 10% have yearly sales exceeding company A's. This is demonstrated in Figure 2.25. Similarly, if the oil company's yearly sales are in the 50th percentile (the median of the data set), 50% of all oil companies would have lower yearly sales and 50% would have higher yearly sales.

Percentile rankings are of practical value only for large data sets. Finding them involves a process similar to the one used in finding a median. The measurements are ranked in order and a rule is selected to define the location of each percentile. Since we are primarily interested in interpreting the percentile rankings of measurements (rather than finding particular percentiles for a data set), we define the *pth percentile* of a data set as shown in Definition 2.11.

DEFINITION 2.11
For any set of n measurements (arranged in ascending or descending order), the pth **percentile** is a number such that $p\%$ of the measurements fall below the pth percentile and $(100 - p)\%$ fall above it.

Another measure of relative standing in popular use is the z-score. As you can see in Definition 2.12, the z-score makes use of the mean and standard deviation of the data set in order to specify the relative location of a measurement:

DEFINITION 2.12
The **sample z-score** for a measurement x is

$$z = \frac{x - \bar{x}}{s}$$

The **population z-score** for a measurement x is

$$z = \frac{x - \mu}{\sigma}$$

FIGURE 2.26
Annual income of steelworkers

$18,000		$22,000	$24,000		$30,000
$\bar{x} - 3s$		Joe Smith's income	$\bar{x}$		$\bar{x} + 3s$

Note that the z-score is calculated by subtracting $\bar{x}$ (or μ) from the measurement x and then dividing the result by s (or σ). The final result, the z-score, represents the distance between a given measurement x and the mean, expressed in standard deviations.

EXAMPLE 2.14

Suppose 200 steelworkers are selected, and the annual income of each is determined. The mean and standard deviation are $\bar{x} = \$24,000$ and $s = \$2,000$. Suppose Joe Smith's annual income is $22,000. What is his sample z-score?

SOLUTION
Joe Smith's annual income lies below the mean income of the 200 steelworkers (see Figure 2.26). We compute

$$z = \frac{x - \bar{x}}{s} = \frac{\$22,000 - \$24,000}{\$2,000} = -1.0$$

which tells us that Joe Smith's annual income is 1.0 standard deviation *below* the sample mean, or, in short, his sample z-score is -1.0.

The numerical value of the z-score reflects the relative standing of the measurement. A large positive z-score implies that the measurement is larger than almost all other measurements, whereas a large negative z-score indicates that the measurement is smaller than almost every other measurement. If a z-score is 0 or near 0, the measurement is located at or near the mean of the sample or population.

We can be more specific if we know that the frequency distribution of the measurements is mound-shaped. In this case, the following interpretation of the z-score can be given.

Interpretation of z-Scores for Mound-Shaped Distributions of Data

1. Approximately 68% of the measurements will have a z-score between -1 and 1.
2. Approximately 95% of the measurements will have a z-score between -2 and 2.
3. Approximately 99.7% (almost all) of the measurements will have a z-score between -3 and 3.

Note that this interpretation of z-scores is identical to that given by the Empirical Rule for mound-shaped distributions (Table 2.8). The statement that a measurement falls in the interval $(\mu - \sigma)$ to $(\mu + \sigma)$ is equivalent to the statement that a measurement has a population z-score between -1 and 1, since all measurements between $(\mu - \sigma)$ and $(\mu + \sigma)$ are within 1 standard deviation of μ. These z-scores are displayed in Figure 2.27.

FIGURE 2.27
Population z-scores
for a mound-shaped
distribution

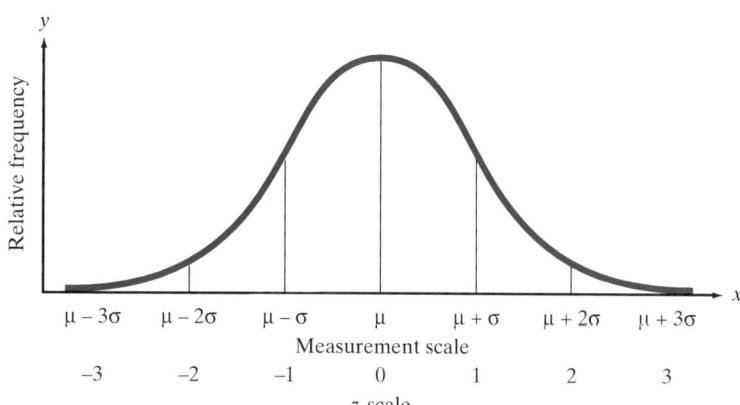

We end this section with an example that indicates how z-scores may be used to accomplish our primary objective—the use of sample information to make inferences about the population.

EXAMPLE 2.15   Suppose a female bank employee believes that her salary is low as a result of sex discrimination. To substantiate her belief, she collects information on the salaries of her male counterparts in the banking business. She finds that their salaries have a mean of $34,000 and a standard deviation of $2,000. Her salary is $27,000. Does this information support her claim of sex discrimination?

SOLUTION
The analysis might proceed as follows: First, we calculate the z-score for the woman's salary with respect to those of her male counterparts. Thus,

$$z = \frac{\$27,000 - \$34,000}{\$2,000} = -3.5$$

The implication is that the woman's salary is 3.5 standard deviations *below* the mean of the male salary distribution. Furthermore, if a check of the male salary data shows that the frequency distribution is mound-shaped, we can infer that very few salaries in this distribution should have a z-score less than -3, as shown in Figure 2.28. Therefore, a z-score of -3.5 represents either a measurement from a distribution different from the male salary distribution or a very unusual (highly improbable) measurement for the male salary distribution.

Which of the two situations do you think prevails? Do you think the woman's salary is simply unusually low in the distribution of salaries, or do you think her

FIGURE 2.28
Male salary
distribution

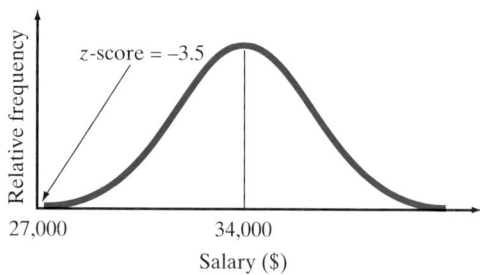

claim of sex discrimination is justified? Most people would probably conclude that her salary does not come from the male salary distribution. However, the careful investigator should require more information before inferring sex discrimination as the cause. We would want to know more about the data collection technique the woman used and more about her competence at her job. Also, perhaps other factors such as length of employment should be considered in the analysis. ▐▙

Examples 2.13 and 2.15 exemplify an approach to statistical inference that might be called the **rare-event approach**. An experimenter hypothesizes a specific frequency distribution to describe a population of measurements. Then a sample of measurements is drawn from the population. If the experimenter finds it unlikely that the sample came from the hypothesized distribution, the hypothesis is concluded to be false. Thus, in Example 2.15 the woman believes her salary reflects sex discrimination. She hypothesizes that her salary should be just another measurement in the distribution of her male counterparts' salaries if no discrimination exists. However, it is so unlikely that the sample (in this case, her salary) came from the male frequency distribution that she rejects that hypothesis, concluding that the distribution from which her salary was drawn is different from the distribution for the men.

This rare-event approach to inference-making is discussed further in later chapters. Proper application of the approach requires a knowledge of probability, the subject of our next chapter.

EXERCISES   2.75–2.86

Learning the Mechanics

2.75 Compute the z-score corresponding to each of the following values of x:
  a. $x = 40, s = 5, \bar{x} = 30$
  b. $x = 90, \mu = 89, \sigma = 2$
  c. $\mu = 50, \sigma = 5, x = 50$
  d. $s = 4, x = 20, \bar{x} = 30$
  e. In parts **a–d**, state whether the z-score locates x within a sample or a population.
  f. In parts **a–d**, state whether each value of x lies above or below the mean and by how many standard deviations.

2.76 Give the percentage of measurements in a data set that are above and below each of the following percentiles:
  a. 75th percentile b. 50th percentile
  c. 20th percentile d. 84th percentile

2.77 What is the 50th percentile of a quantitative data set called?

2.78 Compare the z-scores to decide which of the following x values lie the greatest distance above the mean and the greatest distance below the mean.
  a. $x = 100, \mu = 50, \sigma = 25$
  b. $x = 1, \mu = 4, \sigma = 1$
  c. $x = 0, \mu = 200, \sigma = 100$

  d. $x = 10, \mu = 5, \sigma = 3$

2.79 At one university, the students are given z-scores at the end of each semester rather than the traditional GPAs. The mean and standard deviation of all students' cumulative GPAs, on which the z-scores are based, are 2.7 and .5, respectively.
  a. Translate each of the following z-scores to corresponding GPA: $z = 2.0, z = -1.0, z = .5, z = -2.5$.
  b. Students with z-scores below -1.6 are put on probation. What is the corresponding probationary GPA?
  c. The president of the university wishes to graduate the top 16% of the students with *cum laude* honors and the top 2.5% with *summa cum laude* honors. Where (approximately) should the limits be set in terms of z-scores? In terms of GPAs? What assumption, if any, did you make about the distribution of the GPAs at the university?

2.80 Suppose that 40 and 90 are two elements of a population data set and that their z-scores are -2 and 3, respectively. Using only this information, is it possible to determine the population's mean and standard deviation? If so, find them. If not, explain why it's not possible.

Applying the Concepts

2.81 The U.S. Environmental Protection Agency (EPA) sets a limit on the amount of lead permitted in drinking water. The EPA *Action Level* for lead is .015 milligrams per liter (mg/L) of water. Under EPA guidelines, if 90% of a water system's study samples have a lead concentration less than .015 mg/L, the water is considered safe for drinking. I (co-author Sincich) received a 1994 report on a study of lead levels in the drinking water of homes in my subdivision. The 90th percentile of the study sample had a lead concentration of .00372 mg/L. Are water customers in my subdivision at risk of drinking water with unhealthy lead levels? Explain.

2.82 In *Fortune's* ranking of the 500 largest industrial corporations in the United States, Dell Computer ranked 490th in terms of 1991 sales. In 1996, it ranked 250th. Use percentiles to describe Dell Computer's position in each year's sales distribution.

2.83 In 1994 the United States imported merchandise valued at $664 billion and exported merchandise worth $513 billion. The difference between these two quantities (exports minus imports) is referred to as the *merchandise trade balance*. Since more goods were imported than exported in 1994, the merchandise trade balance was a *negative* $151 billion. The accompanying table lists the U.S. exports to and imports from a sample of ten countries in 1994 (in millions of dollars).

Country	Exports	Imports
Brazil	8,118	8,708
China	9,287	38,781
Egypt	2,844	548
France	13,622	16,775
Italy	7,193	14,711
Japan	53,481	119,149
Mexico	50,840	49,493
Panama	1,276	323
Sweden	2,520	5,044
Singapore	13,022	15,361

Source: Statistical Abstract of the United States: 1995, pp. 819–822.

  a. Calculate the U.S. merchandise trade balance with each of the ten countries. Express your answers in billions of dollars.
  b. Use a z-score to identify the relative position of the U.S. trade balance with Japan within the data set you developed in part **a**. Do the same for the trade balance with Egypt. Write a sentence or two that describes the relative positions of these two trade balances.

2.84 The accompanying table lists the unemployment rate in 1993 for a sample of nine countries.

Country	Percent Unemployed
Australia	10.9
Canada	11.2
France	11.8
Germany	5.8
Great Britain	10.4
Italy	10.5
Japan	2.5
Sweden	8.1
United States	6.8

Source: Statistical Abstract of the United States: 1995, p. 862.

The mean and standard deviation of the nine countries' unemployment rates are 8.67 and 3.12, respectively.
  a. Calculate the z-scores of the unemployment rates of the United States, France, and Japan.
  b. Describe the information conveyed by the sign (positive or negative) of the z-scores you calculated in part **a**.

2.85 Refer to the *Arkansas Business and Economic Review* (Summer 1995) study of hazardous waste sites in Arkansas counties, Exercise 2.38. A SAS descriptive statistics printout for the number of Superfund waste sites in each of the 75 counties is displayed on page 82.
  a. Find the 10th percentile of the data set on the printout. Interpret the result.
  b. Find the 95th percentile of the data set on the printout. Interpret the result.
  c. Use the information on the SAS printout to calculate the z-score for an Arkansas county with 48 Superfund sites.
  d. Based on your answer to part **c**, would you classify 48 as an extreme number of Superfund sites?

2.86 One of the ways the federal government raises money is through the sale of securities such as **Treasury bonds**, **Treasury bills (T-bills)**, and **U.S. savings bonds**. Treasury bonds and bills are marketable (i.e., they can be traded in the securities market) long-term and short-term notes, respectively. U.S. savings bonds are nonmarketable notes; they can be purchased and redeemed only from the U.S. Treasury. On July 5, 1996, the interest rate on three-month T-bills was 5.3%. Periodically *The Wall Street Journal* samples economists and asks them to forecast the interest rate of three-month T-bills. (T-bills are offered for sale weekly by the government, and their interest rates typically vary with each offering.) The forecasts for Sept. 30, 1996, are listed in the table at the bottom of page 82. The mean and standard deviation of the 17 forecasts are 5.4% and .60%, respectively.

```
                    UNIVARIATE PROCEDURE
Variable=NUMSITES
                          Moments
         N               75   Sum Wgts          75
         Mean           5.24   Sum              393
         Std Dev    7.244457   Variance    52.48216
         Skewness    3.46829   Kurtosis    16.41177
         USS            5943   CSS          3883.68
         CV          138.253   Std Mean    0.836518
         T:Mean=0   6.264062   Prob>|T|      0.0001
         Sgn Rank       1008   Prob>|S|      0.0001
         Num ^=0          63

                      Quantiles(Def=5)
         100%   Max        48        99%         48
          75%   Q3          6        95%         21
          50%   Med         3        90%         12
          25%   Q1          1        10%          0
           0%   Min         0         5%          0
                                      1%          0
         Range            48
         Q3-Q1             5
         Mode              2

                          Extremes
         Lowest    Obs        Highest    Obs
              0(    68)          17(    47)
              0(    67)          21(    52)
              0(    66)          21(    75)
              0(    39)          25(    36)
              0(    38)          48(    74)
```

a. Calculate the z-scores of Economist #1's forecast and Economist #17's forecast. What do the z-scores tell you about their forecasts relative to the forecasts of the other economists?

b. Write a sentence or two that summarizes the 17 forecasts. In your summary, use a measure of central tendency and a measure of variability.

Economist	Interest Rate Forecast
1	5.2
2	5.25
3	5.85
4	4.30
5	5.85
6	4.75
7	5.70
8	4.23
9	5.0
10	5.0
11	6.0
12	5.0
13	5.2
14	5.5
15	5.65
16	5.75
17	6.50

2.9 QUARTILES AND BOX PLOTS (OPTIONAL)

The **box plot**, a relatively recent introduction to the methodology of descriptive measures, is based on the **quartiles** of a data set. Quartiles are values that partition the data set into four groups, each containing 25% of the measurements. The lower quartile Q_L is the 25th percentile, the middle quartile is the median m (the 50th percentile), and the upper quartile Q_U is the 75th percentile (see Figure 2.29).

DEFINITION 2.13

The **lower quartile Q_L** is the 25th percentile of a data set. The **middle quartile m** is the median. The **upper quartile Q_U** is the 75th percentile.

A box plot is based on the *interquartile range (IQR)*, the distance between the lower and upper quartiles:

$$IQR = Q_U - Q_L$$

DEFINITION 2.14

The **interquartile range (IQR)** is the distance between the lower and upper quartiles:

$$IQR = Q_U - Q_L$$

The box plot for the 50 companies' percentages of revenues spent on R&D (Table 2.3) is given in Figure 2.30. It was generated by the MINITAB for Windows statistical software package.* Note that a rectangle (the **box**) is drawn, with the top and bottom sides of the rectangle (the **hinges**) drawn at the quartiles Q_L and Q_U. By definition, then, the "middle" 50% of the observations—those between Q_L and Q_U—fall inside the box. For the R&D data, these quartiles appear to be at (approximately) 7.0 and 9.5. Thus,

$$IQR = 9.5 - 7.0 = 2.5 \text{ (approximately)}$$

The median is shown at about 8.0 by a horizontal line within the box.

To guide the construction of the "tails" of the box plot, two sets of limits, called **inner fences** and **outer fences**, are used. Neither set of fences actually appears on the box plot. Inner fences are located at a distance of 1.5(IQR) from the hinges. Emanating from the hinges of the box are vertical lines called the **whiskers**. The two whiskers extend to the most extreme observation inside the inner fences. For

FIGURE 2.29

The quartiles for a data set

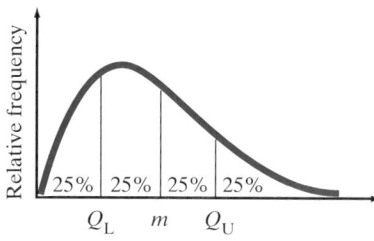

*Although box plots can be generated by hand, the amount of detail required makes them particularly well suited for computer generation. We use computer software to generate the box plots in this section.

FIGURE 2.30
MINITAB box plot
for R&D percentages

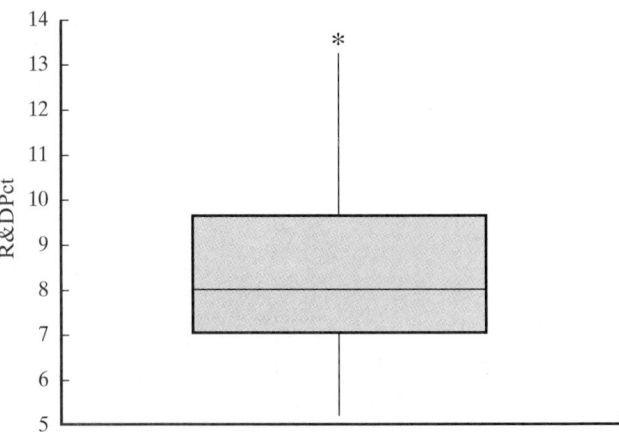

example, the inner fence on the lower side (bottom) of the R&D percentage box plot is (approximately)

Lower inner fence = Lower hinge − 1.5(IQR)

≈ 7.0 − 1.5(2.5)

= 7.0 − 3.75 = 3.25

The smallest measurement in the data set is 5.2, which is well inside this inner fence. Thus, the lower whisker extends to 5.2. Similarly, the upper whisker extends to about (9.5 + 3.75) = 13.25. The largest measurement inside this fence is the third largest measurement, 13.2. Note that the longer upper whisker reveals the rightward skewness of the R&D distribution.

Values that are beyond the inner fences receive special attention because they are extreme values that represent relatively rare occurrences. In fact, for mound-shaped distributions, fewer than 1% of the observations are expected to fall outside the inner fences. Two of the 50 R&D measurements, at 13.5, fall outside the upper inner fence. These measurements are represented by an asterisk (*) and they further emphasize the rightward skewness of the distribution. Note that the box plot does not reveal that there are *two* measurements at 13.5, since only a single symbol is used to represent both observations at that point.

The other two imaginary fences, the outer fences, are defined at a distance 3(IQR) from each end of the box. Measurements that fall beyond the outer fences are represented by 0s and are very extreme measurements that require special analysis. Less than one-hundredth of 1% (.01% or .0001) of the measurements from mound-shaped distributions are expected to fall beyond the outer fences. Since no measurement in the R&D percentage box plot (Figure 2.30) is represented by a 0, we know that no measurements fall outside the outer fences.

Generally, any measurements that fall beyond the inner fences—and certainly any that fall beyond the outer fences—are considered potential **outliers**. Outliers are extreme measurements that stand out from the rest of the sample and may be faulty: They may be incorrectly recorded observations, members of a population different from the rest of the sample, or, at the least, very unusual measurements from the same population. For example, the two R&D measurements at 13.5 (identified by an asterisk) may be considered outliers. When we analyze these measurements, we find that they are correctly recorded. However, it turns out that both represent R&D expenditures of relatively young and fast-growing companies. Thus, the outlier analysis may have revealed important factors that relate to the R&D expenditures of high-tech companies: their age and rate of growth.

Outlier analysis often reveals useful information of this kind and therefore plays an important role in the statistical inference-making process.

The elements (and nomenclature) of box plots are summarized in the next box. Some aids to the interpretation of box plots are also given.

Elements of a Box Plot

1. A rectangle (the **box**) is drawn with the ends (the **hinges**) drawn at the lower and upper quartiles (Q_L and Q_U). The median of the data is shown in the box, usually by a line or a symbol (such as "+").

2. The points at distances 1.5(IQR) from each hinge mark the **inner fences** of the data set. Horizontal lines (the **whiskers**) are drawn from each hinge to the most extreme measurement inside the inner fence.

3. A second pair of fences, the **outer fences**, appear at a distance of 3 interquartile ranges, 3(IQR), from the hinges. One symbol (usually "*") is used to represent measurements falling between the inner and outer fences, and another (usually "0") is used to represent measurements beyond the outer fences. Thus, outer fences are not shown unless one or more measurements lie beyond them.

4. The symbols used to represent the median and the extreme data points (those beyond the fences) will vary depending on the software you use to construct the box plot. (You may use your own symbols if you are constructing a box plot by hand.) You should consult the program's documentation to determine exactly which symbols are used.

Aids to the Interpretation of Box Plots

1. Examine the length of the box. The IQR is a measure of the sample's variability and is especially useful for the comparison of two samples (see Example 2.17).

2. Visually compare the lengths of the whiskers. If one is clearly longer, the distribution of the data is probably skewed in the direction of the longer whisker.

3. Analyze any measurements that lie beyond the fences. Fewer than 5% should fall beyond the inner fences, even for very skewed distributions. Measurements beyond the outer fences are probably outliers, with one of the following explanations:

   a. The measurement is incorrect. It may have been observed, recorded, or entered into the computer incorrectly.

   b. The measurement belongs to a population different from the population that the rest of the sample was drawn from (see Example 2.17).

   c. The measurement is correct *and* from the same population as the rest. Generally, we accept this explanation only after carefully ruling out all others.

EXAMPLE 2.16

In Example 2.2 we analyzed 50 processing times for the development of price quotes by the manufacturer of industrial wheels. The intent was to determine whether the success or failure in obtaining the order was related to the amount of time to process the price quotes. Each quote that corresponds to "lost" business was so classified. The data are repeated in Table 2.9. Use a statistical software package to draw a box plot for these data.

SOLUTION

The SAS box plot printout for these data is shown in Figure 2.31. SAS uses a horizontal dashed line in the box to represent the median, and a plus sign (+) to represent the mean. (SAS shows the mean in box plots, unlike many other statistical programs.) Also, SAS uses the symbol "0" to represent measurements between

TABLE 2.9   Price Quote Processing Time (Days)

Request Number	Processing Time	Lost?	Request Number	Processing Time	Lost?
1	2.36	No	26	3.34	No
2	5.73	No	27	6.00	No
3	6.60	No	28	5.92	No
4	10.05	Yes	29	7.28	Yes
5	5.13	No	30	1.25	No
6	1.88	No	31	4.01	No
7	2.52	No	32	7.59	No
8	2.00	No	33	13.42	Yes
9	4.69	No	34	3.24	No
10	1.91	No	35	3.37	No
11	6.75	Yes	36	14.06	Yes
12	3.92	No	37	5.10	No
13	3.46	No	38	6.44	No
14	2.64	No	39	7.76	No
15	3.63	No	40	4.40	No
16	3.44	No	41	5.48	No
17	9.49	Yes	42	7.51	No
18	4.90	No	43	6.18	No
19	7.45	No	44	8.22	Yes
20	20.23	Yes	45	4.37	No
21	3.91	No	46	2.93	No
22	1.70	No	47	9.95	Yes
23	16.29	Yes	48	4.46	No
24	5.52	No	49	14.32	Yes
25	1.44	No	50	9.01	No

the inner and outer fences and "*" to represent observations beyond the outer fences (the opposite of MINITAB).

Note that the upper whisker is longer than the lower whisker and that the mean lies above the median; these characteristics reveal the rightward skewness of

FIGURE 2.31
SAS box plot for processing time data

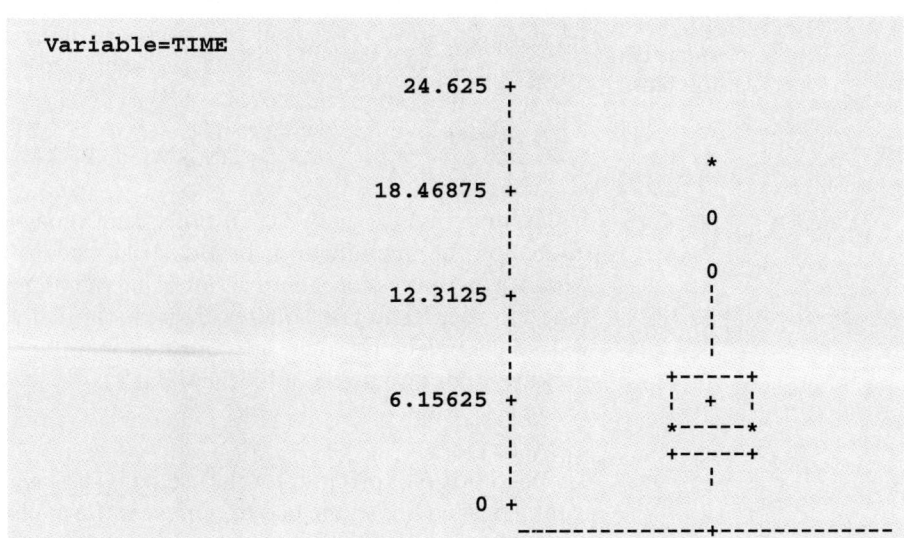

the data. However, the most important feature of the data is made very obvious by the box plot: There are at least two measurements between the inner and outer fences (in fact, there are three, but two are almost equal and are represented by the same "0") and at least one beyond the outer fence, all on the upper end of the distribution. Thus, the distribution is extremely skewed to the right, and several measurements need special attention in our analysis. We offer an explanation for the outliers in the following example.

EXAMPLE 2.17

The box plot for the 50 processing times (Figure 2.31) does not explicitly reveal the differences, if any, between the set of times corresponding to the success and the set of times corresponding to the failure to obtain the business. Box plots corresponding to the 39 "won" and 11 "lost" bids were generated using SAS, and are shown in Figure 2.32. Interpret them.

SOLUTION

The division of the data set into two parts, corresponding to won and lost bids, eliminates any observations that are beyond inner or outer fences. Furthermore, the skewness in the distributions has been reduced, as evidenced by the facts that the upper whiskers are only slightly longer than the lower, and that the means are closer to the medians than for the combined sample. The box plots also reveal that the processing times corresponding to the lost bids tend to exceed those of the won bids. A plausible explanation for the outliers in the combined box plot (Figure 2.31) is that they are from a different population than the bulk of the times. In other words, there are two populations represented by the sample of processing times—one corresponding to lost bids, and the other to won bids.

The box plots lend support to the conclusion that the price quote processing time and the success of acquiring the business are related. However, whether the visual differences between the box plots generalize to inferences about the populations corresponding to these two samples is a matter for inferential statistics, not graphical descriptions. We'll discuss how to use samples to compare two populations using inferential statistics in Chapter 9.

FIGURE 2.32
Box plots of
processing time data:
Won and lost bids

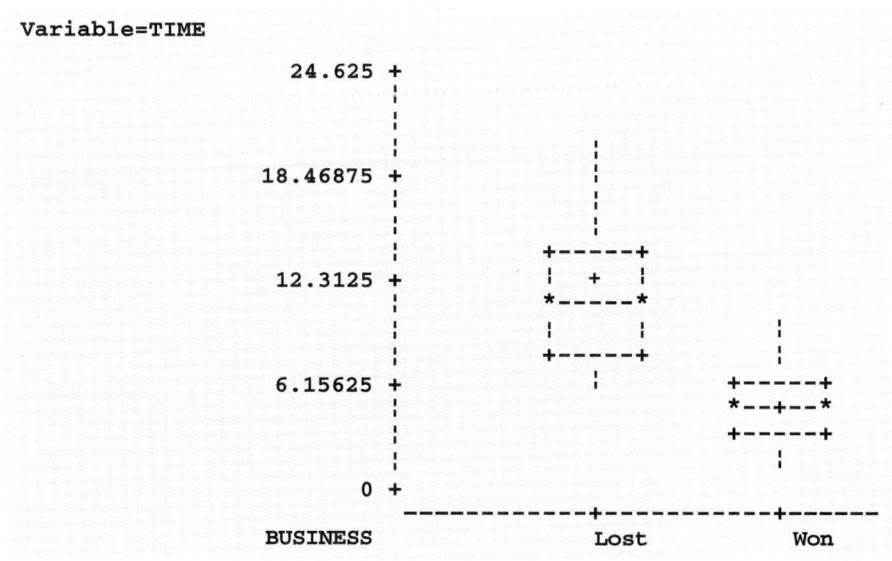

EXERCISES **2.87–2.96**

Note: Exercises marked with 💾 *contain data available for computer analysis on a 3.5" disk (file name in parentheses).*

Learning the Mechanics

2.87 Define the 25th, 50th, and 75th percentiles of a data set. Explain how they provide a description of the data.

2.88 Suppose a data set consisting of exam scores has a lower quartile $Q_L = 60$, a median $m = 75$, and an upper quartile $Q_U = 85$. The scores on the exam range from 18 to 100. Without having the actual scores available to you, construct as much of the box plot as possible.

2.89 MINITAB was used to generate the following horizontal box plot. (*Note:* The hinges are represented by the symbol "I".)

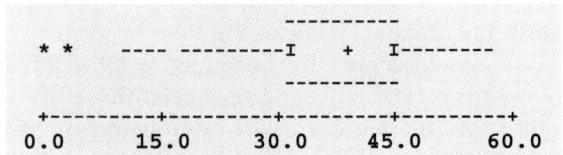

a. What is the median of the data set (approximately)?

b. What are the upper and lower quartiles of the data set (approximately)?

c. What is the interquartile range of the data set (approximately)?

d. Is the data set skewed to the left, skewed to the right, or symmetric?

e. What percentage of the measurements in the data set lie to the right of the median? To the left of the upper quartile?

2.90 MINITAB was used to generate the horizontal box plots below. Compare and contrast the frequency distributions of the two data sets. Your answer should include comparisons of the following characteristics: central tendency, variation, skewness, and outliers.

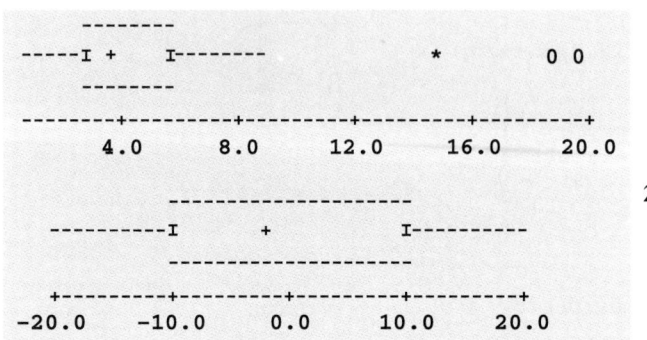

2.91 (**X02.091**) Consider the following two sample data sets:

Sample A			Sample B		
121	171	158	171	152	170
173	184	163	168	169	171
157	85	145	190	183	185
165	172	196	140	173	206
170	159	172	172	174	169
161	187	100	199	151	180
142	166	171	167	170	188

a. Use a statistical software package to construct a box plot for each data set.

b. Using information reflected in your box plots, describe the similarities and differences in the two data sets.

Applying the Concepts

2.92 (**X02.092**) The table contains the top salary offer (in thousands of dollars) received by each member of a sample of 50 MBA students who graduated from the Graduate School of Management at Rutgers, the state university of New Jersey, in 1996.

61.1	48.5	47.0	49.1	43.5
50.8	62.3	50.0	65.4	58.0
53.2	39.9	49.1	75.0	51.2
41.7	40.0	53.0	39.6	49.6
55.2	54.9	62.5	35.0	50.3
41.5	56.0	55.5	70.0	59.2
39.2	47.0	58.2	59.0	60.8
72.3	55.0	41.4	51.5	63.0
48.4	61.7	45.3	63.2	41.5
47.0	43.2	44.6	47.7	58.6

Source: Career Services Office, Graduate School of Management, Rutgers University.

a. The mean and standard deviation are 52.33 and 9.22, respectively. Find and interpret the z-score associated with the highest salary offer, the lowest salary offer, and the mean salary offer. Would you consider the highest offer to be unusually high? Why or why not?

b. Use a statistical software package to construct a box plot for this data set. Which salary offers (if any) are potentially faulty observations? Explain.

2.93 Refer to the *Financial Management* (Spring 1995) study of 49 firms filing for prepackaged bankruptcies, Exercise 2.22. Recall that three types of "prepack" firms exist: (1) those who hold no pre-filing vote; (2) those who vote their preference for a joint solution; and (3) those who vote their preference for a prepack. Box plots, constructed using MINITAB for Windows, for the time in bankruptcy (months) for each type of firm are shown below.

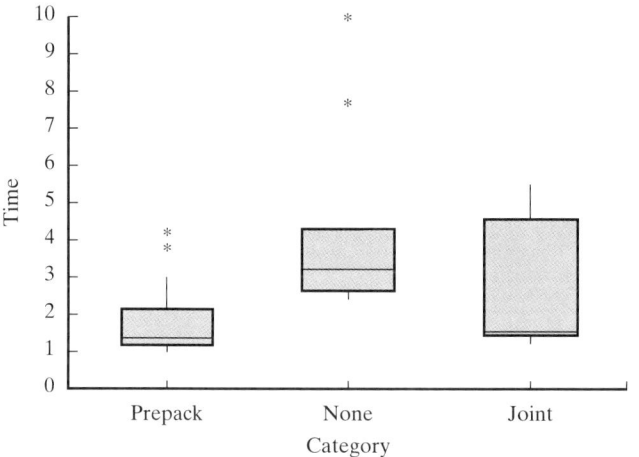

a. How do the median bankruptcy times compare for the three types? [*Hint:* Recall that MINITAB for Windows uses a horizontal line through the box to represent the median.]

b. How do the variabilities of the bankruptcy times compare for the three types?

c. The standard deviations of the bankruptcy times are 2.47 for "none," 1.72 for "joint," and 0.96 for "prepack." Do the standard deviations agree with the interquartile ranges (part **b**) with regard to the comparison of the variabilities of the bankruptcy times?

d. Is there evidence of outliers in any of the three distributions?

2.94   A firm's earnings per share (E/S) of common stock is a measure used by investors to monitor the financial performance of a firm. Thirty firms were sampled from *Fortune's* 1996 listing of the 500 largest corporations in the United States, and their earnings per share for 1995 are recorded in the table (above, to the right).

a. **(X02.094)** Use a statistical software package to construct a box plot for this data set. Identify any outliers that may exist in this data set.

b. For each outlier identified in part **a**, determine how many standard deviations it lies from the mean of the E/S data set.

2.95   A manufacturer of minicomputer systems is interested in improving its customer support services. As a first step, its marketing department has been charged with the responsibility of summarizing the extent of customer problems in terms of system down time. The 40 most recent customers were surveyed to determine the amount of down time (in hours) they had experienced during the previous month. These data are listed in the table to the right.

Firm	E/S
Illinois Tool Works	3.29
Sara Lee	1.62
Reynolds Metals	5.35
Nike	5.44
Phelps Dodge	10.65
Centex	3.04
Avery Dennison	2.70
Warner-Lambert	5.48
Maytag	−0.19
General Electric	3.90
Cooper Industries	0.84
Lockheed	3.28
Kellogg	2.24
FMC	5.72
Hasbro	1.76
Dow Chemical	7.72
Olin	5.50
Avon Products	3.76
Bear Stearns	1.70
American Stores	2.16
Humana	1.17
Asarco	4.00
Office Depot	0.85
DANA	2.84
Exxon	5.18
Georgia-Pacific	11.29
Crown Cork & Seal	0.83
DuPont (E.I.) de Nemours	5.61
McDonald's	1.97
UAL	20.01

Source: Fortune, April 29, 1996, pp. F1–F20.

Customer Number	Down Time	Customer Number	Down Time	Customer Number	Down Time
230	12	244	2	258	28
231	16	245	11	259	19
232	5	246	22	260	34
233	16	247	17	261	26
234	21	248	31	262	17
235	29	249	10	263	11
236	38	250	4	264	64
237	14	251	10	265	19
238	47	252	15	266	18
239	0	253	7	267	24
240	24	254	20	268	49
241	15	255	9	269	50
242	13	256	22		
243	8	257	18		

a. **(X02.095)** Use a statistical software package to construct a box plot for these data. Use the information reflected in the box plot to describe the frequency distribution of the data set. Your description should address central tendency, variation, and skewness.

b. Use your box plot to determine which customers are having unusually lengthy down times.

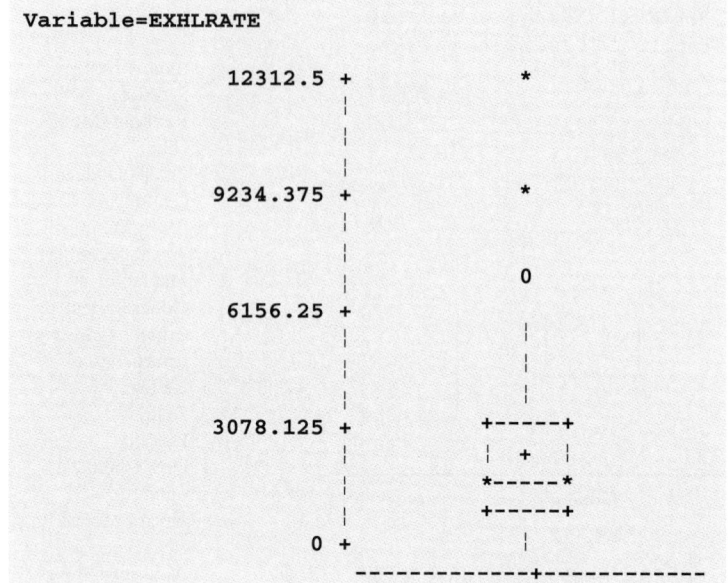

c. Find and interpret the z-scores associated with customers you identified in part **b**.

2.96 In Exercise 2.23 we constructed a stem-and-leaf display for 40 radiation (exhalation rate) measurements on waste gypsum and phosphate mounds in Florida. The figure above, constructed using SAS, is a box plot for the same data.
a. Use the box plot to estimate the lower quartile, median, and upper quartile of these data.

b. Does the distribution appear to be skewed? Explain.

c. Are there any outliers among these data? Explain.

d. Examine the stem-and-leaf display for these data in Exercise 2.23, and the box plot here. Which do you prefer as a description of these radiation measurements?

2.10 GRAPHING BIVARIATE RELATIONSHIPS (OPTIONAL)

The claim is often made that the crime rate and the unemployment rate are "highly correlated." Another popular belief is that the Gross Domestic Product (GDP) and the rate of inflation are "related." Some people even believe that the Dow Jones Industrial Average and the lengths of fashionable skirts are "associated." The words "correlated," "related," and "associated" imply a relationship between two variables—in the examples above, two *quantitative* variables.

One way to describe the relationship between two quantitative variables—called a **bivariate relationship**—is to plot the data in a **scattergram** (or **scatterplot**). A scattergram is a two-dimensional plot, with one variable's values plotted along the vertical axis and the other along the horizontal axis. For example, Figure 2.33 is a scattergram relating (1) the cost of mechanical work (heating, ventilating, and plumbing) to (2) the floor area of the building for a sample of 26 factory and warehouse buildings. Note that the scattergram suggests a general tendency for mechanical cost to increase as building floor area increases.

When an increase in one variable is generally associated with an increase in the second variable, we say that the two variables are "positively related" or "positively correlated."* Figure 2.33 implies that mechanical cost and floor area are positively correlated. Alternatively, if one variable has a tendency to decrease as

*A formal definition of correlation is given in Chapter 10.

FIGURE 2.33
Scattergram of cost vs.
floor area

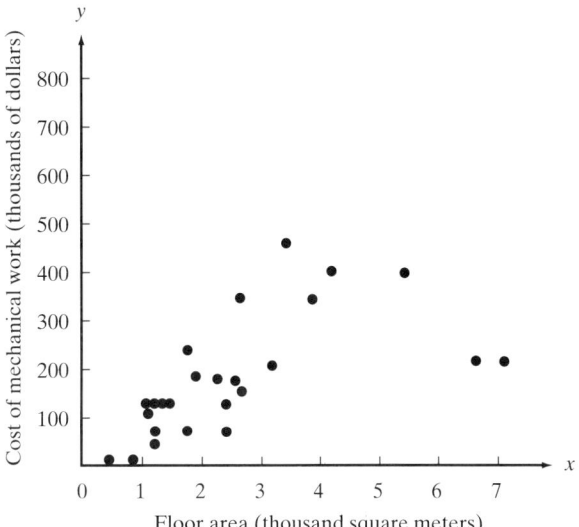

the other increases, we say the variables are "negatively correlated." Figure 2.34 shows several hypothetical scattergrams that portray a positive bivariate relationship (Figure 2.34a), a negative bivariate relationship (Figure 2.34b), and a situation where the two variables are unrelated (Figure 2.34c).

EXAMPLE 2.18

A medical item used to administer to a hospital patient is called a **factor**. For example, factors can be intravenous (IV) tubing, IV fluid, needles, shave kits, bedpans, diapers, dressings, medications, and even code carts. The coronary care unit at Bayonet Point Hospital (St. Petersburg, Florida) recently investigated the relationship between the number of factors administered per patient and the patient's length of stay (in days). Data on these two variables for a sample of 50 coronary care patients are given in Table 2.10. Use a scattergram to describe the relationship between the two variables of interest, number of factors and length of stay.

SOLUTION
Rather than construct the plot by hand, we resort to a statistical software package. The SPSS plot of the data in Table 2.10, with length of stay (LOS) on the vertical axis and number of factors (FACTORS) on the horizontal axis, is shown in Figure 2.35.

As plotting symbols, SPSS uses numbers. Each symbol represents the number of sample points, (e.g., patients) plotted at that particular coordinate. Although the plotted points exhibit a fair amount of variation, the scattergram clearly shows an

FIGURE 2.34
Hypothetical bivariate
relationship

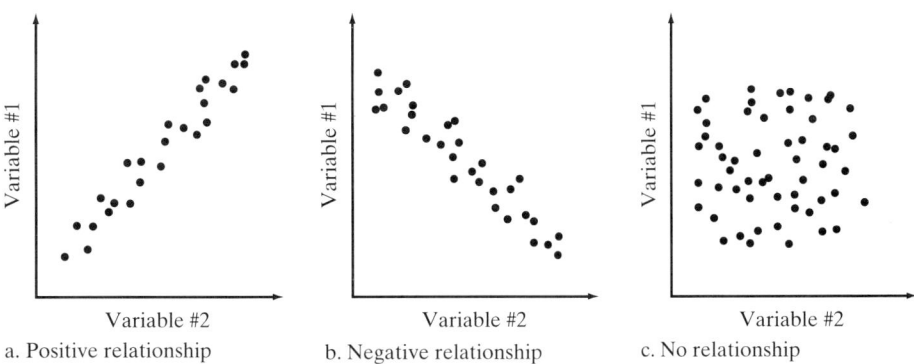

a. Positive relationship   b. Negative relationship   c. No relationship

TABLE 2.10   Data on Patient's Factors and Length of Stay

Number of Factors	Length of Stay (days)	Number of Factors	Length of Stay (days)
231	9	354	11
323	7	142	7
113	8	286	9
208	5	341	10
162	4	201	5
117	4	158	11
159	6	243	6
169	9	156	6
55	6	184	7
77	3	115	4
103	4	202	6
147	6	206	5
230	6	360	6
78	3	84	3
525	9	331	9
121	7	302	7
248	5	60	2
233	8	110	2
260	4	131	5
224	7	364	4
472	12	180	7
220	8	134	6
383	6	401	15
301	9	155	4
262	7	338	8

Source: Bayonet Point Hospital, Coronary Care Unit.

increasing trend. It appears that a patient's length of stay is positively correlated with the number of factors administered to the patient. Hospital administrators may use this information to improve their forecasts of lengths of stay for future patients.

FIGURE 2.35
SPSS scatterplot of data in Table 2.10

STATISTICS IN ACTION

2.2 CAR & DRIVER'S "ROAD TEST DIGEST"

Periodically, *Car & Driver* magazine conducts comprehensive road tests on all new car models. The results of the tests are reported in *Car & Driver's* "Road Test Digest." The "Road Test Digest" includes the following variables for each new car tested:

1. Model
2. List price ($)
3. Elapsed time from 0 to 60 mph (seconds)
4. Elapsed time for $\frac{1}{4}$ mile at full throttle (seconds)
5. Maximum speed (mph)
6. Braking distance from 70 to 0 mph (feet)
7. EPA-estimated city fuel economy (mpg)

8. Road-holding (grip) during cornering (gravitational force, in *g*'s)

Focus

The "Road Test Digest" data from the August 1995 issue of *Car & Driver* is available in ASCII format on a 3.5" diskette that accompanies this text. The name of the file containing the data is CAR.DAT. Your assignment is to completely describe the data for *Car & Driver* magazine. Are there any trends in the data? What are typical values of these variables that a new car buyer can expect? Are there any new car models that have exceptional values of these variables? Are there any relationships among the variables? Your summary results will be reported in a future issue of the magazine.

The scattergram is a simple but powerful tool for describing a bivariate relationship. However, keep in mind that it is only a graph. No measure of reliability can be attached to inferences made about bivariate populations based on scattergrams of sample data. The statistical tools that enable us to make inferences about bivariate relationships are presented in Chapter 10.

2.11 DISTORTING THE TRUTH WITH DESCRIPTIVE TECHNIQUES

A picture may be "worth a thousand words," but pictures can also color messages or distort them. In fact, the pictures in statistics (e.g., histograms, bar charts, time series plots, etc.) are susceptible to distortion, whether unintentional or as a result of unethical statistical practices. In this section, we will mention a few of the pitfalls to watch for when interpreting a chart, graph, or numerical descriptive measure.

One common way to change the impression conveyed by a graph is to change the scale on the vertical axis, the horizontal axis, or both. For example, Figure 2.36 is a bar graph that shows the market share of sales for a company for each of the years 1990 to 1995. If you want to show that the change in firm A's market share over time is moderate, you should pack in a large number of units per inch on the vertical axis—that is, make the distance between successive units on the vertical scale small, as shown in Figure 2.36. You can see that a change in the firm's market share over time is barely apparent.

If you want to use the same data to make the changes in firm A's market share appear large, you should increase the distance between successive units on the vertical axis. That is, stretch the vertical axis by graphing only a few units per inch as in Figure 2.37. A telltale sign of stretching is a long vertical axis, but this is often hidden by starting the vertical axis at some point above 0, as shown in the time

FIGURE 2.36

Firm A's market share from 1990 to 1995— packed vertical axis

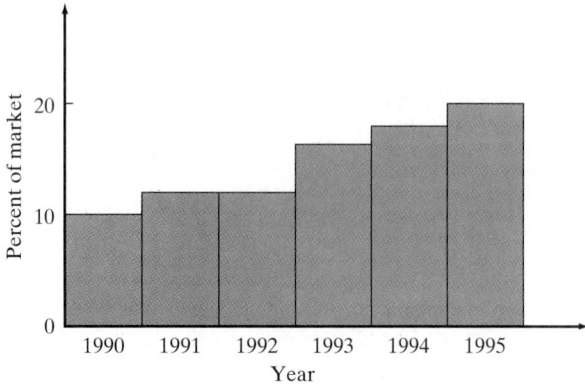

series plot, Figure 2.38a. The same effect can be achieved by using a broken line— called a *scale break*—for the vertical axis, as shown in Figure 2.38b.

Stretching the horizontal axis (increasing the distance between successive units) may also lead you to incorrect conclusions. For example, Figure 2.39a depicts the change in the Gross Domestic Product (GDP) from the first quarter of 1993 to the last quarter of 1994. If you increase the size of the horizontal axis, as in Figure 2.39b, the change in GDP over time seems less pronounced.

The changes in categories indicated by a bar graph can also be emphasized or deemphasized by stretching or shrinking the vertical axis. Another method of achieving visual distortion with bar graphs is by making the width of the bars proportional to the height. For example, look at the bar chart in Figure 2.40a, which depicts the percentage of a year's total automobile sales attributable to each of the four major manufacturers. Now suppose we make both the width and the height grow as the market share grows. This change is shown in Figure 2.40b. The reader may tend to equate the *area* of the bars with the relative market share of each manufacturer. But in fact, the true relative market share is proportional only to the *height* of the bars.

Sometimes we do not need to manipulate the graph to distort the impression it creates. Modifying the verbal description that accompanies the graph can change the interpretation that will be made by the viewer. Figure 2.41 provides a good illustration of this ploy.

Although we've discussed only a few of the ways that graphs can be used to convey misleading pictures of phenomena, the lesson is clear. Look at all graphical descriptions of data with a critical eye. Particularly, check the axes and the size

FIGURE 2.37

Firm A's market share from 1990 to 1995— stretched vertical axis

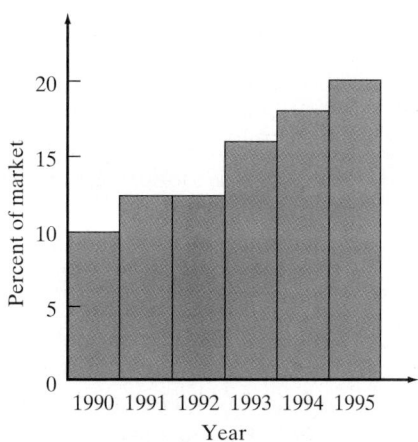

FIGURE 2.38
Changes in money
supply from
January to June

a. Vertical axis started at a point greater
than zero

b. Gap in vertical axis

of the units on each axis. Ignore the visual changes and concentrate on the actual
numerical changes indicated by the graph or chart.

The information in a data set can also be distorted by using numerical descriptive measures, as Example 2.19 indicates.

EXAMPLE 2.19   Suppose you're considering working for a small law firm—one that currently has
a senior member and three junior members. You inquire about the salary you
could expect to earn if you join the firm. Unfortunately, you receive two answers:

Answer A: The senior member tells you that an "average employee" earns
$67,500.

Answer B: One of the junior members later tells you that an "average
employee" earns $55,000.

Which answer can you believe?

SOLUTION
The confusion exists because the phrase "average employee" has not been clearly defined. Suppose the four salaries paid are $55,000 for each of the three junior
members and $105,000 for the senior member. Thus,

$$\text{Mean} = \frac{3(\$55,000) + \$105,000}{4} = \frac{\$270,000}{4} = \$67,500$$

$$\text{Median} = \$55,000$$

FIGURE 2.39
Gross National
Product from 1993
to 1994

a. Small horizontal axis

b. Stretched horizontal axis

FIGURE 2.40
Relative share of the automobile market for each of four major manufacturers

a. Bar chart

b. Width of bars grows with height

You can now see how the two answers were obtained. The senior member reported the mean of the four salaries, and the junior member reported the median. The information you received was distorted because neither person stated which measure of central tendency was being used. ∎

Another distortion of information in a sample occurs when *only* a measure of central tendency is reported. Both a measure of central tendency and a measure of variability are needed to obtain an accurate mental image of a data set.

Suppose you want to buy a new car and are trying to decide which of two models to purchase. Since energy and economy are both important issues, you decide to purchase model A because its EPA mileage rating is 32 miles per gallon in the city, whereas the mileage rating for model B is only 30 miles per gallon in the city.

FIGURE 2.41
Changing the verbal description to change a viewer's interpretation
Source: Adapted from Selazny, G. "Grappling with Graphics," *Management Review,* Oct. 1975, p. 7.

Production continues to decline for second year

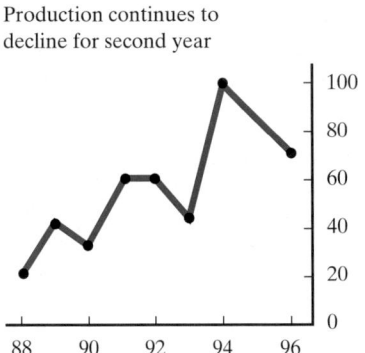

For our production, we need not even change the chart, so we can't be accused of fudging the data. Here we'll simply change the title so that for the Senate subcommittee, we'll indicate that we're not doing as well as in the past...

1996: 3rd best year for production

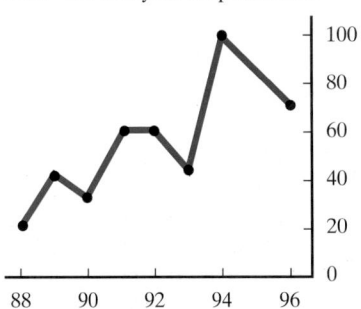

whereas for the general public, we'll tell them that we're still in the prime years.

FIGURE 2.42
Mileage distributions
for two car models

However, you may have acted too quickly. How much variability is associated with the ratings? As an extreme example, suppose that further investigation reveals that the standard deviation for model A mileages is 5 miles per gallon, whereas that for model B is only 1 mile per gallon. If the mileages form a mound-shaped distribution, they might appear as shown in Figure 2.42. Note that the larger amount of variability associated with model A implies that more risk is involved in purchasing model A. That is, the particular car you purchase is more likely to have a mileage rating that will greatly differ from the EPA rating of 32 miles per gallon if you purchase model A, while a model B car is not likely to vary from the 30-miles-per-gallon rating by more than 2 miles per gallon.

We conclude this section with another example on distorting the truth with numerical descriptive measures.

EXAMPLE 2.20

Children Out of School in America is a report on delinquency of school-age children prepared by the Children's Defense Fund (CDF), a government-sponsored organization. Consider the following three reported results of the CDF survey.

Reported result 1: 25 percent of the 16- and 17-year-olds in the Portland, Maine, Bayside East Housing Project were out of school. Fact: *Only eight children were surveyed; two were found to be out of school.*

Reported result 2: Of all the secondary school students who had been suspended more than once in census tract 22 in Columbia, South Carolina, 33% had been suspended two times and 67% had been suspended three or more times. Fact: *CDF found only three children in that entire census tract who had been suspended; one child was suspended twice and the other two children, three or more times.*

Reported result 3: In the Portland Bayside East Housing Project, 50% of all the secondary school children who had been suspended more than once had been suspended three or more times. Fact: *The survey found two secondary school children had been suspended in that area; one of them had been suspended three or more times.*

Identify the potential distortions in the results reported by the CDF.

SOLUTION
In each of these examples the reporting of percentages (i.e., relative frequencies) instead of the numbers themselves is misleading. No inference we might draw from the cited examples would be reliable. (We'll see how to measure the reliability of estimated percentages in Chapter 7.) In short, either the report should state the numbers alone instead of percentages, or, better yet, it should state that the numbers were too small to report by region. If several regions were combined, the numbers (and percentages) would be more meaningful.

QUICK REVIEW

Key Terms

Note: Starred (*) terms are from the optional sections in this chapter.

Bar graph   28
Bivariate relationship*   90
Box plots*   83
Chebyshev's Rule   69
Class frequency   26
Class relative frequency   26
Classes   26
Dot plot   37
Empirical Rule   70
Hinges*   83
Histogram   38
Inner fences*   83
Interquartile range*   83
Lower quartile*   83

Mean   53
Measurement classes   39
Measures of central tendency   53
Measures of relative standing   77
Measures of variation or spread   53
Median   55
Mode   58
Numerical descriptive measures   53
Outer fences*   83
Outliers*   84
Percentile   77
Pie chart   28
Quartiles*   83
Range   63

Rare-event approach   80
Relative frequency histogram   38
Scattergram*   90
Skewness   56
Standard deviation   65
Stem-and-leaf display   37
Time series data*   49
Time series plot*   49
Upper quartile*   83
Variance   65
Whiskers*   83
z-score   77

Key Formulas

$$x = \frac{\sum_{i=1}^{n} x_i}{n}$$
Sample mean   54

$$s^2 = \frac{\sum_{i=1}^{n} (x_i - \bar{x})^2}{n-1} = \frac{\sum_{i=1}^{n} x_i^2 - \frac{\left(\sum_{i=1}^{n} x_i\right)^2}{n}}{n-1}$$
Sample variance   65

$$s = \sqrt{s^2}$$
Sample standard deviation   65

$$z = \frac{x - \bar{x}}{s}$$
Sample z-score   77

$$z = \frac{x - \mu}{\sigma}$$
Population z-score   77

$$IQR = Q_U - Q_L$$
Interquartile range   83

LANGUAGE LAB

Symbol	Pronunciation	Description
Σ	sum of	Summation notation; $\sum_{i=1}^{n} x_i$ represents the sum of the measurements $x_1, x_2, \ldots, x_n$
μ	mu	Population mean
$\bar{x}$	x-bar	Sample mean
σ^2	sigma squared	Population variance
σ	sigma	Population standard deviation
s^2		Sample variance
s		Sample standard deviation
z		z-score for a measurement
m		Median (middle quartile) of a sample data set
Q_L		Lower quartile (25th percentile)
Q_U		Upper quartile (75th percentile)
IQR		Interquartile range

SUPPLEMENTARY EXERCISES 2.97–2.123

Note: Exercises marked with 💾 *contain data available for computer analysis on a 3.5" disk (file name in parentheses). Starred (*) exercises are from the optional sections in this chapter.*

Learning the Mechanics

2.97 Construct a relative frequency histogram for the data summarized in the accompanying table.

Measurement Class	Relative Frequency	Measurement Class	Relative Frequency
.00–.75	.02	5.25–6.00	.15
.75–1.50	.01	6.00–6.75	.12
1.50–2.25	.03	6.75–7.50	.09
2.25–3.00	.05	7.50–8.25	.05
3.00–3.75	.10	8.25–9.00	.04
3.75–4.50	.14	9.00–9.75	.01
4.50–5.25	.19		

2.98 Discuss the conditions under which the median is preferred to the mean as a measure of central tendency.

2.99 Consider the following three measurem   : 50, 70, 80. Find the z-score for each measur   nt if they are from a population with a mean a   tandard deviation equal to
a. $\mu = 60, \sigma = 10$ b. $\mu = 60, \sigma = 5$
c. $\mu = 40, \sigma = 10$ d. $\mu = 40, \sigma = 100$

2.100 If the range of a set of data is 20, find a rough approximation to the standard deviation of the data set.

2.101 For each of the following data sets, compute $\bar{x}, s^2$, and s:
a. $13, 1, 10, 3, 3$ b. $13, 6, 6, 0$
c. $1, 0, 1, 10, 11, 11, 15$ d. $3, 3, 3, 3$

2.102 For each of the following data sets, compute $\bar{x}, s^2$, and s. If appropriate, specify the units in which your answers are expressed.
a. $4, 6, 6, 5, 6, 7$ b. $-\$1, \$4, -\$3, \$0, -\$3, -\$6$
c. $\frac{3}{5}\%, \frac{4}{5}\%, \frac{2}{5}\%, \frac{1}{5}\%, \frac{1}{16}\%$
d. Calculate the range of each data set in parts **a–c**.

2.103 Explain why we generally prefer the standard deviation to the range as a measure of variability for quantitative data.

Applying the Concepts

2.104 U.S. manufacturing executives frequently complain about the high cost of labor in this country. While it may be high relative to many Pacific Rim and South American countries, the table at right indicates that among Western countries, U.S. labor costs are relatively low.

Country	Hourly Manufacturing Labor Rates (in German marks)
Germany	43.97
Switzerland	41.47
Belgium	37.35
Japan	36.01
Austria	35.19
Netherlands	34.87
Sweden	31.00
France	28.92
United States	27.97
Italy	27.21
Ireland	22.17
Britain	22.06
Spain	20.25
Portugal	9.10

Source: The New York Times, October 15, 1995, p. 10.

a. What percentage of countries listed in the table have a higher wage rate than the United States? A lower wage rate than the United States?
b. As of July 5, 1996, one German mark was worth .65 U.S. dollars (*The Wall Street Journal,* July 8, 1996). Convert the data set to U.S. dollars and use the data set to answer the remaining parts of this exercise.
c. What is the mean hourly wage for the 13 Western countries listed in the table? For all 14 countries?
d. Find s^2 and s for all 14 countries.
e. According to Chebyshev's Rule, what percentage of the measurements in the table would you expect to find in the intervals $\bar{x} \pm .75s, \bar{x} \pm 2.5s, \bar{x} \pm 4s$?
f. What percentage of measurements actually fall in the intervals of part **e**? Compare your results with those of part **e**.

2.105 The sequence of pie charts on page 100 portrays the evolution of the structure of the top 500 firms in the United States and the top 200 firms in the United Kingdom over the period 1950–1980.
a. Describe the trends that are revealed by these pie charts.
b. Using your answer to part **a**, draw pie charts for the United Kingdom and the United States that forecast diversification in 2000.

2.106 *Consumer Reports* is a magazine that contains ratings and reports for consumers on goods, services, health, and personal finances. It is published by Consumers Union, a nonprofit organization established in 1936. Consumers Union reported on the testing of 46 brands of toothpaste (*Consumer Reports,* Sept. 1992). Each was rated on: package

Growth of Diversification of Large Companies

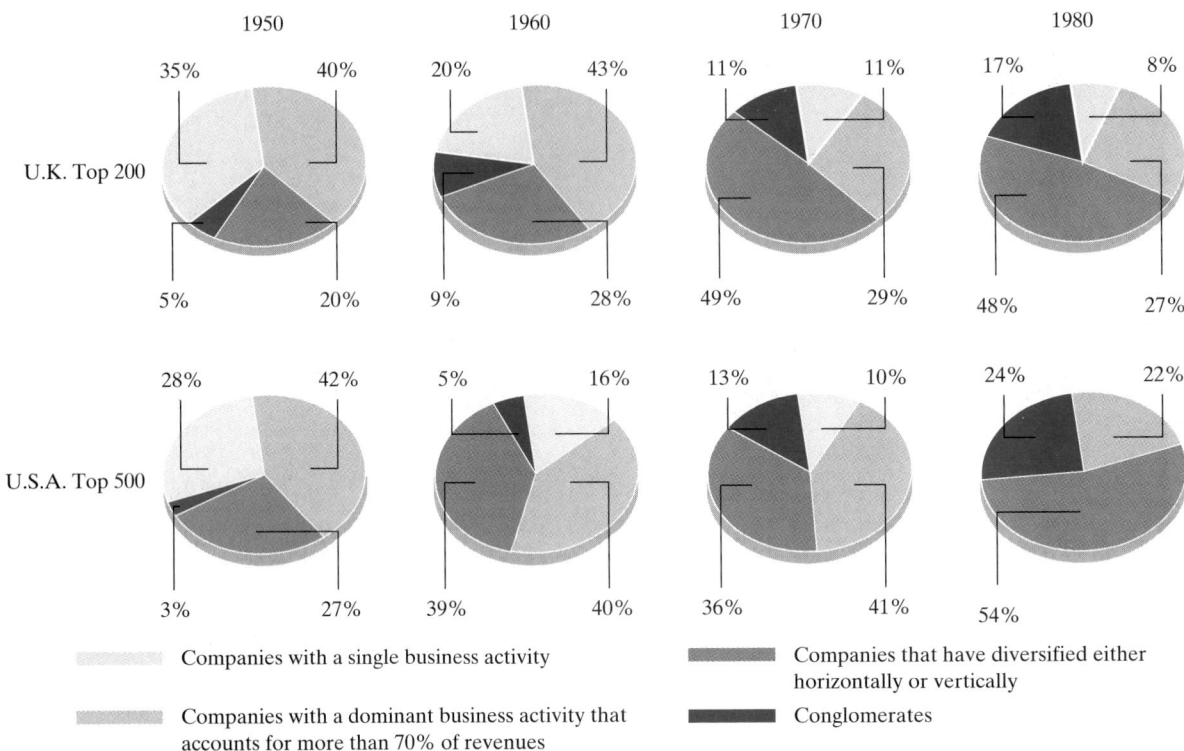

Source: Adapted and reprinted from *Long Range Planning,* Vol. 19, No. 1, pp. 52–60, Copyright 1986, with kind permission from Elsevier Science Ltd., The Boulevard, Langford Lane, Kidlington OX5 1GB UK.

design, flavor, cleaning ability, fluoride content, and cost per month (a cost estimate based on brushing with half-inch of toothpaste twice daily). The data below are costs per month for the 46 brands. Costs marked by an asterisk represent those brands that carry the American Dental Association (ADA) seal verifying effective decay prevention.

a. **(X02.106)** Use a statistical software package to construct a stem-and-leaf display for the data.
b. Circle the individual leaves that represent those brands that carry the ADA seal.
c. What does the pattern of circles suggest about the costs of those brands approved by the ADA?

2.107 A manufacturer of industrial wheels is losing many profitable orders because of the long time it takes the firm's marketing, engineering, and accounting departments to develop price quotes for potential customers. To remedy this problem the firm's management would like to set guidelines for the length of time each department should spend developing price quotes. To help develop these guidelines, 50 requests for price quotes were randomly selected from the set of all price quotes made last year; the processing time was determined for each price quote for each department. These times are displayed in the table on page 101. The price quotes are also classified by whether they were "lost" (i.e., whether or not the customer placed an order after receiving the price quote).

.58	.66	1.02	1.11	1.77	1.40	.73*	.53*	.57*	1.34
1.29	.89*	.49	.53*	.52	3.90	4.73	1.26	.71*	.55*
.59*	.97	.44*	.74*	.51*	.68*	.67	1.22	.39	.55
.62	.66*	1.07	.64	1.32*	1.77*	.80*	.79	.89*	.64
.81*	.79*	.44*	1.09	1.04	1.12				

PRICE QUOTE PROCESSING TIMES (IN DAYS)

Request Number	Marketing	Engineering	Accounting	Lost?	Request Number	Marketing	Engineering	Accounting	Lost?
1	7.0	6.2	.1	No	26	.6	2.2	.5	No
2	.4	5.2	.1	No	27	6.0	1.8	.2	No
3	2.4	4.6	.6	No	28	5.8	.6	.5	No
4	6.2	13.0	.8	Yes	29	7.8	7.2	2.2	Yes
5	4.7	.9	.5	No	30	3.2	6.9	.1	No
6	1.3	.4	.1	No	31	11.0	1.7	3.3	No
7	7.3	6.1	.1	No	32	6.2	1.3	2.0	No
8	5.6	3.6	3.8	No	33	6.9	6.0	10.5	Yes
9	5.5	9.6	.5	No	34	5.4	.4	8.4	No
10	5.3	4.8	.8	No	35	6.0	7.9	.4	No
11	6.0	2.6	.1	No	36	4.0	1.8	18.2	Yes
12	2.6	11.3	1.0	No	37	4.5	1.3	.3	No
13	2.0	.6	.8	No	38	2.2	4.8	.4	No
14	.4	12.2	1.0	No	39	3.5	7.2	7.0	Yes
15	8.7	2.2	3.7	No	40	.1	.9	14.4	No
16	4.7	9.6	.1	No	41	2.9	7.7	5.8	No
17	6.9	12.3	.2	Yes	42	5.4	3.8	.3	No
18	.2	4.2	.3	No	43	6.7	1.3	.1	No
19	5.5	3.5	.4	No	44	2.0	6.3	9.9	Yes
20	2.9	5.3	22.0	No	45	.1	12.0	3.2	No
21	5.9	7.3	1.7	No	46	6.4	1.3	6.2	No
22	6.2	4.4	.1	No	47	4.0	2.4	13.5	Yes
23	4.1	2.1	30.0	Yes	48	10.0	5.3	.1	No
24	5.8	.6	.1	No	49	8.0	14.4	1.9	Yes
25	5.0	3.1	2.3	No	50	7.0	10.0	2.0	No

a. MINITAB stem-and-leaf displays for each of the departments and for the total processing time are shown below and shown on page 102. Note that the units of the leaves for accounting and total processing times are units (1.0), while the leaf units for marketing and engineering processing times are tenths (.1). Shade the leaves that correspond to "lost" orders in each of the displays, and interpret each of the displays.

b. Using your results from part a, develop "maximum processing time" guidelines for each department that, if followed, will help the firm reduce the number of lost orders.

```
Stem-and-leaf of MKT          N = 50
Leaf Unit = 0.10

     6      0  112446
     7      1  3
    14      2  0024699
    16      3  25
    22      4  001577
   (10)     5  0344556889
    18      6  0002224799
     8      7  0038
     4      8  07
     2      9
     2     10  0
     1     11  0
```

```
Stem-and-leaf of ENG          N = 50
Leaf Unit = 0.10

     7      0  4466699
    14      1  3333788
    19      2  12246
    23      3  1568
    (5)     4  24688
    22      5  233
    19      6  01239
    14      7  22379
     9      8
     9      9  66
     7     10  0
     6     11  3
     5     12  023
     2     13  0
     1     14  4
```

```
Stem-and-leaf of ACC        N = 50
Leaf Unit = 1.0

   (31)    0  0000000000000000000000000001111
    19     0  22223333
    11     0  5
    10     0  67
     8     0  89
     6     1  0
     5     1  3
     4     1  4
     3     1
     3     1  8
     2     2
     2     2  2
     1     2
     1     2
     1     2
     1     3  0
```

```
Stem-and-leaf of TOTAL      N = 50
Leaf Unit = 1.0

     4     0  1334
    17     0  5666677888999
   (15)    1  000033333444444
    18     1  555566778999
     6     2  0344
     2     2
     2     3  0
     1     3  6
```

2.108 Refer to Exercise 2.107. Summary statistics for the processing times are given in the MINITAB printout below.

a. Calculate the z-score corresponding to the maximum processing time guideline you developed in Exercise 2.107 for each department, and for the total processing time.

b. Calculate the maximum processing time corresponding to a z-score of 3 for each of the departments. What percentage of the orders exceed these guidelines? How does this agree with Chebyshev's Rule and the Empirical Rule?

c. Repeat part **b** using a z-score of 2.

d. Compare the percentage of "lost" quotes with corresponding times that exceed at least one of the guidelines in part **b** to the same percentage using the guidelines in part **c**. Which set of guidelines would you recommend be adopted? Why?

	N	MEAN	MEDIAN	TRMEAN	STDEV	SEMEAN
MKT	50	4.766	5.400	4.732	2.584	0.365
ENG	50	5.044	4.500	4.798	3.835	0.542
ACC	50	3.652	0.800	2.548	6.256	0.885
TOTAL	50	13.462	13.750	13.043	6.820	0.965

	MIN	MAX	Q1	Q3
MKT	0.100	11.000	2.825	6.250
ENG	0.400	14.400	1.775	7.225
ACC	0.100	30.000	0.200	3.725
TOTAL	1.800	36.200	8.075	16.600

*2.109 A time series plot similar to the one shown here appeared in a recent advertisement for a well-known golf magazine. One person might interpret the plot's message as the longer you subscribe to the magazine, the better golfer you should become. Another person might interpret it as indicating that if you subscribe for 3 years, your game should improve dramatically.

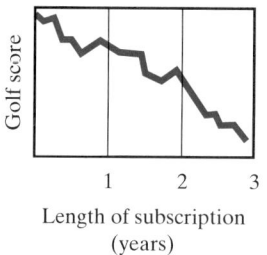

a. Explain why the plot can be interpreted in more than one way.
b. How could the plot be altered to rectify the current distortion?

2.110 A company has roughly the same number of people in each of five departments: Production, Sales, R&D, Maintenance, and Administration. The following table lists the number and type of major injuries that occurred in each department last year.

Type of Injury	Department	Number of Injuries
Burn	Production	3
	Maintenance	6
Back strain	Production	2
	Sales	1
	R&D	1
	Maintenance	5
	Administration	2
Eye damage	Production	1
	Maintenance	2
	Administration	1
Deafness	Production	1
Cuts	Production	4
	Sales	1
	R&D	1
	Maintenance	10
Broken arm	Production	2
	Maintenance	2
Broken leg	Sales	1
	Maintenance	1
Broken finger	Administration	1
Concussion	Maintenance	3
	Administration	1
Hearing loss	Maintenance	2

a. Construct a Pareto diagram to identify which department or departments have the worst safety record.

b. Explode the Pareto diagram of part **a** to identify the most prevalent type of injury in the department with the worst safety record.

2.111 In some locations, radiation levels in homes are measured at well above normal background levels in the environment. As a result, many architects and builders are making design changes to ensure adequate air exchange so that radiation will not be "trapped" in homes. In one such location, 50 homes' levels were measured, and the mean level was 10 parts per billion (ppb), the median was 8 ppb, and the standard deviation was 3 ppb. Background levels in this location are at about 4 ppb.
a. Based on these results, is the distribution of the 50 homes' radiation levels symmetric, skewed to the left, or skewed to the right? Why?
b. Use both Chebyshev's Rule and the Empirical Rule to describe the distribution of radiation levels. Which do you think is most appropriate in this case? Why?
c. Use the results from part **b** to approximate the number of homes in this sample that have radiation levels above the background level.
d. Suppose another home is measured at a location 10 miles from the one sampled, and has a level of 20 ppb. What is the z-score for this measurement relative to the 50 homes sampled in the other location? Is it likely that this new measurement comes from the same distribution of radiation levels as the other 50? Why? How would you go about confirming your conclusion?

2.112 The 1995 Salary Survey by *Working Women* magazine (Jan. 1996) reports that over the 15-year period that ended in 1993, pay for female managers and executives climbed 18.3%, while their male colleagues gained only 1.7%. However, a gap still remains between the genders. For example, they report the median salaries for senior vice presidents/account managers in the advertising field are $122,000 for women and $145,000 for men. These medians were determined from sample data. They are estimates of the medians of their respective populations.
a. Describe the two populations.
b. Is it possible to determine the exact medians of these populations? Explain in detail.
c. Interpret the values of the reported medians.

2.113 Part-time and temporary workers have always represented a large share of employment in Japan. The need for less costly labor and protection against fluctuations in labor demand over the past decade in Japan have raised the number of part-time and temporary workers there. The table on page 104, extracted from *Monthly Labor*

U.S. Peanut Production*
(in billions of pounds)

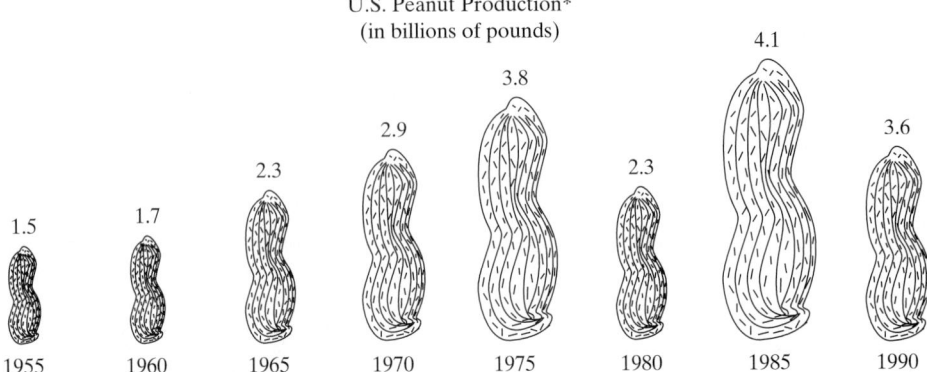

| 1.5 | 1.7 | 2.3 | 2.9 | 3.8 | 2.3 | 4.1 | 3.6 |
| 1955 | 1960 | 1965 | 1970 | 1975 | 1980 | 1985 | 1990 |

Review (Oct. 1995), gives the percentages of all paid employees in Japan in the different job categories for 1982 and 1992. Use a graphical method to demonstrate the increase in part-time and temporary workers in Japan from 1982 to 1992.

Job Category	PERCENT OF TOTAL NUMBER OF PAID WORKERS	
	1982	**1992**
Regular full-time	72.7	68.8
Part-time	11.0	16.1
Temporary	7.9	8.4
Day laborer	3.6	2.8
Other nonregular	4.8	3.9
Totals	100.0	100.0

*2.114 If not examined carefully, the graphical description of U.S. peanut production shown at the top of the page can be misleading.
   a. Explain why the graph may mislead some readers.
   b. Construct an undistorted graph of U.S. peanut production for the given years.

2.115 In experimenting with a new technique for imprinting paper napkins with designs, names, etc., a paper-products company discovered that four different results were possible:
   (A) Imprint successful
   (B) Imprint smeared
   (C) Imprint off-center to the left
   (D) Imprint off-center to the right
To test the reliability of the technique, the company imprinted 1,000 napkins and obtained the results shown in the graph in the next column.
   a. What type of graphical tool is the figure?
   b. What information does the graph convey to you?
   c. From the information provided by the graph, how might you numerically describe the reliability of the imprinting technique?

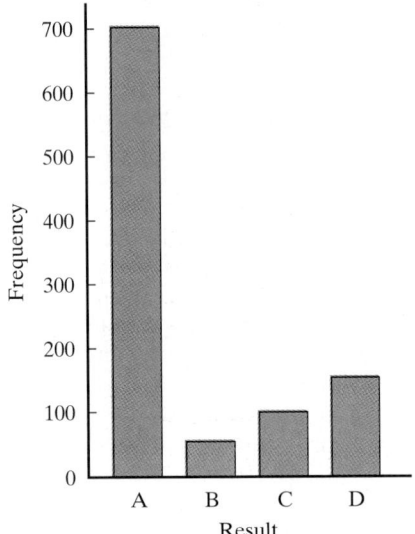

2.116 The data in the table below describe the distribution of rent amounts paid by U.S. apartment dwellers in 1993. Use a relative frequency histogram to describe the data.

Rent (in dollars)	Percent of Renters in Rent Class
Less than $100	2.0
$100–$199	7.0
$200–$299	10.0
$300–$399	15.0
$400–$499	18.0
$500–$599	16.0
$600–$699	12.0
$700–$799	8.0
$800–$899	4.0
$900–$999	3.0
$1000 or more	5.0
Total	100.0

Source: U.S. Bureau of the Census, *Statistical Abstract of the United States: 1995,* p. 738.

2.117 A study by the U.S. Public Research Interest Group found that in Massachusetts bank customers were charged lower fees than the national average for regular checking accounts, NOW accounts, and savings accounts. For regular checking accounts the Massachusetts mean was $190.06 per year, while the national mean was $201.94 (*Boston Globe,* Aug. 9, 1995). The referenced article did not explain how these averages were determined other than to say the national average was estimated from a sample of 271 banks in 25 states. Prepare a report that explains in detail how Massachusetts' mean could have been estimated. There are 245 banks in Massachusetts. Your answer should include a sampling plan, a measurement plan, and a calculation formula.

2.118 Polychlorinated biphenyls (PCBs), considered to be extremely hazardous to humans, are often used in the insulation of large electric transformers. The *Gainesville Sun* (Mar. 24, 1984) reported on the discovery of a particularly high PCB count at a salvage company in Clay County, Florida. The company, which salvaged the copper in electrical transformers, allowed oil contaminated with PCBs to seep into the soil in and around the salvage site. One soil sample in the vicinity registered 200 parts per million (ppm) of PCBs, four times the safe limit established by the Florida Department of Environmental Regulation. Suppose that the PCB count in samples of soil in the vicinity of the salvage operation has a distribution with mean equal to 25 ppm and standard deviation equal to 5 ppm of PCBs. Would a soil sample showing 200 ppm be classified as an extreme observation? Explain.

2.119 The table lists the average inflation rates between 1985 and 1993 for two samples of countries, those with high Gross National Products (GNP) per capita and low GNP per capita.

	High GNP		**Low GNP**
United States	3.5	China	8.1
Sweden	6.3	India	9.7
Germany	3.2	Egypt	16.9
Spain	6.8	Ethiopia	380.0
France	3.0	Ghana	29.4
Italy	6.5	Vietnam	118.7
Japan	1.4	Sudan	55.3
Australia	4.6	Pakistan	8.4

Source: The World Bank Atlas, 1995.

a. For each sample, characterize the magnitude and variability of the inflation rates using appropriate numerical descriptive measures.

b. Justify the measures you used in part **a.** For example, is the mean, median, or mode the most appropriate measure of magnitude?

c. Notice that there is variation in the inflation rates both within each sample and between the samples. Is this surprising? Why or why not?

2.120 The Age Discrimination in Employment Act mandates that workers 40 years of age or older be treated without regard to age in all phases of employment (hiring, promotions, firing, etc.). Age discrimination cases are of two types: *disparate treatment* and *disparate impact*. In the former, the issue is whether workers have been intentionally discriminated against. In the latter, the issue is whether employment practices adversely affect the protected class (i.e., workers 40 and over) even though no such effect was intended by the employer (Zabell, 1989). During the recession of the early 1990s, a small computer manufacturer laid off 10 of its 20 software engineers. The ages of all the engineers at the time of the layoff are shown in the table.

Not laid off:	34	55	42	38	42	32	40	40	46	29
Laid off:	52	35	40	41	40	39	40	64	47	44

Analyze the data to determine whether the company may be vulnerable to a disparate impact claim.

*2.121 A national chain of automobile oil-change franchises claims that "your hood will be open for less than 12 minutes when we service your car." To check their claim, an undercover consumer reporter from a local television station monitored the "hood time" of 25 consecutive customers at one of the chain's franchises. The resulting data follow. Construct a time series plot for these data and describe in words what it reveals.

Customer Number	Hood Open (Minutes)	Customer Number	Hood Open (Minutes)
1	11.50	14	12.50
2	13.50	15	13.75
3	12.25	16	12.00
4	15.00	17	11.50
5	14.50	18	14.25
6	13.75	19	15.50
7	14.00	20	13.00
8	11.00	21	18.25
9	12.75	22	11.75
10	11.50	23	12.50
11	11.00	24	11.25
12	13.00	25	14.75
13	16.25		

2.122 The table on page 106 reports the year-to-date automobile sales in the United States (in thousands of cars) for the "Big Three" U.S. manufacturers (Ford, General Motors, and Chrysler), European manufacturers, and Japanese manufacturers.

a. Construct a relative frequency bar graph for these data.

Manufacturer	November 1995
General Motors	229.7
Ford	131.2
Chrysler	58.3
Japanese	192.6
European	37.0
Total	648.8

Source: Wall Street Journal, December 6, 1995, p. B5.

b. *Stacking* is the combining of all bars in a bar graph into a single bar, by drawing one on top of the other and distinguishing one from another by the use of colors or patterns. Stack the relative frequencies of the five car manufacturers for November 1995.

c. What information about the U.S. automobile market is reflected in your graph of part **a**?

d. What share of the U.S. automobile market has been captured by U.S. manufacturers?

2.123 Computer anxiety is defined as "the mixture of fear, apprehension, and hope that people feel when planning to interact, or when interacting with a computer." Researchers have found computer anxiety in people at all levels of society, including students, doctors, lawyers, secretaries, managers, and college professors. One profession for which little is known about the level and impact of computer anxiety is secondary technical education (STE), since STE teachers have just recently begun to participate in the high-tech computer revolution. The extent of computer anxiety among STE teachers was investigated by H. R. D. Gordon in the *Journal of Studies in Technical Careers* (Vol. 15, 1995). A sample of 116 teachers were administered the Computer Anxiety Scale (COMPAS) designed to measure level of computer anxiety. Scores, ranging from 10 to 50, were categorized as follows: very anxious (37–50); anxious/tense (33–36); some mild anxiety (27–32); generally relaxed/comfortable (20–26); very relaxed/confident (10–19). A summary of the COMPAS anxiety levels for the sample is provided in the following table.

Category	Score Range	Frequency	Relative Frequency
Very anxious	37–50	22	.19
Anxious/tense	33–36	8	.07
Some mild anxiety	27–32	23	.20
Generally relaxed/ comfortable	20–26	24	.21
Very relaxed/confident	10–19	39	.33
Totals		116	1.00

Source: Gordon, H. R. D. "Analysis of the computer anxiety levels of secondary technical education teachers in West Virginia." *Journal of Studies in Technical Careers,* Vol. 15, No. 2, 1995, pp. 26–27 (Table 1).

a. Graph and interpret the results.

b. One of the objectives of the research is to compare the computer anxiety levels of male and female STE teachers. Use the summary information in the following table to make the comparison.

	Male Teachers	Female Teachers	All Teachers
n	68	48	116
$\bar{x}$	26.4	24.5	25.6
s	10.6	11.2	10.8

Source: Gordon, H. R. D. "Analysis of the computer anxiety levels of secondary technical education teachers in West Virginia." *Journal of Studies in Technical Careers,* Vol. 15, No. 2, 1995, pp. 26–27 (Table 2).

THE KENTUCKY MILK CASE—PART I

SHOWCASE

Many products and services are purchased by governments, cities, states, and businesses on the basis of sealed bids, and contracts are awarded to the lowest bidders. This process works extremely well in competitive markets, but it has the potential to increase the cost of purchasing if the markets are noncompetitive or if collusive practices are present. An investigation that began with a statistical analysis of bids in the Florida school milk market in 1986 led to the recovery of more than $33,000,000 from dairies who had conspired to rig the bids there in the 1980s. The investigation spread quickly to other states, and to date settlements and fines from dairies exceed $100,000,000 for school milk bidrigging in twenty other states. This case concerns a school milk bidrigging investigation in Kentucky.

Each year, the Commonwealth of Kentucky invites bids from dairies to supply half-pint containers of fluid milk products for its school districts. The products include whole white milk, low-fat white milk, and low-fat chocolate milk. In 13 school districts in northern Kentucky, the suppliers (dairies) were accused of "price-fixing," that is, conspiring to allocate the districts, so that the "winner" was predetermined. Since these districts are located in Boone, Campbell, and Kenton counties, the geographic market they represent is designated as the "tri-county" market. Between 1983 and 1991, two dairies—Meyer Dairy and Trauth Dairy—were the only bidders on the milk contracts in the school districts in the tri-county market. Consequently, these two companies were awarded all the milk contracts in the market. (In contrast, a large number of different dairies won the milk contracts for the school districts in the remainder of the northern Kentucky market–called the "surrounding" market.) The Commonwealth of Kentucky alleged that Meyer and Trauth conspired to allocate the districts in the tri-county market. To date, one of the dairies (Meyer) has admitted guilt, while the other (Trauth) steadfastly maintains its innocence.

The Commonwealth of Kentucky maintains a database on all bids received from the dairies competing for the milk contracts. Some of these data have been made available to you to analyze to determine whether there is empirical evidence of bid collusion in the tri-county market. The data, available in ASCII format on a 3.5" diskette, is described in detail below. Some background information on the data and important economic theory regarding bid collusion is also provided. Use this information to guide your analysis. Prepare a professional document which presents the results of your analysis and gives your opinion regarding collusion.

DATA.   ASCII file name: **MILK.DAT**
Number of observations: **392**

Variable	Column(s)	Type	Description
YEAR	1–4	QN	Year in which milk contract awarded
MARKET	6–15	QL	Northern Kentucky Market (TRI-COUNTY or SURROUND)
WINNER	17–30	QL	Name of winning dairy
WWBID	32–38	QN	Winning bid price of whole white milk (dollars per half-pint)
WWQTY	40–46	QN	Quantity of whole white milk purchased (number of half-pints)
LFWBID	48–53	QN	Winning bid price of low-fat white milk (dollars per half-pint)
LFWQTY	55–62	QN	Quantity of low-fat white milk purchased (number of half-pints)
LFCBID	64–69	QN	Winning bid price of low-fat chocolate milk (dollars per half-pint)
LFCQTY	71–78	QN	Quantity of low-fat chocolate milk purchased (number of half-pints)
DISTRICT	80–82	QL	School district number
KYFMO	84–89	QN	FMO minimum raw cost of milk (dollars per half-pint)
MILESM	91–93	QN	Distance (miles) from Meyer processing plant to school district
MILEST	95–97	QN	Distance (miles) from Trauth processing plant to school district
LETDATE	99–106	QL	Date on which bidding on milk contract began (month/day/year)

BACKGROUND INFORMATION

Collusive Market Environment. Certain economic features of a market create an environment in which collusion may be found. These basic features include:

1. *Few sellers and high concentration.* Only a few dairies control all or nearly all of the milk business in the market.

2. *Homogeneous products.* The products sold are essentially the same from the standpoint of the buyer (i.e., the school district).

3. *Inelastic demand.* Demand is relatively insensitive to price. (Note: The quantity of milk required by a school district is primarily determined by school enrollment, not price.)

4. *Similar costs.* The dairies bidding for the milk contracts face similar cost conditions. (Note: Approximately 60% of a dairy's production cost is raw milk, which is federally regulated. Meyer and Trauth are dairies of similar size and both bought their raw milk from the same supplier.)

Although these market structure characteristics create an environment which makes collusive behavior easier, they do not necessarily indicate the existence of collusion. An analysis of the actual bid prices may provide additional information about the degree of competition in the market.

Collusive Bidding Patterns. The analyses of patterns in sealed bids reveal much about the level of competition, or lack thereof, among the vendors serving the market. Consider the following bid analyses:

1. *Market shares.* A market share for a dairy is the number of milk half-pints supplied by the dairy over a given school year, divided by the total number of half-pints supplied to the entire market. One sign of potential collusive behavior is stable, nearly equal market shares over time for the dairies under investigation.

2. *Incumbency rates.* Market allocation is a common form of collusive behavior in bidrigging conspiracies. Typically, the same diary controls the same school districts year after year. The incumbency rate for a market in a given school year is defined as the percentage of school districts that are won by the same vendor who won the previous year. An incumbency rate that exceeds 70% has been considered a sign of collusive behavior.

3. *Bid levels and dispersion.* In competitive sealed bid markets vendors do not share information about their bids. Consequently, more dispersion or variability among the bids is observed than in collusive markets, where vendors communicate about their bids and have a tendency to submit bids in close proximity to one another in an attempt to make the bidding appear competitive. Furthermore, in competitive markets the bid dispersion tends to be directly proportional to the level of the bid: When bids are submitted at relatively high levels, there is more variability among the bids than when they are submitted at or near marginal cost, which will be approximately the same among dairies in the same geographic market.

4. *Price versus cost/distance.* In competitive markets, bid prices are expected to track costs over time. Thus, if the market is competitive, the bid price of milk should be highly correlated with the raw milk cost. Lack of such a relationship is another sign of collusion. Similarly, bid price should be correlated to the distance the product must travel from the processing plant to the school (due to delivery costs) in a competitive market.

5. *Bid sequence.* School milk bids are submitted over the spring and summer months, generally at the end of one school year and before the beginning of the next. When the bids are examined in sequence in competitive markets, the level of bidding is expected to fall as the bidding season progresses. (This phenomenon is attributable to the learning process that occurs during the season, with bids adjusted accordingly. Dairies may submit relatively high bids early in the season to "test the market," confident that volume can be picked up later if the early high bids lose. But, dairies who do not win much business early in the season are likely to become more aggressive in their bidding as the season progresses, driving price levels down.) Constant or slightly increasing price patterns of sequential bids in a market where a single dairy wins year after year is considered another indication of collusive behavior.

6. *Comparison of average winning bid prices.* Consider two similar markets, one in which bids are possibly rigged and the other in which bids are competitively determined. In theory, the mean winning price in the "rigged" market will be significantly higher than the mean price in the competitive market for each year in which collusion occurs. ▲

www.int.com
www.int.com
INTERNET LAB
www.int.com

ACCESSING AND SUMMARIZING BUSINESS AND ECONOMIC DATA MAINTAINED BY THE U.S. GOVERNMENT

A vital underpinning of statistical analysis and interpretation of results is the information value of the data used. Data collection is often an expensive undertaking and many studies begin with an examination of external data; that is, data routinely collected and maintained by credible sources. Various government agencies play a major role in producing data across many areas of business and economics. These data constitute a primary starting point for obtaining external data.

Here we will visit three important U.S. government sites, all of which provide data for examining business and economic conditions. Our initial focus is to become acquainted with locating prominent data published by these three agencies and to learn about the variety of different data each of these sources produces. In the process of examining these sites, you will notice links to other government sites where yet other data reside. Visiting these three sites will not give you an exhaustive overview of either U.S. government or Internet resources but hopefully will provide you with a structured introduction to the vast resources available. Later labs will examine in further detail data selections from these three sites, among others.

For each site, perform the following tasks:

1. Note the type of data (quantitative or qualitative) available.

2. Note the format of the data set of interest (ASCII, HTML, SAS, SPSS, etc.) and read any associated notes about downloading and/or formatting the data.

3. Are there subscription fees or other conditions or restrictions on obtaining the data? If so, note what those are.

4. Write down the direct URL address of the requested data.

5. List three or more other major data series available from the parent agency.

6. Are there special formats, subscriptions, and so forth associated with any of these other data sets?

7. Name some other agencies or organizations to which this site provides links.

8. Leave the site completely by typing in the home page address of your school in your address location area (use: *http://www.prenhall.com* if you do not know the school's address).

9. Now type in the direct address of the requested data from step 4. Are you able to locate the data in one step?

10. Save the data set of interest to your statistical applications software (e.g., MINITAB) data files.

11. Summarize and describe the data using your statistical software.

SITE 1: LOCATE GROSS DOMESTIC PRODUCT (GDP) DATA

These data are produced by the U.S. Department of Commerce, located at *http://www.docgov/*

- At the Department of Commerce home page, click on: **U.S. Department of Commerce Agencies**

- At this location, click on: **Bureau of Economic Analysis** (BEA)

- From the main BEA page, click on: **BEA Data and Methodology**

- Here, scroll down to the heading "Please select one of BEA's three program areas," click on: **National**

- From BEA National programs, scroll to the heading/subheading "Data—National Income and Product Accounts," click on: **4. Time Series**

- On the page of Frequently Requested NIPA Data: History, click on: **Real GDP, GNP, and final sales. Annually**

SITE 2: LOCATE UNEMPLOYMENT STATISTICS

These data are produced by the U.S. Department of Labor, Bureau of Labor Statistics, located at *http://stats.bls.gov.80/*

- From the Bureau of Labor Statistics site, click on: **Data**

- Then click on: **Most Requested Series**

- Next, click on: **Overall BLS Most Requested Data**

- Here, scroll down through the selections

SITE 3: LOCATE DATA ON NEW BUSINESS START-UPS

These data are made available from the Federal Reserve Bank of Kansas City, located at *http://www.kc.frb.org/*

- From the Federal Reserve Board of Kansas City home page, click on: **Contents**

- Scroll down to the heading "Special features …," click on: **Regional historical economic data**

- Here, click on: **business activity**

As a final task, pick key words of the requested data set from any of sites 1, 2, or 3. Use those key words in the *Net Search* area of your browser. Try out four or five of the search engines (Yahoo!, Excite, Alta Vista, and so forth). Which of the search engines directs you to the data in the first 25 selections? ○

CHAPTER 3

PROBABILITY

Where We've Been

We've identified inference, from a sample to a population, as the goal of statistics. And we've seen that to reach this goal, we must be able to describe a set of measurements. Thus, we explored the use of graphical and numerical methods for describing both quantitative and qualitative data sets.

Where We're Going

We now turn to the problem of making an inference. What is it that permits us to make the inferential jump from sample to population and then to give a measure of reliability for the inference? As you'll see, the answer is *probability*. This chapter is devoted to a study of probability—what it is and some of the basic concepts of the theory behind it.

Recall that one branch of statistics is concerned with decisions about a population based on sample information. You can see how this is accomplished more easily if you understand the relationship between population and sample—a relationship that becomes clearer if we reverse the statistical procedure of making inferences from sample to population. In this chapter then, we assume that the population is *known* and calculate the chances of obtaining various samples from the population. Thus, we show that probability is the reverse of statistics: In probability, we use the population information to infer the probable nature of the sample.

Probability plays an important role in inference-making. Suppose, for example, you have an opportunity to invest in an oil exploration company. Past records show that out of 10 previous oil drillings (a sample of the company's experiences), all 10 came up dry. What do you conclude? Do you think the chances are better than 50:50 that the company will hit a gusher? Should you invest in this company? Chances are, your answer to these questions will be an emphatic No. If the company's exploratory prowess is sufficient to hit a producing well 50% of the time, a record of 10 dry wells out of 10 drilled is an event that is just too improbable.

Or suppose you're playing poker with what your opponents assure you is a well-shuffled deck of cards. In three consecutive five-card hands, the person on your right is dealt four aces. Based on this sample of three deals, do you think the cards are being adequately shuffled? Again, your answer is likely to be No because dealing three hands of four aces is just too improbable if the cards were properly shuffled.

Note that the decisions concerning the potential success of the oil drilling company and the adequacy of card shuffling both involve knowing the chance—or probability—of a certain sample result. Both situations were contrived so that you could easily conclude that the probabilities of the sample results were small. Unfortunately, the probabilities of many observed sample results aren't so easy to evaluate intuitively. For these cases we will need the assistance of a theory of probability.

3.1 EVENTS, SAMPLE SPACES, AND PROBABILITY

Let's begin our treatment of probability with simple examples that are easily described. With the aid of simple examples, we can introduce important definitions that will help us develop the notion of probability more easily.

Suppose a coin is tossed once and the up face is recorded. The result we see and record is called an *observation,* or *measurement,* and the process of making an observation is called an *experiment.* Notice that our definition of experiment is broader than the one used in the physical sciences, where you would picture test tubes, microscopes, and other laboratory equipment. Among other things, statistical experiments may include recording a customer's preference for one of two computer operating systems (DOS or Macintosh), recording a change in the Dow Jones Industrial Average from one day to the next, recording the weekly sales of a business firm, and counting the number of errors on a page of an accountant's ledger. The point is that a statistical experiment can be almost any act of observation as long as the outcome is uncertain.

DEFINITION 3.1
An **experiment** is an act or process of observation that leads to a single outcome that cannot be predicted with certainty.

Consider another simple experiment consisting of tossing a die and observing the number on the up face. The six basic possible outcomes to this experiment are:

1. Observe a 1
2. Observe a 2
3. Observe a 3
4. Observe a 4
5. Observe a 5
6. Observe a 6

Note that if this experiment is conducted once, *you can observe one and only one of these six basic outcomes, and the outcome cannot be predicted with certainty.* Also, these possibilities cannot be decomposed into more basic outcomes. Because observing the outcome of an experiment is similar to selecting a sample from a population, the basic possible outcomes to an experiment are called *sample points.*[*]

DEFINITION 3.2

A **sample point** is the most basic outcome of an experiment.

EXAMPLE 3.1

Two coins are tossed, and their up faces are recorded. List all the sample points for this experiment.

SOLUTION

Even for a seemingly trivial experiment, we must be careful when listing the sample points. At first glance, we might expect three basic outcomes: Observe two heads, Observe two tails, or Observe one head and one tail. However, further reflection reveals that the last of these, Observe one head and one tail, can be decomposed into two outcomes: Head on coin 1, Tail on coin 2; and Tail on coin 1, Head on coin 2.[†] Thus, we have four sample points:

1. Observe *HH*
2. Observe *HT*
3. Observe *TH*
4. Observe *TT*

where *H* in the first position means "Head on coin 1," *H* in the second position means "Head on coin 2," and so on.   **L**

We often wish to refer to the collection of all the sample points of an experiment. This collection is called the *sample space* of the experiment. For example, there are six sample points in the sample space associated with the die-toss experiment. The sample spaces for the experiments discussed thus far are shown in Table 3.1.

---

[*]Alternatively, the term "simple event" can be used.
[†]Even if the coins are identical in appearance, there are, in fact, two distinct coins. Thus, the designation of one coin as coin 1 and the other coin as coin 2 is legitimate in any case.

TABLE 3.1   Experiments and Their Sample Spaces

Experiment: Observe the up face on a coin.
Sample space: 1. Observe a head
                   2. Observe a tail
This sample space can be represented in set notation as a set containing two sample points:

$$S: \{H, T\}$$

where H represents the sample point Observe a head and T represents the sample point Observe a tail.

Experiment: Observe the up face on a die.
Sample space: 1. Observe a 1
                   2. Observe a 2
                   3. Observe a 3
                   4. Observe a 4
                   5. Observe a 5
                   6. Observe a 6
This sample space can be represented in set notation as a set of six sample points:

$$S: \{1, 2, 3, 4, 5, 6\}$$

Experiment: Observe the up faces on two coins.
Sample space: 1. Observe HH
                   2. Observe HT
                   3. Observe TH
                   4. Observe TT
This sample space can be represented in set notation as a set of four sample points:

$$S: \{HH, HT, TH, TT\}$$

---

a. Experiment: Observe the up face on a coin

b. Experiment: Observe the up face on a die

c. Experiment: Observe the up faces on two coins

FIGURE 3.1
Venn diagrams for the three experiments from Table 3.1

DEFINITION 3.3
The **sample space** of an experiment is the collection of all its sample points.

Just as graphs are useful in describing sets of data, a pictorial method for presenting the sample space will often be useful. Figure 3.1 shows such a representation for each of the experiments in Table 3.1. In each case, the sample space is shown as a closed figure, labeled S, containing all possible sample points. Each sample point is represented by a solid dot (i.e., a "point") and labeled accordingly. Such graphical representations are called **Venn diagrams**.

Now that we know that an experiment will result in *only one* basic outcome—called a sample point—and that the sample space is the collection of all possible sample points, we're ready to discuss the probabilities of the sample points. You've undoubtedly used the term *probability* and have some intuitive idea about its meaning. Probability is generally used synonymously with "chance," "odds," and similar concepts. For example, if a fair coin is tossed, we might reason that both the sample points, Observe a head and Observe a tail, have the same *chance* of occurring. Thus, we might state that "the probability of observing a head is 50%" or "the *odds* of seeing a head are 50:50." Both of these statements are based on an informal knowledge of probability. We'll begin our treatment of probability by using such informal concepts and then solidify what we mean later.

The probability of a sample point is a number between 0 and 1 that measures the likelihood that the outcome will occur when the experiment is performed. This number is usually taken to be the relative frequency of the occurrence of a sample

FIGURE 3.2
The proportion of heads in N tosses of a coin

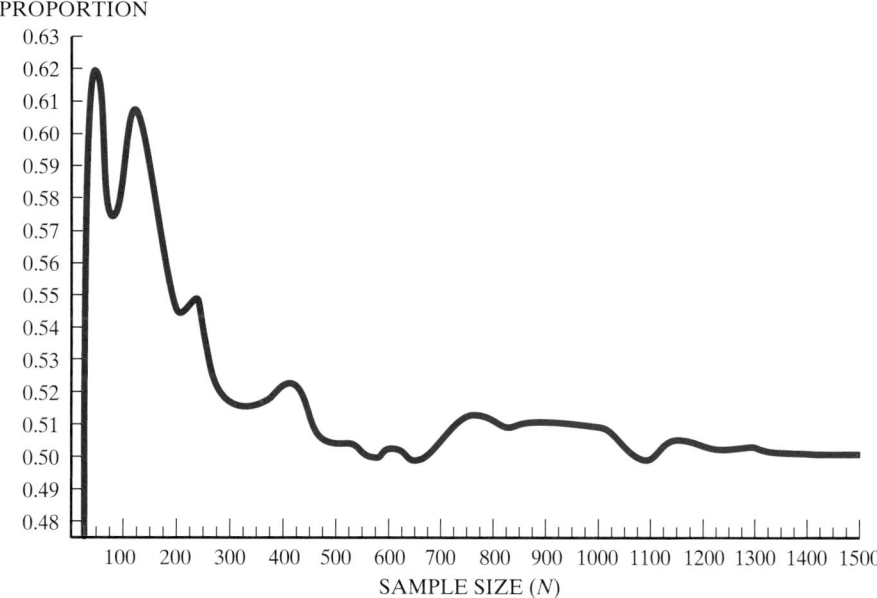

point in a very long series of repetitions of an experiment.* For example, if we are assigning probabilities to the two sample points in the coin-toss experiment (Observe a head and Observe a tail), we might reason that if we toss a balanced coin a very large number of times, the sample points Observe a head and Observe a tail will occur with the same relative frequency of .5.

Our reasoning is supported by Figure 3.2. The figure plots the relative frequency of the number of times that a head occurs when simulating (by computer) the toss of a coin N times, where N ranges from as few as 25 tosses to as many as 1,500 tosses of the coin. You can see that when N is large (i.e., $N = 1,500$), the relative frequency is converging to .5. Thus, the probability of each sample point in the coin-tossing experiment is .5.

For some experiments, we may have little or no information on the relative frequency of occurrence of the sample points; consequently, we must assign probabilities to the sample points based on general information about the experiment. For example, if the experiment is to invest in a business venture and to observe whether it succeeds or fails, the sample space would appear as in Figure 3.3. We are unlikely to be able to assign probabilities to the sample points of this experiment based on a long series of repetitions since unique factors govern each performance of this kind of experiment. Instead, we may consider factors such as the personnel managing the venture, the general state of the economy at the time, the rate of success of similar ventures, and any other pertinent information. If we finally decide that the venture has an 80% chance of succeeding, we assign a probability of .8 to the sample point Success. This probability can be interpreted as a measure of our degree of belief in the outcome of the business venture; that is, it is a subjective probability. Notice, however, that such probabilities should be based on expert information that is carefully assessed. If not, we may be misled on any

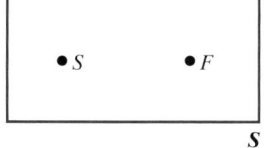

S

FIGURE 3.3
Experiment: Invest in a business venture and observe whether it succeeds (S) or fails (F)

*The result derives from an axiom in probability theory called the **Law of Large Numbers**. Phrased informally, this law states that the relative frequency of the number of times that an outcome occurs when an experiment is replicated over and over again (i.e., a large number of times) approaches the theoretical probability of the outcome.

decisions based on these probabilities or based on any calculations in which they appear. [*Note:* For a text that deals in detail with the subjective evaluation of probabilities, see Winkler (1972) or Lindley (1985).]

No matter how you assign the probabilities to sample points, the probabilities assigned must obey two rules:

Probability Rules for Sample Points
1. All sample point probabilities *must* lie between 0 and 1.
2. The probabilities of all the sample points within a sample space *must* sum to 1.

Assigning probabilities to sample points is easy for some experiments. For example, if the experiment is to toss a fair coin and observe the face, we would probably all agree to assign a probability of $\frac{1}{2}$ to the two sample points, Observe a head and Observe a tail. However, many experiments have sample points whose probabilities are more difficult to assign.

EXAMPLE **3.2**

A retail computer store sells two basic types of personal computers (PCs): standard desktop units and laptop units. Thus the owner must decide how many of each type of PC to stock. An important factor affecting the solution is the proportion of customers who purchase each type of PC. Show how this problem might be formulated in the framework of an experiment with sample points and a sample space. Indicate how probabilities might be assigned to the sample points.

SOLUTION

If we use the term *customer* to refer to a person who purchases one of the two types of PCs, the experiment can be defined as the entrance of a customer and the observation of which type of PC is purchased. There are two sample points in the sample space corresponding to this experiment:

D: {The customer purchases a standard desktop unit}
L: {The customer purchases a laptop unit}

The difference between this and the coin-toss experiment becomes apparent when we attempt to assign probabilities to the two sample points. What probability should we assign to the sample point *D*? If you answer .5, you are assuming that the events *D* and *L* should occur with equal likelihood, just like the sample points Heads and Tails in the coin-toss experiment. But assignment of sample point probabilities for the PC purchase experiment is not so easy. Suppose a check of the store's records indicates that 80% of its customers purchase desktop units. Then it might be reasonable to approximate the probability of the sample point *D* as .8 and that of the sample point *L* as .2. Here we see that sample points are not always equally likely, so assigning probabilities to them can be complicated—particularly for experiments that represent real applications (as opposed to coin- and die-toss experiments).

Although the probabilities of sample points are often of interest in their own right, it is usually probabilities of collections of sample points that are important. Example 3.3 demonstrates this point.

EXAMPLE 3.3

A fair die is tossed, and the up face is observed. If the face is even, you win $1. Otherwise, you lose $1. What is the probability that you win?

SOLUTION

Recall that the sample space for this experiment contains six sample points:

$$S: \{1, 2, 3, 4, 5, 6\}$$

Since the die is balanced, we assign a probability of $\frac{1}{6}$ to each of the sample points in this sample space. An even number will occur if one of the sample points, Observe a 2, Observe a 4, or Observe a 6, occurs. A collection of sample points such as this is called an *event*, which we denote by the letter A. Since the event A contains three sample points—each with probability $\frac{1}{6}$—and since no sample points can occur simultaneously, we reason that the probability of A is the sum of the probabilities of the sample points in A. Thus, the probability of A is $\frac{1}{6} + \frac{1}{6} + \frac{1}{6} = \frac{1}{2}$. This implies that, *in the long run*, you will win $1 half the time and lose $1 half the time.

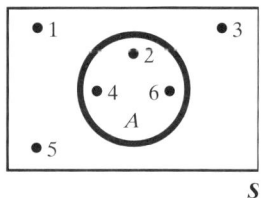

FIGURE 3.4

Die-toss experiment with event A: Observe an even number

Figure 3.4 is a Venn diagram depicting the sample space associated with a die-toss experiment and the event A, Observe an even number. The event A is represented by the closed figure inside the sample space S. This closed figure A contains all the sample points that comprise it.

To decide which sample points belong to the set associated with an event A, test each sample point in the sample space S. If event A occurs, then that sample point is in the event A. For example, the event A, Observe an even number, in the die-toss experiment will occur if the sample point Observe a 2 occurs. By the same reasoning, the sample points Observe a 4 and Observe a 6 are also in event A.

To summarize, we have demonstrated that an event can be defined in words or it can be defined as a specific set of sample points. This leads us to the following general definition of an event:

DEFINITION 3.4

An **event** is a specific collection of sample points.

EXAMPLE 3.4

Consider the experiment of tossing two coins. Suppose the coins are *not* balanced and the correct probabilities associated with the sample points are given in the table. [*Note:* The necessary properties for assigning probabilities to sample points are satisfied.]

Consider the events

$A:$ {Observe exactly one head}

$B:$ {Observe at least one head}

Calculate the probability of A and the probability of B.

Sample Point	Probability
HH	$\frac{4}{9}$
HT	$\frac{2}{9}$
TH	$\frac{2}{9}$
TT	$\frac{1}{9}$

SOLUTION

Event *A* contains the sample points *HT* and *TH*. Since two or more sample points cannot occur at the same time, we can easily calculate the probability of event *A* by summing the probabilities of the two sample points. Thus, the probability of observing exactly one head (event *A*), denoted by the symbol *P(A)*, is

$$P(A) = P(\text{Observe } HT) + P(\text{Observe } TH) = \tfrac{2}{9} + \tfrac{2}{9} = \tfrac{4}{9}$$

Similarly, since *B* contains the sample points *HH, HT,* and *TH,*

$$P(B) = \tfrac{4}{9} + \tfrac{2}{9} + \tfrac{2}{9} = \tfrac{8}{9}$$

The preceding example leads us to a general procedure for finding the probability of an event *A:*

> The probability of an event *A* is calculated by summing the probabilities of the sample points in the sample space for *A*.

Thus, we can summarize the steps for calculating the probability of any event, as indicated in the next box.

> **Steps for Calculating Probabilities of Events**
> 1. Define the experiment; that is, describe the process used to make an observation and the type of observation that will be recorded.
> 2. List the sample points.
> 3. Assign probabilities to the sample points.
> 4. Determine the collection of sample points contained in the event of interest.
> 5. Sum the sample point probabilities to get the event probability.

EXAMPLE 3.5

Diversity training of employees is the latest trend in U.S. business. *USA Today* (Aug. 15, 1995) reported on the primary reasons businesses give for making diversity training part of their strategic planning process. The reasons are summarized in Table 3.2. Assume that one business is selected at random from all U.S. businesses that use diversity training and the primary reason is determined.

a. Define the experiment that generated the data in Table 3.2, and list the sample points.

TABLE 3.2 Primary Reasons for Diversity Training

Reason	Percentage
Comply with personnel policies (CPP)	7
Increase productivity (IP)	47
Stay competitive (SC)	38
Social responsibility (SR)	4
Other (O)	4
Total	100%

Source: USA Today, August 15, 1995.

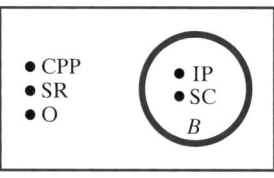

FIGURE 3.5
Venn diagram for
diversity training survey

TABLE 3.3   Sample Point Probabilities for Diversity Training Survey

Sample Point	Probability
CPP	.07
IP	.47
SC	.38
SR	.04
O	.04

b. Assign probabilities to the sample points.

c. What is the probability that the primary reason for diversity training is business related; that is, related to competition or productivity?

d. What is the probability that social responsibility is not a primary reason for diversity training?

SOLUTION

a. The experiment is the act of determining the primary reason for diversity training of employees at a U.S. business. The sample points, the simplest outcomes of the experiment, are the five response categories listed in Table 3.2. These sample points are shown in the Venn diagram in Figure 3.5.

b. If, as in Example 3.1, we were to assign equal probabilities in this case, each of the response categories would have a probability of one-fifth ($\frac{1}{5}$), or .20. But, by examining Table 3.2 you can see that equal probabilities are not reasonable here because the response percentages were not even approximately the same in the five classifications. It is more reasonable to assign a probability equal to the response percentage in each class, as shown in Table 3.3.*

c. Let the symbol B represent the event that the primary reason for diversity training is business related. B is not a sample point because it consists of more than one of the response classifications (the sample points). In fact, as shown in Figure 3.5, B consists of two sample points, IP and SC. The probability of B is defined to be the sum of the probabilities of the sample points in B:

$$P(B) = P(\text{IP}) + P(\text{SC}) = .47 + .38 = .85$$

d. Let NSR represent the event that social responsibility is not a primary reason for diversity training. Then NSR consists of all sample points except SR, and the probability is the sum of the corresponding sample point probabilities:

$$P(NSR) = P(\text{CPP}) + P(\text{IP}) + P(\text{SC}) + P(\text{O})$$
$$= .07 + .47 + .38 + .04 = .96$$

EXAMPLE 3.6

You have the capital to invest in two of four ventures, each of which requires approximately the same amount of investment capital. Unknown to you, two of the investments will eventually fail and two will be successful. You research the four ventures because you think that your research will increase your probability of a successful choice over a purely random selection, and you eventually decide on two. What is the lower limit of your probability of selecting the two best out of four? That is, if you used none of the information generated by your research, and selected two ventures at random, what is the probability that you would select the two successful ventures? At least one?

SOLUTION

Denote the two successful enterprises as S_1 and S_2 and the two failing enterprises as F_1 and F_2. The experiment involves a random selection of two out of the four ventures, and each possible pair of ventures represents a sample point. The six sample points that make up the sample space are

---

*The response percentages were based on a sample of U.S. businesses; consequently, these assigned probabilities are estimates of the true population-response percentages. You'll learn how to measure the reliability of probability estimates in Chapter 7.

1. (S_1, S_2)
2. (S_1, F_1)
3. (S_1, F_2)
4. (S_2, F_1)
5. (S_2, F_2)
6. (F_1, F_2)

The next step is to assign probabilities to the sample points. If we assume that the choice of any one pair is as likely as any other, then the probability of each sample point is $\frac{1}{6}$. Now check to see which sample points result in the choice of two successful ventures. Only one such sample point exists—namely, (S_1, S_2). Therefore, the probability of choosing two successful ventures out of the four is

$$P(S_1, S_2) = \frac{1}{6}$$

The event of selecting at least one of the two successful ventures includes all the sample points except (F_1, F_2).

$$P(\text{Select at least one success}) = P(S_1, S_2) + P(S_1, F_1) + P(S_1, F_2) + P(S_2, F_1) \\ + P(S_2, F_2)$$
$$= \frac{1}{6} + \frac{1}{6} + \frac{1}{6} + \frac{1}{6} + \frac{1}{6} = \frac{5}{6}$$

Therefore, the worst that you could do in selecting two ventures out of four may not be too bad. With a random selection, the probability of selecting two successful ventures will be $\frac{1}{6}$ and the probability of selecting at least one successful venture out of two is $\frac{5}{6}$. ∎

The preceding examples have one thing in common: The number of sample points in each of the sample spaces was small; hence, the sample points were easy to identify and list. How can we manage this when the sample points run into the thousands or millions? For example, suppose you wish to select five business ventures from a group of 1,000. Then each different group of five ventures would represent a sample point. How can you determine the number of sample points associated with this experiment?

One method of determining the number of sample points for a complex experiment is to develop a counting system. Start by examining a simple version of the experiment. For example, see if you can develop a system for counting the number of ways to select two ventures from a total of four (this is exactly what was done in Example 3.6). If the ventures are represented by the symbols V_1, V_2, V_3, and V_4, the sample points could be listed in the following pattern:

(V_1, V_2) (V_2, V_3) (V_3, V_4)
(V_1, V_3) (V_2, V_4)
(V_1, V_4)

Note the pattern and now try a more complex situation—say, sampling three ventures out of five. List the sample points and observe the pattern. Finally, see if you can deduce the pattern for the general case. Perhaps you can program a computer to produce the matching and counting for the number of samples of 5 selected from a total of 1,000.

A second method of determining the number of sample points for an experiment is to use **combinatorial mathematics**. This branch of mathematics is concerned with developing counting rules for given situations. For example, there is a simple rule for finding the number of different samples of five ventures selected from 1,000. This rule, called the **combinations rule**, is given by the formula

$$\binom{N}{n} = \frac{N!}{n!(N-n)!}$$

where N is the number of elements in the population; n is the number of elements in the sample; and the factorial symbol (!) means that, say,

$$n! = n(n-1)(n-2)\cdots(3)(2)(1)$$

Thus, $5! = 5 \cdot 4 \cdot 3 \cdot 2 \cdot 1$. (The quantity 0! is defined to be equal to 1.)

EXAMPLE 3.7

Refer to Example 3.6 in which we selected two ventures from four in which to invest. Use the combinatorial counting rule to determine how many different selections can be made.

SOLUTION
For this example, $N = 4, n = 2$, and

$$\binom{4}{2} = \frac{4!}{2!2!} = \frac{4 \cdot 3 \cdot 2 \cdot 1}{(2 \cdot 1)(2 \cdot 1)} = 6$$

You can see that this agrees with the number of sample points obtained in Example 3.6.

EXAMPLE 3.8

Suppose you plan to invest equal amounts of money in each of five business ventures. If you have 20 ventures from which to make the selection, how many different samples of five ventures can be selected from the 20?

SOLUTION
For this example, $N = 20$ and $n = 5$. Then the number of different samples of 5 that can be selected from the 20 ventures is

$$\binom{20}{5} = \frac{20!}{5!(20-5)!} = \frac{20!}{5!15!}$$

$$= \frac{20 \cdot 19 \cdot 18 \cdots \cdots 3 \cdot 2 \cdot 1}{(5 \cdot 4 \cdot 3 \cdot 2 \cdot 1)(15 \cdot 14 \cdot 13 \cdots \cdots 3 \cdot 2 \cdot 1)} = 15,504$$

The symbol $\binom{N}{n}$, meaning the **number of combinations of N elements taken n at a time,** is just one of a large number of counting rules that have been developed by combinatorial mathematicians. This counting rule applies to situations in which the experiment calls for selecting n elements from a total of N elements, without replacing each element before the next is selected. If you are interested in learning other methods for counting sample points for various types of experiments, you will find a few of the basic counting rules in Appendix A. Others can be found in the chapter references.

STATISTICS IN ACTION

3.1 GAME SHOW STRATEGY: TO SWITCH OR NOT TO SWITCH?

Marilyn vos Savant, who is listed in *Guinness Book of World Records Hall of Fame* for "Highest IQ," writes a monthly column in the Sunday newspaper supplement, *Parade Magazine.* Her column, "Ask Marilyn," is devoted to games of skill, puzzles, and mind-bending riddles. In one issue, vos Savant posed the following question:

Suppose you're on a game show, and you're given a choice of three doors. Behind one door is a car; behind the others, goats. You pick a door—say, #1—and the host, who knows what's behind the doors, opens another door—say #3—which has a goat. He then says to you, "Do you want to pick door #2?" Is it to your advantage to switch your choice?

Vos Savant's answer: "Yes, you should switch. The first door has a $\frac{1}{3}$ chance of winning [the car], but the second has a $\frac{2}{3}$ chance [of winning the car]." Predictably, vos Savant's surprising answer elicited thousands of critical letters, many of them from Ph.D. mathematicians, who disagreed with her. Some of the more interesting and critical letters, which were printed in her next column (*Parade Magazine,* Feb. 24, 1991) are condensed below:

- "May I suggest you obtain and refer to a standard textbook on probability before you try to answer a question of this type again?" (University of Florida)

- "Your logic is in error, and I am sure you will receive many letters on this topic from high school and college students. Perhaps you should keep a few addresses for help with future columns." (Georgia State University)

- "You are utterly incorrect about the game-show question, and I hope this controversy will call some public attention to the serious national crisis in mathematical education. If you can admit your error you will have contributed constructively toward the solution of a deplorable situation. How many irate mathematicians are needed to get you to change your mind?" (Georgetown University)

- "I am in shock that after being corrected by at least three mathematicians, you still do not see your mistake." (Dickinson State University)

- "You are the goat!" (Western State University)

- "You're wrong, but look on the positive side. If all the Ph.D.'s were wrong, the country would be in serious trouble." (U.S. Army Research Institute)

The logic employed by those who disagree with vos Savant is as follows: Once the host shows you door #3 (a goat), only two doors remain. The probability of the car being behind door #1 (your door) is $\frac{1}{2}$; similarly, the probability is $\frac{1}{2}$ for door #2. Therefore, in the long run (i.e., over a long series of trials) it doesn't matter whether you switch to door #2 or keep door #1. Approximately 50% of the time you'll win a car, and 50% of the time you'll get a goat.

Who is correct, the Ph.D.s or vos Savant? By answering the following series of questions, you'll arrive at the correct solution.

Focus

a. Before the show is taped, the host randomly decides the door behind which to put the car; then the goats go behind the remaining two doors. List the sample points for this experiment.

b. Suppose you choose at random door #1. Now, for each sample point in part **a**, circle door #1 and put an X through one of the remaining two doors that hides a goat. (This is the door that the host shows—always a goat.)

c. Refer to the altered sample points in part **b**. Assume your strategy is to keep door #1. Count the number of sample points for which this is a "winning" strategy (i.e., you win the car). Assuming equally likely sample points, what is the probability that you win the car?

d. Repeat part **c**, but assume your strategy is to always switch doors.

e. Based on the probabilities of parts **c** and **d**, is it to your advantage to switch your choice?

EXERCISES   3.1–3.15

Learning the Mechanics

3.1 An experiment results in one of the following sample points: $E_1, E_2, E_3, E_4,$ or E_5.

   a. Find $P(E_3)$ if $P(E_1) = .1, P(E_2) = .2, P(E_4) = .1,$ and $P(E_5) = .1$.

   b. Find $P(E_3)$ if $P(E_1) = P(E_3), P(E_2) = .1,$ $P(E_4) = .2,$ and $P(E_5) = .1$.

   c. Find $P(E_3)$ if $P(E_1) = P(E_2) = P(E_4) = P(E_5)$ $= .1$.

3.2 The accompanying diagram describes the sample space of a particular experiment and events A and B.

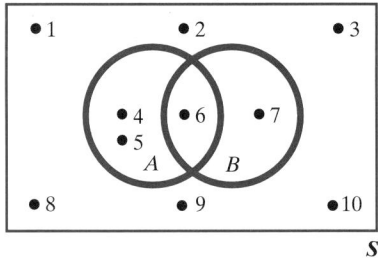

   a. What is this type of diagram called?

   b. Suppose the sample points are equally likely. Find $P(A)$ and $P(B)$.

   c. Suppose $P(1) = P(2) = P(3) = P(4) = P(5) =$ $^1\!/_{20}$ and $P(6) = P(7) = P(8) = P(9) = P(10) =$ $^3\!/_{20}$. Find $P(A)$ and $P(B)$.

3.3 The sample space for an experiment contains five sample points with probabilities as shown in the table. Find the probability of each of the following events:

Sample Points	Probabilities
1	.05
2	.20
3	.30
4	.30
5	.15

   A: {Either 1, 2, or 3 occurs}

   B: {Either 1, 3, or 5 occurs}

   C: {4 does not occur}

3.4 Compute each of the following:

   a. $\binom{9}{4}$ **b.** $\binom{7}{2}$ **c.** $\binom{4}{4}$ **d.** $\binom{5}{0}$ **e.** $\binom{6}{5}$

3.5 Two marbles are drawn at random and without replacement from a box containing two blue marbles and three red marbles. Determine the probability of observing each of the following events:

   A: {Two blue marbles are drawn}

   B: {A red and a blue marble are drawn}

   C: {Two red marbles are drawn}

3.6 Simulate the experiment described in Exercise 3.5 using any five identically shaped objects, two of which are one color and three, another. Mix the objects, draw two, record the results, and then replace the objects. Repeat the experiment a large number of times (at least 100). Calculate the proportion of time events A, B, and C occur. How do these proportions compare with the probabilities you calculated in Exercise 3.5? Should these proportions equal the probabilities? Explain.

Applying the Concepts

3.7 *Total Quality Management* (TQM) has been defined as responsive customer service through continuously improved and redesigned work processes (*Quality Progress,* July 1995). However, as its usage has grown it has been called different names by different organizations. At the University of North Carolina in Charlotte (UNCC), where TQM implementation began in 1992, it is called Continuous Quality Improvement (CQI). In evaluating perceptions of CQI, UNCC professors K. Buch and J. W. Shelnutt asked 159 employees to indicate how strongly they agreed or disagreed with a series of statements including: "I believe that management is committed to CQI." The following responses were received:

Strongly agree	Agree	Neither agree nor disagree	Disagree	Strongly disagree
30	64	41	18	6

Source: Buch, K., and Shelnut, J. W. "UNC Charlotte measures the effects of its quality initiative." *Quality Progress,* July 1995, p. 75 (Table 2).

   a. Define the experiment and list the sample points.

   b. Assign probabilities to the sample points.

   c. What is the probability that an employee agrees or strongly agrees with the above statement?

d. What is the probability that an employee does not strongly agree with the above statement?

3.8 Communications products (telephones, fax machines, etc.) can be designed to operate on either an analog or a digital system. Because of improved accuracy, a digital signal will soon replace the current analog signal used in telephone lines. The result will be a flood of new digital products for consumers to choose from (*Newsweek*, Nov. 16, 1992). Suppose a particular firm plans to produce a new fax machine in both analog and digital forms. Concerned with whether the products will succeed or fail in the marketplace, a market analysis is conducted that results in the sample points and associated probabilities of occurrence listed in the table (S_a: analog succeeds, F_a: analog fails, etc.). Find the probability of each of the following events:

A: {Both new products are successful}

B: {The analog design is successful}

C: {The digital design is successful}

D: {At least one of the two products is successful}

Sample Points	Probabilities
$S_a S_d$	.31
$S_a F_d$	.10
$F_a S_d$	.50
$F_a F_d$	.09

3.9 Of six cars produced at a particular factory between 8 and 10 A.M. last Monday morning, test runs revealed three of them to be "lemons." Nevertheless, three of the six cars were shipped to dealer A and the other three to dealer B. Dealer A received all three lemons. What is the probability of this event occurring if, in fact, the three cars shipped to dealer A were selected at random from the six produced?

3.10 Carbon monoxide (CO) is an odorless, colorless, highly toxic gas which is produced by fires as well as by motor vehicles and appliances that use carbon-based fuels. The *American Journal of Public Health* (July 1995) published a study on unintentional CO poisoning of Colorado residents for the years 1986–1991. A total of 981 cases of CO poisoning were reported during the six-year period. Each case was classified as fatal or nonfatal and by source of exposure. The number of cases occurring in each of the categories is shown in the accompanying table. Assume that one of the 981 cases of unintentional CO poisoning is randomly selected.
a. List all sample points for this experiment.

Source of Exposure	Fatal	Nonfatal	Total
Fire	63	53	116
Auto exhaust	60	178	238
Furnace	18	345	363
Kerosene or spaceheater	9	18	27
Appliance	9	63	72
Other gas-powered motor	3	73	76
Fireplace	0	16	16
Other	3	19	22
Unknown	9	42	51
Total	174	807	981

Source: Cook, M. C., Simon, P. A., and Hoffman, R. E. "Unintentional carbon monoxide poisoning in Colorado, 1986 through 1991." *American Journal of Public Health,* Vol. 85, No. 7, July 1995, p. 989 (Table 1). American Public Health Association.

b. What is the set of all sample points called?
c. Let *A* be the event that the CO poisoning is caused by fire. Find $P(A)$.
d. Let *B* be the event that the CO poisoning is fatal. Find $P(B)$.
e. Let *C* be the event that the CO poisoning is caused by auto exhaust. Find $P(C)$.
f. Let *D* be the event that the CO poisoning is caused by auto exhaust and is fatal. Find $P(D)$.
g. Let *E* be the event that the CO poisoning is caused by fire but is nonfatal. Find $P(E)$.

3.11 The credit card industry depends heavily on mail solicitation to attract new customers. In 1994, the industry sent out 2.4 billion pieces of mail and incurred postage costs of nearly $500 million (*Forbes*, Sept. 11, 1995). The table on page 125 lists the number of credit card accounts outstanding on June 30, 1995, for the top 15 credit card companies. One of these 177.5 million accounts is to be selected at random and the credit card company holding the account is to be identified.
a. List or describe the sample points in this experiment.
b. Find the probability of each sample point.
c. What is the probability that the account selected belongs to a nontraditional bank? A traditional bank?

3.12 *Consumer Reports* magazine annually asks readers to evaluate their experiences in buying a new car during the previous year. More than 120,000 questionnaires were completed for the 1994 sales year. Analysis of the questionnaires revealed that readers' were most satisfied with the following three dealers (in no particular order): Infiniti, Saturn, and Saab (*Consumer Reports*, Apr. 1995).
a. List all possible sets of rankings for these top three dealers.
b. Assuming that each set of rankings in part **a** is equally likely, what is the probability that

	Number of Accounts (in millions)
Citibank	24.3
Discover/Novus*	33.6
MBNA*	12.1
First USA*	7.8
First Chicago	13.2
AT&T Universal*	16.2
Household International*	12.2
Chase Manhattan	9.8
Chemical Bank	6.7
Capital One*	5.8
Bank of America	9.3
Bank One	9.7
Advanta*	4.9
Bank of New York	5.9
Optima (American Express)*	6.0
Total	177.5

*Not a traditional bank

Source: RAM Research Corp./Capital One Financial Corp.

Secondary Source: Novack, J. "The data edge." *Forbes,* September 11, 1995, p. 148.

readers ranked Saturn first? That readers ranked Saturn third? That readers ranked Saturn first and Infiniti second (which is, in fact, what they did)?

3.13 Often, probabilities are expressed in terms of **odds**, especially in gambling settings. For example, handicappers for greyhound races express their belief about the probabilities that each greyhound will win a race in terms of odds. If the probability of event E is $P(E)$, then the *odds in favor of E* are $P(E)$ to $1 - P(E)$. Thus, if a handicapper assesses a probability of .25 that Oxford Shoes will win its next race, the odds in favor of Oxford Shoes are $25/100$ to $75/100$, or 1 to 3. It follows that the *odds against E* are $1 - P(E)$ to $P(E)$, or 3 to 1 against a win by Oxford Shoes. In general, if the odds in favor of event E are a to b, then $P(E) = a/(a + b)$.

a. A second handicapper assesses the probability of a win by Oxford Shoes to be $1/3$. According to the second handicapper, what are the odds in favor of Oxford Shoes winning?

b. A third handicapper assesses the odds in favor of Oxford Shoes to be 1 to 1. According to the third handicapper, what is the probability of Oxford Shoes winning?

c. A fourth handicapper assesses the odds against Oxford Shoes winning to be 3 to 2. Find this handicapper's assessment of the probability that Oxford Shoes will win.

3.14 The Value Line Survey, a service for common stock investors, provides its subscribers with up-to-date evaluations of the prospects and risks associated with the purchase of a large number of common stocks. Each stock is ranked 1 (highest) to 5 (lowest) according to Value Line's estimate of the stock's potential for price appreciation during the next 12 months. Suppose you plan to purchase stock in three electrical utility companies from among seven that possess rankings of 2 for price appreciation. Unknown to you, two of the companies will experience serious difficulties with their nuclear facilities during the coming year. If you randomly select the three companies from among the seven, what is the probability that you select:

a. None of the companies with prospective nuclear difficulties?

b. One of the companies with prospective nuclear difficulties?

c. Both of the companies with prospective nuclear difficulties?

3.15 *Sustainable development* or *sustainable farming* means "finding ways to live and work the Earth without jeopardizing the future" (Schmickle, *Minneapolis Star Tribune,* June 20, 1992). Studies were conducted in five midwestern states to develop a profile of a sustainable farmer. The results revealed that farmers can be classified along a sustainability scale, depending on whether they are likely or unlikely to engage in the following practices: (1) Raise a broad mix of crops; (2) Raise livestock; (3) Use chemicals sparingly; (4) Use techniques for regenerating the soil, such as crop rotation.

a. List the different sets of classifications that are possible.

b. Suppose you are planning to interview farmers across the country to determine the frequency with which they fall into the classification sets you listed for part **a**. Since no information is yet available, assume initially that there is an equal chance of a farmer falling into any single classification set. Using that assumption, what is the probability that a farmer will be classi-

fied as unlikely on all four criteria (i.e., classified as a nonsustainable farmer)?

c. Using the same assumption as in part **b**, what is the probability that a farmer will be classified as likely on at least three of the criteria (i.e., classified as a near-sustainable farmer)?

3.2 UNIONS AND INTERSECTIONS

An event can often be viewed as a composition of two or more other events. Such events, which are called **compound events**, can be formed (composed) in two ways, as defined and illustrated here.

DEFINITION 3.5
The **union** of two events A and B is the event that occurs if either A or B or both occur on a single performance of the experiment. We denote the union of events A and B by the symbol $A \cup B$. $A \cup B$ consists of all the sample points that belong to A or B or both. (See Figure 3.6a.)

DEFINITION 3.6
The **intersection** of two events A and B is the event that occurs if both A and B occur on a single performance of the experiment. We write $A \cap B$ for the intersection of A and B. $A \cap B$ consists of all the sample points belonging to *both A and B*. (See Figure 3.6b.)

EXAMPLE 3.9

Consider the die-toss experiment. Define the following events:

A: {Toss an even number}
B: {Toss a number less than or equal to 3}

a. Describe $A \cup B$ for this experiment.
b. Describe $A \cap B$ for this experiment.
c. Calculate $P(A \cup B)$ and $P(A \cap B)$ assuming the die is fair.

SOLUTION
Draw the Venn diagram as shown in Figure 3.7

a. The union of A and B is the event that occurs if we observe either an even number, a number less than or equal to 3, or both on a single throw of the die. Consequently, the sample points in the event $A \cup B$ are those for which A occurs, B occurs, or both A and B occur. Checking the sample points in the

FIGURE 3.6
Venn diagrams for union and intersection

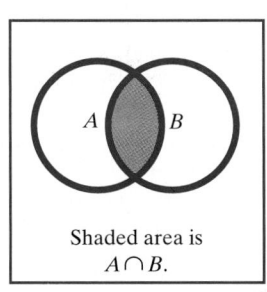

Entire shaded area is $A \cup B$.

Shaded area is $A \cap B$.

a. Union

b. Intersection

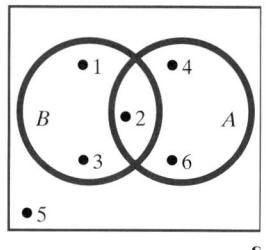

FIGURE 3.7
Venn diagram for die toss

entire sample space, we find that the collection of sample points in the union of A and B is

$$A \cup B = \{1, 2, 3, 4, 6\}$$

b. The intersection of A and B is the event that occurs if we observe *both* an even number and a number less than or equal to 3 on a single throw of the die. Checking the sample points to see which imply the occurrence of *both* events A and B, we see that the intersection contains only one sample point:

$$A \cap B = \{2\}$$

In other words, the intersection of A and B is the sample point Observe a 2.

c. Recalling that the probability of an event is the sum of the probabilities of the sample points of which the event is composed, we have

$$P(A \cup B) = P(1) + P(2) + P(3) + P(4) + P(6)$$
$$= \tfrac{1}{6} + \tfrac{1}{6} + \tfrac{1}{6} + \tfrac{1}{6} + \tfrac{1}{6} = \tfrac{5}{6}$$

and

$$P(A \cap B) = P(2) = \tfrac{1}{6}$$

EXAMPLE 3.10

Many firms undertake direct marketing campaigns to promote their products. The campaigns typically involve mailing information to millions of households. The response rates are carefully monitored to determine the demographic characteristics of respondents. By studying tendencies to respond, the firms can better target future mailings to those segments of the population most likely to purchase their products.

Suppose a distributor of mail-order tools is analyzing the results of a recent mailing. The probability of response is believed to be related to income and age. The percentages of the total number of respondents to the mailing are given by income and age classification in Table 3.4.

Define the following events:

A: {A respondent's income is more than $50,000}

B: {A respondent's age is 30 or more}

a. Find $P(A)$ and $P(B)$.
b. Find $P(A \cup B)$.
c. Find $P(A \cap B)$.

SOLUTION

Following the steps for calculating probabilities of events, we first note that the objective is to characterize the income and age distribution of respondents to the mailing. To accomplish this, we define the experiment to consist of selecting a

TABLE 3.4   Percentage of Respondents in Age-Income Classes

	INCOME		
Age	<$25,000	$25,000–$50,000	>$50,000
< 30 yrs	5%	12%	10%
30–50 yrs	14%	22%	16%
> 50 yrs	8%	10%	3%

respondent from the collection of all respondents and observing which income and age class he or she occupies. The sample points are the nine different age-income classifications:

$$E_1: \{<30 \text{ yrs}, <\$25{,}000\}$$
$$E_2: \{30\text{–}50 \text{ yrs}, <\$25{,}000\}$$
$$\vdots$$
$$E_9: \{>50 \text{ yrs}, >\$50{,}000\}$$

Next, we assign probabilities to the sample points. If we blindly select one of the respondents, the probability that he or she will occupy a particular age-income classification is just the proportion, or relative frequency, of respondents in the classification. These proportions are given (as percentages) in Table 3.4. Thus,

$$P(E_1) = \text{Relative frequency of respondents in age-income class}$$
$$\{<30 \text{ yrs}, <\$25{,}000\} = .05$$

$$P(E_2) = .14$$

and so forth. You may verify that the sample points probabilities add to 1.

a. To find $P(A)$, we first determine the collection of sample points contained in event A. Since A is defined as $\{>\$50{,}000\}$, we see from Table 3.4 that A contains the three sample points represented by the last column of the table. In words, the event A consists of the income classification $\{>\$50{,}000\}$ in all three age classifications. The probability of A is the sum of the probabilities of the sample points in A:

$$P(A) = .10 + .16 + .03 = .29$$

Similarly, B consists of the six sample points in the second and third rows of Table 3.4:

$$P(B) = .14 + .22 + .16 + .08 + .10 + .03 = .73$$

b. The union of events A and B, $A \cup B$, consists of all the sample points in *either A or B or both*. That is, the union of A and B consists of all respondents whose income exceeds \$50,000 *or* whose age is 30 or more. In Table 3.4 this is any sample point found in the third column *or* the last two rows. Thus,

$$P(A \cup B) = .10 + .14 + .22 + .16 + .08 + .10 + .03 = .83$$

c. The intersection of events A and B, $A \cap B$, consists of all sample points in *both A and B*. That is, the intersection of A and B consists of all respondents whose income exceeds \$50,000 *and* whose age is 30 or more. In Table 3.4 this is any sample point found in the third column *and* the last two rows. Thus,

$$P(A \cap B) = .16 + .03 = .19$$

3.3   COMPLEMENTARY EVENTS

A very useful concept in the calculation of event probabilities is the notion of **complementary events**:

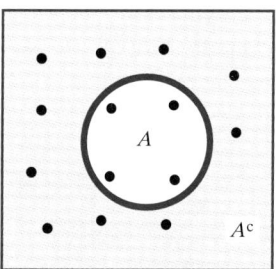

FIGURE 3.8
Venn diagram of
complementary events

DEFINITION 3.7
The **complement** of an event A is the event that A does *not* occur—that is, the event consisting of all sample points that are not in event A. We denote the complement of A by A^c.

An event A is a collection of sample points, and the sample points included in A^c are those not in A. Figure 3.8 demonstrates this idea. Note from the figure that all sample points in S are included in *either* A or A^c and that *no* sample point is in both A and A^c. This leads us to conclude that the probabilities of an event and its complement *must sum to 1:*

The sum of the probabilities of complementary events equals 1; i.e., $P(A) + P(A^c) = 1$.

In many probability problems, calculating the probability of the complement of the event of interest is easier than calculating the event itself. Then, because

$$P(A) + P(A^c) = 1$$

we can calculate $P(A)$ by using the relationship

$$P(A) = 1 - P(A^c).$$

EXAMPLE 3.11 Consider the experiment of tossing two fair coins. Use the complementary relationship to calculate the probability of event A: {Observing at least one head}.

SOLUTION
We know that the event A: {Observing at least one head} consists of the sample points

A: {HH, HT, TH}

The complement of A is defined as the event that occurs when A does not occur. Therefore,

A^c: {Observe no heads} = {TT}

This complementary relationship is shown in Figure 3.9. Assuming the coins are balanced,

$$P(A^c) = P(TT) = \frac{1}{4}$$

and

$$P(A) = 1 - P(A^c) = 1 - \frac{1}{4} = \frac{3}{4}.$$

3.4 THE ADDITIVE RULE AND MUTUALLY EXCLUSIVE EVENTS

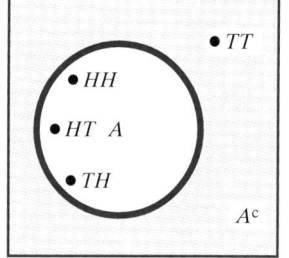

FIGURE 3.9
Complementary events
in the toss of two coins

In Section 3.2 we saw how to determine which sample points are contained in a union and how to calculate the probability of the union by adding the probabilities of the sample points in the union. It is also possible to obtain the probability of the union of two events by using the **additive rule of probability**.

The union of two events will often contain many sample points, since the union occurs if either one or both of the events occur. By studying the Venn diagram in

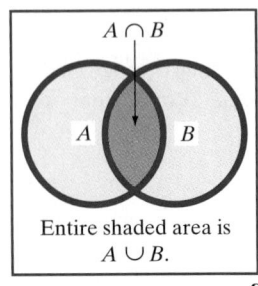

Entire shaded area is
$A \cup B$.

FIGURE 3.10
Venn diagram of union

Figure 3.10, you can see that the probability of the union of two events, A and B, can be obtained by summing $P(A)$ and $P(B)$ and subtracting the probability corresponding to $A \cap B$. Therefore, the formula for calculating the probability of the union of two events is given in the next box.

Additive Rule of Probability

The probability of the union of events A and B is the sum of the probability of events A and B minus the probability of the intersection of events A and B, that is,

$$P(A \cup B) = P(A) + P(B) - P(A \cap B)$$

EXAMPLE 3.12   Hospital records show that 12% of all patients are admitted for surgical treatment, 16% are admitted for obstetrics, and 2% receive both obstetrics and surgical treatment. If a new patient is admitted to the hospital, what is the probability that the patient will be admitted either for surgery, obstetrics, or both? Use the additive rule of probability to arrive at the answer.

SOLUTION
Consider the following events:

A: {A patient admitted to the hospital receives surgical treatment}

B: {A patient admitted to the hospital receives obstetrics treatment}

Then, from the given information,

$$P(A) = .12$$

$$P(B) = .16$$

and the probability of the event that a patient receives both obstetrics and surgical treatment is

$$P(A \cap B) = .02$$

The event that a patient admitted to the hospital receives either surgical treatment, obstetrics treatment, or both is the union $A \cup B$. The probability of $A \cup B$ is given by the additive rule of probability:

$$P(A \cup B) = P(A) + P(B) - P(A \cap B) = .12 + .16 - .02 = .26$$

Thus, 26% of all patients admitted to the hospital receive either surgical treatment, obstetrics treatment, or both.

A very special relationship exists between events A and B when $A \cap B$ contains no sample points. In this case we call the events A and B *mutually exclusive events*.

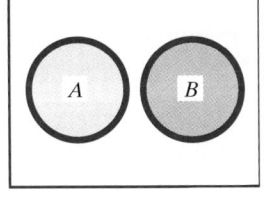

FIGURE 3.11
Venn diagram of mutually exclusive events

DEFINITION 3.8

Events A and B are **mutually exclusive** if $A \cap B$ contains no sample points, that is, if A and B have no sample points in common.

Figure 3.11 shows a Venn diagram of two mutually exclusive events. The events A and B have no sample points in common, that is, A and B cannot occur simultaneously, and $P(A \cap B) = 0$. Thus, we have the important relationship given in the box.

> If two events A and B are *mutually exclusive*, the probability of the union of A and B equals the sum of the probabilities of A and B; that is, $P(A \cup B) = P(A) + P(B)$

Caution: The formula shown above is *false* if the events are *not* mutually exclusive. In this case (i.e., two nonmutually exclusive events), you must apply the general additive rule of probability.

EXAMPLE 3.13

Consider the experiment of tossing two balanced coins. Find the probability of observing *at least* one head.

SOLUTION
Define the events

A: {Observe at least one head}

B: {Observe exactly one head}

C: {Observe exactly two heads}

Note that

$$A = B \cup C$$

and that $B \cap C$ contains no sample points (see Figure 3.12). Thus, B and C are mutually exclusive, so that

$$P(A) = P(B \cup C) = P(B) + P(C) = \tfrac{1}{2} + \tfrac{1}{4} = \tfrac{3}{4}$$

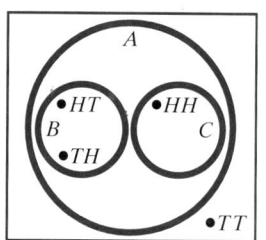

FIGURE 3.12
Venn diagram for coin-toss experiment

Although Example 3.13 is very simple, it shows us that writing events with verbal descriptions that include the phrases "at least" or "at most" as unions of mutually exclusive events is very useful. This practice enables us to find the probability of the event by adding the probabilities of the mutually exclusive events.

EXERCISES 3.16–3.31

Learning the Mechanics

3.16 A fair coin is tossed three times and the events A and B are defined as follows:

A: {At least one head is observed}

B: {The number of heads observed is odd}

    a. Identify the sample points in the events A, B, $A \cup B$, A^c, and $A \cap B$.

    b. Find $P(A)$, $P(B)$, $P(A \cup B)$, $P(A^c)$, and $P(A \cap B)$ by summing the probabilities of the appropriate sample points.

    c. Find $P(A \cup B)$ using the additive rule. Compare your answer to the one you obtained in part **b**.

    d. Are the events A and B mutually exclusive? Why?

3.17 What are mutually exclusive events? Give a verbal description, then draw a Venn diagram.

3.18 A pair of fair dice is tossed. Define the following events:

A: {You will roll a 7} (i.e., the sum of the dots on the up faces of the two dice is equal to 7)

B: {At least one of the two dice shows a 4}

    a. Identify the sample points in the events A, B, $A \cap B$, $A \cup B$, and A^c.

    b. Find $P(A)$, $P(B)$, $P(A \cap B)$, $P(A \cup B)$, and $P(A^c)$ by summing the probabilities of the appropriate sample points.

    c. Find $P(A \cup B)$ using the additive rule. Compare your answer to that for the same event in part **b**.

    d. Are A and B mutually exclusive? Why?

3.19 Consider the accompanying Venn diagram, where $P(E_1) = P(E_2) = P(E_3) = \tfrac{1}{5}$, $P(E_4) = P(E_5) = \tfrac{1}{20}$, $P(E_6) = \tfrac{1}{10}$, and $P(E_7) = \tfrac{1}{5}$. Find each of the following probabilities:

a. $P(A)$ b. $P(B)$ c. $P(A\cup B)$ d. $P(A\cap B)$

e. $P(A^c)$ f. $P(B^c)$ g. $P(A\cup A^c)$ h. $P(A^c\cap B)$

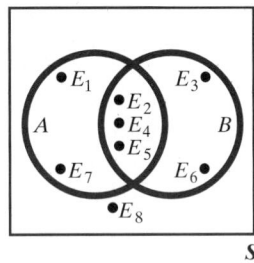

S

3.20 Consider the accompanying Venn diagram, where $P(E_1) = .10, P(E_2) = .05, P(E_3) = P(E_4) = .2,$ $P(E_5) = .06, P(E_6) = .3, P(E_7) = .06,$ and $P(E_8) = .03$. Find the following probabilities:

a. $P(A^c)$ b. $P(B^c)$ c. $P(A^c\cap B)$ d. $P(A\cup B)$

e. $P(A\cap B)$ f. $P(A^c\cup B^c)$

g. Are events A and B mutually exclusive? Why?

S

3.21 The following table describes the adult population of a small suburb of a large southern city. A marketing research firm plans to randomly select one adult from the suburb to evaluate a new food product. For this experiment the nine age-income categories are the sample points. Consider the following events:

$A:$ {Person is under 25}

$B:$ {Person is between 25 and 45}

$C:$ {Person is over 45}

$D:$ {Person has income under \$20,000}

$E:$ {Person has income of \$20,000–\$50,000}

$F:$ {Person has income over \$50,000}

Convert the frequencies in the table to relative frequencies and use them to calculate the following probabilities:

	INCOME		
Age	<\$20,000	\$20,000–\$50,000	>\$50,000
<25	950	1,000	50
25–45	450	2,050	1,500
>45	50	950	1,000

a. $P(B)$ b. $P(F)$ c. $P(C\cap F)$ d. $P(B\cup C)$

e. $P(A^c)$ f. $P(A^c\cap F)$

g. Consider each pair of events (A and B, A and C, etc.) and list the pairs of events that are mutually exclusive. Justify your choices.

3.22 Refer to Exercise 3.21. Use the same event definitions to do the following exercises.

a. Write the event that the person selected is under 25 with an income over \$50,000 as an intersection of two events.

b. Write the event that the person selected is age 25 or older as the union of two mutually exclusive events and as the complement of an event.

Applying the Concepts

3.23 A state energy agency mailed questionnaires on energy conservation to 1,000 homeowners in the state capital. Five hundred questionnaires were returned. Suppose an experiment consists of randomly selecting and reviewing one of the returned questionnaires. Consider the events:

$A:$ {The home is constructed of brick}

$B:$ {The home is more than 30 years old}

$C:$ {The home is heated with oil}

Describe each of the following events in terms of unions, intersections, and complements (i.e., $A\cup B$, $A\cap B$, A^c, etc.):

a. The home is more than 30 years old and is heated with oil.

b. The home is not constructed of brick.

c. The home is heated with oil or is more than 30 years old.

d. The home is constructed of brick and is not heated with oil.

3.24 Corporate downsizing in the United States has caused a significant increase in the demand for temporary and part-time workers. In Japan a similar increase in demand has been fueled by the need for less costly labor and protection against variation in labor demand. The distribution (in percent) of nonregular workers in Japan in 1992 (by age) is provided in the table on page 133 (adapted from *Monthly Labor Review*, Oct. 1995). Column headings are defined below the table.

Suppose a nonregular worker is to be chosen at random from this population. Define the following events:

$A:$ {The worker is 40 or over}

$B:$ {The worker is a teenager and part-time}

$C:$ {The worker is under 40 and either arubaito or dispatched}

$D:$ {The worker is part-time}

a. Find the probability of each of the above events.

b. Find $P(A\cap D)$ and $P(A\cup D)$.

Age	Part-Time	Arubaito	Temporary and Day	Dispatched	Totals
15–19	.3	3.7	2.3	.2	6.5
20–29	3.4	7.8	6.1	4.7	22.0
30–39	8.4	1.6	4.5	2.7	17.2
40–49	15.6	1.6	7.3	1.4	25.9
50–59	9.4	1.1	5.8	.6	16.9
60 and over	4.3	1.8	4.8	.6	11.5
Totals	41.4	17.6	30.8	10.2	100.0

Part-time: Work fewer hours per day or days per week than regular workers; *arubaito:* someone with a "side" job who is in school or has regular employment elsewhere; *temporary:* employed on a contract lasting more than one month but less than one year; *day:* employed on a contract of less than one month's duration; *dispatched:* hired from a temporary-help agency.

Source: Houseman, S., and Osawa, M. "Part-time and temporary employment in Japan." *Monthly Labor Review,* October 1995, pp. 12–13 (Tables 1 and 2).

c. Describe in words the following events: A^c, B^c, and D^c.

d. Find the probability of each of the events you described in part **c**.

3.25 A buyer for a large metropolitan department store must choose two firms from the four available to supply the store's fall line of men's slacks. The buyer has not dealt with any of the four firms before and considers their products equally attractive. Unknown to the buyer, two of the four firms are having serious financial problems that may result in their not being able to deliver the fall line of slacks as soon as promised. The four firms are identified as G_1 and G_2 (firms in good financial condition) and P_1 and P_2 (firms in poor financial condition). Sample points identify the pairs of firms selected. If the probability of the buyer's selecting a particular firm from among the four is the same for each firm, the sample points and their probabilities for this buying experiment are those listed in the following table.

Sample Points	Probability
G_1G_2	$1/6$
G_1P_1	$1/6$
G_1P_2	$1/6$
G_2P_1	$1/6$
G_2P_2	$1/6$
P_1P_2	$1/6$

We define the following events:

A: {At least one of the selected firms is in good financial condition}

B: {Firm P_1 is selected}

a. Define the event $A \cap B$ as a specific collection of sample points.

b. Define the event $A \cup B$ as a specific collection of sample points.

c. Define the event A^c as a specific collection of sample points.

d. Find $P(A)$, $P(B)$, $P(A \cap B)$, $P(A \cup B)$, and $P(A^c)$ by summing the probabilities of the appropriate sample points.

e. Find $P(A \cup B)$ using the additive rule. Are events A and B mutually exclusive? Why?

3.26 *Roulette* is a very popular game in many American casinos. In roulette, a ball spins on a circular wheel that is divided into 38 arcs of equal length, bearing the numbers 00, 0, 1, 2, ..., 35, 36. The number of the arc on which the ball stops is the outcome of one play of the game. The numbers are also colored in the following manner:

Red: 1, 3, 5, 7, 9, 12, 14, 16, 18, 19, 21, 23, 25, 27, 30, 32, 34, 36

Black: 2, 4, 6, 8, 10, 11, 13, 15, 17, 20, 22, 24, 26, 28, 29, 31, 33, 35

Green: 00, 0

Players may place bets on the table in a variety of ways, including bets on odd, even, red, black, high, low, etc. Define the following events:

A: {Outcome is an odd number (00 and 0 are considered neither odd nor even)}

B: {Outcome is a black number}

C: {Outcome is a low number (1–18)}

a. Define the event $A \cap B$ as a specific set of sample points.

b. Define the event $A \cup B$ as a specific set of sample points.

c. Find $P(A)$, $P(B)$, $P(A \cap B)$, $P(A \cup B)$, and $P(C)$ by summing the probabilities of the appropriate sample points.

d. Define the event $A \cap B \cap C$ as a specific set of sample points.

e. Find $P(A \cup B)$ using the additive rule. Are events A and B mutually exclusive? Why?

f. Find $P(A \cap B \cap C)$ by summing the probabilities of the sample points given in part **d**.

g. Define the event $(A \cup B \cup C)$ as a specific set of sample points.

h. Find $P(A \cup B \cup C)$ by summing the probabilities of the sample points given in part **g**.

3.27 After completing an inventory of three warehouses, a manufacturer of golf club shafts described its stock of 20,125 shafts with the percentages given in the table. Suppose a shaft is selected at random from the 20,125 currently in stock and the warehouse number and type of shaft are observed.

		TYPE OF SHAFT		
		Regular	**Stiff**	**Extra Stiff**
	1	41%	6%	0%
Warehouse	2	10%	15%	4%
	3	11%	7%	6%

a. List all the sample points for this experiment.
b. What is the set of all sample points called?
c. Let C be the event that the shaft selected is from warehouse 3. Find $P(C)$ by summing the probabilities of the sample points in C.
d. Let F be the event that the shaft chosen is an extra-stiff type. Find $P(F)$.
e. Let A be the event that the shaft selected is from warehouse 1. Find $P(A)$.
f. Let D be the event that the shaft selected is a regular type. Find $P(D)$.
g. Let E be the event that the shaft selected is a stiff type. Find $P(E)$.

3.28 Refer to Exercise 3.27. Define the characteristics of a golf club shaft portrayed by the following events, and then find the probability of each. For each union, use the additive rule to find the probability. Also, determine whether the events are mutually exclusive.
a. $A \cap F$ **b.** $C \cup E$ **c.** $C \cap D$
d. $A \cup F$ **e.** $A \cup D$

3.29 The types of occupations of the 123,060,000 employed workers (age 16 years and older) in the United States in 1994 are described in the table, and their relative frequencies are listed. A worker is to be selected at random from this population and his or her occupation is to be determined. (Assume that each worker in the population has only one occupation.)
a. What is the probability that the worker will be a male service worker?
b. What is the probability that the worker will be a manager or a professional?
c. What is the probability that the worker will be a female professional or a female operator/fabricator/laborer?
d. What is the probability that the worker will not be in a technical/sales administrative occupation?

Occupation	Relative Frequency	
Male Worker	.54	
Managerial/professional		.14
Technical/sales/administrative		.11
Service		.06
Precision production, craft, and repair		.10
Operators/fabricators/laborers		.11
Farming, forestry, and fishing		.02
Female Worker	.46	
Managerial/professional		.13
Technical/sales/administrative		.19
Service		.08
Precision production, craft, and repair		.01
Operators/fabricators/laborers		.04
Farming, forestry, and fishing		.01

Source: Statistical Abstract of the United States: 1995, p. 411.

3.30 The long-run success of a business depends on its ability to market products with superior characteristics that maximize consumer satisfaction and that give the firm a competitive advantage (Kotler, *Marketing Management*, 1994). Ten new products have been developed by a food-products firm. Market research has indicated that the 10 products have the characteristics described by the Venn diagram shown here.

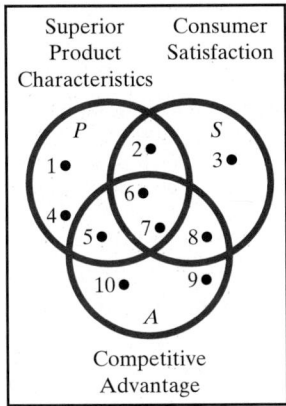

a. Write the event that a product possesses all the desired characteristics as an intersection of the events defined in the Venn diagram. Which products are contained in this intersection?
b. If one of the 10 products were selected at random to be marketed, what is the probability that it would possess all the desired characteristics?
c. Write the event that the randomly selected product would give the firm a competitive advantage or would satisfy consumers as a union of the events defined in the Venn diagram. Find the probability of this union.

d. Write the event that the randomly selected product would possess superior product characteristics and satisfy consumers. Find the probability of this intersection.

3.31 Identifying managerial prospects who are both talented and motivated is difficult. A human-resources director constructed the following two-way table to define nine combinations of talent-motivation levels. The number in a cell is the director's estimate of the probability that a managerial prospect will fall in that category. Suppose the director has decided to hire a new manager. Define the following events:

A: {Prospect places in high-motivation category}

B: {Prospect places in high-talent category}

C: {Prospect is medium or better in both categories}

D: {Prospect places low in at least one category}

E: {Prospect places highest in both categories}

		TALENT	
Motivation	High	Medium	Low
High	.05	.16	.05
Medium	.19	.32	.05
Low	.11	.05	.02

a. Does the sum of the cell probabilities equal 1?

b. List the sample points in each of the events described above and find their probabilities.

c. Find $P(A \cup B)$, $P(A \cap B)$, and $P(A \cup C)$.

d. Find $P(A^c)$ and explain what this means from a practical point of view.

e. Consider each pair of events (*A* and *B*, *A* and *C*, etc.). Which of the pairs are mutually exclusive? Why?

3.5 CONDITIONAL PROBABILITY

The event probabilities we've been discussing give the relative frequencies of the occurrences of the events when the experiment is repeated a very large number of times. Such probabilities are often called **unconditional probabilities** because no special conditions are assumed, other than those that define the experiment.

Often, however, we have additional knowledge that might affect the outcome of an experiment, so we need to alter the probability of an event of interest. A probability that reflects such additional knowledge is called the **conditional probability** of the event. For example, we've seen that the probability of observing an even number (event *A*) on a toss of a fair die is $\frac{1}{2}$. But suppose we're given the information that on a particular throw of the die the result was a number less than or equal to 3 (event *B*). Would the probability of observing an even number on that throw of the die still be equal to $\frac{1}{2}$? It can't be, because making the assumption that *B* has occurred reduces the sample space from six sample points to three sample points (namely, those contained in event *B*). This reduced sample space is as shown in Figure 3.13. Because the sample points for the die-toss experiment are equally likely, each of the three sample points in the reduced sample space is assigned an equal *conditional probability* of $\frac{1}{3}$. Since the only even number of the three in the reduced sample space *B* is the number 2 and the die is fair, we conclude that the probability that *A* occurs *given that B occurs* is $\frac{1}{3}$. We use the symbol $P(A|B)$ to represent the probability of event *A* given that event *B* occurs. For the die-toss example $P(A|B) = \frac{1}{3}$.

To get the probability of event *A* given that event *B* occurs, we proceed as follows. We divide the probability of the part of *A* that falls within the reduced sample space *B*, namely $P(A \cap B)$, by the total probability of the reduced sample space, namely, $P(B)$. Thus, for the die-toss example with event *A:* {Observe an even number} and event *B:* {Observe a number less than or equal to 3}, we find

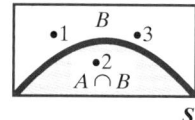

FIGURE 3.13
Reduced sample space for the die-toss experiment given that event *B* has occurred

$\bullet\ B \cap F \qquad B^c \cap F \bullet$

$\bullet\ B \cap F^c \qquad B^c \cap F^c \bullet$

S

FIGURE 3.14
Sample space for contacting a sales product

$$P(A|B) = \frac{P(A \cap B)}{P(B)} = \frac{P(2)}{P(1) + P(2) + P(3)} = \frac{\frac{1}{6}}{\frac{3}{6}} = \frac{1}{3}$$

The formula for $P(A|B)$ is true in general:

> To find the *conditional probability that event A occurs given that event B occurs,* divide the probability that *both* A and B occur by the probability that B occurs, that is,
>
> $$P(A|B) = \frac{P(A \cap B)}{P(B)} \qquad \text{[We assume that } P(B) \neq 0.\text{]}$$

This formula adjusts the probability of $A \cap B$ from its original value in the complete sample space S to a conditional probability in the reduced sample space B. If the sample points in the complete sample space are equally likely, then the formula will assign equal probabilities to the sample points in the reduced sample space, as in the die-toss experiment. If, on the other hand, the sample points have unequal probabilities, the formula will assign conditional probabilities proportional to the probabilities in the complete sample space. This is illustrated by the following examples.

EXAMPLE 3.14

Suppose you are interested in the probability of the sale of a large piece of earth-moving equipment. A single prospect is contacted. Let F be the event that the buyer has sufficient money (or credit) to buy the product and let F^c denote the complement of F (the event that the prospect does not have the financial capability to buy the product). Similarly, let B be the event that the buyer wishes to buy the product and let B^c be the complement of that event. Then the four sample points associated with the experiment are shown in Figure 3.14, and their probabilities are given in Table 3.5.

Find the probability that a single prospect will buy, given that the prospect is able to finance the purchase.

SOLUTION

Suppose you consider the large collection of prospects for the sale of your product and randomly select one person from this collection. What is the probability that the person selected will buy the product? In order to buy the product, the customer must be financially able *and* have the desire to buy, so this probability would correspond to the entry in Table 3.5 below {To buy, B} and next to {Yes, F}, or $P(B \cap F) = .2$. This is called the **unconditional probability** of the event $B \cap F$.

In contrast, suppose you know that the prospect selected has the financial capability for purchasing the product. Now you are seeking the probability that the customer will buy given (the condition) that the customer has the financial ability to pay. This probability, the **conditional probability** of B given that F has occurred and denoted by the symbol $P(B|F)$, would be determined by considering

TABLE 3.5 Probabilities of Customer Desire to Buy and Ability to Finance

		DESIRE	
		To Buy, B	Not to Buy, B^c
Able to Finance	Yes, F	.2	.1
	No, F^c	.4	.3

FIGURE 3.15
Subspace (shaded) containing sample points implying a financially able prospect

only the sample points in the reduced sample space containing the sample points $B \cap F$ and $B^c \cap F$—i.e., sample points that imply the prospect is financially able to buy. (This subspace is shaded in Figure 3.15.) From our definition of conditional probability,

$$P(B|F) = \frac{P(B \cap F)}{P(F)}$$

where $P(F)$ is the sum of the probabilities of the two sample points corresponding to $B \cap F$ and $B^c \cap F$ (given in Table 3.5). Then

$$P(F) = P(B \cap F) + P(B^c \cap F) = .2 + .1 = .3$$

and the conditional probability that a prospect buys, given that the prospect is financially able, is

$$P(B|F) = \frac{P(B \cap F)}{P(F)} = \frac{.2}{.3} = .667$$

As we would expect, the probability that the prospect will buy, given that he or she is financially able, is higher than the unconditional probability of selecting a prospect who will buy.

Note in Example 3.14, that the conditional probability formula assigns a probability to the event $(B \cap F)$ in the reduced sample space that is proportional to the probability of the event in the complete sample space. To see this, note that the two sample points in the reduced sample space, $(B \cap F)$ and $(B^c \cap F)$, have probabilities of .2 and .1, respectively, in the complete sample space S. The formula assigns conditional probabilities $\frac{2}{3}$ and $\frac{1}{3}$ (use the formula to check the second one) to these sample points in the reduced sample space F, so that the conditional probabilities retain the 2 to 1 proportionality of the original sample point probabilities.

EXAMPLE 3.15

The investigation of consumer product complaints by the Federal Trade Commission (FTC) has generated much interest by manufacturers in the quality of their products. A manufacturer of an electromechanical kitchen utensil conducted an analysis of a large number of consumer complaints and found that they fell into the six categories shown in Table 3.6. If a consumer complaint is received, what is the probability that the cause of the complaint was product appearance given that the complaint originated during the guarantee period?

SOLUTION
Let A represent the event that the cause of a particular complaint is product appearance, and let B represent the event that the complaint occurred during the guarantee period. Checking Table 3.6, you can see that $(18 + 13 + 32)\% = 63\%$ of the complaints occur during the guarantee period. Hence, $P(B) = .63$. The

TABLE 3.6 Distribution of Product Complaints

	REASON FOR COMPLAINT			
	Electrical	Mechanical	Appearance	Totals
During Guarantee Period	18%	13%	32%	63%
After Guarantee Period	12%	22%	3%	37%
Totals	30%	35%	35%	100%

percentage of complaints that were caused by the appearance and occurred during the guarantee period (the event $A \cap B$) is 32%. Therefore, $P(A \cap B) = .32$.

Using these probability values, we can calculate the conditional probability $P(A|B)$ that the cause of a complaint is appearance given that the complaint occurred during the guarantee time:

$$P(A|B) = \frac{P(A \cap B)}{P(B)} = \frac{.32}{.63} = .51$$

Consequently, we can see that slightly more than half the complaints that occurred during the guarantee period were due to scratches, dents, or other imperfections in the surface of the kitchen devices. ∎

You will see in later chapters that conditional probability plays a key role in many applications of statistics. For example, we may be interested in the probability that a particular stock gains 10% during the next year. We may assess this probability using information such as the past performance of the stock or the general state of the economy at present. However, our probability may change drastically if we assume that the Gross Domestic Product (GDP) will increase by 10% in the next year. We would then be assessing the *conditional probability* that our stock gains 10% in the next year given that the GDP gains 10% in the same year. Thus, the probability of any event that is calculated or assessed based on an assumption that some other event occurs concurrently is a conditional probability.

3.6 THE MULTIPLICATIVE RULE AND INDEPENDENT EVENTS

The probability of an intersection of two events can be calculated using the multiplicative rule, which employs the conditional probabilities we defined in the previous section. Actually, we have already developed the formula in another context. You will recall that the formula for calculating the conditional probability of B given A is

$$P(B|A) = \frac{P(A \cap B)}{P(A)}$$

If we multiply both sides of this equation by $P(A)$, we get a formula for the probability of the intersection of events A and B:

> **Multiplicative Rule of Probability**
> $P(A \cap B) = P(A)P(B|A)$ or, equivalently, $P(A \cap B) = P(B)P(A|B)$

The second expression in the box is obtained by multiplying both sides of the equation $P(A|B) = P(A \cap B)/P(B)$ by $P(B)$.

EXAMPLE 3.16

An investor in wheat futures is concerned with the following events:

  B: {U.S. production of wheat will be profitable next year}
  A: {A serious drought will occur next year}

Based on available information, the investor believes that the probability is .01 that production of wheat will be profitable *assuming* a serious drought will occur in the same year and that the probability is .05 that a serious drought will occur. That is,

$$P(B|A) = .01 \text{ and } P(A) = .05$$

Based on the information provided, what is the probability that a serious drought will occur *and* that a profit will be made? That is, find $P(A \cap B)$, the probability of the intersection of events A and B.

SOLUTION
We want to calculate $P(A \cap B)$. Using the formula for the multiplicative rule, we obtain:

$$P(A \cap B) = P(A)P(B|A) = (.05)(.01) = .0005$$

The probability that a serious drought occurs *and* the production of wheat is profitable is only .0005. As we might expect, this intersection is a very rare event.

Intersections often contain only a few sample points. In this case, the probability of an intersection is easy to calculate by summing the appropriate sample point probabilities. However, the formula for calculating intersection probabilities is invaluable when the intersection contains numerous sample points, as the next example illustrates.

EXAMPLE 3.17

A county welfare agency employs ten welfare workers who interview prospective food stamp recipients. Periodically the supervisor selects, at random, the forms completed by two workers to audit for illegal deductions. Unknown to the supervisor, three of the workers have regularly been giving illegal deductions to applicants. What is the probability that both of the two workers chosen have been giving illegal deductions?

SOLUTION
Define the following two events:

A: {First worker selected gives illegal deductions}

B: {Second worker selected gives illegal deductions}

We want to find the probability of the event that both selected workers have been giving illegal deductions. This event can be restated as: {First worker gives illegal deductions *and* second worker gives illegal deductions}. Thus, we want to find the probability of the intersection, $A \cap B$. Applying the multiplicative rule, we have

$$P(A \cap B) = P(A)P(B|A)$$

To find $P(A)$ it is helpful to consider the experiment as selecting one worker from the ten. Then the sample space for the experiment contains ten sample points (representing the ten welfare workers), where the three workers giving illegal deductions are denoted by the symbol I (I_1, I_2, I_3), and the seven workers not giving illegal deductions are denoted by the symbol N $(N_1, ..., N_7)$. The resulting Venn diagram is illustrated in Figure 3.16. Since the first worker is selected at random from the ten, it is reasonable to assign equal probabilities to the 10 sample points. Thus, each sample point has a probability of $1/10$. The sample points in event A are $\{I_1, I_2, I_3\}$—the three workers who are giving illegal deductions. Thus,

$$P(A) = P(I_1) + P(I_2) + P(I_3) = \tfrac{1}{10} + \tfrac{1}{10} + \tfrac{1}{10} = \tfrac{3}{10}$$

FIGURE 3.16
Venn diagram for
finding $P(A)$

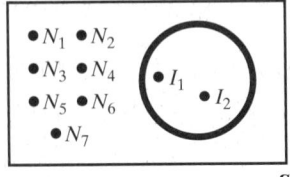

FIGURE 3.17
Venn diagram for
finding $P(B|A)$

To find the conditional probability, $P(B|A)$, we need to alter the sample space S. Since we know A has occurred, i.e., the first worker selected is giving illegal deductions, only two of the nine remaining workers in the sample space are giving illegal deductions. The Venn diagram for this new sample space is shown in Figure 3.17. Each of these 9 sample points are equally likely, so each is assigned a probability of $1/9$. Since the event $(B|A)$ contains the sample points $\{I_1, I_2\}$, we have

$$P(B|A) = P(I_1) + P(I_2) = \tfrac{1}{9} + \tfrac{1}{9} = \tfrac{2}{9}$$

Substituting $P(A) = 3/10$ and $P(B|A) = 2/9$ into the formula for the multiplicative rule, we find

$$P(A \cap B) = P(A)P(B|A) = (\tfrac{3}{10})(\tfrac{2}{9}) = \tfrac{6}{90} = \tfrac{1}{15}$$

Thus, there is a 1 in 15 chance that both workers chosen by the supervisor have been giving illegal deductions to food stamp recipients.

The sample space approach is only one way to solve the problem posed in Example 3.17. An alternative method employs the concept of a **tree diagram**. Tree diagrams are helpful for calculating the probability of an intersection.

To illustrate, a tree diagram for Example 3.17 is displayed in Figure 3.18 The tree begins at the far left with two branches. These branches represent the two possible outcomes N (no illegal deductions) and I (illegal deductions) for the first worker selected. The unconditional probability of each outcome is given (in parentheses) on the appropriate branch. That is, for the first worker selected, $P(N) = 7/10$ and $P(I) = 3/10$. (These can be obtained by summing sample point probabilities as in Example 3.17.)

The next level of the tree diagram (moving to the right) represents the outcomes for the second worker selected. The probabilities shown here are conditional probabilities since the outcome for the first worker is assumed to be known. For example, if the first worker is giving illegal deductions (I), the probability that the second worker is also giving illegal deductions (I) is $2/9$ since of the nine workers left to be selected, only two remain who are giving illegal deductions. This

FIGURE 3.18
Tree diagram for
Example 3.17

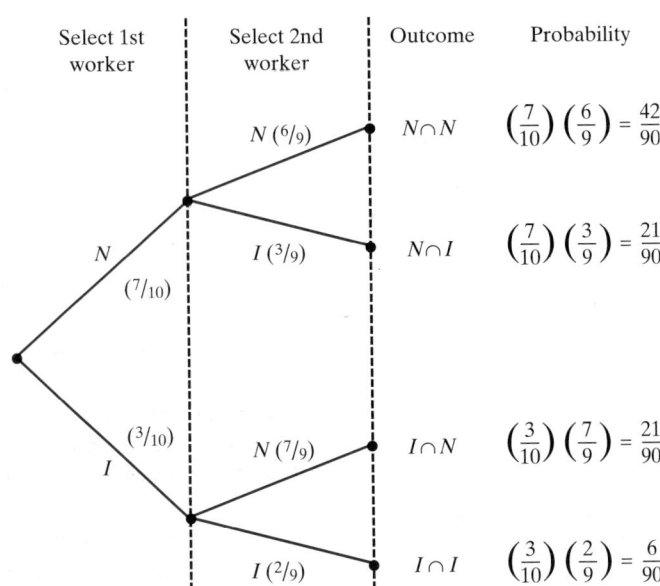

conditional probability, $\frac{2}{9}$, is shown in parentheses on the bottom branch of Figure 3.18.

Finally, the four possible outcomes of the experiment are shown at the end of each of the four tree branches. These events are intersections of two events (outcome of first worker *and* outcome of second worker). Consequently, the multiplicative rule is applied to calculate each probability, as shown in Figure 3.18. You can see that the intersection $\{I \cap I\}$, i.e., the event that both workers selected are giving illegal deductions, has probability $\frac{6}{90} = \frac{1}{15}$—the same value obtained in Example 3.17.

In Section 3.5 we showed that the probability of an event A may be substantially altered by the knowledge that an event B has occurred. However, this will not always be the case. In some instances, the assumption that event B has occurred will *not* alter the probability of event A at all. When this is true, we call events A and B **independent**.

DEFINITION 3.9

Events A and B are **independent events** if the occurrence of B does not alter the probability that A has occurred; that is, events A and B are independent if

$$P(A|B) = P(A)$$

When events A and B are independent, it is also true that

$$P(B|A) = P(B)$$

Events that are not independent are said to be **dependent**.

EXAMPLE 3.18

Consider the experiment of tossing a fair die and let

A: {Observe an even number}

B: {Observe a number less than or equal to 4}

Are events A and B independent?

SOLUTION

The Venn diagram for this experiment is shown in Figure 3.19. We first calculate

$$P(A) = P(2) + P(4) + P(6) = \frac{1}{2}$$

$$P(B) = P(1) + P(2) + P(3) + P(4) = \frac{2}{3}$$

$$P(A \cap B) = P(2) + P(4) = \frac{1}{3}$$

Now assuming B has occurred, the conditional probability of A given B is

$$P(A|B) = \frac{P(A \cap B)}{P(B)} = \frac{\frac{1}{3}}{\frac{2}{3}} = \frac{1}{2} = P(A)$$

Thus, assuming that event B does not alter the probability of observing an even number, it remains $\frac{1}{2}$. Therefore, the events A and B are independent. Note that if we calculate the conditional probability of B given A, our conclusion is the same:

$$P(B|A) = \frac{P(A \cap B)}{P(A)} = \frac{\frac{1}{3}}{\frac{1}{2}} = \frac{2}{3} = P(B)$$

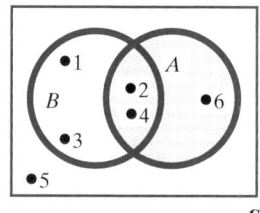

FIGURE 3.19
Venn diagram for die-toss experiment

EXAMPLE 3.19

Refer to the consumer product complaint study in Example 3.15. The percentages of complaints of various types during and after the guarantee period are shown in Table 3.6. Define the following events:

> A: {Cause of complaint is product appearance}
>
> B: {Complaint occurred during the guarantee term}

Are A and B independent events?

SOLUTION

Events A and B are independent if $P(A|B) = P(A)$. We calculated $P(A|B)$ in Example 3.15 to be .51, and from Table 3.6 we see that

$$P(A) = .32 + .03 = .35$$

Therefore, $P(A|B)$ is not equal to $P(A)$, and A and B are dependent events.

To gain an intuitive understanding of independence, think of situations in which the occurrence of one event does not alter the probability that a second event will occur. For example, suppose two small companies are being monitored by a financier for possible investment. If the businesses are in different industries and they are otherwise unrelated, then the success or failure of one company may be *independent* of the success or failure of the other. That is, the event that company A fails may not alter the probability that company B will fail.

As a second example, consider an election poll in which 1,000 registered voters are asked their preference between two candidates. Pollsters try to use procedures for selecting a sample of voters so that the responses are independent. That is, the objective of the pollster is to select the sample so the event that one polled voter prefers candidate A does not alter the probability that a second polled voter prefers candidate A.

We will make three final points about independence. The first is that the property of independence, unlike the mutually exclusive property, cannot be shown on or gleaned from a Venn diagram. This means *you can't trust your intuition*. In general, the only way to check for independence is by performing the calculations of the probabilities in the definition.

The second point concerns the relationship between the mutually exclusive and independence properties. Suppose that events A and B are mutually exclusive, as shown in Figure 3.20, and both events have nonzero probabilities. Are these events independent or dependent? That is, does the assumption that B occurs alter the probability of the occurrence of A? It certainly does, because if we assume that B has occurred, it is impossible for A to have occurred simultaneously. That is, $P(A|B) = 0$. Thus, *mutually exclusive events are dependent events* since $P(A) \neq P(A|B)$.

The third point is that the probability of the intersection of independent events is very easy to calculate. Referring to the formula for calculating the probability of an intersection, we find

$$P(A \cap B) = P(A)P(B|A)$$

Thus, since $P(B|A) = P(B)$ when A and B are independent, we have the following useful rule:

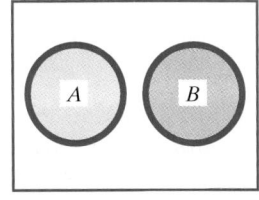

FIGURE 3.20
Mutually exclusive events are dependent events

> *If events A and B are independent,* the probability of the intersection of A and B equals the product of the probabilities of A and B; that is,
>
> $$P(A\cap B) = P(A)P(B)$$
>
> The converse is also true: If $P(A\cap B) = P(A)P(B)$, then events A and B are independent.

In the die-toss experiment, we showed in Example 3.18 that the events A: {Observe an even number} and B: {Observe a number less than or equal to 4} are independent if the die is fair. Thus,

$$P(A\cap B) = P(A)P(B) = (\tfrac{1}{2})(\tfrac{2}{3}) = \tfrac{1}{3}$$

This agrees with the result that we obtained in the example:

$$P(A\cap B) = P(2) + P(4) = \tfrac{2}{6} = \tfrac{1}{3}$$

EXAMPLE 3.20

Almost every retail business has the problem of determining how much inventory to purchase. Insufficient inventory may result in lost business, and excess inventory may have a detrimental effect on profits. Suppose a retail computer store owner is planning to place an order for personal computers (PCs). She is trying to decide how many IBM PCs and how many IBM compatibles to order.

The owner's records indicate that 80% of the previous PC customers purchased IBM PCs and 20% purchased compatibles.

  a. What is the probability that the next two customers will purchase compatibles?

  b. What is the probability that the next ten customers will purchase compatibles?

SOLUTION

  a. Let C_1 represent the event that customer 1 will purchase a compatible and C_2 represent the event that customer 2 will purchase a compatible. The event that *both* customers purchase compatibles is the intersection of the two events, $C_1\cap C_2$. From the records the store owner could reasonably conclude that $P(C_1) = .2$ (based on the fact that 20% of past customers have purchased compatibles), and the same reasoning would apply to C_2. However, in order to compute the probability of $C_1\cap C_2$, we need more information. Either the records must be examined for the occurrence of consecutive purchases of compatibles, or some assumption must be made to allow the calculation of $P(C_1\cap C_2)$ from the multiplicative rule. It seems reasonable to make the assumption that the two events are independent, since the decision of the first customer is not likely to affect the decision of the second customer. Assuming independence, we have

$$P(C_1\cap C_2) = P(C_1)P(C_2) = (.2)(.2) = .04$$

  b. To see how to compute the probability that ten consecutive purchases will be compatibles, first consider the event that three consecutive customers purchase compatibles. If C_3 represents the event that the third customer purchases a compatible, then we want to compute the probability of the intersection $C_1\cap C_2$ with C_3. Again assuming independence of the purchasing decisions, we have

$$P(C_1\cap C_2\cap C_3) = P(C_1\cap C_2)\, P(C_3) = (.2)^2(.2) = .008$$

Similar reasoning leads to the conclusion that the intersection of ten such events can be calculated as follows:

$$P(C_1 \cap C_2 \cap \cdots \cap C_{10}) = P(C_1)P(C_2) \cdots P(C_{10}) = (.2)^{10} = .0000001024$$

Thus, the probability that ten consecutive customers purchase IBM compatibles is about 1 in 10 million, assuming the probability of each customer's purchase of a compatible is .2 and the purchase decisions are independent. ⌐

EXERCISES   3.32–3.51

Learning the Mechanics

3.32 An experiment results in one of three mutually exclusive events, A, B, or C. It is known that $P(A) = .30$, $P(B) = .55$, and $P(C) = .15$. Find each of the following probabilities:
a. $P(A \cup B)$ **b.** $P(A \cap C)$
c. $P(A|B)$ **d.** $P(B \cup C)$
e. Are B and C independent events? Explain.

3.33 Consider the experiment depicted by the Venn diagram, with the sample space S containing five sample points. The sample points are assigned the following probabilities: $P(E_1) = .20$, $P(E_2) = .30$, $P(E_3) = .30$, $P(E_4) = .10$, $P(E_5) = .10$.

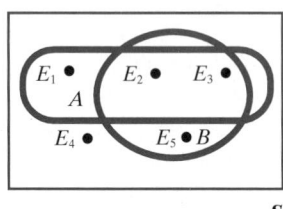

S

a. Calculate $P(A)$, $P(B)$, and $P(A \cap B)$.
b. Suppose we know that event A has occurred, so that the reduced sample space consists of the three sample points in A—namely, E_1, E_2, and E_3. Use the formula for conditional probability to adjust the probabilities of these three sample points for the knowledge that A has occurred [i.e., $P(E_i|A)$]. Verify that the conditional probabilities are in the same proportion to one another as the original sample point probabilities.
c. Calculate the conditional probability $P(B|A)$ in two ways: (1) Add the adjusted (conditional) probabilities of the sample points in the intersection $A \cap B$, since these represent the event that B occurs given that A has occurred; (2) Use the formula for conditional probability:

$$P(B|A) = \frac{P(A \cap B)}{P(A)}$$

Verify that the two methods yield the same result.
d. Are events A and B independent? Why or why not?

3.34 Three fair coins are tossed and the following events are defined:

A: {Observe at least one head}

B: {Observe exactly two heads}

C: {Observe exactly two tails}

D: {Observe at most one head}

a. Sum the probabilities of the appropriate sample points to find: $P(A), P(B), P(C), P(D), P(A \cap B), P(A \cap D), P(B \cap C),$ and $P(B \cap D)$.
b. Use your answers to part **a** to calculate $P(B|A)$, $P(A|D)$, and $P(C|B)$.
c. Which pairs of events, if any, are independent? Why?

3.35 An experiment results in one of five sample points with the following probabilities: $P(E_1) = .22, P(E_2) = .31, P(E_3) = .15, P(E_4) = .22$, and $P(E_5) = .1$. The following events have been defined:

A: $\{E_1, E_3\}$

B: $\{E_2, E_3, E_4\}$

C: $\{E_1, E_5\}$

Find each of the following probabilities:
a. $P(A)$ **b.** $P(B)$ **c.** $P(A \cap B)$
d. $P(A|B)$ **e.** $P(B \cap C)$ **f.** $P(C|B)$
g. Consider each pair of events: A and B, A and C, and B and C. Are any of the pairs of events independent? Why?

3.36 Two fair dice are tossed, and the following events are defined:

A: {Sum of the numbers showing is odd}

B: {Sum of the numbers showing is 9, 11, or 12}

Are events A and B independent? Why?

3.37 A sample space contains six sample points and events A, B, and C as shown in the Venn diagram. The probabilities of the sample points are

$P(1) = .20, P(2) = .05, P(3) = .30, P(4) = .10,$
$P(5) = .10, P(6) = .25.$

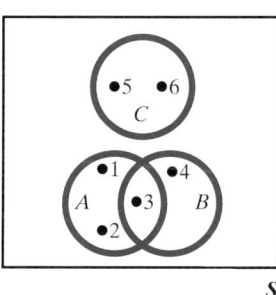

S

a. Which pairs of events, if any, are mutually exclusive? Why?
b. Which pairs of events, if any, are independent? Why?
c. Find $P(A \cup B)$ by adding the probabilities of the sample points and then by using the additive rule. Verify that the answers agree. Repeat for $P(A \cup C)$.

3.38 Defend or refute each of the following statements:
a. Dependent events are always mutually exclusive.
b. Mutually exclusive events are always dependent.
c. Independent events are always mutually exclusive.

3.39 For two events, A and B, $P(A) = .4$ and $P(B) = .2$.
a. If A and B are independent, find $P(A \cap B)$, $P(A|B)$, and $P(A \cup B)$.
b. If A and B are dependent, with $P(A|B) = .6$, find $P(A \cap B)$ and $P(B|A)$.

Applying the Concepts

3.40 "Go" is one of the oldest and most popular strategic board games in the world, especially in Japan and Korea. This two-player game is played on a flat surface marked with 19 vertical and 19 horizontal lines. The objective is to control territory by placing pieces called "stones" on vacant points on the board. Players alternate placing their stones. The player using black stones goes first, followed by the player using white stones. [*Note:* The University of Virginia requires MBA students to learn Go to understand how the Japanese conduct business.] *Chance* (Summer 1995) published an article that investigated the advantage of playing first (i.e., using the black stones) in Go. The results of 577 games recently played by professional Go players were analyzed.

a. In the 577 games, the player with the black stones won 319 times and the player with the white stones won 258 times. Use this information to assess the probability of winning when you play first in Go.
b. Professional Go players are classified by level. Group C includes the top-level players followed by Group B (middle-level) and Group A (low-level) players. The table below describes the number of games won by the player with the black stones, categorized by level of the black player and level of the opponent. Assess the probability of winning when you play first in Go for each combination of player and opponent level.
c. If the player with the black stones is ranked higher than the player with the white stones, what is the probability that black wins?
d. Given the players are of the same level, what is the probability that the player with the black stones wins?

3.41 Businesses that offer credit to their customers are inevitably faced with the task of collecting unpaid bills. A study of collection remedies used by creditors was published in the *Journal of Financial Research* (Spring 1986). As part of the study, creditors in four states were asked about how they deal with past-due bills. Their responses are tallied in the table on page 146. "Tough actions"

Black Player Level	Opponent Level	Number of Wins	Number of Games
C	A	34	34
C	B	69	79
C	C	66	118
B	A	40	54
B	B	52	95
B	C	27	79
A	A	15	28
A	B	11	51
A	C	5	39
Totals		319	577

Source: J. Kim, and H. J. Kim. "The advantage of playing first in Go." *Chance,* Vol. 8, No. 3, Summer 1995, p. 26 (Table 3).

	Wisconsin	Illinois	Arkansas	Louisiana
Take tough action early	0	1	5	1
Take tough action later	37	23	22	21
Never take tough action	9	11	6	15

included filing a legal action, turning the debt over to a third party such as an attorney or collection agency, garnishing wages, and repossessing secured property. Suppose one of the creditors questioned is selected at random.

a. What is the probability that the creditor is from Wisconsin or Louisiana?

b. What is the probability that the creditor is not from Wisconsin or Louisiana?

c. What is the probability that the creditor never takes tough action?

d. What is the probability that the creditor is from Arkansas and never takes tough action?

e. What is the probability that the creditor never takes tough action, given that the creditor is from Arkansas?

f. If the creditor takes tough action early, what is the probability that the creditor is from Arkansas or Louisiana?

g. What is the probability that a creditor from Arkansas never takes tough action?

3.42 In the last decade, increasingly more employees have been offered a variety of health care plans to choose from. This is a direct result of the growing prevalence of preferred provider organizations (PPOs) and health maintenance organizations (HMOs). PPOs permit employees to choose their health care provider, but offer financial incentives when designated doctors and hospitals are chosen. HMOs offer prepaid health care from a particular set of providers (*Monthly Labor Review*, Oct. 1995). A survey of 100 large, 100 medium, and 100 small companies that offer their employees HMOs, PPOs, and fee-for-service plans was conducted; each firm provided information on the plans chosen by their employees. These companies had a total employment of 833,303 people. A breakdown of the number of employees in each category by firm size and plan is provided in the table.

Company Size	Fee-for-Service	PPO	HMO	Totals
Small	1,808	1,757	1,456	5,021
Medium	8,953	6,491	6,983	22,382
Large	330,419	241,770	233,711	805,900
Totals	341,180	250,018	242,105	833,303

Source: Adapted from Bucci, M., and Grant, R. "Employer-sponsored health insurance: What's offered; what's chosen?" *Monthly Labor Review,* October 1995, pp. 38–43.

One employee from the 833,303 total employees is to be chosen at random for further analysis. Define the events A and B as follows:

A: {Observe an employee that chose fee-for-service}

B: {Observe an employee from a small company}

a. Find $P(B)$. **b.** Find $P(A \cap B)$.

c. Find $P(A \cup B)$. **d.** Find $P(A|B)$.

e. Are A and B independent? Justify your answer.

3.43 Refer to the *American Journal of Public Health* study of unintentional carbon monoxide (CO) poisonings in Colorado, Exercise 3.10. The 981 cases were classified in a table, which is reproduced below. A case of unintentional CO poisoning is chosen at random from the 981 cases.

Source of Exposure	Fatal	Nonfatal	Total
Fire	63	53	116
Auto exhaust	60	178	238
Furnace	18	345	363
Kerosene or spaceheater	9	18	27
Appliance	9	63	72
Other gas-powered motor	3	73	76
Fireplace	0	16	16
Other	3	19	22
Unknown	9	42	51
Total	174	807	981

Source: Cook, M. C., Simon, P. A., and Hoffman, R. E. "Unintentional carbon monoxide poisoning in Colorado, 1986 through 1991." *American Journal of Public Health,* Vol. 85, No. 7, July 1995, p. 989 (Table 1). © 1995 American Public Health Association.

a. Given that the source of the poisoning is fire, what is the probability that the case is fatal?

b. Given that the case is nonfatal, what is the probability that it is caused by auto exhaust?

c. If the case is fatal, what is the probability that the source is unknown?

d. If the case is nonfatal, what is the probability that the source is not fire or a fireplace?

3.44 Physicians and pharmacists sometimes fail to inform patients adequately about the proper application of prescription drugs and about the precautions to take in order to avoid potential side effects. This failure is an ongoing problem in the United States. One method of increasing patients' awareness of the problem is for physicians to provide Patient Medication Instruction (PMI) sheets. The American Medical Association, however, has found that only 20% of the doctors who prescribe drugs frequently distribute PMI sheets to their patients. Assume that 20% of all patients receive the PMI sheet with their prescriptions and that 12% receive the PMI sheet and are hospitalized because of a drug-related problem. What is the probability that a person will be hospitalized for a drug-related problem given that the person has received the PMI sheet?

3.45 A soft-drink bottler has two quality control inspectors independently check each case of soft drinks for chipped or cracked bottles before the cases leave the bottling plant. Having observed the work of the two trusted inspectors over several years, the bottler has determined that the probability of a defective case getting by the first inspector is .05 and the probability of a defective case getting by the second inspector is .10. What is the probability that a defective case gets by both inspectors?

3.46 The table describes the 63.1 million U.S. long-form federal tax returns filed with the Internal Revenue Service (IRS) in 1992 and the percentage of those returns that were audited by the IRS.

Income	Number of Tax Filers (millions)	Percentage Audited
Under $25,000	18.7	.6
$25,000–$49,999	27.5	.6
$50,000–$99,999	13.7	1.0
$100,000 or more	3.2	4.9

Source: Statistical Abstract of the United States: 1995, p. 344.

a. If a tax filer is randomly selected from this population of tax filers (i.e., each tax filer has an equal probability of being selected), what is the probability that the tax filer was audited?

b. If a tax filer is randomly selected from this population of tax filers, what is the probability that the tax filer had an income of $25,000–$49,999 in 1992 *and* was audited? What is the probability that the tax filer had an income of $50,000 or more in 1992 *or* was not audited?

3.47 "Channel One" is an education television network that is available to all secondary schools in the United States. Participating schools are equipped with TV sets in every classroom in order to receive the Channel One broadcasts. According to *Educational Technology* (May–June 1995), 40% of all U.S. secondary schools subscribe to the Channel One Communications Network (CCN). Of these subscribers, only 5% never use the CCN broadcasts, while 20% use CCN more than five times per week.

a. Find the probability that a randomly selected U.S. secondary school subscribes to CCN but never uses the CCN broadcasts.

b. Find the probability that a randomly selected U.S. secondary school subscribes to CCN and uses the broadcasts more than five times per week.

3.48 In October 1994, a flaw was discovered in the Pentium chip installed in many new personal computers. The chip produced an incorrect result when dividing two numbers. Intel, the manufacturer of the Pentium chip, initially announced that such an error would occur only once in 9 billion divides, or "once in every 27,000 years" for a typical user; consequently, it did not immediately replace the chip. Assume the probability of a divide error with the Pentium chip is, in fact, $1/9,000,000,000$.

a. For a division performed using the flawed Pentium chip, what is the probability that no error will occur?

b. Consider two successive divisions performed using the flawed chip. What is the probability that neither result will be in error? (Assume that any one division has no impact on the result of any other division performed by the chip.)

c. Depending on the procedure, statistical software packages may perform an extremely large number of divisions to produce the required output. For heavy users of the software, 1 billion divisions over a short time frame is not unusual. Calculate the probability that 1 billion divisions performed using the flawed Pentium chip will result in no errors.

d. Use the result, part **c**, to compute the probability of at least one error in the 1 billion divisions. [*Note:* Two months after the flaw was discovered, Intel agreed to replace all Pentium chips free of charge.]

3.49 The genetic origin and properties of maize (modern-day corn), a domestic plant developed 8,000 years ago in Mexico, was investigated in *Economic Botany* (Jan.–Mar. 1995). Seeds from maize ears carry either single spikelets or paired spikelets, but not both. Progeny tests on approximately 600 maize ears revealed the following information. Forty percent of all seeds carry single spikelets, while 60% carry paired spikelets. A seed with single spikelets will produce maize ears with single spikelets 29% of the time and paired spikelets 71% of the time. A seed with paired spikelets will produce maize ears with single spikelets 26% of the time and paired spikelets 74% of the time.

a. Find the probability that a randomly selected maize ear seed carries a single spikelet and produces ears with single spikelets.

b. Find the probability that a randomly selected maize ear seed produces ears with paired spikelets.

3.50 A particular automatic sprinkler system for high-rise apartment buildings, office buildings, and hotels has two different types of activation devices for each sprinkler head. One type has a reliability of .91 (i.e., the probability that it will activate the sprinkler when it should is .91). The other type, which operates independently of the first type, has a reliability of .87. Suppose a serious fire starts near a particular sprinkler head.

   a. What is the probability that the sprinkler head will be activated?

   b. What is the probability that the sprinkler head will not be activated?

   c. What is the probability that both activation devices will work properly?

   d. What is the probability that only the device with reliability .91 will work properly?

3.51 One definition of *Total Quality Management* (TQM) was given in Exercise 3.7. Another definition is a "management philosophy and a system of management techniques to improve product and service quality and worker productivity." TQM involves such techniques as teamwork, empower-ment of workers, improved communication with customers, evaluation of work processes, and statistical analysis of processes and their output (Benson, *Minnesota Management Review,* Fall 1992). One hundred U.S. companies were surveyed and it was found that 30 had implemented TQM. Among the 100 companies surveyed, 60 reported an increase in sales last year. Of those 60, 20 had implemented TQM. Suppose one of the 100 surveyed companies is to be selected at random for additional analysis.

   a. What is the probability that a firm that implemented TQM is selected? That a firm whose sales increased is selected?

   b. Are the two events {TQM implemented} and {Sales increased} independent or dependent? Explain.

   c. Suppose that instead of 20 TQM implementers among the 60 firms reporting sales increases, there were 18. Now are the events {TQM implemented} and {Sales increased} independent or dependent? Explain.

3.7   RANDOM SAMPLING

How a sample is selected from a population is of vital importance in statistical inference because the probability of an observed sample will be used to infer the characteristics of the sampled population. To illustrate, suppose you deal yourself four cards from a deck of 52 cards and all four cards are aces. Do you conclude that your deck is an ordinary bridge deck, containing only four aces, or do you conclude that the deck is stacked with more than four aces? It depends on how the cards were drawn. If the four aces were always placed at the top of a standard bridge deck, drawing four aces is not unusual—it is certain. On the other hand, if the cards are thoroughly mixed, drawing four aces in a sample of four cards is highly improbable. The point, of course, is that in order to use the observed sample of four cards to draw inferences about the population (the deck of 52 cards), you need to know how the sample was selected from the deck.

One of the simplest and most frequently employed sampling procedures is implied in many of the previous examples and exercises. It is called **random sampling** and produces what is known as a *random sample*.

DEFINITION 3.10
If *n* elements are selected from a population in such a way that every set of *n* elements in the population has an equal probability of being selected, the *n* elements are said to be a **random sample.***

If a population is not too large and the elements can be numbered on slips of paper, poker chips, etc., you can physically mix the slips of paper or chips and remove *n* elements from the total. The numbers that appear on the chips selected would indicate the population elements to be included in the sample. Since it is

*Strictly speaking, this is a **simple random sample**. There are many different types of random samples. The simple random sample is the most common.

often difficult to achieve a thorough mix, such a procedure only provides an approximation to random sampling. Most researchers rely on **random number generators** to automatically generate the random sample. Random number generators are available in table form and they are built into most statistical software packages.

EXAMPLE 3.21

Suppose you wish to randomly sample five households from a population of 100,000 households to participate in a study.

    a. How many different samples can be selected?

    b. Use a random number generator to select a random sample.

SOLUTION

    a. To determine the number of samples, we'll apply the combinatorial rule of Section 3.1. In this case, $N = 100,000$ and $n = 5$. Then,

$$\binom{N}{n} = \binom{100,000}{5} = \frac{100,000!}{5!\,99,995!}$$

$$= \frac{100,000 \cdot 99,999 \cdot 99,998 \cdot 99,997 \cdot 99,996}{5 \cdot 4 \cdot 3 \cdot 2 \cdot 1}$$

$$= 8.33 \times 10^{22}$$

Thus, there are 83.3 billion trillion different samples of five households that can be selected from 100,000.

    b. To ensure that each of the possible samples has an equal chance of being selected, as required for random sampling, we can employ a **random number table**, as provided in Table I of Appendix B. Random number tables are constructed in such a way that every number occurs with (approximately) equal probability. Furthermore, the occurrence of any one number in a position is independent of any of the other numbers that appear in the table. To use a table of random numbers, number the N elements in the population from 1 to N. Then turn to Table I and select a starting number in the table. Proceeding from this number either across the row or down the column, remove and record n numbers from the table.

    To illustrate, first we number the households in the population from 1 to 100,000. Then, we turn to a page of Table I, say the first page. (A partial reproduction of the first page of Table I is shown in Table 3.7.) Now, we arbitrarily select a starting number, say the random number appearing in the third row, second column. This number is 48,360. Then we proceed down the second column to obtain the remaining four random numbers. In this case we have selected five random numbers, which are shaded in Table 3.7. Using the first five digits to represent households from 1 to 99,999 and the number 00000 to represent household 100,000, we can see that the households numbered

    48,360

    93,093

    39,975

    6,907

    72,905

should be included in our sample. *Note:* Use only the necessary number of digits in each random number to identify the element to be included in the sample. If, in

TABLE 3.7   Partial Reproduction of Table I in Appendix B

Column Row	1	2	3	4	5	6
1	10480	15011	01536	02011	81647	91646
2	22368	46573	25595	85393	30995	89198
3	24130	48360	22527	97265	76393	64809
4	42167	93093	06243	61680	07856	16376
5	37570	39975	81837	16656	06121	91782
6	77921	06907	11008	42751	27756	53498
7	99562	72905	56420	69994	98872	31016
8	96301	91977	05463	07972	18876	20922
9	89579	14342	63661	10281	17453	18103
10	85475	36857	53342	53988	53060	59533
11	28918	69578	88231	33276	70997	79936
12	63553	40961	48235	03427	49626	69445
13	09429	93969	52636	92737	88974	33488

the course of recording the n numbers from the table, you select a number that has already been selected, simply discard the duplicate and select a replacement at the end of the sequence. Thus, you may have to record more than n numbers from the table to obtain a sample of n unique numbers.

Can we be perfectly sure that all 83.3 billion trillion samples have an equal chance of being selected? That fact is, we can't; but to the extent that the random number table contains truly random sequences of digits, the sample should be very close to random.

Table I in Appendix B is just one example of a random number generator. For most scientific studies that require a large random sample, computers are used to generate the random sample. The SAS and MINITAB statistical software packages both have easy-to-use random number generators.

For example, suppose we required a random sample of $n = 50$ households from the population of 100,000 households in Example 3.21. Here, we might employ the SAS random number generator. Figure 3.21 shows a SAS printout listing 50 random numbers (from a population of 100,000). The households with these identification numbers would be included in the random sample.

FIGURE 3.21
SAS-generated random sample of 50 households

OBS	HOUSENUM	OBS	HOUSENUM	OBS	HOUSENUM	OBS	HOUSENUM
1	47122	14	47271	27	17098	40	4260
2	94231	15	3642	28	23259	41	58140
3	95531	16	7611	29	30512	42	22903
4	41445	17	81646	30	91548	43	65959
5	80287	18	92158	31	7673	44	13962
6	11731	19	36667	32	68549	45	25819
7	47523	20	71811	33	85433	46	66497
8	84847	21	78988	34	5231	47	79559
9	69822	22	3819	35	13455	48	87017
10	18270	23	21873	36	71666	49	28483
11	52636	24	74938	37	66280	50	91806
12	21750	25	23635	38	66210		
13	63363	26	35807	39	21998		

STATISTICS IN ACTION

3.2 LOTTERY BUSTER

"Welcome to the Wonderful World of Lottery Bu$ters." So begins the premier issue of *Lottery Buster,* a monthly publication for players of the state lottery games. *Lottery Buster* provides interesting facts and figures on the nearly 40 state lotteries currently operating in the United States and purported "tips" on how to increase a player's odds of winning the lottery.

New Hampshire, in 1963, was the first state in modern times to authorize a state lottery as an alternative to increasing taxes. (Prior to this time, beginning in 1895, lotteries were banned in America for fear of corruption.) Since then, lotteries have become immensely popular for two reasons. First, they lure you with the opportunity to win millions of dollars with a $1 investment; second, when you lose, at least you know your money is going to a good cause.

The popularity of the state lottery has brought with it an avalanche of self-proclaimed "experts" and "mathematical wizards" (such as the editors of *Lottery Buster*) who provide advice on how to win the lottery—for a fee, of course! These experts—the legitimate ones, anyway—base their "systems" of winning on their knowledge of probability and statistics.

For example, more experts would agree that the "golden rule" or "first rule" in winning lotteries is *game selection*. State lotteries generally offer three types of games: Instant (scratch-off) tickets, Daily Numbers (Pick-3 and Pick-4), and the weekly Pick-6 Lotto game.

The Instant game involves scratching off the thin, opaque covering on a ticket to determine whether you have won or lost. The cost of a ticket is 50¢, and the amount to be won ranges from $1 to $100,000 in most states, while it reaches $1 million in others. *Lottery Buster* advises against playing the Instant game because it is "a pure chance play, and you can win only by dumb luck. No skill can be applied to this game."

The Daily Numbers game permits you to choose either a three-digit (Pick-3) or four-digit (Pick-4) number at a cost of $1 per ticket. Each night, the winning number is drawn. If your number matches the winning number, you win a large sum of money, usually $100,000. You do have some control over the Daily Numbers game (since you pick the numbers that you play) and, consequently, there are strategies available to increase your chances of winning. However, the Daily Numbers game, like the Instant game, is not available for out-of-state play. For this reason, and because the payoffs are relatively small, lottery experts prefer the weekly Pick-6 Lotto game.

To play Pick-6 Lotto, you select six numbers of your choice from a field of numbers ranging from 1 to *N*, where *N* depends on which state's game you are playing. For example, Florida's Lotto game involves picking six numbers ranging from 1 to 49 (denoted 6/49) as shown on the Florida Lotto ticket, Figure 3.22. Delaware's Lotto is a 6/30 game, and Pennsylvania's is a 6/40 game. The cost of a ticket is $1 and the payoff, if your six numbers match the winning numbers drawn at the end of each week, is $6 million or more, depending on the number of tickets purchased. (To date, Pennsylvania has had the largest weekly payoff of $97 million.) In addition to the grand prize, you can win second-, third-, and fourth-prize payoffs by matching five, four, and three of the six numbers drawn, respectively. And you don't have to be a resident of the state to play the state's Lotto game. Anyone can play by calling a toll-free "hotline" number.

Focus

a. Consider Florida's 6/49 Lotto game. Calculate the number of possible ways in which you can choose the six numbers from the 49 available. If you purchase a single $1 ticket, what is the probability that you win the grand prize (i.e., match all six numbers)?

b. Repeat part **a** for Delaware's 6/30 game.

c. Repeat part **a** for Pennsylvania's 6/40 game.

d. Since you can play any state's Lotto game, which of the three, Florida, Delaware, or Pennsylvania, would you choose to play? Why?

e. One strategy used to increase your odds of winning a Lotto is to employ a *wheeling system*. In a complete wheeling system, you select more than six numbers, say, seven, and play every combination of six of those seven numbers. Suppose you choose to "wheel" the following seven numbers in a 6/40 game: 2, 7, 18, 23, 30, 32, 39. How many tickets would you need to purchase to have every possible combination of the seven numbers? List the six numbers on each of these tickets.

continued

f. Refer to part **e**. What is the probability of winning the 6/40 Lotto when you wheel seven numbers? Does the strategy, in fact, increase your odds of winning?

g. Consider the strategy of playing **neighboring pairs**. Neighboring pairs are two consecutive numbers that come up together on the winning ticket. In one state lottery, for example, 79% of the winning tick-

ets had at least one neighboring pair. Thus, some "experts" feel that you have a better chance of winning if you include at least one neighboring pair in your number selection. Calculate the probability of winning the 6/40 Lotto with the six numbers: 2, 15, 19, 20, 27, 37. [*Note:* 19, 20 is a neighboring pair.] Compare this probability to the one in part **c**. Comment on the neighboring pairs strategy.

FIGURE 3.22
Reproduction of Florida's 6/49 Lotto ticket (Statistics in Action 3.2)

EXERCISES 3.52–3.58

Learning the Mechanics

3.52 Suppose you wish to sample $n = 2$ elements from a total of $N = 10$ elements.

a. Count the number of different samples that can be drawn, first by listing them, and then by using combinatorial mathematics. (See Section 3.1.)

b. If random sampling is to be employed, what is the probability that any particular sample will be selected?

c. Show how to use the random number table, Table I in Appendix B, to select a random sample of 2 elements from a population of 10 elements. Perform the sampling procedure 20 times. Do any two of the samples contain the same 2 elements? Given your answer to part **b**, did you expect repeated samples?

3.53 Suppose you wish to sample $n = 3$ elements from a total of $N = 600$ elements.

a. Count the number of different samples by using combinatorial mathematics (see Section 3.1).

b. If random sampling is to be employed, what is the probability that any particular sample will be selected?

c. Show how to use the random number table, Table I in Appendix B, to select a random

sample of 3 elements from a population of 600 elements. Perform the sampling procedure 20 times. Do any two of the samples contain the same three elements? Given your answer to part **b**, did you expect repeated samples?

d. Use a computer to generate a random sample of 3 from the population of 600 elements.

3.54 Suppose that a population contains $N = 200,000$ elements. Use a computer or Table I of Appendix B to select a random sample of $n = 10$ elements from the population. Explain how you selected your sample.

Applying the Concepts

3.55 In auditing a firm's financial statements, an auditor will (1) assess the capability of the firm's accounting system to accumulate, measure, and synthesize transactional data properly, and (2) assess the operational effectiveness of the accounting system. In performing the second assessment, the auditor frequently relies on a random sample of actual transactions (Stickney and Weil, *Financial Accounting: An Introduction to Concepts, Methods, and Uses*, 1994). A particular firm has 5,382 customer accounts that are numbered from 0001 to 5382.

a. One account is to be selected at random for audit. What is the probability that account number 3,241 is selected?

b. Draw a random sample of ten accounts and explain in detail the procedure you used.

c. Refer to part **b**. The following are two possible random samples of size ten. Is one more likely to be selected than the other? Explain.

Sample Number 1				
5011	0082	0963	0772	3415
2663	1126	0008	0026	4189

Sample Number 2				
0001	0003	0005	0007	0009
0002	0004	0006	0008	0010

3.56 To ascertain the effectiveness of their advertising campaigns, firms frequently conduct telephone interviews with consumers. They may use random samples of telephone numbers that are arbitrarily or systematically selected from telephone directories, or they may employ an innovation called *random-digit dialing*. In this approach, a random number generator mechanically creates the sample of phone numbers to be called. An advantage of random-digit dialing is that it can obtain a representative sample from the population of *all* households with telephones, whereas telephone-directory sampling obtains a sample only from the population of households with *listed* telephone numbers.

a. Explain how the random number table (Table I of Appendix B, or a computer) could be used to generate a sample of 7-digit telephone numbers.

b. Use the procedure you described in part **a** to generate a sample of ten 7-digit telephone numbers.

c. Use the procedure you described in part **a** to generate five 7-digit telephone numbers whose first three digits are 373.

3.57 When a company sells shares of stock to investors, the transaction is said to take place in the *primary market*. To enable investors to resell the stock when they wish, *secondary markets* called *stock exchanges* were created. Stock exchange transactions involve buyers and sellers exchanging cash for shares of stock, with none of the proceeds going to the companies that issued the shares (Radcliffe, *Investment: Concepts, Analysis, Strategy,* 1994). The results of the previous business day's transactions for stocks traded on the New York Stock Exchange (NYSE) and five regional exchanges—the Midwest, Pacific, Philadelphia, Boston, and Cincinnati stock exchanges—are summarized each business day in the NYSE–Composite Transactions table in *The Wall Street Journal.*

a. Examine the NYSE–Composite Transactions table in a recent issue of *The Wall Street Journal* and explain how to draw a random sample of stocks from the table.

b. Use the procedure you described in part **a** to draw a random sample of 20 stocks from a recent NYSE–Composite Transactions table. For each stock in the sample, list its name (i.e., the abbreviation given in the table), its sales volume, and its closing price.

3.58 In addition to its decennial enumeration of the population, the U.S. Bureau of the Census regularly samples the population to estimate level of and changes in a number of other attributes, such as income, family size, employment, and marital status. Suppose the bureau plans to sample 1,000 households in a city that has a total of 534,322 households. Show how the bureau could use the random number table in Appendix B or a computer to generate the sample. Select the first 10 households to be included in the sample.

QUICK REVIEW

Key Terms

Additive rule of probability   130
Combinations rule   121
Combinatorial mathematics   121
Complementary events   128
Compound event   126
Conditional probability   135
Event   117

Experiment   112
Independent events   141
Intersection   126
Multiplicative rule   138
Multiplicative rule of probability   138
Mutually exclusive events   130
Probability rules   116

Random number generator   149
Random sample   148
Sample point   113
Sample space   114
Tree diagram   140
Union   126
Venn diagram   114

Key Formulas

$P(A) + P(A^c) = 1$ Complementary events   129

$P(A \cup B) = P(A) + P(B) - P(A \cap B)$ Additive rule   130

$P(A \cap B) = 0$ Mutually exclusive events   130

$P(A \cup B) = P(A) + P(B)$ Additive rule for mutually exclusive events   131

$P(A|B) = \dfrac{P(A \cap B)}{P(B)}$ Conditional probability   136

$P(A \cap B) = P(A)P(B|A) = P(B)P(A|B)$ Multiplicative rule   138

$P(A|B) = P(A)$ Independent events   141

$P(A \cap B) = P(A)P(B)$ Multiplicative rule for independent events   143

$\dbinom{N}{n} = \dfrac{N!}{n!(N-n)!}$ Combinatorial rule   121

where $N! = N(N-1)(N-2)\cdots(2)(1)$

LANGUAGE LAB

Symbol	Pronunciation	Description
S		Sample space
$S: \{1,2,3,4,5\}$		Set of sample points, 1, 2, 3, 4, 5, in sample space
$A: \{1,2\}$		Set of sample points, 1, 2, in event A
$P(A)$	Probability of A	Probability that event A occurs
$A \cup B$	A union B	Union of events A and B (either A or B or both occur)
$A \cap B$	A intersect B	Intersection of events A and B (both A and B occur)
A^c	A complement	Complement of event A (the event that A does not occur)
$P(A|B)$	Probability of A given B	Conditional probability that event A occurs given that event B occurs
$\dbinom{N}{n}$	N chose n	Number of combinations of N elements taken n at a time
$N!$	N factorial	Multiply $N(N-1)(N-2)\cdots(2)(1)$

SUPPLEMENTARY EXERCISES   3.59–3.88

Learning the Mechanics

3.59 What are the two rules that probabilities assigned to sample points must obey?

3.60 Are mutually exclusive events also dependent events? Explain.

3.61 Given that $P(A \cap B) = .4$ and $P(A|B) = .8$, find $P(B)$.

3.62 Which of the following pairs of events are mutually exclusive? Justify your response.
  a. {The Dow Jones Industrial Average increases on Monday}, {A large New York bank decreases its prime interest rate on Monday}
  b. {The next sale by a PC retailer is an IBM compatible microcomputer}, {The next sale by a PC retailer is an Apple microcomputer}
  c. {You reinvest all your dividend income for 1997 in a limited partnership}, {You reinvest all your dividend income for 1997 in a money market fund}

3.63 The accompanying Venn diagram illustrates a sample space containing six sample points and three events, A, B, and C. The probabilities of the sample points are: $P(1) = .3, P(2) = .2, P(3) = .1, P(4) = .1, P(5) = .1,$ and $P(6) = .2$.

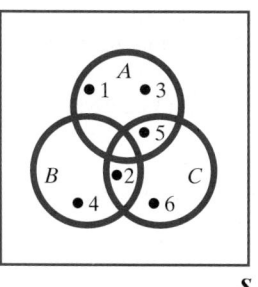

S

  a. Find $P(A \cap B), P(B \cap C), P(A \cup C), P(A \cup B \cup C),$ $P(B^c), P(A^c \cap B), P(B|C),$ and $P(B|A)$.
  b. Are A and B independent? Mutually exclusive? Why?

(continued)

c. Are B and C independent? Mutually exclusive? Why?

3.64 Two events, A and B, are independent, with $P(A) = .3$ and $P(B) = .1$.
  a. Are A and B mutually exclusive? Why?
  b. Find $P(A|B)$ and $P(B|A)$.
  c. Find $P(A \cup B)$.

3.65 Find the numerical value of:
  a. $6!$ **b.** $\binom{10}{9}$ **c.** $\binom{10}{1}$ **d.** $\binom{6}{3}$ **e.** $0!$

3.66 A random sample of five graduate students is to be selected from 50 MBA majors for participation in a case competition.
  a. In how many different ways can the sample be drawn?
  b. Show how the random number table, Table I of Appendix B, can be used to select the sample of students.

Applying the Concepts

3.67 A research and development company surveyed all 200 of its employees over the age of 60 and obtained the information given in the table below. One of these 200 employees is selected at random.
  a. What is the probability that the person selected is on the technical staff?
  b. If the person selected has over 20 years of service with the company, what is the probability that the person plans to retire at age 68?
  c. If the person selected is on the technical staff, what is the probability that the person has been with the company less than 20 years?
  d. What is the probability that the person selected has over 20 years with the company, is on the nontechnical staff, and plans to retire at age 65?
  e. Consider the events A: {Plan to retire at age 68} and B: {On the technical staff}. Are events A and B independent? Explain.
  f. Consider the event D: {Plan to retire at age 68 *and* on the technical staff}. Describe the complement of event D.
  g. Consider the event E: {On the nontechnical staff}. Are events B and E mutually exclusive? Explain.

3.68 Many U.S. manufacturers are adopting the ISO 9000 series of standards for setting up and documenting quality systems, processes, and procedures. However, it is not generally known how managers who have led or participated in the implementation of the standards view them or how the standards were achieved. A sample of 40 ISO 9000–registered companies in Colorado was selected and the manager most responsible for ISO 9000 implementation was interviewed (*Quality Progress*, 1995). The following are some of the data obtained by the study:

Level of Top Management Involvement in the ISO 9000 Registration Process	Frequency
Very involved	9
Moderate involvement	16
Minimal involvement	12
Not involved	3

Length of Time to Achieve ISO 9000 Registration	Frequency
Less than 1 year	5
1–1.5 years	21
1.6–2 years	9
2.1–2.5 years	2
More than 2.5 years	3

Source: Weston, F. C., "What do managers really think of the ISO 9000 registration process?" *Quality Progress*, October 1995, p. 68–69 (Tables 3 and 4).

Suppose one of the 40 managers who were interviewed is to be randomly selected for additional questioning. Consider the events defined below:

A: {The manager was involved in the ISO 9000 registration}

B: {The length of time to achieve ISO 9000 registration was more than 2 years}

  a. Find $P(A)$.
  b. Find $P(B)$.
  c. Explain why the above data are not sufficient to determine whether events A and B are independent.

3.69 The table on page 156 lists the overall percentage of domestic flights of major U.S. airlines that arrived on time during June 1995.
  a. One of these ten airlines is to be selected at random. What is the probability that Southwest is selected? That Continental is selected?
  b. If one of Continental's domestic flights during June 1995 were randomly selected, what is the

	UNDER 20 YEARS WITH COMPANY		OVER 20 YEARS WITH COMPANY	
	Technical Staff	Nontechnical Staff	Technical Staff	Nontechnical Staff
Plan to Retire at Age 65	31	5	45	12
Plan to Retire at Age 68	59	25	15	8

Carrier	Percent Arriving on Time
Southwest	82.9
American	78.5
Northwest	78.4
USAir	77.0
America West	75.8
United	75.4
Delta	74.3
TWA	72.9
Alaska	70.0
Continental	64.1

Source: Aviation Daily, August 7, 1995.

probability that the flight arrived on time? Was late?

c. These data are reported each month by the airlines to the U.S. Department of Transportation. Consequently, some experts question their accuracy. With this in mind, would you recommend that these percentages be treated as upper or lower bounds for the actual on-time percentages? Explain.

3.70 The state legislature has appropriated $1 million to be distributed in the form of grants to individuals and organizations engaged in the research and development of alternative energy sources. You have been hired by the state's energy agency to assemble a panel of five energy experts whose task it will be to determine which individuals and organizations should receive the grant money. You have identified 11 equally qualified individuals who are willing to serve on the panel. How many different panels of five experts could be formed from these 11 individuals?

3.71 A manufacturer of electronic digital watches claims that the probability of its watch running more than 1 minute slow or 1 minute fast after 1 year of use is .05. A consumer protection agency has purchased four of the manufacturer's watches with the intention of testing the claim.

a. Assuming that the manufacturer's claim is correct, what is the probability that none of the watches are as accurate as claimed?

b. Assuming that the manufacturer's claim is correct, what is the probability that exactly two of the four watches are as accurate as claimed?

c. Suppose that only one of the four tested watches is as accurate as claimed. What inference can be made about the manufacturer's claim? Explain.

d. Suppose that none of the watches tested are as accurate as claimed. Is it necessarily true that the manufacturer's claim is false? Explain.

3.72 The corporations in the highly competitive razor blade industry do a tremendous amount of advertising each year. Corporation G gave a supply of three top name brands, G, S, and W, to a consumer and asked her to use them and rank them in order of preference. The corporation was, of course, hoping the consumer would prefer its brand and rank it first, thereby giving them some material for a consumer interview advertising campaign. If the consumer did not prefer one blade over any other, but was still required to rank the blades, what is the probability that:

a. The consumer ranked brand G first?

b. The consumer ranked brand G last?

c. The consumer ranked brand G last and brand W second?

d. The consumer ranked brand W first, brand G second, and brand S third?

3.73 Two marketing research companies, Richard Saunders International and Marketing Intelligence Service, joined forces to create a consumer preference poll called Acupoll. Acupoll is used to predict whether newly developed products will succeed if they are brought to market. The reliability of the Acupoll has been described as follows: The probability that Acupoll predicts the success of a particular product, given that later the product actually is successful, is .89 (*Minneapolis Star Tribune,* Dec. 16, 1992). A company is considering the introduction of a new product and assesses the product's probability of success to be .90. If this company were to have its product evaluated through Acupoll, what is the probability that Acupoll predicts success for the product and the product actually turns out to be successful?

3.74 Use your intuitive understanding of independence to form an opinion about whether each of the following scenarios represents an independent event.

a. The results of consecutive tosses of a coin

b. The opinions of randomly selected individuals in a preelection poll

c. A major league baseball player's results in two consecutive at-bats

d. The amount of gain or loss associated with investments in different stocks if these stocks are bought on the same day and sold on the same day one month later

e. The amount of gain or loss associated with investments in different stocks that are bought and sold in different time periods, five years apart

f. The prices bid by two different development firms in response to a building construction proposal

3.75 A local country club has a membership of 600 and operates facilities that include an 18-hole championship golf course and 12 tennis courts. Before deciding whether to accept new members, the club president would like to know how many members regularly use each facility. A survey of the membership indicates that 70% regularly use the golf course, 50% regularly use the tennis courts, and 5% use neither of these facilities regularly.

a. Construct a Venn diagram to describe the results of the survey.

b. If one club member is chosen at random, what is the probability that the member uses either the golf course or the tennis courts or both?

c. If one member is chosen at random, what is the probability that the member uses both the golf and the tennis facilities?

d. A member is chosen at random from among those known to use the tennis courts regularly. What is the probability that the member also uses the golf course regularly?

3.76 Insurance companies use *mortality tables* to help them determine how large a premium to charge a particular individual for a particular life insurance policy. The accompanying table shows the probability of survival to age 65 for persons of the specified ages.

Age	Probability of Survival to Age 65
0	.72
10	.74
20	.74
30	.75
35	.76
40	.77
45	.79
50	.81
55	.85
60	.90

a. For a person 20 years old, what is the probability that he or she will die before age 65?

b. Describe in words the trend indicated by the increasing probabilities in the second and fourth columns.

3.77 "What are the characteristics of families with young children (under age 6)?" This was one of several questions posed by a University of Michigan researcher in *Children and Youth Services Review* (Vol. 17, 1995). Using data obtained from the National Child Care Survey, the income distribution and employment status of these families are summarized in the table below:

a. Find the probability that a randomly selected family with young children has an income above the poverty line, but less than $25,000.

b. Find the probability that a randomly selected family with young children has unemployed parents or no parents.

c. Find the probability that a randomly selected family with young children has an income below the poverty line.

3.78 All-terrain vehicles (ATVs) came under fire in the 1980s owing to the high number of injuries and deaths attributed to these machines. In response, manufacturers agreed to provide extensive safety warnings to owners, to develop a media safety-awareness program, and to implement a nationwide training program. The *Journal of Risk and Uncertainty* (May 1992) published an article investigating the relationship of injury rate to a variety of factors. One of the more interesting factors studied, age of the driver, was found to have a strong relationship to injury rate. The article reports that prior to the safety-awareness program, 14% of the ATV drivers were under age 12; another 13% were 12–15, and 48% were under age 25. Suppose an ATV driver is selected at random prior to the installation of the safety-awareness program.

a. Find the probability that the ATV driver is 15 years old or younger.

b. Find the probability that the ATV driver is 25 years old or older.

c. Given that the ATV driver is under age 25, what is the probability the driver is under age 12?

d. Are the events Under age 25 and Under age 12 mutually exclusive? Why or why not?

e. Are the events Under age 25 and Under age 12 independent? Why or why not?

3.79 The probability that an Avon salesperson sells beauty products to a prospective customer on the first visit to the customer is .4. If the salesperson fails to make the sale on the first visit, the probability that the sale will be made on the second visit is .65. The salesperson never visits a prospective customer more than twice. What is the probability

Income Characteristic	Percentage
No parent	1
Below poverty line; not employed	7
Below poverty line; employed	7
Above poverty line, but less than $25,000; not employed	2
Above poverty line, but less than $25,000; employed	22
$25,000 or more	61
Total	100

A System Comprised of Three Components in Series

that the salesperson will make a sale to a particular customer?

3.80 The performance of quality inspectors affects both the quality of outgoing products and the cost of the products. A product that passes inspection is assumed to meet quality standards; a product that fails inspection may be reworked, scrapped, or reinspected. Quality engineers at Westinghouse Electric Corporation evaluated performances of inspectors in judging the quality of solder joints by comparing each inspector's classifications of a set of 153 joints with the consensus evaluation of a panel of experts. The results for a particular inspector are shown in the accompanying table.

	INSPECTOR'S JUDGMENT	
Committee's Judgment	**Joint Acceptable**	**Joint Rejectable**
Joint acceptable	101	10
Joint rejectable	23	19

Source: Meagher, J. J., and Scazzero, J. A. "Measuring inspector variability." *39th Annual Quality Congress Transactions,* May 1985, pp. 75–81, American Society for Quality Control.

One of the 153 solder joints is to be selected at random.

a. What is the probability that the inspector judges the joint to be acceptable? That the committee judges the joint to be acceptable?

b. What is the probability that both the inspector and the committee judge the joint to be acceptable? That neither judge the joint to be acceptable?

c. What is the probability that the inspector and the committee disagree? Agree?

3.81 The figure shown above is a schematic representation of a system comprised of three components. The system operates properly only if all three components operate properly. The three components are said to operate *in series*. The components could be mechanical or electrical; they could be work stations in an assembly process; or they could represent the functions of three different

departments in an organization. The probability of failure for each component is listed in the table. Assume the components operate independently of each other.

Component	Probability of Failure
1	.12
2	.09
3	.11

a. Find the probability that the system operates properly.

b. What is the probability that at least one of the components will fail and therefore that the system will fail?

3.82 The figure below is a representation of a system comprised of two subsystems that are said to operate *in parallel*. Each subsystem has two components that operate in series (refer to Exercise 3.81). The system will operate properly as long as at least one of the subsystems functions properly. The probability of failure for each component in the system is .1. Assume the components operate independently of each other.

a. Find the probability that the system operates properly.

b. Find the probability that exactly one subsystem fails.

c. Find the probability that the system fails to operate properly.

d. How many parallel subsystems like the two shown here would be required to guarantee that the system would operate properly at least 99% of the time?

3.83 Consider the population of new savings accounts opened in one business day at a bank, as shown in the table. Suppose you wish to draw a random sample of two accounts from this population.

Account Number	0001	0002	0003	0004	0005
Account Balance	$1,000	$12,500	$850	$1,000	$3,450

A System Comprised of Two Parallel Subsystems

a. List all possible different pairs of accounts that could be obtained.

b. What is the probability of selecting accounts 0001 and 0004?

c. What is the probability of selecting two accounts that each have a balance of $1,000? That each have a balance other than $1,000?

3.84 Two hundred shoppers at a large suburban mall were asked two questions: (1) Did you see a television ad for the sale at department store X during the past two weeks? (2) Did you shop at department store X during the past two weeks? The responses to these questions are summarized in the table. One of the 200 shoppers questioned is to be chosen at random.

	Shopped at X	Did Not Shop at X
Saw ad	100	25
Did not see ad	25	50

a. What is the probability that the person selected saw the ad?

b. What is the probability that the person selected saw the ad and shopped at store X?

c. Find the conditional probability that the person shopped at store X given that the person saw the ad.

d. What is the probability that the person selected shopped at store X?

e. Use your answers to parts **a**, **b**, and **d** to check the independence of the events {Saw ad} and {Shopped at X}.

f. Are the two events {Did not see ad} and {Did not shop at X} mutually exclusive? Explain.

3.85 The National Resident Matching Program (NRMP) is a service provided by the Association of American Medical Colleges to match graduating medical students with residency appointments at hospitals. After students and hospitals have evaluated each other, they submit rank-order lists of their preferences to the NRMP. Using a matching algorithm, the NRMP then generates final, nonnegotiable assignments of students to the residency programs of hospitals (*Academic Medicine*, June 1995). Assume that three graduating medical students (#1, #2, and #3) have applied for positions at three different hospitals (A, B, and C), where each hospital has one and only one resident opening.

a. How many different assignments of medical students to hospitals are possible? List them.

b. Suppose student #1 prefers hospital B. If the NRMP algorithm is entirely random, what is the probability that the student is assigned to hospital B?

3.86 A small brewery has two bottling machines. Machine A produces 75% of the bottles and machine B produces 25%. One out of every 20 bottles filled by A is rejected for some reason, while one out of every 30 bottles from B is rejected. What proportion of bottles is rejected? What is the probability that a randomly selected bottle comes from machine A, given that it is accepted?

3.87 Suppose there are 500 applicants for five equivalent positions at a factory and the company is able to narrow the field to 30 equally qualified applicants. Seven of the finalists are minority candidates. Assume that the five who are chosen are selected at random from this final group of 30.

a. In how many different ways can the selection be made?

b. What is the probability that none of the minority candidates is hired?

c. What is the probability that no more than one minority candidate is hired?

3.88 A fair coin is flipped 20 times and 20 heads are observed. In such cases it is often said that a tail is due on the next flip. Is this statement true or false? Explain.

CHAPTER 4

DISCRETE RANDOM VARIABLES

CONTENTS

STATISTICS IN ACTION

Where We've Been

We saw by illustration in Chapter 3 how probability would be used to make an inference about a population from data contained in an observed sample. We also noted that probability would be used to measure the reliability of the inference.

Where We're Going

Most of the experimental events we encountered in Chapter 3 were events described in words and denoted by capital letters. In real life, most sample observations are numerical—in other words, they are numerical data. In this chapter, we learn that data are observed values of random variables. We study two important random variables and learn how to find the probabilities of specific numerical outcomes.

FIGURE 4.1
Venn diagram for coin-tossing experiment

You may have noticed that many of the examples of experiments in Chapter 3 generated quantitative (numerical) observations. The Consumer Price Index, the unemployment rate, the number of sales made in a week, and the yearly profit of a company are all examples of numerical measurements of some phenomenon. Thus, most experiments have sample points that correspond to values of some numerical variable.

To illustrate, consider the coin-tossing experiment of Chapter 3. Figure 4.1 is a Venn diagram showing the sample points when two coins are tossed and the up faces (heads or tails) of the coins are observed. One possible numerical outcome is the total number of heads observed. These values (0, 1, or 2) are shown in parentheses on the Venn diagram, one numerical value associated with each sample point. In the jargon of probability, the variable "total number of heads observed in two tosses of a coin" is called a **random variable**.

DEFINITION 4.1
A **random variable** is a variable that assumes numerical values associated with the random outcomes of an experiment, where one (and only one) numerical value is assigned to each sample point.

The term *random variable* is more meaningful than the term *variable* because the adjective *random* indicates that the coin-tossing experiment may result in one of the several possible values of the variable—0, 1, and 2—according to the *random* outcome of the experiment, *HH, HT, TH,* and *TT*. Similarly, if the experiment is to count the number of customers who use the drive-up window of a bank each day, the random variable (the number of customers) will vary from day to day, partly because of the random phenomena that influence whether customers use the drive-up window. Thus, the possible values of this random variable range from 0 to the maximum number of customers the window could possibly serve in a day.

We define two different types of random variables, *discrete* and *continuous,* in Section 4.1. Then we spend the remainder of this chapter discussing specific types of discrete random variables and the aspects that make them important in business applications. We discuss continuous random variables in Chapter 5.

4.1 TWO TYPES OF RANDOM VARIABLES

Recall that the sample point probabilities corresponding to an experiment must sum to 1. Dividing one unit of probability among the sample points in a sample space and consequently assigning probabilities to the values of a random variable is not always as easy as the examples in Chapter 3 might lead you to believe. If the number of sample points can be completely listed, the job is straightforward. But if the experiment results in an infinite number of numerical sample points that are impossible to list, the task of assigning probabilities to the sample points is impossible without the aid of a probability model. The next three examples demonstrate the need for different probability models depending on the number of values that a random variable can assume.

EXAMPLE 4.1

A panel of 10 experts for the *Wine Spectator* (a national publication) is asked to taste a new white wine and assign a rating of 0, 1, 2, or 3. A score is then obtained by adding together the ratings of the 10 experts. How many values can this random variable assume?

SOLUTION

A sample point is a sequence of 10 numbers associated with the rating of each expert. For example, one sample point is

$$\{1, 0, 0, 1, 2, 0, 0, 3, 1, 0\}.$$

The random variable assigns a score to each one of these sample points by adding the 10 numbers together. Thus, the smallest score is 0 (if all 10 ratings are 0) and the largest score is 30 (if all 10 ratings are 3). Since every integer between 0 and 30 is a possible score, the random variable denoted by the symbol x can assume 31 values. Note that the value of the random variable for the sample point above is $x = 8$.*

This is an example of a **discrete random variable**, since there is a finite number of distinct possible values. Whenever all the possible values a random variable can assume can be listed (or counted), the random variable is discrete.

EXAMPLE 4.2

Suppose the Environmental Protection Agency (EPA) takes readings once a month on the amount of pesticide in the discharge water of a chemical company. If the amount of pesticide exceeds the maximum level set by the EPA, the company is forced to take corrective action and may be subject to penalty. Consider the following random variable:

Number, x, of months before the company's discharge exceeds the EPA's maximum level

What values can x assume?

SOLUTION

The company's discharge of pesticide may exceed the maximum allowable level on the first month of testing, the second month of testing, etc. It is possible that the company's discharge will *never* exceed the maximum level. Thus, the set of possible values for the number of months until the level is first exceeded is the set of all positive integers

$$1, 2, 3, 4, \ldots$$

If we can list the values of a random variable x, even though the list is never-ending, we call the list **countable** and the corresponding random variable *discrete*. Thus, the number of months until the company's discharge first exceeds the limit is a *discrete random variable*.   ▟

EXAMPLE 4.3

Refer to Example 4.2. A second random variable of interest is the amount x of pesticide (in milligrams per liter) found in the monthly sample of discharge waters from the chemical company. What values can this random variable assume?

---

*The standard mathematical convention is to use a capital letter (e.g., X) to denote the theoretical random variable. The possible values (or realizations) of the random variable are typically denoted with a lowercase letter (e.g., x). Thus, in Example 4.1, the random variable X can take on the values $x = 0, 1, 2, \ldots, 30$. Since this notation can be confusing for introductory statistics students, we simplify the notation by using the lowercase x to represent the random variable throughout.

SOLUTION

Unlike the *number* of months before the company's discharge exceeds the EPA's maximum level, the set of all possible values for the *amount* of discharge *cannot* be listed—i.e., is not countable. The possible values for the amounts of pesticide would correspond to the points on the interval between 0 and the largest possible value the amount of the discharge could attain, the maximum number of milligrams that could occupy 1 liter of volume. (Practically, the interval would be much smaller, say, between 0 and 500 milligrams per liter.) When the values of a random variable are not countable but instead correspond to the points on some interval, we call it a **continuous random variable**. Thus, the *amount* of pesticide in the chemical plant's discharge waters is a *continuous random variable*.

DEFINITION 4.2
Random variables that can assume a *countable* number of values are called **discrete**.

DEFINITION 4.3
Random variables that can assume values corresponding to any of the points contained in one or more intervals are called **continuous**.

Several more examples of discrete random variables follow:

1. The number of sales made by a salesperson in a given week: $x = 0, 1, 2, \ldots$
2. The number of consumers in a sample of 500 who favor a particular product over all competitors: $x = 0, 1, 2, \ldots, 500$
3. The number of bids received in a bond offering: $x = 0, 1, 2, \ldots$
4. The number of errors on a page of an accountant's ledger: $x = 0, 1, 2, \ldots$
5. The number of customers waiting to be served in a restaurant at a particular time: $x = 0, 1, 2, \ldots$

Note that each of the examples of discrete random variables begins with the words "The number of ..." This wording is very common, since the discrete random variables most frequently observed are counts.

We conclude this section with some more examples of continuous random variables:

1. The length of time between arrivals at a hospital clinic: $0 \leqslant x < \infty$ (infinity)
2. For a new apartment complex, the length of time from completion until a specified number of apartments are rented: $0 \leqslant x < \infty$
3. The amount of carbonated beverage loaded into a 12-ounce can in a can-filling operation: $0 \leqslant x \leqslant 12$
4. The depth at which a successful oil drilling venture first strikes oil: $0 \leqslant x \leqslant c$, where c is the maximum depth obtainable
5. The weight of a food item bought in a supermarket: $0 \leqslant x \leqslant 500$ [*Note:* Theoretically, there is no upper limit on x, but it is unlikely that it would exceed 500 pounds.]

Discrete random variables and their probability distributions are discussed in this chapter. Continuous random variables and their probability distributions are the topic of Chapter 5.

EXERCISES   4.1–4.10

Applying the Concepts

4.1   What is a random variable?

4.2   How do discrete and continuous random variables differ?

4.3   Security analysts are professionals who devote full-time efforts to evaluating the investment worth of a narrow list of stocks. For example, one security analyst might specialize in bank stocks while another specializes in evaluating firms in the computer or pharmaceutical industries. The following variables are of interest to security analysts (Radcliffe, *Investments: Concepts, Analysis and Strategy,* 1994). Which are discrete and which are continuous random variables?
  a. The closing price of a particular stock on the New York Stock Exchange.
  b. The number of shares of a particular stock that are traded each business day.
  c. The quarterly earnings of a particular firm.
  d. The percentage change in yearly earnings between 1996 and 1997 for a particular firm.
  e. The number of new products introduced per year by a firm.
  f. The time until a pharmaceutical company gains approval from the U.S. Food and Drug Administration to market a new drug.

4.4   Which of the following describe continuous random variables, and which describe discrete random variables?
  a. The number of newspapers sold by the *New York Times* each month
  b. The amount of ink used in printing a Sunday edition of the *New York Times*
  c. The actual number of ounces in a one-gallon bottle of laundry detergent
  d. The number of defective parts in a shipment of nuts and bolts
  e. The number of people collecting unemployment insurance each month

4.5   Give two examples of a business-oriented discrete random variable. Do the same for a continuous random variable.

4.6   Give an example of a discrete random variable that would be of interest to a banker.

4.7   Give an example of a continuous random variable that would be of interest to an economist.

4.8   Give an example of a discrete random variable that would be of interest to the manager of a hotel.

4.9   Give two examples of discrete random variables that would be of interest to the manager of a clothing store.

4.10   Give an example of a continuous random variable that would be of interest to a stockbroker.

4.2   PROBABILITY DISTRIBUTIONS FOR DISCRETE RANDOM VARIABLES

A complete description of a discrete random variable requires that we *specify the possible values the random variable can assume and the probability associated with each value.* To illustrate, consider Example 4.4.

EXAMPLE 4.4

Recall the experiment of tossing two coins (Section 4.1), and let x be the number of heads observed. Find the probability associated with each value of the random variable x, assuming the two coins are fair.

SOLUTION

The sample space and sample points for this experiment are reproduced in Figure 4.2. Note that the random variable x can assume values 0, 1, 2. Recall (from Chapter 3) that the probability associated with each of the four sample points is $\frac{1}{4}$. Then, identifying the probabilities of the sample points associated with each of these values of x, we have

$$P(x = 0) = P(TT) = \frac{1}{4}$$
$$P(x = 1) = P(TH) + P(HT) = \frac{1}{4} + \frac{1}{4} = \frac{1}{2}$$
$$P(x = 2) = P(HH) = \frac{1}{4}$$

Thus, we now know the values the random variable can assume (0, 1, 2) and how the probability is *distributed over* these values $(\frac{1}{4}, \frac{1}{2}, \frac{1}{4})$. This completely describes the random variable and is referred to as the *probability distribution,*

HH • $x = 2$	*HT* • $x = 1$
TH • $x = 1$	*TT* • $x = 0$

S

FIGURE 4.2
Venn diagram for the two-coin-toss experiment

TABLE 4.1   Probability Distribution for Coin-Toss Experiment: Tabular Form

x	$p(x)$
0	$1/4$
1	$1/2$
2	$1/4$

FIGURE 4.3
Probability distribution for coin-toss experiment: Graphical form

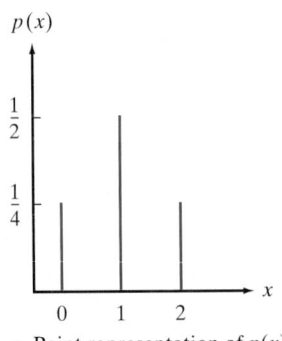

a. Point representation of $p(x)$

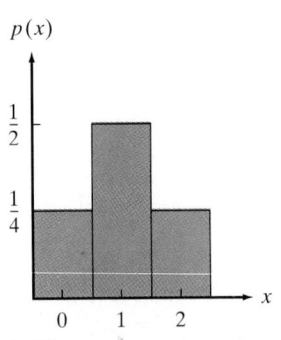

b. Histogram representation of $p(x)$

denoted by the symbol $p(x)$.* The probability distribution for the coin-toss example is shown in tabular form in Table 4.1 and in graphic form in Figure 4.3. Since the probability distribution for a discrete random variable is concentrated at specific points (values of x), the graph in Figure 4.3a represents the probabilities as the heights of vertical lines over the corresponding values of x. Although the representation of the probability distribution as a histogram, as in Figure 4.3b, is less precise (since the probability is spread over a unit interval), the histogram representation will prove useful when we approximate probabilities of certain discrete random variables in Section 4.4.

We could also present the probability distribution for x as a formula, but this would unnecessarily complicate a very simple example. We give the formulas for the probability distributions of some common discrete random variables later in this chapter.

DEFINITION 4.4

The **probability distribution** of a discrete random variable is a graph, table, or formula that specifies the probability associated with each possible value the random variable can assume.

Two requirements must be satisfied by all probability distributions for discrete random variables.

Requirements for the Probability Distribution of a Discrete Random Variable, x

$p(x) \geqslant 0 \qquad$ for all values of x

$$\sum p(x) = 1$$

where the summation of $p(x)$ is over all possible values of x.†

Example 4.4 illustrates how the probability distribution for a discrete random variable can be derived, but for many practical situations the task is much more difficult. Fortunately, many experiments and associated discrete random variables

---

*In standard mathematical notation, the probability that a random variable X takes on a value x is denoted $P(X = x) = p(x)$. Thus, $P(X = 0) = p(0)$, $P(X = 1) = p(1)$, etc. In this introductory text, we adopt the simpler $p(x)$ notation.

†Unless otherwise indicated, summations will always be over all possible values of x.

observed in business possess identical characteristics. Thus, you might observe a random variable in a marketing experiment that would possess the same characteristics as a random variable observed in accounting, economics, or management. We classify random variables according to type of experiment, derive the probability distribution for each of the different types, and then use the appropriate probability distribution when a particular type of random variable is observed in a practical situation. The probability distributions for most commonly occurring discrete random variables have already been derived. This fact simplifies the problem of finding the appropriate probability distributions for the business analyst.

In Sections 4.4 and 4.5, we describe two important types of discrete random variables, give their probability distributions, and explain where and how they can be applied in practice. (Mathematical derivations of the probability distributions will be omitted, but these details can be found in the references at the back of the book.)

But first, in Section 4.3, we discuss some descriptive measures of these sometimes complex probability distributions. Since probability distributions are analogous to the relative frequency distributions of Chapter 2, it should be no surprise that the mean and standard deviation are useful descriptive measures.

EXERCISES   4.11–4.20

Learning the Mechanics

4.11 A discrete random variable x can assume five possible values: 2, 3, 5, 8, and 10. Its probability distribution is shown here:

x	2	3	5	8	10
$p(x)$	.15	.10	—	.25	.25

a. What is $p(5)$?
b. What is the probability that x equals 2 or 10?
c. What is $P(x \leqslant 8)$?

4.12 Explain why each of the following is or is not a valid probability distribution for a discrete random variable x:

a.

x	0	1	2	3
$p(x)$	.1	.3	.3	.2

b.

x	−2	−1	0
$p(x)$	.25	.50	.25

c.

x	4	9	20
$p(x)$	−.3	.4	.3

d.

x	2	3	5	6
$p(x)$	.15	.15	.45	.35

4.13 Toss three fair coins and let x equal the number of heads observed.

a. Identify the sample points associated with this experiment and assign a value of x to each sample point.
b. Calculate $p(x)$ for each value of x.
c. Construct a probability histogram for $p(x)$.
d. What is $P(x = 2 \text{ or } x = 3)$?

4.14 The random variable x has the following discrete probability distribution:

x	1	3	5	7	9
$p(x)$	.1	.2	.4	.2	.1

a. Find $P(x \leqslant 3)$. b. Find $P(x < 3)$.
c. Find $P(x = 7)$. d. Find $P(x \geqslant 5)$.
e Find $P(x > 2)$. f. Find $P(3 \leqslant x \leqslant 9)$.

4.15 A die is tossed. Let x be the number of spots observed on the upturned face of the die.

a. Find the probability distribution of x and display it in tabular form.
b. Display the probability distribution of x in graphical form.

Applying the Concepts

4.16 A team of consultants studied the service operation at the Wendy's Restaurant in the Woodbridge Mall in Woodbridge, New Jersey. They measured the time between customer arrivals to the restaurant over the course of a day and used those data to develop a probability distribution to characterize x,

x	5	6	7	8	9	10	11	12	13	14	15
$p(x)$	.01	.02	.03	.05	.08	.09	.11	.13	.12	.10	.08

x	16	17	18	19	20	21
$p(x)$	.06	.05	.03	.02	.01	.01

Source: Ford, R., Roberts, D., and Saxton, P. *Queuing Models.* Graduate School of Management, Rutgers University, 1992.

the number of customer arrivals per 15-minute period. The distribution is shown above.

a. Does this distribution meet the two requirements for the probability distribution of a discrete random variable? Justify your answer.

b. What is the probability that exactly 16 customers enter the restaurant in the next 15 minutes?

c. Find $p(x \leq 10)$. d. Find $p(5 \leq x \leq 15)$.

4.17 In a study of tax write-offs by the affluent, Peter Dreier of Occidental College (Los Angeles) compiled the relative frequency distribution shown below. The distribution describes the incomes of all households in the United States that filed tax returns in 1995. A household is to be randomly sampled from this population.

a. Explain why the percentages in the table can be interpreted as probabilities. For example, the probability of selecting a household with income under $10,000 is .185.

b. Find the probability that the selected household has income over $200,000; over $100,000; less than $100,000; between $30,000 and $49,999.

c. Together, the income categories (1, 2, 3, …) and the percentages form a discrete probability distribution. Graph this distribution.

d. What is the probability that the randomly selected household will fall in income category 6? In income category 1 or 9?

Income Category	Household Income	Percentage of Households
1	Under $10,000	18.5
2	$10,000 to $19,999	19.0
3	$20,000 to $29,999	15.9
4	$30,000 to $39,999	12.8
5	$40,000 to $49,999	9.1
6	$50,000 to $74,999	13.8
7	$75,000 to $99,999	5.7
8	$100,000 to $199,999	4.1
9	$200,000 and over	1.1

Source: Johnston, D. C. "The Divine Write-off." *New York Times,* January 12, 1996, p. D1.

4.18 In 1993, President Clinton encountered difficulties in appointing an attorney general. One troublesome issue involved the nominees' hiring of illegal aliens and/or failing to pay Social Security taxes for their domestic help. Both of these practices are against the law. Suppose that a study reveals that 10% of households with incomes exceeding $50,000 annually have hired an illegal alien and/or failed to pay Social Security taxes. Let x be the number of households with incomes in that range who are contacted before one that has not broken either law is found.

a. What is the range of possible values for x?

b. Find $P(x < 3)$.

c. Find $P(x > 2)$.

d. Find the probability distribution for values of x from 1 to 10 and graph it over that domain. Can x exceed 10?

4.19 Many real-world systems (e.g., electric power transmission, transportation, telecommunications, and manufacturing systems) can be regarded as capacitated-flow networks, whose arcs have independent but random capacities. A team of Chinese university professors investigated the reliability of several flow networks in the journal *Networks* (May 1995). One network examined in the article, and illustrated on page 169, is a bridge network with arcs a_1, a_2, a_3, a_4, a_5, and a_6. The probability distribution of the capacity x for each of the six arcs is also provided on page 169.

a. Verify that the properties of discrete probability distributions are satisfied for each arc capacity distribution.

b. Find the probability that the capacity for arc a_1 will exceed 1.

c. Repeat part **b** for each of the remaining five arcs.

d. One path from the source node to the sink node is through arcs a_1 and a_2. Find the probability that the system maintains a capacity of more than 1 through the a_1–a_2 path. (Recall that the arc capacities are independent.)

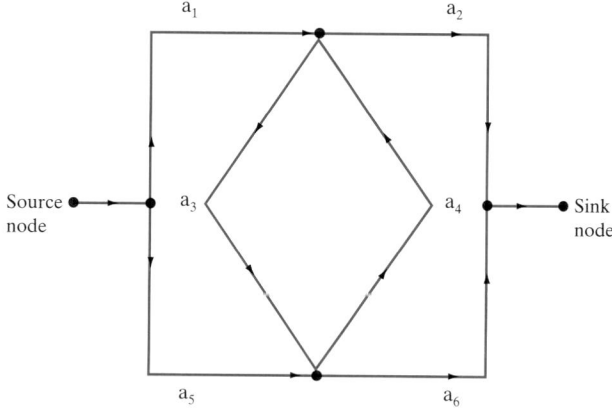

Arc	Capacity (x)	p(x)
a_1	3	.60
	2	.25
	1	.10
	0	.05
a_2	2	.60
	1	.30
	0	.10
a_3	1	.90
	0	.10

Arc	Capacity (x)	p(x)
a_4	1	.90
	0	.10
a_5	1	.90
	0	.10
a_6	2	.70
	1	.25
	0	.05

Source: Lin, J., *et al.* "On reliability evaluation of capacitated-flow network in terms of minimal pathsets." *Networks,* Vol. 25, No. 3, May 1995, p. 135 (Table 1), 1995, John Wiley and Sons.

4.20   Probabilities that are used for forecasting are known as *probability forecasts* or *probabilistic predictions* (Wright and Ayton, *Subjective Probability,* 1994). A team of management scientists used probability forecasts to help the city of Minneapolis (Minnesota) deal with an increased incidence of Dutch elm disease fungus. One year, the fungus had destroyed 16% of all the city's elm trees. To prevent the fungus from spreading, a sanitation program was incorporated to remove all the diseased trees. An integral part of the program proposed by the team involved forecasting the number of elms to be lost in the coming growing season. Because of the scarcity of historical data, the forecast was developed from the opinions of four disease experts. Each expert developed a discrete probability distribution to represent his beliefs regarding the number of elms that would be infected by the disease during the next growing season. These four probability distributions were combined (by averaging using equal weights) to obtain a single discrete probability distribution reflecting the beliefs of all the experts regarding the number of elms to be infected. A slightly modified version of this probability distribution appears in the table below.

Number of Elms That Would Be Infected Next Growing Season (x)	p(x)
5,000–9,999	.02
10,000–14,999	.07
15,000–19,999	.16
20,000–24,999	.17
25,000–29,999	.12
30,000–34,999	.13
35,000–39,999	.11
40,000–44,999	.08
45,000–49,999	.07
50,000 or more	.07

Source: Chervany, N. L., *et. al.* "A management science approach to a Dutch elm disease sanitation program." *Interfaces,* April 10, 1980, p. 108.

a. Using the above probability distribution, make a probability forecast for the following interval: $15,000 \leq x \leq 29,999$.

b. The team of consultants was asked to use an interval of width 5,000 trees to forecast the number of elm trees that would be infected in the coming growing season. Which interval should be selected? Why?

c. It is interesting to note that the actual number of trees lost to Dutch elm disease in the year of interest was 20,817. What does this outcome suggest about the expertise of the forecasters and the forecasting methodology that was employed?

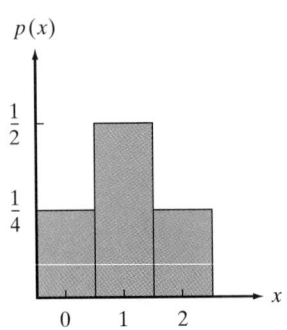

FIGURE 4.4
Probability distribution
for a two-coin toss

4.3   EXPECTED VALUES OF DISCRETE RANDOM VARIABLES

If a discrete random variable x were observed a very large number of times and the data generated were arranged in a relative frequency distribution, the relative frequency distribution would be indistinguishable from the probability distribution for the random variable. Thus, the probability distribution for a random variable is a theoretical model for the relative frequency distribution of a population. To the extent that the two distributions are equivalent (and we will assume they are), the probability distribution for x possesses a mean μ and a variance σ^2 that are identical to the corresponding descriptive measures for the population. This section explains how you can find the mean value for a random variable. We illustrate the procedure with an example.

Examine the probability distribution for x (the number of heads observed in the toss of two fair coins) in Figure 4.4. Try to locate the mean of the distribution intuitively. We may reason that the mean μ of this distribution is equal to 1 as follows: In a large number of experiments, $\frac{1}{4}$ should result in $x = 0$, $\frac{1}{2}$ in $x = 1$, and $\frac{1}{4}$ in $x = 2$ heads. Therefore, the average number of heads is

$$\mu = 0(\tfrac{1}{4}) + 1(\tfrac{1}{2}) + 2(\tfrac{1}{4}) = 0 + \tfrac{1}{2} + \tfrac{1}{2} = 1$$

Note that to get the population mean of the random variable x, we multiply each possible value of x by its probability $p(x)$, and then sum this product over all possible values of x. The *mean of x* is also referred to as the *expected value of x*, denoted $E(x)$.

DEFINITION 4.5
The **mean**, or **expected value**, of a discrete random variable x is

$$\mu = E(x) = \sum x p(x)$$

The term *expected* is a mathematical term and should not be interpreted as it is typically used. Specifically, a random variable might never be equal to its "expected value." Rather, the expected value is the mean of the probability distribution or a measure of its central tendency. You can think of μ as the mean value of x in a *very large* (actually, *infinite*) number of repetitions of the experiment.

EXAMPLE 4.5

Suppose you work for an insurance company, and you sell a $10,000 whole-life insurance policy at an annual premium of $290. Actuarial tables show that the probability of death during the next year for a person of your customer's age, sex, health, etc. is .001. What is the expected gain (amount of money made by the company) for a policy of this type?

SOLUTION
The experiment is to observe whether the customer survives the upcoming year. The probabilities associated with the two sample points, Live and Die, are .999 and .001, respectively. The random variable you are interested in is the gain x, which can assume the values shown in the following table.

Gain, x	Sample Point	Probability
$290	Customer lives	.999
$290–$10,000	Customer dies	.001

If the customer lives, the company gains the $290 premium as profit. If the customer dies, the gain is negative because the company must pay $10,000, for a net "gain" of $(290 − 10,000). The expected gain is therefore

$$\mu = E(x) = \sum_{\text{all } x} x p(x)$$

$$= (290)(.999) + (290 - 10,000)(.001) = \$280$$

In other words, if the company were to sell a very large number of one-year $10,000 policies to customers possessing the characteristics described above, it would (on the average) net $280 per sale in the next year.

Example 4.5 illustrates that the expected value of a random variable x need not equal a possible value of x. That is, the expected value is $280, but x will equal either $290 or −$9,710 each time the experiment is performed (a policy is sold and a year elapses). The expected value is a measure of central tendency—and in this case represents the average over a very large number of one-year policies—but is not a possible value of x.

We learned in Chapter 2 that the mean and other measures of central tendency tell only part of the story about a set of data. The same is true about probability distributions. We need to measure variability as well. Since a probability distribution can be viewed as a representation of a population, we will use the population variance to measure its variability.

The **population variance** σ^2 is defined as the average of the squared distance of x from the population mean μ. Since x is a random variable, the squared distance, $(x - \mu)^2$, is also a random variable. Using the same logic used to find the mean value of x, we find the mean value of $(x - \mu)^2$ by multiplying all possible values of $(x - \mu)^2$ by $p(x)$ and then summing over all possible x values.* This quantity,

$$E[(x - \mu)^2] = \sum_{\text{all } x}(x - \mu)^2 p(x)$$

is also called the **expected value of the squared distance from the mean**; that is, $\sigma^2 = E[(x - \mu)^2]$. The standard deviation of x is defined as the square root of the variance σ^2.

DEFINITION 4.6
The **variance** of a random variable x is
$$\sigma^2 = E[(x - \mu)^2] = \sum(x - \mu)^2 p(x)$$

DEFINITION 4.7
The **standard deviation** of a discrete random variable is equal to the square root of the variance, i.e., $\sigma = \sqrt{\sigma^2}$.

*It can be shown that $E[(x - \mu)^2] = E(x^2) - \mu^2$ where $E(x^2) = \sum x^2 p(x)$. Note the similarity between this expression and the shortcut formula $\sum(x - \bar{x})^2 = \sum x^2 - \left(\sum x\right)^2/n$ given in Chapter 2.

FIGURE 4.5
Shapes of two probability distributions for a discrete random variable x

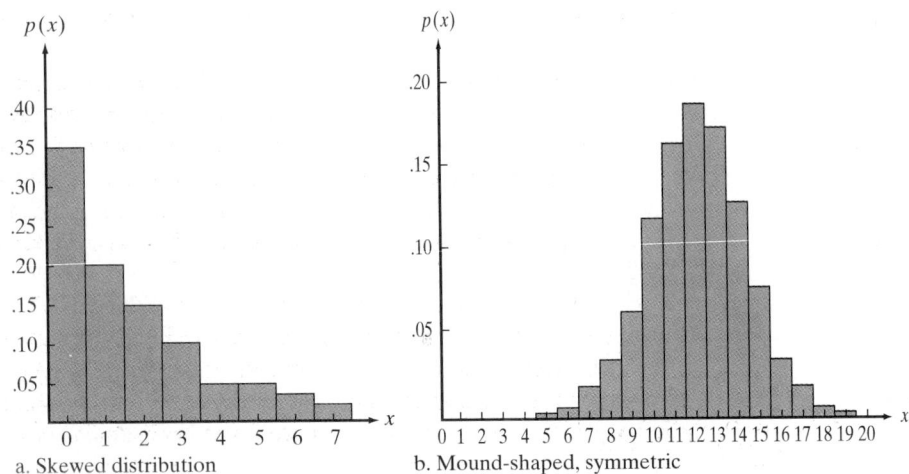

a. Skewed distribution

b. Mound-shaped, symmetric

Knowing the mean μ and standard deviation σ of the probability distribution of x, in conjunction with Chebyshev's Rule (Table 2.7) and the Empirical Rule (Table 2.8), we can make statements about the likelihood that values of x will fall within the intervals $\mu \pm \sigma$, $\mu \pm 2\sigma$, and $\mu \pm 3\sigma$. These probabilities are given in the box.

Chebyshev's Rule and Empirical Rule for a Discrete Random Variable

Let x be a discrete random variable with probability distribution $p(x)$, mean μ, and standard deviation σ. Then, depending on the shape of $p(x)$, the following probability statements can be made:

	Chebyshev's Rule	Empirical Rule
	Applies to any probability distribution (see Figure 4.5a)	Applies to probability distributions that are mound-shaped and symmetric (see Figure 4.5b)
$P(\mu - \sigma < x < \mu + \sigma)$	$\geqslant 0$	$\approx .68$
$P(\mu - 2\sigma < x < \mu + 2\sigma)$	$\geqslant \frac{3}{4}$	$\approx .95$
$P(\mu - 3\sigma < x < \mu + 3\sigma)$	$\geqslant \frac{8}{9}$	≈ 1.00

EXAMPLE 4.6

Suppose you invest a fixed sum of money in each of five business ventures. Assume you know that 70% of such ventures are successful, the outcomes of the ventures are independent of one another, and the probability distribution for the number, x, of successful ventures out of five is:

x	0	1	2	3	4	5
$p(x)$	.002	.029	.132	.309	.360	.168

a. Find $\mu = E(x)$. Interpret the result.

b. Find $\sigma = \sqrt{E[(x - \mu)^2]}$. Interpret the result.

c. Graph $p(x)$. Locate μ and the interval $\mu \pm 2\sigma$ on the graph. Use either Chebyshev's Rule or the Empirical Rule to approximate the probability that x falls in this interval. Compare this result with the actual probability.

d. Would you expect to observe fewer than two successful ventures out of five?

SOLUTION

a. Applying the formula,

$$\mu = E(x) = \sum xp(x) = 0(.002) + 1(.029) + 2(.132) + 3(.309)$$
$$+ 4(.360) + 5(.168) = 3.50$$

On average, the number of successful ventures out of five will equal 3.5. Remember that this expected value only has meaning when the experiment— investing in five business ventures—is repeated a large number of times.

b. Now we calculate the variance of x:

$$\sigma^2 = E[(x - \mu)^2] = \sum (x - \mu)^2 p(x)$$

$$= (0 - 3.5)^2(.002) + (1 - 3.5)^2(.029) + (2 - 3.5)^2(.132)$$
$$+ (3 - 3.5)^2(.309) + (4 - 3.5)^2(.360) + (5 - 3.5)^2(.168)$$

$$= 1.05$$

Thus, the standard deviation is

$$\sigma = \sqrt{\sigma^2} = \sqrt{1.05} = 1.02$$

This value measures the spread of the probability distribution of x, the number of successful ventures out of five.

c. The graph of $p(x)$ is shown in Figure 4.6 with the mean μ and the interval $\mu \pm 2\sigma = 3.50 \pm 2(1.02) = 3.50 \pm 2.04 = (1.46, 5.54)$ shown on the graph. Note particularly that $\mu = 3.5$ locates the center of the probability distribution. Since this distribution is a theoretical relative frequency distribution that is moderately mound-shaped (see Figure 4.6), we expect (from Chebyshev's Rule) at least 75% and, more likely (from the Empirical Rule), approximately 95% of observed x values to fall in the interval $\mu \pm 2\sigma$—that is, between 1.46 and 5.54. You can see from Figure 4.6 that the actual probability that x falls in the interval $\mu \pm 2\sigma$ includes the sum of $p(x)$ for the

FIGURE 4.6
Graph of $p(x)$ for
Example 4.6

STATISTICS IN ACTION

4.1 PORTFOLIO SELECTION

Investors—be they large corporations, banks, pension funds, mutual funds, or individuals—seldom hold a single financial asset; rather, they hold portfolios of financial assets. Thus, the investor should be less concerned with the rate of return achieved by, say, a particular stock in the portfolio* than in the overall rate of return of the portfolio. Since the future rate of return of a portfolio is uncertain, a probability distribution can be used to characterize a portfolio's future rate of return. Two examples of such distributions are shown in Figure 4.7.

Alternatively, we might use just the mean and standard deviation of the probability distribution to characterize the future rate of return. Notice that portfolios A and B have the same mean, but that A has the greater standard deviation. As a result, A has the higher probability of yielding a negative rate of return. (Can you demonstrate this?) Accordingly, it should not be surprising that the standard deviation of a portfolio's rate of return distribution is frequently used as a measure of the risk associated with the portfolio—the higher the standard deviation, the greater the risk of the portfolio (i.e., the greater the uncertainty of the portfolio's rate of return) and vice versa.

Typically, an investor can choose from among many different assets to form a portfolio. Or put another

way, there are many different portfolios for the investor to choose among. But which portfolio should the investor select? This problem was first addressed by Harry M. Markowitz (1952) in a classic article published in the *Journal of Finance*. Characterizing portfolios by the mean and standard deviation of their rates of return, Markowitz proposed a two-step procedure for choosing among portfolios. First, the set of all possible portfolios—the *feasible set*—must be reduced to an *efficient* set of portfolios. An efficient portfolio is one that provides the highest possible mean rate of return for any given degree of risk (i.e., any given standard deviation) or the lowest possible degree of risk for any given mean rate of return. Second, from the efficient set, the investor should choose the portfolio that best suits his or her needs.

The graph in Figure 4.8 shows the mean and standard deviation of the rate of return for various portfolios. Portfolios identified by a value of μ and σ that fall within the ellipse represent the feasible set of portfolios for a particular investor. The efficient set of portfolios is denoted by the boundary line *ABC* and is sometimes called the *efficient frontier*. Portfolios to the left of *ABC* are not obtainable because they fall outside the feasible set. Portfolios to the right of ABC are not efficient because there always exists a portfolio on the efficient frontier that could provide (1) a higher mean return for a given level of standard deviation of

FIGURE 4.7
Rate of return distributions (Statistics in Action 4.1)

a. Portfolio A: $\mu = .050$, $\sigma = .053$

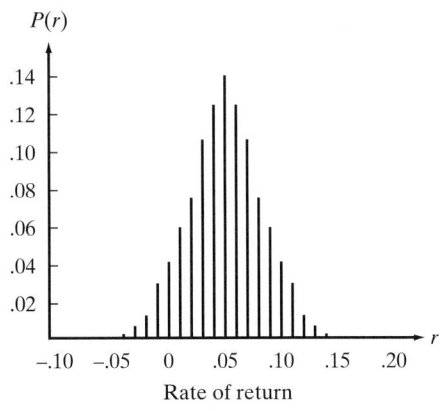

b. Portfolio B: $\mu = .050$, $\sigma = .033$

*If no dividends have been declared on the day in question, a stock's rate of return on day t is defined as $(P_t - P_{t-1})/P_{t-1}$, where P_t is the closing price of the stock on day t and P_{t-1} is its closing price the day before.

returns (compare points B and D), or (2) a lower standard deviation (lower degree of risk) for a given mean return (compare points B and E). For details on how to determine the efficient set of portfolios for an investor, see Alexander, Sharp, and Bailey (1993) or Alexander and Francis (1986).

Focus

The future rates of return of stock portfolios X, Y, and Z can be characterized by the following probability distributions.

a. Which portfolio subjects the investor to the greatest chance of a negative rate of return? Justify your answer.

b. Find μ and σ for each portfolio.

c. Plot the mean and standard deviation for each portfolio on a graph like Figure 4.8.

d. Which portfolio would you choose? Justify your choice.

STOCK PORTFOLIO X		STOCK PORTFOLIO Y		STOCK PORTFOLIO Z	
Rate of Return	**Probability**	**Rate of Return**	**Probability**	**Rate of Return**	**Probability**
.20	.05	.15	.10	.25	.05
.15	.15	.10	.20	.20	.10
.10	.26	.05	.30	.15	.25
.05	.20	.00	.20	.10	.20
.00	.15	−.05	.10	.05	.15
−.05	.10	−.10	.07	.00	.10
−.10	.05	−.15	.03	−.05	.07
−.15	.03			−.10	.05
−.20	.01			−.15	.03

FIGURE 4.8
Efficient set of portfolios (Statistics in Action 4.1)

values $x = 2, x = 3, x = 4$, and $x = 5$. This probability is $p(2) + p(3) + p(4) + p(5) = .132 + .309 + .360 + .168 = .969$. Therefore, 96.9% of the probability distribution lies within 2 standard deviations of the mean. This percentage is consistent with both Chebyshev's Rule and the Empirical Rule.

d. Fewer than two successful ventures out of five implies that $x = 0$ or $x = 1$. Since both these values of x lie outside the interval $\mu \pm 2\sigma$, we know from the Empirical Rule that such a result is unlikely (approximate probability of .05). The exact probability, $P(x \leq 1)$, is $p(0) + p(1) = .002 + .029 = .031$. Consequently, in a single experiment where we invest in five business ventures, we would not expect to observe fewer than two successful ones. ▪

EXERCISES 4.21–4.34

Learning the Mechanics

4.21 Describe the differences in the meanings of the symbols, $\mu, \bar{x}$, and $E(x)$.

4.22 Consider the probability distribution shown here.

x	1	2	4	10
$p(x)$	.2	.4	.2	.2

a. Find $\mu = E(x)$. **b.** Find $\sigma^2 = E[(x - \mu)^2]$.
c. Find σ.
d. Interpret the value you obtained for μ.
e. In this case, can the random variable x ever assume the value μ? Explain.
f. In general, can a random variable ever assume a value equal to its expected value? Explain.

4.23 Consider the probability distribution for the random variable x shown here.

x	10	20	30	40	50	60
$p(x)$	.05	.20	.30	.25	.10	.10

a. Find μ, σ^2, and σ. **b.** Graph $p(x)$.
c. Locate μ and the interval $\mu \pm 2\sigma$ on your graph. What is the probability that x will fall within the interval $\mu \pm 2\sigma$?

4.24 Consider the probability distribution shown here.

x	−4	−3	−2	−1	0	1	2	3	4
$p(x)$	.02	.07	.10	.15	.30	.18	.10	.06	.02

a. Calculate μ, σ^2, and σ.
b. Graph $p(x)$. Locate $\mu, \mu - 2\sigma$, and $\mu + 2\sigma$ on the graph.
c. What is the probability that x is in the interval $\mu \pm 2\sigma$?

4.25 Consider the probability distributions shown here.

x	0	1	2
$p(x)$	.3	.4	.3

y	0	1	2
$p(y)$	.1	.8	.1

a. Use your intuition to find the mean for each distribution. How did you arrive at your choice?

b. Which distribution appears to be more variable? Why?
c. Calculate μ and σ^2 for each distribution. Compare these answers to your answers in parts **a** and **b**.

Applying the Concepts

4.26 Statistics in Action 4.1 dealt with the measurement and analysis of the risk of a portfolio of financial assets. This is sometimes called *investment risk* (Radcliffe, 1994). In general, investment risk is typically measured by computing the variance or standard deviation of the probability distribution that describes the decision-maker's potential outcomes (gains or losses). This follows from the fact that the greater the variation in potential outcomes, the greater the uncertainty faced by the decision-maker; the smaller the variation in potential outcomes, the more predictable the decision-maker's gains or losses. The two discrete probability distributions given in the table were developed from historical data. They describe the potential total physical damage losses next year to the fleets of delivery trucks of two different firms.

FIRM A		FIRM B	
Loss next year	Probability	Loss next year	Probability
$ 0	.01	$ 0	.00
500	.01	200	.01
1,000	.01	700	.02
1,500	.02	1,200	.02
2,000	.35	1,700	.15
2,500	.30	2,200	.30
3,000	.25	2,700	.30
3,500	.02	3,200	.15
4,000	.01	3,700	.02
4,500	.01	4,200	.02
5,000	.01	4,700	.01

a. Verify that both firms have the same expected total physical damage loss.
b. Compute the standard deviation of each probability distribution, and determine which firm faces the greater risk of physical damage to its fleet next year.

4.27 Odds makers try to predict which professional and college football teams will win and by how much (the *spread*). If the odds makers do this accurately, adding the spread to the underdog's score should make the final score a tie. Suppose a bookie will give you $6 for every $1 you risk if you pick the winners in three ballgames (adjusted by the spread) on a "parlay" card. Thus, for every $1 bet you will either lose $1 or gain $5. What is the bookie's expected earnings per dollar wagered?

4.28 In 1965 the U.S. Weather Bureau (now called the National Weather Service) initiated a nationwide program in which precipitation probabilities were included in all public weather forecasts. This was the first time in any field of application that probabilities were issued on such a large scale. The program continues today. Precipitation forecasts indicate the likelihood of measurable precipitation ($\geq .01$ inch) at a specific point (the official rain gauge) during a given time period (Doswell and Brooks, *Probabilistic Forecasting: A Primer*, 1996). Suppose that if a measurable amount of rain falls during the next 24 hours, a river will reach flood stage and a business will incur damages of $300,000. The National Weather Service has indicated that there is a 30% chance of a measurable amount of rain during the next 24 hours.

    a. Construct the probability distribution that describes the potential flood damages.

    b. Find the firm's expected loss due to flood damage.

4.29 The number of training units that must be passed before a complex computer software program is mastered varies from one to five, depending on the student. After much experience, the software manufacturer has determined the probability distribution that describes the fraction of users mastering the software after each number of training units:

Number of Units	1	2	3	4	5
Probability of Mastery	.1	.25	.4	.15	.1

    a. Calculate the mean number of training units necessary to master the program. Calculate the median. Interpret each.

    b. If the firm wants to ensure that at least 75% of the students master the program, what is the minimum number of training units that must be administered? At least 90%?

    c. Suppose the firm develops a new training program that increases the probability that only one unit of training is needed from .1 to .25, increases the probability that only two units are needed to .35, leaves the probability that three units are needed at .4, and completely eliminates the need for four or five units. How do your answers to parts **a** and **b** change for this new program?

4.30 A team of consultants working for a large national supermarket chain based in the New York metropolitan area developed a statistical model for predicting the annual sales of potential new store locations. Part of their analysis involved identifying variables that influence store sales, such as the size of the store (in square feet), the size of the surrounding population, and the number of checkout lanes. They surveyed 52 supermarkets in a particular region of the country and constructed the relative frequency distribution shown below to describe the number of checkout lanes per store, x.

    a. Why do the relative frequencies in the table represent the approximate probabilities of a randomly selected supermarket having x number of checkout lanes?

    b. Find $E(x)$ and interpret its value in the context of the problem.

    c. Find the standard deviation of x.

    d. According to Chebyshev's Rule (Chapter 2), what percentage of supermarkets would be expected to fall within $\mu \pm \sigma$? Within $\mu \pm 2\sigma$?

    e. What is the actual number of supermarkets that fall within $\mu \pm \sigma$? $\mu \pm 2\sigma$? Compare your answers to those of part **d**. Are the answers consistent?

4.31 A capacitated-bridge network with six arcs (*Network*, May 1995) was presented in Exercise 4.19. The probability distributions for the capacities of the six arcs are reproduced on page 178.

x	1	2	3	4	5	6	7	8	9	10
Relative Frequency	.01	.04	.04	.08	.10	.15	.25	.20	.08	.05

Source: Adapted from Chow, W., *et. al.* "A model for predicting a supermarket's annual sales per square foot." Graduate School of Management, Rutgers University, 1994.

Compute the mean capacity of each arc and interpret its value.

Arc	Capacity (x)	$p(x)$
a_1	3	.60
	2	.25
	1	.10
	0	.05
a_2	2	.60
	1	.30
	0	.10
a_3	1	.90
	0	.10

Arc	Capacity (x)	$p(x)$
a_4	1	.90
	0	.10
a_5	1	.90
	0	.10
a_6	2	.70
	1	.25
	0	.05

Source: Lin, J., *et al.* "On reliability evaluation of capacitated-flow network in terms of minimal pathsets." *Networks,* Vol. 25, No. 3, May 1995, p. 135 (Table 1), 1995, John Wiley and Sons.

4.32 Suppose you own a company that bonds financial managers. Based on past experience, you assess the probability that you will have to forfeit any particular bond to be .001. How much should you charge for a $1 million bond in order to break even on all such bonds?

4.33 The success of an organization is determined largely by the caliber of its employees. Thus, it is vital for any organization to have effective recruitment and selection policies. These policies must have the support of top management and be regularly evaluated (Cowling and James, *The Essence of Personnel Management and Industrial Relations,* 1994). A company is interested in hiring a person with an MBA degree and at least two years experience in a marketing department of a computer products firm. The company's personnel department has determined that it will cost the company $1,000 per job candidate to collect the required background information and to interview the candidate. As a result, the company will hire the first qualified person it finds and will interview no more than three candidates. The company has received job applications from four persons who appear to be qualified but, unknown to the company, only one actually possesses the required background. Candidates to be interviewed will be randomly selected from the pool of four applicants.

a. Construct the probability distribution for the total cost to the firm of the interviewing strategy.

b. What is the probability that the firm's interviewing strategy will result in none of the four applicants being hired?

c. Calculate the mean of the probability distribution you constructed in part **a**.

d. What is the expected total cost of the interviewing strategy?

4.34 Most states offer weekly lotteries to generate revenue for the state. Despite the long odds of winning, residents continue to gamble on the lottery each week (see Statistics in Action 3.2). The chance of winning Florida's Pick-6 Lotto game is 1 in approximately 14 million. Suppose you buy a $1 Lotto ticket in anticipation of winning the $7 million grand prize. Calculate your expected net winnings. Interpret the result.

4.4 THE BINOMIAL RANDOM VARIABLE

Many experiments result in *dichotomous* responses—i.e., responses for which there exist two possible alternatives, such as Yes-No, Pass-Fail, Defective-Nondefective, or Male-Female. A simple example of such an experiment is the coin-toss experiment. A coin is tossed a number of times, say 10. Each toss results in one of two outcomes, Head or Tail. Ultimately, we are interested in the probability distribution of x, the number of heads observed. Many other experiments are equivalent to tossing a coin (either balanced or unbalanced) a fixed number n of times and observing the number x of times that one of the two possible outcomes occurs. Random variables that possess these characteristics are called **binomial random variables**.

Public opinion and consumer preference polls (e.g., the Gallup and Harris polls) frequently yield observations on binomial random variables. For example, suppose a sample of 100 current customers is selected from a firm's data base and each person is asked whether he or she prefers the firm's product (a Head) or prefers a competitor's product (a Tail). Ultimately, we are interested in x, the number of customers in the sample who prefer the firm's product. Sampling 100 customers is analogous to tossing the coin 100 times. Thus, you can see that consumer preference polls like the one described here are real-life equivalents of coin-toss experiments. We have been describing a **binomial experiment**; it is identified by the following characteristics.

> **Characteristics of a Binomial Random Variable**
> **1.** The experiment consists of n identical trials.
> **2.** There are only two possible outcomes on each trial. We will denote one outcome by S (for Success) and the other by F (for Failure).
> **3.** The probability of S remains the same from trial to trial. This probability is denoted by p, and the probability of F is denoted by q. Note that $q = 1 - p$.
> **4.** The trials are independent.
> **5.** The binomial random variable x is the number of S's in n trials.

EXAMPLE 4.7   For the following examples, decide whether x is a binomial random variable.

> a. You randomly select three bonds out of a possible ten for an investment portfolio. Unknown to you, eight of the ten will maintain their present value, and the other two will lose value due to a change in their ratings. Let x be the number of the three bonds you select that lose value.
>
> b. Before marketing a new product on a large scale, many companies will conduct a consumer preference survey to determine whether the product is likely to be successful. Suppose a company develops a new diet soda and then conducts a taste preference survey in which 100 randomly chosen consumers state their preferences among the new soda and the two leading sellers. Let x be the number of the 100 who choose the new brand over the two others.
>
> c. Some surveys are conducted by using a method of sampling other than simple random sampling (defined in Chapter 3). For example, suppose a television cable company plans to conduct a survey to determine the fraction of households in the city that would use the cable television service. The sampling method is to choose a city block at random and then survey every household on that block. This sampling technique is called **cluster sampling**. Suppose 10 blocks are so sampled, producing a total of 124 household responses. Let x be the number of the 124 households that would use the television cable service.

SOLUTION

> a. In checking the binomial characteristics in the box, a problem arises with both characteristic 3 (probabilities remaining the same from trial to trial) and characteristic 4 (independence). The probability that the first bond you pick loses value is clearly $2/10$. Now suppose the first bond you picked was one of the two that will lose value. This reduces the chance that the second bond you pick will lose value to $1/9$, since now only one of the nine remaining bonds are in that category. Thus, the choices you make are dependent, and therefore x, the number of the three bonds you select that lose value, is *not* a binomial random variable.
>
> b. Surveys that produce dichotomous responses and use random sampling techniques are classic examples of binomial experiments. In our example, each randomly selected consumer either states a preference for the new diet soda or does not. The sample of 100 consumers is a very small proportion of the totality of potential consumers, so the response of one would be, for all practical purposes, independent of another.* Thus, x is a binomial random variable.

*In most real-life applications of the binomial distribution, the population of interest has a finite number of elements (trials), denoted N. When N is large and the sample size n is small relative to N, say $n/N \leq .05$, the sampling procedure, for all practical purposes, satisfies the conditions of a binomial experiment.

c. This example is a survey with dichotomous responses (Yes or No to the cable service), but the sampling method is not simple random sampling. Again, the binomial characteristic of independent trials would probably not be satisfied. The responses of households within a particular block would be dependent, since the households within a block tend to be similar with respect to income, level of education, and general interests. Thus, the binomial model would not be satisfactory for x if the cluster sampling technique were employed.

EXAMPLE 4.8

A retail computer store sells desktop personal computers (PCs) and laptops. Assume that 80% of the PCs that the store sells are desktops, and 20% are laptops.

a. Use the steps given in Chapter 3 (box on page 118) to find the probability that all of the next four PC purchases are laptops.

b. Find the probability that three of the next four PC purchases are laptops.

c. Let x represent the number of the next four PC purchases that are laptops. Explain why x is a binomial random variable.

d. Use the answers to parts **a** and **b** to derive a formula for $p(x)$, the probability distribution of the binomial random variable, x.

SOLUTION

a. 1. The first step is to define the experiment. Here we are interested in observing the type of PC purchased by each of the next four (buying) customers: desktop (D) or laptop (L).

2. Next, we list the sample points associated with the experiment. Each sample point consists of the purchase decisions made by the four customers. For example, $DDDD$ represents the sample point that all four purchase desktop PCs, while $LDDD$ represents the sample point that customer 1 purchases a laptop, while customers 2, 3, and 4 purchase desktops. The 16 sample points are listed in Table 4.2.

3. We now assign probabilities to the sample points. Note that each sample point can be viewed as the intersection of four customers' decisions and, assuming the decisions are made independently, the probability of each sample point can be obtained using the multiplicative rule, as follows:

$$P(DDDD) = P[(\text{customer 1 chooses desktop}) \cap (\text{customer 2 chooses desktop})$$
$$\cap (\text{customer 3 chooses desktop}) \cap (\text{customer 4 chooses desktop})]$$

$$= P[(\text{customer 1 chooses desktop}) \times P(\text{customer 2 chooses desktop}) \times P(\text{customer 3 chooses desktop}) \times P(\text{customer 4 chooses desktop})]$$

$$= (.8)(.8)(.8)(.8) = (.8)^4 = .4096$$

TABLE 4.2   Sample Points for PC Experiment of Example 4.8

$DDDD$	$LDDD$	$LLDD$	$DLLL$	LLLL
	$DLDD$	$LDLD$	$LDLL$	
	$DDLD$	$LDDL$	$LLDL$	
	$DDDL$	$DLLD$	$LLLD$	
		$DLDL$		
		$DDLL$		

All other sample point probabilities are calculated using similar reasoning. For example,

$$P(LDDD) = (.2)(.8)(.8)(.8) = (.2)(.8)^3 = .1024$$

You can check that this reasoning results in sample point probabilities that add to 1 over the 16 points in the sample space.

4. Finally, we add the appropriate sample point probabilities to obtain the desired event probability. The event of interest is that all four customers purchase laptops. In Table 4.2 we find only one sample point, *LLLL*, contained in this event. All other sample points imply that at least one desktop is purchased. Thus,

$$P(\text{All four purchase laptops}) = P(LLLL) = (.2)^4 = .0016$$

That is, the probability is only 16 in 10,000 that all four customers purchase laptop PCs.

b. The event that three of the next four buyers purchase laptops consists of the four sample points in the fourth column of Table 4.2: *DLLL, LDLL, LLDL,* and *LLLD*. To obtain the event probability we add the sample point probabilities:

$P(3 \text{ of next 4 customers purchase laptops})$
$$= P(DLLL) + P(LDLL) + P(LLDL) + P(LLLD)$$
$$= (.2)^3(.8) + (.2)^3(.8) + (.2)^3(.8) + (.2)^3(.8)$$
$$= 4(.2)^3(.8) = .0256$$

Note that each of the four sample point probabilities is the same, because each sample point consists of three *L*'s and one *D*; the order does not affect the probability because the customers' decisions are (assumed) independent.

c. We can characterize the experiment as consisting of four identical trials—the four customers' purchase decisions. There are two possible outcomes to each trial, *D* or *L*, and the probability of *L*, $p = .2$, is the same for each trial. Finally, we are assuming that each customer's purchase decision is independent of all others, so that the four trials are independent. Then it follows that *x*, the number of the next four purchases that are laptops, is a binomial random variable.

d. The event probabilities in parts **a** and **b** provide insight into the formula for the probability distribution $p(x)$. First, consider the event that three purchases are laptops (part **b**). We found that

$$P(x = 3) = (\text{Number of sample points for which } x = 3) \times$$
$$(.2)^{\text{Number of laptops purchased}} \times (.8)^{\text{Number of desktops purchased}}$$
$$= 4(.2)^3(.8)^1$$

In general, we can use combinatorial mathematics to count the number of sample points. For example,

Number of sample points for which $(x = 3)$
$$= \text{Number of different ways of selecting 3 of the 4 trials for } L \text{ purchases}$$

$$= \binom{4}{3} = \frac{4!}{3!(4 - 3)!} = \frac{4 \cdot 3 \cdot 2 \cdot 1}{(3 \cdot 2 \cdot 1) \cdot 1} = 4$$

The formula that works for any value of x can be deduced as follows:

$$P(x = 3) = \binom{4}{3}(.2)^3(.8)^1 = \binom{4}{x}(.2)^x(.8)^{4-x}$$

The component $\binom{4}{x}$ counts the number of sample points with x laptops and the component $(.2)^x(.8)^{4-x}$ is the probability associated with each sample point having x laptops.

For the general binomial experiment, with n trials and probability of Success p on each trial, the probability of x Successes is

$$p(x) = \binom{n}{x} \cdot p^x(1 - p)^{n-x}$$

$\uparrow$ $\uparrow$

No. of simple   Probability of x S's
events with   and $(n - x)$ F's in
x S's   any simple event

In theory, you could always resort to the principles developed in Example 4.8 to calculate binomial probabilities; list the sample points and sum their probabilities. However, as the number of trials (n) increases, the number of sample points grows very rapidly (the number of sample points is 2^n). Thus, we prefer the formula for calculating binomial probabilities, since its use avoids listing sample points.

The binomial distribution is summarized in the box.

The Binomial Probability Distribution

$$p(x) = \binom{n}{x}p^x q^{n-x} \qquad (x = 0, 1, 2, ..., n)$$

where p = Probability of a success on a single trial
$q = 1 - p$
n = Number of trials
x = Number of successes in n trials
$$\binom{n}{x} = \frac{n!}{x!(n - x)!}$$

As noted in Chapter 3, the symbol 5! means $5 \cdot 4 \cdot 3 \cdot 2 \cdot 1 = 120$. Similarly, $n! = n(n - 1)(n - 2) \cdots 3 \cdot 2 \cdot 1$; remember, $0! = 1$.

The mean, variance, and standard deviation for the binomial random variable x are shown in the box.

Mean, Variance, and Standard Deviation for a Binomial Random Variable

Mean: $\mu = np$

Variance: $\sigma^2 = npq$

Standard deviation: $\sigma = \sqrt{npq}$

As we demonstrated in Chapter 2, the mean and standard deviation provide measures of the central tendency and variability, respectively, of a distribution. Thus, we can use μ and σ to obtain a rough visualization of the probability distribution for x when the calculation of the probabilities is too tedious. To illustrate the use of the binomial probability distribution, consider Examples 4.9 and 4.10.

EXAMPLE 4.9

A machine that produces stampings for automobile engines is malfunctioning and producing 10% defectives. The defective and nondefective stampings proceed from the machine in a random manner. If the next five stampings are tested, find the probability that three of them are defective.

SOLUTION

Let x equal the number of defectives in $n = 5$ trials. Then x is a binomial random variable with p, the probability that a single stamping will be defective, equal to .1, and $q = 1 - p = 1 - .1 = .9$. The probability distribution for x is given by the expression

$$p(x) = \binom{n}{x}p^x q^{n-x} = \binom{5}{x}(.1)^x(.9)^{5-x}$$

$$= \frac{5!}{x!(5-x)!}(.1)^x(.9)^{5-x} \qquad (x = 0, 1, 2, 3, 4, 5)$$

To find the probability of observing $x = 3$ defectives in a sample of $n = 5$, substitute $x = 3$ into the formula for $p(x)$ to obtain

$$p(3) = \frac{5!}{3!(5-3)!}(.1)^3(.9)^{5-3} = \frac{5!}{3!2!}(.1)^3(.9)^2$$

$$= \frac{5\cdot4\cdot3\cdot2\cdot1}{(3\cdot2\cdot1)(2\cdot1)}(.1)^3(.9)^2 = 10(.1)^3(.9)^2$$

$$= .0081$$

Note that the binomial formula tells us that there are 10 sample points having 3 defectives (check this by listing them), each with probability $(.1)^3(.9)^2$.

EXAMPLE 4.10

Refer to Example 4.9 and find the values of $p(0), p(1), p(2), p(4)$, and $p(5)$. Graph $p(x)$. Calculate the mean μ and standard deviation σ. Locate μ and the interval $\mu - 2\sigma$ to $\mu + 2\sigma$ on the graph. If the experiment were to be repeated many times, what proportion of the x observations would fall within the interval $\mu - 2\sigma$ to $\mu + 2\sigma$?

SOLUTION

Again, $n = 5, p = .1$, and $q = .9$. Then, substituting into the formula for $p(x)$:

$$p(0) = \frac{5!}{0!(5-0)!}(.1)^0(.9)^{5-0} = \frac{5\cdot4\cdot3\cdot2\cdot1}{(1)(5\cdot4\cdot3\cdot2\cdot1)}(1)(.9)^5 = .59049$$

$$p(1) = \frac{5!}{1!(5-1)!}(.1)^1(.9)^{5-1} = 5(.1)(.9)^4 = .32805$$

$$p(2) = \frac{5!}{2!(5-2)!}(.1)^2(.9)^{5-2} = (10)(.1)^2(.9)^3 = .07290$$

$$p(4) = \frac{5!}{4!(5-4)!}(.1)^4(.9)^{5-4} = 5(.1)^4(.9) = .00045$$

$$p(5) = \frac{5!}{5!(5-5)!}(.1)^5(.9)^{5-5} = (.1)^5 = .00001$$

The graph of $p(x)$ is shown as a probability histogram in Figure 4.9. [$p(3)$ is taken from Example 4.9 to be .0081.]

To calculate the values of μ and σ, substitute $n = 5$ and $p = .1$ into the following formulas:

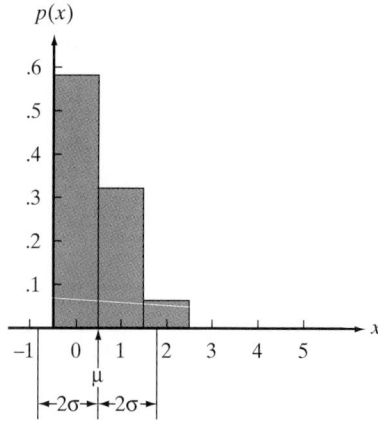

FIGURE 4.9
The binomial
distribution: $n = 5$,
$p = .1$

$$\mu = np = (5)(.1) = .5$$

$$\sigma = \sqrt{npq} = \sqrt{(5)(.1)(.9)} = \sqrt{.45} = .67$$

To find the interval $\mu - 2\sigma$ to $\mu + 2\sigma$, we calculate

$$\mu - 2\sigma = .5 - 2(.67) = -.84$$

$$\mu + 2\sigma = .5 + 2(.67) = 1.84$$

If the experiment were to be repeated a large number of times, what proportion of the x observations would fall within the interval $\mu - 2\sigma$ to $\mu + 2\sigma$? You can see from Figure 4.9 that all observations equal to 0 or 1 will fall within the interval. The probabilities corresponding to these values are .5905 and .3280, respectively. Consequently, you would expect .5905 + .3280 = .9185, or approximately 91.9%, of the observations to fall within the interval $\mu - 2\sigma$ to $\mu + 2\sigma$. This again emphasizes that for most probability distributions, observations rarely fall more than 2 standard deviations from μ.

USING BINOMIAL TABLES

Calculating binomial probabilities becomes tedious when n is large. For some values of n and p the binomial probabilities have been tabulated in Table II of Appendix B. Part of Table II is shown in Table 4.3; a graph of the binomial proba-

TABLE 4.3   Reproduction of Part of Table II of Appendix B: Binomial Probabilities for $n = 10$

k \ p	.01	.05	.10	.20	.30	.40	.50	.60	.70	.80	.90	.95	.99
0	.904	.599	.349	.107	.028	.006	.001	.000	.000	.000	.000	.000	.000
1	.996	.914	.736	.376	.149	.046	.011	.002	.000	.000	.000	.000	.000
2	1.000	.988	.930	.678	.383	.167	.055	.012	.002	.000	.000	.000	.000
3	1.000	.999	.987	.879	.650	.382	.172	.055	.011	.001	.000	.000	.000
4	1.000	1.000	.998	.967	.850	.633	.377	.166	.047	.006	.000	.000	.000
5	1.000	1.000	1.000	.994	.953	.834	.623	.367	.150	.033	.002	.000	.000
6	1.000	1.000	1.000	.999	.989	.945	.828	.618	.350	.121	.013	.001	.000
7	1.000	1.000	1.000	1.000	.998	.988	.945	.833	.617	.322	.070	.012	.000
8	1.000	1.000	1.000	1.000	1.000	.998	.989	.954	.851	.624	.264	.086	.004
9	1.000	1.000	1.000	1.000	1.000	1.000	.999	.994	.972	.893	.651	.401	.096

FIGURE 4.10
Binomial probability
distribution for $n = 10$
and $p = .10$; $P(x \leqslant 2)$
shaded

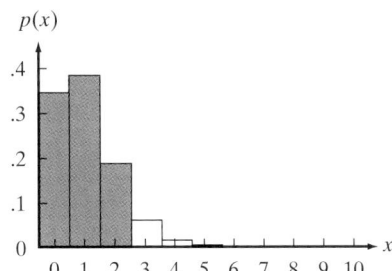

bility distribution for $n = 10$ and $p = .10$ is shown in Figure 4.10. Table II actually contains a total of nine tables, labeled (**a**) through (**i**), one each corresponding to $n = 5, 6, 7, 8, 9, 10, 15, 20$, and 25. In each of these tables the columns correspond to values of p, and the rows correspond to values of the random variable x. The entries in the table represent **cumulative** binomial probabilities. Thus, for example, the entry in the column corresponding to $p = .10$ and the row corresponding to $x = 2$ is .930 (shaded), and its interpretation is

$$P(x \leqslant 2) = P(x = 0) + P(x = 1) + P(x = 2) = .930$$

This probability is also shaded in the graphical representation of the binomial distribution with $n = 10$ and $p = .10$ in Figure 4.10.

You can also use Table II to find the probability that x equals a specific value. For example, suppose you want to find the probability that $x = 2$ in the binomial distribution with $n = 10$ and $p = .10$. This is found by subtraction as follows:

$$P(x = 2) = [P(x = 0) + P(x = 1) + P(x = 2)] - [P(x = 0) + P(x = 1)]$$
$$= P(x \leqslant 2) - P(x \leqslant 1) = .930 - .736 = .194$$

The probability that a binomial random variable exceeds a specified value can be found using Table II and the notion of complementary events. For example, to find the probability that x exceeds 2 when $n = 10$ and $p = .10$, we use

$$P(x > 2) = 1 - P(x \leqslant 2) = 1 - .930 = .070$$

Note that this probability is represented by the unshaded portion of the graph in Figure 4.10.

All probabilities in Table II are rounded to three decimal places. Thus, although none of the binomial probabilities in the table is exactly zero, some are small enough (less than .0005) to round to .000. For example, using the formula to find $P(x = 0)$ when $n = 10$ and $p = .6$, we obtain

$$P(x = 0) = \binom{10}{0}(.6)^0(.4)^{10-0} = .4^{10} = .00010486$$

but this is rounded to .000 in Table II of Appendix B (see Table 4.3).

Similarly, none of the table entries is exactly 1.0, but when the cumulative probabilities exceed .9995, they are rounded to 1.000. The row corresponding to the largest possible value for x, $x = n$, is omitted, because all the cumulative probabilities in that row are equal to 1.0 (exactly). For example, in Table 4.3 with $n = 10$, $P(x \leqslant 10) = 1.0$, no matter what the value of p.

The following example further illustrates the use of Table II.

EXAMPLE 4.11

Suppose a poll of 20 employees is taken in a large company. The purpose is to determine x, the number who favor unionization. Suppose that 60% of all the company's employees favor unionization.

    a. Find the mean and standard deviation of x.

    b. Use Table II of Appendix B to find the probability that $x < 10$.

    c. Use Table II to find the probability that $x > 12$.

    d. Use Table II to find the probability that $x = 11$.

SOLUTION

    a. The number of employees polled is presumably small compared with the total number of employees in this company. Thus, we may treat x, the number of the 20 who favor unionization, as a binomial random variable. The value of p is the fraction of the total employees who favor unionization; i.e., $p = .6$. Therefore, we calculate the mean and variance:

$$\mu = np = 20(.6) = 12$$

$$\sigma^2 = npq = 20(.6)(.4) = 4.8$$

$$\sigma = \sqrt{4.8} = 2.19$$

    b. The tabulated value is

$$P(x \leq 9) = .128$$

    c. To find the probability

$$P(x > 12) = \sum_{x=13}^{20} p(x)$$

we use the fact that for all probability distributions, $\sum_{\text{All } x} p(x) = 1$. Therefore,

$$P(x > 12) = 1 - P(x \leq 12) = 1 - \sum_{x=0}^{12} p(x)$$

Consulting Table II, we find the entry in row $k = 12$, column $p = .6$ to be .584. Thus,

$$P(x > 12) = 1 - .584 = .416$$

    d. To find the probability that exactly 11 employees favor unionization, recall that the entries in Table II are cumulative probabilities and use the relationship

$$P(x = 11) = [p(0) + p(1) + \cdots + p(11)] - [p(0) + p(1) + \cdots + p(10)]$$
$$= P(x \leq 11) - P(x \leq 10)$$

Then

$$P(x = 11) = .404 - .245 = .159$$

The probability distribution for x in this example is shown in Figure 4.11. Note that the interval $\mu \pm 2\sigma$ is $(7.6, 16.4)$.

FIGURE 4.11
The binomial probability distribution for x in Example 4.11: $n = 20, p = .6$

STATISTICS IN ACTION

4.2 THE SPACE SHUTTLE CHALLENGER: CATASTROPHE IN SPACE

On January 28, 1986, at 11:39.13 A.M. (EST), while traveling at mach 1.92 at an altitude of 46,000 feet, the space shuttle *Challenger* was totally enveloped in an explosive burn that destroyed the shuttle and resulted in the deaths of all seven astronauts aboard. What happened? What was the cause of this catastrophe? This was the 25th shuttle mission. The preceding 24 missions had all been successful.

According to *Discover* (Apr. 1986), the report of the presidential commission assigned to investigate the accident concluded that the explosion was caused by the failure of the O-ring seal in the joint between the two lower segments of the right solid-fuel rocket booster. The seal is supposed to prevent superhot gases from leaking through the joint during the propellant burn of the booster rocket. The failure of the seal permitted a jet of white-hot gases to escape and to ignite the liquid fuel of the external fuel tank. The fuel tank fireburst destroyed the *Challenger*.

What were the chances that this event would occur? In a report made one year prior to the catastrophe, the National Aeronautics and Space Administration (NASA) claimed that the probability of such a failure was about $1/60,000$, or about once in every 60,000 flights. But a risk assessment study conducted for the Air Force at about the same time assessed the probability of shuttle catastrophe due to booster rocket "burn-through" to be $1/35$, or about once in every 35 missions.

Focus

a. Assuming NASA's failure-rate estimate was accurate, compute the probability that no disasters would have occurred during 25 shuttle missions.

b. Repeat part **a**, but use the Air Force's failure-rate estimate.

c. What conditions must exist for the probabilities, parts **a** and **b**, to be valid?

d. Given the events of January 28, 1986, which risk assessment—NASA's or the Air Force's—appears to be more appropriate? [*Hint:* Consider the complement of the events, parts **a** and **b**.]

e. After making improvements in the shuttle's systems over the late 1980s and early 1990s, NASA issued a report in 1993 in which the risk of catastrophic failure of the shuttle's main engine was assessed for each mission at 1 in 120. ("Laying Odds on Shuttle Disaster," *Chance*, Fall 1993.) Use this risk assessment and the binomial probability distribution to find the probability of at least one catastrophic failure in the next 10 missions.

EXERCISES 4.35–4.52

Learning the Mechanics

4.35 Compute the following:

a. $\dfrac{6!}{2!(6-2)!}$ b. $\dbinom{5}{2}$ c. $\dbinom{7}{0}$ d. $\dbinom{6}{6}$ e. $\dbinom{4}{3}$

4.36 Consider the following probability distribution:

$$p(x) = \binom{5}{x}(.7)^x(.3)^{5-x} \quad (x = 0, 1, 2, ..., 5)$$

a. Is x a discrete or a continuous random variable?
b. What is the name of this probability distribution?
c. Graph the probability distribution.
d. Find the mean and standard deviation of x.
e. Show the mean and the 2-standard-deviation interval on each side of the mean on the graph you drew in part c.

4.37 If x is a binomial random variable, compute $p(x)$ for each of the following cases:

a. $n = 5, x = 1, p = .2$ b. $n = 4, x = 2, q = .4$
c. $n = 3, x = 0, p = .7$ d. $n = 5, x = 3, p = .1$
e. $n = 4, x = 2, q = .6$ f. $n = 3, x = 1, p = .9$

4.38 Suppose x is a binomial random variable with $n = 3$ and $p = .3$.

a. Calculate the value of $p(x)$, $x = 0, 1, 2, 3$, using the formula for a binomial probability distribution.
b. Using your answers to part a, give the probability distribution for x in tabular form.

4.39 If x is a binomial random variable, calculate μ, σ^2, and σ for each of the following:

a. $n = 25, p = .5$ b. $n = 80, p = .2$
c. $n = 100, p = .6$ d. $n = 70, p = .9$
e. $n = 60, p = .8$ f. $n = 1,000, p = .04$

4.40 If x is a binomial random variable, use Table II in Appendix B to find the following probabilities:

a. $P(x = 2)$ for $n = 10, p = .4$
b. $P(x \le 5)$ for $n = 15, p = .6$
c. $P(x > 1)$ for $n = 5, p = .1$
d. $P(x < 10)$ for $n = 25, p = .7$
e. $P(x \ge 10)$ for $n = 15, p = .9$
f. $P(x = 2)$ for $n = 20, p = .2$

4.41 The binomial probability distribution is a family of probability distributions with each single distribution depending on the values of n and p. Assume that x is a binomial random variable with $n = 4$.

a. Determine a value of p such that the probability distribution of x is symmetric.
b. Determine a value of p such that the probability distribution of x is skewed to the right.
c. Determine a value of p such that the probability distribution of x is skewed to the left.
d. Graph each of the binomial distributions you obtained in parts a, b, and c. Locate the mean for each distribution on its graph.

e. In general, for what values of p will a binomial distribution be symmetric? Skewed to the right? Skewed to the left?

Applying the Concepts

4.42 Lechmere, a division of Chicago-based Montgomery Ward, is a national appliance chain store. Recently, the Massachusetts Division of Standards discovered that checkout scanners at Lechmere stores in five Boston suburbs were registering the wrong price more than $1/3$ of the time for sale items (*Boston Globe,* Aug. 8, 1996). Of the 235 sale items checked by state investigators, 83 scanned incorrectly with 51 resulting in overcharges. (The problem was due to the main computer in Chicago overriding the local scanning systems.) Consider a sample of 10 sale items purchased at the Lechmere stores under investigation. Suppose we are interested in x, the number of items that register the wrong sale price when scanned at the checkout register.

a. Show that x is an approximate binomial random variable.
b. Use the information gathered by the investigators to estimate p for the binomial experiment. (Round the estimate to the nearest .05.)
c. Using the value of p, part b, what is the probability of exactly two scanning errors in the sample of 10 items? At least two?
d. Estimate the probability of observing at least two items resulting in overcharges because of scanning errors.

4.43 According to the Internal Revenue Service (IRS), the chances of your tax return being audited are about 6 in 1,000 if your income is less than $50,000; 10 in 1,000 if your income is between $50,000 and $99,999; and 49 in 1,000 if your income is $100,000 or more (*Statistical Abstract of the United States: 1995*).

a. What is the probability that a taxpayer with income less than $50,000 will be audited by the IRS? With income between $50,000 and $99,999? With income $100,000 or more?
b. If five taxpayers with incomes under $50,000 are randomly selected, what is the probability that exactly one will be audited? That more than one will be audited?
c. Repeat part b assuming that five taxpayers with incomes between $50,000 and $99,999 are randomly selected.
d. If two taxpayers with incomes under $50,000 are randomly selected and two with incomes more than $100,000 are randomly selected, what is the probability that none of these taxpayers will be audited by the IRS?

e. What assumptions did you have to make in order to answer these questions using the methodology presented in this section?

4.44 A problem of considerable economic impact on the economy is the burgeoning cost of Medicare and other public-funded medical services. One aspect of this problem concerns the high percentage of people seeking medical treatment who, in fact, have no physical basis for their ailments. One conservative estimate is that the percentage of people who seek medical assistance and who have no real physical ailment is 10%, and some doctors believe that it may be as high as 40%. Suppose we were to randomly sample the records of a doctor and found that five of 15 patients seeking medical assistance were physically healthy.

a. What is the probability of observing five or more physically healthy patients in a sample of 15 if the proportion, p, that the doctor normally sees is 10%?

b. What is the probability of observing five or more physically healthy patients in a sample of 15 if the proportion, p, that the doctor normally sees is 40%?

c. Why might your answer to part **a** make you believe that p is larger than .10?

4.45 According to the U.S. Golf Association (USGA), "The weight of the [golf] ball shall not be greater than 1.620 ounces avoirdupois (45.93 grams). ...The diameter of the ball shall not be less than 1.680 inches. ...The velocity of the ball shall not be greater than 250 feet per second" (USGA, 1996). The USGA periodically checks the specifications of golf balls sold in the United States by randomly sampling balls from pro shops around the country. Two dozen of each kind are sampled, and if more than three do not meet size and/or velocity requirements, that kind of ball is removed from the USGA's approved-ball list.

a. What assumptions must be made and what information must be known in order to use the binomial probability distribution to calculate the probability that the USGA will remove a particular kind of golf ball from its approved-ball list?

b. Suppose 10% of all balls produced by a particular manufacturer are less than 1.680 inches in diameter, and assume that the number of such balls, x, in a sample of two dozen balls can be adequately characterized by a binomial probability distribution. Find the mean and standard deviation of the binomial distribution.

c. Refer to part **b**. If x has a binomial distribution, then so does the number, y, of balls in the sample that meet the USGA's minimum diameter. [*Note:* $x + y = 24$.] Describe the distribution of y. In particular, what are p, q, and n? Also, find $E(y)$ and the standard deviation of y.

4.46 Unlike older radar systems, Doppler radar can detect air movements and moisture in advance of a storm's arrival. In 1982, before Doppler radar was installed, 80% of the severe storm warnings issued by the National Weather Service for Norman, Oklahoma, were false alarms. In 1994, using Doppler radar, only 22% of the warnings were false alarms (*Newark Star-Ledger*, Nov. 12, 1995).

a. If five severe storm warnings were issued in Norman, Oklahoma, using the old radar system, what is the probability that all five would be false alarms? That none of the five would be false alarms?

b. Answer part **a** again, but assume Doppler radar was in use.

c. What assumptions did you have to make in order to answer these questions using the methodology of this section?

4.47 Suppose you are a purchasing officer for a large company. You have purchased 5 million electrical switches and your supplier has guaranteed that the shipment will contain no more than .1% defectives. To check the shipment, you randomly sample 500 switches, test them, and find that four are defective. If the switches are as represented, calculate μ and σ for this sample of 500. Based on this evidence, do you think the supplier has complied with the guarantee? Explain.

4.48 For a space vehicle to gain reentry into the earth's atmosphere, a particular system must work properly. One component of the system operates successfully only 85% of the time. To increase the reliability of the system, four of these components are installed in such a way that the system will operate successfully if at least one component is working. What is the probability that the system will fail? Assume the components operate independently.

4.49 Every quarter the Food and Drug Administration (FDA) produces a report called the *Total Diet Study*. The FDA's report covers more than 200 food items, each of which is analyzed for potentially harmful chemical compounds. A recent *Total Diet Study* reported that no pesticides at all were found in 65% of the domestically produced food samples (*Consumer's Research*, June 1995). Consider a random sample of 800 food items analyzed for the presence of pesticides.

a. Compute μ and σ for the random variable x, the number of food items found that showed no trace of pesticide.

b. Based on a sample of 800 food items, is it likely you would observe less than half without any traces of pesticide? Explain.

4.50 A study conducted in New Jersey by the Governor's Council for a Drug Free Workplace concluded that 70% of New Jersey's businesses have employees whose performance is affected by drugs and/or alcohol. In those businesses, it was estimated that 8.5% of their workforces have alcohol problems and 5.2% have drug problems. These last two numbers are slightly lower than the national statistics of 10% and 7%, respectively (*Report: The Governor's Council for a Drug Free Workplace*, Spring/Summer 1995).

   a. In a New Jersey company that acknowledges it has performance problems caused by substance abuse, out of every 1,000 employees, approximately how many have drug problems?

   b. In the company referred to in part **a**, if 10 employees are randomly selected to form a committee to address alcohol abuse problems, what is the probability that at least one member of the committee is an alcohol abuser? That exactly two are alcohol abusers?

   c. What assumptions did you have to make in order to answer part **b** using the methodology of this section?

4.51 Many firms utilize sampling plans to control the quality of manufactured items ready for shipment or the quality of incoming items (parts, raw materials, etc.) that have been purchased. To illustrate the use of a sampling plan, suppose you are shipping electrical fuses in lots, each containing 5,000 fuses. The plan specifies that you will randomly sample 25 fuses from each lot and accept (and ship) the lot if the number of defective fuses, x, in the sample is less than 3. If $x \geq 3$, you will reject the lot. Find the probability of accepting a lot ($x = 0$, 1, or 2) if the actual fraction defective in the lot is:

   a. 0   **b.** .01   **c.** .10   **d.** .30
   e. .50   **f.** .80   **g.** .95   **h.** 1

   i. Construct a graph showing $P(A)$, the probability of lot acceptance, as a function of the lot fraction defective, p. This graph is called the **operating characteristic curve** for the sampling plan.

4.52 Refer to Exercise 4.51. Suppose the sampling plan called for sampling $n = 25$ fuses and accepting a lot of $x \leq 3$. Calculate the quantities specified in Exercise 4.51, and construct the operating characteristic curve for this sampling plan. Compare this curve with the curve obtained in Exercise 4.51. (Note how the curve characterizes the ability of the plan to screen bad lots from shipment.)

4.5   THE POISSON RANDOM VARIABLE (OPTIONAL)

A type of probability distribution that is often useful in describing the number of events that will occur in a specific period of time or in a specific area or volume is the **Poisson distribution** (named after the 18th-century physicist and mathematician, Siméon Poisson). Typical examples of random variables for which the Poisson probability distribution provides a good model are

1. The number of industrial accidents per month at a manufacturing plant
2. The number of noticeable surface defects (scratches, dents, etc.) found by quality inspectors on a new automobile
3. The parts per million of some toxin found in the water or air emission from a manufacturing plant
4. The number of customer arrivals per unit of time at a supermarket checkout counter
5. The number of death claims received per day by an insurance company
6. The number of errors per 100 invoices in the accounting records of a company

Characteristics of a Poisson Random Variable

1. The experiment consists of counting the number of times a certain event occurs during a given unit of time or in a given area or volume (or weight, distance, or any other unit of measurement).
2. The probability that an event occurs in a given unit of time, area, or volume is the same for all the units.

3. The number of events that occur in one unit of time, area, or volume is independent of the number that occur in other units.

4. The mean (or expected) number of events in each unit is denoted by the Greek letter lambda, λ.

The characteristics of the Poisson random variable are usually difficult to verify for practical examples. The examples given satisfy them well enough that the Poisson distribution provides a good model in many instances. As with all probability models, the real test of the adequacy of the Poisson model is in whether it provides a reasonable approximation to reality—that is, whether empirical data support it.

The probability distribution, mean, and variance for a Poisson random variable are shown in the next box.

Probability Distribution, Mean, and Variance for a Poisson Random Variable*

$$p(x) = \frac{\lambda^x e^{-\lambda}}{x!} \qquad (x = 0, 1, 2, \ldots)$$

$$\mu = \lambda$$

$$\sigma^2 = \lambda$$

where

λ = Mean number of events during given unit of time, area, volume, etc.

$e = 2.71828\ldots$

The calculation of Poisson probabilities is made easier by the use of Table III in Appendix B, which gives the cumulative probabilities $P(x \leq k)$ for various values of λ. The use of Table III is illustrated in Example 4.12.

EXAMPLE 4.12

Suppose the number, x, of a company's employees who are absent on Mondays has (approximately) a Poisson probability distribution. Furthermore, assume that the average number of Monday absentees is 2.6.

a. Find the mean and standard deviation of x, the number of employees absent on Monday.

b. Use Table III to find the probability that fewer than two employees are absent on a given Monday.

c. Use Table III to find the probability that more than five employees are absent on a given Monday.

d. Use Table III to find the probability that exactly five employees are absent on a given Monday.

SOLUTION

a. The mean and variance of a Poisson random variable are both equal to λ. Thus, for this example,

---

*The Poisson probability distribution also provides a good approximation to a binomial distribution with mean $\lambda = np$ when n is large and p is small (say, $np \leq 7$).

$$\mu = \lambda = 2.6$$

$$\sigma^2 = \lambda = 2.6$$

Then the standard deviation of x is

$$\sigma = \sqrt{2.6} = 1.61$$

Remember that the mean measures the central tendency of the distribution and does not necessarily equal a possible value of x. In this example, the mean is 2.6 absences, and although there cannot be 2.6 absences on a given Monday, the average number of Monday absences is 2.6. Similarly, the standard deviation of 1.61 measures the variability of the number of absences per week. Perhaps a more helpful measure is the interval $\mu \pm 2\sigma$, which in this case stretches from $-.62$ to 5.82. We expect the number of absences to fall in this interval most of the time—with at least 75% relative frequency (according to Chebyshev's Rule) and probably with approximately 95% relative frequency (the Empirical Rule). The mean and the 2-standard-deviation interval around it are shown in Figure 4.12.

b. A partial reproduction of Table III is shown in Table 4.4. The rows of the table correspond to different values of λ, and the columns correspond to different values of the Poisson random variable x. The entries in the table are cumulative probabilities (much like the binomial probabilities in Table II). To find the probability that fewer than two employees are absent on Monday, we first note that

$$P(x < 2) = P(x \leq 1)$$

This probability is a cumulative probability and therefore is the entry in Table III in the row corresponding to $\lambda = 2.6$ and the column corresponding to $x = 1$. The entry is .267, shown shaded in Table 4.4. This probability corresponds to the shaded area in Figure 4.12 and may be interpreted as meaning that there is a 26.7% chance that fewer than two employees will be absent on a given Monday.

c. To find the probability that more than five employees are absent on a given Monday, we consider the complementary event

$$P(x > 5) = 1 - P(x \leq 5) = 1 - .951 = .049$$

where .951 is the entry in Table III corresponding to $\lambda = 2.6$ and $x = 5$ (see Table 4.4). Note from Figure 4.12 that this is the area in the interval $\mu \pm 2\sigma$, or $-.62$ to 5.82. Then the number of absences should exceed 5—or, equivalently, should be more than 2 standard deviations from the mean—during only about 4.9% of all Mondays. Note that this percentage agrees remarkably well with that given by the Empirical Rule for mound-shaped distribu-

FIGURE 4.12
Probability distribution for number of Monday absences

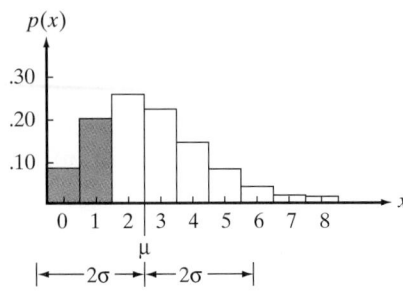

TABLE 4.4 Reproduction of Part of Table III in Appendix B

λ \ x	0	1	2	3	4	5	6	7	8	9
2.2	.111	.355	.623	.819	.928	.975	.993	.998	1.000	1.000
2.4	.091	.308	.570	.779	.904	.964	.988	.997	.999	1.000
2.6	.074	.267	.518	.736	.877	.951	.983	.995	.999	1.000
2.8	.061	.231	.469	.692	.848	.935	.976	.992	.998	.999
3.0	.050	.199	.423	.647	.815	.916	.966	.988	.996	.999
3.2	.041	.171	.380	.603	.781	.895	.955	.983	.994	.998
3.4	.033	.147	.340	.558	.744	.871	.942	.977	.992	.997
3.6	.027	.126	.303	.515	.706	.844	.927	.969	.988	.996
3.8	.022	.107	.269	.473	.668	.816	.909	.960	.984	.994
4.0	.018	.092	.238	.433	.629	.785	.889	.949	.979	.992
4.2	.015	.078	.210	.395	.590	.753	.867	.936	.972	.989
4.4	.012	.066	.185	.359	.551	.720	.844	.921	.964	.985
4.6	.010	.056	.163	.326	.513	.686	.818	.905	.955	.980
4.8	.008	.048	.143	.294	.476	.651	.791	.887	.944	.975
5.0	.007	.040	.125	.265	.440	.616	.762	.867	.932	.968
5.2	.006	.034	.109	.238	.406	.581	.732	.845	.918	.960
5.4	.005	.029	.095	.213	.373	.546	.702	.822	.903	.951
5.6	.004	.024	.082	.191	.342	.512	.670	.797	.886	.941
5.8	.003	.021	.072	.170	.313	.478	.638	.771	.867	.929
6.0	.002	.017	.062	.151	.285	.446	.606	.744	.847	.916

tions, which tells us to expect approximately 5% of the measurements (values of the random variable) to lie farther than 2 standard deviations from the mean.

d. To use Table III to find the probability that *exactly* five employees are absent on a Monday, we must write the probability as the difference between two cumulative probabilities:

$$P(x = 5) = P(x \leq 5) - P(x \leq 4) = .951 - .877 = .074$$

Note that the probabilities in Table III are all rounded to three decimal places. Thus, although in theory a Poisson random variable can assume infinitely large values, the values of x in Table III are extended only until the cumulative probability is 1.000. This does not mean that x *cannot* assume larger values, but only that the likelihood is less than .001 (in fact, less than .0005) that it will do so.

Finally, you may need to calculate Poisson probabilities for values of λ not found in Table III. You may be able to obtain an adequate approximation by interpolation, but if not, consult more extensive tables for the Poisson distribution.

EXERCISES 4.53–4.65

Learning the Mechanics

4.53 Consider the probability distribution shown here:

$$p(x) = \frac{3^x e^{-3}}{x!} \quad (x = 0, 1, 2, \ldots)$$

a. Is x a discrete or continuous random variable? Explain.
b. What is the name of this probability distribution?
c. Graph the probability distribution.

d. Find the mean and standard deviation of x.

e. Find the mean and standard deviation of the probability distribution.

4.54 Given that x is a random variable for which a Poisson probability distribution provides a good approximation, use Table III to compute the following:

a. $P(x \leq 2)$ when $\lambda = 1$

b. $P(x \leq 2)$ when $\lambda = 2$

c. $P(x \leq 2)$ when $\lambda = 3$

d. What happens to the probability of the event $\{x \leq 2\}$ as λ increases from 1 to 3? Is this intuitively reasonable?

4.55 Assume that x is a random variable having a Poisson probability distribution with a mean of 1.5. Use Table III to find the following probabilities:

a. $P(x \leq 3)$ **b.** $P(x \geq 3)$ **c.** $P(x = 3)$

d. $P(x = 0)$ **e.** $P(x > 0)$ **f.** $P(x > 6)$

4.56 Suppose x is a random variable for which a Poisson probability distribution with $\lambda = 5$ provides a good characterization.

a. Graph $p(x)$ for $x = 0, 1, 2, ..., 15$.

b. Find μ and σ for x, and locate μ and the interval $\mu \pm 2\sigma$ on the graph.

c. What is the probability that x will fall within the interval $\mu \pm 2\sigma$?

Applying the Concepts

4.57 The Federal Deposit Insurance Corporation (FDIC), established in 1933, insures deposits of up to $100,000 in banks that are members of the Federal Reserve System (and others that voluntarily join the insurance fund) against losses due to bank failure or theft. From 1988 through 1994 the average number of bank failures per year among insured banks was approximately 128.6 (*Statistical Abstract of the United States: 1995*). Assume that x, the number of bank failures per year among insured banks, can be adequately characterized by a Poisson probability distribution with mean 128.6.

a. Find the expected value and standard deviation of x.

b. In 1993, only 41 insured banks failed. How far (in standard deviations) does $x = 41$ lie below the mean of the Poisson distribution? That is, find the z-score for $x = 41$.

c. In 1992, 122 insured banks failed. Indicate how to calculate $P(x \leq 122)$. Do not actually perform the calculation.

d. Discuss conditions that would make the Poisson assumption plausible.

4.58 As part of a project targeted at improving the services of a local bakery, a management consultant (L. Lei of Rutgers University) monitored customer arrivals for several Saturdays and Sundays. Using the arrival data, she estimated the average number of customer arrivals per 10-minute period on Saturdays to be 6.2. She assumed that arrivals per 10-minute interval followed the Poisson distribution (some of whose values are missing) shown at the bottom of the page.

a. Compute the missing probabilities.

b. Plot the distribution.

c. Find μ and σ and plot the intervals $\mu \pm \sigma$, $\mu \pm 2\sigma$, and $\mu \pm 3\sigma$ on your plot of part **b**.

d. The owner of the bakery claims that more than 75 customers per hour enter the store on Saturdays. Based on the consultant's data, is this likely? Explain.

4.59 The Environmental Protection Agency (EPA), established in 1970 as part of the executive branch of the federal government, issues pollution standards that vitally affect the safety of consumers and the operations of industry (*The United States Government Manual 1995–1996*). For example, the EPA states that manufacturers of vinyl chloride and similar compounds must limit the amount of these chemicals in plant air emissions to no more than 10 parts per million. Suppose the mean emission of vinyl chloride for a particular plant is 4 parts per million. Assume that the number of parts per million of vinyl chloride in air samples, x, follows a Poisson probability distribution.

a. What is the standard deviation of x for the plant?

b. Is it likely that a sample of air from the plant would yield a value of x that would exceed the EPA limit? Explain.

c. Discuss conditions that would make the Poisson assumption plausible.

4.60 U.S. airlines fly approximately 41 billion passenger-miles per month and average about 3.75 fatalities per month (*Statistical Abstract of the United States: 1995*). Assume the probability distribution for x, the number of fatalities per month, can be approximated by a Poisson probability distribution.

a. What is the probability that no fatalities will occur during any given month? [*Hint:* Either

x	0	1	2	3	4	5	6	7	8	9	10	11	12	13
$p(x)$	.002	.013	—	.081	.125	.155	—	.142	.110	.076	—	.026	.014	.007

Source: Lei, L. *Dorsi's Bakery: Modeling Service Operations.* Graduate School of Management, Rutgers University, 1993.

use Table III of Appendix B and interpolate to approximate the probability, or use a calculator or computer to calculate the probability exactly.]

b. Find $E(x)$ and the standard deviation of x.

c. Use your answers to part **b** to describe the probability that as many as 10 fatalities will occur in any given month.

d. Discuss conditions that would make the Poisson assumption plausible.

4.61 The mean number of patients admitted per day to the emergency room of a small hospital is 2.5, If, on a given day, there are only four beds available for new patients, what is the probability the hospital will not have enough beds to accommodate its newly admitted patients?

4.62 As a check on the quality of the wooden doors produced by a company, its owner requested that each door undergo inspection for defects before leaving the plant. The plant's quality control inspector found that one square foot of door surface contains, on the average, .5 minor flaw. Subsequently, one square foot of each door's surface was examined for flaws. The owner decided to have all doors reworked that were found to have two or more minor flaws in the square foot of surface that was inspected. What is the probability that a door will fail inspection and be sent back for reworking? What is the probability that a door will pass inspection?

4.63 The safety supervisor at a large manufacturing plant believes the expected number of industrial accidents per month is 3.4.

a. What is the probability of exactly two accidents occurring next month?

b. What is the probability of three or more accidents occurring next month?

c. What assumptions do you need to make to solve this problem using the methodology of this chapter?

4.64 The number x of people who arrive at a cashier's counter in a bank during a specified period of time often exhibits (approximately) a Poisson probability distribution. If we know the mean arrival rate λ, the Poisson probability distribution can be used to aid in the design of the customer service facility. Suppose you estimate that the mean number of arrivals per minute for cashier service at a bank is one person per minute.

a. What is the probability that in a given minute the number of arrivals will equal three or more?

b. Can you tell the bank manager that the number of arrivals will rarely exceed two per minute?

4.65 A large manufacturing plant has 3,200 incandescent light bulbs illuminating the manufacturing floor. If the rate at which the bulbs fail follows a Poisson distribution with a mean of three bulbs per hour, what is the probability that exactly three light bulbs fail in an hour? What is the probability that no bulbs fail in an hour? That no bulbs fail in an eight-hour shift? What assumption is required to calculate the last probability?

QUICK REVIEW

Key Terms

Note: Starred (*) terms refer to the optional section in this chapter.

Binomial experiment 178	Cumulative binomial	Poisson random variable* 190
Binomial random variable 178	probabilities 185	Probability distribution 166
Continuous random variable 164	Discrete random variable 164	Random variable 162
	Expected value 170	

Key Formulas

Note: Starred (*) formulas refer to the optional section in this chapter.

Probability Distribution	Mean μ	Variance σ^2		
$p(x)$	$\sum\limits_{\text{all } x} xp(x)$	$\sum\limits_{\text{all } x}(x - \mu)^2 p(x)$	General discrete random variable	166, 170, 171
$\binom{n}{x}p^x q^{n-x}$	np	npq	Binomial random variable	182
$\dfrac{\lambda^x e^{-\lambda}}{x!}$	λ	λ	Poisson random variable*	191

LANGUAGE LAB

Symbol	Pronunciation	Description
$p(x)$		Probability distribution of the random variable x
S		The outcome of a binomial trial denoted a "success"
F		The outcome of a binomial trial denoted a "failure"
p		The probability of success (S) in a binomial trial
q		The probability of failure (F) in a binomial trial, where $q = 1 - p$
λ	lambda	The mean (or expected) number of events for a Poisson random variable
e		A constant used in the Poisson probability distribution, where $e = 2.71828\ldots$

SUPPLEMENTARY EXERCISES 4.66–4.86

Note: Starred (*) exercises refer to the optional section in this chapter.

Learning the Mechanics

4.66 For each of the following examples, decide whether x is a binomial random variable and explain your decision:

a. A manufacturer of computer chips randomly selects 100 chips from each hour's production in order to estimate the proportion defective. Let x represent the number of defectives in the 100 sampled chips.

b. Of five applicants for a job, two will be selected. Although all applicants appear to be equally qualified, only three have the ability to fulfill the expectations of the company. Suppose that the two selections are made at random from the five applicants, and let x be the number of qualified applicants selected.

c. A software developer establishes a support hotline for customers to call in with questions regarding use of the software. Let x represent the number of calls received on the support hotline during a specified workday.

d. Florida is one of a minority of states with no state income tax. A poll of 1,000 registered voters is conducted to determine how many would favor a state income tax in light of the state's current fiscal condition. Let x be the number in the sample who would favor the tax.

4.67 Given that x is a binomial random variable, compute $p(x)$ for each of the following cases:

a. $n = 7, x = 3, p = .5$ **b.** $n = 4, x = 3, p = .8$
c. $n = 15, x = 1, p = .1$

4.68 Consider the discrete probability distribution shown here.

x	10	12	18	20
$p(x)$	.2	.3	.1	.4

a. Calculate μ, σ^2, and σ. **b.** What is $P(x < 15)$?

c. Calculate $\mu \pm 2\sigma$.
d. What is the probability that x is in the interval $\mu \pm 2\sigma$?

4.69 Suppose x is a binomial random variable with $n = 20$ and $p = .7$.
a. Find $P(x = 14)$. **b.** Find $P(x \leq 12)$.
c. Find $P(x > 12)$. **d.** Find $P(9 \leq x \leq 18)$.
e. Find $P(8 < x < 18)$. **f.** Find μ, σ^2, and σ.
g. What is the probability that x is in the interval $\mu \pm 2\sigma$?

*4.70 Suppose x is a Poisson random variable. Compute $p(x)$ for each of the following cases:
a. $\lambda = 2, x = 3$ **b.** $\lambda = 1, x = 4$ **c.** $\lambda = .5, x = 2$

4.71 Which of the following describe discrete random variables, and which describe continuous random variables?
a. The number of damaged inventory items
b. The average monthly sales revenue generated by a salesperson over the past year
c. The number of square feet of warehouse space a company rents
d. The length of time a firm must wait before its copying machine is fixed

4.72 Variables x, y, and z are three discrete random variables with the same mean and the same range. Their probability distributions are shown in the figures on page 197. Which has the largest variance? The next largest? The smallest? Explain.

Applying the Concepts

4.73 As part of a study of how pricing decisions are made by fabricare firms (the dry cleaning and laundry industry), 103 fabricare firms were contacted and questioned (*Journal of Small Business Management*, Apr. 1985). The table at the bottom of page 197 describes the sales volumes of these firms. Assume that the sales volume, x, for each of the six intervals can be adequately approximated by the midpoint of the interval. These midpoints are shown in the second column of the table. One of the 103 firms is to be randomly selected for

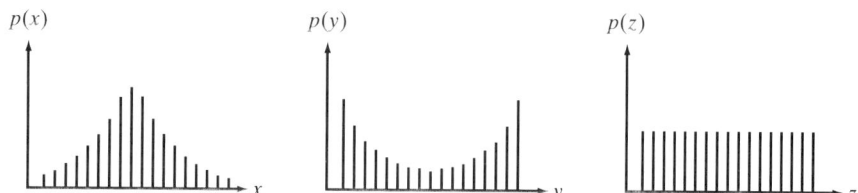

more intensive questioning. In this situation the relative frequencies in the table can be interpreted as probabilities that describe the approximate likelihood the sample firm has sales volume x.
a. Find $E(x)$.   b. Find $\text{Var}(x)$.
c. Interpret the values you obtained in parts **a** and **b** in the context of the problem.

4.74 A national study conducted by Geoffrey Alpert of the University of South Carolina found that 40% of all high-speed police chases end in accidents; 20% of all chases end in injury; and 1% in death. In trying to balance public safety, law enforcement, and liability concerns, many police departments have moved to restrict high-speed chases. One exception is the Tampa Police Department. After restricting chases for three years, management changed their policy and eased the restrictions. Prior to doing so, however, police received safety guidelines and refresher safe-driving courses. The result: high-speed chases increased from 10 in the previous 5 months to 85 in the succeeding 5 months, with 29 of those resulting in accidents. But, auto thefts dropped by 51% and overall crime dropped by 25% (*New York Times*, Dec. 17, 1995). Consider a random sample of five high-speed chases.
a. Demonstrate that x, the number of chases resulting in an accident, is an approximate binomial random variable.
b. Using the Alpert statistics, what is the probability that the five high-speed chases result in at least one accident?
c. Use the Tampa data to estimate the probability of part **b**.
d. Which probability, part **b** or part **c**, best describes high-speed chases in your state? Explain.

4.75 Your firm's accountant believes that 10% of the company's invoices contain arithmetic errors. To check this theory, the accountant randomly sam-

ples 25 invoices and finds that seven contain errors. What is the probability that of the 25 invoices written, seven or more would contain errors if the accountant's theory was valid? What assumptions do you have to make to solve this problem using the methodology of this chapter?

4.76 Anticipating a substantial growth in sales over the next five years, a printing company is planning today for the warehouse space it will need five years hence. It obviously cannot be certain exactly how many square feet of storage space, x, it will need in five years, but the company can project its needs by using a probability distribution such as the following:

x	10,000	15,000	20,000	25,000	30,000	35,000
$p(x)$	.05	.15	.35	.25	.15	.05

What is the expected number of square feet of storage space the printing company will need in five years?

4.77 The Environmental Protection Agency (EPA) tests in-use automobiles to determine whether there were differences between the cars' actual gas mileage and the mileage projected in the EPA's mileage guide. One year the EPA found that only 70% of the cars tested had highway driving fuel economies within 2 miles per gallon of the mileage guide's projection. Assume this figure holds for the population of cars currently in use for which the EPA has determined projected gas mileages. Suppose the EPA is planning to select 20 cars at random from this population and test their fuel economies to determine how many are within 2 miles per gallon of their EPA projections.
a. Decide whether the following statement is true or false and explain: The number of cars in the sample of 20 that have mileages within 2 miles per gallon of their EPA projections is not a

Sales Volume	x	Relative Frequency
Over $0 to $75,000	$ 37,500	.14
Over $75,000 to $150,000	112,500	.30
Over $150,000 to $300,000	225,000	.20
Over $300,000 to $500,000	400,000	.17
Over $500,000 to $1,000,000	750,000	.10
Over $1,000,000 to $5,000,000	3,000,000	.09

binomial random variable but, for convenience, could be treated as a binomial random variable.

b. What is the probability (approximately) that fewer than 10 of the 20 cars selected will be within 2 miles per gallon of their EPA projections?

4.78 A large number of preventable errors are being made by doctors and nurses in U.S. hospitals. From overdoses to botched operations to misdiagnoses, many patients leave the hospital in worse condition than they entered. The on-going debate on health care in the United States has revived calls for systematic approaches for catching errors, approaches that involve management techniques and computer systems to control quality, as is done in industry (*New York Times,* July 18, 1995). A study of a major metropolitan hospital revealed that of every 100 medications prescribed or dispensed, 1 was in error; but, only 1 in 500 resulted in an error that caused significant problems for the patient. It is known that the hospital prescribes and dispenses 60,000 medications per year.

a. What is the expected number of errors per year at this hospital? The expected number of significant errors per year?

b. Within what limits would you expect the number of significant errors per year to fall?

c. What assumptions did you need to make in order to answer these questions?

*4.79 Millions of suburban commuters are finding railroads to be a convenient, time-saving, less stressful alternative to the automobile. While generally perceived as a safe mode of transportation, the average number of deaths per week due to railroad accidents is a surprisingly high 14 (U.S. National Center for Health Statistics, *Vital Statistics of the United States, 1995*).

a. Construct arguments both for and against the use of the Poisson distribution to characterize the number of deaths per week due to railroad accidents.

b. For the remainder of this exercise, assume the Poisson distribution is an adequate approximation for x, the number of deaths per week due to railroad accidents. Find $E(x)$ and the standard deviation of x.

c. Based strictly on your answers to part **b**, is it likely that only 4 or fewer deaths occur next week? Explain.

d. Find $P(x \leq 4)$. Is this probability consistent with your answer to part **c**? Explain.

4.80 The probability that a consumer responds to a marketing department's mailed questionnaire is .4.

a. What is the probability that of 20 questionnaires, more than 15 will be returned?

b. How many questionnaires should be mailed if you want to be reasonably certain that at least 100 will be returned?

4.81 The *Journal of Applied Psychology* (Vol. 71, 1986) reported the results of an extensive survey conducted to determine the extent of whistle blowing among federal employees and to study the factors that are associated with retaliation against whistle blowers. *Whistle blowing* refers to an employee's reporting of wrongdoing by coworkers. Among other things, the survey found that about 5% of employees contacted had reported wrongdoing during the past 12 months. Assume that a sample of 25 employees in one agency are contacted, and let x be the number who have observed and reported wrongdoing in the last 12 months. Assume that the probability of whistle blowing is .05 for any federal employee over the past 12 months.

a. Find the mean and standard deviation of x. Can x be equal to its expected value? Explain.

b. Write the event that at least five of the employees are whistle blowers in terms of x. Find the probability of the event.

c. If five of the 25 contacted have been whistle blowers over the past 12 months, what would you conclude about the applicability of the 5% assumption to this agency? Use your answer to part **b** to justify your conclusion.

4.82 The owner of construction company A bids on jobs so that if awarded the job, company A will make a $10,000 profit. The owner of construction company B makes bids on jobs so that if awarded the job, company B will make a $15,000 profit. Each company describes the probability distribution of the number of jobs the company is awarded per year as shown in the table.

Company A		Company B	
2	.05	2	.15
3	.15	3	.30
4	.20	4	.30
5	.35	5	.20
6	.25	6	.05

a. Find the expected number of jobs each will be awarded in a year.

b. What is the expected profit for each company?

c. Find the variance and standard deviation of the distribution of number of jobs awarded per year for each company.

d. Graph $p(x)$ for both companies A and B. For each company, what proportion of the time will x fall in the interval $\mu \pm 2\sigma$?

4.83 The efficacy of insecticides is often measured by the dose necessary to kill a certain percentage of insects. Suppose a certain dose of a new insecticide is supposed to kill 80% of the insects that receive it. To test the claim, 25 insects are exposed to the insecticide.

a. If the insecticide really kills 80% of the exposed insects, what is the probability that fewer than 15 die?

b. If you observed such a result, what would you conclude about the new insecticide? Explain your logic.

4.84 Every few years in the United States debate arises over whether to increase the minimum wage. Advocates argue that it would significantly help improve the quality of life of low-wage earners. Opponents counter that an increase would force business owners to cut jobs and that the beneficiaries would primarily be teenagers and others who do not really need the raise. The following is a portrait of minimum wage earners:

Number of minimum wage earners	3.66 million
Percentage of minimum wage earners who are:	
Under 20	37
Under 25	54
White	82
Black	14
Women	63
Full-time workers	37
Food service workers	41

Primary Source: U.S. Labor Department.

Secondary Source: "The Minimum Wage: A Portrait." *New York Times,* Apr. 19, 1996, p. A26.

The government is interested in doing an in-depth study of the lives of 6 randomly selected minimum wage earners. Define the following four events:

A: {All 6 are white}

B: {None are full-time workers}

C: {Three are food service workers}

D: {More than half are teenagers}

a. Find $P(A), P(B), P(C),$ and $P(D)$.

b. What assumptions did you make to calculate the probabilities of part **a**?

c. Are the given summary statistics sufficient to determine the probability of obtaining 3 part-time food service workers and 3 full-time workers? Explain.

*4.85 Large bakeries typically have fleets of delivery trucks. One such bakery determined that the expected number of delivery truck breakdowns per day is 1.5. Assume that the number of breakdowns is independent from day to day.

a. What is the probability that there will be exactly two breakdowns today and exactly three tomorrow?

b. Fewer than two today and more than two tomorrow?

4.86 When the price of grain is low, many farmers participate in government-financed, on-farm storage programs rather than selling their grain. But storage invites insect infestations, and grain elevators penalize farmers who sell them insect-infested grain. The U.S. Grain Marketing Research Laboratory estimates that 80% of the storage bins of corn in the country are infested with insects. Suppose 20 storage bins of corn are randomly selected and examined for insect infestation.

a. What is the probability (approximately) that less than one-half of the bins are infested?

b. What assumptions did you make in answering part **a**?

c. Why is your answer to part **a** an approximation?

d. Would you be surprised if all 20 of the bins were infested? Explain.

CHAPTER 5

CONTINUOUS RANDOM VARIABLES

CONTENTS

STATISTICS IN ACTION

Where We've Been

We've seen that because numerical data represent observed values of random variables, we need to find the probabilities associated with specific sample observations. The probability theory of Chapter 3 provided the mechanism for finding the probabilities associated with discrete random variables. Finding and describing this set of probabilities—the probability distribution for a discrete random variable—was the subject of Chapter 4.

Where We're Going

Business data may be derived from observations on continuous as well as discrete random variables. Thus, we need to know about probability distributions associated with continuous random variables and also how to use the mean and standard deviation to describe these distributions. Chapter 5 addresses this problem and, in particular, introduces the *normal probability distribution*. As you'll see, the normal probability distribution is one of the most useful distributions in statistics.

In this chapter we'll consider some continuous random variables that are commonly encountered. Recall that a continuous random variable is one that can assume any value within some interval or intervals. For example, the length of time between a customer's purchase of new automobiles, the thickness of sheets of steel produced in a rolling mill, and the yield of wheat per acre of farmland are all continuous random variables. The methodology we employ to describe continuous random variables will necessarily be somewhat different from that used to describe discrete random variables. We first discuss the general form of *continuous probability distributions*, and then we explore three specific types that are used in making business decisions. The *normal probability distribution*, which plays a basic and important role in both the theory and application of statistics, is essential to the study of most of the subsequent chapters in this book. The other types have practical applications, but a study of these topics is optional.

5.1 CONTINUOUS PROBABILITY DISTRIBUTIONS

The graphical form of the probability distribution for a continuous random variable x is a smooth curve that might appear as shown in Figure 5.1. This curve, a function of x, is denoted by the symbol $f(x)$ and is variously called a **probability density function**, a **frequency function**, or a **probability distribution**.

The areas under a probability distribution correspond to probabilities for x. For example, the area A beneath the curve between the two points a and b, as shown in Figure 5.1, is the probability that x assumes a value between a and b ($a < x < b$). Because there is no area over a point, say $x = a$, it follows that (according to our model) the probability associated with a particular value of x is equal to 0; that is, $P(x = a) = 0$ and hence $P(a < x < b) = P(a \leq x \leq b)$. In other words, the probability is the same whether or not you include the endpoints of the interval. Also, because areas over intervals represent probabilities, it follows that the total area under a probability distribution, the probability assigned to all values of x, should equal 1. Note that probability distributions for continuous random variables possess different shapes depending on the relative frequency distributions of real data that the probability distributions are supposed to model.

The areas under most probability distributions are obtained by using calculus or numerical methods.* Because these methods often involve difficult procedures, we will give the areas for some of the most common probability distributions in tabular form in Appendix B. Then, to find the area between two values of x, say $x = a$ and $x = b$, you simply have to consult the appropriate table.

FIGURE 5.1
A probability distribution $f(x)$ for a continuous random variable x

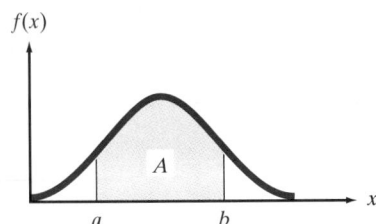

---

*Students with knowledge of calculus should note that the probability that x assumes a value in the interval $a < x < b$ is $P(a < x < b) = \int_a^b f(x)\, dx$, assuming the integral exists. Similar to the requirement for a discrete probability distribution, we require $f(x) \geq 0$ and $\int_{-\infty}^{\infty} f(x)\, dx = 1$.

For each of the continuous random variables presented in this chapter, we will give the formula for the probability distribution along with its mean μ and standard deviation σ. These two numbers will enable you to make some approximate probability statements about a random variable even when you do not have access to a table of areas under the probability distribution.

5.2   THE UNIFORM DISTRIBUTION (OPTIONAL)

All the probability problems discussed in Chapter 3 had sample spaces that contained a finite number of sample points. In many of these problems, the sample points were assigned equal probabilities—for example, the die toss or the coin toss. For continuous random variables, there is an infinite number of values in the sample space, but in some cases the values may appear to be equally likely. For example, if a short exists in a 5-meter stretch of electrical wire, it may have an equal probability of being in any particular 1-centimeter segment along the line. Or if a safety inspector plans to choose a time at random during the 4 afternoon work hours to pay a surprise visit to a certain area of a plant, then each 1-minute time interval in this 4-work-hour period will have an equally likely chance of being selected for the visit.

Continuous random variables that appear to have equally likely outcomes over their range of possible values possess a **uniform probability distribution**, perhaps the simplest of all continuous probability distributions. Suppose the random variable x can assume values only in an interval $c \leq x \leq d$. Then the uniform frequency function has a rectangular shape, as shown in Figure 5.2. Note that the possible values of x consist of all points in the interval between point c and point d. The height of $f(x)$ is constant in that interval and equals $1/(d - c)$. Therefore, the total area under $f(x)$ is given by

$$\text{Total area of rectangle} = (\text{Base})(\text{Height}) = (d - c)\left(\frac{1}{d - c}\right) = 1$$

The uniform probability distribution provides a model for continuous random variables that are *evenly distributed* over a certain interval. That is, a uniform random variable is one that is just as likely to assume a value in one interval as it is to assume a value in any other interval of equal size. There is no clustering of values around any value; instead, there is an even spread over the entire region of possible values.

The uniform distribution is sometimes referred to as the **randomness distribution**, since one way of generating a uniform random variable is to perform an experiment in which a point is *randomly selected* on the horizontal axis between the points c and d. If we were to repeat this experiment infinitely often, we would create a uniform probability distribution like that shown in Figure 5.2. The random selection of points in an interval can also be used to generate random

FIGURE 5.2
The uniform
probability distribution

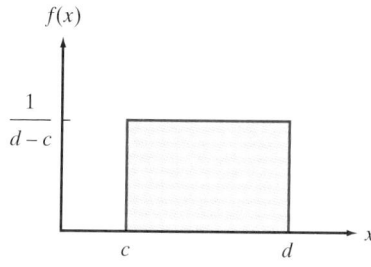

numbers such as those in Table I of Appendix B. Recall that random numbers are selected in such a way that every number would have an equal probability of selection. Therefore, random numbers are realizations of a uniform random variable. (Random numbers were used to draw random samples in Section 3.7.) The formulas for the uniform probability distribution, its mean, and standard deviation are shown in the box.

Probability Distribution, Mean, and Standard Deviation of a Uniform Random Variable x

$$f(x) = \frac{1}{d-c} \qquad c \leq x \leq d$$

$$\mu = \frac{c+d}{2} \qquad \sigma = \frac{d-c}{\sqrt{12}}$$

Suppose the interval $a < x < b$ lies within the domain of x; that is, it falls within the larger interval $c \leq x \leq d$. Then the probability that x assumes a value within the interval $a < x < b$ is equal to the area of the rectangle over the interval, namely, $(b-a)/(d-c)$.*

EXAMPLE 5.1

Suppose the research department of a steel manufacturer believes that one of the company's rolling machines is producing sheets of steel of varying thickness. The thickness is a uniform random variable with values between 150 and 200 millimeters. Any sheets less than 160 millimeters must be scrapped because they are unacceptable to buyers.

a. Calculate the mean and standard deviation of x, the thickness of the sheets produced by this machine. Graph the probability distribution of x, and show the mean on the horizontal axis. Also show 1- and 2-standard-deviation intervals around the mean.

b. Calculate the fraction of steel sheets produced by this machine that have to be scrapped.

SOLUTION

a. To calculate the mean and standard deviation for x, we substitute 150 and 200 millimeters for c and d, respectively, in the formulas for uniform random variables. Thus,

$$\mu = \frac{c+d}{2} = \frac{150 + 200}{2} = 175 \text{ millimeters}$$

and

$$\sigma = \frac{d-c}{\sqrt{12}} = \frac{200 - 150}{\sqrt{12}} = \frac{50}{3.464} = 14.43 \text{ millimeters}$$

The uniform probability distribution is

$$f(x) = \frac{1}{d-c} = \frac{1}{200 - 150} = \frac{1}{50} \qquad (150 \leq x \leq 200)$$

---

*The student with knowledge of calculus should note that

$$P(a < x < b) = \int_a^b f(x)\, d(x) = \int_a^b 1/(d-c)\, dx = (b-a)/(d-c)$$

FIGURE 5.3
Distribution for x
in Example 5.1

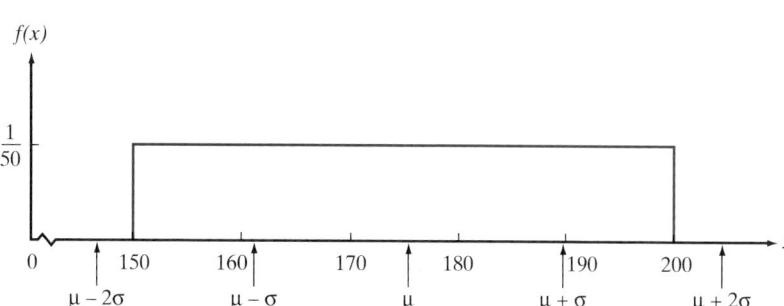

FIGURE 5.4
Probability that sheet
thickness, x, is between
150 and 160
millimeters

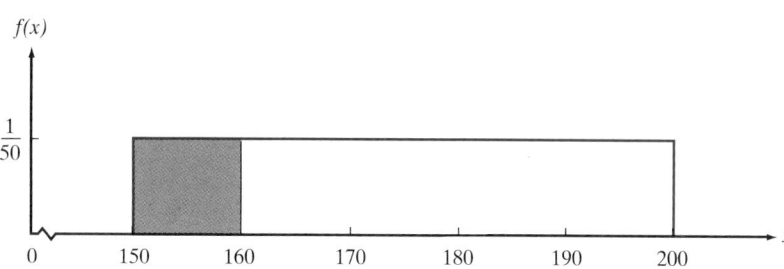

The graph of this function is shown in Figure 5.3. The mean and 1- and 2-standard-deviation intervals around the mean are shown on the horizontal axis.

b. To find the fraction of steel sheets produced by the machine that have to be scrapped, we must find the probability that x, the thickness, is less than 160 millimeters. As indicated in Figure 5.4, we need to calculate the area under the frequency function $f(x)$ between the points $x = 150$ and $x = 160$. This is the area of a rectangle with base $160 - 150 = 10$ and height $\frac{1}{50}$. The fraction that has to be scrapped is then

$$P(x < 160) = (\text{Base})(\text{Height}) = (10)\left(\frac{1}{50}\right) = \frac{1}{5}$$

That is, 20% of all the sheets made by this machine must be scrapped. ◼

EXERCISES   5.1–5.12

Note: Exercises marked with 💾 *contain data available for computer analysis on a 3.5" disk (file name in parentheses).*

Learning the Mechanics

5.1   Suppose x is a random variable best described by a uniform probability distribution with $c = 20$ and $d = 45$.
   a. Find $f(x)$.
   b. Find the mean and standard deviation of x.
   c. Graph $f(x)$ and locate μ and the interval $\mu \pm 2\sigma$ on the graph. Note that the probability that x assumes a value within the interval $\mu \pm 2\sigma$ is equal to 1.

5.2   Refer to Exercise 5.1. Find the following probabilities:

   a. $P(20 \leq x \leq 30)$ **b.** $P(20 < x < 30)$
   c. $P(x \geq 30)$ **d.** $P(x \geq 45)$ **e.** $P(x \leq 40)$
   f. $P(x < 40)$ **g.** $P(15 \leq x \leq 35)$
   h. $P(21.5 \leq x \leq 31.5)$

5.3   Suppose x is a random variable best described by a uniform probability distribution with $c = 3$ and $d = 7$.
   a. Find $f(x)$.
   b. Find the mean and standard deviation of x.
   c. Find $P(\mu - \sigma \leq x \leq \mu + \sigma)$.

5.4   Refer to Exercise 5.3. Find the value of a that makes each of the following probability statements true.
   a. $P(x \geq a) = .6$ **b.** $P(x \leq a) = .25$

c. $P(x \leq a) = 1$ **d.** $P(4 \leq x \leq a) = .5$

5.5 The random variable x is best described by a uniform probability distribution with $c = 100$ and $d = 200$. Find the probability that x assumes a value
a. More than 2 standard deviations from μ.
b. Less than 3 standard deviations from μ.
c. Within 2 standard deviations of μ.

5.6 The random variable x is best described by a uniform probability distribution with mean 10 and standard deviation 1. Find c, d, and $f(x)$. Graph the probability distribution.

Applying the Concepts

5.7 The manager of a local soft-drink bottling company believes that when a new beverage-dispensing machine is set to dispense 7 ounces, it in fact dispenses an amount x at random anywhere between 6.5 and 7.5 ounces inclusive. Suppose x has a uniform probability distribution.
a. Is the amount dispensed by the beverage machine a discrete or a continuous random variable? Explain.
b. Graph the frequency function for x, the amount of beverage the manager believes is dispensed by the new machine when it is set to dispense 7 ounces.
c. Find the mean and standard deviation for the distribution graphed in part **b**, and locate the mean and the interval $\mu \pm 2\sigma$ on the graph.
d. Find $P(x \geq 7)$. **e.** Find $P(x < 6)$.
f. Find $P(6.5 \leq x \leq 7.25)$.
g. What is the probability that each of the next six bottles filled by the new machine will contain more than 7.25 ounces of beverage? Assume that the amount of beverage dispensed in one bottle is independent of the amount dispensed in another bottle.

5.8 Researchers at the University of California–Berkeley have designed, built, and tested a switched-capacitor circuit for generating random signals (*International Journal of Circuit Theory and Applications*, May–June 1990). The circuit's trajectory was shown to be uniformly distributed on the interval $(0, 1)$.
a. Give the mean and variance of the circuit's trajectory.
b. Compute the probability that the trajectory falls between .2 and .4.
c. Would you expect to observe a trajectory that exceeds .995? Explain.

5.9 **(X05.009)** The data set listed below was created using the MINITAB random number generator. Construct a relative frequency histogram for the data. Except for the expected variation in relative frequencies among the class intervals, does your histogram suggest that the data are observa-

tions on a uniform random variable with $c = 0$ and $d = 100$? Explain.

38.8759	98.0716	64.5788	60.8422	.8413
88.3734	31.8792	32.9847	.7434	93.3017
12.4337	11.7828	87.4506	94.1727	23.0892
47.0121	43.3629	50.7119	88.2612	69.2875
62.6626	55.6267	78.3936	28.6777	71.6829
44.0466	57.8870	71.8318	28.9622	23.0278
35.6438	38.6584	46.7404	11.2159	96.1009
95.3660	21.5478	87.7819	12.0605	75.1015

5.10 During the recession of the late 1980s and early 1990s, many companies began tightening their reimbursement expense policies. For example, a survey of 550 companies by the Dartnell Corporation found that in 1992 about half reimbursed their salespeople for home fax machines, but by 1994 only one-fourth continued to do so (*Inc.*, Sept. 1995). One company found that monthly reimbursements to their employees, x, could be adequately modeled by a uniform distribution over the interval $\$10,000 \leq x \leq \$15,000$.
a. Find $E(x)$ and interpret it in the context of the exercise.
b. What is the probability of employee reimbursements exceeding $\$12,000$ next month?
c. For budgeting purposes, the company needs to estimate next month's employee reimbursement expenses. How much should the company budget for employee reimbursements if they want the probability of exceeding the budgeted amount to be only .20?

5.11 A tool-and-die machine shop produces extremely high-tolerance spindles. The spindles are 18-inch slender rods used in a variety of military equipment. A piece of equipment used in the manufacture of the spindles malfunctions on occasion and places a single gouge somewhere on the spindle. However, if the spindle can be cut so that it has 14 consecutive inches without a gouge, then the spindle can be salvaged for other purposes. Assuming that the location of the gouge along the spindle is best described by a uniform distribution, what is the probability that a defective spindle can be salvaged?

5.12 The **reliability** of a piece of equipment is frequently defined to be the probability, p, that the equipment performs its intended function successfully for a given period of time under specific conditions (Render and Heizer, *Principles of Operations Management*, 1995). Because p varies from one point in time to another, some reliability analysts treat p as if it were a random variable. Suppose an analyst characterizes the uncertainty about the reliability of a particular robotic device used in an automobile assembly line using the following distribution:

$$f(p) = \begin{cases} 1 & 0 \leq p \leq 1 \\ 0 & \text{otherwise} \end{cases}$$

a. Graph the analyst's probability distribution for p.
b. Find the mean and variance of p.
c. According to the analyst's probability distribution for p, what is the probability that p is greater than .95? Less than .95?

d. Suppose the analyst receives the additional information that p is definitely between .90 and .95, but that there is complete uncertainty about where it lies between these values. Describe the probability distribution the analyst should now use to describe p.

5.3   THE NORMAL DISTRIBUTION

One of the most commonly observed continuous random variables has a **bell-shaped** probability distribution as shown in Figure 5.5. It is known as a **normal random variable** and its probability distribution is called a **normal distribution**.

The normal distribution plays a very important role in the science of statistical inference. Moreover, many business phenomena generate random variables with probability distributions that are very well approximated by a normal distribution. For example, the monthly rate of return for a particular stock is approximately a normal random variable, and the probability distribution for the weekly sales of a corporation might be approximated by a normal probability distribution. The normal distribution might also provide an accurate model for the distribution of scores on an employment aptitude test. You can determine the adequacy of the normal approximation to an existing population by comparing the relative frequency distribution of a large sample of the data to the normal probability distribution. Tests to detect disagreement between a set of data and the assumption of normality are available, but they are beyond the scope of this book.

The normal distribution is perfectly symmetric about its mean μ, as can be seen in the examples in Figure 5.6. Its spread is determined by the value of its standard deviation σ.

The formula for the normal probability distribution is shown in the box. When plotted, this formula yields a curve like that shown in Figure 5.5.

FIGURE 5.5
A normal probability distribution

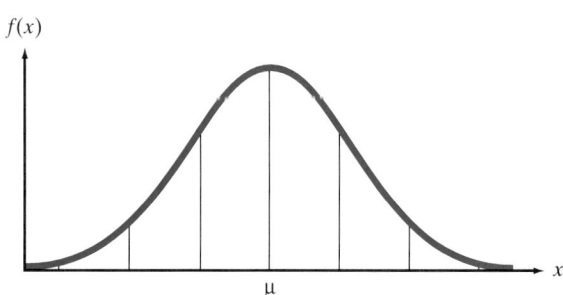

FIGURE 5.6
Several normal distributions with different means and standard deviations

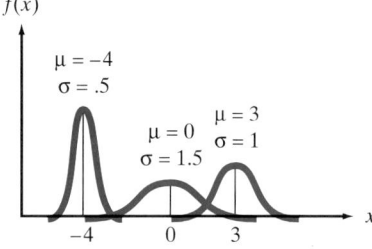

Probability Distribution for a Normal Random Variable x

$$f(x) = \frac{1}{\sigma\sqrt{2\pi}} e^{-(1/2)[(x-\mu)/\sigma]^2}$$

where μ = Mean of the normal random variable x
 σ = Standard deviation
 π = 3.1416...
 e = 2.71828...

Note that the mean μ and standard deviation σ appear in this formula, so that no separate formulas for μ and σ are necessary. To graph the normal curve we have to know the numerical values of μ and σ.

Computing the area over intervals under the normal probability distribution is a difficult task.* Consequently, we will use the computed areas listed in Table IV of Appendix B (and inside the front cover). Although there are an infinitely large number of normal curves—one for each pair of values for μ and σ—we have formed a single table that will apply to any normal curve.

Table IV is based on a normal distribution with mean $\mu = 0$ and standard deviation $\sigma = 1$, called a *standard normal distribution*. A random variable with a standard normal distribution is typically denoted by the symbol z. The formula for the probability distribution of z is given by

$$f(z) = \frac{1}{\sqrt{2\pi}} e^{-(1/2)z^2}$$

Figure 5.7 shows the graph of a standard normal distribution.

Since we will ultimately convert all normal random variables to standard normal in order to use Table IV to find probabilities, it is important that you learn to use Table IV well. A partial reproduction of Table IV is shown in Table 5.1. Note that the values of the standard normal random variable z are listed in the left-hand column. The entries in the body of the table give the area (probability) between 0 and z. Examples 5.2–5.5 illustrate the use of the table.

FIGURE 5.7
Standard normal
distribution: $\mu = 0$,
$\sigma = 1$

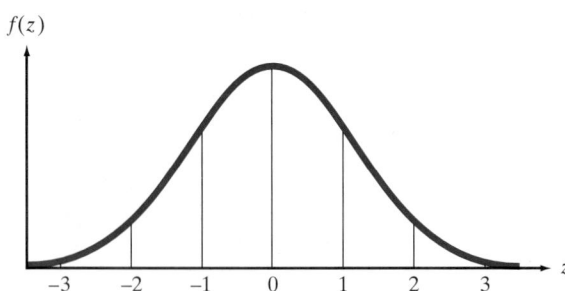

---

*The student with knowledge of calculus should note that there is not a closed-form expression for $P(a < x < b) = \int_a^b f(x)\,dx$ for the normal probability distribution. The value of this definite integral can be obtained to any desired degree of accuracy by numerical approximation procedures. For this reason, it is tabulated for the user.

TABLE 5.1 **Reproduction of Part of Table IV in Appendix B**

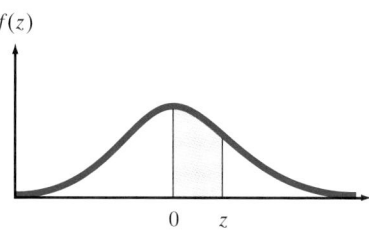

f(z)

z	.00	.01	.02	.03	.04	.05	.06	.07	.08	.09
.0	.0000	.0040	.0080	.0120	.0160	.0199	.0239	.0279	.0319	.0359
.1	.0398	.0438	.0478	.0517	.0557	.0596	.0636	.0675	.0714	.0753
.2	.0793	.0832	.0871	.0910	.0948	.0987	.1026	.1064	.1103	.1141
.3	.1179	.1217	.1255	.1293	.1331	.1368	.1406	.1443	.1480	.1517
.4	.1554	.1591	.1628	.1664	.1700	.1736	.1772	.1808	.1844	.1879
.5	.1915	.1950	.1985	.2019	.2054	.2088	.2123	.2157	.2190	.2224
.6	.2257	.2291	.2324	.2357	.2389	.2422	.2454	.2486	.2517	.2549
.7	.2580	.2611	.2642	.2673	.2704	.2734	.2764	.2794	.2823	.2852
.8	.2881	.2910	.2939	.2967	.2995	.3023	.3051	.3078	.3106	.3133
.9	.3159	.3186	.3212	.3238	.3264	.3289	.3315	.3340	.3365	.3389
1.0	.3413	.3438	.3461	.3485	.3508	.3531	.3554	.3577	.3599	.3621
1.1	.3643	.3665	.3686	.3708	.3729	.3749	.3770	.3790	.3810	.3830
1.2	.3849	.3869	.3888	.3907	.3925	.3944	.3962	.3980	.3997	.4015
1.3	.4032	.4049	.4066	.4082	.4099	.4115	.4131	.4147	.4162	.4177
1.4	.4192	.4207	.4222	.4236	.4251	.4265	.4279	.4292	.4306	.4319
1.5	.4332	.4345	.4357	.4370	.4382	.4394	.4406	.4418	.4429	.4441

EXAMPLE 5.2

Find the probability that the standard normal random variable z falls between -1.33 and $+1.33$.

SOLUTION

The standard normal distribution is shown again in Figure 5.8. Since all probabilities associated with standard normal random variables can be depicted as areas under the standard normal curve, you should always draw the curve and then equate the desired probability to an area.

In this example we want to find the probability that z falls between -1.33 and $+1.33$, which is equivalent to the area between -1.33 and $+1.33$, shown shaded in Figure 5.8. Table IV provides the area between $z = 0$ and any value of z, so that if we look up $z = 1.33$, we find that the area between $z = 0$ and $z = 1.33$ is .4082. This is the area labeled A_1 in Figure 5.8. To find the area A_2 located between $z = 0$ and $z = -1.33$, we note that the symmetry of the normal distribution implies that the area between $z = 0$ and any point to the left is equal to the area between $z = 0$ and the point equidistant to the right. Thus, in this example the area between $z = 0$ and $z = -1.33$ is equal to the area between $z = 0$ and $z = +1.33$. That is,

FIGURE 5.8
Areas under the
standard normal
curve for Example 5.2

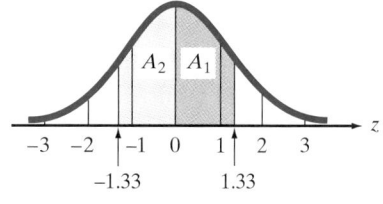

FIGURE 5.9
Areas under the
standard normal curve
for Example 5.3

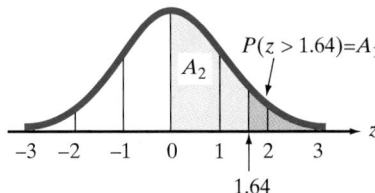

$$A_1 = A_2 = .4082$$

The probability that z falls between -1.33 and $+1.33$ is the sum of the areas of A_1 and A_2. We summarize in probabilistic notation:

$$P(-1.33 < z < 1.33) = P(-1.33 < z < 0) + P(0 < z \leq 1.33)$$
$$= A_1 + A_2 = .4082 + .4082 = .8164$$

Remember that "<" and "≤" are equivalent in events involving z, because the inclusion (or exclusion) of a single point does not alter the probability of an event involving a continuous random variable.

EXAMPLE 5.3   Find the probability that a standard normal random variable exceeds 1.64; that is, find $P(z > 1.64)$.

SOLUTION
The area under the standard normal distribution to the right of 1.64 is the shaded area labeled A_1 in Figure 5.9. This area represents the desired probability that z exceeds 1.64. However, when we look up $z = 1.64$ in Table IV, we must remember that the probability given in the table corresponds to the area between $z = 0$ and $z = 1.64$ (the area labeled A_2 in Figure 5.9). From Table IV we find that $A_2 = .4495$. To find the area A_1 to the right of 1.64, we make use of two facts:

  1. The standard normal distribution is symmetric about its mean, $z = 0$.
  2. The total area under the standard normal probability distribution equals 1.

Taken together, these two facts imply that the areas on either side of the mean $z = 0$ equal .5; thus, the area to the right of $z = 0$ in Figure 5.9 is $A_1 + A_2 = .5$. Then

$$P(z > 1.64) = A_1 = .5 - A_2 = .5 - .4495 = .0505$$

To attach some practical significance to this probability, note that the implication is that the chance of a standard normal random variable exceeding 1.64 is approximately .05.

EXAMPLE 5.4   Find the probability that a standard normal random variable lies to the right of $-.74$.

SOLUTION
We want to find $P(z > -.74)$. The event is shown as the shaded area in Figure 5.10. We divide the shaded area into two parts: the area A_1 between $z = -.74$ and $z = 0$, and the area A_2 to the right of $z = 0$. We must always make such a division

FIGURE 5.10
Areas under the
standard normal curve
for Example 5.4

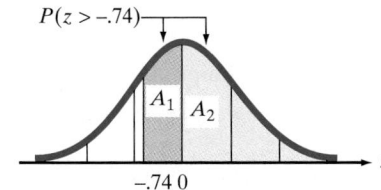

FIGURE 5.11
Areas under the
standard normal curve
for Example 5.5

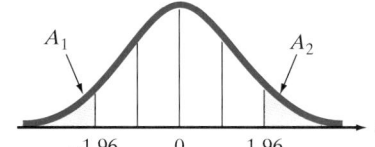

when the desired area lies on both sides of the mean ($z = 0$) because Table IV contains areas between $z = 0$ and the point you look up. To find A_1, we remember that the sign of z is unimportant when determining the area, because the standard normal distribution is symmetric about its mean. We look up $z = .74$ in Table IV to find that $A_1 = .2704$. The symmetry also implies that half the distribution lies on each side of the mean, so the area A_2 to the right of $z = 0$ is .5. Then,

$$P(z > -.74) = A_1 + A_2 = .2704 + .5 = .7704$$

EXAMPLE 5.5

Find the probability that a standard normal random variable exceeds 1.96 in absolute value.

SOLUTION
We want to find

$$P(|z| > 1.96) = P(z < -1.96 \text{ or } z > 1.96)$$

This probability is the shaded area in Figure 5.11. Note that the total shaded area is the sum of two areas, A_1 and A_2—areas that are equal because of the symmetry of the normal distribution.

We look up $z = 1.96$ and find the area between $z = 0$ and $z = 1.96$ to be .4750. Then the area to the right of 1.96, A_2, is $.5 - .4750 = .0250$, so that

$$P(|z| > 1.96) = A_1 + A_2 = .0250 + .0250 = .05$$

To apply Table IV to a normal random variable x with any mean μ and any standard deviation σ, we must first convert the value of x to a z-score. The population z-score for a measurement was defined (in Section 2.6) as the *distance* between the measurement and the population mean, divided by the population standard deviation. Thus, the z-score gives the distance between a measurement and the mean in units equal to the standard deviation. In symbolic form, the z-score for the measurement x is

$$z = \frac{x - \mu}{\sigma}$$

Note that when $x = \mu$, we obtain $z = 0$.

An important property of the normal distribution is that if x is normally distributed with any mean and any standard deviation, z is *always* normally distributed with mean 0 and standard deviation 1. That is, z is a standard normal random variable.

DEFINITION 5.1
The **standard normal distribution** is a normal distribution with $\mu = 0$ and $\sigma = 1$. A random variable with a standard normal distribution, denoted by the symbol z, is called a **standard normal random variable**.

Property of Normal Distributions

If x is a normal random variable with mean μ and standard deviation σ, then the random variable z, defined by the formula

$$z = \frac{x - \mu}{\sigma}$$

has a standard normal distribution. The value z describes the number of standard deviations between x and μ.

Recall from Example 5.5 that $P(|z| > 1.96) = .05$. This probability coupled with our interpretation of z implies that any normal random variable lies more than 1.96 standard deviations from its mean only 5% of the time. Compare this to the Empirical Rule (Chapter 2) which tells us that about 5% of the measurements in mound-shaped distributions will lie beyond 2 standard deviations from the mean. The normal distribution actually provides the model on which the Empirical Rule is based, along with much "empirical" experience with real data that often approximately obey the rule, whether drawn from a normal distribution or not.

EXAMPLE 5.6

Assume that the length of time, x, between charges of a pocket calculator is normally distributed with a mean of 100 hours and a standard deviation of 15 hours. Find the probability that the calculator will last between 80 and 120 hours between charges.

SOLUTION

The normal distribution with mean $\mu = 100$ and $\sigma = 15$ is shown in Figure 5.12. The desired probability that the calculator lasts between 80 and 120 hours is shaded. In order to find the probability, we must first convert the distribution to standard normal, which we do by calculating the z-score:

$$z = \frac{x - \mu}{\sigma}$$

The z-scores corresponding to the important values of x are shown beneath the x values on the horizontal axis in Figure 5.12. Note that $z = 0$ corresponds to the mean of $\mu = 100$ hours, whereas the x values 80 and 120 yield z-scores of -1.33 and $+1.33$, respectively. Thus, the event that the calculator lasts between 80 and 120 hours is equivalent to the event that a standard normal random variable lies between -1.33 and $+1.33$. We found this probability in Example 5.2 (see Figure 5.8) by doubling the area corresponding to $z = 1.33$ in Table IV. That is,

$$P(80 \leq x \leq 120) = P(-1.33 \leq z \leq 1.33) = 2(.4082) = .8164$$

The steps to follow when calculating a probability corresponding to a normal random variable are shown in the box.

FIGURE 5.12
Areas under the normal curve for Example 5.6

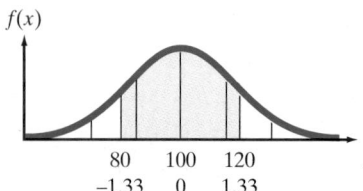

Steps for Finding a Probability Corresponding to a Normal Random Variable

1. Sketch the normal distribution and indicate the mean of the random variable x. Then shade the area corresponding to the probability you want to find.

2. Convert the boundaries of the shaded area from x values to standard normal random variable z values using the formula

$$z = \frac{x - \mu}{\sigma}$$

Show the z values under the corresponding x values on your sketch.

3. Use Table IV in Appendix B (and inside the front cover) to find the areas corresponding to the z values. If necessary, use the symmetry of the normal distribution to find areas corresponding to negative z values and the fact that the total area on each side of the mean equals .5 to convert the areas from Table IV to the probabilities of the event you have shaded.

EXAMPLE **5.7**

Suppose an automobile manufacturer introduces a new model that has an advertised mean in-city mileage of 27 miles per gallon. Although such advertisements seldom report any measure of variability, suppose you write the manufacturer for the details of the tests, and you find that the standard deviation is 3 miles per gallon. This information leads you to formulate a probability model for the random variable x, the in-city mileage for this car model. You believe that the probability distribution of x can be approximated by a normal distribution with a mean of 27 and a standard deviation of 3.

a. If you were to buy this model of automobile, what is the probability that you would purchase one that averages less than 20 miles per gallon for in-city driving? In other words, find $P(x < 20)$.

b. Suppose you purchase one of these new models and it does get less than 20 miles per gallon for in-city driving. Should you conclude that your probability model is incorrect?

SOLUTION

a. The probability model proposed for x, the in-city mileage, is shown in Figure 5.13.

We are interested in finding the area A to the left of 20 since this area corresponds to the probability that a measurement chosen from this distribution falls below 20. In other words, if this model is correct, the area A represents the fraction of cars that can be expected to get less than 20 miles per gallon for in-city driving. To find A, we first calculate the z value corresponding to $x = 20$. That is,

$$z = \frac{x - \mu}{\sigma} = \frac{20 - 27}{3} = -\frac{7}{3} = -2.33$$

FIGURE 5.13
Area under the
normal curve for
Example 5.7

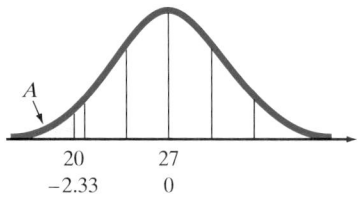

Then

$$P(x < 20) = P(z < -2.33)$$

as indicated by the shaded area in Figure 5.13. Since Table IV gives only areas to the right of the mean (and because the normal distribution is symmetric about its mean), we look up 2.33 in Table IV and find that the corresponding area is .4901. This is equal to the area between $z = 0$ and $z = -2.33$, so we find

$$P(x < 20) = A = .5 - .4901 = .0099 \approx .01$$

According to this probability model, you should have only about a 1% chance of purchasing a car of this make with an in-city mileage under 20 miles per gallon.

b. Now you are asked to make an inference based on a sample—the car you purchased. You are getting less than 20 miles per gallon for in-city driving. What do you infer? We think you will agree that one of two possibilities is true:

1. The probability model is correct. You simply were unfortunate to have purchased one of the cars in the 1% that get less than 20 miles per gallon in the city.

2. The probability model is incorrect. Perhaps the assumption of a normal distribution is unwarranted or the mean of 27 is an overestimate, or the standard deviation of 3 is an underestimate, or some combination of these errors was made. At any rate, the form of the actual probability model certainly merits further investigation.

You have no way of knowing with certainty which possibility is correct, but the evidence points to the second one. We are again relying on the rare-event approach to statistical inference that we introduced earlier. The sample (one measurement in this case) was so unlikely to have been drawn from the proposed probability model that it casts serious doubt on the model. We would be inclined to believe that the model is somehow in error.

Occasionally you will be given a probability and will want to find the values of the normal random variable that correspond to the probability. For example, suppose the scores on a college entrance examination are known to be normally distributed, and a certain prestigious university will consider for admission only those applicants whose scores exceed the 90th percentile of the test score distribution. To determine the minimum score for admission consideration, you will need to be able to use Table IV in reverse, as demonstrated in the following example.

EXAMPLE 5.8   Find the value of z, call it z_0, in the standard normal distribution that will be exceeded only 10% of the time. That is, find z_0 such that $P(z \geq z_0) = .10$.

SOLUTION
In this case we are given a probability, or an area, and asked to find the value of the standard normal random variable that corresponds to the area. Specifically, we want to find the value z_0 such that only 10% of the standard normal distribution exceeds z_0 (see Figure 5.14).

We know that the total area to the right of the mean $z = 0$ is .5, which implies that z_0 must lie to the right of (above) 0. To pinpoint the value, we use the fact that the area to the right of z_0 is .10, which implies that the area between $z = 0$ and z_0 is $.5 - .1 = .4$. But areas between $z = 0$ and some other z value are exactly the

FIGURE 5.14
Areas under the
standard normal curve
for Example 5.8

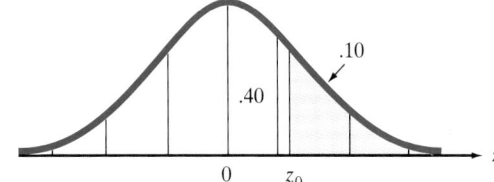

types given in Table IV. Therefore, we look up the area .4000 in the body of Table IV and find that the corresponding z value is (to the closest approximation) $z_0 = 1.28$. The implication is that the point 1.28 standard deviations above the mean is the 90th percentile of a normal distribution.

EXAMPLE 5.9

Find the value of z_0 such that 95% of the standard normal z values lie between $-z_0$ and $+z_0$, i.e., $P(-z_0 \leq z \leq z_0) = .95$.

SOLUTION
Here we wish to move an equal distance z_0 in the positive and negative directions from the mean $z = 0$ until 95% of the standard normal distribution is enclosed. This means that the area on each side of the mean will be equal $\frac{1}{2}(.95) = .475$, as shown in Figure 5.15. Since the area between $z = 0$ and z_0 is .475, we look up .475 in the body of Table IV to find the value $z_0 = 1.96$. Thus, as we found in the reverse order in Example 5.5, 95% of a normal distribution lies between +1.96 and −1.96 standard deviations of the mean.

Now that you have learned to use Table IV to find a standard normal z value that corresponds to a specified probability, we demonstrate a practical application in Example 5.10.

EXAMPLE 5.10

Suppose a paint manufacturer has a daily production, x, that is normally distributed with a mean of 100,000 gallons and a standard deviation of 10,000 gallons. Management wants to create an incentive bonus for the production crew when the daily production exceeds the 90th percentile of the distribution, in hopes that the crew will, in turn, become more productive. At what level of production should management pay the incentive bonus?

SOLUTION
In this example, we want to find a production level, x_0, such that 90% of the daily levels (x values) in the distribution fall below x_0 and only 10% fall above x_0. That is,

$$P(x \leq x_0) = .90$$

Converting x to a standard normal random variable, where $\mu = 100,000$ and $\sigma = 10,000$, we have

FIGURE 5.15
Areas under the
standard normal curve
for Example 5.9

STATISTICS IN ACTION

5.1 IQ, ECONOMIC MOBILITY, AND THE BELL CURVE

In their controversial book *The Bell Curve* (Free Press, 1994), Professors Richard J. Herrnstein (a Harvard psychologist who died while the book was in production) and Charles Murray (a political scientist at MIT) explore, as the subtitle states, "intelligence and class structure in American life." *The Bell Curve* heavily employs statistical analyses in an attempt to support the authors' positions. Since the book's publication, many expert statisticians have raised doubts about the authors' statistical methods and the inferences drawn from them. (See, for example, "Wringing *The Bell Curve:* A cautionary tale about the relationships among race, genes, and IQ," *Chance,* Summer 1995.) In Statistics in Action 11.2, we explore a few of these problems.

One of the many controversies sparked by the book is the authors' tenet that level of intelligence (or lack thereof) is a cause of a wide range of intractable social problems, including constrained economic mobility.

"America has taken great pride in the mobility of generations," state Herrnstein and Murray, "but this mobility has its limits. ...The son of a father whose earnings are in the bottom five percent of the [income] distribution has something like one chance in twenty (or less) of rising to the top fifth of the income distribution and almost a fifty-fifty chance of staying in the bottom fifth. He has less than one chance in four of rising above even the median income. ...Most people at present are stuck near where their parents were on the income distribution in part because [intelligence], which has become a major predictor of income, passes on sufficiently from one generation to the next to constrain economic mobility."

The measure of intelligence chosen by the authors is the well known Intelligent Quotient (IQ). Numerous tests have been developed to measure IQ; Herrnstein and Murray use the Armed Forces Qualification Test (AFQT), originally designed to measure the cognitive ability of military recruits. Psychologists traditionally

$$P(x \leq x_0) = P\left(z \leq \frac{x_0 - \mu}{\sigma}\right)$$

$$= P\left(z \leq \frac{x_0 - 100{,}000}{10{,}000}\right) = .90$$

In Example 5.8 (see Figure 5.14) we found the 90th percentile of the standard normal distribution to be $z_0 = 1.28$. That is, we found $P(z \leq 1.28) = .90$. Consequently, we know the production level x_0 at which the incentive bonus is paid corresponds to a z-score of 1.28; that is,

$$\frac{x_0 - 100{,}000}{10{,}000} = 1.28$$

If we solve this equation for x_0, we find

$$x_0 = 100{,}000 + 1.28(10{,}000) = 100{,}000 + 12{,}800 = 112{,}800$$

This x value is shown in Figure 5.16. Thus, the 90th percentile of the production distribution is 112,800 gallons. Management should pay an incentive bonus when a day's production exceeds this level if its objective is to pay only when production is in the top 10% of the current daily production distribution.

treat IQ as a random variable having a normal distribution with mean $\mu = 100$ and standard deviation $\sigma = 15$. This distribution, or *bell curve*, is shown in Figure 5.17.

In their book, Herrnstein and Murray refer to five cognitive classes of people defined by percentiles of the normal distribution. Class I ("very bright") consists of those with IQs above the 95th percentile; Class II ("bright") are those with IQs between the 75th and 95th percentiles; Class III ("normal") includes IQs between the 25th and 75th percentiles; Class IV ("dull") are those with IQs between the 5th and 25th percentiles; and Class V ("very dull") are IQs below the 5th percentile. These classes are also illustrated in Figure 5.17.

Focus

a. Assuming that the distribution of IQ is accurately represented by the bell curve in Figure 5.17, deter-

mine the proportion of people with IQs in each of the five cognitive classes defined by Herrnstein and Murray.

b. Although the cognitive classes above are defined in terms of percentiles, the authors stress that IQ scores should be compared with z-scores, not percentiles. In other words, it is more informative to give the difference in z-scores for two IQ scores than it is to give the difference in percentiles. To demonstrate this point, calculate the difference in z-scores for IQs at the 50th and 55th percentiles. Do the same for IQs at the 94th and 99th percentiles. What do you observe?

c. Researchers have found that scores on many intelligence tests are decidedly nonnormal. Some distributions are skewed toward higher scores, others toward lower scores. How would the proportions in the five cognitive classes differ for an IQ distribution that is skewed right? Skewed left?

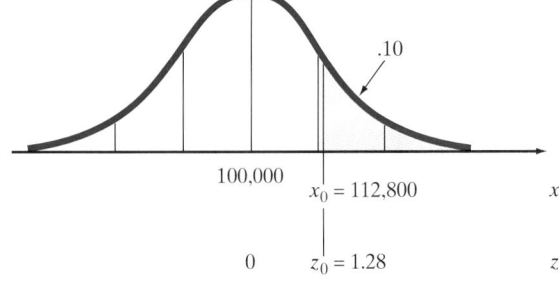

FIGURE 5.16
Area under the normal curve for Example 5.10

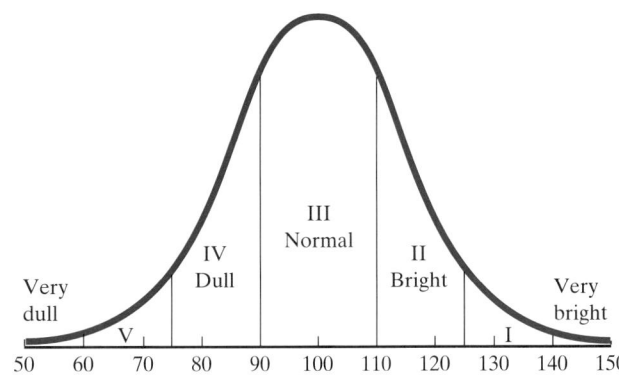

FIGURE 5.17
The distribution of IQ
(Statistics in Action 5.1)

EXERCISES 5.13–5.37

Learning the Mechanics

5.13 Find the area under the standard normal probability distribution between the following pairs of z-scores:
a. $z = 0$ and $z = 2.00$ **b.** $z = 0$ and $z = 3$
c. $z = 0$ and $z = 1.5$ **d.** $z = 0$ and $z = .80$

5.14 Find the following probabilities for the standard normal random variable z:
a. $P(-1 \leq z \leq 1)$ **b.** $P(-2 \leq z \leq 2)$
c. $P(-2.16 \leq z \leq .55)$ **d.** $P(-.42 < z < 1.96)$
e. $P(z \geq -2.33)$ **f.** $P(z < 2.33)$

5.15 Find the following probabilities for the standard normal random variable z:
a. $P(z > 1.46)$ **b.** $P(z < -1.56)$
c. $P(.67 \leq z \leq 2.41)$ **d.** $P(-1.96 \leq z < -.33)$
e. $P(z \geq 0)$ **f.** $P(-2.33 < z < 1.50)$

5.16 Find each of the following probabilities for a standard normal random variable z:
a. $P(z = 1)$ **b.** $P(z \leq 1)$
c. $P(z < 1)$ **d.** $P(z > 1)$

5.17 Find each of the following probabilities for the standard normal random variable z:
a. $P(-1 \leq z \leq 1)$ **b.** $P(-1.96 \leq z \leq 1.96)$
c. $P(-1.645 \leq z \leq 1.645)$ **d.** $P(-2 \leq z \leq 2)$

5.18 Find a value of the standard normal random variable z, call it z_0, such that
a. $P(z \geq z_0) = .05$ **b.** $P(z \geq z_0) = .025$
c. $P(z \leq z_0) = .025$ **d.** $P(z \geq z_0) = .10$
e. $P(z > z_0) = .10$

5.19 Find a value of the standard normal random variable z, call it z_0, such that
a. $P(z \leq z_0) = .2090$ **b.** $P(z \leq z_0) = .7090$
c. $P(-z_0 \leq z < z_0) = .8472$
d. $P(-z_0 \leq z \leq z_0) = .1664$
e. $P(z_0 \leq z \leq 0) = .4798$
f. $P(-1 < z < z_0) = .5328$

5.20 Give the z-score for a measurement from a normal distribution for the following:
a. 1 standard deviation above the mean
b. 1 standard deviation below the mean
c. Equal to the mean
d. 2.5 standard deviations below the mean
e. 3 standard deviations above the mean

5.21 Suppose the random variable x is best described by a normal distribution with $\mu = 30$ and $\sigma = 4$. Find the z-score that corresponds to each of the following x values:
a. $x = 20$ **b.** $x = 30$ **c.** $x = 27.5$
d. $x = 15$ **e.** $x = 35$ **f.** $x = 25$

5.22 The random variable x has a normal distribution with $\mu = 1,000$ and $\sigma = 10$.
a. Find the probability that x assumes a value more than 2 standard deviations from its mean. More than 3 standard deviations from μ.

b. Find the probability that x assumes a value within 1 standard deviation of its mean. Within 2 standard deviations of μ.
c. Find the value of x that represents the 80th percentile of this distribution. The 10th percentile.

5.23 Suppose x is a normally distributed random variable with $\mu = 11$ and $\sigma = 2$. Find each of the following:
a. $P(10 \leq x \leq 12)$ **b.** $P(6 \leq x \leq 10)$
c. $P(13 \leq x \leq 16)$ **d.** $P(7.8 \leq x \leq 12.6)$
e. $P(x \geq 13.24)$ **f.** $P(x \geq 7.62)$

5.24 Suppose x is a normally distributed random variable with $\mu = 50$ and $\sigma = 3$. Find a value of the random variable, call it x_0, such that
a. $P(x \leq x_0) = .8413$ **b.** $P(x > x_0) = .025$
c. $P(x > x_0) = .95$ **d.** $P(41 \leq x < x_0) = .8630$
e. 10% of the values of x are less than x_0.
f. 1% of the values of x are greater than x_0.

5.25 Suppose x is a normally distributed random variable with mean 120 and variance 36. Draw a rough graph of the distribution of x. Locate μ and the interval $\mu \pm 2\sigma$ on the graph. Find the following probabilities:
a. $P(\mu - 2\sigma \leq x \leq \mu + 2\sigma)$ **b.** $P(x \geq 128)$
c. $P(x \leq 108)$ **d.** $P(112 \leq x \leq 130)$
e. $P(114 \leq x \leq 116)$ **f.** $P(115 \leq x \leq 128)$

5.26 The random variable x has a normal distribution with standard deviation 25. It is known that the probability that x exceeds 150 is .90. Find the mean μ of the probability distribution.

Applying the Concepts

5.27 It is vitally important for airlines to appropriately match aircraft to passenger demand on each flight leg. This is called the **flight assignment problem**. If the aircraft is too large, the result is empty seats and, therefore, lost revenue; if the aircraft is too small, business is lost to other airlines. **Spill** is defined as the number of passengers not carried because the aircraft's capacity is insufficient. A solution to the flight assignment problem at Delta Airlines was published in *Interfaces* (Jan.–Feb. 1994). The authors—four Delta Airlines researchers and a Georgia Tech professor (Roy Marsten)—demonstrated their approach with an example in which passenger demand for a particular flight leg is normally distributed with a mean of 125 passengers and a standard deviation of 45. Consider a Boeing 727 with a capacity of 148 passengers and a Boeing 757 with a capacity of 182.
a. What is the probability that passenger demand will exceed the capacity of the Boeing 727? The Boeing 757?

b. If the 727 is assigned to the flight leg, what is the probability that the flight will depart with one or more empty seats? Answer the same question for the Boeing 757.

c. If the 727 is assigned to the flight, what is the probability that the spill will be more than 100 passengers?

5.28 Ideally, a worker seeking a new job in a particular industry should acquire information about wage rates offered by all firms in the industry. However, workers may not find it worthwhile to search until they find the highest available wage rate. The result is that managers may not have to pay top dollar to attract workers. These factors help to explain the existing disparity in wage rates among firms. The latest government data indicate that the mean hourly wage for manufacturing workers in the United States is $13.69 (*Statistical Abstract of the United States: 1995*). Suppose the distribution of manufacturing wage rates nationwide can be approximated by a normal distribution with standard deviation $1.25 per hour. The first manufacturing firm contacted by a particular worker pays $15.00 per hour.

a. If the worker were to undertake a nationwide job search, approximately what proportion of the wage rates would be greater than $15.00 per hour?

b. If the worker were to randomly select a U.S. manufacturing firm, what is the probability the firm would pay more than $15.00 per hour?

c. The population median, call it η, of a continuous random variable x is the value such that $P(x \geq \eta) = P(x \leq \eta) = .5$. That is, the median is the value η such that half the area under the probability distribution lies above η and half lies below it. Find the median of the random variable corresponding to the wage rate and compare it to the mean wage rate.

5.29 In studying the dynamics of fish populations, knowing the length of a species at different ages is critical, especially for commercial fishermen. *Fisheries Science* (Feb. 1995) published a study of the length distributions of sardines inhabiting Japanese waters. At two years of age, fish have a length distribution that is approximately normal with $\mu = 20.20$ centimeters (cm) and $\sigma = .65$ cm.

a. Find the probability that a two-year-old sardine inhabiting Japanese waters is between 20 and 21 cm long.

b. A sardine captured in Japanese waters has a length of 19.84 cm. Is this sardine likely to be two years old?

c. Repeat part **b** for a sardine with a length of 22.01 cm.

5.30 Personnel tests are designed to test a job applicant's cognitive and/or physical abilities. An IQ test is an example of the former; a speed test involving the arrangement of pegs on a peg board is an example of the latter (Cowling and James, *The Essence of Personnel Management and Industrial Relations*, 1994). A particular dexterity test is administered nationwide by a private testing service. It is known that for all tests administered last year the distribution of scores was approximately normal with mean 75 and standard deviation 7.5.

a. A particular employer requires job candidates to score at least 80 on the dexterity test. Approximately what percentage of the test scores during the past year exceeded 80?

b. The testing service reported to a particular employer that one of its job candidate's scores fell at the 98th percentile of the distribution (i.e., approximately 98% of the scores were lower than the candidate's, and only 2% were higher). What was the candidate's score?

5.31 In baseball, a "no-hitter" is a regulation 9-inning game in which the pitcher yields no hits to the opposing batters. *Chance* (Summer 1994) reported on a study of no-hitters in Major League Baseball (MLB). The initial analysis focused on the total number of hits yielded per game per team for all 9-inning MLB games played between 1989 and 1993. The distribution of hits/9-innings is approximately normal with mean 8.72 and standard deviation 1.10.

a. What percentage of 9-inning MLB games result in fewer than 6 hits?

b. Demonstrate, statistically, why a no-hitter is considered an extremely rare occurrence in MLB.

5.32 Before negotiating a long-term construction contract, building contractors must carefully estimate the total cost of completing the project and, thereafter, determine the price they would need to charge in order to make a reasonable profit. The process is complicated by the fact that total cost cannot be known with certainty ahead of time. Wages, salaries, the price of materials, the time to complete the job, etc. are all subject to change. Benzion Barlev of New York University proposed a model for total cost of a long-term contract based on the normal distribution (*Journal of Business Finance and Accounting*, July 1995). For one particular construction contract, Barlev assumed total cost, x, to be normally distributed with mean $850,000 and standard deviation $170,000. The revenue, R, promised to the contractor is $1,000,000.

a. The contract will be profitable if revenue exceeds total cost. What is the probability that the contract will be profitable for the contractor?

b. What is the probability that the project will result in a loss for the contractor?

c. Suppose the contractor has the opportunity to renegotiate the contract. What value of R should the contractor strive for in order to have a .99 probability of making a profit?

5.33 A machine used to regulate the amount of dye dispensed for mixing shades of paint can be set so that it discharges an average of μ milliliters (mL) of dye per can of paint. The amount of dye discharged is known to have a normal distribution with a standard deviation of .4 mL. If more than 6 mL of dye are discharged when making a certain shade of blue paint, the shade is unacceptable. Determine the setting for μ so that only 1% of the cans of paint will be unacceptable.

5.34 An important quality characteristic for soft-drink bottlers is the amount of soft drink injected into each bottle. This volume is determined (approximately) by measuring the height of the soft drink in the neck of the bottle and comparing it to a scale that converts the height measurement to a volume measurement (Montgomery, *Introduction to Statistical Quality Control,* 1991). In a particular filling process, the number of ounces injected into 8-ounce bottles is approximately normally distributed with mean 8.00 ounces and standard deviation .05 ounce. Bottles that contain less than 7.9 ounces do not meet the bottle's quality standard and are sold at a substantial discount.

a. If 20,000 bottles are filled, approximately how many will fail to meet the quality standard?

b. Suppose that, due to the failure of one of the filling system's components, the mean of the filling process shifts to 7.95 ounces. (Assume that the standard deviation remains .05 ounce.) If 20,000 bottles are filled, approximately how many will fail to meet the quality standard?

c. Suppose that a different component fails and, although the mean of the filling process remains 8.00 ounces, the standard deviation increases to .1 ounce. If 20,000 bottles are filled, approximately how many will fail to meet the quality standard?

5.35 The **monthly rate of return** of a stock is a measure investors frequently use for evaluating the behavior of a stock over time. A stock's monthly rate of return generally reflects the amount of money an investor makes (or loses if the return is negative) for every dollar invested in the stock in a given month. In his classic text, *Foundations of Finance* (1976), Eugene Fama demonstrated that the probability distribution for the monthly rate of return of a stock can be approximated by a normal probability distribution. Suppose the monthly rates of return to stock ABC are normally distributed with mean .05 and standard deviation .03, and the monthly rates of return to stock XYZ are normally distributed with mean .07 and standard devia-

tion .05. Assume that you have $100 invested in each stock.

a. Over the long run, which stock will yield the higher average monthly rate of return? Why?

b. Suppose you plan to hold each stock for only one month. What is the expected value of each investment at the end of one month?

c. Which stock offers greater protection against incurring a loss on your investment next month? Why?

5.36 Do security analysts do a good job of forecasting corporate earnings growth and advising their clientele? This question was addressed in an article titled "Astrology might be better" (*Forbes,* Mar. 26, 1984). The basis of the article is a study by Professors Michael Sandretto of Harvard and Sudhir Milkrishnamurthi of the Massachusetts Institute of Technology. The study surveys security analysts' forecasts of annual earnings for the (then) current year for more than 769 companies with five or more forecasts per company per year. The average forecast error for this large number of forecasts was 31.3%. To apply this information to a practical situation, suppose the population of analysts' forecast errors is normally distributed with a mean of 31.3% and a standard deviation of 10%.

a. If you obtain a security analyst's forecast for a particular company, what is the probability that it will be in error by more than 50%?

b. If three analysts make the forecast, what is the probability that at least one of the analysts will err by more than 50%?

5.37 What relationship exists between the standard normal distribution and the box-plot methodology (optional Section 2.9) for describing distributions of data using quartiles? The answer depends on the true underlying probability distribution of the data. Assume for the remainder of this exercise that the distribution is normal.

a. Calculate the values of the standard normal random variable z, call them z_L and z_U, that correspond to the hinges of the box plot—i.e., the lower and upper quartiles, Q_L and Q_U—of the probability distribution.

b. Calculate the z values that correspond to the inner fences of the box plot for a normal probability distribution.

c. Calculate the z values that correspond to the outer fences of the box plot for a normal probability distribution.

d. What is the probability that an observation lies beyond the inner fences of a normal probability distribution? The outer fences?

e. Can you better understand why the inner and outer fences of a box plot are used to detect outliers in a distribution? Explain.

5.4   APPROXIMATING A BINOMIAL DISTRIBUTION WITH A NORMAL DISTRIBUTION

When a binomial random variable can assume a large number of values, the calculation of its probabilities may become very tedious. To contend with this problem, we provide tables in Appendix B to give the probabilities for some values of n and p, but these tables are by necessity incomplete. In particular, the binomial probability table (Table II) can be used only for $n = 5, 6, 7, 8, 9, 10, 15, 20,$ or 25. To deal with this limitation, we seek approximation procedures for calculating the probabilities associated with a binomial probability distribution.

When n is large, a normal probability distribution may be used to provide a good approximation to the probability distribution of a binomial random variable. To show how this approximation works, we refer to Example 4.10, in which we used the binomial distribution to model the number x of 20 employees who favor unionization. We assumed that 60% of all the company's employees favored unionization. The mean and standard deviation of x were found to be $\mu = 12$ and $\sigma = 2.2$. The binomial distribution for $n = 20$ and $p = .6$ is shown in Figure 5.18, and the approximating normal distribution with mean $\mu = 12$ and standard deviation $\sigma = 2.2$ is superimposed.

As part of Example 4.10, we used Table II to find the probability that $x \leq 10$. This probability, which is equal to the sum of the areas contained in the rectangles (shown in Figure 5.18) that correspond to $p(0), p(1), p(2), \ldots, p(10)$, was found to equal .245. The portion of the approximating normal curve that would be used to approximate the area $p(0) + p(1) + p(2) + \cdots + p(10)$ is shaded in Figure 5.18. Note that this shaded area lies to the left of 10.5 (not 10), so we may include all of the probability in the rectangle corresponding to $p(10)$. Because we are approximating a discrete distribution (the binomial) with a continuous distribution (the normal), we call the use of 10.5 (instead of 10 or 11) a **correction for continuity**. That is, we are correcting the discrete distribution so that it can be approximated by the continuous one. The use of the correction for continuity leads to the calculation of the following standard normal z value:

$$z = \frac{x - \mu}{\sigma} = \frac{10.5 - 12}{2.2} = -.68$$

FIGURE 5.10

Binomial distribution for $n = 20, p = .6$ and normal distribution with $\mu = 12, \sigma = 2.2$

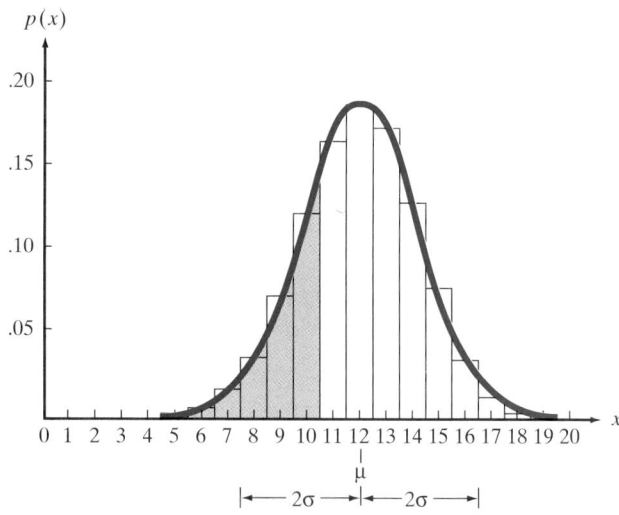

Using Table IV, we find the area between $z = 0$ and $z = .68$ to be .2517. Then the probability that x is less than or equal to 10 is approximated by the area under the normal distribution to the left of 10.5, shown shaded in Figure 5.18. That is,

$$P(x \leq 10) \approx P(z \leq -.68) = .5 - P(-.68 < z \leq 0) = .5 - .2517 = .2438$$

The approximation differs only slightly from the exact binomial probability, .245. Of course, when tables of exact binomial probabilities are available, we will use the exact value rather than a normal approximation.

Use of the normal distribution will not always provide a good approximation for binomial probabilities. The following is a useful rule of thumb to determine when n is large enough for the approximation to be effective: The interval $\mu \pm 3\sigma$ should lie within the range of the binomial random variable x (i.e., 0 to n) in order for the normal approximation to be adequate. The rule works well because almost all of the normal distribution falls within 3 standard deviations of the mean, so if this interval is contained within the range of x values, there is "room" for the normal approximation to work.

As shown in Figure 5.19a for the preceding example with $n = 20$ and $p = .6$, the interval $\mu \pm 3\sigma = 12 \pm 3(2.19) = (5.43, 18.57)$ lies within the range 0 to 20. However, if we were to try to use the normal approximation with $n = 10$ and $p = .1$, the interval $\mu \pm 3\sigma$ is $1 \pm 3(.95)$, or $(-1.85, 3.85)$. As shown in Figure 5.19b, this interval is not contained within the range of x since $x = 0$ is the lower bound for a binomial random variable. Note in Figure 5.19b that the normal dis-

FIGURE 5.19
Rule of thumb for normal approximation to binomial probabilities

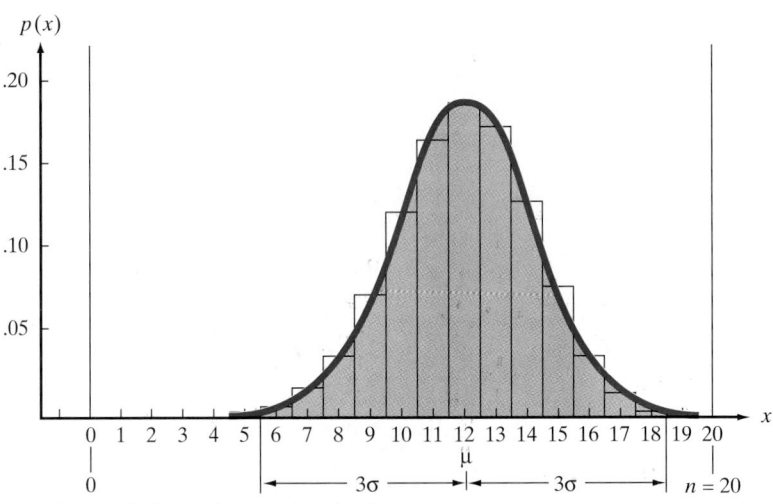

a. $n = 20$, $p = .6$: Normal approximation is good

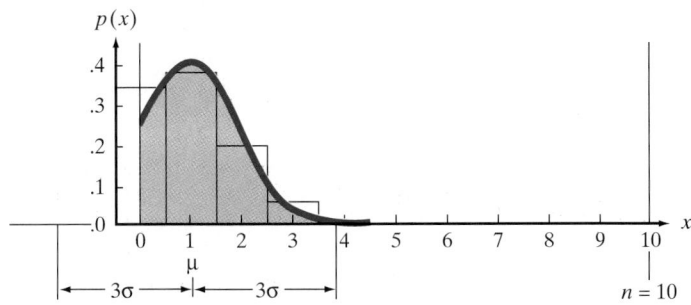

b. $n = 10$, $p = .1$: Normal approximation is poor

tribution will not "fit" in the range of x, and therefore it will not provide a good approximation to the binomial probabilities.

EXAMPLE **5.11**

The pocket calculator has become relatively inexpensive because its solid-state circuitry is stamped by machine, thus making mass production feasible. One problem with anything that is mass-produced is quality control. The process must somehow be monitored or audited to be sure the output of the process conforms to requirements.

One method of dealing with this problem is **lot acceptance sampling**, in which items being produced are sampled at various stages of the production process and are carefully inspected. The lot of items from which the sample is drawn is then accepted or rejected, based on the number of defectives in the sample. Lots that are accepted may be sent forward for further processing or may be shipped to customers; lots that are rejected may be reworked or scrapped. For example, suppose a manufacturer of calculators chooses 200 stamped circuits from the day's production and determines x, the number of defective circuits in the sample. Suppose that up to a 6% rate of defectives is considered acceptable for the process.

a. Find the mean and standard deviation of x, assuming the defective rate is 6%.

b. Use the normal approximation to determine the probability that 20 or more defectives are observed in the sample of 200 circuits (i.e., find the approximate probability that $x \geq 20$).

SOLUTION

a. The random variable x is binomial with $n = 200$ and the fraction defective $p = .06$. Thus,

$$\mu = np = 200(.06) = 12$$

$$\sigma = \sqrt{npq} = \sqrt{200(.06)(.94)} = \sqrt{11.28} = 3.36$$

We first note that

$$\mu \pm 3\sigma = 12 \pm 3(3.36) = 12 \pm 10.08 = (1.92, 22.08)$$

lies completely within the range from 0 to 200. Therefore, a normal probability distribution should provide an adequate approximation to this binomial distribution.

b. Use the rule of complements, $P(x \geq 20) = 1 - P(x \leq 19)$. To find the approximating area corresponding to $x \leq 19$, refer to Figure 5.20. Note that we want to include all the binomial probability histogram from 0 to 19, inclusive. Since the event is of the form $x \leq a$, the proper correction for continuity is $a + .5 = 19 + .5 = 19.5$. Thus, the z value of interest is

FIGURE 5.20
Normal approximation to the binomial distribution with $n = 200, p = .06$

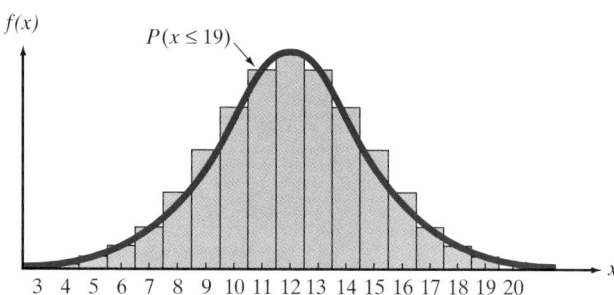

FIGURE 5.21
Standard normal distribution

$$z = \frac{(a + .5) - \mu}{\sigma} = \frac{19.5 - 12}{3.36} = \frac{7.5}{3.36} = 2.23$$

Referring to Table IV in Appendix B, we find that the area to the right of the mean 0 corresponding to $z = 2.23$ (see Figure 5.21) is .4871. So the area $A = P(z \leqslant 2.23)$ is:

$$A = .5 + .4871 = .9871$$

Thus, the normal approximation to the binomial probability we seek is

$$P(x \geqslant 20) = 1 - P(x \leqslant 19) \approx 1 - .9871 = .0129$$

In other words, the probability is extremely small that 20 or more defectives will be observed in a sample of 200 circuits—*if in fact the true fraction of defectives is .06.* If the manufacturer observes $x \geqslant 20$, the likely reason is that the process is producing more than the acceptable 6% defectives. The lot acceptance sampling procedure is another example of using the rare-event approach to make inferences. ∎

The steps for approximating a binomial probability by a normal probability are given in the accompanying box.

Using a Normal Distribution to Approximate Binomial Probabilities

1. After you have determined n and p for the binomial distribution, calculate the interval

$$\mu \pm 3\sigma = np \pm 3\sqrt{npq}$$

If the interval lies in the range 0 to n, the normal distribution will provide a reasonable approximation to the probabilities of most binomial events.

2. Express the binomial probability to be approximated in the form $P(x \leqslant a)$ or $P(x \leqslant b) - P(x \leqslant a)$. For example,

$$P(x < 3) = P(x \leqslant 2)$$

$$P(x \geqslant 5) = 1 - P(x \leqslant 4)$$

$$P(7 \leqslant x \leqslant 10) = P(x \leqslant 10) - P(x \leqslant 6)$$

3. For each value of interest a, the correction for continuity is $(a + .5)$, and the corresponding standard normal z value is

$$z = \frac{(a + .5) - \mu}{\sigma} \quad \text{(See Figure 5.22)}$$

4. Sketch the approximating normal distribution and shade the area corresponding to the probability of the event of interest, as in Figure 5.22. Verify that the rectangles

FIGURE 5.22
Approximating
binomial probabilities
by normal probabilities

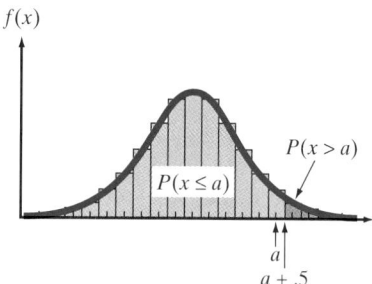

you have included in the shaded area correspond to the event probability you wish to approximate. Using Table IV and the z value(s) you calculated in step 3, find the shaded area. This is the approximate probability of the binomial event.

EXERCISES 5.38–5.51

Learning the Mechanics

5.38 Why might you want to use a normal distribution to approximate a binomial distribution?

5.39 What conditions must be satisfied in order for the normal distribution to provide a good approximation to the binomial probability distribution?

5.40 Assume that x is a binomial random variable with n and p as specified in parts **a–f**. For which cases would it be appropriate to use a normal distribution to approximate the binomial distribution?
  a. $n = 100, p = .05$ **b.** $n = 100, p = .2$
  c. $n = 25, p = .5$ **d.** $n = 1,000, p = .01$
  e. $n = 60, p = .95$ **f.** $n = 1,000, p = .95$

5.41 Suppose x is a binomial random variable with $p = .7$ and $n = 25$.
  a. Would it be appropriate to approximate the probability distribution of x with a normal distribution? Explain.
  b. Assuming that a normal distribution provides an adequate approximation to the distribution of x, what are the mean and variance of the approximating normal distribution?
  c. Use Table II of Appendix B to find the exact value of $P(x \geq 15)$.
  d. Use the normal approximation to find $P(x \geq 15)$.

5.42 Assume that x is a binomial random variable with $n = 100$ and $p = .45$. Use a normal approximation to find the following:
  a. $P(x \leq 45)$ **b.** $P(40 \leq x \leq 50)$ **c.** $P(x \geq 38)$

5.43 Assume that x is a binomial random variable with $n = 1,000$ and $p = .50$. Find each of the following probabilities:

  a. $P(x > 500)$ **b.** $P(490 \leq x < 500)$
  c. $P(x > 1,000)$

Applying the Concepts

5.44 The computer chips in today's notebook and laptop computers are produced from semiconductor wafers. Certain semiconductor wafers are exposed to an environment that generates up to 100 possible defects per wafer. U. Kaempf demonstrates that the number of defects per wafer, x, follows a binomial distribution if the manufacturing process is stable and generates defects that are randomly distributed on the wafers (*IEEE Transactions on Semiconductor Manufacturing*, May 1995). Let p represent the probability that a defect occurs at any one of the 100 points of the wafer. For each of the following cases, determine whether the normal approximation can be used to characterize x.
  a. $p = .01$ **b.** $p = .50$ **c.** $p = .90$

5.45 An article in the *International Journal of Sports Psychology* (July–Sept. 1990) evaluated the relationship between physical fitness and stress. The research revealed that white-collar workers in good physical condition have only a 10% probability of developing a stress-related health problem. What is the probability that more than 60 in a random sample of 400 white-collar employees in good physical condition will develop stress-related illnesses?

5.46 The *Statistical Abstract of the United States: 1995* reports that 24% of the country's households are composed of one person. If 1,000 randomly selected homes are to participate in a Nielsen survey to determine television ratings, find the approximate probability that no more than 240 of these homes are one-person households.

5.47 In Statistics in Action 4.2, the number of shuttle catastrophes caused by booster failure in n missions was treated as a binomial random variable. Using the binomial distribution and the probability of catastrophe determined by the Air Force's risk assessment study ($\frac{1}{35}$), you determined the probability of at least 1 shuttle catastrophe in 25 missions to be .5155.

a. Based on the guidelines presented in this section, would it have been advisable to approximate this probability using the normal approximation to the binomial distribution? Explain.

b. Regardless of your answer to part **a**, use the normal distribution to approximate the binomial probability. Comment on the difference between the exact and approximate probabilities.

c. Refer to part **a**. Would the normal approximation be advisable if $n = 100$? If $n = 500$? If $n = 1,000$?

d. Approximate the probability that more than 25 catastrophes occur in 1,000 flights, assuming that the probability of a catastrophe in any given flight remains $\frac{1}{35}$.

5.48 The *Chronicle of Higher Education Almanac* (Sept. 2, 1996) reports that the percentage of undergraduates in the United States receiving federal financial aid in 1992–1993 was 35% at public four-year institutions and 45% at private four-year institutions. The U.S. Department of Education is interested in questioning a random sample of 100 U.S. undergraduate students to assess their satisfaction with federal financial aid procedures and policies.

a. Explain the difficulties of obtaining the desired random sample.

b. Assume the appropriate percentage above applies to your institution. If a random sample of 100 students from your institution were contacted, what is the approximate probability that 50 or more receive financial aid? Less than 25?

c. What assumptions must be made in order to answer part **b** using the normal approximation to the binomial?

5.49 General Motors Corporation's auto assembly plant in Fremont, California, was shut down 15 years ago and turned over to Toyota Motor Corporation as part of a joint venture with the Japanese firm. Before the shutdown, 5,000 workers produced 240,000 cars a year and had an absentee rate of 20%. After the Japanese took over and introduced their distinctive management style, the same number of cars were produced by only 2,500

workers and the absentee rate dropped to 2% ("The difference Japanese management makes," *Business Week,* July 14, 1986).

a. With an absentee rate of 20%, what is the probability that at least 90% of a random sample of 50 workers will be on the job on a particular day?

b. What assumption must we make in order to use the normal distribution to approximate the probability required in part **a**?

c. If the absentee rate were 2%, should the probability of the event in part **b** be approximated using a normal distribution? Explain.

5.50 According to *New Jersey Business* (Feb. 1996), Newark International Airport's new terminal handles an average of 3,000 international passengers an hour, but is capable of handling twice that number. Also, 80% of arriving international passengers pass through without their luggage being inspected and the remainder are detained for inspection. The inspection facility can handle 600 passengers an hour without unreasonable delays for the travelers.

a. When international passengers arrive at the rate of 1,500 per hour, what is the expected number of passengers who will be detained for luggage inspection?

b. In the future, it is expected that as many as 4,000 international passengers will arrive per hour. When that occurs, what is the expected number of passengers who will be detained for luggage inspection?

c. Refer to part **b**. Find the approximate probability that more than 600 international passengers will be detained for luggage inspection. (This is also the probability that travelers will experience unreasonable luggage inspection delays.)

5.51 Honeywell Corporation manufactures, among other products, smoke detectors. An extensive investigation by the Consumer Product Safety Commission (CPSC) forced Honeywell to recall 770,000 potentially defective smoke detectors in 1983. The commission suggested that about 40% of the Honeywell detectors were defective. However, Honeywell found only four defectives in a random sample of 2,000 detectors and claimed the recall was not justified (*Minneapolis Star Tribune,* May 25, 1983). Let x be the number of defective smoke detectors found in a random sample of 2,000 detectors.

a. What assumptions must be made in order to characterize x as a binomial random variable? Do these assumptions appear to be satisfied?

b. Assume that the conditions of part **a** hold. Determine the approximate probability of finding four or fewer defective smoke detectors in a random sample of 2,000 if, in fact, 40% of all detectors are defective.

c. Assume that Honeywell's sample data had been reported accurately. Is it *likely* that 40%

of their detectors were defective at the time of the investigation by the CPSC? Explain.

d. Refer to part **c**. Is it *possible* that 40% of Honeywell's detectors were defective at the time of the investigation? Explain.

5.5   THE EXPONENTIAL DISTRIBUTION (OPTIONAL)

The length of time between arrivals at a fast-food drive-through restaurant, the length of time between breakdowns of manufacturing equipment, and the length of time between filings of claims in a small insurance office are all business phenomena that we might want to describe probabilistically. The amount of time between occurrences of random events like these can often be described by the **exponential probability distribution**. For this reason, the exponential distribution is sometimes called the **waiting time distribution**. The formula for the exponential probability distribution is shown in the box along with its mean and standard deviation.

Probability Distribution, Mean, and Standard Deviation for an Exponential Random Variable x

$$f(x) = \lambda e^{-\lambda x} \qquad (x > 0)$$

$$\mu = \frac{1}{\lambda}$$

$$\sigma = \frac{1}{\lambda}$$

Unlike the normal distribution which has a shape and location determined by the values of the two quantities μ and σ, the shape of the exponential distribution is governed by a single quantity, λ. Further, it is a probability distribution with the property that its mean equals its standard deviation. Exponential distributions corresponding to $\lambda = .5, 1$, and 2 are shown in Figure 5.23.

To calculate probabilities for exponential random variables, we need to be able to find areas under the exponential probability distribution. Suppose we want to find the area A to the right of some number a, as shown in Figure 5.24. This area can be calculated by using the following formula:

FIGURE 5.23
Exponential distributions

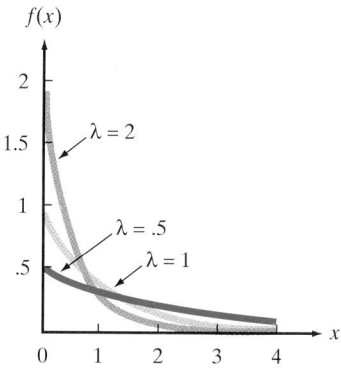

FIGURE 5.24
The area A to the right of a number a for an exponential distribution

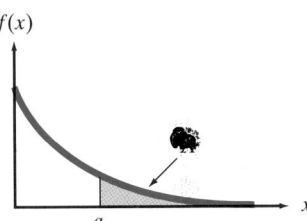

Finding the Area A to the Right of a Number a for an Exponential Distribution*

$$A = P(x \geq a) = e^{-\lambda a}$$

Use Table V in Appendix B or a pocket calculator with an exponential function to find the value of $e^{-\lambda a}$ after substituting the appropriate numerical values for λ and a.

EXAMPLE 5.12

Suppose the length of time (in days) between sales for an automobile salesperson is modeled as an exponential distribution with $\lambda = .5$. What is the probability the salesperson goes more than 5 days without a sale?

SOLUTION
The probability we want is the area A to the right of $a = 5$ in Figure 5.25. To find this probability, use the formula given for area:

$$A = e^{-\lambda a} = e^{-(.5)5} = e^{-2.5}$$

Referring to Table V, we find

$$A = e^{-2.5} = .082085$$

Our exponential model indicates that the probability of going more than 5 days without a sale is about .08 for this automobile salesperson.

EXAMPLE 5.13

A microwave oven manufacturer is trying to determine the length of warranty period it should attach to its magnetron tube, the most critical component in the oven. Preliminary testing has shown that the length of life (in years), x, of a magnetron tube has an exponential probability distribution with $\lambda = .16$.

   a. Find the mean and standard deviation of x.

FIGURE 5.25
Area to the right of $a = 5$ for Example 5.12

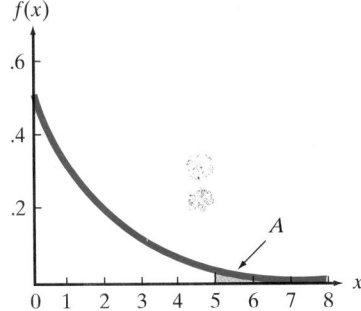

---

*For students with a knowledge of calculus, the shaded area in Figure 5.24 corresponds to the integral

$$\int_a^\infty \lambda e^{-\lambda x}\, dx = -e^{-\lambda x}\Big|_a^\infty = e^{-\lambda a}$$

b. Suppose a warranty period of 5 years is attached to the magnetron tube. What fraction of tubes must the manufacturer plan to replace, assuming that the exponential model with $\lambda = .16$ is correct?

c. Find the probability that the length of life of a magnetron tube will fall within the interval $\mu - 2\sigma$ to $\mu + 2\sigma$.

SOLUTION

a. For this exponential random variable, $\mu = 1/\lambda = \frac{1}{.16} = 6.25$ years. Also, since $\mu = \sigma$, $\sigma = 6.25$ years.

b. To find the fraction of tubes that will have to be replaced before the 5-year warranty period expires, we need to find the area between 0 and 5 under the distribution. This area, A, is shown in Figure 5.26.

To find the required probability, we recall the formula

$$P(x > a) = e^{-\lambda a}$$

Using this formula, we can find

$$P(x > 5) = e^{-\lambda(5)} = e^{-(.16)(5)} = e^{-.80} = .449329$$

(see Table V). To find the area A, we use the complementary relationship:

$$P(x \le 5) = 1 - P(x > 5) = 1 - .449329 = .550671$$

So approximately 55% of the magnetron tubes will have to be replaced during the 5-year warranty period.

c. We would expect the probability that the life of a magnetron tube, x, falls within the interval $\mu - 2\sigma$ to $\mu + 2\sigma$ to be quite large. A graph of the exponential distribution showing the interval $\mu - 2\sigma$ to $\mu + 2\sigma$ is given in Figure 5.27. Since the point $\mu - 2\sigma$ lies below $x = 0$, we need to find only

FIGURE 5.26
Area to the left of
$a = 5$ for Example 5.13

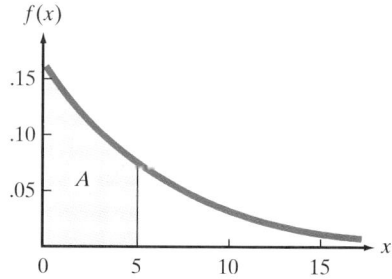

FIGURE 5.27
Area in the interval
$\mu \pm 2\sigma$ for
Example 5.13

STATISTICS IN ACTION

5.2 QUEUEING THEORY

The formation of waiting lines, or *queues,* is a phenomenon that occurs whenever the demand for a service exceeds its supply. We see this daily at bank teller windows, supermarket checkout counters, traffic lights, etc. If long queues develop, it may be an indication that not enough service is being provided. If no queues develop, it may be an indication that too much service is being provided. Either situation can prove costly to the service provider. To assist in planning service capacity, an area of study known as **queueing theory** has been employed to model the characteristics of waiting lines.

In the basic structure assumed by most queueing models, *customers* seeking service are generated over time by an *input source.* These customers enter the *queueing system,* join a queue, and await service. Members of the queue are selected for service by some rule (for example, first-come, first-served or random sampling) known as the *service discipline.* A chosen customer is served by the service *mechanism* and then leaves the queueing system. This process is illustrated in Figure 5.28.

To complete the basic queueing model, certain assumptions must be made to model probabilistically the arrivals to and departures from the queueing system. It has been found that the *interarrival time* (the time between arrivals) of many real queues can be reasonably approximated by an exponential probability distribution. Furthermore, when the specific service required differs among individual customers, the exponential distribution has proved to provide an adequate approximation to the time required to service a customer (i.e., the time that elapses between when service begins and when it ends). Thus, the exponential distribution can be used to describe both the input source and the service mechanism. A more detailed description of the basic queueing theory model and its various assumptions can be found in Camm and Evans (1996).

After developing a queueing model, we can answer such questions as: (1) What is the expected number of customers in the queueing system? (2) What is the expected length of the queue? (3) What is the expected waiting time in the system for an individual customer? (4) What is the expected waiting time in the queue for an individual customer? (5) Are the rates of arrival and departure such that the queue will continue to grow without bound?

Agnihothri and Taylor (*Interfaces,* Vol. 21, 1991) describe how queueing theory was used to improve the centralized telephone scheduling system at Lourdes Hospital in Binghamton, New York. The central system is designed to schedule appointments for outpatients, inpatients, and other ambulatory services requested by patients, physicians, physical therapists, X-ray technicians, the maternity ward, etc. Plagued by complaints of long delays in answering incoming calls, hospital administrators installed an answering machine to queue calls on a first-come, first-served basis. This initial solution, unfortunately, was unacceptable since customers then complained about being put on hold for several minutes.

The problem was eventually solved by applying queueing theory. A sample of almost 1,000 calls to the system revealed that service times could be closely approximated by an exponential distribution with a mean of 3.11 minutes. This information enabled the manager to determine the appropriate staffing level so that no more than 10% of all incoming calls would be put on hold to wait in the queue.

Focus

a. What is λ for this distribution?

b. Graph this exponential distribution and locate the mean on your graph.

c. On average, how many calls per hour are handled by the system? This is called the *service rate.*

d. What is the probability that a randomly selected incoming call will last more than three minutes? Less than one minute?

e. Would you expect this particular exponential distribution to be applicable at all times of day and night? Explain.

FIGURE 5.28
Basic queueing
system (Statistics
in Action 5.2)

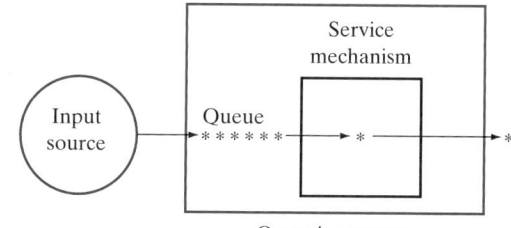

the area between $x = 0$ and $x = \mu + 2\sigma = 6.25 + 2(6.25) = 18.75$. This area, P, which is shaded in Figure 5.27, is

$$P = 1 - P(x > 18.75) = 1 - e^{-\lambda(18.75)} = 1 - e^{-(.16)(18.75)} = 1 - e^{-3}$$

Using Table V or a calculator, we find $e^{-3} = .049787$. Therefore, the probability that the life x of a magnetron tube will fall within the interval $\mu - 2\sigma$
to $\mu + 2\sigma$ is

$$P = 1 - e^{-3} = 1 - .049787 = .950213$$

You can see that this probability agrees very well with the Empirical Rule
even though this probability distribution is not mound-shaped. (It is strongly skewed to the right.)

EXERCISES   5.52–5.65

Learning the Mechanics

5.52   The random variables x and y have exponential
distributions with $\lambda = 3$ and $\lambda = .75$, respectively.
Using Table V in Appendix B, carefully plot both
distributions on the same set of axes.

5.53   Use Table V in Appendix B to determine the
value of $e^{-\lambda a}$ for each of the following cases.
  a. $\lambda = 1, a = 1$ **b.** $\lambda = 1, a = 2.5$
  c. $\lambda = 2.5, a = 3$ **d.** $\lambda = 5, a = .3$

5.54   Suppose x has an exponential distribution with
$\lambda = 3$. Find the following probabilities:
  a. $P(x > 2)$ **b.** $P(x > 1.5)$ **c.** $P(x > 3)$
  d. $P(x > .45)$

5.55   Suppose x has an exponential distribution with λ
$= 2.5$. Find the following probabilities:
  a. $P(x \leq 3)$ **b.** $P(x \leq 4)$ **c.** $P(x \leq 1.6)$
  d. $P(x \leq .4)$

5.56   Suppose the random variable x has an exponential
probability distribution with $\lambda = 2$. Find the mean
and standard deviation of x. Find the probability
that x will assume a value within the interval
$\mu \pm 2\sigma$.

5.57   The random variable x can be adequately approximated by an exponential probability distribution
with $\lambda = 1$. Find the probability that x assumes a
value

  a. More than 3 standard deviations from μ.
  b. Less than 2 standard deviations from μ.
  c. Within .5 standard deviation of μ.

Applying the Concepts

5.58   Cargo transported by ship is normally delivered
directly to a pier in the receiving port. However,
lack of port facilities or shallow water may require
cargo to be transferred at sea to smaller craft that
deliver the cargo to shore. This process may
require the smaller craft to cycle back and forth
from ship to shore many times. Queueing of these
craft may occur at either the ship or the pier or
both. Researchers G. Horne (Center for Naval
Analysis) and T. Irony (George Washington
University) developed models of this transfer
process that provide estimates of ship-to-shore
transfer times (*Naval Research Logistics*, Vol. 41,
1994). They modeled the time between arrivals of
the smaller craft at the pier using an exponential
distribution.

  a. Assume the mean time between arrivals at the
  pier is 17 minutes. Give the value of λ for this
  exponential distribution. Graph the distribution.
  b. Suppose there is only one unloading zone at
  the pier available for the small craft to use. If
  the first craft docks at 10:00 A.M. and doesn't
  finish unloading until 10:15 A.M., what is the

probability that the second craft will arrive at the unloading zone and have to wait before docking?

5.59 In the National Hockey League (NHL), games that are tied at the end of three periods are sent to "sudden-death" overtime. In overtime, the team to score the first goal wins. An analysis of all NHL overtime games played between 1970 and 1993 showed that the length of time elapsed before the winning goal is scored has an exponential distribution with mean 9.15 minutes (*Chance,* Winter 1995).

   a. For a randomly selected overtime NHL game, find the probability that the winning goal is scored in three minutes or less.

   b. In the NHL, each period (including overtime) lasts 20 minutes. If neither team scores a goal in overtime, the game is considered a tie. What is the probability of an NHL game ending in a tie?

5.60 A part processed in a flexible manufacturing system (FMS) is routed through a set of operations, some of which are sequential and some of which are parallel. In addition, an FMS operation can be processed by alternative machines. An article in *IEEE Transactions* (Mar. 1990) gave an example of an FMS with four machines operating independently. The repair rates for the machines (i.e., the time, in hours, it takes to repair a failed machine) are exponentially distributed with means $\mu_1 = 1, \mu_2 = 2, \mu_3 = .5,$ and $\mu_4 = .5,$ respectively.

   a. Find the probability that the repair time for machine 1 exceeds one hour.

   b. Repeat part **a** for machine 2.

   c. Repeat part **a** for machines 3 and 4.

   d. If all four machines fail simultaneously, find the probability that the repair time for the entire system exceeds one hour.

5.61 **Product reliability** has been defined as the probability that a product will perform its intended function satisfactorily for its intended life when operating under specified conditions. The **reliability function**, $R(x)$, for a product indicates the probability of the product's life exceeding x time periods. When the time until failure of a product can be adequately modeled by an exponential distribution, the product's reliability function is $R(x) = e^{-\lambda x}$ (Ross, *Stochastic Processes,* 1996). Suppose that the time to failure (in years) of a particular product is modeled by an exponential distribution with $\lambda = .5$.

   a. What is the product's reliability function?

   b. What is the probability that the product will perform satisfactorily for at least four years?

   c. What is the probability that a particular product will survive longer than the mean life of the product?

   d. If λ changes, will the probability that you calculated in part **c** change? Explain.

   e. If 10,000 units of the product are sold, approximately how many will perform satisfactorily for more than five years? About how many will fail within one year?

   f. How long should the length of the warranty period be for the product if the manufacturer wants to replace no more than 5% of the units sold while under warranty?

5.62 A taxi service based at an airport can be characterized as a transportation system with one source terminal and a fleet of vehicles. Each vehicle takes passengers from the terminal to different destinations; then it returns to the terminal after some random trip time and makes another trip. To improve the vehicle-dispatching decisions involved in such a system (e.g., How many passengers should be allocated to a waiting taxi?), a study was conducted and published in the *European Journal of Operational Research* (Vol. 21, 1985). In modeling the system, the authors assumed travel times of successive trips to be independent exponential random variables. Assume $\lambda = .05$.

   a. What is the mean trip time for the taxi service?

   b. What is the probability that a particular trip will take more than 30 minutes?

   c. Two taxis have just been dispatched. What is the probability that both will be gone for more than 30 minutes? That at least one of the taxis will return within 30 minutes?

5.63 The importance of modeling machine downtime correctly in simulation studies was discussed in *Industrial Engineering* (Aug. 1990). The paper presented simulation results for a single-machine-tool system with the following properties:

- The interarrival times of jobs are exponentially distributed with a mean of 1.25 minutes

- The amount of time the machine operates before breaking down is exponentially distributed with a mean of 540 minutes

   a. Find the probability that two jobs arrive for processing at most one minute apart.

   b. Find the probability that the machine operates for at least 720 minutes (12 hours) before breaking down.

5.64 The shelf-life of a product is a random variable that is related to consumer acceptance and, ultimately, to sales and profit. Suppose the shelf life of bread is best approximated by an exponential distribution with mean equal to 2 days. What fraction of the loaves stocked today would you expect to still be salable (i.e., not stale) three days from now?

5.65 Often, it is important to know whether or not it is better to periodically replace an old component (e.g., a computer chip, halogen light bulb, or compact disk player) with a new component. For example, for certain types of light bulbs, an old bulb that has been in use for a while tends to have a longer life length than a new bulb. Let x represent the life length (in hours) of a new halogen light bulb. Assume that x has an exponential distribution with $\lambda = .004$.

a. Find the mean of x. Interpret its value.
b. Find the probability that the life length of the new halogen bulb exceeds 500 hours.
c. For two independently selected new halogen bulbs, find the probability that one has a life length exceeding 300 hours and the other has a life length exceeding 200 hours.
d. According to *Microelectronics and Reliability* (Jan. 1986), the "life" distribution of x is considered *new better than used* (NBU) if

$$P(x > a + b) \leq P(x > a)P(x > b)$$

Alternatively, a "life" distribution is considered *new worse than used* (NWU) if

$$P(x > a + b) \geq P(x > a)P(x > b)$$

Use the probabilities, parts **b–c**, to show that when $a = 300$ and $b = 200$ the exponential distribution is both NBU and NWU.

e. Choose any two positive numbers a and b, where $a > 0$ and $b > 0$, and repeat part **d**.
f. Show that, in general, for any a and b ($a > 0$ and $b > 0$), the exponential distribution with mean $1/\lambda$ is both NBU and NWU. Such a "life" distribution is said to be *new same as used* or *memoryless*. Explain why.

QUICK REVIEW

Key Terms

Note: Starred (*) terms refer to the optional sections in this chapter.

Bell curve   207
Continuous probability
 distribution   202
Correction for continuity   221

Exponential distribution*   227
Frequency function   202
Normal distribution   207
Probability density function   202

Standard normal distribution   211
Uniform distribution*   203
Waiting time distribution*   227

Key Formulas

Note: Starred (*) formulas refer to the optional sections in this chapter.

Random Variable	Density Function	Mean	Standard Deviation	
Uniform, x*	$f(x) = \dfrac{1}{d - c}$ $(c \leq x \leq d)$	$\mu = \dfrac{c + d}{2}$	$\sigma = \dfrac{d - c}{\sqrt{12}}$	204
Normal, x	$f(x) = \dfrac{1}{\sigma\sqrt{2\pi}}e^{-(1/2)[(x - \mu)/\sigma]^2}$	μ	σ	208
Standard Normal, $z = \left(\dfrac{x - \mu}{\sigma}\right)$	$f(z) = \dfrac{1}{\sqrt{2\pi}}e^{-(1/2)z^2}$	$\mu = 0$	$\sigma = 1$	208
Exponential, x*	$f(x) = \lambda e^{-\lambda x}$ $(x > 0)$	$\mu = \dfrac{1}{\lambda}$	$\sigma = \dfrac{1}{\lambda}$	227

$$P(x \leq a) = P\left[z \leq \frac{(a + .5) - \mu}{\sigma}\right] \quad \text{Normal Approximation to Binomial}\ \ 224$$

LANGUAGE LAB

Symbol	Pronunciation	Description
$f(x)$	f of x	Probability density function for a continuous random variable x
λ	lambda	Parameter for an exponential random variable

SUPPLEMENTARY EXERCISES 5.66–5.88

Note: Starred (*) exercises refer to the optional sections in this chapter.

Learning the Mechanics

5.66 Find the following probabilities for the standard normal random variable z:
  a. $P(z \leq 2.1)$ **b.** $P(z \geq 2.1)$
  c. $P(z \geq -1.65)$ **d.** $P(-2.13 \leq z \leq -.41)$
  e. $P(-1.45 \leq z \leq 2.15)$ **f.** $P(z \leq -1.43)$

*5.67 Assume that x is a random variable best described by a uniform distribution with $c = 10$ and $d = 90$.
  a. Find $f(x)$.
  b. Find the mean and standard deviation of x.
  c. Graph the probability distribution for x and locate its mean and the interval $\mu \pm 2\sigma$ on the graph.
  d. Find $P(x \leq 60)$.   **e.** Find $P(x \geq 90)$.
  f. Find $P(x \leq 80)$.
  g. Find $P(\mu - \sigma \leq x \leq \mu + \sigma)$.
  h. Find $P(x > 75)$.

5.68 The random variable x has a normal distribution with $\mu = 75$ and $\sigma = 10$. Find the following probabilities:
  a. $P(x \leq 80)$ **b.** $P(x \geq 85)$
  c. $P(70 \leq x \leq 75)$ **d.** $P(x > 80)$
  e. $P(x = 78)$ **f.** $P(x \leq 110)$

5.69 Find a z-score, call it z_0, such that
  a. $P(z \leq z_0) = .5080$ **b.** $P(z \geq z_0) = .5517$
  c. $P(z \geq z_0) = .1492$
  d. $P(z_0 \leq z \leq .59) = .4773$

5.70 The random variable x has a normal distribution with $\mu = 40$ and $\sigma^2 = 36$. Find a value of x, call it x_0, such that
  a. $P(x \geq x_0) = .10$ **b.** $P(\mu \leq x < x_0) = .40$
  c. $P(x < x_0) = .05$ **d.** $P(x \geq x_0) = .40$
  e. $P(x_0 \leq x < \mu) = .45$

5.71 Assume that x is a binomial random variable with $n = 100$ and $p = .5$. Use the normal probability distribution to approximate the following probabilities:
  a. $P(x \leq 48)$ **b.** $P(50 \leq x \leq 65)$
  c. $P(x \geq 70)$ **d.** $P(55 \leq x \leq 58)$
  e. $P(x = 62)$ **f.** $P(x \leq 49 \text{ or } x \geq 72)$

*5.72 Assume that x has an exponential distribution with $\lambda = 3.0$. Find
  a. $P(x \leq 2)$ **b.** $P(x > 3)$ **c.** $P(x = 1)$
  d. $P(x \leq 7)$ **e.** $P(4 \leq x \leq 12)$

Applying the Concepts

5.73 The **tolerance limits** for a particular quality characteristic (e.g., length, weight, or strength) of a product are the minimum and/or maximum values at which the product will operate properly. Tolerance limits are set by the engineering design function of the manufacturing operation (Moss,

Applying TQM to Product Design and Development, 1996). The tensile strength of a particular metal part can be characterized as being normally distributed with a mean of 25 pounds and a standard deviation of 2 pounds. The upper and lower tolerance limits for the part are 30 pounds and 21 pounds, respectively. A part that falls within the tolerance limits results in a profit of $10. A part that falls below the lower tolerance limit costs the company $2; a part that falls above the upper tolerance limit costs the company $1. Find the company's expected profit per metal part produced.

5.74 The distribution of the demand (in number of units per unit time) for a product can often be approximated by a normal probability distribution. For example, a bakery has determined that the number of loaves of its white bread demanded daily has a normal distribution with mean 7,200 loaves and standard deviation 300 loaves. Based on cost considerations, the company has decided that its best strategy is to produce a sufficient number of loaves so that it will fully supply demand on 94% of all days.
  a. How many loaves of bread should the company produce?
  b. Based on the production in part **a**, on what percentage of days will the company be left with more than 500 loaves of unsold bread?

5.75 The metropolitan airport commission is considering the establishment of limitations on noise pollution around a local airport. At the present time, the noise level per jet takeoff in one neighborhood near the airport is approximately normally distributed with a mean of 100 decibels and a standard deviation of 6 decibels.
  a. What is the probability that a randomly selected jet will generate a noise level greater than 108 decibels in this neighborhood?
  b. What is the probability that a randomly selected jet will generate a noise level of exactly 100 decibels?
  c. Suppose a regulation is passed that requires jet noise in this neighborhood to be lower than 105 decibels 95% of the time. Assuming the standard deviation of the noise distribution remains the same, how much will the mean level of noise have to be lowered to comply with the regulation?

*5.76 Probability distributions and event probabilities can be used to express uncertainty about future events. For example, security analysts use probability distributions to forecast stock prices and quarterly earnings; weather forecasters use event probabilities to forecast precipitation, temperature ranges, and the location of a hurricane's landfall. Such forecasts are known as **probability forecasts**. Probability forecasts can be derived from sample data, expert judgment, or a combination of both (Wright and Ayton, *Subjective Probability,* 1994). When a forecaster possesses relatively little information about the future value of a random variable, the uniform distribution is frequently used to make a probability forecast. Suppose a security analyst believes that the closing price of a particular stock three months from today will be between $30 and $40, but has no idea where within the interval the price will be.

  a. Graph the uniform distribution the security analyst should use as a probability forecast.

  b. According to the analyst's forecast, what is the probability that the stock will close higher than $35? Higher than $38? Between $34 and $36, inclusive? Higher than $50?

*5.77 The length of time between arrivals at a hospital clinic and the length of clinical service time are two random variables that play important roles in designing a clinic and deciding how many physicians and nurses are needed for its operation. The probability distributions of both the length of time between arrivals and the length of service time are often approximately exponential. Suppose the mean time between arrivals for patients at a clinic is 4 minutes.

  a. What is the probability that a particular interarrival time (the time between the arrival of two patients) is less than 1 minute?

  b. What is the probability that the next four interarrival times are all less than 1 minute?

  c. What is the probability that an interarrival time will exceed 10 minutes?

5.78 The net weight per package of a certain brand of corn chips is listed as 10 ounces. The weight actually delivered to each package by an automated machine is a normal random variable with mean 10.5 ounces and standard deviation .2 ounce. Suppose 1,500 packages are chosen at random and the net weights are ascertained. Let x be the number of the 1,500 selected packages that contain at least 10 ounces of corn chips. Then x is a binomial random variable with $n = 1,500$ and $p =$ probability that a randomly selected package contains at least 10 ounces. What is the probability that they all contain at least 10 ounces of corn chips? What is the probability that at least 90% of the packages contain 10 ounces or more?

5.79 To help highway planners anticipate the need for road repairs and design future construction projects, data are collected on the volume and weight of truck traffic on specific roadways (Edwards, *Transportation Planning Handbook,* 1992).

Equipment has been developed that can be built into road surfaces to measure traffic volumes and to weigh trucks without requiring them to stop at roadside weigh stations. As with any measuring device, however, the "weigh-in-motion" equipment does not always record truck weights accurately. In an experiment performed by the Minnesota Department of Transportation involving repeated weighing of a 27,907-pound truck, it was found that the weights recorded by the weigh-in-motion equipment were approximately normally distributed with mean 27,315 and a standard deviation of 628 pounds (Minnesota Department of Transportation). It follows that the difference between the actual weight and recorded weight, the error of measurement, is normally distributed with mean 592 pounds and standard deviation 628 pounds.

  a. What is the probability that the weigh-in-motion equipment understates the actual weight of the truck?

  b. If a 27,907-pound truck were driven over the weigh-in-motion equipment 100 times, approximately how many times would the equipment overstate the truck's weight?

  c. What is the probability that the error in the weight recorded by the weigh-in-motion equipment for a 27,907-pound truck exceeds 400 pounds?

  d. It is possible to adjust (or *calibrate*) the weigh-in-motion equipment to control the mean error of measurement. At what level should the mean error be set so the equipment will understate the weight of a 27,907-pound truck 50% of the time? Only 40% of the time?

5.80 If you are attracted to lotteries, one of the best is run by the U.S. government. Furthermore, with some research you can improve your chances of winning. We refer to the Interior Department's lottery for oil and gas leases. *The Wall Street Journal* reported on abuses in the lottery that occurred in the past—particularly the tendency of the Interior Department to include valuable oil leases, some worth millions of dollars, among the many included in the lottery. The Interior Department claims that only 5% to 10% of the leases included in the $75 per ticket lottery should be salable to an oil company. Yet 184 of 328 winners in the July 1980 lottery of Wyoming lands were able to sell their leases to oil companies. Suppose as many as 10% of all leases awarded by the Interior Department are salable to oil companies to answer the following questions:

  a. What is the probability that as many as 50 leases (i.e., 50 or more) would be salable to oil companies?

b. If 184 of the 328 leases awarded in the July 1980 Wyoming lottery were in fact salable to oil companies, would you regard this as a rare event? Explain.

c. Given the outcome of the Wyoming lottery and considering your answer to part **b**, do you believe the Interior Department's claim? Explain.

5.81 A company has a lump-sum incentive plan for salespeople that is dependent on their level of sales. If they sell less than $100,000 per year, they receive a $1,000 bonus; from $100,000 to $200,000, they receive $5,000; and above $200,000, they receive $10,000. Suppose the annual sales per salesperson has approximately a normal distribution with $\mu = \$180,000$ and $\sigma = \$50,000$.

a. Find p_1, the proportion of salespeople who receive a $1,000 bonus.

b. Find p_2, the proportion of salespeople who receive a $5,000 bonus.

c. Find p_3, the proportion of salespeople who receive a $10,000 bonus.

d. What is the mean value of the bonus payout for the company? [*Hint:* See the definition for the expected value of a random variable in Chapter 4.]

*5.82 The Jacksonville, Florida, *Times Union* (Mar. 11, 1984) reported on the unexplained crash of a small plane on takeoff and the resulting injury to its 24-year-old student pilot. The article noted that Shields Aviation, the renter of the plane, inspected (and presumably performed maintenance on) the aircraft every 100 flight hours. The plane had flown 30 hours since its last inspection. Suppose x, the time between malfunctions for this particular plane, has an exponential distribution with mean equal to 300 hours. What is the probability that a plane of this type will malfunction within 30 hours after the last inspection?

5.83 A. K. Shah published a simple approximation for areas under the normal curve in the *American Statistician* (Feb. 1985). Shah showed that the area A under the standard normal curve between 0 and z is

$$A \approx \begin{cases} z(4.4 - z)/10 & \text{for } 0 \le z \le 2.2 \\ .49 & \text{for } 2.2 < z < 2.6 \\ .50 & \text{for } z \ge 2.6 \end{cases}$$

a. Use the approximation to find
  (i) $P(0 < z < 1.2)$
  (ii) $P(0 < z < 2.5)$
  (iii) $P(z > .8)$
  (iv) $P(z < 1.0)$

b. Find the exact probabilities in part **a**.

c. Shah showed that the approximation has a maximum absolute error of .0052. Verify this for the approximations in part **a**.

*5.84 Based on sample data collected in the Denver area, a study found that in some cases the exponential distribution is an adequate approximation for the distribution of the time (in weeks) an individual is unemployed (*Journal of Economics*, Vol. 28, 1985). In particular, the author found the exponential distribution to be appropriate for white and African American workers but not for Hispanics. Use $\lambda = \frac{1}{13}$ to answer the following questions.

a. What is the mean time workers are unemployed according to the exponential distribution?

b. Find the probability that a white worker who just lost her job will be unemployed for at least 2 weeks. For more than 6 weeks.

c. What is the probability that an unemployed worker will find a new job within 12 weeks?

5.85 Contrary to our intuition, very reliable decisions concerning the proportion of a large group of consumers favoring a certain product or a certain social issue can be based on relatively small samples. For example, suppose the target population of consumers contains 50 million people and we wish to decide whether the proportion of consumers, p, in the population that favor some product (or issue) is as large as some value, say .2. Suppose you randomly select a sample as small as 1,600 from the 50 million and you observe the number, x, of consumers in the sample who favor the new product. Assuming that $p = .2$, find the mean and standard deviation of x. Suppose that 400 (or 25%) of the sample of 1,600 consumers favor the new product. Why might this sample result lead you to conclude that p (the proportion of consumers favoring the product in the population of 50 million) is at least as large as .2? [*Hint:* Find the values of μ and σ for $p = .2$, and use them to decide whether the observed value of x is unusually large.]

*5.86 A bus is scheduled to stop at a certain bus stop every half hour on the hour and the half hour. At the end of the day, buses still stop after every 30 minutes, but due to delays that often occur earlier in the day, the bus is likely to be late. The director of the bus line claims that the length of time a bus is late is uniformly distributed and the maximum time that a bus is late is 20 minutes.

a. If the director's claim is true, what is the expected number of minutes a bus will be late?

b. If the director's claim is true, what is the probability that the last bus on a given day will be more than 19 minutes late?

c. If you arrive at the bus stop at the end of a day at exactly half past the hour and must wait more than 19 minutes for the bus, what would you conclude about the director's claim? Why?

*5.87 The number of serious accidents in a manufacturing plant has (approximately) a Poisson probability distribution with a mean of two serious accidents per month. [If x, the number of events per unit time, has a Poisson distribution with mean λ, then it can be shown that the time between two successive events has an exponential probability distribution with mean $1/\lambda$.]

a. If an accident occurs today, what is the probability that the next serious accident will not occur within the next month?

b. What is the probability that more than one serious accident will occur within the next month?

5.88 A manufacturer of 3.5-inch computer disks claims that 99.4% of its disks are defect free. A large software company that buys and uses large numbers of the disks wants to verify this claim, and selects 1,600 disks to be tested. The tests reveal 12 disks to be defective. Assuming that the disk manufacturer's claim is correct, what is the probability of finding 12 or more defective disks in a sample of 1,600? Does your answer cast doubt on the manufacturer's claim? Explain.

CHAPTER 6

SAMPLING DISTRIBUTIONS

CONTENTS

STATISTICS IN ACTION

Where We've Been

We've learned that the objective of most statistical investigations is inference—that is, making decisions or predictions about a population based on information in a sample. To actually make the decision, we use the sample data to compute sample statistics, such as the sample mean or variance. The knowledge of random variables and their probability distributions enables us to construct theoretical models of populations.

Where We're Going

Because sample measurements are observed values of random variables, the value for a sample statistic will vary in a random manner from sample to sample. In other words, since sample statistics are random variables, they possess probability distributions that are either discrete or continuous. In this chapter, we'll explore these probability distributions, which are called *sampling distributions*. You'll learn why many sampling distributions tend to be approximately normal, and you'll see how sampling distributions can be used to evaluate the reliability of inferences made using the statistics.

In Chapters 4 and 5 we assumed that we knew the probability distribution of a random variable, and using this knowledge we were able to compute the mean, variance, and probabilities associated with the random variable. However, in most practical applications, this information is not available. To illustrate, in Example 4.11 we calculated the probability that the binomial random variable x, the number of 20 polled employees who favor unionization, assumed specific values. To do this, it was necessary to assume some value for p, the proportion of the employees in the population who favor unionization. Thus, for the purposes of illustration, we assumed $p = .6$ when, in all likelihood, the exact value of p would be unknown. In fact, the probable purpose of taking the poll is to estimate p. Similarly, when we modeled the in-city gas mileage of a certain automobile model in Example 5.7, we used the normal probability distribution with an *assumed* mean and standard deviation of 27 and 3 miles per gallon, respectively. In reality, the true mean and standard deviation are unknown quantities that would have to be estimated. Numerical quantities that describe probability distributions are called *parameters*. Thus, p, the probability of a success in a binomial experiment, and μ and σ, the mean and standard deviation of a normal distribution, are examples of parameters.

DEFINITION 6.1
A **parameter** is a numerical descriptive measure of a population. Because it is based on the observations in the population, its value is almost always unknown.

We have also discussed the sample mean $\bar{x}$, sample variance s^2, sample standard deviation s, etc., which are numerical descriptive measures calculated from the sample. We will often use the information contained in these *sample statistics* to make inferences about the parameters of a population.

DEFINITION 6.2
A **sample statistic** is a numerical descriptive measure of a sample. It is calculated from the observations in the sample.

Note that the term *statistic* refers to a *sample* quantity and the term *parameter* refers to a *population* quantity.

Before we can show you how to use sample statistics to make inferences about population parameters, we need to be able to evaluate their properties. Does one sample statistic contain more information than another about a population parameter? On what basis should we choose the "best" statistic for making inferences about a parameter? The purpose of this chapter is to answer these questions.

6.1 THE CONCEPT OF SAMPLING DISTRIBUTIONS

If we want to estimate a parameter of a population—say, the population mean μ—we could use a number of sample statistics for our estimate. Two possibilities are the sample mean $\bar{x}$ and the sample median m. Which of these do you think will provide a better estimate of μ?

FIGURE 6.1
Comparing the sample mean ($\bar{x}$) and sample median (m) as estimators of the population mean (μ)

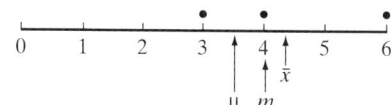

a. Sample 1: $\bar{x}$ is closer than m to μ b. Sample 2: m is closer than $\bar{x}$ to μ

Before answering this question, consider the following example: Toss a fair die, and let x equal the number of dots showing on the up face. Suppose the die is tossed three times, producing the sample measurements 2, 2, 6. The sample mean is $\bar{x} = 3.33$ and the sample median is $m = 2$. Since the population mean of x is $\mu = 3.5$, you can see that for this sample of three measurements, the sample mean $\bar{x}$ provides an estimate that falls closer to μ than does the sample median (see Figure 6.1a). Now suppose we toss the die three more times and obtain the sample measurements 3, 4, 6. The mean and median of this sample are $\bar{x} = 4.33$ and $m = 4$, respectively. This time m is closer to μ (see Figure 6.1b).

This simple example illustrates an important point: Neither the sample mean nor the sample median will *always* fall closer to the population mean. Consequently, we cannot compare these two sample statistics, or, in general, any two sample statistics, on the basis of their performance for a single sample. Instead, we need to recognize that sample statistics are themselves random variables, because different samples can lead to different values for the sample statistics. As random variables, sample statistics must be judged and compared on the basis of their probability distributions, i.e., the *collection* of values and associated probabilities of each statistic that would be obtained if the sampling experiment were repeated a *very large number of times*. We will illustrate this concept with another example.

Suppose it is known that the connector module manufactured for a certain brand of pacemaker has a mean length of $\mu = .3$ inch and a standard deviation of .005 inch. Consider an experiment consisting of randomly selecting 25 recently manufactured connector modules, measuring the length of each, and calculating the sample mean length $\bar{x}$. If this experiment were repeated a very large number of times, the value of $\bar{x}$ would vary from sample to sample. For example, the first sample of 25 length measurements might have a mean $\bar{x} = .301$, the second sample a mean $\bar{x} = .298$, the third sample a mean $\bar{x} = .303$, etc. If the sampling experiment were repeated a very large number of times, the resulting histogram of sample means would be approximately the probability distribution of $\bar{x}$. If $\bar{x}$ is a good estimator of μ, we would expect the values of $\bar{x}$ to cluster around μ as shown in Figure 6.2. This probability distribution is called a *sampling distribution* because it is generated by repeating a sampling experiment a very large number of times.

FIGURE 6.2
Sampling distribution for $\bar{x}$ based on a sample of $n = 25$ length measurements

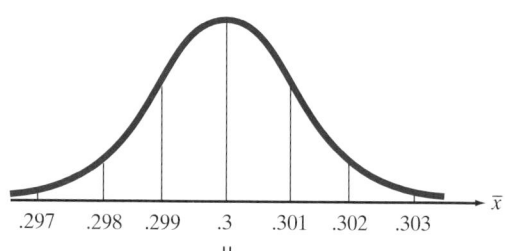

FIGURE 6.3
Two sampling
distributions for
estimating the
population variance, σ^2

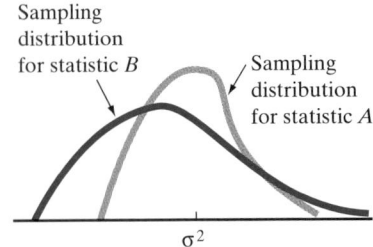

In actual practice, the sampling distribution of a statistic is obtained mathematically or (at least approximately) by simulating the sample on a computer using a procedure similar to that just described.

If $\bar{x}$ has been calculated from a sample of $n = 25$ measurements selected from a population with mean $\mu = .3$ and standard deviation $\sigma = .005$, the sampling distribution (Figure 6.2) provides information about the behavior of $\bar{x}$ in repeated sampling. For example, the probability that you will draw a sample of 25 length measurements and obtain a value of $\bar{x}$ in the interval $.299 \leqslant \bar{x} \leqslant .3$ will be the area under the sampling distribution over that interval.

Since the properties of a statistic are typified by its sampling distribution, it follows that to compare two sample statistics you compare their sampling distributions. For example, if you have two statistics, A and B, for estimating the same parameter (for purposes of illustration, suppose the parameter is the population variance σ^2) and if their sampling distributions are as shown in Figure 6.3, you would choose statistic A in preference to statistic B. You would make this choice because the sampling distribution for statistic A centers over σ^2 and has less spread (variation) than the sampling distribution for statistic B. When you draw a single sample in a practical sampling situation, the probability is higher that statistic A will fall nearer σ^2.

Remember that in practice we will not know the numerical value of the unknown parameter σ^2, so we will not know whether statistic A or statistic B is closer to σ^2 for a sample. We have to rely on our knowledge of the theoretical sampling distributions to choose the best sample statistic and then use it sample after sample. The procedure for finding the sampling distribution for a statistic is demonstrated in Example 6.1.

DEFINITION 6.3
The **sampling distribution** of a sample statistic calculated from a sample of n measurements is the probability distribution of the statistic.

EXAMPLE 6.1

Consider a population consisting of the measurements 0, 3, and 12 and described by the probability distribution shown here. A random sample of $n = 3$ measurements is selected from the population.

a. Find the sampling distribution of the sample mean $\bar{x}$.

b. Find the sampling distribution of the sample median m.

x	0	3	12
$p(x)$	$^1/_3$	$^1/_3$	$^1/_3$

TABLE 6.1 All Possible Samples of $n = 3$ Measurements, Example 6.1

Possible Samples	$\bar{x}$	m	Probability
0, 0, 0	0	0	$1/27$
0, 0, 3	1	0	$1/27$
0, 0, 12	4	0	$1/27$
0, 3, 0	1	0	$1/27$
0, 3, 3	2	3	$1/27$
0, 3, 12	5	3	$1/27$
0, 12, 0	4	0	$1/27$
0, 12, 3	5	3	$1/27$
0, 12, 12	8	12	$1/27$
3, 0, 0	1	0	$1/27$
3, 0, 3	2	3	$1/27$
3, 0, 12	5	3	$1/27$
3, 3, 0	2	3	$1/27$
3, 3, 3	3	3	$1/27$
3, 3, 12	6	3	$1/27$
3, 12, 0	5	3	$1/27$
3, 12, 3	6	3	$1/27$
3, 12, 12	9	12	$1/27$
12, 0, 0	4	0	$1/27$
12, 0, 3	5	3	$1/27$
12, 0, 12	8	12	$1/27$
12, 3, 0	5	3	$1/27$
12, 3, 3	6	3	$1/27$
12, 3, 12	9	12	$1/27$
12, 12, 0	8	12	$1/27$
12, 12, 3	9	12	$1/27$
12, 12, 12	12	12	$1/27$

SOLUTION
Every possible sample of $n = 3$ measurements is listed in Table 6.1 along with the sample mean and median. Also, because any one sample is as likely to be selected as any other (random sampling), the probability of observing any particular sample is $1/27$. The probability is also listed in Table 6.1.

a. From Table 6.1 you can see that $\bar{x}$ can assume the values 0, 1, 2, 3, 4, 5, 6, 8, 9, and 12. Because $\bar{x} = 0$ occurs in only one sample, $P(\bar{x} = 0) = 1/27$. Similarly, $\bar{x} = 1$ occurs in three samples: (0, 0, 3) (0, 3, 0), and (3, 0, 0). Therefore, $P(\bar{x} = 1) = 3/27 = 1/9$. Calculating the probabilities of the remaining values of $\bar{x}$ and arranging them in a table, we obtain the probability distribution shown here.

x	0	1	2	3	4	5	6	8	9	12
$p(\bar{x})$	$1/27$	$3/27$	$3/27$	$1/27$	$3/27$	$6/27$	$3/27$	$3/27$	$3/27$	$1/27$

This is the sampling distribution for $\bar{x}$ because it specifies the probability associated with each possible value of $\bar{x}$.

b. In Table 6.1 you can see that the median m can assume one of the three values 0, 3, or 12. The value $m = 0$ occurs in seven different samples. Therefore, $P(m = 0) = 7/27$. Similarly, $m = 3$ occurs in 13 samples and $m = 12$

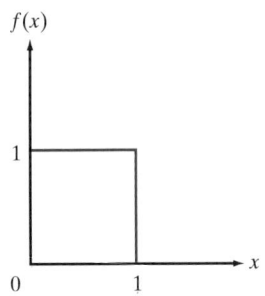

$f(x)$

1

0   1 x

FIGURE 6.4
Uniform distribution
from 0 to 1

occurs in seven samples. Therefore, the probability distribution (i.e., the sampling distribution) for the median m is as shown below.

m	0	3	12
$p(m)$	$7/27$	$13/27$	$7/27$

Example 6.1 demonstrates the procedure for finding the exact sampling distribution of a statistic when the number of different samples that could be selected from the population is relatively small. In the real world, populations often consist of a large number of different values, making samples difficult (or impossible) to enumerate. When this situation occurs, we may choose to obtain the approximate sampling distribution for a statistic by simulating the sampling over and over again and recording the proportion of times different values of the statistic occur. Example 6.2 illustrates this procedure.

 EXAMPLE 6.2

Suppose we perform the following experiment over and over again: Take a sample of 11 measurements from the distribution shown in Figure 6.4. This distribution, known as the **uniform distribution**, was discussed in optional Section 5.2. Calculate the two sample statistics

$$\bar{x} = \text{Sample mean} = \frac{\sum x}{11}$$

m = Median = Sixth sample measurement when the 11 measurements are arranged in ascending order

Obtain approximations to the sampling distributions of $\bar{x}$ and m.

SOLUTION
We use a computer to generate 1,000 samples, each with $n = 11$ observations. Then we compute $\bar{x}$ and m for each sample. Our goal is to obtain approximations to the sampling distributions of $\bar{x}$ and m to find out which sample statistic ($\bar{x}$ or m) contains more information about μ. [*Note:* In this particular example, we *know* the population mean is $\mu = .5$. (See optional Section 5.2.)] The first 10 of the 1,000 samples generated are presented in Table 6.2. For instance, the first computer-generated sample from the uniform distribution (arranged in ascending order) contained the following measurements: .125, .138, .139, .217, .419, .506, .516, .757, .771, .786, and .919. The sample mean $\bar{x}$ and median m computed for this sample are

TABLE 6.2   First 10 Samples of $n = 11$ Measurements from a Uniform Distribution

Sample	Measurements										
1	.217	.786	.757	.125	.139	.919	.506	.771	.138	.516	.419
2	.303	.703	.812	.650	.848	.392	.988	.469	.632	.012	.065
3	.383	.547	.383	.584	.098	.676	.091	.535	.256	.163	.390
4	.218	.376	.248	.606	.610	.055	.095	.311	.086	.165	.665
5	.144	.069	.485	.739	.491	.054	.953	.179	.865	.429	.648
6	.426	.563	.186	.896	.628	.075	.283	.549	.295	.522	.674
7	.643	.828	.465	.672	.074	.300	.319	.254	.708	.384	.534
8	.616	.049	.324	.700	.803	.399	.557	.975	.569	.023	.072
9	.093	.835	.534	.212	.201	.041	.889	.728	.466	.142	.574
10	.957	.253	.983	.904	.696	.766	.880	.485	.035	.881	.732

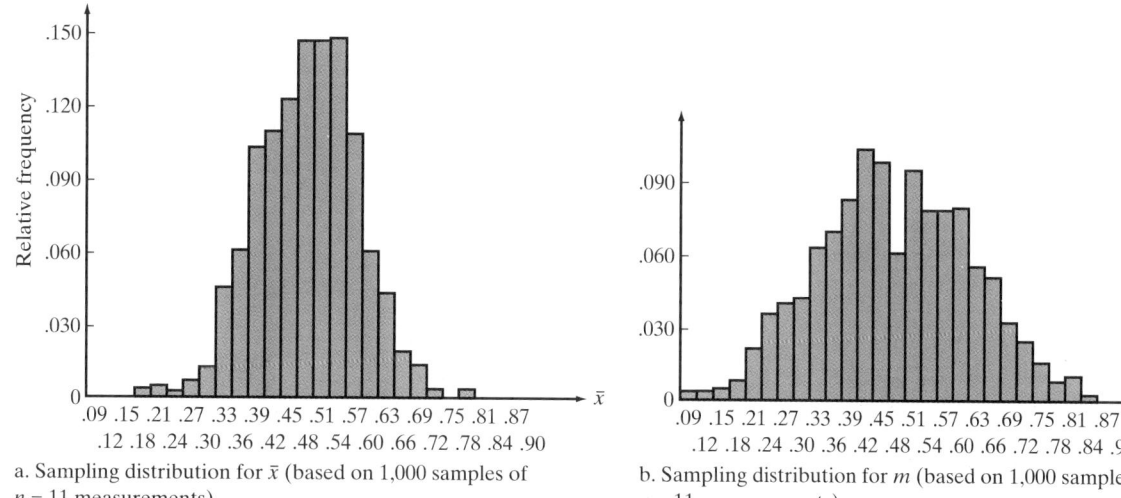

a. Sampling distribution for $\bar{x}$ (based on 1,000 samples of $n = 11$ measurements)

b. Sampling distribution for m (based on 1,000 samples of $n = 11$ measurements)

FIGURE 6.5   Relative frequency histograms for $\bar{x}$ and m, Example 6.2

$$x = \frac{.125 + .138 + \cdots + .919}{11} = .481$$

$$m = \text{Sixth ordered measurement} = .506$$

The relative frequency histograms for $\bar{x}$ and m for the 1,000 samples of size $n = 11$ are shown in Figure 6.5.

You can see that the values of $\bar{x}$ tend to cluster around μ to a greater extent than do the values of m. Thus, on the basis of the observed sampling distributions, we conclude that $\bar{x}$ contains more information about μ than m does—at least for samples of $n = 11$ measurements from the uniform distribution. ◣

As noted earlier, many sampling distributions can be derived mathematically, but the theory necessary to do this is beyond the scope of this text. Consequently, when we need to know the properties of a statistic, we will present its sampling distribution and simply describe its properties. Several of the important properties we look for in sampling distributions are discussed in the next section.

EXERCISES   6.1–6.7

Note: Exercises marked with 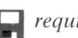 *require the use of a computer.*

Learning the Mechanics

6.1   The probability distribution shown here describes a population of measurements that can assume values of 0, 2, 4, and 6, each of which occurs with the same relative frequency:

x	0	2	4	6
$p(x)$	¼	¼	¼	¼

a. List all the different samples of $n = 2$ measurements that can be selected from this population.

b. Calculate the mean of each different sample listed in part **a**.

c. If a sample of $n = 2$ measurements is randomly selected from the population, what is the probability that a specific sample will be selected?

d. Assume that a random sample of $n = 2$ measurements is selected from the population. List the different values of $\bar{x}$ found in part **b**, and find the probability of each. Then give the sampling distribution of the sample mean $\bar{x}$ in tabular form.

e. Construct a probability histogram for the sampling distribution of $\bar{x}$.

6.2 Simulate sampling from the population described in Exercise 6.1 by marking the values of x, one on each of four identical coins (or poker chips, etc.). Place the coins (marked 0, 2, 4, and 6) into a bag, randomly select one, and observe its value. Replace this coin, draw a second coin, and observe its value. Finally, calculate the mean $\bar{x}$ for this sample of $n = 2$ observations randomly selected from the population (Exercise 6.1, part **b**). Replace the coins, mix, and using the same procedure, select a sample of $n = 2$ observations from the population. Record the numbers and calculate $\bar{x}$ for this sample. Repeat this sampling process until you acquire 100 values of $\bar{x}$. Construct a relative frequency distribution for these 100 sample means. Compare this distribution to the exact sampling distribution of $\bar{x}$ found in part **e** of Exercise 6.1. [*Note:* The distribution obtained in this exercise is an approximation to the exact sampling distribution. But, if you were to repeat the sampling procedure, drawing two coins not 100 times but 10,000 times, the relative frequency distribution for the 10,000 sample means would be almost identical to the sampling distribution of $\bar{x}$ found in Exercise 6.1, part **e**.]

6.3 Consider the population described by the probability distribution shown here.

x	1	2	3	4	5
$p(x)$	.2	.3	.2	.2	.1

The random variable x is observed twice. If these observations are independent, verify that the different samples of size 2 and their probabilities are as shown here.

Sample	Probability	Sample	Probability
1, 1	.04	3, 4	.04
1, 2	.06	3, 5	.02
1, 3	.04	4, 1	.04
1, 4	.04	4, 2	.06
1, 5	.02	4, 3	.04
2, 1	.06	4, 4	.04
2, 2	.09	4, 5	.02
2, 3	.06	5, 1	.02
2, 4	.06	5, 2	.03
2, 5	.03	5, 3	.02
3, 1	.04	5, 4	.02
3, 2	.06	5, 5	.01
3, 3	.04		

a. Find the sampling distribution of the sample mean $\bar{x}$.
b. Construct a probability histogram for the sampling distribution of $\bar{x}$.
c. What is the probability that $\bar{x}$ is 4.5 or larger?
d. Would you expect to observe a value of $\bar{x}$ equal to 4.5 or larger? Explain.

6.4 Refer to Exercise 6.3 and find $E(x) = \mu$. Then use the sampling distribution of $\bar{x}$ found in Exercise 6.3 to find the expected value of $\bar{x}$. Note that $E(\bar{x}) = \mu$.

6.5 Refer to Exercise 6.3. Assume that a random sample of $n = 2$ measurements is randomly selected from the population.
a. List the different values that the sample median m may assume and find the probability of each. Then give the sampling distribution of the sample median.
b. Construct a probability histogram for the sampling distribution of the sample median and compare it with the probability histogram for the sample mean (Exercise 6.3, part **b**).

6.6 In Example 6.2 we used the computer to generate 1,000 samples, each containing $n = 11$ observations, from a uniform distribution over the interval from 0 to 1. For this exercise, generate 500 samples, each containing $n = 15$ observations, from this population.
a. Calculate the sample mean for each sample. To approximate the sampling distribution of $\bar{x}$, construct a relative frequency histogram for the 500 values of $\bar{x}$.
b. Repeat part **a** for the sample median. Compare this approximate sampling distribution with the approximate sampling distribution of $\bar{x}$ found in part **a**.

6.7 Consider a population that contains values of x equal to 00, 01, 02, 03, ..., 96, 97, 98, 99. Assume that these values of x occur with equal probability. Generate 500 samples, each containing $n = 25$ measurements, from this population. Calculate the sample mean $\bar{x}$ and sample variance s^2 for each of the 500 samples.
a. To approximate the sampling distribution of $\bar{x}$, construct a relative frequency histogram for the 500 values of $\bar{x}$.
b. Repeat part **a** for the 500 values of s^2.

6.2   PROPERTIES OF SAMPLING DISTRIBUTIONS: UNBIASEDNESS AND MINIMUM VARIANCE

The simplest type of statistic used to make inferences about a population parameter is a *point estimator*. A point estimator is a rule or formula that tells us how to use the sample data to calculate a single number that is intended to estimate the value of some population parameter. For example, the sample mean $\bar{x}$ is a point estimator of the population mean μ. Similarly, the sample variance s^2 is a point estimator of the population variance σ^2.

> ### DEFINITION 6.4
> A **point estimator** of a population parameter is a rule or formula that tells us how to use the sample data to calculate a single number that can be used as an *estimate* of the population parameter.

Often, many different point estimators can be found to estimate the same parameter. Each will have a sampling distribution that provides information about the point estimator. By examining the sampling distribution, we can determine how large the difference between an estimate and the true value of the parameter (called the **error of estimation**) is likely to be. We can also tell whether an estimator is more likely to overestimate or to underestimate a parameter.

EXAMPLE 6.3

Suppose two statistics, A and B, exist to estimate the same population parameter, θ (theta). (Note that θ could be any parameter, μ, σ^2, σ, etc.) Suppose the two statistics have sampling distributions as shown in Figure 6.6. Based on these sampling distributions, which statistic is more attractive as an estimator of θ?

SOLUTION

As a first consideration, we would like the sampling distribution to center over the value of the parameter we wish to estimate. One way to characterize this property is in terms of the mean of the sampling distribution. Consequently, we say that a statistic is *unbiased* if the mean of the sampling distribution is equal to the parameter it is intended to estimate. This situation is shown in Figure 6.6a, where the mean μ_A of statistic A is equal to θ. If the mean of a sampling distribution is not equal to the parameter it is intended to estimate, the statistic is said to be *biased*. The sampling distribution for a biased statistic is shown in Figure 6.6b. The mean

FIGURE 6.6

Sampling distributions of unbiased and biased estimators

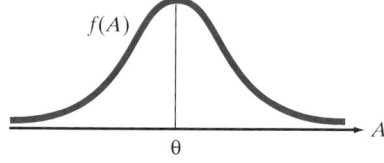

a. Unbiased sample statistic for the parameter θ

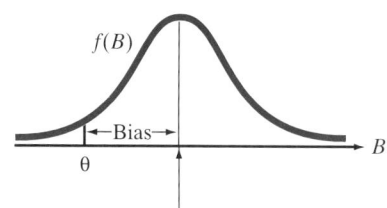

b. Biased sample statistic for the parameter θ

μ_B of the sampling distribution for statistic B is not equal to θ; in fact, it is shifted to the right of θ.

You can see that biased statistics tend either to overestimate or to underestimate a parameter. Consequently, when other properties of statistics tend to be equivalent, we will choose an unbiased statistic to estimate a parameter of interest.*

DEFINITION 6.5

If the sampling distribution of a sample statistic has a mean equal to the population parameter the statistic is intended to estimate, the statistic is said to be an **unbiased estimate** of the parameter.

If the mean of the sampling distribution is not equal to the parameter, the statistic is said to be a **biased estimate** of the parameter.

The standard deviation of a sampling distribution measures another important property of statistics—the spread of these estimates generated by repeated sampling. Suppose two statistics, A and B, are both unbiased estimators of a population parameter θ. Since the means of the two sampling distributions are the same, we turn to their standard deviations in order to decide which will provide estimates that fall closer to the unknown population parameter we are estimating. Naturally, we will choose the sample statistic that has the smaller standard deviation. Figure 6.7 depicts sampling distributions for A and B. Note that the standard deviation of the distribution of A is smaller than the standard deviation for B, indicating that over a large number of samples, the values of A cluster more closely around θ than do the values of B. Stated differently, the probability that A is close to the parameter value is higher than the probability that B is close to the parameter value.

In summary, to make an inference about a population parameter, we use the sample statistic with a sampling distribution that is unbiased and has a small standard deviation (usually smaller than the standard deviation of other unbiased sample statistics). The derivation of this sample statistic will not concern us, because the "best" statistic for estimating specific parameters is a matter of record. We will simply present an unbiased estimator with its standard deviation for each population parameter we consider. [*Note:* The standard deviation of the sampling distribution of a statistic is also called the **standard error of the statistic**.]

FIGURE 6.7
Sampling distributions for two unbiased estimators

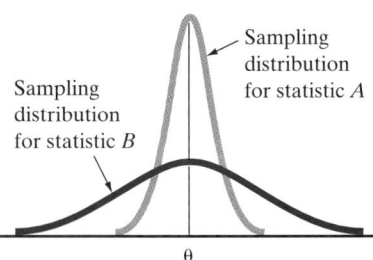

*Unbiased statistics do not exist for all parameters of interest, but they do exist for the parameters considered in this text.

EXAMPLE 6.4   In Example 6.1, we found the sampling distributions of the sample mean $\bar{x}$ and the sample median m for a random sample of $n = 3$ measurements from a population defined by the probability distribution shown here.

x	0	3	12
$p(x)$	$1/3$	$1/3$	$1/3$

The sampling distributions of $\bar{x}$ and m were found to be as shown below.

x	0	1	2	3	4	5	6	8	9	12
$p(x)$	$1/27$	$3/27$	$3/27$	$1/27$	$3/27$	$6/27$	$3/27$	$3/27$	$3/27$	$1/27$

m	0	3	12
$p(m)$	$7/27$	$13/27$	$7/27$

a. Show that $\bar{x}$ is an unbiased estimator of μ in this situation.

b. Show that m is a biased estimator of μ in this situation.

SOLUTION

a. The expected value of a discrete random variable x (see Section 4.3) is defined to be $E(x) = \Sigma x p(x)$, where the summation is over all values of x. Then

$$E(x) = \mu = \sum x p(x) = (0)(1/3) + (3)(1/3) + (12)(1/3) = 5$$

The expected value of the discrete random variable $\bar{x}$ is

$$E(\bar{x}) = \sum (\bar{x}) p(\bar{x})$$

summed over all values of $\bar{x}$. Or

$$E(\bar{x}) = (0)(1/27) + (1)(1/27) + (2)(1/27) + \cdots + (12)(1/27) = 5$$

Since $E(\bar{x}) = \mu$, we see that $\bar{x}$ is an unbiased estimator of μ.

b. The expected value of the sample median m is

$$E(m) = \sum m p(m) = (0)(7/27) + (3)(13/27) + (12)(7/27) = 4.56$$

Since the expected value of m is not equal to μ ($\mu = 5$), the sample median m is a biased estimator of μ. ◾

EXAMPLE 6.5   Refer to Example 6.4 and find the standard deviations of the sampling distributions of $\bar{x}$ and m. Which statistic would appear to be a better estimator of μ?

SOLUTION

The variance of the sampling distribution of $\bar{x}$ (we denote it by the symbol $\sigma_{\bar{x}}^2$) is found to be

$$\sigma_{\bar{x}}^2 = E\{[\bar{x} - E(\bar{x})]^2\} = \sum (\bar{x} - \mu)^2 p(\bar{x})$$

where, from Example 6.4,

$$E(\bar{x}) = \mu = 5$$

STATISTICS IN ACTION

6.1 REDUCING INVESTMENT RISK THROUGH DIVERSIFICATION

In Statistics in Action 4.1, it was noted that the variance of the monthly rate of return of a security is used by many investors as a measure of the risk or uncertainty involved in investing in the security. In this application, we investigate what happens to the risk faced by an investor when he or she invests in more than one security—that is, when the investor **diversifies** his or her holding.

A number of studies by financial analysts have shown that the total risk (total variation) of a stock, as measured by the variance of the stock's rates of return over time, is comprised of two components: **systematic risk** and **unsystematic risk**. Systematic risk (systematic variability) is the portion of total risk caused by factors that simultaneously influence the prices of all stocks. Examples of such factors are changes in federal economic policies and changes in the national political climate. These factors explain why the prices of all stocks tend to move together over time (i.e., generally upward or generally downward). Unsystematic risk (unsystematic variability) is the portion of the total risk of a particular stock due to factors that influence the firm in question but generally do not influence other firms. Examples of such factors are labor strikes, management errors, and lawsuits. Although the proportions of systematic and unsystematic risk vary from firm to firm, it has been determined that, for many of the stocks listed on the New York Stock Exchange, systematic risk comprises about 25% and unsystematic risk comprises about 75% of the stock's total risk (Blume, 1971). Here, we examine the effects of diversification on the unsystematic portion of the total investment risk faced by an investor.

Consider an investor who wants to invest a total of $5,000 in one or more of five different stocks. We denote the monthly rates of return of these stocks by r_1, r_2, r_3, r_4, and r_5. For simplicity, we assume these monthly returns are independent and identically dis-tributed random variables with mean $\mu = 10\%$ and standard deviation $\sigma = 4\%$. Suppose the investor has narrowed the choice to two options: (1) invest $5,000 in stock 1 or (2) invest $1,000 in each of the five stocks.

Under the first option, the investor's monthly rate of return is r_1. Under the second option, since equal amounts of money were invested in each stock, the investor's monthly rate of return is

$$\bar{r} = \sum_{i=1}^{5} r_i / 5$$

Focus

a. If the first option is chosen, what is the investor's expected monthly rate of return? What is the variance of the monthly rate of return (i.e., the risk faced by the investor)?

b. Is r_1 an unbiased estimator of μ? Explain.

c. It can be shown that $\bar{r}$ is an unbiased estimate of μ. Use this information to find the expected monthly rate of return under the second option.

d. It can further be shown that since $\bar{r}$ is the sum of $n = 5$ independent and identically distributed random variables, each with mean μ and variance σ^2, the variance of $\bar{r}$ is

$$\sigma_{\bar{r}}^2 = \frac{\sigma^2}{n}$$

Use this fact to find the risk associated with the second option.

e. Compare your answers to parts **b** and **d** and discuss the implications for investors who diversify versus those who put "all their eggs in one basket."

For a more detailed discussion of investment risk and the effects of diversification, see Alexander, Sharpe, and Bailey (1993) or Radcliffe (1994).

Then
$$\sigma_{\bar{x}}^2 = (0-5)^2(\tfrac{1}{27}) + (1-5)^2(\tfrac{3}{27}) + (2-5)^2(\tfrac{3}{27}) + \cdots + (12-5)^2(\tfrac{1}{27})$$
$$= 8.6667$$

and
$$\sigma_{\bar{x}} = \sqrt{8.6667} = 2.94$$

Similarly, the variance of the sampling distribution of m (we denote it by σ_m^2) is
$$\sigma_m^2 = E\{[m - E(m)]^2\}$$

where, from Example 6.4, the expected value of m is $E(m) = 4.56$. Then

$$\sigma_m^2 = E\{[m - E(m)]^2\} = \sum[m - E(m)]^2 p(m)$$

$$= (0 - 4.56)^2(\tfrac{7}{27}) + (3 - 4.56)^2(\tfrac{13}{27}) + (12 - 4.56)^2(\tfrac{7}{27}) = 20.9136$$

and
$$\sigma_m = \sqrt{20.9136} = 4.57$$

Which statistic appears to be the better estimator for the population mean μ: the sample mean $\bar{x}$ or the median m? To answer this question, we compare the sampling distributions of the two statistics. The sampling distribution of the sample median m is biased (i.e., it is located to the left of the mean μ) and its standard deviation $\sigma_m = 4.57$ is much larger than the standard deviation of the sampling distribution of $\bar{x}$, $\sigma_{\bar{x}} = 2.94$. Consequently, the sample mean $\bar{x}$ would be a better estimator of the population mean μ, for the population in question, than would the sample median m.

EXERCISES   6.8–6.14

Note: Exercises marked with 💾 *require the use of a computer.*

Learning the Mechanics

6.8   Consider the probability distribution shown here.

x	0	1	4
$p(x)$	$\tfrac{1}{3}$	$\tfrac{1}{3}$	$\tfrac{1}{3}$

a. Find μ and σ^2.
b. Find the sampling distribution of the sample mean $\bar{x}$ for a random sample of $n = 2$ measurements from this distribution.
c. Show that $\bar{x}$ is an unbiased estimator for μ.

   [*Hint:* Show that $E(\bar{x}) = \sum \bar{x}p(\bar{x}) = \mu$.]

d. Find the sampling distribution of the sample variance s^2 for a random sample of $n = 2$ measurements from this distribution.

e. Show that s^2 is an unbiased estimator for σ^2.

6.9   Consider the probability distribution shown here.

x	2	4	9
$p(x)$	$\tfrac{1}{3}$	$\tfrac{1}{3}$	$\tfrac{1}{3}$

a. Calculate μ for this distribution.
b. Find the sampling distribution of the sample mean $\bar{x}$ for a random sample of $n = 3$ measurements from this distribution, and show that $\bar{x}$ is an unbiased estimator of μ.
c. Find the sampling distribution of the sample median m for a random sample of $n = 3$ measurements from this distribution, and show that the median is a biased estimator of μ.
d. If you wanted to estimate μ using a sample of three measurements from this population, which estimator would you use? Why?

6.10 Consider the probability distribution shown here.

x	0	1	2
$p(x)$	$\frac{1}{3}$	$\frac{1}{3}$	$\frac{1}{3}$

a. Find μ.
b. For a random sample of $n = 3$ observations from this distribution, find the sampling distribution of the sample mean.
c. Find the sampling distribution of the median of a sample of $n = 3$ observations from this population.
d. Refer to parts **b** and **c** and show that both the mean and median are unbiased estimators of μ for this population.
e. Find the variances of the sampling distributions of the sample mean and the sample median.
f. Which estimator would you use to estimate μ? Why?

6.11 Generate 500 samples, each containing $n = 25$ measurements, from a population that contains values of x equal to 1, 2, ..., 48, 49, 50. Assume that these values of x are equally likely. Calculate the sample mean $\bar{x}$ and median m for each sample.

Construct relative frequency histograms for the 500 values of $\bar{x}$ and the 500 values of m. Use these approximations to the sampling distributions of $\bar{x}$ and m to answer the following questions:
a. Does it appear that $\bar{x}$ and m are unbiased estimators of the population mean? [*Note:* $\mu = 25.5$.]
b. Which sampling distribution displays greater variation?

6.12 Refer to Exercise 6.3.
a. Show that $\bar{x}$ is an unbiased estimator of μ.
b. Find $\sigma_{\bar{x}}^2$.
c. Find the probability that $\bar{x}$ will fall within $2\sigma_{\bar{x}}$ of μ.

6.13 Refer to Exercise 6.3.
a. Find the sampling distribution of s^2.
b. Find the population variance σ^2.
c. Show that s^2 is an unbiased estimator of σ^2.
d. Find the sampling distribution of the sample standard deviation s.
e. Show that s is a biased estimator of σ.

6.14 Refer to Exercise 6.5, where we found the sampling distribution of the sample median. Is the median an unbiased estimator of the population mean μ?

6.3 THE SAMPLING DISTRIBUTION OF THE SAMPLE MEAN

Estimating the mean useful life of automobiles, the mean monthly sales for all computer dealers in a large city, and the mean breaking strength of a new plastic are practical problems with something in common. In each case we are interested in making an inference about the mean μ of some population. As we mentioned in Chapter 2, the sample mean $\bar{x}$ is, in general, a good estimator of μ. We now develop pertinent information about the sampling distribution for this useful statistic.

EXAMPLE 6.6 Suppose a population has the uniform probability distribution given in Figure 6.8. The mean and standard deviation of this probability distribution are $\mu = .5$ and $\sigma = .29$. (See optional Section 5.2 for the formulas for μ and σ.) Now suppose a sample of 11 measurements is selected from this population. Describe the sam-

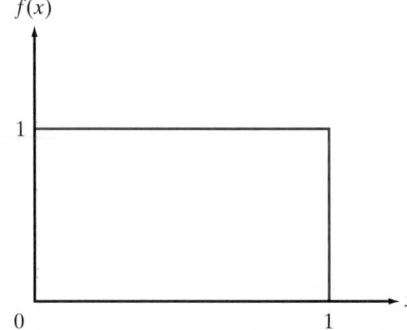

FIGURE 6.8
Sampled uniform population

FIGURE 6.9
Relative frequency histogram for $\bar{x}$ in 1,000 samples of $n = 11$ measurements with normal distribution superimposed

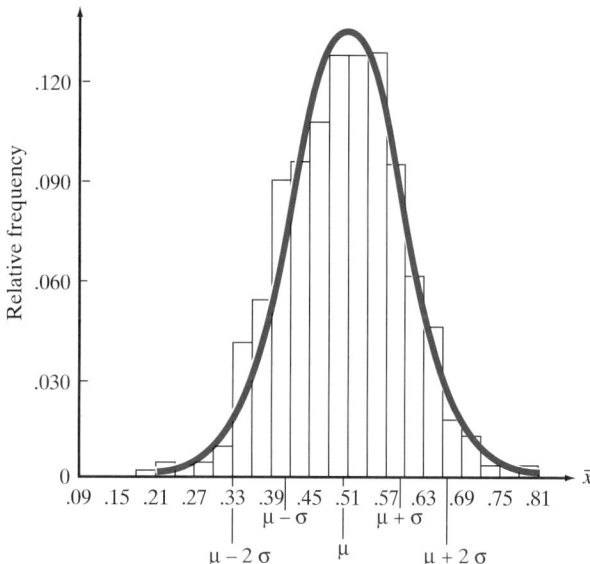

pling distribution of the sample mean $\bar{x}$ based on the 1,000 sampling experiments discussed in Example 6.2.

SOLUTION
You will recall that in Example 6.2 we generated 1,000 samples of $n = 11$ measurements each. The relative frequency histogram for the 1,000 sample means is shown in Figure 6.9 with a normal probability distribution superimposed. You can see that this normal probability distribution approximates the computer-generated sampling distribution very well.

To fully describe a normal probability distribution, it is necessary to know its mean and standard deviation. Inspection of Figure 6.9 indicates that the mean of the distribution of $\bar{x}$, $\mu_{\bar{x}}$, appears to be very close to .5, the mean of the sampled uniform population. Furthermore, for a mound-shaped distribution such as that shown in Figure 6.9, almost all the measurements should fall within 3 standard deviations of the mean. Since the number of values of $\bar{x}$ is very large (1,000), the range of the observed $\bar{x}$'s divided by 6 (rather than 4) should give a reasonable approximation to the standard deviation of the sample mean, $\sigma_{\bar{x}}$. The values of $\bar{x}$ range from about .2 to .8, so we calculate

$$\sigma_{\bar{x}} \approx \frac{\text{Range of } \bar{x}\text{'s}}{6} = \frac{.8 - .2}{6} = .1$$

To summarize our findings based on 1,000 samples, each consisting of 11 measurements from a uniform population, the sampling distribution of $\bar{x}$ appears to be approximately normal with a mean of about .5 and a standard deviation of about .1.

The sampling distribution of $\bar{x}$ has the properties given in the next box, assuming only that a random sample of n observations has been selected from *any* population.

Properties of the Sampling Distribution of $\bar{x}$

1. Mean of sampling distribution equals mean of sampled population. That is, $\mu_{\bar{x}} = E(\bar{x}) = \mu$.

2. Standard deviation of sampling distribution equals

$$\frac{\text{Standard deviation of sampled population}}{\text{Square root of sample size}}$$

That is, $\sigma_{\bar{x}} = \sigma/\sqrt{n}$.*

The standard deviation $\sigma_{\bar{x}}$ is often referred to as the **standard error of the mean**.

You can see that our approximation to $\mu_{\bar{x}}$ in Example 6.6 was precise, since property 1 assures us that the mean is the same as that of the sampled population: .5. Property 2 tells us how to calculate the standard deviation of the sampling distribution of $\bar{x}$. Substituting $\sigma = .29$, the standard deviation of the sampled uniform distribution, and the sample size $n = 11$ into the formula for $\sigma_{\bar{x}}$, we find

$$\sigma_{\bar{x}} = \frac{\sigma}{\sqrt{n}} = \frac{.29}{\sqrt{11}} = .09$$

Thus, the approximation we obtained in Example 6.6, $\sigma_{\bar{x}} \approx .1$, is very close to the exact value, $\sigma_{\bar{x}} = .09$.

What can be said about the shape of the sampling distribution of $\bar{x}$? Two important theorems provide this information.

Theorem 6.1

If a random sample of n observations is selected from a population with a normal distribution, the sampling distribution of $\bar{x}$ will be a normal distribution.

Theorem 6.2 (Central Limit Theorem)

Consider a random sample of n observations selected from a population (*any* population) with mean μ and standard deviation σ. Then, when n is sufficiently large, the sampling distribution of x will be approximately a normal distribution with mean $\mu_{\bar{x}} = \mu$ and standard deviation $\sigma_{\bar{x}} = \sigma/\sqrt{n}$. The larger the sample size, the better will be the normal approximation to the sampling distribution of $\bar{x}$.†

Thus, for sufficiently large samples the sampling distribution of $\bar{x}$ is approximately normal. How large must the sample size n be so that the normal distribution provides a good approximation for the sampling distribution of $\bar{x}$? The answer depends on the shape of the distribution of the sampled population, as shown by Figure 6.10. Generally speaking, the greater the skewness of the sampled population distribution, the larger the sample size must be before the normal distribution is an adequate approximation for the sampling distribution of $\bar{x}$. For most sampled populations, sample sizes of $n \geq 30$ will suffice for the normal

---

*If the sample size, n, is large relative to the number, N, of elements in the population, (e.g., 5% or more), $\sigma/\sqrt{n}$ must be multiplied by a finite population correction factor, $\sqrt{(N-n)/(N-1)}$. For most sampling situations, this correction factor will be close to 1 and can be ignored.

†Moreover, because of the Central Limit Theorem, the sum of a random sample of n observations, Σx, will possess a sampling distribution that is approximately normal for large samples. This distribution will have a mean equal to $n\mu$ and a variance equal to $n\sigma^2$. Proof of the Central Limit Theorem is beyond the scope of this book, but it can be found in many mathematical statistics texts.

FIGURE 6.10

Sampling distributions of $\bar{x}$ for different populations and different sample sizes

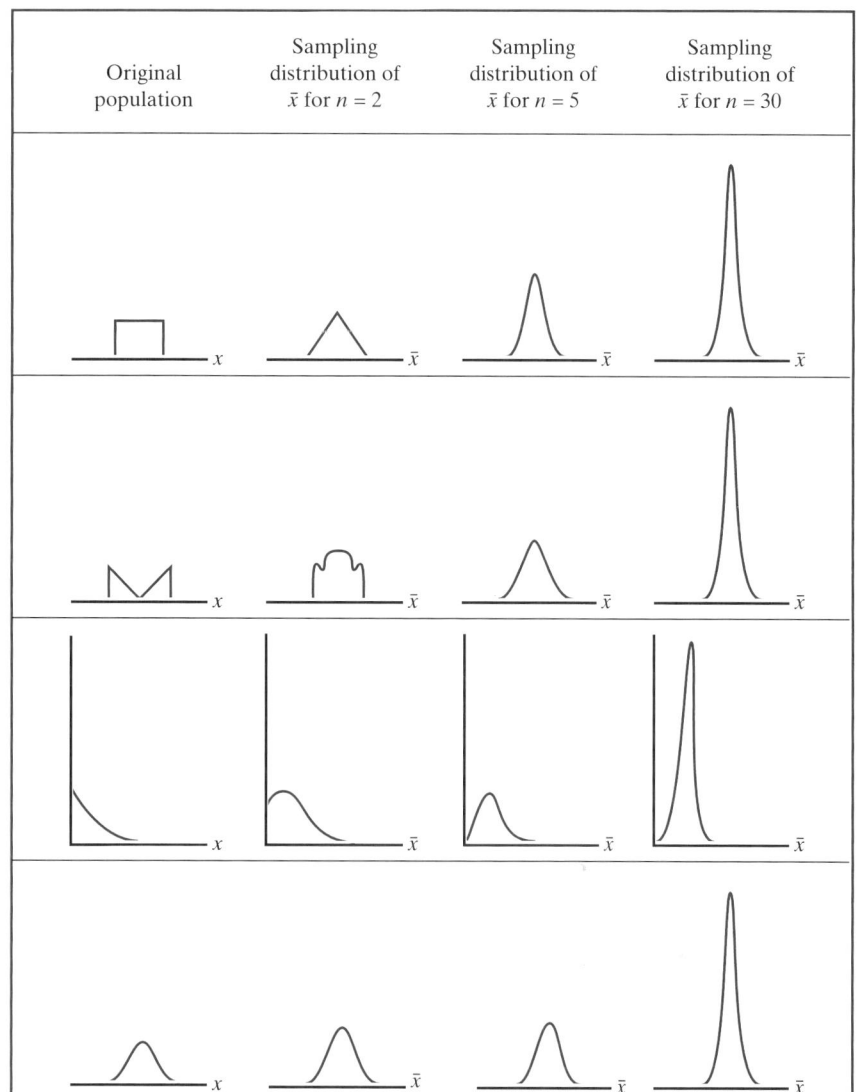

Original population	Sampling distribution of $\bar{x}$ for $n = 2$	Sampling distribution of $\bar{x}$ for $n = 5$	Sampling distribution of $\bar{x}$ for $n = 30$

approximation to be reasonable. We will use the normal approximation for the sampling distribution of $\bar{x}$ when the sample size is at least 30.

EXAMPLE 6.7   Suppose we have selected a random sample of $n = 25$ observations from a population with mean equal to 80 and standard deviation equal to 5. It is known that the population is not extremely skewed.

   a. Sketch the relative frequency distributions for the population and for the sampling distribution of the sample mean, $\bar{x}$.

   b. Find the probability that $\bar{x}$ will be larger than 82.

SOLUTION

   a. We do not know the exact shape of the population relative frequency distribution, but we do know that it should be centered about $\mu = 80$, its spread should be measured by $\sigma = 5$, and it is not highly skewed. One possibility is shown in Figure 6.11a. From the Central Limit Theorem, we know that the sampling distribution of $\bar{x}$ will be approximately normal since the sampled

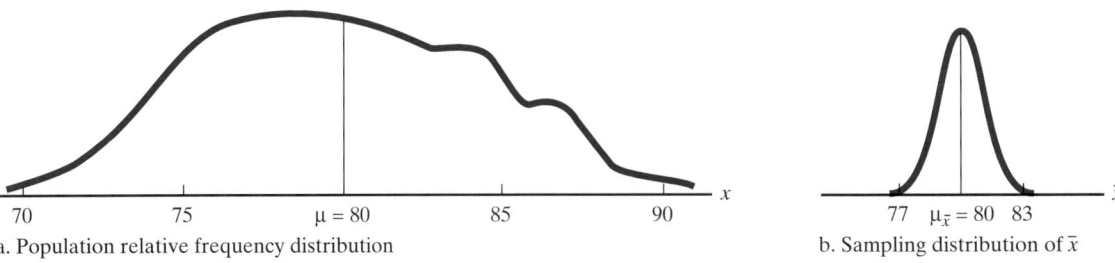

a. Population relative frequency distribution

b. Sampling distribution of $\bar{x}$

FIGURE 6.11 A population relative frequency distribution and the sampling distribution for $\bar{x}$

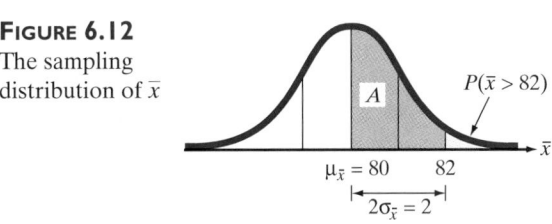

FIGURE 6.12
The sampling
distribution of $\bar{x}$

population distribution is not extremely skewed. We also know that the sampling distribution will have mean and standard deviation

$$\mu_{\bar{x}} = \mu = 80 \qquad \text{and} \qquad \sigma_{\bar{x}} = \frac{\sigma}{\sqrt{n}} = \frac{5}{\sqrt{25}} = 1$$

The sampling distribution of $\bar{x}$ is shown in Figure 6.11b.

b. The probability that $\bar{x}$ will exceed 82 is equal to the lightly shaded area in Figure 6.12. To find this area, we need to find the z value corresponding to $\bar{x} = 82$. Recall that the standard normal random variable z is the difference between any normally distributed random variable and its mean, expressed in units of its standard deviation. Since $\bar{x}$ is a normally distributed random variable with mean $\mu_{\bar{x}} = \mu$ and $\sigma_{\bar{x}} = \sigma/\sqrt{n}$, it follows that the standard normal z value corresponding to the sample mean, $\bar{x}$, is

$$z = \frac{(\text{Normal random variable}) - (\text{Mean})}{\text{Standard deviation}} = \frac{\bar{x} - \mu_{\bar{x}}}{\sigma_{\bar{x}}}$$

Therefore, for $\bar{x} = 82$, we have

$$z = \frac{\bar{x} - \mu_{\bar{x}}}{\sigma_{\bar{x}}} = \frac{82 - 80}{1} = 2$$

The area A in Figure 6.12 corresponding to $z = 2$ is given in the table of areas under the normal curve (see Table IV of Appendix B) as .4772. Therefore, the tail area corresponding to the probability that $\bar{x}$ exceeds 82 is

$$P(\bar{x} > 82) = P(z > 2) = .5 - .4772 = .0228. \qquad \blacksquare$$

EXAMPLE **6.8**

A manufacturer of automobile batteries claims that the distribution of the lengths of life of its best battery has a mean of 54 months and a standard deviation of 6 months. Suppose a consumer group decides to check the claim by purchasing a sample of 50 of these batteries and subjecting them to tests that determine battery life.

a. Assuming that the manufacturer's claim is true, describe the sampling distribution of the mean lifetime of a sample of 50 batteries.

FIGURE 6.13
Sampling distribution
of $\bar{x}$ in Example 6.8 for
$n = 50$

$P(\bar{x} \leq 52)$

A

52   54 $\bar{x}$

b. Assuming that the manufacturer's claim is true, what is the probability the consumer group's sample has a mean life of 52 or fewer months?

SOLUTION

a. Even though we have no information about the shape of the probability distribution of the lives of the batteries, we can use the Central Limit Theorem to deduce that the sampling distribution for a sample mean lifetime of 50 batteries is approximately normally distributed. Furthermore, the mean of this sampling distribution is the same as the mean of the sampled population, which is $\mu = 54$ months according to the manufacturer's claim. Finally, the standard deviation of the sampling distribution is given by

$$\sigma_{\bar{x}} = \frac{\sigma}{\sqrt{n}} = \frac{6}{\sqrt{50}} = .85 \text{ month}$$

Note that we used the claimed standard deviation of the sampled population, $\sigma = 6$ months. Thus, if we assume that the claim is true, the sampling distribution for the mean life of the 50 batteries sampled is as shown in Figure 6.13.

b. If the manufacturer's claim is true, the probability that the consumer group observes a mean battery life of 52 or fewer months for their sample of 50 batteries, $P(x \leq 52)$, is equivalent to the lightly shaded area in Figure 6.13. Since the sampling distribution is approximately normal, we can find this area by computing the standard normal z value:

$$z = \frac{\bar{x} - \mu_{\bar{x}}}{\sigma_{\bar{x}}} = \frac{\bar{x} - \mu}{\sigma_{\bar{x}}} = \frac{52 - 54}{.85} = -2.35$$

where $\mu_{\bar{x}}$, the mean of the sampling distribution of $\bar{x}$, is equal to μ, the mean of the lives of the sampled population, and $\sigma_{\bar{x}}$ is the standard deviation of the sampling distribution of $\bar{x}$. Note that z is the familiar standardized distance (z-score) of Section 2.7 and, since $\bar{x}$ is approximately normally distributed, it will possess the standard normal distribution of Section 5.3.

The area A shown in Figure 6.13 between $\bar{x} = 52$ and $\bar{x} = 54$ (corresponding to $z = -2.35$) is found in Table IV of Appendix B to be .4906. Therefore, the area to the left of $\bar{x} = 52$ is

$$P(\bar{x} \leq 52) = .5 - A = .5 - .4906 = .0094$$

Thus, the probability the consumer group will observe a sample mean of 52 or less is only .0094 if the manufacturer's claim is true. If the 50 tested batteries do exhibit a mean of 52 or fewer months, the consumer group will have strong evidence that the manufacturer's claim is untrue, because such an event is very unlikely to occur if the claim is true. (This is still another application of the *rare-event approach to statistical inference*.) ◣

STATISTICS IN ACTION

6.2 THE INSOMNIA PILL

A research report published in the *Proceedings of the National Academy of Sciences* (Mar. 1994) brought encouraging news to insomniacs and international business travelers who suffer from jet lag. Neuroscientists at the Massachusetts Institute of Technology (MIT) have been experimenting with melatonin—a hormone secreted by the pineal gland in the brain—as a sleep-inducing hormone. Since the hormone is naturally produced, it is nonaddictive. The researchers believe melatonin may be effective in treating jet lag—the body's response to rapid travel across many time zones so that a daylight-darkness change disrupts sleep patterns.

In the MIT study, young male volunteers were given various doses of melatonin or a placebo (a dummy medication containing no melatonin). Then they were placed in a dark room at midday and told to close their eyes for 30 minutes. The variable of interest was the time (in minutes) elapsed before each volunteer fell asleep.

According to the lead investigator, Professor Richard Wurtman, "Our volunteers fall asleep in five or six minutes on melatonin, while those on placebo take about 15 minutes." Wurtman warns, however, that uncontrolled doses of melatonin could cause mood-altering side effects. (Melatonin is sold in some health food stores. However, sales are unregulated, and the purity and strength of the hormone are often uncertain.)

Focus

With the placebo (i.e., no hormone) the researchers found that the mean time to fall asleep was 15 minutes. Assume that with the placebo treatment $\mu = 15$ and $\sigma = 5$. Now, consider a random sample of 40 young males, each of whom is given a dosage of the sleep-inducing hormone, melatonin. The times (in minutes) to fall asleep for these 40 males are listed in Table 6.3.* Use the data to make an inference about the true value of μ for those taking the melatonin. Does melatonin appear to be an effective drug against insomnia?

*These are simulated sleep times based on summary information provided in the MIT study.

TABLE 6.3 **Times (in Minutes) for 40 Male Volunteers to Fall Asleep (Statistics in Action 6.2)**

6.4	6.0	3.2	4.4	6.2	1.7	5.1
5.9	1.6	4.4	16.2	4.8	8.3	7.5
4.8	3.3	4.0	6.2	6.3	5.0	6.3
5.1	6.4	15.6	3.4	3.1	6.1	6.0
5.0	1.8	6.1	4.5	4.5	1.5	4.7
7.6	8.2	4.9	6.1	3.9		

We conclude this section with two final comments on the sampling distribution of $\bar{x}$. First, from the formula $\sigma_{\bar{x}} = \sigma/\sqrt{n}$, we see that the standard deviation of the sampling distribution of $\bar{x}$ gets smaller as the sample size n gets larger. For example, we computed $\sigma_{\bar{x}} = .85$ when $n = 50$ in Example 6.8. However, for $n = 100$ we obtain $\sigma_{\bar{x}} = \sigma/\sqrt{n} = 6/\sqrt{100} = .60$. This relationship will hold true for most of the sample statistics encountered in this text. That is: *The standard deviation of the sampling distribution decreases as the sample size increases.* Consequently, the larger the sample size, the more accurate the sample statistic (e.g., $\bar{x}$) is in estimating a population parameter (e.g., μ). We will use this result in Chapter 7 to help us determine the sample size needed to obtain a specified accuracy of estimation.

Our second comment concerns the Central Limit Theorem. In addition to providing a very useful approximation for the sampling distribution of a sample mean, the Central Limit Theorem offers an explanation for the fact that many relative frequency distributions of data possess mound-shaped distributions. Many of the measurements we take in business are really means or sums of a large number of small phenomena. For example, a company's sales for one year are the total of the many individual sales the company made during the year. Similarly, we can view the length of time a construction company takes to build a house as the total of the times taken to complete a multitude of the distinct jobs, and we can regard the monthly demand for blood at a hospital as the total of the many individual patients' needs. Whether or not the observations entering into these sums satisfy the assumptions basic to the Central Limit Theorem is open to question. However, it is a fact that many distributions of data in nature are mound-shaped and possess the appearance of normal distributions.

EXERCISES   6.15–6.30

Note: Exercises marked with 💾 require the use of a computer.

Learning the Mechanics

6.15 Suppose a random sample of n measurements is selected from a population with mean $\mu = 100$ and variance $\sigma^2 = 100$. For each of the following values of n, give the mean and standard deviation of the sampling distribution of the sample mean $\bar{x}$.
a. $n = 4$ **b.** $n = 25$ **c.** $n = 100$
d. $n = 50$ **e.** $n = 500$ **f.** $n = 1,000$

6.16 Suppose a random sample of $n = 25$ measurements is selected from a population with mean μ and standard deviation σ. For each of the following values of μ and σ, give the values of $\mu_{\bar{x}}$ and $\sigma_{\bar{x}}$.
a. $\mu = 10, \sigma = 3$ **b.** $\mu = 100, \sigma = 25$
c. $\mu = 20, \sigma = 40$ **d.** $\mu = 10, \sigma = 100$

6.17 Consider the probability distribution shown here.

x	1	2	3	8
$p(x)$	.1	.4	.4	.1

a. Find μ, σ^2, and σ.
b. Find the sampling distribution of $\bar{x}$ for random samples of $n = 2$ measurements from this distribution by listing all possible values of $\bar{x}$, and find the probability associated with each.
c. Use the results of part **b** to calculate $\mu_{\bar{x}}$ and $\sigma_{\bar{x}}$. Confirm that $\mu_{\bar{x}} = \mu$ and $\sigma_{\bar{x}} = \sigma/\sqrt{n} = \sigma/\sqrt{2}$.

6.18 Will the sampling distribution of $\bar{x}$ always be approximately normally distributed? Explain.

6.19 A random sample of $n = 64$ observations is drawn from a population with a mean equal to 20 and standard deviation equal to 16.
a. Give the mean and standard deviation of the (repeated) sampling distribution of $\bar{x}$.
b. Describe the shape of the sampling distribution of $\bar{x}$. Does your answer depend on the sample size?

c. Calculate the standard normal z-score corresponding to a value of $\bar{x} = 15.5$.
d. Calculate the standard normal z-score corresponding to $\bar{x} = 23$.

6.20 Refer to Exercise 6.19. Find the probability that
a. $\bar{x}$ is less than 16   **b.** $\bar{x}$ is greater than 23
c. $\bar{x}$ is greater than 25
d. $\bar{x}$ falls between 16 and 22   **e.** $\bar{x}$ is less than 14

6.21 A random sample of $n = 100$ observations is selected from a population with $\mu = 30$ and $\sigma = 16$. Approximate the following probabilities:
a. $P(\bar{x} \geq 28)$ **b.** $P(22.1 \leq \bar{x} \leq 26.8)$
c. $P(\bar{x} \leq 28.2)$ **d.** $P(\bar{x} \geq 27.0)$

6.22 A random sample of $n = 900$ observations is selected from a population with $\mu = 100$ and $\sigma = 10$.
a. What are the largest and smallest values of $\bar{x}$ that you would expect to see?
b. How far, at the most, would you expect $\bar{x}$ to deviate from μ?
c. Did you have to know μ to answer part **b**? Explain.

6.23 💾 Consider a population that contains values of x equal to 0, 1, 2, ..., 97, 98, 99. Assume that the values of x are equally likely. For each of the following values of n, generate 500 random samples and calculate $\bar{x}$ for each sample. For each sample size, construct a relative frequency histogram of the 500 values of $\bar{x}$. What changes occur in the histograms as the value of n increases? What similarities exist? Use $n = 2, n = 5, n = 10, n = 30$, and $n = 50$.

Applying the Concepts

6.24 The *College Student Journal* (Dec. 1992) investigated differences in traditional and nontraditional students, where nontraditional students are generally defined as those 25 years or older and who are working full or part-time. Based on the study results, we can assume that the population mean and standard deviation for the GPA of all nontraditional students is $\mu = 3.5$ and $\sigma = .5$. Suppose that a random sample of $n = 100$ nontraditional students is selected from the population of all nontraditional students, and the GPA of each student is determined. Then $\bar{x}$, the sample mean, will be approximately normally distributed (because of the Central Limit Theorem).

a. Calculate $\mu_{\bar{x}}$ and $\sigma_{\bar{x}}$.
b. What is the approximate probability that the nontraditional student sample has a mean GPA between 3.40 and 3.60?
c. What is the approximate probability that the sample of 100 nontraditional students has a mean GPA that exceeds 3.62?
d. How would the sampling distribution of $\bar{x}$ change if the sample size n were doubled from 100 to 200? How do your answers to parts **b** and **c** change when the sample size is doubled?

6.25 Filling processes are used in the production of a wide variety of products including beverages, food, soaps, cleaners, chemicals, paints, and pharmaceuticals. They involve inserting a specific amount of a product into a container, subject to certain specifications. However, because of both the physical properties of the product and the design of the filling process, the amount of "fill" dispensed is a random variable. University of Louisville researchers J. Usher, S. Alexander, and D. Duggins examined the process of filling plastic pouches of dry blended biscuit mix (*Quality Engineering*, Vol. 9, 1996). The current fill mean of the process is set at $\mu = 406$ grams and the process fill standard deviation is $\sigma = 10.1$ grams. (According to the researchers, "The high level of variation is due to the fact that the product has poor flow properties and is, therefore, difficult to fill consistently from pouch to pouch.") Operators monitor the process by randomly sampling 36 pouches each day and measuring the amount of biscuit mix in each. Consider $\bar{x}$, the main fill amount of the sample of 36 products.

a. Describe the sampling distribution of $\bar{x}$. (Give the values of $\mu_{\bar{x}}$ and $\sigma_{\bar{x}}$, and the shape of the probability distribution.)
b. Find $P(\bar{x} \leq 400.8)$.
c. Suppose that on one particular day, the operators observe $\bar{x} = 400.8$. One of the operators believes that this indicates that the true process fill mean μ for that day is less than 406 grams. Another operator argues that $\mu = 406$ and the small value of $\bar{x}$ observed is due to random variation in the fill process. Which operator do you agree with? Why?

6.26 Last year a company began a program to compensate its employees for unused sick days, paying each employee a bonus of one-half the usual wage earned for each unused sick day. The question that naturally arises is: "Did this policy motivate employees to use fewer sick days?" *Before* last year, the number of sick days used by employees had a distribution with a mean of 7 days and a standard deviation of 2 days.

a. Assuming that these parameters did not change last year, find the approximate probability that the sample mean number of sick days used by 100 employees chosen at random was less than or equal to 6.4 last year.
b. How would you interpret the result if the sample mean for the 100 employees was 6.4?

6.27 The ocean quahog is a type of clam found in the coastal waters of New England and the mid-Atlantic states. Extensive beds of ocean quahogs along the New Jersey shore gave rise to the development of the largest U.S. shellfish harvesting program. A federal survey of offshore ocean quahog harvesting in New Jersey, conducted from 1980 to 1992, revealed an average catch per unit effort (CPUE) of 89.34 clams. The CPUE standard deviation was 7.74 (*Journal of Shellfish Research*, June 1995). Let $\bar{x}$ represent the mean CPUE for a sample of 35 attempts to catch ocean quahogs off the New Jersey shore.

a. Compute $\mu_{\bar{x}}$ and $\sigma_{\bar{x}}$. Interpret their values.
b. Sketch the sampling distribution of $\bar{x}$.
c. Find $P(\bar{x} > 88)$.   d. Find $P(\bar{x} < 87)$.

6.28 In determining when to place orders to replenish depleted product inventories, a retailer should take into consideration the lead times for the products. **Lead time** is the time between placing the order and having the product available to satisfy customer demand. It includes time for placing the order, receiving the shipment from the supplier, inspecting the units received, and placing them in inventory (Clauss, *Applied Management Science and Spreadsheet Modeling*, 1996). Interested in the average lead time, μ, for a particular supplier of men's apparel, the purchasing department of a national department store chain randomly sampled 50 of the supplier's lead times and found $\bar{x} = 44$ days.

a. Describe the shape of the sampling distribution of $\bar{x}$.
b. If μ and σ are really 40 and 12, respectively, what is the probability that a second random sample of size 50 would yield $\bar{x}$ greater than or equal to 44?
c. Using the values for μ and σ in part **b**, what is the probability that a sample of size 50 would yield a sample mean within the interval $\mu \pm 2\sigma/\sqrt{n}$?

6.29 A soft-drink bottler purchases glass bottles from a vendor. The bottles are required to have an internal pressure strength of at least 150 pounds per square inch (psi). A prospective bottle vendor claims that its production process yields bottles with a mean internal pressure strength of 157 psi and a standard deviation of 3 psi. The bottler strikes an agreement with the vendor that permits the bottler to sample from the vendor's production process to verify the vendor's claim. The bottler randomly selects 40 bottles from the last 10,000 produced, measures the internal pressure of each, and finds the mean pressure for the sample to be 1.3 psi below the process mean cited by the vendor.

a. Assuming the vendor's claim to be true, what is the probability of obtaining a sample mean this far or farther below the process mean? What does your answer suggest about the validity of the vendor's claim?

b. If the process standard deviation were 3 psi as claimed by the vendor, but the mean were 156 psi, would the observed sample result be more or less likely than in part **a**? What if the mean were 158 psi?

c. If the process mean were 157 psi as claimed, but the process standard deviation were 2 psi, would the sample result be more or less likely than in part **a**? What if instead the standard deviation were 6 psi?

6.30 National Car Rental Systems, Inc. commissioned USAC Properties, Inc. [the performance testing/ endorsement arm of the United States Automobile Club (USAC)] to conduct a survey of the general condition of the cars rented to the public by Hertz, Avis, National, and Budget Rent-a-Car.*

USAC officials evaluate each company's cars on appearance and cleanliness, accessory performance, mechanical functions, and vehicle safety using a demerit point system designed specifically for this survey. Each car starts with a perfect score of 0 points and incurs demerit points for each discrepancy noted by the inspectors. One measure of the overall condition of a company's cars is the mean of all scores received by the company, i.e., the company's *fleet mean score*. To estimate the fleet mean score of each rental car company, 10 major airports were randomly selected, and 10 cars from each company were randomly rented for inspection from each airport by USAC officials; i.e., a sample of size $n = 100$ cars from each company's fleet was drawn and inspected.

a. Describe the sampling distribution of $\bar{x}$, the mean score of a sample of $n = 100$ rental cars.

b. Interpret the mean of $\bar{x}$ in the context of this problem.

c. Assume $\mu = 30$ and $\sigma = 60$ for one rental car company. For this company, find $P(\bar{x} \geq 45)$.

d. Refer to part **c**. The company claims that their true fleet mean score "couldn't possibly be as high as 30." The sample mean score tabulated by USAC for this company was $\bar{x} = 45$. Does this result tend to support or refute the claim? Explain.

*Information by personal communication with Rajiv Tandon, Corporate Vice President and General Manager of the Car Rental Division, National Car Rental Systems, Inc., Minneapolis, Minnesota.

QUICK REVIEW

Key Terms

Biased estimate   248
Central Limit Theorem   254
Error of estimation   247

Parameter   240
Point estimator   247
Sample statistic   240

Sampling distribution   242
Standard error of the mean   254
Unbiased estimate   248

Key Formulas

Mean	Standard Deviation	z-score	
$\mu_{\bar{x}} = \mu$	$\sigma_{\bar{x}} = \dfrac{\sigma}{\sqrt{n}}$	$z = \dfrac{\bar{x} - \mu_{\bar{x}}}{\sigma_{\bar{x}}} = \dfrac{\bar{x} - \mu}{\sigma/\sqrt{n}}$	Sampling distribution of $\bar{x}$ 254, 256

LANGUAGE LAB

Symbol	Pronunciation	Description
θ	theta	Population parameter (general)
$\mu_{\bar{x}}$	mu of x-bar	True mean of sampling distribution of $\bar{x}$
$\sigma_{\bar{x}}$	sigma of x-bar	True standard deviation of sampling distribution of $\bar{x}$

SUPPLEMENTARY EXERCISES 6.31–6.51

Note: Exercises marked with 💾 *require the use of a computer.*

Learning the Mechanics

6.31 Consider a sample statistic A. As with all sample statistics, A is computed by utilizing a specified function (formula) of the sample measurements. (For example, if A were the sample mean, the specified formula would be to sum the measurements and divide by the number of measurements.)

a. Describe what we mean by the phrase "the sampling distribution of the sample statistic A."

b. Suppose A is to be used to estimate a population parameter α. What is meant by the assertion that A is an unbiased estimator of α?

c. Consider another sample statistic, B. Assume that B is also an unbiased estimator of the population parameter α. How can we use the sampling distributions of A and B to decide which is the better estimator of α?

d. If the sample sizes on which A and B are based are large, can we apply the Central Limit Theorem and assert that the sampling distributions of A and B are approximately normal? Why or why not?

6.32 The standard deviation (or, as it is usually called, the *standard error*) of the sampling distribution for the sample mean, $\bar{x}$, is equal to the standard deviation of the population from which the sample was selected divided by the square root of the sample size. That is,

$$\sigma_{\bar{x}} = \frac{\sigma}{\sqrt{n}}$$

a. As the sample size is increased, what happens to the standard error of $\bar{x}$? Why is this property considered important?

b. Suppose that a sample statistic has a standard error that is not a function of the sample size. In other words, the standard error remains constant as n changes. What would this imply about the statistic as an estimator of a population parameter?

c. Suppose another unbiased estimator (call it A) of the population mean is a sample statistic with a standard error equal to

$$\sigma_A = \frac{\sigma}{\sqrt[3]{n}}$$

Which of the sample statistics, $\bar{x}$ or A, is preferable as an estimator of the population mean? Why?

d. Suppose that the population standard deviation σ is equal to 10 and that the sample size is 64. Calculate the standard errors of $\bar{x}$ and A. Assuming that the sampling distribution of A is approximately normal, interpret the standard errors. Why is the assumption of (approximate) normality unnecessary for the sampling distribution of $\bar{x}$?

6.33 A random sample of $n = 68$ observations is selected from a population with $\mu = 19.6$ and $\sigma = 3.2$. Approximate each of the following probabilities.

a. $P(\bar{x} \leq 19.6)$ **b.** $P(\bar{x} \leq 19)$
c. $P(\bar{x} \geq 20.1)$ **d.** $P(19.2 \leq \bar{x} \leq 20.6)$

6.34 A random sample of 40 observations is to be drawn from a large population of measurements. It is known that 30% of the measurements in the population are 1's, 20% are 2's, 20% are 3's, and 30% are 4's.

a. Give the mean and standard deviation of the (repeated) sampling distribution of $\bar{x}$, the sample mean of the 40 observations.

b. Describe the shape of the sampling distribution of $\bar{x}$. Does your answer depend on the sample size?

6.35 💾 Use a statistical software package to generate 100 random samples of size $n = 2$ from a population characterized by a uniform probability distribution (optional Section 5.2) and $c = 0$ and $d = 10$. Compute $\bar{x}$ for each sample, and plot a frequency distribution for the 100 $\bar{x}$ values. Repeat this process for $n = 5, 10, 30$, and 50. Explain how your plots illustrate the Central Limit Theorem.

6.36 💾 Use a statistical software package to generate 100 random samples of size $n = 2$ from a population characterized by a normal probability distribution with mean 100 and standard deviation 10. Compute $\bar{x}$ for each sample and plot a frequency distribution for the 100 values of $\bar{x}$. Repeat this process for $n = 5, 10, 30$, and 50. How does the fact that the sampled population is normal affect the sampling distribution of $\bar{x}$?

6.37 A random sample of size n is to be drawn from a large population with mean 100 and standard deviation 10, and the sample mean $\bar{x}$ is to be calculated. To see the effect of different sample sizes on the standard deviation of the sampling distribution of $\bar{x}$, plot $\sigma/\sqrt{n}$ against n for $n = 1, 5, 10, 20, 30, 40$, and 50.

Applying the Concepts

6.38 The fourth *Annual Report: Florida Employer Opinion Survey* (1992) gives the results of an extensive survey of employer opinions in Florida. Each employer was asked to rate his or her satisfaction with the preparation of employees by the public education system. Responses were 1, 1.5, or 2, representing very dissatisfied, neither satisfied nor dissatisfied, and very satisfied, respectively. A sample of 651 employers was selected. Assume that the mean for all employers in Florida is 1.50 (the "dividing line" between satisfied and dissatisfied) and the standard deviation is .45.

a. Which type of distribution describes the individual survey responses, continuous or discrete?

b. Describe the distribution that best approximates the sample mean response of 651 employers. What are the mean and standard deviation of this distribution? What assumptions, if any, are necessary to ensure the validity of your answers?

c. What is the approximate probability that the sample mean will be 1.45 or less?

d. The mean of the sample of 651 employers surveyed in 1992 was 1.36. Given this result, do you think it is likely that all Florida employers' opinions were evenly divided on the effectiveness of public education? That is, do you think the assumption that the population mean is 1.50 is correct? Why or why not?

6.39   One measure of elevator performance is cycle time. Elevator cycle time is the time between successive elevator starts, which includes the time when the car is moving and the time when it is standing at a floor. Researchers have found that simulation is necessary to determine the average cycle time of a system of elevators in complex traffic situations.

Simulation (Oct. 1993) published a study on the use of a microcomputer-based simulator for elevators. The simulator produced an average cycle time μ of 26 seconds when traffic intensity was set at 50 persons every five minutes. Consider a sample of 200 simulated elevator runs and let $\bar{x}$ represent the mean cycle time of this sample.

a. What do you know about the distribution of x, the time between successive elevator starts? (Give the value of the mean and standard deviation of x and the shape of the distribution, if possible.)

b. What do you know about the distribution of $\bar{x}$? (Give the value of the mean and standard deviation of $\bar{x}$ and the shape of the distribution, if possible.)

c. Assume σ, the standard deviation of cycle time x, is 20 seconds. Use this information to calculate $P(\bar{x} > 26.8)$.

d. Repeat part **c** but assume $\sigma = 10$.

6.40   Refer to the *Simulation* (Oct. 1993) study of elevator cycle times, Exercise 6.39. Cycle time is related to the distance (measured by number of floors) the elevator covers on a particular run, called *running distance*. The simulated distribution of running distance, x, during a down-peak period in elevator traffic intensity is shown in the accompanying figure. The distribution has mean μ = 5.5 floors and standard deviation σ = 7 floors. Consider a random sample of 80 simulated elevator runs during a down-peak in traffic intensity. Of interest is the sample mean running distance, $\bar{x}$.

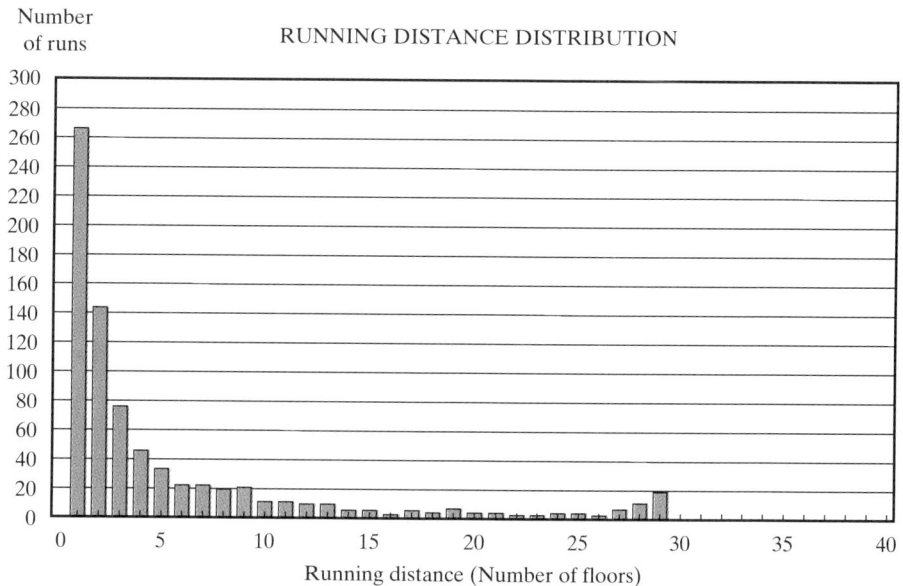

RUNNING DISTANCE DISTRIBUTION

Source: Siikonen, M. L. "Elevator traffic simulation." *Simulation,* Vol. 61, No. 4, Oct. 1993, p. 266 (Figure 8). Copyright © 1993 by Simulation Councils, Inc. Reprinted by permission.

a. Find $\mu_{\bar{x}}$ and $\sigma_{\bar{x}}$.

b. Is the shape of the distribution of $\bar{x}$ similar to the figure? If not, sketch the distribution.

c. During a down-peak in traffic intensity, is it likely to observe a sample mean running distance of $\bar{x} = 5.3$ floors? Explain.

6.41 Steven Hartley (1983) conducted an experiment to evaluate the forecasting skills of 140 retail buyers of two large midwestern retail organizations. In one part of the experiment, 61 of the buyers were given historical sales data for the previous 30 months and asked to forecast sales six months from now. For each buyer, Hartley calculated the difference between the actual number of units sold six months later and the buyer's forecast. This difference is sometimes called **forecast error** and is denoted here as x. In order to characterize the accuracy of this group of 61 buyers, Hartley calculated $\bar{x}$, the mean forecast error for the sample.

a. Assume the sample of 61 buyers was randomly selected from a large population of buyers whose forecast errors have a distribution with mean 10 and standard deviation 16. Describe the sampling distribution of $\bar{x}$.

b. Hartley found $\bar{x} = 13.49$. Given the information in part **a** about the population of buyers, is this a likely result? Explain.

c. Suppose $\bar{x} = 0$ and $s^2 = 1$. What do these statistics tell you about the accuracy of the forecasts of the 61 buyers?

6.42 In Statistics in Action 6.1, an individual was considering investing $1,000 in each of $n = 5$ different stocks. The monthly rate of return on each stock had mean $\mu = 10\%$ and standard deviation $\sigma = 4\%$. The investor's monthly rate of return for the portfolio of five stocks was $\bar{r} = \Sigma r_i/5$. It was shown that the variance of the investor's monthly rate of return was $\sigma_{\bar{r}}^2 = \sigma^2/n = 3.2$ and that this number is a measure of the risk faced by the investor.

a. If instead the individual were to invest $1,000 in only three of the five stocks, would the risk faced by the investor increase or decrease? Explain.

b. Suppose $1,000 was invested in each of 10 stocks with rate-of-return characteristics identical to those described above. Measure the risk faced by the investor and compare it to the risk associated with investing in just five of the stocks.

6.43 It was not until the 1950s that manufacturing companies began to measure and account for the costs of their quality functions. In general, quality costs are those associated with producing, identifying, avoiding, or repairing products that do not meet requirements. They are often divided into four categories: prevention costs, appraisal costs, internal failure costs, and external failure costs (Stevenson, *Production/Operations Management,* 1996). This exercise is concerned with an inspection and evaluation activity that would generate appraisal costs.

A particular manufacturing process requires steel rods that are at least 3 meters in length. The rods are purchased in lots of 50,000. To determine whether the lot meets the required quality standards, 100 rods are randomly sampled from each incoming lot and the mean length of rods in the sample is calculated. The quality manager has decided to accept lots whose sample mean is 3.005 meters or more. Assume that the standard deviation of the rod lengths in a lot is .03 meter.

a. If in fact each lot has a mean length of 3 meters, what percentage of the lots received by the manufacturer will be returned to the vendor (i.e., the supplier)?

b. If in fact all of the rods in all of the lots received by the manufacturer are between 2.999 and 3.004 meters in length, what percentage of the lots will be returned to the vendor?

6.44 A manufacturer produces safety jackets for competitive fencers. These jackets are rated by the minimum force, in newtons, that will allow a weapon to pierce the jacket. When this process is operating correctly, it produces jackets that have ratings with an average of 840 newtons and a standard deviation of 15 newtons. FIE, the international governing body for fencing, requires jackets to be rated at a minimum of 800 newtons. To check whether the process is operating correctly, a manager takes a sample of 50 jackets from the process, rates them, and calculates $\bar{x}$, the mean rating for jackets in the sample. She assumes that the standard deviation of the process is fixed, but is worried that the mean rating of the process may have changed.

a. What is the sampling distribution of $\bar{x}$ if the process is still operating correctly?

b. Suppose the manager's sample has a mean rating of 830 newtons. What is the probability of getting an $\bar{x}$ of 830 newtons or lower if the process is operating correctly?

c. Given the manager's assumption that the standard deviation of the process is fixed, what does your answer to part **b** suggest about the current state of the process (i.e., does it appear that the mean jacket rating is still 840 newtons)?

d. Now suppose that the mean of the process has not changed, but the standard deviation of the process has increased from 15 newtons to 45 newtons. What is the sampling distribution of $\bar{x}$ in this case? What is the probability of getting an $\bar{x}$ of 830 newtons or lower when $\bar{x}$ has this distribution?

6.45 To determine whether a metal lathe that produces machine bearings is properly adjusted, a random sample of 36 bearings is collected and the diameter of each is measured.

a. If the standard deviation of the diameters of the bearings measured over a long period of time is .001 inch, what is the approximate probability that the mean diameter $\bar{x}$ of the sample of 36 bearings will lie within .0001 inch of the population mean diameter of the bearings?

b. If the population of diameters has an extremely skewed distribution, how will your approximation in part **a** be affected?

6.46 Refer to Exercise 6.45. The mean diameter of the bearings produced by the machine is supposed to be .5 inch. The company decides to use the sample mean (from Exercise 6.45) to decide whether the process is in control; i.e., whether it is producing bearings with a mean diameter of .5 inch. The machine will be considered out of control if the mean of the sample of $n = 36$ diameters is less than .4994 inch or larger than .5006 inch. If the true mean diameter of the bearings produced by the machine is .501 inch, what is the approximate probability that the test will imply that the process is out of control?

6.47 In any production process, some variation in the quality of the product is unavoidable. Variation in product can be divided into two categories: **variation due to special causes** and **variation due to common causes**. The former includes variation due to a specific worker or group of workers, a specific machine, or a specific local condition. The latter includes variation due to faults of the overall production system, such as poor working conditions for workers, use of raw materials of inferior quality, poor design of the product, etc. The discovery and removal of special causes is generally the responsibility of a person directly involved with the pro-

duction operation in question. In contrast, common causes are the responsibility of management.

A production process in which all special causes of variation have been eliminated is said to be **stable** or **in statistical control**. The variation that remains is simply random variation. If the magnitude of the random variation is unacceptable to management, it can be reduced through the elimination of common causes (Deming, 1982, 1986; DeVor, Chang, and Sutherland, 1992).

It is common practice to monitor the variation in the quality characteristic of a product over time by plotting the quality characteristic on a **control chart**. For example, the amount of alkali in soap might be monitored each hour by randomly selecting from the production process and measuring the quantity of alkali in $n = 5$ test specimens of soap. The mean, $\bar{x}$, of the sample alkaline measurements would be plotted against time, as shown in the accompanying figure. If the process is in statistical control, $\bar{x}$ should assume a distribution with a mean equal to the process mean, μ, and with a standard deviation equal to the process standard deviation divided by the square root of the sample size, $\sigma_{\bar{x}} = \sigma/\sqrt{n}$. The control chart shown here includes a horizontal line to locate the process mean and two lines, called **control limits**, located $3\sigma_{\bar{x}}$ above and below μ. If $\bar{x}$ is outside the limits, there is strong evidence that special causes of variation are present, and the process is deemed to be out of control. We discuss control charts in detail in Chapter 13.

When the production process is in statistical control, the percentage of alkali in a test specimen of soap follows approximately a normal distribution with $\mu = 2\%$ and $\sigma = 1\%$.

a. If $n = 4$, how far from μ should the upper and lower control limits be located?

b. If the process is in control, what is the probability that $\bar{x}$ will fall outside the control limits?

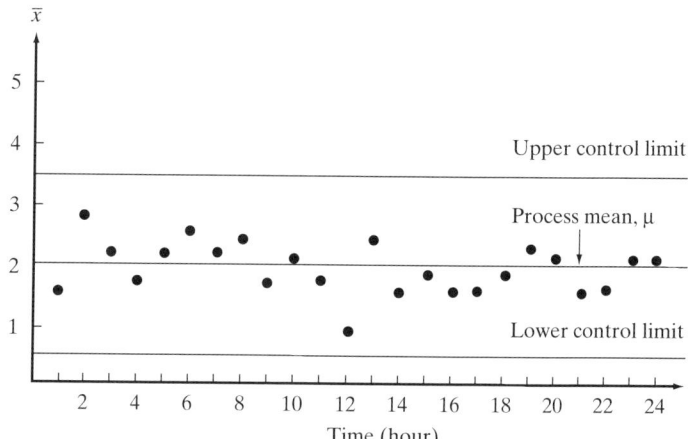

c. If the process mean shifts to $\mu = 3\%$ before the sample is drawn, what is the probability that the sample will lead to the (correct) conclusion that the process is out of control?

6.48   Refer to Exercise 6.47. The soap company has decided to set tighter control limits than the $3\sigma_{\bar{x}}$ limits described in Exercise 6.47. In particular, when the process is in control, the company is willing to risk a .10 probability that $\bar{x}$ falls outside the control limits.

   a. The company still wants the control limits to be located at equal distances above and below the process mean and is still planning to use $n = 4$ measurements in each hourly sample. Where should the control limits be located?

   b. Suppose the control limits developed in part **a** are implemented, but unknown to the company, μ is currently 3% (not 2%). What is the probability that $\bar{x}$ will fall outside the control limits if $n = 4$? If $n = 9$?

6.49   Refer to Exercise 6.48. To improve the sensitivity of control charts, **warning limits** are sometimes included on the chart along with the control limits. These limits are typically set at $\mu \pm 1.96\sigma_{\bar{x}}$. If two successive data points fall outside the warning limits, the process is deemed to be out of control (Montgomery, 1991).

   a. If the soap process is in control (i.e., it follows a normal distribution with $\mu = 2\%$ and $\sigma = 1\%$), what is the probability that the next value of $\bar{x}$ will fall outside the warning limits?

   b. If the soap process is in control, how many of the next 40 values of $\bar{x}$ plotted on the control chart would be expected to fall above the upper warning limit?

   c. If the soap process is in control, what is the probability that the next two values of $\bar{x}$ will fall below the lower warning limit?

6.50   [*Note:* This exercise refers to the optional section in Chapter 4.] A building contractor has decided to purchase a load of factory-reject aluminum siding as long as the average number of flaws per piece of siding in a sample of size 35 from the factory's reject pile is 2.1 or less. If it is known that the number of flaws per piece of siding in the factory's reject pile has a Poisson probability distribution with a mean of 2.5, find the approximate probability that the contractor will not purchase a load of siding. [*Hint:* If x is a Poisson random variable with mean λ, then σ_x^2 also equals λ.]

6.51   [*Note:* This exercise refers to the optional section on exponential distributions in Chapter 5.] An article in *Industrial Engineering* (Aug. 1990) discussed the importance of modeling machine downtime correctly in simulation studies. As an illustration, the researcher considered a single-machine-tool system with repair times (in minutes) that can be modeled by an exponential distribution with $\lambda = \frac{1}{60}$ (see Section 5.5). Of interest is the mean repair time, $\bar{x}$, of a sample of 100 machine breakdowns.

   a. Find $E(\bar{x})$ and the variance of $\bar{x}$.

   b. What probability distribution provides the best model of the sampling distribution of $\bar{x}$? Why?

   c. Calculate the probability that the mean repair time, $\bar{x}$, is no longer than 30 minutes.

THE FURNITURE FIRE CASE

A wholesale furniture retailer stores in-stock items at a large warehouse located in Tampa, Florida. In early 1992, a fire destroyed the warehouse and all the furniture in it. After determining the fire was an accident, the retailer sought to recover costs by submitting a claim to its insurance company.

As is typical in a fire insurance policy of this type, the furniture retailer must provide the insurance company with an estimate of "lost" profit for the destroyed items. Retailers calculate profit margin in percentage form using the Gross Profit Factor (GPF). By definition, the GPF for a single sold item is the ratio of the profit to the item's selling price measured as a percentage, i.e.,

$$\text{Item GPF} = (\text{Profit/Sales price}) \times 100$$

Of interest to both the retailer and the insurance company is the average GPF for all of the items in the warehouse. Since these furniture pieces were all destroyed, their eventual selling prices and profit values are obviously unknown. Consequently, the average GPF for all the warehouse items is unknown.

One way to estimate the mean GPF of the destroyed items is to use the mean GPF of similar, recently sold items. The retailer sold 3,005 furniture items in 1991 (the year prior to the fire) and kept paper invoices on all sales. Rather than calculate the mean GPF for all 3,005 items (the data were not computerized), the retailer sampled a total of 253 of the invoices and computed the mean GPF for these items. The 253 items were obtained by first selecting a sample of 134 items and then augmenting this sample with a second sample of 119 items. The mean GPFs for the two subsamples were calculated to be 50.6% and 51.0%, respectively, yielding an overall average GPF of 50.8%. This average GPF can be applied to the costs of the furniture items destroyed in the fire to obtain an estimate of the "lost" profit.

According to experienced claims adjusters at the insurance company, the GPF for sale items of the type destroyed in the fire rarely exceeds 48%. Consequently, the estimate of 50.8% appeared to be unusually high. (A 1% increase in GPF for items of this type equates to, approximately, an additional $16,000 in profit.) When the insurance company questioned the retailer on this issue, the retailer responded, "Our estimate was based on selecting two independent, random samples from the population of 3,005 invoices in 1991. Since the samples were selected randomly and the total sample size is large, the mean GPF estimate of 50.8% is valid."

A dispute arose between the furniture retailer and the insurance company, and a lawsuit was filed. In one portion of the suit, the insurance company accused the retailer of fraudulently representing their sampling methodology. Rather than selecting the samples randomly, the retailer was accused of selecting an unusual number of "high profit" items from the population in order to increase the average GPF of the overall sample.

To support their claim of fraud, the insurance company hired a CPA firm to independently assess the retailer's 1991 Gross Profit Factor. Through the discovery process, the CPA firm legally obtained the paper invoices for the entire population of 3,005 items sold and input the information into a computer. The selling price, profit, profit margin, and month sold for these 3,005 furniture items are available in ASCII format on a 3.5-inch diskette, as described below.

Your objective in this case is to use these data to determine the likelihood of fraud. Is it likely that a random sample of 253 items selected from the population of 3,005 items would yield a mean GPF of at least 50.8%? Or, is it likely that two independent, random samples of size 134 and 119 will yield mean GPFs of at least 50.6% and 51.0%, respectively? (These were the questions posed to a statistician retained by the CPA firm.) Use the ideas of probability and sampling distributions to guide your analysis.

Prepare a professional document that presents the results of your analysis and gives your opinion regarding fraud. Be sure to describe the assumptions and methodology used to arrive at your findings.

DATA   ASCII file name: FIRE.DAT
   Number of observations: 3005

Variable	Column(s)	Type	Description
MONTH	17–19	QL	Month in which item was sold in 1991
INVOICE	25–29	QN	Invoice number
SALES	35–42	QN	Sales price of item in dollars
PROFIT	47–54	QN	Profit amount of item in dollars
MARGIN	59–64	QN	Profit margin of item = (Profit/Sales) × 100

www.int.com
www.int.com
INTERNET LAB
www.int.com

ANALYZING MONTHLY BUSINESS START-UPS

A pulse of economic health regionally, and nationally, is the rate of new business start-ups. Strategic planners follow this business activity as a guide to timing the introduction of new ventures.

Here we examine the distribution of the monthly data on business start-ups provided by the Federal Reserve Board of Kansas City: *http://www.kc.frb.org/* (refer to your notes or the Internet Lab that follows Chapter 2).

1. Obtain monthly national business start-up data for the past eight or nine full years.

2. Save the data in your statistical applications software data files.

3. Calculate the mean and standard deviation of the monthly number of start-ups over all the years of data you have. Assume these values represent the population parameters, μ and σ, respectively.

4. For each full year of data, calculate the mean number of start-ups. Also, compute the standard error for this distribution of start-ups.

5. For each month (January, February, and so forth), calculate the mean number of start-ups. Also, compare the standard error for this distribution of means.

6. Sequentially, plot the means obtained in each of steps 4 and 5. Do either or both of these distributions show evidence of bias? How might that bias be interpreted in terms of changing, seasonal, or cyclical economic activity? ○

CHAPTER 7

INFERENCES BASED ON A SINGLE SAMPLE
Estimation with Confidence Intervals

CONTENTS

STATISTICS IN ACTION

Where We've Been

We've learned that populations are characterized by numerical descriptive measures (called *parameters*) and that decisions about their values are based on sample statistics computed from sample data. Since statistics vary in a random manner from sample to sample, inferences based on them will be subject to uncertainty. This property is reflected in the sampling (probability) distribution of a statistic.

Where We're Going

In this chapter, we'll put all the preceding material into practice; that is, we'll estimate population means and proportions based on a single sample selected from the population of interest. Most importantly, we use the sampling distribution of a sample statistic to assess the reliability of an estimate.

The estimation of the mean gas mileage for a new car model, the estimation of the expected life of a computer monitor, and the estimation of the mean yearly sales for companies in the steel industry are problems with a common element. In each case, we're interested in estimating the mean of a population of quantitative measurements. This important problem constitutes the primary topic of this chapter.

You'll see that different techniques are used for estimating a mean, depending on whether a sample contains a large or small number of measurements. Nevertheless, our objectives remain the same: We want to use the sample information to estimate the mean and to assess the reliability of the estimate.

First, we consider a method of estimating a population mean using a large random sample (Section 7.1) and a small random sample (Section 7.2). Then, we consider estimation of population proportions (Section 7.3). Next, we see how to determine the sample sizes necessary for reliable estimates based on random sampling (Section 7.4). Finally, we describe several other more complex sample survey designs (Sections 7.5 and 7.6).

7.1 LARGE-SAMPLE CONFIDENCE INTERVAL FOR A POPULATION MEAN

We illustrate the **large-sample method** of estimating a population mean with an example. Suppose a large bank wants to estimate the average amount of money owed by its delinquent debtors—i.e., debtors who are more than two months behind in payment. To accomplish this objective, the bank plans to randomly sample 100 of its delinquent accounts and to use the sample mean, $\bar{x}$, of the amounts overdue to estimate μ, the mean for *all* delinquent accounts. The sample mean $\bar{x}$ represents a *point estimator* of the population mean μ (Definition 6.4). How can we assess the accuracy of this point estimator?

According to the Central Limit Theorem, the sampling distribution of the sample mean is approximately normal for large samples, as shown in Figure 7.1. Let us calculate the interval

$$\bar{x} \pm 2\sigma_{\bar{x}} = \bar{x} \pm \frac{2\sigma}{\sqrt{n}}$$

That is, we form an interval 4 standard deviations wide—from 2 standard deviations below the sample mean to 2 standard deviations above the mean. Prior to drawing the sample, what are the chances that this interval will enclose μ, the population mean?

To answer this question, refer to Figure 7.1. If the 100 measurements yield a value of $\bar{x}$ that falls between the two lines on either side of μ—i.e., within 2 standard deviations of μ—then the interval $\bar{x} \pm 2\sigma_{\bar{x}}$ will contain μ; if $\bar{x}$ falls outside these boundaries, the interval $\bar{x} \pm 2\sigma_{\bar{x}}$ will not contain μ. Since the area under the

FIGURE 7.1
Sampling distribution of $\bar{x}$

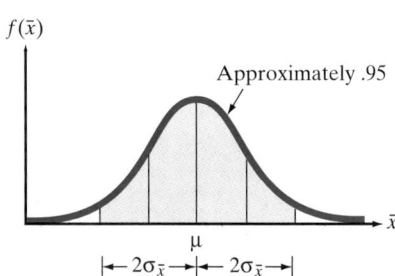

TABLE 7.1   Overdue Amounts (in Dollars) for 100 Delinquent Accounts

195	243	132	133	209	400	142	312	221	289
221	162	134	275	355	293	242	458	378	148
278	222	236	178	202	222	334	208	194	135
363	221	449	265	146	215	113	229	221	243
512	193	134	138	209	207	206	310	293	310
237	135	252	365	371	238	232	271	121	134
203	178	180	148	162	160	86	234	244	266
119	259	108	289	328	331	330	227	162	354
304	141	158	240	82	17	357	187	364	268
368	274	278	190	344	157	219	77	171	280

normal curve (the sampling distribution of $\bar{x}$) between these boundaries is about .95 (more precisely, from Table IV in Appendix B the area is .9544), we know that the interval $\bar{x} \pm 2\sigma_{\bar{x}}$ will contain μ with a probability approximately equal to .95.

For instance, consider the overdue amounts for 100 delinquent accounts shown in Table 7.1. A SAS printout of summary statistics for the sample of 100 overdue amounts is shown in Figure 7.2. From the printout, we find $\bar{x} = \$233.28$ and $s = \$90.34$. To achieve our objective, we must construct the interval

$$\bar{x} \pm 2\sigma_{\bar{x}} = 233.28 \pm 2\frac{\sigma}{\sqrt{100}}$$

But now we face a problem. You can see that without knowing the standard deviation σ of the original population—that is, the standard deviation of the overdue amounts of *all* delinquent accounts—we cannot calculate this interval. However, since we have a large sample ($n = 100$ measurements), we can approximate the interval by using the sample standard deviation s to approximate σ. Thus,

$$\bar{x} \pm 2\frac{\sigma}{\sqrt{100}} \approx \bar{x} \pm 2\frac{s}{\sqrt{100}} = 233.28 \pm 2\left(\frac{90.34}{10}\right) = 233.28 \pm 18.07$$

That is, we estimate the mean amount of delinquency for all accounts to fall within the interval \$215.21 to \$251.35.

Can we be sure that μ, the true mean, is in the interval (215.21, 251.35)? We cannot be certain, but we can be reasonably confident that it is. This confidence is derived from the knowledge that if we were to draw repeated random samples of 100 measurements from this population and form the interval $\bar{x} \pm 2\sigma_{\bar{x}}$ each time, approximately 95% of the intervals would contain μ. We have no way of knowing (without looking at all the delinquent accounts) whether our sample interval is one of the 95% that contain μ or one of the 5% that do not, but the odds certainly favor its containing μ. Consequently, the interval \$215.21 to \$251.35 provides a reliable estimate of the mean delinquency per account.

The formula that tells us how to calculate an interval estimate based on sample data is called an *interval estimator*, or *confidence interval*. The probability, .95, that measures the confidence we can place in the interval estimate is called a

FIGURE 7.2
SAS summary statistics for the overdue amounts of 100 delinquent accounts

```
Analysis Variable : AMOUNT

N Obs    N      Minimum        Maximum           Mean       Std Dev
-------------------------------------------------------------------
 100    100   17.0000000    512.0000000    233.2800000    90.3398835
-------------------------------------------------------------------
```

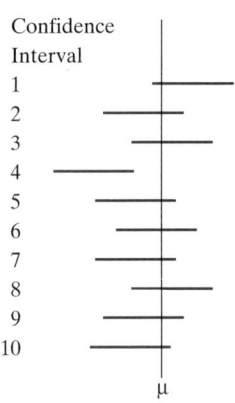

FIGURE 7.3
Confidence intervals for μ:
10 samples

confidence coefficient. The percentage, 95%, is called the *confidence level* for the interval estimate. It is not usually possible to assess precisely the reliability of point estimators because they are single points rather than intervals. So, because we prefer to use estimators for which a measure of reliability can be calculated, we will generally use interval estimators.

DEFINITION 7.1

An **interval estimator** (or **confidence interval**) is a formula that tells us how to use sample data to calculate an interval that estimates a population parameter.

DEFINITION 7.2

The **confidence coefficient** is the probability that a confidence interval encloses the population parameter—that is, the relative frequency with which the interval encloses the population parameter when the estimator is used repeatedly a very large number of times. The **confidence level** is the confidence coefficient expressed as a percentage.

Now we have seen how an interval can be used to estimate a population mean. When we use an interval estimator, we can usually calculate the probability that the estimation *process* will result in an interval that contains the true value of the population mean. That is, the probability that the interval contains the parameter in repeated usage is usually known. Figure 7.3 shows what happens when 10 different samples are drawn from a population, and a confidence interval for μ is calculated from each. The location of μ is indicated by the vertical line in the figure. Ten confidence intervals, each based on one of 10 samples, are shown as horizontal line segments. Note that the confidence intervals move from sample to sample—sometimes containing μ and other times missing μ. If our confidence level is 95%, then in the long run, 95% of our sample confidence intervals will contain μ and 5% will not.

Suppose you wish to choose a confidence coefficient other than .95. Notice in Figure 7.1 that the confidence coefficient .95 is equal to the total area under the sampling distribution, less .05 of the area, which is divided equally between the two tails. Using this idea, we can construct a confidence interval with any desired confidence coefficient by increasing or decreasing the area (call it α) assigned to the tails of the sampling distribution (see Figure 7.4). For example, if we place area $\alpha/2$ in each tail and if $z_{\alpha/2}$ is the z value such that the area $\alpha/2$ lies to its right, then the confidence interval with confidence coefficient $(1 - \alpha)$ is

$$\bar{x} \pm z_{\alpha/2}\sigma_{\bar{x}}$$

To illustrate, for a confidence coefficient of .90 we have $(1 - \alpha) = .90, \alpha = .10$, and $\alpha/2 = .05$; $z_{.05}$ is the z value that locates area .05 in the upper tail of the sampling distribution. Recall that Table IV in Appendix B gives the areas between the mean and a specified z value. Since the total area to the right of the mean is .5, we

FIGURE 7.4
Locating $z_{\alpha/2}$ on the standard normal curve

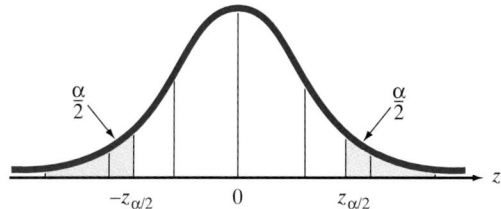

FIGURE 7.5

The z value ($z_{.05}$) corresponding to an area equal to .05 in the upper tail of the z-distribution

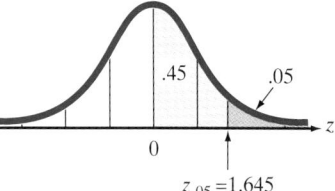

find that $z_{.05}$ will be the z value corresponding to an area of $.5 - .05 = .45$ to the right of the mean (see Figure 7.5). This z value is $z_{.05} = 1.645$.

Confidence coefficients used in practice usually range from .90 to .99. The most commonly used confidence coefficients with corresponding values of α and $z_{\alpha/2}$ are shown in Table 7.2.

Large-Sample 100(1 − α)% Confidence Interval for μ

$$\bar{x} \pm z_{\alpha/2}\sigma_{\bar{x}} = \bar{x} \pm z_{\alpha/2}\frac{\sigma}{\sqrt{n}}$$

where $z_{\alpha/2}$ is the z value with an area $\alpha/2$ to its right (see Figure 7.4) and $\sigma_{\bar{x}} = \sigma/\sqrt{n}$. The parameter σ is the standard deviation of the sampled population and n is the sample size.

Note: When σ is unknown (as is almost always the case) and n is large (say, $n \geq 30$), the confidence interval is approximately equal to

$$\bar{x} \pm z_{\alpha/2}\left(\frac{s}{\sqrt{n}}\right)$$

where s is the sample standard deviation.

Assumptions: None, since the Central Limit Theorem guarantees that the sampling distribution of $\bar{x}$ is approximately normal.

EXAMPLE 7.1

Unoccupied seats on flights cause airlines to lose revenue. Suppose a large airline wants to estimate its average number of unoccupied seats per flight over the past year. To accomplish this, the records of 225 flights are randomly selected, and the number of unoccupied seats is noted for each of the sampled flights. The sample mean and standard deviation are

$$\bar{x} = 11.6 \text{ seats} \qquad s = 4.1 \text{ seats}$$

Estimate μ, the mean number of unoccupied seats per flight during the past year, using a 90% confidence interval.

TABLE 7.2   Commonly Used Values of $z_{\alpha/2}$

CONFIDENCE LEVEL

$100(1-\alpha)$	α	$\alpha/2$	$z_{\alpha/2}$
90%	.10	.05	1.645
95%	.05	.025	1.96
99%	.01	.005	2.575

SOLUTION
The general form of the 90% confidence interval for a population mean is

$$\bar{x} \pm z_{\alpha/2}\sigma_{\bar{x}} = \bar{x} \pm z_{.05}\sigma_{\bar{x}} = \bar{x} \pm 1.645\left(\frac{\sigma}{\sqrt{n}}\right)$$

For the 225 records sampled, we have

$$11.6 \pm 1.645\left(\frac{\sigma}{\sqrt{225}}\right)$$

Since we do not know the value of σ (the standard deviation of the number of unoccupied seats per flight for all flights of the year), we use our best approximation—the sample standard deviation s. Then the 90% confidence interval is, approximately,

$$11.6 \pm 1.645\left(\frac{4.1}{\sqrt{225}}\right) = 11.6 \pm .45$$

or from 11.15 to 12.05. That is, at the 90% confidence level, we estimate the mean number of unoccupied seats per flight to be between 11.15 and 12.05 during the sampled year. This result is verified on the MINITAB printout of the analysis shown in Figure 7.6.

We stress that the confidence level for this example, 90%, refers to the procedure used. If we were to apply this procedure repeatedly to different samples, approximately 90% of the intervals would contain μ. We do not know whether this particular interval (11.15, 12.05) is one of the 90% that contain μ or one of the 10% that do not.

The interpretation of confidence intervals for a population mean is summarized in the accompanying box.

Interpretation of a Confidence Interval for a Population Mean
When we form a $100(1 - \alpha)\%$ confidence interval for μ, we usually express our confidence in the interval with a statement such as, "We can be $100(1 - \alpha)\%$ confident that μ lies between the lower and upper bounds of the confidence interval," where for a particular application, we substitute the appropriate numerical values for the confidence and for the lower and upper bounds. *The statement reflects our confidence in the estimation process rather than in the particular interval that is calculated from the sample data.* We know that repeated application of the same procedure will result in different lower and upper bounds on the interval. Furthermore, we know that $100(1 - \alpha)\%$ of the resulting intervals will contain μ. There is (usually) no way to determine whether any particular interval is one of those that contain μ, or one that does not. However, unlike point estimators, confidence intervals have some measure of reliability, the confidence coefficient, associated with them. For that reason they are generally preferred to point estimators.

Sometimes, the estimation procedure yields a confidence interval that is too wide for our purposes. In this case, we will want to reduce the width of the interval

FIGURE 7.6
MINITAB printout for the confidence intervals in Example 7.1

	N	MEAN	STDEV	SE MEAN	90.0 PERCENT C.I.
NoSeats	225	11.6	4.1	0.273	(11.15, 12.05)

to obtain a more precise estimate of μ. One way to accomplish this is to decrease the confidence coefficient, $1 - \alpha$. For example, reconsider the problem of estimating the mean amount owed, μ, for all delinquent accounts. Recall that for a sample of 100 accounts, $\bar{x} = \$233.28$ and $s = \$90.34$. A 90% confidence interval for μ is

$$\bar{x} \pm 1.645\sigma/\sqrt{n} \approx 233.28 \pm (1.645)\left(90.34/\sqrt{100}\right) = 233.28 \pm 14.86$$

or ($218.42, $248.14). You can see that this interval is narrower than the previously calculated 95% confidence interval, ($215.21, $251.35). Unfortunately, we also have "less confidence" in the 90% confidence interval. An alternative method used to decrease the width of an interval without sacrificing "confidence" is to increase the sample size n. We demonstrate this method in Section 7.4.

EXERCISES   7.1–7.17

Note: Exercises marked with 💾 *contain data available for computer analysis on a 3.5" disk (file name in parentheses).*

Learning the Mechanics

7.1 Find $z_{\alpha/2}$ for each of the following:
 a. $\alpha = .10$ **b.** $\alpha = .01$ **c.** $\alpha = .05$ **d.** $\alpha = .20$

7.2 What is the confidence level of each of the following confidence intervals for μ?
 a. $\bar{x} \pm 1.96\left(\dfrac{\sigma}{\sqrt{n}}\right)$ **b.** $\bar{x} \pm 1.645\left(\dfrac{\sigma}{\sqrt{n}}\right)$
 c. $\bar{x} \pm 2.575\left(\dfrac{\sigma}{\sqrt{n}}\right)$ **d.** $\bar{x} \pm 1.282\left(\dfrac{\sigma}{\sqrt{n}}\right)$
 e. $\bar{x} \pm .99\left(\dfrac{\sigma}{\sqrt{n}}\right)$

7.3 A random sample of n measurements was selected from a population with unknown mean μ and standard deviation σ. Calculate a 95% confidence interval for μ for each of the following situations:
 a. $n = 75, \bar{x} = 28, s^2 = 12$
 b. $n = 200, \bar{x} = 102, s^2 = 22$
 c. $n = 100, \bar{x} = 15, s = .3$
 d. $n = 100, \bar{x} = 4.05, s = .83$
 e. Is the assumption that the underlying population of measurements is normally distributed necessary to ensure the validity of the confidence intervals in parts **a–d**? Explain.

7.4 A random sample of 90 observations produced a mean $\bar{x} = 25.9$ and a standard deviation $s = 2.7$.
 a. Find a 95% confidence interval for the population mean μ.
 b. Find a 90% confidence interval for μ.
 c. Find a 99% confidence interval for μ.

7.5 A random sample of 70 observations from a normally distributed population possesses a mean equal to 26.2 and a standard deviation equal to 4.1.
 a. Find a 95% confidence interval for μ.
 b. What do you mean when you say that a confidence coefficient is .95?

 c. Find a 99% confidence interval for μ.
 d. What happens to the width of a confidence interval as the value of the confidence coefficient is increased while the sample size is held fixed?
 e. Would your confidence intervals of parts **a** and **c** be valid if the distribution of the original population was not normal? Explain.

7.6 Explain what is meant by the statement, "We are 95% confident that an interval estimate contains μ."

7.7 Explain the difference between an interval estimator and a point estimator for μ.

7.8 The mean and standard deviation of a random sample of n measurements are equal to 33.9 and 3.3, respectively.
 a. Find a 95% confidence interval for μ if $n = 100$.
 b. Find a 95% confidence interval for μ if $n = 400$.
 c. Find the widths of the confidence intervals found in parts **a** and **b**. What is the effect on the width of a confidence interval of quadrupling the sample size while holding the confidence coefficient fixed?

7.9 Will a large-sample confidence interval be valid if the population from which the sample is taken is not normally distributed? Explain.

Applying the Concepts

7.10 The *Journal of the American Medical Association* (Apr. 21, 1993) reported on the results of a National Health Interview Survey designed to determine the prevalence of smoking among U.S. adults. More than 40,000 adults responded to questions such as "Have you smoked at least 100 cigarettes in your lifetime?" and "Do you smoke cigarettes now?" Current smokers (more than 11,000 adults in the survey) were also asked: "On the average, how many cigarettes do you now smoke a day?" The results yielded a mean of 20.0 cigarettes per day with an associated 95% confidence interval of (19.7, 20.3).

a. Carefully describe the population from which the sample was drawn.

b. Interpret the 95% confidence interval.

c. State any assumptions about the target population of current cigarette smokers that must be satisfied for inferences derived from the interval to be valid.

d. A tobacco industry researcher claims that the mean number of cigarettes smoked per day by regular cigarette smokers is less than 15. Comment on this claim.

7.11 (X07.011) At the end of 1992, 1993, and 1994, the average prices of a share of stock on the New York Stock Exchange (NYSE) were $34.83, $34.65, and $31.26, respectively (*Statistical Abstract of the United States: 1995*). To investigate the average share price at the end of 1995, a random sample of 30 NYSE stocks was drawn. Their closing prices on December 29, 1995, are listed (by their NYSE abbreviations) in the table. A SAS descriptive statistics printout is at the bottom of the page.

Stock	Price	Stock	Price
Litton	$44\frac{1}{2}$	MCN	$23\frac{1}{4}$
Morton	$35\frac{7}{8}$	Premdor	$7\frac{3}{4}$
Deere	$35\frac{1}{4}$	Clorox	$71\frac{5}{8}$
Tremont	$16\frac{5}{8}$	ToysRUs	$21\frac{3}{4}$
Munivest PA	$11\frac{1}{2}$	Penn Entr	$37\frac{7}{8}$
Case Cp	$45\frac{3}{4}$	Ameron	$37\frac{5}{8}$
TriMas	$18\frac{3}{4}$	MDC	$7\frac{1}{8}$
Pac Ent	$28\frac{1}{4}$	Dean Food	$27\frac{1}{2}$
Pepsi Co	$55\frac{7}{8}$	PubSvcEnt	$30\frac{5}{8}$
DeVry	27	CocaCola	$74\frac{1}{4}$
Loctite	$47\frac{1}{2}$	Morgan	$80\frac{1}{4}$
Lyondell	$27\frac{7}{8}$	Dana Cp	$29\frac{1}{4}$
Moore Cp	$18\frac{3}{4}$	CV REIT	$11\frac{1}{4}$
MrgnStnAtr	$12\frac{7}{8}$	PLC Cap MPS	$26\frac{1}{2}$
Alco Std	$45\frac{5}{8}$	Progrsv Cp	$48\frac{7}{8}$

Source: Wall Street Journal, January 2, 1996.

a. Use the information in the SAS printout to estimate the average price of a share of stock at the end of 1995 with a 90% confidence interval.

b. Use the latest edition of the *Statistical Abstract of the United States* to find the actual average price of a stock on the NYSE at the end of 1995. Is this figure in agreement with your con-

fidence interval? Explain. If not, provide a possible explanation for the disagreement.

7.12 Research indicates that bicycle helmets save lives. A study reported in *Public Health Reports* (May–June 1992) was intended to identify ways of encouraging helmet use in children. One of the variables measured was the children's perception of the risk involved in bicycling. A four-point scale was used, with scores ranging from 1 (no risk) to 4 (very high risk). A sample of 797 children in grades 4–6 yielded the following results on the perception of risk variable: $\bar{x} = 3.39, s = .80$.

a. Calculate a 90% confidence interval for the average perception of risk for all students in grades 4–6. What assumptions did you make to ensure the validity of the confidence interval?

b. If the population mean perception of risk exceeds 2.50, the researchers will conclude that students in these grades exhibit an awareness of the risk involved with bicycling. Interpret the confidence interval constructed in part **a** in this context.

7.13 An auditor was hired to verify the accuracy of a company's new billing system. The auditor randomly sampled 35 invoices produced since the system was installed. Each invoice was compared against the relevant internal records to determine by how much the invoice was in error. The amount of the error, x, was defined as $(A - I)$, where A is the actual amount owed the company and I is the amount indicated on the invoice. The auditor found that $\bar{x} = \$1$ and $s = \$124$.

a. Identify the population the auditor studied.

b. Describe the variable that the auditor measured.

c. Construct a 98% confidence interval for the mean error per invoice.

d. Interpret the confidence interval.

e. Comment on the accuracy of the billing system.

7.14 The trade magazine *Quality Progress* randomly sampled 9,117 of its more than 100,000 subscribers and mailed them a salary questionnaire. A week after the first mailing, a postcard was sent to the same people reminding them to complete the questionnaire. Two weeks after the postcard was mailed, a duplicate questionnaire was sent to all those people who hadn't yet responded. A week later another reminder postcard was sent. In the end, 4,828 usable responses were received, yielding a response rate of 53%. (*Note:* This high response rate could not have been achieved with-

```
Analysis Variable : PRICE

N Obs    N      Minimum       Maximum          Mean       Std Dev
----------------------------------------------------------------------
   30   30    7.1250000    80.2500000    33.5833333    19.1494613
----------------------------------------------------------------------
```

Title	Sample Size	Mean	Standard Deviation
Inspector	251	26,098	7,395
Technician	397	27,384	5,956
Coordinator	176	36,919	13,178
Specialist	373	42,110	13,449
Supervisor	456	42,699	14,187
Engineer	651	46,816	12,557
Manager	1,142	55,076	17,910
Consultant (in-house)	260	60,601	20,561
Director	670	67,339	23,211
Consultant (independent)	163	69,355	26,871
Vice president	284	93,247	33,740

Source: "1994 Salary Survey." *Quality Progress*, November 1994, pp. 27–49.

out the extensive follow-up procedures that were employed.) The survey yielded the data shown above concerning salary and job title.

a. The column labeled MEAN reports point estimators for certain parameters. Carefully describe both the relevant populations and parameters.

b. Construct and interpret a 95% confidence interval for the mean salary for managers.

c. Repeat part **b** for vice presidents.

d. Explain why the confidence intervals of parts **b** and **c** are preferred over the point estimates when describing the mean salaries of managers and vice presidents.

7.15 Nasser Arshadi and Edward Lawrence investigated the profiles (i.e., career patterns, social backgrounds, and so forth) of the top executives in the U.S. banking industry (*Journal of Retail Banking,* Winter 1983–1984). They sampled 96 executives and found that 80% studied business or economics and that 45% had a graduate degree. With respect to the number of years of service, x, at the same bank, the group had a mean of 23.43 years and a standard deviation of 10.82 years.

a. Construct a 90% confidence interval for $E(x) = \mu$.

b. Interpret your interval in the context of the problem.

c. What assumption(s) was it necessary to make in order to construct the confidence interval of part **a**?

d. Is your interval estimate for $E(x)$ also an interval estimate for $E(\bar{x})$? Explain. [*Hint:* See Chapter 6.]

7.16 Named for the section of the 1978 Internal Revenue Code that authorized them, 401(k) plans permit employees to shift part of their before-tax

salaries into investments such as mutual funds. Employers typically match 50% of the employee's contribution up to about 6% of salary (*Fortune,* Dec. 28, 1992). One company, concerned with what it believed was a low employee participation rate in its 401(k) plan, sampled 30 other companies with similar plans and asked for their 401(k) participation rates. The following rates (in percentages) were obtained:

80 76 81 77 82 80 85 60 80 79 82 70
88 85 80 79 83 75 87 78 80 84 72 75
90 84 82 77 75 86

Descriptive statistics for the data are given in the SPSS printout at the bottom of the page:

a. Use the information on the SPSS printout to construct a 95% confidence interval for the mean participation rate for all companies that have 401(k) plans.

b. Interpret the interval in the context of this problem.

c. What assumption is necessary to ensure the validity of this confidence interval?

d. If the company that conducted the sample has a 71% participation rate, can it safely conclude that its rate is below the population mean rate for all companies with 401(k) plans? Explain.

e. If in the data set the 60% had been 80%, how would the center and width of the confidence interval you constructed in part **a** be affected?

7.17 Research reported in the *Journal of Psychology and Aging* (May 1992) studied the role that the age of workers has in determining their level of job satisfaction. The researcher hypothesized that both younger and older workers would have a higher job satisfaction rating than middle-age workers. Each of a sample of 1,686 adults was given a job satisfaction score based on answers to

```
Number of Valid Observations (Listwise) =      30.00
Variable      Mean     Std Dev   Minimum    Maximum    N Label
PARTRATE     79.73       5.96     60.00      90.00     30
```

a series of questions. Higher job satisfaction scores indicate higher levels of job satisfaction. The data are given in the accompanying table, arranged by age group.

| | AGE GROUP | | |
	Younger 18–24	Middle-Age 25–44	Older 45–64
$\bar{x}$	4.17	4.04	4.31
s	.75	.81	.82
n	241	768	677

a. Construct 95% confidence intervals for the mean job satisfaction scores of each age group. Carefully interpret each interval.

b. In the construction of three 95% confidence intervals, is it more or less likely that at least one of them will *not* contain the population mean it is intended to estimate than it is for a single confidence interval to miss the population mean? [*Hint:* Assume the three intervals are independent and calculate the probability that at least one of them will not contain the population mean it estimates. Compare this probability to the probability that a single interval fails to enclose the mean.]

c. Based on these intervals, does it appear that the researcher's hypothesis is supported? [*Caution:* We will learn how to use sample information to compare population means in Chapter 9, and will return to this exercise at that time. Here, simply base your opinion on the individual confidence intervals you constructed in part **a.**]

7.2 SMALL-SAMPLE CONFIDENCE INTERVAL FOR A POPULATION MEAN

Federal legislation requires pharmaceutical companies to perform extensive tests on new drugs before they can be marketed. Initially, a new drug is tested on animals. If the drug is deemed safe after this first phase of testing, the pharmaceutical company is then permitted to begin human testing on a limited basis. During this second phase, inferences must be made about the safety of the drug based on information in very small samples.

Suppose a pharmaceutical company must estimate the average increase in blood pressure of patients who take a certain new drug. Assume that only six patients (randomly selected from the population of all patients) can be used in the initial phase of human testing. The use of a **small sample** in making an inference about μ presents two immediate problems when we attempt to use the standard normal z as a test statistic.

Problem 1. The shape of the sampling distribution of the sample mean $\bar{x}$ (and the z statistic) now depends on the shape of the population that is sampled. We can no longer assume that the sampling distribution of $\bar{x}$ is approximately normal, because the Central Limit Theorem ensures normality only for samples that are sufficiently large.

Solution to Problem 1. According to Theorem 6.1, the sampling distribution of $\bar{x}$ (and z) is exactly normal even for relatively small samples if the sampled population is normal. It is approximately normal if the sampled population is approximately normal.

Problem 2. The population standard deviation σ is almost always unknown. Although it is still true that $\sigma_{\bar{x}} = \sigma/\sqrt{n}$, the sample standard deviation s may provide a poor approximation for σ when the sample size is small.

Solution to Problem 2. Instead of using the standard normal statistic

$$z = \frac{\bar{x} - \mu}{\sigma_{\bar{x}}} = \frac{\bar{x} - \mu}{\sigma/\sqrt{n}}$$

which requires knowledge of or a good approximation to σ, we define and use the statistic

$$t = \frac{\bar{x} - \mu}{s/\sqrt{n}}$$

in which the sample standard deviation, s, replaces the population standard deviation, σ.

The distribution of the ***t* statistic** in repeated sampling was discovered by W. S. Gosset, a chemist in the Guinness brewery in Ireland, who published his discovery in 1908 under the pen name of Student. The main result of Gosset's work is that if we are sampling from a normal distribution, the t statistic has a sampling distribution very much like that of the z statistic: mound-shaped, symmetric, with mean 0. The primary difference between the sampling distributions of t and z is that the t statistic is more variable than the z, which follows intuitively when you realize that t contains two random quantities ($\bar{x}$ and s), whereas z contains only one ($\bar{x}$).

The actual amount of variability in the sampling distribution of t depends on the sample size n. A convenient way of expressing this dependence is to say that the t statistic has $(n - 1)$ **degrees of freedom (df).** Recall that the quantity $(n - 1)$ is the divisor that appears in the formula for s^2. This number plays a key role in the sampling distribution of s^2 and appears in discussions of other statistics in later chapters. In particular, the smaller the number of degrees of freedom associated with the t statistic, the more variable will be its sampling distribution.

In Figure 7.7 we show both the sampling distribution of z and the sampling distribution of a t statistic with 4 df. You can see that the increased variability of the t statistic means that the t value, t_α, that locates an area α in the upper tail of the t-distribution is larger than the corresponding value z_α. For any given value of α, the t value t_α increases as the number of degrees of freedom (df) decreases. Values of t that will be used in forming small-sample confidence intervals of μ are given in Table VI of Appendix B and inside the back cover of the text. A partial reproduction of this table is shown in Table 7.3.

Note that t_α values are listed for degrees of freedom from 1 to 29, where α refers to the tail area under the t-distribution to the right of t_α. For example, if we want the t value with an area of .025 to its right and 4 df, we look in the table under the column $t_{.025}$ for the entry in the row corresponding to 4 df. This entry is $t_{.025} = 2.776$, as shown in Figure 7.8. The corresponding standard normal z-score is $z_{.025} = 1.96$.

Note that the last row of Table VI, where df $= \infty$ (infinity), contains the standard normal z values. This follows from the fact that as the sample size n grows very large, s becomes closer to σ and thus t becomes closer in distribution to z. In fact, when df $= 29$, there is little difference between corresponding tabulated values of z and t. Thus, we choose the arbitrary cutoff of $n = 30$ (df $= 29$) to distinguish between the large-sample and small-sample inferential techniques.

FIGURE 7.7
Standard normal (z) distribution and t-distribution with 4 df

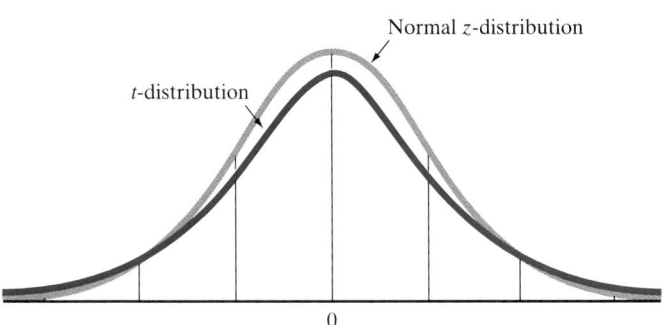

TABLE 7.3   **Reproduction of Part of Table VI in Appendix B**

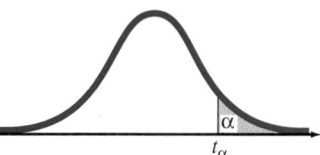

Degrees of Freedom	$t_{.100}$	$t_{.050}$	$t_{.025}$	$t_{.010}$	$t_{.005}$	$t_{.001}$	$t_{.0005}$
1	3.078	6.314	12.706	31.821	63.657	318.31	636.62
2	1.886	2.920	4.303	6.965	9.925	22.326	21.598
3	1.638	2.353	3.182	4.541	5.841	10.213	12.924
4	1.533	2.132	2.776	3.747	4.604	7.173	8.610
5	1.476	2.015	2.571	3.365	4.032	5.893	6.869
6	1.440	1.943	2.447	3.132	3.707	5.208	5.959
7	1.415	1.895	2.365	2.998	3.499	4.785	5.408
8	1.397	1.860	2.306	2.896	3.355	4.501	5.041
9	1.383	1.833	2.262	2.821	3.250	4.297	4.781
10	1.372	1.812	2.228	2.764	3.169	4.144	4.587
11	1.363	1.796	2.201	2.718	3.106	4.025	4.437
12	1.356	1.782	2.179	2.681	3.055	3.930	4.318
13	1.350	1.771	2.160	2.650	3.012	3.852	4.221
14	1.345	1.761	2.145	2.624	2.977	3.787	4.140
15	1.341	1.753	2.131	2.602	2.947	3.733	4.073
⋮	⋮	⋮	⋮	⋮	⋮	⋮	⋮
∞	1.282	1.645	1.960	2.326	2.576	3.090	3.291

Returning to the example of testing a new drug, suppose that the six test patients have blood pressure increases of 1.7, 3.0, .8, 3.4, 2.7, and 2.1 points. How can we use this information to construct a 95% confidence interval for μ, the mean increase in blood pressure associated with the new drug for all patients in the population?

First, we know that we are dealing with a sample too small to assume that the sample mean $\bar{x}$ is approximately normally distributed by the Central Limit Theorem. That is, we do not get the normal distribution of $\bar{x}$ "automatically" from the Central Limit Theorem when the sample size is small. Instead, the measured variable, in this case the increase in blood pressure, must be normally distributed in order for the distribution of $\bar{x}$ to be normal.

Second, unless we are fortunate enough to know the population standard deviation σ, which in this case represents the standard deviation of *all* the patients' increases in blood pressure when they take the new drug, we cannot use the stan-

FIGURE 7.8
The $t_{.025}$ value in a t-distribution with 4 df and the corresponding $z_{.025}$ value

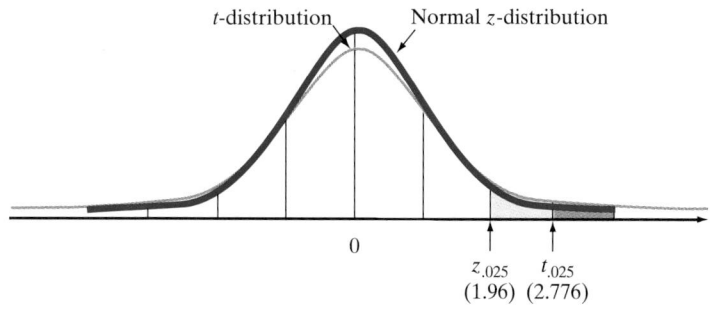

FIGURE 7.9
MINITAB analysis
of six blood
pressure increases

	N	MEAN	STDEV	SE MEAN	95.0 PERCENT C.I.
BPIncr	6	2.283	0.950	0.388	(1.287, 3.280)

dard normal z statistic to form our confidence interval for μ. Instead, we must use the t-distribution, with $(n - 1)$ degrees of freedom.

In this case, $n - 1 = 5$ df, and the t value is found in Table 7.3 to be $t_{.025} = 2.571$ with 5 df. Recall that the large-sample confidence interval would have been of the form

$$\bar{x} \pm z_{\alpha/2}\sigma_{\bar{x}} = \bar{x} \pm z_{\alpha/2}\frac{\sigma}{\sqrt{n}} = \bar{x} \pm z_{.025}\frac{\sigma}{\sqrt{n}}$$

where 95% is the desired confidence level. To form the interval for a small sample from *a normal distribution, we simply substitute* t *for z and* s *for* σ *in the preceding formula:*

$$\bar{x} \pm t_{\alpha/2}\frac{s}{\sqrt{n}}$$

A MINITAB printout showing descriptive statistics for the six blood pressure increases is displayed in Figure 7.9. Note that $\bar{x} = 2.283$ and $s = .950$. Substituting these numerical values into the confidence interval formula, we get

$$2.283 \pm (2.571)\left(\frac{.950}{\sqrt{6}}\right) = 2.283 \pm .997$$

or 1.286 to 3.280 points. Note that this interval agrees (except for rounding) with the confidence interval generated by MINITAB in Figure 7.9.

We interpret the interval as follows: We can be 95% confident that the mean increase in blood pressure associated with taking this new drug is between 1.286 and 3.28 points. As with our large-sample interval estimates, our confidence is in the process, not in this particular interval. We know that if we were to repeatedly use this estimation procedure, 95% of the confidence intervals produced would contain the true mean μ, *if the probability distribution of changes in blood pressure from which our sample was selected is normal.* If the distribution is nonnormal, the small-sample interval is not valid.

What price did we pay for having to utilize a small sample to make the inference? First, we had to assume the underlying population is normally distributed, and if the assumption is invalid, our interval might also be invalid.* Second, we had to form the interval using a t value of 2.571 rather than a z value of 1.96, resulting in a wider interval to achieve the same 95% level of confidence. If the interval from 1.286 to 3.28 is too wide to be of use, then we know how to remedy the situation: increase the number of patients sampled to decrease the interval width (on average).

The procedure for forming a small-sample confidence interval is summarized in the accompanying box.

---

*By *invalid,* we mean that the probability that the procedure will yield an interval that contains μ is not equal to $(1 - \alpha)$. Generally, if the underlying population is approximately normal, then the confidence coefficient will approximate the probability that the interval contains μ.

Small-Sample Confidence Interval * for μ

$$\bar{x} \pm t_{\alpha/2}\left(\frac{s}{\sqrt{n}}\right)$$

where $t_{\alpha/2}$ is based on $(n - 1)$ degrees of freedom

Assumptions: A random sample is selected from a population with a relative frequency distribution that is approximately normal.

EXAMPLE 7.2

Some quality control experiments require *destructive sampling* (i.e., the test to determine whether the item is defective destroys the item) in order to measure some particular characteristic of the product. The cost of destructive sampling often dictates small samples. For example, suppose a manufacturer of printers for personal computers wishes to estimate the mean number of characters printed before the printhead fails. Suppose the printer manufacturer tests $n = 15$ randomly selected printheads and records the number of characters printed until failure for each. These 15 measurements (in millions of characters) are listed in Table 7.4, followed by an EXCEL summary statistics printout in Figure 7.10.

a. Form a 99% confidence interval for the mean number of characters printed before the printhead fails. Interpret the result.

b. What assumption is required for the interval, part **a**, to be valid? Is it reasonably satisfied?

TABLE 7.4   Number of Characters (in Millions) for $n = 15$ Printhead Tests

1.13	1.55	1.43	.92	1.25
1.36	1.32	.85	1.07	1.48
1.20	1.33	1.18	1.22	1.29

FIGURE 7.10
EXCEL summary statistics printout for data in Table 7.4

Number	
Mean	1.238667
Standard Error	0.049875
Median	1.25
Mode	#N/A
Standard Deviation	0.193164
Sample Variance	0.037312
Kurtosis	0.063636
Skewness	-0.49126
Range	0.7
Minimum	0.85
Maximum	1.55
Sum	18.58
Count	15
Confidence Level(95.000%)	0.097753

*The procedure given in the box assumes that the population standard deviation σ is unknown, which is almost always the case. If σ is known, we can form the small-sample confidence interval just as we would a large-sample confidence interval using a standard normal z value instead of t. However, we must still assume that the underlying population is approximately normal.

SOLUTION

a. For this small sample ($n = 15$), we use the t statistic to form the confidence interval. We use a confidence coefficient of .99 and $n - 1 = 14$ degrees of freedom to find $t_{\alpha/2}$ in Table VI:

$$t_{\alpha/2} = t_{.005} = 2.977$$

[*Note:* The small sample forces us to extend the interval almost 3 standard deviations (of $\bar{x}$) on each side of the sample mean in order to form the 99% confidence interval.] From the EXCEL printout, Figure 7.10, we find $\bar{x} = 1.239$ and $s = .193$. Substituting these values into the confidence interval formula, we obtain:

$$\bar{x} \pm t_{.005}\left(\frac{s}{\sqrt{n}}\right) = 1.239 \pm 2.977\left(\frac{.193}{\sqrt{15}}\right)$$

$$= 1.239 \pm .148 \quad \text{or} \quad (1.091, 1.387)$$

Thus, the manufacturer can be 99% confident that the printhead has a mean life of between 1.091 and 1.387 million characters. If the manufacturer were to advertise that the mean life of its printheads is (at least) 1 million characters, the interval would support such a claim. Our confidence is derived from the fact that 99% of the intervals formed in repeated applications of this procedure would contain μ.

b. Since n is small, we must assume that the number of characters printed before printhead failure is a random variable from a normal distribution. That is, we assume that the population from which the sample of 15 measurements is selected is distributed normally. One way to check this assumption is to graph the distribution of data in Table 7.4. If the sample data are approximately normal, then the population from which the sample is selected is very likely to be normal. A MINITAB stem-and-leaf plot for the sample data is displayed in Figure 7.11. The distribution is mound-shaped and nearly symmetric. Therefore, the assumption of normality appears to be reasonably satisfied.   ▙

We have emphasized throughout this section that an assumption that the population is approximately normally distributed is necessary for making small-sample inferences about μ when using the t statistic. Although many phenomena do have approximately normal distributions, it is also true that many random phenomena have distributions that are not normal or even mound-shaped. Empirical evidence acquired over the years has shown that the t-distribution is

FIGURE 7.11
MINITAB stem-and-leaf display of data in Table 7.4

```
Stem-and-leaf of NUMBER    N = 15
Leaf Unit = 0.010

    1      8 5
    2      9 2
    3     10 7
    5     11 38
  (4)     12 0259
    6     13 236
    3     14 38
    1     15 5
```

STATISTICS IN ACTION

7.1 SCALLOPS, SAMPLING, AND THE LAW

Arnold Bennett, a Sloan School of Management professor at the Massachusetts Institute of Technology (MIT), describes a recent legal case in which he served as a statistical "expert" in *Interfaces* (Mar.–Apr. 1995). The case involved a ship that fishes for scallops off the coast of New England. In order to protect baby scallops from being harvested, the U.S. Fisheries and Wildlife Service requires that "the average meat per scallop weigh at least $1/36$ of a pound." The ship was accused of violating this weight standard. Bennett lays out the scenario:

The vessel arrived at a Massachusetts port with 11,000 bags of scallops, from which the harbormaster randomly selected 18 bags for weighing. From each such bag, his agents took a large scoopful of scallops; then, to estimate the bag's average meat per scallop, they divided the total weight of meat in the scoopful by the number of scallops it contained. Based on the 18 [numbers] thus generated, the harbormaster estimated that each of the ship's scallops possessed an average $1/39$ of a pound of meat (that is, they were about seven percent lighter than the minimum requirement). Viewing this outcome as conclusive evidence that the weight standard had been violated, federal authorities at once confiscated *95 percent* of the catch (which they then sold at auction). The fishing voyage was thus transformed into a financial catastrophe for its participants.

Bennett provided the actual scallop weight measurements for each of the 18 sampled bags in the article.

The data are listed in Table 7.5. For ease of exposition, Bennett expressed each number as a multiple of $1/36$ of a pound, the minimum permissible average weight per scallop. Consequently, numbers below one indicate individual bags that do not meet the standard.

The ship's owner filed a lawsuit against the federal government, declaring that his vessel had fully complied with the weight standard. A Boston law firm was hired to represent the owner in legal proceedings and Bennett was retained by the firm to provide statistical litigation support and, if necessary, expert witness testimony.

Focus

a. Recall that the harbormaster sampled only 18 of the ship's 11,000 bags of scallops. One of the questions the lawyers asked Bennett was: "Can a reliable estimate of the mean weight of all the scallops be obtained from a sample of size 18?" Give your opinion on this issue.

b. As stated in the article, the government's decision rule is to confiscate a scallop catch if the sample mean weight of the scallops is less than $1/36$ of a pound. Do you see any flaws in this rule?

c. Develop your own procedure for determining whether a ship is in violation of the minimum weight restriction. Apply your rule to the data in Table 7.5. Draw a conclusion about the ship in question.

TABLE 7.5 Scallop Weight Measurements for 18 Bags Sampled (Statistics in Action 7.1)

.93	.88	.85	.91	.91	.84	.90	.98	.88
.89	.98	.87	.91	.92	.99	1.14	1.06	.93

Source: Bennett, A. "Misapplications review: Jail terms." *Interfaces,* Vol. 25, No. 2, March–April 1995, p. 20.

rather insensitive to moderate departures from normality. That is, use of the *t* statistic when sampling from mound-shaped populations generally produces credible results; however, for cases in which the distribution is distinctly nonnormal, we must either take a large sample or use a *nonparametric method* (the topic of Chapter 17).

> **What Do You Do When the Population Relative Frequency Distribution Departs Greatly from Normality?**
> *Answer:* Use the nonparametric statistical methods of Chapter 17.

EXERCISES   7.18–7.31

Note: Exercises marked with ▣ *contain data available for computer analysis on a 3.5" disk (file name in parentheses).*

Learning the Mechanics

7.18 Explain the differences in the sampling distributions of $\bar{x}$ for large and small samples under the following assumptions.
   a. The variable of interest, x, is normally distributed.
   b. Nothing is known about the distribution of the variable x.

7.19 Suppose you have selected a random sample of $n = 5$ measurements from a normal distribution. Compare the standard normal z values with the corresponding t values if you were forming the following confidence intervals.
   a. 80% confidence interval
   b. 90% confidence interval
   c. 95% confidence interval
   d. 98% confidence interval
   e. 99% confidence interval
   f. Use the table values you obtained in parts **a–e** to sketch the z- and t-distributions. What are the similarities and differences?

7.20 Let t_0 be a specific value of t. Use Table VI in Appendix B to find t_0 values such that the following statements are true.
   a. $P(t \geq t_0) = .025$ where df $= 11$
   b. $P(t \geq t_0) = .01$ where df $= 9$
   c. $P(t \leq t_0) = .005$ where df $= 6$
   d. $P(t \leq t_0) = .05$ where df $= 18$

7.21 Let t_0 be a particular value of t. Use Table VI of Appendix B to find t_0 values such that the following statements are true.
   a. $P(-t_0 < t < t_0) = .95$ where df $= 10$
   b. $P(t \leq -t_0 \text{ or } t \geq t_0) = .05$ where df $= 10$
   c. $P(t \leq t_0) = .05$ where df $= 10$
   d. $P(t \leq -t_0 \text{ or } t \geq t_0) = .10$ where df $= 20$
   e. $P(t \leq -t_0 \text{ or } t \geq t_0) = .01$ where df $= 5$

7.22 The following random sample was selected from a normal distribution: 4, 6, 3, 5, 9, 3.
   a. Construct a 90% confidence interval for the population mean μ.
   b. Construct a 95% confidence interval for the population mean μ.
   c. Construct a 99% confidence interval for the population mean μ.

   d. Assume that the sample mean $\bar{x}$ and sample standard deviation s remain exactly the same as those you just calculated but that they are based on a sample of $n = 25$ observations rather than $n = 6$ observations. Repeat parts **a–c**. What is the effect of increasing the sample size on the width of the confidence intervals?

7.23 The following sample of 16 measurements was selected from a population that is approximately normally distributed:

91 80   99 110 95 106 78 121 106 100 97 82
100 83 115 104

   a. Construct an 80% confidence interval for the population mean.
   b. Construct a 95% confidence interval for the population mean and compare the width of this interval with that of part **a**.
   c. Carefully interpret each of the confidence intervals and explain why the 80% confidence interval is narrower.

Applying the Concepts

7.24 Health insurers and the federal government are both putting pressure on hospitals to shorten the average length of stay (LOS) of their patients. In 1993, the average LOS for men in the United States was 6.5 days and the average for women was 5.6 days (*Statistical Abstract of the United States: 1995*). A random sample of 20 hospitals in one state had a mean LOS for women in 1996 of 3.8 days and a standard deviation of 1.2 days.
   a. Use a 90% confidence interval to estimate the population mean LOS for women for the state's hospitals in 1996.
   b. Interpret the interval in terms of this application.
   c. What is meant by the phrase "90% confidence interval"?

7.25 Accidental spillage and misguided disposal of petroleum wastes have resulted in extensive contamination of soils across the country. A common hazardous compound found in the contaminated soil is benzo(a)pyrene [B(a)p]. An experiment was conducted to determine the effectiveness of a method designed to remove B(a)p from soil (*Journal of Hazardous Materials,* June 1995). Three soil specimens contaminated with a known amount of B(a)p were treated with a toxin that inhibits microbial growth. After 95 days of incubation, the percentage of B(a)p removed from each soil specimen was measured. The experiment produced the following summary statistics: $\bar{x} = 49.3$ and $s = 1.5$.

a. Use a 99% confidence interval to estimate the mean percentage of B(a)p removed from a soil specimen in which the toxin was used.

b. Interpret the interval in terms of this application.

c. What assumption is necessary to ensure the validity of this confidence interval?

7.26 **(X07.026)** A *mortgage* is a type of loan that is secured by a designated piece of property. If the borrower defaults on the loan, the lender can sell the property to recover the outstanding debt. In a home mortgage, the borrower pledges the home in question as security for the loan (Alexander, Sharpe, and Bailey, 1993). A federal bank examiner is interested in estimating the mean outstanding principal balance of all home mortgages foreclosed by the bank due to default by the borrower during the last three years. A random sample of 20 foreclosed mortgages yielded the following data (in dollars):

95,982	81,422	39,888	46,836	66,899	69,110
59,200	62,331	105,812	55,545	56,635	72,123
60,044	75,267	71,490	65,273	42,871	68,100
84,525	79,006				

a. Describe the population from which the bank examiner collected the sample data. What characteristic must this population possess to enable us to construct a confidence interval for the mean outstanding principal balance using the method described in this section? Check this graphically.

b. A 90% confidence interval for the mean of interest is displayed in the MINITAB printout below. Locate the interval.

c. Carefully interpret the confidence interval in the context of the problem.

7.27 Kitchens are frequently the most expensive room for homeowners to remodel. The job requires electricians, carpenters, and plumbers and can cost as much as $600 a square foot, compared to $60 a square foot for a bedroom. The average cost of a major kitchen remodeling job in each of a sample of 11 U.S. cities is shown in the next table.

a. Describe possible causes for the variation in the sample data.

City	Average Cost
Atlanta	$20,427
Boston	27,255
Des Moines	22,115
Kansas City, Mo.	23,256
Louisville	21,887
Portland, Ore.	24,255
Raleigh-Durham	19,852
Reno, Nev.	23,624
Ridgewood, N.J.	25,885
San Francisco	28,999
Tulsa	20,836

Source: Auerbach, J. "A guide to what's cooking in kitchens." *Wall Street Journal,* November 17, 1995, p. B10.

b. Use a 95% confidence interval to estimate the mean kitchen remodeling cost per city in the United States.

c. Why are you so confident that the true mean kitchen remodeling cost per city in the United States falls within the interval, part **b**?

7.28 It is customary practice in the United States to base roadway design on the 30th highest hourly volume in a year. Thus, all roadway facilities are expected to operate at acceptable levels of service for all but 29 hours of the year. The Florida Department of Transportation (DOT), however, has shifted from the 30th highest hour to the 100th highest hour as the basis for level-of-service determinators. Florida Atlantic University researcher Reid Ewing investigated whether this shift was warranted in the *Journal of STAR Research* (July 1994). The table on page 287 gives the traffic counts at the 30th highest hour and the 100th highest hour of a recent year for 20 randomly selected DOT permanent count stations. MINITAB stem-and-leaf plots for the two variables are provided on page 287 as well as summary statistics and 95% confidence interval printouts.

a. Describe the population from which the sample data is selected.

b. Does the sample appear to be representative of the population? Explain.

c. Locate and interpret the 95% confidence interval for the mean traffic count at the 30th highest hour.

d. What assumption is necessary for the confidence interval to be valid? Does it appear to be satisfied? Explain.

e. Repeat parts **c** and **d** for the 100th highest hour.

```
                 N      MEAN      STDEV   SE MEAN     90.0 PERCENT C.I.
    prinbal     20    67918.0   16552.4    3701.2    ( 61516.5, 74319.4)
```

Station	Type of Route	30th Highest Hour	100th Highest Hour
0117	small city	1,890	1,736
0087	recreational	2,217	2,069
0166	small city	1,444	1,345
0013	rural	2,105	2,049
0161	urban	4,905	4,815
0096	urban	2,022	1,958
0145	rural	594	548
0149	rural	252	229
0038	urban	2,162	2,048
0118	rural	1,938	1,748
0047	rural	879	811
0066	urban	1,913	1,772
0094	rural	3,494	3,403
0105	small city	1,424	1,309
0113	small city	4,571	4,425
0151	urban	3,494	3,359
0159	rural	2,222	2,137
0160	small city	1,076	989
0164	recreational	2,167	2,039
0165	recreational	3,350	3,123

Source: Ewing, R. "Roadway levels of service in an era of growth management." *Journal of STAR Research*, Vol. 3, July 1994, p. 103 (Table 2).

```
Stem-and-leaf of Hour30    N = 20
Leaf Unit = 100

    1      0 2
    3      0 58
    6      1 044
    9      1 899
   (6)     2 011122
    5      2
    5      3 344
    2      3
    2      4
    2      4 59


Stem-and-leaf of Hour100   N = 20
Leaf Unit = 100
    1      0 2
    4      0 589
    6      1 33
   10      1 7779
   10      2 00001
    5      2
    5      3 134
    2      3
    2      4 4
    1      4 8


              N      MEAN     STDEV   SE MEAN    95.0 PERCENT C.I.
Hour30       20   2205.95   1223.81    273.65   ( 1633.05, 2778.85)
Hour100      20   2095.60   1203.12    269.02   ( 1532.39, 2658.81)
```

| 50 | 78 | 41 | 32 | 35 | 12 | 12 | 15 | 5 | 3 | 5 |
| 23 | 16 | 24 | 24 | 15 | 12 | 11 | 30 | 43 | 4 | 4 |

Source: Tampa Bay Business Journal, June 21–27, 1996, p. 27.

```
Analysis Variable : NUMEMPLY

N Obs   N    Minimum      Maximum           Mean      Std Dev
------------------------------------------------------------------
   22  22   3.0000000   78.0000000     22.4545455   18.5182722
------------------------------------------------------------------
```

7.29 Private and public colleges and universities rely on money contributed by individuals, corporations, and foundations for both salaries and operating expenses. Much of this money is put into a fund called an *endowment,* and the college spends only the interest earned by the fund. A random sample of eight college endowments drawn from the list of endowments in the *Chronicle of Higher Education Almanac* (Sept. 2, 1996) yielded the following endowments (in millions of dollars): 148.6, 66.1, 340.8, 500.2, 212.8, 55.4, 72.6, 83.4. Estimate the mean endowment for this population of colleges and universities using a 95% confidence interval. List any assumptions you make.

7.30 One of the continuing concerns of U.S. industry is the increasing cost of health insurance for its workers. In 1993 the average cost of health premiums per employee was $2,851, up 10.5% from 1992 (*Nation's Business,* Feb. 1995). In 1997, a random sample of 23 U.S. companies had a mean health insurance premium per employee of $3,321 and a standard deviation of $255.

a. Use a 95% confidence interval to estimate the mean health insurance premium per employee for all U.S. companies.
b. What assumption is necessary to ensure the validity of the confidence interval?
c. Make an inference about whether the true mean health insurance premium per employee in 1997 exceeds $2,851—the 1993 mean.

7.31 (**X07.031**) The table above lists the number of full-time employees at each of 22 office furniture dealers serving Tampa, Florida, and its surrounding communities. Summary statistics for the data are provided in the SAS printout.

a. Construct a 99% confidence interval for the true mean number of full-time employees at office furniture dealers in Tampa.
b. Interpret the interval, part **a**.
c. Comment on the assumption required for the interval to be valid.
d. The 22 dealers in the sample were the top-ranked furniture dealers in Tampa based on sales volume in 1995. How does this fact impact the validity of the confidence interval? Explain.

7.3 LARGE-SAMPLE CONFIDENCE INTERVAL FOR A POPULATION PROPORTION

The number of public opinion polls has grown at an astounding rate in recent years. Almost daily, the news media report the results of some poll. Pollsters regularly determine the percentage of people who approve of the president's on-the-job performance, the fraction of voters in favor of a certain candidate, the fraction of customers who prefer a particular product, and the proportion of households that watch a particular TV program. In each case, we are interested in estimating the percentage (or proportion) of some group with a certain characteristic. In this section we consider methods for making inferences about population proportions when the sample is large.

EXAMPLE 7.3

A food-products company conducted a market study by randomly sampling and interviewing 1,000 consumers to determine which brand of breakfast cereal they prefer. Suppose 313 consumers were found to prefer the company's brand. How would you estimate the true fraction of *all* consumers who prefer the company's cereal brand?

SOLUTION

What we have really asked is how you would estimate the probability p of success in a binomial experiment, where p is the probability that a chosen consumer prefers the company's brand. One logical method of estimating p for the population is to use the proportion of successes in the sample. That is, we can estimate p by calculating

$$\hat{p} = \frac{\text{Number of consumers sampled who prefer the company's brand}}{\text{Number of consumers sampled}}$$

where $\hat{p}$ is read "p hat." Thus, in this case,

$$\hat{p} = \frac{313}{1,000} = .313$$

To determine the reliability of the estimator $\hat{p}$, we need to know its sampling distribution. That is, if we were to draw samples of 1,000 consumers over and over again, each time calculating a new estimate $\hat{p}$, what would be the frequency distribution of all the $\hat{p}$ values? The answer lies in viewing $\hat{p}$ as the average, or mean, number of successes per trial over the n trials. If each success is assigned a value equal to 1 and a failure is assigned a value of 0, then the sum of all n sample observations is x, the total number of successes, and $\hat{p} = x/n$ is the average, or mean, number of successes per trial in the n trials. The Central Limit Theorem tells us that the relative frequency distribution of the sample mean for any population is approximately normal for sufficiently large samples. ⌐

The repeated sampling distribution of $\hat{p}$ has the characteristics listed in the next box and shown in Figure 7.12.

Sampling Distribution of $\hat{p}$

1. The mean of the sampling distribution of $\hat{p}$ is p; that is, $\hat{p}$ is an unbiased estimator of p.

2. The standard deviation of the sampling distribution of $\hat{p}$ is $\sqrt{pq/n}$; that is, $\sigma_{\hat{p}} = \sqrt{pq/n}$, where $q = 1 - p$.

3. For large samples, the sampling distribution of $\hat{p}$ is approximately normal. A sample size is considered large if the interval $\hat{p} \pm 3\sigma_{\hat{p}}$ does not include 0 or 1. [*Note:* This requirement is almost equivalent to that given in Section 5.4 for approximating a binomial distribution with a normal one. The difference is that we assumed p to be known in Section 5.4; now we are trying to make inferences about an unknown p, so we use $\hat{p}$ to estimate p in checking the adequacy of the normal approximation.]

The fact that $\hat{p}$ is a "sample mean fraction of successes" allows us to form confidence intervals about p in a manner that is completely analogous to that used for large-sample estimation of μ.

FIGURE 7.12
Sampling distribution
of $\hat{p}$

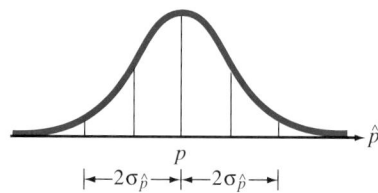

TABLE 7.6 **Values of pq for Several Different Values of p**

p	pq	$\sqrt{pq}$
.5	.25	.50
.6 or .4	.24	.49
.7 or .3	.21	.46
.8 or .2	.16	.40
.9 or .1	.09	.30

Large-Sample Confidence Interval for p

$$\hat{p} \pm z_{\alpha/2}\sigma_{\hat{p}} = \hat{p} \pm z_{\alpha/2}\sqrt{\frac{pq}{n}} \approx \hat{p} \pm z_{\alpha/2}\sqrt{\frac{\hat{p}\hat{q}}{n}}$$

where $\hat{p} = \dfrac{x}{n}$ and $\hat{q} = 1 - \hat{p}$

Note: When n is large, $\hat{p}$ can approximate the value of p in the formula for $\sigma_{\hat{p}}$.

Thus, if 313 of 1,000 consumers prefer the company's cereal brand, a 95% confidence interval for the proportion of *all* consumers who prefer the company's brand is

$$\hat{p} \pm z_{\alpha/2}\sigma_{\hat{p}} = .313 \pm 1.96\sqrt{\frac{pq}{1,000}}$$

where $q = 1 - p$. Just as we needed an approximation for σ in calculating a large-sample confidence interval for μ, we now need an approximation for p. As Table 7.6 shows, the approximation for p does not have to be especially accurate, because the value of $\sqrt{pq}$ needed for the confidence interval is relatively insensitive to changes in p. Therefore, we can use $\hat{p}$ to approximate p. Keeping in mind that $\hat{q} = 1 - \hat{p}$, we substitute these values into the formula for the confidence interval:

$$\hat{p} \pm 1.96\sqrt{\frac{pq}{1,000}} \approx \hat{p} \pm 1.96\sqrt{\frac{\hat{p}\hat{q}}{1,000}}$$

$$= .313 \pm 1.96\sqrt{\frac{(.313)(.687)}{1,000}}$$

$$= .313 \pm .029$$

$$= (.284, .342)$$

The company can be 95% confident that the interval from 28.4% to 34.2% contains the true percentage of *all* consumers who prefer its brand. That is, in repeated construction of confidence intervals, approximately 95% of all samples would produce confidence intervals that enclose p. Note that the guidelines for interpreting a confidence interval about μ also apply to interpreting a confidence interval for p because p is the "population mean fraction of successes" in a binomial experiment.

EXAMPLE 7.4

Many public polling agencies conduct surveys to determine the current consumer sentiment concerning the state of the economy. For example, the Bureau of Economic and Business Research (BEBR) at the University of Florida conducts quarterly surveys to gauge consumer sentiment in the Sunshine State. Suppose that BEBR randomly samples 484 consumers and finds that 257 are optimistic about the state of the economy. Use a 90% confidence interval to estimate the proportion of all consumers in Florida who are optimistic about the state of the economy. Based on the confidence interval, can BEBR infer that the majority of Florida consumers are optimistic about the economy?

SOLUTION
The number, x, of the 484 sampled consumers who are optimistic about the Florida economy is a binomial random variable if we can assume that the sample was randomly selected from the population of Florida consumers and that the poll was conducted identically for each sampled consumer.

The point estimate of the proportion of Florida consumers who are optimistic about the economy is

$$\hat{p} = \frac{x}{n} = \frac{257}{484} = .531$$

We first check to be sure that the sample size is sufficiently large that the normal distribution provides a reasonable approximation for the sampling distribution of $\hat{p}$. We check the 3-standard-deviation interval around $\hat{p}$:

$$\hat{p} \pm 3\sigma_{\hat{p}} \approx \hat{p} \pm 3\sqrt{\frac{\hat{p}\hat{q}}{n}}$$

$$= .531 \pm 3\sqrt{\frac{(.531)(.469)}{484}} = .531 \pm .068 = (.463, .599)$$

Since this interval is wholly contained in the interval $(0, 1)$, we may conclude that the normal approximation is reasonable.

We now proceed to form the 90% confidence interval for p, the true proportion of Florida consumers who are optimistic about the state of the economy:

$$\hat{p} \pm z_{\alpha/2}\sigma_{\hat{p}} = \hat{p} \pm z_{\alpha/2}\sqrt{\frac{pq}{n}} \approx \hat{p} \pm z_{\alpha/2}\sqrt{\frac{\hat{p}\hat{q}}{n}}$$

$$= .531 \pm 1.645\sqrt{\frac{(.531)(.469)}{484}} = .531 \pm .037 = (.494, .568)$$

Thus, we can be 90% confident that the proportion of all Florida consumers who are confident about the economy is between .494 and .568. As always, our confidence stems from the fact that 90% of all similarly formed intervals will contain the true proportion p and not from any knowledge about whether this particular interval does.

Can we conclude that the majority of Florida consumers are optimistic about the economy based on this interval? If we wished to use this interval to infer that a majority is optimistic, the interval would have to support the inference that p exceeds .5—that is, that more than 50% of the Florida consumers are optimistic about the economy. Note that the interval contains some values below .5 (as low as .494) as well as some above .5 (as high as .568). Therefore, we cannot conclude that the true value of p exceeds .5 based on this 90% confidence interval.   ■

In Example 7.4 we used the confidence interval to make an inference about whether the true value of p exceeds .5. That is, we used the sample to **test** whether p exceeds .5. When we want to use sample information to test the value of a population parameter, we usually conduct a *test of hypothesis,* the subject of Chapter 8. But first, we'll conclude Chapter 7 with a section showing how to determine the sample size necessary to estimate either a population mean or a population proportion.

EXERCISES   7.32–7.46

Note: Exercises marked with ▣ contain data available for computer analysis on a 3.5" disk (file name in parentheses).

Learning the Mechanics

7.32 Describe the sampling distribution of $\hat{p}$ based on large samples of size n. That is, give the mean, the standard deviation, and the (approximate) shape of the distribution of $\hat{p}$ when large samples of size n are (repeatedly) selected from the binomial distribution with probability of success p.

7.33 Explain the meaning of the phrase "$\hat{p}$ is an unbiased estimator of p."

7.34 A random sample of size $n = 121$ yielded $\hat{p} = .88$.

a. Is the sample size large enough to use the methods of this section to construct a confidence interval for p? Explain.

b. Construct a 90% confidence interval for p.

c. What assumption is necessary to ensure the validity of this confidence interval?

7.35 For the binomial sample information summarized in each part, indicate whether the sample size is large enough to use the methods of this chapter to construct a confidence interval for p.

a. $n = 400, \hat{p} = .10$ b. $n = 50, \hat{p} = .10$
c. $n = 20, \hat{p} = .5$ d. $n = 20, \hat{p} = .3$

7.36 A random sample of 50 consumers taste tested a new snack food. Their responses were coded (0: do not like; 1: like; 2: indifferent) and recorded as follows:

1	0	0	1	2	0	1	1	0	0
0	1	0	2	0	2	2	0	0	1
1	0	0	0	0	1	0	2	0	0
0	1	0	0	1	0	0	1	0	1
0	2	0	0	1	1	0	0	0	1

a. Use an 80% confidence interval to estimate the proportion of consumers who like the snack food.

b. Provide a statistical interpretation for the confidence interval you constructed in part **a**.

7.37 A random sample of size $n = 225$ yielded $\hat{p} = .46$.

a. Is the sample size large enough to use the methods of this section to construct a confidence interval for p? Explain.

b. Construct a 95% confidence interval for p.

c. Interpret the 95% confidence interval.

d. Explain what is meant by the phrase "95% confidence interval."

Applying the Concepts

7.38 According to the U.S. Bureau of Labor Statistics, one of every 80 American workers (i.e., 1.3%) was fired or laid off in 1995. Are employees with cancer fired or laid off at the same rate? To answer this question, *Working Women* magazine and Amgen—a company that makes drugs to lessen chemotherapy side effects—conducted a telephone survey of 100 cancer survivors who worked while undergoing treatment (*Tampa Tribune*, Sept. 25, 1996). Of these 100 cancer patients, 7 were fired or laid off due to their illness.

a. Construct a 90% confidence interval for the true percentage of all cancer patients who are fired or laid off due to their illness.

b. Give a practical interpretation of the interval, part **a**.

c. Are employees with cancer fired or laid off at the same rate as all U.S. workers? Explain.

7.39 Substance abuse problems are widespread at New Jersey businesses, according to the *Governor's Council for a Drug Free Workplace Report* (Spring/Summer 1995). A questionnaire on the issue was mailed to all New Jersey businesses that were members of the Governor's Council. Of the 72 companies that responded to the survey, 50 admitted that they had employees whose performance was affected by drugs or alcohol.

a. Use a 95% confidence interval to estimate the proportion of all New Jersey companies with substance abuse problems.

b. What assumptions are necessary to ensure the validity of the confidence interval?

c. Interpret the interval in the context of the problem.

d. In interpreting the confidence interval, what does it mean to say you are "95% confident"?

e. Would you use the interval of part **a** to estimate the proportion of all U.S. companies with substance abuse problems? Why or why not?

7.40 Obstructive sleep apnea is a sleep disorder that causes a person to stop breathing momentarily and then awaken briefly. These sleep interruptions, which may occur hundreds of times in a night, can drastically reduce the quality of rest and cause fatigue during waking hours. Researchers at Stanford University studied 159 commercial truck drivers and found that 124 of them suffered from obstructive sleep apnea (*Chest*, May 1995).

a. Use the study results to estimate, with 90% confidence, the fraction of truck drivers who suffer from the sleep disorder.

b. Sleep researchers believe that about 25% of the general population suffer from obstructive sleep apnea. Comment on whether or not this value represents the true percentage of truck drivers who suffer from the sleep disorder.

7.41 Past research has clearly indicated that the stress produced by today's lifestyles results in health problems for a large proportion of society. An article in the *International Journal of Sports Psychology* (July–Sept. 1992) evaluates the relationship between physical fitness and stress. Employees of companies that participate in the Health Examination Program offered by Health Advancement Services (HAS) were classified into three fitness levels: poor, average, and good. Each person was tested for signs of stress. The results for the three groups are reported below:

Fitness Level	Sample Size	Proportion with Signs of Stress
Poor	242	.155
Average	212	.133
Good	95	.108

a. Check to see whether each of these samples is large enough to construct a confidence interval for the true proportion of all employees at each fitness level exhibiting signs of stress.

b. Assuming each sample represents a random sample from its corresponding population, calculate and interpret a 95% confidence interval for the proportion of people with signs of stress within each of the three fitness levels.

c. Interpret each of the confidence intervals constructed in part **b** using the terminology of this exercise.

7.42 Family-owned companies are notorious for having difficulties in transferring control from one generation to the next. Part of this problem can be traced to lack of a well-documented strategic business plan. In a survey of 3,900 privately held family firms with revenues exceeding $1,000,000 a year, Arthur Andersen, the international accounting and consulting firm, found that 1,911 had no strategic business plan (*Minneapolis Star Tribune*, Sept. 4, 1995).

a. Describe the population studied by Arthur Andersen.

b. Assume the 3,900 firms were randomly sampled from the population. Use a 90% confidence interval to estimate the proportion of family-owned companies without strategic business plans.

c. How wide is the 90% confidence interval you constructed in part **b**? Would an 80% confidence interval be wider or narrower? Justify your answer.

7.43 For the last five years, the accounting firm Price Waterhouse has monitored the U.S. Postal Service's performance. One parameter of interest is the percentage of mail delivered on time. In a sample of 332,000 items mailed between Dec. 10, 1994, and Mar. 3, 1995—the most difficult delivery season due to bad weather and holidays—Price Waterhouse determined that 282,200 items were delivered on time (*Tampa Tribune*, Mar. 26, 1995). Use this information to estimate with 99% confidence the true percentage of items delivered on time by the U.S. Postal Service. Interpret the result.

7.44 In August 1995 the Gallup organization conducted interviews with a random sample of 1,002 people who operate businesses in their homes. The most common reason given for starting a home business

was wanting to be one's own boss (170 respondents); being laid off was the least common reason (30 respondents) (*New York Times*, Oct. 15, 1995).

a. Describe the population of interest to the Gallup organization.

b. Is the sample size large enough to construct a valid confidence interval for the proportion of home business operators who started their business because they were laid off? Justify your answer.

c. Repeat part **b** for the proportion wanting to be their own boss.

d. Estimate the proportion referred to in part **c** using a 95% confidence interval and interpret your result.

7.45 (**X07.045**) Refer to the *Marine Technology* (Jan. 1995) study of the causes of fifty recent major oil spills from tankers and carriers, Exercise 2.10. The data is reproduced in the table on page 294.

a. Give a point estimate for the proportion of major oil spills that are caused by hull failure.

b. Form a 95% confidence interval for the estimate, part **a**. Interpret the result.

7.46 Performark, Inc., a sales and marketing consulting company located in Minneapolis, Minn., provides its clients with sales programs designed to maximize efficiency and control. The sales programs are based on Performark's extensive research on product advertisements. One study, conducted over a five-year period, examined advertisements for products that cost at least $5,000. Each of these ads were in the form of inquiry cards, bingo cards, or reader-response cards (see Exercise 2.5) in which the potential buyer returns the card with the information requested. Of the 15,324 ad inquiries that were returned to the advertiser, Performark found that 3,371, or 22%, of the advertisers never bothered to respond to or contact the potential buyer (*The Current State of Inquiry Management*, Performark, Inc., 1995).

a. Describe the population of interest to Performark in this study.

b. Construct a 99% confidence interval for the true proportion of advertisers that do not respond to their own ad inquiries.

c. Interpret the interval, part **b**.

7.4 DETERMINING THE SAMPLE SIZE

Recall (Section 1.5) that one way to collect the relevant data for a study used to make inferences about the population is to implement a designed (planned) experiment. Perhaps the most important design decision faced by the analyst is to determine the size of the sample. We show in this section that the appropriate sample size for making an inference about a population mean or proportion depends on the desired reliability.

Tanker	Spillage (metric tons, thousands)	Collision	Grounding	Fire/ Explosion	Hull Failure	Unknown
			CAUSE OF SPILLAGE			
Atlantic Empress	257	X				
Castillo De Bellver	239			X		
Amoco Cadiz	221				X	
Odyssey	132			X		
Torrey Canyon	124		X			
Sea Star	123	X				
Hawaiian Patriot	101				X	
Independento	95	X				
Urquiola	91		X			
Irenes Serenade	82			X		
Khark 5	76			X		
Nova	68	X				
Wafra	62		X			
Epic Colocotronis	58		X			
Sinclair Petrolore	57			X		
Yuyo Maru No 10	42	X				
Assimi	50			X		
Andros Patria	48			X		
World Glory	46				X	
British Ambassador	46				X	
Metula	45		X			
Pericles G.C.	44			X		
Mandoil II	41	X				
Jacob Maersk	41		X			
Burmah Agate	41	X				
J. Antonio Lavalleja	38		X			
Napier	37		X			
Exxon Valdez	36		X			
Corinthos	36	X				
Trader	36				X	
St. Peter	33			X		
Gino	32	X				
Golden Drake	32			X		
Ionnis Angelicoussis	32			X		
Chryssi	32				X	
Irenes Challenge	31				X	
Argo Merchant	28		X			
Heimvard	31	X				
Pegasus	25					X
Pacocean	31				X	
Texaco Oklahoma	29				X	
Scorpio	31		X			
Ellen Conway	31		X			
Caribbean Sea	30				X	
Cretan Star	27					X
Grand Zenith	26				X	
Athenian Venture	26			X		
Venoil	26	X				
Aragon	24				X	
Ocean Eagle	21		X			

Source: Daidola, J. C. "Tanker structure behavior during collision and grounding." *Marine Technology*, Vol. 32, No. 1, Jan. 1995, p. 22 (Table 1). Reprinted with permission of The Society of Naval Architects and Marine Engineers (SNAME), 601 Pavonia Ave., Jersey City, NJ 07306, USA, (201) 798-4800. Material appearing in The Society of Naval Architect and Marine Engineers (SNAME) publications cannot be reprinted without obtaining written permission.

a. $n = 100$

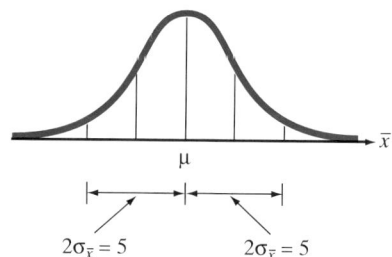

b. $n = 867$

FIGURE 7.13   Relationship between sample size and width of confidence interval: Delinquent creditors example

ESTIMATING A POPULATION MEAN

Consider the example from Section 7.1 in which we estimated the mean overdue amount for all delinquent accounts in a large credit corporation. A sample of 100 delinquent accounts produced the 95% confidence interval: $\bar{x} \pm 2\sigma_{\bar{x}} \approx 233.28 \pm 18.07$. Consequently, our estimate $\bar{x}$ was within \$18.07 of the true mean amount due, μ, for all the delinquent accounts at the 95% confidence level. That is, the 95% confidence interval for μ was $2(18.07) = \$36.14$ wide when 100 accounts were sampled. This is illustrated in Figure 7.13a.

Now suppose we want to estimate μ to within \$5 with 95% confidence. That is, we want to narrow the width of the confidence interval from \$36.14 to \$5, as shown in Figure 7.13b. How much will the sample size have to be increased to accomplish this? If we want the estimator $\bar{x}$ to be within \$5 of μ, we must have

$$2\sigma_{\bar{x}} = 5 \qquad \text{or, equivalently,} \qquad 2\left(\frac{\sigma}{\sqrt{n}}\right) = 5$$

The necessary sample size is obtained by solving this equation for n. To do this we need an approximation for σ. We have an approximation from the initial sample of 100 accounts—namely, the sample standard deviation, $s = 90.34$. Thus,

$$2\left(\frac{\sigma}{\sqrt{n}}\right) \approx 2\left(\frac{s}{\sqrt{n}}\right) = 2\left(\frac{90.34}{\sqrt{n}}\right) = 5$$

$$\sqrt{n} = \frac{2(90.34)}{5} = 36.136$$

$$n = (36.136)^2 = 1{,}305.81 \approx 1{,}306$$

Approximately 1,306 accounts will have to be randomly sampled to estimate the mean overdue amount μ to within \$5 with (approximately) 95% confidence. The confidence interval resulting from a sample of this size will be approximately \$10 wide (see Figure 7.13b).

In general, we express the reliability associated with a confidence interval for the population mean μ by specifying the **bound**, B, within which we want to

FIGURE 7.14
Specifying the bound
B as the half-width of
a confidence interval

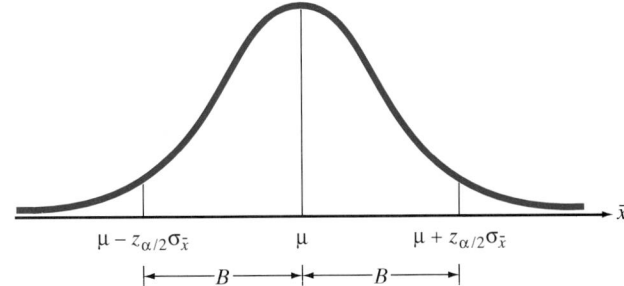

estimate μ with $100(1 - \alpha)\%$ confidence. The bound B then is equal to the half-width of the confidence interval, as shown in Figure 7.14.

The procedure for finding the sample size necessary to estimate μ to within a given bound B is given in the box.

Sample Size Determination for $100(1 - \alpha)\%$ Confidence Intervals for μ
In order to estimate μ to within a **bound B** with $100(1 - \alpha)\%$ confidence, the required sample size is found as follows:

$$z_{\alpha/2}\left(\frac{\sigma}{\sqrt{n}}\right) = B$$

The solution can be written in terms of B as follows:

$$n = \frac{(z_{\alpha/2})^2 \sigma^2}{B^2}$$

The value of σ is usually unknown. It can be estimated by the standard deviation, s, from a prior sample. Alternatively, we may approximate the range R of observations in the population, and (conservatively) estimate $\sigma \approx R/4$. In any case, you should round the value of n obtained *upward* to ensure that the sample size will be sufficient to achieve the specified reliability.

EXAMPLE 7.5

The manufacturer of official NFL footballs uses a machine to inflate its new balls to a pressure of 13.5 pounds. When the machine is properly calibrated, the mean inflation pressure is 13.5 pounds, but uncontrollable factors cause the pressures of individual footballs to vary randomly from about 13.3 to 13.7 pounds. For quality control purposes, the manufacturer wishes to estimate the mean inflation pressure to within .025 pound of its true value with a 99% confidence interval. What sample size should be used?

SOLUTION
We desire a 99% confidence interval that estimates μ to within $B = .025$ pound of its true value. For a 99% confidence interval, we have $z_{\alpha/2} = z_{.005} = 2.575$. To estimate σ, we note that the range of observations is $R = 13.7 - 13.3 = .4$ and use $\sigma \approx R/4 = .1$. Now we use the formula derived in the box to find the sample size n:

$$n = \frac{(z_{\alpha/2})^2 \sigma^2}{B^2} \approx \frac{(2.575)^2(.1)^2}{(.025)^2} = 106.09$$

We round this up to $n = 107$. Realizing that σ was approximated by $R/4$, we might even advise that the sample size be specified as $n = 110$ to be more certain of attaining the objective of a 99% confidence interval with bound $B = .025$ pound or less.

Sometimes the formula will yield a small sample size ($n < 30$). Unfortunately, this solution is invalid because the procedures and assumptions for small samples differ from those for large samples, as we discovered in Section 7.2. Therefore, if the formulas yield a small sample size, one simple strategy is to select a sample size $n \geq 30$.

ESTIMATING A POPULATION PROPORTION

The method outlined above is easily applied to a population proportion p. For example, in Section 7.3 a company used a sample of 1,000 consumers to calculate a 95% confidence interval for the proportion of consumers who preferred its cereal brand, obtaining the interval .313 ± .029. Suppose the company wishes to estimate its market share more precisely, say to within .015 with a 95% confidence interval.

The company wants a confidence interval with a bound B on the estimate of p of $B = .015$. The sample size required to generate such an interval is found by solving the following equation for n:

$$z_{\alpha/2}\sigma_{\hat{p}} = B \qquad \text{or} \qquad z_{\alpha/2}\sqrt{\frac{pq}{n}} = .015 \qquad \text{(see Figure 7.15)}$$

Since a 95% confidence interval is desired, the appropriate z value is $z_{\alpha/2} = z_{.025} = 1.96 \approx 2$. We must approximate the value of the product pq before we can solve the equation for n. As shown in Table 7.6, the closer the values of p and q to .5, the larger the product pq. Thus, to find a conservatively large sample size that will generate a confidence interval with the specified reliability, we generally choose an approximation of p close to .5. In the case of the tobacco company, however, we have an initial sample estimate of $\hat{p} = .313$. A conservatively large estimate of pq can therefore be obtained by using, say, $p = .35$. We now substitute into the equation and solve for n:

$$2\sqrt{\frac{(.35)(.65)}{n}} = .015$$

$$n = \frac{(2)^2(.35)(.65)}{(.015)^2}$$

$$= 4{,}044.44 \approx 4{,}045$$

The company must sample about 4,045 consumers to estimate the percentage who prefer its brand to within .015 with a 95% confidence interval.

The procedure for finding the sample size necessary to estimate a population proportion p to within a given bound B is given in the box.

FIGURE 7.15
Specifying the bound B of a confidence interval for a population proportion p

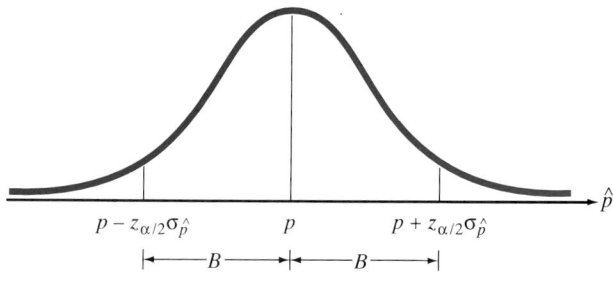

Sample Size Determination for 100(1 − α)% Confidence Interval for p

In order to estimate a binomial probability p to within a bound B with $100(1 - \alpha)\%$ confidence, the required sample size is found by solving the following equation for n:

$$z_{\alpha/2}\sqrt{\frac{pq}{n}} = B$$

The solution can be written in terms of B:

$$n = \frac{(z_{\alpha/2})^2(pq)}{B^2}$$

Since the value of the product pq is unknown, it can be estimated by using the sample fraction of successes, $\hat{p}$, from a prior sample. Remember (Table 7.6) that the value of pq is at its maximum when p equals .5, so that you can obtain conservatively large values of n by approximating p by .5 or values close to .5. In any case, you should round the value of n obtained *upward* to ensure that the sample size will be sufficient to achieve the specified reliability.

EXAMPLE 7.6

A small telephone manufacturer that entered the postregulation market too quickly has an initial problem with excessive customer complaints and consequent returns of the phones for repair or replacement. The manufacturer wants to determine the magnitude of the problem in order to estimate its warranty liability. How many telephones should the company randomly sample from its warehouse and check in order to estimate the fraction defective, p, to within .01 with 90% confidence?

SOLUTION

In order to estimate p to within a bound of .01, we set the half-width of the confidence interval equal to $B = .01$, as shown in Figure 7.16.

The equation for the sample size n requires an estimate of the product pq. We could most conservatively estimate $pq = .25$ (i.e., use $p = .5$), but this may be overly conservative when estimating a fraction defective. A value of .1, corresponding to 10% defective, will probably be conservatively large for this application. The solution is therefore

$$n = \frac{(z_{\alpha/2})^2(pq)}{B^2} = \frac{(1.645)^2(.1)(.9)}{(.01)^2} = 2,435.4 \approx 2,436$$

Thus, the manufacturer should sample 2,436 telephones in order to estimate the fraction defective, p, to within .01 with 90% confidence. Remember that this answer depends on our approximation for pq, where we used .09. If the fraction defective is closer to .05 than .10, we can use a sample of 1,286 telephones (check this) to estimate p to within .01 with 90% confidence. ◣

FIGURE 7.16
Specified reliability for estimate of fraction defective in Example 7.6

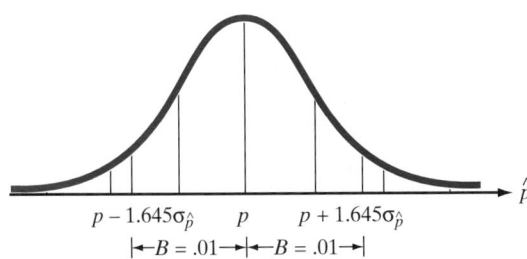

$p - 1.645\sigma_{\hat{p}}$ p $p + 1.645\sigma_{\hat{p}}$
|←$B = .01$→|←$B = .01$→|

STATISTICS IN ACTION

7.2 IS CAFFEINE ADDICTIVE?

Scientific research has established that certain substances, when taken in excess, can become addictive. These substances range from heavy narcotic drugs such as heroine and cocaine to alcohol in beer and wine and nicotine in cigarettes. Media blitzes have made drug users, drinkers, and smokers well aware of the dangers of these addictions. But what about the millions of Americans who regularly drink coffee, tea, or cola products each day? Does the caffeine in coffee, tea, and cola induce an addiction similar to that induced by alcohol, tobacco, heroine, and cocaine?

In an attempt to answer this question, researchers at Johns Hopkins University recently examined 27 caffeine drinkers and found 25 who displayed some type of withdrawal symptoms when abstaining from caffeine. [*Note:* The 27 caffeine drinkers volunteered for the study.] Furthermore, of 11 caffeine drinkers who were diagnosed as caffeine dependent, 8 displayed dramatic withdrawal symptoms (including impairment in normal functioning) when they consumed a caffeine-free diet in a controlled setting.

The National Coffee Association claimed, however, that the study group was too small to draw conclusions. "It is inappropriate to overgeneralize the results of this ... study, since caffeine as normally consumed poses no health risk to the average consumer and cannot be described as a substance of dependence" (*Los Angeles Times,* Oct. 5, 1994).

Focus

Give your (supported) opinion on the issue. If the sample size is deemed satisfactory, establish confidence intervals for the parameters of interest. If not, how large a sample should be selected?

The cost of sampling will also play an important role in the final determination of the sample size to be selected to estimate either μ or p. Although more complex formulas can be derived to balance the reliability and cost considerations, we will solve for the necessary sample size and note that the sampling budget may be a limiting factor. Consult the references for a more complete treatment of this problem.

EXERCISES   7.47–7.63

Learning the Mechanics

7.47   If you wish to estimate a population mean to within a bound $B = .3$ using a 95% confidence interval and you know from prior sampling that σ^2 is approximately equal to 7.2, how many observations would have to be included in your sample?

7.48   If nothing is known about p, .5 can be substituted for p in the sample-size formula for a population proportion. But when this is done, the resulting sample size may be larger than needed. Under what circumstances will using $p = .5$ in the sample-size formula yield a sample size larger than needed to construct a confidence interval for p with a specified bound and a specified confidence level?

7.49   Suppose you wish to estimate a population mean correct to within a bound $B = .20$ with probability equal to .90. You do not know σ^2, but you know

that the observations will range in value between 30 and 34.

    a. Find the approximate sample size that will produce the desired accuracy of the estimate. You wish to be conservative to ensure that the sample size will be ample to achieve the desired accuracy of the estimate. [*Hint:* Using your knowledge of data variation from Section 2.6, assume that the range of the observations will equal 4σ.]

    b. Calculate the approximate sample size making the less conservative assumption that the range of the observations is equal to 6σ.

7.50   In each case, find the approximate sample size required to construct a 95% confidence interval for p that has bound $B = .08$.

    a. Assume p is near .2.

    b. Assume you have no prior knowledge about p, but you wish to be certain that your sample is large enough to achieve the specified accuracy for the estimate.

7.51 The following is a 90% confidence interval for p: (.26, .54). How large was the sample used to construct this interval?

7.52 It costs you $10 to draw a sample of size $n = 1$ and measure the attribute of interest. You have a budget of $1,500.

    a. Do you have sufficient funds to estimate the population mean for the attribute of interest with a 95% confidence interval 5 units in width? Assume $\sigma = 14$.

    b. If you used a 90% confidence level, would your answer to part **a** change? Explain.

7.53 Suppose you wish to estimate the mean of a normal population using a 95% confidence interval, and you know from prior information that $\sigma^2 \approx 1$.

    a. To see the effect of the sample size on the width of the confidence interval, calculate the width of the confidence interval for $n = 16, 25, 49, 100,$ and 400.

    b. Plot the width as a function of sample size n on graph paper. Connect the points by a smooth curve and note how the width decreases as n increases.

Applying the Concepts

7.54 The 1994 salary survey of quality professionals described in Exercise 7.14 generated responses from 1,142 quality managers. The lowest salary reported by a manager was $18,500; the highest was $167,000 ("1994 Salary Survey," *Quality Progress*, Nov. 1994).

    a. Plans are being made to repeat the survey this year. Use the above information to determine how large a sample would need to be drawn to estimate the mean income of managers to within $5,000 with 95% confidence.

    b. In the 1994 survey, the standard deviation of managers' salaries was $17,910. Use this information and recalculate the sample size asked for in part **a**.

    c. Compare your answers to parts **a** and **b**. Which sample size would you use to estimate this year's mean salary? Justify your answer.

7.55 As businesses around the world rush to cash in on the popularity of the World Wide Web (WWW), questions have arisen as to what WWW services users would be willing to pay for. In 1995, Georgia Institute of Technology's Graphics Visualization and Usability Center surveyed 13,000 WWW users and asked them about their willingness to pay fees for access to web sites. Of these, 2,938 were definitely not willing to pay such fees (*Inc. Technology*, No. 3, 1995).

    a. Assume the 13,000 users were randomly selected. Construct a 95% confidence interval for the proportion definitely unwilling to pay fees.

    b. What is the width of the interval you constructed in part **a**? For most applications, this width is unnecessarily narrow. What does that suggest about the survey's sample size?

    c. How large a sample size is necessary to estimate the proportion of interest to within 2% with 95% confidence?

7.56 Although corporate executives are probably not as highly stressed as air-traffic controllers or inner-city police, research has indicated that they are among the more highly pressured work groups. In order to estimate p, the proportion of managers who perceive themselves to be frequently under stress, one study sampled 532 managers in western Australian corporations (*Harvard Business Review*, Jan.–Feb. 1986). One hundred ninety of these managers fell into the high-stress group. Assume that random sampling was used in this study. Was the sample size large enough to estimate p to within .03 with 95% confidence? Explain.

7.57 A large food-products company receives about 100,000 phone calls a year from consumers on its toll-free number. A computer monitors and records how many rings it takes for an operator to answer, how much time each caller spends "on hold," and other data. However, the reliability of the monitoring system has been called into question by the operators and their labor union. As a check on the computer system, approximately how many calls should be manually monitored during the next year to estimate the true mean time that callers spend on hold to within 3 seconds with 95% confidence? Answer this question for the following values of the standard deviation of waiting times (in seconds): 10, 20, and 30.

7.58 According to estimates made by the General Accounting Office, the Internal Revenue Service (IRS) answered 18.3 million telephone inquiries during a recent tax season, and 17% of the IRS offices provided answers that were wrong. These estimates were based on data collected from sample calls to numerous IRS offices. How many IRS offices should be randomly selected and contacted in order to estimate the proportion of IRS offices that fail to correctly answer questions about gift taxes with a 90% confidence interval of width .06?

7.59 Refer to Exercise 7.17, in which workers' level of job satisfaction was related to age. Suppose that we want to estimate the mean job-level satisfaction for younger workers (age 18–24) to within .04 with 95% confidence. How large a sample should be selected? Recall that the standard deviation for this age group was .75.

7.60 In a survey conducted for *Money* magazine by the ICR Survey Research Group, 26% of parents with college-bound high school children reported not having saved any money for college. The poll had a "… margin of error of plus or minus 4 percentage points" (*Newark Star-Ledger,* Aug. 16, 1996).

a. Assume that random sampling was used in conducting the survey and that the researchers wanted to have 95% confidence in their results. Estimate the sample size used in the survey.

b. Repeat part **a**, but this time assume the researchers wanted to be 99% confident.

7.61 The United States Golf Association (USGA) tests all new brands of golf balls to ensure that they meet USGA specifications. One test conducted is intended to measure the average distance traveled when the ball is hit by a machine called "Iron Byron," a name inspired by the swing of the famous golfer Byron Nelson. Suppose the USGA wishes to estimate the mean distance for a new brand to within 1 yard with 90% confidence. Assume that past tests have indicated that the standard deviation of the distances Iron Byron hits golf balls is approximately 10 yards. How many golf balls should be hit by Iron Byron to achieve the desired accuracy in estimating the mean?

7.62 It costs more to produce defective items—since they must be scrapped or reworked—than it does to produce nondefective items. This simple fact suggests that manufacturers should ensure the quality of their products by perfecting their production processes rather than through inspection of finished products (Deming, 1986). In order to better understand a particular metal-stamping process, a manufacturer wishes to estimate the mean length of items produced by the process during the past 24 hours.

a. How many parts should be sampled in order to estimate the population mean to within .1 millimeter (mm) with 90% confidence? Previous studies of this machine have indicated that the standard deviation of lengths produced by the stamping operation is about 2 mm.

b. Time permits the use of a sample size no larger than 100. If a 90% confidence interval for μ is constructed using $n = 100$, will it be wider or narrower than would have been obtained using the sample size determined in part **a**? Explain.

c. If management requires that μ be estimated to within .1 mm and that a sample size of no more than 100 be used, what is (approximately) the maximum confidence level that could be attained for a confidence interval that meets management's specifications?

7.63 Refer to the *International Journal of Sports Psychology* study, Exercise 7.41, where a sample of 95 workers in good physical condition was used to estimate the proportion of all workers in good condition who showed signs of stress. Recall that the point estimate of the proportion was .108. How many workers from this category must be sampled to estimate the true proportion who are stressed to within .01 with 95% confidence?

7.5 FINITE POPULATION CORRECTION FOR SIMPLE RANDOM SAMPLING (OPTIONAL)

The large-sample confidence intervals for a population mean μ and a population proportion p presented in the previous sections are based on a simple random sample selected from the target population. Although we did not state it, the procedure also assumes that the number N of measurements (i.e., sampling units) in the population is large relative to the sample size n.

In some sampling situations, the sample size n may represent 5% or perhaps 10% of the total number N of sampling units in the population. When the sample size is large relative to the number of measurements in the population (see the next box), the standard errors of the estimators of μ and p given in Sections 7.1 and 7.3, respectively, should be multiplied by a **finite population correction factor**.

The form of the finite population correction factor depends on how the population variance σ^2 is defined. In order to simplify the formulas of the standard errors, it is common to define σ^2 as division of the sum of squares of deviations by $N - 1$ rather than by N (analogous to the way we defined the sample variance). If we adopt this convention, the finite population correction factor becomes $\sqrt{(N - n)/N}$. Then the estimated standard errors of $\bar{x}$ (the estimator of μ) and $\hat{p}$ (the estimator of p) are as shown in the box.*

---

*For most surveys and opinion polls, the finite population correction factor is approximately equal to 1 and, if desired, can be safely ignored. However, if $n/N > .05$, the finite population correction factor should be included in the calculation of the standard error.

Rule of Thumb for Finite Population Correction Factor
Use the finite population correction factor (shown in the next box) when $n/N > .05$.

Simple Random Sampling with Finite Population of Size N
Estimation of the Population Mean
Estimated standard error:

$$\hat{\sigma}_{\bar{x}} = \frac{s}{\sqrt{n}}\sqrt{\frac{N-n}{N}}$$

Approximate 95% confidence interval: $\bar{x} \pm 2\hat{\sigma}_{\bar{x}}$

Estimation of the Population Proportion
Estimated standard error:

$$\hat{\sigma}_{\hat{p}} = \sqrt{\frac{\hat{p}(1-\hat{p})}{n}}\sqrt{\frac{N-n}{N}}$$

Approximate 95% confidence interval: $\hat{p} \pm 2\hat{\sigma}_{\hat{p}}$

EXAMPLE 7.7

A specialty manufacturer wants to purchase remnants of sheet aluminum foil. The foil, all of which is the same thickness, is stored on 1,462 rolls, each containing a varying amount of foil. To obtain an estimate of the total number of square feet of foil on all the rolls, the manufacturer randomly sampled 100 rolls and measured the number of square feet on each roll. The sample mean was 47.4, and the sample standard deviation was 12.4.

   a. Find an approximate 95% confidence interval for the mean amount of foil on the 1,462 rolls.

   b. Estimate the total number of square feet of foil on all the rolls by multiplying the confidence interval, part **a**, by 1,462. Interpret the result.

SOLUTION

   a. Each roll of foil is a sampling unit, and there are $N = 1,462$ units in the population, and the sample size is $n = 100$. Since $n/N = 100/1,462 = .068$ exceeds .05, we need to apply the finite population correction. We have $n = 100$, $\bar{x} = 47.4$ and $s = 12.4$. Substituting these quantities, we obtain the approximate 95% confidence interval

$$\bar{x} \pm 2\frac{s}{\sqrt{n}}\sqrt{\frac{(N-n)}{N}} = (47.4) \pm 2\frac{12.4}{\sqrt{100}}\sqrt{\frac{(1,462-100)}{1,462}}$$

$$= 47.4 \pm 2.39$$

or (45.01, 49.79).

   b. For finite populations of size N, the sum of all measurements in the population—called a population total—is

$$\sum_{i=1}^{N} x_i = N\mu$$

Since the confidence interval, part **a**, estimates μ, an estimate of the population total is obtained by multiplying the endpoints of the interval by N. For $N = 1,462$ we have

$$\text{Lower Limit} = N(45.01) = 1{,}462(45.01) = 65{,}804.6$$
$$\text{Upper Limit} = N(49.79) = 1{,}462(49.79) = 72{,}793.0$$

Consequently, the manufacturer estimates the total amount of foil to be in the interval 65,805 square feet to 72,793 square feet with 95% confidence. If the manufacturer wants to adopt a conservative approach, the bid for the foil will be based on the lower confidence limit, 65,805 square feet of foil.

EXERCISES 7.64–7.76

Learning the Mechanics

7.64 Calculate the percentage of the population sampled and the finite population correction factor for each of the following situations.
 a. $n = 1{,}000, N = 2{,}500$ **b.** $n = 1{,}000, N = 5{,}000$
 c. $n = 1{,}000, N = 10{,}000$
 d. $n = 1{,}000, N = 100{,}000$

7.65 Suppose the standard deviation of the population is known to be $\sigma = 200$. Calculate the standard error of $\bar{x}$ for each of the situations described in Exercise 7.64.

7.66 Suppose $N = 5{,}000, n = 64$, and $s = 24$.
 a. Compare the size of the standard error of $\bar{x}$ computed with and without the finite population correction factor.
 b. Repeat part **a**, but this time assume $n = 400$.
 c. Theoretically, when sampling from a finite population, the finite population correction factor should always be used in computing the standard error of $\bar{x}$. However, when n is small relative to N, the finite population correction factor is close to 1 and can safely be ignored. Explain how parts **a** and **b** illustrate this point.

7.67 Suppose $N = 10{,}000, n = 2{,}000$, and $s = 50$.
 a. Compute the standard error of $\bar{x}$ using the finite population correction factor.
 b. Repeat part **a** assuming $n = 4{,}000$.
 c. Repeat part **a** assuming $n = 10{,}000$.
 d. Compare parts **a**, **b**, and **c**, and describe what happens to the standard error of $\bar{x}$ as n increased.
 e. The answer to part **c** is 0. This indicates that there is no sampling error in this case. Explain.

7.68 Suppose you want to estimate a population mean, μ, and $\bar{x} = 422, s = 14, N = 375$, and $n = 40$. Find an approximate 95% confidence interval for μ.

7.69 Suppose you want to estimate a population proportion, p, and $\hat{p} = .42, N = 6{,}000$, and $n = 1{,}600$. Find an approximate 95% confidence interval for p.

7.70 A random sample of size $n = 30$ was drawn from a population of size $N = 3{,}000$. The following measurements were obtained:

21	33	19	29	22	38	58	29	52	36	37	30
53	37	29	18	35	42	36	41	35	36	33	38
29	38	39	54	42	42

 a. Estimate μ with an approximate 95% confidence interval.
 b. Estimate p, the proportion of measurements in the population that are greater than 30, with an approximate 95% confidence interval.

Applying the Concepts

7.71 Organizations hire independent public accountants to perform audit examinations of their financial statements and to judge the fairness with which the statements characterize their financial position. Since the early 1950s, auditors have relied to a great extent on sampling techniques, rather than 100% audits, to help them test and evaluate financial records. For example, sampling is frequently used to obtain an estimate of the total dollar value of an account—the account balance. The estimate can be used to check the account balance reported in the organization's financial statements. Such an examination of an account balance is known as a *substantive test* (Arkin, *Sampling Methods for the Auditor,* 1982). In order to evaluate the reasonableness of a firm's stated total value of its parts inventory, an auditor randomly samples 100 of the total of 5,000 parts in stock, prices each part, and reports the results shown in the accompanying table. Descriptive statistics for the data follow in the SPSS printout on page 304.

Part Number	Part Price	Sample Size
002	$ 108	3
101	55	2
832	500	1
077	73	10
688	300	1
910	54	4
839	92	6
121	833	5
271	50	9
399	125	12
761	1,000	2
093	62	8
505	205	7
597	88	11
830	100	19

```
Number of Valid Observations (Listwise) =      100.00

Variable        Mean      Std Dev   Minimum    Maximum      N Label

PARTPRIC       156.46     209.10     50.00     1000.00     100
```

a. Give a point estimate of the mean value of the parts inventory.

b. Find the estimated standard error of the point estimate of part **a**.

c. Construct an approximate 95% confidence interval for the mean value of the parts inventory.

d. The firm reported a mean parts inventory value of $300. What does your confidence interval of part **c** suggest about the reasonableness of the firm's reported figure? Explain.

7.72 The U.S. Environmental Protection Agency (EPA) bans use of the cancer-causing pesticide ethylene dibromide (EDB) as a fumigant for grain- and flour-milling equipment. EDB was once used to protect against infestation by microscopic roundworms called nematodes. The EPA sets maximum safe levels for EDB presence in raw grain, flour, cake mixes, cereals, bread, and other grain products on supermarket shelves and in warehouses. Of the 3,000 corn-related products sold in one state, tests indicated that 15 of a random sample of 175 had EDB residues above the safe level.

a. In the context of the problem, describe the population parameter p for which $\hat{p} = 15/175$ is a point estimate.

b. Calculate the standard error of $\hat{p}$.

c. Construct an approximate 95% confidence interval for p.

d. Will more than 7% of the corn-related products in this state have to be removed from shelves and warehouses? Explain.

7.73 Refer to the study of invoice errors in a company's new billing system, Exercise 7.13. Recall that an auditor randomly sampled 35 invoices produced by the new system and recorded actual amount (A), invoice amount (I), and the difference (or error), $x = (A - I)$. The results were $\bar{x} = \$1$ and $s = \$124$. At the time that the sample was drawn, the new system had produced 1,500 invoic-

es. Use this information to find an approximate 95% confidence interval for the true mean error per invoice of the new system. Interpret the result.

7.74 Refer to the *Quality Progress* (Nov. 1994) study of subscribers' salaries, Exercise 7.14. The 284 vice presidents sampled had a mean salary of $93,247 and a standard deviation of $33,740. Suppose the goal of the study is to estimate the true mean salary of all vice presidents who subscribe to *Quality Progress*.

a. If 2,193 vice presidents subscribe to *Quality Progress*, estimate the mean with an approximate 95% confidence interval. Interpret the result.

b. Compare the interval, part **a**, to the result obtained in Exercise 7.14c.

7.75 Refer to the New Jersey *Governor's Council for a Drug Free Workplace Report* (Spring/Summer 1995), Exercise 7.39. Recall that 50 of the 72 businesses that are members of the council admitted that they had employees with substance abuse problems. At the time of the survey, 251 New Jersey businesses were members of the Governor's Council. Based on this information, find a 95% confidence interval for the proportion of all New Jersey Governor's Council business members that have employees with substance abuse problems. Interpret the resulting interval.

7.76 A sample survey is undertaken to determine the proportion of voters in a county who favor a proposal to create urban enterprise zones that would seek to attract new business and job opportunities in declining areas of the county's cities. A random sample of 1,000 voters is selected from 50,840 eligible voters in the county. Of the 1,000 voters, 620 said they would favor the proposal. Use the techniques outlined in this section to find an approximate 95% confidence interval for the true proportion of the county's voters who favor the creation of urban enterprise zones.

7.6 SAMPLE SURVEY DESIGNS (OPTIONAL)

The confidence interval methodology developed in Sections 7.1–7.4 is based on simple random sampling (Chapter 3). A (simple) random sample is just one of several different sampling designs used in *sample surveys*.

The term **sample survey** is used in conjunction with the sampling of populations, i.e., collections of people, households, businesses, etc. A consumer preference poll is an example of a sample survey. Samplings conducted to estimate the general level of business inventories or to estimate the proportion of households that watched a particular television program are also examples of sample surveys.

Sample surveys cost time and money, and sometimes they are almost impossible to conduct. For example, suppose we want to obtain an estimate of the proportion of households in the United States that plan to purchase new television sets next year, and we plan to base our estimate on the intentions of a random sample of 3,000 households. What are the problems associated with collecting these data? In order to use a random number generator (Chapter 3) to select the sample, we would need a list of all the households in the United States. Obtaining such a list would be a monumental obstacle. After we obtain a list of households, we need to contact each of the 3,000 selected for the sample. Will all be at home when the surveyor reaches the household? And will all answer the surveyor's question? You can see that collecting a random sample is easier said than done.

The large body of knowledge underlying **survey sampling** or **sample survey design** was developed to help solve some of the problems we have noted. It includes sample survey designs that help reduce the cost and time involved in conducting a sample survey, and it includes the confidence interval procedures associated with those designs. Since survey sampling is a course in itself, we will present only a few of the most widely used sample survey designs and address only a few of the problems you might encounter in this optional section. Further information on this important subject can be found in the references at the end of the text.

One of the most common sampling designs (besides random sampling) is called *stratified random sampling*. **Stratified random sampling** is used when the sampling units (i.e., the units that are sampled) associated with the population can be physically separated into two or more groups of sampling units (called **strata**) where the within-stratum response variation is less than the variation within the entire population. For example, suppose we want to estimate the average amount of rent paid for a two-bedroom apartment in New York City. Since the variation in rent paid within New York City is likely to be large, we may want to divide the city into regions (strata) where the rents within each stratum are relatively homogeneous. Then we would estimate the population mean by selecting random samples from within each stratum and combining the stratum estimates.

Stratified random sampling often produces estimators with smaller standard errors than those achieved using simple random sampling. Furthermore, by sampling from each stratum we are more likely to obtain a sample representative of the entire population. In addition, the administrative and labor costs of selecting the stratum samples are often less than those for simple random sampling.

Sometimes it is difficult or too costly to select random samples. For example, it would be easier to obtain a sample of student opinions at a large university by systematically selecting every hundredth name from the student directory. This type of sample design is called a **systematic sample**. Although systematic samples are usually easier to select than other types of samples, one difficulty is the possibility of a systematic sampling bias. For example, if every fifth item in an assembly line is selected for quality control inspection, and if five different machines are sequentially producing the items, all the items sampled may have been manufactured by the same machine. If we use systematic sampling we must be certain that no cycles (like every fifth item manufactured by the same machine) exist in the list of the sampling units.

A third alternative to the simple random sampling design is *randomized response sampling*. **Randomized response sampling** is particularly useful when the questions of the pollsters are likely to elicit false answers. For example, suppose each person in a sample of wage earners is asked whether he or she cheated on an income tax return. A person who has not cheated most likely would give an honest answer to this question. A cheater might lie, thus biasing an estimate of what proportion of persons cheats on their income tax return.

One method of coping with the false responses produced by sensitive questions is randomized response sampling. Each person is presented *two* questions; one question is the object of the survey and the other is an innocuous question to which the interviewee will give an honest answer. For example, each person might be asked these two questions:

1. Did you cheat on your income tax return?
2. Did you drink coffee this morning?

Then a procedure is used to select randomly which of the two questions the person is to answer. For example, the interviewee might be asked to flip a coin. If the coin shows a head, the interviewee answers the sensitive question, 1. If the coin shows a tail, the interviewee answers the innocuous question, 2. Since the interviewer never has the opportunity to see the coin, the interviewee can answer the question and feel assured that his or her guilt (if guilty) will not be exposed. Consequently, the random response procedure can elicit an honest response to a sensitive question. Sophisticated methodology is then used to derive an estimate of the percentage of "yes" responses to the sensitive question.

As mentioned earlier, in any sample survey design, cost (either in time, manpower, or money) may be an issue. Two methods for reducing the cost of random sampling are to use a telephone survey or a mailed survey. Although this type of sampling eliminates transportation costs and reduces labor costs, it introduces a serious difficulty—the problem of **nonresponse**. By this, we mean that sampling units contained in a sample do not produce sample observations. For example, an individual may not be at home when telephoned or may refuse to complete and mail back a questionnaire.

Nonresponse is a serious problem because it may lead to very biased results. There may be a high correlation between the type of response and whether or not a person responds. For example, most citizens in a community might have an opinion on a school bond issue, but the respondents in a mail survey might very well be those with vested interests in the outcome of the survey—say, parents with children of school age, or school teachers, or those whose taxes might be substantially affected. Others with no vested interests might have opinions on the issue but might not take the time to respond. For this example, the absence of the non-respondents' data could lead to a larger estimate of the percentage in favor of the issue than was actually the case. In other words, the absence of the nonrespondents' data could lead to a biased estimate.

Nonresponse is a very important sampling problem. If your sampling plan calls for a specific collection of sampling units, failure to acquire the responses from those units may violate your sampling plan and lead to biased estimates. If you intend to select a random sample and you cannot obtain the responses from some of the sampling units, then your sampling procedure is *no longer random,* and the methodology based on it (e.g., confidence intervals) and the product of the methodology (e.g., inferences) are suspect.

There are ways for coping with nonresponse. Most involve tracking down and questioning all or part of the nonrespondents and using the additional information to adjust for the missing nonrespondent data. For mailed surveys, however, it has been found that the inclusion of a monetary incentive with the question-naire—even as little as 25¢—will substantially increase the response rate of the survey (Armstrong, 1975).

There are many sampling designs available to a sample surveyor; some are variations on simple random sampling and stratified random sampling, and others are completely different. In addition, different types of estimators can be used with these designs. In this brief introduction to survey sampling, our intent was to present only a few of the most important sample survey designs and some of their inherent problems. Thorough presentations of the different sample survey designs are given in textbooks devoted to this topic (see the references at the end of this text).

STATISTICS IN ACTION

7.3 SAMPLING ERROR VERSUS NONSAMPLING ERROR

In Chapter 6, we learned that the behavior of the sample mean, $\bar{x}$, in repeated sampling can be described by its sampling distribution. We described the difference between a particular value of the estimator, $\bar{x}$, and the true value of the population parameter, μ, as **estimation error**. This difference is also known as **sampling error**. It is not error in the sense that anyone or anything is at fault or deserves blame; it is simply due to the fact that $\bar{x}$ is computed from a subset of the population rather than from the entire population. The standard error of the sampling distribution of $\bar{x}$ is a measure of the magnitude of the sampling error (estimation error) that may be present in the results of a survey that has been conducted to estimate μ. Accordingly, the standard error of $\bar{x}$ is used to place a bound on the sampling error associated with $\bar{x}$. As we saw in Section 7.4, this bound can be tightened simply by increasing the sample size of the survey.

Unfortunately, the other types of errors that plague surveys—known as **nonsampling errors**—are not so easily measured or controlled. Nonsampling errors are any phenomena other than sampling errors that cause a difference between an estimate and the true value of the population parameter. Nonsampling errors can be classified into two groups: **random errors**, whose effects approximately cancel out if large samples are used, and **biases** that tend to create errors in the same direction and thus do not cancel out over the entire sample.

Biases can arise from any aspect of the survey operation. Some of the main contributing causes are out-lined in an American Statistical Association brochure titled "What are the Main Sources of Survey Error?" (1995). These include:

1. *Sampling operations* Mistakes are made in drawing the sample or part of the population is omitted from the list of all sampling units.

2. *Noninterviews* Information is obtained for only part of the sample due to, for example, "not-at-homes" or nonresponse to mail questionnaires. This causes a problem because, typically, there are differences between the noninterviewed part of the sample and the part that is interviewed. (See Section 7.6.)

3. *Adequacy of respondent* Sometimes respondents cannot be interviewed, so information is obtained about them from others; the proxy respondent is not always as knowledgeable about the facts.

4. *Understanding the concepts* Some respondents do not understand what is wanted.

5. *Lack of knowledge* Respondents do not always know the information requested or do not try to obtain the correct information.

6. *Concealment of the truth* Out of fear or suspicion, respondents conceal the truth. This concealment may reflect a desire to answer in a way that is socially acceptable, such as claiming to follow an energy conservation program when this is not actually so.

7. *Loaded questions* The question as worded influences the respondents to answer in a specific (not necessarily correct) way.

continued

8. *Processing errors* These include coding errors, data keying, computer programming errors, etc.

9. *Conceptual problems* What is desired may differ from what the survey actually covers. For example, the population or the time period may not be the one for which information is needed, but may have to be used to meet a deadline.

10. *Interviewer errors* Interviewers who misread the question or recast the answers in their own words thereby introduce bias.

Although not every survey will be subject to all these biases, a good survey statistician is aware of them and will attempt to control as many as possible. For example, the U.S. Bureau of the Census conducts its *Current Population Survey* to provide information on the social and economic health of our society. Each month approximately 1,500 interviewers visit or telephone about 60,000 households in the United States and question the occupants over 14 years of age about such matters as income, employment status, etc. Many safeguards have been built into the survey process to protect against biases due to interviewer errors (Taeuber, 1978):

1. The survey's 1,500 interviewers are continuously trained and retrained.

2. Each interviewer's work is reviewed each month.

3. Periodically, interviewers are accompanied by supervisory personnel.

4. Approximately twice each year, a sample of the addresses assigned to an interviewer is reinterviewed by a supervisor. The interviewers have no way of knowing when their work will be checked or which addresses will be reinterviewed.

These precautions not only protect against interviewer error but also provide a measure of quality of the *Current Population Survey*.

Focus

Below are two polls, one recent and one conducted 60 years ago, that were very likely to have been plagued by nonsampling error. Identify the source of this error and suggest an alternative sampling method to reduce the bias.

a. In 1936, the *Literary Digest,* a popular magazine, mailed 10 million questionnaires to voters in the United States. The questionnaire asked which presidential candidate was preferred, the Democratic incumbent, F. D. Roosevelt, or the Republican governor of Kansas, Alfred Landon. The *Digest* had previously predicted the winner of the presidency in every election since 1916. Prior to receiving the responses to its questionnaire, the *Digest* boasted, "When the last figure has been totted and checked, if past experience is a criterion, the country will know to within a fraction of 1% the actual popular vote of forty million" (Aug. 22, 1936). The *Digest* received 2.4 million responses—a sample size approximately 800 times larger than is currently used by the Gallup poll. The sample results indicated Landon would win by a landslide: Landon 57% and FDR 43%. Unfortunately for Landon and the *Literary Digest,* the actual election results yielded a landslide for FDR: FDR 62% and Landon 38%. [*Notes:* (1) The *Literary Digest* obtained its list of voters to sample from sources such as telephone directories, club membership lists, magazine subscriptions, and car registrations. (2) The country was split politically along economic lines in 1936—Republicans were generally wealthier than Democrats. (3) The *Literary Digest* relied on *voluntary response* to its poll.]

b. It has become popular for television networks to conduct surveys of their viewers by telephone. The TV network typically provides two or more "900" telephone numbers (each corresponding to a different opinion) which the viewer can dial at a cost of 50¢ per call. Several times in 1995, the cable news network CNN provided "900" phone numbers for viewers of its popular "Larry King Live" talk show to voice their opinion on the guilt or innocence of O. J. Simpson, the former NFL star, TV sportscaster, and actor accused of murder. [The results indicated a strong racial divide on the issue—most African Americans who responded believed Simpson to be innocent while most whites who responded believed he was guilty.]

QUICK REVIEW

Key Terms

Note: Starred (*) terms are from the optional sections in this chapter.

Bound on the error of estimation   295
Confidence coefficient   272
Confidence interval   272
Confidence level   272
Degrees of freedom   279

Finite population correction factor*   301
Interval estimator   272
Nonresponse*   306
Randomized response sampling*   305

Sample survey design*   305
Strata*   305
Stratified random sampling*   305
Survey sampling*   305
Systematic sampling*   305
t statistic   279

Key Formulas

$\hat{\theta} \pm (z_{\alpha/2})\sigma_{\hat{\theta}}$ Large-sample confidence interval for population parameter θ where $\hat{\theta}$ and $\sigma_{\hat{\theta}}$ are obtained from the table below

Parameter θ	Estimator $\hat{\theta}$	Standard Error $\sigma_{\hat{\theta}}$	
Mean, μ	$\bar{x}$	$\dfrac{\sigma}{\sqrt{n}}$	273
Proportion, p	$\hat{p}$	$\sqrt{\dfrac{pq}{n}}$	290

$\bar{x} \pm t_{\alpha/2}\left(\dfrac{s}{\sqrt{n}}\right)$ Small-sample confidence interval for population mean μ 282

$n = \dfrac{(z_{\alpha/2})^2 \sigma^2}{B^2}$ Determining the sample size n for estimating μ 296

$n = \dfrac{(z_{\alpha/2})^2 (pq)}{B^2}$ Determining the sample size n for estimating p 298

$n/N \geqslant .05$ Rule of thumb for using finite population correction factor*   302

$\hat{\sigma}_{\bar{x}} = \dfrac{s}{\sqrt{n}}\sqrt{\dfrac{N-n}{n}}$ Finite population correction for estimating μ*   302

$\hat{\sigma}_{\hat{p}} = \sqrt{\dfrac{\hat{p}\hat{q}}{n}}\sqrt{\dfrac{N-n}{n}}$ Finite population correction for estimating p*   302

LANGUAGE LAB

Note: Starred (*) symbols are from the optional sections in this chapter.

Symbol	Pronunciation	Description
θ	theta	General population parameter
μ	mu	Population mean
p		Population proportion
B		Bound on error of estimation
α	alpha	$(1 - \alpha)$ represents the confidence coefficient
$z_{\alpha/2}$	z of alpha over 2	z value used in a $100(1 - \alpha)\%$ large-sample confidence interval
$t_{\alpha/2}$	t of alpha over 2	t value used in a $100(1 - \alpha)\%$ small-sample confidence interval
$\bar{x}$	x-bar	Sample mean; point estimate of μ
$\hat{p}$	p-hat	Sample proportion; point estimate of p
σ	sigma	Population standard deviation
s		Sample standard deviation; point estimate of σ
$\sigma_{\bar{x}}$	sigma of $\bar{x}$	Standard deviation of sampling distribution of $\bar{x}$
$\sigma_{\hat{p}}$	sigma of $\hat{p}$	Standard deviation of sampling distribution of $\hat{p}$
N*		Total number of measurements in the target population

SUPPLEMENTARY EXERCISES 7.77–7.101

Note: List the assumptions necessary for the valid implementation of the statistical procedures you use in solving all these exercises. Exercises marked with 💾 *contain data available for computer analysis on a 3.5" disk (file name in parentheses). Starred (*) exercises are from the optional sections in this chapter.*

Learning the Mechanics

7.77 Let t_0 represent a particular value of t from Table VI of Appendix B. Find the table values such that the following statements are true.
   a. $P(t \leq t_0) = .05$ where df = 20
   b. $P(t \geq t_0) = .005$ where df = 9
   c. $P(t \leq -t_0$ or $t \geq t_0) = .10$ where df = 8
   d. $P(t \leq -t_0$ or $t \geq t_0) = .01$ where df = 17

7.78 In each of the following instances, determine whether you would use a z or t statistic (or neither) to form a 95% confidence interval, and then look up the appropriate z or t value.
   a. Random sample of size $n = 23$ from a normal distribution with unknown mean μ and standard deviation σ
   b. Random sample of size $n = 135$ from a normal distribution with unknown mean μ and standard deviation σ
   c. Random sample of size $n = 10$ from a normal distribution with unknown mean μ and standard deviation $\sigma = 5$
   d. Random sample of size $n = 73$ from a distribution about which nothing is known
   e. Random sample of size $n = 12$ from a distribution about which nothing is known

7.79 A random sample of 225 measurements is selected from a population, and the sample mean and standard deviation are $\bar{x} = 32.5$ and $s = 30.0$, respectively.
   a. Use a 99% confidence interval to estimate the mean of the population, μ.
   b. How large a sample would be needed to estimate μ to within .5 with 99% confidence?
   c. What is meant by the phrase "99% confidence" as it is used in this exercise?

7.80 In a random sample of 400 measurements, 227 of the measurements possess the characteristic of interest, A.
   a. Use a 95% confidence interval to estimate the true proportion p of measurements in the population with characteristic A.
   b. How large a sample would be needed to estimate p to within .02 with 95% confidence?

*7.81 Calculate the finite population correction factor for each of the following situations:
   a. $n = 50, N = 2{,}000$ **b.** $n = 20, N = 100$
   c. $n = 300, N = 1{,}500$

Applying the Concepts

7.82 A large New York City bank is interested in estimating (1) the proportion of weeks in which it processes more than 100,000 checks and (2) the average number of checks it processes per week. The bank maintains records of x, the number of checks processed each week. Suppose the bank records the number of checks, x, processed per week for 50 weeks randomly sampled from among the past 6 years. Define each of the following *in the context of the problem.*
   a. $\bar{x}$ **b.** $\hat{p}$ **c.** $\mu_{\bar{x}}$ **d.** n **e.** $\sigma_{\bar{x}}$ **f.** p **g.** s_x

7.83 (X07.083) As part of a study of residential property values in Cedar Grove, New Jersey, the county tax assessor sampled 20 single-family homes that sold during the first half of 1996 and recorded their sales prices (in thousands of dollars; see table below). A stem-and-leaf display and descriptive statistics for these data are shown in the MINITAB printout on page 311.
   a. On the MINITAB printout, locate a 95% confidence interval for the mean sale price of all single-family homes in Cedar Grove, New Jersey.
   b. Give a practical interpretation of the interval, part **a**.
   c. What is meant by the phrase "95% confidence" as it is used in this exercise?
   d. Comment on the validity of any assumptions required to properly apply the estimation procedure.

7.84 The Centers for Disease Control and Prevention (CDCP) in Atlanta, Georgia, conducts an annual survey of the general health of the U.S. population as part of its Behavioral Risk Factor Surveillance System (*New York Times,* Mar. 29, 1995). Using random-digit dialing, the CDCP telephones U.S. citizens over 18 years of age and asks them the following four questions:

   (1) Is your health generally excellent, very good, good, fair, or poor?
   (2) How many days during the previous 30 days was your physical health not good because of injury or illness?

189.9	235.0	159.0	190.9	239.0	559.0	875.0	635.0
265.0	330.0	669.0	935.0	210.0	179.9	334.9	219.0
1,190.0	739.0	424.7	229.0				

Source: Multiple Listing Service of Suburban Essex County, May 17, 1996.

```
Stem-and-leaf of SalePric   N = 20
Leaf Unit = 10
     4     1  5789
    10     2  112336
    10     3  33
     8     4  2
     7     5  5
     6     6  36
     4     7  3
     3     8  7
     2     9  3
     1    10
     1    11  9
```

```
                N      MEAN    STDEV   SE MEAN    95.0 PERCENT C.I.
SalePric       20     440.4    303.0     67.8    (   298.6,    582.3)
```

(3) How many days during the previous 30 days was your mental health not good because of stress, depression, or emotional problems?

(4) How many days during the previous 30 days did your physical or mental health prevent you from performing your usual activities?

Identify the parameter of interest for each question.

7.85 Refer to Exercise 7.84. According to the CDCP, 89,582 of 102,263 adults interviewed stated their health was good, very good, or excellent.

a. Use a 99% confidence interval to estimate the true proportion of U.S. adults who believe their health to be good to excellent. Interpret the interval.

b. Why might the estimate, part **a**, be overly optimistic (i.e., biased high)?

7.86 A firm's president, vice presidents, department managers, and others use financial data generated by the firm's accounting system to help them make decisions regarding such things as pricing, budgeting, and plant expansion. To provide reasonable certainty that the system provides reliable data, internal auditors periodically perform various checks of the system (Horngren, Foster, and Datar, *Cost Accounting: A Managerial Emphasis*, 1994). Suppose an internal auditor is interested in determining the proportion of sales invoices in a population of 5,000 sales invoices for which the "total sales" figure is in error. She plans to estimate the true proportion of invoices in error based on a random sample of size 100.

a. Assume that the population of invoices is numbered from 1 to 5,000 and that every invoice ending with a 0 is in error (i.e., 10% are in error). Use a random number generator to draw a random sample of 100 invoices from the population of 5,000 invoices. For example,

random number 456 stands for invoice number 456. List the invoice numbers in your sample and indicate which of your sampled invoices are in error (i.e., those ending in a 0).

b. Use the results of your sample of part **a** to construct a 90% confidence interval for the true proportion of invoices in error.

c. Recall that the true population proportion of invoices in error is equal to .1. Compare the true proportion with the estimate of the true proportion you developed in part **b**. Does your confidence interval include the true proportion?

7.87 Research reported in the *Professional Geographer* (May 1992) investigates the hypothesis that the disproportionate housework responsibility of women in two-income households is a major factor in determining the proximity of a woman's place of employment. The researcher studied the distance (in miles) to work for both men and women in two-income households. Random samples of men and women yielded the following results:

	CENTRAL CITY RESIDENCE		SUBURBAN RESIDENCE	
	Men	Women	Men	Women
Sample Size	159	119	138	93
Mean	7.4	4.5	9.3	6.6
Std. Deviation	6.3	4.2	7.1	5.6

a. For central city residences, calculate a 95% confidence interval for the average distance to work for men and women in two-income households. Interpret the intervals.

b. Repeat part **a** for suburban residences.

[*Note:* We will show how to use statistical techniques to compare two population means in Chapter 9.]

7.88 Refer to the *Journal of the American Medical Association* (Apr. 21, 1993) report on the prevalence of cigarette smoking among U.S. adults, Exercise 7.10. Of the 43,732 survey respondents, 11,239 indicated that they were current smokers and 10,539 indicated they were former smokers.

a. Construct and interpret a 90% confidence interval for the percentage of U.S. adults who currently smoke cigarettes.

b. Construct and interpret a 90% confidence interval for the percentage of U.S. adults who are former cigarette smokers.

7.89 A company is interested in estimating μ, the mean number of days of sick leave taken by all its employees. The firm's statistician selects at random 100 personnel files and notes the number of sick days taken by each employee. The following sample statistics are computed: $\bar{x} = 12.2$ days, $s = 10$ days.

a. Estimate μ using a 90% confidence interval.

b. How many personnel files would the statistician have to select in order to estimate μ to within 2 days with a 99% confidence interval?

7.90 In the United States, people over age 50 represent 25% of the population, yet they control 70% of the wealth. Research indicates the highest priority of retirees is travel. A study in the *Annals of Tourism Research* (Vol. 19, 1992) investigates the relationship of retirement status (pre- and post-retirement) to various items of interest to the travel industry. As one part of the study, a sample of 323 retirees was selected, and the number of nights each typically stayed away from home on trips was determined. One hundred seventy-two (172) responded that their typical stays ranged from 4 to 7 nights. Use a 90% confidence interval to estimate the true proportion of postretirement travelers who stay between 4 and 7 nights on a typical trip. Interpret the interval.

7.91 The primary determinant of the amount of vacation time U.S. employees receive is their length of service. According to data released by Hewitt Associates (*Management Review,* Nov. 1995), more than 8 of 10 employers provide two weeks of vacation after the first year. After five years, 75% of employers provide three weeks and after 15 years most provide four-week vacations. To more accurately estimate p, the proportion of U.S. employers who provide only two weeks of vacation to new hires, a random sample of 24 major U.S. companies was contacted. The following vacation times were reported (in days):

10	12	10	10	10	10
15	10	10	10	10	10
10	10	10	10	10	15
10	10	15	10	10	10

a. Is the sample size large enough to ensure that the normal distribution provides a reasonable approximation to the sampling distribution of $\hat{p}$? Justify your answer.

b. How large a sample would be required to estimate p to within .02 with 95% confidence?

7.92 (X07.092) One of the most important ways to measure the performance of a business is to evaluate how well it has treated its stockholders. After all, it is the stockholders who provided the capital to launch and/or expand the business; it is the stockholders who own the business. This can be done by examining the rate of return received by stockholders. To evaluate the performance of U.S. corporations in 1995 and over the five-year period 1991–1995, a random sample of 15 corporations was drawn from the 1,000 major U.S. corporations listed in *The Wall Street Journal's* Shareholder Scoreboard (Feb. 29, 1996):

Corporation	Stockholder's Return: 1995	Stockholder's Return: 1991–1995
Andrew	9.8%	51.2%
Bank One	54.4	19.3
Gannett	18.1	14.2
Hasbro	7.5	25.4
Alco Standard	47.5	25.0
Ceridian	53.5	39.9
Teledyne	32.8	15.2
Snap-On	40.0	10.7
Salomon	−4.0	9.7
New York Times	37.0	9.9
Jostens	34.5	−2.2
Ogden	20.7	8.8
UAL	104.3	17.7
Merck	76.4	20.1
Liz Claiborne	65.4	−0.1

a. Find point estimates for the mean rate of return of the 1,000 companies in 1995 and over the period 1991–1995.

b. Construct 90% confidence intervals for the two parameters described in part **a** and list any assumptions that are needed to ensure the validity of the confidence intervals.

c. Interpret the confidence intervals in the context of the problem.

d. Which method of estimation is better, point estimation or interval estimation? Justify your answer.

*e. Since a finite number of major corporations (1,000) are listed in the Shareholder Scoreboard, a finite population correction factor should be applied to the confidence interval, part **b**. Explain why the finite population correction will yield, for all practical purposes, an identical result.

10	0	5	18	0	5	22	0	50	60	35	0	0
18	35	0	40	10	50	20	150	15	0	0	30	15
0	20	15	10									

7.93 *Management Accounting* (June 1995) reported the results of its sixth annual salary survey of the members of the Institute of Management Accountants (IMA). The 2,112 members responding had a salary distribution with a 20th percentile of $35,100; a median of $50,000; and an 80th percentile of $73,000.

   a. Use this information to determine the minimum sample size that could be used in next year's survey to estimate the mean salary of IMA members to within $2,000 with 98% confidence.

   b. Explain how you estimated the standard deviation required for the sample size calculation.

   c. List any assumptions you make.

7.94 For decades, U.S. companies have tied a portion of the compensation of many upper-management employees to the performance of the firm. In the last few years, however, a growing number of companies have begun offering similar performance incentives to all of their employees. What instigated this change in pay structures? Of 46 companies (surveyed by the American Compensation Association) that had modified their traditional pay structures, 26 reported making the modification in response to profound market changes in the last decade: global competition, consumer demand for high-quality goods and services, etc. They needed new ways to improve performance and cut costs (*Minneapolis Star Tribune,* June 29, 1992). For the population of U.S. firms that have switched to nontraditional pay structures, estimate the proportion that have done so in response to market forces (rather than to growth, downsizing, or some other reason). Use a 90% confidence interval and specify whatever assumptions are necessary to ensure the validity of the estimate.

7.95 In 1989, the American Society for Quality Control began publishing a journal called *Quality Engineering.* In 1994, the journal distributed a questionnaire to its 8,521 subscribers. A total of 202 replies were received. To the question "How long have you been a subscriber?" they got the responses shown below:

   a. What assumption(s) would need to be made in order to apply the confidence interval methodology described in this chapter to the problem of estimating the mean subscription length for the population of 8,521 journal subscribers?

   b. Use a 98% confidence interval to estimate the population mean referred to in part **a**.

   ****c.** Describe potential nonsampling errors that may plague this survey.

****7.96** Corporations, labor unions, and trade and medical associations can set up organizations known as political action committees (PACs) to raise money from their members for support of political candidates believed to represent their best interests. Approximately 3,500 PACs currently exist. Federal law limits the amount a PAC can contribute to a presidential candidate to $5,000 per election. However, a loophole in the law permits committees to spend as much as they want to elect or defeat a candidate as long as there is no cooperation or contact with the candidate or the candidate's authorized agents. In early 1996, in order to estimate the amount of money that would be spent in support of Bill Clinton in the 1996 presidential election, a political economist hired by the Republican party randomly sampled 30 PACs and asked them how much they expected to spend in support of Clinton. The results (in thousands of dollars) are shown above. An SPSS analysis of the data is provided on page 314.

   a. Estimate the total amount that PACs expected to spend in support of Clinton in 1996.

   b. Use an approximate 95% confidence interval to estimate the proportion of PACs that planned to support Clinton.

   c. In addition to sampling error, what might cause your estimate for part **a** to be inaccurate?

****7.97** When a poll reports, for example, that 61% of the public supports a program of national health insurance, it usually also reports the sampling error. For example, a poll might report that the estimate is accurate to within plus or minus 3%. An essay in *Time* magazine ("How not to read polls," Apr. 28, 1980) points out:

Readers consistently misinterpret the meaning of this "warning label."... [The sampling error warning] says nothing about errors that might be caused by a sloppily worded question or a biased one or a single question that evokes

Years	1	2	3	4	5	6	7	8	9	10	11	12	No reply
No. of Responses	44	39	27	17	12	38	1	1	0	0	0	1	22

Source: Adapted from "Quality engineering reader survey." *Quality Engineering,* Vol. 7, No. 4, 1995, p. ix.

```
        AMOUNT
Valid cases:        30.0   Missing cases:        .0   Percent Missing:      .0

Mean          21.1000  Std Err     5.4299  Min          .0000  Skewness    3.0392
Median        15.0000  Variance  884.5069  Max       150.0000  S E Skew     .4269
5% Trim       16.7778  Std Dev    29.7407  Range     150.0000  Kurtosis   11.9488
                                           IQR        31.2500  S E Kurt     .8327

Frequency     Stem &  Leaf
   11.00        0  .  00000000055
    8.00        1  .  00055588
    3.00        2  .  002
    3.00        3  .  055
    1.00        4  .  0
    2.00        5  .  00
    1.00        6  .  0
    1.00 Extremes    (150)

Stem width:      10.00
Each leaf:        1 case(s)
```

complex feelings. Example: "Are you satisfied with your job?" Most important of all, warning labels about sampling error say nothing about whether or not the public is conflict-ridden or has given a subject much thought. This is the most serious source of opinion poll misinterpretation.

Carefully explain the difference between sampling error and nonsampling error, both in general and in the context of the above quote.

*7.98 Publishers of a weekly nationwide business magazine believe that a large proportion of their Florida subscribers invest in the stock market. They would like to be able to use this information to persuade brokerage firms in Florida to advertise in their magazine. The publishers send each of the 500,000 subscribers in Florida a questionnaire about stock investments. A total of 10,000 of the questionnaires are returned, and of these, 9,296 subscribers respond that they do currently have stock market investments.

a. Use this information to estimate the proportion of Florida subscribers who invest in the stock market with an approximate 95% confidence interval.

b. Should a brokerage firm in Florida consider the estimate in part a to be reliable? Explain.

7.99 When companies employ control charts to monitor the quality of their products, a series of small samples is typically used to determine if the process is "in control" during the period of time in which each sample is selected. (We cover quality control charts in Chapter 13.) Suppose a concrete-block manufacturer samples nine blocks per hour and tests the breaking strength of each. During one hour's test

the mean and standard deviation are 985.6 pounds per square inch (psi) and 22.9 psi, respectively.

a. Construct a 99% confidence interval for the mean breaking strength of blocks produced during the hour in which the sample was selected.

b. The process is to be considered "out of control" if the mean strength differs from 1,000 psi. What would you conclude based on the confidence interval constructed in part a?

c. Repeat parts a and b using a 90% confidence interval.

d. The manufacturer wants to be reasonably certain that the process is really out of control before shutting down the process and trying to determine the problem. Which interval, the 99% or 90% confidence interval, is more appropriate for making the decision? Explain.

e. Which assumptions are necessary to ensure the validity of the confidence intervals?

7.100 Recently, a case of salmonella (bacterial) poisoning was traced to a particular brand of ice cream bar, and the manufacturer removed the bars from the market. Despite this response, many consumers refused to purchase *any* brand of ice cream bars for some period of time after the event (McClave, personal consulting). One manufacturer conducted a survey of consumers 6 months after the outbreak. A sample of 244 ice cream bar consumers was contacted, and 23 respondents indicated that they would not purchase ice cream bars because of the potential for food poisoning.

a. What is the point estimate of the true fraction of the entire market who refuse to purchase bars 6 months after the outbreak?

b. Is the sample size large enough to use the normal approximation for the sampling distribution of the estimator of the binomial probability? Justify your response.

c. Construct a 95% confidence interval for the true proportion of the market who still refuse to purchase ice cream bars 6 months after the event.

d. Interpret both the point estimate and confidence interval in terms of this application.

7.101 Refer to Exercise 7.100. Suppose it is now 1 year after the outbreak of food poisoning was traced to ice cream bars. The manufacturer wishes to estimate the proportion who still will not purchase bars to within .02 using a 95% confidence interval. How many consumers should be sampled?

CHAPTER 8

INFERENCES BASED ON A SINGLE SAMPLE
Tests of Hypothesis

Where We've Been

We saw how to use sample information to estimate population parameters in Chapter 7. The sampling distribution of a statistic is used to assess the reliability of an estimate, which we express in terms of a confidence interval.

Where We're Going

We'll see how to utilize sample information to test what the value of a population parameter may be. This type of inference is called a *test of hypothesis*. We'll also see how to conduct a test of hypothesis about a population mean μ and a population proportion p. And, just as with estimation, we'll stress the measurement of the reliability of the inference. An inference without a measure of reliability is little more than a guess.

Suppose you wanted to determine whether the mean waiting time in the drive-through line of a fast-food restaurant is less than five minutes, or whether the majority of consumers are optimistic about the economy. In both cases you are interested in making an inference about how the value of a parameter relates to a specific numerical value. Is it less than, equal to, or greater than the specified number? This type of inference, called a **test of hypothesis**, is the subject of this chapter.

We introduce the elements of a test of hypothesis in Section 8.1. We then show how to conduct a large-sample test of hypothesis about a population mean in Sections 8.2 and 8.3. In Section 8.4 we utilize small samples to conduct tests about means. Large-sample tests about binomial probabilities are the subject of Section 8.5, and some advanced methods for determining the reliability of a test are covered in optional Section 8.6.

8.1 THE ELEMENTS OF A TEST OF HYPOTHESIS

Suppose building specifications in a certain city require that the average breaking strength of residential sewer pipe be more than 2,400 pounds per foot of length (i.e., per linear foot). Each manufacturer who wants to sell pipe in this city must demonstrate that its product meets the specification. Note that we are again interested in making an inference about the mean μ of a population. However, in this example we are less interested in estimating the value of μ than we are in testing a *hypothesis* about its value. That is, we want to decide whether the mean breaking strength of the pipe exceeds 2,400 pounds per linear foot.

The method used to reach a decision is based on the rare-event concept explained in earlier chapters. We define two hypotheses: (1) The **null hypothesis** is that which represents the status quo to the party performing the sampling experiment—the hypothesis that will be accepted unless the data provide convincing evidence that it is false. (2) The **alternative**, or **research**, **hypothesis** is that which will be accepted only if the data provide convincing evidence of its truth. From the point of view of the city conducting the tests, the null hypothesis is that the manufacturer's pipe does *not* meet specifications unless the tests provide convincing evidence otherwise. The null and alternative hypotheses are therefore

Null hypothesis (H_0): $\mu \leq 2,400$ (i.e., the manufacturer's pipe does not meet specifications)

Alternative (research) hypothesis (H_a): $\mu > 2,400$ (i.e., the manufacturer's pipe meets specifications)

How can the city decide when enough evidence exists to conclude that the manufacturer's pipe meets specifications? Since the hypotheses concern the value of the population mean μ, it is reasonable to use the sample mean $\bar{x}$ to make the inference, just as we did when forming confidence intervals for μ in Sections 7.1 and 7.2. The city will conclude that the pipe meets specifications only when the sample mean $\bar{x}$ convincingly indicates that the population mean exceeds 2,400 pounds per linear foot.

"Convincing" evidence in favor of the alternative hypothesis will exist when the value of $\bar{x}$ exceeds 2,400 by an amount that cannot be readily attributed to sampling variability. To decide, we compute a **test statistic**, which is the z value that measures the distance between the value of $\bar{x}$ and the value of μ specified in the null hypothesis. When the null hypothesis contains more than one value of μ, as in this case (H_0: $\mu \leq 2,400$), we use the value of μ closest to the values specified in the alternative hypothesis. The idea is that if the hypothesis that μ *equals* 2,400 can

FIGURE 8.1
The sampling
distribution of $\bar{x}$,
assuming $\mu = 2{,}400$

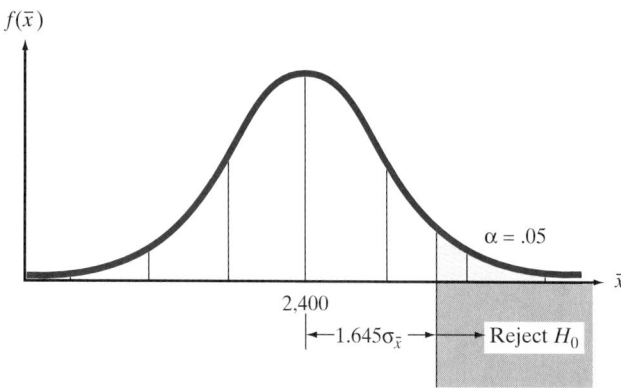

be rejected in favor of $\mu > 2{,}400$, then μ *less than or equal to* 2,400 can certainly be rejected. Thus, the test statistic is

$$z = \frac{\bar{x} - 2{,}400}{\sigma_{\bar{x}}} = \frac{\bar{x} - 2{,}400}{\sigma/\sqrt{n}}$$

Note that a value of $z = 1$ means that $\bar{x}$ is 1 standard deviation above $\mu = 2{,}400$; a value of $z = 1.5$ means that $\bar{x}$ is 1.5 standard deviations above $\mu = 2{,}400$, etc. How large must z be before the city can be convinced that the null hypothesis can be rejected in favor of the alternative and conclude that the pipe meets specifications?

If you examine Figure 8.1, you will note that the chance of observing $\bar{x}$ more than 1.645 standard deviations above 2,400 is only .05—*if in fact the true mean μ is 2,400.* Thus, if the sample mean is more than 1.645 standard deviations above 2,400, either H_0 is true and a relatively rare event has occurred (.05 probability) or H_a is true and the population mean exceeds 2,400. Since we would most likely reject the notion that a rare event has occurred, we would reject the null hypothesis ($\mu \leq 2{,}400$) and conclude that the alternative hypothesis ($\mu > 2{,}400$) is true. What is the probability that this procedure will lead us to an incorrect decision?

Such an incorrect decision—deciding that the null hypothesis is false when in fact it is true—is called a **Type I error**. As indicated in Figure 8.1, the risk of making a Type I error is denoted by the symbol α. That is,

$\alpha = P(\text{Type I error})$

$\qquad = P(\text{Rejecting the null hypothesis when in fact the null hypothesis is true})$

In our example

$$\alpha = P(z > 1.645 \text{ when in fact } \mu = 2{,}400) = .05$$

We now summarize the elements of the test:

$H_0: \mu \leq 2{,}400$

$H_a: \mu > 2{,}400$

Test statistic: $z = \dfrac{\bar{x} - 2{,}400}{\sigma_{\bar{x}}}$

Rejection region: $z > 1.645$, which corresponds to $\alpha = .05$

Note that the **rejection region** refers to the values of the test statistic for which we will *reject the null hypothesis.*

FIGURE 8.2
Location of the test
statistic for a test of
the hypothesis
$H_0: \mu = 2,400$

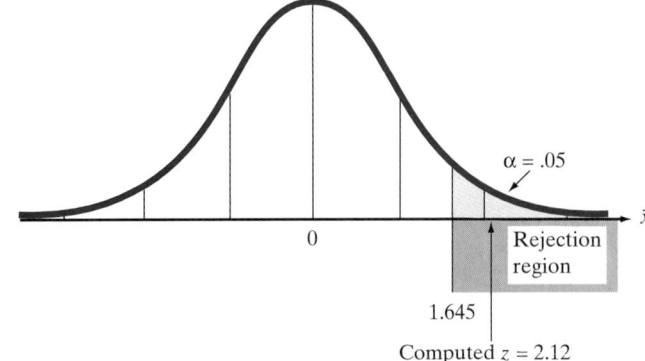

To illustrate the use of the test, suppose we test 50 sections of sewer pipe and find the mean and standard deviation for these 50 measurements to be

$$\bar{x} = 2,460 \text{ pounds per linear foot}$$

$$s = 200 \text{ pounds per linear foot}$$

As in the case of estimation, we can use s to approximate σ when s is calculated from a large set of sample measurements.

The test statistic is

$$z = \frac{\bar{x} - 2,400}{\sigma_{\bar{x}}} = \frac{\bar{x} - 2,400}{\sigma/\sqrt{n}} \approx \frac{\bar{x} - 2,400}{s/\sqrt{n}}$$

Substituting $\bar{x} = 2,460$, $n = 50$, and $s = 200$, we have

$$z \approx \frac{2,460 - 2,400}{200/\sqrt{50}} = \frac{60}{28.28} = 2.12$$

Therefore, the sample mean lies $2.12\sigma_{\bar{x}}$ above the hypothesized value of μ, 2,400, as shown in Figure 8.2. Since this value of z exceeds 1.645, it falls in the rejection region. That is, we reject the null hypothesis that $\mu = 2,400$ and conclude that $\mu > 2,400$. Thus, it appears that the company's pipe has a mean strength that exceeds 2,400 pounds per linear foot.

How much faith can be placed in this conclusion? What is the probability that our statistical test could lead us to reject the null hypothesis (and conclude that the company's pipe meets the city's specifications) when in fact the null hypothesis is true? The answer is $\alpha = .05$. That is, we selected the level of risk, α, of making a Type I error when we constructed the test. Thus, the chance is only 1 in 20 that our test would lead us to conclude the manufacturer's pipe satisfies the city's specifications when in fact the pipe does *not* meet specifications.

Now, suppose the sample mean breaking strength for the 50 sections of sewer pipe turned out to be $\bar{x} = 2,430$ pounds per linear foot. Assuming that the sample standard deviation is still $s = 200$, the test statistic is

$$z = \frac{2,430 - 2,400}{200/\sqrt{50}} = \frac{30}{28.28} = 1.06$$

Therefore, the sample mean $\bar{x} = 2,430$ is only 1.06 standard deviations above the null hypothesized value of $\mu = 2,400$. As shown in Figure 8.3, this value does not fall into the rejection region ($z > 1.645$). Therefore, we know that we cannot reject H_0 using $\alpha = .05$. Even though the sample mean exceeds the city's specification of 2,400 by 30 pounds per linear foot, it does not exceed the specification by enough to provide *convincing* evidence that the *population mean* exceeds 2,400.

FIGURE 8.3
Location of test statistic when $\bar{x} = 2,430$

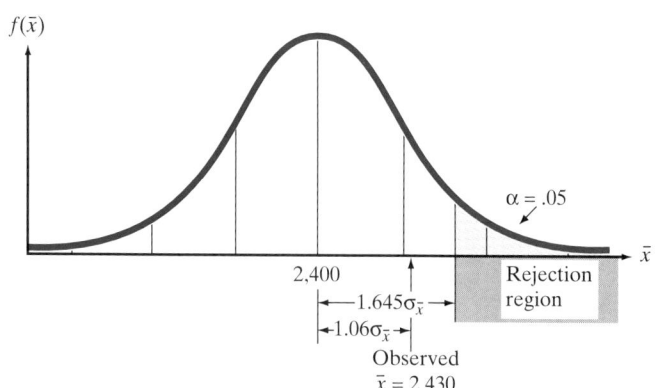

Should we accept the null hypothesis H_0: $\mu \leq 2,400$ and conclude that the manufacturer's pipe does not meet specifications? To do so would be to risk a **Type II error**—that of concluding that the null hypothesis is true (the pipe does not meet specifications) when in fact it is false (the pipe does meet specifications). We denote the probability of committing a Type II error by β, and we show in optional Section 8.6 that β is often difficult to determine precisely. Rather than make a decision (accept H_0) for which the probability of error (β) is unknown, we avoid the potential Type II error by avoiding the conclusion that the null hypothesis is true. Instead, we will simply state that *the sample evidence is insufficient to reject H_0 at $\alpha = .05$*. Since the null hypothesis is the "status-quo" hypothesis, the effect of not rejecting H_0 is to maintain the status quo. In our pipe-testing example, the effect of having insufficient evidence to reject the null hypothesis that the pipe does not meet specifications is probably to prohibit the utilization of the manufacturer's pipe unless and until there is sufficient evidence that the pipe does meet specifications. That is, until the data indicate convincingly that the null hypothesis is false, we usually maintain the status quo implied by its truth.

Table 8.1 summarizes the four possible outcomes of a test of hypothesis. The "true state of nature" columns in Table 8.1 refer to the fact that either the null hypothesis H_0 is true or the alternative hypothesis H_a is true. Note that the true state of nature is unknown to the researcher conducting the test. The "decision" rows in Table 8.1 refer to the action of the researcher, assuming that he or she will either conclude that H_0 is true or that H_a is true, based on the results of the sampling experiment. Note that a Type I error can be made *only* when the null hypothesis is rejected in favor of the alternative hypothesis, and a Type II error can be made *only* when the null hypothesis is accepted. Our policy will be to make a decision only when we know the probability of making the error that corresponds to that decision. Since α is usually specified by the analyst, we will generally be able to reject H_0 (accept H_a) when the sample evidence supports that decision. However, since β is usually not specified, we will generally avoid the

TABLE 8.1 Conclusions and Consequences for a Test of Hypothesis

		TRUE STATE OF NATURE	
		H_0 **True**	H_a **True**
Conclusion	H_0 True	Correct decision	Type II error (probability β)
	H_a True	Type I error (probability α)	Correct decision

STATISTICS IN ACTION

8.1 STATISTICS IS MURDER!

Statistics and probability can play a key role in establishing credible evidence in a trial by jury. For example, statistics similar to those you produced for the Kentucky Milk Case (Case 1) ultimately led to the conviction of one dairy owner for bid collusion. Sometimes, the outcome of a jury trial defies belief from the general public (e.g., the O.J. Simpson verdict in the "Trial of the Century"). Such a verdict is more understandable when you realize that the jury trial of an accused murderer is analogous to the statistical hypothesis-testing process. Each of the elements of a test of hypothesis applies to the jury system of deciding the guilt or innocence of the accused:

1. *Null hypothesis H_0:* The null hypothesis in a jury trial is that the accused is innocent. The status quo hypothesis in the U.S. system of justice is innocence, which in a murder trial is assumed to be true until proven *beyond a reasonable doubt*.

2. *Alternative hypothesis H_a:* The alternative hypothesis is guilt, which is accepted only when sufficient evidence exists to establish its truth.

3. *Test statistic:* The test statistic in a trial is the final vote of the jury—that is, the number of the jury members who vote "guilty."

4. *Rejection region:* In a murder trial the jury vote must be unanimous in favor of guilt before the null hypothesis of innocence is rejected in favor of the alternative hypothesis of guilt. Thus, for a 12-member jury trial, the rejection region is $x = 12$, where x is the number of "guilty" votes.

5. *Assumption:* The primary assumption made in trials concerns the method of selecting the jury. The jury is assumed to represent a random sample of citizens who have no prejudice concerning the case.

6. *Experiment and calculation of the test statistic:* The sampling experiment is analogous to the jury selec-

tion, the trial, and the jury deliberations. The final vote of the jury is analogous to the calculation of the test statistic.

7. *Conclusion:*
   a. If the vote of the jury is unanimous in favor of guilt, the null hypothesis of innocence is rejected and the court concludes that the accused murderer is guilty.
   b. Any vote other than a unanimous one for guilt results in the court's reserving judgment about the hypotheses, either by declaring the accused "not guilty," or by declaring a mistrial and repeating the "test" with a new jury. (The latter is analogous to collecting more data and repeating a statistical test of hypothesis.) The court never accepts the null hypothesis; that is, the court never declares the accused "innocent." A "not guilty" verdict (as in the O. J. Simpson case) implies that the court could not find the defendant guilty **beyond a reasonable doubt**.

Focus

a. Define Type I and Type II errors in a murder trial.
b. Which of the two errors is the more serious? Explain.
c. The court does not, in general, know the values of α and β; but ideally, both should be small. One of these probabilities is assumed to be smaller than the other in a jury trial. Which one, and why?
d. The court system relies on the belief that the value of α is made very small by requiring a unanimous vote before guilt is concluded. Explain why this is so.
e. For a jury prejudiced against a guilty verdict as the trial begins, will the value of α increase or decrease? Explain.
f. For a jury prejudiced against a guilty verdict as the trial begins, will the value of β increase or decrease? Explain.

decision to accept H_0, preferring instead to state that the sample evidence is insufficient to reject H_0 when the test statistic is not in the rejection region.

The elements of a test of hypothesis are summarized in the following box. Note that the first four elements are all specified *before* the sampling experiment is performed. In no case will the results of the sample be used to determine the hypotheses—the data are collected to test the predetermined hypotheses, not to formulate them.

Elements of a Test of Hypothesis

1. *Null hypothesis* (H_0): A theory about the values of one or more population parameters. The theory generally represents the status quo, which we adopt until it is proven false.

2. *Alternative (research) hypothesis* (H_a): A theory that contradicts the null hypothesis. The theory generally represents that which we will adopt only when sufficient evidence exists to establish its truth.

3. *Test statistic:* A sample statistic used to decide whether to reject the null hypothesis.

4. *Rejection region:* The numerical values of the test statistic for which the null hypothesis will be rejected. The rejection region is chosen so that the probability is α that it will contain the test statistic when the null hypothesis is true, thereby leading to a Type I error. The value of α is usually chosen to be small (e.g., .01, .05, or .10), and is referred to as the **level of significance** of the test.

5. *Assumptions:* Clear statement(s) of any assumptions made about the population(s) being sampled.

6. *Experiment and calculation of test statistic:* Performance of the sampling experiment and determination of the numerical value of the test statistic.

7. *Conclusion:*

   a. If the numerical value of the test statistic falls in the rejection region, we reject the null hypothesis and conclude that the alternative hypothesis is true. We know that the hypothesis-testing process will lead to this conclusion incorrectly (Type I error) only $100\alpha\%$ of the time when H_0 is true.

   b. If the test statistic does not fall in the rejection region, we do not reject H_0. Thus, we reserve judgment about which hypothesis is true. We do not conclude that the null hypothesis is true because we do not (in general) know the probability β that our test procedure will lead to an incorrect acceptance of H_0 (Type II error).*

*In many practical business applications of hypothesis testing, nonrejection leads management to behave as if the null hypothesis were accepted. Accordingly, the distinction between acceptance and nonrejection is frequently blurred in practice. We discuss the issues connected with the acceptance of the null hypothesis and the calculation of β in more detail in (optional) Section 8.6.

EXERCISES   8.1–8.10

Learning the Mechanics

8.1   Which hypothesis, the null or the alternative, is the status-quo hypothesis? Which is the research hypothesis?

8.2   Which element of a test of hypothesis is used to decide whether to reject the null hypothesis in favor of the alternative hypothesis?

8.3   What is the level of significance of a test of hypothesis?

8.4   What is the difference between Type I and Type II errors in hypothesis testing? How do α and β relate to Type I and Type II errors?

8.5   List the four possible results of the combinations of decisions and true states of nature for a test of hypothesis.

8.6   We (generally) reject the null hypothesis when the test statistic falls in the rejection region, but we do not accept the null hypothesis when the test statistic does not fall in the rejection region. Why?

8.7   If you test a hypothesis and reject the null hypothesis in favor of the alternative hypothesis, does your test prove that the alternative hypothesis is correct? Explain.

Applying the Concepts

8.8   In 1895 an Italian criminologist, Cesare Lombroso, proposed that blood pressure be used to test for truthfulness. In the 1930s, William Marston added the measurements of respiration and perspiration to the process, built a machine to do the measuring, and called his invention the *polygraph*, or *lie detector*. Today, the federal court system will not consider polygraph results as evidence, but nearly half the state courts do permit polygraph tests under certain circumstances. In addition, its use in screening job applicants is on the rise. Physicians Michael Phillips, Allan Brett, and John Beary subjected the polygraph to the same careful testing given to medical diagnostic tests. They found that if 1,000 people were subjected to the polygraph and 500 told the truth and 500 lied, the polygraph would indicate that approximately 185 of the truth tellers were liars and that approximately 120 of the liars were truth tellers ("Lie detectors can make a liar of you," *Discover*, June 1986).

a. In the application of a polygraph test, an individual is presumed to be a truth teller (H_0) until "proven" a liar (H_a). In this context, what is a Type I error? A Type II error?

b. According to Phillips, Brett, and Beary, what is the probability (approximately) that a polygraph test will result in a Type I error? A Type II error?

8.9 According to *Chemical Marketing Reporter* (Feb. 20, 1995), pharmaceutical companies spend $15 billion per year on research and development of new drugs. The pharmaceutical company must subject each new drug to lengthy and involved testing before receiving the necessary permission from the Food and Drug Administration (FDA) to market the drug. The FDA's policy is that the pharmaceutical company must provide substantial evidence that a new drug is safe prior to receiving FDA approval, so that the FDA can confidently certify the safety of the drug to potential consumers.

a. If the new drug testing were to be placed in a test of hypothesis framework, would the null hypothesis be that the drug is safe or unsafe? The alternative hypothesis?

b. Given the choice of null and alternative hypotheses in part **a**, describe Type I and Type II errors in terms of this application. Define α and β in terms of this application.

c. If the FDA wants to be very confident that the drug is safe before permitting it to be market-

ed, is it more important that α or β be small? Explain.

8.10 One of the most pressing problems in high-technology industries is computer security. Computer security is typically achieved by use of a *password*—a collection of symbols (usually letters and numbers) that must be supplied by the user before the computer permits access to the account. The problem is that persistent hackers can create programs that enter millions of combinations of symbols into a target system until the correct password is found. The newest systems solve this problem by requiring authorized users to identify themselves by unique body characteristics. For example, a system developed by Palmguard, Inc. tests the hypothesis

H_0: The proposed user is authorized

versus

H_a: The proposed user is unauthorized

by checking characteristics of the proposed user's palm against those stored in the authorized users' data bank (*Omni*, 1984).

a. Define a Type I error and Type II error for this test. Which is the more serious error? Why?

b. Palmguard reports that the Type I error rate for its system is less than 1%, whereas the Type II error rate is .00025%. Interpret these error rates.

c. Another successful security system, the EyeDentifyer, "spots authorized computer users by reading the one-of-a-kind patterns formed by the network of minute blood vessels across the retina at the back of the eye." The EyeDentifyer reports Type I and II error rates of .01% (1 in 10,000) and .005% (5 in 100,000), respectively. Interpret these rates.

8.2 LARGE-SAMPLE TEST OF HYPOTHESIS ABOUT A POPULATION MEAN

In Section 8.1 we learned that the null and alternative hypotheses form the basis for a test of hypothesis inference. The null and alternative hypotheses may take one of several forms. In the sewer pipe example we tested the null hypothesis that the population mean strength of the pipe is less than or equal to 2,400 pounds per linear foot against the alternative hypothesis that the mean strength exceeds 2,400. That is, we tested

$$H_0: \mu \leq 2,400$$

$$H_a: \mu > 2,400$$

This is a **one-tailed** (or **one-sided**) **statistical test** because the alternative hypothesis specifies that the population parameter (the population mean μ, in this example) is strictly greater than a specified value (2,400, in this example). If the null hypothesis had been $H_0: \mu \geq 2,400$ and the alternative hypothesis had been $H_a: \mu < 2,400$, the test would still be one-sided, because the parameter is still specified to be on "one

FIGURE 8.4
Rejection regions corresponding to one- and two-tailed tests

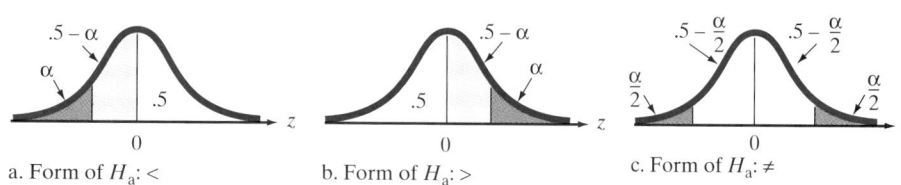

a. Form of H_a: <   b. Form of H_a: >   c. Form of H_a: ≠

side" of the null hypothesis value. Some statistical investigations seek to show that the population parameter is *either larger or smaller* than some specified value. Such an alternative hypothesis is called a **two-tailed** (or **two-sided**) **hypothesis**.

While alternative hypotheses are always specified as strict inequalities, such as $\mu < 2{,}400$, $\mu > 2{,}400$, or $\mu \neq 2{,}400$, null hypotheses are usually specified as equalities, such as $\mu = 2{,}400$. Even when the null hypothesis is an inequality, such as $\mu \leq 2{,}400$, we specify $H_0: \mu = 2{,}400$, reasoning that if sufficient evidence exists to show that $H_a: \mu > 2{,}400$ is true when tested against $H_0: \mu = 2{,}400$, then surely sufficient evidence exists to reject $\mu < 2{,}400$ as well. Therefore, the null hypothesis is specified as the value of μ closest to a one-sided alternative hypothesis and as the only value *not* specified in a two-tailed alternative hypothesis. The steps for selecting the null and alternative hypotheses are summarized in the accompanying box.

Steps for Selecting the Null and Alternative Hypotheses

1. Select the *alternative hypothesis* as that which the sampling experiment is intended to establish. The alternative hypothesis will assume one of three forms:

   a. One-tailed, upper-tailed   *Example:* $H_a: \mu > 2{,}400$

   b. One-tailed, lower-tailed   *Example:* $H_a: \mu < 2{,}400$

   c. Two-tailed   *Example:* $H_a: \mu \neq 2{,}400$

2. Select the *null hypothesis* as the status quo, that which will be presumed true unless the sampling experiment conclusively establishes the alternative hypothesis. The null hypothesis will be specified as that parameter value closest to the alternative in one-tailed tests, and as the complementary (or only unspecified) value in two-tailed tests.

Example: $H_0: \mu = 2{,}400$

The rejection region for a two-tailed test differs from that for a one-tailed test. When we are trying to detect departure from the null hypothesis in *either* direction, we must establish a rejection region in both tails of the sampling distribution of the test statistic. Figures 8.4a and 8.4b show the one-tailed rejection regions for lower- and upper-tailed tests, respectively. The two-tailed rejection region is illustrated in Figure 8.4c. Note that a rejection region is established in each tail of the sampling distribution for a two-tailed test.

The rejection regions corresponding to typical values selected for α are shown in Table 8.2 for one-and two-tailed tests. Note that the smaller α you select, the more evidence (the larger z) you will need before you can reject H_0.

TABLE 8.2   Rejection Regions for Common Values of α

	Lower-Tailed	**Upper-Tailed**	**Two-Tailed**
	\multicolumn{3}{c}{**ALTERNATIVE HYPOTHESES**}	
$\alpha = .10$	$z < -1.28$	$z > 1.28$	$z < -1.645$ or $z > 1.645$
$\alpha = .05$	$z < -1.645$	$z > 1.645$	$z < -1.96$ or $z > 1.96$
$\alpha = .01$	$z < -2.33$	$z > 2.33$	$z < -2.575$ or $z > 2.575$

EXAMPLE 8.1

A manufacturer of cereal wants to test the performance of one of its filling machines. The machine is designed to discharge a mean amount of $\mu = 12$ ounces per box, and the manufacturer wants to detect any departure from this setting. This quality study calls for randomly sampling 100 boxes from today's production run and determining whether the mean fill for the run is 12 ounces per box. Set up a test of hypothesis for this study, using $\alpha = .01$. (In Statistics in Action 8.2 and in Chapter 13, we describe how this problem can be addressed using control charts.)

SOLUTION

Since the manufacturer wishes to detect a departure from the setting of $\mu = 12$ in either direction, $\mu < 12$ or $\mu > 12$, we conduct a two-tailed statistical test. Following the procedure for selecting the null and alternative hypotheses, we specify as the alternative hypothesis that the mean differs from 12 ounces, since detecting the machine's departure from specifications is the purpose of the quality control study. The null hypothesis is the presumption that the fill machine is operating properly unless the sample data indicate otherwise. Thus,

$$H_0: \mu = 12$$

$$H_a: \mu \neq 12 \text{ (i.e., } \mu < 12 \text{ or } \mu > 12)$$

The test statistic measures the number of standard deviations between the observed value of $\bar{x}$ and the null hypothesized value $\mu = 12$:

$$\text{Test statistic: } \frac{\bar{x} - 12}{\sigma_{\bar{x}}}$$

The rejection region must be designated to detect a departure from $\mu = 12$ in *either* direction, so we will reject H_0 for values of z that are either too small (negative) or too large (positive). To determine the precise values of z that comprise the rejection region, we first select α, the probability that the test will lead to incorrect rejection of the null hypothesis. Then we divide α equally between the lower and upper tail of the distribution of z, as shown in Figure 8.5. In this example, $\alpha = .01$, so $\alpha/2 = .005$ is placed in each tail. The areas in the tails correspond to $z = -2.575$ and $z = 2.575$, respectively (from Table 8.2):

$$\text{Rejection region: } z < -2.575 \text{ or } z > 2.575 \qquad \text{(see Figure 8.5)}$$

Assumptions: Since the sample size of the experiment is large enough ($n > 30$), the Central Limit Theorem will apply, and no assumptions need be made about the population of fill measurements. The sampling distribution of the sample mean fill of 100 boxes will be approximately normal regardless of the distribution of the individual boxes' fills.

FIGURE 8.5
Two-tailed rejection region: $\alpha = .01$

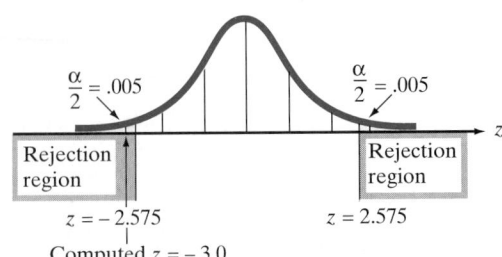

$\frac{\alpha}{2} = .005$ $\frac{\alpha}{2} = .005$

Rejection region Rejection region

$z = -2.575$ $z = 2.575$

Computed $z = -3.0$

Note that the test in Example 8.1 is set up *before* the sampling experiment is conducted. The data are not used to develop the test. Evidently, the manufacturer does not want to disrupt the filling process to adjust the machine unless the sample data provide very convincing evidence that it is not meeting specifications, because the value of α has been set quite low at .01. If the sample evidence results in the rejection of H_0, the manufacturer can be 99% confident that the machine needs adjustment.

Once the test is set up, the manufacturer is ready to perform the sampling experiment and conduct the test. The test is performed in Example 8.2.

EXAMPLE 8.2

Refer to the quality control test set up in Example 8.1. Suppose the sample yields the following results:

$$n = 100 \text{ observations} \qquad \bar{x} = 11.85 \text{ ounces} \qquad s = .5 \text{ ounce}$$

Use these data to conduct the test of hypothesis.

SOLUTION

Since the test is completely specified in Example 8.1, we simply substitute the sample statistics into the test statistic:

$$z = \frac{\bar{x} - 12}{\sigma_{\bar{x}}} = \frac{\bar{x} - 12}{\sigma/\sqrt{n}} = \frac{11.85 - 12}{\sigma/\sqrt{100}}$$

$$\approx \frac{11.85 - 12}{s/10} = \frac{-.15}{.5/10} = -3.0$$

The implication is that the sample mean, 11.85, is (approximately) 3 standard deviations below the null hypothesized value of 12.0 in the sampling distribution of $\bar{x}$. You can see in Figure 8.5 that this value of z is in the lower-tail rejection region, which consists of all values of $z < -2.575$. These sample data provide sufficient evidence to reject H_0 and conclude, at the $\alpha = .01$ level of significance, that the mean fill differs from the specification of $\mu = 12$ ounces. It appears that the machine is, on average, underfilling the boxes. ∎

Two final points about the test of hypothesis in Example 8.2 apply to all statistical tests:

1. Since z is less than -2.575, it is tempting to state our conclusion at a significance level lower than $\alpha = .01$. We resist the temptation because the level of α is determined *before* the sampling experiment is performed. If we decide that we are willing to tolerate a 1% Type I error rate, the result of the sampling experiment should have no effect on that decision. *In general, the same data should not be used both to set up and to conduct the test.*

2. When we state our conclusion at the .01 level of significance, we are referring to the failure rate of the *procedure,* not the result of this particular test. We know that the test procedure will lead to the rejection of the null hypothesis only 1% of the time when in fact $\mu = 12$. *Therefore, when the test statistic falls in the rejection region, we infer that the alternative $\mu \neq 12$ is true and express our confidence in the procedure by quoting the α level of significance, or the $100(1 - \alpha)\%$ confidence level.*

The setup of a large-sample test of hypothesis about a population mean is summarized in the following box. Both the one- and two-tailed tests are shown.

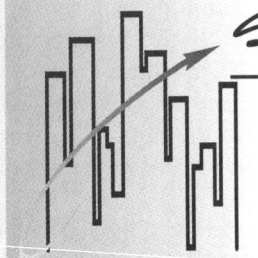

STATISTICS IN ACTION

8.2 STATISTICAL QUALITY CONTROL, PART I

In Exercise 6.47 we described a graphical device, known as a control chart, that can be used in business operations to monitor the variation over time in the quality of products and services being produced. The control chart was developed by Walter A. Shewhart of Bell Telephone Laboratories in 1924 and has become a basic tool of quality control engineers and operations managers the world over. Japan's emergence as an industrial superpower is due in part to its early adoption and refinement of quality control techniques, such as the control chart (Duncan, 1986). In this Statistics in Action and Statistics in Action 8.3, we expand the discussion of control charts and demonstrate that they are simply vehicles for conducting hypothesis tests. We discuss control charts in detail in Chapter 13.

Suppose it is desired to monitor the pitch diameter of the threads on a particular aircraft fitting. When the process is in control, the pitch diameters follow a normal distribution with mean μ_0 and standard deviation σ_0. Recall from Exercise 6.47 that such monitoring can be accomplished by (1) sampling n items from the production process at regular time intervals, (2) measuring the pitch diameter of each item sampled, and

(3) plotting the mean diameter of each sample, $\bar{x}$, on a control chart like that in Figure 8.6. Such a control chart is called an **$\bar{x}$-chart**. If a value of $\bar{x}$ falls above the upper control limit or below the lower control limit, there is strong evidence that the process is out of control—i.e., that the quality of the product being produced does not meet established standards. Otherwise, the process is deemed to be in control.

In effect, each time an analyst plots a sample mean on an $\bar{x}$-chart and observes where it falls in relation to the control limits, the analyst is conducting a two-tailed hypothesis test.

Focus

Describe the analyst's decision process in the language of hypothesis testing by answering the following questions.

a. What are the null and alternative hypotheses of interest?

b. What is the test statistic?

c. Specify the rejection region.

d. What is the probability of committing a Type I error?

Large-Sample Test of Hypothesis About μ

One-Tailed Test

$H_0: \mu = \mu_0$*

$H_a: \mu < \mu_0$:
  (or $H_a: \mu > \mu_0$)

Test statistic: $z = \dfrac{\bar{x} - \mu_0}{\sigma_{\bar{x}}}$

Rejection region: $z < -z_\alpha$
  (or $z > z_\alpha$ when $H_a: \mu > \mu_0$)

where z_α is chosen so that
  $P(z > z_\alpha) = \alpha$

Two-Tailed Test

$H_0: \mu = \mu_0$*

$H_a: \mu \neq \mu_0$

Test statistic: $z = \dfrac{\bar{x} - \mu_0}{\sigma_{\bar{x}}}$

Rejection region: $z < -z_{\alpha/2}$
  or $z > z_{\alpha/2}$

where $z_{\alpha/2}$ is chosen so that
  $P(z > z_{\alpha/2}) = \alpha/2$

Assumptions: None, since the Central Limit Theorem assures us that the sampling distribution of $\bar{x}$ (and, hence, the test statistic z) will be approximately normal.

*Note: μ_0 is the symbol for the numerical value assigned to μ under the null hypothesis.

FIGURE 8.6
$\bar{x}$-chart (Statistics in Action 8.2)

Once the test has been set up, the sampling experiment is performed and the test statistic calculated. The next box contains possible conclusions for a test of hypothesis, depending on the result of the sampling experiment.

Possible Conclusions for a Test of Hypothesis

1. If the calculated test statistic falls in the rejection region, reject H_0 and conclude that the alternative hypothesis H_a is true. State that you are rejecting H_0 at the α level of significance. Remember that the confidence is in the testing *process*, not the particular result of a single test.

2. If the test statistic does not fall in the rejection region, conclude that the sampling experiment does not provide sufficient evidence to reject H_0 at the α level of significance. [Generally, we will not "accept" the null hypothesis unless the probability β of a Type II error has been calculated (see optional Section 8.6).]

EXERCISES   8.11–8.23

Note: Exercises marked with ▨ contain data for computer analysis on a 3.5" disk (file name in parentheses).

Learning the Mechanics

8.11   For each of the following rejection regions, sketch the sampling distribution for z and indicate the location of the rejection region.
   a. $z > 1.96$ **b.** $z > 1.645$ **c.** $z > 2.575$
   d. $z < -1.28$ **e.** $z < -1.645$ or $z > 1.645$
   f. $z < -2.575$ or $z > 2.575$
   g. For each of the rejection regions specified in parts **a–f**, what is the probability that a Type I error will be made?

8.12   Suppose you are interested in conducting the statistical test of $H_0: \mu = 255$ against $H_a: \mu > 255$, and you have decided to use the following decision rule: Reject H_0 if the sample mean of a random sample of 81 items is more than 270. Assume that the standard deviation of the population is 63.

   a. Express the decision rule in terms of z.
   b. Find α, the probability of making a Type I error, by using this decision rule.

8.13   A random sample of 100 observations from a population with standard deviation 60 yielded a sample mean of 110.
   a. Test the null hypothesis that $\mu = 100$ against the alternative hypothesis that $\mu > 100$ using $\alpha = .05$. Interpret the results of the test.
   b. Test the null hypothesis that $\mu = 100$ against the alternative hypothesis that $\mu \neq 100$ using $\alpha = .05$. Interpret the results of the test.
   c. Compare the results of the two tests you conducted. Explain why the results differ.

8.14   A random sample of 64 observations produced the following summary statistics: $\bar{x} = .323$ and $s^2 = .034$.
   a. Test the null hypothesis that $\mu = .36$ against the alternative hypothesis that $\mu < .36$ using $\alpha = .10$.

b. Test the null hypothesis that $\mu = .36$ against the alternative hypothesis that $\mu \neq .36$ using $\alpha = .10$. Interpret the result.

Applying the Concepts

8.15 Most major corporations have psychologists available to help employees who suffer from stress. One problem that is difficult to diagnose is post-traumatic stress disorder (PTSD). Researchers studying PTSD often use as subjects former prisoners of war (POWs). *Psychological Assessment* (Mar. 1995) published the results of a study of World War II aviators who were captured by German forces after they were shot down. Having located a total of 239 World War II aviator POW survivors, the researchers asked each veteran to participate in the study; 33 responded to the letter of invitation. Each of the 33 POW survivors were administered the Minnesota Multiphasic Personality Inventory, one component of which measures level of PTSD. [*Note:* The higher the score, the higher the level of PTSD.] The aviators produced a mean PTSD score of $\bar{x} = 9.00$ and a standard deviation of $s = 9.32$.

a. Set up the null and alternative hypotheses for determining whether the true mean PTSD score of all World War II aviator POWs is less than 16. [*Note:* The value, 16, represents the mean PTSD score established for Vietnam POWs.]

b. Conduct the test, part **a**, using $\alpha = .10$. What are the practical implications of the test?

c. Discuss the representativeness of the sample used in the study and its ramifications.

8.16 A study reported in the *Journal of Occupational and Organizational Psychology* (Dec. 1992) investigated the relationship of employment status to mental health. A sample of 49 unemployed men was given a mental health examination using the General Health Questionnaire (GHQ). The GHQ is a widely recognized measure of present mental health, with lower values indicating better mental health. The mean and standard deviation of the GHQ scores were $\bar{x} = 10.94$ and $s = 5.10$, respectively.

a. Specify the appropriate null and alternative hypotheses if we wish to test the research hypothesis that the mean GHQ score for all unemployed men exceeds 10. Is the test one-tailed or two-tailed? Why?

b. If we specify $\alpha = .05$, what is the appropriate rejection region for this test?

c. Conduct the test, and state your conclusion clearly in the language of this exercise.

8.17 (X08.017) In quality control applications of hypothesis testing (see Statistics in Action 8.2), the null and alternative hypotheses are frequently specified as

H_0: The production process is performing satisfactorily

H_a: The process is performing in an unsatisfactory manner

Accordingly, α is sometimes referred to as the **producer's risk**, while β is called the **consumer's risk** (Stevenson, *Production/Operations Management*, 1996). An injection molder produces plastic golf tees. The process is designed to produce tees with a mean weight of .250 ounce. To investigate whether the injection molder is operating satisfactorily, 40 tees were randomly sampled from the last hour's production. Their weights (in ounces) are listed in the table below. Summary statistics for the data are shown in the SAS printout that follows.

a. Do the data provide sufficient evidence to conclude that the process is not operating satisfactorily? Test using $\alpha = .01$.

b. In the context of this problem, explain why it makes sense to call α the producer's risk and β the consumer's risk.

8.18 What factors inhibit the learning process in the classroom? To answer this question, researchers at Murray State University surveyed 40 students from a senior-level marketing class (*Marketing Education Review,* Fall 1994). Each student was given a list of factors and asked to rate the extent to which each factor inhibited the learning process in courses offered in their department. A 7-point rating scale was used, where 1 = "not at all" and 7 = "to a great extent." The factor with the highest rating was instructor-related: "Professors who place too much emphasis on a single right answer rather than overall thinking and creative ideas."

.247	.251	.254	.253	.253	.248	.253	.255	.256	.252
.253	.252	.253	.256	.254	.256	.252	.251	.253	.251
.253	.253	.248	.251	.253	.256	.254	.250	.254	.255
.249	.250	.254	.251	.251	.255	.251	.253	.252	.253

```
Analysis Variable : WEIGHT

N Obs   N     Minimum        Maximum           Mean        Std Dev
     40  40   0.2470000      0.2560000       0.2524750     0.0022302
```

Summary statistics for the student ratings of this factor are: $\bar{x} = 4.70, s = 1.62$.

a. Conduct a test to determine if the true mean rating for this instructor-related factor exceeds 4. Use $\alpha = .05$. Interpret the test results.

b. Because the variable of interest, rating, is measured on a 7-point scale, it is unlikely that the population of ratings will be normally distributed. Consequently, some analysts may perceive the test, part **a**, to be invalid and search for alternative methods of analysis. Defend or refute this argument.

8.19 In 1993 U.S. banks handled 61 billion individual and corporate checks, compared to 46 billion ten years ago. The increase in check writing has apparently led to an increase in check fraud. An American Bankers Association 1993 survey of 50 midsized banks found a mean loss due to check fraud of $37,443 per bank (*Bank Security Report*, Feb. 1995). Losses at the 50 individual banks ranged from $208 to $400,000. Assume that ten years ago, the true mean loss per midsized bank due to check fraud was $15,100. Conduct a test at $\alpha = .10$ to determine whether the true mean loss due to check fraud of midsized banks in 1993 exceeds $15,100 per bank.

8.20 (**X08.020**) The introduction of printed circuit boards (PCBs) in the 1950s revolutionized the electronics industry. However, solder-joint defects on PCBs have plagued electronics manufacturers since the introduction of the PCB. A single PCB may contain thousands of solder joints. Current technology uses X-rays and lasers for inspection (*Quality Congress Transactions*, 1986). A particular manufacturer of laser-based inspection equipment claims that its product can inspect on average at least 10 solder joints per second when the joints are spaced .1 inch apart. The equipment was tested by a potential buyer on 48 different PCBs. In each case, the equipment was operated for exactly 1 second. The number of solder joints inspected on each run follows:

10	9	10	10	11	9	12	8	8	9	6	10
7	10	11	9	9	13	9	10	11	10	12	8
9	9	9	7	12	6	9	10	10	8	7	9
11	12	10	0	10	11	12	9	7	9	9	10

a. The potential buyer wants to know whether the sample data refute the manufacturer's claim. Specify the null and alternative hypotheses that the buyer should test.

b. In the context of this exercise, what is a Type I error? A Type II error?

c. Conduct the hypothesis test you described in part **a**, and interpret the test's results in the context of this exercise. Use $\alpha = .05$ and the SPSS descriptive statistics printout below.

8.21 A company has devised a new ink-jet cartridge for its plain-paper fax machine that it believes has a longer lifetime (on average) than the one currently being produced. To investigate its length of life, 225 of the new cartridges were tested by counting the number of high-quality printed pages each was able to produce. The sample mean and standard deviation were determined to be 1,511.4 pages and 35.7 pages, respectively. The historical average lifetime for cartridges produced by the current process is 1,502.5 pages; the historical standard deviation is 97.3 pages.

a. What are the appropriate null and alternative hypotheses to test whether the mean lifetime of the new cartridges exceeds that of the old cartridges?

b. Use $\alpha = .005$ to conduct the test in part **a**. Do the new cartridges have an average lifetime that is statistically significantly longer than the cartridges currently in production?

c. Does the difference in average lifetimes appear to be of practical significance from the perspective of the consumer? Explain.

d. Should the apparent decrease in the standard deviation in lifetimes associated with the new cartridges be viewed as an improvement over the old cartridges? Explain.

8.22 Nutritionists stress that weight control generally requires significant reductions in the intake of fat. A random sample of 64 middle-aged men on weight control programs is selected to determine whether their mean intake of fat exceeds the recommended 30 grams per day. The sample mean and standard deviation are $\bar{x} = 37$ and $s = 32$, respectively.

a. Considering the sample mean and standard deviation, would you expect the distribution for fat intake per day to be symmetric or skewed? Explain.

b. Do the sample results indicate that the mean intake for middle-aged men on weight control programs exceeds 30 grams? Test using $\alpha = .10$.

c. Would you reach the same conclusion as in part **b** using $\alpha = .05$? Using $\alpha = .01$? Why can the conclusion of a test change when the value of α is changed?

8.23 The pain reliever currently used in a hospital is known to bring relief to patients in a mean time of

Variable	Mean	Std Dev	Minimum	Maximum	N Label
NUMBER	9.29	2.10	.00	13.00	48

3.5 minutes. To compare a new pain reliever with the current one, the new drug is administered to a random sample of 50 patients. The mean time to relief for the sample of patients is 2.8 minutes and the standard deviation is 1.14 minutes. Do the

data provide sufficient evidence to conclude that the new drug was effective in reducing the mean time until a patient receives relief from pain? Test using $\alpha = .10$.

8.3 OBSERVED SIGNIFICANCE LEVELS: P-VALUES

According to the statistical test procedure described in Section 8.2, the rejection region and, correspondingly, the value of α are selected prior to conducting the test, and the conclusions are stated in terms of rejecting or not rejecting the null hypothesis. A second method of presenting the results of a statistical test is one that reports the extent to which the test statistic disagrees with the null hypothesis and leaves to the reader the task of deciding whether to reject the null hypothesis. This measure of disagreement is called the *observed significance level* (or *p-value*) for the test.

DEFINITION 8.1
The **observed significance level**, or **p-value**, for a specific statistical test is the probability (assuming H_0 is true) of observing a value of the test statistic that is at least as contradictory to the null hypothesis, and supportive of the alternative hypothesis, as the actual one computed from the sample data.

For example, the value of the test statistic computed for the sample of $n = 50$ sections of sewer pipe was $z = 2.12$. Since the test is one-tailed—i.e., the alternative (research) hypothesis of interest is $H_a: \mu > 2,400$—values of the test statistic even more contradictory to H_0 than the one observed would be values larger than $z = 2.12$. Therefore, the observed significance level (p-value) for this test is

$$p\text{-value} = P(z \geq 2.12)$$

or, equivalently, the area under the standard normal curve to the right of $z = 2.12$ (see Figure 8.7).

The area A in Figure 8.7 is given in Table IV in Appendix B as .4830. Therefore, the upper-tail area corresponding to $z = 2.12$ is

$$p\text{-value} = .5 - .4830 = .0170$$

Consequently, we say that these test results are "very significant"; i.e., they disagree rather strongly with the null hypothesis, $H_0: \mu = 2,400$, and favor $H_a: \mu > 2,400$. The probability of observing a z value as large as 2.12 is only .0170, if in fact the true value of μ is 2,400.

If you are inclined to select $\alpha = .05$ for this test, then you would reject the null hypothesis because the p-value for the test, .0170, is less than .05. In contrast, if you choose $\alpha = .01$, you would not reject the null hypothesis because the p-value

FIGURE 8.7
Finding the p-value for an upper-tailed test when $z = 2.12$

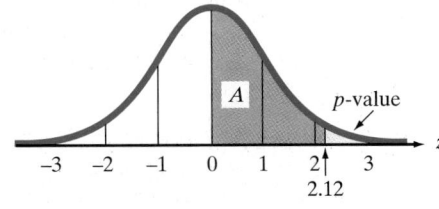

FIGURE 8.8
Finding the *p*-value for a one-tailed test

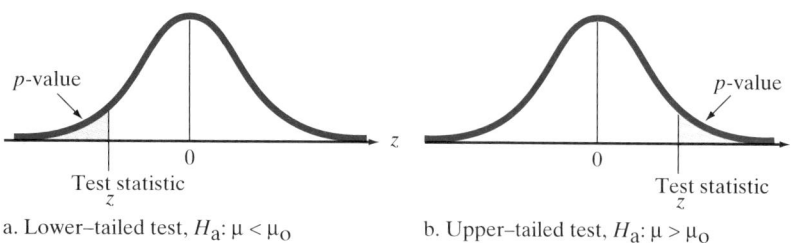

a. Lower–tailed test, H_a: $\mu < \mu_0$ b. Upper–tailed test, H_a: $\mu > \mu_0$

for the test is larger than .01. Thus, the use of the observed significance level is identical to the test procedure described in the preceding sections except that the choice of α is left to you.

The steps for calculating the *p*-value corresponding to a test statistic for a population mean are given in the next box.

Steps for Calculating the *p*-value for a Test of Hypothesis

1. Determine the value of the test statistic z corresponding to the result of the sampling experiment.

2. **a.** If the test is one-tailed, the *p*-value is equal to the tail area beyond z in the same direction as the alternative hypothesis. Thus, if the alternative hypothesis is of the form $>$, the *p*-value is the area to the right of, or above, the observed z value. Conversely, if the alternative is of the form $<$, the *p*-value is the area to the left of, or below, the observed z value. (See Figure 8.8.)

   b. If the test is two-tailed, the *p*-value is equal to twice the tail area beyond the observed z value in the direction of the sign of z. That is, if z is positive, the *p*-value is twice the area to the right of, or above, the observed z value. Conversely, if z is negative, the *p*-value is twice the area to the left of, or below, the observed z value. (See Figure 8.9.)

EXAMPLE 8.3   Find the observed significance level for the test of the mean filling weight in Examples 8.1 and 8.2.

SOLUTION
Example 8.1 presented a two-tailed test of the hypothesis

$$H_0: \mu = 12 \text{ ounces}$$

against the alternative hypothesis

$$H_a: \mu \neq 12 \text{ ounces}$$

The observed value of the test statistic in Example 8.2 was $z = -3.0$, and any value of z less than -3.0 or greater than $+3.0$ (because this is a two-tailed test) would be even more contradictory to H_0. Therefore, the observed significance level for the test is

$$p\text{-value} = P(z < -3.0 \text{ or } z > +3.0) = P(|z| > 3.0)$$

FIGURE 8.9
Finding the *p*-value for a two-tailed test: *p*-value = 2(*p*/2)

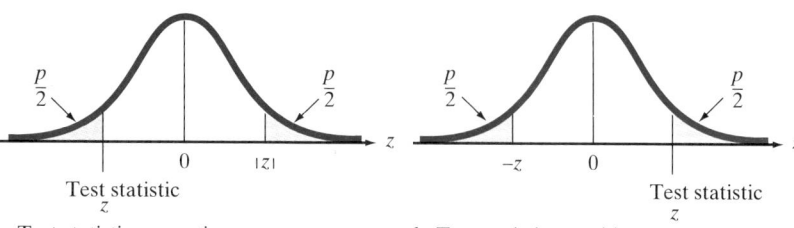

a. Test statistic z negative   b. Test statistic z positive

Thus, we calculate the area below the observed z value, $z = -3.0$, and double it. Consulting Table IV in Appendix B, we find that $P(z < -3.0) = .5 - .4987 = .0013$. Therefore, the p-value for this two-tailed test is

$$2P(z < -3.0) = 2(.0013) = .0026$$

We can interpret this p-value as a strong indication that the machine is not filling the boxes according to specifications, since we would observe a test statistic this extreme or more extreme only 26 in 10,000 times if the machine were meeting specifications ($\mu = 12$). The extent to which the mean differs from 12 could be better determined by calculating a confidence interval for μ. ◣

When publishing the results of a statistical test of hypothesis in journals, case studies, reports, etc., many researchers make use of p-values. Instead of selecting α beforehand and then conducting a test, as outlined in this chapter, the researcher computes (usually with the aid of a statistical software package) and reports the value of the appropriate test statistic and its associated p-value. It is left to the reader of the report to judge the significance of the result—i.e., the reader must determine whether to reject the null hypothesis in favor of the alternative hypothesis, based on the reported p-value. Usually, the null hypothesis is rejected if the observed significance level is *less than* the fixed significance level, α, chosen by the reader. The inherent advantage of reporting test results in this manner are twofold: (1) Readers are permitted to select the maximum value of α that they would be willing to tolerate if they actually carried out a standard test of hypothesis in the manner outlined in this chapter, and (2) a measure of the degree of significance of the result (i.e., the p-value) is provided.

> **Reporting Test Results as p-values: How to Decide Whether to Reject H_0**
> **1.** Choose the maximum value of α that you are willing to tolerate.
> **2.** If the observed significance level (p-value) of the test is less than the chosen value of α, reject the null hypothesis. Otherwise, do not reject the null hypothesis.

EXAMPLE 8.4

Knowledge of the amount of time a patient occupies a hospital bed—called length of stay (LOS)—is important for allocating resources. At one hospital, the mean length of stay was determined to be 5 days. A hospital administrator believes that the mean LOS may now be less than 5 days due to a newly adopted managed care system. To check this, the LOSs (in days) for 100 randomly selected hospital patients were recorded; these are listed in Table 8.3. Test the hypothesis that the true mean LOS at the hospital is less than 5 days, i.e.,

---

TABLE 8.3 Lengths of Stay for 100 Hospital Patients

2	3	8	6	4	4	6	4	2	5
8	10	4	4	4	2	1	3	2	10
1	3	2	3	4	3	5	2	4	1
2	9	1	7	17	9	9	9	4	4
1	1	1	3	1	6	3	3	2	5
1	3	3	14	2	3	9	6	6	3
5	1	4	6	11	22	1	9	6	5
2	2	5	4	3	6	1	5	1	6
17	1	2	4	5	4	4	3	2	3
3	5	2	3	3	2	10	2	4	2

FIGURE 8.10
MINITAB printout for the lower-tailed test in Example 8.4

```
TEST OF MU = 5.000 VS MU L.T. 5.000
THE ASSUMED SIGMA = 3.68
                 N      MEAN    STDEV    SE MEAN        Z    P VALUE
LOS            100     4.530    3.678      0.368    -1.28       0.10
```

$$H_0: \mu = 5$$
$$H_a: \mu < 5$$

Use the data in the table to conduct the test at $\alpha = .05$.

SOLUTION

Instead of performing the computations by hand, we will use a statistical software package. The data were entered into a computer and MINITAB was used to conduct the analysis. The MINITAB printout for the lower-tailed test is displayed in Figure 8.10. Both the test statistic, $z = -1.28$, and p-value of the test, $p = .10$, are highlighted on the MINITAB printout. Since the p-value exceeds our selected α value, $\alpha = .05$, we cannot reject the null hypothesis. Hence, there is insufficient evidence (at $\alpha = .05$) to conclude that the true mean LOS at the hospital is less than 5 days.

Note: MINITAB provides an option for selecting one-tailed or two-tailed tests and reports the appropriate p-value. Some statistical software packages such as SAS and SPSS will conduct only two-tailed tests of hypothesis. For these packages, you obtain the p-value for a one-tailed test as follows:

$$p = \frac{\text{Reported } p\text{-value}}{2} \quad \text{if} \begin{cases} H_a \text{ is of form} > \text{and } z \text{ is positive} \\ H_a \text{ is of form} < \text{and } z \text{ is negative} \end{cases}$$

$$p = 1 - \left(\frac{\text{Reported } p\text{-value}}{2}\right) \quad \text{if} \begin{cases} H_a \text{ is of form} > \text{and } z \text{ is negative} \\ H_a \text{ is of form} < \text{and } z \text{ is positive} \end{cases}$$

EXERCISES   8.24–8.38

Note: Exercises marked with 💾 *contain data for computer analysis on a 3.5" disk (file name in parentheses).*

Learning the Mechanics

8.24   If a hypothesis test were conducted using $\alpha = .05$, for which of the following p-values would the null hypothesis be rejected?
   a. .06   **b.** .10   **c.** .01   **d.** .001   **e.** .251   **f.** .042

8.25   For each α and observed significance level (p-value) pair, indicate whether the null hypothesis would be rejected.
   a. $\alpha = .05, p\text{-value} = .10$
   b. $\alpha = .10, p\text{-value} = .05$
   c. $\alpha = .01, p\text{-value} = .001$
   d. $\alpha = .025, p\text{-value} = .05$
   e. $\alpha = .10, p\text{-value} = .45$

8.26   An analyst tested the null hypothesis $\mu \geq 20$ against the alternative hypothesis that $\mu < 20$. The analyst reported a p value of .06. What is the smallest value of α for which the null hypothesis would be rejected?

8.27   In a test of $H_0: \mu = 100$ against $H_a: \mu > 100$, the sample data yielded the test statistic $z = 2.17$. Find the p-value for the test.

8.28   In a test of $H_0: \mu = 100$ against $H_a: \mu \neq 100$, the sample data yielded the test statistic $z = 2.17$. Find the p-value for the test.

8.29   In a test of the hypothesis $H_0: \mu = 50$ versus $H_a: \mu > 50$, a sample of $n = 100$ observations possessed mean $\bar{x} = 49.4$ and standard deviation $s = 4.1$. Find and interpret the p-value for this test.

8.30   In a test of the hypothesis $H_0: \mu = 10$ versus $H_a: \mu \neq 10$, a sample of $n = 50$ observations possessed mean $\bar{x} = 10.7$ and standard deviation $s = 3.1$. Find and interpret the p-value for this test.

8.31 Consider a test of H_0: $\mu = 75$ performed using the computer. SAS reports a two-tailed p-value of .1032. Make the appropriate conclusion for each of the following situations:
a. H_a: $\mu < 75$, $z = -1.63$, $\alpha = .05$
b. H_a: $\mu < 75$, $z = 1.63$, $\alpha = .10$
c. H_a: $\mu > 75$, $z = 1.63$, $\alpha = .10$
d. H_a: $\mu \neq 75$, $z = -1.63$, $\alpha = .01$

Applying the Concepts

8.32 Refer to the *Psychological Assessment* study of World War II aviator POWs, Exercise 8.15. You tested whether the true mean post-traumatic stress disorder score of World War II aviator POWs is less than 16. Recall that $\bar{x} = 9.00$ and $s = 9.32$ for a sample of $n = 33$ POWs. Compute the p-value of the test and interpret the result.

8.33 (X08.033) The one-year rate of return to shareholders in 1995 was calculated for each in a sample of 63 electric utility stocks. The data, extracted from *The Wall Street Journal* (Feb. 29, 1996), are shown in the table below.

Summary statistics for the data are computed using EXCEL. The resulting printout is given below.

Return	
Mean	31.92857143
Standard Error	1.696482051
Median	32
Mode	31.8
Standard Deviation	13.46540883
Sample Variance	181.317235
Kurtosis	5.231651006
Skewness	-1.083676944
Range	90.4
Minimum	-27.1
Maximum	63.3
Sum	2011.5
Count	63
Confidence Level(95.000%)	3.325038797

Electric Utilities	Rate of Return (%)
Pinnacle West Capital	52.4
DPL Inc	27.7
Nipsco Industries Inc	34.8
Cipsco Inc	53.8
Southern Co	30.3
DQE Inc	63.3
Scana Corp	44.4
Western Resources Inc	24.2
Portland General Corp	59.0
Peco Energy Co	30.5
Allegheny Power System	40.6
New England Electric System	31.8
Public Service Co of Colo	28.4
FPL Group Inc	38.1
CiNergy Corp	39.2
Illinova Corp	42.8
LG&E Energy Corp	21.0
Baltimore Gas & Electric	36.8
American Electric Power	31.9
Kansas City Power & Light	19.8
Boston Edison Co	32.0
General Public Utilities	38.0
Carolina Power & Light	37.5
Duke Power Co	30.4
Ohio Edison Co	35.9
KU Energy Corp	17.9
Northern States Power	18.4
Ipalco Enterprises Inc	35.3
Union Electric Co	25.9
UtiliCorp United Inc	17.8
Teco Energy Inc	32.7
Houston Industries Inc	46.1
Florida Progress Corp	25.5
Consolidated Edison of NY	32.3

Electric Utilities	Rate of Return (%)
Wisconsin Energy Corp	24.6
Potomac Electric Power	54.4
Dominion Resources Inc	22.6
Delmarva Power & Light	35.4
Northeast Utilities	20.8
Energy Corp	43.8
Central & South West Corp	31.8
Detroit Edison Co	41.2
Hawaiian Electric Inds	27.8
Public Service Entrp	24.5
Puget Sound Power & Light	25.7
Texas Utilities Co	38.8
Southwestern Public Svc Co	32.9
Idaho Power Co	37.4
PP&L Resources Inc	42.0
Oklahoma Gas & Electric	39.7
Pacific Gas & Electric	24.8
Montana Power Co	5.5
San Diego Gas & Electric	32.4
New York State Elec & Gas	44.8
Unicom Corp	44.5
MidAmerican Energy Co	31.8
PacifiCorp	23.4
SCEcorp	26.1
CMS Energy Corp	35.4
Long Island Lighting	19.0
Niagara Mohawk Power	-27.1
Centerior Energy Corp	8.6
AES Corp	22.4

```
TEST OF MU = 10.00 VS MU G.T. 10.00
THE ASSUMED SIGMA = 5.10

        N    MEAN   STDEV   SE MEAN    Z    P VALUE
GHQ    49   10.94   5.10      0.73   1.29    .0985
```

a. Specify the null and alternative hypotheses tested for determining whether the true mean one-year rate of return for electric utility stocks exceeded 30%.

b. Calculate the observed significance level of the test.

c. Interpret the result, part **b**, in the words of the problem.

8.34 Refer to Exercise 8.16, in which a random sample of 49 unemployed men were administered the General Health Questionnaire (GHQ). The sample mean and standard deviation were 10.94 and 5.10, respectively. Denoting the population mean GHQ for unemployed workers by μ, we wish to test the null hypothesis H_0: $\mu = 10$ versus the one-tailed alternative H_a: $\mu > 10$.

a. When the data are run through MINITAB, the results (in part) are as shown above. Check the program's results for accuracy.

b. What conclusion would you reach about the test based on the computer analysis?

8.35 In Exercise 7.12 we examined research about bicycle helmets reported in *Public Health Reports* (May–June 1992). One of the variables measured was the children's perception of the risk involved in bicycling. A random sample of 797 children in grades 4–6 were asked to rate their perception of bicycle risk without wearing a helmet, ranging from 1 (no risk) to 4 (very high risk). The mean and standard deviation of the sample were $\bar{x} = 3.39, s = .80$, respectively.

a. Assume that a mean score, μ, of 2.5 is indicative of indifference to risk, and values of μ exceeding 2.5 indicate a perception that a risk exists. What are the appropriate null and alternative hypotheses for testing the research hypothesis that children in this age group perceive a risk associated with failure to wear helmets?

b. Calculate the p-value for the data collected in this study.

c. Interpret the p-value in the context of this research.

8.36 In Exercise 8.17 you tested H_0: $\mu = .250$ versus H_a: $\mu \neq .250$, where μ is the population mean weight of plastic golf tees. A SAS printout for the hypothesis test is shown below. Locate the p-value on the printout and interpret its value.

8.37 An article published in the *Journal of the American Medical Association* (Oct. 16, 1995) calls smoking in China "a public health emergency." The researchers found that smokers in China smoke an average of 16.5 cigarettes a day. The high smoking rate is one reason why the tobacco industry is the central government's largest source of tax revenue. Has the average number of cigarettes smoked per day by Chinese smokers increased over the past two years? Consider that in a random sample of 200 Chinese smokers in 1997, the number of cigarettes smoked per day had a mean of 17.05 and a standard deviation of 5.21.

a. Set up the null and alternative hypotheses for testing whether Chinese smokers smoke, on average, more cigarettes a day in 1997 than in 1995. (Assume that the population mean for 1995 is $\mu = 16.5$.)

b. Compute and interpret the observed significance level of the test.

c. Why is a two-tailed test inappropriate for this problem?

8.38 In Exercise 8.20 you tested H_0: $\mu \geq 10$ versus H_a: $\mu < 10$, where μ is the average number of solder joints inspected per second when the joints are spaced .1 inch apart. An SPSS printout of the hypothesis test is shown on page 338.

a. Locate the two-tailed p-value of the test shown on the printout.

b. Adjust the p-value for the one-tailed test (if necessary) and interpret its value.

```
Analysis Variable : WT_250 (Test Mean Weight=.250)

N Obs         Mean        Std Dev          T    Prob>|T|
---------------------------------------------------------
  40      0.0024750     0.0022302    7.0188284    0.0001
---------------------------------------------------------
```

Variable	Number of Cases	Mean	Standard Deviation	Standard Error
NUMBER	48	9.2917	2.103	.304
MU	48	10.0000	.	.

(Difference) Mean	Standard Deviation	Standard Error	t Value	Degrees of Freedom	2-Tail Prob.
-.7083	2.103	.304	-2.33	47	.024

8.4 SMALL-SAMPLE TEST OF HYPOTHESIS ABOUT A POPULATION MEAN

A manufacturing operation consists of a single-machine-tool system that produces an average of 15.5 transformer parts every hour. After undergoing a complete overhaul, the system was monitored by observing the number of parts produced in each of seventeen randomly selected one-hour periods. The mean and standard deviation for the 17 production runs are:

$$\bar{x} = 15.42 \qquad s = .16$$

Does this sample provide sufficient evidence to conclude that the true mean number of parts produced every hour by the overhauled system differs from 15.5?

This inference can be placed in a test of hypothesis framework. We establish the preoverhaul mean as the null hypothesized value and utilize a two-tailed alternative that the true mean of the overhauled system differs from the preoverhaul mean:

$$H_0: \mu = 15.5$$

$$H_a: \mu \neq 15.5$$

Recall from Section 7.3 that when we are faced with making inferences about a population mean using the information in a small sample, two problems emerge:

1. The normality of the sampling distribution for $\bar{x}$ does not follow from the Central Limit Theorem when the sample size is small. We must assume that the distribution of measurements from which the sample was selected is approximately normally distributed in order to ensure the approximate normality of the sampling distribution of $\bar{x}$.

2. If the population standard deviation σ is unknown, as is usually the case, then we cannot assume that s will provide a good approximation for σ when the sample size is small. Instead, we must use the t-distribution rather than the standard normal z-distribution to make inferences about the population mean μ.

Therefore, as the test statistic of a small-sample test of a population mean, we use the t statistic:

$$\textit{Test statistic:} \; t = \frac{\bar{x} - \mu_0}{s/\sqrt{n}} = \frac{\bar{x} - 15.5}{s/\sqrt{n}}$$

where μ_0 is the null hypothesized value of the population mean, μ. In our example, $\mu_0 = 15.5$.

To find the rejection region, we must specify the value of α, the probability that the test will lead to rejection of the null hypothesis when it is true, and then con-

FIGURE 8.11
Two-tailed rejection
region for small-
sample *t*-test

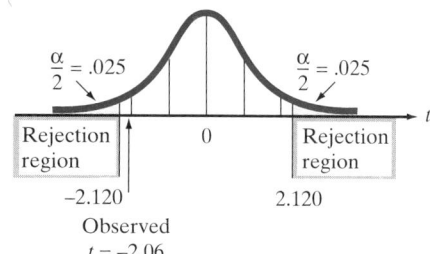

sult the *t*-table (Table VI of Appendix B). Using $\alpha = .05$, the two-tailed rejection region is

> *Rejection region:* $t_{\alpha/2} = t_{.025} = 2.120$ with $n - 1 = 16$ degrees of freedom

> Reject H_0 if $t < -2.120$ or $t > 2.120$

The rejection region is shown in Figure 8.11.

We are now prepared to calculate the test statistic and reach a conclusion:

$$t = \frac{\bar{x} - \mu_0}{s/\sqrt{n}} = \frac{15.42 - 15.50}{.16/\sqrt{17}} = \frac{-.08}{.0388} = -2.06$$

Since the calculated value of *t* does not fall in the rejection region (Figure 8.11), we cannot reject H_0 at the $\alpha = .05$ level of significance. Based on the sample evidence, we should not conclude that the mean number of parts produced per hour by the overhauled system differs from 15.5.

It is interesting to note that the calculated *t* value, -2.06, is *less than* the .05 level *z* value, -1.96. The implication is that if we had *incorrectly* used a *z* statistic for this test, we would have rejected the null hypothesis at the .05 level, concluding that the mean production per hour of the overhauled system differs from 15.5 parts. The important point is that the statistical procedure to be used must always be closely scrutinized and all the assumptions understood. Many statistical distortions are the result of misapplications of otherwise valid procedures.

The technique for conducting a small-sample test of hypothesis about a population mean is summarized in the following box.

Small-Sample Test of Hypothesis About μ

One-Tailed Test

$H_0\colon \mu = \mu_0$

$H_a\colon \mu < \mu_0$
  (or $H_a\colon \mu > \mu_0$)

Test statistic: $t = \dfrac{\bar{x} - \mu_0}{s/\sqrt{n}}$

Rejection region: $t < -t_\alpha$
  (or $t > t_\alpha$ when $H_a\colon \mu > \mu_0$)

Two-Tailed Test

$H_0\colon \mu = \mu_0$

$H_a\colon \mu \neq \mu_0$

Test statistic: $t = \dfrac{\bar{x} - \mu_0}{s/\sqrt{n}}$

Rejection region: $t < -t_{\alpha/2}$
  or $t > t_{\alpha/2}$

where t_α and $t_{\alpha/2}$ are based on $(n - 1)$ degrees of freedom

Assumption: A random sample is selected from a population with a relative frequency distribution that is approximately normal.

EXAMPLE 8.5

A major car manufacturer wants to test a new engine to determine whether it meets new air pollution standards. The mean emission μ of all engines of this type must be less than 20 parts per million of carbon. Ten engines are manufactured for testing purposes, and the emission level of each is determined. The data (in parts per million) are listed below:

15.6 16.2 22.5 20.5 16.4 19.4 16.6 17.9 12.7 13.9

Do the data supply sufficient evidence to allow the manufacturer to conclude that this type of engine meets the pollution standard? Assume that the production process is stable and the manufacturer is willing to risk a Type I error with probability $\alpha = .01$.

SOLUTION

The manufacturer wants to support the research hypothesis that the mean emission level μ for all engines of this type is less than 20 parts per million. The elements of this small-sample one-tailed test are

$$H_0: \mu = 20$$

$$H_a: \mu < 20$$

$$\text{Test statistic: } t = \frac{\bar{x} - 20}{s/\sqrt{n}}$$

Assumption: The relative frequency distribution of the population of emission levels for all engines of this type is approximately normal.

Rejection region: For $\alpha = .01$ and df $= n - 1 = 9$, the one-tailed rejection region (see Figure 8.12) is $t < -t_{.01} = -2.821$.

To calculate the test statistic, we entered the data into a computer and analyzed it using SAS. The SAS descriptive statistics printout is shown in Figure 8.13. From the printout, we obtain $\bar{x} = 17.17, s = 2.98$. Substituting these values into the test statistic formula, we get

$$t = \frac{\bar{x} - 20}{s/\sqrt{n}} = \frac{17.17 - 20}{2.98/\sqrt{10}} = -3.00$$

Since the calculated t falls in the rejection region (see Figure 8.12), the manufacturer concludes that $\mu < 20$ parts per million and the new engine type meets the pollution standard. Are you satisfied with the reliability associated with this infer-

FIGURE 8.12
A t-distribution with 9 df and the rejection region for Example 8.5

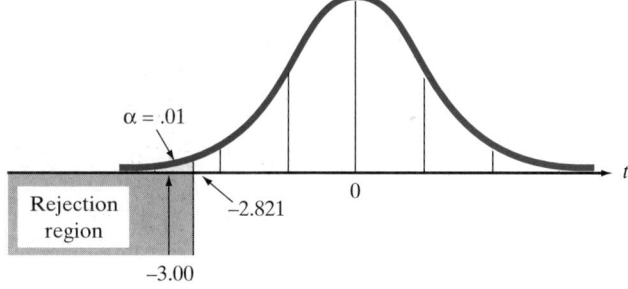

FIGURE 8.13
SAS descriptive statistics for 10 emission levels

```
Analysis Variable : EMIT

N Obs   N       Minimum         Maximum            Mean          Std Dev
-------------------------------------------------------------------------
   10   10    12.7000000      22.5000000      17.1700000        2.9814426
-------------------------------------------------------------------------
```

FIGURE 8.14
The observed
significance level for
the test of Example 8.5

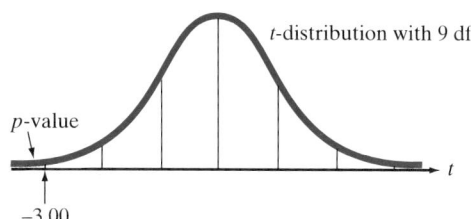

ence? The probability is only $\alpha = .01$ that the test would support the research hypothesis if in fact it were false.

EXAMPLE 8.6 Find the observed significance level for the test described in Example 8.5. Interpret the result.

SOLUTION
The test of Example 8.5 was a lower-tailed test: H_0: $\mu = 20$ versus H_a: $\mu < 20$. Since the value of t computed from the sample data was $t = -3.00$, the observed significance level (or p-value) for the test is equal to the probability that t would assume a value less than or equal to -3.00 if in fact H_0 were true. This is equal to the area in the lower tail of the t-distribution (shaded in Figure 8.14).

One way to find this area—i.e., the p-value for the test—is to consult the t-table (Table VI in Appendix B). Unlike the table of areas under the normal curve, Table VI gives only the t values corresponding to the areas .100, .050, .025, .010, .005, .001, and .0005. Therefore, we can only approximate the p-value for the test. Since the observed t value was based on 9 degrees of freedom, we use the df = 9 row in Table VI and move across the row until we reach the t values that are closest to the observed $t = -3.00$. [*Note:* We ignore the minus sign.] The t values corresponding to p-values of .010 and .005 are 2.821 and 3.250, respectively. Since the observed t value falls between $t_{.010}$ and $t_{.005}$, the p-value for the test lies between .005 and .010. In other words, $.005 < p$-value $< .01$. Thus, we would reject the null hypothesis, H_0: $\mu = 20$ parts per million, for any value of α larger than .01 (the upper bound of the p-value).

A second, more accurate, way to obtain the p-value is to use a statistical software package to conduct the test of hypothesis. The SAS printout for the test of H_0: $\mu = 20$ is displayed in Figure 8.15. Both the test statistic (-3.00) and p-value (.0149) are highlighted in Figure 8.15. Recall (from Section 8.3) that SAS conducts, by default, a two-tailed test. That is, SAS tests the alternative H_a: $\mu \neq 20$. Thus, the p-value reported on the printout must be adjusted to obtain the appropriate p-value for our lower-tailed test. Since the value of the test statistic is negative and H_a is of the form $<$ (i.e., the value of t agrees with the direction specified in H_a), the p-value is obtained by dividing the printout value in half:

$$\text{One-tailed } p\text{-value} = \frac{\text{Reported } p\text{-value}}{2} = \frac{.0149}{2} = .00745$$

You can see that the actual p-value of the test falls within the bounds obtained from Table VI. Thus, the two methods agree; we will reject H_0: $\mu = 20$ in favor of H_a: $\mu < 20$ for any α level larger than .01.

FIGURE 8.15
SAS test of H_0: $\mu = 20$
for Example 8.6

```
Analysis Variable : EMIT_20

N Obs          Mean        Std Dev              T  Prob>|T|
------------------------------------------------------------
  10     -2.8300000     2.9814426      -3.0016495    0.0149
------------------------------------------------------------
```

Small-sample inferences typically require more assumptions and provide less information about the population parameter than do large-sample inferences. Nevertheless, the t-test is a method of testing a hypothesis about a population mean of a normal distribution when only a small number of observations are available. What can be done if you know that the population relative frequency distribution is decidedly nonnormal, say highly skewed?

> **What Can Be Done If the Population Relative Frequency Distribution Departs Greatly from Normal?**
> *Answer:* Use one of the nonparametric statistical methods of Chapter 17.

EXERCISES 8.39–8.52

Learning the Mechanics

8.39 Under what circumstances should you use the t-distribution in testing a hypothesis about a population mean?

8.40 In what ways are the distributions of the z statistic and t-test statistic alike? How do they differ?

8.41 For each of the following rejection regions, sketch the sampling distribution of t, and indicate the location of the rejection region on your sketch:
a. $t > 1.440$ where df $= 6$
b. $t < -1.782$ where df $= 12$
c. $t < -2.060$ or $t > 2.060$ where df $= 25$

8.42 For each of the rejection regions defined in Exercise 8.41, what is the probability that a Type I error will be made?

8.43 A random sample of n observations is selected from a normal population to test the null hypothesis that $\mu = 10$. Specify the rejection region for each of the following combinations of H_a, α, and n:
a. $H_a: \mu \neq 10$; $\alpha = .05$; $n = 14$
b. $H_a: \mu > 10$; $\alpha = .01$; $n = 24$
c. $H_a: \mu > 10$; $\alpha = .10$; $n = 9$
d. $H_a: \mu < 10$; $\alpha = .01$; $n = 12$
e. $H_a: \mu \neq 10$; $\alpha = .10$; $n = 20$
f. $H_a: \mu < 10$; $\alpha = .05$; $n = 4$

8.44 A sample of five measurements, randomly selected from a normally distributed population, resulted in the following summary statistics: $\bar{x} = 4.8$, $s = 1.3$.
a. Test the null hypothesis that the mean of the population is 6 against the alternative hypothesis, $\mu < 6$. Use $\alpha = .05$.

b. Test the null hypothesis that the mean of the population is 6 against the alternative hypothesis, $\mu \neq 6$. Use $\alpha = .05$.
c. Find the observed significance level for each test.

8.45 MINITAB is used to conduct a t-test for the null hypothesis $H_0: \mu = 1,000$ versus the alternative hypothesis $H_a: \mu > 1,000$ based on a sample of 17 observations. The software's output is shown below.
a. What assumptions are necessary for the validity of this procedure?
b. Interpret the results of the test.
c. Suppose the alternative hypothesis had been the two-tailed $H_a: \mu \neq 1,000$. If the t statistic were unchanged, then what would the p-value be for this test? Interpret the p-value for the two-tailed test.

Applying the Concepts

8.46 The Cleveland Casting Plant is a large, highly automated producer of gray and nodular iron automotive castings for Ford Motor Company. Since Cleveland Casting ships 400,000 tons of iron-cast automobile parts per year, periodic monitoring of the settings for the casting process is required to achieve acceptable performance levels. Researchers B. Price and B. Barth studied process data collected at Cleveland Casting (*Quality Engineering*, Vol. 7, 1995). One process variable of interest to the researchers was the pouring temperature of the molten iron. The pouring temperatures (in degrees Fahrenheit) for a sample of 10 crankshafts are listed in the table on page 343. The

```
TEST OF MU = 1,000 VS MU G.T. 1,000

              N       MEAN     STDEV    SE MEAN       T    P VALUE
   X         17       1020     43.54      10.56    1.894     .0382
```

target setting for the pouring temperature is set at 2,550 degrees. Assuming the process is stable, conduct a test to determine whether the true mean pouring temperature differs from the target setting. Test using $\alpha = .01$.

| 2,543 | 2,541 | 2,544 | 2,620 | 2,560 | 2,559 | 2,562 |
| 2,553 | 2,552 | 2,553 | | | | |

Source: Price, B., and Barth, B. "A structural model relating process inputs and final product characteristics." *Quality Engineering,* Vol. 7, No. 4, 1995, p. 696 (Table 2).

8.47 Organochlorine pesticides (OCPs), like polychlorinated biphenyls (PCBs), are highly toxic organic compounds that are often found in fish. By law, the levels of OCPs and PCBs in fish are constantly monitored, so it is important to be able to accurately measure the amounts of these compounds in fish specimens. A new technique, called matrix solid-phase dispersion (MSPD), has been developed for chemically extracting trace organic compounds from solids (*Chromatographia,* Mar. 1995). The MSPD method was tested as follows. Uncontaminated fish fillets were injected with a known amount of OCP or PCB. The MSPD method was then used to extract the contaminant and the percentage of the toxic compound recovered was measured. The recovery percentages for $n = 5$ fish fillets injected with the OCP Aldrin are listed below:

99 102 94 99 95

Do the data provide sufficient evidence to indicate that the mean recovery percentage of Aldrin exceeds 85% using the new MSPD method? Test using $\alpha = .05$.

8.48 To instill customer loyalty, airlines, hotels, rental car companies, and credit card companies (among others) have initiated **frequency marketing programs** that reward their regular customers. In the United States alone, 30 million people are members of the frequent flier programs of the airline industry (*Fortune,* Feb. 22, 1993). A large fast-food restaurant chain wished to explore the profitability of such a program. They randomly selected 12 of their 1,200 restaurants nationwide and instituted a frequency program that rewarded customers with a $5.00 gift certificate after every 10 meals purchased at full price. They ran the trial program for three months. The restaurants not in the sample had an average increase in profits of $1,047.34 over the previous three months, whereas the restaurants in the sample had the following changes in profit:

$2,232.90 $545.47 $3,440.70 $1,809.10
$6,552.70 $4,798.70 $2,965.00 $2,610.70
$3,381.30 $1,591.40 $2,376.20   −$2,191.00

Note that the last number is negative, representing a decrease in profits. Summary statistics and

graphs for the data are given in the SPSS printout at the top of page 344.
a. Specify the appropriate null and alternative hypotheses for determining whether the mean profit change for restaurants with frequency programs is significantly greater (in a statistical sense) than $1,047.34.
b. Conduct the test of part **b** using $\alpha = .05$. Does it appear that the frequency program would be profitable for the company if adopted nationwide?

8.49 The changing ecology of the Everglades National Park in Florida, considered a national treasure by many, has been the subject of much environmental research. One water-quality parameter of concern in the park is the total phosphorus level. Suppose that the EPA makes 12 measurements in one section of the park, yielding a mean level of total phosphorus at 12.3 parts per billion (ppb) and a standard deviation of 5.4 ppb. The EPA wants to test whether the data support the conclusion that the mean level is less than 15 ppb.
a. What are the null and alternative hypotheses appropriate for the EPA's test?
b. The EPA statistician analyzed the data using SAS, with the results shown. Find and adjust (if necessary) the p-value of the test.
c. Interpret the results of the test.

```
Analysis Variable : PHOS_15

  N Obs          T     Prob>|T|
-------------------------------------
    12      -1.732       0.1112
-------------------------------------
```

8.50 The Occupational Safety and Health Act (OSHA) allows issuance of engineering standards to ensure safe workplaces for all Americans. The maximum allowable mean level of arsenic in smelters, herbicide production facilities, and other places where arsenic is used is .004 milligram per cubic meter of air. Suppose smelters at two plants are being investigated to determine whether they are meeting OSHA standards. Two analyses of the air are made at each plant, and the results (in milligrams per cubic meter of air) are shown in the table.

PLANT 1		PLANT 2	
Observation	Arsenic Level	Observation	Arsenic Level
1	.01	1	.05
2	.005	2	.09

a. What are the appropriate null and alternative hypotheses if we wish to test whether the plants meet the current OSHA standard?

```
        PROFIT
Valid cases:        12.0   Missing cases:        .0    Percent missing:        .0

Mean       2509.431  Std Err   620.4388  Min     -2191.00   Skewness     -.3616
Median     2493.450  Variance  4619332   Max      6552.700  S E Skew      .6373
5% Trim    2545.940  Std Dev   2149.263  Range    8743.700  Kurtosis    1.8750
                                         IQR      1780.025  S E Kurt    1.2322
------------------------------------------------------------------------------
Frequency    Stem &  Leaf
    1.00 Extremes      (-2191)
    1.00      0 .  5
    2.00      1 .  58
    4.00      2 .  2369
    2.00      3 .  34
    1.00      4 .  7
    1.00 Extremes      (6553)

Stem width:    1000.00
Each leaf:        1 case(s)
------------------------------------------------------------------------------
  8000.00 ─

                    (O) CASE5

  4000.00 ─         ┌─┬─┐
                    │ * │
                    └─┴─┘
     .00 ─

                    (O) CASE12
 -4000.00 ─


Variables       PROFIT

N of Cases       12.00

    Symbol Key:        *    - Median    (O)  - Outlier    (E)  - Extreme
```

b. These data are analyzed by MINITAB, with the results shown below. Check the calculations of the t statistics and p-values.

c. Interpret the results of the two tests.

8.51 Periodic assessment of stress in paved highways is important to maintaining safe roads. The Mississippi Department of Transportation recently collected data on number of cracks (called *crack intensity*) in an undivided two-lane highway using van-mounted state-of-the-art video technology (*Journal of Infrastructure Systems*, Mar. 1995). The mean number of cracks found in a sample of eight 50-meter sections of the highway was $\bar{x} = .210$, with a variance of $s^2 = .011$. Suppose the American Association of State Highway and Transportation Officials (AASHTO) recommends a maximum mean crack intensity of .100 for safety purposes. Test the hypothesis that the true mean crack intensity of the Mississippi highway exceeds the AASHTO recommended maximum. Use $\alpha = .01$.

```
TEST OF MU = 0.00400 VS MU G.T. 0.00400

           N      MEAN     STDEV   SE MEAN       T   P VALUE
Plant1     2   0.00750   0.00354   0.00250    1.40      0.20
Plant2     2   0.07000   0.02828   0.02000    3.30     0.094
```

8.52 One way of evaluating a measuring instrument is to repeatedly measure the same item and compare the average of these measurements to the item's known measured value. The difference is used to assess the instrument's accuracy (*Quality Progress,* Jan. 1993). To evaluate a particular Metlar scale, an item whose weight is known to be 16.01 ounces is weighed five times by the same operator. The measurements, in ounces, are as follows:

15.99   16.00   15.97   16.01   15.96

a. In a statistical sense, does the average measurement differ from 16.01? Conduct the appropriate hypothesis test. What does your analysis suggest about the accuracy of the instrument?

b. List any assumptions you make in conducting the hypothesis test.

8.5 LARGE-SAMPLE TEST OF HYPOTHESIS ABOUT A POPULATION PROPORTION

Inferences about population proportions (or percentages) are often made in the context of the probability, p, of "success" for a binomial distribution. We saw how to use large samples from binomial distributions to form confidence intervals for p in Section 7.3. We now consider tests of hypotheses about p.

For example, consider the problem of *insider trading* in the stock market. Insider trading is the buying and selling of stock by an individual privy to inside information in a company, usually a high-level executive in the firm. The Securities and Exchange Commission (SEC) imposes strict guidelines about insider trading so that all investors can have equal access to information that may affect the stock's price. An investor wishing to test the effectiveness of the SEC guidelines monitors the market for a period of a year and records the number of times a stock price increases the day following a significant purchase of stock by an insider. For a total of 576 such transactions, the stock increased the following day 327 times. Does this sample provide evidence that the stock price may be affected by insider trading?

We first view this as a binomial experiment, with the 576 transactions as the trials, and success representing an increase in the stock's price the following day. Let p represent the probability that the stock price will increase following a large insider purchase. If the insider purchase has no effect on the stock price (that is, if the information available to the insider is identical to that available to the general market), then the investor expects the probability of a stock increase to be the same as that of a decrease, or $p = .5$. On the other hand, if insider trading affects the stock price (indicating that the market has not fully accounted for the information known to the insiders), then the investor expects the stock either to decrease or to increase more than half the time following significant insider transactions; that is, $p \neq .5$.

We can now place the problem in the context of a test of hypothesis:

$$H_0: p = .5$$
$$H_a: p \neq .5$$

Recall that the sample proportion, $\hat{p}$ is really just the sample mean of the outcomes of the individual binomial trials and, as such, is approximately normally distributed (for large samples) according to the Central Limit Theorem. Thus, for large samples we can use the standard normal z as the test statistic:

$$\text{Test statistic: } z = \frac{\text{Sample proportion} - \text{Null hypothesized proportion}}{\text{Standard deviation of sample proportion}}$$

$$= \frac{\hat{p} - p_0}{\sigma_{\hat{p}}}$$

where we use the symbol p_0 to represent the null hypothesized value of p.

FIGURE 8.16
Rejection region for insider trading example

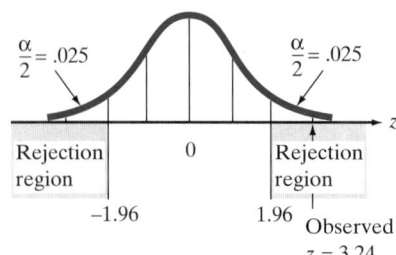

Rejection region: We use the standard normal distribution to find the appropriate rejection region for the specified value of α. Using $\alpha = .05$, the two-tailed rejection region is

$$z < -z_{\alpha/2} = -z_{.025} = -1.96 \quad \text{or} \quad z > z_{\alpha/2} = z_{.025} = 1.96$$

See Figure 8.16.

We are now prepared to calculate the value of the test statistic. Before doing so, we want to be sure that the sample size is large enough to ensure that the normal approximation for the sampling distribution of $\hat{p}$ is reasonable. To check this, we calculate a 3-standard-deviation interval around the null hypothesized value, p_0, which is assumed to be the true value of p until our test procedure indicates otherwise. Recall that $\sigma_{\hat{p}} = \sqrt{pq/n}$ and that we need an estimate of the product pq in order to calculate a numerical value of the test statistic z. Since the null hypothesized value is generally the accepted-until-proven-otherwise value, we use the value of p_0q_0 (where $q_0 = 1 - p_0$) to estimate pq in the calculation of z. Thus,

$$\sigma_{\hat{p}} = \sqrt{\frac{pq}{n}} = \sqrt{\frac{p_0q_0}{n}} = \sqrt{\frac{(.5)(.5)}{576}} = .021$$

and the 3-standard-deviation interval around p_0 is

$$p_0 \pm 3\sigma_{\hat{p}} \approx .5 \pm 3(.021) = (.437, .563)$$

As long as this interval does not contain 0 or 1 (i.e., is completely contained in the interval 0 to 1), as is the case here, the normal distribution will provide a reasonable approximation for the sampling distribution of $\hat{p}$.

Returning to the hypothesis test at hand, the proportion of the sampled transactions that resulted in a stock increase is

$$\hat{p} = \frac{327}{576} = .568$$

Finally, we calculate the number of standard deviations (the z value) between the sampled and hypothesized value of the binomial proportion:

$$z = \frac{\hat{p} - p_0}{\sigma_{\hat{p}}} = \frac{\hat{p} - p_0}{\sqrt{p_0q_0/n}} = \frac{.568 - .5}{.021} = \frac{.068}{.021} = 3.24$$

The implication is that the observed sample proportion is (approximately) 3.24 standard deviations above the null hypothesized proportion .5 (Figure 8.16). Therefore, we reject the null hypothesis, concluding at the .05 level of significance that the true probability of an increase or decrease in a stock's price differs from .5 the day following insider purchase of the stock. It appears that an insider purchase significantly increases the probability that the stock price will increase the following day. (To estimate the magnitude of the probability of an increase, a confidence interval can be constructed.)

The test of hypothesis about a population proportion p is summarized in the next box. Note that the procedure is entirely analogous to that used for conducting large-sample tests about a population mean.

Large-Sample Test of Hypothesis About p

One-Tailed Test

$H_0: p = p_0$
  (p_0 = hypothesized value of p)

$H_a: p < p_0$
  (or $H_a: p > p_0$)

Test statistic: $z = \dfrac{\hat{p} - p_0}{\sigma_{\hat{p}}}$

Two-Tailed Test

$H_0: p = p_0$

$H_a: p \neq p_0$

Test statistic: $z = \dfrac{\hat{p} - p_0}{\sigma_{\hat{p}}}$

where, according to H_0, $\sigma_{\hat{p}} = \sqrt{p_0 q_0 / n}$ and $q_0 = 1 - p_0$

Rejection region: $z < -z_\alpha$
  (or $z > z_\alpha$ when $H_a: p > p_0$)

Rejection region: $z < -z_{\alpha/2}$
  or $z > z_{\alpha/2}$

Assumption: The experiment is binomial, and the sample size is large enough that the interval $p_0 \pm 3\sigma_{\hat{p}}$ does not include 0 or 1.

EXAMPLE 8.7

The reputations (and hence sales) of many businesses can be severely damaged by shipments of manufactured items that contain a large percentage of defectives. For example, a manufacturer of alkaline batteries may want to be reasonably certain that fewer than 5% of its batteries are defective. Suppose 300 batteries are randomly selected from a very large shipment; each is tested and 10 defective batteries are found. Does this provide sufficient evidence for the manufacturer to conclude that the fraction defective in the entire shipment is less than .05? Use $\alpha = .01$.

SOLUTION

Before conducting the test of hypothesis, we check to determine whether the sample size is large enough to use the normal approximation for the sampling distribution of $\hat{p}$. The criterion is tested by the interval

$$p_0 \pm 3\sigma_{\hat{p}} = p_0 \pm 3\sqrt{\frac{p_0 q_0}{n}} = .05 \pm 3\sqrt{\frac{(.05)(.95)}{300}}$$

$$= .05 \pm .04 \qquad \text{or} \qquad (.01, .09)$$

Since the interval lies within the interval $(0, 1)$, the normal approximation will be adequate.

The objective of the sampling is to determine whether there is sufficient evidence to indicate that the fraction defective, p, is less than .05. Consequently, we will test the null hypothesis that $p = .05$ against the alternative hypothesis that $p < .05$. The elements of the test are

$$H_0: p = .05$$

$$H_a: p < .05$$

FIGURE 8.17
Rejection region
for Example 8.7

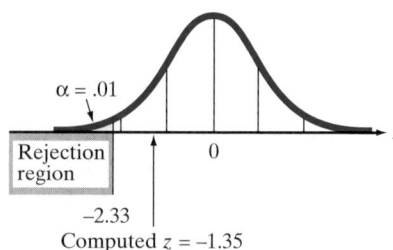

$\alpha = .01$

Rejection region

0

z

−2.33

Computed $z = -1.35$

Test statistic: $z = \dfrac{\hat{p} - p_0}{\sigma_{\hat{p}}}$

Rejection region: $z < -z_{.01} = -2.33$ (see Figure 8.17)

We now calculate the test statistic:

$$z = \frac{\hat{p} - .05}{\sigma_{\hat{p}}} = \frac{(10/300) - .05}{\sqrt{p_0 q_0/n}} = \frac{.033 - .05}{\sqrt{p_0 q_0/300}}$$

Notice that we use p_0 to calculate $\sigma_{\hat{p}}$ because, in contrast to calculating $\sigma_{\hat{p}}$ for a confidence interval, the test statistic is computed on the assumption that the null hypothesis is true—that is, $p = p_0$. Therefore, substituting the values for $\hat{p}$ and p_0 into the z statistic, we obtain

$$z \approx \frac{-.017}{\sqrt{(.05)(.95)/300}} = \frac{-.017}{.0126} = -1.35$$

As shown in Figure 8.17, the calculated z value does not fall in the rejection region. Therefore, there is insufficient evidence at the .01 level of significance to indicate that the shipment contains fewer than 5% defective batteries. ◼

EXAMPLE 8.8

In Example 8.7 we found that we did not have sufficient evidence, at the $\alpha = .01$ level of significance, to indicate that the fraction defective p of alkaline batteries was less than $p = .05$. How strong was the weight of evidence favoring the alternative hypothesis ($H_a: p < .05$)? Find the observed significance level for the test.

SOLUTION
The computed value of the test statistic z was $z = -1.35$. Therefore, for this lower-tailed test, the observed significance level is

$$\text{Observed significance level} = P(z \leq -1.35)$$

This lower-tail area is shown in Figure 8.18. The area between $z = 0$ and $z = 1.35$ is given in Table IV in Appendix B as .4115. Therefore, the observed significance level is $.5 - .4115 = .0885$. Note that this probability is quite small. Although we did not reject $H_0: p = .05$ at $\alpha = .01$, the probability of observing a z value as small as or smaller than -1.35 is only .0885 if in fact H_0 is true. Therefore, we would reject H_0 if we choose $\alpha = .10$ (since the observed significance level is less than .10), and we would not reject H_0 (the conclusion of Example 8.7) if we choose $\alpha = .05$ or $\alpha = .01$. ◼

FIGURE 8.18
The observed
significance level
for Example 8.8

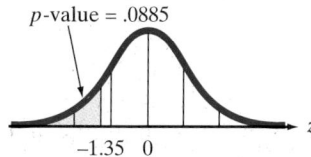

p-value = .0885

−1.35 0

z

STATISTICS IN ACTION

8.3 STATISTICAL QUALITY CONTROL, PART II

In complicated assembly operations (such as railway-car assembly), many quality variables could be measured (e.g., strength of welds, degree of corrosion, and number of paint flaws), and in principle, each could be monitored over time using control charts, as described in Statistics in Action 8.2. In some situations, however, an alternative, simpler procedure may be more appropriate. For example, n finished products could be randomly sampled at regular time intervals, inspected for defects, and simply classified as being defective or nondefective products. Then $\hat{p}$, the proportion of defectives in each sample, could be determined and plotted on a control chart called a **p-chart**, as illustrated in Figure 8.19. In this way, the proportion of defective products produced and, therefore, product quality and the current capability of the production process could be monitored over time (Montgomery, 1991).

In order to construct the control chart shown in Figure 8.19, it is necessary to know (i.e., have a good estimate for) p_0, the proportion of defectives produced when the process is operating properly (i.e., in control). Then, assuming n is large enough to use the normal distribution to approximate the sampling distribution of $\hat{p}$, the control limits are located $3\sigma_{\hat{p}}$ above and below p_0. If a value of $\hat{p}$ falls above the upper limit or below the lower limit, there is strong evidence that the process is out of control.

Focus

Describe this control chart decision procedure in the language of hypothesis testing by answering the following questions:

a. What are the null and alternative hypotheses of interest?

b. What is the test statistic?

c. Specify the rejection region.

d. What is the probability of committing a Type I error?

e. If a value of $\hat{p}$ falls above the upper limit, it is a signal that the process is turning out more defectives than usual. But what is the significance of the lower control limit? Why should the manufacturer be concerned if fewer defectives than usual are being produced? [*Hint:* There are two important reasons. One is related to the problem of inspection error; the other has to do with acquiring new knowledge to improve the production process.]

Small-sample test procedures are also available for p. These are omitted from our discussion because most surveys use samples that are large enough to employ the large-sample tests presented in this section.

FIGURE 8.19
p-chart for proportion defective (Statistics in Action 8.3)

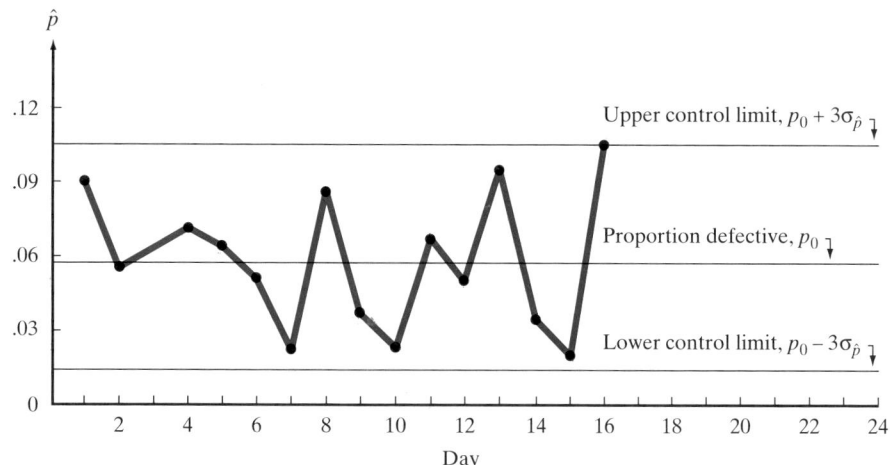

Note: Exercises marked with 💾 *contain data for computer analysis on a 3.5" disk (file name in parentheses).*

Learning the Mechanics

8.53 For the binomial sample sizes and null hypothesized values of p in each part, determine whether the sample size is large enough to use the normal approximation methodology presented in this section to conduct a test of the null hypothesis H_0: $p = p_0$.
a. $n = 900, p_0 = .975$ **b.** $n = 125, p_0 = .01$
c. $n = 40, p_0 = .75$ **d.** $n = 15, p_0 = .75$
e. $n = 12, p_0 = .62$

8.54 Suppose a random sample of 100 observations from a binomial population gives a value of $\hat{p} = .63$ and you wish to test the null hypothesis that the population parameter p is equal to .70 against the alternative hypothesis that p is less than .70.
a. Noting that $\hat{p} = .63$, what does your intuition tell you? Does the value of $\hat{p}$ appear to contradict the null hypothesis?
b. Use the large-sample z-test to test H_0: $p = .70$ against the alternative hypothesis, H_a: $p < .70$. Use $\alpha = .05$. How do the test results compare with your intuitive decision from part **a**?
c. Find and interpret the observed significance level of the test you conducted in part **b**.

8.55 Suppose the sample in Exercise 8.54 has produced $\hat{p} = .83$ and we wish to test H_0: $p = .9$ against the alternative H_a: $p < .9$.
a. Calculate the value of the z statistic for this test.
b. Note that the numerator of the z statistic $(\hat{p} - p_0 = .83 - .90 = -.07)$ is the same as for Exercise 8.54. Considering this, why is the absolute value of z for this exercise larger than that calculated in Exercise 8.54?
c. Complete the test using $\alpha = .05$ and interpret the result.
d. Find the observed significance level for the test and interpret its value.

8.56 A statistics student used a computer program to test the null hypothesis H_0: $p = .5$ against the one-tailed alternative, H_a: $p > .5$. A sample of 500

observations are input into SPSS, which returns the output shown at the bottom of the page.
a. The student concludes, based on the p-value, that there is a 33% chance that the alternative hypothesis is true. Do you agree? If not, correct the interpretation.
b. How would the p-value change if the alternative hypothesis were two-tailed, H_a: $p \neq .5$? Interpret this p-value.

8.57 (X08.057) Refer to Exercise 7.36, in which 50 consumers taste tested a new snack food. Their responses (where 0 = do not like; 1 = like; 2 = indifferent) are reproduced below.

1	0	0	1	2	0	1	1	0	0	0	1
0	2	0	2	2	0	0	1	1	0	0	0
0	1	0	2	0	0	0	1	0	0	1	0
0	1	0	1	0	2	0	0	1	1	0	0
0	1										

a. Test H_0: $p = .5$ against H_a: $p > .5$, where p is the proportion of customers who do not like the snack food. Use $\alpha = .10$.
b. Find the observed significance level of your test.

Applying the Concepts

8.58 In 1895, druggist Asa Candler began distributing handwritten tickets to his customers for free glasses of Coca-Cola at his soda fountain. That was the genesis of the discount coupon. In 1975 it was estimated that 69% of U.S. consumers regularly used discount coupons when shopping. Today more than 3,000 manufacturers distribute more than 310 billion coupons per year. In a 1995 consumer survey, 71% said they regularly redeem coupons (*Newark Star-Ledger*, Oct. 9, 1995). Assume the 1995 survey consisted of a random sample of 1,000 shoppers.
a. Does the 1995 survey provide sufficient evidence that the percentage of shoppers using cents-off coupons exceeds 69%? Test using $\alpha = .05$.
b. Is the sample size large enough to use the inferential procedures presented in this section? Explain.
c. Find the observed significance level for the test you conducted in part **a**, and interpret its value.

```
- - - - - - Binomial Test
       Cases
                                Test Prop. =   .5000
          220   = 1            Obs. Prop. =   .4400
          280   = 0
          --                   Z Approximation
          500   Total          2-Tailed P =  0.3300
```

8.59 If you live in California, the decision to purchase earthquake insurance is a critical one. An article in the *Annals of the Association of American Geographers* (June 1992) investigated many factors that California residents consider when purchasing earthquake insurance. The survey revealed that only 133 of 337 randomly selected residences in Los Angeles County were protected by earthquake insurance.

   a. What are the appropriate null and alternative hypotheses to test the research hypothesis that less than 40% of the residents of Los Angeles County were protected by earthquake insurance?

   b. Do the data provide sufficient evidence to support the research hypothesis? Use $\alpha = .10$.

   c. Calculate and interpret the *p*-value for the test.

8.60 **(X08.060)** *Consumer Reports* (Sept. 1992) recently evaluated and rated 46 brands of toothpaste. (See Exercise 2.106.) One attribute examined in the study was whether or not a toothpaste brand carries an American Dental Association (ADA) seal verifying effective decay prevention. The data for the 46 brands (coded 1 = ADA seal, 0 = no ADA seal) are reproduced below.

```
0  0  0  0  0  0  1  1  1  0  0  1
0  1  0  0  0  0  1  1  1  0  1  1
1  1  0  0  0  0  1  0  0  1  1
1  0  1  0  1  1  1  0  0  0
```

   a. Give the null and alternative hypotheses for testing whether the true proportion of toothpaste brands with the ADA seal verifying effective decay prevention is less than .5.

   b. The data were analyzed in SPSS; the results of the test are shown in the SPSS printout below. Interpret the results.

8.61 A placebo is a pill that looks and tastes real but contains no medically active chemicals. The *placebo effect* describes the phenomenon of improvement in the condition of a patient taking placebos. For the placebo effect to occur, both doctors and patients must believe that the placebo being administered is really a drug. Such was the case at a clinic in La Jolla, California. Physicians gave what they thought were drugs to 7,000 asthma, ulcer, and herpes patients. Although the doctors later learned that the drugs were really placebos, 70% of the patients reported an improved condition (*Forbes,* May 22, 1995). Use this information to test (at $\alpha = .05$) if there is a placebo effect at the clinic. Assume that if the placebo is ineffective, the probability of a patient's condition improving is .5.

8.62 "Take the Pepsi Challenge" was a marketing campaign used recently by the Pepsi-Cola Company. Coca-Cola drinkers participated in a blind taste test where they were asked to taste unmarked cups of Pepsi and Coke and were asked to select their favorite. In one Pepsi television commercial, an announcer states that "in recent blind taste tests, more than half the Diet Coke drinkers surveyed said they preferred the taste of Diet Pepsi" (*Consumer's Research,* May 1993). Suppose 100 Diet Coke drinkers took the Pepsi Challenge and 56 preferred the taste of Diet Pepsi. Test the hypothesis that more than half of all Diet Coke drinkers will select Diet Pepsi in the blind taste test. Use $\alpha = .05$. What are the consequences of the test results from Coca-Cola's perspective?

8.63 Refer to the *Chest* (May 1995) study of obstructive sleep apnea, Exercise 7.40. Recall that the disorder causes a person to stop breathing and awaken briefly during a sleep cycle. Stanford University researchers found that 124 of 159 commercial truck drivers suffered from obstructive sleep apnea.

   a. Sleep researchers theorize that 25% of the general population suffer from obstructive sleep apnea. Use a test of hypothesis (at $\alpha = .10$) to determine whether this percentage differs for commercial truck drivers.

   b. Find the observed significance level of the test and interpret its value.

   c. In part **b** of Exercise 7.40, you used a 90% confidence interval to make the inference of part **a**. Explain why these two inferences must necessarily agree.

8.64 In gambling, a *system* is a strategy for playing a game that is thought to improve one's chances of winning. A professional gambler sells videotapes that teach his system for playing casino blackjack. His televised advertisements on late-night cable

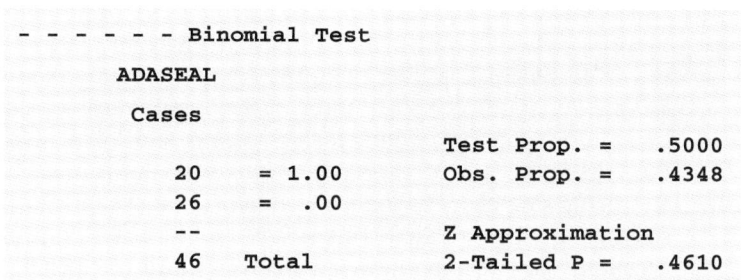

TV claim that the "system guarantees winning results on average." A customer who lost thousands of dollars while using the system decided to sue the professional gambler for false advertising. To test the gambler's claim, the customer's lawyer commissioned a computer simulation study. The computer "played" 1,000,000 independent games of blackjack with the "player" following the gambler's system and the "dealer" obeying the standard house rules. The "player" won 497,584 of the simulated games.

a. Letting p represent the long-run proportion of games won by players using the system, test $H_0: p \geq .50$ versus $H_a: p < .50$ using $\alpha = .01$.

b. Do the results of this test contradict the advertised claim? Explain.

c. Suppose the simulation had been run only 10,000 times. Would the results of the test be the same if the "player" won the same proportion of the simulated games (i.e., 4,976)?

d. List any assumptions that you made in answering parts **a** and **c**.

e. Find the observed significance levels for the tests you conducted in parts **a** and **c** and interpret their values.

8.6 CALCULATING TYPE II ERROR PROBABILITIES: MORE ABOUT β (OPTIONAL)

In our introduction to hypothesis testing in Section 8.1, we showed that the probability of committing a Type I error, α, can be controlled by the selection of the rejection region for the test. Thus, when the test statistic falls in the rejection region and we make the decision to reject the null hypothesis, we do so knowing the error rate for incorrect rejections of H_0. The situation corresponding to accepting the null hypothesis, and thereby risking a Type II error, is not generally as controllable. For that reason, we adopted a policy of nonrejection of H_0 when the test statistic does not fall in the rejection region, rather than risking an error of unknown magnitude.

To see how β, the probability of a Type II error, can be calculated for a test of hypothesis, recall the example in Section 8.1 in which a city tests a manufacturer's pipe to see whether it meets the requirement that the mean strength exceeds 2,400 pounds per linear foot. The setup for the test is as follows:

$$H_0: \mu = 2,400$$
$$H_a: \mu > 2,400$$
$$\text{Test statistic: } z = \frac{\bar{x} - 2,400}{\sigma/\sqrt{n}}$$

Rejection region: $z > 1.645$ for $\alpha = .05$

Figure 8.20a shows the rejection region for the **null distribution**—that is, the distribution of the test statistic assuming the null hypothesis is true. The area in the rejection region is .05, and this area represents α, the probability that the test statistic leads to rejection of H_0 when in fact H_0 is true.

The Type II error probability β is calculated assuming that the null hypothesis is false, because it is defined as the *probability of accepting H_0 when it is false*. Since H_0 is false for any value of μ exceeding 2,400, one value of β exists for each possible value of μ greater than 2,400 (an infinite number of possibilities). Figures 8.20b, 8.20c, and 8.20d show three of the possibilities, corresponding to alternative hypothesis values of μ equal to 2,425, 2,450, and 2,475, respectively. Note that β is the area in the *nonrejection* (or *acceptance*) *region* in each of these distributions and that β decreases as the true value of μ moves farther from the null hypothesized value of $\mu = 2,400$. This is sensible because the probability of incorrectly accepting the null hypothesis should decrease as the distance between the null and alternative values of μ increases.

FIGURE 8.20
Values of α and β for various values of μ

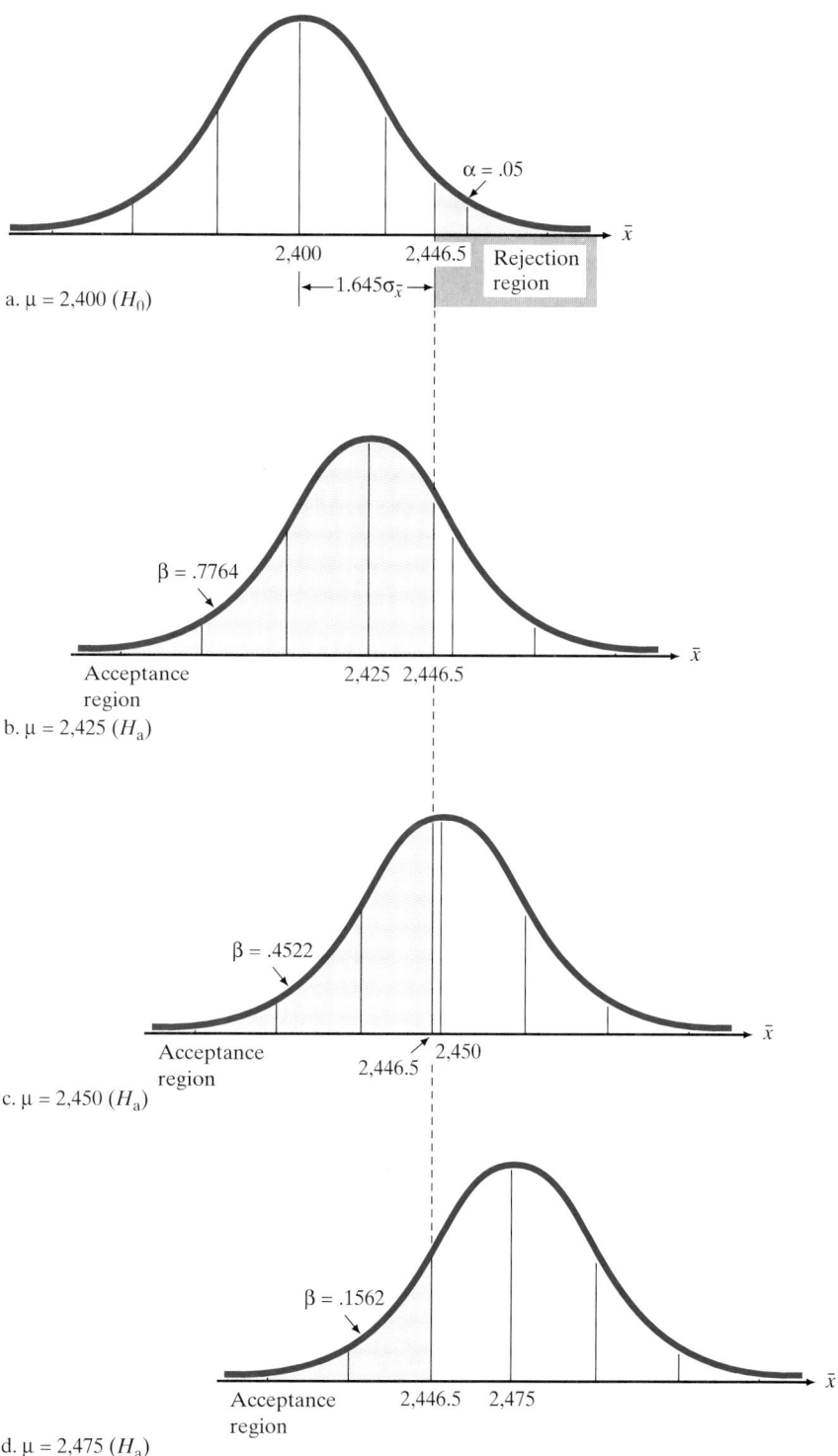

a. $\mu = 2{,}400$ (H_0)

b. $\mu = 2{,}425$ (H_a)

c. $\mu = 2{,}450$ (H_a)

d. $\mu = 2{,}475$ (H_a)

In order to calculate the value of β for a specific value of μ in H_a, we proceed as follows:

1. Calculate the value of $\bar{x}$ that corresponds to the border between the acceptance and rejection regions. For the sewer pipe example, this is the value of $\bar{x}$

that lies 1.645 standard deviations above $\mu = 2{,}400$ in the sampling distribution of $\bar{x}$. Denoting this value by $\bar{x}_0$, corresponding to the largest value of $\bar{x}$ that supports the null hypothesis, we find (recalling that $s = 200$ and $n = 50$)

$$\bar{x}_0 = \mu_0 + 1.645\sigma_{\bar{x}} = 2{,}400 + 1.645\left(\frac{\sigma}{\sqrt{n}}\right)$$

$$\approx 2{,}400 + 1.645\left(\frac{s}{\sqrt{n}}\right) = 2{,}400 + 1.645\left(\frac{200}{\sqrt{50}}\right)$$

$$= 2{,}400 + 1.645(28.28) = 2{,}446.5$$

2. For a particular alternative distribution corresponding to a value of μ, denoted by μ_a, we calculate the z value corresponding to $\bar{x}_0$, the border between the rejection and acceptance regions. We then use this z value and Table IV of Appendix B to determine the area in the *acceptance region* under the alternative distribution. This area is the value of β corresponding to the particular alternative μ_a. For example, for the alternative $\mu_a = 2{,}425$, we calculate

$$z = \frac{\bar{x}_0 - 2{,}425}{\sigma_{\bar{x}}} = \frac{\bar{x}_0 - 2{,}425}{\sigma/\sqrt{n}}$$

$$\approx \frac{\bar{x}_0 - 2{,}425}{s/\sqrt{n}} = \frac{2{,}446.5 - 2{,}425}{28.28} = .76$$

Note in Figure 8.20b that the area in the acceptance region is the area to the left of $z = .76$. This area is

$$\beta = .5 + .2764 = .7764$$

Thus, the probability that the test procedure will lead to an incorrect acceptance of the null hypothesis $\mu = 2{,}400$ when in fact $\mu = 2{,}425$ is about .78. As the average strength of the pipe increases to 2,450, the value of β decreases to .4522 (Figure 8.20c). If the mean strength is further increased to 2,475, the value of β is further decreased to .1562 (Figure 8.20d). Thus, even if the true mean strength of the pipe exceeds the minimum specification by 75 pounds per linear foot, the test procedure will lead to an incorrect acceptance of the null hypothesis (rejection of the pipe) approximately 16% of the time. The upshot is that the pipe must be manufactured so that the mean strength well exceeds the minimum requirement if the manufacturer wants the probability of its acceptance by the city to be large (i.e., β to be small).

The steps for calculating β for a large-sample test about a population mean are summarized in the next box.

Steps for Calculating β for a Large-Sample Test About μ

1. Calculate the value(s) of $\bar{x}$ corresponding to the border(s) of the rejection region. There will be one border value for a one-tailed test, and two for a two-tailed test. The formula is one of the following, corresponding to a test with level of significance α:

$$\text{Upper-tailed test: } \bar{x}_0 = \mu_0 + z_\alpha\sigma_{\bar{x}} \approx \mu_0 + z_\alpha\left(\frac{s}{\sqrt{n}}\right)$$

$$\text{Lower-tailed test: } \bar{x}_0 = \mu_0 - z_\alpha\sigma_{\bar{x}} \approx \mu_0 - z_\alpha\left(\frac{s}{\sqrt{n}}\right)$$

$$\text{Two-tailed test:} \quad \bar{x}_{0,L} = \mu_0 - z_{\alpha/2}\sigma_{\bar{x}} \approx \mu_0 - z_{\alpha/2}\left(\frac{s}{\sqrt{n}}\right)$$

$$\bar{x}_{0,U} = \mu_0 + z_{\alpha/2}\sigma_{\bar{x}} \approx \mu_0 + z_{\alpha/2}\left(\frac{s}{\sqrt{n}}\right)$$

2. Specify the value of μ_a in the alternative hypothesis for which the value of β is to be calculated. Then convert the border value(s) of $\bar{x}_0$ to z value(s) using the alternative distribution with mean μ_a. The general formula for the z value is

$$z = \frac{\bar{x}_0 - \mu_a}{\sigma_{\bar{x}}}$$

Sketch the alternative distribution (centered at μ_a), and shade the area in the acceptance (nonrejection) region. Use the z statistic(s) and Table IV of Appendix B to find the shaded area, which is β.

Following the calculation of β for a particular value of μ_a, you should interpret the value in the context of the hypothesis testing application. It is often useful to interpret the value of $1 - \beta$, which is known as the *power of the test* corresponding to a particular alternative, μ_a. Since β is the probability of accepting the null hypothesis when the alternative hypothesis is true with $\mu = \mu_a$, $1 - \beta$ is the probability of the complementary event, or the probability of rejecting the null hypothesis when the alternative $H_a: \mu = \mu_a$ is true. That is, the power $1 - \beta$ measures the likelihood that the test procedure will lead to the correct decision (reject H_0) for a particular value of the mean in the alternative hypothesis.

DEFINITION 8.2

The **power of a test** is the probability that the test will correctly lead to the rejection of the null hypothesis for a particular value of μ in the alternative hypothesis. The power is equal to $1 - \beta$ for the particular alternative considered.

For example, in the sewer pipe example we found that $\beta = .7764$ when $\mu = 2,425$. This is the probability that the test leads to the (incorrect) acceptance of the null hypothesis when $\mu = 2,425$. Or, equivalently, the power of the test is $1 - .7764 = .2236$, which means that the test will lead to the (correct) rejection of the null hypothesis only 22% of the time when the pipe exceeds specifications by 25 pounds per linear foot. When the manufacturer's pipe has a mean strength of 2,475 (that is, 75 pounds per linear foot in excess of specifications), the power of the test increases to $1 - .1562 = .8438$. That is, the test will lead to the acceptance of the manufacturer's pipe 84% of the time if $\mu = 2,475$.

EXAMPLE 8.9   Recall the quality control study in Examples 8.1 and 8.2, in which we tested to determine whether a cereal box filling machine was deviating from the specified mean fill of $\mu = 12$ ounces. The test setup is repeated here:

$$H_0: \mu = 12$$

$$H_a: \mu \neq 12 \text{ (i.e., } \mu < 12 \text{ or } \mu > 12)$$

$$\text{Test statistic: } z = \frac{\bar{x} - 12}{\sigma_{\bar{x}}}$$

$$\text{Rejection region: } z < -1.96 \quad \text{or} \quad z > 1.96 \qquad \text{for } \alpha = .05$$

$$z < -2.575 \quad \text{or} \quad z > 2.575 \qquad \text{for } \alpha = .01$$

Note that two rejection regions have been specified corresponding to values of $\alpha = .05$ and $\alpha = .01$, respectively. Assume that $n = 100$ and $s = .5$.

a. Suppose the machine is underfilling the boxes by an average of .1 ounce, i.e., $\mu = 11.9$. Calculate the values of β corresponding to the two rejection regions. Discuss the relationship between the values of α and β.

b. Calculate the power of the test for each of the rejection regions when $\mu = 11.9$.

SOLUTION

a. We first consider the rejection region corresponding to $\alpha = .05$. The first step is to calculate the border values of $\bar{x}$ corresponding to the two-tailed rejection region, $z < -1.96$ or $z > 1.96$:

$$\bar{x}_{0,L} = \mu_0 - 1.96\sigma_{\bar{x}} \approx \mu_0 - 1.96\left(\frac{s}{\sqrt{n}}\right) = 12 - 1.96\left(\frac{.5}{10}\right) = 11.902$$

$$\bar{x}_{0,U} = \mu_0 + 1.96\sigma_{\bar{x}} \approx \mu_0 + 1.96\left(\frac{s}{\sqrt{n}}\right) = 12 + 1.96\left(\frac{.5}{10}\right) = 12.098$$

These border values are shown in Figure 8.21.

Next, we convert these values to z values in the alternative distribution with $\mu_a = 11.9$:

$$z_L = \frac{x_{0,L} - \mu_a}{\sigma_{\bar{x}}} \approx \frac{11.902 - 11.9}{.05} = .04$$

$$z_U = \frac{x_{0,U} - \mu_a}{\sigma_{\bar{x}}} \approx \frac{12.098 - 11.9}{.05} = 3.96$$

These z values are shown in Figure 8.21b. You can see that the acceptance (or nonrejection) region is the area between them. Using Table IV of Appendix B, we find that the area between $z = 0$ and $z = .04$ is .0160, and the area between $z = 0$ and $z = 3.96$ is (approximately) .5 (since $z = 3.96$ is off the scale of Table IV). Then the area between $z = .04$ and $z = 3.96$ is, approximately,

$$\beta = .5 - .0160 = .4840$$

Thus, the test with $\alpha = .05$ will lead to a Type II error about 48% of the time when the machine is underfilling, on average, by .1 ounce.

For the rejection region corresponding to $\alpha = .01$, $z < -2.575$ or $z > 2.575$, we find

$$\bar{x}_{0,L} = 12 - 2.575\left(\frac{.5}{10}\right) = 11.871$$

$$\bar{x}_{0,U} = 12 + 2.575\left(\frac{.5}{10}\right) = 12.129$$

These border values of the rejection region are shown in Figure 8.21c.

FIGURE 8.21
Calculation of β
for filling machine
example

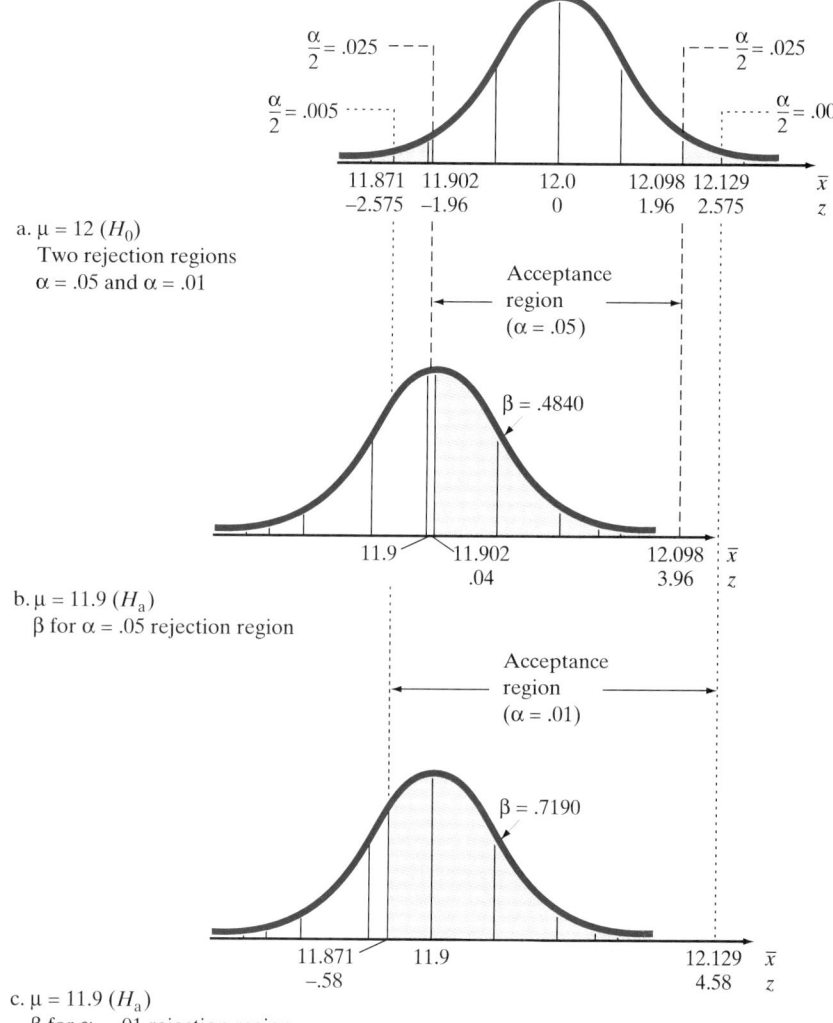

a. $\mu = 12$ (H_0)
   Two rejection regions
   $\alpha = .05$ and $\alpha = .01$

b. $\mu = 11.9$ (H_a)
   β for $\alpha = .05$ rejection region

c. $\mu = 11.9$ (H_a)
   β for $\alpha = .01$ rejection region

Converting these to z values in the alternative distribution with $\mu_a = 11.9$, we find $z_L = -.58$ and $z_U = 4.58$. The area between these values is, approximately,

$$\beta = .2190 + .5 = .7190$$

Thus, the chance that the test procedure with $\alpha = .01$ will lead to an incorrect acceptance of H_0 is about 72%.

Note that the value of β increases from .4840 to .7190 when we decrease the value of α from .05 to .01. This is a general property of the relationship between α and β: *as α is decreased (increased), β is increased (decreased).*

b. The power is defined to be the probability of (correctly) rejecting the null hypothesis when the alternative is true. When $\mu = 11.9$ and $\alpha = .05$, we find

$$\text{Power} = 1 - \beta = 1 - .4840 = .5160$$

When $\mu = 11.9$ and $\alpha = .01$, we find

$$\text{Power} = 1 - \beta = 1 - .7190 = .2810$$

FIGURE 8.22
Relationship between
α, β, and n

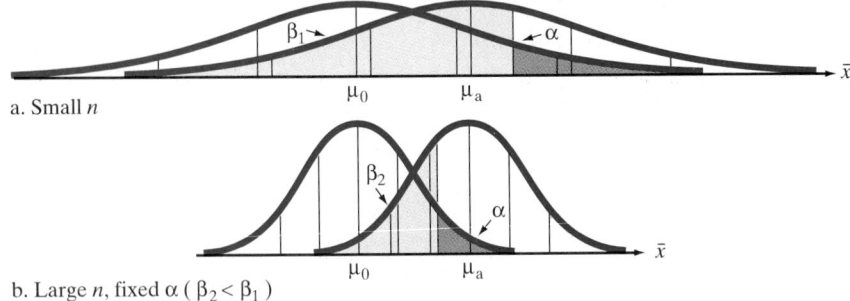

a. Small n

b. Large n, fixed α ($\beta_2 < \beta_1$)

You can see that the power of the test is decreased as the level of α is decreased. This means that as the probability of incorrectly rejecting the null hypothesis is decreased, the probability of correctly accepting the null hypothesis for a given alternative is also decreased. Thus, the value of α must be selected carefully, with the realization that a test is made less capable of detecting departures from the null hypothesis when the value of α is decreased. ▟

We have shown that the probability of committing a Type II error, β, is inversely related to α (Example 8.9), and that the value of β decreases as the value of μ_a moves farther from the null hypothesis value (sewer pipe example). The sample size n also affects β. Remember that the standard deviation of the sampling distribution of $\bar{x}$ is inversely proportional to the square root of the sample size ($\sigma_{\bar{x}} = \sigma/\sqrt{n}$). Thus, as illustrated in Figure 8.22, the variability of both the null and alternative sampling distributions is decreased as n is increased. If the value of α is specified and remains fixed, the value of β decreases as n increases, as illustrated in Figure 8.22. Conversely, the power of the test for a given alternative hypothesis is increased as the sample size is increased. The properties of β and power are summarized in the box.

Properties of β and Power

1. For fixed n and α, the value of β decreases and the power increases as the distance between the specified null value μ_0 and the specified alternative value μ_a increases (see Figure 8.20).

2. For fixed n and values of μ_0 and μ_a, the value of β increases and the power decreases as the value of α is decreased (see Figure 8.21).

3. For fixed α and values of μ_0 and μ_a, the value of β decreases and the power increases as the sample size n is increased (see Figure 8.22).

EXERCISES   **8.65–8.75**

Learning the Mechanics

8.65 List three factors that will increase the power of a test.

8.66 What is the relationship between β, the probability of committing a Type II error, and the power of a test?

8.67 Suppose you want to test H_0: $\mu = 500$ against H_a: $\mu > 500$ using $\alpha = .05$. The population in question is normally distributed with standard deviation 100. A random sample of size $n = 25$ will be used.
  a. Sketch the sampling distribution of $\bar{x}$ assuming that H_0 is true.

b. Find the value of $\bar{x}_0$, that value of $\bar{x}$ above which the null hypothesis will be rejected. Indicate the rejection region on your graph of part **a**. Shade the area above the rejection region and label it α.

c. On your graph of part **a**, sketch the sampling distribution of $\bar{x}$ if $\mu = 550$. Shade the area under this distribution that corresponds to the probability that $\bar{x}$ falls in the nonrejection region when $\mu = 550$. Label this area β.

d. Find β.

e. Compute the power of this test for detecting the alternative $H_a: \mu = 550$.

8.68   Refer to Exercise 8.67.

a. If $\mu = 575$ instead of 550, what is the probability that the hypothesis test will incorrectly fail to reject H_0? That is, what is β?

b. If $\mu = 575$, what is the probability that the test will correctly reject the null hypothesis? That is, what is the power of the test?

c. Compare β and the power of the test when $\mu = 575$ to the values you obtained in Exercise 8.67 for $\mu = 550$. Explain the differences.

8.69   It is desired to test $H_0: \mu = 75$ against $H_a: \mu < 75$ using $\alpha = .10$. The population in question is uniformly distributed with standard deviation 15. A random sample of size 49 will be drawn from the population.

a. Describe the (approximate) sampling distribution $\bar{x}$ under the assumption that H_0 is true.

b. Describe the (approximate) sampling distribution $\bar{x}$ under the assumption that the population mean is 70.

c. If μ were really equal to 70, what is the probability that the hypothesis test would lead the investigator to commit a Type II error?

d. What is the power of this test for detecting the alternative $H_a: \mu = 70$?

8.70   Refer to Exercise 8.69.

a. Find β for each of the following values of the population mean: 74, 72, 70, 68, and 66.

b. Plot each value of β you obtained in part **a** against its associated population mean. Show β on the vertical axis and μ on the horizontal axis. Draw a curve through the five points on your graph.

c. Use your graph of part **b** to find the approximate probability that the hypothesis test will lead to a Type II error when $\mu = 73$.

d. Convert each of the β values you calculated in part **a** to the power of the test at the specified value of μ. Plot the power on the vertical axis against μ on the horizontal axis. Compare the graph of part **b** to the *power curve* of this part.

e. Examine the graphs of parts **b** and **d**. Explain what they reveal about the relationships among the distance between the true mean μ

and the null hypothesized mean μ_0, the value of β, and the power.

8.71   Suppose you want to conduct the two-tailed test of $H_0: \mu = 30$ against $H_a: \mu \neq 30$ using $\alpha = .05$. A random sample of size 121 will be drawn from the population in question. Assume the population has a standard deviation equal to 1.2.

a. Describe the sampling distribution of $\bar{x}$ under the assumption that H_0 is true.

b. Describe the sampling distribution of $\bar{x}$ under the assumption that $\mu = 29.8$.

c. If μ were really equal to 29.8, find the value of β associated with the test.

d. Find the value of β for the alternative $H_a: \mu = 30.4$.

Applying the Concepts

8.72   If a manufacturer (the vendee) buys all items of a particular type from a particular vendor, the manufacturer is practicing *sole sourcing*. Sole sourcing is a purchasing policy that is generally recognized as an important component of a firm's quality system. One of the major benefits of sole sourcing for the vendee is the improved communication that results from the closer vendee/vendor relationship (Schonberger and Knod, *Operations Management*, 1994). As part of a sole-sourcing arrangement, a vendor agrees to periodically supply its vendee with sample data from its production process. The vendee uses the data to investigate whether the mean length of rods produced by the vendor's production process is truly 5.0 millimeters (mm) or more, as claimed by the vendor and desired by the vendee.

a. If the production process has a standard deviation of .01 mm, the vendor supplies $n = 100$ items to the vendee, and the vendee uses $\alpha = .05$ in testing $H_0: \mu = 5.0$ mm against $H_a: \mu < 5.0$ mm, what is the probability that the vendee's test will fail to reject the null hypothesis when in fact $\mu = 4.9975$ mm? What is the name given to this type of error?

b. Refer to part **a**. What is the probability that the vendee's test will reject the null hypothesis when in fact $\mu = 5.0$? What is the name given to this type of error?

c. What is the power of the test to detect a departure of .0025 mm below the specified mean rod length of 5.0 mm?

8.73   A salary survey conducted on behalf of the Institute of Management Accountants (IMA) and the publication *Management Accounting* revealed that the average salary for all members of the IMA was \$56,391. A random sample of 122 IMA members from New York were questioned and found to have a mean salary of $\bar{x} = \$62,770$ and a standard deviation of $s = \$28,972$ (*Management Accounting*, June 1995).

a. Assume that the national mean is known with certainty. Do the sample data provide sufficient evidence to conclude that the true mean salary of IMA members in New York is higher than the national average? Test using $\alpha = .05$.

b. Suppose the true mean salary for all New York IMA members is $66,391. What is the power of the test in part **a** to detect this $10,000 difference?

8.74 The Environmental Protection Agency (EPA) estimated that the 1997 Cirrus automobile obtains a mean of 35 miles per gallon (mpg) on the highway. However, the company that manufactures the car claims that the EPA has underestimated the Cirrus' mileage. To support its assertion, the company selects 36 1997 Cirrus cars and records the mileage obtained for each car over a driving course similar to the one used by the EPA. The following data resulted: $\bar{x} = 37.3$ mpg, $s = 6.4$ mpg.

a. If the auto manufacturer wishes to show that the mean mpg for 1997 Cirrus autos is greater than 35 mpg, what should the alternative hypothesis be? The null hypothesis?

b. Do the data provide sufficient evidence to support the auto manufacturer's claim? Test using $\alpha = .05$. List any assumptions you make in conducting the test.

c. Calculate the power of the test for the mean values of 35.5, 36.0, 36.5, 37.0, and 37.5, assuming $s = 6.4$ is a good estimate of σ.

d. Plot the power of the test on the vertical axis against the mean on the horizontal axis. Draw a curve through the points.

e. Use the power curve of part **d** to estimate the power for the mean value $\mu = 36.75$. Calculate the power for this value of μ, and compare it to your approximation.

f. Use the power curve to approximate the power of the test when $\mu = 40$. If the true value of the mean mpg for this model is really 40, what (approximately) are the chances that the test will fail to reject the null hypothesis that the mean is 35?

8.75 Refer to Exercise 8.20, in which the performance of a particular type of laser-based inspection equipment was investigated. Assume that the standard deviation of the number of solder joints inspected on each run is 1.2. If $\alpha = .05$ is used in conducting the hypothesis test of interest using a sample of 48 circuit boards, and if the true mean number of solder joints that can be inspected is really equal to 9.5, what is the probability that the test will result in a Type II error?

QUICK REVIEW

Key Terms

Alternative (research) hypothesis 318
Conclusion 323
Level of significance 323
Lower-tailed test 325
Null hypothesis 318

Observed significance level (*p*-value) 332
One-tailed test 324
Power of the test 355
Rejection region 319
Test statistic 318

Two-tailed test 325
Type I error 319
Type II error 321
Upper-tailed test 325

Key Formulas

Note: Starred (*) formulas are from the optional section in this chapter.

For testing H_0: $\theta = \theta_0$, the **large-sample test statistic** is

$$z = \frac{\hat{\theta} - \theta_0}{\sigma_{\hat{\theta}}}$$

where $\hat{\theta}$, θ_0, and $\sigma_{\hat{\theta}}$ are obtained from the table below:

Parameter, θ	Hypothesized Parameter Value, θ_0	Estimator, $\hat{\theta}$	Standard Error of Estimator, $\sigma_{\hat{\theta}}$	
μ	μ_0	$\bar{x}$	$\dfrac{\sigma}{\sqrt{n}}$	319, 328
p	p_0	$\hat{p}$	$\sqrt{\dfrac{p_0 q_0}{n}}$	347

For testing H_0: $\mu = \mu_0$, the **small-sample test statistic** is

$$t = \frac{\bar{x} - \mu_0}{s/\sqrt{n}}$$ 339

$\beta = P(\hat{\theta}$ falls in acceptance region $| \theta = \theta_a)^*$ 352
Power $= 1 - \beta^*$ 355

LANGUAGE LAB

Symbol	Pronunciation	Description
H_0	H-oh	Null hypothesis
H_a	H-a	Alternative hypothesis
α	alpha	Probability of Type I error
β	beta	Probability of Type II error

SUPPLEMENTARY EXERCISES 8.76–8.104

Note: List the assumptions necessary for the valid implementation of the statistical procedures you use in solving all these exercises. Starred (*) exercises refer to the optional section in this chapter.

Learning the Mechanics

8.76 Specify the differences between a large-sample and small-sample test of hypothesis about a population mean μ. Focus on the assumptions and test statistics.

8.77 *Complete the following statement:* The smaller the p-value associated with a test of hypothesis, the stronger the support for the _____ hypothesis. Explain your answer.

8.78 Which of the elements of a test of hypothesis can and should be specified *prior* to analyzing the data that are to be utilized to conduct the test?

8.79 If you select a very small value for α when conducting a hypothesis test, will β tend to be big or small? Explain.

8.80 If the rejection of the null hypothesis of a particular test would cause your firm to go out of business, would you want α to be small or large? Explain.

8.81 A random sample of 20 observations selected from a normal population produced $\bar{x} = 72.6$ and $s^2 = 19.4$.

a. Test H_0: $\mu = 80$ against H_a: $\mu < 80$. Use $\alpha = .05$.
b. Test H_0: $\mu = 80$ against H_a: $\mu \neq 80$. Use $\alpha = .01$.

8.82 A random sample of $n = 200$ observations from a binomial population yields $\hat{p} = .29$.

a. Test H_0: $p = .35$ against H_a: $p < .35$. Use $\alpha = .05$.
b. Test H_0: $p = .35$ against H_a: $p \neq .35$. Use $\alpha = .05$.

8.83 A random sample of 175 measurements possessed a mean $\bar{x} = 8.2$ and a standard deviation $s = .79$.

a. Test H_0: $\mu = 8.3$ against H_a: $\mu \neq 8.3$. Use $\alpha = .05$.
b. Test H_0: $\mu = 8.4$ against H_a: $\mu \neq 8.4$. Use $\alpha = .05$.

8.84 A t-test is conducted for the null hypothesis H_0: $\mu = 10$ versus the alternative H_a: $\mu > 10$ for a random sample of $n = 17$ observations. The data are analyzed using MINITAB, with the results shown below.

a. Interpret the p-value.
b. What assumptions are necessary for the validity of this test?
c. Calculate and interpret the p-value assuming the alternative hypothesis was instead H_a: $\mu \neq 10$.

Applying the Concepts

8.85 Medical tests have been developed to detect many serious diseases. A medical test is designed to minimize the probability that it will produce a "false positive" or a "false negative." A false positive

```
TEST OF MU = 10.000 VS MU G.T. 10.000

            N      MEAN     STDEV    SE MEAN        T    P VALUE
    X      17     12.50      8.78       2.13    1.174      .1288
```

refers to a positive test result for an individual who does not have the disease, whereas a false negative is a negative test result for an individual who does have the disease.

a. If we treat a medical test for a disease as a statistical test of hypothesis, what are the null and alternative hypotheses for the medical test?

b. What are the Type I and Type II errors for the test? Relate each to false positives and false negatives.

c. Which of the errors has graver consequences? Considering this error, is it more important to minimize α or β? Explain.

8.86 The Lincoln Tunnel (under the Hudson River) connects suburban New Jersey to midtown Manhattan. On Mondays at 8:30 A.M., the mean number of cars waiting in line to pay the Lincoln Tunnel toll is 1,220. Because of the substantial wait during rush hour, the Port Authority of New York and New Jersey is considering raising the amount of the toll between 7:30 and 8:30 A.M. to encourage more drivers to use the tunnel at an earlier or later time. Such peak-hour pricing is already used successfully in Paris, Singapore, and Milan (*Newark Star-Ledger,* Aug. 27, 1995). Suppose the Port Authority experiments with peak-hour pricing for six months, increasing the toll from $4 to $7 during the rush hour peak. On 10 different workdays at 8:30 A.M. aerial photographs of the tunnel queues are taken and the number of vehicles counted. The results follow:

1,260   1,052   1,201   942   1,062   999   931   849   867   735

Analyze the data for the purpose of determining whether peak-hour pricing succeeded in reducing the average number of vehicles attempting to use the Lincoln Tunnel during the peak rush hour. Utilize the information in the accompanying EXCEL printout.

Count	
Mean	989.8
Standard Error	50.81006025
Median	970.5
Mode	#N/A
Standard Deviation	160.6755184
Sample Variance	25816.62222
Kurtosis	-0.339458911
Skewness	0.276807237
Range	525
Minimum	735
Maximum	1260
Sum	9898
Count	10
Confidence Level(95.000%)	99.58574067

8.87 The trade publication *Potentials in Marketing* (Nov./Dec. 1995) surveyed its readers concerning their opinions of electronic marketing (i.e., marketing via the Internet, e-mail, CD-ROMS, etc.). A questionnaire was faxed to 1,500 randomly selected U.S. readers in August and September 1995. Of the 195 questionnaires that were returned, 37 reported that their company already has a World Wide Web site and 59 indicated that their company had plans to create one.

a. Do these data provide sufficient evidence to reject the claim by a producer of a well-known Web browser that "more than 25% of all U.S. businesses will have Web sites by the middle of 1995"?

b. Discuss potential problems associated with the sampling methodology and the appropriateness of the sample for making generalizations about all U.S. businesses.

8.88 Failure to meet payments on student loans guaranteed by the U.S. government has been a major problem for both banks and the government. Approximately 50% of all student loans guaranteed by the government are in default. A random sample of 350 loans to college students in one region of the United States indicates that 147 loans are in default.

a. Do the data indicate that the proportion of student loans in default in this area of the country differs from the proportion of all student loans in the United States that are in default? Use $\alpha = .01$.

b. Find the observed significance level for the test and interpret its value.

8.89 In order to be effective, the mean length of life of a certain mechanical component used in a spacecraft must be larger than 1,100 hours. Owing to the prohibitive cost of this component, only three can be tested under simulated space conditions. The lifetimes (hours) of the components were recorded and the following statistics were computed: $\bar{x} = 1,173.6$ and $s = 36.3$. These data were analyzed using MINITAB, with the results shown on page 363.

a. Verify that the software has correctly calculated the t statistic and determine whether the p-value is in the appropriate range.

b. Interpret the p-value.

c. Which type of error, I or II, is of greater concern for this test? Explain.

d. Would you recommend that this component be passed as meeting specifications?

8.90 A consumer protection group is concerned that a ketchup manufacturer is filling its 20-ounce family-size containers with less than 20 ounces of ketchup. The group purchases 10 family-size

```
TEST OF MU = 1100 VS MU G.T. 1100
              N      MEAN    STDEV   SE MEAN      T    P VALUE
   COMP       3    1,173.6    36.3    20.96    3.512    .0362
```

bottles of this ketchup, weighs the contents of each, and finds that the mean weight is equal to 19.86 ounces, and the standard deviation is equal to .22 ounce.

a. Do the data provide sufficient evidence for the consumer group to conclude that the mean fill per family-size bottle is less than 20 ounces? Test using $\alpha = .05$.

b. If the test in part **a** were conducted on a periodic basis by the company's quality control department, is the consumer group more concerned about making a Type I error or a Type II error? (The probability of making this type of error is called the *consumer's risk.*)

c. The ketchup company is also interested in the mean amount of ketchup per bottle. It does not wish to overfill them. For the test conducted in part **a**, which type of error is more serious from the company's point of view—a Type I error or a Type II error? (The probability of making this type of error is called the *producer's risk.*)

8.91 Sales promotions that are used by manufacturers to entice retailers to carry, feature, or push the manufacturer's products are called *trade promotions.* A survey of 250 manufacturers conducted by Cannondale Associates, a sales and marketing consulting firm, found that 91% of the manufacturers believe their spending for trade promotions is inefficient (*Potentials in Marketing,* June 1995). Is this sufficient evidence to reject a previous claim by the American Marketing Association that no more than half of all manufacturers are dissatisfied with their trade promotion spending?

a. Conduct the appropriate hypothesis test at $\alpha = .02$. Begin your analysis by determining whether the sample size is large enough to apply the testing methodology presented in this section.

b. Report the observed significance level of the test and interpret its meaning in the context of the problem.

*c. Calculate β, the probability of a Type II error, if in fact 55% of all manufacturers are dissatisfied with their trade promotion spending.

8.92 According to the Internal Revenue Service (IRS), in 1980, 4,414 taxpayers reported earning more than $1 million in adjusted gross income. By 1994 that number had grown to 68,064.

Interestingly, as the number of millionaires rose dramatically, their charitable contributions nose-dived from an average of $207,089 in 1980 to $98,500 in 1994 (Internal Revenue Service, *Statistics of Income Bulletin,* Spring 1996). Will this trend continue into the late 1990s? The IRS sampled six 1997 tax returns of millionaires and found the following charitable contributions (in thousands of dollars):

91.1   103.2   62.9   150.4   209.5   31.7

Do the sample data indicate that annual charitable contributions by millionaires have increased since 1994? Conduct the test using $\alpha = .05$.

8.93 The EPA sets an airborne limit of 5 parts per million (ppm) on vinyl chloride, a colorless gas used to make plastics, adhesives, and other chemicals. It is both a carcinogen and a mutagen (New Jersey Department of Health, *Hazardous Substance Fact Sheet,* Dec. 1994). A major plastics manufacturer, attempting to control the amount of vinyl chloride its workers are exposed to, has given instructions to halt production if the mean amount of vinyl chloride in the air exceeds 3.0 ppm. A random sample of 50 air specimens produced the following statistics: $\bar{x} = 3.1$ ppm, $s = .5$ ppm.

a. Do these statistics provide sufficient evidence to halt the production process? Use $\alpha = .01$.

b. If you were the plant manager, would you want to use a large or a small value for α for the test in part **a**? Explain.

c. Find the p-value for the test and interpret its value.

*8.94 Refer to Exercise 8.93.

a. In the context of the problem, define a Type II error.

b. Calculate β for the test described in part **a** of Exercise 8.93, assuming that the true mean is $\mu = 3.1$ ppm.

c. What is the power of the test to detect a departure from the manufacturer's 3.0 ppm limit when the mean is 3.1 ppm?

d. Repeat parts **b** and **c** assuming that the true mean is 3.2 ppm. What happens to the power of the test as the plant's mean vinyl chloride level departs further from the limit?

*8.95 Refer to Exercises 8.93 and 8.94.

a. Suppose an α value of .05 is used to conduct the test. Does this change favor halting production? Explain.

```
TEST OF MU = 12432 VS MU G.T. 12432
THE ASSUMED SIGMA = 1721

                  N      MEAN    STDEV    SE MEAN       Z    P VALUE
   TUITION       30     13016     1721     314.03    1.86     .0314
```

b. Determine the value of β and the power for the test when $\alpha = .05$ and $\mu = 3.1$.

c. What happens to the power of the test when α is increased?

8.96 One study (*Journal of Political Economy*, Feb. 1988) of gambling newsletters that purport to improve a bettor's odds of winning bets on NFL football games indicates that the newsletters' betting schemes were not profitable. Suppose a random sample of 50 games is selected to test one gambling newsletter. Following the newsletter's recommendations, 30 of the 50 games produced winning wagers.

a. Test whether the newsletter can be said to significantly increase the odds of winning over what one could expect by selecting the winner at random. Use $\alpha = .05$.

b. Calculate and interpret the *p*-value for the test.

*8.97 Refer to Exercise 8.96.

a. Describe a Type II error in terms of this application.

b. Calculate the probability β of a Type II error for this test assuming that the newsletter really does increase the probability of winning a wager on an NFL game to $p = .55$.

c. Suppose the number of games sampled is increased from 50 to 100. How does this affect the probability of a Type II error for $p = .55$?

8.98 Twenty years ago, personal computers (PCs) didn't even exist. Today they are fast becoming as common in the home as television sets and toasters. In 1995, Roper Starch Worldwide surveyed 2,000 middle-class Americans and found that 860 had used a PC in the past 12 months (*USA Today Special Newsletter Edition*, Dec. 1995). Is this sufficient evidence for Roper Starch Worldwide to claim that "one in two middle-class Americans has used a PC within the past year"? Test using $\alpha = .10$.

8.99 The *Chronicle of Higher Education Almanac* (Sept. 2, 1996) reported that for the 1995–1996 academic year, four-year private colleges charged students an average of $12,432 for tuition and fees, whereas at four-year public colleges the average was $2,860. Suppose that for 1996–1997 a random sample of 30 private colleges yielded the following data on tuition and fees: $\bar{x} = \$13,016$ and $s = \$1,721$. Assume that $12,432 is the population mean for 1995–1996.

a. Specify the null and alternative hypotheses you would use to investigate whether the mean amount for tuition and fees in 1996–1997 was significantly larger (in the statistical sense) than it was in 1995–1996.

b. The data are submitted to MINITAB, and the results obtained are shown above. Check these calculations, and interpret the result.

c. Explain the difference between statistical significance and practical significance in the context of this exercise.

8.100 The "beta coefficient" of a stock is a measure of the stock's volatility (or risk) relative to the market as a whole. Stocks with beta coefficients greater than 1 generally bear greater risk (more volatility) than the market, whereas stocks with beta coefficients less than 1 are less risky (less volatile) than the overall market (Alexander, Sharpe, and Bailey, *Fundamentals of Investments*, 1993). A random sample of 15 high-technology stocks was selected at the end of 1996, and the mean and standard deviation of the beta coefficients were calculated: $\bar{x} = 1.23, s = .37$.

a. Set up the appropriate null and alternative hypotheses to test whether the average high-technology stock is riskier than the market as a whole.

b. Establish the appropriate test statistic and rejection region for the test. Use $\alpha = .10$.

c. What assumptions are necessary to ensure the validity of the test?

d. Calculate the test statistic and state your conclusion.

e. What is the approximate *p*-value associated with this test? Interpret it.

8.101 Refer to Exercise 8.100. SAS was used to analyze the data, and the output was as follows:

```
Analysis Variable : BETA_1

  N Obs                 T    Prob>|T|
  ---------------------------------------
     15      2.4080000      0.0304
  ---------------------------------------
```

a. Interpret the *p*-value on the computer output. (**Prob** > |**T**| on the SAS printout corresponds to a two-tailed test of the null hypothesis $\mu = 1$.)

b. If the alternative hypothesis of interest is $\mu > 1$, what is the appropriate *p*-value of the test?

8.102 In the past, a chemical company produced 880 pounds of a certain type of plastic per day. Now, using a newly developed and less expensive process, the mean daily yield of plastic for the first 50 days of production is 871 pounds; the standard deviation is 21 pounds.

a. Do the data provide sufficient evidence to indicate that the mean daily yield for the new process is less than that for the old procedure? (Test using $\alpha = .01$.)

b. What assumptions must you make in order to use the statistical test you employed?

*8.103 Refer to Exercise 8.102. Calculate the probability β that the test fails to reject the null hypothesis that the new process has a mean daily yield of 880 when in fact the true mean is 875. What is the power of the test to determine the $\mu < 880$ when $\mu = 875$?

8.104 The manufacturer of an over-the-counter analgesic claims that its product brings pain relief to headache sufferers in less than 3.5 minutes, on average. In order to be able to make this claim in its television advertisements, the manufacturer was required by a particular television network to present statistical evidence in support of the claim. The manufacturer reported that for a random sample of 50 headache sufferers, the mean time to relief was 3.3 minutes and the standard deviation was 1.1 minutes.

a. Do these data support the manufacturer's claim? Test using $\alpha = .05$.

b. Report the p-value of the test.

c. In general, do large p-values or small p-values support the manufacturer's claim? Explain.

CHAPTER 9

INFERENCES BASED ON TWO SAMPLES
Confidence Intervals and Tests of Hypotheses

Where We've Been

We explored two methods for making statistical inferences, confidence intervals, and tests of hypotheses in Chapters 7 and 8. In particular, we studied confidence intervals and tests of hypotheses concerning a single population mean μ and a single population proportion p. We also learned how to select the sample size necessary to obtain a specified amount of information concerning a parameter.

Where We're Going

Now that we've learned to make inferences about a single population, we'll learn how to compare two populations. For example, we may wish to compare the mean gas mileages for two models of automobiles or the proportion of consumers who prefer a product before and after an advertising campaign. In this chapter we'll see how to decide whether differences exist and how to estimate the differences between population means and proportions.

Many experiments involve a comparison of two populations. For instance, a consumer group may want to test whether two major brands of food freezers differ in the mean amount of electricity they use. A television market researcher may want to estimate the difference in the proportions of younger and older viewers who watch a certain TV program regularly. A golf ball supplier may wish to compare the variability in the distance that two competing brands of golf balls travel when struck with the same club. In this chapter we consider techniques for using two samples to compare the populations from which they were selected.

9.1   COMPARING TWO POPULATION MEANS: INDEPENDENT SAMPLING

Many of the same procedures that are used to estimate and test hypotheses about a single parameter can be modified to make inferences about two parameters. Both the z and t statistics may be adapted to make inferences about the difference between two population means.

In this section we develop both large-sample and small-sample methodologies for comparing two population means. In the large-sample case we use the z statistic, while in the small-sample case we use the t statistic.

LARGE SAMPLES

EXAMPLE 9.1

In recent years, the United States and Japan have engaged in intense negotiations regarding restrictions on trade between the two countries. One of the claims made repeatedly by U.S. officials is that many Japanese manufacturers price their goods higher in Japan than in the United States, in effect subsidizing low prices in the United States by extremely high prices in Japan. According to the U.S. argument, Japan accomplishes this by keeping competitive U.S. goods from reaching the Japanese marketplace.

An economist decided to test the hypothesis that higher retail prices are being charged for Japanese automobiles in Japan than in the United States. She obtained random samples of 50 retail sales in the United States and 30 retail sales in Japan over the same time period and for the same model of automobile, converted the Japanese sales prices from yen to dollars using current conversion rates, and obtained the summary information shown in Table 9.1. Form a 95% confidence interval for the difference between the population mean retail prices of this automobile model for the two countries. Interpret the result.

SOLUTION

Recall that the general form of a large-sample confidence interval for a single mean μ is $\bar{x} \pm z_{\alpha/2}\sigma_{\bar{x}}$. That is, we add and subtract $z_{\alpha/2}$ standard deviations of the sample estimate, $\bar{x}$, to the value of the estimate. We employ a similar procedure to form the confidence interval for the difference between two population means.

TABLE 9.1   **Summary Statistics for Automobile Retail Price Study**

	U.S. Sales	Japan Sales
Sample Size	50	30
Sample Mean	$14,545	$15,243
Sample Standard Deviation	$ 1,989	$ 1,843

FIGURE 9.1
Sampling distribution
of $(\bar{x}_1 - \bar{x}_2)$

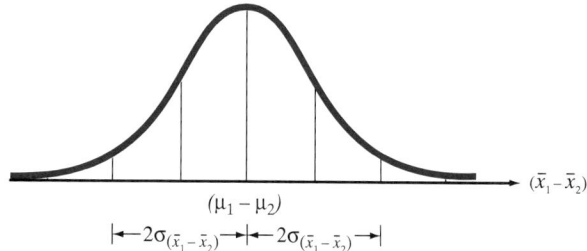

$(\mu_1 - \mu_2)$

$\longmapsto 2\sigma_{(\bar{x}_1 - \bar{x}_2)} \longrightarrow \longmapsto 2\sigma_{(\bar{x}_1 - \bar{x}_2)} \longrightarrow$

$(\bar{x}_1 - \bar{x}_2)$

Let μ_1 represent the mean of the population of retail sales prices for this car model sold in the United States. Let μ_2 be similarly defined for retail sales in Japan. We wish to form a confidence interval for $(\mu_1 - \mu_2)$. An intuitively appealing estimator for $(\mu_1 - \mu_2)$ is the difference between the sample means, $(\bar{x}_1 - \bar{x}_2)$. Thus, we will form the confidence interval of interest by

$$(\bar{x}_1 - \bar{x}_2) \pm z_{\alpha/2}\sigma_{(\bar{x}_1 - \bar{x}_2)}$$

Assuming the two samples are independent, the standard deviation of the difference between the sample means is

$$\sigma_{(\bar{x}_1 - \bar{x}_2)} = \sqrt{\frac{\sigma_1^2}{n_1} + \frac{\sigma_2^2}{n_2}} \approx \sqrt{\frac{s_1^2}{n_1} + \frac{s_2^2}{n_2}}$$

Using the sample data and noting that $\alpha = .05$ and $z_{.025} = 1.96$, we find that the 95% confidence interval is, approximately,

$$(14{,}545 - 15{,}243) \pm 1.96\sqrt{\frac{(1{,}989)^2}{50} + \frac{(1{,}843)^2}{30}} = -698 \pm (1.96)(438.57)$$

$$= -698 \pm 860$$

or $(-1{,}558, 162)$. Using this estimation procedure over and over again for different samples, we know that approximately 95% of the confidence intervals formed in this manner will enclose the difference in population means $(\mu_1 - \mu_2)$. Therefore, we are highly confident that the difference in mean retail prices in the United States and Japan is between $-\$1{,}558$ and $\$162$. Since 0 falls in this interval, the economist cannot conclude that a significant difference exists between the mean retail prices in the two countries. 🔲

The justification for the procedure used in Example 9.1 to estimate $(\mu_1 - \mu_2)$ relies on the properties of the sampling distribution of $(\bar{x}_1 - \bar{x}_2)$. The performance of the estimator in repeated sampling is pictured in Figure 9.1, and its properties are summarized in the box.

Properties of the Sampling Distribution of $(\bar{x}_1 - \bar{x}_2)$

1. The mean of the sampling distribution $(\bar{x}_1 - \bar{x}_2)$ is $(\mu_1 - \mu_2)$.

2. If the two samples are independent, the standard deviation of the sampling distribution is

$$\sigma_{(\bar{x}_1 - \bar{x}_2)} = \sqrt{\frac{\sigma_1^2}{n_1} + \frac{\sigma_2^2}{n_2}}$$

continued

where σ_1^2 and σ_2^2 are the variances of the two populations being sampled and n_1 and n_2 are the respective sample sizes. We also refer to $\sigma_{(\bar{x}_1 - \bar{x}_2)}$ as the **standard error** of the statistic $(\bar{x}_1 - \bar{x}_2)$.

3. The sampling distribution of $(\bar{x}_1 - \bar{x}_2)$ is approximately normal for *large samples* by the Central Limit Theorem.

In Example 9.1, we noted the similarity in the procedures for forming a large-sample confidence interval for one population mean and a large-sample confidence interval for the difference between two population means. When we are testing hypotheses, the procedures are again very similar. The general large-sample procedures for forming confidence intervals and testing hypotheses about $(\mu_1 - \mu_2)$ are summarized in the next two boxes.

Large-Sample Confidence Interval for $(\mu_1 - \mu_2)$

$$(\bar{x}_1 - \bar{x}_2) \pm z_{\alpha/2}\sigma_{(\bar{x}_1 - \bar{x}_2)} = (\bar{x}_1 - \bar{x}_2) \pm z_{\alpha/2}\sqrt{\frac{\sigma_1^2}{n_1} + \frac{\sigma_2^2}{n_2}}$$

Assumptions: The two samples are randomly selected in an independent manner from the two populations; the sample sizes n_1 and n_2 are large (i.e., $n_1 \geqslant 30$ and $n_2 \geqslant 30$).

Large-Sample Test of Hypothesis for $(\mu_1 - \mu_2)$

One-Tailed Test

$H_0: (\mu_1 - \mu_2) = D_0$

$H_a: (\mu_1 - \mu_2) < D_0$
 $[\text{or } H_a: (\mu_1 - \mu_2) > D_0]$

Two-Tailed Test

$H_0: (\mu_1 - \mu_2) = D_0$

$H_a: (\mu_1 - \mu_2) \neq D_0$

where D_0 = Hypothesized difference between the means (this difference is often hypothesized to be equal to 0)

Test statistic:

$$z = \frac{(\bar{x}_1 - \bar{x}_2) - D_0}{\sigma_{(\bar{x}_1 - \bar{x}_2)}} \quad \text{where} \quad \sigma_{(\bar{x}_1 - \bar{x}_2)} = \sqrt{\frac{\sigma_1^2}{n_1} + \frac{\sigma_2^2}{n_2}}$$

Rejection region: $z < -z_\alpha$

 $[\text{or } z > z_\alpha \text{ when } H_a: (\mu_1 - \mu_2) > D_0]$

Rejection region: $|z| > z_{\alpha/2}$

Assumptions: Same as for the large-sample confidence interval.

EXAMPLE **9.2** Refer to the study of retail prices of an automobile sold in the United States and Japan, Example 9.1. Another way to compare the mean retail prices for the two countries is to conduct a test of hypothesis. Use the summary data in Table 9.1 to conduct the test. Use $\alpha = .05$.

SOLUTION

Again, we let μ_1 and μ_2 represent the population mean retail sales prices in the United States and Japan, respectively. If the claim made by the U.S. government is

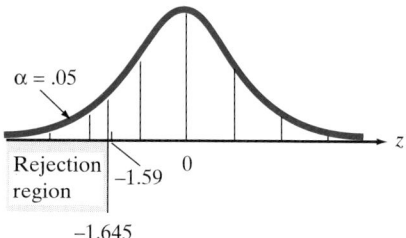

FIGURE 9.2
Rejection region
for Example 9.2

true, then the mean retail price in Japan will exceed the mean in the U.S., i.e., $\mu_1 < \mu_2$ or $(\mu_1 - \mu_2) < 0$.

Thus, the elements of the test are as follows:

$H_0: (\mu_1 - \mu_2) = 0$ (i.e., $\mu_1 = \mu_2$; note that $D_0 = 0$ for this hypothesis test)

$H_a: (\mu_1 - \mu_2) < 0$ (i.e., $\mu_1 < \mu_2$)

Test statistic: $z = \dfrac{(\bar{x}_1 - \bar{x}_2) - D_0}{\sigma_{(\bar{x}_1 - \bar{x}_2)}} = \dfrac{\bar{x}_1 - \bar{x}_2 - 0}{\sigma_{(\bar{x}_1 - \bar{x}_2)}}$

Rejection region: $z < -z_{.05} = -1.645$ (see Figure 9.2)

Substituting the summary statistics given in Table 9.1 into the test statistic, we obtain

$$z = \frac{(\bar{x}_1 - \bar{x}_2) - 0}{\sigma_{(\bar{x}_1 - \bar{x}_2)}} = \frac{(14{,}545 - 15{,}243)}{\sqrt{\dfrac{\sigma_1^2}{n_1} + \dfrac{\sigma_2^2}{n_2}}}$$

$$\approx \frac{-698}{\sqrt{\dfrac{s_1^2}{n_1} + \dfrac{s_2^2}{n_2}}} = \frac{-698}{\sqrt{\dfrac{(1{,}989)^2}{50} + \dfrac{(1{,}843)^2}{30}}} = \frac{-698}{438.57} = -1.59$$

As you can see in Figure 9.2, the calculated z value does not fall in the rejection region. Therefore, the samples do not provide sufficient evidence, at $\alpha = .05$, for the economist to conclude that the mean retail price in Japan exceeds that in the United States.

Note that this conclusion agrees with the inference drawn from the 95% confidence interval in Example 9.1. ∎

EXAMPLE 9.3 Find the observed significance level for the test in Example 9.2. Interpret the result.

SOLUTION
The alternative hypothesis in Example 9.2, $H_a: (\mu_1 - \mu_2) < 0$, required a lower one-tailed test using

$$z = \frac{\bar{x}_1 - \bar{x}_2}{\sigma_{(\bar{x}_1 - \bar{x}_2)}}$$

as a test statistic. Since the value z calculated from the sample data was -1.59, the observed significance level (p-value) for the lower-tailed test is the probability of observing a value of z at least as contradictory to the null hypothesis as $z = -1.59$; that is,

$$p\text{-value} = P(z \leqslant -1.59)$$

This probability is computed assuming H_0 is true and is equal to the shaded area shown in Figure 9.3.

FIGURE 9.3

The observed significance level for Example 9.2

p-value = .0559

FIGURE 9.4

MINITAB printout for the hypothesis test of Example 9.2

```
Two sample T for US vs JAPAN
            N        Mean       StDev     SE Mean
US          50       14545      1989      281.29
JAPAN       30       15243      1843      336.48

95% CI for mu US - mu JAPAN: (-1558, 162)
T-Test mu US = mu JAPAN (vs <): T= -1.59 P=0.056 DF= 78
```

The tabulated area corresponding to $z = 1.59$ in Table IV of Appendix B is .4441. Therefore, the observed significance level of the test is

$$p\text{-value} = .5 - .4441 = .0559$$

Since our selected α value, .05, is less than this *p*-value, we have insufficient evidence to reject $H_0: (\mu_1 - \mu_2) = 0$ in favor of $H_a: (\mu_1 - \mu_2) < 0$.

The *p*-value of the test is more easily obtained from a statistical software package. A MINITAB printout for the hypothesis test is displayed in Figure 9.4. The one-tailed *p*-value, highlighted on the printout, is .056. [Note that MINITAB also gives a 95% confidence interval for $(\mu_1 - \mu_2)$. This interval agrees with the interval calculated in Example 9.1.]

Reminder: The SAS and SPSS software packages conduct only two-tailed hypothesis tests. For these packages, obtain the *p*-value for a one-tailed test as follows:

$$p = \frac{\text{Reported } p\text{-value}}{2} \quad \text{if form of } H_a \text{ (e.g., <) agrees with sign of test statistic (e.g., negative)}$$

$$p = 1 - \frac{\text{Reported } p\text{-value}}{2} \quad \text{if form of } H_a \text{ (e.g., <) disagrees with sign of test statistic (e.g., positive)}$$

SMALL SAMPLES

When comparing two population means with small samples (say, $n_1 < 30$ and $n_2 < 30$), the methodology of the previous three examples is invalid. The reason? When the sample sizes are small, estimates of σ_1^2 and σ_2^2 are unreliable and the Central Limit Theorem (which guarantees that the z statistic is normal) can no longer be applied. But as in the case of a single mean (Section 8.4), we use the familiar Student's *t*-distribution described in Chapter 7.

To use the t-distribution, both sampled populations must be approximately normally distributed with equal population variances, and the random samples must be selected independently of each other.

The normality and equal variances assumptions imply relative frequency distributions for the populations that would appear as shown in Figure 9.5.

Since we assume the two populations have equal variances ($\sigma_1^2 = \sigma_2^2 = \sigma^2$), it is reasonable to use the information contained in both samples to construct a **pooled sample estimator** of σ^2 for use in confidence intervals and test statistics.

FIGURE 9.5
Assumptions for the
two-sample t:
(1) normal populations,
(2) equal variances

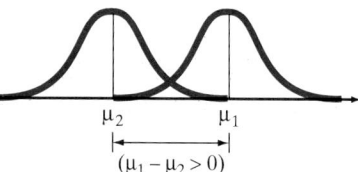

Thus, if s_1^2 and s_2^2 are the two sample variances (both estimating the variance σ^2 common to both populations), the pooled estimator of σ^2, denoted as s_p^2, is

$$s_p^2 = \frac{(n_1 - 1)s_1^2 + (n_2 - 1)s_2^2}{(n_1 - 1) + (n_2 - 1)} = \frac{(n_1 - 1)s_1^2 + (n_2 - 1)s_2^2}{n_1 + n_2 - 2}$$

or

$$s_p^2 = \frac{\overbrace{\sum(x_1 - \bar{x}_1)^2}^{\text{From sample 1}} + \overbrace{\sum(x_2 - \bar{x}_2)^2}^{\text{From sample 2}}}{n_1 + n_2 - 2}$$

where x_1 represents a measurement from sample 1 and x_2 represents a measurement from sample 2. Recall that the term *degrees of freedom* was defined in Section 7.2 as 1 less than the sample size. Thus, in this case, we have $(n_1 - 1)$ degrees of freedom for sample 1 and $(n_2 - 1)$ degrees of freedom for sample 2. Since we are pooling the information on σ^2 obtained from both samples, the degrees of freedom associated with the pooled variance s_p^2 is equal to the sum of the degrees of freedom for the two samples, namely, the denominator of s_p^2; that is, $(n_1 - 1) + (n_2 - 1) = n_1 + n_2 - 2$.

Note that the second formula given for s_p^2 shows that the pooled variance is simply a **weighted average** of the two sample variances, s_1^2 and s_2^2. The weight given each variance is proportional to its degrees of freedom. If the two variances have the same number of degrees of freedom (i.e., if the sample sizes are equal), then the pooled variance is a simple average of the two sample variances. The result is an average or "pooled" variance that is a better estimate of σ^2 than either s_1^2 or s_2^2 alone.

Both the confidence interval and the test of hypothesis procedures for comparing two population means with small samples are summarized in the accompanying boxes.

Small-Sample Confidence Interval for $(\mu_1 - \mu_2)$ (Independent Samples)

$$(\bar{x}_1 - \bar{x}_2) \pm t_{\alpha/2}\sqrt{s_p^2\left(\frac{1}{n_1} + \frac{1}{n_2}\right)}$$

where $s_p^2 = \dfrac{(n_1 - 1)s_1^2 + (n_2 - 1)s_2^2}{n_1 + n_2 - 2}$

and $t_{\alpha/2}$ is based on $(n_1 + n_2 - 2)$ degrees of freedom.

Assumptions: **1.** Both sampled populations have relative frequency distributions that are approximately normal.

2. The population variances are equal.

3. The samples are randomly and independently selected from the population.

Small-Sample Test of Hypothesis for $(\mu_1 - \mu_2)$ (Independent Samples)

One-Tailed Test

$H_0: (\mu_1 - \mu_2) = D_0$

$H_a: (\mu_1 - \mu_2) < D_0$
   [or $H_a: (\mu_1 - \mu_2) > D_0$]

Two-Tailed Test

$H_0: (\mu_1 - \mu_2) = D_0$

$H_a: (\mu_1 - \mu_2) \neq D_0$

Test statistic:
$$t = \frac{(\bar{x}_1 - \bar{x}_2) - D_0}{\sqrt{s_p^2\left(\dfrac{1}{n_1} + \dfrac{1}{n_2}\right)}}$$

Rejection region: $t < -t_\alpha$
   [or $t > t_\alpha$ when $H_a: (\mu_1 - \mu_2) > D_0$]

Rejection region: $|t| > t_{\alpha/2}$

where t_α and $t_{\alpha/2}$ are based on $(n_1 + n_2 - 2)$ degrees of freedom.

Assumptions: Same as for the small-sample confidence interval for $(\mu_1 - \mu_2)$ in the previous box.

EXAMPLE 9.4

Behavioral researchers have developed an index designed to measure managerial success. The index (measured on a 100-point scale) is based on the manager's length of time in the organization and his or her level within the firm; the higher the index, the more successful the manager. Suppose a researcher wants to compare the average success index for two groups of managers at a large manufacturing plant. Managers in group 1 engage in a high volume of interactions with people outside the manager's work unit. (Such interactions include phone and face-to-face meetings with customers and suppliers, outside meetings, and public relations work.) Managers in group 2 rarely interact with people outside their work unit. Independent random samples of 12 and 15 managers are selected from groups 1 and 2, respectively, and the success index of each recorded. The results of the study are given in Table 9.2.

a. Use the data in the table to estimate the true mean difference between the success indexes of managers in the two groups. Use a 95% confidence interval, and interpret the interval.

b. What assumptions must be made in order that the estimate be valid? Are they reasonably satisfied?

SOLUTION

a. For this experiment, let μ_1 and μ_2 represent the mean success index of group 1 and group 2 managers, respectively. Then, the objective is to obtain a 95% confidence interval for $(\mu_1 - \mu_2)$.

TABLE 9.2   Managerial Success Indexes for Two Groups of Managers

GROUP 1						GROUP 2					
Interaction with Outsiders						Few Interactions					
65	58	78	60	68	69	62	53	36	34	56	50
66	70	53	71	63	63	42	57	46	68	48	42
						52	53	43			

FIGURE 9.6
SAS printout for
Example 9.4

```
Analysis Variable : SUCCESS
-------------------------------- GROUP=1 -----------------------------------

N Obs   N      Minimum        Maximum            Mean      Std Dev
--------------------------------------------------------------------------
    12  12   53.0000000    78.0000000    65.3333333    6.6103683


-------------------------------- GROUP=2 -----------------------------------

N Obs   N      Minimum        Maximum            Mean      Std Dev
--------------------------------------------------------------------------
    15  15   34.0000000    68.0000000    49.4666667    9.3340136
```

The first step in constructing the confidence interval is to obtain summary statistics (e.g., $\bar{x}$ and s) on the success index for each group of managers. The data of Table 9.2 were entered into a computer, and SAS used to obtain these descriptive statistics. The SAS printout appears in Figure 9.6. Note that $\bar{x}_1 = 65.33$, $s_1 = 6.61$, $\bar{x}_2 = 49.47$, and $s_2 = 9.33$.

Next, we calculate the pooled estimate of variance:

$$s_p^2 = \frac{(n_1 - 1)s_1^2 + (n_2 - 1)s_2^2}{n_1 + n_2 - 2}$$

$$= \frac{(12 - 1)(6.61)^2 + (15 - 1)(9.33)^2}{12 + 15 - 2} = 67.97$$

where s_p^2 is based on $(n_1 + n_2 - 2) = (12 + 15 - 2) = 25$ degrees of freedom. Also, we find $t_{\alpha/2} = t_{.025} = 2.06$ (based on 25 degrees of freedom) from Table VI of Appendix B.

Finally, the 95% confidence interval for $(\mu_1 - \mu_2)$, the difference between mean managerial success indexes for the two groups, is

$$(\bar{x}_1 - \bar{x}_2) \pm t_{\alpha/2}\sqrt{s_p^2\left(\frac{1}{n_1} + \frac{1}{n_2}\right)} = 65.33 - 49.47 \pm t_{.025}\sqrt{67.97\left(\frac{1}{12} + \frac{1}{15}\right)}$$

$$= 15.86 \pm (2.06)(3.19)$$

$$= 15.86 \pm 6.58$$

or (9.28, 22.44). Note that the interval includes only positive differences. Consequently, we are 95% confident that $(\mu_1 - \mu_2)$ exceeds 0. In fact, we estimate the mean success index, μ_1, for managers with a high volume of outsider interaction (group 1) to be anywhere between 9.28 and 22.44 points higher than the mean success index, μ_2, of managers with few interactions (group 2).

b. To properly use the small-sample confidence interval, the following assumptions must be satisfied:

1. The samples of managers are randomly and independently selected from the populations of group 1 and group 2 managers.

2. The success indexes are normally distributed for both groups of managers.

3. The variance of the success indexes are the same for the two populations, i.e., $\sigma_1^2 = \sigma_2^2$.

Variable=SUCCESS

```
----------------------------------GROUP=1 -------------------------------------

        Stem Leaf                          #          Boxplot
          7 8                              1             |
          7 01                             2          +------+
          6 5689                           4          *--+--*
          6 033                            3          +------+
          5 8                              1             |
          5 3                              1             |
            ----+----+----+----+
        Multiply Stem.Leaf by 10**+1




----------------------------------GROUP=2 -------------------------------------

        Stem Leaf                          #          Boxplot
          6 8                              1             |
          6 2                              1             |
          5 67                             2          +------+
          5 0233                           4          *------*
          4 68                             2          |  +  |
          4 223                            3          +------+
          3 6                              1             |
          3 4                              1             |
            ----+----+----+----+
        Multiply Stem.Leaf by 10**+1
```

FIGURE 9.7   SAS graphs for Example 9.4

The first assumption is satisfied, based on the information provided about the sampling procedure in the problem description. To check the plausibility of the remaining two assumptions, we resort to graphical methods. Figure 9.7 is a portion of the SAS printout that gives stem-and-leaf displays for the success indexes of the two samples of managers. Both plots reveal distributions that are approximately mound-shaped and symmetric. Consequently, each sample data set appears to come from a population that is approximately normal.

One way to check assumption #3 is to test the null hypothesis $H_0: \sigma_1^2 = \sigma_2^2$. This test is covered in Section 9.5. Another approach is to examine box plots for the sample data. Figure 9.8 is a SAS printout that shows side-by-side vertical box plots for the success indexes in the two samples. Recall, from Section 2.9, that the box plot represents the "spread" of a data set. The two box plots appear to have about the same spread; thus, the samples appear to come from populations with approximately the same variance.

All three assumptions, then, appear to be reasonably satisfied for this application of the small-sample confidence interval.

FIGURE 9.8   SAS box plots for Example 9.4

The two-sample t statistic is a powerful tool for comparing population means when the assumptions are satisfied. It has also been shown to retain its usefulness when the sampled populations are only approximately normally distributed. And when the sample sizes are equal, the assumption of equal population variances

STATISTICS IN ACTION

9.1 THE EFFECT OF SELF-MANAGED WORK TEAMS ON FAMILY LIFE

To improve quality, productivity, and timeliness, more and more American industries are adopting a new participative management style utilizing self-managed work teams (SMWTs). A team typically consists of five to 15 workers who are collectively responsible for making decisions and performing all tasks related to a particular project. For example, a SMWT may be responsible for scheduling work hours, interfacing with customers, disciplining team members, and participating in hiring. Studies reveal that SMWTs have positive impacts on both a firm's performance and employee attitudes.

SMWTs require that employees be trained in interpersonal skills such as listening, decision-making, and conflict resolution. Consequently, SMWTs can have potential positive spillover effects on a worker's family life. Researchers L. Stanley-Stevens (Tarleton State University), D. E. Yeatts, and R. R. Seward (both University of North Texas) investigated the connection between SMWT work characteristics and workers' perceptions of positive spillover into family life (*Quality Management Journal*, Summer 1995).

Survey data were collected from 114 AT&T employees who work in one of fifteen SMWTs at an AT&T technical division. The workers were divided into two groups: (1) those who reported positive spillover of work skills to family life and (2) those who did not report positive work spillover. The two groups were compared on a variety of job and demographic characteristics, several of which are shown in Table 9.3. All but the demographic characteristics were measured on a 7-point scale, ranging from 1 = "strongly disagree" to 7 = "strongly agree"; thus, the larger the number, the more of the job characteristic indicated.

Focus

For each characteristic, the sample means of the two groups are shown in Table 9.3, as well as the observed significance level (*p*-value) for a test to compare the group means. Fully interpret these results. Which job-related characteristics are most highly associated with positive work spillover?

---

can be relaxed. That is, if $n_1 = n_2$, then σ_1^2 and σ_2^2 can be quite different and the test statistic will still possess, approximately, a Student's *t*-distribution. When the assumptions are not satisfied, you can select larger samples from the populations or you can use other available statistical tests (nonparametric statistical tests, which are described in Chapter 17).

> **What Should You Do If the Assumptions Are Not Satisfied?**
> *Answer:* If you are concerned that the assumptions are not satisfied, use the Wilcoxon rank sum test for independent samples to test for a shift in population distributions. See Chapter 17.

EXERCISES 9.1–9.26

Note: Exercises marked with 💾 *contain data for computer analysis on a 3.5" disk (file name in parentheses).*

Learning the Mechanics

9.1 The purpose of this exercise is to compare the variability of $\bar{x}_1$ and $\bar{x}_2$ with the variability of $(\bar{x}_1 - \bar{x}_2)$.

a. Suppose the first sample is selected from a population with mean $\mu_1 = 150$ and variance $\sigma_1^2 = 900$. Within what range should the sample mean vary about 95% of the time in repeated samples of 100 measurements from this distribution? That is, construct an interval extending 2 standard deviations of $\bar{x}_1$ on each side of μ_1.

TABLE 9.3 Results of Tests to Compare Two Groups of SMWT Employees (Statistics in Action 9.1)

		MEANS		
	Characteristic	No Positive Work Spillover ($n = 67$)	Positive Work Spillover ($n = 47$)	p-Value
Information Flow (7-point scale)	Use of creative ideas	4.4	5.3	$p < .001$
	Communication	3.6	4.4	$.001 < p < .01$
	Cooperation	4.6	5.5	$p < .001$
	Utilization of information	4.7	5.2	$p > .05$
Decision-Making (7-point scale)	Participation in decisions regarding personnel matters	2.7	3.3	$.01 < p < .05$
	Participation in decisions regarding work conditions	4.2	5.0	$.001 < p < .01$
Job (7-point scale)	Good use of skills	4.8	5.9	$p < .001$
	Task significance	5.3	6.0	$.001 < p < .01$
	Task identity	4.2	4.8	$.01 < p < .05$
Demographics	Age (years)	45.0	46.2	$p > .05$
	Education (years)	13.1	13.0	$p > .05$
	Gender (percent female)	12.0	17.0	$p > .05$

Source: Stanley-Stevens, L., Yeatts, D. E., and Seward, R. R. "Positive effects of work on family-life: A case for self-managed work teams." *Quality Management Journal,* Summer 1995, p. 38 (Table 1).

b. Suppose the second sample is selected independently of the first from a second population with mean $\mu_2 = 150$ and variance $\sigma_2^2 = 1{,}600$. Within what range should the sample mean vary about 95% of the time in repeated samples of 100 measurements from this distribution? That is, construct an interval extending 2 standard deviations of $\bar{x}_2$ on each side of μ_2.

c. Now consider the difference between the two sample means $(\bar{x}_1 - \bar{x}_2)$. What are the mean and standard deviation of the sampling distribution of $(\bar{x}_1 - \bar{x}_2)$?

d. Within what range should the difference in sample means vary about 95% of the time in repeated independent samples of 100 measurements each from the two populations?

e. What, in general, can be said about the variability of the difference between independent sample means relative to the variability of the individual sample means?

9.2 Independent random samples of 64 observations each are chosen from two normal populations with the following means and standard deviations:

Population 1	Population 2
$\mu_1 = 12$	$\mu_2 = 10$
$\sigma_1 = 4$	$\sigma_2 = 3$

Let $\bar{x}_1$ and $\bar{x}_2$ denote the two sample means.
a. Give the mean and standard deviation of the sampling distribution of $\bar{x}_1$.
b. Give the mean and standard deviation of the sampling distribution of $\bar{x}_2$.

c. Suppose you were to calculate the difference $(\bar{x}_1 - \bar{x}_2)$ between the sample means. Find the mean and standard deviation of the sampling distribution of $(\bar{x}_1 - \bar{x}_2)$.
d. Will the statistic $(\bar{x}_1 - \bar{x}_2)$ be normally distributed? Explain.

9.3 In order to compare the means of two populations, independent random samples of 400 observations are selected from each population, with the following results:

Sample 1	Sample 2
$\bar{x}_1 = 5{,}275$	$\bar{x}_2 = 5{,}240$
$s_1 = 150$	$s_2 = 200$

a. Use a 95% confidence interval to estimate the difference between the population means $(\mu_1 - \mu_2)$. Interpret the confidence interval.
b. Test the null hypothesis $H_0: (\mu_1 - \mu_2) = 0$ versus the alternative hypothesis $H_a: (\mu_1 - \mu_2) \neq 0$. Give the significance level of the test, and interpret the result.
c. Suppose the test in part **b** was conducted with the alternative hypothesis $H_a: (\mu_1 - \mu_2) > 0$. How would your answer to part **b** change?
d. Test the null hypothesis $H_0: (\mu_1 - \mu_2) = 25$ versus $H_a: (\mu_1 - \mu_2) \neq 25$. Give the significance level, and interpret the result. Compare your answer to the test conducted in part **b**.
e. What assumptions are necessary to ensure the validity of the inferential procedures applied in parts **a–d**?

9.4 To use the t statistic to test for a difference between the means of two populations, what assumptions

```
Two sample Z for X1 vs X2
              N        Mean      StDev     SE Mean
X1           233        473        84        15.26
X2           312        485        93        17.66

Z-Test mu X1 = mu X2 (vs n.e.): T= -1.576   P=0.1150
```

must be made about the two populations? About the two samples?

9.5 Two populations are described in each of the following cases. In which cases would it be appropriate to apply the small-sample t-test to investigate the difference between the population means?
   a. Population 1: Normal distribution with variance σ_1^2. Population 2: Skewed to the right with variance $\sigma_2^2 = \sigma_1^2$.
   b. Population 1: Normal distribution with variance σ_1^2. Population 2: Normal distribution with variance $\sigma_2^2 \neq \sigma_1^2$.
   c. Population 1: Skewed to the left with variance σ_1^2. Population 2: Skewed to the left with variance $\sigma_2^2 = \sigma_1^2$.
   d. Population 1: Normal distribution with variance σ_1^2. Population 2: Normal distribution with variance $\sigma_2^2 = \sigma_1^2$.
   e. Population 1: Uniform distribution with variance σ_1^2. Population 2: Uniform distribution with variance $\sigma_2^2 = \sigma_1^2$.

9.6 In the t-tests of this section, σ_1^2 and σ_2^2 are assumed to be equal. Thus, we say $\sigma_1^2 = \sigma_2^2 = \sigma^2$. Why is a pooled estimator of σ^2 used instead of either s_1^2 or s_2^2?

9.7 Assume that $\sigma_1^2 = \sigma_2^2 = \sigma^2$. Calculate the pooled estimator of σ^2 for each of the following cases:
   a. $s_1^2 = 120, s_2^2 = 100, n_1 = n_2 = 25$
   b. $s_1^2 = 12, s_2^2 = 20, n_1 = 20, n_2 = 10$
   c. $s_1^2 = .15, s_2^2 = .20, n_1 = 6, n_2 = 10$
   d. $s_1^2 = 3,000, s_2^2 = 2,500, n_1 = 16, n_2 = 17$
   e. Note that the pooled estimate is a weighted average of the sample variances. To which of the variances does the pooled estimate fall nearer in each of the above cases?

9.8 Independent random samples from normal populations produced the results shown below:

Sample 1	Sample 2
1.2	4.2
3.1	2.7
1.7	3.6
2.8	3.9
3.0	

   a. Calculate the pooled estimate of σ^2.
   b. Do the data provide sufficient evidence to indicate that $\mu_2 > \mu_1$? Test using $\alpha = .10$.
   c. Find a 90% confidence interval for $(\mu_1 - \mu_2)$.

   d. Which of the two inferential procedures, the test of hypothesis in part **b** or the confidence interval in part **c**, provides more information about $(\mu_1 - \mu_2)$?

9.9 Two independent random samples have been selected, 100 observations from population 1 and 100 from population 2. Sample means $\bar{x}_1 = 15.5$ and $\bar{x}_2 = 26.6$ were obtained. From previous experience with these populations, it is known that the variances are $\sigma_1^2 = 9$ and $\sigma_2^2 = 16$.
   a. Find $\sigma_{(\bar{x}_1 - \bar{x}_2)}$.
   b. Sketch the approximate sampling distribution for $(\bar{x}_1 - \bar{x}_2)$ assuming $(\mu_1 - \mu_2) = 10$.
   c. Locate the observed value of $(\bar{x}_1 - \bar{x}_2)$ on the graph you drew in part **b**. Does it appear that this value contradicts the null hypothesis $H_0: (\mu_1 - \mu_2) = 10$?
   d. Use the z-table on the inside of the front cover to determine the rejection region for the test of $H_0: (\mu_1 - \mu_2) = 10$ against $H_0: (\mu_1 - \mu_2) \neq 10$. Use $\alpha = .05$.
   e. Conduct the hypothesis test of part **d** and interpret your result.

9.10 Refer to Exercise 9.9. Construct a 95% confidence interval for $(\mu_1 - \mu_2)$. Interpret the interval. Which inference provides more information about the value of $(\mu_1 - \mu_2)$—the test of hypothesis in Exercise 9.9 or the confidence interval in this exercise?

9.11 Independent random samples are selected from two populations and used to test the hypothesis $H_0: (\mu_1 - \mu_2) = 0$ against the alternative $H_a: (\mu_1 - \mu_2) \neq 0$. A total of 233 observations from population 1 and 312 from population 2 are analyzed by using MINITAB, with the results shown above.
   a. Interpret the results of the computer analysis.
   b. If the alternative hypothesis had been $H_a: (\mu_1 - \mu_2) < 0$, how would the p-value change? Interpret the p-value for this one-tailed test.

9.12 (X09.012) Independent random samples from approximately normal populations produced the results shown below:

Sample 1				Sample 2			
52	33	42	44	52	43	47	56
41	50	44	51	62	53	61	50
45	38	37	40	56	52	53	60
44	50	43		50	48	60	55

a. Do the data provide sufficient evidence to conclude that $(\mu_2 - \mu_1) > 10$? Test using $\alpha = .01$.

b. Construct a 98% confidence interval for $(\mu_2 - \mu_1)$. Interpret your result.

9.13 Independent random samples selected from two normal populations produced the sample means and standard deviations shown below:

Sample 1	Sample 2
$n_1 = 17$	$n_2 = 12$
$\bar{x}_1 = 5.4$	$\bar{x}_2 = 7.9$
$s_1 = 3.4$	$s_2 = 4.8$

a. The test H_0: $(\mu_1 - \mu_2) = 0$ against H_a: $(\mu_1 - \mu_2) \neq 0$ was conducted using SAS, with the results shown below. Check and interpret the results.

b. Estimate $(\mu_1 - \mu_2)$ using a 95% confidence interval.

Applying the Concepts

9.14 Some college professors make bound lecture notes available to their classes in an effort to improve teaching effectiveness. Because students pay the additional cost, educators want to know whether the students find the lecture notes to be of good educational value. *Marketing Educational Review* (Fall 1994) published a study of business students' opinions of lecture notes. Two groups of students were surveyed—86 students enrolled in a promotional strategy class that required the purchase of lecture notes, and 35 students enrolled in a sales/retailing elective that did not offer lecture notes. In both courses, the instructor used lectures as the main method of delivery. At the end of the semester, the students were asked to respond to the statement: "Having a copy of the lecture notes was [would be] helpful in understanding the material." Responses were measured on a 9-point semantic difference scale, where 1 = "strongly disagree" and 9 = "strongly agree." A summary of the results are reported in the next table.

a. Describe the two populations involved in the comparison.

b. Do the samples provide sufficient evidence to conclude that there is a difference in the mean responses of the two groups of students? Test using $\alpha = .01$.

c. Construct a 99% confidence interval for $(\mu_1 - \mu_2)$. Interpret the result.

d. Would a 95% confidence interval for $(\mu_1 - \mu_2)$ be narrower or wider than the one you found in part **c**? Why?

Classes Buying Lecture Notes	Classes Not Buying Lecture Notes
$n_1 = 86$	$n_2 = 35$
$\bar{x}_1 = 8.48$	$\bar{x}_2 = 7.80$
$s_1^2 = 0.94$	$s_2^2 = 2.99$

Source: Gray, J. I., and Abernathy, A. M. "Pros and cons of lecture notes and handout packages: Faculty and student opinions," *Marketing Education Review,* Vol. 4, No. 3, Fall 1984, p. 25 (Table 4), American Marketing Association.

9.15 (X09.015) Marketing strategists would like to predict consumer response to new products and their accompanying promotional schemes. Consequently, studies that examine the differences between buyers and nonbuyers of a product are of interest. One classic study conducted by Shuchman and Riesz (*Journal of Marketing Research,* Feb. 1975) was aimed at characterizing the purchasers and nonpurchasers of Crest toothpaste. Purchasers were defined as households that converted to Crest following its endorsement by the Council on Dental Therapeutics of the American Dental Association on August 1, 1960, and remained "loyal" to Crest until at least April 1963. Nonpurchasers were defined as households that did not convert to Crest during the same time period. Using demographic data collected from a sample of 499 purchasers and 499 nonpurchasers, Shuchman and Riesz demonstrated that both the mean household size (number of persons) and mean household income were significantly larger for purchasers than for nonpurchasers. A similar study utilized independent random samples of size 20 and yielded the data shown in the table (page 382) on the age of the householder primarily responsible for buying toothpaste. An analysis of the data is provided in the SAS printout on page 382.

```
Variable: X

SAMPLE    N    Mean    Std Dev    Std Error
-------------------------------------------------
   1      17    5.4      3.4        4.123
   2      12    7.9      4.8        3.464

Variances        T      DF     Prob>|T|
-------------------------------------------------
Equal         -1.646    27      .1114
```

Purchasers						Nonpurchasers					
34	35	23	44	52	46	28	22	44	33	55	63
28	48	28	34	33	52	45	31	60	54	53	58
41	32	34	49	50	45	52	52	66	35	25	48
29	59					59	61				

```
                          TTEST PROCEDURE

Variable: AGE

BUYER            N              Mean          Std Dev         Std Error
-------------------------------------------------------------------------
NONPURCH         20          47.20000000    13.62119092       3.04579088
PURCHASE         20          39.80000000    10.03992032       2.24499443

Variances        T        DF      Prob>|T|
-------------------------------------------------------------------------
Unequal        1.9557    34.9      0.0585
Equal          1.9557    38.0      0.0579

For HO: Variances are equal, F' = 1.84  DF =  (19,19)  Prob>F' = 0.1927
```

a. Do the data present sufficient evidence to conclude there is a difference in the mean age of purchasers and nonpurchasers? Use $\alpha = .10$.

b. What assumptions are necessary in order to answer part **a**?

c. Find the observed significance level for the test on the printout, and interpret its value.

d. Calculate and interpret a 90% confidence interval for the difference between the mean ages of purchasers and nonpurchasers.

9.16 Valparaiso University professors D. L. Schroeder and K. E. Reichardt conducted a salary survey of members of the Institute of Management Accountants (IMA) and reported the results in *Management Accounting* (June 1995). A salary questionnaire was mailed to a random sample of 4,800 IMA members; 2,287 were returned and form the database for the study. The researchers compared average salaries by management level, education, and gender. Some of the results for entry level managers are shown in the following table.

a. Suppose you want to make an inference about the difference between salaries of male and female entry-level managers who earned a CPA degree, at a 95% level of confidence. Why is this impossible to do using the information in the table?

b. Make the inference, part **a**, assuming the salary standard deviation for male and female entry-level managers with CPAs are $4,000 and $3,000, respectively.

c. Repeat part **b**, but assume the male and female salary standard deviations are $16,000 and $12,000, respectively.

d. Compare the two inferences, parts **b** and **c**.

e. Suppose you want to compare the mean salaries of male entry-level managers with a CPA to the mean salary of male entry-level managers without a CPA degree. Give sample standard deviation values that will yield a significant difference between the two means, at $\alpha = .05$.

f. In your opinion, are the sample standard deviations, part **e**, reasonable values for the salary data? Explain.

9.17 When Firm A combines with Firm B and only Firm A survives, this is called a *merger*. When Firm A and Firm B combine to form Firm C, a new company, this is called a *consolidation*. A third form of business combination occurs when Firm A buys Firm B and both remain in existence.

	CPA DEGREE		BACCALAUREATE DEGREE NO CPA	
	Men	**Women**	**Men**	**Women**
Mean Salary	$40,084	$35,377	$39,268	$33,159
Number of Respondents	48	39	205	177

Source: Schroeder, D. L., and Reichardt, K. E. "Salaries 1994." *Management Accounting,* Vol. 76, No. 12, June 1995, p. 34 (Table 12).

	Merged Firms	Nonmerged Firms
Sample Mean	7.295	14.666
Sample Standard Deviation	7.374	16.089

Source: Wansley, J. W., Roenfeldt, R. L., and Corley, P. L. "Abnormal returns from merger profiles." *Journal of Financial and Quantitative Analysis,* Vol. 18, No. 2, June 1983, pp. 149–162.

This is called an *acquisition* (Lee, Finnerty, and Norton, *Foundations of Financial Management,* 1997). During a recent wave of merger activity, researchers compared the profiles of a sample of 44 firms that merged with those of a sample of 44 firms that did not merge. The table above displays information obtained on the firms' price-earnings ratios (P/E):

a. The analysis indicated that merged firms generally have smaller price-earnings ratios. Do you agree? Test using $\alpha = .05$.

b. Report and interpret the *p*-value of the test you conducted in part **a**.

c. Do you think that the distributions of the price-earnings ratios for the populations from which these samples were drawn are normally distributed? Why or why not? [*Hint:* Note the relative values of the sample means and standard deviations.]

d. How does your answer to part **c** impact the validity of the inference drawn from the analysis? Explain.

9.18 As a country's standard of living increases, so does its production of solid waste. The attendant environmental threat makes solid-waste management an important national problem in many countries of the world. The *International Journal of Environmental Health Research* (Vol. 4, 1994) reported on the solid-waste generation rates (in kilograms per capita per day) for samples of cities from industrialized and middle-income countries. The data are provided in the next table.

Industrialized Countries		Middle-Income Countries	
New York (USA)	2.27	Singapore	0.87
Phoenix (USA)	2.31	Hong Kong	0.85
London (UK)	2.24	Medellin (Colombia)	0.54
Hamburg (Germany)	2.18	Kano (Nigeria)	0.46
Rome (Italy)	2.15	Manila (Philippines)	0.50
		Cairo (Egypt)	0.50
		Tunis (Tunisia)	0.56

a. Based on only a visual inspection of the data, does it appear that the mean waste generation rates of cities in industrialized and middle-income countries differ?

b. Conduct a test of hypothesis (at $\alpha = .05$) to support your observation in part **a**. Use the EXCEL printout below to make your conclusion.

9.19 A recent rash of retirements from the U.S. Senate prompted Middlebury College researchers J. E. Trickett and P. M. Sommers to study the ages and lengths of service of members of Congress (*Chance,* Spring 1996). One question of interest to the researchers is: "Did the 13 senators who decided to retire in 1995–1996 begin their careers at a younger average age than did the rest of their colleagues in the Senate?"

a. The average age at which the 13 retiring senators began their service is 45.783 years; the corresponding average for all other senators is 47.201 years. Is this sufficient information to answer the researchers' question? Explain.

t-Test: Two-Sample Assuming Equal Variances		
	INDUST	MIDDLE
Mean	2.23	0.611428571
Variance	0.00425	0.029880952
Observations	5	7
Pooled Variance	0.019628571	
Hypothesized Mean Difference	0	
df	10	
t Stat	19.73017433	
P(T<=t) one-tail	1.22537E-09	
t Critical one-tail	1.812461505	
P(T<=t)two-tail	2.45073E-09	
t Critical two-tail	2.228139238	

b. The researchers conducted a two-sample *t*-test on the difference between the two means. Specify the null and alternative hypothesis for this test. Clearly define the parameter of interest.

c. The observed significance level for the test, part **b**, was reported as *p* = .55. Interpret this result.

9.20 One way corporations raise money for expansion is to issue *bonds*, loan agreements to repay the purchaser a specified amount with a fixed rate of interest paid periodically over the life of the bond. The sale of bonds is usually handled by an underwriting firm. Does it pay for companies to shop around for an underwriter? The reason for the question is that the price of a bond may rise or fall after its issuance. Therefore, whether a corporation receives the market price for a bond depends on the skill of its underwriter (Radcliffe, 1994). The mean change in the prices of 27 bonds handled over a 12-month period by one underwriter and in the prices of 23 bonds handled by another are shown.

	Underwriter 1	Underwriter 2
Sample size	27	23
Sample mean	−.0491	−.0307
Sample variance	.009800	.002465

a. Do the data provide sufficient evidence to indicate a difference in the mean change in bond prices handled by the two underwriters? Test using α = .05.

b. Find a 95% confidence interval for the mean difference for the two underwriters, and interpret it.

9.21 Since the emergence of Japan as an industrial superpower in the 1970s and 1980s, U.S. businesses have paid close attention to Japanese management styles and philosophies. Some of the credit for the high quality of Japanese products is attributed to the Japanese system of permanent employment for their workers. In the United States, high job turnover rates are common in many industries and are associated with high product defect rates. High turnover rates mean U.S. plants have more inexperienced workers who are unfamiliar with the company's product lines than Japan has (Stevenson, *Production/Operations*

Management, 1996). For example, in a study of the air conditioner industry in Japan and the United States, the difference in the average annual turnover rate of workers between U.S. plants and Japanese plants was reported as 3.1% (*Harvard Business Review,* Sept.–Oct. 1983). In a more recent study, five Japanese and five U.S. plants that manufacture air conditioners were randomly sampled; their turnover rates are listed in the table, with a MINITAB descriptive statistics printout at the bottom of the page.

U.S. Plants	Japanese Plants
7.11%	3.52%
6.06	2.02
8.00	4.91
6.87	3.22
4.77	1.92

a. Do the data provide sufficient evidence to indicate that the mean annual percentage turnover for U.S. plants exceeds the corresponding mean percentage for Japanese plants? Test using α = .05.

b. Report and interpret the observed significance level of the test you conducted in part **a**.

c. List any assumptions you made in conducting the hypothesis test of part **a**. Comment on their validity for this application.

9.22 *Sales quotas* are volume objectives assigned to specific sales units, such as regions, districts, or salespersons' territories. Sometimes to achieve manufacturing efficiency or long-term goals, sales managers set quotas for specific products at challenging levels. The underlying idea is that setting challenging quotas and attaching significant rewards will direct salespersons' efforts along desired paths (Guiltinan and Paul, 1994). The Universal Products Company (real company, fictitious name) manufactures and markets electronic and electromechanical industrial equipment. It has a sales force of over 1,000, organized in 10 districts and 135 branch offices. Salespersons have sales quotas on two specific products, Dataprinters and Micromagnetics, as well as an overall sales volume quota. Many salespersons have complained that having to make the quota on Dataprinters takes so much time that it keeps them

```
TWOSAMPLE T FOR US VS JAPAN
           N      MEAN    STDEV   SE MEAN
US         5      6.56    1.22     0.54
JAPAN      5      3.12    1.23     0.55

95 PCT CI FOR MU US - MU JAPAN: (1.62, 5.27)

TTEST MU US = MU JAPAN (VS NE): T= 4.46   P=0.0031   DF= 7
```

from generating a higher overall sales volume. To determine how reducing the Dataprinter quota would affect total sales volume, the sales volumes of a sample of branch offices whose salespersons all worked under the standard quota were compared with the sales volumes of a sample of branch offices whose salespersons all were given a lower Dataprinter quota. Data were collected for a seven-month period and are reported in the table in terms of total sales per worker-month (in thousands of dollars).

Branch	Lower Quota	Standard Quota
1		17.7
2	15.6	
3		15.1
4	14.0	
5		12.3
6		12.0
7	11.2	
8	11.0	
9		10.5
10	10.3	
11		10.0
12	9.4	

Source: Adapted from Winer, L. "The effect of product sales quotas on sales force productivity." *Journal of Marketing Research*, Vol. 10, May 1973.

a. What are the appropriate null and alternative hypotheses for testing whether salespersons on the two types of quotas differ in their mean sales per worker-month? Define any symbols you use.

b. The data in the table are submitted to MINITAB, with results as shown below. What do you conclude about the test set up in part **a**?

c. Interpret the confidence interval. Does its width imply that little or much information about the difference in mean sales is contained in these data? How could the amount of information be increased?

9.23 Helping smokers kick the habit is a big business in today's no-smoking environment. One of the more commonly used treatments according to an article in the *Journal of Imagination, Cognition and Personality* (Vol. 12, 1992/93) is Spiegel's three-point message:

1. For your body, smoking is a poison.
2. You need your body to live.
3. You owe your body this respect and protection.

To determine the effectiveness of this treatment, the authors conducted a study consisting of a sample of 52 smokers placed in two groups, a Spiegel treatment group or a control group (no treatment). Each participant was asked to record the number of cigarettes he or she smoked each week. The results for the study are shown below for the beginning period and four follow-up time periods.

	NUMBER OF CIGARETTES SMOKED IN WEEK		
	n	$\bar{x}$	s
Beginning			
Treatment	35	165.09	71.20
Control	17	159.00	67.45
First follow-up (2 wks)			
Treatment	35	105.00	69.08
Control	17	157.24	66.80
Second follow-up (4 wks)			
Treatment	35	111.11	69.08
Control	17	159.52	65.73
Third follow-up (8 wks)			
Treatment	35	120.20	67.59
Control	17	157.88	64.41
Fourth follow-up (12 wks)			
Treatment	35	123.63	74.09
Control	17	162.17	67.01

a. Create 95% confidence intervals for the difference in the average number of cigarettes smoked per week for the two groups for the beginning and each follow-up period. Interpret the results.

b. What assumptions are necessary for the validity of these confidence intervals?

9.24 Suppose you manage a plant that purifies its liquid waste and discharges the water into a local river. An EPA inspector has collected water specimens of the discharge of your plant and also water specimens in the river upstream from your plant. Each water specimen is divided into five parts, the bacteria count is read on each, and the mean count for each specimen is reported. The average bacteria

```
TWOSAMPLE T FOR LOWER VS STANDARD
              N       MEAN      STDEV    SE MEAN
LOWER         6       11.92      2.38      0.97
STANDARD      6       12.93      2.94      1.2

95 PCT CI FOR MU LOWER - MU STANDARD: (-4.51, 2.5)

TTEST MU LOWER = MU STANDARD (VS NE): T= -0.66   P=0.53   DF= 9
```

counts for each of six specimens are reported in the following table for the two locations.

Plant Discharge			Upstream		
30.1	36.2	33.4	29.7	30.3	26.4
28.2	29.8	34.9	27.3	31.7	32.3

a. Why might the bacteria counts shown here tend to be approximately normally distributed?

b. What are the appropriate null and alternative hypotheses to test whether the mean bacteria count for the plant discharge exceeds that for the upstream location? Be sure to define any symbols you use.

c. When the data are submitted to SPSS, part of the output is shown at the bottom of the page. Carefully interpret this output.

d. What assumptions are necessary to ensure the validity of this test?

9.25 While cable television companies in Minnesota are prohibited from holding exclusive rights to an area, the laws do not demand that a company face competition (*Minneapolis Star-Tribune,* Jan. 10, 1993). Many subscribers feel that these de facto monopolies exploit consumers by charging excessive monthly cable fees. Suppose a congressional subcommittee considering regulation of the cable industry investigates whether cable rates are higher in areas with no competition than in areas with competition. They randomly sample basic rates for six cable companies that have no competition and for six companies that face competition (but not from each other). The observed rates are shown in the table.

a. What are the appropriate null and alternative hypotheses to test the research hypothesis of the subcommittee?

b. Conduct the test of part **a** using $\alpha = .05$. Report and interpret the approximate significance level of the test.

c. What assumptions are necessary to ensure the validity of the test? Why does it matter that none of the companies in the sample compete against each other?

9.26 Research reported in the *Professional Geographer* (May 1992) examines the hypothesis that the disproportionate housework responsibility of women in two-income households is a major factor in determining the proximity of a woman's place of employment. The distance to work for both men and women in two-income households was reported for random samples of both central city and suburban residences:

	CENTRAL CITY RESIDENCE		SUBURBAN RESIDENCE	
	Men	Women	Men	Women
n	159	119	138	93
$\bar{x}$	7.4	4.5	9.3	6.6
s	6.3	4.2	7.1	5.6

a. For central city residences, calculate a 99% confidence interval for the difference in average distance to work for men and women in two-income households. Interpret the interval.

b. Repeat part **a** for suburban residences.

c. Interpret the confidence intervals. Do they indicate that women tend to work closer to home than men?

d. What assumptions have you made to assure the validity of the confidence intervals constructed in parts **a** and **b**?

No competition	$18.44	$26.88	$22.87	$25.78	$23.34	$27.52
Competition	$18.95	$23.74	$17.25	$20.14	$18.98	$20.14

```
Independent samples of  LOCATION

Group 1:  LOCATION EQ        1.00          Group 2:  LOCATION EQ        2.00
t-test for:  BACOUNT

                       Number                 Standard     Standard
                      of Cases    Mean        Deviation     Error
           Group 1       6        32.1000       3.189        1.302
           Group 2       6        29.6167       2.355         .961

                   | Pooled Variance Estimate | Separate Variance Estimate
      F    2-Tail  |   t     Degrees of 2-Tail |   t     Degrees of 2-Tail
    Value  Prob.   | Value   Freedom    Prob.  | Value   Freedom    Prob.
    1.83    .522   | 1.53      10        .156   | 1.53     9.20       .159
```

9.2   COMPARING TWO POPULATION MEANS: PAIRED DIFFERENCE EXPERIMENTS

Suppose you want to compare the mean daily sales of two restaurants located in the same city. If you were to record the restaurants' total sales for each of 12 randomly selected days during a six-month period, the results might appear as shown in Table 9.4. An SPSS printout of descriptive statistics for the data is displayed in Figure 9.9. Do these data provide evidence of a difference between the mean daily sales of the two restaurants?

We want to test the null hypothesis that the mean daily sales, μ_1 and μ_2, for the two restaurants are equal against the alternative hypothesis that they differ, i.e.,

$$H_0: (\mu_1 - \mu_2) = 0$$

$$H_a: (\mu_1 - \mu_2) \neq 0$$

If we employ the t statistic for independent samples (Section 9.1) we first calculate s_p^2 using the values of s_1 and s_2 highlighted on the SPSS printout:

$$s_p^2 = \frac{(n_1 - 1)s_1^2 + (n_2 - 1)s_2^2}{n_1 + n_2 - 2}$$

$$= \frac{(12 - 1)(530.07)^2 + (12 - 1)(516.04)^2}{12 + 12 - 2} = 273{,}630.6$$

Then we substitute the values of $\bar{x}_1$ and $\bar{x}_2$, also highlighted on the printout, to form the test statistic:

$$t = \frac{(\bar{x}_1 - \bar{x}_2) - 0}{\sqrt{s_p^2 \left(\frac{1}{n_1} + \frac{1}{n_2} \right)}} = \frac{(1{,}349.00 - 1{,}267.00)}{\sqrt{273{,}630.6 \left(\frac{1}{12} + \frac{1}{12} \right)}} = \frac{82.0}{213.54} = .38$$

TABLE 9.4   Daily Sales for Two Restaurants

Day	Restaurant 1	Restaurant 2
1 (Wednesday)	$1,005	$ 918
2 (Saturday)	2,073	1,971
3 (Tuesday)	873	825
4 (Wednesday)	1,074	999
5 (Friday)	1,932	1,827
6 (Thursday)	1,338	1,281
7 (Thursday)	1,449	1,302
8 (Monday)	759	678
9 (Friday)	1,905	1,782
10 (Monday)	693	639
11 (Saturday)	2,106	2,049
12 (Tuesday)	981	933

FIGURE 9.9
SPSS printout for daily restaurant sales

```
Number of Valid Observations (Listwise) =         12.00

Variable       Mean      Std Dev    Minimum    Maximum    N   Label

REST1        1349.00     530.07     693.00     2106.00    12
REST2        1267.00     516.04     639.00     2049.00    12
```

This small t value will not lead to rejection of H_0 when compared to the t-distribution with $n_1 + n_2 - 2 = 22$ df, even if α were chosen as large as .20 ($t_{\alpha/2} = t_{.10} = 1.321$). Thus, from *this* analysis we might conclude that insufficient evidence exists to infer that there is a difference in mean daily sales for the two restaurants.

However, if you examine the data in Table 9.4 more closely, you will find this conclusion difficult to accept. The sales of restaurant 1 exceed those of restaurant 2 *for every one of the randomly selected 12 days.* This, in itself, is strong evidence to indicate that μ_1 differs from μ_2, and we will subsequently confirm this fact. Why, then, was the t-test unable to detect this difference? The answer is: *The independent samples t-test is not a valid procedure to use with this set of data.*

The t-test is inappropriate because the assumption of independent samples is invalid. We have randomly chosen *days,* and thus, once we have chosen the sample of days for restaurant 1, we have *not* independently chosen the sample of days for restaurant 2. The dependence between observations within days can be seen by examining the pairs of daily sales, which tend to rise and fall together as we go from day to day. This pattern provides strong visual evidence of a violation of the assumption of independence required for the two-sample t-test of Section 9.1. In this situation, you will note the *large variation within samples* (reflected by the large value of s_p^2) in comparison to the relatively *small difference between the sample means.* Because s_p^2 is so large, the t-test of Section 9.1 is unable to detect a possible difference between μ_1 and μ_2.

We now consider a valid method of analyzing the data of Table 9.4. In Table 9.5 we add the column of differences between the daily sales of the two restaurants. We can regard these daily differences in sales as a random sample of all daily differences, past and present. Then we can use this sample to make inferences about the mean of the population of differences, μ_D, which is equal to the difference $(\mu_1 - \mu_2)$. That is, the mean of the population (and sample) of differences equals the difference between the population (and sample) means. Thus, our test becomes

$$H_0: \mu_D = 0 \qquad (\mu_1 - \mu_2) = 0$$
$$H_a: \mu_D \neq 0 \qquad (\mu_1 - \mu_2) \neq 0$$

The test statistic is a one-sample t (Section 8.4), since we are now analyzing a single sample of differences for small n:

$$\text{Test statistic: } t = \frac{\bar{x}_D - 0}{s_D/\sqrt{n_D}}$$

TABLE 9.5 Daily Sales and Differences for Two Restaurants

Day	Restaurant 1	Restaurant 2	Restaurant 1 − Restaurant 2
1 (Wednesday)	$1,005	$ 918	$ 87
2 (Saturday)	2,073	1,971	102
3 (Tuesday)	873	825	48
4 (Wednesday)	1,074	999	75
5 (Friday)	1,932	1,827	105
6 (Thursday)	1,338	1,281	57
7 (Thursday)	1,449	1,302	147
8 (Monday)	759	678	81
9 (Friday)	1,905	1,782	123
10 (Monday)	693	639	54
11 (Saturday)	2,106	2,049	57
12 (Tuesday)	981	933	48

FIGURE 9.10

Rejection region for restaurant sales example

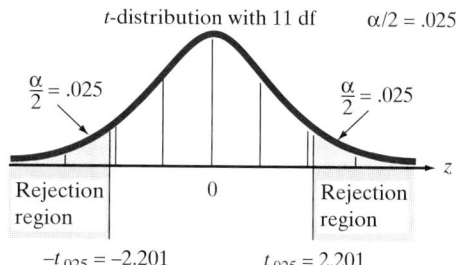

where $\bar{x}_D$ = Sample mean difference
s_D = Sample standard deviation of differences
n_D = Number of differences = Number of pairs

> *Assumptions:* The population of differences in daily sales is approximately normally distributed. The sample differences are randomly selected from the population differences. [*Note:* We do not need to make the assumption that $\sigma_1^2 = \sigma_2^2$.]
>
> *Rejection region:* At significance level $\alpha = .05$, we will reject H_0 if $|t| > t_{.05}$, where $t_{.05}$ is based on $(n_D - 1)$ degrees of freedom.

Referring to Table IV in Appendix B, we find the t value corresponding to $\alpha = .025$ and $n_D - 1 = 12 - 1 = 11$ df to be $t_{.025} = 2.201$. Then we will reject the null hypothesis if $|t| > 2.201$, (see Figure 9.10). Note that the number of degrees of freedom has decreased from $n_1 + n_2 - 2 = 22$ to 11 when we use the paired difference experiment rather than the two independent random samples design.

Summary statistics for the $n = 12$ differences are shown on the MINITAB printout, Figure 9.11. Note that $\bar{x}_D = 82.0$ and $s_D = 32.0$ (rounded). Substituting these values into the formula for the test statistic, we have

$$t = \frac{\bar{x}_D - 0}{s_D/\sqrt{n_D}} = \frac{82}{32/\sqrt{12}} = 8.88$$

Because this value of t falls in the rejection region, we conclude (at $\alpha = .05$) that the difference in population mean daily sales for the two restaurants differs from 0. We can reach the same conclusion by noting that the p-value of the test, highlighted in Figure 9.11, is approximately 0. The fact that $\bar{x}_1 - \bar{x}_2 = \bar{x}_D = \$82.00$ strongly suggests that the mean daily sales for restaurant 1 exceeds the mean daily sales for restaurant 2.

This kind of experiment, in which observations are paired and the differences are analyzed, is called a **paired difference experiment**. In many cases, a paired difference experiment can provide more information about the difference between population means than an independent samples experiment. The idea is to compare population means by comparing the differences between pairs of experimental units (objects, people, etc.) that were very similar prior to the experiment. The differencing removes sources of variation that tend to inflate σ^2. For instance, in the restaurant example, the day-to-day variability in daily sales is removed by analyzing the differences between the restaurants' daily sales. Making comparisons within groups of similar experimental units is called **blocking**, and the paired

FIGURE 9.11

MINITAB analysis of differences in Table 9.5

	N	MEAN	STDEV	SE MEAN	T	P VALUE
TEST OF MU = 0.000 VS MU N.E. 0.000						
DIFF	12	82.000	31.989	9.234	8.88	0.0000

difference experiment is an example of a **randomized block experiment**. In our example, the days represent the blocks.

Some other examples for which the paired difference experiment might be appropriate are the following:

1. Suppose you want to estimate the difference $(\mu_1 - \mu_2)$ in mean price per gallon between two major brands of premium gasoline. If you choose two independent random samples of stations for each brand, the variability in price due to geographic location may be large. To eliminate this source of variability you could choose pairs of stations of similar size, one station for each brand, in close geographic proximity and use the sample of differences between the prices of the brands to make an inference about $(\mu_1 - \mu_2)$.

2. A college placement center wants to estimate the difference $(\mu_1 - \mu_2)$ in mean starting salaries for men and women graduates who seek jobs through the center. If it independently samples men and women, the starting salaries may vary because of their different college majors and differences in grade point averages. To eliminate these sources of variability, the placement center could match male and female job seekers according to their majors and grade point averages. Then the differences between the starting salaries of each pair in the sample could be used to make an inference about $(\mu_1 - \mu_2)$.

3. To compare the performance of two automobile salespeople, we might test a hypothesis about the difference $(\mu_1 - \mu_2)$ in their respective mean monthly sales. If we randomly choose n_1 months of salesperson 1's sales and independently choose n_2 months of salesperson 2's sales, the month-to-month variability caused by the seasonal nature of new car sales might inflate s_p^2 and prevent the two-sample t statistic from detecting a difference between μ_1 and μ_2, if such a difference actually exists. However, by taking the difference in monthly sales for the two salespeople for each of n months, we eliminate the month-to-month variability (seasonal variation) in sales, and the probability of detecting a difference between μ_1 and μ_2, if a difference exists, is increased.

The hypothesis-testing procedures and the method of forming confidence intervals for the difference between two means using a paired difference experiment are summarized in the boxes for both large and small n.

Paired Difference Confidence Interval for $\mu_D = \mu_1 - \mu_2$

Large Sample

$$\bar{x}_D \pm z_{\alpha/2}\frac{\sigma_D}{\sqrt{n_D}} \approx \bar{x}_D \pm z_{\alpha/2}\frac{s_D}{\sqrt{n_D}}$$

Assumption: The sample differences are randomly selected from the population of differences.

Small Sample

$$\bar{x}_D \pm t_{\alpha/2}\frac{s_D}{\sqrt{n_D}}$$

where $t_{\alpha/2}$ is based on $(n_D - 1)$ degrees of freedom

Assumptions: **1.** The relative frequency distribution of the population of differences is normal.

2. The sample differences are randomly selected from the population of differences.

Paired Difference Test of Hypothesis for $\mu_D = \mu_1 - \mu_2$

One-Tailed Test

$H_0: \mu_D = D_0$

$H_a: \mu_D < D_0$
    [or $H_a: \mu_D > D_0$]

Two-Tailed Test

$H_0: \mu_D = D_0$

$H_a: \mu_D \neq D_0$

Large Sample

Test statistic:
$$z = \frac{\bar{x}_D - D_0}{\sigma_D/\sqrt{n_D}} \approx \frac{\bar{x}_D - D_0}{s_D/\sqrt{n_D}}$$

Rejection region: $z < -z_\alpha$
    [or $z > z_\alpha$ when $H_a: \mu_D > D_0$]

Rejection region: $|z| > z_{\alpha/2}$

Assumption: The differences are randomly selected from the population of differences.

Small Sample

Test statistic:
$$t = \frac{\bar{x}_D - D_0}{s_D/\sqrt{n_D}}$$

Rejection region: $t < -t_\alpha$
    [or $t > t_\alpha$ when $H_a: \mu_D > D_0$]

Rejection region: $|t| > t_{\alpha/2}$

where t_α and $t_{\alpha/2}$ are based on $(n_D - 1)$ degrees of freedom

Assumptions: **1.** The relative frequency distribution of the population of differences is normal.

2. The differences are randomly selected from the population of differences.

EXAMPLE 9.5

An experiment is conducted to compare the starting salaries of male and female college graduates who find jobs. Pairs are formed by choosing a male and a female with the same major and similar grade point averages (GPAs). Suppose a random sample of 10 pairs is formed in this manner and the starting annual salary of each person is recorded. The results are shown in Table 9.6. Compare the mean starting salary, μ_1, for males to the mean starting salary, μ_2, for females using a 95% confidence interval. Interpret the results.

TABLE 9.6   Data on Annual Salaries for Matched Pairs of College Graduates

Pair	Male	Female	Difference (Male–Female)	Pair	Male	Female	Difference (Male–Female)
1	$29,300	$28,800	$ 500	6	$27,800	$28,000	$−200
2	31,500	31,600	−100	7	29,500	29,200	300
3	30,400	29,800	600	8	31,200	30,100	1,100
4	28,500	28,500	0	9	28,400	28,200	200
5	33,500	32,600	900	10	29,200	28,500	700

FIGURE 9.12
MINITAB analysis of differences in Table 9.6

	N	MEAN	STDEV	SE MEAN	95.0 PERCENT C.I.
DIFF	10	400.000	434.613	137.437	(89.013, 710.987)

SOLUTION

Since the data on annual salary are collected in pairs of males and females matched on GPA and major, a paired difference experiment is performed. To conduct the analysis, we first compute the differences between the salaries, as shown in Table 9.6. Summary statistics for these $n = 10$ differences are displayed in the MINITAB printout, Figure 9.12.

The 95% confidence interval for $\mu_D = (\mu_1 - \mu_2)$ for this small sample is

$$\bar{x}_D \pm t_{\alpha/2}\frac{s_D}{\sqrt{n_D}}$$

where $t_{\alpha/2} = t_{.025} = 2.262$ (obtained from Table VI, Appendix B) is based on $n - 2 = 8$ degrees of freedom. Substituting the values of $\bar{x}_D$ and s_D shown on the printout, we obtain

$$\bar{x}_D \pm 2.262\frac{s_D}{\sqrt{n_D}} = 400 \pm 2.262\left(\frac{434.613}{\sqrt{10}}\right)$$

$$= 400 \pm 310.88 \approx 400 \pm 311 = (\$89, \$711)$$

[*Note:* This interval is also shown on the MINITAB printout, Figure 9.12.] Our interpretation is that the true mean difference between the starting salaries of males and females falls between $89 and $711, with 95% confidence. Since the interval falls above 0, we infer that $\mu_1 - \mu_2 > 0$, that is, that the mean salary for males exceeds the mean salary for females. ◣

To measure the amount of information about $(\mu_1 - \mu_2)$ gained by using a paired difference experiment in Example 9.5 rather than an independent samples experiment, we can compare the relative widths of the confidence intervals obtained by the two methods. A 95% confidence interval for $(\mu_1 - \mu_2)$ using the paired difference experiment is, from Example 9.5, ($89, $711). If we analyzed the same data as though this were an independent samples experiment,* we would first obtain the descriptive statistics shown in the MINITAB printout, Figure 9.13.

Then we substitute the sample means and standard deviations shown on the printout into the formula for a 95% confidence interval for $(\mu_1 - \mu_2)$ using independent samples:

FIGURE 9.13
MINITAB analysis of data in Table 9.6, assuming independent samples

```
TWOSAMPLE T FOR C1 VS C2
        N        MEAN       STDEV   SE MEAN
C1  10         29930        1735       549
C2  10         29530        1527       483

95 PCT CI FOR MU C1 - MU C2: (-1136, 1936)

TTEST MU C1 = MU C2 (VS NE): T= 0.55  P=0.59  DF=  18

POOLED STDEV =        1634
```

*This is done only to provide a measure of the increase in the amount of information obtained by a paired design in comparison to an unpaired design. Actually, if an experiment is designed using pairing, an unpaired analysis would be invalid because the assumption of independent samples would not be satisfied.

$$(\bar{x}_1 - \bar{x}_2) \pm t_{.025} \sqrt{s_p^2 \left(\frac{1}{n_1} + \frac{1}{n_2} \right)}$$

where

$$s_p^2 = \frac{(n_1 - 1)s_1^2 + (n_2 - 1)s_2^2}{n_1 + n_2 - 2}$$

MINITAB performed these calculations and obtained the interval ($-$\$1,136, \$1,936). This interval is highlighted on Figure 9.13.

Notice that the independent samples interval includes 0. Consequently, if we were to use this interval to make an inference about ($\mu_1 - \mu_2$), we would incorrectly conclude that the mean starting salaries of males and females do not differ! You can see that the confidence interval for the independent sampling experiment is about five times wider than for the corresponding paired difference confidence interval. Blocking out the variability due to differences in majors and grade point averages significantly increases the information about the difference in male and female mean starting salaries by providing a much more accurate (smaller confidence interval for the same confidence coefficient) estimate of ($\mu_1 - \mu_2$).

You may wonder whether conducting a paired difference experiment is always superior to an independent samples experiment. The answer is: Most of the time, but not always. We sacrifice half the degrees of freedom in the t statistic when a paired difference design is used instead of an independent samples design. This is a loss of information, and unless this loss is more than compensated for by the reduction in variability obtained by blocking (pairing), the paired difference experiment will result in a net loss of information about ($\mu_1 - \mu_2$). Thus, we should be convinced that the pairing will significantly reduce variability before performing the paired difference experiment. Most of the time this will happen.

One final note: The pairing of the observations is determined before the experiment is performed (that is, by the *design* of the experiment). A paired difference experiment is *never* obtained by pairing the sample observations after the measurements have been acquired.

What Do You Do When the Assumption of a Normal Distribution for the Population of Differences Is Not Satisfied?

Answer: Use the Wilcoxon signed rank test for the paired difference design (Chapter 17).

EXERCISES   9.27–9.39

Note: Exercises marked with ▣ contain data for computer analysis on a 3.5" disk (file name in parentheses).

Learning the Mechanics

9.27 A paired difference experiment yielded n_D pairs of observations. In each case, what is the rejection region for testing H_0: $\mu_D > 2$?
  a. $n_D = 12, \alpha = .05$ **b.** $n_D = 24, \alpha = .10$
  c. $n_D = 4, \alpha = .025$ **d.** $n_D = 8, \alpha = .01$

9.28 The data for a random sample of six paired observations are shown in the next table.

Pair	Sample from Population 1 Observation 1	Sample from Population 2 Observation 2
1	7	4
2	3	1
3	9	7
4	6	2
5	4	4
6	8	7

  a. Calculate the difference between each pair of observations by subtracting observation 2 from observation 1. Use the differences to calculate $\bar{x}_D$ and s_D^2.

b. If μ_1 and μ_2 are the means of populations 1 and 2, respectively, express μ_D in terms of μ_1 and μ_2.

c. Form a 95% confidence interval for μ_D.

d. Test the null hypothesis $H_0: \mu_D = 0$ against the alternative hypothesis $H_a: \mu_D \neq 0$. Use $\alpha = .05$.

9.29 The data for a random sample of 10 paired observations are shown in the accompanying table.

Pair	Sample from Population 1	Sample from Population 2
1	19	24
2	25	27
3	31	36
4	52	53
5	49	55
6	34	34
7	59	66
8	47	51
9	17	20
10	51	55

a. If you wish to test whether these data are sufficient to indicate that the mean for population 2 is larger than that for population 1, what are the appropriate null and alternative hypotheses? Define any symbols you use.

b. The data are analyzed using MINITAB, with the results shown below. Interpret these results.

c. The output of MINITAB also included a confidence interval. Interpret this output.

d. What assumptions are necessary to ensure the validity of this analysis?

9.30 A paired difference experiment produced the following data:

$$n_D = 18 \quad \bar{x}_1 = 92 \quad \bar{x}_2 = 95.5 \quad \bar{x}_D = -3.5 \quad s_D^2 = 21$$

a. Determine the values of t for which the null hypothesis, $\mu_1 - \mu_2 = 0$, would be rejected in favor of the alternative hypothesis, $\mu_1 - \mu_2 < 0$. Use $\alpha = .10$.

b. Conduct the paired difference test described in part **a**. Draw the appropriate conclusions.

c. What assumptions are necessary so that the paired difference test will be valid?

d. Find a 90% confidence interval for the mean difference μ_D.

e. Which of the two inferential procedures, the confidence interval of part **d** or the test of hypothesis of part **b**, provides more information about the differences between the population means?

9.31 A paired difference experiment yielded the data shown in the next table.

Pair	x	y	Pair	x	y
1	55	44	5	75	62
2	68	55	6	52	38
3	40	25	7	49	31
4	55	56			

a. Test $H_0: \mu_D = 10$ against $H_a: \mu_D \neq 10$, where $\mu_D = (\mu_1 - \mu_2)$. Use $\alpha = .05$.

b. Report the p-value for the test you conducted in part **a**. Interpret the p-value.

Applying the Concepts

9.32 It has been estimated that U.S. companies spend more than $500 million annually on service recognition programs for their employees. Such programs reward workers for such things as years of service, attendance, high-quality work, customer service, suggestions, and safety ("Dispelling the myths about service recognition programs," *Potentials in Marketing,* Feb. 1996). Before instituting a new employee service recognition program in its manufacturing plant, a company randomly sampled eight workers and measured their productivity in terms of the number of items produced per day. A year after the start of the service recognition program the productivity of seven of these workers was reevaluated. (The eighth had been promoted in the interim.) These productivity data are shown in the table.

Employee ID Number	August 1996	August 1997
1011	10	9
0033	9	11
0998	12	14
0006	8	9
1802	10	9
0246	11	14
0777	14	—
1112	11	13

```
TEST OF MU = 0.000 VS MU L.T. 0.000

           N       MEAN     STDEV   SE MEAN        T    P VALUE
DIFF      10     -3.700     2.214     0.700    -5.29     0.0002

------------------------------------------------------------

           N       MEAN     STDEV   SE MEAN    95.0 PERCENT C.I.
DIFF      10     -3.700     2.214     0.700   (  -5.284,   -2.116)
```

a. Do these data provide evidence that the service recognition program has helped to increase worker productivity? Test using $\alpha = .10$, and clearly state any assumptions you make in conducting the test.

b. Discuss how the one-year gap between productivity evaluations could weaken the results of the study.

9.33 Facility layout and material flowpath design are major factors in the productivity analysis of automated manufacturing systems. Facility layout is concerned with the location arrangement of machines and buffers for work-in-process. Flowpath design is concerned with the direction of manufacturing material flows (e.g., unidirectional or bidirectional) (Lee, Lei, and Pinedo, *Annals of Operations Research,* 1997). A manufacturer of printed circuit boards (PCBs) is interested in evaluating two alternative existing layout and flowpath designs. The output of each design was monitored for eight consecutive working days.

Working Days	Design 1	Design 2
8/16	1,220 units	1,273 units
8/17	1,092 units	1,363 units
8/18	1,136 units	1,342 units
8/19	1,205 units	1,471 units
8/20	1,086 units	1,299 units
8/23	1,274 units	1,457 units
8/24	1,145 units	1,263 units
8/25	1,281 units	1,368 units

a. Construct a 95% confidence interval for the difference in mean daily output of the two designs.

b. What assumptions must hold to ensure the validity of the confidence interval?

c. Design 2 appears to be superior to Design 1. Is this confirmed by the confidence interval? Explain.

9.34 A manufacturer of automobile shock absorbers was interested in comparing the durability of its shocks with that of the shocks produced by its biggest competitor. To make the comparison, one of the manufacturer's and one of the competitor's shocks were randomly selected and installed on the rear wheels of each of six cars. After the cars had been driven 20,000 miles, the strength of each test shock was measured, coded, and recorded. Results of the examination are shown in the table.

Car Number	Manufacturer's Shock	Competitor's Shock
1	8.8	8.4
2	10.5	10.1
3	12.5	12.0
4	9.7	9.3
5	9.6	9.0
6	13.2	13.0

a. Do the data present sufficient evidence to conclude that there is a difference in the mean strength of the two types of shocks after 20,000 miles of use? Use $\alpha = .05$.

b. Find the approximate observed significance level for the test, and interpret its value.

c. What assumptions are necessary to apply a paired difference analysis to the data?

d. Construct a 95% confidence interval for $(\mu_1 - \mu_2)$. Interpret the confidence interval.

9.35 Suppose the data in Exercise 9.34 are based on independent random samples.

a. Do the data provide sufficient evidence to indicate a difference between the mean strengths for the two types of shocks? Use $\alpha = .05$.

b. Construct a 95% confidence interval for $(\mu_1 - \mu_2)$. Interpret your result.

c. Compare the confidence intervals you obtained in Exercise 9.34 and in part **b** of this exercise. Which is wider? To what do you attribute the difference in width? Assuming in each case that the appropriate assumptions are satisfied, which interval provides you with more information about $(\mu_1 - \mu_2)$? Explain.

d. Are the results of an unpaired analysis valid if the data come from a paired experiment?

9.36 (**X09.036**) A *pupillometer* is a device used to observe changes in pupil dilations as the eye is exposed to different visual stimuli. Since there is a direct correlation between the amount an individual's pupil dilates and his or her interest in the stimuli, marketing organizations sometimes use pupillometers to help them evaluate potential consumer interest in new products, alternative package designs, and other factors (McLaren, Fjerstad, and Brubaker, *Optical Engineering,* Mar. 1995). The Design and Market Research Laboratories of the Container Corporation of America used a pupillometer to evaluate consumer reaction to different silverware patterns for a client (McGuire, 1973). Suppose 15 consumers were chosen at random, and each was shown two silverware patterns. Their pupillometer readings (in millimeters) are shown in the table at the top of page 396.

a. What are the appropriate null and alternative hypotheses to test whether the mean amount of pupil dilation differs for the two patterns? Define any symbols you use.

b. The data were analyzed using MINITAB, with the results shown in the printout on page 396. Interpret these results.

c. Is the paired difference design used for this study preferable to an independent samples design? For independent samples we could select 30 consumers, divide them into two groups of 15, and show each group a different pattern. Explain your preference.

Consumer	Pattern 1	Pattern 2	Consumer	Pattern 1	Pattern 2
1	1.00	.80	9	.98	.91
2	.97	.66	10	1.46	1.10
3	1.45	1.22	11	1.85	1.60
4	1.21	1.00	12	.33	.21
5	.77	.81	13	1.77	1.50
6	1.32	1.11	14	.85	.65
7	1.81	1.30	15	.15	.05
8	.91	.32			

```
TEST OF MU = 0.000 VS MU N.E. 0.000

          N      MEAN     STDEV    SE MEAN      T     P VALUE
DIFF     15      .239     .161     .0415      5.76    0.0000

          N      MEAN     STDEV    SE MEAN    95.0 PERCENT CI
DIFF     15      .239     .161     .0415       (.150, .328)
```

	INFLATION FORECASTS (IN PERCENT)	
	June 1995 Forecast for 11/95	January 1996 Forecast for 11/96
Maureen Allyn	3.1	2.4
Wayne Angell	3.4	3.1
David Blitzer	3.0	3.1
Michael Cosgrove	4.0	3.5
Gail Fosler	3.7	3.8
Irwin Kellner	3.3	2.3
Donald Ratajczak	3.5	2.9
Thomas Synott	3.5	3.2
John Williams	3.3	2.6

Source: Wall Street Journal, January 2, 1996.

9.37 Twice a year *The Wall Street Journal* asks a panel of economists to forecast interest rates, inflation rates, growth in Gross Domestic Product, and other economic variables. The table above reports the inflation forecasts made in June 1995 and in January 1996 by nine randomly selected members of the panel.

a. As a group, were the economists more optimistic about the prospects for low inflation in late 1996 than they were for late 1995? Specify the hypotheses to be tested.

b. Conduct the hypothesis testing using $\alpha = .05$ and answer the question proposed in part a.

9.38 A study reported in the *Journal of Psychology* (Mar. 1991) measures the change in female students' self-concepts as they move from high school to college. A sample of 133 Boston College first-year female students was selected for the study. Each was asked to evaluate several aspects of her life at two points in time: at the end of her senior year of high school, and during her sophomore year of college. Each student was asked to evaluate where she believed she stood on a scale that ranged from top 10% of class (1) to lowest 10% of class (5). The results for three of the traits evaluated are reported in the table below.

Trait	n	SENIOR YEAR OF HIGH SCHOOL $\bar{x}$	SOPHOMORE YEAR OF COLLEGE $\bar{x}$
Leadership	133	2.09	2.33
Popularity	133	2.48	2.69
Intellectual self-confidence	133	2.29	2.55

a. What null and alternative hypotheses would you test to determine whether the mean self-concept of females decreases between the senior year of high school and the sophomore year of college as measured by each of these three traits?

b. Are these traits more appropriately analyzed using an independent samples test or a paired difference test? Explain.

c. Noting the size of the sample, what assumptions are necessary to ensure the validity of the tests?

d. The article reports that the leadership test results in a *p*-value greater than .05, while the tests for popularity and intellectual self-confidence result in *p*-values less than .05. Interpret these results.

9.39 **(X09.039)** Merck Research Labs conducted an experiment to evaluate the effect of a new drug using the single-T swim maze. Nineteen impregnated dam rats were captured and allocated a dosage of 12.5 milligrams of the drug. One male and one female rat pup were randomly selected from each resulting litter to perform in the swim maze. Each pup was placed in the water at one end of the maze and allowed to swim until it escaped at the opposite end. If the pup failed to escape after a certain period of time, it was placed at the beginning of the maze and given another chance. The experiment was repeated until each pup accomplished three successful escapes. The accompanying table reports the number of swims required by each pup to perform three successful escapes. Is there sufficient evidence of a difference between the mean number of swims required by male and female pups? Use the accompanying MINITAB printout to conduct the test (at α = .10). Comment on the assumptions required for the test to be valid.

Litter	Male	Female	Litter	Male	Female
1	8	5	11	6	5
2	8	4	12	6	3
3	6	7	13	12	5
4	6	3	14	3	8
5	6	5	15	3	4
6	6	3	16	8	12
7	3	8	17	3	6
8	5	10	18	6	4
9	4	4	19	9	5
10	4	4			

Source: Thomas E. Bradstreet, Merck Research Labs, BL 3-2, West Point, PA 19486

```
TEST OF MU = 0.000 VS MU N.E. 0.000

              N     MEAN   STDEV   SE MEAN     T  P VALUE
SwimDiff     19    0.368   3.515     0.806  0.46     0.65
```

9.5 COMPARING TWO POPULATION PROPORTIONS: INDEPENDENT SAMPLING

Suppose a manufacturer of camper vans wants to compare the potential market for its products in the northeastern United States to the market in the southeastern United States. Such a comparison would help the manufacturer decide where to concentrate sales efforts. Using telephone directories, the company randomly chooses 1,000 households in the northeast (NE) and 1,000 households in the southeast (SE) and determines whether each household plans to buy a camper within the next five years. The objective is to use this sample information to make an inference about the difference $(p_1 - p_2)$ between the proportion p_1 of *all* households in the NE and the proportion p_2 of *all* households in the SE that plan to purchase a camper within five years.

The two samples represent independent binomial experiments. (See Section 4.4 for the characteristics of binomial experiments.) The binomial random variables are the numbers x_1 and x_2 of the 1,000 sampled households in each area that indicate they will purchase a camper within five years. The results are summarized below.

NE	SE
$n_1 = 1{,}000$	$n_2 = 1{,}000$
$x_1 = 42$	$x_2 = 24$

We can now calculate the sample proportions $\hat{p}_1$ and $\hat{p}_2$ of the households in the NE and SE, respectively, that are prospective buyers:

$$\hat{p}_1 = \frac{x_1}{n_1} = \frac{42}{1,000} = .042$$

$$\hat{p}_2 = \frac{x_2}{n_2} = \frac{24}{1,000} = .024$$

The difference between the sample proportions $(\hat{p}_1 - \hat{p}_2)$ makes an intuitively appealing point estimator of the difference between the population parameters $(p_1 - p_2)$. For our example, the estimate is

$$(\hat{p}_1 - \hat{p}_2) = .042 - .024 = .018$$

To judge the reliability of the estimator $(\hat{p}_1 - \hat{p}_2)$, we must observe its performance in repeated sampling from the two populations. That is, we need to know the sampling distribution of $(\hat{p}_1 - \hat{p}_2)$. The properties of the sampling distribution are given in the following box. Remember that $\hat{p}_1$ and $\hat{p}_2$ can be viewed as means of the number of successes per trial in the respective samples, so the Central Limit Theorem applies when the sample sizes are large.

Properties of the Sampling Distribution of $(\hat{p}_1 - \hat{p}_2)$

1. The mean of the sampling distribution of $(\hat{p}_1 - \hat{p}_2)$ is $(p_1 - p_2)$; that is,

$$E(\hat{p}_1 - \hat{p}_2) = p_1 - p_2$$

Thus, $(\hat{p}_1 - \hat{p}_2)$ is an unbiased estimator of $(p_1 - p_2)$.

2. The standard deviation of the sampling distribution of $(\hat{p}_1 - \hat{p}_2)$ is

$$\sigma_{(\hat{p}_1 - \hat{p}_2)} = \sqrt{\frac{p_1 q_1}{n_1} + \frac{p_2 q_2}{n_2}}$$

3. If the sample sizes n_1 and n_2 are large (see Section 7.3 for a guideline), the sampling distribution of $(\hat{p}_1 - \hat{p}_2)$ is approximately normal.

Since the distribution of $(\hat{p}_1 - \hat{p}_2)$ in repeated sampling is approximately normal, we can use the z statistic to derive confidence intervals for $(p_1 - p_2)$ or to test a hypothesis about $(p_1 - p_2)$.

For the camper example, a 95% confidence interval for the difference $(p_1 - p_2)$ is

$$(\hat{p}_1 - \hat{p}_2) \pm 1.96\sigma_{(\hat{p}_1 - \hat{p}_2)} \quad \text{or} \quad (\hat{p}_1 - \hat{p}_2) \pm 1.96\sqrt{\frac{p_1 q_1}{n_1} + \frac{p_2 q_2}{n_2}}$$

The quantities $p_1 q_1$ and $p_2 q_2$ must be estimated in order to complete the calculation of the standard deviation $\sigma_{(\hat{p}_1 - \hat{p}_2)}$ and hence the calculation of the confidence interval. In Section 7.3 we showed that the value of pq is relatively insensitive to the value chosen to approximate p. Therefore, $\hat{p}_1 \hat{q}_1$ and $\hat{p}_2 \hat{q}_2$ will provide satisfactory estimates to approximate $p_1 q_1$ and $p_2 q_2$, respectively. Then

$$\sqrt{\frac{p_1 q_1}{n_1} + \frac{p_2 q_2}{n_2}} \approx \sqrt{\frac{\hat{p}_1 \hat{q}_1}{n_1} + \frac{\hat{p}_2 \hat{q}_2}{n_2}}$$

and we will approximate the 95% confidence interval by

$$(\hat{p}_1 - \hat{p}_2) \pm 1.96 \sqrt{\frac{\hat{p}_1 \hat{q}_1}{n_1} + \frac{\hat{p}_2 \hat{q}_2}{n_2}}$$

Substituting the sample quantities yields

$$(.042 - .024) \pm 1.96 \sqrt{\frac{(.042)(.958)}{1,000} + \frac{(.024)(.976)}{1,000}}$$

or $.018 \pm .016$. Thus, we are 95% confident that the interval from .002 to .034 contains $(p_1 - p_2)$.

We infer that there are between .2% and 3.4% more households in the northeast than in the southeast that plan to purchase campers in the next five years.

The general form of a confidence interval for the difference $(p_1 - p_2)$ between population proportions is given in the following box.

Large-Sample $100(1 - \alpha)$% Confidence Interval for $(p_1 - p_2)$

$$(\hat{p}_1 - \hat{p}_2) \pm z_{\alpha/2} \sigma_{(\hat{p}_1 - \hat{p}_2)} = (\hat{p}_1 - \hat{p}_2) \pm z_{\alpha/2} \sqrt{\frac{p_1 q_1}{n_1} + \frac{p_2 q_2}{n_2}}$$

$$\approx (\hat{p}_1 - \hat{p}_2) \pm z_{\alpha/2} \sqrt{\frac{\hat{p}_1 \hat{q}_1}{n_1} + \frac{\hat{p}_2 \hat{q}_2}{n_2}}$$

Assumptions: The two samples are independent random samples. Both samples should be large enough that the normal distribution provides an adequate approximation to the sampling distribution of $\hat{p}_1$ and $\hat{p}_2$ (see Section 8.5).

The z statistic,

$$z = \frac{(\hat{p}_1 - \hat{p}_2) - (p_1 - p_2)}{\sigma_{(\hat{p}_1 - \hat{p}_2)}}$$

is used to test the null hypothesis that $(p_1 - p_2)$ equals some specified difference, say D_0. For the special case where $D_0 = 0$, that is, where we want to test the null hypothesis $H_0: (p_1 - p_2) = 0$ (or, equivalently, $H_0: p_1 = p_2$), the best estimate of $p_1 = p_2 = p$ is obtained by dividing the total number of successes $(x_1 + x_2)$ for the two samples by the total number of observations $(n_1 + n_2)$; that is

$$\hat{p} = \frac{x_1 + x_2}{n_1 + n_2} \qquad \text{or} \qquad \hat{p} = \frac{n_1 \hat{p}_1 + n_2 \hat{p}_2}{n_1 + n_2}$$

The second equation shows that $\hat{p}$ is a weighted average of $\hat{p}_1$ and $\hat{p}_2$, with the larger sample receiving more weight. If the sample sizes are equal, then $\hat{p}$ is a simple average of the two sample proportions of successes.

We now substitute the weighted average $\hat{p}$ for both p_1 and p_2 in the formula for the standard deviation of $(\hat{p}_1 - \hat{p}_2)$:

$$\sigma_{(\hat{p}_1 - \hat{p}_2)} = \sqrt{\frac{p_1 q_1}{n_1} + \frac{p_2 q_2}{n_2}} \approx \sqrt{\frac{\hat{p}\hat{q}}{n_1} + \frac{\hat{p}\hat{q}}{n_2}} = \sqrt{\hat{p}\hat{q}\left(\frac{1}{n_1} + \frac{1}{n_2}\right)}$$

The test is summarized in the next box.

Large-Sample Test of Hypothesis About $(p_1 - p_2)$

One-Tailed Test

$H_0: (p_1 - p_2) = 0^*$

$H_a: (p_1 - p_2) < 0$
   $[\text{or } H_a: (p_1 - p_2) > 0]$

Two-Tailed Test

$H_0: (p_1 - p_2) = 0$

$H_a: (p_1 - p_2) \neq 0$

Test statistic:
$$z = \frac{\hat{p}_1 - \hat{p}_2}{\sigma_{(\hat{p}_1 - \hat{p}_2)}}$$

Rejection region: $z < -z_\alpha$
   $[\text{or } z > z_\alpha \text{ when } H_a: (p_1 - p_2) > 0]$

Rejection region: $|z| > z_{\alpha/2}$

Note: $\sigma_{(\hat{p}_1 - \hat{p}_2)} = \sqrt{\dfrac{p_1 q_1}{n_1} + \dfrac{p_2 q_2}{n_2}} \approx \sqrt{\hat{p}\hat{q}\left(\dfrac{1}{n_1} + \dfrac{1}{n_2}\right)}$ where $\hat{p} = \dfrac{x_1 + x_2}{n_1 + n_2}$

Assumption: Same as for large-sample confidence interval for $(p_1 - p_2)$.

EXAMPLE 9.6

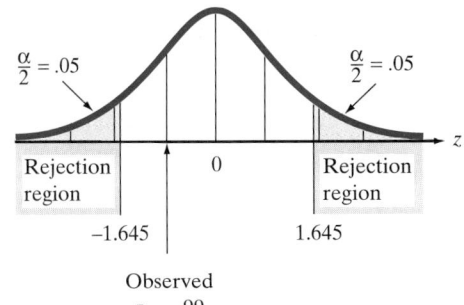

A consumer advocacy group wants to determine whether there is a difference between the proportions of the two leading automobile models that need major repairs (more than $500) within two years of their purchase. A sample of 400 two-year owners of model 1 is contacted, and a sample of 500 two-year owners of model 2 is contacted. The numbers x_1 and x_2 of owners who report that their cars needed major repairs within the first two years are 53 and 78, respectively. Test the null hypothesis that no difference exists between the proportions in populations 1 and 2 needing major repairs against the alternative that a difference does exist. Use $\alpha = .10$.

SOLUTION

If we define p_1 and p_2 as the true proportions of model 1 and model 2 owners, respectively, whose cars need major repairs within two years, the elements of the test are

$H_0: (p_1 - p_2) = 0$

$H_a: (p_1 - p_2) \neq 0$

Test statistic: $z = \dfrac{(\hat{p}_1 - \hat{p}_2) - 0}{\sigma_{(\hat{p}_1 - \hat{p}_2)}}$

Rejection region $(\alpha = .10)$: $|z| > z_{\alpha/2} = z_{.05} = 1.645$ (see Figure 9.14)

FIGURE 9.14
Rejection region for Example 9.6

$\frac{\alpha}{2} = .05$ $\frac{\alpha}{2} = .05$

Rejection region

0

Rejection region

z

-1.645 1.645

Observed $z = -.99$

---

*The test can be adapted to test for a difference $D_0 \neq 0$. Because most applications call for a comparison of p_1 and p_2, implying $D_0 = 0$, we will confine our attention to this case.

We now calculate the sample proportions of owners who need major car repairs,

$$\hat{p}_1 = \frac{x_1}{n_1} = \frac{53}{400} = .1325$$

$$\hat{p}_2 = \frac{x_2}{n_2} = \frac{78}{500} = .1560$$

Then

$$z = \frac{(\hat{p}_1 - \hat{p}_2) - 0}{\sigma_{(\hat{p}_1 - \hat{p}_2)}} \approx \frac{(\hat{p}_1 - \hat{p}_2)}{\sqrt{\hat{p}\hat{q}\left(\dfrac{1}{n_1} + \dfrac{1}{n_2}\right)}}$$

where

$$\hat{p} = \frac{x_1 + x_2}{n_1 + n_2} = \frac{53 + 78}{400 + 500} = .1456$$

Note that $\hat{p}$ is a weighted average of $\hat{p}_1$ and $\hat{p}_2$, with more weight given to the larger sample of model 2 owners.

Thus, the computed value of the test statistic is

$$z = \frac{.1325 - .1560}{\sqrt{(.1456)(.8544)\left(\dfrac{1}{400} + \dfrac{1}{500}\right)}} = \frac{-.0235}{.0237} = -.99$$

The samples provide insufficient evidence at $\alpha = .10$ to detect a difference between the proportions of the two models that need repairs within two years. Even though 2.35% more sampled owners of model 2 found they needed major repairs, this difference is less than 1 standard deviation ($z = -.99$) from the hypothesized zero difference between the true proportions.

EXAMPLE 9.7   Find the observed significance level for the test in Example 9.6.

SOLUTION

The observed value of z for this two-tailed test was $z = -.99$. Therefore, the observed significance level is

$$p\text{-value} = P(|z| > .99) = P(z < -.99 \text{ or } z > .99)$$

This probability is equal to the shaded area shown in Figure 9.15. The area corresponding to $z = .99$ is given in Table IV of Appendix B as .3389. Therefore, the observed significance level for the test, the sum of the two shaded tail areas under the standard normal curve, is

$$p\text{-value} = 2(.5 - .3389) = .3222$$

The probability of observing a z as large as .99 or less than $-.99$ if in fact $p_1 = p_2$ is .3222. This large p-value indicates that there is little or no evidence of a difference between p_1 and p_2.

FIGURE 9.15

The observed significance level for the test of Example 9.6

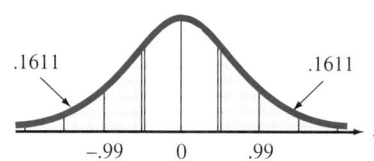

EXERCISES 9.40–9.56

Learning the Mechanics

9.40 What are the characteristics of a binomial experiment?

9.41 Explain why the Central Limit Theorem is important in finding an approximate distribution for $(\hat{p}_1 - \hat{p}_2)$.

9.42 In each case, determine whether the sample sizes are large enough to conclude that the sampling distribution of $(\hat{p}_1 - \hat{p}_2)$ is approximately normal.
 a. $n_1 = 12, n_2 = 14, \hat{p}_1 = .42, \hat{p}_2 = .57$
 b. $n_1 = 12, n_2 = 14, \hat{p}_1 = .92, \hat{p}_2 = .86$
 c. $n_1 = n_2 = 30, \hat{p}_1 = .70, \hat{p}_2 = .73$
 d. $n_1 = 100, n_2 = 250, \hat{p}_1 = .93, \hat{p}_2 = .97$
 e. $n_1 = 125, n_2 = 200, \hat{p}_1 = .08, \hat{p}_2 = .12$

9.43 For each of the following values of α, find the values of z for which $H_0: (p_1 - p_2) = 0$ would be rejected in favor of $H_a: (p_1 - p_2) < 0$.
 a. $\alpha = .01$ b. $\alpha = .025$
 c. $\alpha = .05$ d. $\alpha = .10$

9.44 Independent random samples, each containing 800 observations, were selected from two binomial populations. The samples from populations 1 and 2 produced 320 and 400 successes, respectively.
 a. Test $H_0: (p_1 - p_2) = 0$ against $H_a: (p_1 - p_2) \neq 0$. Use $\alpha = .05$.
 b. Test $H_0: (p_1 - p_2) = 0$ against $H_a: (p_1 - p_2) \neq 0$. Use $\alpha = .01$.
 c. Test $H_0: (p_1 - p_2) = 0$ against $H_a: (p_1 - p_2) < 0$. Use $\alpha = .01$.
 d. Form a 90% confidence interval for $(p_1 - p_2)$.

9.45 Construct a 95% confidence interval for $(p_1 - p_2)$ in each of the following situations:
 a. $n_1 = 400, \hat{p}_1 = .65; n_2 = 400, \hat{p}_2 = .58$
 b. $n_1 = 180, \hat{p}_1 = .31; n_2 = 250, \hat{p}_2 = .25$
 c. $n_1 = 100, \hat{p}_1 = .46; n_2 = 120, \hat{p}_2 = .61$

9.46 Sketch the sampling distribution of $(\hat{p}_1 - \hat{p}_2)$ based on independent random samples of $n_1 = 100$ and $n_2 = 200$ observations from two binomial populations with success probabilities $\hat{p}_1 = .1$ and $\hat{p}_2 = .5$, respectively.

9.47 Random samples of size $n_1 = 55$ and $n_2 = 65$ were drawn from populations 1 and 2, respectively. The samples yielded $\hat{p}_1 = .7$ and $\hat{p}_2 = .6$. Test $H_0: (p_1 - p_2) = 0$ against $H_a: (p_1 - p_2) > 0$ using $\alpha = .05$.

Applying the Concepts

9.48 Since the early 1990s marketers have wrestled with the appropriateness of using ads that appeal to children to sell adult products. One controversial advertisement campaign is Camel cigarettes' use of the cartoon character "Joe Camel" as its brand symbol. The Federal Trade Commission has considered banning ads featuring Joe Camel because they supposedly encourage young people to smoke. Lucy L. Henke, a marketing professor at the University of New Hampshire, assessed young children's abilities to recognize cigarette brand advertising symbols. She found that 15 out of 28 children under the age of 6, and 46 out of 55 children age 6 and over recognized Joe Camel, the brand symbol of Camel cigarettes (*Journal of Advertising*, Winter 1995).
 a. Use a 95% confidence interval to estimate the proportion of all children that recognize Joe Camel. Interpret the interval.
 b. Do the data indicate that recognition of Joe Camel increases with age? Test using $\alpha = .05$.

9.49 Price scanners are widely used in U.S. supermarkets. While they are fast and easy to use, they also make mistakes. Over the years, various consumer advocacy groups have complained that scanners routinely gouge the customer by overcharging. A recent Federal Trade Commission study found that supermarket scanners erred 3.47% of the time and department store scanners erred 9.15% of the time ("Scan Errors Help Public," *Newark Star-Ledger*, Oct. 23, 1996).
 a. Assume the above error rates were determined from merchandise samples of size 800 and 900, respectively. Are these sample sizes large enough to apply the methods of this section to estimate the difference in the error rates? Justify your answer.
 b. Use a 98% confidence interval to estimate the difference in the error rates. Interpret your result.
 c. What assumptions must hold to ensure the validity of the confidence interval of part **b**?

9.50 Do you have an insatiable craving for chocolate or some other food? Since many North Americans apparently do, psychologists are designing scientific studies to examine the phenomenon. According to the *New York Times* (Feb. 22, 1995), one of the largest studies of food cravings involved a survey of 1,000 McMaster University (Canada) students. The survey revealed that 97% of the women in the study acknowledged specific food cravings while only 67% of the men did. Assume that 600 of the respondents were women and 400 were men.
 a. Is there sufficient evidence to claim that the true proportion of women who acknowledge having food cravings exceeds the corresponding proportion of men? Test using $\alpha = .01$.
 b. Why is it dangerous to conclude from the study that women have a higher incidence of food cravings than men?

9.51 Most large consumer and industrial products companies assign a *product manager* to each product/brand they sell. The overall responsibility of the product manager is to integrate the various segments of the business—including design, production, marketing, and sales—to ensure the success of the product or product line. *Industrial Marketing Management* (Vol. 25, 1996) published a study that examined the demographics, decision-making roles, and time demands of product managers. Independent samples of $n_1 = 93$ consumer/commercial product managers and $n_2 = 212$ industrial product managers took part in the study. In the consumer/commercial group, 40% of the product managers are 40 years of age or older; in the industrial group, 54% are 40 or more years old. Use the method outlined in this section to make an inference about the difference between the true proportions of consumer/commercial and industrial product managers who are at least 40 years old. Justify your choice of method (confidence interval or hypothesis test) and α level. Do industrial product managers tend to be older than consumer/commercial product managers?

9.52 Many female undergraduates at four-year colleges and universities switch from science, mathematics, and engineering (SME) majors into disciplines that are not science based, such as journalism, marketing, and sociology. When female undergraduates switch majors, are their reasons different from those of their male counterparts? This question was investigated in *Science Education* (July 1995). A sample of 335 junior/senior undergraduates—172 females and 163 males—at two large research universities were identified as "switchers," that is, they left a declared SME major for a non-SME major. Each student listed one or more factors that contributed to their switching decision.

a. Of the 172 females in the sample, 74 listed lack or loss of interest in SME (i.e., "turned off" by science) as a major factor, compared to 72 of the 163 males. Conduct a test (at $\alpha = .10$) to determine whether the proportion of female switchers who give "lack of interest in SME" as a major reason for switching differs from the corresponding proportion of males.

b. Thirty-three of the 172 females in the sample admitted they were discouraged or lost confidence due to low grades in SME during their early years, compared to 44 of 163 males. Construct a 90% confidence interval for the difference between the proportions of female and male switchers who lost confidence due to low grades in SME. Interpret the result.

9.53 Despite company policies allowing unpaid family leave for new fathers, many men fear that exercising this option would be held against them by their superiors (*Minneapolis Star-Tribune*, Feb. 14, 1993). In a random sample of 100 male workers planning to become fathers, 35 agreed with the statement, "If I knew there would be no repercussions, I would choose to participate in the family leave program after the birth of a son or daughter." However, of 96 men who became fathers in the previous 16 months, only nine participated in the program.

a. Specify the appropriate null and alternative hypotheses to test whether the sample data provide sufficient evidence to reject the hypothesis that the proportion of new fathers participating in the program is the same as the proportion that would like to participate. Define any symbols you use.

b. Are the sample sizes large enough to conclude that the sampling distribution of $(\hat{p}_1 - \hat{p}_2)$ is approximately normal?

c. Conduct the hypothesis test using $\alpha = .05$. Report the observed significance level of the test.

d. What assumptions must be satisfied for the test to be valid?

9.54 Women are filling managerial positions in increasing numbers, although there is much dissension about whether progress has been fast enough. Does marriage hinder the career progression of women to a greater degree than that of men? An article in the *Journal of Applied Psychology* (Vol. 77, 1992) investigates this and other questions relating to managerial careers of men and women in today's workforce. In a random sample of 795 male managers and 223 female managers from 20 *Fortune* 500 corporations, 86% of the male managers and 45% of the female managers were married.

a. Use a 95% confidence interval to estimate the difference between the proportions of men and women managers who are married.

b. Interpret the interval. State your conclusion in terms of the populations from which the samples were drawn.

9.55 Refer to Exercise 7.41, in which we examined data from an article in the *International Journal of Sports Psychology* (1990) studying the relationship between levels of fitness and stress among employees of companies offering health and fitness programs. Random samples of employees were selected from each of three fitness-level categories, and each was evaluated for signs of stress. The data are shown in the table on page 404.

a. What are the appropriate null and alternative hypotheses to test whether a greater proportion of employees in the poor fitness category show signs of stress than those in the average fitness category? Define any symbols you use.

Fitness Level	Sample Size	Proportion with Signs of Stress
Poor	242	.155
Average	212	.133
Good	95	.108

b. Conduct the test constructed in part **a** using $\alpha = .10$. Interpret the result.

c. How would your null and alternative hypotheses change if you wanted to compare the proportions showing signs of stress in the poor and good fitness categories?

d. To conduct the test in part **c**, the data are analyzed by a statistical software package with the results shown below. Based on these results, state whether you would be willing to support the following statement: "Fitness level has no bearing on whether an individual shows signs of stress." Explain.

```
Z = 1.11        P-VALUE = .1335
```

9.56 When recruiting sales representatives, sales managers sometimes advertise for these positions in local newspapers, and then invite applicants to interviews which are frequently held in hotel rooms. An article in *Sloan Management Review* (Spring 1982) examined the effects of the hotel interview site on prospective sales representatives, and on women in particular. Each in a sample of 74 female college students from Rutgers University, Montclair State College, and Union College was asked whether she would agree to a job interview in a room at a local hotel; 62% said they would. Another sample of 74 college women were asked whether they would agree to a job interview in a room of a local office building, and 98% said yes. Use this information to make an inference about $(p_1 - p_2)$, where p_1 represents the proportion of female college students who, if offered a job interview in a room of a local office building, would say they would attend the interview and p_2 represents the proportion of female college students who, if offered a job interview in a room of a local hotel, would say they would attend the interview.

9.4 DETERMINING THE SAMPLE SIZE FOR COMPARING MEANS OR PROPORTIONS

You can find the appropriate sample size to estimate the difference between a pair of parameters with a specified degree of reliability by using the method described in Section 7.4. That is, to estimate the difference between a pair of parameters correct to within B units with probability $(1 - \alpha)$, let $z_{\alpha/2}$ standard deviations of the sampling distribution of the estimator equal B. Then solve for the sample size. To do this, you have to solve the problem for a specific ratio between n_1 and n_2. Most often, you will want to have equal sample sizes, that is, $n_1 = n_2 = n$. We will illustrate the procedure with two examples.

EXAMPLE 9.8

New fertilizer compounds are often advertised with the promise of increased crop yields. Suppose we want to compare the mean yield μ_1 of wheat when a new fertilizer is used to the mean yield μ_2 with a fertilizer in common use. The estimate of the difference in mean yield per acre is to be correct to within .25 bushel with a confidence coefficient of .95. If the sample sizes are to be equal, find $n_1 = n_2 = n$, the number of one-acre plots of wheat assigned to each fertilizer.

SOLUTION

To solve the problem, you need to know something about the variation in the bushels of yield per acre. Suppose from past records you know the yields of wheat possess a range of approximately 10 bushels per acre. You could then approximate $\sigma_1 = \sigma_2 = \sigma$ by letting the range equal 4σ. Thus,

$$4\sigma \approx 10 \text{ bushels}$$

$$\sigma \approx 2.5 \text{ bushels}$$

The next step is to solve the equation

$$z_{\alpha/2}\sigma_{(\bar{x}_1 - \bar{x}_2)} = B \qquad \text{or} \qquad z_{\alpha/2}\sqrt{\frac{\sigma_1^2}{n_1} + \frac{\sigma_2^2}{n_2}} = B$$

for n, where $n = n_1 = n_2$. Since we want the estimate to lie within $B = .25$ of $(\mu_1 - \mu_2)$ with confidence coefficient equal to .95, we have $z_{\alpha/2} = z_{.025} = 1.96$. Then, letting $\sigma_1 = \sigma_2 = 2.5$ and solving for n, we have

$$1.96\sqrt{\frac{(2.5)^2}{n} + \frac{(2.5)^2}{n}} = .25$$

$$1.96\sqrt{\frac{2(2.5)^2}{n}} = .25$$

$$n = 768.32 \approx 769 \text{ (rounding up)}$$

Consequently, you will have to sample 769 acres of wheat for each fertilizer to estimate the difference in mean yield per acre to within .25 bushel. Since this would necessitate extensive and costly experimentation, you might decide to allow a larger bound (say, $B = .50$ or $B = 1$) in order to reduce the sample size, or you might decrease the confidence coefficient. The point is that we can obtain an idea of the experimental effort necessary to achieve a specified precision in our final estimate by determining the approximate sample size *before* the experiment is begun. ∎

EXAMPLE 9.9

A production supervisor suspects a difference exists between the proportions p_1 and p_2 of defective items produced by two different machines. Experience has shown that the proportion defective for each of the two machines is in the neighborhood of .03. If the supervisor wants to estimate the difference in the proportions to within .005 using a 95% confidence interval, how many items must be randomly sampled from the production of each machine? (Assume that the supervisor wants $n_1 = n_2 = n$.)

SOLUTION

In this sampling problem, $B = .005$, and for the specified level of reliability, $z_{\alpha/2} = z_{.025} = 1.96$. Then, letting $p_1 = p_2 = .03$ and $n_1 = n_2 = n$, we find the required sample size per machine by solving the following equation for n.

$$z_{\alpha/2}\sigma_{(\hat{p}_1 - \hat{p}_2)} = B$$

or

$$z_{\alpha/2}\sqrt{\frac{p_1 q_1}{n_1} + \frac{p_2 q_2}{n_2}} = B$$

$$1.96\sqrt{\frac{(.03)(.97)}{n} + \frac{(.03)(.97)}{n}} = .005$$

$$1.96\sqrt{\frac{2(.03)(.97)}{n}} = .005$$

$$n = 8{,}943.2$$

You can see that this may be a tedious sampling procedure. If the supervisor insists on estimating $(p_1 - p_2)$ correct to within .005 with 95% confidence, approximately 9,000 items will have to be inspected for each machine. ∎

STATISTICS IN ACTION

9.2 UNPAID OVERTIME AND THE FAIR LABOR STANDARDS ACT

In 1938, Congress passed and President Roosevelt signed a wage and hour law called the Fair Labor Standards Act (FLSA). It was part of Roosevelt's "New Deal," a program aimed at ending the Great Depression. The law applies to employees of companies that do business in more than one state and have annual sales of more than $500,000. It established a minimum wage (then $.25 per hour; now $5.15 per hour); set a limit on the number of hours of labor per week per individual worker (then 44 hours; now 40 hours); and discouraged oppressive child labor practices. The act also requires employees to be paid for *overtime*—the time worked beyond the regular 40-hour work week—at a rate one and one-half times their regular hourly wage. The act has been amended many times. An amendment passed in 1963, called the Equal Pay Act, requires employers to pay men and women equally for doing equal work. The act is enforced by the U.S. Department of Labor (Twomey, *Labor and Employment Law,* 1994).

This application involves a well-known U.S. fast-food restaurant chain with 10,000 employees and restaurants in 20 midwestern and southwestern states. (For reasons of confidentiality, the name of the restaurant is withheld.) The chain has three levels of employees in its restaurants: crew, shift leaders, and managers. In early 1996, a group of 75 crew-level employees from 10 different Arizona restaurants charged that management frequently required them to work overtime without pay in order to be considered for promotion to shift leader. They filed suit under the Fair Labor Standards Act seeking an award of back wages, attorneys' fees, and other related costs. Top management at the restaurant chain strongly denied the charges.

As part of the investigation of this claim, a federal judge appointed an examiner to compare the average number of hours of unpaid overtime worked per week per employee for Arizona-based crew members to the corresponding average for Illinois-based crew members using independent random samples of crew members from both states. The examiner planned to use equal sample sizes and to depose (question under oath) each sampled employee concerning overtime worked "off the clock." These data would then be used to estimate the difference in the average number of hours of unpaid overtime worked per week per employee in the two states to within one-half hour with 95% confidence. [*Note:* Pilot samples indicated that the standard deviation for the Illinois employees was about 1.5 hours and the standard deviation for the Arizona employees was about 3.6 hours.]

Focus

a. Your goal is to develop a sampling plan for the examiner in order to achieve the objective outlined by the federal judge. The plan should address each of the following:

1. the target population(s)
2. the parameter of interest
3. the desired level of confidence
4. the required sample sizes
5. a method of obtaining the samples

b. Due to time constraints, the examiner may only be able to depose between 60 and 80 employees, total. Develop a contingency sampling plan should this occur.

You can see from the calculations in Example 9.9 that $\sigma_{(\hat{p}_1 - \hat{p}_2)}$ (and hence the solution, $n_1 = n_2 = n$) depends on the actual (but unknown) values of p_1 and p_2. In fact, the required sample size $n_1 = n_2 = n$ is largest when $p_1 = p_2 = .5$. Therefore, if you have no prior information on the approximate values of p_1 and p_2, use $p_1 = p_2 = .5$ in the formula for $\sigma_{(\hat{p}_1 - \hat{p}_2)}$. If p_1 and p_2 are in fact close to .5, then the values of n_1 and n_2 that you have calculated will be correct. If p_1 and p_2 differ substantially from .5, then your solutions for n_1 and n_2 will be larger than needed. Consequently, using $p_1 = p_2 = .5$ when solving for n_1 and n_2 is a conservative procedure because the sample sizes n_1 and n_2 will be at least as large as (and probably larger than) needed.

The procedures for determining sample sizes necessary for estimating $(\mu_1 - \mu_2)$ or $(p_1 - p_2)$ for the case $n_1 = n_2$ are given in the following box.

Determination of Sample Size for Two-Sample Procedures

1. To estimate $(\mu_1 - \mu_2)$ to within a given bound B with probability $(1 - \alpha)$, use the following formula to solve for equal sample sizes that will achieve the desired reliability:

$$n_1 = n_2 = \frac{(z_{\alpha/2})^2(\sigma_1^2 + \sigma_2^2)}{B^2}$$

You will need to substitute estimates for the values of σ_1^2 and σ_2^2 before solving for the sample size. These estimates might be sample variances s_1^2 and s_2^2 from prior sampling (e.g., a pilot sample), or from an educated (and conservatively large) guess based on the range—that is, $s \approx R/4$.

2. To estimate $(p_1 - p_2)$ to within a given bound B with probability $(1 - \alpha)$, use the following formula to solve for equal sample sizes that will achieve the desired reliability:

$$n_1 = n_2 = \frac{(z_{\alpha/2})^2(p_1 q_1 + p_2 q_2)}{B^2}$$

You will need to substitute estimates for the values of p_1 and p_2 before solving for the sample size. These estimates might be based on prior samples, obtained from educated guesses or, most conservatively, specified as $p_1 = p_2 = .5$.

EXERCISES   9.57–9.67

Learning the Mechanics

9.57 Suppose you want to estimate the difference between two population means correct to within 1.8 with a 95% confidence interval. If prior information suggests that the population variances are approximately equal to $\sigma_1^2 = \sigma_2^2 = 14$ and you want to select independent random samples of equal size from the populations, how large should the sample sizes, n_1 and n_2, be?

9.58 Find the appropriate values of n_1 and n_2 (assume $n_1 = n_2$) needed to estimate $(\mu_1 - \mu_2)$ with:

   a. A bound on the error of estimation equal to 3.2 with 95% confidence. From prior experience it is known that $\sigma_1 \approx 15$ and $\sigma_2 \approx 17$.

   b. A bound on the error of estimation equal to 8 with 99% confidence. The range of each population is 60.

   c. A 90% confidence interval of width 1.0. Assume that $\sigma_1^2 \approx 5.8$ and $\sigma_2^2 \approx 7.5$.

9.59 Assuming that $n_1 = n_2$, find the sample sizes needed to estimate $(p_1 - p_2)$ for each of the following situations:

   a. Bound $= .01$ with 99% confidence. Assume that $p_1 \approx .4$ and $p_2 \approx .7$.

   b. A 90% confidence interval of width .05. Assume that there is no prior information available to obtain approximate values of p_1 and p_2.

   c. Bound $= .03$ with 90% confidence. Assume that $p_1 \approx .2$ and $p_2 \approx .3$.

9.60 Enough money has been budgeted to collect independent random samples of size $n_1 = n_2 = 100$ from populations 1 and 2 in order to estimate $(\mu_1 - \mu_2)$. Prior information indicates that $\sigma_1 = \sigma_2 = 10$. Have sufficient funds been allocated to construct a 90% confidence interval for $(\mu_1 - \mu_2)$ of width 5 or less? Justify your answer.

Applying the Concepts

9.61 A pollster wants to estimate the difference between the proportions of men and women who favor a particular national candidate using a 90% confidence interval of width .04. Suppose the pollster has no prior information about the proportions. If equal numbers of men and women are to be polled, how large should the sample sizes be?

9.62 Is housework hazardous to your health? A study in the *Public Health Reports* (July–Aug. 1992) compares the life expectancies of 25-year-old white women in the labor force to those who are housewives. How large a sample would have to be taken from each group in order to be 95% confident that the estimate of difference in average life expectancies for the two groups is within one year of the true difference in average life expectancies? Assume that equal sample sizes will be selected from the two groups, and that the standard deviation for both groups is approximately 15 years.

9.63 After an extended period of downsizing and restructuring in which U.S. corporations laid off workers in record numbers, a 1996 national survey of 1,441 firms by the American Management Association revealed that only 20% plan to eliminate jobs within the next year, while nearly 50% plan to add jobs. They concluded that downsizing was no longer the dominant theme in the workplace (*Newark Star-Ledger*, Oct. 22, 1996). But are there regional differences in this phenomenon? Is there more growth in jobs in the Sunbelt than the Rustbelt? Assuming equal sample sizes for the two regions, how large would the samples need to be to estimate the difference in the proportion of firms that plan to add new jobs in the next year in the two regions? A 90% confidence interval of width no more than .10 is desired.

9.64 Nationally televised home shopping was introduced in 1985. Overnight it became the hottest craze in television programming. Today, nearly all cable companies carry at least one home shopping channel. Who uses these home shopping services? Are the shoppers primarily men or women? Suppose you want to estimate the difference in the proportions of men and women who say they have used or expect to use televised home shopping using an 80% confidence interval of width .06 or less.

  a. Approximately how many people should be included in your samples?

  b. Suppose you want to obtain individual estimates for the two proportions of interest. Will the sample size found in part **a** be large enough to provide estimates of each proportion correct to within .02 with probability equal to .90? Justify your response.

9.65 Rat damage creates a large financial loss in the production of sugarcane. One aspect of the problem that has been investigated by the U.S. Department of Agriculture concerns the optimal place to locate rat poison. To be most effective in reducing rat damage, should the poison be located in the middle of the field or on the outer perimeter? One way to answer this question is to determine where the greater amount of damage occurs. If damage is measured by the proportion of cane stalks that have been damaged by rats, how many stalks from each section of the field should be sampled in order to estimate the true difference between proportions of stalks damaged in the two sections to within .02 with 95% confidence?

9.66 Even though Japan is an economic superpower, Japanese workers are in many ways worse off than their U.S. and European counterparts. For example, in 1991 the estimated average housing space per person (in square feet) was 665.2 in the United States, 400.4 in Germany, and only 269 in Japan (*Minneapolis Star-Tribune*, Jan. 31, 1993). Next year a team of economists and sociologists from the United Nations plans to reestimate the difference in the mean housing space per person for U.S. and Japanese workers. Assume that equal sample sizes will be used for each country and that the standard deviation is 35 square feet for Japan and 80 for the United States. How many people should be sampled in each country to estimate the difference to within 10 square feet with 95% confidence?

9.67 Refer to Exercise 9.55, where we examined data relating levels of fitness and stress (*International Journal of Sports Psychology*, July–Sept. 1990). Essentially, we failed to reject the null hypothesis that those in poor physical condition exhibit signs of stress in the same proportion as those in good physical condition, even though the sample proportions differed by nearly .05. (That is, of those sampled, almost 5% more of those in poor condition exhibited signs of stress than those in good condition.)

  a. How large would the samples have to be to estimate the difference in the proportions showing signs of stress to within .04 with 95% confidence? Assume the sample sizes for the two groups will be equal, and remember that the first samples selected resulted in proportions of .155 and .108 for the poor and good fitness levels, respectively.

  b. Suppose samples of the size you calculated in part **a** were selected from each group, and the sample proportions again turned out to be .155 and .108. Test the null hypothesis $H_0: (p_1 - p_2) = 0$ against the alternative $H_a: (p_1 - p_2) > 0$, where p_1 is the proportion of all employees at the poor fitness level who show signs of stress and p_2 is the proportion of all employees at the good fitness level who show signs of stress. Calculate and interpret the observed significance level.

9.5 **COMPARING TWO POPULATION VARIANCES: INDEPENDENT SAMPLING**

Many times it is of practical interest to use the techniques developed in this chapter to compare the means or proportions of two populations. However, there are also important instances when we wish to compare two population variances. For example, when two devices are available for producing precision measurements (scales, calipers, thermometers, etc.), we might want to compare the variability of the measurements of the devices before deciding which one to purchase. Or when two standardized tests can be used to rate job applicants, the variability of the scores for both tests should be taken into consideration before deciding which test to use.

For problems like these we need to develop a statistical procedure to compare population variances. The common statistical procedure for comparing population variances, σ_1^2 and σ_2^2, makes an inference about the ratio σ_1^2/σ_2^2. In this section, we will show how to test the null hypothesis that the ratio σ_1^2/σ_2^2 equals 1 (the variances are equal) against the alternative hypothesis that the ratio differs from 1 (the variances differ):

$$H_0: \frac{\sigma_1^2}{\sigma_2^2} = 1 \qquad (\sigma_1^2 = \sigma_2^2)$$

$$H_a: \frac{\sigma_1^2}{\sigma_2^2} \neq 1 \qquad (\sigma_1^2 \neq \sigma_2^2)$$

To make an inference about the ratio σ_1^2/σ_2^2, it seems reasonable to collect sample data and use the ratio of the sample variances, s_1^2/s_2^2. We will use the test statistic

$$F = \frac{s_1^2}{s_2^2}$$

To establish a rejection region for the test statistic, we need to know the sampling distribution of s_1^2/s_2^2. As you will subsequently see, the sampling distribution of s_1^2/s_2^2 is based on two of the assumptions already required for the *t*-test:

1. The two sampled populations are normally distributed.
2. The samples are randomly and independently selected from their respective populations.

When these assumptions are satisfied and when the null hypothesis is true (that is, $\sigma_1^2 = \sigma_2^2$), the sampling distribution of $F = s_1^2/s_2^2$ is the **F-distribution** with $(n_1 - 1)$ numerator degrees of freedom and $(n_2 - 1)$ denominator degrees of freedom, respectively. The shape of the F-distribution depends on the degrees of freedom associated with s_1^2 and s_2^2—that is, on $(n_1 - 1)$ and $(n_2 - 1)$. An F-distribution with 7 and 9 df is shown in Figure 9.16. As you can see, the distribution is skewed to the right, since s_1^2/s_2^2 cannot be less than 0 but can increase without bound.

We need to be able to find F values corresponding to the tail areas of this distribution in order to establish the rejection region for our test of hypothesis because we expect the ratio F of the sample variances to be either very large or very small when the population variances are unequal. The upper-tail F values for $\alpha = .10, .05, .025,$ and $.01$ can be found in Tables VII, VIII, IX, and X of Appendix B.

FIGURE 9.16
An *F*-distribution with 7 numerator and 9 denominator degrees of freedom

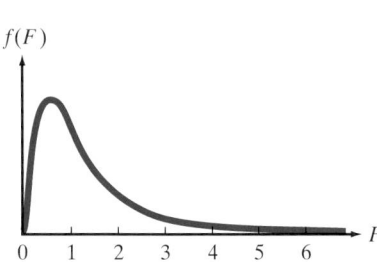

TABLE 9.7   **Reproduction of Part of Table VIII in Appendix B:**
Percentage Points of the *F*-Distribution, $\alpha = .05$

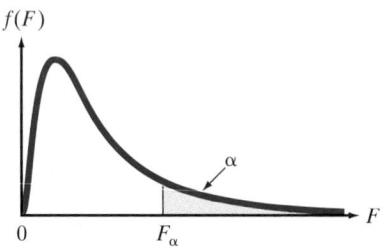

		NUMERATOR DEGREES OF FREEDOM								
ν_2 / ν_1	**1**	**2**	**3**	**4**	**5**	**6**	**7**	**8**	**9**
1	161.4	199.5	215.7	224.6	230.2	234.0	236.8	238.9	240.5
2	18.51	19.00	19.16	19.25	19.30	19.33	19.35	19.37	19.38
3	10.13	9.55	9.28	9.12	9.01	8.94	8.89	8.85	8.81
4	7.71	6.94	6.59	6.39	6.26	6.16	6.09	6.04	6.00
5	6.61	5.79	5.41	5.19	5.05	4.95	4.88	4.82	4.77
6	5.99	5.14	4.76	4.53	4.39	4.28	4.21	4.15	4.10
7	5.59	4.74	4.35	4.12	3.97	3.87	3.79	3.73	3.68
8	5.32	4.46	4.07	3.84	3.69	3.58	3.50	3.44	3.39
9	5.12	4.26	3.86	3.63	3.48	3.37	3.29	3.23	3.18
10	4.96	4.10	3.71	3.48	3.33	3.22	3.14	3.07	3.02
11	4.84	3.98	3.59	3.36	3.20	3.09	3.01	2.95	2.90
12	4.75	3.89	3.49	3.25	3.11	3.00	2.91	2.85	2.80
13	4.67	3.81	3.41	3.18	3.03	2.92	2.83	2.77	2.71
14	4.60	3.74	3.34	3.11	2.96	2.85	2.76	2.70	2.65

(DENOMINATOR DEGREES OF FREEDOM — row labels ν_2)

Table VIII is partially reproduced in Table 9.7. It gives F values that correspond to $\alpha = .05$ upper-tail areas for different degrees of freedom ν_1 for the numerator sample variance, s_1^2, whereas the rows correspond to the degrees of freedom ν_2 for the denominator sample variance, s_2^2. Thus, if the numerator degrees of freedom is $\nu_1 = 7$ and the denominator degrees of freedom is $\nu_2 = 9$, we look in the seventh column and ninth row to find $F_{.05} = 3.29$. As shown in Figure 9.17, $\alpha = .05$ is the tail area to the right of 3.29 in the F-distribution with 7 and 9 df. That is, if $\sigma_1^2 = \sigma_2^2$, then the probability that the F statistic will exceed 3.29 is $\alpha = .05$.

FIGURE 9.17
An F-distribution for
$\nu_1 = 7$ and $\nu_2 = 9$ df;
$\alpha = .05$

EXAMPLE 9.10

A manufacturer of paper products wants to compare the variation in daily production levels at two paper mills. Independent random samples of days are selected from each mill and the production levels (in units) recorded. The following summary information was obtained:

Mill 1	Mill 2
$n_1 = 13$ days	$n_2 = 18$ days
$\bar{x}_1 = 26.3$	$\bar{x}_2 = 19.7$
$s_1 = 8.2$	$s_2 = 4.7$

Do these data provide sufficient evidence to indicate a difference in the variability of production levels at the two paper mills? (Use $\alpha = .10$.)

SOLUTION
Let

$$\sigma_1^2 = \text{Population variance of production levels at mill 1}$$

$$\sigma_2^2 = \text{Population variance of production levels at mill 2}$$

The hypotheses of interest then are

$$H_0: \frac{\sigma_1^2}{\sigma_2^2} = 1 \quad (\sigma_1^2 = \sigma_2^2)$$

$$H_a: \frac{\sigma_1^2}{\sigma_2^2} \neq 1 \quad (\sigma_1^2 \neq \sigma_2^2)$$

The nature of the F-tables given in Appendix B affects the form of the test statistic. To form the rejection region for a two-tailed F-test, we want to make certain that the upper tail is used, because only the upper-tail values of F are shown in Tables VII, VIII, IX, and X. To accomplish this, *we will always place the larger sample variance in the numerator of the* F-*test statistic.* This has the effect of doubling the tabulated value for α, since we double the probability that the F-ratio will fall in the upper tail by always placing the larger sample variance in the numerator. That is, we establish a one-tailed rejection region by putting the larger variance in the numerator rather than establishing rejection regions in both tails.

Thus, for our example, we have a numerator s_1^2 with df $= \nu_1 = n_1 - 1 = 12$ and a denominator s_2^2 with df $= \nu_2 = n_2 - 1 = 17$. Therefore, the test statistic will be

$$F = \frac{\text{Larger sample variance}}{\text{Smaller sample variance}} = \frac{s_1^2}{s_2^2}$$

and we will reject $H_0: \sigma_1^2 = \sigma_2^2$ for $\alpha = .10$ when the calculated value of F exceeds the tabulated value:

$$F_{\alpha/2} = F_{.05} = 2.38 \quad \text{(see Figure 9.18)}$$

We can now calculate the value of the test statistic and complete the analysis:

$$F = \frac{s_1^2}{s_2^2} = \frac{(8.2)^2}{(4.7)^2} = 3.04$$

When we compare this result to the rejection region shown in Figure 9.18, we see that $F = 3.04$ falls in the rejection region. Therefore, the data provide sufficient evidence to indicate that the population variances differ. It appears that the variation in production levels at mill 1 tends to be higher than the variation at mill 2. ▪

FIGURE 9.18
Rejection region
for Example 9.10

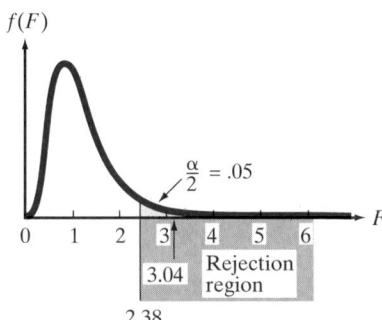

What would you have concluded if the value of F calculated from the samples had not fallen in the rejection region? Would you conclude that the null hypothesis of equal variances is true? No, because then you risk the possibility of a Type II error (accepting H_0 if H_a is true) without knowing the value of β, the probability of accepting $H_0: \sigma_1^2 = \sigma_2^2$ if in fact it is false. Since we will not consider the calculation of β for specific alternatives in this text, when the F statistic does not fall in the rejection region we simply conclude that insufficient sample evidence exists to refute the null hypothesis that $\sigma_1^2 = \sigma_2^2$.

The F-test for equal population variances is summarized in the next box.*

F-Test for Equal Population Variances

One-Tailed Test

$H_0: \sigma_1^2 = \sigma_2^2$

$H_a: \sigma_1^2 < \sigma_2^2$
(or $H_a: \sigma_1^2 > \sigma_2^2$)

Test statistic:

$F = \dfrac{s_2^2}{s_1^2}$

$\left(\text{or } F = \dfrac{s_1^2}{s_2^2} \text{ when } H_a: \sigma_1^2 > \sigma_2^2\right)$

Rejection region:
$F > F_\alpha$

Two-Tailed Test

$H_0: \sigma_1^2 = \sigma_2^2$

$H_a: \sigma_1^2 \neq \sigma_2^2$

Test statistic:

$F = \dfrac{\text{Larger sample variance}}{\text{Smaller sample variance}}$

$= \dfrac{s_1^2}{s_2^2} \text{ when } s_1^2 > s_2^2$

$\left(\text{or } \dfrac{s_2^2}{s_1^2} \text{ when } s_2^2 > s_1^2\right)$

Rejection region:
$F > F_{\alpha/2}$

where F_α and $F_{\alpha/2}$ are based on $\nu_1 = $ numerator degrees of freedom and $\nu_2 = $ denominator degrees of freedom; ν_1 and ν_2 are the degrees of freedom for the numerator and denominator sample variances, respectively.

Assumptions: **1.** Both sampled populations are normally distributed.

2. The samples are random and independent.

---

*Although a test of a hypothesis of equality of variances is the most common application of the F-test, it can also be used to test a hypothesis that the ratio between the population variances is equal to some specified value, $H_0: \sigma_1^2/\sigma_2^2 = k$. The test is conducted in exactly the same way as specified in the box, except that we use the test statistic

$$F = \frac{s_1^2}{s_2^2}\left(\frac{1}{k}\right)$$

EXAMPLE 9.11

Find the *p*-value for the test in Example 9.10 using the *F*-tables in Appendix B.

SOLUTION

Since the observed value of the *F* statistic in Example 9.10 was 3.04, the observed significance level of the test would equal the probability of observing a value of *F* at least as contradictory to H_0: $\sigma_1^2 = \sigma_2^2$ as $F = 3.04$, if in fact H_0 is true. Since we give the *F*-tables in Appendix B only for values of α equal to .10, .05, .025, and .01, we can only approximate the observed significance level. Checking Tables IX and X, we find $F_{.025} = 2.82$ and $F_{.01} = 3.46$. Since the observed value of *F* exceeds $F_{.025}$ but is less than $F_{.01}$, the observed significance level for the test is less than 2(.025) = .05, but greater than 2(.01) = .02, that is,

$$.02 < p\text{-value} < .05$$

(Note that we double the α value shown in Table X and XI because this is a two-tailed test.)

EXAMPLE 9.12

An investor believes that although the price of stock 1 usually exceeds that of stock 2, stock 1 represents a riskier investment, where the risk of a given stock is measured by the variation in daily price changes. Suppose we obtain a random sample of 25 daily price changes for stock 1 and 25 for stock 2. The sample results are summarized in the table below.

a. Compare the risks associated with the two stocks by testing the null hypothesis that the variances of the price changes for the stocks are equal against the alternative that the price variance of stock 1 exceeds that of stock 2. Use $\alpha = .05$.

b. Find the *p*-value of the test.

Stock 1	**Stock 2**
$n_1 = 25$	$n_2 = 25$
$\bar{x}_1 = .250$	$\bar{x}_2 = .125$
$s_1 = .76$	$s_2 = .46$

SOLUTION

a.

$$H_0: \sigma_1^2 = \sigma_2^2$$

$$H_a: \sigma_1^2 > \sigma_2^2$$

$$\text{Test statistic: } F = \frac{s_1^2}{s_2^2}$$

Assumptions:

1. The changes in daily stock prices have relative frequency distributions that are approximately normal.

2. The stock samples are randomly and independently selected from a set of daily stock reports.

Rejection region: $F > F_\alpha = F_{.05} = 1.98$, where $F_{.05}$ is based on $\nu_1 = 24$ df and $\nu_2 = 24$ df.

We calculate

$$F = \frac{s_1^2}{s_2^2} = \frac{(.76)^2}{(.46)^2} = 2.73$$

The calculated *F* exceeds the rejection value of 1.98. Therefore, we conclude that the variance of the daily price change for stock 1 exceeds that for stock 2.

It appears that stock 1 is a riskier investment than stock 2. How much reliability can we place in this inference? Only one time in 20 (since $\alpha = .05$), on the average, would this statistical test lead us to conclude erroneously that σ_1^2 exceeds σ_2^2 if in fact they are equal.

b. Since this is a one-tailed test, the p-value is equal to the probability that F exceeds the computed value, 2.73; that is,

$$p\text{-value} = P(F > 2.73)$$

Checking Tables IX and X, we find that $F_{.025} = 2.27$ and $F_{.01} = 2.66$. Since the computed value of the F statistic exceeds 2.66, the observed significance level for the test is slightly less:

$$\text{Approximate } p\text{-value} = .01$$

As a final example of an application, consider the comparison of population variances as a check of the assumption $\sigma_1^2 = \sigma_2^2$ needed for the two-sample t-test. Rejection of the null hypothesis $\sigma_1^2 = \sigma_2^2$ would indicate that the assumption is invalid. [*Note:* Nonrejection of the null hypothesis does *not* imply that the assumption is valid.] We illustrate with an example.

EXAMPLE 9.13

In Example 9.4 (Section 9.1) we used the two-sample t statistic to compare the success indexes of two groups of managers. The data are repeated in Table 9.8 for convenience. The use of the t statistic was based on the assumption that the population variances of the managerial success indexes were equal for the two groups. Use the computer to check this assumption at $\alpha = .10$.

SOLUTION
We want to test

$$H_0: \sigma_1^2 = \sigma_2^2$$
$$H_a: \sigma_1^2 \neq \sigma_2^2$$

This F-test is shown on the SAS printout, Figure 9.19. Both the test statistic, $F = 1.99$, and two-tailed p-value, .2554, are highlighted on the printout. Since $\alpha = .10$ is less than the p-value, we do not reject the null hypothesis that the population variances of the success indexes are equal. It is here that the temptation to misuse the F-test is strongest. *We cannot conclude that the data justify the use of the* t *statistic.* This is equivalent to accepting H_0, and we have repeatedly warned against this conclusion because the probability of a Type II error, β, is unknown. The α level of .10 protects us only against rejecting H_0 if it is true. This use of the F-test may prevent us from abusing the t procedure when we obtain a value of F that leads to a rejection of the assumption that $\sigma_1^2 = \sigma_2^2$. But when the F statistic does not fall in the rejection region, we know little more about the validity of the assumption than before we conducted the test.

TABLE 9.8   Managerial Success Indexes for Two Groups of Managers

GROUP 1						GROUP 2					
Interaction with Outsiders						Few Interactions					
65	58	78	60	68	69	62	53	36	34	56	50
66	70	53	71	63	63	42	57	46	68	48	42
						52	53	43			

```
                        TTEST PROCEDURE

Variable: SUCCESS

GROUP      N        Mean       Std Dev     Std Error    Minimum       Maximum
----------------------------------------------------------------------------
  1       12   65.33333333   6.61036835   1.90824897   53.00000000   78.00000000
  2       15   49.46666667   9.33401358   2.41003194   34.00000000   68.00000000

Variances          T        DF      Prob>|T|
----------------------------------------------------------------------------
Unequal       5.1615       24.7      0.0001
Equal         4.9675       25.0      0.0000

For HO: Variances are equal, F' = 1.99    DF = (14,11)    Prob>F' = 0.2554
```

FIGURE 9.19   SAS F-test for the data in Table 9.8

What Do You Do If the Assumption of Normal Population Distributions Is Not Satisfied?

Answer: The F-test is much less robust (i.e., much more sensitive) to departures from normality than the t-test for comparing the population means (Section 9.1). If you have doubts about the normality of the population frequency distributions, use a **nonparametric method** for comparing the two population variances. A method can be found in the nonparametric statistics texts listed in the references.

EXERCISES   9.68–9.80

Note: Exercises marked with 💾 *contain data for computer analysis on a 3.5" disk (file name in parentheses).*

Learning the Mechanics

9.68   Under what conditions is the sampling distribution of s_1^2/s_2^2 an F-distribution?

9.69   Use Tables VII, VIII, IX, and X of Appendix B to find each of the following F values:
a. $F_{.05}$ where $\nu_1 = 9$ and $\nu_2 = 6$
b. $F_{.01}$ where $\nu_1 = 18$ and $\nu_2 = 14$
c. $F_{.025}$ where $\nu_1 = 11$ and $\nu_2 = 4$
d. $F_{.10}$ where $\nu_1 = 20$ and $\nu_2 = 5$

9.70   Given ν_1 and ν_2, find the following probabilities:
a. $\nu_1 = 2, \nu_2 = 30, P(F \geq 5.39)$
b. $\nu_1 = 24, \nu_2 = 10, P(F < 2.74)$
c. $\nu_1 = 7, \nu_2 = 1, P(F \leq 236.8)$
d. $\nu_1 = 40, \nu_2 = 40, P(F > 2.11)$

9.71   For each of the following cases, identify the rejection region that should be used to test $H_0: \sigma_1^2 = \sigma_2^2$ against $H_a: \sigma_1^2 > \sigma_2^2$. Assume $\nu_1 = 30$ and $\nu_2 = 20$.
a. $\alpha = .10$ b. $\alpha = .05$
c. $\alpha = .025$ d. $\alpha = .01$

9.72   For each of the following cases, identify the rejection region that should be used to test $H_0: \sigma_1^2 = \sigma_2^2$ against $H_a: \sigma_1^2 \neq \sigma_2^2$. Assume $\nu_1 = 10$ and $\nu_2 = 12$.

a. $\alpha = .20$ b. $\alpha = .10$ c. $\alpha = .05$ d. $\alpha = .02$

9.73   Specify the appropriate rejection region for testing $H_0: \sigma_1^2 = \sigma_2^2$ in each of the following situations:
a. $H_a: \sigma_1^2 > \sigma_2^2; \alpha = .05, n_1 = 25, n_2 = 20$
b. $H_a: \sigma_1^2 < \sigma_2^2; \alpha = .05, n_1 = 10, n_2 = 15$
c. $H_a: \sigma_1^2 \neq \sigma_2^2; \alpha = .10, n_1 = 21, n_2 = 31$
d. $H_a: \sigma_1^2 < \sigma_2^2; \alpha = .01, n_1 = 31, n_2 = 41$
e. $H_a: \sigma_1^2 \neq \sigma_2^2; \alpha = .05, n_1 = 7, n_2 = 16$

9.74   Independent random samples were selected from each of two normally distributed populations, $n_1 = 12$ from population 1 and $n_2 = 27$ from population 2. The means and variances for the two samples are shown in the table.

Sample 1	Sample 2
$n_1 = 12$	$n_2 = 27$
$\bar{x}_1 = 31.7$	$\bar{x}_2 = 37.4$
$s_1^2 = 3.87$	$s_2^2 = 8.75$

a. Test the null hypothesis $H_0: \sigma_1^2 = \sigma_2^2$ against the alternative hypothesis $H_a: \sigma_1^2 \neq \sigma_2^2$. Use $\alpha = .10$.
b. Find the approximate p-value of the test.

9.75 Independent random samples were selected from each of two normally distributed populations, $n_1 = 6$ from population 1 and $n_2 = 5$ from population 2. The data are shown in the table below, followed by an SPSS descriptive statistics printout at the bottom of the page.

Sample 1	Sample 2
3.1	2.3
4.4	1.4
1.2	3.7
1.7	8.9
.7	5.5
3.4	

a. Test $H_0: \sigma_1^2 = \sigma_2^2$ against $H_a: \sigma_1^2 < \sigma_2^2$. Use $\alpha = .01$.

b. Find the approximate p-value of the test.

Applying the Concepts

9.76 A study in the *Journal of Occupational and Organizational Psychology* (Dec. 1992) investigated the relationship of employment status and mental health. A sample of working and unemployed people was selected, and each person was given a mental health examination using the General Health Questionnaire (GHQ), a widely recognized measure of mental health. Although the article focused on comparing the mean GHQ levels, a comparison of the variability of GHQ scores for employed and unemployed men and women is of interest as well.

a. In general terms, what does the amount of variability in GHQ scores tell us about the group?

b. What are the appropriate null and alternative hypotheses to compare the variability of the mental health scores of the employed and unemployed groups? Define any symbols you use.

c. The standard deviation for a sample of 142 employed men was 3.26, while the standard deviation for 49 unemployed men was 5.10. Conduct the test you set up in part **b** using $\alpha = .05$. Interpret the results.

d. What assumptions are necessary to ensure the validity of the test?

9.77 (X09.077) Tests of product quality can be completely automated or can be conducted using human inspectors or human inspectors aided by mechanical devices. Although human inspection is frequently the most economical alternative, it can lead to serious inspection error problems. Numerous studies have demonstrated that inspectors often cannot detect as many as 85% of the defective items that they inspect; moreover, performance varies from inspector to inspector (*Journal of Quality Technology,* Apr. 1986). To evaluate the performance of inspectors in a new company, a quality manager had a sample of 12 novice inspectors evaluate 200 finished products. The same 200 items were evaluated by 12 experienced inspectors. The quality of each item—whether defective or nondefective—was known to the manager. The table lists the number of inspection errors (classifying a defective item as nondefective or vice versa) made by each inspector. A SAS printout with descriptive statistics for the two types of inspectors is shown at the top of page 417.

Novice Inspectors				Experienced Inspectors			
30	35	26	40	31	15	25	19
36	20	45	31	28	17	19	18
33	29	21	48	24	10	20	21

a. Prior to conducting this experiment, the manager believed the variance in inspection errors was lower for experienced inspectors than for novice inspectors. Do the sample data support her belief? Test using $\alpha = .05$.

b. What is the appropriate p-value of the test you conducted in part **a**?

9.78 Refer to the *International Journal of Environmental Health Research* (Vol. 4, 1994) study, Exercise 9.18, in which the mean solid-waste generation rates for middle-income and industrialized countries were compared. The data are reproduced in the next table on page 417.

```
Summaries of     X
By levels of     SAMPLE

Variable          Value   Label                        Mean      Std Dev    Cases

For Entire Population                                  3.3000     2.3656       11

SAMPLE            1.00                                 2.4167     1.4359        6
SAMPLE            2.00                                 4.3600     2.9729        5

   Total Cases =          11
```

```
Analysis Variable : ERRORS

------------------------INSPECT=EXPER------------------------

N Obs   N      Minimum         Maximum              Mean        Std Dev
-----------------------------------------------------------------------
   12  12   10.0000000      31.0000000       20.5833333      5.7439032
-----------------------------------------------------------------------


------------------------INSPECT=NOVICE-----------------------

N Obs   N      Minimum         Maximum              Mean        Std Dev
-----------------------------------------------------------------------
   12  12   20.0000000      48.0000000       32.8333333      8.6427409
-----------------------------------------------------------------------
```

Industrialized Countries		Middle-Income Countries	
New York (USA)	2.27	Singapore	0.87
Phoenix (USA)	2.31	Hong Kong	0.85
London (UK)	2.24	Medellin (Colombia)	0.54
Hamburg (Germany)	2.18	Kano (Nigeria)	0.46
Rome (Italy)	2.15	Manila (Philippines)	0.50
		Cairo (Egypt)	0.50
		Tunis (Tunisia)	0.56

a. In order to conduct the two-sample *t*-test in Exercise 9.18, it was necessary to assume that the two population variances were equal. Test this assumption at $\alpha = .05$. Use the SAS printout below to conduct the test.

b. What does your test indicate about the appropriateness of applying a two-sample *t*-test?

9.79 Following the Persian Gulf War, the Pentagon changed its logistics processes to be more corporate-like. The extravagant "just-in-case" mentality was replaced with "just-in-time" systems. Emulating Federal Express and United Parcel Service, deliveries from factories to foxholes are now expedited using bar codes, laser cards, radio tags, and databases to track supplies. The following table contains order-to-delivery times for a sample of shipments from the United States to the Persian Gulf in 1991 and a sample of shipments to Bosnia in 1995.

ORDER-TO-DELIVERY TIMES (IN DAYS)

Persian Gulf 1991	Bosnia 1995
28.0	15.1
20.0	6.4
26.5	5.0
10.6	11.4
9.1	6.5
35.2	6.5
29.1	3.0
41.2	7.0
27.5	5.5

Source: Adapted from Crock, S. "The Pentagon goes to B-school." *Business Week,* December 11, 1995, p. 98.

a. Use the accompanying SPSS printout on page 418 to test whether the variances in order-to-delivery times for Persian Gulf and Bosnia shipments are equal. Use $\alpha = .05$.

b. Given your answer to part **a**, is it appropriate to construct a confidence interval for the difference between the mean order-to-delivery times? Explain.

9.80 The quality control department of a paper company measures the brightness (a measure of

```
                        TTEST PROCEDURE

Variable: WASTE

COUNTRY       N              Mean             Std Dev         Std Error
-----------------------------------------------------------------------
INDUS         5        2.23000000          0.06519202       0.02915476
MIDDLE        7        0.61142857          0.17286108       0.06533535

Variances          T     DF    Prob>|T|
-----------------------------------------------------------------------
Unequal      22.6231    8.1     0.0001
Equal        19.7302   10.0     0.0000

For HO: Variances are equal, F' = 7.03    DF = (6,4)    Prob>F' = 0.0800
```

```
Independent samples of    LOCATION

Group 1:  LOCATION  EQ        1.00          Group 2:  LOCATION  EQ        2.00

t-test for:   TIME

                    Number                Standard    Standard
                    of Cases    Mean      Deviation    Error

        Group 1        9        25.2444    10.520       3.507
        Group 2        9         7.3778     3.654       1.218

                 | Pooled Variance Estimate  | Separate Variance Estimate
                 |                            |
   F    2-Tail   |   t    Degrees of 2-Tail  |   t    Degrees of  2-Tail
 Value   Prob.   | Value   Freedom   Prob.   | Value   Freedom    Prob.
                 |                            |
 8.29    .007    | 4.81      16      .000     | 4.81     9.90      .001
```

reflectance) of finished paper on a periodic basis throughout the day. Two instruments that are available to measure the paper specimens are subject to error, but they can be adjusted so that the mean readings for a control paper specimen are the same for both instruments. Suppose you are concerned about the precision of the two instruments and want to compare the variability in the readings of instrument 1 to those of instrument 2. Five brightness measurements were made on a single paper specimen using each of the two instruments. The data are shown in the table.

a. Form a 95% confidence interval for the ratio of the variance of the measurements obtained

Instrument 1	Instrument 2
29	26
28	34
30	30
28	32
30	28

by instrument 1 to the variance of the measurements obtained using instrument 2.

b. Interpret the interval you found in part **a** in terms of the precision of the two instruments.

c. What assumptions must be satisfied for the confidence interval in part **a** to be valid?

QUICK REVIEW

Key Terms

Blocking 389
F-distribution 409
Nonparametric method 415

Paired difference experiment 389
Pooled sample variance 372
Randomized block experiment 390

Standard error 370
Weighted average 373

Key Formulas

$(1 - \alpha)100\%$ confidence interval for θ: (see table on page 419)

Large samples: $\hat{\theta} \pm z_{\alpha/2}\sigma_{\hat{\theta}}$

Small samples: $\hat{\theta} \pm t_{\alpha/2}\sigma_{\hat{\theta}}$

For testing H_0: $\theta = D_0$: (see table on page 419)

Large samples: $z = \dfrac{\hat{\theta} - D_0}{\sigma_{\hat{\theta}}}$

Small samples: $t = \dfrac{\hat{\theta} - D_0}{\sigma_{\hat{\theta}}}$

Parameter, θ	Estimator, $\hat{\theta}$	Standard Error of Estimator, $\sigma_{\hat{\theta}}$	Estimated Standard Error	
$(\mu_1 - \mu_2)$ (independent samples)	$(\bar{x}_1 - \bar{x}_2)$	$\sqrt{\dfrac{\sigma_1^2}{n_1} + \dfrac{\sigma_2^2}{n_2}}$	Large n: $\sqrt{\dfrac{s_1^2}{n_1} + \dfrac{s_2^2}{n_2}}$	370
			Small n: $\sqrt{s_p^2\left(\dfrac{1}{n_1} + \dfrac{1}{n_2}\right)}$	373, 374
μ_D (paired sample)	$\bar{x}_D$	$\dfrac{\sigma_D}{\sqrt{n_D}}$	$\dfrac{s_D}{\sqrt{n_D}}$	390, 391
$(p_1 - p_2)$ (large, independent samples)	$(\hat{p}_1 - \hat{p}_2)$	$\sqrt{\dfrac{p_1 q_1}{n_1} + \dfrac{p_2 q_2}{n_2}}$	Hypothesis tests: $\sqrt{\hat{p}\hat{q}\left(\dfrac{1}{n_1} + \dfrac{1}{n_2}\right)}$	400
			Confidence intervals: $\sqrt{\dfrac{\hat{p}_1 \hat{q}_1}{n_1} + \dfrac{\hat{p}_2 \hat{q}_2}{n_2}}$	399

$s_p^2 = \dfrac{(n_1 - 1)s_1^2 + (n_2 - 1)s_2^2}{n_1 + n_2 - 2}$ Pooled sample variance   373

$\hat{p} = \dfrac{x_1 + x_2}{n_1 + n_2}, \hat{q} = 1 - \hat{p}$ Pooled sample proportion   399

$n_1 = n_2 = \dfrac{(z_{\alpha/2})^2(\sigma_1^2 + \sigma_2^2)}{B^2}$ Determining the sample size for estimating $(\mu_1 - \mu_2)$ 407

$n_1 = n_2 = \dfrac{(z_{\alpha/2})^2(p_1 q_1 + p_2 q_2)}{B^2}$ Determining the sample size for estimating $(p_1 - p_2)$ 407

$F = \dfrac{\text{larger } s^2}{\text{smaller } s^2}$ if $H_a: \dfrac{\sigma_1^2}{\sigma_2^2} \neq 1$ Test statistic for testing $H_0: \dfrac{\sigma_1^2}{\sigma_2^2}$ 412

$F = \dfrac{s_1^2}{s_2^2}$ if $H_a: \dfrac{\sigma_1^2}{\sigma_2^2} > 1$

LANGUAGE LAB

Symbol	Pronunciation	Description
$(\mu_1 - \mu_2)$	mu-1 minus mu-2	Difference between population means
$(\bar{x}_1 - \bar{x}_2)$	x-bar 1 minus x-bar-2	Difference between sample means
$\sigma_{(\bar{x}_1 - \bar{x}_2)}$	sigma of x-bar-1 minus x-bar-2	Standard deviation of the sampling distribution of $(\bar{x}_1 - \bar{x}_2)$
s_p^2	s-p squared	Pooled sample variance
D_0	D naught	Hypothesized value of difference
μ_D	mu D	Difference between population means, paired data
$\bar{x}_D$	x-bar D	Mean of sample differences
s_D	s-D	Standard deviation of sample differences
n_D	n-D	Number of differences in sample
$(p_1 - p_2)$	p-1 minus p-2	Difference between population proportions
$(\hat{p}_1 - \hat{p}_2)$	p-1 hat minus p-2 hat	Difference between sample proportions
$\sigma_{(\hat{p}_1 - \hat{p}_2)}$	sigma of p-1 hat minus p-2 hat	Standard deviation of the sampling distribution of $(\hat{p}_1 - \hat{p}_2)$
F_{α}	F-alpha	Critical value of F associated with tail area α
ν_1	nu-1	Numerator degrees of freedom for F statistic
ν_2	nu-2	Denominator degrees of freedom for F statistic
$\dfrac{\sigma_1^2}{\sigma_2^2}$	sigma-1 squared over sigma-2 squared	Ratio of two population variances

SUPPLEMENTARY EXERCISES 9.81–9.106

Note: List the assumptions necessary to ensure the validity of the statistical procedures you use to work these exercises. Exercises marked with 💾 contain data for computer analysis on a 3.5" disk (file name in parentheses).

Learning the Mechanics

9.81 Independent random samples were selected from two normally distributed populations with means μ_1 and μ_2, respectively. The sample sizes, means, and variances are shown in the following table.

Sample 1	Sample 2
$n_1 = 12$	$n_2 = 14$
$\bar{x}_1 = 17.8$	$\bar{x}_2 = 15.3$
$s_1^2 = 74.2$	$s_2^2 = 60.5$

  a. Test $H_0: (\mu_1 - \mu_2) = 0$ against $H_a: (\mu_1 - \mu_2) > 0$. Use $\alpha = .05$.

  b. Form a 99% confidence interval for $(\mu_1 - \mu_2)$.

  c. How large must n_1 and n_2 be if you wish to estimate $(\mu_1 - \mu_2)$ to within 2 units with 99% confidence? Assume that $n_1 = n_2$.

9.82 Two independent random samples were selected from normally distributed populations with means and variances (μ_1, σ_1^2) and (μ_2, σ_2^2), respectively. The sample sizes, means, and variances are shown in the table below.

Sample 1	Sample 2
$n_1 = 20$	$n_2 = 15$
$\bar{x}_1 = 123$	$\bar{x}_2 = 116$
$s_1^2 = 31.3$	$s_2^2 = 120.1$

  a. Test $H_0: \sigma_1^2 = \sigma_2^2$ against $H_a: \sigma_1^2 \neq \sigma_2^2$. Use $\alpha = .05$.

  b. Would you be willing to use a t-test to test the null hypothesis $H_0: (\mu_1 - \mu_2) = 0$ against the alternative hypothesis $H_a: (\mu_1 - \mu_2) \neq 0$? Why?

9.83 Two independent random samples are taken from two populations. The results of these samples are summarized in the following table.

Sample 1	Sample 2
$n_1 = 135$	$n_2 = 148$
$\bar{x}_1 = 12.2$	$\bar{x}_2 = 8.3$
$s_1^2 = 2.1$	$s_2^2 = 3.0$

  a. Form a 90% confidence interval for $(\mu_1 - \mu_2)$.

  b. Test $H_0: (\mu_1 - \mu_2) = 0$ against $H_a: (\mu_1 - \mu_2) \neq 0$. Use $\alpha = .01$.

  c. What sample sizes would be required if you wish to estimate $(\mu_1 - \mu_2)$ to within .2 with 90% confidence? Assume that $n_1 = n_2$.

9.84 Independent random samples were selected from two binomial populations. The sizes and number of observed successes for each sample are shown in the table below.

Sample 1	Sample 2
$n_1 = 200$	$n_2 = 200$
$x_1 = 110$	$x_2 = 130$

  a. Test $H_0: (p_1 - p_2) = 0$ against $H_a: (p_1 - p_2) < 0$. Use $\alpha = .10$.

  b. Form a 95% confidence interval for $(p_1 - p_2)$.

  c. What sample sizes would be required if we wish to use a 95% confidence interval of width .01 to estimate $(p_1 - p_2)$?

9.85 A random sample of five pairs of observations were selected, one of each pair from a population with mean μ_1, the other from a population with mean μ_2. The data are shown in the accompanying table.

Pair	Value from Population 1	Value from Population 2
1	28	22
2	31	27
3	24	20
4	30	27
5	22	20

  a. Test the null hypothesis $H_0: \mu_D = 0$ against $H_a: \mu_D \neq 0$, where $\mu_D = \mu_1 - \mu_2$. Use $\alpha = .05$.

  b. Form a 95% confidence interval for μ_D.

  c. When are the procedures you used in parts **a** and **b** valid?

9.86 List the assumptions necessary for each of the following inferential techniques:

  a. Large-sample inferences about the difference $(\mu_1 - \mu_2)$ between population means using a two-sample z statistic

  b. Small-sample inferences about $(\mu_1 - \mu_2)$ using an independent samples design and a two-sample t statistic

  c. Small-sample inferences about $(\mu_1 - \mu_2)$ using a paired difference design and a single-sample t statistic to analyze the differences

  d. Large-sample inferences about the differences $(p_1 - p_2)$ between binomial proportions using a two-sample z statistic

  e. Inferences about the ratio σ_1^2 / σ_2^2 of two population variances using an F-test.

9.87 Suppose you use either the SAS or SPSS statistical program package to test the null hypothesis $H_0: (\mu_1 - \mu_2) = 0$ against $H_a: (\mu_1 - \mu_2) \neq 0$ with independent samples of size 12 and 10, respectively. Assuming you are using $\alpha = .05$, what conclusion would you reach in each of the following instances of observed significance level reported by the program? (Recall that both SAS and SPSS report the two-tailed p-value.)

a. P-VALUE = .0429   b. P-VALUE = .1984
c. P-VALUE = .0001   d. P-VALUE = .0344
e. P-VALUE = .0545   f. P-VALUE = .9633
g. What assumptions are necessary to ensure the validity of this test?

Applying the Concepts

9.88   Was the average amount spent by firms in the pharmaceutical industry on company-sponsored research and development (R&D) higher in 1995 than in 1994? The table below lists R&D expenditures (in millions of dollars) for a sample of firms in the pharmaceutical industry.

Firm	1994	1995
Alza	18.1	20.9
American Home Products	817.1	1,355.0
Bristol Myers Squibb	1,108.0	1,199.0
Johnson and Johnson	1,278.0	1,634.0
Merck	1,230.6	1,331.4
Pfizer	1,139.4	1,442.4
Warner-Lambert	456.0	501.2

Source: Standard and Poor's Compustat 1996.

a. A securities analyst who follows the pharmaceutical industry believes that mean R&D expenditures have increased by more than $100 million per firm. Do the data support the analyst's belief? Use the EXCEL printout below to answer the question.
b. What are the Type I and Type II errors associated with your hypothesis test of part **a**?
c. What assumptions must hold in order for your test of part **a** to be valid?

9.89   Refer to Exercise 9.88. Use a 95% confidence interval to estimate the mean difference between 1995 and 1994 R&D expenditures. Interpret the interval.

9.90   Nontraditional university students, generally defined as those at least 25 years old, comprise an increasingly large proportion of undergraduate student bodies at most universities. A study reported in the *College Student Journal* (Dec. 1992) compared traditional and nontraditional students on a number of factors, including grade point average (GPA). The table below summarizes the information from the sample.

GPA	Traditional Students	Nontraditional Students
n	94	73
$\bar{x}$	2.90	3.50
s	.50	.50

a. What are the appropriate null and alternative hypotheses if we want to test whether the mean GPAs of traditional and nontraditional students differ?
b. Conduct the test using $\alpha = .01$, and interpret the result.
c. What assumptions are necessary to ensure the validity of the test?

9.91   Advertising companies often try to characterize the average user of a client's product so ads can be targeted at particular segments of the buying community. A new movie is about to be released, and the advertising company wants to determine whether to aim the ad campaign at people under or over 25 years of age. It plans to arrange an advance showing of the movie to an audience from each group, then obtain an opinion about the movie from each individual. How many individuals should be included in each sample if the advertising company wants to estimate the difference in the proportions of viewers in each age group who will like the movie to within .05 with 90% confidence? Assume the sample size for each group will be the same and about half of each group will like the movie.

t-Test: Paired Two Sample for Means		
	year94	**year95**
Mean	863.8857143	1069.128571
Variance	220897.1748	341185.4424
Observations	7	7
Pearson Correlation	0.952837714	
Hypothesized Mean Difference	0	
df	6	
t Stat	-2.75263003	
P(T<=t) one-tail	0.016588005	
t Critical one-tail	1.943180905	
P(T<=t) two-tail	0.03317601	
t Critical two-tail	2.446913641	

9.92 In a study of the effectiveness of a new TV commercial, shoppers were randomly selected as they entered a large Phoenix supermarket and asked their preferences for several product brands. One was brand XYZ, whose new TV commercial was the object of the study. Ostensibly in exchange for their time, the shoppers were given a packet of "cents-off" coupons for various products sold in the supermarket, including XYZ. The coupons could be used only in that store and only on that day. A second sample of 387 shoppers were given the same interview, but were also asked to watch four television commercials in a trailer parked outside the supermarket. One commercial was the newly developed ad for XYZ. Following the viewing, the shoppers were asked for their reactions to the commercials, then were given the same packet of coupons. Of the 392 shoppers not exposed to the television commercials, 57 redeemed the coupon for XYZ. Of the 387 shoppers who saw XYZ's commercial, 84 redeemed the XYZ coupon.

a. Do the sample data provide sufficient evidence to conclude that the new XYZ commercial motivates shoppers to purchase the XYZ brand? Use $\alpha = .05$.

b. Find and interpret the observed significance level for the test.

9.93 **(X09.093)** It has been known for a number of years that the tailings (waste) of gypsum and phosphate mines in Florida contain radioactive radon 222. The radiation levels in waste gypsum and phosphate mounds in Polk County, Florida, are regularly monitored by the Eastern Environmental Radiation Facility (EERF) and by the Polk County Health Department (PCHD), Winter Haven, Florida. The following table shows measurements of the exhalation rate (a measure of radiation) for 15 soil samples obtained from waste mounds in Polk County, Florida. The exhalation rate was measured for each soil sample by both the PCHD and the EERF. The objective of selecting the paired measurements was to determine whether there is a bias—a difference in the mean readings—between PCHD and EERF. The data in the table represent part of the data contained in a report by Thomas R. Horton of EERF.

a. Considering the relative size of the measurements from canister to canister, explain why a paired difference experiment was conducted rather than an independent samples experiment.

b. Given that the mean difference (PCHD − EERF) for the 15 sampled canisters is 84.17 with standard deviation 408.92, do the data provide sufficient evidence to indicate a differ-

Charcoal Canister No.	PCHD	EERF
71	1,709.79	1,479.0
58	357.17	257.8
84	1,150.94	1,287.0
91	1,572.69	1,395.0
44	558.33	416.5
43	4,132.28	3,993.0
79	1,489.86	1,351.0
61	3,017.48	1,813.0
85	393.55	187.7
46	880.84	630.4
4	2,996.49	3,707.0
20	2,367.40	2,791.0
36	599.84	706.8
42	538.37	618.5
55	2,770.23	2,639.0

Source: Horton, T. R. "Preliminary radiological assessment of radon exhalation from phosphate gypsum piles and inactive uranium mill tailings piles." EPA-520/5-79-004. Washington, D.C.: Environmental Protection Agency, 1979.

ence in the mean exhalation rates between PCHD and EERF? Test using $\alpha = .05$.

c. Find a 95% confidence interval for the difference in mean measurements between PCHD and EERF. Interpret the interval. Does it support the result of the test in part **a**?

9.94 An important interaction occurs when a consumer dissatisfied with a purchase returns to the retailer to obtain satisfaction. The action taken by the retailer, however, may not conform to the consumer's expectations, and the resulting frustration and ill will benefit neither party. In a classic study published in the *Journal of Consumer Affairs* (Summer 1975), a hypothesis test was conducted to determine whether differences exist between retailers' and consumers' perceptions regarding actions taken by retailers in market transactions. A random sample of 300 consumers selected from the Cincinnati Metropolitan Area Telephone Directory were asked via mail questionnaire to react to scenarios like the following:

- A customer calls the retailer to report that her refrigerator purchased two weeks ago is not cooling properly and all the food has spoiled.

- Action that should be taken by the retailer: The customer should be reimbursed for the value of the spoiled food.

One hundred usable questionnaires were returned. The same questionnaire was presented in person to 100 managers and assistant managers of a random sample of 40 retail establishments drawn from the yellow pages of the Cincinnati Telephone Directory. For the preceding scenario, 89 consumers agreed with the action prescribed for the

Variable	STAYERS ($n_1 = 174$)		LEAVERS ($n_2 = 355$)	
	$\bar{x}_1$	s_1	$\bar{x}_2$	s_2
Initial performance	3.51	.51	3.24	.52
Rate of career advancement	.43	.20	.31	.31
Final performance appraisal	3.78	.62	3.15	.68

retailer, 3 disagreed, and 8 had no opinion. Thirty-seven retailers (managers or assistant managers) agreed with the prescribed action, 54 disagreed, and 9 had no opinion.

a. Use a 95% confidence interval to estimate the difference in the proportions of consumers and retailers who agree with the action prescribed. Draw appropriate conclusions regarding the hypothesis of interest to the researchers.

b. What assumption(s), if any, must be made in constructing the confidence interval?

c. Discuss the implications of the composition of the sample of retailers for the validity of the conclusions you made in part **a**. How would you improve the sampling procedure?

9.95 One theory regarding the mobility of college and university faculty members is that those who publish the most scholarly articles are also the most mobile. The logic behind this theory is that good researchers who publish frequently receive more job offers and are therefore more likely to move from one university to another. The *Academy of Management Journal* (Vol. 25, 1982) examined this relationship for persons employed in industry. Using the personnel records of a large national oil company, the researchers obtained the early career performance records for 529 of the company's employees. Of these, 174 were classified as *stayers*, those who stayed with the company; the other 355, who left the company at varying points during a 15-year period, were classified as *leavers* Summary statistics on three variables—initial performance, rate of career advancement (number of promotions per year), and final performance appraisals—for both stayers and leavers are shown in the table at the top of the page. For each variable, compare the means of stayers and leavers using an appropriate statistical method. Interpret the results.

9.96 A study in the *Journal of Psychology and Marketing* (Jan. 1992) investigates the degree to which American consumers are concerned about product tampering. Large random samples of male and female consumers were asked to rate their concern about product tampering on a scale of 1 (little or no concern) to 9 (very concerned).

a. What are the appropriate null and alternative hypotheses to determine whether a difference exists in the mean level of concern about product tampering between men and women? Define any symbols you use.

b. The statistics reported include those shown in the MINITAB printout below. Interpret these results.

c. What assumptions are necessary to ensure the validity of this test?

9.97 Management training programs are often instituted to teach supervisory skills and thereby increase productivity. Suppose a company psychologist administers a set of examinations to each of ten supervisors before such a training program begins and then administers similar examinations at the end of the program. The examinations are designed to measure supervisory skills, with higher scores indicating increased skill. The results of the tests are shown in the table.

Supervisor	Pre-Test	Post-Test
1	63	78
2	93	92
3	84	91
4	72	80
5	65	69
6	72	85
7	91	99
8	84	82
9	71	81
10	80	87

```
TWOSAMPLE T FOR MSCORE VS FSCORE
           N     MEAN    STDEV   SE MEAN
MSCORE    200    3.209    2.33    0.165
FSCORE    200    3.923    2.94    0.208

TTEST MU MSCORE = MU FSCORE (VS NE): T= -2.69 P=0.0072 DF=398
```

```
TEST OF MU = 0.000 VS MU N.E. 0.000

               N      MEAN    STDEV   SE MEAN        T    P VALUE
PRE-POST      10    -6.900    5.425     1.716    -4.02     0.0030
```

a. Do the data provide evidence that the training program is effective in increasing supervisory skills, as measured by the examination scores? Use $\alpha = .10$.

b. Find and interpret the approximate p-value for the test on the MINITAB printout shown above.

9.98 Some power plants are located near rivers or oceans so that the available water can be used for cooling the condensers. Suppose that, as part of an environmental impact study, a power company wants to estimate the difference in mean water temperature between the discharge of its plant and the offshore waters. How many sample measurements must be taken at each site in order to estimate the true difference between means to within .2°C with 95% confidence? Assume that the range in readings will be about 4°C at each site and the same number of readings will be taken at each site.

9.99 As part of a study of participative management, workers from two types of New Zealand sociocultural backgrounds were sampled: those who believed in the existence of a class system and those who believed that they lived and worked in a classless society (*Academy of Management Journal*, Vol. 17, 1974). Each worker in the sample was selected from a work environment with participatory management. Do workers who consider themselves to be social equals with their management superiors possess different levels of job satisfaction than those workers who see themselves as socially different from management? Each worker in the independent random samples was asked to answer this question by rating his or her job satisfaction on a scale of 1 (poor) to 7 (excellent). Using the results shown in the table below, what can you say about the differences in job satisfaction for the two different sociocultural types of workers?

	BELIEF IN EXISTENCE OF A CLASS SYSTEM	
	Yes	No
Sample size	175	277
Mean	5.42	5.19
Standard deviation	1.24	1.17

Source: Excerpted from Hines, G. H. "Influences on employee expectancy and participative management." *Academy of Management Journal*, 1974, Vol. 17.

9.100 Does the time of day during which one works affect job satisfaction? A study in the *Journal of Occupational Psychology* (Sept. 1991) examined differences in job satisfaction between day-shift and night-shift nurses. Nurses' satisfaction with their hours of work, free time away from work, and breaks during work were measured. The following table shows the mean scores for each measure of job satisfaction (higher scores indicate greater satisfaction), along with the observed significance level comparing the means for the day-shift and night-shift samples:

	MEAN SATISFACTION		
	Day Shift	Night Shift	p-Value
Satisfaction with:			
Hours of work	3.91	3.56	.813
Free time	2.55	1.72	.047
Breaks	2.53	3.75	.0073

a. Specify the null and alternative hypotheses if we wish to test whether a difference in job satisfaction exists between day-shift and night-shift nurses on each of the three measures. Define any symbols you use.

b. Interpret the p-value for each of the tests. (Each of the p-values in the table is two-tailed.)

c. Assume that each of the tests is based on small samples of nurses from each group. What assumptions are necessary for the tests to be valid?

9.101 An economist wants to investigate the difference in unemployment rates between an urban industrial community and a university community in the same state. She interviews 525 potential members of the work force in the industrial community and 375 in the university community. Of these, 47 and 22, respectively, are unemployed. Use a 95% confidence interval to estimate the difference in unemployment rates in the two communities.

9.102 When new instruments are developed to perform chemical analyses of products (food, medicine, etc.), they are usually evaluated with respect to two criteria: accuracy and precision. *Accuracy* refers to the ability of the instrument to identify correctly the nature and amounts of a product's components. *Precision* refers to the consistency with which the instrument will identify the components of the same material. Thus, a large variability in the identification of a single batch of a product indicates a lack of precision. Suppose a pharmaceutical firm is considering two brands of an instrument designed to identify the components of certain drugs. As part of a comparison of precision, 10 test-tube samples of a well-mixed batch of a drug are selected and then five are analyzed by instrument A and five by instrument B. The data shown below are the percentages of the primary component of the drug given by the instruments. Do these data provide evidence of a difference in the precision of the two machines? Use $\alpha = .10$.

Instrument A	Instrument B
43	46
48	49
37	43
52	41
45	48

9.103 The threat of earthquakes is a part of life for homeowners in California. Scientists have been warning about "the big one" for decades. An article in the *Annals of the Association of American Geographers* (June 1992) explored some factors that are considered when California homeowners purchase earthquake insurance, including the proximity to a major earthquake fault. Surveys were mailed to residents in four California counties. The data collected are shown in the table below.
   a. Los Angeles County is the closest of the four to a major earthquake fault. Calculate 95% confidence intervals for the difference in the proportions of earthquake-insured residents in Los Angeles County and each of the other counties.
   b. Do these results support the contention that closer proximities to major earthquake faults result in higher proportions of earthquake-insured residents?

9.104 Refer to Exercise 9.103. How large would the samples from Los Angeles and San Bernardino counties have to be in order to estimate the difference between earthquake-insured proportions to within .03 with 95% confidence?

9.105 How does gender affect the type of advertising that proves to be most effective? An article in the *Journal of Advertising Research* (May/June 1990) makes reference to numerous studies that conclude males tend to be more competitive with others than with themselves. To apply this conclu-

sion to advertising, the author creates two ads promoting a new brand of soft drink:

Ad 1: Four men are shown competing in racquetball

Ad 2: One man is shown competing against himself in racquetball

The author hypothesized that the first ad will be more effective when shown to males. To test this hypothesis, 43 males were shown both ads and asked to measure their attitude toward the advertisement (Aad), their attitude toward the brand of soft drink (Ab), and their intention to purchase the soft drink (Intention). Each variable was measured using a 7-point scale, with higher scores indicating a more favorable attitude. The results are shown here:

	SAMPLE MEANS		
	Aad	**Ab**	**Intention**
Ad 1	4.465	3.311	4.366
Ad 2	4.150	2.902	3.813
Level of significance	$p = .091$	$p = .032$	$p = .050$

   a. What are the appropriate null and alternative hypotheses to test the author's research hypothesis? Define any symbols you use.
   b. Based on the information provided about this experiment, do you think this is an independent samples experiment or a paired difference experiment? Explain.
   c. Interpret the *p*-value for each test.
   d. What assumptions are necessary for the validity of the tests?

9.106 What makes entrepreneurs different from chief executive officers (CEOs) of *Fortune* 500 companies? The *Wall Street Journal* hired the Gallup organization to investigate this question. For the study, entrepreneurs were defined as chief executive officers of companies listed by *Inc.* magazine as among the 500 fastest-growing smaller companies in the United States. The Gallup organization sampled 207 CEOs of *Fortune* 500 companies and 153 entrepreneurs. They obtained the results shown in the table on page 426.
   a. In each of the three areas—age, education, and employment record—are the sample sizes large enough to use the inferential methods of this section to investigate the differences

	Contra Costa	Santa Clara	Los Angeles	San Bernardino
Sample size	521	556	337	372
Number with earthquake insurance	117	222	133	109

Variable	*Fortune* 500 CEOs	Entrepreneurs
Age Under 45 years old	19	96
Education Completed 4 years of college	195	116
Employment record Have been fired or dismissed from a job	19	47

Source: Graham, E. "The entrepreneurial mystique." *Wall Street Journal,* May 20, 1985.

between *Fortune* 500 CEOs and entrepreneurs? Justify your answer.

b. Test to determine whether the data indicate that the fractions of CEOs and entrepreneurs who have been fired or dismissed from a job differ at the $\alpha = .01$ level of significance.

c. Construct a 99% confidence interval for the difference between the fractions of CEOs and

entrepreneurs who have been fired or dismissed from a job.

d. Which inferential procedure provides more information about the difference between employment records, the test of part **b** or the interval of part **c**? Explain.

THE KENTUCKY MILK CASE—PART II

SHOWCASE

In The Kentucky Milk Case—Part I, you used graphical and numerical descriptive statistics to investigate bid collusion in the Kentucky school milk market. This case expands your previous analyses, incorporating inferential statistical methodology. The three areas of your focus are described below. [See page 107 for the file layout of the data available on disk for analysis.] Again, you should prepare a professional document which presents the results of the analyses and any implications regarding collusionary practices in the tri-county Kentucky milk market.

1. *Incumbency rates.* Recall from Part I that market allocation (where the same dairy controls the same school districts year after year) is a common form of collusive behavior in bidrigging conspiracies. Market allocation is typically gauged by the incumbency rate for a market in a given school year—defined as the percentage of school districts that are won by the same milk vendor who won the previous year. Past experience with milk bids in a competitive market reveals that a "normal" incumbency rate is about .7. That is, 70% of the school districts are expected to purchase their milk from the same vendor who supplied the milk the previous year. In the 13-district tri-county Kentucky market, 13 vendor transitions potentially exist each year. Over the 1985–1988 period (when bid collusion was alleged to have occurred), there are 52 potential vendor transitions. Based on the actual number of vendor transitions that occurred each year and over the 1985–1988 period, make an inference regarding bid collusion.

2. *Bid price dispersion.* Recall that in competitive sealed-bid markets, more dispersion or variability among the bids is observed than in collusive markets. (This is due to conspiring vendors sharing information about their bids.) Consequently, if collusion exists, the variation in bid prices in the tri-county market should be significantly smaller than the corresponding variation in the surrounding market. For each milk product, conduct an analysis to compare the bid price variances of the two markets each year. Make the appropriate inferences.

3. *Average winning bid price.* According to collusion theorists, the mean winning bid price in the "rigged" market will exceed the mean winning bid price in the competitive market for each year in which collusion occurs. In addition, the difference between the competitive average and the "rigged" average tends to grow over time when collusionary tactics are employed over several consecutive years. For each milk product, conduct an analysis to compare the winning bid price means of the tri-county and surrounding markets each year. Make the appropriate inferences. ▲

www.int.com
www.int.com
INTERNET LAB
www.int.com

CHOOSING BETWEEN ECONOMIC INDICATORS

The Gross Domestic Product (GDP) data that was located in the Internet Lab on page 109 is a measure of all product revenues produced by U.S. business concerns, within and outside the borders of the United States. Another economic indicator, the Gross National Product (GNP), measures all product revenues produced within the borders of the United States by either domestic or foreign-owned business concerns. Prior to 1991, the United States relied on GNP information as the basis for measuring productivity growth, and many businesses used that measure in negotiating union labor contracts. A change to using GDP occurred in 1991 for two primary reasons: (1) other advanced countries in the world used GDP exclusively; and (2) some economists argued that the GNP overstated U.S. economic growth, and thus wage and price increases based on it.

Here we will examine whether these two different measures behave the same statistically or which might have the greater information value if used in business forecasting models of revenues, materials, prices, labor costs, and so forth. Data is provided by the U.S. Department of Commerce: *http://doc.gov/* (refer to your notes from the Internet Lab on page 109).

1. Obtain annual GDP and GNP data from 1980 to present.

2. Save the data in your statistical applications software data files.

3. Formulate and test the hypothesis that the average economic growth measured by the two methods over this time period is equal against the alternative hypothesis that the average GNP is higher than the average GDP. If you are able to reject the null hypothesis, what further business and economic implications do you think this would have other than the level of wage and benefits adjustments? ○

CHAPTER 10

SIMPLE LINEAR REGRESSION

Where We've Been

We've learned how to estimate and test hypotheses about population parameters based on a random sample of observations from the population. We've also seen how to extend these methods to allow for a comparison of parameters from two populations.

Where We're Going

Suppose we want to predict the assessed value of a house in a particular community. We could select a single random sample of n houses from the community, use the methods of Chapter 7 to estimate the mean assessed value μ, and then use this quantity to predict the house's assessed value. A better method uses information that is available to any property appraiser, e.g., square feet of floor space and age of the house. If we measure square footage and age at the same time as assessed value, we can establish the relationship between these variables—one that lets us use these variables for prediction. This chapter covers the simplest situation—relating two variables. The more complex problem of relating more than two variables is the topic of Chapter 11.

In Chapters 7–9 we described methods for making inferences about population means. The mean of a population was treated as a *constant,* and we showed how to use sample data to estimate or to test hypotheses about this constant mean. In many applications, the mean of a population is not viewed as a constant, but rather as a variable. For example, the mean sale price of residences in a large city during 1997 can be treated as a constant and might be equal to $150,000. But we might also treat the mean sale price as a variable that depends on the square feet of living space in the residence. For example, the relationship might be

Mean sale price = $30,000 + $60(Square feet)

This formula implies that the mean sale price of 1,000-square-foot homes is $90,000, the mean sale price of 2,000-square-foot homes is $150,000, and the mean sale price of 3,000-square-foot homes is $210,000.

What do we gain by treating the mean as a variable rather than a constant? In many practical applications we will be dealing with highly variable data, data for which the standard deviation is so large that a constant mean is almost "lost" in a sea of variability. For example, if the mean residential sale price is $150,000 but the standard deviation is $75,000, then the actual sale prices will vary considerably, and the mean price is not a very meaningful or useful characterization of the price distribution. On the other hand, if the mean sale price is treated as a variable that depends on the square feet of living space, the standard deviation of sale prices for any given size of home might be only $10,000. In this case, the mean price will provide a much better characterization of sale prices when it is treated as a variable rather than a constant.

In this chapter we discuss situations in which the mean of the population is treated as a variable, dependent on the value of another variable. The dependence of residential sale price on the square feet of living space is one illustration. Other examples include the dependence of mean sales revenue of a firm on advertising expenditure, the dependence of mean starting salary of a college graduate on the student's GPA, and the dependence of mean monthly production of automobiles on the total number of sales in the previous month.

In this chapter we discuss the simplest of all models relating a population mean to another variable, *the straight-line model.* We show how to use the sample data to estimate the straight-line relationship between the mean value of one variable, *y*, as it relates to a second variable, *x*. The methodology of estimating and using a straight-line relationship is referred to as *simple linear regression analysis.*

10.1 PROBABILISTIC MODELS

An important consideration in merchandising a product is the amount of money spent on advertising. Suppose you want to model the monthly sales revenue of an appliance store as a function of the monthly advertising expenditure. The first question to be answered is this: "Do you think an exact relationship exists between these two variables?" That is, do you think it is possible to state the exact monthly sales revenue if the amount spent on advertising is known? We think you will agree with us that this is *not* possible for several reasons. Sales depend on many variables other than advertising expenditure—for example, time of year, the state of the general economy, inventory, and price structure. Even if many variables are included in a model (the topic of Chapter 11), it is still unlikely that we would be able to predict the monthly sales *exactly.* There will almost certainly be some variation in response times due strictly to *random phenomena* that cannot be modeled or explained.

FIGURE 10.1
Possible sales revenues, y, for five different months, x

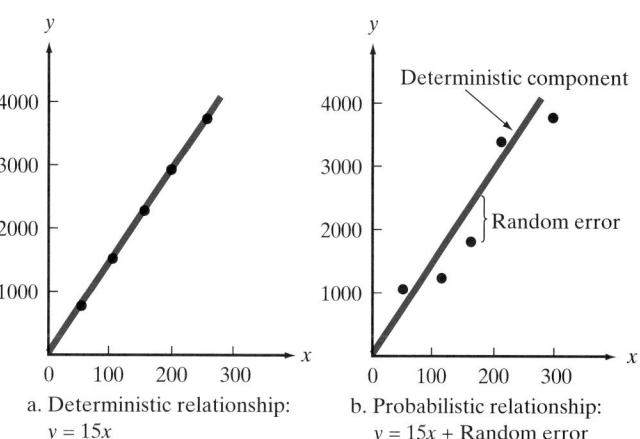

a. Deterministic relationship:
$y = 15x$

b. Probabilistic relationship:
$y = 15x$ + Random error

If we were to construct a model that hypothesized an exact relationship between variables, it would be called a **deterministic model**. For example, if we believe that y, the monthly sales revenue, will be exactly fifteen times x, the monthly advertising expenditure, we write

$$y = 15x$$

This represents a **deterministic relationship** between the variables y and x. It implies that y can always be determined exactly when the value of x is known. *There is no allowance for error in this prediction.*

If, on the other hand, we believe there will be unexplained variation in monthly sales—perhaps caused by important but unincluded variables or by random phenomena—we discard the deterministic model and use a model that accounts for this **random error**. This **probabilistic model** includes both a deterministic component and a random error component. For example, if we hypothesize that the sales y is related to advertising expenditure x by

$$y = 15x + \text{Random error}$$

we are hypothesizing a **probabilistic relationship** between y and x. Note that the deterministic component of this probabilistic model is $15x$.

Figure 10.1a shows the possible values of y and x for five different months, when the model is deterministic. All the pairs of (x, y) data points must fall exactly on the line because a deterministic model leaves no room for error.

Figure 10.1b shows a possible set of points for the same values of x when we are using a probabilistic model. Note that the deterministic part of the model (the straight line itself) is the same. Now, however, the inclusion of a random error component allows the monthly sales to vary from this line. Since we know that the sales revenue does vary randomly for a given value of x, the probabilistic model provides a more realistic model for y than does the deterministic model.

General Form of Probabilistic Models

$$y = \text{Deterministic component} + \text{Random error}$$

where y is the variable of interest. We always assume that the mean value of the random error equals 0. This is equivalent to assuming that the mean value of y, $E(y)$, equals the deterministic component of the model; that is

$$E(y) = \text{Deterministic component}$$

We begin with the simplest of probabilistic models—the **straight-line model**—which derives its name from the fact that the deterministic portion of the model graphs as a straight line. Fitting this model to a set of data is an example of **regression analysis**, or **regression modeling**. The elements of the straight-line model are summarized in the next box.

A First-Order (Straight-Line) Probabilistic Model

$$y = \beta_0 + \beta_1 x + \epsilon$$

where

y = *Dependent or response variable* (variable to be modeled)

x = *Independent or predictor variable* (variable used as a predictor of y)*

$E(y) = \beta_0 + \beta_1 x$ = Deterministic component

ϵ (epsilon) = Random error component

β_0 (beta zero) = *y-intercept of the line,* that is, the point at which the line intercepts or cuts through the y-axis (see Figure 10.2)

β_1 (beta one) = *Slope of the line,* that is, the amount of increase (or decrease) in the deterministic component of y for every 1-unit increase in x. [As you can see in Figure 10.2, $E(y)$ increases by the amount β_1 as x increases from 2 to 3.]

In the probabilistic model, the deterministic component is referred to as the **line of means**, because the mean of y, $E(y)$, is equal to the straight-line component of the model. That is,

$$E(y) = \beta_0 + \beta_1 x$$

Note that the Greek symbols β_0 and β_1, respectively, represent the y-intercept and slope of the model. They are population parameters that will be known only if we have access to the entire population of (x, y) measurements. Together with a specific value of the independent variable x, they determine the mean value of y, which is just a specific point on the line of means (Figure 10.2).

FIGURE 10.2
The straight-line model

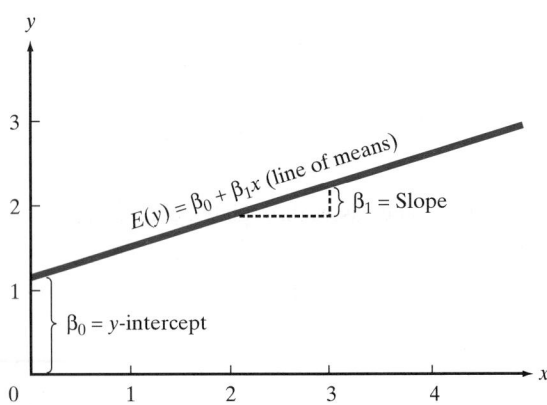

*The word *independent* should not be interpreted in a probabilistic sense, as defined in Chapter 3. The phrase *independent variable* is used in regression analysis to refer to a predictor variable for the response y.

The values of β_0 and β_1 will be unknown in almost all practical applications of regression analysis. The process of developing a model, estimating the unknown parameters, and using the model can be viewed as the five-step procedure shown in the next box.

Step 1	Hypothesize the deterministic component of the model that relates the mean, $E(y)$, to the independent variable x (Section 10.1).
Step 2	Use the sample data to estimate unknown parameters in the model (Section 10.2).
Step 3	Specify the probability distribution of the random error term and estimate the standard deviation of this distribution (Sections 10.3 and 10.4).
Step 4	Statistically evaluate the usefulness of the model (Sections 10.5, 10.6, and 10.7).
Step 5	When satisfied that the model is useful, use it for prediction, estimation, and other purposes (Section 10.8).

In this chapter only the straight-line model is discussed; more complex models are addressed in Chapters 11 and 12.

EXERCISES   10.1–10.9

Learning the Mechanics

10.1 In each case, graph the line that passes through the given points.
  a. $(1, 1)$ and $(5, 5)$ **b.** $(0, 3)$ and $(3, 0)$
  c. $(-1, 1)$ and $(4, 2)$ **d.** $(-6, -3)$ and $(2, 6)$

10.2 Give the slope and y-intercept for each of the lines graphed in Exercise 10.1.

10.3 The equation for a straight line (deterministic model) is

$$y = \beta_0 + \beta_1 x$$

If the line passes through the point $(-2, 4)$, then $x = -2, y = 4$ must satisfy the equation; that is,

$$4 = \beta_0 + \beta_1(-2)$$

Similarly, if the line passes through the point $(4, 6)$, then $x = 4, y = 6$ must satisfy the equation; that is,

$$6 = \beta_0 + \beta_1(4)$$

Use these two equations to solve for β_0 and β_1; then find the equation of the line that passes through the points $(-2, 4)$ and $(4, 6)$.

10.4 Refer to Exercise 10.3. Find the equations of the lines that pass through the points listed in Exercise 10.1.

10.5 Plot the following lines:
  a. $y = 4 + x$ **b.** $y = 5 - 2x$ **c.** $y = -4 + 3x$
  d. $y = -2x$ **e.** $y = x$ **f.** $y = .50 + 1.5x$

10.6 Give the slope and y-intercept for each of the lines defined in Exercise 10.5.

10.7 Why do we generally prefer a probabilistic model to a deterministic model? Give examples for which the two types of models might be appropriate.

10.8 What is the line of means?

10.9 If a straight-line probabilistic relationship relates the mean $E(y)$ to an independent variable x, does it imply that every value of the variable y will always fall exactly on the line of means? Why or why not?

10.2   FITTING THE MODEL: THE LEAST SQUARES APPROACH

After the straight-line model has been hypothesized to relate the mean $E(y)$ to the independent variable x, the next step is to collect data and to estimate the (unknown) population parameters, the y-intercept β_0 and the slope β_1.

TABLE 10.1   Advertising–Sales Data

Month	Advertising Expenditure, x ($100s)	Sales Revenue, y ($1,000s)
1	1	1
2	2	1
3	3	2
4	4	2
5	5	4

To begin with a simple example, suppose an appliance store conducts a five-month experiment to determine the effect of advertising on sales revenue. The results are shown in Table 10.1. (The number of measurements and the measurements themselves are unrealistically simple in order to avoid arithmetic confusion in this introductory example.) This set of data will be used to demonstrate the five-step procedure of regression modeling given in Section 10.1. In this section we hypothesize the deterministic component of the model and estimate its unknown parameters (steps 1 and 2). The model assumptions and the random error component (step 3) are the subjects of Sections 10.3 and 10.4, whereas Sections 10.5–10.7 assess the utility of the model (step 4). Finally, we use the model for prediction and estimation (step 5) in Section 10.8.

Step 1   *Hypothesize the deterministic component of the probabilistic model.* As stated before, we will consider only straight-line models in this chapter. Thus, the complete model to relate mean sales revenue $E(y)$ to advertising expenditure x is given by

$$E(y) = \beta_0 + \beta_1 x$$

Step 2   *Use sample data to estimate unknown parameters in the model.* This step is the subject of this section—namely, how can we best use the information in the sample of five observations in Table 10.1 to estimate the unknown y-intercept β_0 and slope β_1?

To determine whether a linear relationship between y and x is plausible, it is helpful to plot the sample data in a **scattergram** (see optional Section 2.10). The scattergram for the five data points of Table 10.1 is shown in Figure 10.3. Note that the scattergram suggests a general tendency for y to increase as x increases. If you place a ruler on the scattergram, you will see that a line may be drawn through three of the five points, as shown in Figure 10.4. To obtain the equation of this visually fitted line, note that the line intersects the y-axis at $y = -1$, so the y-intercept is -1. Also, y increases exactly 1 unit for every 1-unit increase in x, indicating that the slope is $+1$. Therefore, the equation is

$$\tilde{y} = -1 + 1(x) = -1 + x$$

where $\tilde{y}$ is used to denote the predicted y from the visual model.

FIGURE 10.3
Scattergram for data in Table 10.1

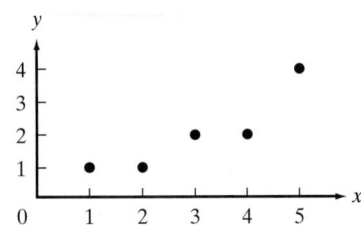

FIGURE 10.4
Visual straight line fitted to the data in Figure 10.3

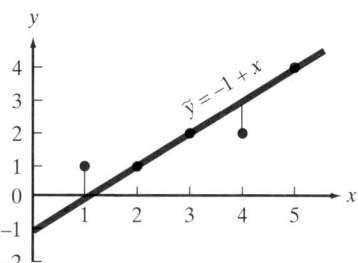

One way to decide quantitatively how well a straight line fits a set of data is to note the extent to which the data points deviate from the line. For example, to evaluate the model in Figure 10.4, we calculate the magnitude of the **deviations**, i.e., the differences between the observed and the predicted values of y. These deviations, or **errors**, are the vertical distances between observed and predicted values (see Figure 10.4). The observed and predicted values of y, their differences, and their squared differences are shown in Table 10.2. Note that the *sum of errors* equals 0 and the *sum of squares of the errors* (SSE), which gives greater emphasis to large deviations of the points from the line, is equal to 2.

You can see by shifting the ruler around the graph that it is possible to find many lines for which the sum of errors is equal to 0, but it can be shown that there is one (and only one) line for which the SSE is a *minimum*. This line is called the **least squares line**, the **regression line**, or the **least squares prediction equation**.

To find the least squares prediction equation for a set of data, assume that we have a sample of n data points consisting of pairs of values of x and y, say (x_1, y_1), (x_2, y_2), ..., (x_n, y_n). For example, the $n = 5$ data points shown in Table 10.2 are $(1, 1), (2, 1), (3, 2), (4, 2)$, and $(5, 4)$. The fitted line, which we will calculate based on the five data points, is written as

$$\hat{y} = \hat{\beta}_0 + \hat{\beta}_1 x$$

The "hats" indicate that the symbols below them are estimates: $\hat{y}$ (y-hat) is an estimator of the mean value of y, $E(y)$, and a predictor of some future value of y; and $\hat{\beta}_0$ and $\hat{\beta}_1$ are estimators of β_0 and β_1, respectively.

For a given data point, say the point (x_i, y_i), the observed value of y is y_i and the predicted value of y would be obtained by substituting x_i into the prediction equation:

$$\hat{y}_i = \hat{\beta}_0 + \hat{\beta}_1 x_i$$

And the deviation of the ith value of y from its predicted value is

$$(y_i - \hat{y}_i) = [y_i - (\hat{\beta}_0 + \hat{\beta}_1 x_i)]$$

TABLE 10.2 Comparing Observed and Predicted Values for the Visual Model

x	y	$\tilde{y} = -1 + x$	$(y - \tilde{y})$	$(y - \tilde{y})^2$
1	1	0	$(1 - 0) =$ 1	1
2	1	1	$(1 - 1) =$ 0	0
3	2	2	$(2 - 2) =$ 0	0
4	2	3	$(2 - 3) = -1$	1
5	4	4	$(4 - 4) =$ 0	0
			Sum of errors = 0	Sum of squared errors (SSE) = 2

Then the sum of squares of the deviations of the y-values about their predicted values for all the n points is

$$\text{SSE} = \sum[y_i - (\hat{\beta}_0 + \hat{\beta}_1 x_i)]^2$$

The quantities $\hat{\beta}_0$ and $\hat{\beta}_1$ that make the SSE a minimum are called the **least squares estimates** of the population parameters β_0 and β_1, and the prediction equation $\hat{y} = \hat{\beta}_0 + \hat{\beta}_1 x$ is called the *least squares line.*

DEFINITION 10.1

The **least squares line** is one that has the following two properties:

1. the sum of the errors (SE) equals 0
2. the sum of squared errors (SSE) is smaller than for any other straight-line model

---

The values of $\hat{\beta}_0$ and $\hat{\beta}_1$ that minimize the SSE are (proof omitted) given by the formulas in the box.*

Formulas for the Least Squares Estimates

Slope: $\qquad \hat{\beta}_1 = \dfrac{\text{SS}_{xy}}{\text{SS}_{xx}}$

y-intercept: $\quad \hat{\beta}_0 = \bar{y} - \hat{\beta}_1 \bar{x}$

where $\quad \text{SS}_{xy} = \sum(x_i - \bar{x})(y_i - \bar{y}) = \sum x_i y_i - \dfrac{\left(\sum x_i\right)\left(\sum y_i\right)}{n}$

$\qquad \text{SS}_{xx} = \sum(x_i - \bar{x})^2 = \sum x_i^2 - \dfrac{\left(\sum x_i\right)^2}{n}$

$\qquad n = \text{Sample size}$

Preliminary computations for finding the least squares line for the advertising–sales example are presented in Table 10.3. We can now calculate

$$\text{SS}_{xy} = \sum x_i y_i - \frac{\left(\sum x_i\right)\left(\sum y_i\right)}{5} = 37 - \frac{(15)(10)}{5} = 37 - 30 = 7$$

$$\text{SS}_{xx} = \sum x_i^2 - \frac{\left(\sum x_i\right)^2}{5} = 55 - \frac{(15)^2}{5} = 55 - 45 = 10$$

Then the slope of the least squares line is

$$\hat{\beta}_1 = \frac{\text{SS}_{xy}}{\text{SS}_{xx}} = \frac{7}{10} = .7$$

---

*Students who are familiar with calculus should note that the values of β_0 and β_1 that minimize SSE $= \Sigma(y_i - \hat{y}_i)^2$ are obtained by setting the two partial derivatives $\partial\text{SSE}/\partial\beta_0$ and $\partial\text{SSE}/\partial\beta_1$ equal to 0. The solutions to these two equations yield the formulas shown in the box. Furthermore, we denote the *sample* solutions to the equations by $\hat{\beta}_0$ and $\hat{\beta}_1$, where the "hat" denotes that these are sample estimates of the true population intercept β_0 and true population slope β_1.

TABLE 10.3   **Preliminary Computations for Advertising–Sales Example**

x_i	y_i	x_i^2	$x_i y_i$
1	1	1	1
2	1	4	2
3	2	9	6
4	2	16	8
5	4	25	20
Totals $\sum x_i = 15$	$\sum y_i = 10$	$\sum x_i^2 = 55$	$\sum x_i y_i = 37$

and the y-intercept is

$$\hat{\beta}_0 = \bar{y} - \hat{\beta}_1 \bar{x} = \frac{\sum y_i}{5} - \hat{\beta}_1 \frac{\sum x_i}{5}$$

$$= \frac{10}{5} - (.7)\left(\frac{15}{5}\right) = 2 - (.7)(3) = 2 - 2.1 = -.1$$

The least squares line is thus

$$\hat{y} = \hat{\beta}_0 + \hat{\beta}_1 x = -.1 + .7x$$

The graph of this line is shown in Figure 10.5.

The predicted value of y for a given value of x can be obtained by substituting into the formula for the least squares line. Thus, when $x = 2$ we predict y to be

$$\hat{y} = -.1 + .7x = -.1 + .7(2) = 1.3$$

We show how to find a prediction interval for y in Section 10.8.

The observed and predicted values of y, the deviations of the y values about their predicted values, and the squares of these deviations are shown in Table 10.4. Note that the sum of squares of the deviations, SSE, is 1.10, and (as we

FIGURE 10.5
The line $\hat{y} = -.1 + .7x$
fit to the data

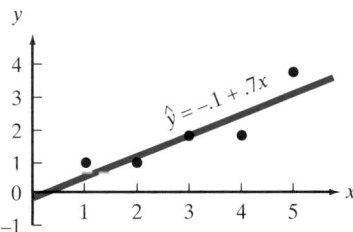

TABLE 10.4   **Comparing Observed and Predicted Values for the Least Squares Prediction Equation**

x	y	$\hat{y} = -.1 + .7x$	$(y - \hat{y})$	$(y - \hat{y})^2$
1	1	.6	$(1 - .6) = .4$	.16
2	1	1.3	$(1 - 1.3) = -.3$	.09
3	2	2.0	$(2 - 2.0) = 0$	.00
4	2	2.7	$(2 - 2.7) = -.7$	.49
5	4	3.4	$(4 - 3.4) = .6$	.36
			Sum of errors = 0	SSE = 1.10

Dependent Variable: Y

                        Analysis of Variance

                              Sum of   Mean
        Source   DF   Squares   Square   F Value   Prob>F

        Model   1   4.90000   4.90000   13.364   0.0354
        Error   3   1.10000   0.36667
        C Total   4   6.00000

            Root MSE   0.60553   R-square   0.8167
            Dep Mean   2.00000   Adj R-sq   0.7556
            C.V.   30.27650

                        Parameter Estimates

                        Parameter   Standard   T for HO:
        Variable   DF   Estimate   Error   Parameter=0   Prob>|T|

        INTERCEP   1   -0.100000   0.63508530   -0.157   0.8849
        X   1   0.700000   0.19148542   3.656   0.0354

FIGURE 10.6 SAS printout for advertising–sales regression

would expect) this is less than the SSE = 2.0 obtained in Table 10.2 for the visually fitted line.

The calculations required to obtain $\hat{\beta}_0, \hat{\beta}_1$, and SSE in simple linear regression, although straightforward, can become rather tedious. Even with the use of a pocket calculator, the process is laborious and susceptible to error, especially when the sample size is large. Fortunately, the use of a statistical software package can significantly reduce the labor involved in regression calculations. The SAS output for the simple linear regression of the data in Table 10.1 is displayed in Figure 10.6. The values of $\hat{\beta}_0$ and $\hat{\beta}_1$ are highlighted on the SAS printout under the **Parameter Estimate** column in the rows labeled **INTERCEP** and **X**, respectively. These values, $\hat{\beta}_0 = -.1$ and $\hat{\beta}_1 = .7$, agree exactly with our hand-calculated values. The value of SSE = 1.10 is also highlighted in Figure 10.6, under the **Sum of Squares** column in the row labeled **Error**.

Whether you use a hand calculator or a computer, it is important that you be able to interpret the intercept and slope in terms of the data being utilized to fit the model. In the advertising–sales example, the estimated y-intercept, $\hat{\beta}_0 = -.1$, appears to imply that the estimated mean sales revenue is equal to −.1, or −$100, when the advertising expenditure, x, is equal to $0. Since negative sales revenues are not possible, this seems to make the model nonsensical. However, *the model parameters should be interpreted only within the sampled range of the independent variable*—in this case, for advertising expenditures between $100 and $500. Thus, the y-intercept—which is, by definition, at x = 0 ($0 advertising expenditure)—is not within the range of the sampled values of x and is not subject to meaningful interpretation.

The slope of the least squares line, $\hat{\beta}_1 = -.7$, implies that for every unit increase of x, the mean value of y is estimated to increase by .7 unit. In terms of this example, for every $100 increase in advertising, the mean sales revenue is estimated to increase by $700 *over the sampled range of advertising expenditures from $100 to $500.* Thus, the model does not imply that increasing the advertising expenditures from $500 to $1,000 will result in an increase in mean sales of $3,500, because the range of x in the sample does not extend to $1,000 (x = 10). Be careful to interpret the estimated parameters only within the sampled range of x.

Even when the interpretations of the estimated parameters are meaningful, we need to remember that they are only estimates based on the sample. As such, their values will typically change in repeated sampling. How much confidence do we have that the estimated slope, $\hat{\beta}_1$, accurately approximates the true slope, β_1? This requires statistical inference, in the form of confidence intervals and tests of hypotheses, which we address in Section 10.5.

To summarize, we defined the best-fitting straight line to be the one that minimizes the sum of squared errors around the line, and we called it the least squares line. We should interpret the least squares line only within the sampled range of the independent variable. In subsequent sections we show how to make statistical inferences about the model.

EXERCISES   10.10–10.21

Note: Exercises marked with 💾 *contain data for computer analysis on a 3.5" disk (file name in parentheses).*

Learning the Mechanics

10.10 The following table is similar to Table 10.3. It is used for making the preliminary computations for finding the least squares line for the given pairs of x and y values.

x_i	y_i	x_i^2	$x_i y_i$
7	2		
4	4		
6	2		
2	5		
1	7		
1	6		
3	5		

Totals	$\sum x_i =$	$\sum y_i =$	$\sum x_i^2 =$	$\sum x_i y_i =$

a. Complete the table. **b.** Find SS_{xy}.
c. Find SS_{xx}. **d.** Find $\hat{\beta}_1$.
e. Find $\bar{x}$ and $\bar{y}$. **f.** Find $\hat{\beta}_0$.
g. Find the least squares line.

10.11 Refer to Exercise 10.10. After the least squares line has been obtained, the table below (which is similar to Table 10.4) can be used for (1) comparing the observed and the predicted values of y, and (2) computing SSE.

x	y	$\hat{y}$	$(y - \hat{y})$	$(y - \hat{y})^2$
7	2			
4	4			
6	2			
2	5			
1	7			
1	6			
3	5			

			$\sum(y - \hat{y}) =$	$SSE = \sum(y - \hat{y})^2 =$

a. Complete the table.
b. Plot the least squares line on a scattergram of the data. Plot the following line on the same graph: $\hat{y} = 14 - 2.5x$.
c. Show that SSE is larger for the line in part **b** than it is for the least squares line.

10.12 Construct a scattergram for the data in the following table.

x	.5	1	1.5
y	2	1	3

a. Plot the following two lines on your scattergram:
$$y = 3 - x \quad \text{and} \quad y = 1 + x$$
b. Which of these lines would you choose to characterize the relationship between x and y? Explain.
c. Show that the sum of errors for both of these lines equals 0.
d. Which of these lines has the smaller SSE?
e. Find the least squares line for the data and compare it to the two lines described in part **a**.

10.13 Consider the following pairs of measurements:

x	8	5	4	6	2	5	3
y	1	3	6	3	7	2	5

a. Construct a scattergram for these data.
b. What does the scattergram suggest about the relationship between x and y?
c. Find the least squares estimates of β_0 and β_1 on the MINITAB printout on page 440.
d. Plot the least squares line on your scattergram. Does the line appear to fit the data well? Explain.
e. Interpret the y-intercept and slope of the least squares line. Over what range of x are these interpretations meaningful?

```
The regression equation is
Y = 8.54 - 0.994 X

Predictor        Coef       Stdev      t-ratio        p
Constant        8.543       1.117         7.65     0.001
X             -0.9939      0.2208        -4.50     0.006

s = 1.069        R-sq = 80.2%      R-sq(adj) = 76.2%

Analysis of Variance

SOURCE          DF          SS          MS          F          p
Regression       1      23.144      23.144      20.25      0.006
Error            5       5.713       1.143
Total            6      28.857
```

10.14 Suppose that $n = 100$ recent residential home sales in a city are used to fit a least squares straight-line model relating the sale price, y, to the square feet of living space, x. Homes in the sample range from 1,500 square feet to 4,000 square feet of living space, and the resulting least squares equation is

$$\hat{y} = -30,000 + 70x$$

a. What is the underlying hypothesized probabilistic model for this application? What does it imply about the relationship between the mean sale price and living space?
b. Identify the least squares estimates of the y-intercept and slope of the model.
c. Interpret the least squares estimate of the y-intercept. Is it meaningful for this application? Why?
d. Interpret the least squares estimate of the slope of the model. Over what range of x is the interpretation meaningful?
e. Use the least squares model to estimate the mean sale price of a 3,000-square-foot home. Is the estimate meaningful? Explain.
f. Use the least squares model to estimate the mean sale price of a 5,000-square-foot home. Is the estimate meaningful? Explain.

[*Note:* We show how to measure the statistical reliability of these least squares estimates in subsequent sections.]

Applying the Concepts

10.15 (X10.015) Individuals who report perceived wrongdoing of a corporation or public agency are known as *whistle blowers*. Two researchers developed an index to measure the extent of retaliation against a whistle blower (*Journal of Applied Psychology*, 1986). The index was based on the number of forms of reprisal actually experienced, the number of forms of reprisal threatened, and the number of people within the organization (e.g., coworkers or immediate supervisor) who retaliated against them. The table lists the retalia-

tion index (higher numbers indicate more extensive retaliation) and salary for a sample of 15 whistle blowers from federal agencies.

Retaliation Index	Salary	Retaliation Index	Salary
301	$62,000	535	$19,800
550	36,500	455	44,000
755	21,600	615	46,600
327	24,000	700	15,100
500	30,100	650	70,000
377	35,000	630	21,000
290	47,500	360	16,900
452	54,000		

Source: Data adapted from Near, J. P., and Miceli, M. P. "Retaliation against whistle blowers: Predictors and effects." *Journal of Applied Psychology*, Vol. 71, No. 1, 1986, pp. 137–145.

a. Construct a scattergram for the data. Does it appear that the extent of retaliation increases, decreases, or stays the same with an increase in salary? Explain.
b. Use the method of least squares to fit a straight line to the data.
c. Graph the least squares line on your scattergram. Does the least squares line support your answer to the question in part **a**? Explain.
d. Interpret the y-intercept, $\hat{\beta}_0$, of the least squares line in terms of this application. Is the interpretation meaningful?
e. Interpret the slope, $\hat{\beta}_1$, of the least squares line in terms of this application. Over what range of x is this interpretation meaningful?

10.16 (X10.016) Due primarily to the price controls of the Organization of Petroleum Exporting Countries (OPEC), a cartel of crude-oil suppliers, the price of crude oil rose dramatically from the mid-1970s to the mid-1980s. As a result, motorists saw an upward spiral in gasoline prices. The data in the table on page 441 are typical prices for a gallon of regular leaded gasoline and a barrel of crude oil (refiner acquisition cost) for the indicated years.
a. Use the data to calculate the least squares line that describes the relationship between

Year	Gasoline, y (¢/gal.)	Crude Oil, x ($/bbl.)
1975	57	10.38
1976	59	10.89
1977	62	11.96
1978	63	12.46
1979	86	17.72
1980	119	28.07
1981	131	35.24
1982	122	31.87
1983	116	28.99
1984	113	28.63
1985	112	26.75
1986	86	14.55
1987	90	17.90
1988	90	14.67
1989	100	17.97
1990	115	22.23
1991	72	16.54
1992	71	15.99
1993	75	14.24

Source: U.S. Bureau of the Census, *Statistical Abstract of the United States: 1982–1995.*

Team	Games Won, y	Team Batting Average, x
Cleveland	99	.293
New York	92	.288
Boston	85	.283
Toronto	74	.259
Texas	90	.284
Detroit	53	.256
Minnesota	78	.288
Baltimore	88	.274
California	70	.276
Milwaukee	80	.279
Seattle	85	.287
Kansas City	75	.267
Oakland	78	.265
Chicago	85	.281

Source: Compiled by the Major League Baseball (MLB) Baseball Information System, 1996.

the price of a gallon of gasoline and the price of a barrel of crude oil over the period 1975–1985.

b. Construct a scattergram of *all* the data.

c. Plot your least squares line on the scattergram. Does your least squares line appear to be an appropriate characterization of the relationship between *y* and *x* over the period 1975–1985?

d. According to your model, if the price of crude oil fell to $15 per barrel, to what level (approximately) would the price of regular leaded gasoline fall? Justify your answer.

10.17 Baseball wisdom says if you can't hit, you can't win. But is the number of games won by a major league baseball team in a season related to the team's batting average? The table (upper right) shows the number of games won and the batting averages for the 14 teams in the American League for the 1996 season, for games played through September 29.

a. If you were to model the relationship between the mean (or expected) number of games won by a major league team and the team's batting average *x*, using a straight line, would you expect the slope of the line to be positive or negative? Explain.

b. Construct a scattergram of the data. Does the pattern revealed by the scattergram agree with your answer to part **a**?

c. An SPSS printout of the simple linear regression is provided at the top of page 442. Find the estimates of the β's on the printout and write the equation of the least squares line.

d. Graph the least squares line on your scattergram. Does your least squares line seem to fit the points on your scattergram?

e. Does the mean (or expected) number of games won appear to be strongly related to a team's batting average? Explain.

f. Interpret the values of $\hat{\beta}_0$ and $\hat{\beta}_1$ in the words of the problem.

10.18 (X10.018) The long jump is a track and field event in which a competitor attempts to jump a maximum distance into a sandpit after a running start. At the edge of the sandpit is a takeoff board. Jumpers usually try to plant their toes at the front edge of this board to maximize jumping distance. The absolute distance between the front edge of the takeoff board and the spot where the toe actually lands on the board prior to jumping is called "takeoff error." Is takeoff error in the long jump linearly related to best jumping distance? To answer this question, kinesiology researchers videotaped the performances of 18 novice long jumpers at a high school track meet (*Journal of Applied Biomechanics,* May 1995). The average takeoff error, *x*, and best jumping distance (out of three jumps), *y*, for each jumper are recorded in the table on page 442.

a. Propose a straight-line model relating *y* to *x*.

b. Construct a scattergram for the data. Is there visual evidence of a linear relationship between *y* and *x*?

c. A MINITAB printout of the simple linear regression analysis is given below the table. Find the estimates of β_0 and β_1 on the printout.

d. Graph the least squares line on the scattergram. Does the least squares line seem to fit the points on the scattergram?

e. Interpret the least squares intercept and slope.

10.19 A recent winner of Britain's Best Factory Award, NCR Ltd., manufactures automated teller

```
* * * *     M U L T I P L E      R E G R E S S I O N    * * * *
Equation Number 1 Dependent Variable..   WINS

Variable(s) Entered on Step Number
   1.. BATAVE

Multiple R              .78592
R Square                .61767
Adjusted R Square       .58581
Standard Error         7.21028

Analysis of Variance
                    DF        Sum of Squares        Mean Square
Regression           1           1007.85692         1007.85692
Residual            12            623.85737           51.98811

F =     19.38630          Signif F =  .0009

-------------------Variables in the Equation ---------------------

Variable             B           SE B         Beta           T   Sig T

BATAVE        765.101228    173.768675     .785918       4.403   .0009
(Constant)   -131.185197     48.197286                  -2.722   .0185
```

Jumper	Best Jumping Distance y (meters)	Average Takeoff Error, x (meters)	Jumper	Best Jumping Distance y (meters)	Average Takeoff Error, x (meters)
1	5.30	.09	10	5.77	.09
2	5.55	.17	11	5.12	.13
3	5.47	.19	12	5.77	.16
4	5.45	.24	13	6.22	.03
5	5.07	.16	14	5.82	.50
6	5.32	.22	15	5.15	.13
7	6.15	.09	16	4.92	.04
8	4.70	.12	17	5.20	.07
9	5.22	.09	18	5.42	.04

Source: W. P. Berg and N. L. Greer, "A kinematic profile of the approach run of novice long jumpers." *Journal of Applied Biomechanics,* Vol. 11, No. 2, May 1995, p. 147 (Table 1).

```
The regression equation is
DISTANCE = 5.35 + 0.530 TAKOFFER

Predictor      Coef      Stdev      t-ratio         p
Constant     5.3480     0.1635       32.71     0.000
TAKOFFER     0.5299     0.9254        0.57     0.575

s = 0.4115      R-sq = 2.0%      R-sq(adj) = 0.0%

Analysis of Variance

SOURCE       DF         SS          MS        F         p
Regression    1      0.0555      0.0555     0.33     0.575
Error        16      2.7091      0.1693
Total        17      2.7646
```

machines. NCR attributes its success to Total Quality Management (TQM) strategies, including reducing inventory levels through just-in-time (JIT) inventory ordering policies, instructing operators to stop the assembly line when quality problems are detected, and using only high-quality suppliers. This last strategy helped NCR cut the number of suppliers from 430 to 180 between 1980 and 1989. It saw a corresponding increase in the percentage of products that passed final

	1980	1982	1985	1987	1989
Number of Suppliers, x	430	395	360	270	180
Products Passing Inspection, y (%)	40	60	80	88	98

Source: Lee-Mortimer, A. "Best of the best." *Total Quality Management,* December 1990, p. 317.

inspection, from 40% to 98%. Data on number of suppliers x and percent of products passing inspection y for five years between 1980 and 1989 are shown in the table above.

a. Give the equation of the straight-line model relating y to x.

b. Find the least squares line.

c. Plot the data and graph the least squares line as a check on your calculations.

d. Interpret the least squares estimates $\hat{\beta}_0$ and $\hat{\beta}_1$ in the context of the problem.

10.20 Each year *Sales and Marketing Management* determines the "effective buying income" (EBI) of the average household in a state. Can the EBI be used to predict retail sales per household in the store-group category "eating and drinking places"?

a. Use the data for 13 states given in the table below to find the least squares line relating retail sales per household (y) to average household EBI (x).

b. Plot the least squares line, as well as the actual data points, on a scattergram.

c. Based on the graph, part **b**, give your opinion regarding the predictive ability of the least squares line.

10.21 The downsizing and restructuring that took place in corporate America during the first half of the 1990s encouraged both laid off middle managers and recent graduates of business schools to become entrepreneurs and start their own businesses. Assuming a business start-up does well, how fast will it grow? Can it expect to need 10 employees in

three years or 50 or 100? To answer these questions, a random sample of 12 firms were drawn from the *Inc. Magazine's* "1996 Ranking of the Fastest-Growing Private Companies in America." The age (in years since 1995), x, and number of employees (in 1995), y, of each firm are recorded in the table. SAS was used to conduct a simple linear regression analysis for the model, $E(y) = \beta_0 + \beta_1 x$. The printout is on page 444.

Firm	Age, x (years)	Number of Employees, y
General Shelters of Texas	5	43
Productivity Point International	5	52
K.C. Oswald	4	9
Multimax	7	40
Pay + Benefits	5	6
Radio Spirits	6	12
KRA	14	200
Consulting Partners	5	76
Apex Instruments	7	15
Portable Products	6	40
Progressive System Technology	5	65
Viking Components	7	175

Source: Inc. 500, October 22, 1996, pp. 103–132.

a. Plot the data in a scattergram. Does the number of employees at a fast-growing firm appear to increase linearly as the firm's age increases?

b. Find the estimates of β_0 and β_1 in the SAS printout. Interpret their values.

State	Average Household Buying Income ($)	Retail Sales: Eating and Drinking Places ($ per household)
Connecticut	60,998	2,553.8
New Jersey	63,853	2,154.8
Michigan	46,915	2,523.3
Minnesota	44,717	2,278.6
Florida	42,442	2,475.8
South Carolina	37,848	2,358.4
Mississippi	34,490	1,538.4
Oklahoma	34,830	2,063.1
Texas	44,729	2,363.5
Colorado	44,571	3,214.9
Utah	43,421	2,653.8
California	50,713	2,215.0
Oregon	40,597	2,144.0

Source: Sales and Marketing Management, 1995.

```
Dependent Variable: NUMBER
                        Analysis of Variance

                            Sum of          Mean
        Source          DF  Squares         Square       F Value     Prob>F

        Model           1   23536.50149   23536.50149     11.451     0.0070
        Error          10   20554.41518    2055.44152
        C Total        11   44090.91667

            Root MSE       45.33698      R-square        0.5338
            Dep Mean       61.08333      Adj R-sq        0.4872
            C.V.           74.22152

                        Parameter Estimates

                       Parameter       Standard      T for HO:
        Variable   DF   Estimate          Error     Parameter=0    Prob > |T|

        INTERCEP    1   -51.361607     35.71379104      -1.438        0.1809
        AGE         1    17.754464      5.24673562       3.384        0.0070
```

10.3   MODEL ASSUMPTIONS

In Section 10.2 we assumed that the probabilistic model relating the firm's sales revenue y to the advertising dollars is

$$y = \beta_0 + \beta_1 x + \epsilon$$

We also recall that the least squares estimate of the deterministic component of the model, $\beta_0 + \beta_1 x$ is

$$\hat{y} = \hat{\beta}_0 + \hat{\beta}_1 x = -.1 + .7x$$

Now we turn our attention to the random component ϵ of the probabilistic model and its relation to the errors in estimating β_0 and β_1. We will use a probability distribution to characterize the behavior of ϵ. We will see how the probability distribution of ϵ determines how well the model describes the relationship between the dependent variable y and the independent variable x.

Step 3 in a regression analysis requires us to specify the probability distribution of the random error ϵ. We will make four basic assumptions about the general form of this probability distribution:

Assumption 1: The mean of the probability distribution of ϵ is 0. That is, the average of the values of ϵ over an infinitely long series of experiments is 0 for each setting of the independent variable x. This assumption implies that the mean value of y, $E(y)$, for a given value of x is $E(y) = \beta_0 + \beta_1 x$.

Assumption 2: The variance of the probability distribution of ϵ is constant for all settings of the independent variable x. For our straight-line model, this assumption means that the variance of ϵ is equal to a constant, say σ^2, for all values of x.

Assumption 3: The probability distribution of ϵ is normal.

Assumption 4: The values of ϵ associated with any two observed values of y are independent. That is, the value of ϵ associated with one value of y has no effect on the values of ϵ associated with other y values.

The implications of the first three assumptions can be seen in Figure 10.7, which shows distributions of errors for three values of x, namely, x_1, x_2, and x_3. Note that the relative frequency distributions of the errors are normal with a

FIGURE 10.7
The probability
distribution of ϵ

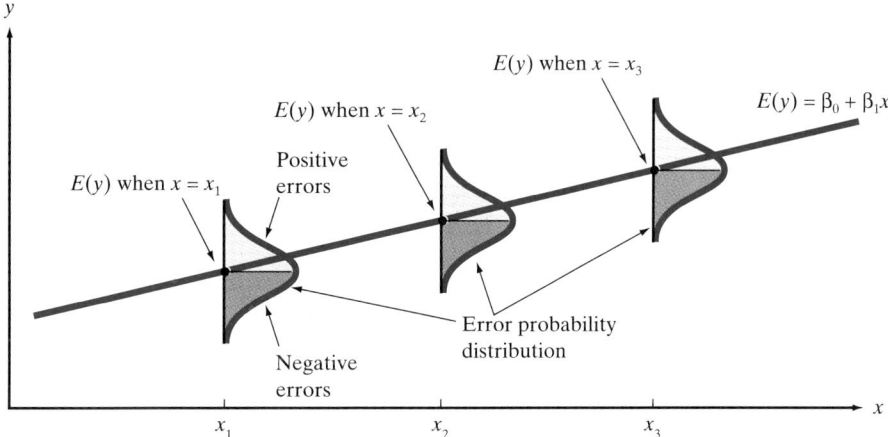

mean of 0 and a constant variance σ^2. (All the distributions shown have the same amount of spread or variability.) The straight line shown in Figure 10.7 is the line of means. It indicates the mean value of y for a given value of x. We denote this mean value as $E(y)$. Then, the line of means is given by the equation

$$E(y) = \beta_0 + \beta_1 x$$

These assumptions make it possible for us to develop measures of reliability for the least squares estimators and to develop hypothesis tests for examining the usefulness of the least squares line. We have various techniques for checking the validity of these assumptions, and we have remedies to apply when they appear to be invalid. Several of these remedies are discussed in Chapters 11 and 12. Fortunately, the assumptions need not hold exactly in order for least squares estimators to be useful. The assumptions will be satisfied adequately for many applications encountered in practice.

10.4   AN ESTIMATOR OF σ^2

It seems reasonable to assume that the greater the variability of the random error ϵ (which is measured by its variance σ^2), the greater will be the errors in the estimation of the model parameters β_0 and β_1 and in the error of prediction when $\hat{y}$ is used to predict y for some value of x. Consequently, you should not be surprised, as we proceed through this chapter, to find that σ^2 appears in the formulas for all confidence intervals and test statistics that we will be using.

Estimation of σ^2 for a (First-Order) Straight-Line Model

$$s^2 = \frac{\text{SSE}}{\text{Degrees of freedom for error}} = \frac{\text{SSE}}{n-2}$$

where $\text{SSE} = \sum(y_i - \hat{y}_i)^2 = \text{SS}_{yy} - \hat{\beta}_1 \text{SS}_{xy}$

$$\text{SS}_{yy} = \sum(y_i - \bar{y})^2 = \sum y_i^2 - \frac{\left(\sum y_i\right)^2}{n}$$

---

continued

To estimate the standard deviation σ of ϵ, we calculate

$$s = \sqrt{s^2} = \sqrt{\frac{\text{SSE}}{n-2}}$$

We will refer to s as the **estimated standard error of the regression model**.

Warning: When performing these calculations, you may be tempted to round the calculated values of SS_{yy}, $\hat{\beta}_1$, and SS_{xy}. Be certain to carry at least six significant figures for each of these quantities to avoid substantial errors in calculation of the SSE.

In most practical situations, σ^2 is unknown and we must use our data to estimate its value. The best estimate of σ^2, denoted by s^2, is obtained by dividing the sum of squares of the deviations of the y values from the prediction line,

$$\text{SSE} = \sum(y_i - \hat{y}_i)^2$$

by the number of degrees of freedom associated with this quantity. We use 2 df to estimate the two parameters β_0 and β_1 in the straight-line model, leaving $(n-2)$ df for the error variance estimation.

In the advertising–sales example, we previously calculated SSE = 1.10 for the least squares line $\hat{y} = -.1 + .7x$. Recalling that there were $n = 5$ data points, we have $n - 2 = 5 - 2 = 3$ df for estimating σ^2. Thus,

$$s^2 = \frac{\text{SSE}}{n-2} = \frac{1.10}{3} = .367$$

is the estimated variance, and

$$s = \sqrt{.367} = .61$$

is the standard error of the regression model.

The values of s^2 and s can also be obtained from a simple linear regression printout. The SAS printout for the advertising–sales example is reproduced in Figure 10.8. The value of s^2 is highlighted on the printout in the **Mean Square** column in the row labeled **Error**. (In regression, the estimate of σ^2 is called Mean Square for Error, or MSE.) The value, $s^2 = .36667$, rounded to three decimal places agrees with the one calculated by hand. The value of s is highlighted in Figure 10.8 next to the heading **Root MSE**. This value, $s = .60553$, agrees (except for rounding) with our hand-calculated value.

You may be able to grasp s intuitively by recalling the interpretation of a standard deviation given in Chapter 2 and remembering that the least squares line estimates the mean value of y for a given value of x. Since s measures the spread of the distribution of y values about the least squares line, we should not be surprised to find that most of the observations lie within $2s$, or $2(.61) = 1.22$, of the least squares line. For this simple example (only five data points), all five sales revenue values fall within $2s$ (or \$1,220) of the least squares line. In Section 10.8, we use s to evaluate the error of prediction when the least squares line is used to predict a value of y to be observed for a given value of x.

Interpretation of s, the Estimated Standard Deviation of ϵ

We expect most of the observed y values to lie within $2s$ of their respective least squares predicted values, $\hat{y}$.

Dependent Variable: Y

Analysis of Variance

Source	DF	Sum of Squares	Mean Square	F Value	Prob>F
Model	1	4.90000	4.90000	13.364	0.0354
Error	3	1.10000	0.36667		
C Total	4	6.00000			

Root MSE	0.60553	R-square	0.8167	
Dep Mean	2.00000	Adj R-sq	0.7556	
C.V.	30.27650			

Parameter Estimates

Variable	DF	Parameter Estimate	Standard Error	T for HO: Parameter=0	Prob > |T|
INTERCEP	1	-0.100000	0.63508530	-0.157	0.8849
X	1	0.700000	0.19148542	3.656	0.0354

FIGURE 10.8   SAS printout for advertising expenditure–sales revenue example

---

EXERCISES   10.22–10.30

Note: Exercises marked with 💾 *contain data for computer analysis on a 3.5" disk (file name in parentheses).*

Learning the Mechanics

10.22   Calculate SSE and s^2 for each of the following cases:
   a. $n = 20, \text{SS}_{yy} = 95, \text{SS}_{xy} = 50, \hat{\beta}_1 = .75$
   b. $n = 40, \ \Sigma y^2 = 860, \ \Sigma y = 50, \ \text{SS}_{xy} = 2{,}700, \ \hat{\beta}_1 = .2$
   c. $n = 10, \Sigma(y_i - \bar{y})^2 = 58, \text{SS}_{xy} = 91, \text{SS}_{xx} = 170$

10.23   Suppose you fit a least squares line to 26 data points and the calculated value of SSE is 8.34.
   a. Find s^2, the estimator of σ^2 (the variance of the random error term ϵ).
   b. What is the largest deviation that you might expect between any one of the 26 points and the least squares line?

10.24   Visually compare the scattergrams shown below. If a least squares line were determined for each data set, which do you think would have the smallest variance, s^2? Explain.

10.25   Refer to Exercises 10.10 and 10.13. Calculate SSE, s^2, and s for the least squares lines obtained in these exercises. Interpret the standard error of the regression model, s, for each.

Applying the Concepts

10.26   Prior to the 1970s the developing countries played a small role in world trade because their own economic policies hindered integration with the world economy. However, many of these countries have since changed their policies and vastly improved their importance to the global economy (*World Economy,* July 1992). Data for investigating the relationship between developing coun-

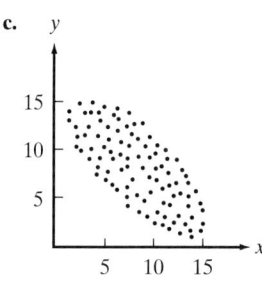

	1950	1960	1970	1980	1990
Industrial Countries' Imports, x	39.8	85.4	226.9	1,370.2	2,237.9
Developing Countries' Imports, y	21.1	40.1	75.6	556.4	819.4

tries and industrial countries in annual import levels is shown in the table above (given in billions of U.S. dollars).

a. Given that $SS_{xx} = 3,809,368.452$, $SS_{xy} = 1,419,492.796$, $SS_{yy} = 531,174.148$, $\bar{x} = 792.04$, and $\bar{y} = 302.52$, fit a least squares line to the data. Plot the data points and graph the least squares line as a check on your calculations.

b. According to your least squares line, approximately what would you expect annual imports for developing countries to be if annual imports for industrial countries were $1,600 billion?

c. Calculate SSE and s^2.

d. Interpret the standard deviation s in the context of this problem.

10.27 Refer to the simple linear regression relating games won by a major league baseball team y to team batting average x, Exercise 10.17. The SPSS printout is reproduced below.

a. Find SSE, s^2, and s on the printout.

b. Interpret the value of s.

10.28 Refer to the simple linear regression relating number of employees y to age x of a fast-growing firm, Exercise 10.21. The SAS printout is reproduced on page 449.

a. Find SSE, s^2, and s on the printout.

b. Interpret the value of s.

10.29 A much larger proportion of U.S. teenagers are working while attending high school than was the case a decade ago. These heavy workloads often result in underachievement in the classroom and lower grades. As a result, many states are imposing tighter child labor laws. A study of high school students in California and Wisconsin showed that those who worked only a few hours per week had the highest grade point averages (*Newsweek*, Nov. 16, 1992). The following table shows grade point averages (GPAs) and number of hours worked per week for a sample of five students. Consider a simple linear regression relating GPA (y) to hours worked (x).

Grade Point Average, y	2.93	3.00	2.86	3.04	2.66
Hours Worked per Week, x	12	0	17	5	21

a. Find the equation of the least squares line.

b. Plot the data and graph the least squares line.

c. Predict the grade point average of a high school student who works 10 hours per week. Repeat this for one who works 16 hours per week.

d. Compute SSE and s.

```
        * * * *   MULTIPLE   REGRESSION   * * * *
Equation Number 1      Dependent Variable..    WINS

Variable(s) Entered on Step Number
    1..    BATAVE

Multiple R            .78592
R Square              .61767
Adjusted R Square     .58581
Standard Error       7.21028

Analysis of Variance
                   DF      Sum of Squares      Mean Square
Regression          1         1007.85692       1007.85692
Residual           12          623.85737         51.98811

F =      19.38630      Signif F =   .0009

------------------ Variables in the Equation --------------------

Variable          B         SE B        Beta         T    Sig T

BATAVE     765.101228   173.768675    .785918     4.403   .0009
(Constant) -131.185197   48.197286               -2.722   .0185
```

Dependent Variable: NUMBER

Analysis of Variance

Source	DF	Sum of Squares	Mean Square	F Value	Prob>F
Model	1	23536.50149	23536.50149	11.451	0.0070
Error	10	20554.41518	2055.44152		
C Total	11	44090.91667			

Root MSE	45.33698	R-square	0.5338
Dep Mean	61.08333	Adj R-sq	0.4872
C.V.	74.22152		

Parameter Estimates

Variable	DF	Parameter Estimate	Standard Error	T for HO: Parameter=0	Prob > |T|
INTERCEP	1	-51.361607	35.71379104	-1.438	0.1809
AGE	1	17.754464	5.24673562	3.384	0.0070

e. Within what approximate distance do you expect your predictions in part **c** to fall from the student's true grade point average? [*Note:* A more precise measure of reliability for these predictions is discussed in Section 10.8.]

10.30 **(X10.030)** To improve the quality of the output of any production process, it is necessary first to understand the capabilities of the process (Gitlow, *et al., Quality Management: Tools and Methods for Improvement,* 1995). In a particular manufacturing process, the useful life of a cutting tool is related to the speed at which the tool is operated. It is necessary to understand this relationship in order to predict when the tool should be replaced and how many spare tools should be available. The data in the table below were derived from life tests for the two different brands of cutting tools currently used in the production process.

a. Construct a scattergram for each brand of cutting tool.
b. For each brand, the method of least squares was used to model the relationship between useful life and cutting speed. Find the least squares line for each brand on the EXCEL printouts shown on page 450.
c. Locate SSE, s^2, and s for each least squares line on the printouts.
d. For a cutting speed of 70 meters per minute, find $\hat{y} \pm 2s$ for each least squares line.
e. For which brand would you feel more confident in using the least squares line to predict useful life for a given cutting speed? Explain.

	USEFUL LIFE (HOURS)	
Cutting Speed (meters per minute)	Brand A	Brand B
30	4.5	6.0
30	3.5	6.5
30	5.2	5.0
40	5.2	6.0
40	4.0	4.5
40	2.5	5.0
50	4.4	4.5
50	2.8	4.0
50	1.0	3.7
60	4.0	3.8
60	2.0	3.0
60	1.1	2.4
70	1.1	1.5
70	.5	2.0
70	3.0	1.0

EXCEL Output: Brand A

SUMMARY OUTPUT

Regression Statistics	
Multiple R	0.6737515
R Square	0.453941084
Adjusted R Square	0.411936552
Standard Error	1.210721336
Observations	15

ANOVA

	df	SS	MS	F	Significance F
Regression	1	15.84133333	15.84133333	10.80695494	0.00588884
Residual	13	19.056	1.465846154		
Total	14	34.89733333			

	Coefficients	Standard Error	t Stat	P-value	Lower 95%	Upper 95%
Intercept	6.62	1.14859111	5.763582829	6.55988E-05	4.138620245	9.101379755
Speed(x)	-0.072666667	0.022104646	-3.287393335	0.00588884	-0.120420842	-0.024912491

EXCEL Output: Brand B

SUMMARY OUTPUT

Regression Statistics	
Multiple R	0.937007633
R Square	0.877983304
Adjusted R Square	0.868597404
Standard Error	0.609728817
Observations	15

ANOVA

	df	SS	MS	F	Significance F
Regression	1	34.77633333	34.77633333	93.5427961	2.64643E-07
Residual	13	4.833	0.371769231		
Total	14	39.60933333			

	Coefficients	Standard Error	t Stat	P-value	Lower 95%	Upper 95%
Intercept	9.31	0.578439545	16.09502683	5.7707E-10	8.060357577	10.55964242
Speed(x)	-0.10766667	0.011132074	-9.67175248	2.6464E-07	-0.1317605	-0.08361729

10.5 ASSESSING THE UTILITY OF THE MODEL: MAKING INFERENCES ABOUT THE SLOPE β_1

Now that we have specified the probability distribution of ϵ and found an estimate of the variance σ^2, we are ready to make statistical inferences about the model's usefulness for predicting the response y. This is step 4 in our regression modeling procedure.

Refer again to the data of Table 10.1 and suppose the appliance store's sales revenue is *completely unrelated* to the advertising expenditure. What could be said about the values of β_0 and β_1 in the hypothesized probabilistic model

$$y = \beta_0 + \beta_1 x + \epsilon$$

if x contributes no information for the prediction of y? The implication is that the mean of y—that is, the deterministic part of the model $E(y) = \beta_0 + \beta_1 x$—does not change as x changes. In the straight-line model, this means that the true slope, β_1, is equal to 0 (see Figure 10.9). Therefore, to test the null hypothesis that the linear model contributes no information for the prediction of y against the alternative hypothesis that the linear model is useful for predicting y, we test

$$H_0: \beta_1 = 0$$

$$H_a: \beta_1 \neq 0$$

If the data support the alternative hypothesis, we will conclude that x does contribute information for the prediction of y using the straight-line model (although the true relationship between $E(y)$ and x could be more complex than a straight line). Thus, in effect, this is a test of the usefulness of the hypothesized model.

The appropriate test statistic is found by considering the sampling distribution of $\hat{\beta}_1$, the least squares estimator of the slope β_1, as shown in the following box.

Sampling Distribution of $\hat{\beta}_1$

If we make the four assumptions about ϵ (see Section 10.3), the sampling distribution of the least squares estimator $\hat{\beta}_1$ of the slope will be normal with mean β_1 (the true slope) and standard deviation

$$\sigma_{\hat{\beta}_1} = \frac{\sigma}{\sqrt{SS_{xx}}} \qquad \text{(see Figure 10.10)}$$

We estimate $\sigma_{\hat{\beta}_1}$ by $s_{\hat{\beta}_1} = \dfrac{s}{\sqrt{SS_{xx}}}$ and refer to this quantity as the estimated standard error of the least squares slope $\hat{\beta}_1$.

FIGURE 10.9
Graphing the model
$y = \beta_0 + \epsilon$ ($\beta_1 = 0$)

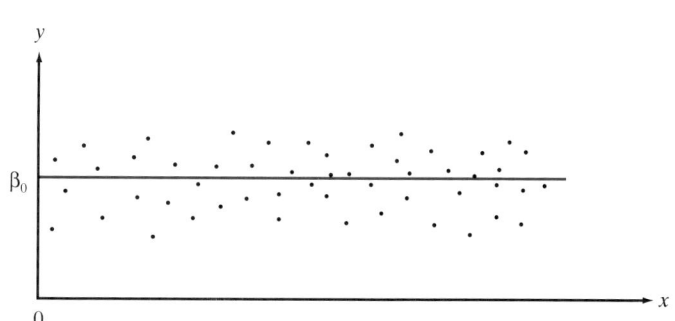

FIGURE 10.10
Sampling distribution
of $\hat{\beta}_1$

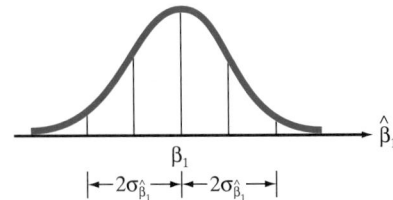

Since σ is usually unknown, the appropriate test statistic is a t statistic, formed as follows:

$$t = \frac{\hat{\beta}_1 - \text{Hypothesized value of } \beta_1}{s_{\hat{\beta}_1}} \qquad \text{where } s_{\hat{\beta}_1} = \frac{s}{\sqrt{\text{SS}_{xx}}}$$

Thus,

$$t = \frac{\hat{\beta}_1 - 0}{s/\sqrt{\text{SS}_{xx}}}$$

Note that we have substituted the estimator s for σ and then formed the estimated standard error $s_{\hat{\beta}_1}$ by dividing s by $\sqrt{\text{SS}_{xx}}$. The number of degrees of freedom associated with this t statistic is the same as the number of degrees of freedom associated with s. Recall that this number is $(n - 2)$ df when the hypothesized model is a straight line (see Section 10.4). The setup of our test of the usefulness of the straight-line model is summarized in the next box.

A Test of Model Utility: Simple Linear Regression

One-Tailed Test

$H_0: \beta_1 = 0$

$H_a: \beta_1 < 0 \quad (\text{or } H_a: \beta_1 > 0)$

Test statistic:

Two-Tailed Test

$H_0: \beta_1 = 0$

$H_a: \beta_1 \neq 0$

$$t = \frac{\hat{\beta}_1}{s_{\hat{\beta}_1}} = \frac{\hat{\beta}_1}{s/\sqrt{\text{SS}_{xx}}}$$

Rejection region: $t < -t_\alpha$
  (or $t > t_\alpha$ when $H_a: \beta_1 > 0$)

Rejection region: $|t| > t_{\alpha/2}$

where t_α and $t_{\alpha/2}$ are based on $(n - 2)$ degrees of freedom

Assumptions: The four assumptions about ϵ listed in Section 10.3.

For the advertising–sales example, we will choose $\alpha = .05$ and, since $n = 5$, t will be based on $n - 2 = 3$ df and the rejection region will be

$$|t| > t_{.025} = 3.182$$

We previously calculated $\hat{\beta}_1 = .7, s = .61$, and $\text{SS}_{xx} = 10$. Thus,

$$t = \frac{\hat{\beta}_1}{s/\sqrt{\text{SS}_{xx}}} = \frac{.7}{.61\sqrt{10}} = \frac{.7}{.19} = 3.7$$

Since this calculated t value falls in the upper-tail rejection region (see Figure 10.11), we reject the null hypothesis and conclude that the slope β_1 is not 0. The

FIGURE 10.11
Rejection region and calculated t value for testing $H_0: \beta_1 = 0$ versus $H_a: \beta_1 \neq 0$

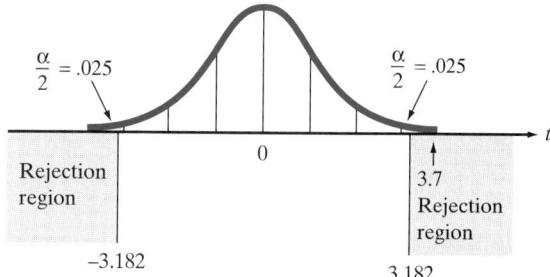

sample evidence indicates that advertising expenditure x contributes information for the prediction of sales revenue y when a linear model is used.

We can reach the same conclusion by using the observed significance level (p-value) of the test from a computer printout. The SAS printout for the advertising–sales example is reproduced in Figure 10.12. The test statistic is highlighted on the printout under the **T for HO: Parameter=0** column in the row corresponding to **X**, while the two-tailed p-value is highlighted under the column labeled **Prob >|T|**. Since the p-value $= .0354$ is smaller than $\alpha = .05$, we will reject H_0.

What conclusion can be drawn if the calculated t value does not fall in the rejection region or if the observed significance level of the test exceeds α? We know from previous discussions of the philosophy of hypothesis testing that such a t value does *not* lead us to accept the null hypothesis. That is, we do not conclude that $\beta_1 = 0$. Additional data might indicate that β_1 differs from 0, or a more complex relationship may exist between x and y, requiring the fitting of a model other than the straight-line model. We discuss several such models in Chapter 11.

Another way to make inferences about the slope β_1 is to estimate it using a confidence interval. This interval is formed as shown in the next box.

Dependent Variable: Y

Analysis of Variance

Source	DF	Sum of Squares	Mean Square	F Value	Prob>F
Model	1	4.90000	4.90000	13.364	0.0354
Error	3	1.10000	0.36667		
C Total	4	6.00000			

Root MSE	0.60553	R-square	0.8167	
Dep Mean	2.00000	Adj R-sq	0.7556	
C.V.	30.27650			

Parameter Estimates

Variable	DF	Parameter Estimate	Standard Error	T for HO: Parameter=0	Prob > |T|
INTERCEP	1	-0.100000	0.63508530	-0.157	0.8849
X	1	0.700000	0.19148542	3.656	0.0354

FIGURE 10.12 SAS printout for advertising–sales example

> **A 100(1 − α)% Confidence Interval for the Simple Linear Regression Slope β_1**
>
> $$\hat{\beta}_1 \pm t_{\alpha/2} s_{\hat{\beta}_1}$$
>
> where the estimated standard error $\hat{\beta}_1$ is calculated by
>
> $$s_{\hat{\beta}_1} = \frac{s}{\sqrt{SS_{xx}}}$$
>
> and $t_{\alpha/2}$ is based on $(n − 2)$ degrees of freedom.
>
> *Assumptions:* The four assumptions about ϵ listed in Section 10.3.

For the advertising–sales example, $t_{\alpha/2}$ is based on $(n − 2) = 3$ degrees of freedom. Therefore, a 95% confidence interval for the slope β_1, the expected change in sales revenue for a $100 increase in advertising expenditure, is

$$\hat{\beta}_1 \pm t_{.025}\, s_{\hat{\beta}_1} = .7 \pm 3.182\left(\frac{s}{\sqrt{SS_{xx}}}\right) = .7 \pm 3.182\left(\frac{.61}{\sqrt{10}}\right) = .7 \pm .61$$

Thus, the interval estimate of the slope parameter β_1 is .09 to 1.31. In terms of this example, the implication is that we can be 95% confident that the *true* mean increase in monthly sales revenue per additional $100 of advertising expenditure is between $90 and $1,310. This inference is meaningful only over the sampled range of x—that is, from $100 to $500 of advertising expenditures.

Since all the values in this interval are positive, it appears that β_1 is positive and that the mean of y, $E(y)$, increases as x increases. However, the rather large width of the confidence interval reflects the small number of data points (and, consequently, a lack of information) in the experiment. Particularly bothersome is the fact that the lower end of the confidence interval implies that we are not even recovering our additional expenditure, since a $100 increase in advertising may produce as little as a $90 increase in mean sales. If we wish to tighten this interval, we need to increase the sample size.

STATISTICS IN ACTION

10.1 NEW JERSEY BANKS— SERVING MINORITIES?

Bankers and community leaders both agree that financial institutions have a legal and social responsibility to serve all communities. But is this obligation being met? Do banks adequately serve both inner city and suburban neighborhoods, both poor and wealthy communities? In New Jersey, banks have been charged with withdrawing from urban areas with a high percentage of minorities. Some surprising statistics: Three out of four minority areas in New Jersey have no bank branches whatsoever, while two out of three white areas have at least one branch.

To examine this charge, a regional New Jersey newspaper, the *Asbury Park Press,* compiled county-by-county data on (1) the number of people in each county per branch bank in the county and (2) the percentage of the population in each county that is minority. These data for each of New Jersey's 21 counties are provided in Table 10.5.

Focus

Use the methods of this chapter to determine whether these data support or refute the charge made against the New Jersey banking community. Summarize your analysis and findings in a report addressed to New Jersey's Commissioner of Banking. *[Note:* The data is available on a 3.5" disk under the file name TAB10.005.]

TABLE 10.5   Data on New Jersey Banks (Statistics in Action 10.1)

County	Number of People per Bank Branch	Percentage of Minority Population
Atlantic	3,073	23.3
Bergen	2,095	13.0
Burlington	2,905	17.8
Camden	3,330	23.4
Cape May	1,321	7.3
Cumberland	2,557	26.5
Essex	3,474	48.8
Gloucester	3,068	10.7
Hudson	3,683	33.2
Hunterdon	1,998	3.7
Mercer	2,607	24.9
Middlesex	3,154	18.1
Monmouth	2,609	12.6
Morris	2,253	8.2
Ocean	2,317	4.7
Passaic	3,307	28.1
Salem	2,511	16.7
Somerset	2,333	12.0
Sussex	2,568	2.4
Union	3,048	25.6
Warren	2,349	2.8

Source: D'Ambrosio, P., and Chambers, S. "No checks and balances." *Asbury Park Press,* September 10, 1995.

EXERCISES   10.31–10.43

Note: Exercises marked with 💾 *contain data for computer analysis on a 3.5″ disk (file name in parentheses).*

Learning the Mechanics

10.31 Construct both a 95% and a 90% confidence interval for β_1 for each of the following cases:
  a. $\hat{\beta}_1 = 31, s = 3, SS_{xx} = 35, n = 10$
  b. $\hat{\beta}_1 = 64, SSE = 1,960, SS_{xx} = 30, n = 14$
  c. $\hat{\beta}_1 = -8.4, SSE = 146, SS_{xx} = 64, n = 20$

10.32 Consider the following pairs of observations:

x	1	4	3	2	5	6	0
y	1	3	3	1	4	7	2

  a. Construct a scattergram for the data.
  b. Use the method of least squares to fit a straight line to the seven data points in the table.
  c. Plot the least squares line on your scattergram of part **a**.
  d. Specify the null and alternative hypotheses you would use to test whether the data provide sufficient evidence to indicate that x contributes information for the (linear) prediction of y.
  e. What is the test statistic that should be used in conducting the hypothesis test of part **d**? Specify the degrees of freedom associated with the test statistic.

  f. Conduct the hypothesis test of part **d** using $\alpha = .05$.

10.33 Refer to Exercise 10.32. Construct an 80% and a 98% confidence interval for β_1.

10.34 Do the accompanying data provide sufficient evidence to conclude that a straight line is useful for characterizing the relationship between x and y?

y	4	2	4	3	2	4
x	1	6	5	3	2	4

10.35 Suppose that $n = 100$ recent residential home sales in a city are used to fit a least squares straight-line model relating the sale price, y, to the square feet of living space, x. Homes in the sample range from 1,500 square feet to 4,000 square feet of living space, and the resulting least squares equation is

$$\hat{y} = -30,000 + 70x$$

  a. When the null hypothesis that the true slope is zero is tested, the result is a t value of 6.572. Give the appropriate p-value of this test, and interpret the result in the context of this application.
  b. The 95% confidence interval for the slope is calculated to be 49.1 to 90.9. Interpret this interval in the context of this application. What can be done to obtain a narrower confidence interval?

Applying the Concepts

10.36 The U.S. Department of Agriculture has developed and adopted the Universal Soil Loss Equation (USLE) for predicting water erosion of soils. In geographical areas where runoff from melting snow is common, the USLE requires an accurate estimate of snowmelt runoff erosion. An article in the *Journal of Soil and Water Conservation* (Mar.–Apr. 1995) used simple linear regression to develop a snowmelt erosion index. Data for 54 climatological stations in Canada were used to model the McCool winter-adjusted rainfall erosivity index, *y*, as a straight-line function of the once-in-five-year snowmelt runoff amount, *x* (measured in millimeters).

a. The data points are plotted in the scattergram shown below. Is there visual evidence of a linear trend?

b. The data for seven stations were removed from the analysis due to lack of snowfall during the study period. Why is this strategy advisable?

c. The simple linear regression on the remaining $n = 47$ data points yielded the following results:

$$\hat{y} = -6.72 + 1.39x; s_{\hat{\beta}_1} = .06$$

Use this information to construct a 90% confidence interval for β_1.

d. Interpret the interval, part **c**.

10.37 One of the most common types of "information retrieval" processes is document-database searching. An experiment was conducted to investigate the variables that influence search performance in the Medline database and retrieval system (*Journal of Information Science,* Vol. 21, 1995).

Simple linear regression was used to model the fraction *y* of the set of potentially informative documents that are retrieved using Medline as a function of the number *x* of terms in the search query, based on a sample of $n = 124$ queries. The results are summarized below:

$$\hat{y} = .202 + .135x \qquad t \text{ (for testing } H_0: \beta_1 = 0) = 4.98$$

Two-tailed *p*-value = .001

a. Is there sufficient evidence to indicate that *x* and *y* are linearly related? Test using $\alpha = .01$.

b. If appropriate, use the model to predict the fraction of documents retrieved for a search query with $x = 3$ terms.

10.38 (**X10.038**) Successful U.S. investors, no longer focusing exclusively on U.S. securities, have developed global investment strategies. One of the most difficult tasks of developing and managing a global portfolio is assessing the risks of potential foreign investments. Duke University researcher C. R. Henry collaborated with two First Chicago Investment Management Company directors to examine the use of country credit ratings as a means of evaluating foreign investments (*Journal of Portfolio Management,* Winter 1995). To be effective, such a measure should help explain and predict the volatility of the foreign market in question. The researchers analyzed data on annualized risk (*y*) and average credit rating (*x*) for the 40 countries shown in the table on page 458. An SPSS printout for a simple linear regression analysis conducted on the data is shown at the top of page 457.

a. Locate the least squares estimates of β_0 and β_1 on the printout.

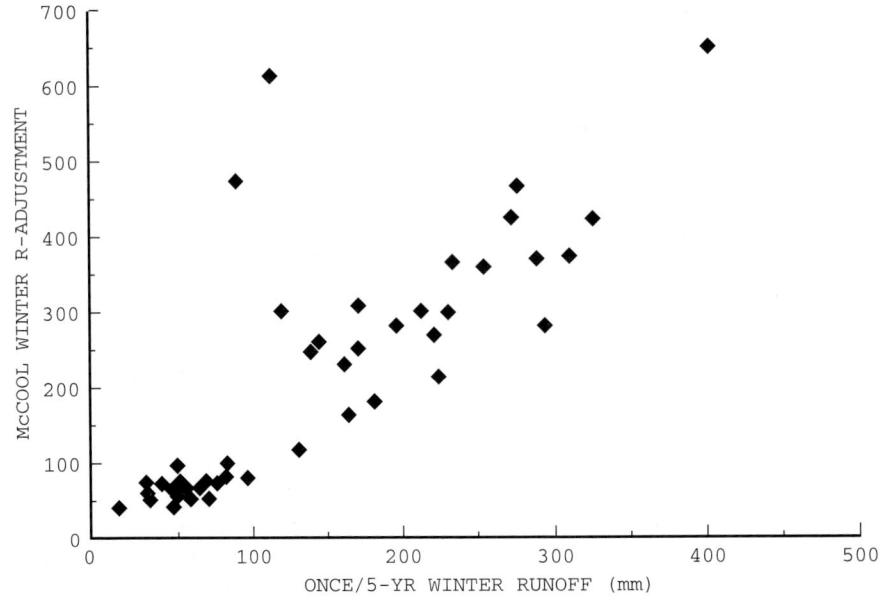

```
* * * *   M U L T I P L E   R E G R E S S I O N   * * * *

Equation Number 1    Dependent Variable..   RISK

Variable(s) Entered on Step Number
   1..     RATING

Multiple R              .57802
R Square                .33411
Adjusted R Square       .31658
Standard Error        12.67770

Analysis of Variance
                    DF        Sum of Squares        Mean Square
Regression           1            3064.40538        3064.40538
Residual            38            6107.51862         160.72417

F =      19.06624        Signif F =  .0001

----------------- Variables in the Equation ---------------------

Variable              B           SE B         Beta          T     Sig T

RATING          -.399606        .091516     -.578020     -4.366    .0001
(Constant)     57.755060       6.127836                   9.425    .0000
```

```
Dependent Variable:  NUMBER

                        Analysis of Variance
                          Sum of          Mean
   Source       DF        Squares        Square      F Value      Prob>F

   Model         1     23536.50149    23536.50149     11.451      0.0070
   Error        10     20554.41518     2055.44152
   C Total      11     44090.91667

        Root MSE       45.33698      R-square      0.5338
        Dep Mean       61.08333      Adj R-sq      0.4872
        C.V.           74.22152

                       Parameter Estimates

                  Parameter        Standard      T for HO:
   Variable   DF   Estimate          Error     Parameter=0    Prob > |T|

   INTERCEP    1   -51.361607     35.71379104     -1.438        0.1809
   AGE         1    17.754464      5.24673562      3.384        0.0070
```

b. Plot the data in a scattergram, then sketch the least squares line on the graph.

c. Do the data provide sufficient evidence to conclude that country credit risk (x) contributes information for the prediction of market volatility (y)?

d. Use the plot, part **b**, to locate any unusual data points (outliers).

e. Eliminate the outlier(s), part **d**, from the data set and rerun the simple linear regression analysis. Note any dramatic changes in the results.

10.39 Refer to Exercises 10.21 and 10.28. The SAS simple linear regression printout relating number

of employees y to age of a fast-growing firm x is reproduced directly above.

a. Test to determine whether y is positively linearly related to x. Use $\alpha = .01$.

b. Construct a 99% confidence interval for β_1. Practically interpret the result.

10.40 (X10.040) H. Mintzberg's classic book, *The Nature of Managerial Work* (1973), identified the roles found in all managerial jobs. An observational study of 19 managers from a medium-sized manufacturing plant extended Mintzberg's work by investigating which activities *successful* managers actually perform (*Journal of Applied Behavioral*

Country	Annualized Risk (%)	Average Credit Rating
Argentina	87.0	31.8
Australia	26.9	78.2
Austria	26.3	83.8
Belgium	22.0	78.4
Brazil	64.8	36.2
Canada	19.2	87.1
Chile	31.6	38.6
Colombia	31.5	44.4
Denmark	20.6	72.6
Finland	26.1	76.0
France	23.8	85.3
Germany	23.0	93.4
Greece	39.6	51.9
Hong Kong	34.3	69.6
India	30.0	46.6
Ireland	23.4	66.4
Italy	28.0	75.5
Japan	25.7	94.5
Jordan	17.6	33.6
Korea	30.7	62.2
Malaysia	26.7	64.4
Mexico	46.3	43.3
Netherlands	18.5	87.6
New Zealand	26.3	68.9
Nigeria	41.4	30.6
Norway	28.3	83.0
Pakistan	24.4	26.4
Philippines	38.4	29.6
Portugal	47.5	56.7
Singapore	26.4	77.6
Spain	24.8	70.8
Sweden	24.5	79.5
Switzerland	19.6	94.7
Taiwan	53.7	72.9
Thailand	27.0	55.8
Turkey	74.1	32.6
United Kingdom	21.8	87.6
United States	15.4	93.4
Venezuela	46.0	45.0
Zimbabwe	35.6	24.5

Source: Erb, C. B., Harvey, C. R., and Viskanta, T. E. "Country risk and global equity selection." *Journal of Portfolio Management,* Vol. 21, No. 2, Winter 1995, p. 76. This copyrighted material is reprinted with permission from *The Journal of Portfolio Management,* a publication of Institutional Investor, Inc., 488 Madison Ave., New York, NY 10022.

Science, Aug. 1985). To measure success, the researchers devised an index based on the manager's length of time in the organization and his or her level within the firm; the higher the index, the more successful the manager. The table at the top of page 459 presents data (which are representative of the data collected by the researchers) that can be used to determine whether managerial success is related to the extensiveness of a manger's network-building interactions with people outside the manager's work unit. Such interactions include phone and face-to-face meetings with customers and suppliers, attending outside meetings, and doing public

relations work. A MINITAB printout of the simple linear regression follows the table.

a. Construct a scattergram for the data.
b. Find the prediction equation for managerial success.
c. Find *s* for your prediction equation. Interpret the standard deviation *s* in the context of this problem.
d. Plot the least squares line on your scattergram of part **a**. Does it appear that the number of interactions with outsiders contributes information for the prediction of managerial success? Explain.

Manager	Manager Success Index, y	Number of Interactions with Outsiders, x
1	40	12
2	73	71
3	95	70
4	60	81
5	81	43
6	27	50
7	53	42
8	66	18
9	25	35
10	63	82
11	70	20
12	47	81
13	80	40
14	51	33
15	32	45
16	50	10
17	52	65
18	30	20
19	42	21

```
The regression equation is
SUCCESS = 44.1 + 0.237 INTERACT

Predictor      Coef       Stdev      t-ratio        p
Constant     44.130      9.362         4.71      0.000
INTERACT     0.2366      0.1865         1.27      0.222

s = 19.40        R-sq = 8.6%       R-sq(adj) = 3.3%

Analysis of Variance

SOURCE        DF          SS          MS          F        p
Regression     1       606.0       606.0       1.61    0.222
Error         17      6400.6       376.5
Total         18      7006.6
```

e. Conduct a formal statistical hypothesis test to answer the question posed in part **d**. Use $\alpha = .05$.

f. Construct a 95% confidence interval for β_1. Interpret the interval in the context of the problem.

10.41 The expenses involved in a manufacturing operation may be categorized as being for *raw material, direct labor,* and *overhead.* Direct labor refers to the persons employed to transform the raw materials into the finished product. Overhead refers to all expenses other than those for raw materials and direct labor that are involved with running the factory (e.g., supervisory labor, maintenance of equipment, and office supplies) (Horngren, *et al., Cost Accounting,* 1994). A manufacturer of 10-speed racing bicycles is interested in estimating the relationship between its monthly factory overhead and the total number of bicycles produced per month. The estimate will be used to help develop the manufacturing budget for next year.

The data in the table below have been collected for the previous 12 months.

Month	Production Level (1,000's of units)	Overhead ($1,000s)
1	16.9	41.4
2	15.6	35.0
3	17.4	38.3
4	11.6	29.5
5	17.7	39.6
6	17.6	37.4
7	16.3	37.5
8	15.5	37.0
9	23.4	47.9
10	28.4	55.6
11	27.1	53.1
12	19.2	40.6

a. Find the least squares prediction equation relating monthly overhead y to monthly production level x on the EXCEL printout on page 460.

SUMMARY OUTPUT						
Regression Statistics						
Multiple R	0.985330898					
R Square	0.970876979					
Adjusted R Square	0.967964677					
Standard Error	1.350376282					
Observations	12					

ANOVA						
	df	SS	MS	F	Significance F	
Regression	1	607.907339	607.907339	333.3709739	5.2194E-09	
Residual	10	18.23516102	1.823516102			
Total	11	626.1425				

	Coefficients	Standard Error	t Stat	P-value	Lower 95%	Upper 95%
Intercept	12.71272173	1.601544156	7.937790339	1.26074E-05	9.144258354	16.2811851
Prodlevel	1.501311598	0.08222558	18.25844938	5.2194E-09	1.318101556	1.68452164

460

b. Does the straight-line model contribute information for predicting overhead costs? Test at $\alpha = .05$.

c. Which of the four assumptions we make about the random error ϵ may be inappropriate in this problem? Explain.

10.42 During June, July, and early August of 1981, 10 bids were made by DuPont, Seagram, and Mobil to take over Conoco. Finally, on August 5, DuPont announced success. The total value of the offer accepted by Conoco was $7.54 billion, making it the largest takeover in the history of American business at that time. A study of the Conoco takeover used regression analysis to examine whether movements in the rate of return of the contending companies' common stock could be explained by movements in the return rate of the stock market as a whole. The model was $y = \beta_0 + \beta_1 x + \epsilon$, where y is the daily rate of return of a stock, x is the daily rate of return of the stock market as a whole (based on Standard & Poor's 500 Composite Index), and ϵ is believed to satisfy the assumptions of Section 10.3. (This model is known in the finance literature as the *market model*. Note that the parameter β_1 reflects the sensitivity of the stock's return rate to movements in the stock market as a whole.) Daily data from early 1979 through 1980 ($n = 504$) yielded the least squares lines shown in the table for the four firms in question. The t statistics and p-values associated with the values of β_1 are also shown.

Firm	Estimated Market Model	t Statistics	p-Values
Conoco	$\hat{y} = .0010 + 1.40x$	$t = 21.93$	.000
DuPont	$\hat{y} = -.0005 + 1.21x$	$t = 18.76$	.000
Mobil	$\hat{y} = .0010 + 1.62x$	$t = 16.21$	.000
Seagram	$\hat{y} = .0013 + .76x$	$t = 6.05$	.000

Source: Ruback, R. S. "The Conoco takeover and stockholder returns." *Sloan Management Review,* Vol. 23, Winter 1982, pp. 13–33.

a. For each of the models, test $H_0: \beta_1 = 0$ versus $H_a: \beta_1 \neq 0$. Use $\alpha = .01$. Draw the appropriate conclusion regarding the usefulness of the market model in each case.

b. If the rate of return of Standard & Poor's 500 Composite Index increased by .10, how much change would occur in the mean rate of return for Conoco's common stock? For Seagram's?

c. Which of the two stocks, Conoco or Seagram, appears to be more responsive to changes in the market as a whole? Explain.

10.43 Refer to Exercise 10.15, in which the extent of retaliation against whistle blowers was investigated. Since salary is a reasonably good indicator of a person's power within an organization, the data of Exercise 10.15 can be used to investigate whether the extent of retaliation is related to the power of the whistle blower in the organization. The researchers were unable to reject the hypothesis that the extent of retaliation is unrelated to power. Do you agree? Test using $\alpha = .05$.

10.6   THE COEFFICIENT OF CORRELATION

Recall (from optional Section 2.10) that a **bivariate relationship** describes a relationship between two variables, x and y. Scattergrams are used to graphically describe a bivariate relationship. In this section we will discuss the concept of **correlation** and show how it can be used to measure the linear relationship between two variables x and y. A numerical descriptive measure of correlation is provided by the *Pearson product moment coefficient of correlation, r.*

DEFINITION 10.2

The **Pearson product moment coefficient of correlation**, r, is a measure of the strength of the *linear* relationship between two variables x and y. It is computed (for a sample of n measurements on x and y) as follows:

$$r = \frac{SS_{xy}}{\sqrt{SS_{xx}SS_{yy}}}$$

Note that the computational formula for the correlation coefficient r given in Definition 10.2 involves the same quantities that were used in computing the least squares prediction equation. In fact, since the numerators of the expressions for $\hat{\beta}_1$ and r are identical, you can see that $r = 0$ when $\hat{\beta}_1 = 0$ (the case where x

FIGURE 10.13
Values of r and their implications

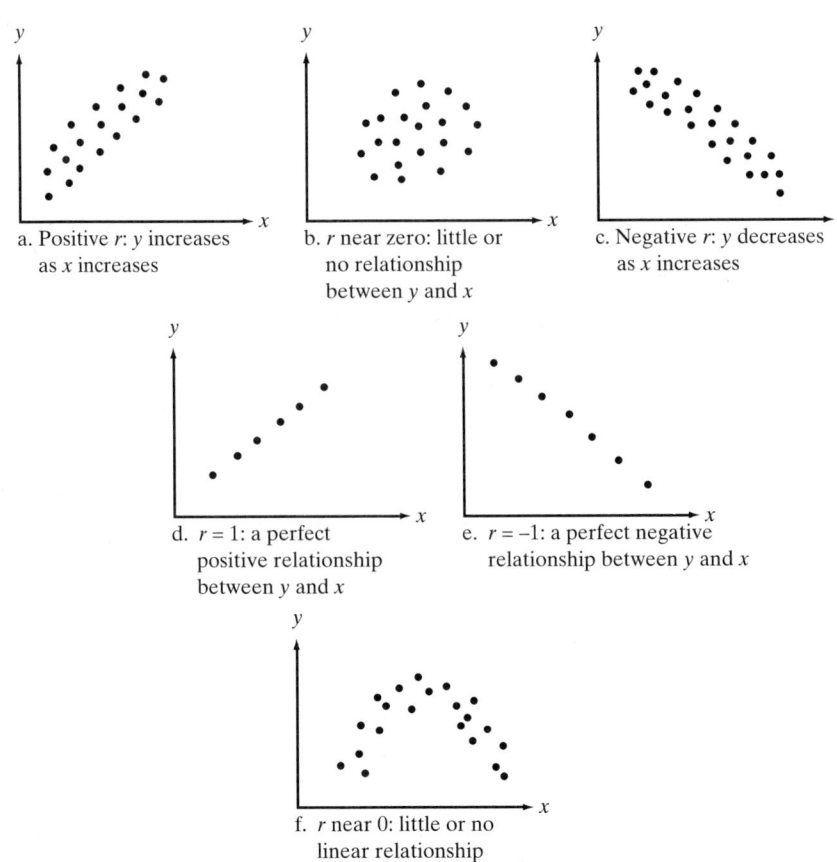

a. Positive r: y increases as x increases

b. r near zero: little or no relationship between y and x

c. Negative r: y decreases as x increases

d. $r = 1$: a perfect positive relationship between y and x

e. $r = -1$: a perfect negative relationship between y and x

f. r near 0: little or no linear relationship between y and x

contributes no information for the prediction of y) and that r is positive when the slope is positive and negative when the slope is negative. Unlike $\hat{\beta}_1$, the correlation coefficient r is *scaleless* and assumes a value between -1 and $+1$, regardless of the units of x and y.

A value of r near or equal to 0 implies little or no linear relationship between y and x. In contrast, the closer r comes to 1 or -1, the stronger the linear relationship between y and x. And if $r = 1$ or $r = -1$, all the sample points fall exactly on the least squares line. Positive values of r imply a positive linear relationship between y and x; that is, y increases as x increases. Negative values of r imply a negative linear relationship between y and x; that is, y decreases as x increases. Each of these situations is portrayed in Figure 10.13.

We demonstrate how to calculate the coefficient of correlation r using the data in Table 10.1 for the advertising–sales example. The quantities needed to calculate r are SS_{xy}, SS_{xx}, and SS_{yy}. The first two quantities have been calculated previously and are repeated here for convenience:

$$SS_{xy} = 7 \qquad SS_{xx} = 10 \qquad SS_{yy} = \sum y^2 - \frac{\left(\sum y\right)^2}{n}$$

$$= 26 - \frac{(10)^2}{5} = 26 - 20 = 6$$

We now find the coefficient of correlation:

$$r = \frac{SS_{xy}}{\sqrt{SS_{xx}SS_{yy}}} = \frac{7}{\sqrt{(10)(6)}} = \frac{7}{\sqrt{60}} = .904$$

The fact that r is positive and near 1 in value indicates that the sales revenue y tends to increase as advertising expenditure x increases—*for this sample of five months.* This is the same conclusion we reached when we found the calculated value of the least squares slope to be positive.

EXAMPLE 10.1

Legalized gambling is available on several riverboat casinos operated by a city in Mississippi. The mayor of the city wants to know the correlation between the number of casino employees and the yearly crime rate. The records for the past 10 years are examined, and the results listed in Table 10.6 are obtained. Calculate the coefficient of correlation r for the data.

SOLUTION

Rather than use the computing formula given in Definition 10.2, we resort to a statistical software package. The data of Table 10.6 were entered into a computer and MINITAB was used to compute r. The MINITAB printout is shown in Figure 10.14.

The coefficient of correlation, highlighted on the printout, is $r = .987$. Thus, the size of the casino workforce and crime rate in this city are very highly correlated—at least over the past 10 years. The implication is that a strong positive linear relationship exists between these variables (see Figure 10.15). We must be careful, however, not to jump to any unwarranted conclusions. For instance, the mayor may be tempted to conclude that hiring more casino workers next year will increase the crime rate—that is, that there is a *causal relationship* between the two variables. However, high correlation does not imply causality. The fact is, many things have probably contributed both to the increase in the casino workforce and to the increase in crime rate. The city's tourist trade has undoubtedly grown since legalizing riverboat casinos and it is likely that the casinos have expanded both in services offered and in number. *We cannot infer a causal relationship on the basis of high sample correlation. When a high correlation is observed in the sample data, the only safe conclusion is that a linear trend may exist between* x *and* y. Another variable, such as the increase in tourism, may be the underlying cause of the high correlation between x and y.

TABLE 10.6   Data on Casino Employees and Crime Rate, Example 10.1

Year	Number of Casino Employees x, thousands	Crime Rate y, number of crimes per 1,000 population
1987	15	1.35
1988	18	1.63
1989	24	2.33
1990	22	2.41
1991	25	2.63
1992	29	2.93
1993	30	3.41
1994	32	3.26
1995	35	3.63
1996	38	4.15

FIGURE 10.14
MINITAB printout for
Exercise 10.1

`Correlation of NOEMPLOY and CRIMERAT = 0.987`

FIGURE 10.15
Scattergram for
Example 10.1

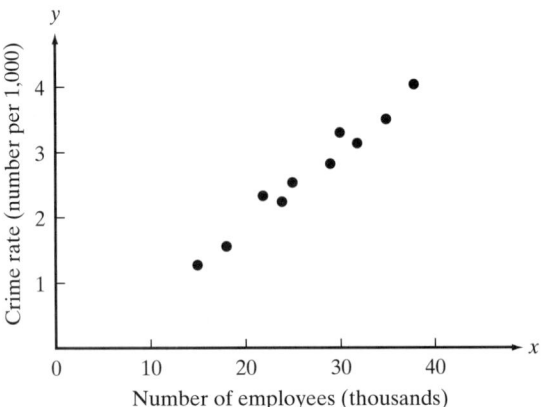

Keep in mind that the correlation coefficient r measures the linear correlation between x values and y values in the sample, and a similar linear coefficient of correlation exists for the population from which the data points were selected. The **population correlation coefficient** is denoted by the symbol ρ (rho). As you might expect, ρ is estimated by the corresponding sample statistic, r. Or, instead of estimating ρ, we might want to test the null hypothesis H_0: $\rho = 0$ against H_a: $\rho \neq 0$—that is, we can test the hypothesis that x contributes no information for the prediction of y by using the straight-line model against the alternative that the two variables are at least linearly related.

However, we already performed this *identical* test in Section 10.5 when we tested H_0: $\beta_1 = 0$ against H_a: $\beta_1 \neq 0$. That is, the null hypothesis H_0: $\rho = 0$ is equivalent to the hypothesis H_0: $\beta_1 = 0$.* When we tested the null hypothesis H_0: $\beta_1 = 0$ in connection with the advertising–sales example, the data led to a rejection of the null hypothesis at the $\alpha = .05$ level. This rejection implies that the null hypothesis of a 0 linear correlation between the two variables (sales revenue and advertising expenditure) can also be rejected at the $\alpha = .05$ level. The only real difference between the least squares slope $\hat{\beta}_1$ and the coefficient of correlation r is the measurement scale. Therefore, the information they provide about the usefulness of the least squares model is to some extent redundant. For this reason, we will use the slope to make inferences about the existence of a positive or negative linear relationship between two variables.

10.7 THE COEFFICIENT OF DETERMINATION

Another way to measure the usefulness of the model is to measure the contribution of x in predicting y. To accomplish this, we calculate how much the errors of prediction of y were reduced by using the information provided by x. To illustrate, consider the sample shown in the scattergram of Figure 10.16a. If we assume that x contributes no information for the prediction of y, the best prediction for a value of y is the sample mean $\bar{y}$, which is shown as the horizontal line in Figure 10.16b. The vertical line segments in Figure 10.16b are the deviations of the points about the mean $\bar{y}$. Note that the sum of squares of deviations for the prediction equation $\hat{y} = \bar{y}$ is

---

*The correlation test statistic that is equivalent to $t = \hat{\beta}_1/s_{\hat{\beta}_1}$ is $t = \dfrac{r}{\sqrt{(1 - r^2)/(n - 2)}}$.

FIGURE 10.16
A comparison of
the sum of squares
of deviations for
two models

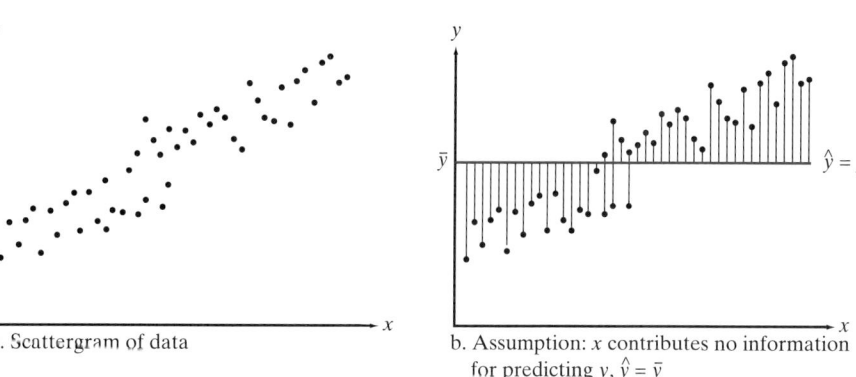

a. Scattergram of data

b. Assumption: x contributes no information for predicting y, $\hat{y} = \bar{y}$

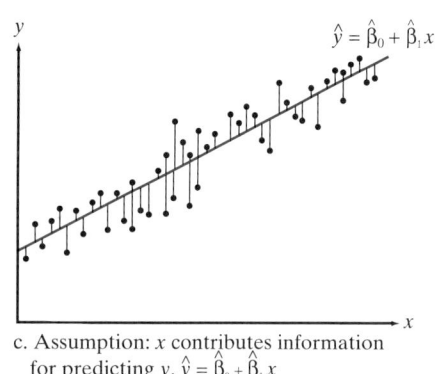

c. Assumption: x contributes information for predicting y, $\hat{y} = \hat{\beta}_0 + \hat{\beta}_1 x$

$$SS_{yy} = \sum (y_i - \bar{y})^2$$

Now suppose you fit a least squares line to the same set of data and locate the deviations of the points about the line as shown in Figure 10.16c. Compare the deviations about the prediction lines in Figures 10.16b and 10.16c. You can see that

1. If x contributes little or no information for the prediction of y, the sums of squares of deviations for the two lines,

$$SS_{yy} = \sum (y_i - \bar{y})^2 \quad \text{and} \quad SSE = \sum (y_i - \hat{y}_i)^2$$

   will be nearly equal.

2. If x does contribute information for the prediction of y, the SSE will be smaller than SS_{yy}. In fact, if all the points fall on the least squares line, then SSE = 0.

Then the reduction in the sum of squares of deviations that can be attributed to x, expressed as a proportion of SS_{yy}, is

$$\frac{SS_{yy} - SSE}{SS_{yy}}$$

Note that SS_{yy} is the "total sample variation" of the observations around the mean $\bar{y}$ and that SSE is the remaining "unexplained sample variability" after fitting the line $\hat{y}$. Thus, the difference ($SS_{yy} - SSE$) is the "explained sample variability" attributable to the linear relationship with x. Then a verbal description of the proportion is

$$\frac{\text{SS}_{yy} - \text{SSE}}{\text{SS}_{yy}} = \frac{\text{Explained sample variability}}{\text{Total sample variability}}$$

$$= \text{Proportion of total sample variability explained}$$
$$\text{by the linear relationship}$$

In simple linear regression, it can be shown that this proportion is equal to the square of the simple linear coefficient of correlation r (the Pearson product moment coefficient of correlation.)

DEFINITION 10.3

The **coefficient of determination** is

$$r^2 = \frac{\text{SS}_{yy} - \text{SSE}}{\text{SS}_{yy}} = 1 - \frac{\text{SSE}}{\text{SS}_{yy}}$$

It represents the proportion of the total sample variability around $\bar{y}$ that is explained by the linear relationship between y and x. (In simple linear regression, it may also be computed as the square of the coefficient of correlation r.)

Note that r^2 is always between 0 and 1, because r is between -1 and $+1$. Thus, an r^2 of .60 means that the sum of squares of deviations of the y values about their predicted values has been reduced 60% by the use of the least squares equation $\hat{y}$, instead of $\bar{y}$, to predict y.

EXAMPLE 10.2   Calculate the coefficient of determination for the advertising–sales example. The data are repeated in Table 10.7 for convenience. Interpret the result.

SOLUTION
From previous calculations,

$$\text{SS}_{yy} = 6 \quad \text{and} \quad \text{SSE} = \sum(y - \hat{y})^2 = 1.10$$

Then, from Definition 10.3, the coefficient of determination is given by

$$r^2 = \frac{\text{SS}_{yy} - \text{SSE}}{\text{SS}_{yy}} = \frac{6.0 - 1.1}{6.0} = \frac{4.9}{6.0} = .82$$

Another way to compute r^2 is to recall (Section 10.6) that $r = .904$. Then we have $r^2 = (.904)^2 = .82$. A third way to obtain r^2 is from a computer printout. This value is highlighted on the SAS printout reproduced in Figure 10.17 next to the

---

TABLE 10.7 Advertising Expenditure–Sales Revenue Data

Advertising Expenditure, x ($100s)	Sales Revenue, y ($1,000s)
1	1
2	1
3	2
4	2
5	4

```
Dependent Variable: Y
                        Analysis of Variance

                            Sum of          Mean
        Source       DF     Squares        Square    F Value     Prob>F

        Model         1     4.90000       4.90000     13.364     0.0354
        Error         3     1.10000       0.36667
        C Total       4     6.00000

            Root MSE          0.60553     R-square     0.8167
            Dep Mean          2.00000     Adj R-sq     0.7556
            C.V.             30.27650

                        Parameter Estimates

                      Parameter      Standard     T for HO:
        Variable  DF    Estimate        Error    Parameter=0    Prob > |T|

        INTERCEP   1   -0.100000     0.63508530      -0.157       0.8849
        X          1    0.700000     0.19148542       3.656       0.0354
```

FIGURE 10.17   SAS printout for advertising–sales example

heading **R-square**. Our interpretation is as follows: We know that using advertising expenditure, x, to predict y with the least squares line

$$\hat{y} = -.1 + .7x$$

accounts for 82% of the total sum of squares of deviations of the five sample y values about their mean. Or, stated another way, 82% of the sample variation in sales revenue (y) can be "explained" by using advertising expenditure (x) in a straight-line model.

> **Practical Interpretation of the Coefficient of Determination, r^2**
> About $100(r^2)\%$ of the sample variation in y (measured by the total sum of squares of deviations of the sample y values about their mean $\bar{y}$) can be explained by (or attributed to) using x to predict y in the straight-line model.

EXERCISES   10.44–10.56

Note: Exercises marked with 💾 *contain data for computer analysis on a 3.5" disk (file name in parentheses).*

Learning the Mechanics

10.44   Explain what each of the following sample correlation coefficients tells you about the relationship between the x and y values in the sample:
a. $r = 1$ **b.** $r = -1$ **c.** $r = 0$
d. $r = .90$ **e.** $r = .10$ **f.** $r = -.88$

10.45   Describe the slope of the least squares line if
a. $r = .7$ **b.** $r = -.7$ **c.** $r = 0$ **d.** $r^2 = .64$

10.46   Construct a scattergram for each data set. Then calculate r and r^2 for each data set. Interpret their values.

a.

x	−2	−1	0	1	2
y	−2	1	2	5	6

b.

x	−2	−1	0	1	2
y	6	5	3	2	0

c.

x	1	2	2	3	3	3	4
y	2	1	3	1	2	3	2

d.

x	0	1	3	5	6
y	0	1	2	1	0

10.47 Calculate r^2 for the least squares line in each of the following exercises. Interpret their values.
  a. Exercise 10.10 **b.** Exercise 10.13

Applying the Concepts

10.48 **(X10.048)** The table below reports the average daily hotel room rate and average car-rental rate during a week in October 1995 for a sample of 20 U.S. cities.

City	Daily Room Rate	Daily Car-Rental Rate
Atlanta	$118	$56
Boston	192	49
Chicago	168	57
Cleveland	77	51
Dallas	118	45
Denver	94	37
Detroit	114	53
Houston	115	62
Los Angeles	136	42
Miami	138	32
Minneapolis	98	49
New Orleans	136	55
New York	177	69
Orlando	95	41
Phoenix	135	45
Pittsburgh	133	47
St. Louis	109	77
San Francisco	181	49
Seattle	124	45
Washington, D.C.	167	53

Source: The Wall Street Journal, October 20, 1995, p. B6.

  a. Construct a scatterplot for the data.
  b. Based on a visual inspection of the plot, describe in words the strength of the linear relationship between the two variables.
  c. Find and interpret the coefficient of correlation for these data.

10.49 Many high school students experience "math anxiety," which has been shown to have a negative effect on their learning achievement. Does such an attitude carry over to learning computer skills? A math and computer science researcher at Duquesne University investigated this question and published her results in *Educational Technology* (May–June 1995). A sample of 1,730 high school students—902 boys and 828 girls—from public schools in Pittsburgh, Pennsylvania, participated in the study. Using 5-point Likert scales, where 1 = "strongly disagree" and 5 = "strongly agree," the researcher measured the students' interest and confidence in both mathematics and computers.

  a. For boys, math confidence and computer interest were correlated at $r = .14$. Fully interpret this result.
  b. For girls, math confidence and computer interest were correlated at $r = .33$. Fully interpret this result.

10.50 Studies of Asian (particularly Japanese) and U.S. managers in the 1970s and 1980s found sharp differences of opinion and attitude toward quality management. Do these differences continue to exist? To find out, two California State University researchers (B. F. Yavas and T. M. Burrows) surveyed 100 U.S. and 96 Asian managers in the electronics manufacturing industry (*Quality Management Journal,* Fall 1994). The accompanying table gives the percentages of U.S. and Asian managers who agree with each of 13 randomly selected statements regarding quality. (For example, one statement is "Quality is a problem in my company." Another is "Improving quality is expensive.")

	PERCENTAGE OF MANAGERS WHO AGREE	
Statement	United States	Asian
1	36	38
2	31	42
3	28	43
4	27	48
5	78	58
6	74	49
7	43	46
8	50	56
9	31	65
10	66	58
11	18	21
12	61	69
13	53	45

Source: Yavas, B. F., and Burrows, T. M. "A comparative study of attitudes of U.S. and Asian managers toward product quality." *Quality Management Journal,* Fall 1994, p. 49 (Table 5).

  a. Find the coefficient of correlation r for these data on the MINITAB printout below.

`Correlation of USA and ASIAN = 0.570`

  b. Interpret r in the context of the problem. Do U.S. and Asian managers tend to have similar attitudes toward quality and quality management?

10.51 Refer to Exercise 10.50. Using the coefficient of correlation r to make inferences about the difference in attitudes between U.S. and Asian managers regarding quality can be misleading. The value of r measures the strength of the linear relationship between two variables; it does not

	PERCENTAGE OF MANAGERS WHO AGREE	
Quality Statement	U.S.	Asian
1	20	50
2	30	65
3	40	70
4	50	80
5	55	90

account for a difference between the means of the variables. To illustrate this, consider the hypothetical data shown in the table above.

a. Show that the coefficient of correlation r is near 1.

b. Examine the hypothetical data and note that the Asian percentage is approximately 30 points higher for each quality statement. In this case, does $r = 1$ imply that the attitudes of U.S. and Asian managers are similar? Explain.

10.52 **(X10.052)** The fertility rate of a country is defined as the number of children a woman citizen bears, on average, in her lifetime. *Scientific American* (Dec. 1993) reported on the declining fertility rate in developing countries. The researchers found that family planning can have a great effect on fertility rate. The table below gives the fertility rate, y, and contraceptive prevalence, x (measured as the percentage of married women who use contraception), for each of 27 developing countries. A SAS printout of the simple linear regression analysis is on page 470.

a. According to the researchers, "the data reveal that differences in contraceptive prevalence explain about 90% of the variation in fertility rates." Do you concur?

b. The researchers also concluded that "if contraceptive use increases by 15 percent, women bear, on average, one fewer child." Is this statement supported by the data? Explain.

10.53 **(X10.053)** A negotiable certificate of deposit is a marketable receipt for funds deposited in a bank for a specified period of time at a specified rate of interest (Lee, Finnerty, and Norton, 1997). The table on page 470 lists the end-of-quarter interest rate for three-month certificates of deposit from January 1982 through December 1995 with the concurrent end-of-quarter values of Standard & Poor's 500 Stock Composite Average (an indicator of stock market activity). Find the coefficient of determination and the correlation coefficient for the data and interpret those results. Use the SPSS printout at the top of page 471 to arrive at your answer.

10.54 Refer to the *Journal of Information Science* study of the relationship between the fraction y of documents retrieved using Medline and the number x of terms in the search query, Exercise 10.37.

a. The value of r was reported in the article as $r = .679$. Interpret this result.

b. Calculate the coefficient of determination, r^2, and interpret the result.

Country	Contraceptive Prevalence, x	Fertility Rate, y
Mauritius	76	2.2
Thailand	69	2.3
Colombia	66	2.9
Costa Rica	71	3.5
Sri Lanka	63	2.7
Turkey	62	3.4
Peru	60	3.5
Mexico	55	4.0
Jamaica	55	2.9
Indonesia	50	3.1
Tunisia	51	4.3
El Salvador	48	4.5
Morocco	42	4.0
Zimbabwe	46	5.4

Country	Contraceptive Prevalence, x	Fertility Rate, y
Egypt	40	4.5
Bangladesh	40	5.5
Botswana	35	4.8
Jordan	35	5.5
Kenya	28	6.5
Guatemala	24	5.5
Cameroon	16	5.8
Ghana	14	6.0
Pakistan	13	5.0
Senegal	13	6.5
Sudan	10	4.8
Yemen	9	7.0
Nigeria	7	5.7

Source: Robey, B., *et al.* "The fertility decline in developing countries." *Scientific American,* December 1993, p. 62. [*Note:* The data values are estimated from a scatterplot.]

```
Dependent Variable: FERTRATE
                       Analysis of Variance

                           Sum of            Mean
        Source      DF     Squares          Square    F Value    Prob>F

        Model        1     35.96633        35.96633    74.309    0.0001
        Error       25     12.10033         0.48401
        C Total     26     48.06667

            Root MSE        0.69571     R-square    0.7483
            Dep Mean        4.51111     Adj R-sq    0.7382
            C.V.           15.42216

                       Parameter Estimates
                     Parameter       Standard      T for HO:
        Variable  DF   Estimate         Error    Parameter=0    Prob > |T|

        INTERCEP   1   6.731929      0.29034252      23.186       0.0001
        CONTPREV   1  -0.054610      0.00633512      -8.620       0.0001
```

Year	Quarter	Interest Rate, x	S&P 500, y	Year	Quarter	Interest Rate, x	S&P 500, y
1982	I	14.21	111.96	1989	I	10.09	294.87
	II	14.46	109.61		II	9.20	317.98
	III	10.66	120.42		III	8.78	349.15
	IV	8.66	135.28		IV	8.32	353.40
1983	I	8.69	152.96	1990	I	8.27	339.94
	II	9.20	168.11		II	8.33	358.02
	III	9.39	166.07		III	8.08	306.05
	IV	9.69	164.93		IV	7.96	330.22
1984	I	10.08	159.18	1991	I	6.71	375.22
	II	11.34	153.18		II	6.01	371.16
	III	11.29	166.10		III	5.70	387.86
	IV	8.60	167.24		IV	4.91	417.09
1985	I	9.02	180.66	1992	I	4.25	403.69
	II	7.44	191.85		II	3.86	408.14
	III	7.93	182.08		III	3.13	417.80
	IV	7.80	211.28		IV	3.48	435.71
1986	I	7.24	238.90	1993	I	3.11	451.67
	II	6.73	250.84		II	3.21	450.53
	III	5.71	231.32		III	3.12	458.93
	IV	6.04	242.17		IV	3.17	466.45
1987	I	6.17	291.70	1994	I	3.77	445.77
	II	6.94	304.00		II	4.52	444.27
	III	7.37	321.83		III	5.03	462.69
	IV	7.66	247.08		IV	6.29	459.27
1988	I	6.63	258.89	1995	I	6.15	500.71
	II	7.51	273.50		II	5.90	544.75
	III	8.23	271.91		III	5.73	584.41
	IV	9.25	277.72		IV	5.62	615.93

Source: Standard & Poor's Statistical Service, Current Statistics. Standard & Poor's Corporation, 1992, 1996.

10.55 The Minnesota Department of Transportation installed a state-of-the-art weigh-in-motion scale in the concrete surface of the eastbound lanes of Interstate 494 in Bloomington, Minnesota. After installation, a study was undertaken to determine whether the scale's readings correspond with the static weights of the vehicles being monitored. (Studies of this type are known as *calibration stud-*

```
Correlations:  SP500

   INTRATE      -.7607**

N of cases:    56          1-tailed Signif:  * - .01  ** - .001
--------------------------------------------------------------------------
              * * * *  M U L T I P L E   R E G R E S S I O N  * * * *
Equation Number 1    Dependent Variable..  SP500

Variable(s) Entered on Step Number
    1..     INTRATE

Multiple R           .76074
R Square             .57873
Adjusted R Square    .57093
Standard Error    84.49296

Analysis of Variance
                  DF      Sum of Squares       Mean Square
Regression         1        529604.21837      529604.21837
Residual          54        385509.26034        7139.06038

F =      74.18402      Signif F = .0000

------------------ Variables in the Equation -------------------

Variable             B           SE B        Beta        T    Sig T

INTRATE       -37.887641     4.398883    -.760743    -8.613   .0000
(Constant)    587.662145    33.878984                17.346   .0000
```

Trial Number	Static Weight of Truck x (thousand pounds)	Weigh-in-Motion Reading Prior to Calibration Adjustment, y_1 (thousand pounds)	Weigh-in-Motion Reading After Calibration Adjustment, y_2 (thousand pounds)
1	27.9	26.0	27.8
2	29.1	29.9	29.1
3	38.0	39.5	37.8
4	27.0	25.1	27.1
5	30.3	31.6	30.6
6	34.5	36.2	34.3
7	27.8	25.1	26.9
8	29.6	31.0	29.6
9	33.1	35.6	33.0
10	35.5	40.2	35.0

Source: Adapted from data in Wright J. L., Owen, F., and Pena, D. "Status of MN/DOT's weigh-in-motion program." St. Paul: Minnesota Department of Transportation, January 1983.

ies.) After some preliminary comparisons using a two-axle, six-tire truck carrying different loads (see the table above), calibration adjustments were made in the software of the weigh-in-motion system and the scales were reevaluated.

a. Construct two scattergrams, one of y_1 versus x and the other of y_2 versus x.

b. Use the scattergrams of part **a** to evaluate the performance of the weigh-in-motion scale both before and after the calibration adjustment.

c. Calculate the correlation coefficient for both sets of data and interpret their values. Explain

how these correlation coefficients can be used to evaluate the weigh-in-motion scale.

d. Suppose the sample correlation coefficient for y_2 and x was 1. Could this happen if the static weights and the weigh-in-motion readings disagreed? Explain.

10.56 A firm's *demand curve* describes the quantity of its product that can be sold at various prices, other things being equal (Mansfield, *Applied Microeconomics,* 1994). Over the period of a year, a tire company varied the price of a radial tire to estimate its demand curve. When the price was set very low or very high, few tires sold. The latter result the firm understood, the former it attributed to consumer misperception that low price implies poor quality. The data in the table describe the tire's sales over the experimental period. A simple linear regression analysis was conducted using MINITAB. The printout follows.

Price, x ($)	Sales, y (100s)
20	13
35	57
45	85
60	43
70	17

a. Find the least squares line to approximate the firm's demand curve.

b. Construct a scattergram and plot the least squares line on the graph.
c. Test $H_0: \beta_1 = 0$ using a two-tailed test and $\alpha = .05$. Draw the appropriate conclusion in the context of the problem.
d. Does the nonrejection of H_0 in part c imply that no relationship exists between tire price and sales volume?
e. Find the coefficient of determination for the least squares line of part a and interpret its value in the context of the problem.
f. Find the coefficient of correlation for the least squares line of part a and interpret its value in the context of the problem.

```
The regression equation is
SALES = 44.2 -  0.025 PRICE

Predictor        Coef       Stdev      t-ratio        p
Constant        44.17       42.71         1.03    0.377
PRICE         -0.0255       0.8663        -0.03    0.978

s = 34.33         R-sq = 0.0%       R-sq(adj) = 0.0%

Analysis of Variance

SOURCE        DF         SS          MS          F          p
Regression     1          1           1       0.00      0.978
Error          3       3535        1178
Total          4       3536

------------------------------------------------------------

Correlation of PRICE and SALES = -0.017
```

10.8 USING THE MODEL FOR ESTIMATION AND PREDICTION

If we are satisfied that a useful model has been found to describe the relationship between x and y, we are ready for step 5 in our regression modeling procedure: using the model for estimation and prediction.

The most common uses of a probabilistic model for making inferences can be divided into two categories. The first is the use of the model for estimating the mean value of y, E(y), *for a specific value of* x.

For our advertising–sales example, we may want to estimate the mean sales revenue for *all* months during which $400 ($x = 4$) is expended on advertising.

The second use of the model entails predicting a new individual y *value for a given* x.

That is, if we decide to expend $400 in advertising next month, we may want to predict the firm's sales revenue for that month.

In the first case, we are attempting to estimate the mean value of y for a very large number of experiments at the given x value. In the second case, we are trying to predict the outcome of a single experiment at the given x value. Which of these model uses—estimating the mean value of y or predicting an individual new value of y (for the same value of x)—can be accomplished with the greater accuracy?

Before answering this question, we first consider the problem of choosing an estimator (or predictor) of the mean (or a new individual) y value. We will use the least squares prediction equation

$$\hat{y} = \hat{\beta}_0 + \hat{\beta}_1 x$$

both to estimate the mean value of y and to predict a specific new value of y for a given value of x. For our example, we found

$$\hat{y} = -.1 + .7x$$

so that the estimated mean sales revenue for all months when $x = 4$ (advertising is 400) is

$$\hat{y} = -.1 + .7(4) = 2.7$$

or $2,700$. (Recall that the units of y are thousands of dollars.) The same value is used to predict a new y value when $x = 4$. That is, both the estimated mean and the predicted value of y are $\hat{y} = 2.7$ when $x = 4$, as shown in Figure 10.18.

The difference between these two model uses lies in the relative accuracy of the estimate and the prediction. These accuracies are best measured by using the sampling errors of the least squares line when it is used as an estimator and as a predictor, respectively. These errors are reflected in the standard deviations given in the next box.

Sampling Errors for the Estimator of the Mean of y and the Predictor of an Individual New Value of y

1. The standard deviation of the sampling distribution of the estimator $\hat{y}$ of the mean value of y at a specific value of x, say x_p, is

$$\sigma_{\hat{y}} = \sigma \sqrt{\frac{1}{n} + \frac{(x_p - \bar{x})^2}{SS_{xx}}}$$

where σ is the standard deviation of the random error ϵ. We refer to $\sigma_{\hat{y}}$ as the standard error of $\hat{y}$.

2. The standard deviation of the prediction error for the predictor $\hat{y}$ of an individual new y value at a specific value of x is

$$\sigma_{(y-\hat{y})} = \sigma \sqrt{1 + \frac{1}{n} + \frac{(x_p - \bar{x})^2}{SS_{xx}}}$$

where σ is the standard deviation of the random error ϵ. We refer to $\sigma_{(y-\hat{y})}$ as the standard error of the prediction.

FIGURE 10.18
Estimated mean value and predicted individual value of sales revenue y for $x = 4$

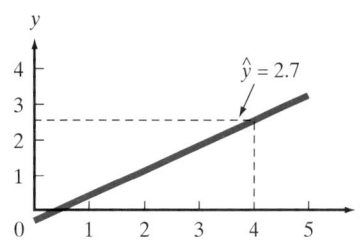

The true value of σ is rarely known, so we estimate σ by s and calculate the estimation and prediction intervals as shown in the next two boxes.

A 100(1 − α)% Confidence Interval for the Mean Value of y at x = x_p

$$\hat{y} \pm t_{\alpha/2} \cdot (\text{Estimated standard error of } \hat{y})$$

or

$$\hat{y} \pm t_{\alpha/2} s \sqrt{\frac{1}{n} + \frac{(x_p - \bar{x})^2}{SS_{xx}}}$$

where $t_{\alpha/2}$ is based on $(n - 2)$ degrees of freedom.

A 100(1 − α)% Prediction Interval* for an Individual New Value of y at x = x_p

$$\hat{y} \pm t_{\alpha/2} \cdot (\text{Estimated standard error of prediction})$$

or

$$\hat{y} \pm t_{\alpha/2} s \sqrt{1 + \frac{1}{n} + \frac{(x_p - \bar{x})^2}{SS_{xx}}}$$

where $t_{\alpha/2}$ is based on $(n - 2)$ degrees of freedom.

EXAMPLE 10.3

Find a 95% confidence interval for the mean monthly sales when the appliance store spends $400 on advertising.

SOLUTION

For a $400 advertising expenditure, $x = 4$ and the confidence interval for the mean value of y is

$$\hat{y} \pm t_{\alpha/2} s \sqrt{\frac{1}{n} + \frac{(x_p - \bar{x})^2}{SS_{xx}}} = \hat{y} \pm t_{.025} s \sqrt{\frac{1}{5} + \frac{(4 - \bar{x})^2}{SS_{xx}}}$$

where $t_{.025}$ is based on $n - 2 = 5 - 2 = 3$ degrees of freedom. Recall that $\hat{y} = 2.7$, $s = .61, \bar{x} = 3$, and $SS_{xx} = 10$. From Table VI in Appendix B, $t_{.025} = 3.182$. Thus, we have

$$2.7 \pm (3.182)(.61) \sqrt{\frac{1}{5} + \frac{(4 - 3)^2}{10}} = 2.7 \pm (3.182)(.61)(.55)$$

$$= 2.7 \pm (3.182)(.34)$$

$$= 2.7 \pm 1.1 = (1.6, 3.8)$$

Therefore, when the store spends $400 a month on advertising, we are 95% confident that the mean sales revenue is between $1,600 and $3,800. Note that we used a small amount of data (small in size) for purposes of illustration in fitting the least squares line. The interval would probably be narrower if more information had been obtained from a larger sample. ∎

---

*The term *prediction interval* is used when the interval formed is intended to enclose the value of a random variable. The term *confidence interval* is reserved for estimation of population parameters (such as the mean).

EXAMPLE 10.4

Predict the monthly sales for next month, if $400 is spent on advertising. Use a 95% prediction interval.

SOLUTION

To predict the sales for a particular month for which $x_p = 4$, we calculate the 95% prediction interval as

$$\hat{y} \pm t_{\alpha/2}s\sqrt{1 + \frac{1}{n} + \frac{(x_p - \bar{x})^2}{SS_{xx}}} = 2.7 \pm (3.182)(.61)\sqrt{1 + \frac{1}{5} + \frac{(4-3)^2}{10}}$$

$$= 2.7 \pm (3.182)(.61)(1.14)$$

$$= 2.7 \pm (3.182)(.70)$$

$$= 2.7 \pm 2.2 = (.5, 4.9)$$

Therefore, we predict with 95% confidence that the sales revenue next month (a month in which we spend $400 in advertising) will fall in the interval from $500 to $4,900. Like the confidence interval for the mean value of y, the prediction interval for y is quite large. This is because we have chosen a simple example (only five data points) to fit the least squares line. The width of the prediction interval could be reduced by using a larger number of data points.

Both the confidence interval for $E(y)$ and prediction interval for y can be obtained using a statistical software package. Figures 10.19 and 10.20 are SAS printouts showing confidence intervals and prediction intervals, respectively, for the data in the advertising–sales example.

The 95% confidence interval for $E(y)$ when $x = 4$ is highlighted in Figure 10.19 in the row corresponding to **4** under the columns labeled **Lower95% Mean** and **Upper95% Mean**. The interval shown on the printout, (1.6445, 3.7555), agrees (except for rounding) with the interval calculated in Example 10.3. The 95% prediction interval for y when $x = 4$ is highlighted in Figure 10.20 under the columns **Lower95% Predict** and **Upper95% Predict**. Again, except for rounding, the SAS interval (.5028, 4.8972) agrees with the one computed in Example 10.4.

Obs	X		Dep Var Y	Predict Value	Std Err Predict	Lower95% Mean	Upper95% Mean	Residual
1	1	1	1.0000	0.6000	0.469	-0.8927	2.0927	0.4000
2	2	2	1.0000	1.3000	0.332	0.2445	2.3555	-0.3000
3	3	3	2.0000	2.0000	0.271	1.1382	2.8618	0
4	4	4	2.0000	2.7000	0.332	1.6445	3.7555	-0.7000
5	5	5	4.0000	3.4000	0.469	1.9073	4.8927	0.6000

FIGURE 10.19   SAS printout giving 95% confidence intervals for $E(y)$

Obs	X		Dep Var Y	Predict Value	Std Err Predict	Lower95% Predict	Upper95% Predict	Residual
1	1	1	1.0000	0.6000	0.469	-1.8376	3.0376	0.4000
2	2	2	1.0000	1.3000	0.332	-0.8972	3.4972	-0.3000
3	3	3	2.0000	2.0000	0.271	-0.1110	4.1110	0
4	4	4	2.0000	2.7000	0.332	0.5028	4.8972	-0.7000
5	5	5	4.0000	3.4000	0.469	0.9624	5.8376	0.6000

FIGURE 10.20   SAS printout giving 95% prediction intervals for y

FIGURE 10.21
A 95% confidence interval for mean sales and a prediction interval for sales when $x = 4$

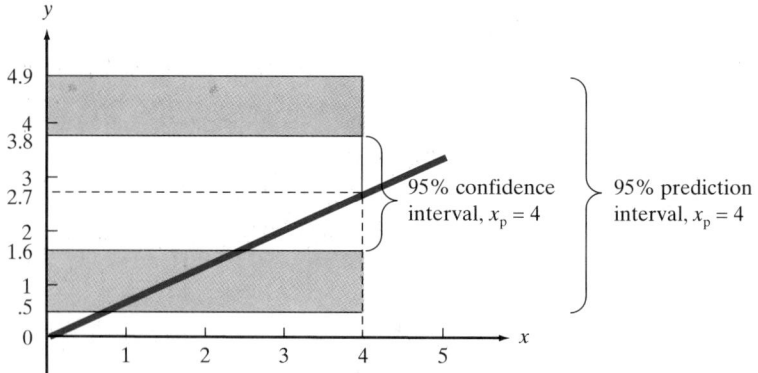

A comparison of the confidence interval for the mean value of y and the prediction interval for a new value of y when $x = 4$ is illustrated in Figure 10.21. Note that the prediction interval for an individual new value of y is always wider than the corresponding confidence interval for the mean value of y. You can see this by examining the formulas for the two intervals and by studying Figure 10.21.

The error in estimating the mean value of y, $E(y)$, for a given value of x, say x_p, is the distance between the least squares line and the true line of means, $E(y) = \beta_0 + \beta_1 x$. This error, $[\hat{y} - E(y)]$, is shown in Figure 10.22. In contrast, *the error* $(y_p - \hat{y})$ *in predicting some future value of y is the sum of two errors*—the error of estimating the mean of y, $E(y)$, shown in Figure 10.22, plus the random error that is a component of the value of y to be predicted (see Figure 10.23). Consequently, the error of predicting a particular value of y will be larger than the error of estimating the mean value of y for a particular value of x. Note from their formulas that both the error of estimation and the error of prediction take their smallest values when $x_p = \bar{x}$. The farther x_p lies from $\bar{x}$, the larger will be the errors of estimation and prediction. You can see why this is true by noting the deviations for different values of x_p between the line of means $E(y) = \beta_0 + \beta_1 x$ and the predicted line of means $\hat{y} = \hat{\beta}_0 + \hat{\beta}_1 x$ shown in Figure 10.23. The deviation is larger at the extremes of the interval where the largest and smallest values of x in the data set occur.

Both the confidence intervals for mean values and the prediction intervals for new values are depicted over the entire range of the regression line in Figure

FIGURE 10.22
Error of estimating the mean value of y for a given value of x

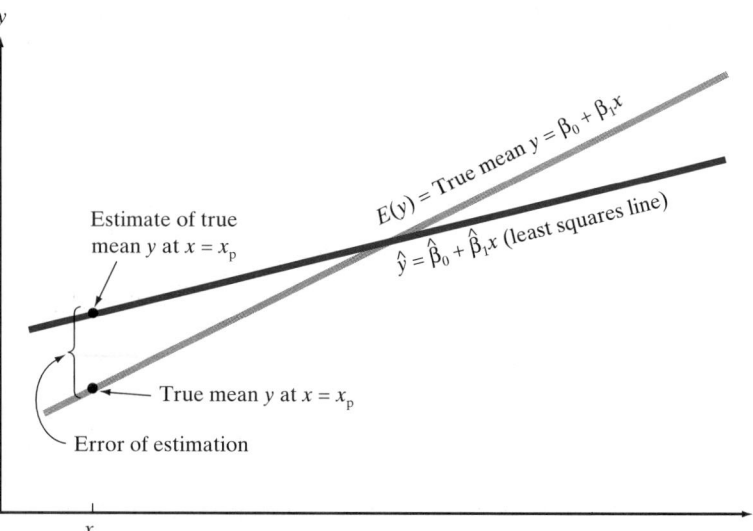

FIGURE 10.23
Error of predicting a
future value of y for a
given value of x

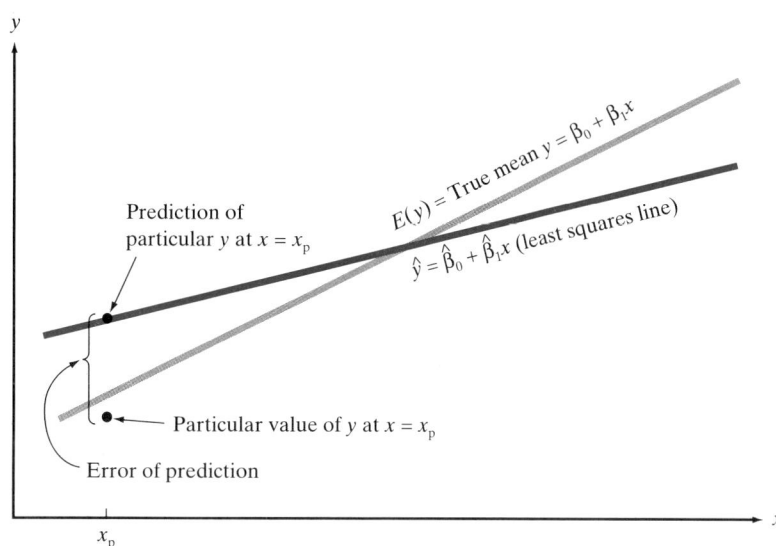

10.24. You can see that the confidence interval is always narrower than the prediction interval, and that they are both narrowest at the mean $\bar{x}$, increasing steadily as the distance $|x - \bar{x}|$ increases. In fact, when x is selected far enough away from $\bar{x}$ so that it falls outside the range of the sample data, it is dangerous to make any inferences about $E(y)$, or y.

> **Warning**
> Using the least squares prediction equation to estimate the mean value of y or to predict a particular value of y for values of x that fall *outside the range* of the values of x contained in your sample data may lead to errors of estimation or prediction that are much larger than expected. Although the least squares model may provide a very good fit to the data over the range of x values contained in the sample, it could give a poor representation of the true model for values of x outside this region.

The confidence interval width grows smaller as n is increased; thus, in theory, you can obtain as precise an estimate of the mean value of y as desired (at any given x) by selecting a large enough sample. The prediction interval for a new value of y also grows smaller as n increases, but there is a lower limit on its width.

FIGURE 10.24
Confidence intervals
for mean values and
prediction intervals for
new values

STATISTICS IN ACTION

10.2 STATISTICAL ASSESSMENT OF DAMAGE TO BRONX BRICKS

This case concerns an actual civil suit, described in *Chance* (Summer 1994), in which statistics played a key role in the jury's decision. The suit revolved around a five-building apartment complex located in the Bronx, New York. The buildings were constructed in the late 1970s from custom-designed jumbo (35-pound) bricks. Nearly three-quarters of a million bricks were used in the construction.

Over time, the bricks began to suffer *spalling* damage, i.e., separation of some portion of the face of a brick from its body. Experts agreed that the cause of the spalling was winter month freeze-thaw cycles in which water absorbed in the brick face alternates between freezing and thawing. The owner of the complex alleged that the bricks were defective. The brick manufacturer countered that poor design and shoddy management of water runoff caused the water to be trapped and absorbed in the bricks, leading to the damage. Ultimately, the suit required an estimate of the spall rate—the rate of damage per 1,000 bricks.

The owner estimated the spall rate using several *scaffold-drop* surveys. With this method, an engineer lowers a scaffold to selected places on building walls and counts the number of visible spalls for every 1,000 bricks in the observation area. The estimated spall rate is then multiplied by the total number of bricks (in thousands) in the entire complex to determine the total number of damaged bricks. When properly designed, the scaffold-drop survey, although extremely time-consuming and tedious to perform, is considered the "gold standard" for measuring spall damage. However, the owner did not drop the scaffolds at randomly selected wall areas. Instead, scaffolds were dropped primarily in areas of high spall concentration, leading to a substantially biased high estimate of total spall damage.

In an attempt to obtain an unbiased estimate of spall rate, the brick manufacturer conducted its own survey of the walls of the complex. The walls were divided into 83 wall segments and a photograph of each wall segment was taken. The number of spalled bricks that could be made out from each photo was recorded and the sum over all 83 wall segments was used as an estimate of total spall damage.

When the data from the two methods were compared, major discrepancies were discovered. At eleven locations that had been painstakingly surveyed by the scaffold drops, the spalls visible from the photos did not include all of the spalls identified on the drops. For these wall segments, the photo method provided a serious underestimate of the spall rate, as shown in Table 10.8. Consequently, the total spall damage estimated by the photo survey will also be underestimated.

In this court case, the jury was faced with the following dilemma: The scaffold-drop survey provided the most accurate estimate of spall rate in a given wall segment. Unfortunately, the drop areas were not selected at random from the entire complex; rather, drops were made at areas with high spall concentrations, leading to an overestimate of the total damage. On the other hand, the photo survey was complete in that all 83 wall segments in the complex were checked for spall damage. But the spall rate estimated by the photos, at least in areas of high spall concentration, was biased low, leading to an underestimate of the total damage.

Focus

Use the data in Table 10.8, as did expert statisticians who testified in the case, to help the jury estimate the true spall rate at a given wall segment. Then explain how this information, coupled with the data (not given here) on all 83 wall segments, can provide a reasonable estimate of the total spall damage (i.e., total number of damaged bricks). *[Note:* The data in Table 10.8 is available on a 3.5" disk in the file named TAB10.008.]

If you examine the formula for the prediction interval, you will see that the interval can get no smaller than $\hat{y} \pm z_{\alpha/2}\sigma$.* Thus, the only way to obtain more accurate predictions for new values of y is to reduce the standard deviation of the regression model, σ. This can be accomplished only by improving the model, either by

---

*The result follows from the facts that, for large n, $t_{\alpha/2} \approx z_{\alpha/2}$, $s \approx \sigma$, and the last two terms under the radical in the standard error of the predictor are approximately 0.

TABLE 10.8   **Comparison of Spall Rates Estimated by Two Methods (Statistics in Action 10.2)**

Drop Location	Drop Spall Rate (per 1,000 bricks)	Photo Spall Rate (per 1,000 bricks)
1	0	0
2	5.1	0
3	6.6	0
4	1.1	.8
5	1.8	1.0
6	3.9	1.0
7	11.5	1.9
8	22.1	7.7
9	39.3	14.9
10	39.9	13.9
11	43.0	11.8

Source: Fairley, W. B., et al. "Bricks, buildings, and the Bronx: Estimating masonry deterioration." Chance, Vol. 7, No. 3, Summer 1994, p. 36 (Figure 3). [Note: The data points are estimated from the points shown on a scatterplot.]

---

using a curvilinear (rather than linear) relationship with x or by adding new independent variables to the model, or both. Methods of improving the model are discussed in Chapters 11 and 12.

EXERCISES   10.57–10.66

Note: Exercises marked with 💾 *contain data for computer analysis on a 3.5" disk (file name in parentheses).*

Learning the Mechanics

10.57 Consider the following pairs of measurements:

x	−2	0	2	4	6	8	10
y	0	3	2	3	8	10	11

  a. Construct a scattergram for these data.
  b. Find the least squares line, and plot it on your scattergram.
  c. Find s^2.
  d. Find a 90% confidence interval for the mean value of y when $x = 3$. Plot the upper and lower bounds of the confidence interval on your scattergram.
  e. Find a 90% prediction interval for a new value of y when $x = 3$. Plot the upper and lower bounds of the prediction interval on your scattergram.
  f. Compare the widths of the intervals you constructed in parts **d** and **e**. Which is wider and why?

10.58 Consider the pairs of measurements shown in the next table.

x	4	6	0	5	2	3	2	6	2	1
y	3	5	−1	4	3	2	0	4	1	1

For these data, $SS_{xx} = 38.9000$, $SS_{yy} = 33.600$, $SS_{xy} = 32.8$, and $\hat{y} = -.414 + .843x$.
  a. Construct a scattergram for these data.
  b. Plot the least squares line on your scattergram.
  c. Use a 95% confidence interval to estimate the mean value of y when $x_p = 6$. Plot the upper and lower bounds of the interval on your scattergram.
  d. Repeat part **c** for $x_p = 3.2$ and $x_p = 0$.
  e. Compare the widths of the three confidence intervals you constructed in parts **c** and **d** and explain why they differ.

10.59 Refer to Exercise 10.58.
  a. Using no information about x, estimate and calculate a 95% confidence interval for the mean value of y. [*Hint:* Use the one-sample t methodology of Section 7.3.]
  b. Plot the estimated mean value and the confidence interval as horizontal lines on your scattergram.
  c. Compare the confidence intervals you calculated in parts **c** and **d** of Exercise 10.58 with the one you calculated in part **a** of this exercise. Does x appear to contribute information about the mean value of y?
  d. Check the answer you gave in part **c** with a statistical test of the null hypothesis $H_0: \beta_1 = 0$ against $H_a: \beta_1 \neq 0$. Use $\alpha = .05$.

10.60 In fitting a least squares line to $n = 10$ data points, the following quantities were computed:

$$SS_{xx} = 32$$
$$\bar{x} = 3$$
$$SS_{yy} = 26$$
$$\bar{y} = 4$$
$$SS_{xy} = 28$$

a. Find the least squares line.
b. Graph the least squares line.
c. Calculate SSE. d. Calculate s^2.
e. Find a 95% confidence interval for the mean value of y when $x_p = 2.5$.
f. Find a 95% prediction interval for y when $x_p = 4$.

Applying the Concepts

10.61 **(X10.061)** Many variables influence the sales of existing single-family homes. One of these is the interest rate charged for mortgage loans. Shown in the table below are the total number of existing single-family homes sold annually, y, and the average annual conventional mortgage interest rate, x, for 1982–1994. A MINITAB printout of the simple linear regression follows the table.

a. Plot the data points on graph paper.
b. Find the least squares line relating y to x on the printout. Plot the line on your graph from part **a** to see if the line appears to model the relationship between y and x.
c. Do the data provide sufficient evidence to indicate that mortgage interest rates contribute information for the prediction of annual sales of existing single-family homes? Use $\alpha = .05$.
d. Locate r^2 and interpret its value.
e. A 95% confidence interval for the mean annual number of existing single-family homes sold when the average annual mortgage interest rate is 10.0% is shown under **95% C.I.** on the printout. Interpret this interval.
f. A 95% prediction interval for the annual number of existing single-family homes sold when the average annual mortgage interest rate is 10.0% is shown under **95% P.I.** on the printout. Interpret this interval.
g. Explain why the widths of the intervals found in parts **e** and **f** differ.

10.62 Refer to the simple linear regression of number of employees y and age x for fast-growing firms, Exercises 10.21, 10.28, and 10.39. The SAS printout of the analysis is reproduced on page 481.

Year	Homes Sold y (1,000s)	Interest Rate x (%)	Year	Homes Sold y (1,000s)	Interest Rate x (%)
1982	1,990	15.82	1989	3,346	10.22
1983	2,719	13.44	1990	3,211	10.08
1984	2,868	13.81	1991	3,220	9.20
1985	3,214	12.29	1992	3,520	8.43
1986	3,565	10.09	1993	3,802	7.36
1987	3,526	10.17	1994	3,946	8.59
1988	3,594	10.31			

Source: U.S. Bureau of the Census, *Statistical Abstract of the United States: 1995,* pp. 529, 730.

```
The regression equation is
HOMES = 5342 - 193 INTRATE

Predictor       Coef       Stdev      t-ratio        p
Constant       5341.9      298.9        17.87      0.000
INTRATE        -192.58      27.17       -7.09      0.000

s = 227.8      R-sq = 82.0%      R-sq(adj) = 80.4%

Analysis of Variance

SOURCE          DF          SS           MS          F          p
Regression       1       2607650      2607650      50.25      0.000
Error           11        570876        51898
Total           12       3178526

    Fit   Stdev.Fit          95% C.I.            95% P.I.
 3416.2        66.4     ( 3269.9, 3562.4) ( 2893.7, 3938.6)
```

Dependent Variable: NUMBER

Analysis of Variance

Source	DF	Sum of Squares	Mean Square	F Value	Prob>F
Model	1	23536.50149	23536.50149	11.451	0.0070
Error	10	20554.41518	2055.44152		
C Total	11	44090.91667			

Root MSE	45.33698	R-square	0.5338	
Dep Mean	61.08333	Adj R-sq	0.4872	
C.V.	74.22152			

Parameter Estimates

Variable	DF	Parameter Estimate	Standard Error	T for HO: Parameter=0	Prob > |T|
INTERCEP	1	-51.361607	35.71379104	-1.438	0.1809
AGE	1	17.754464	5.24673562	3.384	0.0070

Obs	AGE	Dep Var NUMBER	Predict Value	Std Err Predict	Lower95% Predict	Upper95% Predict	Residual
1	5	43.0000	37.4107	14.840	-68.8810	143.7	5.5893
2	5	52.0000	37.4107	14.840	-68.8810	143.7	14.5893
3	4	9.0000	19.6563	17.921	-88.9672	128.3	-10.6562
4	7	40.0000	72.9196	13.547	-32.5114	178.4	-32.9196
5	5	6.0000	37.4107	14.840	-68.8810	143.7	-31.4107
6	6	12.0000	55.1652	13.204	-50.0496	160.4	-43.1652
7	14	200.0	197.2	42.301	59.0415	335.4	2.7991
8	5	76.0000	37.4107	14.840	-68.8810	143.7	38.5893
9	7	15.0000	72.9196	13.547	-32.5114	178.4	-57.9196
10	6	40.0000	55.1652	13.204	-50.0496	160.4	-15.1652
11	5	65.0000	37.4107	14.840	-68.8810	143.7	27.5893
12	7	175.0	72.9196	13.547	-32.5114	178.4	102.1
13	10	.	126.2	23.268	12.6384	239.7	.

a. A 95% prediction interval for y when $x = 10$ is shown at the bottom of the printout. Interpret this interval.

b. How would the width of a 95% confidence interval for $E(y)$ when $x = 10$ compare to the interval, part **a**?

c. Would you recommend using the model to predict the number of employees at a firm that has been in business two years? Explain.

10.63 **(X10.063)** Managers are an important part of any organization's resource base. Accordingly, the organization should be just as concerned about forecasting its future managerial needs as it is with forecasting its needs for, say, the natural resources used in its production process (Northcraft and Neale, *Organizational Behavior: A Management Challenge*, 1994). A common forecasting procedure is to model the relationship between sales and the number of managers needed, since the demand for managers is the result of the increases and decreases in the demand for products and ser-

vices that a firm offers its customers. To develop this relationship, the data shown in the table at the top of page 482 are collected from a firm's records. An SPSS printout of the simple linear regression follows the table.

a. Test the usefulness of the model. Use $\alpha = .05$. State your conclusion in the context of the problem.

b. The company projects that it will sell 39 units in May of 1997. Use the least squares model to construct a 90% prediction interval for the number of managers needed in May 1997.

c. Interpret the interval in part **b**. Use the interval to determine the reliability of the firm's projection.

10.64 The reasons given by workers for quitting their jobs generally fall into one of two categories: (1) worker quits to seek or take a different job, or (2) worker quits to withdraw from the labor force. Economic theory suggests that wages and quit rates are related. The table below lists quit rates

Month	Units Sold, x	Managers, y
3/92	5	10
6/92	4	11
9/92	8	10
12/92	7	10
3/93	9	9
6/93	15	10
9/93	20	11
12/93	21	17
3/94	25	19
6/94	24	21

Month	Units Sold, x	Managers, y
9/94	30	22
12/94	31	25
3/95	36	30
6/95	38	30
9/95	40	31
12/95	41	31
3/96	51	32
6/96	40	30
9/96	48	32
12/96	47	32

```
* * * *   M U L T I P L E   R E G R E S S I O N   * * * *

Equation Number 1    Dependent Variable..    MANAGERS

Variable(s) Entered on Step Number
   1..    UNITS

Multiple R              .96386
R Square                .92903
Adjusted R Square       .92509
Standard Error         2.56642

Analysis of Variance
                     DF        Sum of Squares        Mean Square
Regression            1           1551.99292         1551.99292
Residual             18            118.55708            6.58650

F =     235.63225      Signif F =  .0000

------------------ Variables in the Equation ------------------

Variable              B          SE B         Beta          T    Sig T

UNITS             .586100     .038182      .963863     15.350   .0000
(Constant)       5.325299    1.179868                   4.513   .0003
```

(quits per 100 employees) and the average hourly wage in a sample of 15 manufacturing industries. A MINITAB printout of the simple linear regression of quit rate y on average wage x is shown on page 483.

Industry	Quit Rate, y	Average Wage, x
1	1.4	$ 8.20
2	.7	10.35
3	2.6	6.18
4	3.4	5.37
5	1.7	9.94
6	1.7	9.11
7	1.0	10.59
8	.5	13.29
9	2.0	7.99
10	3.8	5.54
11	2.3	7.50
12	1.9	6.43
13	1.4	8.83
14	1.8	10.93
15	2.0	8.80

a. Do the data present sufficient evidence to conclude that average hourly wage rate contributes useful information for the prediction of quit rates? What does your model suggest about the relationship between quit rates and wages?

b. A 95% prediction interval for the quit rate in an industry with an average hourly wage of $9.00 is given at the bottom of the MINITAB printout. Interpret the result.

c. A 95% confidence interval for the mean quit rate for industries with an average hourly wage of $9.00 is also shown on the printout. Interpret this result.

10.65 **(X10.065)** Managers are interested in modeling past cost behavior in order to make more accurate predictions of future costs. Models of past cost behavior are called *cost functions*. Factors that influence costs are called *cost drivers* (Horngren, Foster, and Datar, *Cost Accounting,* 1994). The cost data on page 483 are from a rug manufacturer. Indirect manufacturing labor costs consist of

```
The regression equation is
QuitRate = 4.86 - 0.347 AveWage

Predictor        Coef        Stdev      t-ratio         p
Constant       4.8615       0.5201         9.35     0.000
AveWage       -0.34655      0.05866       -5.91     0.000

s = 0.4862     R-sq = 72.9%      R-sq(adj) = 70.8%

Analysis of Variance

SOURCE          DF          SS          MS         F         p
Regression       1       8.2507      8.2507     34.90     0.000
Error           13       3.0733      0.2364
Total           14      11.3240

     Fit   Stdev.Fit        95% C.I.              95% P.I.
   1.743      0.128    (  1.467, 2.018)    (  0.656, 2.829)
```

machine maintenance costs and setup labor costs. The latter are the costs of preparing the machines to produce a particular carpet pattern.

Week	Indirect Manufacturing Labor Costs	Cost Driven: Machine Hours
1	$1,190	68
2	1,211	88
3	1,004	62
4	917	72
5	770	60
6	1,456	96
7	1,180	78
8	710	46
9	1,316	82
10	1,032	94
11	752	68
12	963	48

Source: Horngren, Foster, and Datar, *Cost Accounting,* 1994.

a. In developing a cost function from these data, which variable should be the dependent variable? Why?
b. Construct a scatterplot for these data. What does the scatterplot suggest about the relationship between cost and machine hours?
c. Use the method of least squares to estimate the cost function.
d. Is the least squares model statistically useful? Conduct the appropriate hypothesis test. Use $\alpha = .05$.
e. Calculate r^2 and interpret its value in the context of the problem.
f. Find a 95% prediction interval for y for a selected value of x. Interpret the interval.

10.66 The data for Exercise 10.30 are reproduced below.
a. Use a 90% confidence interval to estimate the mean useful life of a brand A cutting tool when the cutting speed is 45 meters per minute.

	USEFUL LIFE (HOURS)	
Cutting Speed (meters per minute)	Brand A	Brand B
30	4.5	6.0
30	3.5	6.5
30	5.2	5.0
40	5.2	6.0
40	4.0	4.5
40	2.5	5.0
50	4.4	4.5
50	2.8	4.0
50	1.0	3.7
60	4.0	3.8
60	2.0	3.0
60	1.1	2.4
70	1.1	1.5
70	.5	2.0
70	3.0	1.0

Repeat for brand B. Compare the widths of the two intervals and comment on the reasons for any difference.

b. Use a 90% prediction interval to predict the useful life of a brand A cutting tool when the cutting speed is 45 meters per minute. Repeat for brand B. Compare the widths of the two intervals to each other, and to the two intervals you calculated in part **a**. Comment on the reasons for any differences.

c. Note that the estimation and prediction you performed in parts **a** and **b** were for a value of x that was not included in the original sample. That is, the value x = 45 was not part of the sample. However, the value is within the range of x values in the sample, so that the regres-

sion model spans the x value for which the estimation and prediction were made. In such situations, estimation and prediction represent **interpolations**. Suppose you were asked to predict the useful life of a brand A cutting tool for a cutting speed of x = 100 meters per minute. Since the given value of x is outside the range of the sample x values, the prediction is an example of **extrapolation**. Predict the useful life of a brand A cutting tool that is operated at 100 meters per minute, and construct a 95% confidence interval for the actual useful life of the tool. What additional assumption do you have to make in order to ensure the validity of an extrapolation?

10.9 SIMPLE LINEAR REGRESSION: AN EXAMPLE

In the preceding sections we have presented the basic elements necessary to fit and use a straight-line regression model. In this section we will assemble these elements by applying them in an example with the aid of a computer.

Suppose a fire insurance company wants to relate the amount of fire damage in major residential fires to the distance between the burning house and the nearest fire station. The study is to be conducted in a large suburb of a major city; a sample of 15 recent fires in this suburb is selected. The amount of damage, y, and the distance between the fire and the nearest fire station, x, are recorded for each fire. The results are given in Table 10.9.

Step 1 First, we hypothesize a model to relate fire damage, y, to the distance from the nearest fire station, x. We hypothesize a straight-line probabilistic model:

$$y = \beta_0 + \beta_1 x + \epsilon$$

TABLE 10.9 Fire Damage Data

Distance From Fire Station, x (miles)	Fire Damage, y (thousands of dollars)
3.4	26.2
1.8	17.8
4.6	31.3
2.3	23.1
3.1	27.5
5.5	36.0
.7	14.1
3.0	22.3
2.6	19.6
4.3	31.3
2.1	24.0
1.1	17.3
6.1	43.2
4.8	36.4
3.8	26.1

```
Dep Variable: Y

                        Analysis of Variance

                      Sum of            Mean
    Source      DF    Squares          Square     F Value    Prob>F

    Model        1   841.76636       841.76636    156.886    0.0001
    Error       13    69.75098         5.36546
    C Total     14   911.51733

            Root MSE     2.31635       R-Square      0.9235
            Dep Mean    26.41333       Adj R-Sq      0.9176
            C.V.         8.76961

                        Parameter Estimates

                  Parameter      Standard      T for HO:
    Variable   DF  Estimate        Error     Parameter=0   Prob > |T|

    INTERCEP    1  10.277929     1.42027781      7.237       0.0001
    X           1   4.919331     0.39274775     12.525       0.0001

                              Predict                Lower95%  Upper95%
       Obs   X           Y     Value   Residual     Predict   Predict

        1   3.4    26.2000   27.0037    -0.8037     21.8344   32.1729
        2   1.8    17.8000   19.1327    -1.3327     13.8141   24.4514
        3   4.6    31.3000   32.9068    -1.6068     27.6186   38.1951
        4   2.3    23.1000   21.5924     1.5076     16.3577   26.8271
        5   3.1    27.5000   25.5279     1.9721     20.3573   30.6984
        6   5.5    36.0000   37.3342    -1.3342     31.8334   42.8351
        7   0.7    14.1000   13.7215     0.3785      8.1087   19.3342
        8   3.0    22.3000   25.0359    -2.7359     19.8622   30.2097
        9   2.6    19.6000   23.0682    -3.4682     17.8678   28.2686
       10   4.3    31.3000   31.4311    -0.1311     26.1908   36.6713
       11   2.1    24.0000   20.6085     3.3915     15.3442   25.8729
       12   1.1    17.3000   15.6892     1.6108     10.1999   21.1785
       13   6.1    43.2000   40.2858     2.9142     34.5906   45.9811
       14   4.8    36.4000   33.8907     2.5093     28.5640   39.2175
       15   3.8    26.1000   28.9714    -2.8714     23.7843   34.1585
       16   3.5             27.4956                 22.3239   32.6672

Sum of Residuals           -3.73035E-14
Sum of Squared Residuals      69.7510
Predicted Resid SS (Press)    93.2117
```

FIGURE 10.25   SAS printout for fire damage regression analysis

Step 2   Next, we enter the data of Table 10.9 into a computer and use a statistical software package to estimate the unknown parameters in the deterministic component of the hypothesized model. The SAS printout for the simple linear regression analysis is shown in Figure 10.25. The least squares estimate of the slope β_1 and intercept β_0, highlighted on the printout, are

$$\hat{\beta}_1 = 4.919331$$
$$\hat{\beta}_0 = 10.277929$$

and the least squares equation is (rounded)

$$\hat{y} = 10.278 + 4.919x$$

FIGURE 10.26
Least squares
model for the fire
damage data

This prediction equation is graphed in Figure 10.26 along with a plot of the data points.

The least squares estimate of the slope, $\hat{\beta}_1 = 4.919$, implies that the estimated mean damage increases by \$4,919 for each additional mile from the fire station. This interpretation is valid over the range of x, or from .7 to 6.1 miles from the station. The estimated y-intercept, $\hat{\beta}_0 = 10.278$, has the interpretation that a fire 0 miles from the fire station has an estimated mean damage of \$10,278. Although this would seem to apply to the fire station itself, remember that the y-intercept is meaningfully interpretable only if $x = 0$ is within the sampled range of the independent variable, which it is not in this case.

Step 3 Now we specify the probability distribution of the random error component ϵ. The assumptions about the distribution are identical to those listed in Section 10.3. Although we know that these assumptions are not completely satisfied (they rarely are for practical problems), we are willing to assume they are approximately satisfied for this example. The estimate of the standard deviation σ of ϵ, highlighted on the printout, is:

$$s = 2.31635$$

This implies that most of the observed fire damage (y) values will fall within approximately $2s = 4.64$ thousand dollars of their respective predicted values when using the least squares line.

Step 4 We can now check the usefulness of the hypothesized model—that is, whether x really contributes information for the prediction of y using the straight-line model. First, test the null hypothesis that the slope β_1 is 0, that is, that there is no linear relationship between fire damage and the distance from the nearest fire station, against the alternative hypothesis that fire damage increases as the distance increases. We test

$$H_0: \beta_1 = 0$$

$$H_a: \beta_1 > 0$$

The observed significance level for testing $H_a: \beta_1 \neq 0$, highlighted on the printout, is .0001. Thus, the p-value for our one-tailed test is $p = .0001/2 = .00005$. This small p-value leaves little doubt that mean fire damage and distance between the fire and station are at least linearly related, with mean fire damage increasing as the distance increases.

We gain additional information about the relationship by forming a confidence interval for the slope β_1. A 95% confidence interval is

$$\hat{\beta}_1 \pm t_{.025} s_{\hat{\beta}_1}$$

where $\hat{\beta}_1 = 4.919$ and its standard error, $s_{\hat{\beta}_1} = .393$ are both obtained from the printout. The value $t_{.025}$, based on $n - 2 = 13$ df, is 2.160. Therefore, the 95% confidence interval is

$$\hat{\beta}_1 \pm t_{.025} s_{\hat{\beta}_1} = 4.919 \pm (2.160)(.393) = 4.919 \pm .849 = (4.070, 5.768)$$

We estimate that the interval from \$4,070 to \$5,768 encloses the mean increase (β_1) in fire damage per additional mile distance from the fire station.

Another measure of the utility of the model is the coefficient of determination, r^2. The value (highlighted on the printout) is $r^2 = .9235$, which implies that about 92% of the sample variation in fire damage (y) is explained by the distance (x) between the fire and the fire station.

The coefficient of correlation, r, that measures the strength of the linear relationship between y and x is not shown on the SAS printout and must be calculated. Using the facts that $r = \sqrt{r^2}$ in simple linear regression and that r and $\hat{\beta}_1$ have the same sign, we find

$$r = +\sqrt{r^2} = \sqrt{.9235} = .96$$

The high correlation confirms our conclusion that β_1 is greater than 0; it appears that fire damage and distance from the fire station are positively correlated. All signs point to a strong linear relationship between y and x.

Step 5 We are now prepared to use the least squares model. Suppose the insurance company wants to predict the fire damage if a major residential fire were to occur 3.5 miles from the nearest fire station. The predicted value (highlighted at the bottom of the printout) is $\hat{y} = 27.4956$, while the 95% prediction interval (also highlighted) is (22.3239, 32.6672). Therefore, with 95% confidence we predict fire damage in a major residential fire 3.5 miles from the nearest station to be between \$22,324 and \$32,667.

One caution before closing: We would not use this prediction model to make predictions for homes less than .7 mile or more than 6.1 miles from the nearest fire station. A look at the data in Table 10.9 reveals that all the x values fall between .7 and 6.1. It is dangerous to use the model to make predictions outside the region in which the sample data fall. A straight line might not provide a good model for the relationship between the mean value of y and the value of x when stretched over a wider range of x values.

QUICK REVIEW

Key Terms

Bivariate relationship   461
Coefficient of correlation   461
Coefficient of determination   466
Confidence interval for mean of y 474

Dependent variable   432
Deterministic model   431
Independent variable   432
Least squares line   435

Key Formulas

$$\hat{\beta}_1 = \frac{SS_{xy}}{SS_{xx}}, \quad \hat{\beta}_0 = \bar{y} - \hat{\beta}_1 \bar{x}$$ Least squares estimates of β's   436

$$\text{where} \quad SS_{xy} = \sum xy - \frac{(\Sigma x)(\Sigma y)}{n}$$

$$SS_{xx} = \sum x^2 - \frac{(\Sigma x)^2}{n}$$

$$\hat{y} = \hat{\beta}_0 + \hat{\beta}_1 x$$ Least squares line   435

$$SSE = \sum(y_i - \hat{y}_i)^2 = SS_{yy} - \hat{\beta}_1 SS_{xy}$$ Sum of squared errors   445

$$\text{where } SS_{yy} = \sum y^2 - \frac{(\Sigma y)^2}{n}$$

$$s^2 = \frac{SSE}{n-2}$$ Estimated variance of σ^2 of ϵ 445

$$s_{\hat{\beta}_1} = \frac{s}{\sqrt{SS_{xx}}}$$ Estimated standard error of $\hat{\beta}_1$ 451

$$\hat{\beta}_1 \pm (t_{\alpha/2})s_{\hat{\beta}_1}$$ $(1-\alpha)100\%$ confidence interval for β_1 454

$$t = \frac{\hat{\beta}_1}{s_{\hat{\beta}_1}}$$ Test statistic for $H_0: \beta_1 = 0$ 452

$$r^2 = \frac{SS_{yy} - SSE}{SS_{yy}}$$ Coefficient of determination   466

$$r = \frac{SS_{xy}}{\sqrt{SS_{xx}SS_{yy}}} = \pm\sqrt{r^2} \text{ (same sign as } \hat{\beta}_1)$$ Coefficient of correlation   461

$$\hat{y} \pm (t_{\alpha/2})s\sqrt{\frac{1}{n} + \frac{(x_p - \bar{x})^2}{SS_{xx}}}$$ $(1-\alpha)100\%$ confidence interval for $E(y)$ when $x = x_p$ 474

$$\hat{y} \pm (t_{\alpha/2})s\sqrt{1 + \frac{1}{n} + \frac{(x_p - \bar{x})^2}{SS_{xx}}}$$ $(1-\alpha)100\%$ prediction interval for y when $x = x_p$ 474

LANGUAGE LAB

Symbol	Pronunciation	Description
y		Dependent variable (variable to be predicted or modeled)
x		Independent (predictor) variable
$E(y)$		Expected (mean) value of y
β_0	beta-zero	y-intercept of true line
β_1	beta-one	Slope of true line
$\hat{\beta}_0$	beta-zero hat	Least squares estimate of y-intercept
$\hat{\beta}_1$	beta-one hat	Least squares estimate of slope
ϵ	epsilon	Random error
$\hat{y}$	y-hat	Predicted value of y
$(y - \hat{y})$		Error of prediction

SE		Sum of errors (will equal zero with least squares line)
SSE		Sum of squared errors (will be smallest for least squares line)
SS_{xx}		Sum of squares of x-values
SS_{yy}		Sum of squares of y-values
SS_{xy}		Sum of squares of cross-products, $x \cdot y$
r		Coefficient of correlation
r^2	R-squared	Coefficient of determination
x_p		Value of x used to predict y

SUPPLEMENTARY EXERCISES 10.67–10.82

Note: Exercises marked with 💾 *contain data for computer analysis on a 3.5" disk (file name in parentheses).*

Learning the Mechanics

10.67 In fitting a least squares line to $n = 15$ data points, the following quantities were computed: $SS_{xx} = 55$, $SS_{yy} = 198$, $SS_{xy} = -88$, $\bar{x} = 1.3$, and $\bar{y} = 35$.
  a. Find the least squares line.
  b. Graph the least squares line.
  c. Calculate SSE.
  d. Calculate s^2.
  e. Find a 90% confidence interval for β_1. Interpret this estimate.
  f. Find a 90% confidence interval for the mean value of y when $x = 15$.
  g. Find a 90% prediction interval for y when $x = 15$.

10.68 Consider the following sample data:

y	5	1	3
x	5	1	3

  a. Construct a scattergram for the data.
  b. It is possible to find many lines for which $\Sigma(y - \hat{y}) = 0$. For this reason, the criterion $\Sigma(y - \hat{y}) = 0$ is not used for identifying the "best-fitting" straight line. Find two lines that have $\Sigma(y - \hat{y}) = 0$.
  c. Find the least squares line.
  d. Compare the value of SSE for the least squares line to that of the two lines you found in part **b**. What principle of least squares is demonstrated by this comparison?

10.69 Consider the following 10 data points:

x	3	5	6	4	3	7	6	5	4	7
y	4	3	2	1	2	3	3	5	4	2

  a. Plot the data on a scattergram.
  b. Calculate the values of r and r^2.

  c. Is there sufficient evidence to indicate that x and y are linearly correlated? Test at the $\alpha = .10$ level of significance.

Applying the Concepts

10.70 **(X10.070)** 💾 Emotional exhaustion, or *burnout,* is a significant problem for people with careers in the field of human services. It seriously affects productivity and feelings of job satisfaction. Regression analysis was used to investigate the relationship between burnout and aspects of the human services professional's job and job-related behavior (*Journal of Applied Behavioral Science,* Vol. 22, 1986). Emotional exhaustion was measured with the Maslach Burnout Inventory, a questionnaire. One of the independent variables considered, called *concentration,* was the proportion of social contacts with individuals who belong to a person's work group. The table at the top of page 490 lists the values of the emotional exhaustion index (higher values indicate greater exhaustion) and concentration for a sample of 25 human services professionals who work in a large public hospital. An SPSS printout of the simple linear regression follows the table.
  a. Construct a scattergram for the data. Do the variables x and y appear to be related?
  b. Find the correlation coefficient for the data and interpret its value. Does your conclusion mean that concentration causes emotional exhaustion? Explain.
  c. Test the usefulness of the straight-line relationship with concentration for predicting burnout. Use $\alpha = .05$.
  d. Find the coefficient of determination for the model and interpret it.
  e. Find a 95% confidence interval for the slope β_1. Interpret the result.
  f. Use a 95% confidence interval to estimate the mean exhaustion level for all professionals who have 80% of their social contacts within their work groups. Interpret the interval.

10.71 *Work standards* specify time, cost, and efficiency norms for the performance of work tasks. They

Exhaustion Index, y	Concentration, x	Exhaustion Index, y	Concentration, x
100	20%	493	86%
525	60	892	83
300	38	527	79
980	88	600	75
310	79	855	81
900	87	709	75
410	68	791	77
296	12	718	77
120	35	684	77
501	70	141	17
920	80	400	85
810	92	970	96
506	77		

```
Correlations:    CONCEN

  EXHAUST        .7825**

N of cases:      25          1-tailed Signif:  * - .01  ** - .001

-------------------------------------------------------------------------------

         * * * *   M U L T I P L E   R E G R E S S I O N   * * * *

Equation Number 1    Dependent Variable..   EXHAUST

Variable(s) Entered on Step Number
   1..     CONCEN

Multiple R           .78250
R Square             .61231
Adjusted R Square    .59545
Standard Error    174.20742

Analysis of Variance
                  DF       Sum of Squares      Mean Square
Regression         1         1102408.24475    1102408.24475
Residual          23          698009.19525      30348.22588

F =     36.32529      Signif F =  .0000

--------------------- Variables in the Equation ------------------------

Variable           B          SE B      95% Confdnce Intrvl B        T    Sig T

CONCEN        8.865471    1.470948      5.822584     11.908359     6.027   .0000
(Constant)  -29.496718  106.697163   -250.216617    191.223182     -.276   .7847
```

are typically used to monitor job performance. In the distribution center of McCormick and Co., Inc., data were collected to develop work standards for the time to assemble or fill customer orders. The table at right contains data for a random sample of 9 orders.

a. Construct a scattergram for these data and interpret it.

b. Fit a least squares line to these data using time as the dependent variable.

c. In general, we would expect the mean time to fill an order to increase with the size of the order. Do the data support this theory? Test using $\alpha = .05$.

Time (mins.)	Order Size (cases)
27	36
15	34
71	255
35	103
8	4
60	555
3	6
10	60
10	96

Source: Boyle, D., Ray, B. A., and Kahan, G. "Work standards—the quality way." *Production and Inventory Management Journal,* Second Quarter, 1991, p. 67.

d. Find a 95% confidence interval for the mean time to fill an order consisting of 150 cases.

10.72 Common maize rust is a serious disease of sweet corn. Although fungicides are effective in controlling maize rust, the timing of the application is crucial. Researchers in New York state have developed an action threshold for initiation of fungicide applications based on a regression equation relating maize rust incidence to severity of the disease (*Phytopathology,* Vol. 80, 1990). In one particular field, data were collected on more than 100 plants of the sweet corn hybrid Jubilee. For each plant, incidence was measured as the percentage of leaves infected (x) and severity was calculated as the log (base 10) of the average number of infections per leaf (y). A simple linear regression analysis of the data produced the following results:

$$\hat{y} = -.939 + .020x$$
$$r^2 = .816$$
$$s = .288$$

a. Interpret the value of $\hat{\beta}_1$.
b. Interpret the value of r^2.
c. Interpret the value of s.
d. Calculate the value of r and interpret it.
e. Use the result, part **d**, to test the utility of the model. Use $\alpha = .05$. (Assume $n = 100$.)
f. Predict the severity of the disease when the incidence of maize rust for a plant is 80%. [*Note:* Take the antilog (base 10) of $\hat{y}$ to obtain the predicted average number of infections per leaf.]

10.73 In 1995, nearly half of all eating places in the United States were fast-food restaurants. These include nontraditional sites, such as hospitals, airports, gas stations, and department stores. For a sample of eight well-known fast-food chains, the table below reports the year each began franchising and the number of outlets each had in 1996. Is there a linear relationship between age of a fast-food chain and its number of outlets? Answer the question by conducting a complete simple linear regression analysis of the data.

10.74 The precision of $\hat{\beta}_1$ as an estimator of β_1 is generally measured by its standard deviation $\sigma_{\hat{\beta}_1}$. In general, the larger the value of $\sigma_{\hat{\beta}_1}$, the wider (less precise) are confidence intervals for β_1; the smaller the value of $\sigma_{\hat{\beta}_1}$, the narrower (more precise) are confidence intervals for β_1.

a. Examine the formula for $\sigma_{\hat{\beta}_1}$ and explain how the observed values of the independent variable influence the size of $\sigma_{\hat{\beta}_1}$.
b. Sometimes it is possible to obtain data for a regression study by setting the independent variable x at different levels and observing the resulting values of the dependent variable y. For example, suppose a supermarket chain is studying the relationship between the sales of a product and how many square feet of display space it is given. Data for such a study will be generated by utilizing display areas of different sizes in different stores and observing the resulting sales. If you were designing such a study, how would your answer to part **a** influence the choice of display area sizes?

10.75 (X10.075) In the late 1970s and early 1980s, the prices of single-family homes in the United States rose faster than the rate of inflation. As a result, many investors directed their funds to the housing market as a hedge against inflation. One way an investor can assess the value of a specific house is to compare it to recent sale prices for similar houses. Another popular approach is to use a regression analysis to model the relationship between price and the variables that influence price. Independent variables that could be utilized are total living area, number of rooms, number of baths, age of property, and so on. Of these factors, total living area provides the most information for determining the worth of a house. The table on page 492 lists the final selling price and total living area for a sample of 24 homes in suburban Essex county, New Jersey, that were sold during the first three months of 1996. The SAS regression printout for a straight-line model relating price to area for these data is given below the table.

a. Construct a scattergram for the data.

Restaurant	Year Began Franchising	Number of Outlets in 1996
McDonald's	1955	8,282
Dunkin' Donuts	1955	2,927
Wendy's	1971	3,002
Pizza Hut	1959	2,738
Taco Bell	1964	1,704
KFC	1971	5,142
TCBY	1982	1,148
Blimpie	1977	986

Source: Franchise Times, October 1996, pp. 14–55.

Area (sq. ft.)	Price	Area (sq. ft.)	Price
2,306	$145,541	1,753	129,900
2,677	179,900	3,206	235,000
2,324	149,000	2,474	129,900
1,447	113,900	2,933	199,500
3,333	189,000	3,987	319,000
3,004	184,500	2,598	185,500
4,142	339,717	4,934	375,000
2,923	228,000	2,253	169,000
2,902	209,000	2,998	185,900
1,847	133,000	2,791	189,800
2,148	168,000	2,865	192,000
2,819	205,000	4,417	379,900

Source: Adapted from data compiled by the Multiple Listing Service, Suburban Essex County, New Jersey, 1996.

Dependent Variable: PRICE

Analysis of Variance

Source	DF	Sum of Squares	Mean Square	F Value	Prob>F
Model	1	115571437221	115571437221	194.384	0.0001
Error	22	13080132976	594551498.89		
C Total	23	128651570197			

Root MSE	24383.42673	R-square	0.8983
Dep Mean	205623.25000	Adj R-sq	0.8937
C.V.	11.85830		

Parameter Estimates

Variable	DF	Parameter Estimate	Standard Error	T for HO: Parameter=0	Prob > |T|
INTERCEP	1	-39001	18237.940955	-2.138	0.0438
AREA	1	84.986976	6.09567579	13.942	0.0001

Obs	AREA	Dep Var PRICE	Predict Value	Std Err Predict	Lower95% Mean	Upper95% Mean	Residual
25	3000	.	215960	5032.160	205524	226396	.

b. Find the least squares line and plot it on your scattergram.

c. Find r^2 and interpret its value in the context of the problem.

d. Do the data provide evidence that living area contributes information for predicting the price of a home? Use $\alpha = .05$.

e. Find a 95% confidence interval for β_1. Does your confidence interval support the conclusion you reached in part **d**? Explain.

f. Find the observed significance level for the test in part **d**, and interpret its value.

g. Estimate the mean selling price for homes with a total living area of 3,000 square feet. Use a 95% confidence interval.

10.76 Refer to Exercise 10.40, in which managerial success, y, was modeled as a function of the number of contacts a manager makes with people outside his or her work unit, x, during a specific period of time. The data are repeated in the table at the upper left of page 493, followed by the MINITAB simple linear regression printout.

a. A particular manager was observed for two weeks, as in the *Journal of Applied Behavioral Science* (1985) study. She made 55 contacts with people outside her work unit. Predict the value of the manager's success index. Use a 90% prediction interval.

b. A second manager was observed for two weeks. This manager made 110 contacts with people outside his work unit. Give two reasons why caution should be exercised in using the least squares model developed from the given data set to construct a prediction interval for this manager's success index.

Manager	Manager Success Index, y	Number of Interactions with Outsiders, x
1	40	12
2	73	71
3	95	70
4	60	81
5	81	43
6	27	50
7	53	42
8	66	18
9	25	35
10	63	82
11	70	20
12	47	81
13	80	40
14	51	33
15	32	45
16	50	10
17	52	65
18	30	20
19	42	21

BTU/Year (thousands)	Shell Area (square feet)
3,870,000	30,001
1,371,000	13,530
2,422,000	26,060
672,200	6,355
233,100	4,576
218,900	24,680
354,000	2,621
3,135,000	23,350
1,470,000	18,770
1,408,000	12,220
2,201,000	25,490
2,680,000	23,680
337,500	5,650
567,500	8,001
555,300	6,147
239,400	2,660
2,629,000	19,240
1,102,000	10,700
423,500	9,125
423,500	6,510
1,691,000	13,530
1,870,000	18,860

c. In the context of this problem, determine the value of x for which the associated prediction interval for y is the narrowest.

10.77 **(X10.077)** Firms planning to build new plants or make additions to existing facilities have become very conscious of the energy efficiency of proposed new structures and are interested in the relation between yearly energy consumption and the number of square feet of building shell. The next table lists the energy consumption in British thermal units (a BTU is the amount of heat required to raise 1 pound of water 1°F) for 22 buildings that were all subjected to the same climatic conditions. The SAS printout that fits the straight-line model relating BTU consumption, y, to building shell area, x, is on page 494.

a. Find the least squares estimates of the intercept β_0 and the slope β_1.

b. Investigate the usefulness of the model you developed in part **a**. Is yearly energy consump-

tion positively linearly related to the shell area of the building? Test using $\alpha = .10$.

c. Calculate the observed significance level of the test of part **b** using the printout. Interpret its value.

d. Find the coefficient of determination r^2 and interpret its value.

e. A company wishes to build a new warehouse that will contain 8,000 square feet of shell area. Find the predicted value of energy consumption and a 95% prediction interval on the printout. Comment on the usefulness of this interval.

f. The application of the model you developed in part **a** to the warehouse problem of part **e** is appropriate only if certain assumptions can be made about the new warehouse. What are these assumptions?

```
The regression equation is
SUCCESS = 44.1 + 0.237 INTERACT

Predictor       Coef      Stdev     t-ratio        p
Constant      44.130      9.362        4.71    0.000
INTERACT      0.2366      0.1865        1.27    0.222

s = 19.40        R-sq = 8.6%      R-sq(adj) = 3.3%

Analysis of Variance

SOURCE        DF         SS          MS         F        p
Regression     1       606.0       606.0      1.61    0.222
Error         17      6400.6       376.5
Total         18      7006.6
```

```
Dep Variable: BTU

                        Analysis of Variance

                        Sum of          Mean
    Source      DF      Squares         Square      F Value     Prob>F

    Model        1   1.658498E+13   1.658498E+13    42.028      0.0001
    Error       20   7.89232E+12    394616010047
    C Total     21   2.44773E+13

         Root MSE     628184.69422      R-Square     0.6776
         Dep Mean   1357904.54545      Adj R-Sq     0.6614
         C.V.            46.26133

                        Parameter Estimates

                     Parameter       Standard     T for HO:
    Variable   DF     Estimate         Error    Parameter=0   Prob > |T|

    INTERCEP    1       -99045     261617.65980     -0.379       0.7090
    AREA        1     102.814048    15.85924082      6.483       0.0001

                                 Predict                  Lower95%  Upper95%
    Obs   AREA          BTU        Value     Residual     Predict   Predict

     1    30001      3870000     2985479      884521      1546958   4424000
     2    13530      1371000     1292029      78971.2    -47949.3   2632007
     3    26060      2422000     2580289     -158289      1183940   3976637
     4     6355       672200      554338      117862      -810192   1918868
     5     4576       233100      371432     -138332     -1005463   1748327
     6    24680       218900     2438405    -2219505      1054223   3822588
     7     2621       354000      170430      183570     -1222796   1563657
     8    23350      3135000     2301663      833337       927871   3675455
     9    18770      1470000     1830774     -360774       482352   3179196
    10    12220      1408000     1157342      250658      -184021   2498706
    11    25490      2201000     2521685     -320685      1130530   3912840
    12    23680      2680000     2335591      344409       959345   3711838
    13     5650       337500      481854     -144354      -887287   1850995
    14     8001       567500      723570     -156070      -631698   2078838
    15     6147       555300      532953      22347.3     -832898   1898804
    16     2660       239400      174440      64959.9    -1218433   1567313
    17    19240      2629000     1879097      749903       528832   3229362
    18    10700      1102000     1001065      100935      -343656   2345786
    19     9125       423500      839133     -415633      -511035   2189301
    20     6510       423500      570274     -146774      -793294   1933842
    21    13530      1691000     1292029      398971     -47949.3   2632007
    22    18860      1870000     1840028      29972.3      491266   3188789
    23     8000          .        723467         .        -631806   2078740

Sum of Residuals              1.6298145E-9
Sum of Squared Residuals      7.89232E+12
Predicted Resid SS (Press)  1.012747E+13
```

10.78 (X10.078) Sometimes it is known from theoretical considerations that the straight-line relationship between two variables, x and y, passes through the origin of the xy-plane. Consider the relationship between the total weight of a shipment of 50-pound bags of flour, y, and the number of bags in the shipment, x. Since a shipment containing $x = 0$ bags (i.e., no shipment at all) has a total weight of $y = 0$, a straight-line model of the relationship between x and y should pass through the point $x = 0$, $y = 0$. In such a case you could assume $\beta_0 = 0$ and characterize the relationship between x and y with the following model:

$$y = \beta_1 x + \epsilon$$

The least squares estimate of β_1 for this model is

$$\hat{\beta}_1 = \frac{\Sigma x_i y_i}{\Sigma x_i^2}$$

From the records of past flour shipments, 15 shipments were randomly chosen and the data shown in the table were recorded.

Weight of Shipment	Number of 50-Pound Bags in Shipment
5,050	100
10,249	205
20,000	450
7,420	150
24,685	500
10,206	200
7,325	150
4,958	100
7,162	150
24,000	500
4,900	100
14,501	300
28,000	600
17,002	400
16,100	400

a. Find the least squares line for the given data under the assumption that $\beta_0 = 0$. Plot the least squares line on a scattergram of the data.

b. Find the least squares line for the given data using the model

$$y = \beta_0 + \beta_1 x + \epsilon$$

(i.e., do not restrict β_0 to equal 0). Plot this line on the same scatterplot you constructed in part **a**.

c. Refer to part **b**. Why might $\hat{\beta}_0$ be different from 0 even though the true value of β_0 is known to be 0?

d. The estimated standard error of $\hat{\beta}_0$ is equal to

$$s\sqrt{\frac{1}{n} + \frac{\bar{x}^2}{\mathrm{SS}_{xx}}}$$

Use the t statistic

$$t = \frac{\hat{\beta}_0 - 0}{s\sqrt{(1/n) + (\bar{x}^2/\mathrm{SS}_{xx})}}$$

to test the null hypothesis $H_0: \beta_0 = 0$ against the alternative $H_a: \beta_0 \neq 0$. Use $\alpha = .10$. Should you include β_0 in your model?

10.79 **(X10.079)** *Comparable worth* is a compensation plan designed to eliminate pay inequities among jobs of similar worth. A number of state and municipal governments have adopted comparable-worth plans, and some unions have attempted to negotiate comparable-worth clauses into their contracts. To develop such a plan, a sample of benchmark jobs are evaluated and assigned points, x, based on factors such as responsibility, skill, effort, and working conditions. A market survey is conducted to determine the market rates (or salaries), y, of the benchmark jobs. A regression analysis is then used to characterize the relationship between salary and job evaluation points (*Public Personnel Management,* Vol. 20, 1991). The table below gives the job evaluation points and salaries for a set of 21 benchmark jobs.

a. Construct a scattergram for these data. What does it suggest about the relationship between salary and job evaluation points?

Job Evaluation Points, x	Salary, y	
970	$15,704	Electrician
500	13,984	Semiskilled laborer
370	14,196	Motor equipment operator
220	13,380	Janitor
250	13,153	Laborer
1,350	18,472	Senior engineering technician
470	14,193	Senior janitor
2,040	20,642	Revenue agent
370	13,614	Engineering aide
1,200	16,869	Electrician supervisor
820	15,184	Senior maintenance technician
1,865	17,341	Registered nurse
1,065	15,194	Licensed practical nurse
880	13,614	Principal clerk typist
340	12,594	Clerk typist
540	13,126	Senior clerk stenographer
490	12,958	Senior clerk typist
940	13,894	Principal clerk stenographer
600	13,380	Institutional attendant
805	15,559	Eligibility technician
220	13,844	Cook's helper

Dependent Variable: Y

Analysis of Variance

Source	DF	Sum of Squares	Mean Square	F Value	Prob>F
Model	1	66801750.334	66801750.334	74.670	0.0001
Error	19	16997968.904	894629.94232		
C Total	20	83799719.238			

Root MSE	945.84879	R-square	0.7972
Dep Mean	14804.52381	Adj R-sq	0.7865
C.V.	6.38892		

Parameter Estimates

Variable	DF	Parameter Estimate	Standard Error	T for HO: Parameter=0	Prob > |T|
INTERCEP	1	12024	382.31829064	31.449	0.0001
X	1	3.581616	0.41448305	8.641	0.0001

Obs	X	Dep Var Y	Predict Value	Std Err Predict	Lower95% Predict	Upper95% Predict	Residual
1	970	15704.0	15497.8	221.447	13464.6	17531.0	206.2
2	500	13984.0	13814.5	236.070	11774.1	15854.9	169.5
3	370	14196.0	13348.9	266.420	11292.1	15405.6	847.1
4	220	13380.0	12811.6	309.502	10728.6	14894.6	568.4
5	250	13153.0	12919.1	300.351	10842.0	14996.2	233.9
6	1350	18472.0	16858.8	314.833	14772.4	18945.3	1613.2
7	470	14193.0	13707.0	242.349	11663.4	15750.6	486.0
8	2040	20642.0	19330.2	562.933	17026.4	21633.9	1311.8
9	370	13614.0	13348.9	266.420	11292.1	15405.6	265.1
10	1200	16869.0	16321.6	270.968	14262.3	18380.9	547.4
11	820	15184.0	14960.6	207.190	12934.0	16987.2	223.4
12	1865	17341.0	18703.4	496.193	16467.8	20938.9	-1362.4
13	1065	15194.0	15838.1	238.553	13796.4	17879.8	-644.1
14	880	13614.0	15175.5	210.818	13147.2	17203.7	-1561.5
15	340	12594.0	13241.4	274.451	11180.1	15302.7	-647.4
16	540	13126.0	13957.7	228.483	11921.1	15994.4	-831.7
17	490	12958.0	13778.6	238.109	11737.2	15820.1	-820.6
18	940	13894.0	15390.4	217.251	13359.1	17421.6	-1496.4
19	600	13380.0	14172.6	218.972	12140.6	16204.7	-792.6
20	805	15559.0	14906.9	206.741	12880.4	16933.3	652.1
21	220	13844.0	12811.6	309.502	10728.6	14894.6	1032.4
22	800	.	14888.9	206.632	12862.6	16915.3	.

b. The SAS printout above shows the results of a straight-line model fit to these data. Identify and interpret the least squares equation.

c. Interpret the value of r^2 for this least squares equation.

d. Is there sufficient evidence to conclude that a straight-line model provides useful information about the relationship in question? Interpret the p-value for this test.

e. A job outside the set of benchmark jobs is evaluated and receives a score of 800 points.

Under the comparable-worth plan, what is a reasonable range within which a fair salary for this job should be found?

10.80 (X10.080) The table on page 496 lists the 1994 sales y (in millions of dollars) and number of employees x (in thousands) for a random sample of 20 *Fortune* 500 companies. Perform a regression analysis that follows the five steps presented in this chapter; be sure to state all assumptions you make. Give a prediction interval for a *Fortune* 500 company with 50,000 employees.

Company	Sales, y (in millions of dollars)	Employees, x (in thousands)
Time Warner	7,396	28.8
AGWAY	3,017	7.9
Boeing	21,924	115.0
QVC	1,390	6.7
Fruit of the Loom	2,298	37.4
Lennar	818	1.5
ILLINOVA	1,590	4.3
Adolph Coors	1,663	6.3
Sara Lee	15,536	145.9
Bear Stearns	3,441	7.3
Hercules	2,821	11.9
Valspar	787	2.5
Teledyne	2,391	18.0
U.S. BANCORP	1,936	10.6
First Security Corp.	980	7.6
ITT	23,767	110.0
Equifax	1,422	14.2
Atlantic Energy	816	1.7
UNISYS	7,400	46.3
Detroit Edison	3,519	8.4

Source: "The Fortune 500." *Fortune,* May 15, 1995.

10.81 Refer to Exercise 10.65, in which a cost function for a rug manufacturer was estimated. The table below provides data on a second cost driver—"direct manufacturing labor-hours"—for this company.

Week	Indirect Manufacturing Labor Costs	Machine-Hours	Direct Manufacturing Labor-Hours
1	$1,190	68	30
2	1,211	88	35
3	1,004	62	36
4	917	72	20
5	770	60	47
6	1,456	96	45
7	1,180	78	44
8	710	46	38
9	1,316	82	70
10	1,032	94	30
11	752	68	29
12	963	48	38

Source: Data and exercise adapted from Horngren, C. T., Foster, G., and Datar, S. M. *Cost Accounting,* Englewood Cliffs, N.J.: Prentice-Hall, 1994.

Your task is to estimate and compare two alternative cost functions. In the first, machine-hours is the independent variable; in the second, direct manufacturing labor-hours is the independent variable. Prepare a report that compares the two cost functions and recommends which should be used to explain and predict indirect manufacturing labor costs. Be sure to justify your choice.

10.82 A problem of economic and social concern in the United States is the importation and sale of illicit drugs. The data shown in the table below are part of a larger body of data collected by the Florida attorney general's office in an attempt to relate the incidence of drug seizures and drug arrests to the characteristics of the Florida counties. Given are the number, y, of drug arrests per county in a particular year, the density, x_1, of the county (population per square mile), and the number, x_2, of law enforcement employees. In order to simplify the calculations, we show data for only 10 counties.

a. Fit a least squares line to relate the number, y, of drug arrests per county to the county population density, x_1.

b. We might expect the mean number of arrests to increase as the population density increases. Do the data support this theory? Test using $\alpha = .05$.

c. Calculate the coefficient of determination for this regression analysis and interpret its value.

d. Repeat parts **a**, **b**, and **c** using the number x_2 of county law enforcement employees as the independent variable.

e. Which least squares line has the lower SSE?

f. Which independent variable explains more of the variation in y? Explain.

	COUNTY									
	1	2	3	4	5	6	7	8	9	10
Population Density, x_1	169	68	278	842	18	42	112	529	276	613
Number of Law Enforcement Employees, x_2	498	35	772	5,788	18	57	300	1,762	416	520
Number of Arrests, y	370	44	716	7,416	25	50	189	1,097	256	432

CHAPTER 11

MULTIPLE REGRESSION

Where We've Been

In Chapter 10 we saw how to model the relationship between a dependent variable y and an independent variable x using a straight line. We fit the straight line to the data points, used r and r^2 to measure the strength of the relationship between y and $x,$ and used the resulting prediction equation to estimate the mean value of y or to predict some future value of y for a given value of x.

Where We're Going

This chapter extends the basic concept of Chapter 10, converting it into a powerful estimation and prediction device by modeling the mean value of y as a function of two or more independent variables. The techniques developed will enable you to model a response, y, as a function of both quantitative and qualitative variables. As in the case of a simple linear regression, a multiple regression analysis involves fitting the model to a data set, testing the utility of the model, and using it for estimation and prediction.

11.1 MULTIPLE REGRESSION: THE MODEL AND THE PROCEDURE

Most practical applications of regression analysis utilize models that are more complex than the simple straight-line model. For example, a realistic probabilistic model for monthly sales revenue would include more than just advertising expenditures. Factors such as season, inventory on hand, size of sales force, and price are a few of the many variables that might influence sales. Thus, we would want to incorporate these and other potentially important independent variables into the model in order to make accurate predictions.

Probabilistic models that include terms involving x^2, x^3 (or higher-order terms), or more than one independent variable are called **multiple regression models**. The general form of these models is

$$y = \beta_0 + \beta_1 x_1 + \beta_2 x_2 + \cdots + \beta_k x_k + \epsilon$$

The dependent variable y is now written as a function of k independent variables, $x_1, x_2, \ldots, x_k$. The random error term is added to make the model probabilistic rather than deterministic. The value of the coefficient β_i determines the contribution of the independent variable x_i, and β_0 is the y-intercept. The coefficients $\beta_0, \beta_1, \ldots, \beta_k$ are usually unknown because they represent population parameters.

At first glance it might appear that the regression model shown above would not allow for anything other than straight-line relationships between y and the independent variables, but this is not true. Actually, $x_1, x_2, \ldots, x_k$ can be functions of variables as long as the functions do not contain unknown parameters. For example, the dollar sales, y, in new housing in a region could be a function of the independent variables

$$x_1 = \text{Mortgage interest rate}$$
$$x_2 = (\text{Mortgage interest rate})^2 = x_1^2$$
$$x_3 = \text{Unemployment rate in the region}$$

and so on. You could even insert a cyclical term (if it would be useful) of the form $x_4 = \sin t$, where t is a time variable. The multiple regression model is quite versatile and can be made to model many different types of response variables.

The General Linear Model

$$y = \beta_0 + \beta_1 x_1 + \beta_2 x_2 + \cdots + \beta_k x_k + \epsilon$$

where

y is the dependent variable

$x_1, x_2, \ldots, x_k$ are the independent variables

$E(y) = \beta_0 + \beta_1 x_1 + \beta_2 x_2 + \cdots + \beta_k x_k$ is the deterministic portion of the model

β_i determines the contribution of the independent variable x_i

Note: The symbols $x_1, x_2, \ldots, x_k$ may represent higher-order terms. For example, x_1 might represent the current interest rate, x_2 might represent x_1^2, and so forth.

As shown in the next box, we use the same steps to develop the multiple regression model as we used for the simple regression model.

Analyzing a Multiple Regression Model

Step 1 Hypothesize the deterministic component of the model. This component relates the mean, $E(y)$, to the independent variables $x_1, x_2, ..., x_k$. This involves the choice of the independent variables to be included in the model (Chapter 12).

Step 2 Use the sample data to estimate the unknown model parameters $\beta_0, \beta_1, \beta_2, ..., \beta_k$ in the model (Section 11.2).

Step 3 Specify the probability distribution of the random error term, ϵ, and estimate the standard deviation of this distribution, σ (Sections 11.3 and 11.8).

Step 4 Statistically evaluate the usefulness of the model (Sections 11.4 and 11.5).

Step 5 When satisfied that the model is useful, use it for prediction, estimation, and other purposes (Section 11.6).

Although we introduce several different types of models in this chapter, we defer formal discussion of model building (step 1) until Chapter 12.

11.2   FITTING THE MODEL: THE LEAST SQUARES APPROACH

The method of fitting multiple regression models is identical to that of fitting the simple straight-line model: the method of least squares. That is, we choose the estimated model

$$\hat{y} = \hat{\beta}_0 + \hat{\beta}_1 x_1 + \cdots + \hat{\beta}_k x_k$$

that minimizes

$$\text{SSE} = \sum (y - \hat{y})^2$$

As in the case of the simple linear model, the sample estimates $\hat{\beta}_0, \hat{\beta}_1, ..., \hat{\beta}_k$ are obtained as a solution to a set of simultaneous linear equations.*

The primary difference between fitting the simple and multiple regression models is computational difficulty. The $(k + 1)$ simultaneous linear equations that must be solved to find the $(k + 1)$ estimated coefficients $\hat{\beta}_0, \hat{\beta}_1, ..., \hat{\beta}_k$ are difficult (sometimes nearly impossible) to solve with a calculator. Consequently, we resort to the use of computers exclusively, presenting output from the SAS, SPSS, MINITAB, and EXCEL statistical software packages. We demonstrate the SAS regression output with the following example.

In all-electric homes the amount of electricity expended is of interest to consumers, builders, and groups involved with energy conservation. Suppose we wish to investigate the monthly electrical usage, y, in all-electric homes and its relationship to the size, x, of the home. Moreover, suppose we think that monthly electrical usage in all-electric homes is related to the size of the home by the model

$$y = \beta_0 + \beta_1 x + \beta_2 x^2 + \epsilon$$

To estimate the unknown parameters β_0, β_1, and β_2, values of y and x are collected for 10 homes during a particular month. The data are shown in Table 11.1.

*Students who are familiar with calculus should note that $\hat{\beta}_0, \hat{\beta}_1, ..., \hat{\beta}_k$ are the solutions to the set of equations $\partial\text{SSE}/\partial\hat{\beta}_0 = 0, \partial\text{SSE}/\partial\hat{\beta}_1 = 0, ..., \partial\text{SSE}/\partial\hat{\beta}_k = 0$. The solution is usually given in matrix form, but we do not present the details here. See the references for details.

TABLE 11.1 Home Size–Electrical Usage Data

Size of Home x (sq. ft.)	Monthly Usage y (kilowatt-hours)
1,290	1,182
1,350	1,172
1,470	1,264
1,600	1,493
1,710	1,571
1,840	1,711
1,980	1,804
2,230	1,840
2,400	1,956
2,930	1,954

Notice that we include a term involving x^2 in this model because we expect curvature in the graph of the response model relating y to x. The term involving x^2 is called a **quadratic term**. Figure 11.1 illustrates that the electrical usage appears to increase in a curvilinear manner with the size of the home. This provides some support for the inclusion of the quadratic term x^2 in the model.

Part of the output from the SAS multiple regression routine for the data in Table 11.1 is reproduced in Figure 11.2. The least squares estimates of the β parameters appear in the column labeled **Parameter Estimate**. You can see that $\hat{\beta}_0 = -1,216.1, \hat{\beta}_1 = 2.3989$, and $\hat{\beta}_2 = -.00045$. Therefore, the equation that minimizes the SSE for the data is

$$\hat{y} = -1,216.1 + 2.3989x - .00045x^2$$

The minimum value of the SSE, 15,332.6, also appears (highlighted) in the printout. [*Note:* Throughout this chapter we highlight the aspects of the printout that are under discussion.]

Note that the graph of the multiple regression model (Figure 11.3, a response curve) provides a good fit to the data of Table 11.1. Furthermore, the small value of $\hat{\beta}_2$ does *not* imply that the curvature is insignificant, since the numerical value of $\hat{\beta}_2$ depends on the scale of the measurements. We will test the contribution of the quadratic coefficient $\hat{\beta}_2$ in Section 11.4.

The ultimate goal of this multiple regression analysis is to use the fitted model to predict electrical usage y for a home of a specific size (area) x. And, of course, we will want to give a prediction interval for y so that we will know how much faith we can place in the prediction. That is, if the prediction model is used to pre-

FIGURE 11.1

Scattergram of the home size–electrical usage data

Dep Variable: Y

Analysis of Variance

Source	DF	Sum of Squares	Mean Square	F Value	Prob>F
Model	2	831069.54637	415534.77319	189.710	0.0001
Error	7	15332.55363	2190.36480		
C Total	9	846402.10000			

Root MSE	46.80133	R-square	0.9819
Dep Mean	1594.70000	Adj R-sq	0.9767
C.V.	2.93480		

Parameter Estimates

Variable	DF	Parameter Estimate	Standard Error	T for H0: Parameter=0	Prob > |T|
INTERCEP	1	-1216.143887	242.80636850	-5.009	0.0016
X	1	2.398930	0.24583560	9.758	0.0001
XSQ	1	-0.000450	0.00005908	-7.618	0.0001

FIGURE 11.2   SAS output for the home size–electrical usage data

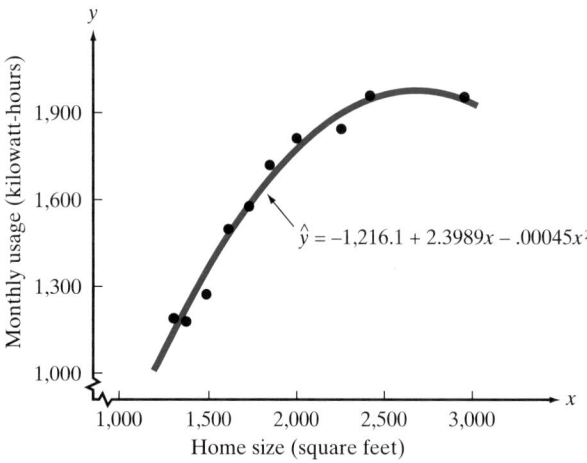

FIGURE 11.3
Least squares model
for the home size–
electrical usage data

$\hat{y} = -1,216.1 + 2.3989x - .00045x^2$

dict electrical usage y for a given size of home, x, what will be the error of prediction? To answer this question, we need to estimate σ^2, the variance of ϵ.

The interpretation of the estimated coefficients in a quadratic model must be undertaken cautiously. First, the estimated y-intercept, $\hat{\beta}_0$, can be meaningfully interpreted only if the range of the independent variables includes zero—that is, if $x = 0$ is included in the sampled range of x. In the electrical usage example, $\hat{\beta}_0 = -1,216.1$, which would seem to imply that the estimated electrical usage is negative when $x = 0$, but this zero point represents a home with 0 square feet. The zero point is, of course, not in the range of the sample (the lowest value of x is 1,290 square feet), and thus the interpretation of $\hat{\beta}_0$ is not meaningful.

The estimated coefficient of x is $\hat{\beta}_1$, but it no longer represents a slope in the presence of the quadratic term x^2.* The estimated coefficient of the linear term x will not, in general, have a meaningful interpretation in the quadratic model.

---

*For students with knowledge of calculus, note that the slope of the quadratic model is the first derivative $\partial y / \partial x = \beta_1 + 2\beta_2 x$. Thus, the slope varies as a function of x, rather than the constant slope associated with the straight-line model.

FIGURE 11.4
Potential misuse
of model

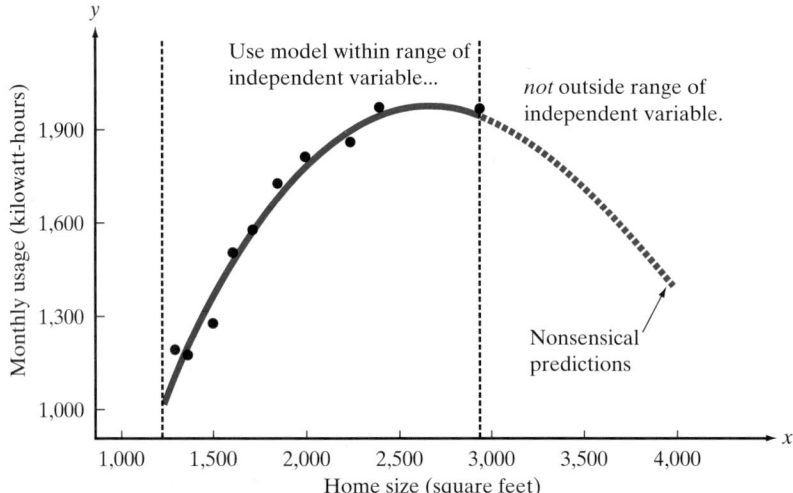

The sign of the coefficient, $\hat{\beta}_2$, of the quadratic term, x^2, is the indicator of whether the curve is concave downward (mound-shaped) or concave upward (bowl-shaped). A negative $\hat{\beta}_2$ implies downward concavity, as in the electrical usage example (Figure 11.3), and a positive $\hat{\beta}_2$ implies upward concavity. Rather than interpreting the numerical value of $\hat{\beta}_2$ itself, we utilize a graphical representation of the model, as in Figure 11.3, to describe the model.

Note that Figure 11.3 implies that the estimated electrical usage is leveling off as the home sizes increase beyond 2,500 square feet. In fact, the convexity of the model would lead to decreasing usage estimates if we were to display the model out to 4,000 square feet and beyond (see Figure 11.4). However, model interpretations are not meaningful outside the range of the independent variable, which has a maximum value of 2,930 square feet in this example. Thus, although the model appears to support the hypothesis that the *rate of increase* per square foot *decreases* for the home sizes near the high end of the sampled values, the conclusion that usage will actually begin to decrease for very large homes would be a *misuse* of the model, since no homes of 3,000 square feet or more were included in the sample.

All the interpretations of the electrical usage model were based on the sample estimates of unknown model parameters. As has been our theme throughout, we want to measure the reliability of these interpretations with regard to the real relationship between usage and home size. Additionally, we will want to use the model to estimate usage for homes not included in the sample, and to measure the reliability of these estimates. All this requires an assessment of the error in the model—that is, of the probability distribution of the random error component, ϵ. This is the subject of the next section.

11.3 MODEL ASSUMPTIONS

We noted in Section 11.1 that the multiple regression model is of the form

$$y = \beta_0 + \beta_1 x_1 + \beta_2 x_2 + \cdots + \beta_k x_k + \epsilon$$

where y is the response variable that we wish to predict; $\beta_0, \beta_1, \ldots, \beta_k$ are parameters with unknown values; $x_1, x_2, \ldots, x_k$ are information-contributing variables that are measured without error; and ϵ is a random error component. Since $\beta_0, \beta_1, \ldots, \beta_k$, and $x_1, x_2, \ldots, x_k$ are nonrandom, the quantity

$$\beta_0 + \beta_1 x_1 + \beta_2 x_2 + \cdots + \beta_k x_k$$

represents the deterministic portion of the model. Therefore, y is composed of two components—one fixed and one random—and, consequently, y is a random variable.

$$y = \underbrace{\beta_0 + \beta_1 x_1 + \cdots + \beta_k x_k}_{\substack{\text{Deterministic} \\ \text{portion of model}}} + \underbrace{\epsilon}_{\substack{\text{Random} \\ \text{error}}}$$

We will assume (as in Chapter 10) that the random error can be positive or negative and that for any setting of the x values, $x_1, x_2, ..., x_k$, the random error ϵ has a normal probability distribution with mean equal to 0 and variance equal to σ^2. Further, we assume that the random errors associated with any (and every) pair of y values are probabilistically independent. That is, the error, ϵ, associated with any one y value is independent of the error associated with any other y value. These assumptions are summarized in the next box.

Assumptions for Random Error ϵ

1. For any given set of values of $x_1, x_2, ..., x_k$, the random error ϵ has a normal probability distribution with mean equal to 0 and variance equal to σ^2.

2. The random errors are independent (in a probabilistic sense).

Note that σ^2 represents the variance of the random error, ϵ. As such, σ^2 is an important measure of the usefulness of the model for the estimation of the mean and the prediction of actual values of y. If $\sigma^2 = 0$, all the random errors will equal 0 and the predicted values, $\hat{y}$, will be identical to $E(y)$; that is $E(y)$ will be estimated without error. In contrast, a large value of σ^2 implies large (absolute) values of ϵ and larger deviations between the predicted values, $\hat{y}$, and the mean value, $E(y)$. Consequently, the larger the value of σ^2, the greater will be the error in estimating the model parameters $\beta_0, \beta_1, ..., \beta_k$ and the error in predicting a value of y for a specific set of values $x_1, x_2, ..., x_k$. Thus, σ^2 plays a major role in making inferences about $\beta_0, \beta_1, ..., \beta_k$ in estimating $E(y)$, and in predicting y for specific values of $x_1, x_2, ..., x_k$.

Since the variance, σ^2, of the random error, ϵ, will rarely be known, we must use the results of the regression analysis to estimate its value. Recall that σ^2 is the variance of the probability distribution of the random error, ϵ, for a given set of values for $x_1, x_2, ..., x_k$; hence it is the mean value of the deviations of the y values (for given values of $x_1, x_2, ..., x_k$) about the mean value $E(y)$.* Since the predicted value, $\hat{y}$, estimates $E(y)$ for each of the data points, it seems natural to use

$$\text{SSE} = \sum (y_i - \hat{y}_i)^2$$

to construct an estimator of σ^2.

For example, in the second-order (quadratic) model describing electrical usage as a function of home size, we found that SSE = 15,332.6. We now want to use this quantity to estimate the variance of ϵ. Recall that the estimator for the straight-line model is $s^2 = \text{SSE}/(n - 2)$ and note that the denominator is $(n - \text{Number of}$

---

*Since $y = E(y) + \epsilon$, ϵ is equal to the deviation $y - E(y)$. Also, by definition, the variance of a random variable is the expected value of the square of the deviation of the random variable from its mean. According to our model, $E(\epsilon) = 0$. Therefore, $\sigma^2 = E(\epsilon^2)$.

estimated β parameters), which is $(n - 2)$ in the first-order (straight-line) model. Since we must estimate one more parameter, β_2, for the second-order model, the estimator of σ^2 is

$$s^2 = \frac{SSE}{n - 3}$$

That is, the denominator becomes $(n - 3)$ because there are now three β parameters in the model. The numerical estimate for this example is

$$s^2 = \frac{SSE}{10 - 3} = \frac{15,332.6}{7} = 2,190.36$$

In many computer printouts and textbooks, s^2 is called the **mean square for error (MSE)**. This estimate of σ^2 is shown in the column titled **Mean Square** in the SAS printout in Figure 11.2.

The units of the estimated variance are squared units of the dependent variable, y. In the electrical usage example, the units of s^2 are (kilowatt-hours)^2. This makes meaningful interpretation of s^2 difficult, so we use the standard deviation s to provide a more meaningful measure of variability. In the electrical usage example,

$$s = \sqrt{2,190.36} = 46.8,$$

which is given on the SAS printout in Figure 11.2 under **Root MSE**. One useful interpretation of the estimated standard deviation s is that the interval $\pm 2s$ will provide a rough approximation to the accuracy with which the model will predict future values of y for given values of x. Thus, in the electrical usage example, we expect the model to provide predictions of electrical usage to within $\pm 2s = \pm 93.6$ kilowatt-hours.*

For the general multiple regression model

$$y = \beta_0 + \beta_1 x_1 + \beta_2 x_2 + \cdots + \beta_k x_k + \epsilon$$

we must estimate the $(k + 1)$ parameters $\beta_0, \beta_1, \beta_2, ..., \beta_k$. Thus, the estimator of σ^2 is SSE divided by the quantity $(n - \text{Number of estimated } \beta \text{ parameters})$.

We will use the estimator of σ^2 both to check the utility of the model (Sections 11.4 and 11.5) and to provide a measure of reliability of predictions and estimates when the model is used for those purposes (Section 11.6). Thus, you can see that the estimation of σ^2 plays an important part in the development of a regression model.

Estimator of σ^2 for Multiple Regression Model with k Independent Variables

$$s^2 = MSE = \frac{SSE}{n - \text{Number of estimated } \beta \text{ parameters}} = \frac{SSE}{n - (k + 1)}$$

11.4 INFERENCES ABOUT THE β PARAMETERS

Sometimes the individual β parameters in a model have practical significance and we want to estimate their values or test hypotheses about them. For example, if electrical usage y is related to home size x by the straight-line relationship

$$y = \beta_0 + \beta_1 x + \epsilon$$

---

*The $\pm 2s$ approximation will improve as the sample size is increased. We will provide more precise methodology for the construction of prediction intervals in Section 11.6.

FIGURE 11.5

The interpretation of β_2 for a second-order model

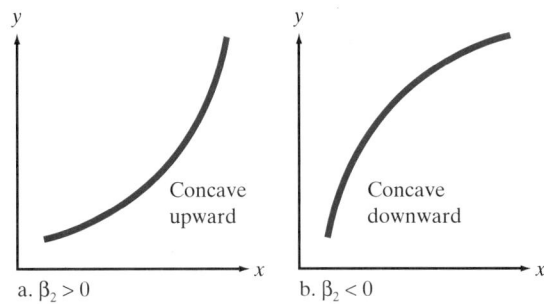

then β_1 has a very practical interpretation. That is, you saw in Chapter 10 that β_1 is the mean increase in electrical usage, y, for a 1-unit increase in home size x.

As proposed in the preceding sections, suppose that electrical usage y is related to home size x by the quadratic model

$$y = \beta_0 + \beta_1 x + \beta_2 x^2 + \epsilon$$

Then the mean value of y for a given value of x is

$$E(y) = \beta_0 + \beta_1 x + \beta_2 x^2$$

What is the practical interpretation of β_2? As noted earlier, the parameter β_2 measures the curvature of the response curve shown in Figure 11.3. If $\beta_2 > 0$, the slope of the curve will increase as x increases (upward concavity), as shown in Figure 11.5a. If $\beta_2 < 0$, the slope of the curve will decrease as x increases (downward concavity), as shown in Figure 11.5b.

Intuitively, we would expect the electrical usage, y, to rise almost proportionally to home size, x. Then, eventually, as the size of the home increases, the increase in electrical usage for a 1-unit increase in home size might begin to decrease. Thus, a forecaster of electrical usage would want to determine whether this type of curvature actually was present in the response curve or, equivalently, the forecaster would want to test the null hypothesis

$$H_0: \beta_2 = 0 \quad \text{(No curvature in the response curve)}$$

against the alternative hypothesis

$$H_a: \beta_2 < 0 \quad \text{(Downward concavity exists in the response curve)}$$

A test of this hypothesis can be performed using a t-test.

The t-test utilizes a test statistic analogous to that used to make inferences about the slope of the straight-line model (Section 10.5). The t statistic is formed by dividing the sample estimate, $\hat{\beta}_2$, of the parameter β_2 by the estimated standard deviation of the sampling distribution of $\hat{\beta}_2$:

$$\textit{Test statistic: } \frac{\hat{\beta}_2}{s_{\hat{\beta}_2}}$$

We use the symbol $s_{\hat{\beta}_2}$ to represent the estimated standard deviation of $\hat{\beta}_2$. The formula for computing $s_{\hat{\beta}_2}$ is very complex and its presentation is beyond the scope of this text,* but this omission will not cause difficulty. Most computer packages list

*Because most of the formulas in a multiple regression analysis are so complex, the only reasonable way to present them is by using matrix algebra. We do not assume a prerequisite of matrix algebra for this text and, in any case, we think the formulas can be omitted in an introductory course without serious loss. They are programmed into almost all statistical software packages with multiple regression routines and are presented in some of the texts listed in the references.

FIGURE 11.6
Rejection region for
test of β_2

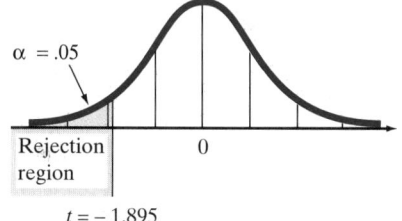

$t = -1.895$

the estimated standard deviation $s_{\hat{\beta}_i}$ for each of the estimated model coefficients $\hat{\beta}_i$. Moreover, they usually give the calculated t values for each coefficient.

The rejection region for the test is found in exactly the same way as the rejection regions for the t-tests in previous chapters. That is, we consult Table VI in Appendix B to obtain an upper-tail value of t. This is a value t_α such that $P(t > t_\alpha) = \alpha$. We can then use this value to construct rejection regions for either one-tailed or two-tailed tests. To illustrate, in the electrical usage example the error degrees of freedom is $(n - 3) = 7$, the denominator of the estimate of σ^2. Then the rejection region (shown in Figure 11.6) for a one-tailed test with $\alpha = .05$ is

$$Rejection\ region: t < -t_\alpha$$

$$t < -1.895$$

In Figure 11.7, we again show a portion of the SAS printout for the electrical usage example. The following quantities are highlighted:

1. The estimated coefficients $\hat{\beta}_0$, $\hat{\beta}_1$, and $\hat{\beta}_2$.
2. The SSE and MSE (estimate of σ^2, variance of ϵ)
3. The t statistic, observed significance level, and standard error of $\hat{\beta}_2$ for testing $H_0: \beta_2 = 0$

Dep Variable: Y

Analysis of Variance

Source	DF	Sum of Squares	Mean Square	F Value	Prob>F
Model	2	831069.54637	415534.77319	189.710	0.0001
Error	7	15332.55363	2190.36480		
C Total	9	846402.10000			

Root MSE	46.80133	R-square	0.9819	
Dep Mean	1594.70000	Adj R-sq	0.9767	
C.V.	2.93480			

Parameter Estimates

Variable	DF	Parameter Estimate	Standard Error	T for HO: Parameter=0	Prob > |T|
INTERCEP	1	-1216.143887	242.80636850	-5.009	0.0016
X	1	2.398930	0.24583560	9.758	0.0001
XSQ	1	-0.000450	0.00005908	-7.618	0.0001

FIGURE 11.7 SAS multiple regression output

The estimated standard deviations for the model coefficients appear under the column labeled **Standard Error**. The t statistics for testing the null hypothesis that the true coefficients are equal to 0 appear under the column headed **T for HO: Parameter=0**. The t value corresponding to the test of the null hypothesis $H_0: \beta_2 = 0$ is found at the bottom of that column, that is, $t = -7.618$. Since this value is less than -1.895, we conclude that the quadratic term $\beta_2 x^2$ makes a contribution to the prediction model of electrical usage.

The SAS printout shown in Figure 11.7 also lists the two-tailed significance levels for each t value under the column headed **Prob > |T|**. The significance level .0001 corresponds to the quadratic term, and this implies that we would reject $H_0: \beta_2 = 0$ in favor of $H_a: \beta_2 \neq 0$ at any α level larger than .0001. Since our alternative was one-sided, $H_a: \beta_2 < 0$, and $\hat{\beta}_2$ is negative, the significance level is half that given in the printout, that is, $\frac{1}{2}(.0001) = .00005$. Thus, there is very strong evidence that the mean electrical usage increases more slowly per square foot for large houses than for small houses.

We can also form a confidence interval for the parameter β_2 as follows:

$$\hat{\beta}_2 \pm t_{\alpha/2} s_{\hat{\beta}_2} = -.000450 \pm (2.365)(.0000591)$$

or $(-.000590, -.000310)$. Note that the t value 2.365 corresponds to $\alpha/2 = .025$ and $(n - 3) = 7$ df. This interval constitutes a 95% confidence interval for β_2 and can be used to estimate the rate of curvature in mean electrical usage as home size is increased. Note that all values in the interval are negative, reconfirming the conclusion of our test.

Note that the SAS printout in Figure 11.7 also provides the t-test statistic and corresponding two-tailed p-values for the tests of $H_0: \beta_0 = 0$ and $H_0: \beta_1 = 0$. Since the interpretation of these parameters is not meaningful for this model, the tests are not of interest.

Testing a hypothesis about a single β parameter that appears in any multiple regression model is accomplished in exactly the same manner as described for the quadratic electrical usage model. The t-test and a confidence interval for a β parameter are shown in the next two boxes.

Test of an Individual Parameter Coefficient in the Multiple Regression Model

One-Tailed Test	**Two-Tailed Test**
$H_0: \beta_i = 0$	$H_0: \beta_i = 0$
$H_a: \beta_i < 0 \quad$ (or $H_a: \beta_i > 0$)	$H_a: \beta_i \neq 0$

$$\text{Test statistic: } t = \frac{\hat{\beta}_i}{s_{\hat{\beta}_i}}$$

Rejection region: $t < t_\alpha$ (or $t > t_\alpha$ when $H_a: -\beta_i > 0$)	Rejection region: $|t| > t_{\alpha/2}$

where t_α and $t_{\alpha/2}$ are based on $n - (k + 1)$ degrees of freedom and

$\quad n = $ Number of observations

$k + 1 = $ Number of β parameters in the model

Assumptions: See Section 11.3 for assumptions about the probability distribution for the random error component ϵ.

A 100(1 − α)% Confidence Interval for a β Parameter

$$\hat{\beta}_i \pm t_{\alpha/2} s_{\hat{\beta}_i}$$

where $t_{\alpha/2}$ is based on $n - (k + 1)$ degrees of freedom and

n = Number of observations

$k + 1$ = Number of β parameters in the model

EXAMPLE 11.1

A collector of antique grandfather clocks knows that the price received for the clocks increases linearly with the age of the clocks. Moreover, the collector hypothesizes that the auction price of the clocks will increase linearly as the number of bidders increases. Thus, the following model is hypothesized:

$$y = \beta_0 + \beta_1 x_1 + \beta_2 x_2 + \epsilon$$

where

y = Auction price

x_1 = Age of clock (years)

x_2 = Number of bidders

A sample of 32 auction prices of grandfather clocks, along with their age and the number of bidders, is given in Table 11.2. The model $y = \beta_0 + \beta_1 x_1 + \beta_2 x_2 + \epsilon$ is fit to the data, and a portion of the MINITAB printout is shown in Figure 11.8.

a. Test the hypothesis that the mean auction price of a clock increases as the number of bidders increases when age is held constant, that is, $\beta_2 > 0$. Use $\alpha = .05$.

b. Interpret the estimates of the β coefficients in the model.

SOLUTION

a. The hypotheses of interest concern the parameter β_2. Specifically,

$$H_0: \beta_2 = 0$$

$$H_a: \beta_2 > 0$$

TABLE 11.2   Auction Price Data

Age x_1	Number of Bidders x_2	Auction Price y	Age x_1	Number of Bidders x_2	Auction Price y
127	13	$1,235	170	14	$2,131
115	12	1,080	182	8	1,550
127	7	845	162	11	1,884
150	9	1,522	184	10	2,041
156	6	1,047	143	6	845
182	11	1,979	159	9	1,483
156	12	1,822	108	14	1,055
132	10	1,253	175	8	1,545
137	9	1,297	108	6	729
113	9	946	179	9	1,792
137	15	1,713	111	15	1,175
117	11	1,024	187	8	1,593
137	8	1,147	111	7	785
153	6	1,092	115	7	744
117	13	1,152	194	5	1,356
126	10	1,336	168	7	1,262

FIGURE 11.8
MINITAB printout for
Example 11.1

```
The regression equation is
Y = -1339 + 12.7 X1 + 86.0 X2

Predictor        Coef       Stdev    t-ratio        p
Constant      -1339.0       173.8      -7.70    0.000
X1            12.7406      0.9047      14.08    0.000
X2            85.953        8.729       9.85    0.000

s = 133.5      R-sq = 89.2%      R-sq(adj) = 88.5%

Analysis of Variance

SOURCE          DF          SS         MS         F        p
Regression       2     4283063    2141532    120.19    0.000
Error           29      516727      17818
Total           31     4799789
```

Test statistic: $t = \dfrac{\hat{\beta}_2}{s_{\hat{\beta}_2}} = 9.85$

Rejection region: For $\alpha = .05$ and $n - (k + 1) = 32 - (2 + 1) = 29$ df,
reject H_0 if $t > 1.699$ (see Figure 11.9).

The calculated t-value, $t = 9.85$, is highlighted on the MINITAB printout, Figure 11.8. This value falls in the rejection region shown in Figure 11.9. Thus, the collector can conclude that the mean auction price of a clock increases as the number of bidders increases, when age is held constant. Note that the observed significance level (p-value) of the test is 0. Therefore, any nonzero α will lead us to reject H_0.

b. The values $\hat{\beta}_1 = 12.74$ and $\hat{\beta}_2 = 85.95$ (highlighted in Figure 11.8) are easily interpreted. We estimated that the mean auction price increases \$12.74 per year of age of the clock (when the number of bidders is held constant), and that the mean price increases by \$85.95 per additional bidder (when the age of the clock is held constant).

Be careful not to interpret the estimated intercept $\hat{\beta}_0 = -1,339$ in the same way $\hat{\beta}_1$ and $\hat{\beta}_2$ are interpreted. You might think that this negative value implies a negative price for clocks 0 years of age with 0 bidders. However, these zeros are meaningless numbers in this example, since the ages range from 108 to 194 and the number of bidders ranges from 5 to 15. Interpretations of predicted y values for values of the independent variables outside their sampled range can be very misleading.

Note: Some computer programs use an F statistic to conduct two-tailed tests concerning the individual β parameters, because the square of a Student t with ν degrees of freedom is equal to an F statistic with 1 degree of freedom in the numerator and ν degrees of freedom in the denominator. If you conduct a two-tailed t-test and reject the null hypothesis if $|t| > t_{\alpha/2}$, the corresponding F-test

FIGURE 11.9
Rejection region for
$H_0: \beta_2 = 0$

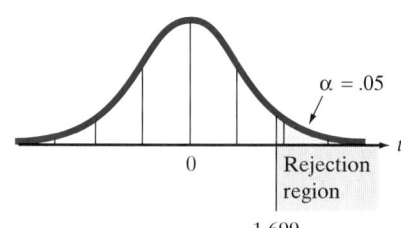

implies rejection if the computed value of F (which is equal to the square of the computed t statistic) is larger than F_α. Thus,

$$t_{\alpha/2}^2 = F_\alpha$$

For example, when we tested a hypothesis about the curvature parameter β_2 in the quadratic model relating electrical usage to home size, the computed t value was -7.62 (see Figure 11.7). The equivalent F-test yields a value $F = t^2 = (-7.62)^2 = 58.06$. And the upper-tail rejection region for a two-tailed test with $\alpha = .05$, 1 df in the numerator, and 7 df in the denominator is

$$F > F_{.05} = 5.59$$

Note that the F value, 5.59, is equal to the square of 2.365, the value of t that corresponds to $t_{.025}$ based on 7 df. You can see that the conclusion is the same no matter which test statistic is used: There is very strong evidence that curvature is present in the model.

EXERCISES   11.1–11.12

Note: Exercises marked with ▢ contain data for computer analysis on a 3.5" disk (file name in parentheses).

Learning the Mechanics

11.1 SAS was used to fit the model $y = \beta_0 + \beta_1 x_1 + \beta_2 x_2 + \epsilon$ to $n = 20$ data points and the printout shown below was obtained.
  a. What are the sample estimates of β_0, β_1, and β_2?
  b. What is the least squares prediction equation?
  c. Find SSE, MSE, and s. Interpret the standard deviation in the context of the problem.
  d. Test $H_0: \beta_1 = 0$ against $H_a: \beta_1 \neq 0$. Use $\alpha = .05$.
  e. Use a 95% confidence interval to estimate β_2.

11.2 Suppose you fit the multiple regression model

$$y = \beta_0 + \beta_1 x_1 + \beta_2 x_2 + \epsilon$$

to $n = 30$ data points and obtain the following result:

$$\hat{y} = 3.4 - 4.6x_1 + 2.7x_2 + .93x_3$$

The estimated standard errors of $\hat{\beta}_2$ and $\hat{\beta}_3$ are 1.86 and .29, respectively.
  a. Test the null hypothesis $H_0: \beta_2 = 0$ against the alternative hypothesis $H_a: \beta_2 \neq 0$. Use $\alpha = .05$.
  b. Test the null hypothesis $H_0: \beta_3 = 0$ against the alternative hypothesis $H_a: \beta_3 \neq 0$. Use $\alpha = .05$.

Dep Variable: Y

Analysis of Variance

Source	DF	Sum of Squares	Mean Square	F Value	Prob>F
Model	2	128329.27624	64164.63812	7.223	0.0054
Error	17	151015.72376	8883.27787		
C Total	19	279345.00000			

Root MSE	94.25114	R-square	0.4594
Dep Mean	360.50000	Adj R-sq	0.3958
C.V.	26.14456		

Parameter Estimates

Variable	DF	Parameter Estimate	Standard Error	T for H0: Parameter=0	Prob > |T|
INTERCEP	1	506.346067	45.16942487	11.210	0.0001
X1	1	-941.900226	275.08555975	-3.424	0.0032
X2	1	-429.060418	379.82566485	-1.130	0.2743

c. The null hypothesis $H_0: \beta_2 = 0$ is not rejected. In contrast, the null hypothesis $H_0: \beta_3 = 0$ is rejected. Explain how this can happen even though $\hat{\beta}_2 > \hat{\beta}_3$.

11.3 Suppose you fit the second-order model

$$y = \beta_0 + \beta_1 x + \beta_2 x^2 + \epsilon$$

to $n = 25$ data points. Your estimate of β_2 is $\hat{\beta}_2 = .47$, and the estimated standard error of the estimate is

$$s_{\hat{\beta}_2} = .15$$

a. Test the null hypothesis that the mean value of y is related to x by the (*first-order*) linear model

$$E(y) = \beta_0 + \beta_1 x$$

($H_0: \beta_2 = 0$) against the alternative hypothesis that the true relationship is given by the (*second-order*) quadratic model

$$E(y) = \beta_0 + \beta_1 x + \beta_2 x^2$$

($H_a: \beta_2 \neq 0$). Use $\alpha = .05$.

b. Suppose you want to determine only whether the quadratic curve opens upward; that is, as x increases, the slope of the curve increases. Give the test statistic and the rejection region for the test for $\alpha = .05$. Do the data support the theory that the slope of the curve increases as x increases? Explain.

c. What is the value of the F statistic for testing the null hypothesis $H_0: \beta_2 = 0$ against the alternative hypothesis $H_a: \beta_2 \neq 0$?

d. Could the F statistic in part **c** be used to conduct the test in part **b**? Explain.

11.4 How is the number of degrees of freedom available for estimating σ^2 (the variance of ϵ) related to the number of independent variables in a regression model?

11.5 (**X11.005**) Use a computer to fit a second-order model to the following data:

x	0	1	2	3	4	5	6
y	1	2.7	3.8	4.5	5.0	5.3	5.2

a. Find SSE and s^2.

b. Do the data provide sufficient evidence to indicate that the second-order term provides information for the prediction of y? [*Hint:* Test $H_0: \beta_2 = 0$.]

c. Find the least squares prediction equation.

d. Plot the data points and graph $\hat{y}$. Does your prediction equation provide a good fit to the data?

Applying the Concepts

11.6 (**X11.006**) Economists have two major types of data available to them: *time series data* and *cross-*

sectional data. For example, an economist estimating a consumption function, say, household food consumption as a function of household income and household size, might measure the variables of interest for one sample of households at one point in time. In this case, the economist is using *cross-sectional data.* If instead, the economist is interested in how total consumption in the United States is related to national income, the economist probably would track these variables over time, using *time series data* (Mansfield, *Applied Microeconomics,* 1994). The data in the table on page 514 were collected for a random sample of 25 households in Washington, D.C., during 1996, and therefore are cross-sectional data.

a. It has been hypothesized that household food consumption y is related to household income x_1 and to household size x_2 as follows:

$$y = \beta_0 + \beta_1 x_1 + \beta_2 x_2 + \epsilon$$

The SPSS printout for fitting the model to the data is shown on page 514. Give the least squares prediction equation.

b. Do the data provide sufficient evidence to conclude that the mean food consumption increases with household income? Test using $\alpha = .01$.

c. As a check on your conclusion of part **b**, construct a scattergram of household food consumption versus household income. Does the plot support your conclusion in part **b**? Explain.

d. In Chapter 10, we used the method of least squares to fit a straight line to a set of data points that were plotted in two dimensions. In this exercise, we are fitting a plane to a set of points plotted in three dimensions. We are attempting to determine the plane, $\hat{y} = \hat{\beta}_0 + \hat{\beta}_1 x_1 + \hat{\beta}_2 x_2$, that, according to the principle of least squares, best fits the data points. Sketch the least squares plane you developed in part **a**. Be sure to label all three axes of your graph.

11.7 Location is one of the most important decisions for hotel chains and lodging firms. A hotel chain that can select good sites more accurately and quickly than its competition has a distinct competitive advantage. Researchers S. E. Kimes (Cornell University) and J. A. Fitzsimmons (University of Texas) studied the site selection process of La Quinta Motor Inns, a moderately priced hotel chain (*Interfaces,* Mar.–Apr. 1990). Using data collected on 57 mature inns owned by La Quinta, the researchers built a regression model designed to predict the profitability for sites under construction. The least squares model is given below:

$$\hat{y} = 39.05 - 5.41 x_1 + 5.86 x_2 - 3.09 x_3 + 1.75 x_4$$

where

Household	1996 Food Consumption ($1,000s)	1996 Income ($1,000s)	Household Size (Dec. 1996)
1	4.2	41.1	4
2	3.4	30.5	2
3	4.8	52.3	4
4	2.9	28.9	1
5	3.5	36.5	2
6	4.0	29.8	4
7	3.6	44.3	3
8	4.2	38.1	4
9	5.1	92.0	5
10	2.7	36.0	1
11	4.0	76.9	3
12	2.7	69.9	1
13	5.5	43.1	7
14	4.1	95.2	2
15	5.5	45.6	9
16	4.5	78.5	3
17	5.0	20.5	5
18	4.5	31.6	4
19	2.8	39.9	1
20	3.9	38.6	3
21	3.6	30.2	2
22	4.6	48.7	5
23	3.8	21.2	3
24	4.5	24.3	7
25	4.0	26.9	5

```
* * * *   M U L T I P L E   R E G R E S S I O N   * * * *
Equation Number 1      Dependent Variable..    FOOD

Variable(s) Entered on Step Number
   1..     SIZE
   2..     INCOME

Multiple R            .90872
R Square              .82578
Adjusted R Square     .80994
Standard Error        .35014

Analysis of Variance
                   DF      Sum of Squares      Mean Square
Regression          2          12.78439           6.39219
Residual           22           2.69721            .12260

F =      52.13842        Signif F =   .0000

------------------ Variables in the Equation ------------------

Variable           B          SE B         Beta          T    Sig T

SIZE          .353964      .035183      .899604     10.061    .0000
INCOME        .009193      .003375      .243540      2.724    .0124
(Constant)   2.369646      .218135                  10.863    .0000
```

y = operating margin (measured as a percentage)

$= \dfrac{(\text{profit} + \text{interest expenses} + \text{depreciation})}{\text{total revenue}}$

x_1 = state population (in thousands) divided by the total number of inns in the state

x_2 = room rate ($) for the inn

x_3 = square root of the median income of the area (in $ thousands)

x_4 = number of college students within four miles of the inn

[*Note:* All variables were "standardized" to have a mean of 0 and a standard deviation of 1.]

```
The regression equation is
ENE = 13.7 - 0.102 WEIGHT +0.000273 WGHTSQ

Predictor        Coef        Stdev      t-ratio         p
Constant       13.713        1.306        10.50     0.000
WEIGHT       -0.10184      0.02881        -3.53     0.010
WGHTSQ      0.0002735    0.0001016         2.69     0.031

s = 2.194       R-sq = 73.7%      R-sq(adj) = 66.2%

Analysis of Variance

SOURCE        DF          SS          MS         F         p
Regression     2      94.659      47.329      9.83     0.009
Error          7      33.705       4.815
Total          9     128.364
```

Interpret the β estimates of the model. Comment on the effect of each independent variable on operating margin, y. [*Note:* A profitable inn is defined as one with an operating margin of over 50%.]

11.8 Fish reared in captivity for commercial purposes must be fed a diet containing an appropriate balance of nutrients and adequate energy to permit efficient growth. The amount of nitrogen excreted through the gills of a fish is one way to measure fish energy metabolism. *Fisheries Science* (Feb. 1995) reported on a study of the variables that affect endogenous nitrogen excretion (ENE) in carp raised in Japan. Carp were divided into groups of 2 to 15 fish each according to body weight and each group placed in a separate tank. The carp were then fed a protein-free diet three times daily for a period of 20 days. One day after terminating the feeding experiment, the amount of ENE in each tank was measured. The table gives the mean body weight (in grams) and ENE amount (in milligrams per 100 grams of body weight per day) for each carp group.

Tank	Body Weight, x	ENE, y
1	11.7	15.3
2	25.3	9.3
3	90.2	6.5
4	213.0	6.0
5	10.2	15.7
6	17.6	10.0
7	32.6	8.6
8	81.3	6.4
9	141.5	5.6
10	285.7	6.0

Source: Watanabe, T., and Ohta, M. "Endogenous nitrogen excretion and non-fecal energy losses in carp and rainbow trout." *Fisheries Science,* Vol. 61, No. 1, February 1995, p. 56 (Table 5).

a. Plot the data in a scattergram. Do you detect a pattern?
b. The quadratic model, $E(y) = \beta_0 + \beta_1 x + \beta_2 x^2$, was fit to the data using MINITAB. The MINI-

TAB printout is displayed above. Use the printout information to test $H_0: \beta_2 = 0$ against $H_a: \beta_2 \neq 0$ using $\alpha = .10$. Give the conclusion in the words of the problem.

11.9 (X11.009) Running a manufacturing operation efficiently requires knowledge of the time it takes employees to manufacture the product, otherwise the cost of making the product cannot be determined. Furthermore, management would not be able to establish an effective incentive plan for its employees because it would not know how to set work standards (Chase and Aquilano, *Production and Operations Management,* 1992). Estimates of production time are frequently obtained using time studies. The data in the accompanying table came from a recent time study of a sample of 15 employees performing a particular task on an automobile assembly line.

Time to Assemble, y (minutes)	Months of Experience, x
10	24
20	1
15	10
11	15
11	17
19	3
11	20
13	9
17	3
18	1
16	7
16	9
17	7
18	5
10	20

a. The SAS printout for fitting the model $y = \beta_0 + \beta_1 x + \beta_2 x^2 + \epsilon$ is shown on page 516. Find the least squares prediction equation.
b. Plot the fitted equation on a scattergram of the data. Is there sufficient evidence to support the inclusion of the quadratic term in the model? Explain.

```
Dep Variable: TIME

                         Analysis of Variance

                             Sum of        Mean
        Source        DF     Squares       Square     F Value    Prob>F

        Model          2    156.11948    78.05974     65.594     0.0001
        Error         12     14.28052     1.19004
        C Total       14    170.40000

              Root MSE          1.09089      R-square    0.9162
              Dep Mean         14.80000      Adj R-sq    0.9022
              C.V.              7.37089

                          Parameter Estimates

                     Parameter      Standard     T for HO:
        Variable  DF  Estimate         Error   Parameter=0    Prob > |T|

        INTERCEP   1  20.091108    0.72470507     27.723        0.0001
        EXP        1  -0.670522    0.15470634     -4.334        0.0010
        EXPSQ      1   0.009535    0.00632580      1.507        0.1576
```

c. Test the null hypothesis that $\beta_2 = 0$ against the alternative that $\beta_2 \neq 0$. Use $\alpha = .01$. Does the quadratic term make an important contribution to the model?

d. Your conclusion in part c should have been to drop the quadratic term from the model. Do so and fit the "reduced model," $y = \beta_0 + \beta_1 x + \epsilon$, to the data.

e. Define β_1 in the context of this exercise. Find a 90% confidence interval for β_1 in the reduced model of part d.

11.10 Empirical research was conducted to investigate the variables that impact the size distribution of manufacturing firms in international markets (*World Development,* Vol. 20, 1992). Data collected on $n = 54$ countries were used to model a country's size distribution, y, measured as the share of manufacturing firms in the country with 100 or more workers. The model studied was $E(y) = \beta_0 + \beta_1 x_1 + \beta_2 x_2 + \beta_3 x_3 + \beta_4 x_4 + \beta_5 x_5$, where

x_1 = natural logarithm of Gross National Product (LGNP)

x_2 = geographic area per capita (in thousands of square meters) (AREAC)

x_3 = share of heavy industry in manufacturing value added (SVA)

x_4 = ratio of credit claims on the private sector to Gross Domestic Product (CREDIT)

x_5 = ratio of stock equity shares to Gross Domestic Product (STOCK)

a. The researchers hypothesized that the higher the credit ratio of a country, the smaller the size distribution of manufacturing firms. Explain how to test this hypothesis.

b. The researchers hypothesized that the higher the stock ratio of a country, the larger the size distribution of manufacturing firms. Explain how to test this hypothesis.

11.11 (X11.011) Many variables influence the price of a company's common stock, including company-specific internal variables such as product quality and financial performance, and external market variables such as interest rates and stock market performance. The table on page 517 contains quarterly data on three such external variables (x_1, x_2, x_3) and the price y of Ford Motor Company's Common stock (adjusted for a stock split). The Japanese Yen Exchange Rate (the value of a U.S. dollar expressed in yen), x_1, measures the strength of the yen versus the U.S. dollar. The higher the rate, the cheaper are Japanese imports—such as the automobiles of Toyota, Nissan, Honda, and Subaru—to U.S. consumers. Similarly, the higher the deutsche mark exchange rate, x_2, the less expensive are BMW's and Mercedes Benz's to U.S. consumers. The S&P 500 Index, x_3, is a general measure of the performance of the market for stocks in U.S. firms.

a. Fit the first-order model $y = \beta_0 + \beta_1 x_1 + \beta_2 x_2 + \beta_3 x_3 + \epsilon$ to the data. Report the least squares prediction equation.

b. Find the standard deviation of the regression model and interpret its value in the context of this problem.

c. Do the data provide sufficient evidence to conclude that the price of Ford stock decreases as

Date		Ford Motor Co. Common Stock y	Yen Exchange Rate x_1	Deutsche Mark Exchange Rate x_2	S&P 500 x_3
1992	I	$38\frac{3}{8}$	133.2	1.64	407.36
	II	$45\frac{7}{8}$	125.5	1.53	408.21
	III	$39\frac{1}{2}$	119.2	1.41	418.48
	IV	$42\frac{7}{8}$	124.7	1.61	435.64
1993	I	52	121.0	1.61	450.16
	II	$52\frac{1}{4}$	110.1	1.69	447.29
	III	$55\frac{1}{4}$	105.2	1.62	459.24
	IV	$64\frac{1}{2}$	111.9	1.73	465.95
1994	I	$58\frac{3}{4}$	103.2	1.67	463.81
	II	59	99.1	1.60	454.83
	III	$27\frac{3}{4}$	98.5	1.55	466.96
	IV	$27\frac{7}{8}$	99.7	1.55	455.19
1995	I	$26\frac{7}{8}$	89.4	1.38	493.15
	II	$29\frac{3}{4}$	84.6	1.38	539.35
	III	$31\frac{1}{8}$	98.3	1.42	578.77
	IV	$28\frac{7}{8}$	102.8	1.43	614.57
1996	I	$34\frac{3}{8}$	106.3	1.48	647.07
	II	$32\frac{3}{8}$	109.4	1.52	668.50

Sources: 1. International Financial Statistics, International Monetary Fund, Washington, D.C., 1993–1996, 2. Economic Indicators, Congress, Joint Economic Committee, Washington, D.C., 1992–1996, 3. Dow Jones News/Retrieval database, Dow Jones and Company, New York, 1996.

the yen rate increases? Report the observed significance level and reach a conclusion using $\alpha = .05$.

d. Interpret the value of $\hat{\beta}_2$ in terms of these data. Remember that your interpretation must recognize the presence of the other variables in the model.

11.12 A researcher wished to investigate the effects of several factors on production-line supervisors' attitudes toward disabled workers. A study was conducted involving 40 randomly selected supervisors. The response y, a supervisor's attitude toward disabled workers, was measured with a standardized attitude scale. Independent variables used in the study were

$$x_1 = \begin{cases} 1 & \text{if the supervisor is female} \\ 0 & \text{if the supervisor is male} \end{cases}$$
(This is called a dummy variable.)

$x_2 = $ Number of years of experience in a supervisory job

The researcher fit the model

$$y = \beta_0 + \beta_1 x_1 + \beta_2 x_2 + \beta_3 x_2^2 + \epsilon$$

to the data with the following results:

$$\hat{y} = 50 + 5x_1 + 5x_2 - .1x_2^2$$

a. Is there sufficient evidence to indicate that the quadratic term in years of experience, x_2^2, is useful for predicting attitude score? Use $\alpha = .05$.

b. Sketch the predicted attitude score $\hat{y}$ as a function of the number of years of experience x_2 for male supervisors ($x_1 = 0$). Next, substitute $x_1 = 1$ into the least squares equation and thereby obtain a plot of the prediction equation for female supervisors. [*Note:* For both males and females, plotting $\hat{y}$ for $x_2 = 0, 2, 4, 6, 8$, and 10 will produce a good picture of the prediction equations. The vertical distance between the males' and females' prediction curves is the same for all values of x_2.]

11.5   CHECKING THE USEFULNESS OF A MODEL: R^2 AND THE ANALYSIS OF VARIANCE F-TEST

Conducting t-tests on each β parameter in a model is *not* a good way to determine whether a model is contributing information for the prediction of y. If we were to conduct a series of t-tests to determine whether the independent variables are contributing to the predictive relationship, we would be very likely to make one or more errors in deciding which terms to retain in the model and which to exclude.

For example, even if all the β parameters (except β_0) are equal to 0, $100(\alpha)\%$ of the time you will reject the null hypothesis and conclude that some β parameter differs from 0. Thus, in multiple regression models for which a large number of independent variables are being considered, conducting a series of t-tests may include a large number of insignificant variables and exclude some useful ones. If we want to test the utility of a multiple regression model, we will need a global test (one that encompasses all the β parameters). We would also like to find some statistical quantity that measures how well the model fits the data.

We commence with the easier problem—finding a measure of how well a linear model fits a set of data. For this we use the multiple regression equivalent of r^2, the coefficient of determination for the straight-line model (Chapter 10). Thus, we define the **multiple coefficient of determination**, R^2, as

$$R^2 = 1 - \frac{\sum(y - \hat{y})^2}{\sum(y - \bar{y})^2} = 1 - \frac{\text{SSE}}{\text{SS}_{yy}} = \frac{\text{SS}_{yy} - \text{SSE}}{\text{SS}_{yy}} = \frac{\text{Explained variability}}{\text{Total variability}}$$

where $\hat{y}$ is the predicted value of y for the model. Just as for the simple linear model, R^2 represents the fraction of the sample variation of the y values (measured by SS_{yy}) that is explained by the least squares prediction equation. Thus, $R^2 = 0$ implies a complete lack of fit of the model to the data and $R^2 = 1$ implies a perfect fit with the model passing through every data point. In general, the larger the value of R^2, the better the model fits the data.

To illustrate, the value $R^2 = .9819$ for the electrical usage example is indicated in Figure 11.10. This very high value of R^2 implies that using the independent variable home size in a quadratic model explains approximately 98% of the total **sample variation** (measured by SS_{yy}) of electrical usage y. Thus, R^2 is a sample statistic that tells how well the model fits the data and thereby represents a measure of the usefulness of the entire model.

```
Dep Variable: Y

                       Analysis of Variance

                            Sum of          Mean
     Source        DF      Squares         Square     F Value    Prob>F

     Model          2   831069.54637   415534.77319   189.710    0.0001
     Error          7    15332.55363     2190.36480
     C Total        9   846402.10000

           Root MSE       46.80133     R-square     0.9819
           Dep Mean     1594.70000     Adj R-sq     0.9767
           C.V.            2.93480

                      Parameter Estimates

                     Parameter     Standard     T for HO:
     Variable  DF     Estimate        Error   Parameter=0   Prob > |T|

     INTERCEP   1  -1216.143887  242.80636850     -5.009       0.0016
     X          1      2.398930    0.24583560      9.758       0.0001
     XSQ        1     -0.000450    0.00005908     -7.618       0.0001
```

FIGURE 11.10   SAS printout for electrical usage example

The fact that R^2 is a sample statistic implies that it can be used to make inferences about the usefulness of the entire model for predicting the population of y values at each setting of the independent variables. In particular, for the electrical usage data, the test

$$H_0: \beta_1 = \beta_2 = 0$$

$$H_a: \text{At least one of the coefficients is nonzero}$$

would formally test the global usefulness of the model.

The test statistic used to test this hypothesis is an F statistic, and several equivalent versions of the formula can be used (although we will usually rely on the computer to calculate the F statistic):

$$\textit{Test statistic: } F = \frac{(SS_{yy} - SSE)/k}{SSE/[n - (k + 1)]} = \frac{R^2/k}{(1 - R^2)/[n - (k + 1)]}$$

Both these formulas indicate that the F statistic is the ratio of the *explained* variability divided by the error degrees of freedom. Thus, the larger the proportion of the total variability accounted for by the model, the larger the F statistic.

To determine when the ratio becomes large enough that we can confidently reject the null hypothesis and conclude that the model is more useful than no model at all for predicting y, we compare the calculated F statistic to a tabulated F value with k df in the numerator and $[n - (k + 1)]$ df in the denominator. Tabulations of the F-distribution for various values of α are given in Tables VIII, IX, X, and XI of Appendix B.

Rejection region: $F > F_\alpha$, where F is based on k numerator and $n - (k + 1)$ denominator degrees of freedom.

For the electrical usage example [$n = 10, k = 2, n - (k + 1) = 7$, and $\alpha = .05$], we will reject $H_0: \beta_1 = \beta_2 = 0$ if

$$F > F_{.05} = 4.74$$

From the SAS printout (Figure 11.10), we find that the computed F is 189.71. Since this value greatly exceeds the tabulated value of 4.74, we conclude that at least one of the model coefficients β_1 and β_2 is nonzero. Therefore, this global F-test indicates that the quadratic model $y = \beta_0 + \beta_1 x + \beta_2 x^2 + \epsilon$ is useful for predicting electrical usage.

The F statistic is also given as a part of most regression printouts, usually in a portion of the printout called the "Analysis of Variance." This is an appropriate descriptive term, since the F statistic relates the explained and unexplained portions of the total variance of y. For example, the elements of the SAS printout in Figure 11.10 that lead to the calculation of the F value are:

$$F \text{ Value} = \frac{\text{Sum of Squares(Model)}/\text{df(Model)}}{\text{Sum of Squares(Error)}/\text{df(Error)}} = \frac{\text{Mean Square(Model)}}{\text{Mean Square(Error)}}$$

From Figure 11.10 we see that **F Value** = 189.71. Note, too, that the observed significance level for the F statistic is given under the heading **Prob>F** as .0001, which means that we would reject the null hypothesis $H_0: \beta_1 = \beta_2 = 0$ at any α value greater than .0001.

The analysis of variance F-test for testing the usefulness of the model is summarized in the next box.

Testing Global Usefulness of the Model: The Analysis of Variance F-Test

$H_0: \beta_1 = \beta_2 = \cdots = \beta_k = 0$ (All model terms are unimportant for predicting y)

H_a: At least one $\beta_i \neq 0$ (At least one model term is useful for predicting y)

Test statistic: $F = \dfrac{(SS_{yy} - SSE)/k}{SSE/[n - (k + 1)]} = \dfrac{R^2/k}{(1 - R^2)/[n - (k + 1)]}$

$= \dfrac{\text{Mean Square(Model))}}{\text{Mean Square(Error)}}$

where n is the sample size and k is the number of terms in the model.

Rejection region: $F > F_\alpha$, with k numerator degrees of freedom and $[n - (k + 1)]$ denominator degrees of freedom.

Assumptions: The standard regression assumptions about the random error component (Section 11.3).

Caution: A rejection of the null hypothesis leads to the conclusion [with $100(1 - \alpha)\%$ confidence] that the model is useful. However, "useful" does not necessarily mean "best." Another model may prove even more useful in terms of providing more reliable estimates and predictions. This global F-test is usually regarded as a test that the model *must* pass to merit further consideration.

EXAMPLE 11.2

Refer to Example 11.1, in which an antique collector modeled the auction price y of grandfather clocks as a function of the age of the clock, x_1, and the number of bidders, x_2. The hypothesized model is

$$y = \beta_0 + \beta_1 x_1 + \beta_2 x_2 + \epsilon$$

A sample of 32 observations is obtained, with the results summarized in the MINITAB printout repeated in Figure 11.11.

a. Find and interpret the coefficient of determination R^2 for this example.
b. Conduct the global F-test of model usefulness at the $\alpha = .05$ level of significance.

SOLUTION

a. The R^2 value (highlighted in Figure 11.11) is .892. This implies that the least squares model has explained about 89% of the total sample variation in y values (auction prices).

FIGURE 11.11
MINITAB printout for Example 11.2

```
The regression equation is
Y = -1339 + 12.7 X1 + 86.0 X2

Predictor      Coef      Stdev    t-ratio       p
Constant    -1339.0      173.8      -7.70   0.000
X1          12.7406     0.9047      14.08   0.000
X2           85.953      8.729       9.85   0.000

s = 133.5     R-sq = 89.2%     R-sq(adj) = 88.5%

Analysis of Variance

SOURCE       DF        SS         MS        F       p
Regression    2    4283063    2141532   120.19   0.000
Error        29     516727      17818
Total        31    4799789
```

b. The elements of the global test of the model follow:

$H_0: \beta_1 = \beta_2 = 0$ [*Note:* $k = 2$]

H_a: At least one of the two model coefficients is nonzero

Test statistic: $F = \dfrac{R^2/k}{(1 - R^2)/[n - (k + 1)]} = 120.19$ (see Figure 11.11)

Rejection region: $F > F_\alpha$

For this example, $n = 32$, $k = 2$, and $n - (k + 1) = 32 - 3 = 29$. Then, for $\alpha = .05$, we will reject $H_0: \beta_1 = \beta_2 = 0$ if $F > F_{.05}$, where F is based on $k = 2$ numerator and $n - (k + 1) = 29$ denominator degrees of freedom—that is, if $F > 3.33$. Since the computed value of the F-test statistic falls in the rejection region ($F = 120.19$ greatly exceeds $F_{.05} = 3.33$, and $\alpha = .05$ exceeds $p = .000$), the data provide strong evidence that at least one of the model coefficients is nonzero. The model appears to be useful for predicting auction prices. ◼

Can we be sure that the best prediction model has been found if the global F-test indicates that a model is useful? Unfortunately, we cannot. The addition of other independent variables may improve the usefulness of the model, as Example 11.3 demonstrates.

EXAMPLE 11.3

Refer to Examples 11.1 and 11.2. Suppose the collector, having observed many auctions, believes that the *rate of increase* of the auction price with age will be driven upward by a large number of bidders. Thus, instead of a relationship like that shown in Figure 11.12a, in which the rate of increase in price with age is the same for any number of bidders, the collector believes the relationship is like that shown in Figure 11.12b. Note that as the number of bidders increases from 5 to 15, the slope of the price versus age line increases. When the slope of the relationship between y and one independent variable (x_1) depends on the value of a second independent variable (x_2), as is the case here, we say that x_1 and x_2 **interact**.* The **interaction model** is written

$$y = \beta_0 + \beta_1 x_1 + \beta_2 x_2 + \beta_3 x_1 x_2 + \epsilon$$

Note that the increase in the mean price, $E(y)$, for each one-year increase in age, x_1, is no longer given by the constant β_1 but is now $\beta_1 + \beta_3 x_2$. *That is, the amount*

FIGURE 11.12
Examples of no-interaction and interaction models

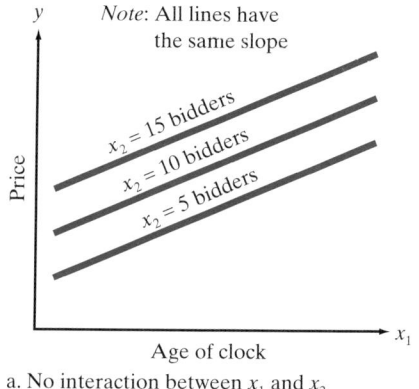

a. No interaction between x_1 and x_2

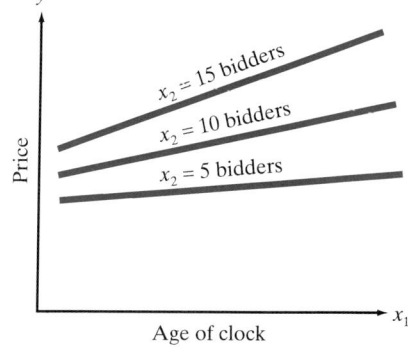

b. Interaction between x_1 and x_2

*A detailed discussion of interaction is given in Chapter 12.

FIGURE 11.13
MINITAB printout for the model with interaction

```
The regression equation is
Y = 320 + 0.88 X1 - 93.3 X2 + 1.30 X1X2

Predictor       Coef       Stdev     t-ratio         p
Constant       320.5       295.1        1.09     0.287
X1             0.878       2.032        0.43     0.669
X2            -93.26       29.89       -3.12     0.004
X1X2          1.2978      0.2123        6.11     0.000

s = 88.91     R-sq = 95.4%      R-sq(adj) = 94.9%

Analysis of Variance

SOURCE       DF          SS         MS         F         p
Regression    3     4578428    1526142    193.04     0.000
Error        28      221362       7906
Total        31     4799789
```

$E(y)$ *increases for each 1-unit increase in* x_1 *is dependent on the number of bidders,* x_2. *Thus, the two variables* x_1 *and* x_2 *interact to affect* y.

The 32 data points listed in Table 11.2 were used to fit the model with interaction. A portion of the MINITAB printout is shown in Figure 11.13. Test the hypothesis that the price-age slope increases as the number of bidders increases—that is, that age and number of bidders, x_2, interact positively.

SOLUTION
The model is

$$y = \beta_0 + \beta_1 x_1 + \beta_2 x_2 + \beta_3 x_1 x_2 + \epsilon$$

and the hypotheses of interest to the collector concern the parameter β_3. Specifically,

$$H_0: \beta_3 = 0$$

$$H_a: \beta_3 > 0$$

Test statistic: $t = \dfrac{\hat{\beta}_3}{s_{\hat{\beta}_3}}$

Rejection region: For $\alpha = .05, t > t_{.05}$

where $n = 32, k = 3$, and $t_{.05} = 1.701$, based on $n - (k + 1) = 28$ df. [*Remember:* $(k + 1) = 4$ is the number of parameters in the regression model.]

The t value corresponding to $\hat{\beta}_3$ is highlighted in Figure 11.13. The value $t = 6.11$ exceeds 1.701 and therefore falls in the rejection region. Thus, the collector can conclude that the rate of change of the mean price of the clocks with age increases as the number of bidders increases; that is, x_1 and x_2 interact. (The same conclusion can be reached by noting that the p-value of the test is 0.) Thus, it appears that the interaction term should be included in the model.

One note of caution: Although the coefficient of x_2 is negative ($\hat{\beta}_2 = -93.26$) in Example 11.3, this does *not* imply that auction price decreases as the number of bidders increases. Since interaction is present, the rate of change (slope) of mean auction price with the number of bidders *depends* on x_1, the age of the clock. Thus, for example, the estimated rate of change of y for a unit increase in x_2 (one new bidder) for a 150-year-old clock is

$$\text{Estimated } x_2 \text{ slope} = \hat{\beta}_2 + \hat{\beta}_3 x_1 = -93.26 + 1.30(150) = 101.74$$

In other words, we estimate that the auction price of a 150-year-old clock will *increase* by about \$101.74 for every additional bidder. Although the rate of increase will vary as x_1 is changed, it will remain positive for the range of values of x_1 included in the sample. Extreme care is needed in interpreting the signs and sizes of coefficients in a multiple regression model.

To summarize the discussion in this section, the value of R^2 is an indicator of how well the prediction equation fits the data. More importantly, it can be used in the F statistic to determine whether the data provide sufficient evidence to indicate that the model contributes information for the prediction of y. Intuitive evaluations of the contribution of the model based on the computed value of R^2 must be examined with care. The value of R^2 increases as more and more variables are added to the model. Consequently, you could force R^2 to take a value very close to 1 even though the model contributes no information for the prediction of y. In fact, R^2 equals 1 when the number of terms in the model equals the number of data points. Therefore, you should not rely solely on the value of R^2 to tell you whether the model is useful for predicting y. Use the F-test.

After we have determined that the overall model is useful for predicting y using the F-test, we may elect to conduct one or more t-tests on the individual β parameters (see Section 11.4). However, the test (or tests) to be conducted should be decided *a priori*, that is, prior to fitting the model. Also, we should limit the number of t-tests conducted to avoid the potential problem of making too many Type I errors. Generally, the regression analyst will conduct t-tests only on the "most important" β's. We provide insight in identifying the most important β's in a linear model in Chapter 12.

Recommendation for Checking the Utility of a Multiple Regression Model

1. Conduct a test of overall model adequacy using the F-test, that is, test

$$H_0: \beta_1 = \beta_2 = \cdots = \beta_k = 0$$

If the model is deemed adequate (that is, if you reject H_0), then proceed to step 2. Otherwise, you should hypothesize and fit another model. The new model may include more independent variables or higher-order terms.

2. Conduct t-tests on those β parameters in which you are particularly interested (that is, the "most important" β's). These usually involve only the β's associated with higher-order terms (x^2, x_1x_2, etc.). However, it is a safe practice to limit the number of β's that are tested. Conducting a series of t-tests leads to a high overall Type I error rate α.

EXERCISES   11.13–11.28

Note: Exercises marked with 🖥 *contain data for computer analysis on a 3.5" disk (file name in parentheses).*

Learning the Mechanics

11.13 Suppose you fit the model

$$y = \beta_0 + \beta_1 x_1 + \beta_2 x_2 + \beta_3 x_1 x_2 + \beta_4 x_1^2 + \beta_5 x_2^2 + \epsilon$$

to $n = 30$ data points and obtain

$$SSE = .46 \qquad R^2 = .87$$

a. Do the values of SSE and R^2 suggest that the model provides a good fit to the data? Explain.

b. Is the model of any use in predicting y? Test the null hypothesis that $E(y) = \beta_0$; that is, test

```
Dep Variable: Y

                          Analysis of Variance

                        Sum of          Mean
        Source    DF     Squares         Square      F Value    Prob>F

        Model      2     24.22335       12.11167      65.478     0.0001
        Error     16      2.95955        0.18497
        C Total   18     27.18289

                  Root MSE      0.43008     R-square      0.8911
                  Dep Mean      3.56053     Adj R-sq      0.8775
                  C.V.         12.07921

                          Parameter Estimates

                        Parameter      Standard      T for H0:
        Variable   DF    Estimate        Error      Parameter=0   Prob > |T|

        INTERCEP    1    0.734606      0.29313351      2.506       0.0234
        X           1    0.765179      0.08754136      8.741       0.0001
        XSQ         1   -0.030810      0.00452890     -6.803       0.0001
```

$H_0: \beta_1 = \beta_2 = \cdots = \beta_5 = 0$

against the alternative hypothesis

H_a: At least one of the parameters $\beta_1, \beta_2, ..., \beta_5$ is nonzero

Use $\alpha = .05$.

11.14 The model $y = \beta_0 + \beta_1 x + \beta_2 x^2 + \epsilon$ was fit to $n = 19$ data points with the results shown in the SAS printout above.
   a. Find R^2 and interpret its value.
   b. Test the null hypothesis that $\beta_1 = \beta_2 = 0$ against the alternative hypothesis that at least one of β_1 and β_2 is nonzero. Calculate the test statistic using the two formulas given in this section, and compare your results to each other and to that given on the printout. Use $\alpha = .05$ and interpret the result of your test.
   c. Find the observed significance level for this test on the printout and interpret it.
   d. Test $H_0: \beta_2 = 0$ against $H_a: \beta_2 \neq 0$. Use $\alpha = .05$ and interpret the result of your test. Report and interpret the observed significance level of the test.

11.15 Suppose you fit the model

$y = \beta_0 + \beta_1 x_1 + \beta_2 x_2 + \epsilon$

to $n = 20$ data points and obtain

$\sum(y_i - \hat{y}_i)^2 = 12.37 \qquad \sum(y_i - \bar{y})^2 = 23.75$

   a. Construct an analysis of variance table for this regression analysis, using the printout in Exercise 11.14 as a model. Be sure to include the sources of variability, the degrees of freedom, the sums of squares, the mean squares, and the F statistic. Calculate R^2 for the regression analysis.
   b. Test the null hypothesis that $\beta_1 = \beta_2 = 0$ against the alternative hypothesis that at least one of the parameters differs from 0. Calculate the test statistic in two different ways and compare the results. Use $\alpha = .05$ to reach a conclusion about whether the model contributes information for the prediction of y.

11.16 If the analysis of variance F-test leads to the conclusion that at least one of the model parameters is nonzero, can you conclude that the model is the best predictor for the dependent variable y? Can you conclude that all of the terms in the model are important for predicting y? What is the appropriate conclusion?

Applying the Concepts

11.17 External auditors are hired to review and analyze the financial and other records of an organization and to attest to the integrity of the organization's financial statements. In recent years, the fees charged by auditors have come under increasing scrutiny. S. Butterworth and K. A. Houghton, two University of Melbourne (Australia) researchers, investigated the effects of several variables on the fee charged by auditors. (*Journal of Business Finance and Accounting,* April 1995.) These variables are described at the top of page 525. The multiple regression model, $E(y) = \beta_0 + \beta_1 x_1 + \beta_2 x_2 + \beta_3 x_3 + \cdots + \beta_7 x_7$ was fit to data collected for $n = 268$ companies. The results are summarized in the table on page 525.
   a. Write the least squares prediction equation.
   b. Assess the overall fit of the model.
   c. Interpret the estimate of β_3.

y = Logarithm of audit fee charged to auditee (FEE)

$x_1 = \begin{cases} 1 & \text{if auditee changed auditors after one year (CHANGE)} \\ 0 & \text{if not} \end{cases}$

x_2 = Logarithm of auditee's total assets (SIZE)

x_3 = Number of subsidiaries of auditee (COMPLEX)

$x_4 = \begin{cases} 1 & \text{if auditee receives an audit qualification (RISK)} \\ 0 & \text{if not} \end{cases}$

$x_5 = \begin{cases} 1 & \text{if auditee in mining industry (INDUSTRY)} \\ 0 & \text{if not} \end{cases}$

$x_6 = \begin{cases} 1 & \text{if auditor is a member of a "Big 8" firm (BIG8)} \\ 0 & \text{if not} \end{cases}$

x_7 = Logarithm of dollar-value of non-audit services provided by auditor (NAS)

Independent Variable	Expected Sign of β	β Estimate	t Value	Level of Significance (p-value)
Constant	−	−4.30	−3.45	.001 (two-tailed)
CHANGE	+	−.002	−0.049	.961 (one-tailed)
SIZE	+	.336	9.94	.000 (one-tailed)
COMPLEX	+	.384	7.63	.000 (one-tailed)
RISK	+	.067	1.76	.079 (one-tailed)
INDUSTRY	−	−.143	−4.05	.000 (one-tailed)
BIG8	+	.081	2.18	.030 (one-tailed)
NAS	+/−	.134	4.54	.000 (two-tailed)
$R^2 = .712$		$F = 111.1$		

Source: Butterworth, S., and Houghton, K. A. "Auditor switching: The pricing of audit services." *Journal of Business Finance and Accounting,* Vol. 22, No. 3, April 1995, p. 334 (Table 4).

d. The researchers hypothesized the direction of the effect of each independent variable on audit fees. These hypotheses are given in the "Expected Sign of β" column in the table. (For example, if the expected sign is negative, the alternative hypothesis is $H_a: \beta_i < 0$.) Interpret the results of the hypothesis test for β_4. Use $\alpha = .05$.

e. The main objective of the analysis was to determine whether new auditors charge less than incumbent auditors in a given year. If this hypothesis is true, then the true value of β_1 is negative. Is there evidence to support this hypothesis? Explain.

11.18 The *Journal of Quantitative Criminology* (Vol. 8, 1992) published a paper on the determinants of regional property crime levels in the United Kingdom. Several multiple regression models for property crime prevalence, y, measured as the percentage of residents in a geographic region who were victims of at least one property crime, were examined. The results for one of the models, based on a sample of n = 313 responses collected for the British Crime Survey, are shown in the table on page 526. [*Note:* All variables except Density are expressed as a percentage of the base region.]

a. Test the hypothesis that the density (x_1) of a region is positively linearly related to crime prevalence (y), holding the other independent variables constant.

b. Do you advise conducting t-tests on each of the 18 independent variables in the model to determine which variables are important predictors of crime prevalence? Explain.

c. The model yielded $R^2 = .411$. Use this information to conduct a test of the global utility of the model. Use $\alpha = .05$.

11.19 Refer to the *Interfaces* (Mar.–Apr. 1990) study of La Quinta Motor Inns, Exercise 11.7. The researchers used state population per inn (x_1), inn room rate (x_2), median income of the area (x_3), and college enrollment (x_4) to build a first-order model for operating margin (y) of a La Quinta inn. Based on a sample of n = 57 inns, the model yielded $R^2 = .51$.

a. Give a descriptive measure of model adequacy.

Variable	$\hat{\beta}$	t	p-Value
x_1 = Density (population per hectare)	.331	3.88	$p < .01$
x_2 = Unemployed male population	−.121	−1.17	$p > .10$
x_3 = Professional population	−.187	−1.90	$.01 < p < .10$
x_4 = Population aged less than 5	−.151	−1.51	$p > .10$
x_5 = Population aged between 5 and 15	.353	3.42	$p < .01$
x_6 = Female population	.095	1.31	$p > .10$
x_7 = 10-year change in population	.130	1.40	$p > .10$
x_8 = Minority population	−.122	−1.51	$p > .10$
x_9 = Young adult population	.163	5.62	$p < .01$
x_{10} = 1 if North region, 0 if not	.369	1.72	$.01 < p < .10$
x_{11} = 1 if Yorkshire region, 0 if not	−.210	−1.39	$p > .10$
x_{12} = 1 if East Midlands region, 0 if not	−.192	−0.78	$p > .10$
x_{13} = 1 if East Anglia region, 0 if not	−.548	−2.22	$.01 < p < .10$
x_{14} = 1 if South East region, 0 if not	.152	1.37	$p > .10$
x_{15} = 1 if South West region, 0 if not	−.151	−0.88	$p > .10$
x_{16} = 1 if West Midlands region, 0 if not	−.308	−1.93	$.01 < p < .10$
x_{17} = 1 if North West region, 0 if not	.311	2.13	$.01 < p < .10$
x_{18} = 1 if Wales region, 0 if not	−.019	−0.08	$p > .10$

Source: Osborn, D. R., Tickett, A., and Elder, R. "Area characteristics and regional variates as determinants of area property crime." *Journal of Quantitative Criminology,* Vol. 8, No. 3, 1992, Plenum Publishing Corp.

b. Make an inference about model adequacy by conducting the appropriate test. Use $\alpha = .05$.

11.20 An important goal in occupational safety is "active caring." Employees demonstrate active caring (AC) about the safety of their coworkers when they identify environmental hazards and unsafe work practices and then implement appropriate corrective actions for these unsafe conditions or behaviors. Three factors hypothesized to increase the propensity for an employee to actively care for safety are (1) high self-esteem, (2) optimism, and (3) group cohesiveness. A study published in *Applied and Preventive Psychology* (Winter 1995) attempted to establish empirical support for the AC hypothesis by fitting the model

$$E(y) = \beta_0 + \beta_1 x_1 + \beta_2 x_2 + \beta_3 x_3,$$

where

y = AC score (measuring active caring on a 15-point scale)

x_1 = Self-esteem score

x_2 = Optimism score

x_3 = Group cohesion score

The regression analysis, based on data collected for $n = 31$ hourly workers at a large fiber-manufacturing plant, yielded a multiple coefficient of determination of $R^2 = .362$.

a. Interpret the value of R^2.

b. Use the R^2-value to test the global utility of the model. Use $\alpha = .05$.

11.21 *Trichuristrichiura,* a parasitic worm, affects millions of school-age children each year, especially children from developing countries. A study was conducted by a pharmaceutical company to determine the effects of treatment of the parasite on school achievement in 407 school-age Jamaican children infected with the disease (*Journal of Nutrition,* July 1995). About half the children in the sample received the treatment, while the others received a placebo. Multiple regression was used to model spelling test score y, measured as number correct, as a function of the following independent variables:

Treatment (T):

$$x_1 = \begin{cases} 1 & \text{if treatment} \\ 0 & \text{if placebo} \end{cases}$$

Disease Intensity (I):

$$x_2 = \begin{cases} 1 & \text{if more than 7,000 eggs per gram of stool} \\ 0 & \text{if not} \end{cases}$$

a. Propose a model for $E(y)$ that includes interaction between treatment and disease intensity.

b. The estimates of the β's in the model, part **a**, and the respective p-values for t-tests on the β's are given in the table. Is there sufficient evidence to indicate that the effect of the treatment on spelling score depends on disease intensity? Test using $\alpha = .05$.

Variable	β Estimate	p-Value
Treatment (x_1)	−.1	.62
Intensity (x_2)	−.3	.57
T × I ($x_1 x_2$)	1.6	.02

[*Note:* The actual model fit in the study included several other variables such as age, gender, and socioeconomic status.]

c. Based on the result, part **b**, explain why the analyst should avoid conducting t-tests for the treatment (x_1) and intensity (x_2) β's or interpreting these β's individually.

11.22 **(X11.022)** Multiple regression is used by accountants in cost analysis to shed light on the factors that cause costs to be incurred and the magnitudes of their effects. The independent variables of such a regression model are the factors believed to be related to cost, the dependent variable. Assuming no interactions between the independent variables, the estimates of the coefficients of the regression model provide measures of the magnitude of the factors' effects on cost. In some instances, however, it is desirable to use physical units instead of cost as the dependent variable in a cost analysis. This would be the case if most of the cost associated with the activity of interest is a function of some physical unit, such as hours of labor. The advantage of this approach is that the regression model will provide estimates of the number of labor hours required under different circumstances and these hours can then be costed at the current labor rate (Horngren, Foster, and Datar, 1994; Benston, 1966). The sample data shown in the table below have been collected from a firm's accounting and production records to provide cost information about the firm's shipping department. The EXCEL computer printout for fitting the model $y = \beta_0 + \beta_1 x_1 + \beta_2 x_2 + \beta_3 x_3 + \epsilon$ is shown on page 528.

a. Find the least squares prediction equation.

b. Use an F-test to investigate the usefulness of the model specified in part **a**. Use $\alpha = .01$, and state your conclusion in the context of the problem.

c. Test H_0: $\beta_2 = 0$ versus H_a: $\beta_2 \neq 0$ using $\alpha = .05$. What do the results of your test suggest about the magnitude of the effects of x_2 on labor costs?

d. Find R^2, and interpret its value in the context of the problem.

e. If shipping department employees are paid \$7.50 per hour, how much less, on average, will it cost the company per week if the average number of pounds per shipment increases from a level of 20 to 21? Assume that x_1 and x_2 remain unchanged. Your answer is an estimate of what is known in economics as the *expected marginal cost* associated with a one-pound increase in x_3.

f. With what approximate precision can this model be used to predict the hours of labor? [*Note:* The precision of multiple regression predictions is discussed in Section 11.6.]

g. Can regression analysis alone indicate what factors *cause* costs to increase? Explain.

11.23 **(X11.023)** Many nonprofit and public hospitals are struggling to survive in the face of the new market forces of managed health care and the extreme fiscal pressures on local governments ("Hard cases at the hospital door," *New York Times*, Sept. 17, 1995). Regression analysis was employed to investigate the determinants of survival size of nonprofit hospitals. For a given sample of hospitals, survival size, y, is defined as the largest size hospital (in terms of number of beds) exhibiting growth in market share over a specific time interval. Suppose 10 states are randomly selected and the survival size for all nonprofit hospitals in each state is determined for two

Week	Labor y (hrs.)	Pounds Shipped x_1 (1,000s)	Percentage of Units Shipped by Truck x_2	Average Shipment Weight x_3 (lbs.)
1	100	5.1	90	20
2	85	3.8	99	22
3	108	5.3	58	19
4	116	7.5	16	15
5	92	4.5	54	20
6	63	3.3	42	26
7	79	5.3	12	25
8	101	5.9	32	21
9	88	4.0	56	24
10	71	4.2	64	29
11	122	6.8	78	10
12	85	3.9	90	30
13	50	3.8	74	28
14	114	7.5	89	14
15	104	4.5	90	21
16	111	6.0	40	20
17	110	8.1	55	16
18	100	2.9	64	19
19	82	4.0	35	23
20	85	4.8	58	25

SUMMARY OUTPUT

Regression Statistics	
Multiple R	0.87755597
R Square	0.77010448
Adjusted R Square	0.72699907
Standard Error	9.810345853
Observations	20

ANOVA

	df	SS	MS	F	Significance F
Regression	3	5158.313828	1719.437943	17.86561083	2.32332E-05
Residual	16	1539.886172	96.24288576		
Total	19	6698.2			

	Coefficients	Standard Error	t Stat	P-value	Lower 95%	Upper 95%
Intercept	131.9242521	25.69321439	5.134595076	9.98597E-05	77.45708304	186.3914211
Ship(x1)	2.72608977	2.275004884	1.198278645	0.24825743	-2.096704051	7.548883591
Truck(x2)	0.047218412	0.093348559	0.505829045	0.6198742	-0.150671647	0.245108472
Weight(x3)	-2.587443905	0.642818185	-4.025156669	0.000978875	-3.950157275	-1.224730536

time periods five years apart, yielding two observations per state. The 20 survival sizes are listed in the accompanying table, along with the following data for each state, for the second year in each time interval:

x_1 = Percentage of beds that are in for-profit hospitals

x_2 = Ratio of the number of persons enrolled in health maintenance organizations (HMOs) to the number of persons covered by hospital insurance

x_3 = State population (in thousands)

x_4 = Percentage of state that is urban

The following model characterizes the relationship between survival size and the four variables just listed:

$$y = \beta_0 + \beta_1 x_1 + \beta_2 x_2 + \beta_3 x_3 + \beta_4 x_4 + \epsilon$$

a. The model was fit to the data in the table using SAS, with the results given in the printout below. Report the least squares prediction equation.

b. Find the regression standard deviation s and interpret its value in the context of the problem.

State	Time Period	Survival Size y	x_1	x_2	x_3	x_4
1	1	370	.13	.09	5,800	89
1	2	390	.15	.09	5,955	87
2	1	455	.08	.11	17,648	87
2	2	450	.10	.16	17,895	85
3	1	500	.03	.04	7,332	79
3	2	480	.07	.05	7,610	78
4	1	550	.06	.005	11,731	80
4	2	600	.10	.005	11,790	81
5	1	205	.30	.12	2,932	44
5	2	230	.25	.13	3,100	45
6	1	425	.04	.01	4,148	36
6	2	445	.07	.02	4,205	38
7	1	245	.20	.01	1,574	25
7	2	200	.30	.01	1,560	28
8	1	250	.07	.08	2,471	38
8	2	275	.08	.10	2,511	38
9	1	300	.09	.12	4,060	52
9	2	290	.12	.20	4,175	54
10	1	280	.10	.02	2,902	37
10	2	270	.11	.05	2,925	38

```
Dep Variable: Y

                        Analysis of Variance

                         Sum of           Mean
    Source      DF       Squares         Square       F Value      Prob>F

    Model        4   246537.05939     61634.26485      28.180      0.0001
    Error       15    32807.94061      2187.19604
    C Total     19   279345.00000

           Root MSE     46.76747        R-square      0.8826
           Dep Mean    360.50000        Adj R-sq      0.8512
           C.V.         12.97295

                         Parameter Estimates

                     Parameter       Standard       T for H0:
    Variable    DF    Estimate         Error      Parameter=0    Prob > |T|

    INTERCEP     1    295.327091     40.17888737       7.350        0.0001
    X1           1   -480.837576    150.39050364      -3.197        0.0060
    X2           1   -829.464955    196.47303539      -4.222        0.0007
    X3           1      0.007934      0.00355335       2.233        0.0412
    X4           1      2.360769      0.76150774       3.100        0.0073
```

c. Use an F-test to investigate the usefulness of the hypothesized model. Report the observed significance level, and use $\alpha = .025$ to reach your conclusion.

d. Prior to collecting the data it was hypothesized that increases in the number of for-profit hospital beds would decrease the survival size of nonprofit hospitals. Do the data support this hypothesis? Test using $\alpha = .05$.

11.24 Because the coefficient of determination R^2 always increases when a new independent variable is added to the model, it is tempting to include many variables in a model to force R^2 to be near 1. However, doing so reduces the degrees of freedom available for estimating σ^2, which adversely affects our ability to make reliable inferences. Suppose you want to use 18 economic indicators to predict next year's Gross Domestic Product (GDP). You fit the model

$$y = \beta_0 + \beta_1 x_1 + \beta_2 x_2 + \cdots + \beta_{17} x_{17} + \beta_{18} x_{18} + \epsilon$$

where $y =$ GDP and $x_1, x_2, ..., x_{18}$ are indicators. Only 20 years of data ($n = 20$) are used to fit the model, and you obtain $R^2 = .95$. Test to see whether this impressive-looking R^2 is large enough for you to infer that the model is useful, that is, that at least one term in the model is important for predicting GDP. Use $\alpha = .05$.

11.25 Refer to Exercise 11.12. The dependent variable being modeled was production-line supervisors' scores on a test designed to measure attitudes toward handicapped workers. The independent variables were the sex of the supervisor ($x_1 = 1$ if female, 0 if male) and the supervisor's years of experience (x_2). Suppose the model proposed adds an interaction between x_1 and x_2; i.e.,

$$y = \beta_0 + \beta_1 x_1 + \beta_2 x_2 + \beta_3 x_2^2 + \beta_4 x_1 x_2 + \epsilon$$

This model is fit to the same data (40 observations) as in Exercise 11.12 with the results

$$\hat{y} = 50 + 5x_1 + 6x_2 - .2x_2^2 - x_1 x_2$$

$$s_{\hat{\beta}_4} = .02$$

$$R^2 = .87$$

a. Interpret the value of R^2.
b. Is there sufficient evidence to indicate that this model is useful for predicting attitude score? Test $H_0: \beta_1 = \beta_2 = \beta_3 = \beta_4 = 0$ using $\alpha = .05$.
c. Is there evidence that the interaction between sex and years of experience is useful in the prediction model?
d. Sketch the predicted attitude score $\hat{y}$ as a function of the number of years of experience x_2 for males ($x_1 = 0$). Next, substitute $x_1 = 1$ into

the least squares equation to obtain a plot of the prediction equation for females. Compare these sketches with those obtained when the model without interaction was fit in Exercise 11.12. [*Note:* For both sexes, plotting $\hat{y}$ for $x_2 = 0, 2, 4, 6, 8,$ and 10 will produce a good picture of the prediction equations. The interaction term allows the vertical distance between the males' and females' prediction curves to change as x_2 changes.]

11.26 **(X11.026)** A company that services copy machines is interested in developing a regression model that will assist in personnel planning. It needs a model that describes the relationship between the time spent on a preventive maintenance service call to a customer, y, and two independent variables: the number of copy machines to be serviced, x_1, and the service person's experience in preventive maintenance, x_2. Company records were sampled and the data in the table were obtained.

Hours of Maintenance	Number of Copy Machines	Months of Experience
1.0	1	12
3.1	3	8
17.0	10	5
14.0	8	2
6.0	5	10
1.8	1	1
11.5	10	10
9.3	5	2
6.0	4	6
12.2	10	18

a. Fit the model $y = \beta_0 + \beta_1 x_1 + \beta_2 x_2 + \epsilon$ to the data.
b. Investigate whether the model is useful. Test using $\alpha = .10$.
c. Find R^2 for the fitted model. Interpret your result.
d. Fit the model $y = \beta_0 + \beta_1 x_1 + \beta_2 x_2 + \beta_3 x_1 x_2 + \epsilon$ to the data.
e. Find R^2 for the model of part **d**.
f. Explain why you should not rely solely on a comparison of the two R^2 values for drawing conclusions about which model is more useful for predicting y.
g. Do the data provide sufficient evidence to indicate that the interaction term, $x_1 x_2$, contributes information for the prediction of y? [*Hint:* Test $H_0: \beta_3 = 0$.] Which model is more useful for predicting y?
h. Can you be certain that the model you selected in part **g** is the best model to use in predicting maintenance time? Explain.

11.27 Much research—and much litigation—has been conducted on the disparity between the salary levels of men and women. Research reported in

Work and Occupations (Nov. 1992) analyzes the salaries for a sample of 191 Illinois managers using a regression analysis with the following independent variables:

$$x_1 = \text{Gender of manager} = \begin{cases} 1 & \text{if male} \\ 0 & \text{if not} \end{cases}$$

$$x_2 = \text{Race of manager} = \begin{cases} 1 & \text{if white} \\ 0 & \text{if not} \end{cases}$$

x_3 = Education level (in years)

x_4 = Tenure with firm (in years)

x_5 = Number of hours worked per week

The regression results are shown below as they were reported in the article.

Variable	$\hat{\beta}$	p-Value
x_1	12.774	<.05
x_2	.713	>.10
x_3	1.519	<.05
x_4	.320	<.05
x_5	.205	<.05
Constant	15.491	—
$R^2 = .240$	$n = 191$	

a. Write the hypothesized model that was used, and interpret each of the β parameters in the model.

b. Write the least squares equation that estimates the model in part **a**, and interpret each of the β estimates.

c. Interpret the value of R^2. Test to determine whether the model is useful for predicting annual salary. Test using $\alpha = .05$.

d. Test to determine whether the gender variable indicates that male managers are paid more than female managers, even after adjusting for and holding constant the other four factors in the model. Test using $\alpha = .05$. [*Note:* The p-values given in the table are two-tailed.]

e. Why would one want to adjust for these other factors before conducting a test for salary discrimination?

f. Discuss how the interaction between gender (x_1) and tenure with the firm (x_4) might affect the results of the analysis. [*Note:* We will discuss the use and implications of this type of interaction term more fully in Chapter 12.]

11.28 Does extensive media coverage of a military crisis influence public opinion on how to respond to the crisis? Political scientists at UCLA researched this question and reported their results in *Communication Research* (June 1993). The military crisis of interest was the 1990 Persian Gulf War, precipitated by Iraqi leader Saddam Hussein's invasion of Kuwait. The researchers used multiple regression analysis to model the level y of U.S. public support for a military (rather than a diplomatic) response to the crisis. Values of y ranged from 0 (preference for a diplomatic response) to 4 (preference for a military response). The independent variables used in the model are described below.

x_1 = Level of TV news exposure in a selected week (number of days)

x_2 = Knowledge of seven political figures (1 point for each correct answer)

x_3 = Gender (1 if male, 0 if female)

x_4 = Race (1 if nonwhite, 0 if white)

x_5 = Partisanship (0–6 scale, where 0 = strong Democrat and 6 = strong Republican)

x_6 = Defense-spending attitude (1–7 scale, where 1 = greatly decrease spending and 7 = greatly increase spending)

x_7 = Education level (1–7 scale, where 1 = less than eight grades and 7 = college)

Data from a survey of 1,763 U.S. citizens were used to fit the model

$$E(y) = \beta_0 + \beta_1 x_1 + \beta_2 x_2 + \beta_3 x_3 + \beta_4 x_4 + \beta_5 x_5 + \beta_6 x_6 + \beta_7 x_7 + \beta_8 x_2 x_3 + \beta_9 x_2 x_4$$

The regression results are shown in the accompanying table.

Variable	β Estimate	Standard Error	Two-Tailed p-Value
TV news exposure (x_1)	.02	.01	.03
Political knowledge (x_2)	.07	.03	.03
Gender (x_3)	.67	.11	<.001
Race (x_4)	−.76	.13	<.001
Partisanship (x_5)	.07	.01	<.001
Defense Spending (x_6)	.20	.02	<.001
Education (x_7)	.07	.02	<.001
Knowledge × Gender ($x_2 x_3$)	−.09	.04	.02
Knowledge × Race ($x_2 x_4$)	.10	.06	.08

Source: Iyengar, S., and Simon, A. "News coverage of the Gulf Crisis and public opinion." *Communication Research,* Vol. 20, No. 3, June 1993, p. 380 (Table 2), Sage Publications.

a. Interpret the β estimate for the variable x_1, TV news exposure.

b. Conduct a test to determine whether an increase in TV news exposure is associated with an increase in support for a military resolution of the crisis. Use $\alpha = .05$.

c. Is there sufficient evidence to indicate that the relationship between support for a military resolution (y) and gender (x_3) depends on political knowledge (x_2)? Test using $\alpha = .05$.

d. Is there sufficient evidence to indicate that the relationship between support for a military resolution (y) and race (x_4) depends on political knowledge (x_2)? Test using $\alpha = .05$.

e. The coefficient of determination for the model was $R^2 = .194$. Interpret this value.

f. Use the value of R^2, part **e**, to conduct a global test for model utility. Use $\alpha = .05$

11.6 USING THE MODEL FOR ESTIMATION AND PREDICTION

In Section 10.8 we discussed the use of the least squares line for estimating the mean value of y, $E(y)$, for some particular value of x, say $x = x_p$. We also showed how to use the same fitted model to predict, when $x = x_p$, some new value of y to be observed in the future. Recall that the least squares line yielded the same value for both the estimate of $E(y)$ and the prediction of some future value of y. That is, both are the result of substituting x_p into the prediction equation $\hat{y} = \hat{\beta}_0 + \hat{\beta}_1 x$ and calculating $\hat{y}_p$. There the equivalence ends. The confidence interval for the mean $E(y)$ is narrower than the prediction interval for y because of the additional uncertainty attributable to the random error ϵ when predicting some future value of y.

These same concepts carry over to the multiple regression model. Suppose we want to estimate the mean electrical usage for a given home size, say $x_p = 1,500$ square feet. Assuming that the quadratic model represents the true relationship between electrical usage and home size, we want to estimate

$$E(y) = \beta_0 + \beta_1 x_p + \beta_2 x_p^2 = \beta_0 + \beta_1(1,500) + \beta_2(1,500)^2$$

Substituting into the least squares prediction equation, we find the estimate of $E(y)$ to be

$$\hat{y} = \hat{\beta}_0 + \hat{\beta}_1(1,500) + \hat{\beta}_2(1,500)^2$$

$$= -1,216.144 + 2.3989(1,500) - .00045004(1,500)^2 = 1,369.7$$

Obs	X	Dep Var Y	Predict Value	Std Err Predict	Lower95% Mean	Upper95% Mean	Residual
1	1290	1182.0	1129.6	30.072	1058.5	1200.7	52.4359
2	1350	1172.0	1202.2	25.851	1141.1	1263.3	-30.2136
3	1470	1264.0	1337.8	19.832	1290.9	1384.7	-73.7916
4	1600	1493.0	1470.0	17.392	1428.9	1511.2	22.9586
5	1710	1571.0	1570.1	17.976	1527.6	1612.6	0.9359
6	1840	1711.0	1674.2	19.919	1627.1	1721.3	36.7685
7	1980	1804.0	1769.4	21.887	1717.6	1821.2	34.5998
8	2230	1840.0	1895.5	23.348	1840.3	1950.7	-55.4654
9	2400	1956.0	1949.1	23.611	1893.2	2004.9	6.9431
10	2930	1954.0	1949.2	44.734	1843.4	2055.0	4.8287
11	1500	.	1369.7	18.892	1325.0	1414.3	.

FIGURE 11.14 SAS printout for estimated mean values and corresponding confidence intervals

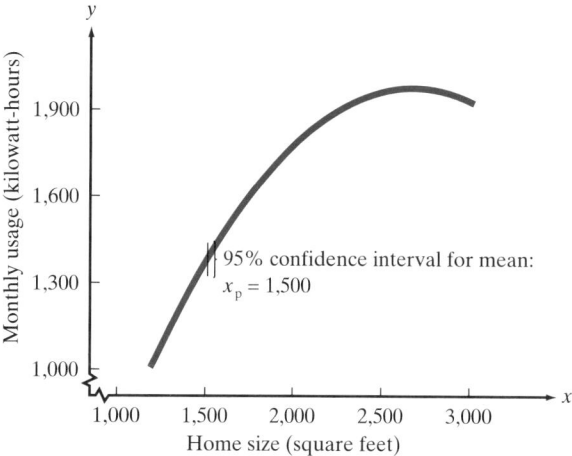

FIGURE 11.15
Confidence interval for mean electrical usage when $x_p = 1,500$

To form a confidence interval for the mean, we need to know the standard deviation of the sampling distribution for the estimator $\hat{y}$. For multiple regression models, the form of this standard deviation is rather complex. However, some regression packages allow us to obtain the confidence intervals for mean values of y for any given combination of values of the independent variables. A portion of the SAS output for the electrical usage example is shown in Figure 11.14 (page 532). The mean value and corresponding 95% confidence interval for the x-values in the sample are shown in the columns labeled **Predict Value**, **Lower95% Mean**, and **Upper95% Mean**. In the last row, corresponding to $x_p = 1,500$, we observe that $\hat{y} = 1,369.7$, which agrees with our earlier calculation. The corresponding 95% confidence interval for the true mean of y, highlighted on the printout, is 1,325.0 to 1,414.3. (This interval is shown graphically in Figure 11.15.)

If we were interested in predicting the electrical usage for a particular 1,500-square-foot home, we would use $\hat{y} = 1,369.7$ as the predicted value. However, the prediction interval for a new value of y is wider than the confidence interval for the mean value. This is reflected by the SAS printout shown in Figure 11.16, which gives the predicted values of y and corresponding 95% prediction intervals under the columns **Lower95% Predict** and **Upper95% Predict**. Note that the prediction interval for $x_p = 1,500$ (highlighted in the last row) is 1,250.3 to 1,489.0. (This interval is shown graphically in Figure 11.17.)

Obs	X	Dep Var Y	Predict Value	Std Err Predict	Lower95% Predict	Upper95% Predict	Residual
1	1290	1182.0	1129.6	30.072	998.0	1261.1	52.4359
2	1350	1172.0	1202.2	25.851	1075.8	1328.6	-30.2136
3	1470	1264.0	1337.8	19.832	1217.6	1458.0	-73.7916
4	1600	1493.0	1470.0	17.392	1352.0	1588.1	22.9586
5	1710	1571.0	1570.1	17.976	1451.5	1688.6	0.9359
6	1840	1711.0	1674.2	19.919	1554.0	1794.5	36.7685
7	1980	1804.0	1769.4	21.887	1647.2	1891.6	34.5998
8	2230	1840.0	1895.5	23.348	1771.8	2019.1	-55.4654
9	2400	1956.0	1949.1	23.611	1825.1	2073.0	6.9431
10	2930	1954.0	1949.2	44.734	1796.1	2102.3	4.8287
11	1500	.	1369.7	18.892	1250.3	1489.0	.

FIGURE 11.16   SAS printout for predicted values and corresponding prediction intervals

FIGURE 11.17
Prediction interval for
electrical usage when
$x_p = 1,500$

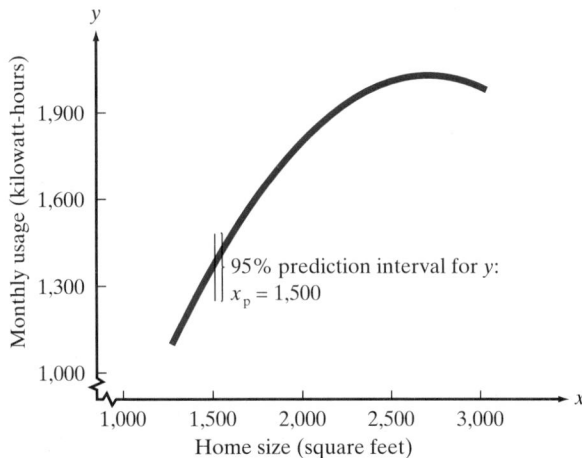

Unfortunately, not all statistical software packages have the capability to produce confidence intervals for means and prediction intervals for specific y values. This is a rather serious oversight, since the estimation of mean values and the prediction of specific values represent the culmination of our model-building efforts: using the model to make inferences about the dependent variable y.

11.7   MULTIPLE REGRESSION: AN EXAMPLE

Towers, Perrin, Forster & Crosby (TPF&C), an international management consulting firm, offers a unique service to its clients. Many firms are interested in evaluating their management salary structure, and TPF&C accomplishes this evaluation using multiple regression models. The Compensation Management Service, as TPF&C calls it, measures both the internal and external consistency of a company's pay policies to determine whether they reflect the management's intent.

The dependent variable y used to measure executive compensation is annual salary. The independent variables used to explain salary structure include the executive's age, education, rank, and bonus eligibility; number of employees under the executive's direct supervision; as well as variables that describe the company for which the executive works, such as annual sales, profit, and total assets.

The initial step in developing models for executive compensation is to obtain a sample of executives from various client firms, which TPF&C calls the Compensation Data Bank. The data for these executives are used to estimate the model coefficients (the β parameters), and these estimates are then substituted into the linear model to form a prediction equation. To predict a particular executive's compensation, TPF&C substitutes into the prediction equation the values of the independent variables that pertain to the executive (age, rank, etc.).

We will use this application of multiple regression to demonstrate all the ideas we have introduced in this chapter. Suppose the list of independent variables given in Table 11.3 is to be used to build a model for the salaries of corporate executives.

Step 1   The first step is to hypothesize a model relating executive salary to the independent variables listed in Table 11.3. TPF&C has found that executive compensation models that use the logarithm of salary as the dependent variable provide better predictive power than those using the salary as the dependent variable. This is probably because salaries tend to be incremented in *percentages* rather than dollar values. When a response variable undergoes percentage changes as the independent

---

TABLE 11.3   **List of Independent Variables for Executive Compensation Example**

Independent Variable	Description
x_1	Years of experience
x_2	Years of education
x_3	1 if male; 0 if female
x_4	Number of employees supervised
x_5	Corporate assets (millions of dollars)
x_6	x_1^2
x_7	$x_3 x_4$

---

variables are varied, the logarithm of the response variable will be more suitable as a dependent variable. The model we propose is

$$y = \beta_0 + \beta_1 x_1 + \beta_2 x_2 + \beta_3 x_3 + \beta_4 x_4 + \beta_5 x_5 + \beta_6 x_6 + \beta_7 x_7 + \epsilon$$

where $y = \log(\text{executive salary})$, $x_6 = x_1^2$ (quadratic term in years of experience), and $x_7 = x_3 x_4$ (cross product or interaction term between sex and number of employees supervised). The variable x_3 is a **dummy variable**; it is used to describe an independent variable that is not measured on a numerical scale but instead is qualitative (categorical) in nature. Sex is such a variable, since its values, male and female, are categories rather than numbers. Thus, we assign the value $x_3 = 1$ if the executive is male and $x_3 = 0$ if the executive is female. For more detail on the use and interpretation of dummy variables, see Chapter 12. The interaction term $x_3 x_4$ accounts for the fact that the relationship between corporate salary and the number of employees supervised, x_4, is dependent on sex, x_3. That is, as the number of supervised employees increases, a woman's salary (with all other factors being equal) might rise more (or less) rapidly than a man's. This concept (interaction), too, is explained in more detail in Chapter 12.

Step 2 Now we estimate the model coefficients $\beta_0, \beta_1, ..., \beta_7$. Suppose a sample of 100 executives is selected, and the variables y and $x_1, x_2, ..., x_7$ are recorded (or, in the case of x_6 and x_7, calculated). The sample is then used as input for the SPSS regression routine; the output is shown in Figure 11.18. The estimated betas are highlighted under the **B** column in the **Variables in the Equation** portion of the printout. The least squares model is

$$\hat{y} = 9.88 + .045 x_1 + .033 x_2 + .119 x_3 + .00033 x_4 +$$
$$.0020 x_5 - .00071 x_6 + .00031 x_7$$

Step 3 The next step is to specify the probability distribution of ϵ, the random error component. We assume that ϵ is normally distributed with a mean of 0 and a constant variance σ^2. Furthermore, we assume that the errors are independent. The estimate of the variance σ^2, shown (and highlighted) on the SPSS printout as **Mean Square (Residual)**, is

$$s^2 = \frac{\text{SSE}}{n - (k + 1)} = \frac{27.06425}{100 - (7 + 1)} = .00212$$

The estimate of the standard deviation σ, shown (and also highlighted) on the printout as **Standard Error**, is $s = \sqrt{s^2} = .0461$. Our interpretation is that most of the observed y values (logarithms of salaries) lie within $2s = 2(.0461) = .0922$ of the least squares predicted values.

```
        * * * *   M U L T I P L E   R E G R E S S I O N   * * * *

Equation Number 1     Dependent Variable..    Y

Multiple R              .9964
R Square                .9928
Adjusted R Square       .9923
Standard Error          .0461

Analysis of Variance
                    DF        Sum of Squares        Mean Square
Regression           7           27.06425            3.86632
Residual            92            0.19551            0.00212

F =     1823.73         Signif F =   .0000
----------------- Variables in the Equation --------------------

Variable             B          SE B          T   Sig T
X1             0.04460       0.00166       26.83   .0000
X2             0.03326       0.00270       12.31   .0000
X3             0.11892       0.01724        6.89   .0001
X4             0.00033       0.00001       19.97   .0000
X5             0.00201       0.00002       73.25   .0000
X1X1          -0.00071       0.00004      -15.11   .0000
X3X4           0.00031       0.00002       16.16   .0000
(Constant)     9.87878       0.04612      214.15   .0000

   Case #        *PRED            *ICIN
                        Lower Bnd  Upper Bnd
      101        11.298       11.203       11.392
```

FIGURE 11.18 SPSS printout for executive compensation example

Step 4 We now want to see how well the model predicts salaries. First, note that the coefficient of determination (highlighted on the printout) is $R^2 = .9928$. This implies that over 99% of the variation in y (the logarithm of salaries) for these 100 sampled executives is accounted for by the model. The significance of this can be tested:

$$H_0: \beta_1 = \beta_2 = \cdots = \beta_7 = 0$$

H_a: At least one of the model coefficients is nonzero

Test statistic: $F = \dfrac{\text{Mean Square (Model)}}{\text{MSE}} = 1{,}823.73$
(highlighted on Figure 11.18)

Rejection region: For $\alpha = .05, F > F_{.05}$

Here the tabulated value of F for $\alpha = .05$ based on $k = 7$ and $n - (k + 1) = 92$ df is $F_{.05} \approx 2.1$ (from Table IX of Appendix B). Since $F = 1{,}823.73$ exceeds the tabulated value of F and, in fact, has an observed significance level of .0000 (highlighted on the printout), we conclude that the model does contribute information for predicting executive salaries. It appears that at least one of the β parameters in the model differs from 0.

If the firm is discriminating (knowingly or unknowingly) against newly hired female executives, then the mean salary for newly hired males

x_1 = 12 years of experience
x_2 = 16 years of education
x_3 = 0 (female)
x_4 = 400 employees supervised
x_5 = \$160.1 million
(the firm's asset value)
$x_6 = x_1^2 = 144$
$x_7 = x_3 x_4 = 0$

will exceed the mean for newly hired females with the same qualifications. Therefore, we may be particularly interested in whether the data provide evidence that the mean salary of executives depends on sex when all other variables (experience, education, etc.) are held constant. In Chapter 12 we will learn that when the dummy variable x_3 is in the model and has a positive β coefficient, the mean salary of males exceeds the mean for females. Thus, one way to test the sex discrimination hypothesis is to test:*

$$H_0: \beta_3 = 0$$

$$H_a: \beta_3 > 0$$

Test statistic: $t = \dfrac{\hat{\beta}_3}{s_{\hat{\beta}_3}} = 6.89$ (highlighted on Figure 11.18)

For $\alpha = .05$, $n = 100$, $k = 7$, and $n - (k + 1) = 92$, we will reject H_0 if $t > t_{.05}$, where (because the degrees of freedom, 92, of t is so large) $t_{.05} \approx z_{.05} = 1.645$. Thus, we reject H_0 if $t > 1.645$.

Since the test statistic exceeds 1.645 (and has an observed significance level of $.0001/2 = .00005$), we find evidence that the mean salaries of newly hired male executives do exceed the corresponding mean for females.

Step 5 The culmination of the modeling effort is to use it for estimation and/or prediction. Suppose a firm is trying to determine fair compensation for an executive with the characteristics shown in Table 11.4. The least squares model can be used to obtain a predicted value for the logarithm of salary.

That is,

$$\hat{y} = \hat{\beta}_0 + \hat{\beta}_1(12) + \hat{\beta}_2(16) + \hat{\beta}_3(0) + \hat{\beta}_4(400) + \hat{\beta}_5(160.1) + \hat{\beta}_6(144) + \hat{\beta}_7(0)$$

The predicted value for this observation, $\hat{y} = 11.298$, is given at the bottom of Figure 11.18 under the ***PRED** column. The corresponding 95% prediction interval, highlighted on the printout, is 11.203 to 11.392. To predict the salary of an executive with these characteristics we take the antilog of these values. That is, the predicted salary is $e^{11.298} = \$80,700$ (rounded to the nearest hundred) and the 95% prediction interval is from $e^{11.203}$ to $e^{11.392}$ (from \$73,400 to \$88,600). Thus, an executive with the characteristics in Table 11.4 should be paid between \$73,400 and \$88,600 to be consistent with the sample data.

11.8 RESIDUAL ANALYSIS: CHECKING THE REGRESSION ASSUMPTIONS

When we apply regression analysis to a set of data, we never know for certain whether the assumptions of Section 11.3 are satisfied. How far can we deviate from the assumptions and still expect regression analysis to yield results that will have the reliability stated in this chapter? How can we detect departures (if they exist) from the assumptions of Section 11.3 and what can we do about them? We

---

*This test assumes that x_4, the n‌   ‌er of employees supervised, is held fixed at 0. A better way to test the discrimination hypothesis i‌   ‌st all β's associated with the dummy variable x_3 simultaneously, that is, test $H_0: \beta_3 = \beta_7 = 0$. Th‌   ‌on a partial set of β's is discussed in Chapter 12.

STATISTICS IN ACTION

11.1 PREDICTING THE PRICE OF VINTAGE RED BORDEAUX WINE

The vineyards in the Bordeaux region of France are known for producing excellent red wines. Wine experts agree that weather during the grape growing season is critical to producing good wines. The best vineyards in Europe are usually located near a large body of water (to delay spring frosts, prolong fall ripening, and reduce temperature fluctuations), on a slope with a southern exposure to the sun (to enhance spring ripening), and in a soil with good drainage (to overcome the dilution of the grapes that accompanies fall rains). The seaport city of Bordeaux, located on the Garonne River, meets all these desired conditions. Consequently, red Bordeaux wines are some of the most expensive wines in the world.

Usually, the more a wine ages, the more expensive it is. This is because young wines—even young wines produced from the best Bordeaux vineyards—are astringent and many wine drinkers find astringent wines unpalatable. As these wines age, they lose their astringency. Since older wines taste better than younger wines, they are deemed more valuable. Thus, both wine sellers and wine drinkers have an incentive to store young wines until they mature.

The combination of factors—the uncertainty of the weather during the growing season, the phenomenon that wine tastes better with age, and the fact that some vineyards produce better wines than others—encourages speculation concerning the value of a case of wine produced by a certain vineyard during a certain year (or vintage). As a result, many wine experts attempt to predict the auction price of a case of wine (on the London market). Trade magazines such as *Wine* and the *Wine Spectator* provide these opinions regularly, based on subjective assessments of the weather and general knowledge about the reputation of the vineyard.

Recently, a newsletter titled *Liquid Assets: The International Guide to Fine Wines* introduced a quantitative approach to predicting wine prices. The method, which employs statistics and multiple regression analysis to analyze wine prices, has sent the wine trade press into a frenzy. The front page headline in the *New York Times* (Mar. 4, 1995) read, "Wine Equation Puts Some Noses Out of Joint." In the article, the most influential wine critic in America called the approach "a Neanderthal way of looking at wine." According to Britain's *Wine* magazine, "the formula's self-evident silliness invited disrespect." Why has the use of multiple regression to predict wine prices engendered such controversy? One reason is simply that the theory behind the method is misunderstood. For example, the *Wine Spectator* condemned the multiple regression model because "the predictions come exactly true only 3 times in the 27 vintages since 1961 that were calculated, even though the formula was specifically designed to fit price data that already existed. The predicted prices are both under and over the actual prices." Obviously, the *Wine Spectator* does not understand that least squares regression proposes a probabilistic (not a deterministic) model that minimizes SSE and yields an average prediction error of 0.

The publishers of *Liquid Assets* discussed the multiple regression approach to predicting the London auction price of red Bordeaux wine in *Chance* (Fall 1995). The natural logarithm of the price y (in dollars) of a case containing a dozen bottles of red wine* was

*The price of a case is an index based on the wines of several Bordeaux vineyards. The bottles in the case were deliberately selected to represent the most expensive wines as well as a selection of less expensive wines.

provide some partial answers to these questions in this section and direct you to further discussion in the next chapter.

Remember from Section 11.3 that

$$y = E(y) + \epsilon$$

where the expected value $E(y)$ of y for a given set of values of $x_1, x_2, \ldots, x_k$ is

$$E(y) = \beta_0 + \beta_1 x_1 + \beta_2 x_2 + \cdots + \beta_k x_k$$

and ϵ is a random error. The first assumption we made was that the mean value of the random error for *any* given set of values $x_1, x_2, \ldots, x_k$ is $E(\epsilon) = 0$. One conmodeled as a function of weather during growing season and age of vintage using data collected for the vintages of 1952–1980.* The natural log of price, denoted $\ln(y)$, was selected in order to measure increases (or decreases) in price as a percentage, as stated in Section 11.7. Three models were proposed:

Model 1:

$$\ln(y) = \beta_0 + \beta_1 x_1 + \epsilon,$$

where

$x_1 = $ Age of the vintage (year)

Model 2:

$$\ln(y) = \beta_0 + \beta_1 x_1 + \beta_2 x_2 + \beta_3 x_3 + \beta_4 x_4 + \epsilon,$$

where

$x_1 = $ Age of the vintage (year)

$x_2 = $ Average temperature (°C) over growing season (Apr.–Sept.)

$x_3 = $ Rainfall (cm) in September and August

$x_4 = $ Rainfall (cm) in the months preceding the vintage (Oct.–Mar.)

Model 3:

$$\ln(y) = \beta_0 + \beta_1 x_1 + \beta_2 x_2 + \beta_3 x_3 + \beta_4 x_4 + \beta_5 x_5 + \epsilon,$$

where

$x_1 = $ Age of the vintage (year)

$x_2 = $ Average temperature (°C) over growing season (Apr.–Sept.)

*The 1954 and 1956 vintages were excluded because they are now rarely sold.

$x_3 = $ Rainfall (cm) in September and August

$x_4 = $ Rainfall (cm) in the months preceding the vintage (Oct.–Mar.)

$x_5 = $ Average temperature (°C) in September.

The results of the regressions are summarized in Table 11.5 on page 540.

Focus

a. Which of the three models would you use to predict red Bordeaux wine prices? Explain.

b. Interpret R^2 and s for the model you selected, part **a**.

c. Conduct a t-test for each of the β parameters in the model you selected, part **a**. Interpret the results.

d. When $\ln(y)$ is used as a dependent variable, the antilogarithm of a β coefficient minus 1, that is, $e^{\beta_i} - 1$, represents the percentage change in y for every 1-unit increase in the associated x value.* Use this information to interpret the β estimates of the model you selected in part **a**.

*The result is derived by expressing the percentage change in price y as $(y_1 - y_0)/y_0$, where $y_1 = $ the value of y when, say, $x = 1$, and $y_0 = $ the value of y when $x = 0$. Now let $y^* = \ln(y)$ and assume the model is $y^* = \beta_0 + \beta_1 x$. Then

$$y = e^{y^*} = e^{\beta_0} e^{\beta_1 x} = \begin{cases} e^{\beta_0} & \text{when } x = 0 \\ e^{\beta_0} e^{\beta_1} & \text{when } x = 1 \end{cases}$$

Substituting, we have

$$\frac{y_1 - y_0}{y_0} = \frac{e^{\beta_0} e^{\beta_1} - e^{\beta_0}}{e^{\beta_0}} = e^{\beta_1} - 1$$

sequence of this assumption is that the mean $E(y)$ for a specific set of values of $x_1, x_2, \ldots, x_k$ is

$$E(y) = \beta_0 + \beta_1 x_1 + \beta_2 x_2 + \cdots + \beta_k x_k$$

That is,

		Mean value of y for specific values of $x_1, x_2, \ldots, x_k$		**Random error**
y	$=$	$E(y)$	$+$	ϵ

TABLE 11.5 **Regression of In(Price) of Red Bourdeaux Wine (Statistics in Action 11.1)**

Independent Variables in Model	BETA ESTIMATES (STANDARD ERRORS)		
	Model 1	**Model 2**	**Model 3**
Vintage (x_1)	.0354 (.0137)	.0238 (.00717)	.0240 (.00747)
Growing season temperature (x_2)	—	.616 (.0952)	.608 (.116)
Sept./Aug. rain (x_3)	—	−.00386 (.00081)	−.00380 (.00095)
Pre-rain (x_4)	—	.0001173 (.000482)	.00115 (.000505)
Sept. temperature (x_5)	—	—	.00765 (.0565)
R^2	.212	.828	.828
s	.575	.287	.293

Source: Ashenfelter, O., Ashmore, D., and LaLonde, R. "Bourdeaux wine vintage quality and weather." *Chance,* Vol. 8, No. 4, Fall 1995, p. 116 (Table 2).

The second consequence of the assumption is that the least squares estimators of the model parameters, $\beta_0, \beta_1, \beta_2, ..., \beta_k$, will be unbiased regardless of the remaining assumptions that we attribute to the random errors and their probability distributions.

The properties of the sampling distributions of the parameter estimators $\hat{\beta}_0, \hat{\beta}_1, ..., \hat{\beta}_k$ will depend on the remaining assumptions that we specify concerning the probability distributions of the random errors. Recall that we assumed that for any given set of values of $x_1, x_2, ..., x_k$, ϵ has a normal probability distribution with mean equal to 0 and variance equal to σ^2. Also, we assumed that the random errors are probabilistically independent.

It is unlikely that these assumptions are ever satisfied exactly in a practical application of regression analysis. Fortunately, experience has shown that least squares regression analysis produces reliable statistical tests, confidence intervals, and prediction intervals as long as the departures from the assumptions are not too great. In this section we present some methods for determining whether the data indicate significant departures from the assumptions.

Because the assumptions all concern the random error component, ϵ, of the model, the first step is to estimate the random error. Since the actual random error associated with a particular value of y is the difference between the actual y value and its unknown mean, we estimate the error by the difference between the actual y value and the *estimated* mean. This estimated error is called the **regression residual**, or simply the **residual**, and is denoted by $\hat{\epsilon}$. The actual error ϵ and residual $\hat{\epsilon}$ are shown in Figure 11.19.

Actual random error $= \epsilon$

$$= (\text{Actual } y \text{ value}) - (\text{Mean of } y)$$

$$= y - E(y) = y - (\beta_0 + \beta_1 x_1 + \beta_2 x_2 + \cdots + \beta_k x_k)$$

Estimated random error (residual) $= \hat{\epsilon}$

$$= (\text{Actual } y \text{ value}) - (\text{Estimated mean of } y)$$

$$= y - \hat{y} = y - (\hat{\beta}_0 + \hat{\beta}_1 x_1 + \hat{\beta}_2 x_2 + \cdots + \hat{\beta}_k x_k)$$

Since the true mean of y (that is, the true regression model) is not known, the actual random error cannot be calculated. However, because the residual is based

FIGURE 11.19
Actual random error
and regression
residual

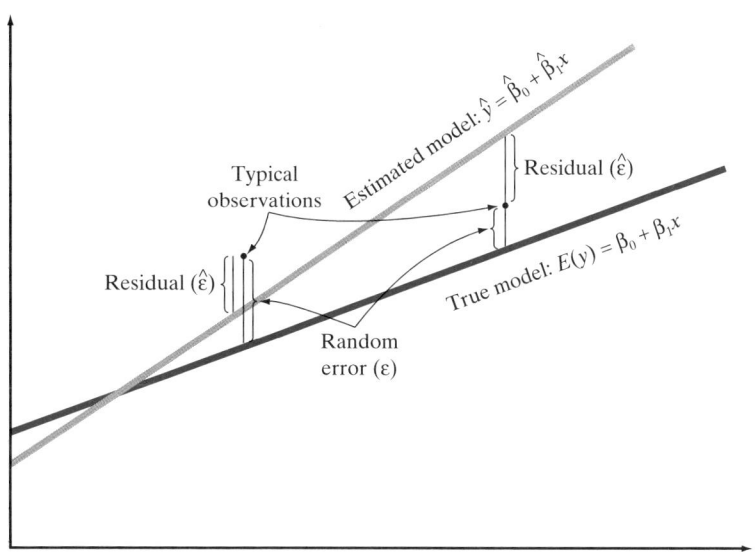

on the estimated mean (the least squares regression model), it can be calculated and used to estimate the random error and to check the regression assumptions. Such checks are generally referred to as **residual analyses**. Some useful properties of residuals are given in the next box.

Properties of Regression Residuals

1. A residual is equal to the difference between the observed y value and its estimated (regression) mean:

$$\text{Residual} = y - \hat{y}$$

2. The mean of the residuals is equal to 0. This property follows from the fact that the sum of the differences between the observed y values and their least squares predicted $(\hat{y})$ values is equal to 0.

$$\sum(\text{Residuals}) = \sum(y - \hat{y}) = 0$$

3. The standard deviation of the residuals is equal to the standard deviation of the fitted regression model, s. This property follows from the fact that the sum of the squared residuals is equal to SSE, which when divided by the error degrees of freedom is equal to the variance of the fitted regression model, s^2. The square root of the variance is both the standard deviation of the residuals and the standard deviation of the regression model.

$$\sum(\text{Residuals})^2 = \sum(y - \hat{y})^2 = \text{SSE}$$

$$s = \sqrt{\frac{\sum(\text{Residuals})^2}{n - (k + 1)}} = \sqrt{\frac{\text{SSE}}{n - (k + 1)}}$$

The following examples show how the analysis of regression residuals can be used to verify the assumptions associated with the model and to improve the model when the assumptions do not appear to be satisfied. Although the residuals can be calculated and plotted by hand, we rely on the computer for these tasks in

TABLE 11.6 Home Size–Electrical Usage Data

Size of Home x (sq. ft.)	Monthly Usage y (kilowatt-hours)
1,290	1,182
1,350	1,172
1,470	1,264
1,600	1,493
1,710	1,571
1,840	1,711
1,980	1,804
2,230	1,840
2,400	1,956
2,930	1,954

the examples and exercises. Most statistical computer packages now include residual analyses as a standard component of their regression modeling programs.

EXAMPLE 11.4

The data for the home size–electrical usage example used throughout this chapter are repeated in Table 11.6. EXCEL printouts for a straight-line model and a quadratic model fit to the data are shown in Figures 11.20a and 11.20b, respectively. The residuals from these models are highlighted in the printouts. The residuals are then plotted on the vertical axis against the variable x, size of home, on the horizontal axis in Figures 11.21a and 11.21b (see page 545), respectively.

a. Verify that each residual is equal to the difference between the observed y value and the estimated mean value, $\hat{y}$.

b. Analyze the residual plots.

SOLUTION

a. For the straight-line model the residual is calculated for the first y value as follows:

$$\text{Residual} = (\text{Observed } y \text{ value}) - (\text{Estimated mean})$$
$$= y - \hat{y} = 1,182 - 1,275.92 = -93.92$$

where the estimated mean is the first number in the column labeled **Predicted Usage(y)** (highlighted) on the EXCEL printout in Figure 11.20a. Similarly, the residual for the first y value using the quadratic model is

$$\text{Residual} = 1,182 - 1,129.56 = 52.44$$

Both residuals agree (after rounding) with the first values given in the column labeled **Residuals** in Figures 11.20a and 11.20b, respectively. Although the residuals both correspond to the same observed y value, 1,182, they differ because the estimated mean value changes depending on whether the straight-line model or quadratic model is used. Similar calculations produce the remaining residuals.

b. The plot of the residuals for the straight-line model (Figure 11.21a) reveals a nonrandom pattern. The residuals exhibit a curved shape, with the residuals for the small values of x below the horizontal 0 (mean of the residuals) line, the residuals corresponding to the middle values of x above the 0 line, and the residual for the largest value of x again below the 0 line. The indication is that the mean value of the random error ϵ *within* each of these ranges of x (small, medium, large) may not be equal to 0. Such a pattern usually indicates that curvature needs to be added to the model.

SUMMARY OUTPUT

Regression Statistics

Multiple R	0.911978829
R Square	0.831705384
Adjusted R Square	0.810668557
Standard Error	133.4376805
Observations	10

ANOVA

	df	SS	MS	F	Significance F
Regression	1	703957.1834	703957.1834	39.53568581	0.000235885
Residual	8	142444.9166	17805.61457		
Total	9	846402.1			

	Coefficients	Standard Error	t Stat	P-value	Lower 95%	Upper 95%
Intercept	578.9277515	166.9680571	3.467296448	0.008476357	193.8984723	963.9570307
Size(x)	0.54304387	0.085929811	6.287740915	0.000235885	0.3214976	0.738459015

RESIDUAL OUTPUT

Observation	Predicted Usage(y)	Residuals
1	1275.920411	-93.92041138
2	1308.338675	-136.3386746
3	1373.175201	-109.1752011
4	1443.414772	49.5852285
5	1502.848254	68.15174587
6	1573.087825	137.9121755
7	1648.730439	155.2695613
8	1783.806536	56.19346438
9	1875.658281	80.3417185
10	2162.019607	-208.0196069

FIGURE 11.20A   EXCEL printout for electrical usage example: Straight-line model

SUMMARY OUTPUT

Regression Statistics	
Multiple R	0.990901117
R Square	0.981885024
Adjusted R Square	0.976709317
Standard Error	46.80133336
Observations	10

ANOVA

	df	SS	MS	F	Significance F
Regression	2	831069.5464	415534.7732	189.7103041	8.00078E-07
Residual	7	15332.55363	2190.364804		
Total	9	846402.1			

	Coefficients	Standard Error	t Stat	P-value	Lower 95%	Upper 95%
Intercept	-1216.143887	242.8063685	-5.008698472	0.00155025	-1790.289304	-641.9984703
size(x)	2.39893017	0.245835602	9.758269998	2.51335E-05	1.817621767	2.980238587
SizeSq(x2)	-0.00045004	5.90766E-05	-7.617907059	0.000124415	-0.000589734	-0.000310346

RESIDUAL OUTPUT

Observation	Predicted Usage(y)	Residuals
1	1129.564114	52.43588588
2	1202.213554	-30.21355416
3	1337.791566	-73.79156553
4	1470.041437	22.95856259
5	1570.064113	0.935886603
6	1674.231476	36.76852434
7	1769.400192	34.59980832
8	1895.465406	-55.46540615
9	1949.05688	6.943119595
10	1949.171261	4.828738521

FIGURE 11.20B EXCEL printout for electrical usage example: Quadratic model

FIGURE 11.21A
EXCEL residual
plot for electrical
usage example:
Straight-line model

FIGURE 11.21B
EXCEL residual
plot for electrical
usage example:
Quadratic model

When the second-order term is added to the model, the nonrandom pattern disappears. In Figure 11.21b, the residuals appear to be randomly distributed around the 0 line, as expected. Note, too, that the value of $2s$ for the quadratic model is $2(46.8) = 93.6$, compared to $2s = 2(133.4) = 266.8$ for the straight-line model. The implication is that the quadratic model provides a considerably better model for predicting electrical usage, verifying our conclusions from previous analyses in this chapter.

Residual analyses are also useful for detecting one or more observations that deviate significantly from the regression model. We expect approximately 95% of the residuals to fall within 2 standard deviations of the 0 line, and all or almost all of them to lie within 3 standard deviations of their mean of 0. Residuals that are

TABLE 11.7 **Auction Price Data**

Age x_1	Number of Bidders x_2	Auction Price y	Age x_1	Number of Bidders x_2	Auction Price y
127	13	$1,235	170	14	$1,131
115	12	1,080	182	8	1,550
127	7	845	162	11	1,884
150	9	1,522	184	10	2,041
156	6	1,047	143	6	845
182	11	1,979	159	9	1,483
156	12	1,822	108	14	1,055
132	10	1,253	175	8	1,545
137	9	1,297	108	6	729
113	9	946	179	9	1,792
137	15	1,713	111	15	1,175
117	11	1,024	187	8	1,593
137	8	1,147	111	7	785
153	6	1,092	115	7	744
117	13	1,152	194	5	1,356
126	10	1,336	168	7	1,262

extremely far from the 0 line, and disconnected from the bulk of the other residuals, are called **outliers**, and should receive special attention from the regression analyst.

EXAMPLE 11.5

The data for the grandfather clock example used throughout this chapter are repeated in Table 11.7, with one important difference: The auction price of the clock at the top of the second column has been changed from $2,131 to $1,131 (shaded in Table 11.7). The interaction model

$$E(y) = \beta_0 + \beta_1 x_1 + \beta_2 x_2 + \beta_3 x_1 x_2$$

is again fit to these (modified) data, with the MINITAB printout shown in Figure 11.22. The residuals are shown highlighted in the printout and then plotted against the number of bidders, x_2, in Figure 11.23. Analyze the residual plot.

SOLUTION

The residual plot dramatically reveals the one altered measurement. Note that one of the two residuals at $x_2 = 14$ bidders falls more than 3 standard deviations below 0. Note that no other residual falls more than 2 standard deviations from 0.

What do we do with outliers once we identify them? First, we try to determine the cause. Were the data entered into the computer incorrectly? Was the observation recorded incorrectly when the data were collected? If so, we correct the observation and rerun the program. Another possibility is that the observation is not representative of the conditions we are trying to model. For example, in this case the low price may be attributable to extreme damage to the clock, or to a clock of inferior quality compared to the others. In these cases we probably would exclude the observation from the analysis. In many cases you may not be able to determine the cause of the outlier. Even so, you may want to rerun the regression analysis excluding the outlier in order to assess the effect of that observation on the results of the analysis.

Figure 11.24 on page 548 shows the printout when the outlier observation is excluded from the grandfather clock analysis, and Figure 11.25 on page 549 shows the new plot of the residuals against the number of bidders. Now only one of the residuals lies beyond 2 standard deviations from 0, and none of them lies beyond 3 standard deviations. Also, the model statistics indicate a much better model without

```
The regression equation is
PRICE = - 513 + 8.17 AGE = 19.9 BIDDERS + 0.320 AGE-BID

Predictor        Coef       Stdev      t-ratio        p
Constant        -512.8       665.9       -0.77      0.448
AGE             8.165        4.585        1.78       0.086
BIDDERS         19.89        67.44        0.29       0.770
AGE-BID         0.3196       0.4790       0.67       0.510

s = 200.6     R-sq = 72.9%    R-sq(adj) = 70.0%

Analysis of Variance

SOURCE          DF          SS           MS          F         p
Regression       3       3033587      1011196       25.13     0.000
Error           28       1126703        40239
Total           31       4160289

Obs.     AGE      PRICE        Fit    Stdev.Fit    Residual    St.Resid
  1      127     1235.0     1310.4       59.3        -75.4      -0.39
  2      115     1080.0     1105.9       62.1        -25.9      -0.14
  3      127      845.0      947.5       61.1       -102.5      -0.54
  4      150     1522.0     1322.5       37.1        199.5       1.01
  5      156     1047.0     1179.5       60.3       -132.5      -0.69
  6      182     1979.0     1831.9       82.9        147.1       0.81
  7      156     1822.0     1598.0       61.9        224.0       1.17
  8      132     1253.0     1185.8       39.7         67.2       0.34
  9      137     1297.0     1178.9       39.0        118.1       0.60
 10      113      946.0      913.9       58.6         32.1       0.17
 11      137     1713.0     1561.0       78.4        152.0       0.82
 12      117     1024.0     1072.6       53.1        -48.6      -0.25
 13      137     1147.0     1115.2       44.3         31.8       0.16
 14      153     1092.0     1149.2       59.0        -57.2      -0.30
 15      117     1152.0     1187.2       69.7        -35.2      -0.19
 16      126     1336.0     1117.6       43.4        218.4       1.12
 17      170     1131.0     1914.4      116.7       -783.4      -4.80R
 18      182     1550.0     1597.7       62.8        -47.7      -0.25
 19      162     1884.0     1598.3       57.0        285.7       1.49
 20      184     2041.0     1776.6       70.7        264.4       1.41
 21      143      845.0     1048.4       58.9       -203.4      -1.06
 22      159     1483.0     1421.8       40.6         61.2       0.31
 23      108     1055.0     1130.7       97.9        -75.7      -0.43
 24      175     1545.0     1522.7       55.4         22.3       0.12
 25      108      729.0      695.5       99.6         33.5       0.19
 26      179     1792.0     1642.7       57.6        149.3       0.78
 27      111     1175.0     1224.0      107.2        -49.0      -0.29
 28      187     1593.0     1651.3       68.6        -58.3      -0.31
 29      111      785.0      781.1       80.9          3.9       0.02
 30      115      744.0      822.7       75.5        -78.7      -0.42
 31      194     1356.0     1480.7      133.6       -124.7      -0.83 X
 32      168     1262.0     1374.0       57.7       -112.0      -0.58

R denotes an obs. with a large st. resid.
X denotes an obs. whose X value gives it large influence.
```

FIGURE 11.22 MINITAB printout for grandfather clock example with altered data

the outlier. Most notably, the standard deviation (s) has decreased from 200.6 to 85.83, indicating a model that will provide more precise estimates and predictions (narrower confidence and prediction intervals) for clocks that are similar to those

FIGURE 11.23
MINITAB residual plot against number of bidders

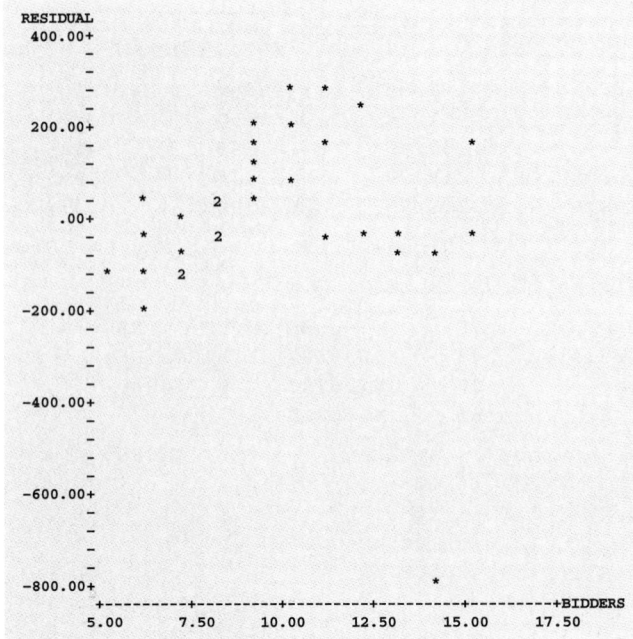

FIGURE 11.24
MINITAB printout for Example 11.5: Outlier deleted

```
The regression equation is
PRICE = 474 - 0.46 AGE - 114 BIDDERS + 1.48 AGE-BID

Predictor        Coef       Stdev    t-ratio        p
Constant        474.0       298.2       1.59    0.124
AGE            -0.465       2.107      -0.22    0.827
BIDDERS       -114.12       31.23      -3.65    0.001
AGE-BID        1.4781      0.2295       6.44    0.000

s = 85.83     R-sq = 95.2%     R-sq(adj) = 94.7%

Analysis of Variance

SOURCE       DF          SS          MS        F        p
Regression    3     3933417     1311139   177.99    0.000
Error        27      198897        7367
Total        30     4132314
```

in the reduced sample. But remember that if the outlier is removed from the analysis when in fact it belongs to the same population as the rest of the sample, the resulting model may provide misleading estimates and predictions.

Outlier analysis is another example of testing the assumption that the expected (mean) value of the random error component is 0, since this assumption is in doubt for the error terms corresponding to the outliers. The last example in this section checks the assumption of the normality of the random error component.

EXAMPLE 11.6

Refer to Example 11.5. Use a stem-and-leaf display (Section 2.2) to plot the frequency distribution of the residuals in the grandfather clock example, both before and after the outlier residual is removed. Analyze the plots and determine whether the assumption of normality of the error distribution is reasonable.

FIGURE 11.25
MINITAB residual
plot for Example 11.5:
Outlier deleted

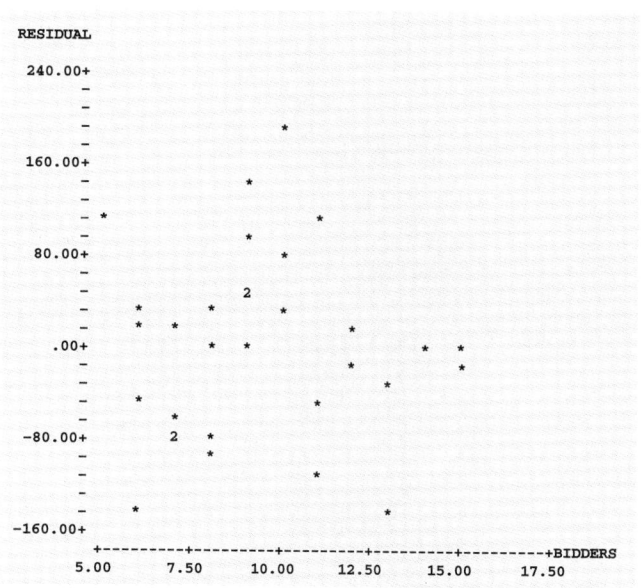

FIGURE 11.26A
MINITAB stem-and-
leaf displays for grand-
father clock example:
Outlier included

```
STEM-AND-LEAF DISPLAY OF RESIDUAL
LEAF DIGIT UNIT =  10.0000
1 2 REPRESENTS 120.

        STEM   LEAF

    1    -7    8
    1    -6
    1    -5
    1    -4
    1    -3
    1    -2
    6    -1    93210
   16    -0    7775544432
   16     0    0233366
    9     1    14459
    4     2    1268
```

SOLUTION

The stem-and-leaf displays for the two sets of residuals are constructed using MINITAB and are shown in Figure 11.26.* Note that the outlier appears to skew the frequency distribution in Figure 11.26a, whereas the stem-and-leaf display in Figure 11.26b appears to be more mound-shaped. Although the displays do not provide formal statistical tests of normality, they do provide a descriptive display. Relative frequency histograms can also be used to check the normality assumption. In this example the normality assumption appears to be more plausible after the outlier is removed. Consult the references for methods to conduct statistical tests of normality using the residuals. ■

---

*Recall that the left column of the MINITAB printout shows the number of measurements at least as extreme as the stem. In Figure 11.26a, for example, the 6 corresponding to the STEM = −1 means that six measurements are less than or equal to −100. If one of the numbers in the leftmost column is enclosed in parentheses, the number in parentheses is the number of measurements in that row, and the median is contained in that row.

FIGURE 11.26B
MINITAB stem-and-leaf displays for grandfather clock example: Outlier excluded

```
STEM-AND-LEAF DISPLAY OF RESIDUAL
LEAF DIGIT UNIT =   10.0000
1 2 REPRESENTS 120.

    3    -1*  331
    9    -0.  987765
   (7)   -0*  4321000
   15    +0*  011223344
    6    +0.  79
    4     1*  004
    1     1.  9
```

Residual analysis is a useful tool for the regression analyst, not only to check the assumptions, but also to provide information about how the model can be improved. A summary of the residual analyses presented in this section to check the assumption that the random error ϵ is normally distributed with mean 0 is presented in the next box.

Steps in a Residual Analysis

1. Calculate and plot the residuals against each of the independent variables, preferably with the assistance of a statistical software program.

2. Analyze each plot, looking for curvature—either a mound or bowl shape. Both shapes are distinguished by groups of residuals at the low and high values of the x variable on one side of the 0 line, with the residuals for the medium x values on the opposite side of the 0 line. This shape signals the need for a curvature term in the model. Try a second-order term in the variable against which the residuals are plotted.

3. Examine the residual plots for outliers. Draw lines on the residual plots at 2- and 3-standard-deviation distances below and above the 0 line. Examine residuals outside the 3-standard-deviation lines as potential outliers, and check to see that approximately 5% of the residuals exceed the 2-standard-deviation lines. Determine whether each outlier can be explained as an error in data collection or transcription, or corresponds to a member of a population different from that of the remainder of the sample, or simply represents an unusual observation. If the observation is determined to be an error, fix it or remove it. Even if you can't determine the cause, you may want to rerun the regression analysis without the observation to determine its effect on the analysis.

4. Plot a frequency distribution of the residuals, using a stem-and-leaf display or a histogram. Check to see if obvious departures from normality exist. Extreme skewness of the frequency distribution may indicate the need for a transformation of the dependent variable. This topic is beyond the scope of this book, but you can find it in the references.

11.9 SOME PITFALLS: ESTIMABILITY, MULTICOLLINEARITY, AND EXTRAPOLATION

You should be aware of several potential problems when constructing a prediction model for some response y. A few of the most important are discussed in this section.

PROBLEM I PARAMETER ESTIMABILITY

Suppose you want to fit a model relating annual crop yield y to the total expenditure for fertilizer, x. We propose the first-order model

$$E(y) = \beta_0 + \beta_1 x$$

FIGURE 11.27
Yield and fertilizer
expenditure data:
Three years

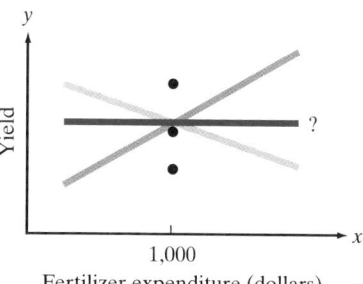

FIGURE 11.28
Only two x values
observed—quadratic
model is not estimable

Now suppose we have three years of data and \$1,000 is spent on fertilizer each year. The data are shown in Figure 11.27. You can see the problem: The parameters of the model cannot be estimated when all the data are concentrated at a single x value. Recall that it takes two points (x values) to fit a straight line. Thus, the parameters are not estimable when only one x is observed.

A similar problem would occur if we attempted to fit the quadratic model

$$E(y) = \beta_0 + \beta_1 x + \beta_2 x^2$$

to a set of data for which only one or two different x values were observed (see Figure 11.28). At least three different x values must be observed before a quadratic model can be fit to a set of data (that is, before all three parameters are estimable). *In general, the number of levels of observed* x *values must be one more than the order of the polynomial in* x *that you want to fit.*

For controlled experiments, the researcher can select experimental designs that will permit estimation of the model parameters. Even when the values of the independent variables cannot be controlled by the researcher, the independent variables are almost always observed at a sufficient number of levels to permit estimation of the model parameters. When the computer program you use suddenly refuses to fit a model, however, the problem is probably inestimable parameters.

PROBLEM 2 MULTICOLLINEARITY

Often, two or more of the independent variables used in the model for $E(y)$ contribute redundant information. That is, the independent variables are correlated with each other. Suppose we want to construct a model to predict the gas mileage rating of a truck as a function of its load, x_1, and the horsepower, x_2, of its engine. In general, we would expect heavy loads to require greater horsepower and to result in lower mileage ratings. Thus, although both x_1 and x_2 contribute information for the prediction of mileage rating, some of the information is overlapping because x_1 and x_2 are correlated.

552 CHAPTER 11 Multiple Regression

If the model

$$E(y) = \beta_0 + \beta_1 x_1 + \beta_2 x_2$$

were fit to a set of data, we might find that the t values for both $\hat{\beta}_1$ and $\hat{\beta}_2$ (the least squares estimates) are nonsignificant. However, the F-test for H_0: $\beta_1 = \beta_2 = 0$ would probably be highly significant. The tests may seem to produce contradictory conclusions, but really they do not. The t-tests indicate that the contribution of one variable, say x_1 = Load, is not significant after the effect of x_2 = Horsepower has been taken into account (because x_2 is also in the model). The significant F-test, on the other hand, tells us that at least one of the two variables is making a contribution to the prediction of y (that is, either β_1 or β_2, or both, differ from 0). In fact, both are probably contributing, but the contribution of one overlaps with that of the other.

When highly correlated independent variables are present in a regression model, the results are confusing. The researcher may want to include only one of the variables in the final model. One way of deciding which one to include is by using a technique called **stepwise regression** (Chapter 12). Generally, only one of a set of multicollinear independent variables is included in a stepwise regression model, since at each step every variable is tested in the presence of all the variables already in the model. For example, if at one step the variable Load is included as a significant variable in the prediction of the mileage rating, the variable Horsepower will probably never be added in a future step. Thus, if a set of independent variables is thought to be multicollinear, some screening by stepwise regression may be helpful.

Note that it would be fallacious to conclude that an independent variable x_1 is unimportant for predicting y *only* because it is not chosen by a stepwise regression procedure. The independent variable x_1 may be correlated with another one, x_2, that the stepwise procedure did select. The implication is that x_2 contributes *more* for predicting y (in the sample being analyzed), but it may still be true that x_1 alone contributes information for the prediction of y.

PROBLEM 3 PREDICTION OUTSIDE THE EXPERIMENTAL REGION

By the late 1960s many research economists had developed highly technical models to relate the state of the economy to various economic indices and other independent variables. Many of these models were multiple regression models, where, for example, the dependent variable y might be next year's growth in GDP and the independent variables might include this year's rate of inflation, this year's Consumer Price Index (CPI), etc. In other words, the model might be constructed to predict next year's economy using this year's knowledge.

Unfortunately, these models were almost all unsuccessful in predicting the recession in the early 1970s. What went wrong? One of the problems was that many of the regression models were used for **extrapolation**, i.e., to predict y for values of the independent variables that were outside the region in which the model was developed. For example, the inflation rate in the late 1960s, when the models were developed, ranged from 6% to 8%. When the double-digit inflation of the early 1970s became a reality, some researchers attempted to use the same models to predict future growth in GDP. As you can see in Figure 11.29, the model may be very accurate for predicting y when x is in the range of experimentation, but the use of the model outside that range is a dangerous practice.

FIGURE 11.29
Using a regression
model outside the
experimental region

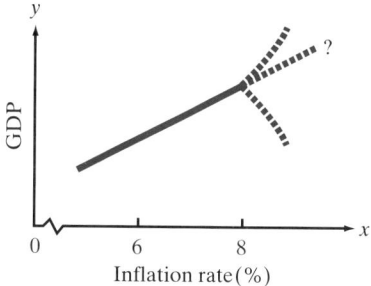

PROBLEM 4   CORRELATED ERRORS

Another problem associated with using a regression model to predict a variable y based on independent variables $x_1, x_2, ..., x_k$ arises from the fact that the data are frequently **time series**. That is, the values of both the dependent and independent variables are observed sequentially over a period of time. The observations tend to be correlated over time, which in turn often causes the prediction errors of the regression model to be correlated. Thus, the assumption of independent errors is violated, and the model tests and prediction intervals are no longer valid. One solution to this problem is to construct a **time series model**; this is the subject of Chapter 14.

STATISTICS IN ACTION

11.2 "WRINGING" THE BELL CURVE

In Statistics in Action 5.1, we introduced *The Bell Curve* (Free Press, 1994) by Richard Herrnstein and Charles Murray, a controversial book about race, genes, IQ, and economic mobility. The book heavily employs statistics and statistical methodology in an attempt to support the authors' positions on the relationships among these variables and their social consequences. The main theme of *The Bell Curve* can be summarized as follows:

1. Measured intelligence (IQ) is largely genetically inherited.

2. IQ is correlated positively with a variety of socioeconomic status success measures, such as prestigious job, high annual income, and high educational attainment.

3. From 1 and 2, it follows that socioeconomic successes are largely genetically caused and therefore resistant to educational and environmental interventions (such as affirmative action).

With the help of a major marketing campaign, the book became a best-seller shortly after its publication in October 1994. The underlying theme of the book—that intelligence is hereditary and tied to race and class—apparently appealed to many readers. However, reviews of *The Bell Curve* in popular magazines and newspapers were mostly negative. Social critics have described the authors as "un-American" and "pseudo-scientific racists," and their book as "alien and repellant." (On the other hand, there were defenders who labeled the book as "powerfully written" and "overwhelmingly convincing.") This Statistics in Action is based on two reviews of *The Bell Curve* that critique the statistical methodology employed by the authors and the inferences derived from the statistics. Both reviews, one published in *Chance* (Summer 1995) and the other in the *Journal of the American Statistical Association* (Dec. 1995), were written by Carnegie Mellon University professors Bernie Devlin, Stephen Fienberg, Daniel Resnick, and Kathryn Roeder. (Devlin, Fienberg, and Roeder are all statisticians; Resnick, a historian.)

continued

Here, our focus is on the statistical method used repeatedly by Herrnstein and Murray (H&M) to support their conclusions in *The Bell Curve:* regression analysis. The following are just a few of the problems with H&M's use of regression that are identified by the Carnegie Mellon professors:

Problem 1

H&M consistently use a trio of independent variables—IQ, socioeconomic status, and age—in a series of first-order models designed to predict dependent social outcome variables such as income and unemployment. (Only on a single occasion are interaction terms incorporated.) Consider, for example, the model

$$E(y) = \beta_0 + \beta_1 x_1 + \beta_2 x_2 + \beta_3 x_3$$

where y = income, x_1 = IQ, x_2 = socioeconomic status, and x_3 = age. H&M utilize t-tests on the individual β parameters to assess the importance of the independent variables. As with most of the models considered in *The Bell Curve*, the estimate of β_1 in the income model is positive and statistically significant at $\alpha = .05$, and the associated t value is larger (in absolute value) than the t values associated with the other independent variables. Consequently, *H&M claim that IQ is a better predictor of income than the other two independent variables.* No attempt was made to determine whether the model was properly specified or whether the model provides an adequate fit to the data.

Problem 2

In an appendix, the authors describe multiple regression as a "mathematical procedure that yields coefficients for each of [the independent variables], indicating how much of a change in [the dependent variable] can be anticipated for a given change in any particular [independent] variable, with all the others held constant." Armed with this information and the fact that the estimate of β_1 in the model above is positive, *H&M infer that a high IQ necessarily implies (or causes) a high income, and a low IQ inevitably leads to a low*

income. (Cause-and-effect inferences like this are made repeatedly throughout the book.)

Problem 3

The title of the book refers to the normal distribution and its well-known "bell-shaped" curve. There is a misconception among the general public that scores on intelligence tests (IQ) are normally distributed. In fact, most IQ scores have distributions that are decidedly skewed. Traditionally, psychologists and psychometricians have transformed these scores so that the resulting numbers have a precise normal distribution. H&M make a special point to do this. Consequently, *the measure of IQ used in all the regression models is normalized (i.e., transformed so that the resulting distribution is normal), despite the fact that regression methodology does not require predictor (independent) variables to be normally distributed.*

Problem 4

A variable that is not used as a predictor of social outcome in any of the models in *The Bell Curve* is level of education. H&M purposely omit education from the models, arguing that IQ causes education, not the other way around. Other researchers who have examined H&M's data report that *when education is included as an independent variable in the model, the effect of IQ on the dependent variable (say, income) is diminished.*

Focus

a. Comment on each of the problems identified by the Carnegie Mellon University professors in their review of *The Bell Curve*. Why do each of these problems cast a shadow on the inferences made by the authors?

b. Using the variables specified in the model above, describe how you would conduct the multiple regression analysis. (Propose a more complex model and describe the appropriate model tests, including a residual analysis.)

EXERCISES   11.29–11.41

Note: Exercises marked with 💾 *contain data for computer analysis on a 3.5" disk (file name in parentheses).*

Learning the Mechanics

11.29   When a multiple regression model is used for estimating the mean of the dependent variable and for predicting a particular value of y, which will be narrower, the confidence interval for the mean or the prediction interval for the particular y value? Explain.

11.30   Refer to Exercise 11.1, in which the model

$$y = \beta_0 + \beta_1 x_1 + \beta_2 x_2 + \epsilon$$

was fit to $n = 20$ data points. The MINITAB regression printout for these data is shown on page 555. Both a confidence interval for $E(y)$ and a prediction interval for y when $x_1 = .5$ and $x_2 = .2$ are shown at the bottom of the printout.

a. Interpret the confidence interval for $E(y)$.

b. Interpret the prediction interval for y.

```
The regression equation is
Y = 508 - 942 X1 + 429 X2

Predictor        Coef        Stdev      t-ratio        p
Constant       506.35        45.17        11.21      0.000
X1            -941.9        275.11        -3.42      0.004
X2             429.1        379.80         1.13      0.252

s = 94.25      R-sq = 45.9%      R-sq(adj) = 39.6%

Analysis of Variance

SOURCE          DF          SS          MS          F          p
Regression       2        128329       64165       7.22      0.003
Error           17        151016        8883
Total           19        279345

      Fit   Stdev.Fit        95% C.I.            95% P.I.
    121.22       46.0    ( 91.7, 150.7)     ( 29.2, 213.2)
```

11.31 Refer to Exercise 11.14, in which a quadratic model was fit to $n = 19$ data points. Two SAS residual plots are shown on page 556—the top one corresponds to the fitting of a straight-line model to the data, and the other to the quadratic model fit in Exercise 11.14. Analyze the two plots. Is the need for a quadratic term evident from the residual plot for the straight-line model? Does your conclusion agree with your test of the quadratic term in Exercise 11.14?

11.32 Consider fitting the multiple regression model

$$E(y) = \beta_0 + \beta_1 x_1 + \beta_2 x_2 + \beta_3 x_3 + \beta_4 x_4 + \beta_5 x_5.$$

A matrix of correlations for all pairs of independent variables is shown in the next column. Do you detect a multicollinearity problem? Explain.

	x_1	x_2	x_3	x_4	x_5
x_1	—	.17	.02	−.23	.19
x_2		—	.45	.93	.02
x_3			—	.22	−.01
x_4				—	.86
x_5					—

Applying the Concepts

11.33 **(X11.033)** A Wall Street security analyst who specializes in the pharmaceutical industry is interested in better understanding the relationship between a firm's sales and its research and development (R&D) expenditures. The table below presents 1995 data on sales revenue (y), number of employees (x_1), and R&D expenditures (x_2) for a sample of 15 pharmaceutical companies.

a. Fit the multiple regression model $E(y) = \beta_0 + \beta_1 x_1 + \beta_2 x_2$ to the data using a statistical software package.

b. Use the software to generate a 95% confidence interval for the mean sales revenue of companies with 1,000 employees and R&D

Company	Sales y (millions of $)	Number of Employees x_1 (thousands)	R&D Expense x_2 (millions of $)
Abbott Laboratories	10,012	50.24	1,072
Alza	326	1.44	20
American Home Products Corp.	13,376	64.71	1,354
Bristol Myers Squibb	13,767	49.14	1,199
Carter-Wallace Inc.	662	3.61	26
Genentech Inc.	857	2.84	503
IVAX Corp.	1,259	7.89	64
Johnson & Johnson	18,842	82.30	1,634
Lilly (Eli) & Co.	6,763	26.80	4,239
Merck & Co.	16,681	45.20	5,269
Pharmacia & Upjohn Inc.	7,094	35.00	3,383
Pfizer	10,021	43.80	3,472
Rhone-Poulenc Roren	5,142	28.00	1,621
Schering-Plough	5,104	20.10	2,098
Warner-Lambert Co.	7,039	37.00	2,006

Source: Compuserve, 1996.

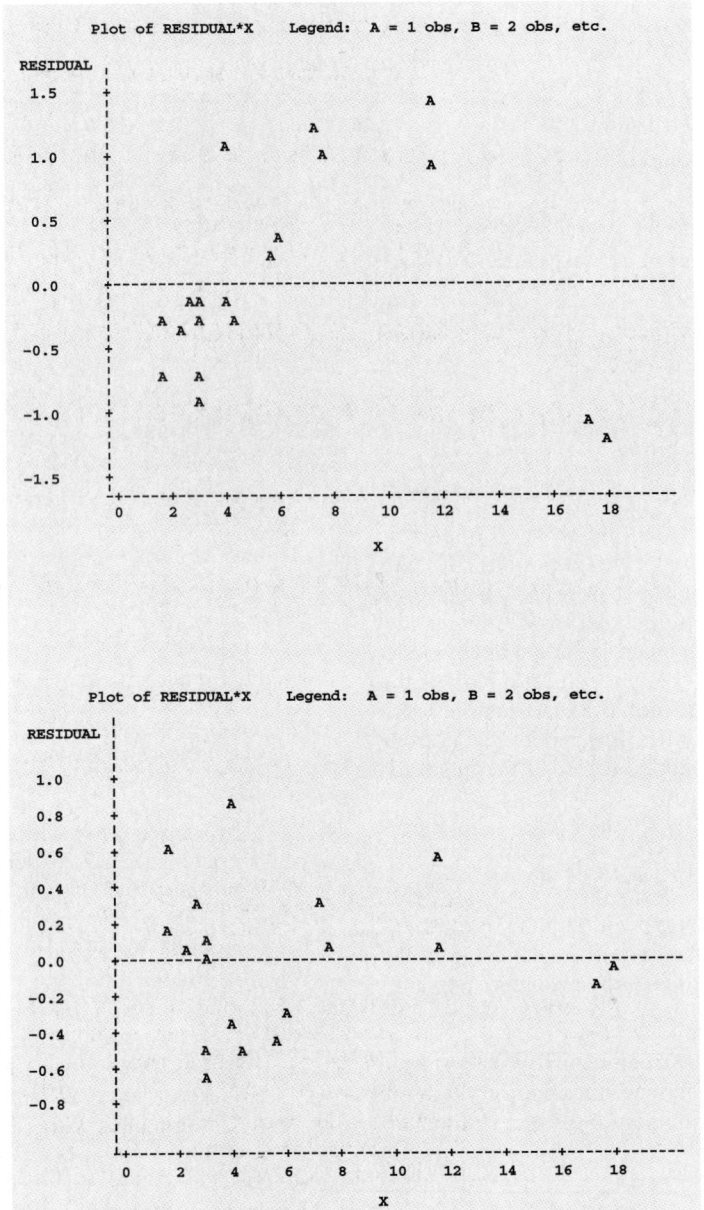

expenditures of $500 million. Interpret the interval.

c. Do you detect any signs of multicollinearity? Explain.

d. Verify your answer to part **c** by finding the correlation between number of employees (x_1) and R&D expenditures (x_2).

11.34 Refer to Exercise 11.6, in which the 1996 food consumption expenditure y of a sample of 25 households in Washington, D.C., was related to

the household income x_1 and size of household x_2 by the model

$$y = \beta_0 + \beta_1 x_1 + \beta_2 x_2 + \epsilon$$

SPSS plots of the standardized residuals from this model are shown on page 557—one versus x_1 and one versus x_2. Analyze the plots. Is there visual evidence of a need for a quadratic term in either x_1 or x_2? Explain.

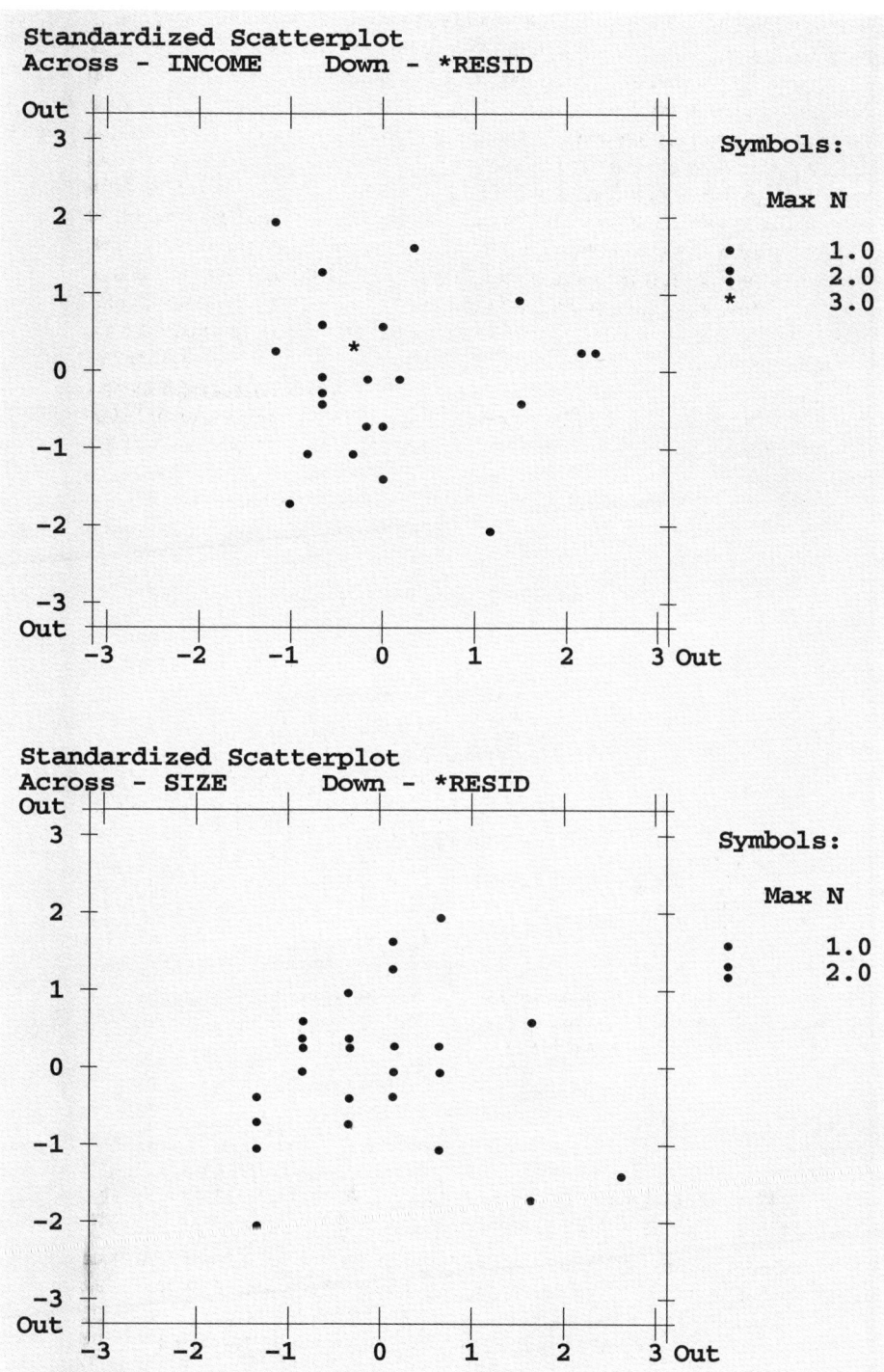

11.35 Refer to Exercise 11.34. Suppose a 26th household is added to the sample, with the following characteristics:

Food consumption: 7.5
Income: 7.3
Household size: 5

Model: MODEL1
Dependent Variable: FOOD

Analysis of Variance

Source	DF	Sum of Squares	Mean Square	F Value	Prob>F
Model	2	12.78439	6.39219	52.138	0.0001
Error	22	2.69721	0.12260		
C Total	24	15.48160			

Root MSE	0.35014	R-square	0.8258
Dep Mean	4.05600	Adj R-sq	0.8099
C.V.	8.63273		

Parameter Estimates

Variable	DF	Parameter Estimate	Standard Error	T for H0: Parameter=0	Prob > |T|
INTERCEP	1	2.369646	0.21813514	10.863	0.0001
INCOME	1	0.009193	0.00337540	2.724	0.0124
SIZE	1	0.353964	0.03518275	10.061	0.0001

Obs	INCOME	SIZE	Dep Var FOOD	Predict Value	Std Err Predict	Lower95% Predict	Upper95% Predict	Residual
1	41.1	4	4.2000	4.1633	0.072	3.4219	4.9048	0.0367

Model: MODEL2
Dependent Variable: FOOD

Analysis of Variance

Source	DF	Sum of Squares	Mean Square	F Value	Prob>F
Model	2	17.79867	8.89934	22.523	0.0001
Error	23	9.08786	0.39512		
C Total	25	26.88654			

Root MSE	0.62859	R-square	0.6620
Dep Mean	4.18846	Adj R-sq	0.6326
C.V.	15.00764		

Parameter Estimates

Variable	DF	Parameter Estimate	Standard Error	T for H0: Parameter=0	Prob > |T|
INTERCEP	1	2.036250	0.38272822	5.320	0.0001
INCOME	1	0.015560	0.00584915	2.660	0.0140
SIZE	1	0.393637	0.06238612	6.310	0.0001

Obs	INCOME	SIZE	Dep Var FOOD	Predict Value	Std Err Predict	Lower95% Predict	Upper95% Predict	Residual
1	41.1	4	4.2000	4.2503	0.128	2.9233	5.5773	-0.0503

Two SAS printouts are shown above—one for the same model fit to the first 25 observations, the second fit to all 26 observations.

a. Record the least squares estimates of the model parameters for each model, and note differences in the estimates. Interpret each estimate.

b. Find and interpret the standard deviation for each model.

c. Conduct the analysis of variance F-test for each model using $\alpha = .05$.

d. Place a 95% confidence interval on the mean rate of change in food consumption per additional person in the household for each model, assuming household income is constant.

e. For each model, interpret the 95% prediction interval for y shown at the bottom of the printout.

f. According to the results of parts **a–d**, how much influence does the additional observation have on the model?

11.36 Refer to Exercises 11.34 and 11.35. MINITAB residual plots against household income and size of household for the models corresponding to 26 observations are shown.

   a. Analyze the plots. Are there any outliers? If so, identify them.

   b. What are possible explanations for any outliers you identified in part **a**?

11.37 Refer to Exercises 11.34 –11.36. The MINITAB stem-and-leaf displays shown on page 560 represent the frequency distributions of the residuals for the two data sets, one with $n = 25$ and one with

$n = 26$. Analyze the displays, especially with regard to the normality assumption.

11.38 Refer to the *World Development* study of the variables impacting the size distribution of manufacturing firms in international markets, Exercise 11.10. Five independent variables, LGNP, AREAC, SVA, CREDIT, and STOCK, were used to model the share, *y*, of firms with 100 or more workers. The researchers detected a high correlation between pairs of the following independent variables: LGNP and SVA, LGNP and STOCK, and CREDIT and STOCK. Describe the problems that may arise if these high correlations are ignored in the multiple regression analysis of the model.

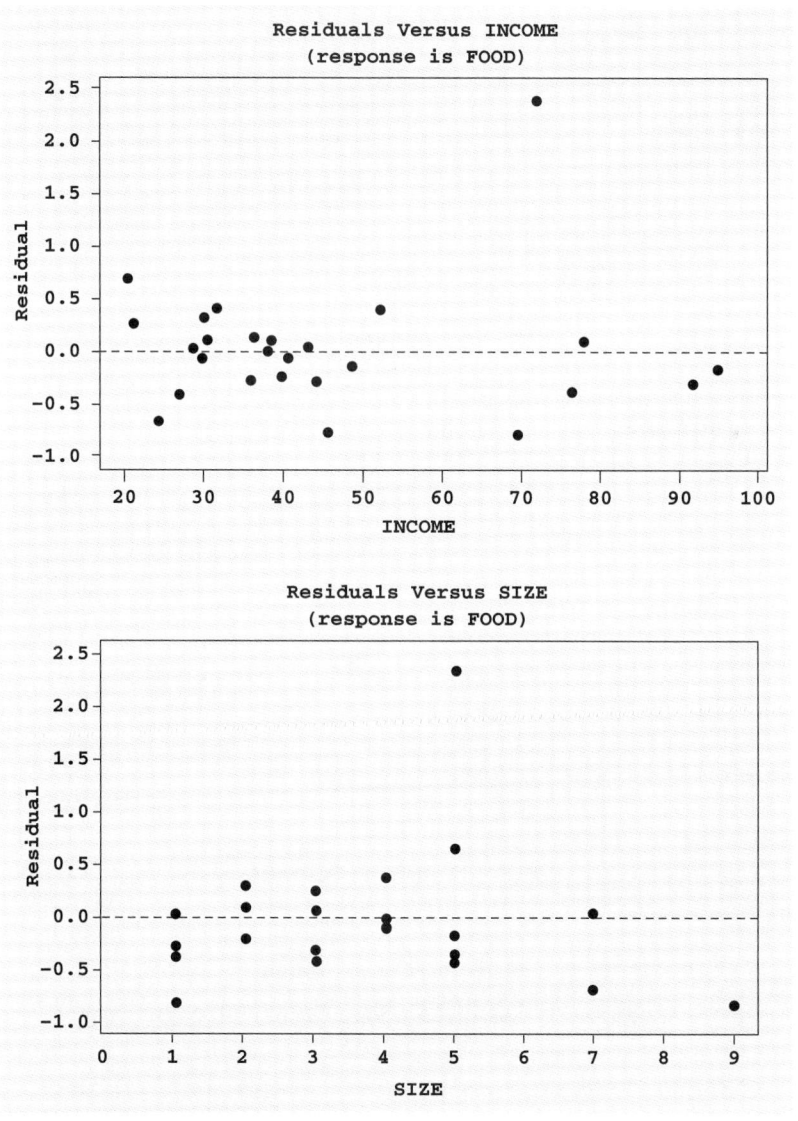

```
Stem-and-leaf of RESID25    N = 25
Leaf Unit = 0.010
     1    -6  6
     2    -5  7
     3    -4  7
     5    -3  85
     7    -2  93
     8    -1  3
    10    -0  85
    (5)    0  13468
    10     1  1147
     6     2  45
     4     3  4
     3     4  2
     2     5  3
     1     6  7
------------------------------------
Stem-and-leaf of RESID26    N = 26
Leaf Unit = 0.10
     3    -0  876
   (11)   -0  44332221000
    12     0  0000112333
     2     0  6
     1     1
     1     1
     1     2  3
```

11.39 **(X11.039)** Passive exposure to environmental tobacco smoke has been associated with growth suppression and an increased frequency of respiratory tract infections in normal children. Is this association more pronounced in children with cystic fibrosis? To answer this question, a study was conducted on 43 children (18 girls and 25 boys) attending a two-week summer camp for cystic fibrosis patients (*New England Journal of Medicine*, Sept. 20, 1990). Researchers investigated the correlation between a child's weight percentile (y) and the number of cigarettes smoked per day in the child's home (x). The accompanying table lists the data for the 25 boys. A MINITAB printout (with residuals) for the straight-line model relating y to x is shown on page 561. Examine the residuals. Do you detect any outliers?

Weight Percentile y	No. of Cigarettes Smoked per Day x
6	0
6	15
2	40
8	23
11	20
17	7
24	3
25	0
17	25
25	20
25	15
31	23
35	10
43	0
49	0
50	0
49	22
46	30
54	0
58	0
62	0
66	0
66	23
83	0
87	44

Source: Rubin, B. K. "Exposure of children with cystic fibrosis to environmental tobacco smoke." *New England Journal of Medicine*, Vol. 323, No. 12, September 20, 1990, p. 785 (data extracted from Figure 3).

```
Multiple R            .94886
R Square              .90033
Adjusted R Square     .89266
Standard Error       1.14301

Analysis of Variance
                 DF      Sum of Squares      Mean Square
Regression        1         153.41583        153.41583
Residual         13          16.98417          1.30647

F =     117.42733         Signif F = .0000

----------------- Variables in the Equation ------------------

Variable              B         SE B         Beta         T     Sig T

X               -.44494       .04106      -.94886    -10.836    .0000
(Constant)     19.27908       .50788                  37.960    .0000
```

```
The regression equation is
WTPCTILE = 41.2 - 0.262 SMOKED

Predictor        Coef        Stdev      t-ratio        p
Constant       41.153        6.843         6.01    0.000
SMOKED        -0.2619        0.3702        -0.71    0.486

s = 24.68      R-sq = 2.1%    R-sq(adj) = 0.0%

Analysis of Variance

SOURCE          DF           SS          MS        F       p
Regression       1         304.9       304.9     0.50   0.486
Error           23       14011.1       609.2
Total           24       14316.0
```

Obs.	SMOKED	WTPCTILE	Fit	Stdev.Fit	Residual	St.Resid
1	0.0	6.00	41.15	6.84	-35.15	-1.48
2	15.0	6.00	37.22	5.00	-31.22	-1.29
3	40.0	2.00	30.68	11.22	-28.68	-1.30
4	23.0	8.00	35.13	6.22	-27.13	-1.14
5	20.0	11.00	35.91	5.61	-24.91	-1.04
6	7.0	17.00	39.32	5.38	-22.32	-0.93
7	3.0	24.00	40.37	6.13	-16.37	-0.68
8	0.0	25.00	41.15	6.84	-16.15	-0.68
9	25.0	17.00	34.60	6.69	-17.60	-0.74
10	20.0	25.00	35.91	5.61	-10.91	-0.45
11	15.0	25.00	37.22	5.00	-12.22	-0.51
12	23.0	31.00	35.13	6.22	-4.13	-0.17
13	10.0	35.00	38.53	5.04	-3.53	-0.15
14	0.0	43.00	41.15	6.84	1.85	0.08
15	0.0	49.00	41.15	6.84	7.85	0.33
16	0.0	50.00	41.15	6.84	8.85	0.37
17	22.0	49.00	35.39	6.00	13.61	0.57
18	30.0	46.00	33.29	8.06	12.71	0.54
19	0.0	54.00	41.15	6.84	12.85	0.54
20	0.0	58.00	41.15	6.84	16.85	0.71
21	0.0	62.00	41.15	6.84	20.85	0.88
22	0.0	66.00	41.15	6.84	24.85	1.05
23	23.0	66.00	35.13	6.22	30.87	1.29
24	0.0	83.00	41.15	6.84	41.85	1.76
25	44.0	87.00	29.63	12.56	57.37	2.70

11.40 Refer to Exercise 11.9, in which a quadratic model was used to relate the time to complete a task, y, to the months of experience, x, for a sample of 15 employees on an automobile assembly line. Suppose a straight-line model has been fit instead. The SPSS printout for the straight-line model is shown at the bottom of page 560. A residual plot is shown on page 562. Does the residual analysis support the statistical test you conducted in part **c** of Exercise 11.9?

11.41 *Teaching Sociology* (July 1995) developed a model for the professional socialization of graduate students working toward their doctorate. One of the dependent variables modeled was professional confidence, y, measured on a 5-point scale. The model included more than 20 independent variables and was fit to data collected for a sample of 309 graduate students. One concern is whether multicollinearity exists in the data. A matrix of Pearson product moment correlations for 10 of the independent variables is shown on page 562. [*Note:* Each entry in the table is the correlation coefficient r between the variable in the corresponding row and corresponding column.]

a. Examine the correlation matrix and find the independent variables that are moderately or highly correlated.

b. What modeling problems may occur if the variables, part **a**, are left in the model? Explain.

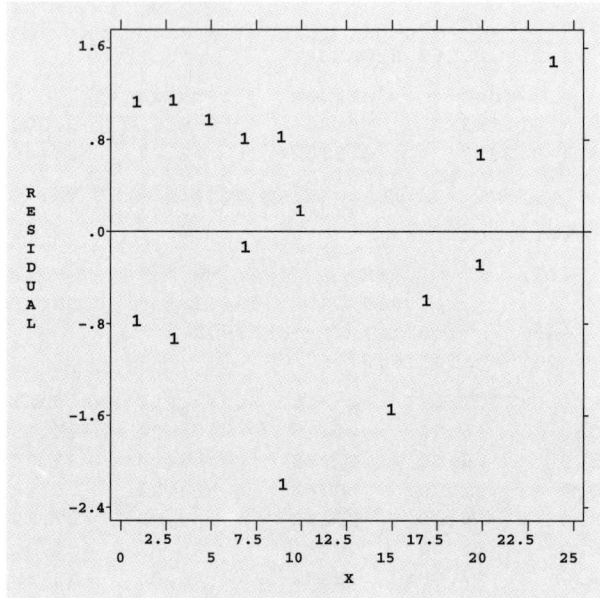

Independent Variable	(1)	(2)	(3)	(4)	(5)	(6)	(7)	(8)	(9)	(10)
(1) Father's occupation	1.000	.363	.099	−.110	−.047	−.053	−.111	.178	.078	.049
(2) Mother's education	.363	1.000	.228	−.139	−.216	.084	−.118	.192	.125	.068
(3) Race	.099	.228	1.000	.036	−.515	.014	−.120	.112	.117	.337
(4) Sex	−.110	−.139	.036	1.000	.165	−.256	.173	−.106	−.117	.073
(5) Foreign status	−.047	−.216	−.515	.165	1.000	−.041	.159	−.130	−.165	−.171
(6) Undergraduate GPA	−.053	.084	.014	−.256	−.041	1.000	.032	.028	−.034	.092
(7) Year GRE taken	−.111	−.118	−.120	.173	.159	.032	1.000	−.086	−.602	.016
(8) Verbal GRE score	.178	.192	.112	−.106	−.130	.028	−.086	1.000	.132	.087
(9) Years in graduate program	.078	.125	.117	−.117	−.165	−.034	−.602	.132	1.000	−.071
(10) First-year graduate GPA	.049	.068	.337	.073	−.171	.092	.016	.087	−.071	1.000

Source: Keith, B., and Moore, H. A. "Training sociologists: An assessment of professional socialization and the emergence of career aspirations."
Teaching Sociology, Vol. 23, No. 3, July 1995, p. 205 (Table 1).

Quick Review

Key Terms

Key Formulas

$$s^2 = \text{MSE} = \frac{\text{SSE}}{n - (k + 1)}$$

Estimator of σ^2 for a model with k independent variables   506

$$t = \frac{\hat{\beta}_i}{s_{\hat{\beta}_i}}$$

Test statistic for testing $H_0: \beta_i = 0$ 509

$$\hat{\beta}_i \pm (t_{\alpha/2})s_{\hat{\beta}_i},$$
where t depends on $n - (k + 1)$ df

$(1 - \alpha)$ 100% confidence interval for β_i 510

$$F = \frac{\text{MS(Model)}}{\text{MSE}} = \frac{R^2/k}{(1 - R^2)/[n - (k + 1)]}$$

Test statistic for testing $H_0: \beta_1 = \beta_2 = \cdots = \beta_k = 0$ 520

$$R^2 = \frac{\text{SS}_{yy} - \text{SSE}}{\text{SS}_{yy}}$$

Multiple coefficient of determination   518

$$y - \hat{y}$$

Regression residual   541

LANGUAGE LAB

Symbol	Pronunciation	Description
x_1^2	x-1 squared	Quadratic term that allows for curvature in the relationship between y and x
$x_1 x_2$	x-1 x-2	Interaction term
MSE	M-S-E	Mean square for error (estimates σ^2)
β_i	beta-i	Coefficient of x_i in the model
$\hat{\beta}_i$	beta-i-hat	Least squares estimate of β_i
$s_{\hat{\beta}_i}$	s of beta-i-hat	Estimated standard error of $\hat{\beta}_i$
R^2	R-squared	Multiple coefficient of determination
F		Test statistic for testing global usefulness of model
$\hat{\epsilon}$	epsilon-hat	Estimated random error, or residual

SUPPLEMENTARY EXERCISES 11.42–11.64

Note: Exercises marked with 💾 *contain data for computer analysis on a 3.5" disk (file name in parentheses).*

Learning the Mechanics

11.42 Suppose you used MINITAB to fit the model

$$y = \beta_0 + \beta_1 x_1 + \beta_2 x_2 + \epsilon$$

to $n = 15$ data points and you obtained the printout shown below.

a. What is the least squares prediction equation?
b. Find R^2 and interpret its value.

c. Is there sufficient evidence to indicate that the model is useful for predicting y? Conduct an F-test using $\alpha = .05$.
d. Test the null hypothesis $H_0: \beta_1 = 0$ against the alternative hypothesis $H_a: \beta_1 \neq 0$. Test using $\alpha = .05$. Draw the appropriate conclusions.
e. Find the standard deviation of the regression model and interpret it.

11.43 Suppose you fit the model

$$y = \beta_0 + \beta_1 x_1 + \beta_2 x_1^2 + \beta_3 x_2 + \beta_4 x_1 x_2 + \epsilon$$

to $n = 25$ data points and find that

```
The regression equation is
Y = 90.1 - 1.84 X1 + .285 X2

Predictor        Coef       Stdev      t-ratio          p
Constant        90.10       23.10         3.90      0.002
X1             -1.836       0.367        -5.01      0.001
X2              0.285       0.231         1.24      0.465

s = 10.68      R-sq = 91.6%      R-sq(adj) = 90.2%

Analysis of Variance

SOURCE         DF          SS           MS         F         p
Regression      2       14801         7400     64.91     0.001
Error          12        1364          114
Total          14       16165
```

$\hat{\beta}_0 = 1.26$ $\hat{\beta}_1 = -2.43$ $\hat{\beta}_2 = .05$ $\hat{\beta}_3 = .62$

$\hat{\beta}_4 = 1.81$ SSE $= .41$ $R^2 = .83$

$s_{\hat{\beta}_1} = 1.21$ $s_{\hat{\beta}_2} = .16$ $s_{\hat{\beta}_3} = .26$ $s_{\hat{\beta}_4} = 1.49$

a. Is there sufficient evidence to conclude that at least one of the parameters $\beta_1, \beta_2, \beta_3$, or β_4 is nonzero? Test using $\alpha = .05$.

b. Test $H_0: \beta_1 = 0$ against $H_a: \beta_1 < 0$. Use $\alpha = .05$.

c. Test $H_0: \beta_2 = 0$ against $H_a: \beta_2 > 0$. Use $\alpha = .05$.

d. Test $H_0: \beta_3 = 0$ against $H_a: \beta_3 \neq 0$. Use $\alpha = .05$.

11.44 When a multiple regression model is used for estimating the mean of the dependent variable and for predicting a new value of y, which will be narrower—the confidence interval for the mean or the prediction interval for the new y value?

11.45 After a regression model is fit to a set of data, a confidence interval for the mean value of y at a given setting of the independent variables is *always* narrower than the corresponding prediction interval for a particular value of y at the same setting of the independent variables. Why?

11.46 Suppose you have developed a regression model to explain the relationship between y and x_1, x_2, and x_3. A set of $n = 15$ data points is used to find the least squares prediction equation. The ranges of the variables you observed were as follows: $10 \leq y \leq 100, 5 \leq x_1 \leq 55, .5 \leq x_2 \leq 1$, and $1,000 \leq x_3 \leq 2,000$. Will the error of prediction be smaller when you use the least squares equation to predict y when $x_1 = 30, x_2 = .6$, and $x_3 = 1,300$, or when $x_1 = 60, x_2 = .4$, and $x_3 = 900$? Why?

11.47 **(X11.047)** A response variable y was observed for $n = 15$ settings of two independent variables, x_1 and x_2. The data are shown in the table below.

a. Fit the model $y = \beta_0 + \beta_1 x_1 + \beta_2 x_2 + \epsilon$ to the data.

b. Fit the model $y = \beta_0 + \beta_1 x_1 + \beta_2 x_2 + \beta_3 x_1 x_2 + \epsilon$ to the data.

c. Which of the models in parts **a** and **b** best describes the relationship between y and x_1 and x_2? Explain.

d. Repeat part **a** using a different statistical program package. For example, if you originally used MINITAB, now use SAS, SPSS, or EXCEL. Compare these results with those found in part **a**.

11.48 Refer to Exercise 11.14, in which a quadratic model was fit to $n = 19$ data points. Two residual plots are shown on page 565—the top one corresponds to the fitting of a straight-line model to the data and the other to the quadratic model fit in Exercise 11.14. Analyze the two plots. Is the need for a quadratic term evident from the residual plot for the straight-line model? Does your conclusion agree with your test of the quadratic term in Exercise 11.14?

Applying the Concepts

11.49 Emergency services (EMS) personnel are constantly exposed to traumatic situations; consequently, they may experience severe psychological stress. The *Journal of Consulting and Clinical Psychology* (June 1995) reported on a study of EMS rescue workers who responded to the I-880 freeway collapse during the 1989 San Francisco earthquake. The goal of the study was to identify the predictors of symptomatic distress in the EMS workers. With this knowledge, EMS personnel managers can anticipate potential problems and assign workers accordingly. One of the distress variables studied was the Global Symptom Index (GSI). Several models for GSI, y, were considered based on the following independent variables:

$x_1 = $ Critical Incident Exposure scale (CIE)

$x_2 = $ Hogan Personality Inventory-Adjustment scale (HPI-A)

$x_3 = $ Years of experience (EXP)

$x_4 = $ Locus of Control scale (LOC)

$x_5 = $ Social Support scale (SS)

$x_6 = $ Dissociative Experiences scale (DES)

$x_7 = $ Peritraumatic Dissociation Experiences Questionnaire, self-report (PDEQ-SR)

a. Write a first-order model for $E(y)$ as a function of the first five independent variables, x_1–x_5.

b. The model of part **a**, fit to data collected for $n = 147$ EMS workers, yielded the following results: $R^2 = .469, F = 34.47, p$-value $< .001$. Interpret these results.

c. Write a first-order model for $E(y)$ as a function of all seven independent variables, x_1–x_7.

d. The model, part **c**, yielded $R^2 = .603$. Interpret this result.

y	-12	28	-15	-25	2	-11	25	-47	-28	12	-29	-3	5	7	6
x_1	3	8	3	2	9	5	7	0	1	5	1	5	7	6	5
x_2	9	7	1	6	1	1	7	8	6	9	4	5	3	4	9

Plot of RESIDUAL*X   Legend: A = 1 obs, B = 2 obs, etc.

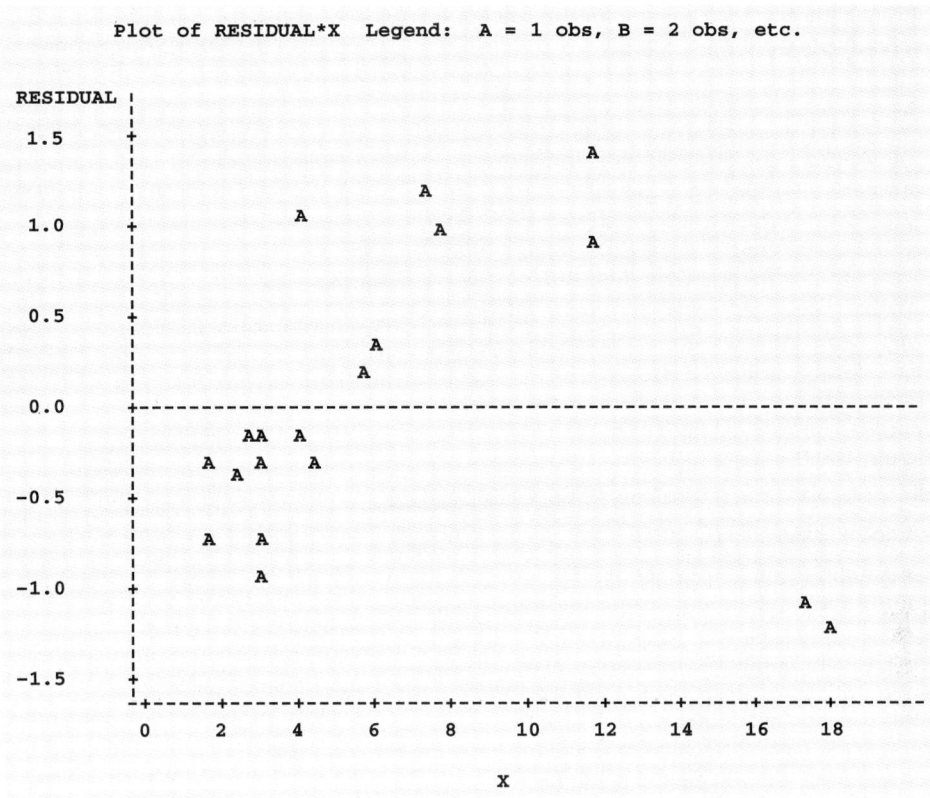

Plot of RESIDUAL*X   Legend: A = 1 obs, B = 2 obs, etc.

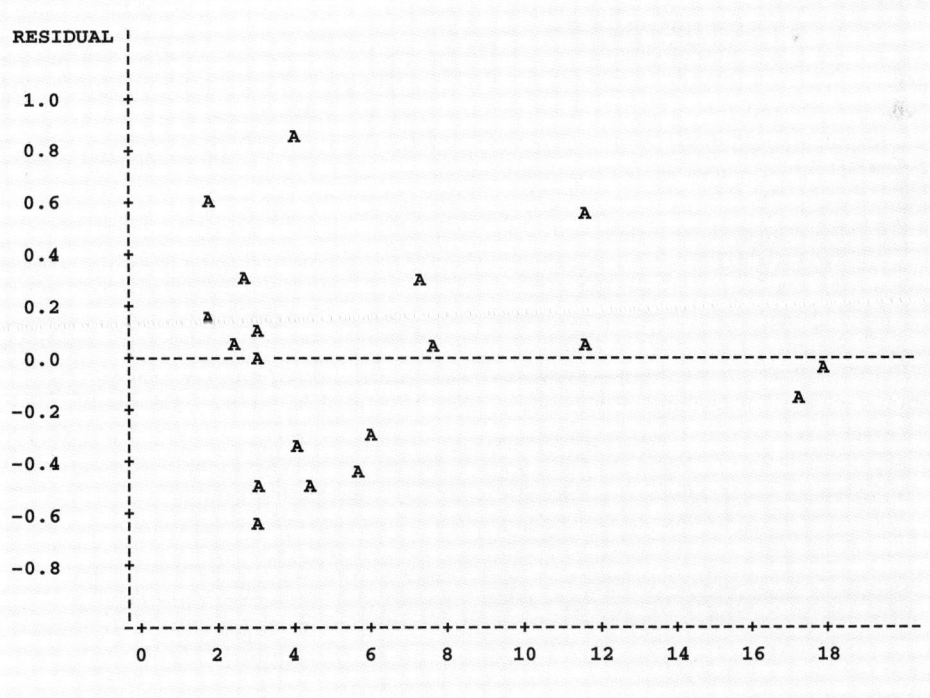

e. The t-tests for testing the DES and PDEQ-SR variables both yielded a p-value of .001. Interpret these results.

11.50 Since the Great Depression of the 1930s, the link between the suicide rate and the state of the economy has been the subject of much research. Research exploring this link using regression analysis was reported in an article in the *Journal of Socio-Economics* (Spring 1992). The researchers collected data from a 45-year period on the following variables:

y = Suicide rate

x_1 = Unemployment rate

x_2 = Percentage of females in the labor force

x_3 = Divorce rate

x_4 = Logarithm of Gross Domestic Product (GDP)

x_5 = Annual percent change in GDP

One of the models explored by the researchers was a multiple regression model relating y to linear terms in x_1 through x_5. The least squares model shown below resulted (the observed significance levels of the β estimates are shown in parentheses beneath the estimates).

a. Interpret the value of R^2. Is there sufficient evidence to indicate that the model is useful for predicting the suicide rate? Use $\alpha = .05$.

b. Interpret each of the coefficients in the model, and each of the corresponding significance levels.

c. Is there sufficient evidence to indicate that the unemployment rate is a useful predictor of the suicide rate? Use $\alpha = .05$.

d. Discuss each of the following terms with respect to potential problems with the above model: curvature (second-order terms), interaction, and multicollinearity.

11.51 To meet the increasing demand for new software products, many systems development experts have adopted a prototyping methodology. The effects of prototyping on the system development life cycle (SDLC) were investigated in the *Journal of Computer Information Systems* (Spring 1993). A survey of 500 randomly selected corporate-level MIS managers was conducted. Three potential independent variables were (1) *importance* of prototyping to each phase of the SDLC; (2) degree of *support* prototyping provides for the SDLC; and

(3) degree to which prototyping *replaces* each phase of the SDLC. The accompanying table gives the pairwise correlations of the three variables in the survey data for one particular phase of the SDLC. Use this information to assess the degree of multicollinearity in the survey data. Would you recommend using all three independent variables in a regression analysis? Explain.

Variable Pairs	Correlation Coefficient, r
Importance—Replace	.2682
Importance—Support	.6991
Replace—Support	−.0531

Source: Hardgrave, B. C., Doke, E. R., and Swanson, N. E. "Prototyping effects on the system development life cycle: An empirical study." *Journal of Computer Information Systems*, Vol. 33, No. 3, Spring 1993, p. 16 (Table 1).

11.52 Most companies institute rigorous safety programs to ensure employee safety. Suppose accident reports over the last year at a company are sampled, and the number of hours the employee had worked before the accident occurred, x, and the amount of time the employee lost from work, y, are recorded. A quadratic model is proposed to investigate a fatigue hypothesis that more serious accidents occur near the end of workdays than occur near the beginning, but that the rate of increase of time lost with hours worked is slower near the end of day. Thus, the proposed model is

$$E(y) = \beta_0 + \beta_1 x + \beta_2 x^2$$

A total of 60 accident reports are examined and the model fit to the data. The regression results are shown here:

$$\hat{y} = 12.3 + .25x - .0033x^2 \qquad R^2 = .0430$$

$$F = 1.28 \ (p\text{-value} = .8711) \qquad s_{\hat{\beta}_2} = .0469$$

a. According to the fatigue hypothesis, what is the expected sign of β_2?

b. Test the fatigue hypothesis at $\alpha = .05$.

c. Conduct a test of overall model adequacy at $\alpha = .05$.

d. Use the model to predict the number of days missed by an employee who has an accident after six hours of work.

e. Suppose the 95% prediction interval for the predicted value in part **d** is determined to be

$$\hat{y} = .002 + .0204x_1 + (-.0231)x_2 + .0765x_3 + .2760x_4 + .0018x_5$$
$$\phantom{\hat{y} = .002 + } (.002) \qquad (.02) \qquad (>.10) \quad (>.10) \quad (>.10)$$

$$R^2 = .45$$

(1.35, 26.01). Interpret this interval. Does this interval support your conclusion about the model in part **c**?

11.53 To increase the motivation and productivity of workers, an electronics manufacturer decides to experiment with a new pay incentive structure at one of two plants. The experimental plan will be tried at plant A for six months, whereas workers at plant B will remain on the original pay plan. To evaluate the effectiveness of the new plan, the average assembly time for part of an electronic system was measured for employees at both plants at the beginning and end of the six-month period. Suppose the model proposed was

$$y = \beta_0 + \beta_1 x_1 + \beta_2 x_2 + \epsilon$$

where

y = Assembly time (hours) at end of six-month period

x_1 = Assembly time (hours) at beginning of six-month period

$$x_2 = \begin{cases} 1 & \text{if plant A} \\ 0 & \text{if plant B} \end{cases} \quad \text{(dummy variable)}$$

A sample of $n = 42$ observations yielded

$$\hat{y} = .11 + .98x_1 - .53x_2$$

where

$$s_{\hat{\beta}_1} = .231 \qquad s_{\hat{\beta}_2} = .48$$

Test to see whether, after allowing for the effect of initial assembly time, plant A had a lower mean assembly time than plant B. Use $\alpha = .01$. [*Note:* When the {0, 1} coding is used to define a dummy variable, the coefficient of the variable represents the difference between the mean response at the two levels represented by the variable. Thus, the coefficient β_2 is the difference in mean assembly time between plant A and plant B at the end of the six-month period, and $\hat{\beta}_2$ is the sample estimator of that difference.]

11.54 A large government agency would like to predict the number of people it will hire within the next year to fill the 30 positions that are currently open. Historically, the agency has been unable to fill all its job openings. It has been decided to model the number of positions filled in a year, y, as a function of the number of positions open, x_1, and the recruiting budget (in dollars) for the year, x_2 (e.g., for advertising the positions, paying travel expenses, etc.). A random sample of 10 years of recruiting records was drawn from the agency's 30 years of records. The model

$$E(y) = \beta_0 + \beta_1 x_1 + \beta_2 x_2$$

was fit to the data using MINITAB. The results shown in the printout below were obtained.

a. Identify the least squares prediction equation.
b. Is there sufficient evidence to indicate that the model contributes information for predicting the number y of positions that will be filled? Conduct an F-test using $\alpha = .05$.
c. Test the null hypothesis $H_0: \beta_2 = 0$ against the alternative hypothesis $H_a: \beta_2 \neq 0$ using $\alpha = .05$. Interpret the results of your test in the context of the problem.
d. Use the least squares prediction equation to predict how many of the 30 positions the agency will fill next year if the recruiting budget is $10,000.
e. Can you think of a situation for which the prediction in part **d** might possibly be inaccurate? Explain.
f. Which (if any) of the assumptions we make about ϵ in a regression analysis are likely to be violated in this problem? Explain.

```
The regression equation is
Y =    .056 + .273 X1 + .0006 X2

Predictor      Coef      Stdev    t-ratio        p
Constant     0.0562      0.902       0.06    0.998
X1           0.2733      0.0971      2.81    0.036
X2         0.000560    0.000129      4.34    0.007

s = 1.33       R-sq = 97.9%    R-sq(adj) = 97.3%

Analysis of Variance

SOURCE       DF        SS        MS         F        p
Regression    2    583.18   -291.59    164.74    0.001
Error         7     12.42      1.77
Total         9    595.60
```

$$\hat{y} = 0 - .0945x_1 - .032x_2 + .009x_3 - .0028x_4 + .007x_5 + .105x_6 + .469x_7$$
$$\quad\quad (-2.61)\quad (-.96)\quad (2.74)\quad (-2.23)\quad (5.71)\quad (4.02)\quad (2.21)$$

where

y = Future wages

x_1 = Amount of business course work in high school

x_2 = Amount of college prep work in high school

x_3 = Math aptitude

x_4 = High school GPA

x_5 = Measure of socioeconomic status

x_6 = 1 if the individual is married, 0 if not

x_7 = Amount of on-the-job training

11.55 Research was conducted to discover the factors in a person's education that determine future wages (*Southern Economic Journal*, Vol. 50, 1983). A first-order model was fit to a set of $n = 60$ data points and the prediction equation and t-test values were obtained (see the table above). The t values used to test the individual model parameters are shown in parentheses below their respective estimates.
a. What are the interpretations of the coefficients?
b. Are they statistically significant at the $\alpha = .01$ level?

c. The standard error for the estimate of β_5 is .001225. Use this information to construct a 99% confidence interval for β_5.
d. Interpret the interval, part **c**.

11.56 **(X11.056)** In Exercise 10.75 you used simple regression to model the relationship between the sales prices (y) of existing homes in suburban Essex county, New Jersey, and their square footage (x_1). These data are reproduced below along with the number of bathrooms (x_2) and yearly property taxes (x_3). Consider the multiple regression model

Area (sq. ft.)	Price ($)	Number of Bathrooms	1995 Property Taxes ($)
2306	145,541	1	3,611
2677	179,900	2	4,433
2324	149,000	1	4,132
1447	113,900	2	2,668
3333	189,000	3	6,089
3004	184,500	2	5,867
4142	339,717	4	5,094
2923	228,000	2	3,776
2902	209,000	3	6,200
1847	133,000	1	3,205
2148	168,000	2	6,034
2819	205,000	2	2,985
1753	129,900	1	2,586
3206	235,000	3	7,184
2474	129,900	2	3,458
2933	199,500	2	5,646
3987	319,000	3	5,669
2598	185,500	2	4,211
4934	375,000	4	9,896
2253	169,000	3	5,502
2998	185,900	1	3,962
2791	189,800	3	4,295
2865	192,000	2	4,416
4417	379,900	4	8,121

Source: Adapted from data compiled by the Multiple Listing Service, Suburban Essex County, New Jersey, 1996.

$$E(y) = \beta_0 + \beta_1 x_1 + \beta_2 x_2 + \beta_3 x_3 + \beta_4 x_1 x_2 + \beta_5 x_1 x_3 + \beta_6 x_2 x_3$$

a. Use a statistical software package to fit the model to the data.

b. Is there evidence (at $\alpha = .05$) that the overall model is useful for predicting price (y)?

c. Is there evidence (at $\alpha = .05$) that the linear relationship between price (y) and square footage (x_1) is dependent on the yearly property taxes (x_3)?

d. Conduct a residual analysis for the model. Identify any outliers in the data and any assumptions that may be violated.

11.57 **(X11.057)** In the oil industry, water mixes with crude oil during production and transportation resulting in tiny oil particles suspended within the water. This water and oil (w/o) suspension is called an emulsion. Chemists have found that the oil can be extracted from the w/o emulsion electrically. Researchers at the University of Bergen (Norway) conducted a series of experiments to study the factors that influence the voltage required to separate the water from the oil in w/o emulsions (*Journal of Colloid and Interface Science*, Aug. 1995). The seven independent variables investigated in the study are described here. Each variable was measured at two levels—a "low" level and a "high" level.

x_1: Volume fraction of disperse phase (as a percentage of weight); Low = 40%, High = 80%

x_2: Salinity of emulsion (as a percentage of weight); Low = 1%, High = 4%

x_3: Temperature of emulsion (in °C); Low = 4°, High = 23°

x_4: Time delay after emulsification (in hours); Low = .25 hour, High = 24 hours

x_5: Concentration of surface-active agent, or "surfactant" (as a percentage of weight); Low = 2%, High = 4%

x_6: Ratio of two chemicals (Span and Triton) used as surfactants; Low = .25, High = .75

x_7: Amount of solid particles added (as a percentage of weight); Low = .5%, High = 2%

Sixteen w/o emulsions were prepared using different combinations of the independent variables listed above; then each emulsion was exposed to a high electric field. In addition, three w/o emulsions were tested when all independent variables were set to 0. For all 19 emulsions, the amount of voltage (Kilovolts per centimeter) where the first sign of macroscopic activity is observed was measured; this value represents the dependent variable, y. The data for the study are provided in the table.

a. Propose a model for y as a function of all seven independent variables. Assume that a linear relationship exists between y and x_i, $i = 1, 2, ..., 7$.

b. Use a statistical software package to fit the model to the data in the table.

Experiment Number	Voltage y	Disperse Phase Volume x_1	Salinity x_2	Temperature x_3	Time Delay x_4	Surfactant Concentration x_5	S:T Ratio x_6	Solid Particles x_7
1	.64	40	1	4	.25	2	.25	.5
2	.80	80	1	4	.25	4	.25	2
3	3.20	40	4	4	.25	4	.75	.5
4	.48	80	4	4	.25	2	.75	2
5	1.72	40	1	23	.25	4	.75	2
6	.32	80	1	23	.25	2	.75	.5
7	.64	40	4	23	.25	2	.25	2
8	.68	80	4	23	.25	4	.25	.5
9	.12	40	1	4	24	2	.75	2
10	.88	80	1	4	24	4	.75	.5
11	2.32	40	4	4	24	4	.25	2
12	.40	80	4	4	24	2	.25	.5
13	1.04	40	1	23	24	4	.25	.5
14	.12	80	1	23	24	2	.25	2
15	1.28	40	4	23	24	2	.75	.5
16	.72	80	4	23	24	4	.75	2
17	1.08	0	0	0	0	0	0	0
18	1.08	0	0	0	0	0	0	0
19	1.04	0	0	0	0	0	0	0

Source: Førdedal, H., *et al.* "A multivariate analysis of W/O emulsions in high external electric fields as studied by means of dielectric time domain spectroscopy." *Journal of Colloid and Interface Science*, Vol. 173, No. 2, August 1995, p. 398 (Table 2).

c. Fully interpret the results of the regression. Part of the analysis should include an interpretation of the β estimates.

d. According to the researchers, the model predicts a negative value for the voltage y for experiment #14. Verify this result.

e. The researchers state that the result, part **d**, "is physically not acceptable, and a model with interaction terms must be proposed." The model the researchers selected is

$$E(y) = \beta_0 + \beta_1 x_1 + \beta_2 x_2 + \beta_3 x_5 + \beta_4 x_1 x_2 + \beta_5 x_1 x_5.$$

Note that the model includes interaction between disperse phase volume (x_1) and salinity (x_2) as well as interaction between disperse phase volume (x_1) and surfactant concentration (x_5). Discuss how these interaction terms impact the hypothetical relationship between y and x_1. Draw a sketch to support your answer.

f. Fit the interaction model, part **e**, to the data. Does the model appear to fit the data better than the model, part **a**? Explain.

g. Interpret the β estimates of the interaction model, part **e**.

h. The researchers concluded that "in order to break an emulsion with the lowest possible voltage, the volume fraction of the disperse phase (x_1) should be high, while the salinity (x_2) and the amount of surfactant (x_5) should be low." Use this information and the interaction model to find a 95% prediction interval for this "low" voltage y. Interpret the interval.

11.58 To determine whether extra personnel are needed for the day, the owners of a water adventure park would like to find a model that would allow them to predict the day's attendance each morning before opening based on the day of the week and weather conditions. The model is of the form

$$E(y) = \beta_0 + \beta_1 x_1 + \beta_2 x_2 + \beta_3 x_3$$

where

y = Daily admissions

$x_1 = \begin{cases} 1 & \text{if weekend} \\ 0 & \text{otherwise} \end{cases}$ (dummy variable)

$x_2 = \begin{cases} 1 & \text{if sunny} \\ 0 & \text{if overcast} \end{cases}$ (dummy variable)

x_3 = Predicted daily high temperature (°F)

These data were recorded for a random sample of 30 days, and a regression model was fit to the data. The least squares analysis produced the following results:

$$\hat{y} = -105 + 25x_1 + 100x_2 + 10x_3$$

with

$$s_{\hat{\beta}_1} = 10 \quad s_{\hat{\beta}_2} = 30 \quad s_{\hat{\beta}_3} = 4 \quad R^2 = .65$$

a. Interpret the estimated model coefficients.

b. Is there sufficient evidence to conclude that this model is useful for the prediction of daily attendance? Use $\alpha = .05$.

c. Is there sufficient evidence to conclude that the mean attendance increases on weekends? Use $\alpha = .10$.

d. Use the model to predict the attendance on a sunny weekday with a predicted high temperature of 95°F.

e. Suppose the 90% prediction interval for part **d** is (645, 1,245). Interpret this interval.

11.59 Refer to Exercise 11.58. The owners of the water adventure park are advised that the prediction model could probably be improved if interaction terms were added. In particular, it is thought that the *rate* at which mean attendance increases as predicted high temperature increases will be greater on weekends than on weekdays. The following model is therefore proposed:

$$E(y) = \beta_0 + \beta_1 x_1 + \beta_2 x_2 + \beta_3 x_5 + \beta_4 x_1 x_3$$

The same 30 days of data used in Exercise 11.58 are again used to obtain the least squares model

$$\hat{y} = 250 - 700x_1 + 100x_2 + 5x_3 + 15x_1 x_3$$

with

$$s_{\hat{\beta}_4} = 3.0 \quad R^2 = .96$$

a. Graph the predicted day's attendance, y, against the day's predicted high temperature, x_3, for a sunny weekday and for a sunny weekend day. Plot both on the same paper for x_3 between 70 and 100°F. Note the increase in slope for the weekend day. Interpret this.

b. Do the data indicate that the interaction term is a useful addition to the model? Use $\alpha = .05$.

c. Use this model to predict the attendance for a sunny weekday with a predicted high temperature of 95°F.

d. Suppose the 90% prediction interval for part **c** is (800, 850). Compare this result with the prediction interval for the model without interaction in Exercise 11.58, part **e**. Do the relative widths of the confidence intervals support or refute your conclusion about the utility of the interaction term (part **b**)?

e. The owners, noting that the coefficient $\hat{\beta}_1 = -700$, conclude the model is ridiculous because it seems to imply that the mean attendance will be 700 less on weekends than on weekdays. Explain why this is *not* the case.

11.60 **(X11.060)** Many colleges and universities develop regression models for predicting the GPA of incoming freshmen. This predicted GPA can then be used to make admission decisions. Although most models use many independent variables to predict GPA, we will illustrate by choosing two variables:

x_1 = Verbal score on college entrance examination (percentile)

x_2 = Mathematics score on college entrance examination (percentile)

The data in the table are obtained for a random sample of 40 freshmen at one college. The SPSS printout corresponding to the model $y = \beta_0 + \beta_1 x_1 + \beta_2 x_2 + \epsilon$ is shown below.

a. Interpret the least squares estimates $\hat{\beta}_1$ and $\hat{\beta}_2$ in the context of this application.

b. Interpret the standard deviation and the coefficient of determination of the regression model in the context of this application.

c. Is this model useful for predicting GPA? Conduct a statistical test to justify your answer.

d. Sketch the relationship between predicted GPA, $\hat{y}$, and verbal score, x_1, for the following mathematics scores: $x_2 = 60, 75,$ and 90.

11.61 Refer to Exercise 11.60. The residuals from the first-order model are plotted against x_1 and x_2. Analyze the two plots shown on page 572, and determine whether visual evidence exists that curvature (a quadratic term) for either x_1 or x_2 should be added to the model.

Verbal x_1	Mathematics x_2	GPA y	Verbal x_1	Mathematics x_2	GPA y	Verbal x_1	Mathematics x_2	GPA y
81	87	3.49	83	76	3.75	97	80	3.27
68	99	2.89	64	66	2.70	77	90	3.47
57	86	2.73	83	72	3.15	49	54	1.30
100	49	1.54	93	54	2.28	39	81	1.22
54	83	2.56	74	59	2.92	87	69	3.23
82	86	3.43	51	75	2.48	70	95	3.82
75	74	3.59	79	75	3.45	57	89	2.93
58	98	2.86	81	62	2.76	74	67	2.83
55	54	1.46	50	69	1.90	87	93	3.84
49	81	2.11	72	70	3.01	90	65	3.01
64	76	2.69	54	52	1.48	81	76	3.33
66	59	2.16	65	79	2.98	84	69	3.06
80	61	2.60	56	78	2.58			
100	85	3.30	98	67	2.73			

```
Multiple R              .82527
R Square                .68106
Adjusted R Square       .66382
Standard Error          .40228

Analysis of Variance
                  DF      Sum of Squares      Mean Square
Regression         2          12.78595           6.39297
Residual          37           5.98755            .16183

F =     39.50530     Signif F =   .0000

------------------Variables in the Equation--------------------

Variable            B          SE B         Beta          T    Sig T

X1             .02573  4.02357E-03        .59719      6.395   .0000
X2             .03361  4.92751E-03        .63702      6.822   .0000
(Constant)   -1.57054        .49375                  -3.181   .0030
```

11.62 Refer to Exercises 11.60 and 11.61. The complete second-order model

$$y = \beta_0 + \beta_1 x_1 + \beta_2 x_2 + \beta_3 x_1^2 + \beta_4 x_2^2 + \beta_5 x_1 x_2 + \epsilon$$

is fit to the data given in Exercise 11.60. The resulting SPSS printout is shown at the top of page 573.

a. Compare the standard deviations of the first-order and second-order regression models. With what relative precision will these two models predict GPA?

b. Test whether this model is useful for predicting GPA. Use $\alpha = .05$.

```
Multiple R              .96777
R Square                .93657
Adjusted R Square       .92724
Standard Error          .18714

Analysis of Variance
                    DF      Sum of Squares      Mean Square
Regression           5          17.58274          3.51655
Residual            34           1.19076           .03502

F =     100.40901      Signif F =   .0000

------------------Variables in the Equation------------------

Variable            B           SE B         Beta          T    Sig T
X1               .16681         .02124     3.87132      7.852    .0000
X2               .13760         .02673     2.60754      5.147    .0000
X1SQ       -1.10825E-03   1.17288E-04    -3.71359     -9.449    .0000
X2SQ       -8.43267E-04   1.59423E-04    -2.37284     -5.290    .0000
X1X2       2.410891E-04   1.43974E-04      .49600      1.675    .1032
(Constant)     -9.91676       1.35441                 -7.322    .0000
```

c. Test whether the interaction term, $\beta_5 x_1 x_2$, is important for the prediction of GPA. Use $\alpha = .10$.

11.63 Refer to Exercises 11.60 and 11.61. The residuals of the second-order model are plotted against x_1 and x_2 below and at the top of page 574. Compare the residual plots to those of the first-order model in Exercises 11.60 and 11.61. Which of the two models do you think is preferable as a predictor of GPA: the first- or second-order model? [*Note:* In Chapter 12 we show how to conduct a statistical test to compare two models.]

11.64 **(X11.064)** An economist is interested in estimating the demand function for passenger car motor fuel in the United States. While demand is clearly a function of many variables, the economist

40 cases plotted.

initially wants to model demand as a function of consumer income and the price of gasoline and plans to estimate the model using yearly time series data over the period 1970–1993. The measure of income will be the average gross weekly earnings per year for production or nonsupervisory workers on private nonagricultural payrolls. These data are available from the Bureau of Labor Statistics (BLS). However, since both earnings and the cost of living increased over this period, the BLS earnings data do not reflect actual purchasing power. Accordingly, the earnings data—originally expressed in *current dollars* (i.e., the number of dollars actually earned)—are converted to 1982 dollars by dividing each figure by the Consumer Price Index (CPI) for that year and multiplying the result by 100. (This procedure is described in detail in Chapter 14.) The resulting earnings data—called *real earnings*—are the number of dollars that would have been earned in 1982 to equal the purchasing power of current-year weekly earnings. These data appear at the top of page 575. Data on the actual price of gasoline and the relative price of gasoline (the CPI for gasoline divided by the CPI for all items) also appear in the table. The *relative price* data reflect the price of gasoline relative to the prices of other consumer goods. The economist believes the relative price may have a substantial influence on demand. For example, even though actual gasoline prices increase, consumers may

actually increase their demand for gasoline if the relative price decreases. Finally, data are collected on motor fuel consumed per year and the population of the United States. The population data are included so that the effects of the growing U.S. population on demand for motor fuel can be removed if desired. This is done by dividing the total motor fuel consumed in a year by the population that year. The result is called *per capita* motor fuel consumption. By using per capita consumption as the measure of demand, the economist can distinguish the effects on demand of factors such as price and income from the effects of population growth.

a. Explain what is being measured by the yearly per capita motor fuel consumption variable.

b. Initially, the economist hypothesizes that per capita motor fuel consumption is a linear function of the relative price of gasoline. Use the method of least squares to estimate this model.

c. Investigate the usefulness of the preliminary model. Use $\alpha = .05$. Also, find R^2.

d. Next, the economist would like to expand the model described in part **b** to include a second independent variable, average gross real weekly earnings. Use the method of least squares to fit this expanded model.

e. Investigate the usefulness of the expanded model of part **d**. Use $\alpha = .05$. Also, find R^2.

f. From an economic (or intuitive) perspective, do the signs of the estimated coefficients of the

Year	Car Fuel Consumed (billion gals.)	U.S. Population (millions)	Average Gross Real Weekly Earnings (1982 $)	Price of Regular Gasoline ($/gal.)	Relative Price of Gasoline
1970	67.8	205.1	308.84	.36	.689
1971	69.5	207.1	314.35	.36	.672
1972	73.5	209.9	327.51	.37	.641
1973	78.0	211.9	327.45	.40	.633
1974	74.2	213.9	313.91	.53	.786
1975	76.5	216.0	303.96	.57	.794
1976	78.8	218.0	308.35	.59	.775
1977	80.7	220.2	311.88	.62	.763
1978	83.8	222.6	312.42	.63	.715
1979	80.2	225.1	302.91	.86	.852
1980	71.9	227.7	285.32	1.19	1.074
1981	71.0	230.0	280.75	1.31	1.125
1982	70.1	232.3	276.95	1.22	1.033
1983	69.9	234.5	281.83	1.24	.998
1984	68.7	236.3	281.87	1.21	.942
1985	69.3	238.5	277.96	1.20	.917
1986	71.4	240.7	278.15	.93	.703
1987	70.6	242.8	275.09	.95	.706
1988	71.9	245.0	272.21	.95	.683
1989	72.7	247.3	269.55	1.02	.713
1990	72.0	249.9	264.23	1.16	.774
1991	70.7	252.6	259.90	1.14	.729
1992	73.9	255.4	259.17	1.12	.705
1993	75.1	258.1	258.57	1.10	.678

Sources: U.S. Bureau of the Census, *Statistical Abstract of the United States,* various years; average gross real weekly earnings from U.S. Department of Labor, Bureau of Labor Statistics, *Employment and Earnings,* December 1996.

expanded model seem to be appropriate? Explain.

g. Using the expanded model, estimate the mean per capita demand for motor fuel when average gross weekly earnings are $340.24 and the relative price of a gallon of gasoline is 1.201. What reservations (if any) do you have about the goodness of your estimate?

h. Calculate the residuals of the expanded model, and plot them against both independent variables. Check for evidence of curvature and for outliers.

i. Note that the data for the study is time series data. Which regression assumption is likely to be violated with time series data? Why?

CHAPTER 12

MODEL BUILDING

CONTENTS

STATISTICS IN ACTION

Where We've Been

One of the most important topics in applied statistics—regression analysis—was presented in the last two chapters. Simple linear regression was the topic of Chapter 10, while multiple regression was the topic of Chapter 11. In both chapters, we learned how to fit regression models to a set of data and how to use the model to estimate the mean value of y or to predict a future value of y for a given value of x.

Where We're Going

Although we discussed, in general, how to use regression analysis to solve many practical problems, we skipped over one important problem—how to select a model that is appropriate for the given data. No matter how much you know about regression analysis, or how well you can fit a model to a set of data and interpret the results, the information will be of little value if you choose an inappropriate model. In this chapter, then, we take up the topic of model building, in which we choose a reasonable model and use the data to modify and improve it.

As indicated in Chapters 10 and 11, the first step in the construction of a regression model is to hypothesize the form of the deterministic portion of the probabilistic model. This *model building,* or model construction, is the key to the success (or failure) of the regression analysis. If the regression model does not reflect, at least approximately, the true nature of the relationship between the mean response $E(y)$ and the independent variables $x_1, x_2, ..., x_k$, the modeling effort will usually be unrewarded.

12.1 INTRODUCTION

By **model building**, we mean developing a model that provides a good fit to a set of data, giving good estimates of the mean value of y and good predictions of future values of y for given values of the independent variables. Suppose, for example, you wish to relate an employee's performance rating y to years of experience x and that (unknown to you) the second-order model

$$E(y) = \beta_0 + \beta_1 x + \beta_2 x^2$$

would permit you to predict y with a very small error of prediction (see Figure 12.1a). But suppose you erroneously choose the first-order model

$$E(y) = \beta_0 + \beta_1 x$$

to explain the relationship between y and x; see Figure 12.1b.

The consequence of choosing the wrong model is clearly demonstrated by comparing Figures 12.1a and 12.1b. The errors of prediction for the second-order model in Figure 12.1a are relatively small in comparison to those for the first-order model shown in Figure 12.1b. The lesson to be learned from this simple example is very clear. Choosing a good set of independent (predictor) variables $x_1, x_2, ..., x_k$, does not guarantee a good multivariable prediction equation. In addition to selecting independent variables that contain information about y, you must also develop an equation relating y to $x_1, x_2, ..., x_k$ that will provide a good fit to your data.

In the following sections, we present several useful models for relating a response y to one or more predictor variables. In addition, we provide tests and procedures for determining which model is appropriate.

FIGURE 12.1

Two models for relating performance rating y to experience x

a. Second-order model

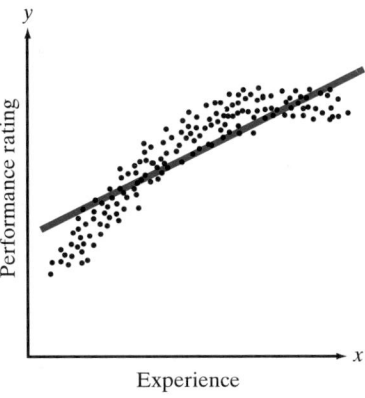

b. First-order model

12.2 THE TWO TYPES OF INDEPENDENT VARIABLES: QUANTITATIVE AND QUALITATIVE

In Chapter 1 we defined two types of data and, correspondingly, two types of variables that may be observed: quantitative and qualitative. In a regression analysis the dependent variable is always quantitative, but the independent variables may be either quantitative or qualitative. As you will see, the way in which an independent variable enters the model depends on its type.

Recall from Chapter 1 that quantitative variables are measured on a natural numerical scale, whereas qualitative variables are measured on a nonnumerical (categorical) scale. Thus, the Gross Domestic Product, prime interest rate, number of defects in a product, and kilowatt-hours of electricity used per day are all examples of quantitative variables. On the other hand, the gender, race, job title, and style of packaging are all examples of qualitative variables.

Quantitative variables always assume numerical values, whereas qualitative variables usually assume nonnumerical values. The possible values of independent variables are also referred to as *levels*. For example, the style of packaging might have three possible levels: A, B, and C. And even if we designate these values arbitrarily as 1, 2, and 3, the numbers still represent categories and the variable is still qualitative. In addition, a variable we normally think of as quantitative, such as income, can sometimes be reported as a level, say low, medium, or high; this makes the variable qualitative for that application. Thus, the distinction between quantitative and qualitative variables is often a function of the type of information available.

DEFINITION 12.1
The possible values of an independent variable are called its **levels**.

EXAMPLE 12.1

In Chapter 11 we considered the problem of predicting executive salaries as a function of several independent variables. Consider the following four independent variables that may affect executive salaries:

a. Number of years of experience

b. Gender of the employee

c. Firm's net asset value

d. Rank of the employee

For each of these independent variables, give its type and describe the nature of the levels you would expect each to observe.

SOLUTION

a. The independent variable for the number of years of experience is quantitative since its values are numerical. We would expect to observe levels ranging from 0 to 40 (approximately) years.

b. The independent variable for gender is qualitative since its levels can be described only by the nonnumerical labels "female" and "male."

c. The independent variable for the firm's net asset value is quantitative, with a very large number of possible levels corresponding to various firms' net asset values.

d. Suppose the independent variable for the rank of the employee has three possible levels: supervisor, manager, and vice president. Since this is a categorical scale, rank is a qualitative independent variable. ∎

Quantitative independent variables are treated differently from qualitative variables in regression modeling. In the next section, we begin our discussion of how quantitative variables are used.

EXERCISES 12.1–12.6

Applying the Concepts

12.1 Multiple regression was employed to model the difference between the actual number and expected number of industrial plants involved in foreign direct investments (FDIs) in 95 Italian provinces (*Journal of International Business Studies,* Fourth Quarter, 1995). Several of the independent variables considered in the study are listed below. Identify the type (quantitative or qualitative) of each variable.

a. Minimum road distance between the province's capital and Rome/Milan

b. Length of time between year of the first FDI in the province and 1985

c. Percentage of workers employed in industrial plants in the province

d. Whether or not the province borders France or Switzerland

e. Rate of unemployment in the province

f. Ratio of union members to population in the province

g. The product sector (oil, textile, etc.) with the most FDIs in the province

12.2 *New Scientist* (Apr. 3, 1993) published an article on strategies for foiling assassination attempts on politicians. The strategies are based on the findings of researchers at Middlesex University (United Kingdom), who used a multiple regression model for predicting the level *y* of assassination risk. Several of the variables used in the model are listed below. Identify each variable as quantitative or qualitative.

a. Number of potential assailants

b. Frequency of exposure (hours per day)

c. Probability that the assailant will succeed in inflicting injury

d. Economic status of country

e. Political status of country

12.3 An Educational Testing Service (ETS) research scientist used multiple regression analysis to model the final grade point average (GPA) of business and management doctoral students (*Journal of Educational Statistics,* Spring 1993). A list of the potential independent variables measured for each doctoral student in the study is given below.

1. Quantitative Graduate Management Aptitude Test (GMAT) score
2. Verbal GMAT score
3. Undergraduate GPA
4. First-year graduate GPA
5. Student cohort (i.e., year in which student entered doctoral program: 1977, 1979, 1981, 1983, or 1985)

a. Identify the variables as quantitative or qualitative.

b. For each quantitative variable, give your opinion on whether the variable is positively or negatively related to final GPA.

c. As we will learn (in Section 12.6), if a qualitative variable is an important predictor of *y*, each level of the variable yields a different value of $E(y)$. For each of the qualitative variables identified in part **a**, determine the number of different mean GPAs that are possible.

12.4 J. R. Rinehart and J. J. Pompe, a pair of Francis Marion University (South Carolina) professors, used multiple regression to model the selling price (*y*) of a home located on the South Carolina coast (*Appraisal Journal,* Oct. 1994). Several of the independent variables employed in the model are listed below. Determine the type (qualitative or quantitative) of each. For quantitative variables, give reasonable units of measurement (e.g., feet, dollars); for qualitative variables, list the response categories.

a. Age of the house b. Living space in the house

c. Number of bathrooms d. View of the ocean

e. Distance to the nearest beach

f. Sold after or before Hurricane Hugo

12.5 *Benefits Quarterly* (First Quarter, 1995) published a study of entry-level job preferences. A number of independent variables were used to model the job preferences (measured on a 10-point scale) of 164 business school graduates. Identify each independent variable as quantitative or qualitative.

a. Flextime of the position applied for (yes/no)

b. Level of day care support required (none, referral, or on-premise)

c. Spousal transfer support required (none, counseling, or active search)

d. Number of days allowed for family sick leave

e. Marital status of applicant

f. Number of children of applicant

g. Gender of applicant

12.6 The process of quality planning and control requires a continuous interaction between the customer and the manufacturer. To design, monitor, and control the quality of a product, the manufacturer needs to know which attributes of the product most influence the customer's decisions to buy and use the product (Schroeder, *Operations Management: Decision Making in the Operating Function*, 1993). The following quality attributes were identified for a product:

a. Weight **b.** Color

c. Age **d.** Hardness

e. Package design

Regression analysis can be used to explore the relationship between these variables and sales of the product. Classify each of the variables as quantitative or qualitative and describe the levels that the variables may assume.

12.3 MODELS WITH A SINGLE QUANTITATIVE INDEPENDENT VARIABLE

The most common linear models relating y to a single quantitative independent variable x are those derived from a **pth-order polynomial** expression of the type shown in the accompanying box. Specific models, obtained by assigning values to p, are listed next.

Formula for a pth-Order Polynomial with One Independent Variable

$$E(y) = \beta_0 + \beta_1 x + \beta_2 x^2 + \beta_3 x^3 + \cdots + \beta_p x^p$$

where p is an integer and $\beta_0, \beta_1, ..., \beta_p$ are unknown parameters that must be estimated.

---

1. FIRST-ORDER MODEL

$$E(y) = \beta_0 + \beta_1 x \qquad \text{(Figure 12.2)}$$

Comments on model parameters

β_0: y-intercept

β_1: Slope of the line

General comments The first-order model is used when you expect the rate of change in y per unit change in x to remain fairly stable over the range of values of x over which you wish to predict y.* Most relationships between $E(y)$ and x are curvilinear, but the curvature over the range of values of x for which you wish to

FIGURE 12.2
Graph of a first-order model

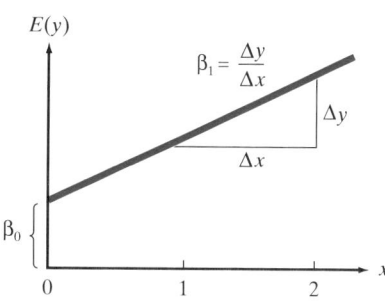

*The symbol Δy represents the change in y corresponding to a change in x equal to Δx.

FIGURE 12.3
Graphs for two
second-order
models

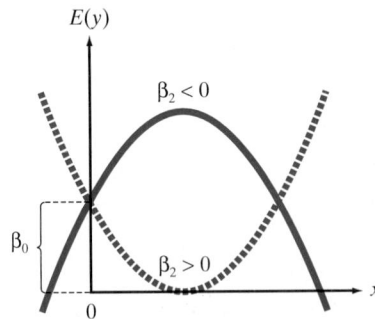

predict y may be very slight. When this occurs, a first-order (straight-line) model should provide a good fit to your data.

2. SECOND-ORDER MODEL

$$E(y) = \beta_0 + \beta_1 x + \beta_2 x^2 \qquad \text{(Figure 12.3)}$$

Comments on model parameters

β_0: y-intercept

β_1: Shift parameter: changing the value of β_1 shifts the parabola to the right or left (increasing the value of β_1 causes the parabola to shift to the left)

β_2: Rate of curvature

General comments A second-order model traces a parabola, one that opens either downward ($\beta_2 < 0$) or upward ($\beta_2 > 0$). Since most relationships possess some curvature, a second-order model is often a good choice to relate y to x.

3. THIRD-ORDER MODEL

$$E(y) = \beta_0 + \beta_1 x + \beta_2 x^2 + \beta_3 x^3 \qquad \text{(Figure 12.4)}$$

Comments on model parameters

β_0: y-intercept

β_3: The magnitude of β_3 controls the rate of reversal of curvature for the curve

General comments Reversals in curvature are not common, but such relationships can be modeled by third- and higher-order polynomials. As can be seen in Figure 12.3, a second-order model contains no reversal in curvature. The slope either continues to increase or continues to decrease as x increases and produces

FIGURE 12.4
Graphs for two third-
order models

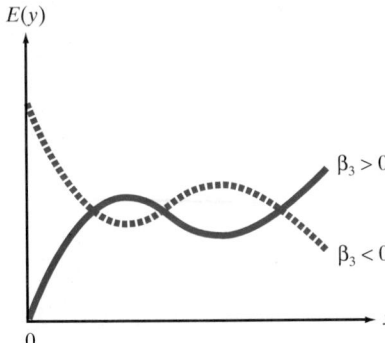

either a trough or a peak. A third-order model (see Figure 12.4) contains one reversal in curvature and produces one peak and one trough. In general, the graph of a kth-order polynomial contains a total of $(k - 1)$ peaks and troughs.

Most functional relationships in nature seem to be smooth (except for random error); that is, they are not subject to rapid and irregular reversals in direction. Consequently, the second-order polynomial model is perhaps the most useful of those described here. To develop a better understanding of how this model is employed, consider the following example.

EXAMPLE 12.2

Power companies have to be able to predict the peak power load at their various stations in order to operate efficiently. The peak power load is the maximum amount of power that must be generated each day in order to meet demand.

Suppose a power company in the southern part of the United States decides to model daily peak power load, y, as a function of the daily high temperature, x, and the model is to be constructed for the summer months when demand is greatest. Although we would expect the peak power load to increase as the high temperature increases, the *rate* of increase in $E(y)$ might also increase as x increases. That is, a 1-unit increase in high temperature from 100 to 101°F might result in a larger increase in power demand than would a 1-unit increase from 80 to 81°F. Therefore, we postulate the second-order model

$$E(y) = \beta_0 + \beta_1 x + \beta_2 x^2$$

and we expect β_2 to be positive.

A random sample of 25 summer days is selected, and the data are shown in Table 12.1. Fit a second-order model using these data, and test the hypothesis that the power load increases at an increasing *rate* with temperature—i.e., that $\beta_2 > 0$.

SOLUTION
The EXCEL printout shown in Figure 12.5 gives the least squares fit of the second-order model using the data in Table 12.1. The estimates of β_0, β_1, and β_2 are highlighted in the **Coefficients** column. After rounding, we obtain the prediction equation

$$\hat{y} = 385.048 - 8.29x + .05982x^2$$

TABLE 12.1   Power Load Data

Temperature (°F)	Peak Load (megawatts)	Temperature (°F)	Peak Load (megawatts)
94	136.0	100	151.9
96	131.7	79	106.2
95	140.7	97	153.2
108	189.3	98	150.1
67	96.5	87	114.7
88	116.4	76	100.9
89	118.5	68	96.3
84	113.4	92	135.1
90	132.0	100	143.6
106	178.2	85	111.4
67	101.6	89	116.5
71	92.5	74	103.9
		86	105.1

SUMMARY OUTPUT

Regression Statistics	
Multiple R	0.979470618
R Square	0.959362691
Adjusted R Square	0.95566839
Standard Error	5.376203469
Observations	25

ANOVA

	df	SS	MS	F	Significance F
Regression	2	15011.772	7505.885999	259.687216	4.99085E-16
Residual	22	635.8784022	28.90356374		
Total	24	15647.6504			

	Coefficients	Standard Error	t Stat	P-value	Lower 95%	Upper 95%
Intercept	385.0480932	55.17243578	6.978993909	5.2661E-07	270.6273418	499.4688447
Temp(x)	-8.292526804	1.29904502	-6.383556132	2.00975E-06	-10.9865418	-5.598469431
TempSq	0.059823368	0.007548554	7.925142711	6.8979E-08	0.04416809	0.075478128

FIGURE 12.5 Portion of the EXCEL printout for the second-order model of Example 12.2

FIGURE 12.6
Plot of the observations
and the second-order
least squares fit,
Example 12.2

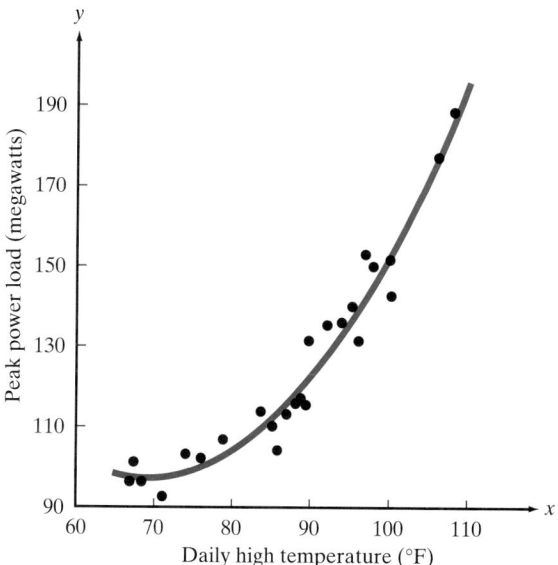

A plot of this equation and the observed values are given in Figure 12.6.

We now test to determine whether the sample value, $\hat{\beta}_2 = .05982$, is large enough to conclude, *in general*, that the power load increases at an increasing rate with temperature:

$$H_0: \beta_2 = 0$$

$$H_a: \beta_2 > 0$$

$$\textit{Test statistic:} \frac{\hat{\beta}_2}{s_{\hat{\beta}_2}} = 7.925 \qquad \text{(highlighted in Figure 12.5)}$$

For $\alpha = .05, n = 25$, and $k = 2$, we will reject H_0 if

$$t > t_{.05}$$

where $t_{.05} = 1.717$ (from Table VI in Appendix B) possesses $n - (k + 1) = 22$ degrees of freedom. Since the test statistic exceeds $t_{.05} = 1.717$, we reject H_0 and conclude that the mean power load increases at an increasing rate with temperature. From Figure 12.5, the observed significance level (highlighted) of the upper-tailed test is $p = .000000069/2 \approx 0$, which supports our conclusion.*

*EXCEL uses E-notation to represent extremely large or small numbers on the printout. For example, "E−08" requires the user to move the decimal point 8 places to the left. Similarly, "E+05" requires the user to move the decimal 5 places to the right.

EXERCISES   12.7–12.20

Note: Exercises marked with 💾 *contain data for computer analysis on a 3.5" disk (file name in parentheses).*

Learning the Mechanics

12.7   The accompanying graphs depict pth-order polynomials with one independent variable. For each graph, identify the order of the polynomial. Find the value of β_0 and β_1 for each.

a. $E(y)$

b. $E(y)$

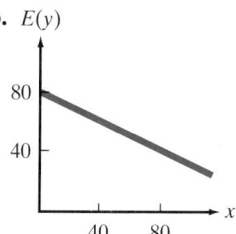

12.8 The accompanying graphs depict pth-order polynomials for one independent variable. For each graph, identify the order of the polynomial, the value of β_0, and the sign of β_2.

a. $E(y)$

b. $E(y)$
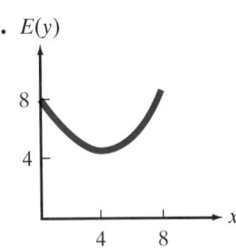

12.9 Graph the following polynomials and identify the order of each on your graph:
a. $E(y) = 2 + 3x$ **b.** $E(y) = 2 + 3x^2$
c. $E(y) = 1 + 2x + 2x^2 + x^3$
d. $E(y) = 2x + 2x^2 + x^3$
e. $E(y) = 2 - 3x^2$ **f.** $E(y) = -2 + 3x$

12.10 The following graphs depict pth-order polynomials for one independent variable:

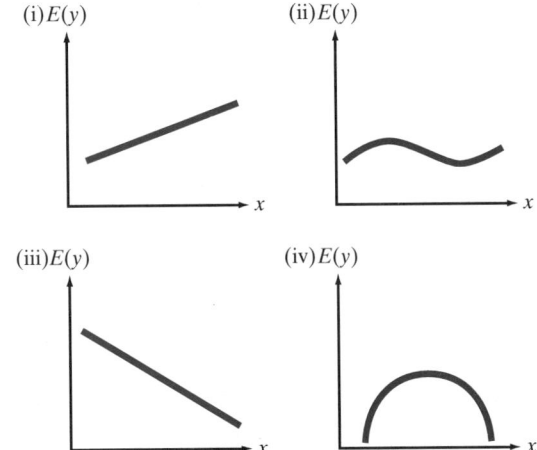

(i)$E(y)$ (ii)$E(y)$ (iii)$E(y)$ (iv)$E(y)$

a. For each graph, identify the order of the polynomial.
b. Using the parameters, β_0, β_1, β_2, etc., write an appropriate model relating $E(y)$ to x for each graph.
c. By examining the graphs, you can determine the signs ($+$ or $-$) of many of the parameters in the models of part **b**. Give the signs of those parameters that can be determined.

12.11 MINITAB was used to fit the model
$$y = \beta_0 + \beta_1 x + \beta_2 x^2 + \epsilon$$
to $n = 17$ data points. The printout is shown below.
a. Identify the least squares prediction equation on the printout.
b. Plot the prediction equation.
c. Specify the null and alternative hypotheses you would use to determine whether y decreases at an increasing rate as x increases.
d. Conduct the hypothesis test of part **c** using $\alpha = .05$. Interpret your result.

12.12 Suppose $E(y)$ can best be modeled by a second-order polynomial in x, where x is a quantitative variable. Write the probabilistic model for y.

Applying the Concepts

12.13 A company that sells and services copy machines conducted a study to relate the number of service calls per month required for a particular brand of table-top copier to the age of the copier (in months). All copiers used in the study were utilized by their owners to produce between 10,000 and 12,000 copies per month. The company suspects that new and old copiers require more service calls than those of middle age.
a. Based on this information, propose an appropriate model relating the mean number of service calls per month to the copier's age. Define all variables in your proposed model.

```
The regression equation is
Y = 63.1 + 1.17 X - 0.0374 XX

Predictor      Coef      Stdev    t-ratio        p
Constant      63.11      11.92       5.30    0.000
X            1.1683     0.8276       1.41    0.148
XX         -0.03742    0.01234      -3.03    0.005

s = 9.289     R-sq = 86.0%     R-sq(adj) = 84.0%

Analysis of Variance

SOURCE      DF        SS         MS        F        p
Regression   2    7434.4     3717.2    43.08    0.000
Error       14    1208.1       86.3
Total       16    8642.5
```

b. Indicate whether you think β_0 and β_2 assume positive or negative values, and explain the reasons for your decisions.

12.14 After spillage, light crude oil and refined oil can lose up to 75% of their volume to evaporation. Consequently, an understanding of the evaporation process is important for cleaning up oil spills. The *Journal of Hazardous Materials* (July 1995) presented a literature review of models designed to predict oil spill evaporation. One of the models presented is the polynomial model

$$E(y) = \beta_0 + \beta_1 x + \beta_2 x^2 + \beta_3 x^3$$

where y represents an oil spill variable and x represents the equivalent paraffin carbon number (that is, the number of carbon atoms characteristic of the type of oil).

a. What is the order of the polynomial model?

b. Give a rough sketch of the relationship between y and x hypothesized by the model.

c. Explain how you could determine whether the cubic term, x^3, is necessary in the model.

12.15 The amount of pressure used to produce a certain plastic is thought to be related to the strength of the plastic. Researchers hypothesize that, below a certain level, increases in pressure increase the strength of the plastic; at some point, however, additional increases in pressure will have a detrimental effect on its strength. Write a model in which the relationship of the plastic strength y to pressure x reflects this hypothesis. Sketch the model.

12.16 **(X12.016)** In early 1994, a chilled orange juice warehousing operation in New York City was experiencing too many out-of-stock situations with its 96-ounce containers. To better understand current and future demand for this product, the company examined the last 40 days of sales, which are shown in the table. One of the company's objectives is to model demand, y, as a function of sale day, x (where $x = 1, 2, 3, ..., 40$).

a. Construct a scatterplot for these data.

b. Does it appear that a second- or third-order model might better explain the variation in demand than a first-order model? Explain.

c. Fit a first-order model to these data.

d. Fit a second-order model to these data.

e. Fit a third-order model to these data.

f. Compare the results in parts **c**, **d**, and **e** and decide which model better explains variation in demand. Justify your choice.

12.17 A company is considering adopting an assembly-line schedule of 4 10-hour days per week instead of 5 8-hour days. However, management believes that the effect of fatigue due to longer afternoons of work might increase assembly times to an

Sale Day x	Demand for 96 oz. Containers y (in cases)
1	4,581
2	4,239
3	2,754
4	4,501
5	4,016
6	4,680
7	4,950
8	3,303
9	2,367
10	3,055
11	4,248
12	5,067
13	5,201
14	5,133
15	4,211
16	3,195
17	5,760
18	5,661
19	6,102
20	6,099
21	5,902
22	2,295
23	2,682
24	5,787
25	3,339
26	3,798
27	2,007
28	6,282
29	3,267
30	4,779
31	9,000
32	9,531
33	3,915
34	8,964
35	6,984
36	6,660
37	6,921
38	10,005
39	10,153
40	11,520

Source: Personal Communication from Rick Campbell, Dave Metzler, and Tom Nelson, Rutgers University, 1994.

unsatisfactory level. An experiment with the 4-day week is planned in which time studies will be conducted on some of the workers during the afternoons. It is believed that an adequate model of the relationship between assembly time, y, and time since lunch, x, should allow for the average assembly time to decrease for a while after lunch (as workers get back in the groove) before it starts to increase as the workers tire.

a. Propose a model to relate $E(y)$ and x that would reflect management's belief. Define all terms in your model.

b. Sketch the shape of the function described by your hypothesized model.

12.18 **(X12.018)** Many studies confirm that manufacturing productivity increases as a result of learning. As more units are produced, the workforce becomes more proficient at the task and each successive unit takes less time to complete, up to a point. Generally, productivity steadily rises following the initiation of a manufacturing process, then levels off and stabilizes. However, some evidence suggests this may not be the case in less developed countries. The table presents data collected on the sacking production of the Victory Jute Mill, Chittagong, Bangladesh, a jute spinning and weaving plant.

Age of Mill (yrs.)	Productivity (kgs./hr.)
2	4.08
3	4.18
4	4.42
5	4.48
6	4.55
7	4.58
8	4.63
9	4.65
10	4.67
11	4.66
12	4.57
13	4.56
14	4.59
15	4.51
16	4.46
22	4.32
23	4.28
24	4.24
25	4.17
26	4.13

Source: Kibria, M., and Tisdell, C. "International comparisons of learning curves and productivity." *Management International Review,* Vol. 25, No. 4, 1985, pp. 66–72.

a. Construct a scattergram for these data. What does your scattergram reveal about the productivity of the mill as it aged?

b. Based on the pattern revealed in your scattergram, propose a model to relate productivity y to the age of the mill x.

c. Fit your model of part **b** to the data. Report the least squares prediction equation and plot it on the scattergram of part **a**.

d. Do the data provide sufficient evidence to conclude that the model proposed in part **b** provides information for the prediction of productivity? Test using $\alpha = .05$.

12.19 An economist has proposed the following model to describe the relationship between the number of items produced per day (output) and the number of work-hours expended per day (input) in a particular production process:

$$y = \beta_0 + \beta_1 x + \beta_2 x^2 + \epsilon$$

where

y = Number of items produced per day

x = Number of work-hours per day

A portion of the MINITAB computer printout that results from fitting this model to a sample of 25 weeks of production data is shown below. Do the data provide sufficient evidence to indicate that the *rate* of increase in output per unit increase of input decreases as the input increases? Test using $\alpha = .05$.

12.20 **(X12.020)** The Federal Reserve System (FRS) was established in 1913 to provide central banking facilities for the United States. It is often referred to as the "banker's bank." One of its major responsibilities is to control the flow of the

```
The regression equation is
Y = -6.17 + 2.04 X - 0.0323 XX

Predictor      Coef      Stdev    t-ratio        p
Constant     -6.173      1.666      -3.71    0.003
X             2.026      0.185      11.02    0.000
XX          -0.03231    0.00489     -6.60    0.000

s = 1.243    R-sq = 95.5%     R-sq(adj) = 95.1%

Analysis of Variance

SOURCE        DF        SS         MS         F        p
Regression     2     718.168    359.084    232.42    0.000
Error         22      33.992      1.545
Total         24     752.160
```

Month	Prime Rate	M1 ($ billions)	Month	Prime Rate	M1 ($ billions)
1/94	6.00	1,132.5	1/95	8.50	1,149.0
2/94	6.00	1,137.0	2/95	8.50	1,147.3
3/94	6.00	1,141.1	3/95	9.00	1,147.9
4/94	6.25	1,142.8	4/95	9.00	1,149.7
5/94	6.75	1,143.5	5/95	9.00	1,143.0
6/94	7.25	1,147.0	6/95	9.00	1,143.9
7/94	7.25	1,152.2	7/95	9.00	1,145.0
8/94	7.25	1,150.8	8/95	8.75	1,143.4
9/94	7.75	1,151.0	9/95	8.75	1,139.8
10/94	7.75	1,148.2	10/95	8.75	1,129.9
11/94	7.75	1,147.6	11/95	8.75	1,126.5
12/94	8.50	1,148.0	12/95	8.75	1,123.0

Source: Economic Report of the President, Feb. 1996, pp. 355, 361.

nation's money supply in order to facilitate orderly economic growth. One way this is done is through buying and selling government securities. The sale of securities to the public draws money from the commercial banking system; the purchase of securities by the FRS from the public moves money into the commercial banking system. This ebb and flow of the money supply affects the level of interest rates (the prices paid for borrowed money) in the economy (Lee, *et al.*, *Foundations of Financial Management*, 1997). Data on the money supply and the prime interest rate are given in the accompanying table. The money supply, M1, is the total sum of all currency, demand deposits, traveler's checks, and other checkable deposits.

a. Construct a scattergram for the data.
b. Based on your observations in part **a**, hypothesize a probabilistic model relating prime interest rate (y) to money supply (x).
c. The SAS computer printout for fitting the model to the data is also shown below. Is there sufficient evidence to indicate that the model provides information for the prediction of y? Test using $\alpha = .05$.
d. Give the observed significance level for the test of part **c**, and interpret it.
e. Does the second-order term contribute information for the prediction of y? Test using $\alpha = .05$.
f. Give the observed significance level for the test of part **e**, and interpret it.

Dependent Variable: PRIMRATE

Analysis of Variance

Source	DF	Sum of Squares	Mean Square	F Value	Prob>F
Model	2	1.73068	0.86534	0.721	0.4979
Error	21	25.20422	1.20020		
C Total	23	26.93490			

Root MSE	1.09554	R-square	0.0643
Dep Mean	7.92708	Adj R-sq	-0.0249
C.V.	13.82018		

Parameter Estimates

Variable	DF	Parameter Estimate	Standard Error	T for HO: Parameter=0	Prob > |T|
INTERCEP	1	5607.767719	4663.6655088	1.202	0.2426
MI	1	-9.837893	8.19361505	-1.201	0.2432
MISQ	1	0.004321	0.00359867	1.201	0.2433

12.4 MODELS WITH TWO OR MORE QUANTITATIVE INDEPENDENT VARIABLES

The best way to understand how to write models relating a mean response $E(y)$ to a set of quantitative independent variables is to examine the different types of models in which only two independent variables are involved. If you can see geometrically (using three-dimensional figures) the relationships implied by these two-variable models, you will more easily understand the relationships in models that contain three or more quantitative independent variables.

1. FIRST-ORDER MODEL WITH TWO INDEPENDENT VARIABLES

$$E(y) = \beta_0 + \beta_1 x_1 + \beta_2 x_2$$

Comments on the parameters

β_0: y-intercept, the value of $E(y)$ when $x_1 = x_2 = 0$

β_1: Change in $E(y)$ for a 1-unit increase in x_1 when x_2 is held fixed

β_2: Change in $E(y)$ for a 1-unit increase in x_2 when x_1 is held fixed

General comments The graph in Figure 12.7 traces a **response surface** [in contrast to the response *curve* that is used to relate $E(y)$ to a single quantitative variable]. Particularly, a first-order model relating $E(y)$ to two independent quantitative variables, x_1 and x_2, graphs as a plane in a three-dimensional space. The plane traces the value of $E(y)$ for every combination of values (x_1, x_2) that correspond to points in the x_1, x_2-plane. Many response surfaces in the real world are well-behaved (i.e., smooth), and they possess curvature. Consequently, a first-order model is appropriate only if the response surface is fairly flat over the (x_1, x_2) region that is of interest.

The assumption that a first-order model will adequately characterize the relationship between $E(y)$ and the variables x_1 and x_2 is equivalent to assuming that x_1 and x_2 do not interact; i.e., you assume that the effect on $E(y)$ of changes in x_1 are the same, regardless of the value of x_2 (and vice versa). Thus, no interaction means that the effect of changes in one variable (say x_1) on $E(y)$ is *independent* of the value of the second variable (say x_2). For example, if we assign values to x_2 in a first-order model, the graph of $E(y)$ as a function of x_1 would produce parallel lines as shown in Figure 12.8. These lines, called **contour lines**, show the contours of the surface when it is sliced by three planes, each of which is parallel to the $E(y), x_1$-plane, at distances $x_2 = 1, 2$, and 3 from the origin.

FIGURE 12.7
Graph of a first-order model

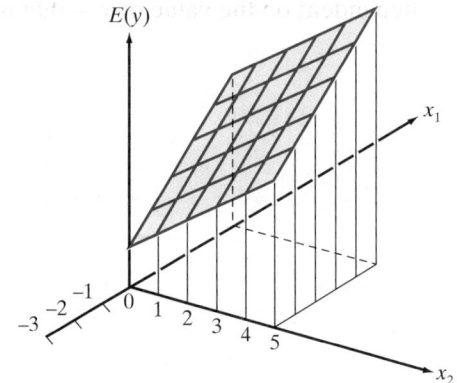

FIGURE 12.8

Graph indicating no interaction between x_1 and x_2

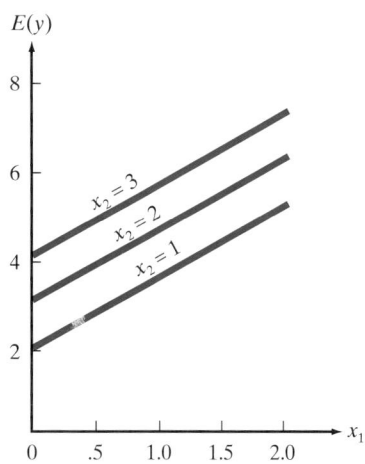

DEFINITION 12.2

Two variables x_1 and x_2 are said to **interact** if the change in $E(y)$ for a 1-unit increase in x_1 (when x_2 is held fixed) is dependent on the value of x_2.

2. INTERACTION MODEL (SECOND-ORDER) WITH TWO INDEPENDENT VARIABLES

$$E(y) = \beta_0 + \beta_1 x_1 + \beta_2 x_2 + \beta_3 x_1 x_2$$

Comments on the parameters

β_0: y-intercept, the value of $E(y)$ when $x_1 = x_2 = 0$

β_1, β_2: Changing β_1 and β_2 causes the surface to shift along the x_1- and x_2-axes

β_3: Controls the rate of twist in the surface (Figure 12.9)

$\beta_1 + \beta_3 x_2$: Change in $E(y)$ for a 1-unit increase in x_1, when x_2 is held fixed

$\beta_2 + \beta_3 x_1$: Change in $E(y)$ for a 1-unit increase in x_2, when x_1 is held fixed

General comments　The model described here is said to be second-order because the highest-order term ($x_1 x_2$) in x_1 and x_2 is of order 2; that is, the sum of the exponents of x_1 and x_2 equals 2.* This interaction model traces a twisted surface in a three-dimensional space (Figure 12.9). A graph of $E(y)$ as a function of x_1 for given values of x_2 (say $x_2 = 1, 2,$ and 3) produces nonparallel contour lines (see Figure 12.10), thus indicating that the change in $E(y)$ for a given change in x_1 is dependent on the value of x_2—that is, x_1 and x_2 interact.

　It is extremely important to keep interaction in mind because it is too easy to get in the habit of fitting first-order models and individually examining the relationships between $E(y)$ and a set of independent variables, $x_1, x_2, \ldots, x_k$. Because such a procedure is meaningless when interaction exists (which is, at least to some extent, almost always the case), it can lead to gross errors in interpretation. For example, suppose the relationship between $E(y)$ and x_1 and x_2 is as shown in Figure 12.10 and you have observed y for each of the $n = 9$ combinations of values of x_1 and $x_2, x_1 = 1, 2, 3$ and $x_2 = 1, 2, 3$. If you were to fit a first-order model

---

*The *order of a term* is equal to the sum of the exponents of the variables included in the term, while the *order of a model* is determined by its highest-order term. Therefore, the interaction model is second-order.

FIGURE 12.9
Graph for an
interaction model
(second-order)

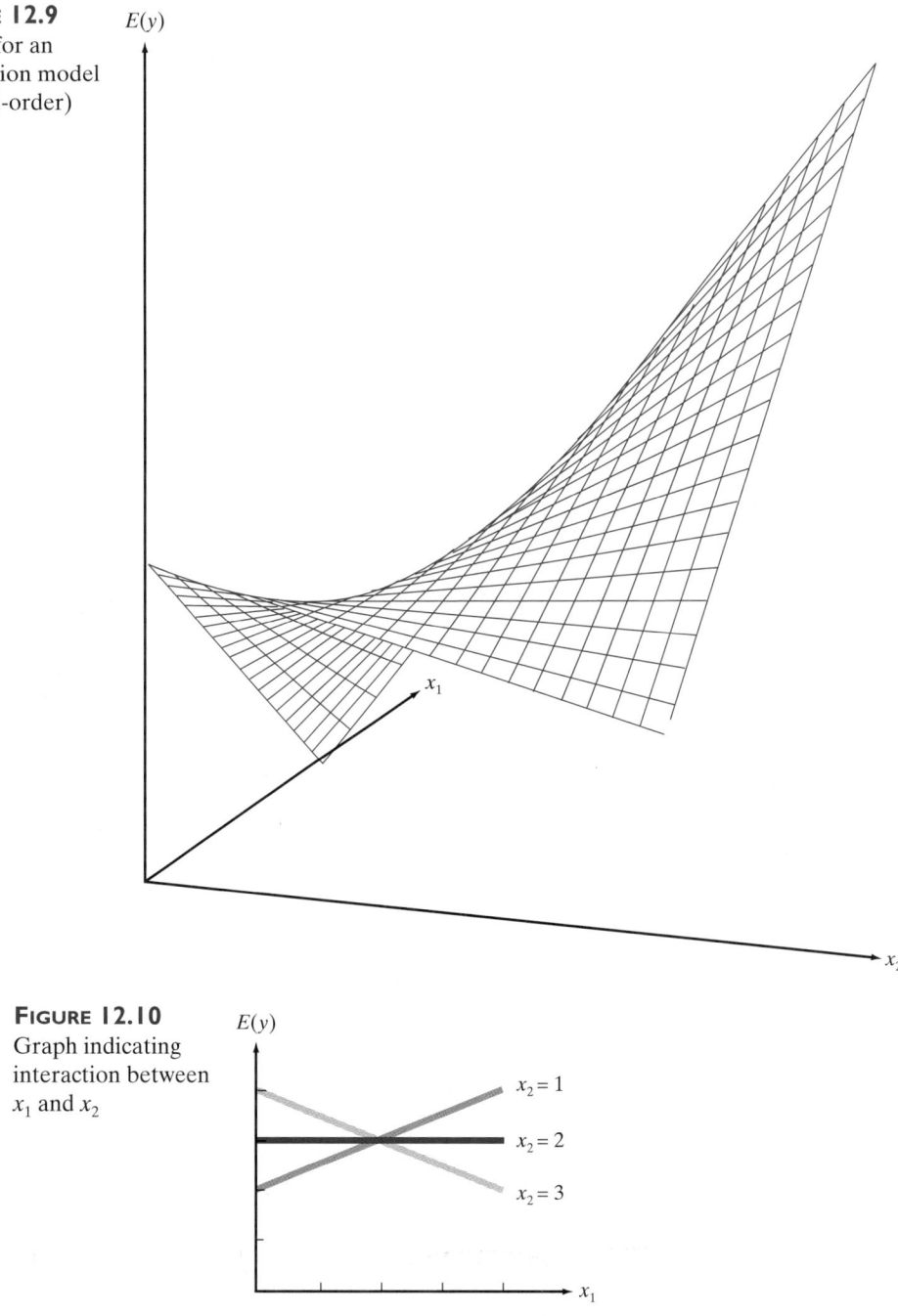

FIGURE 12.10
Graph indicating
interaction between
x_1 and x_2

in x_1 and x_2 to the data, the fitted plane would be (except for random error) approximately parallel to the x_1, x_2-plane, thus suggesting that x_1 and x_2 contribute very little information about $E(y)$. Figure 12.10 clearly indicates that this is not the case. Fitting a first-order model to the data would not allow for the twist in the true surface and would therefore give a false impression of the relationship between $E(y)$ and x_1 and x_2. The procedure for detecting interaction between two independent variables can be seen by examining the model. The interaction model differs from the noninteraction first-order model only in the inclusion of the $\beta_3 x_1 x_2$ term.

Interaction model: $E(y) = \beta_0 + \beta_1 x_1 + \beta_2 x_2 + \beta_3 x_1 x_2$

First-order model: $E(y) = \beta_0 + \beta_1 x_1 + \beta_2 x_2$

Therefore, to test for the presence of interaction we test

$$H_0: \beta_3 = 0 \text{ (No interaction)}$$

against the alternative hypothesis

$$H_a: \beta_3 \neq 0 \text{ (Interaction)}$$

using the familiar Student t-test of Section 11.4.

3. COMPLETE SECOND-ORDER MODEL WITH TWO INDEPENDENT VARIABLES

$$E(y) = \beta_0 + \beta_1 x_1 + \beta_2 x_2 + \beta_3 x_1 x_2 + \beta_4 x_1^2 + \beta_5 x_2^2$$

Comments on the parameters

β_0: y-intercept, the value of $E(y)$ when $x_1 = x_2 = 0$

β_1, β_2: Changing β_1 and β_2 causes the surface to shift along the x_1- and x_2-axes

β_3: Controls the rotation of the surface

β_4, β_5: Signs and values of these parameters control the type of surface and the rates of curvature

Three types of surfaces are produced by a second-order model:* a **paraboloid** that opens upward (Figure 12.11a), a paraboloid that opens downward (Figure 12.11b), and a **saddle-shaped surface** (Figure 12.11c).

General comments   A complete second-order model is the three-dimensional equivalent of a second-order model in a single quantitative variable. Instead of tracing parabolas, it traces paraboloids and saddle surfaces. Since only a portion of the complete surface is used to fit the data, this model provides a very large variety of gently curving surfaces that can be used to fit data. It is a good choice for a model if you expect curvature in the response surface relating $E(y)$ to x_1 and x_2.

FIGURE 12.11
Graphs for three
second-order surfaces

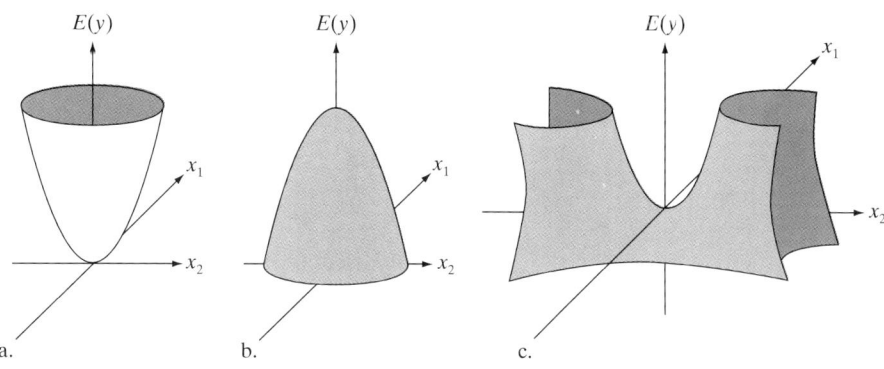

a.   b.   c.

*The saddle-shaped surface (Figure 12.11c) is produced when $\beta_3^2 > 4\beta_4\beta_5$; the paraboloid opens upward (Figure 12.11a) when $\beta_4 + \beta_5 > 0$, and opens downward (Figure 12.11b) when $\beta_4 + \beta_5 < 0$.

EXAMPLE 12.3   An economist would like to relate the number of hours worked per week (outside the home) by a married woman to the number of years of formal education she has completed and the number of children in her family.

a. Identify the dependent variable and the independent variables.
b. Write the first-order model for this example.
c. Modify the model in part **b** to include an interaction term.
d. Write a complete second-order model for $E(y)$.

SOLUTION

a. The dependent variable is

$$y = \text{Number of hours worked per week by a married woman}$$

The two independent variables, both quantitative in nature, are

$$x_1 = \text{Number of years of formal education completed by the woman}$$

$$x_2 = \text{Number of children in the family}$$

b. The first-order model is

$$E(y) = \beta_0 + \beta_1 x_1 + \beta_2 x_2$$

This model would probably not be appropriate in this situation because x_1 and x_2 may interact and/or second-order terms corresponding to x_1^2 and x_2^2 may be needed to obtain a good model for $E(y)$.

c. Adding the interaction term, we obtain

$$E(y) = \beta_0 + \beta_1 x_1 + \beta_2 x_2 + \beta_3 x_1 x_2$$

This model should be better than the model in part **b**, since we have now allowed for interaction between x_1 and x_2.

d. The complete second-order model is

$$E(y) = \beta_0 + \beta_1 x_1 + \beta_2 x_2 + \beta_3 x_1 x_2 + \beta_4 x_1^2 + \beta_5 x_2^2$$

Since it would not be surprising to find curvature in the response surface, the complete second-order model would be preferred to the models in parts **b** and **c**. How can we tell whether the complete second-order model really does provide better predictions of hours worked than the models in parts **b** and **c**? The answers to these and similar questions are examined in Section 12.5. ◾

Models relating a mean response $E(y)$ to more than two quantitative variables are extensions of the corresponding models in two quantitative variables. For example, a first-order model for three quantitative independent variables, $x_1, x_2,$ and $x_3,$ is

$$\textit{First-order model: } E(y) = \beta_0 + \beta_1 x_1 + \beta_2 x_2 + \beta_3 x_3$$

As in the case of two independent variables, this model implies that the relationship between $E(y)$ and any one variable, say x_1, is linear when x_2 and x_3 are held constant. Further, it implies that there is no interaction among $x_1, x_2,$ and x_3; that is, the slope of the linear relation is exactly the same, regardless of the values of x_2 and x_3. If one of the independent variables, say x_3, is held constant, the graph of $E(y)$ as a function of x_1 and x_2 is a plane. (See Figure 12.7.) Thus, for given values of $\beta_0, \beta_1, \beta_2,$ and $\beta_3, E(y)$ will graph as a set of parallel planes, one for each different value of x_3.

Similarly, as in the case of two quantitative independent variables, we can add second-order cross-product terms, $x_1x_2, x_1x_3,$ and x_2x_3, to the first-order model and obtain a second-order model that allows interaction among $x_1, x_2,$ and x_3.

Interaction model: $E(y) = \beta_0 + \beta_1x_1 + \beta_2x_2 + \beta_3x_3 + \beta_4x_1x_2 + \beta_5x_1x_3 + \beta_6x_2x_3$

If one of the independent variables, say x_3, is held constant, the graph of $E(y)$ as a function of x_1 and x_2 is a twisted plane of the type shown in Figure 12.9.

Finally, we could add second-order terms involving $x_1^2, x_2^2,$ and x_3^2 to the interaction model and obtain the complete second-order model:

Complete second-order model: $E(y) = \beta_0 + \beta_1x_1 + \beta_2x_2 + \beta_3x_3 + \beta_4x_1x_2 +$
$$\beta_5x_1x_3 + \beta_6x_2x_3 + \beta_7x_1^2 + \beta_8x_2^2 + \beta_9x_3^2$$

If one of the independent variables, say x_3, is held constant, the graph of $E(y)$ as a function of x_1 and x_2 will trace a conic surface. (See Figure 12.11.)

Most relationships between $E(y)$ and two or more quantitative independent variables are second-order and require the use of either the interactive or the complete second-order model to obtain a good fit to a data set. As in the case of a single quantitative independent variable, however, the curvature in the response surface may be very slight over the range of values of the variables in the data set. When this happens, a first-order model may provide a good fit to the data.

How can you tell which model to use in a particular situation? We answer this question in Section 12.5.

EXERCISES   12.21–12.32

Note: Exercises marked with 💾 *contain data for computer analysis on a 3.5" disk (file name in parentheses).*

Learning the Mechanics

12.21   Consider an application in which you are trying to relate a response y to two independent variables, x_1 and x_2.
a. Write a first-order model relating $E(y)$ to x_1 and x_2.
b. Modify the model you constructed in part **a** to include an interaction term.
c. Modify the model you constructed in part **b** to make it a complete second-order model.

12.22   Suppose the true relationship between $E(y)$ and the quantitative independent variables x_1 and x_2 is described by the first-order model
$$E(y) = 4 - x_1 + 2x_2$$
a. Describe the corresponding response surface.
b. Plot the contour lines of the response surface for $x_1 = 2, 3, 4$, where $0 \le x_2 \le 5$.
c. Plot the contour lines of the response surface for $x_2 = 2, 3, 4$, where $0 \le x_1 \le 5$.

d. Use the contour lines you plotted in parts **b** and **c** to explain how changes in the settings of x_1 and x_2 affect $E(y)$.
e. Use your graph from part **b** to determine how much $E(y)$ changes when x_1 is changed from 4 to 2 and x_2 is simultaneously changed from 1 to 2.

12.23   Suppose the true relationship between $E(y)$ and the quantitative independent variables x_1 and x_2 is
$$E(y) = 4 - x_1 + 2x_2 + x_1x_2$$
a. Describe the corresponding response surface.
b. Plot the contour lines of the response surface for $x_1 = 0, 1, 2$, where $0 \le x_2 \le 5$.
c. Explain why the contour lines you plotted in part **b** are not parallel.
d. Use the contour lines you plotted in part **b** to explain how changes in the settings of x_1 and x_2 affect $E(y)$.
e. Use your graph from part **b** to determine how much $E(y)$ changes when x_1 is changed from 2 to 0 and x_2 is simultaneously changed from 4 to 5.

```
The regression equation is
Y  = -2.55 + 3.82 X1 + 2.63 X2 - 1.29 X1X2

Predictor        Coef        Stdev       t-ratio          p
Constant       -2.550        1.142         -2.23       0.043
X1              3.815        0.529          7.22       0.000
X2              2.630        0.344          7.64       0.000
X1X2           -1.285        0.159         -8.06       0.000

s = 0.713      R-sq = 85.6%    R-sq(adj) = 81.6%

Analysis of Variance

SOURCE          DF          SS          MS          F          p
Regression       3       33.149      11.050      21.75      0.000
Error           11        5.587       0.508
Total           14       38.736
```

12.24 If two variables, x_1 and x_2, do not interact, how would you describe their effect on the mean response $E(y)$?

12.25 The above MINITAB printout provides the results of the model

$$y = \beta_0 + \beta_1 x_1 + \beta_2 x_2 + \beta_3 x_1 x_2 + \epsilon$$

fit to $n = 15$ data points.

a. What is the prediction equation for the response surface?

b. Describe the geometric form of the response surface of part **a**.

c. Plot the prediction equation for the case when $x_2 = 1$. Do this twice more on the same graph for the cases when $x_2 = 3$ and $x_2 = 5$.

d. Explain what it means to say that x_1 and x_2 interact. Explain why your graph of part **c** suggests that x_1 and x_2 interact.

e. Specify the null and alternative hypotheses you would use to test whether x_1 and x_2 interact.

f. Conduct the hypothesis test of part **e** using $\alpha = .01$.

Applying the Concepts

12.26 The Department of Energy (DOE) wants to develop a regression model to help forecast annual gasoline consumption in the United States, y. It decides to model $E(y)$ as a function of two independent variables:

x_1 = Number of cars (millions) in use during year

x_2 = Number of trucks (millions) in use during year

a. Identify the independent variables as quantitative or qualitative.

b. Write the first-order model for $E(y)$.

c. Write the complete second-order model for $E(y)$.

d. Write a model for $E(y)$ that hypothesizes (i) that the relationships are linear and (ii) that the relationship between gas consumption y and number of cars x_1 depends on number of trucks x_2.

12.27 Refer to the *Journal of Hazardous Materials* study of oil spill evaporation, Exercise 12.14. Another model discussed in the article used boiling point (x_1) and API specific gravity (x_2) to predict molecular weight (y) of oil that is spilled. A complete second-order model for y was proposed.

a. Write the equation of the model.

b. Identify the terms in the model that allow for curvilinear relationships.

12.28 Do managers who actively participate in their firm's budget decisions perform better than those who do not? A field study was undertaken to examine the relationship between budgetary participation and managerial performance (*Accounting and Business Research*, Spring 1995). The dependent variable, managerial performance (y), was measured using a self-evaluation questionnaire that asked managers to rate (on a 9-point scale) their own perceived performance. The independent variable, budgetary participation (x_1), measured (on a 7-point scale) the amount of influence and involvement a manager had on a jointly set budget.

a. One theory suggests that managerial performance is positively linearly related to budgetary participation. Hypothesize a model that corresponds to this theory. What are the expected signs of the β coefficients in the model?

b. Another theory suggests that the level of decentralization at a firm moderates the budgetary participation–performance relationship. Specifically, the theory states that participation and performance are positively linearly related in decentralized firms and negatively related in centralized firms. Hypothesize a model that corresponds to this theory. Assume that level of decentralization (x_2) is measured on a

Variable	Estimated β Value	Standard Error	t Value	p-Value	Overall Model Statistics
x_1	-1.02	.33	-3.09	.004	$F = 5.84$
x_2	$-.49$	.27	-1.82	nonsignificant	p-value $< .002$
x_1x_2	.22	.09	2.43	.025	$R^2_{adj} = .34$

Source: Gul, F., *et al.* "Decentralization as a moderating factor in the budgetary participation–performance relationship: Some Hong-Kong evidence." *Accounting and Business Research,* Vol. 25, No. 98, Spring 1995, p. 110 (Table 3).

7-point scale (where 1 = a highly centralized firm and 7 = a highly decentralized firm). What are the expected signs of the β coefficients in the model?

c. In the field study, data collected for $n = 37$ managers at manufacturing companies are summarized in the table above. Interpret the statistics for the overall model.

d. Refer to the regression results, part **c**. Do the individual parameter statistics support the theory outlined in part **b**? Explain.

12.29 Baseball fans are involved in a never-ending search for variables (and a model) that will enable them to predict a professional baseball team's success for a given baseball season. In a *New York Times* review of the book *The Hidden Game of Baseball* (Doubleday, 1984), the reviewer wrote that the book's authors "measure players' offensive contributions by what they call a linear weights measure, which gives separate values to at-bats, singles, doubles, …, home runs, …, stolen bases, and times caught stealing."

a. Would regression analysis, using a first-order model, produce the *New York Times* description of a "linear weights measure"? Explain.

b. List some of the independent variables that you think might be related to a professional baseball team's percentage of games won. Construct a first-order model to relate percentage of games won to these variables.

c. Can you propose a better model than the model in part **b**? Explain.

12.30 (X12.030) Operations managers often use *work sampling* to estimate how much time workers spend on each operation. Work sampling involves observing workers' activities at random points in time. Random times are used to keep workers from changing their behavior—either consciously or subconsciously—in anticipation of being observed (Starr, *Operations Management*, 1996). Work sampling was applied to the staff of the catalog sales department of a clothing manufacturer. Among the activities observed were order taking, order processing, order correction, personal phone calls, and socializing. The department's

manager believes that due to a lack of staff, workers are not spending enough time with customers on the phone taking orders. The time estimates in the table were determined via work sampling. All other data is from company records.

Day	Total Time Spent Taking Telephone Orders y (hours)	Number of Telephone Orders per Day x_1	Size of Staff x_2
1	20.0	210	5
2	22.3	255	4
3	18.6	203	4
4	34.7	341	6
5	21.3	186	6
6	30.5	402	6
7	36.2	350	8
8	20.1	209	5
9	17.8	156	5
10	27.3	390	5
11	33.6	415	8
12	35.9	327	8
13	26.1	309	5
14	21.8	175	6
15	24.2	236	7
16	26.0	246	8
17	28.3	399	5
18	22.6	183	6
19	32.1	333	6
20	36.5	468	8

a. Write a complete second-order model relating time taking orders (y) to number of orders (x_1) and staff size (x_2).

b. Fit the model to the data using a statistical software package.

c. Is the overall model useful for predicting time taking phone orders, y?

d. Do the regression results support the manager's belief? Explain.

12.31 An economist is interested in modeling the relationship between quarterly sales of central-air-conditioning systems (in $ thousands) for single-family homes in the United States and two quantitative independent variables, housing starts in the previous quarter (in thousands), x_1, and the Gross Domestic Product (in billions of 1972 dollars), x_2. Data were collected, and a second-order

```
The regression equation is
Y  = 149.5 + .47 X1 + .10 X2 - .0005 X3 + .0000 X4

Predictor         Coef       Stdev      t-ratio        p
Constant        148.50       224.5         0.66     0.662
X1               0.472       0.126         3.74     0.014
X2              -0.099       0.162        -0.61     0.708
X3           -0.000535    0.000359        -1.49     0.152
X4            0.0000153   0.0000294         0.52     0.887

s = 6.884      R-sq = 92.0%    R-sq(adj) = 89.1%

Analysis of Variance

SOURCE         DF          SS          MS          F        p
Regression      4     6002.08     1500.52      31.66    0.000
Error          11      521.36       47.40
Total          15     6523.44
```

model was fit. The MINITAB printout above describes the least squares prediction equation. In the prediction equation, $x_3 = x_1^2$ and $x_4 = x_2^2$.

a. Write the prediction equation for the response surface.

b. Describe the geometric form of the response surface of part **a**.

c. Do the data provide sufficient evidence to conclude that the model hypothesized by the economist is useful for predicting quarterly sales of central-air-conditioning systems? Test using $\alpha = .01$.

d. Does it appear that the variation in air-conditioner sales could be adequately explained by a less complex regression model? Explain. [*Note:* In the next section we discuss a formal procedure for making this inference.]

12.32 (X12.032) A supermarket chain is interested in exploring the relationship between the sales of its store-brand canned vegetables (y), the amount spent on promotion of the vegetables in local newspapers (x_1), and the amount of shelf space allocated to the brand (x_2). One of the chain's supermarkets was randomly selected, and over a 20-week period x_1 and x_2 were varied, as reported in the next table.

a. Fit the following model to the data:

$$y = \beta_0 + \beta_1 x_1 + \beta_2 x_2 + \beta_3 x_1 x_2 + \epsilon$$

b. Conduct an F-test to investigate the overall usefulness of this model. Use $\alpha = .05$.

Week	Sales ($)	Advertising Expenditures ($)	Shelf Space (sq. ft.)
1	2,010	201	75
2	1,850	205	50
3	2,400	355	75
4	1,575	208	30
5	3,550	590	75
6	2,015	397	50
7	3,908	820	75
8	1,870	400	30
9	4,877	997	75
10	2,190	515	30
11	5,005	996	75
12	2,500	625	50
13	3,005	860	50
14	3,480	1,012	50
15	5,500	1,135	75
16	1,995	635	30
17	2,390	837	30
18	4,390	1,200	50
19	2,785	990	30
20	2,989	1,205	30

c. Test for the presence of interaction between advertising expenditure and shelf space. Use $\alpha = .05$.

d. Explain what it means to say that advertising expenditures and shelf space interact.

e. Explain how you could be misled by using a first-order model instead of an interaction model to explain how advertising expenditure and shelf space influence sales.

12.5 TESTING PORTIONS OF A MODEL

The presentation of models with one and two quantitative independent variables raises a very general question. Do certain terms in the model contribute information for the prediction of y?

To illustrate, suppose you have collected data on a response y and two independent quantitative variables, x_1 and x_2, and you are considering the use of either a first-order or a second-order model to relate $E(y)$ to x_1 and x_2. Will the second-order model provide better predictions of y than the first-order model? To answer this question, examine the two models. Note that the second-order model contains all terms present in the first-order model plus three additional terms, those involving β_3, β_4, and β_5:

First-order model: $E(y) = \beta_0 + \beta_1 x_1 + \beta_2 x_2$

$$\text{Second-order model: } E(y) = \beta_0 + \beta_1 x_1 + \beta_2 x_2 + \overbrace{\beta_3 x_1 x_2 + \beta_4 x_1^2 + \beta_5 x_2^2}^{\text{Second-order terms}}$$

Therefore, asking whether the second-order model contributes more information for the prediction of y than the first-order model is equivalent to asking whether $\beta_3 = \beta_4 = \beta_5 = 0$; that is, whether the terms involving β_3, β_4, and β_5 should be retained in the model. To test whether the second-order terms should be included in the model, we test the null hypothesis

$$H_0: \beta_3 = \beta_4 = \beta_5 = 0$$

(i.e., the second-order terms do not contribute information for the prediction of y) against the alternative hypothesis

$$H_a: \text{At least one of the parameters, } \beta_3, \beta_4, \text{ or } \beta_5, \text{ differs from 0}$$

(i.e., at least one of the second-order terms contributes information for the prediction of y).

In Section 11.4 we presented the t-test for a single coefficient, and in Section 11.5 we gave the F-test for *all* the β parameters (except β_0) in the model. We now need a test for *some* of the β parameters in the model. The test procedure is intuitive: First, we use the method of least squares to fit the first-order model—called the **reduced model** because it is the smaller of the two models—and calculate the corresponding sum of squares for error, SSE_r (the sum of squares of the deviations between observed and predicted values). Next, we fit the second-order model—called the **complete model** because it is the larger of the two models—and calculate its sum of squares for error, SSE_c. Then, we compare SSE_r to SSE_c by calculating $\text{SSE}_r - \text{SSE}_c$. If the second-order terms contribute to the model, then SSE_c should be much smaller than SSE_r and the difference ($\text{SSE}_r - \text{SSE}_c$) will be large. The larger the difference, the greater the weight of evidence that the second-order (complete) model provides better predictions of y than does the first-order (reduced) model.

The sum of squares for error always decreases when new terms are added to the model. That is, the complete-model SSE_c is always smaller than a reduced-model SSE_r. The question is whether this decrease is large enough to conclude that it is due to more than just an increase in the number of model terms and to chance. To test the null hypothesis that the parameters of the second-order terms, β_3, β_4, and β_5, simultaneously equal 0, we use an F statistic calculated as follows:

$$F = \frac{(\text{SSE}_r - \text{SSE}_c)/3}{\text{SSE}_c/[n - (5 + 1)]}$$

$$= \frac{\text{Drop in SSE/Number of } \beta \text{ parameters being tested}}{s^2 \text{ for the larger model}}$$

FIGURE 12.12
Rejection region for the F-test of H_0: $\beta_3 = \beta_4 = \beta_5$

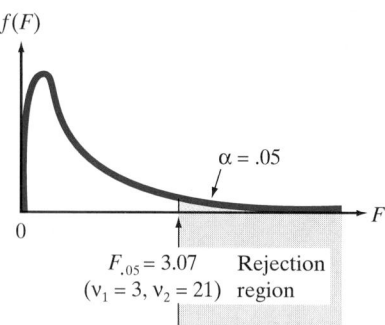

When the assumptions listed in Section 11.3 about the error term ϵ are satisfied and the β parameters for the second-order terms are all 0 (H_0 is true), this F statistic has an F-distribution with $\nu_1 = 3$ numerator df and $\nu_2 = n - 6$ denominator df. Note that ν_1 is the number of β parameters being tested and ν_2 is the number of degrees of freedom associated with s^2 in the complete second-order model.

If the second-order terms do contribute to the model (H_a is true), we expect the F statistic to be large. Thus, we use a one-tailed test and reject H_0 when F exceeds some critical value, F_α, as shown in Figure 12.12. The steps employed in testing the null hypothesis that a set of model parameters are all equal to 0 are summarized in the next box.

F-Test for Testing the Null Hypothesis: Subset of β Parameters Equal to 0

Reduced model: $E(y) = \beta_0 + \beta_1 x_1 + \cdots + \beta_g x_g$

Complete model: $E(y) = \beta_0 + \beta_1 x_1 + \cdots + \beta_g x_g + \beta_{g+1} x_{g+1} + \cdots + \beta_k x_k$

H_0: $\beta_{g+1} = \beta_{g+2} = \cdots = \beta_k = 0$

H_a: At least one of the β parameters being tested is nonzero

Test Statistic:
$$F = \frac{(SSE_r - SSE_c)/(k - g)}{SSE_c/[n - (k + 1)]}$$
$$= \frac{(SSE_r - SSE_c)/\text{Number of } \beta\text{'s tested}}{MSE_c}$$

where

SSE_r = Sum of squared errors for the reduced model

SSE_c = Sum of squared errors for the complete model

MSE_c = Mean square error (or s^2) for the complete model

$k - g$ = Number of β parameters specified in H_0 (i.e., number of β's tested)

$k + 1$ = Number of β parameters in the complete model (including β_0)

n = Total sample size

Rejection region: $F > F_\alpha$

where F_α is based on $\nu_1 = (k - g)$ numerator df and $\nu_2 = [n - (k + 1)]$ denominator df.

TABLE 12.2 **Temperature (x_1), Pressure (x_2), and Quality (y) of the Finished Product**

x_1 (°F)	x_2 (psi)	y	x_1 (°F)	x_2 (psi)	y	x_1 (°F)	x_2 (psi)	y
80	50	50.8	90	50	63.4	100	50	46.6
80	50	50.7	90	50	61.6	100	50	49.1
80	50	49.4	90	50	63.4	100	50	46.4
80	55	93.7	90	55	93.8	100	55	69.8
80	55	90.9	90	55	92.1	100	55	72.5
80	55	90.9	90	55	97.4	100	55	73.2
80	60	74.5	90	60	70.9	100	60	38.7
80	60	73.0	90	60	68.8	100	60	42.5
80	60	71.2	90	60	71.3	100	60	41.4

EXAMPLE 12.4

Many companies manufacture products (e.g., steel, paint, gasoline) that are at least partially chemically produced. In many instances, the quality of the finished product is a function of the temperature and pressure at which the chemical reactions take place. Suppose you want to model the quality y of a product as a function of the temperature x_1 and the pressure x_2 at which it is produced. Four inspectors independently assign a quality score between 0 and 100 to each product, and then the quality y is calculated by averaging the four scores. An experiment is conducted by varying temperature between 80°F and 100°F and pressure between 50 and 60 pounds per square inch (psi). The resulting data are given in Table 12.2.

a. Fit a complete second-order model to the data.

b. Sketch the response surface.

c. Do the data provide sufficient evidence to indicate that the second-order terms contribute information for the prediction of y?

SOLUTION

a. The complete second-order model is

$$E(y) = \beta_0 + \beta_1 x_1 + \beta_2 x_2 + \beta_3 x_1 x_2 + \beta_4 x_1^2 + \beta_5 x_2^2$$

The data in Table 12.2 were used to fit this model, and a portion of the SAS output is shown in Figure 12.13.

The least squares prediction equation is

$$\hat{y} = -5,127.90 + 31.10 x_1 + 139.75 x_2 - .146 x_1 x_2 - .133 x_1^2 - 1.14 x_2^2$$

b. A three-dimensional graph of this prediction model is shown in Figure 12.14. Note that the quality seems to be greatest for temperatures of about 85–90°F and for pressures of about 55–57 pounds per square inch.* Further experimentation in these ranges might lead to a more precise determination of the optimal temperature–pressure combination.

*Students with knowledge of calculus should note that we can solve for the exact temperature and pressure that maximize quality in the least squares model by solving $\partial \hat{y} / \partial x_1 = 0$ and $\partial \hat{y} / \partial x_2 = 0$ for x_1 and x_2. Sample estimates of these estimated optimal values are $x_1 = 86.25$°F and $x_2 = 55.58$ psi. Remember, however, that these represent only sample estimates of the coordinates for the optimal value.

```
Dependent Variable: Y

                        Analysis of Variance

                        Sum of           Mean
        Source      DF    Squares         Square      F Value      Prob>F

        Model        5   8402.26454    1680.45291     596.324      0.0001
        Error       21     59.17843       2.81802
        C Total     26   8461.44296

             Root MSE        1.67870    R-square      0.9930
             Dep Mean       66.96296    Adj R-sq      0.9913
             C.V.            2.50690

                        Parameter Estimates

                     Parameter      Standard      T for HO:
        Variable  DF  Estimate        Error     Parameter=0    Prob > |T|

        INTERCEP   1 -5127.899074  110.29601493    -46.492       0.0001
        X1         1    31.096389    1.34441322     23.130       0.0001
        X2         1   139.747222    3.14005412     44.505       0.0001
        X1X2       1    -0.145500    0.00969196    -15.012       0.0001
        X1SQ       1    -0.133389    0.00685325    -19.464       0.0001
        X2SQ       1    -1.144222    0.02741299    -41.740       0.0001
```

FIGURE 12.13   Portion of the SAS printout for Example 12.4

c. To determine whether the data provide sufficient information to indicate that the second-order terms contribute information for the prediction of y, we wish to test

$$H_0: \beta_3 = \beta_4 = \beta_5 = 0$$

against the alternative hypothesis

H_a: At least one of the parameters, $\beta_3, \beta_4, \beta_5$, differs from 0

The first step in conducting the test is to drop the second-order terms out of the complete (second-order) model and fit the reduced model

$$E(y) = \beta_0 + \beta_1 x_1 + \beta_2 x_2$$

to the data. The SAS printout for this procedure is shown in Figure 12.15.

You can see that the sums of squares for error, highlighted in Figures 12.13 and 12.15 for the complete and reduced models, respectively, are

FIGURE 12.14
Plot of second-order
least squares model
for Example 12.4

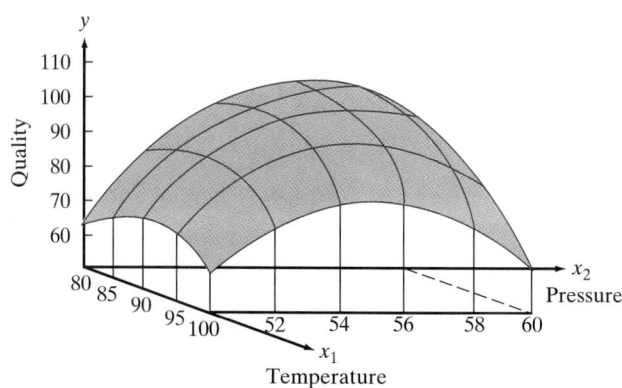

```
Dependent Variable: Y
                          Analysis of Variance

                              Sum of          Mean
        Source         DF     Squares        Square     F Value    Prob>F

        Model           2    1789.93444     894.96722      3.22     0.0577
        Error          24    6671.50852     277.97952
        C Total        26    8461.44296

              Root MSE          16.67272    R-square     0.2115
              Dep Mean          66.96296    Adj R-sq     0.1458
              C.V.              24.89840

                         Parameter Estimates

                        Parameter     Standard     T for HO:
        Variable   DF    Estimate       Error    Parameter=0   Prob > |T|

        INTERCEP    1   106.085185   55.94500427      1.90        0.0700
        X1          1    -0.916111    0.39297973     -2.33        0.0285
        X2          1     0.787778    0.78595946      1.00        0.3262
```

FIGURE 12.15   SAS computer printout for the reduced (first-order) model, Example 12.4

$$SSE_c = 59.17843$$

$$SSE_r = 6,671.50852$$

and that s^2 for the complete model is

$$s^2 = MSE_c = 2.81802$$

Recall that $n = 27$, $k = 5$, and $g = 2$. Therefore, the calculated value of the F statistic, based on $\nu_1 = (k - g) = 3$ numerator df and $\nu_2 = [n - (k + 1)] = 21$ denominator df, is

$$F = \frac{(SSE_r - SSE_c)/(k - g)}{SSE_c/[n - (k + 1)]} = \frac{(SSE_r - SSE_c)/(k - g)}{MSE_c}$$

where $\nu_1 = (k - g)$ is equal to the number of parameters involved in H_0. Therefore,

$$F = \frac{(6,671.50852 - 59.17843)/3}{2.81802} = 782.1$$

The final step in the test is to compare this computed value of F with the tabulated value based on $\nu_1 = 3$ and $\nu_2 = 21$ df. If we choose $\alpha = .05$, then $F_{.05} = 3.07$. Since the computed value of F falls in the rejection region (see Figure 12.12), i.e., it exceeds $F_{.05} = 3.07$, we reject H_0 and conclude that at least one of the second-order terms contributes information for the prediction of y. In other words, the data support the contention that the curvature we see in the response surface is not due simply to random variation in the data. The second-order model appears to provide better predictions of y than a first-order model.

Example 12.4 demonstrates the motivation for testing a hypothesis that each one of a subset of β parameters equals 0; it also demonstrates the procedure. Other applications of this test appear in the following sections.

EXERCISES **12.33–12.43**

Note: Exercises marked with 💾 *contain data for computer analysis on a 3.5" disk (file name in parentheses).*

Learning the Mechanics

12.33 Suppose you fit the regression model

$$y = \beta_0 + \beta_1 x_1 + \beta_2 x_2 + \beta_3 x_1 x_2 + \beta_4 x_1^2 + \beta_5 x_2^2 + \epsilon$$

to $n = 30$ data points and you wish to test

$$H_0: \beta_3 = \beta_4 = \beta_5 = 0$$

a. State the alternative hypothesis H_a.
b. Explain in detail how you would find the quantities necessary to compute the F statistic for this test of hypothesis.
c. What are the numerator and denominator degrees of freedom associated with the F statistic?

12.34 Suppose you fit the complete and reduced models for the hypothesis test described in Exercise 12.33

and obtain $SSE_r = 246.1$ and $SSE_c = 215.2$. Conduct the hypothesis test and interpret the results of your test. Test using $\alpha = .05$.

12.35 Explain why the F-test used to compare complete and reduced models is a one-tailed, upper-tailed test.

12.36 MINITAB was used to fit the complete model

$$y = \beta_0 + \beta_1 x_1 + \beta_2 x_2 + \beta_3 x_3 + \beta_4 x_4 + \epsilon$$

to $n = 20$ data points. Then the independent variables x_3 and x_4 were dropped and MINITAB was used to fit the reduced model. The results are shown below.

a. Report the least squares prediction equations for the complete and reduced models.
b. Find SSE_r and SSE_c. Interpret each of the quantities.
c. How many β parameters are in the complete model? The reduced model?

```
Complete Model
The regression equation is
Y  = 14.6 - 0.611 X1 + 0.439 X2 - 0.080 X3 - 0.064 X4

Predictor        Coef        Stdev      t-ratio         p
Constant       14.575        4.887         2.98     0.010
X1            -0.6113       0.1775        -3.44     0.005
X2             0.4388       0.2199         2.00     0.062
X3            -0.0796       0.1083        -0.74     0.866
X4            -0.0636       0.1247        -0.51     0.921

s = 3.190      R-sq = 84.5%      R-sq(adj) = 80.3%

Analysis of Variance

SOURCE         DF          SS           MS         F         p
Regression      4      831.09       207.77     20.41     0.002
Error          15      152.66        10.18
Total          19      983.75
```

```
Reduced Model
The regression equation is
Y = 14.0 - 0.642 X1 + 0.396 X2

Predictor        Coef        Stdev      t-ratio         p
Constant       13.968        4.626         3.02     0.006
X1            -0.6422       0.1675        -3.84     0.001
X2             0.3959       0.2061         1.92     0.072

s = 3.072      R-sq = 83.7%      R-sq(adj) = 81.8%

Analysis of Variance

SOURCE         DF          SS           MS         F         p
Regression      2      823.31       411.66     43.61     0.000
Error          17      160.44         9.44
Total          19      983.75
```

d. Specify the null and alternative hypotheses you would use to investigate whether the complete model contributes more information for the prediction of y than the reduced model.

e. Conduct the hypothesis test of part **d**. Use $\alpha = .05$.

f. What is the approximate p-value of the test of part **e**?

Applying the Concepts

12.37 A large research and development firm rates the performance of each member of its technical staff once a year. Each person is rated on a scale of 0 to 100 by his or her immediate supervisor, and this merit rating is used to determine the size of the person's pay raise for the coming year. The firm's personnel department is interested in developing a regression model to help them forecast the merit rating that an applicant for a technical position will receive after being employed three years. The firm proposes to use the following model to forecast the merit ratings of applicants who have just completed their graduate studies and have no prior related job experience:

$$E(y) = \beta_0 + \beta_1 x_1 + \beta_2 x_2 + \beta_3 x_1 x_2 + \beta_4 x_1^2 + \beta_5 x_2^2$$

where

y = Applicant's merit rating after three years

x_1 = Applicant's GPA in graduate school

x_2 = Applicant's total score (verbal plus quantitative) on the Graduate Record Examination (GRE)

A random sample of $n = 40$ employees who have been on the technical staff of the firm more than three years is selected. Each employee's merit rating after three years, graduate school GPA, and total score on the GRE are recorded. The model is fit to these data with the aid of a computer. A portion of the resulting computer printout is shown below.

The reduced model $E(y) = \beta_0 + \beta_1 x_1 + \beta_2 x_2$ is also fit to the same data. The resulting computer printout is also shown below.

a. Identify the appropriate null and alternative hypotheses to test whether the complete (second-order) model contributes information for the prediction of y.

b. Conduct the test of hypothesis given in part **a**. Test using $\alpha = .05$. Interpret the results in the context of this problem.

c. Identify the appropriate null and alternative hypotheses to test whether the complete model contributes more information than the reduced (first-order) model for the prediction of y.

d. Conduct the test of hypothesis given in part **c**. Test using $\alpha = .05$. Interpret the results in the context of this problem.

e. Which model, if either, would you use to predict y? Explain.

12.38 A study in the *Journal of Family Issues* (Mar. 1983) investigated the impact of a wife's employment on the number of hours available for household tasks. Some 206 families were included in the study. One independent variable measured for each family was the total time y (in minutes per day) that the wife spent on household chores. Two independent variables were also recorded:

WEMP: x_1 = Wife's hours of employment per week

YAGE: x_2 = Age of the youngest child in the family

The computer printout for the regression analysis is shown on page 606.

The sums of squares shown under **SEQUENTIAL S.S.** are those you would obtain by sequentially adding variables to the model. For example, the sum of squares opposite WEMP is for the model

$$E(y) = \beta_0 + \beta_1 x_1$$

```
Complete model
SOURCE    DF    SUM OF SQUARES    MEAN SQUARE

MODEL      5         4911.56          982.31
ERROR     34         1830.44           53.84
TOTAL     39         6742.00        R-SQUARE
                                        0.73
```

```
Reduced model
SOURCE    DF    SUM OF SQUARES    MEAN SQUARE

MODEL      2         3544.84         1772.42
ERROR     37         3197.16           86.41
TOTAL     39         6742.00        R-SQUARE
                                        0.53
```

DEPENDENT VARIABLE: WIFE'S HOUSEHOLD WORK			(MEAN=401.3[a])		
SOURCE OF VARIATION	DF	SUMS OF SQUARES	MEAN SQUARE	F	R[2]
TOTAL	205	5,432,296		62.10***	0.38
MODEL	2	2,061,918	1,030,959		
ERROR	203	3,370,378	16,603		
SOURCE WITHIN MODEL	DF	SEQUENTIAL S.S.	PARTIAL S.S.	b-ESTIMATES	
WEMP	1	1,810,154***	1,110,288***	-4.08	
YAGE	1	251,765***	251,765***	-7.02	

DEPENDENT VARIABLE: HUSBAND'S WORK	(MEAN=105.2[a])
REGRESSION ANALYSIS NOT SIGNIFICANT	

[*Note:* In this particular printout, "b-estimate" is our β estimate, or parameter estimate. Also, the asterisks indicate the level of significance of test statistics (or sum of squares to compute test statistics). Here, *** means $p < .001$.]

[a]Minutes per day.

Source: Fox, K. D., and Nickols, S. Y. "The time crunch." *Journal of Family Issues,* Mar. 1983, Vol. 4, No. 1, pp. 61–82. Copyright 1983 by Sage Publications. Reprinted by permission of Sage Publications, Inc.

The sum of squares opposite YAGE is the drop in SSE for the model obtained by adding x_2, that is, for

$$E(y) = \beta_0 + \beta_1 x_1 + \beta_2 x_2$$

Therefore, this sum of squares can be used in the F statistic to test H_0: $\beta_2 = 0$.

In contrast, the sums of squares shown under **PARTIAL S.S.** are the differences in the sums of squares between reduced and complete models. These are the quantities needed to conduct individual F-tests on both of the parameters, β_1 and β_2. For example, 1,110,288 is the difference in the SSE values for the models

$$E(y) = \beta_0 + \beta_2 x_2 \text{ and } E(y) = \beta_0 + \beta_1 x_1 + \beta_2 x_2$$

Therefore, it can be used to compute the F statistic for testing H_0: $\beta_1 = 0$. [*Note:* This sum of squares differs substantially from the corresponding sum of squares, 1,810,154, shown under the **SEQUENTIAL S.S.** column.]

a. Use the information in the printout to test H_0: $\beta_1 = 0$. Test using $\alpha = .05$ and interpret your results.

b. State the alternative hypothesis implied in the test in part **a**.

c. Use the information in the printout to test H_0: $\beta_2 = 0$. Test using $\alpha = .05$ and interpret your results.

d. In concluding, the researchers state that "the wife's employment explained substantially more variation in the wife's housework time than age of the younger child." Do you agree? Explain.

12.39 **(X12.039)** A medium-sized automobile insurance company is interested in developing a regression model to help predict the monthly collision claims of its policyholders. A company analyst has proposed modeling monthly collision claims (y) in the Middle Atlantic States as a function of the percentage of claims by drivers under age 30 (x_1) and the average daily temperature during the month (x_2). She believes that as the percentage of claims by drivers under age 30 increases, claims will rise since younger drivers are usually involved in more serious accidents than older drivers. She also believes that claims will rise as the average daily temperature decreases, since lower temperatures are associated with icy, hazardous driving conditions. In order to develop a preliminary model, data were collected for the state of New Jersey over the period 1987–1990. The data are provided in the next table.

a. Use a statistical software package to fit the complete second-order model

$$E(y) = \beta_0 + \beta_1 x_1 + \beta_2 x_2 + \beta_3 x_1 x_2 + \beta_4 x_1^2 + \beta_5 x_2^2$$

b. Test the hypothesis H_0: $\beta_4 = \beta_5 = 0$ using $\alpha = .05$. Interpret the results in practical terms.

c. Do the results support the analysts' beliefs? Explain. (You may need to conduct further tests of hypotheses to answer this question.)

12.40 Refer to Exercise 12.26. Recall that the DOE wants to develop a model that will estimate the mean annual gasoline consumption y in the United States (in millions of barrels) as a function of number of cars (x_1) and number of trucks (x_2) in use during the year. Consider the complete second-order model for $E(y)$.

a. Specify the null and alternative hypotheses you would employ in testing for the presence of curvature in the model.

Month	Monthly Collision Claims y ($)	Percentage of Monthly Claimants Under the Age of 30 x_1	Newark, N.J., Average Daily Temperature During the Month x_2 (°F)
1	116,250	50.0	31.5
2	217,180	60.8	33.0
3	43,436	45.1	45.0
4	159,265	56.4	53.9
5	130,308	53.3	63.9
6	72,393	46.9	74.5
7	174,740	57.8	79.4
8	101,351	50.6	75.3
9	144,787	55.0	68.7
10	28,957	35.8	53.7
11	173,744	57.9	47.6
12	86,872	49.9	38.4
13	108,420	51.0	28.7
14	203,288	62.9	34.4
15	40,658	45.1	43.9
16	149,078	55.2	51.1
17	121,973	53.7	63.4
18	67,763	47.2	73.0
19	163,130	56.1	80.5
20	94,858	48.3	79.8
21	135,525	54.7	68.0
22	27,105	45.4	52.6
23	162,631	56.5	48.9
24	81,315	47.7	35.5
25	114,890	51.3	37.0
26	217,726	61.6	34.2
27	43,084	45.9	42.4
28	157,973	55.2	52.5
29	129,910	53.6	63.2
30	71,808	46.9	74.3
31	172,005	58.2	77.2
32	103,166	51.1	76.3
33	143,612	55.4	69.9
34	28,722	28.2	59.1
35	175,335	57.5	45.0
36	87,157	48.2	25.6
37	154,886	56.9	40.4
38	290,411	66.5	39.8
39	58,082	45.9	44.9
40	212,966	61.4	53.3
41	174,247	57.7	61.1
42	96,804	48.9	73.4
43	230,329	64.3	77.8
44	136,528	53.1	76.6
45	193,608	59.8	68.6
46	38,722	45.6	62.4
47	212,309	63.9	50.0
48	118,796	52.3	42.3

Sources: Anonymous insurance company; New Jersey Department of Insurance; *Weather of U.S. Cities,* 4th ed., Gale Research Inc., Detroit, 1992.

b. Based on a sample of $n = 15$ years, the resulting values of SSE_r and SSE_c were 1,065.9 and 400.6, respectively. Conduct the test to deter-

mine whether the data present sufficient evidence to indicate curvature. Test using $\alpha = .05$.

12.41 **(X12.041)** A firm would like to be able to forecast its yearly sales in each of its sales regions. The firm has decided to base its forecasts on regional population size and its yearly regional advertising expenditures. The population data in the table were obtained from the U.S. Bureau of the Census, and the advertising and sales data were obtained from the firm's internal records.

Sales Region	Sales (thousands of units)	Population of Region (thousands)	Advertising Expenditures (thousands of dollars)
1	65	200	8
2	80	210	10
3	85	205	9
4	100	300	8.5
5	108	320	12
6	114	290	10
7	40	90	6
8	45	85	8
9	150	450	9
10	42	87	9
11	220	480	13
12	200	500	15

a. Fit a complete second-order model to these data.

b. Is the complete second-order model useful for forecasting sales? Test using $\alpha = .05$.

c. The firm is planning to market its product in a new sales region next year. The region has a population of 400,000, and the firm plans to spend $12,000 on advertising. Use the fitted model you obtained in part **a** to forecast next year's sales in this new region. [*Note:* We would want to express this estimate as a prediction interval, but its computation is beyond the scope of this text. The procedure is described in the references. You may also find that it can be obtained using your statistical software package.]

12.42 Refer to Exercise 12.41, in which a firm would like to develop a regression model to forecast its yearly sales in each of its sales regions. The model under consideration is a complete second-order model:

$$E(y) = \beta_0 + \beta_1 x_1 + \beta_2 x_2 + \beta_3 x_1 x_2 + \beta_4 x_1^2 + \beta_5 x_2^2$$

where

y = Yearly regional sales

x_1 = Population of sales region

x_2 = Yearly regional advertising expenditures

```
Complete model

SOURCE      DF    SUM OF SQUARES    MEAN SQUARE

MODEL       5         38638.97        7727.79
ERROR       6           159.94          26.66
TOTAL      11         38798.91        R-SQUARE
                                        0.996


Reduced model

SOURCE      DF    SUM OF SQUARES    MEAN SQUARE

MODEL       2         36704.5        18352.2
ERROR       9          2094.4          232.7
TOTAL      11         38798.9        R-SQUARE
                                       0.946
```

A portion of the computer printout that results from fitting this model to the $n = 12$ data points given in Exercise 12.41 is shown above.

The reduced first-order model

$$E(y) = \beta_0 + \beta_1 x_1 + \beta_2 x_2$$

was fit to the same data, and the resulting computer printout is partially reproduced above.

Do these data present sufficient evidence to conclude that a second-order model contributes more information for the prediction of y than does a first-order model? Test using $\alpha = .05$.

12.43 In Exercise 11.22 we found that a first-order model was useful for explaining the variation in the number of hours worked per week in the shipping department of a particular firm. The data used to fit the model are repeated in the accompanying table.

a. Write a complete second-order model for the data.

b. Write a first-order model for the data.

c. The SAS printouts for the models, parts **a** and **b**, are shown on page 609. Give the prediction equation for each model.

d. Is there sufficient evidence to indicate that the second-order terms are useful for predicting labor, y? Test using $\alpha = .10$.

Week	Labor y (hrs.)	Pounds Shipped x_1 (1,000s)	Percentage of Units Shipped by Truck x_2	Shipment Weight x_3 (lbs.)
1	100	5.1	90	20
2	85	3.8	99	22
3	108	5.3	58	19
4	116	7.5	16	15
5	92	4.5	54	20
6	63	3.3	42	26
7	79	5.3	12	25
8	101	5.9	32	21
9	88	4.0	56	24
10	71	4.2	64	29
11	122	6.8	78	10
12	85	3.9	90	30
13	50	3.8	74	28
14	114	7.5	89	14
15	104	4.5	90	21
16	111	6.0	40	20
17	110	8.1	55	16
18	100	2.9	64	19
19	82	4.0	35	23
20	85	4.8	58	25

```
Model: MODEL1
Dependent Variable: Y
```

Analysis of Variance

Source	DF	Sum of Squares	Mean Square	F Value	Prob>F
Model	9	6043.40530	671.48948	10.255	0.0006
Error	10	654.79470	65.47947		
C Total	19	6698.20000			

Root MSE	8.09194	R-square	0.9022
Dep Mean	93.30000	Adj R-sq	0.8143
C.V.	8.67303		

Parameter Estimates

Variable	DF	Parameter Estimate	Standard Error	T for H0: Parameter=0	Prob > |T|
INTERCEP	1	655.807226	226.28033719	2.898	0.0159
X1	1	-57.326658	33.08376144	-1.733	0.1138
X2	1	-3.389616	1.91983172	-1.766	0.1079
X3	1	-28.270729	10.61901566	-2.662	0.0238
X1X2	1	0.224034	0.14691511	1.525	0.1583
X1X3	1	2.201422	0.90189596	2.441	0.0348
X2X3	1	0.088586	0.03966598	2.233	0.0496
X1SQ	1	0.453276	1.33580032	0.339	0.7414
X2SQ	1	0.003712	0.00404162	0.918	0.3800
X3SQ	1	0.208330	0.12683455	1.643	0.1315

```
Model: MODEL2
Dependent Variable: Y
```

Analysis of Variance

Source	DF	Sum of Squares	Mean Square	F Value	Prob>F
Model	3	5158.31383	1719.43794	17.866	0.0001
Error	16	1539.88617	96.24289		
C Total	19	6698.20000			

Root MSE	9.81035	R-square	0.7701
Dep Mean	93.30000	Adj R-sq	0.7270
C.V.	10.51484		

Parameter Estimates

Variable	DF	Parameter Estimate	Standard Error	T for H0: Parameter=0	Prob > |T|
INTERCEP	1	131.924252	25.69321439	5.135	0.0001
X1	1	2.726090	2.27500488	1.198	0.2483
X2	1	0.047218	0.09334856	0.506	0.6199
X3	1	-2.587444	0.64281819	-4.025	0.0010

12.6 MODELS WITH ONE QUALITATIVE INDEPENDENT VARIABLE

Suppose we want to develop a model for the mean operating cost per mile, $E(y)$, of compact cars as a function of the car's manufacturer. (For the purpose of explanation, we ignore other independent variables that might affect the response.) Further suppose there are three manufacturers of interest, which we identify as A, B, and C. Then the automobile manufacturer is a single qualitative variable with three levels, A, B, and C. Note that with a qualitative independent variable, we cannot attach a quantitative measure to a given level. Even if we were to call the manufacturers 1, 2, and 3, the numbers would simply be identifiers of the manufacturers and would have no meaningful quantitative interpretation.

To simplify our notation, let μ_A be the mean cost per mile for compact cars produced by manufacturer A, and let μ_B and μ_C be the corresponding mean costs per mile for those produced by B and C. Our objective is to write a single equation that will give the mean value of y (cost per mile) for the three manufacturers. This can be done as follows:

$$E(y) = \beta_0 + \beta_1 x_1 + \beta_2 x_2$$

where

$$x_1 = \begin{cases} 1 & \text{if the car is manufactured by B} \\ 0 & \text{if the car is not manufactured by B} \end{cases}$$

$$x_2 = \begin{cases} 1 & \text{if the car is manufactured by C} \\ 0 & \text{if the car is not manufactured by C} \end{cases}$$

The variables x_1 and x_2 are not meaningful independent variables as they are in the case of the models with quantitative independent variables. Instead, they are **dummy** (or **indicator**) **variables** that make the model work. To illustrate, let $x_1 = 0$ and $x_2 = 0$. This condition will apply when we are seeking the mean response A. (Neither B nor C will be the manufacturer; hence, it must be A.) Then the mean cost per mile, $E(y)$, when A is the manufacturer is

$$\mu_A = E(y) = \beta_0 + \beta_1(0) + \beta_2(0) = \beta_0$$

This tells us that the mean cost per mile for A is β_0. Or, using our notation, it means that $\mu_A = \beta_0$.

Now suppose we want to represent the mean cost per mile, $E(y)$, for manufacturer B. Checking the dummy variable definitions, we see that we should let $x_1 = 1$ and $x_2 = 0$:

$$\mu_B = E(y) = \beta_0 + \beta_1 x_1 + \beta_2 x_2 = \beta_0 + \beta_1(1) + \beta_2(0) = \beta_0 + \beta_1$$

or, since $\beta_0 = \mu_A$,

$$\mu_B = \mu_A + \beta_1$$

Then it follows that the interpretation of β_1 is

$$\beta_1 = \mu_B - \mu_A$$

which is the difference between the mean costs per mile for manufacturers B and A.

Finally, if we want the mean value of y when C is the manufacturer, we let $x_1 = 0$ and $x_2 = 1$:

$$\mu_C = E(y) = \beta_0 + \beta_1(0) + \beta_2(1) = \beta_0 + \beta_2$$

FIGURE 12.16
Bar chart comparing $E(y)$ for three automobile manufacturers

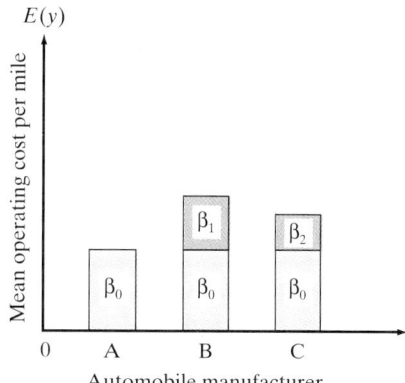

or, since $\beta_0 = \mu_A$,

$$\mu_C = \mu_A + \beta_2$$

Then it follows that the interpretation of β_2 is

$$\beta_2 = \mu_C - \mu_A$$

Note that we were able to describe *three levels* of the qualitative variable with only *two dummy variables*. This is because the mean of the base level (manufacturer A, in this case) is accounted for by the intercept β_0.

Since the automobile manufacturer is a qualitative variable, we will use a bar graph to show the value of mean operating cost per mile $E(y)$ for the three levels of automobile manufacturer (see Figure 12.16). Particularly, note that the height of the bar, $E(y)$, for each level of automobile manufacturer is equal to the sum of the model parameters shown in the preceding equations. You can see that the height of the bar corresponding to manufacturer A is β_0, that is, $E(y) = \beta_0$. Similarly, the heights of the bars corresponding to manufacturers B and C are $E(y) = \beta_0 + \beta_1$ and $E(y) = \beta_0 + \beta_2$, respectively.*

Now carefully examine the model with a single qualitative independent variable at three levels, because we will use exactly the same pattern for any number of levels. Moreover, the interpretation of the parameters will always be the same.

One level is selected as the **base level**. (We used manufacturer A as the base level.) Then for the 1-0 system of coding† for the dummy variables,

$$\mu_A = \beta_0$$

The coding for all dummy variables is as follows: To represent the mean value of y for a particular level, let that dummy variable equal 1; otherwise, the dummy variable is set equal to 0. Using this system of coding,

$$\mu_B = \beta_0 + \beta_1$$

$$\mu_C = \beta_0 + \beta_2$$

---

*Note that either β_1, β_2, or both, could be negative. If, for example, β_1 were negative, the height of the bar corresponding to manufacturer B would be *reduced* (rather than increased) from the height of the bar for manufacturer A by the amount β_1. Figure 12.16 is constructed assuming that β_1 and β_2 are positive quantities.

†You do not have to use a 1-0 system of coding for the dummy variables. Any two-value system will work, but the interpretation given to the model parameters will depend on the code. Using the 1-0 system makes the model parameters easy to interpret.

and so on. Because $\mu_A = \beta_0$, any other model parameter will represent the difference between means for that level and the base level.

$$\beta_1 = \mu_B - \mu_A$$

$$\beta_2 = \mu_C - \mu_A$$

and so on.

Procedure for Writing a Model with One Qualitative Independent Variable with k Levels

Always use a number of dummy variables that is one less than the number of levels of the qualitative variable. Thus, for a qualitative variable with k levels, use $k - 1$ dummy variables:

$$y = \beta_0 + \beta_1 x_1 + \beta_2 x_2 + \cdots + \beta_{k-1} x_{k-1} + \epsilon$$

where x_i is the dummy variable for level $i + 1$ and

$$x_i = \begin{cases} 1 & \text{if } y \text{ is observed at level } i + 1 \\ 0 & \text{otherwise} \end{cases}$$

Then, for this system of coding

$$\mu_A = \beta_0 \qquad \text{and} \qquad \beta_1 = \mu_B - \mu_A$$

$$\mu_B = \beta_0 + \beta_1 \qquad\qquad \beta_2 = \mu_C - \mu_A$$

$$\mu_C = \beta_0 + \beta_2 \qquad\qquad \beta_3 = \mu_D - \mu_A$$

$$\mu_D = \beta_0 + \beta_3 \qquad\qquad \vdots$$

$$\vdots$$

Level 1, or the A level, is the **base level** for this coding system.

EXAMPLE 12.5

Suppose the manager of a department store chain wants to compare the mean dollar amounts owed by delinquent credit card customers in three different annual income groups: less than \$25,000, \$25,000–\$60,000, and more than \$60,000. A sample of 10 customers with delinquent accounts is selected from each group, and the amount owed by each is recorded, as shown in Table 12.3. Do the data

---

TABLE 12.3   Dollars Owed, by Income Group

Group 1 Less than \$25,000	Group 2 \$25,000–\$60,000	Group 3 More than \$60,000
\$148	\$513	\$335
76	264	643
393	433	216
520	94	536
236	535	128
134	327	723
55	214	258
166	135	380
415	280	594
153	304	465

provide sufficient evidence to indicate that the mean dollar amounts owed by customers differ for the three annual income groups?

SOLUTION

Note that income is ordinarily a quantitative variable, but in this example only the group (low, medium, high) in which the customer's income falls is known. We therefore treat income as a qualitative variable (measured on an ordinal scale). For a three-level qualitative variable, we need two dummy variables in the regression model. The model relating $E(y)$ to this single qualitative variable, annual income group, is

$$E(y) = \beta_0 + \beta_1 x_1 + \beta_2 x_2$$

where

$$x_1 = \begin{cases} 1 & \text{if group 2} \\ 0 & \text{if not} \end{cases} \qquad x_2 = \begin{cases} 1 & \text{if group 3} \\ 0 & \text{if not} \end{cases}$$

and

$$\beta_1 = \mu_2 - \mu_1 \qquad \beta_2 = \mu_3 - \mu_1$$

where μ_1, μ_2, and μ_3 are the mean responses for income groups 1, 2, and 3, respectively. Testing the null hypothesis that the means for the three groups are equal, that is, $\mu_1 = \mu_2 = \mu_3$, is equivalent to testing

$$H_0: \beta_1 = \beta_2 = 0$$

because if $\beta_1 = \mu_2 - \mu_1 = 0$ and $\beta_2 = \mu_3 - \mu_1 = 0$, then μ_1, μ_2, and μ_3 must be equal. The alternative hypothesis is

$$H_a: \text{At least one of the parameters, } \beta_1 \text{ or } \beta_2, \text{ differs from 0}$$

which implies that at least two of the three means (μ_1, μ_2, and μ_3) differ.

   There are two ways to conduct this test. We can fit the complete model shown above and the reduced model (deleting the terms involving β_1 and β_2)

$$E(y) = \beta_0$$

and conduct the F-test described in the preceding section. (We leave this as an exercise for you.) Or we can use the F-test of the complete model (Section 11.5), which tests the null hypothesis that all parameters in the model, with the exception of β_0, equal 0. Either way you conduct the test, you will obtain the same computed value of F, the value shown on the SAS printout. The SAS printout for fitting the complete model,

$$E(y) = \beta_0 + \beta_1 x_1 + \beta_2 x_2$$

is shown in Figure 12.17; the value of the F statistic for testing the complete model, $F = 3.482$, is highlighted. If we choose $\alpha = .05$, we will reject H_0: $\beta_1 = \beta_2 = 0$ because the computed value of F, $F = 3.482$, has an observed significance level of .0452 (also highlighted). We therefore reject H_0 and conclude that at least one of the parameters, β_1 and β_2, differs from 0. Or, equivalently, we conclude that the data provide sufficient evidence to indicate that the mean indebtedness does vary from one income group to another.   ⌐

   Note: If you analyze the data by fitting complete and reduced models (Section 12.5), you will find that the least squares estimate of β_0 in the reduced model

```
Dependent Variable: Y
                         Analysis of Variance
                              Sum of          Mean
         Source       DF      Squares        Square    F Value   Prob>F
         Model         2   198772.46667   99386.23333    3.482    0.0452
         Error        27   770670.90000   28543.36667
         C Total      29   969443.36667

              Root MSE       168.94782    R-square     0.2050
              Dep Mean       312.43333    Adj R-sq     0.1462
              C.V.            54.07484

                         Parameter Estimates
                       Parameter     Standard     T for H0:
         Variable  DF   Estimate        Error    Parameter=0   Prob > |T|
         INTERCEP   1  229.600000   53.42599243      4.30        0.0002
         X1         1   80.300000   75.55576307      1.06        0.2973
         X2         1  198.200000   75.55576307      2.62        0.0141
```

FIGURE 12.17 SAS computer printout for Example 12.5

$$E(y) = \beta_0$$

is $\bar{y}$, the mean of all $n = 30$ observations, and the sum of squares for error for the reduced model is

$$SSE_r = \sum(y_i - \hat{y}_i)^2 = \sum(y_i - \bar{y})^2 = 969{,}443.367$$

This value is shown in the SAS printout (Figure 12.17) as the sum of squares corresponding to **C Total**. We leave the remaining steps—calculating the drop in SSE and the resulting F statistic—to you. You will find that the value you obtain is exactly the same as the value of F shown in the SAS printout.*

*An alternative method of finding the F statistic is to use a procedure known as **analysis of variance** (the topic of Chapter 15).

EXERCISES 12.44–12.55

Note: Exercises marked with 💾 *contain data for computer analysis on a 3.5" disk (file name in parentheses).*

Learning the Mechanics

12.44 Write a regression model relating the mean value of y to a qualitative independent variable that can assume two levels. Interpret all the terms in the model.

12.45 Write a regression model relating $E(y)$ to a qualitative independent variable that can assume three levels. Interpret all the terms in the model.

12.46 The following model was used to relate $E(y)$ to a single qualitative variable with four levels:

$$E(y) = \beta_0 + \beta_1x_1 + \beta_2x_2 + \beta_3x_3$$

where

$$x_1 = \begin{cases} 1 & \text{if level 2} \\ 0 & \text{if not} \end{cases}$$

$$x_2 = \begin{cases} 1 & \text{if level 3} \\ 0 & \text{if not} \end{cases}$$

$$x_3 = \begin{cases} 1 & \text{if level 4} \\ 0 & \text{if not} \end{cases}$$

This model was fit to $n = 30$ data points and the following result was obtained:

$$\hat{y} = 10.2 - 4x_1 + 12x_2 + 2x_3$$

a. Use the least squares prediction equation to find the estimate of $E(y)$ for each level of the qualitative independent variable.

b. Specify the null and alternative hypotheses you would use to test whether $E(y)$ is the same for all four levels of the independent variable.

12.47 MINITAB (see printout below) was used to fit the following model to $n = 15$ data points:

$$y = \beta_0 + \beta_1 x_1 + \beta_2 x_2 + \epsilon$$

where

$$x_1 = \begin{cases} 1 & \text{if level 2} \\ 0 & \text{if not} \end{cases} \qquad x_2 = \begin{cases} 1 & \text{if level 3} \\ 0 & \text{if not} \end{cases}$$

a. Report the least squares prediction equation.
b. Interpret the values of $\hat{\beta}_1$ and $\hat{\beta}_2$.
c. Interpret the following hypotheses in terms of $\mu_1, \mu_2,$ and μ_3:

$H_0: \beta_1 = \beta_2 = 0$

$H_a:$ At least one of the parameters β_1 and β_2 differs from 0

d. Conduct the hypothesis test of part **c**.

Applying the Concepts

12.48 In 1995–1996, four-year private colleges charged an average of $12,432 for tuition and fees for the year; four-year public colleges charged $2,860 (*Chronicle of Higher Education Almanac,* Sept. 2, 1996). In order to estimate the difference in the mean amounts charged for the 1997–1998 academic year, random samples of 40 private colleges and 40 public colleges were contacted and questioned about their tuition structures.

a. Which of the procedures described in Chapter 9 could be used to estimate the difference in mean charges between private and public colleges?

b. Propose a regression model involving the qualitative independent variable Type of college that could be used to investigate the difference between the means. Be sure to specify the coding scheme for the dummy variable in the model.

c. Explain how the regression model you developed in part **b** could be used to estimate the difference between the population means.

12.49 Refer to the *Benefits Quarterly* (First Quarter, 1995) study of entry-level job preferences, Exercise 12.5. One qualitative independent variable used to model the job preference score, y, of business school graduates is the level of day care support required. The independent variable was measured at three levels: None, Referral, and On premise.

a. Hypothesize a model for $E(y)$ as a function of level of day care support.
b. Interpret the β's in the model, part **a**.
c. Specify the null hypothesis for testing whether the mean job preference scores differ among the three levels of day care support.

12.50 (X12.050) A firm's debt/capital ratio is a measure of a firm's long-term debt divided by total invested capital (*Industry Surveys,* Apr. 1996). To potential lenders to the firm, a high debt/capital ratio signals that in case of default, the lender is unlikely to recover outstanding loans to the firm, since insufficient capital may exist to cover all the firm's obligations. In addition, the higher the debt, the more funds that are required to service the debt. As a result, if business falls off, the firm may lack sufficient operating funds to meet debt service payments (Diamond, *Financial Accounting,* 1996). The debt/capital ratios (expressed as a percentage) for firms in four industries are given in the next table for the fiscal year ending during 1995.

a. Propose a regression model involving the qualitative independent variable Industry that could be used to investigate whether the mean

```
The regression equation is
Y = 80.0 + 16.8 X1 + 40.4 X2

Predictor      Coef       Stdev     t-ratio        p
Constant       80.000     4.082       19.60     0.000
X1             16.800     5.774        2.91     0.013
X2             40.400     5.774        7.00     0.000

s = 9.129     R-sq = 80.5%    R-sq(adj) = 77.2%
Analysis of Variance

SOURCE         DF         SS          MS         F        p
Regression      2       4118.9      2059.5     24.72    0.000
Error          12       1000.0        83.3
Total          14       5118.9
```

Industry	Firm	Debt/Capital (%)
Aerospace and Defense	Raytheon	26.1
	Boeing	19.7
	Textron	76.8
	Thiokol	0.6
	Lockheed Martin	31.5
	Rohr	75.4
Electric Utilities	Pacific G & E	37.3
	Houston Ind.	37.4
	Florida Progress	34.5
	Duke Power	31.2
	North States Power	32.1
	Ohio Edison	37.7
	Hawaiian Electric	38.5
Retailing	Rite Aid	46.3
	Kmart	38.6
	Bradlees	59.8
	Spiegel	65.5
	Fay's	43.7
Chemical	Olin	32.7
	Valspar	44.9
	Dow Chemical	32.5
	FMC	59.7
	Union Carbide	41.5

Source: "Annual report on American industry." *Forbes,* Jan. 1, 1996.

debt/capital ratio varies among the four industries. Be sure to specify the coding scheme for the dummy variable in your model.

b. Compute estimates of the β's in the model, part **a**, without the aid of a computer. (Use your knowledge of the relationships between the β's and the means of the four industry groups.)

c. The model, part **a**, is fit to the data using SPSS (printout shown below). Test the null hypothesis that the mean debt/capital ratios are equal in the four industries. Use $\alpha = .05$.

12.51 **(X12.051)** Five varieties of peas are currently being tested by a large agribusiness cooperative to determine which is best suited for production. A field was divided into 20 plots, with each variety of peas planted in four plots. The yields (in bushels of peas) produced from each plot are shown in the table.

VARIETY OF PEAS

A	B	C	D	E
26.2	29.2	29.1	21.3	20.1
24.3	28.1	30.8	22.4	19.3
21.8	27.3	33.9	24.3	19.9
28.1	31.2	32.8	21.8	22.1

SAS was used to fit the model

$$y = \beta_0 + \beta_1 x_1 + \beta_2 x_2 + \beta_3 x_3 + \beta_4 x_4 + \epsilon$$

to these data, using the coding $x_1 = 1$ for variety A, $x_2 = 1$ for variety B, $x_3 = 1$ for variety C, and $x_4 = 1$

```
* * * *  M U L T I P L E   R E G R E S S I O N  * * * *

Equation Number 1    Dependent Variable..  Y

Variable(s) Entered on Step Number
    1..    X3
    2..    X1
    3..    X2

Multiple R            .33371
R Square              .11136
Adjusted R Square    -.02895
Standard Error      17.60330

Analysis of Variance
                    DF      Sum of Squares      Mean Square
Regression          3           737.82724       245.94241
Residual           19          5887.64929       309.87628

F =        .79368      Signif F =   .5124

------------------Variables in the Equation------------------

Variable            B          SE B         Beta        T    Sig T

X3            8.520000    11.133306      .207056     .765   .4535
X1           -3.910000    10.659329     -.101159    -.367   .7178
X2           -6.731429    10.307439     -.182492    -.653   .5215
(Constant)   42.260000     7.872436                 5.368   .0000
```

```
Dep Variable: Y

                        Analysis of Variance

                          Sum of              Mean
     Source        DF     Squares            Square    F Value    Prob>F

     Model          4     342.0400          85.51000    23.966    0.0001
     Error         15      53.52000          3.56800
     C Total       19     395.56000

              Root MSE       1.88892      R-Square     0.8647
              Dep Mean      25.70000      Adj R-Sq     0.8286
              C.V.           7.34986

                        Parameter Estimates

                     Parameter      Standard      T for H0:
     Variable   DF   Estimate        Error      Parameter=0    Prob > |T|

     INTERCEP    1   20.350000     0.94445752      21.547         0.0001
     X1          1    4.750000     1.33566463       3.556         0.0029
     X2          1    8.600000     1.33566463       6.439         0.0001
     X3          1   11.300000     1.33566463       8.460         0.0001
     X4          1    2.100000     1.33566463       1.572         0.1367
```

for variety D. The resulting printout is shown at the top of the page.

a. Write the model relating mean yield to pea variety, and interpret all the parameters in the model.

b. Report the least squares model from the SAS printout.

c. What null and alternative hypotheses are tested by the global F-test for this model? Interpret the hypotheses both in terms of the β parameters and the mean yields for the five varieties of peas.

d. Test the hypotheses of part **c** using $\alpha = .05$.

e. Place a 95% confidence interval on the differences in the mean yields of varieties D and E.

12.52 (X12.052) As large U.S. companies flattened their management hierarchies during the early and mid-1990s, many of the middle managers who were laid off gave up on "corporate life" and started their own companies or bought franchise operations. This talent migration, along with the fact that most new jobs in the United States were being created by small businesses, cast entrepreneurism into the national spotlight in the 1990s. The businesses listed in the table on page 618 are among the fastest growing in the franchise industry.

a. Propose a regression model that will enable you to compare the mean number of new franchises for the four types of franchises (food, cleaning, accounting/consulting, hospitality).

b. Without the aid of a computer, find estimates of the β's in the model.

c. Use a statistical software package to fit the model, part **a**, to the data. Interpret the regression results. Specifically, are there differences in the mean number of franchises for the four franchise types?

12.53 The manager of a convenience store wants to model the total weekly sales of beer, y, as a function of brand. This model will enable the manager to plan the store's inventory. The market carries three brands, B_1, B_2, and B_3.

a. What type of independent variable is Brand of beer?

b. Write the model relating mean weekly beer sales $E(y)$ as a function of Brand of beer. Use brand B_1 as the base level in coding the dummy variables. Be sure to explain any dummy variables you use.

c. Interpret the β parameters of your model in part **b**.

d. In terms of the model parameters, what are the mean weekly sales for brand B_3?

12.54 Refer to Exercise 12.53. Suppose the manager uses brand B_1 as the base level and obtains the prediction equation

$$\hat{y} = 450 + 60x_1 - 30x_2$$

where

$$x_1 = \begin{cases} 1 & \text{if brand } B_2 \\ 0 & \text{otherwise} \end{cases}$$

$$x_2 = \begin{cases} 1 & \text{if brand } B_3 \\ 0 & \text{otherwise} \end{cases}$$

Franchise	Type	Number of New Franchises (1994–1995)
Blimpie	Food	330
Tower Cleaning	Cleaning	55
CleanNet USA	Cleaning	430
KFC	Food	169
Comprehensive Business Services	Accounting/Consulting	58
Jani-King	Cleaning	451
Coverall Cleaning Concepts	Cleaning	435
McDonald's	Food	744
Applebee's	Food	124
Padgett Business Services	Accounting/Consulting	47
Super 8 Motels	Hospitality	181
General Business Services	Accounting/Consulting	44
LedgerPlus	Accounting/Consulting	79
Sonic Drive-In	Food	73
Pizza Inn	Food	39
Holiday Inn Worldwide	Hospitality	150
Choice Hotels Int'l	Hospitality	93
Merry Maids	Cleaning	102
Checkers Drive-In	Food	45

Source: Entrepreneur, Apr. 1996, p. 150.

a. What is the difference between the estimated mean weekly sales for brands B_2 and B_1?

b. What is the estimated mean weekly sales for brand B_2? [*Note:* We would generally form confidence intervals for the true means in order to assess the reliability of these estimates. Our objective in these exercises is to develop the ability to use the models to obtain the estimates.]

12.55 The director of marketing of a company that sells business machines is interested in modeling mean monthly sales (in thousands of dollars) per salesperson, $E(y)$, as a function of the type of sales incentive plan that is in effect: commission only, straight salary, or salary plus commission on each sale. The director has proposed the following model:

$$E(y) = \beta_0 + \beta_1 x_1 + \beta_2 x_2$$

where

$$x_1 = \begin{cases} 1 & \text{if salesperson is paid a straight salary} \\ 0 & \text{otherwise} \end{cases}$$

$$x_2 = \begin{cases} 1 & \text{if salesperson is paid a salary plus commission} \\ 0 & \text{otherwise} \end{cases}$$

MINITAB was used to fit this model to the sales data collected from a sample of 15 salespersons (five from each incentive plan). The printout is shown below.

```
The regression equation is
Y  = 20.0 - 8.60 X1 + 3.80 X2

Predictor       Coef        Stdev      t-ratio         p
Constant       20.00        2.898         6.90     0.000
X1             -8.60        4.100        -2.10     0.055
X2              3.80        4.100         0.93     0.386

s = 6.481       R-sq = 44.5%      R-sq(adj) = 35.2%

Analysis of Variance

SOURCE          DF           SS           MS         F         p
Regression       2        403.6       201.80      4.80     0.033
Error           12        504.0        42.00
Total           14        907.6
```

a. Do the data provide sufficient evidence to conclude that there is a difference in mean monthly sales among the three incentive plans? Test using $\alpha = .05$.

b. Use the least squares prediction equation to estimate the mean sales for salespersons working on a straight-salary basis.

c. Use the least squares prediction equation to estimate the mean sales for salespersons working on a commission-only basis.

[*Note:* We would prefer to use confidence intervals for the estimates in parts **b** and **c**, but their calculation is beyond the scope of this text. This procedure can be found in references at the end of the book.]

12.7   COMPARING THE SLOPES OF TWO OR MORE LINES

Suppose you wish to relate the mean monthly sales $E(y)$ of a company to monthly advertising expenditure x for three different advertising media (say newspaper, radio, and television), and you wish to use first-order (straight-line) models to model the responses for all three media. Graphs of these three relationships might appear as shown in Figure 12.18.

Since the lines in Figure 12.18 are hypothetical, a number of practical questions arise. Is one advertising medium as effective as any other? That is, do the three mean sales lines differ for the three advertising media? Do the increases in mean sales per dollar input in advertising differ for the three advertising media? That is, do the slopes of the three lines differ? Note that the two practical questions have been rephrased into questions about the parameters that define the three lines of Figure 12.18. To answer them, we must write a single linear statistical model that will characterize the three lines of Figure 12.18 and that will allow us to test hypotheses about the lines.

The response described previously, monthly sales, is a function of *two* independent variables, one quantitative (advertising expenditure x_1) and one qualitative (type of medium). We will proceed, in stages, to build a model relating $E(y)$ to these variables; then we will show graphically the interpretation we would give to the model at each stage. This will help you to see the contributions of the various terms in the model.

1. The straight-line relationship between mean sales $E(y)$ and advertising expenditure is the same for all three media—that is, a single line will describe the relationship between $E(y)$ and advertising expenditure x_1 for all the media (see Figure 12.19).

$$E(y) = \beta_0 + \beta_1 x$$

where

$$x_1 = \text{Advertising expenditure}$$

FIGURE 12.18
Graphs of the relationship between mean sales $E(y)$ and advertising expenditure x

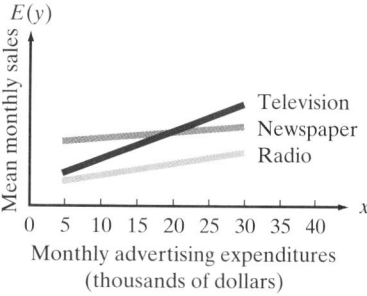

FIGURE 12.19

The relationship between $E(y)$ and x_1 is the same for all media

2. The straight lines relating mean sales $E(y)$ to advertising expenditure x_1 differ from one medium to another, but the rate of increase in mean sales per increase in dollar advertising expenditure x_1 is the same for all media—that is, the lines are parallel but possess different y-intercepts (see Figure 12.20).

$$E(y) = \beta_0 + \beta_1 x + \beta_2 x_2 + \beta_3 x_3$$

where

$$x_1 = \text{Advertising expenditure}$$

$$x_2 = \begin{cases} 1 & \text{if radio medium} \\ 0 & \text{if not} \end{cases}$$

$$x_3 = \begin{cases} 1 & \text{if television medium} \\ 0 & \text{if not} \end{cases}$$

Notice that this model is essentially a combination of a first-order model with a single quantitative variable and the model with a single qualitative variable:

First-order model with a single quantitative variable: $E(y) = \beta_0 + \beta_1 x_1$

Model with a single qualitative variable at three levels: $E(y) = \beta_0 + \beta_2 x_2 + \beta_3 x_3$

where x_1, x_2, and x_3 are as just defined. The model described here implies no interaction between the two independent variables, advertising expenditure x_1, and the qualitative variable, type of advertising medium. The change in $E(y)$ for a 1-unit increase in x_1 is identical (the slopes of the lines are equal) for all three advertising media. The terms corresponding to each of the independent variables are called **main effect terms** because they imply no interaction.

3. The straight lines relating mean sales $E(y)$ to advertising expenditure x_1 differ for the three advertising media—that is, both the line intercepts and the slopes differ (see Figure 12.21). As you will see, this interaction model is

FIGURE 12.20

Parallel response lines for the three media

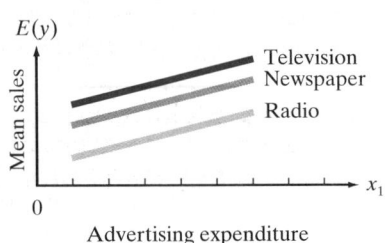

FIGURE 12.21
Different response
lines for the three
media

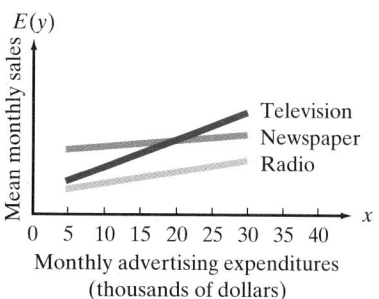

obtained by adding terms involving the cross-product terms, one each from
each of the two independent variables:

Main effect, advertising expenditure	Main effect, type of medium	Interaction

$$E(y) = \beta_0 + \overbrace{\beta_1 x_1} + \overbrace{\beta_2 x_2 + \beta_3 x_3} + \overbrace{\beta_4 x_1 x_2 + \beta_5 x_1 x_3}$$

Note that each of the preceding models is obtained by adding terms to model
1, the single first-order model used to model the responses for all three media.
Model 2 is obtained by adding the main effect terms for type of medium, the qualitative variable. Model 3 is obtained by adding the interaction terms to model 2.

Will a single line (Figure 12.19) characterize the responses for all three media?
Or do all three response lines differ as shown in Figure 12.21? A test of the null
hypothesis that a single first-order model adequately describes the relationship
between $E(y)$ and advertising expenditure x_1 for all three media is a test of the
null hypothesis that the parameters of model 3, β_2, β_3, β_4, and β_5 equal 0; that is,

$$H_0: \beta_2 = \beta_3 = \beta_4 = \beta_5 = 0$$

This hypothesis can be tested by fitting the complete model (model 3) and the
reduced model (model 1) and conducting an F-test.

Suppose we assume that the response lines for the three media will differ but
wonder whether the data present sufficient evidence to indicate a difference among
the slopes of the lines. To test the null hypothesis that model 2 adequately describes
the relationship between $E(y)$ and advertising expenditure x_1, we wish to test

$$H_0: \beta_4 = \beta_5 = 0$$

that is, that the two independent variables, advertising expenditure x_1 and type of
medium, do not interact. This test can be conducted by fitting the complete model
(model 3) and the reduced model (model 2), calculating the drop in the sum of
squares for error, and conducting an F-test as described in Section 12.5.

EXAMPLE 12.6   Substitute the appropriate values of the dummy variables in model 3 to obtain the
equations of the three response lines in Figure 12.21.

SOLUTION
The complete model that characterizes the three lines in Figure 12.21 is

$$E(y) = \beta_0 + \beta_1 x_1 + \beta_2 x_2 + \beta_3 x_3 + \beta_4 x_1 x_2 + \beta_5 x_1 x_3$$

where

$$x_1 = \text{Advertising expenditure}$$

$$x_2 = \begin{cases} 1 & \text{if radio medium} \\ 0 & \text{if not} \end{cases}$$

$$x_3 = \begin{cases} 1 & \text{if television medium} \\ 0 & \text{if not} \end{cases}$$

Examining the coding, you can see that $x_2 = x_3 = 0$ when the advertising medium is newspaper. Substituting these values into the expression for $E(y)$, we obtain the newspaper medium line:

$$E(y) = \beta_0 + \beta_1 x_1 + \beta_2(0) + \beta_3(0) + \beta_4 x_1(0) + \beta_5 x_1(0) = \beta_0 + \beta_1 x_1$$

Similarly, we substitute the appropriate values of x_2 and x_3 into the expression for $E(y)$ to obtain the radio medium line:

$$E(y) = \beta_0 + \beta_1 x_1 + \beta_2(1) + \beta_3(0) + \beta_4 x_1(1) + \beta_5 x_1(0)$$

$$= \underbrace{(\beta_0 + \beta_2)}_{\textbf{y-intercept}} + \underbrace{(\beta_1 + \beta_4)x_1}_{\textbf{Slope}}$$

and the television medium line:

$$E(y) = \beta_0 + \beta_1 x_1 + \beta_2(0) + \beta_3(1) + \beta_4 x_1(0) + \beta_5 x_1(1)$$

$$= \underbrace{(\beta_0 + \beta_3)}_{\textbf{y-intercept}} + \underbrace{(\beta_1 + \beta_5)x_1}_{\textbf{Slope}}$$

If you were to fit the general equation (model 3), obtain estimates of $\beta_0, \beta_1, \beta_2, \ldots, \beta_5$, and substitute them into the equations for the three media lines shown, you would obtain exactly the same prediction equations as you would obtain if you were to fit three separate straight lines, one to each of the three sets of media data. You may ask why we would not fit the three lines separately. Why bother fitting a model that combines all three lines (model 3) into the same equation? The answer is that you need to use this procedure if you wish to use statistical tests to compare the three media lines. We need to be able to express a practical question about the lines in terms of a hypothesis that a set of parameters in the model equal 0. You could not do this if you were to perform three separate regression analyses and fit a line to each set of media data.

EXAMPLE 12.7

An industrial psychologist conducted an experiment to investigate the relationship between worker productivity and a measure of salary incentive for two manufacturing plants; one, plant A, had union representation and the other, plant B, had nonunion representation. The productivity y per worker was measured by recording the number of machined castings that a worker could produce in a four-week period of 40 hours per week. The incentive was the amount x_1 of bonus (in cents per casting) paid for all castings produced in excess of 1,000 per worker for the four-week period. Nine workers were selected from each plant, and three from each group of nine were assigned to receive a 20¢ bonus per casting, three a 30¢ bonus, and three a 40¢ bonus. The productivity data for the nine workers, three for each plant type and incentive combination, are shown in Table 12.4.

a. Assume that the relationship between mean productivity and incentive is first-order. Plot the data points and graph the prediction equations for the two productivity lines.

TABLE 12.4   **Productivity Data for Example 12.7**

Type of Plant	INCENTIVE		
	20¢/casting	30¢/casting	40¢/casting
Union	1,435, 1,512, 1,491	1,583, 1,529, 1,610	1,601, 1,574, 1,636
Nonunion	1,575, 1,512, 1,488	1,635, 1,589, 1,661	1,645, 1,616, 1,689

FIGURE 12.22
MINITAB printout for the complete model, Example 12.7

```
The regression equation is
Y  = 1365 + 6.22 X1 + 47.8 X2 + .03 X1X2

Predictor        Coef        Stdev     t-ratio        p
Constant      1365.833       51.836       26.35    0.000
X1               6.217        1.667        3.73    0.002
X2              47.778       73.308        0.65    0.525
X1X2            0.0333        2.358        0.01    0.989

s = 40.839      R-sq = 71.1%      R-sq(adj) = 64.8%

Analysis of Variance

SOURCE         DF          SS          MS        F        p
Regression      3    57332.38    19110.80    11.46    0.001
Error          14    23349.23     1667.80
Total          17    80681.61
```

b. Do the data provide sufficient evidence to indicate a difference in mean worker responses to incentives between the two plants?

SOLUTION

If we assume that a first-order model* is adequate to detect a change in mean productivity as a function of incentive x_1, then the model that produces two productivity lines, one for each plant, is

$$E(y) = \beta_0 + \beta_1 x_1 + \beta_2 x_2 + \beta_3 x_1 x_2$$

where

$$x_1 = \text{Incentive} \qquad x_2 = \begin{cases} 1 & \text{if nonunion plant} \\ 0 & \text{if union plant} \end{cases}$$

a. The MINITAB printout for the regression analysis is shown in Figure 12.22. Reading the parameter estimates from the printout, you can see that

$$\hat{y} = 1{,}365.833 + 6.217 x_1 + 47.778 x_2 + .033 x_1 x_2$$

The prediction equation for the union plant can be obtained (see the coding) by substituting $x_2 = 0$ into the general prediction equation. Then

$$\hat{y} = \hat{\beta}_0 + \hat{\beta}_1 x_1 + \hat{\beta}_2(0) + \hat{\beta}_3 x_1(0) = \hat{\beta}_0 + \hat{\beta}_1 x_1$$
$$= 1{,}365.833 + 6.217 x_1$$

---

*Although the model contains a term involving $x_1 x_2$, it is first order (graphs as a straight line) in the quantitative variable x_1. The variable x_2 is a dummy variable that introduces or deletes terms in the model. The order of a model is determined only by the quantitative variables that appear in the model.

FIGURE 12.23
Graphs of the prediction equations for the two productivity lines, Example 12.7

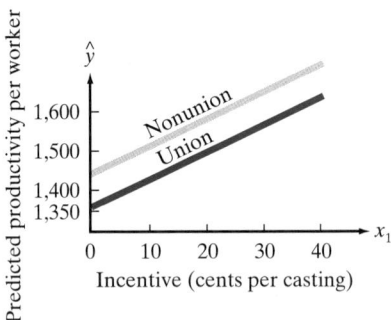

Similarly, the prediction equation for the nonunion plant can be obtained by substituting $x_2 = 1$ into the general prediction equation. Then

$$\hat{y} = \hat{\beta}_0 + \hat{\beta}_1 x_1 + \hat{\beta}_2 x_2 + \hat{\beta}_3 x_1 x_2$$
$$= \hat{\beta}_0 + \hat{\beta}_1 x_1 + \hat{\beta}_2(1) + \hat{\beta}_3 x_1(1)$$

$$= \overbrace{(\hat{\beta}_0 + \hat{\beta}_2)}^{\text{y-intercept}} + \overbrace{(\hat{\beta}_1 + \hat{\beta}_3)x_1}^{\text{Slope}}$$
$$= (1{,}365.833 + 47.778) + (6.217 + .033)x_1$$
$$= 1{,}413.611 + 6.250x_1$$

A graph of these prediction equations is shown in Figure 12.23. Note that the slopes of the two lines are nearly identical (6.217 for union and 6.250 for nonunion).

b. To determine whether the data provide sufficient evidence to indicate a difference in mean worker responses to incentives for the two plants, we test the null hypothesis that a *single* line characterizes the relationship between productivity per worker y and the amount of incentive x_1 against the alternative hypothesis that we need two separate lines to characterize the relationship—one for each plant. If there is no difference in mean response $E(y)$ to x_1 between the two plants, then we do not need the variable Type of plant in the model, i.e., we do not need the terms involving x_2. Therefore, we wish to test

$$H_0: \beta_2 = \beta_3 = 0$$

against the alternative hypothesis

H_a: At least one of the two parameters, β_2 or β_3, is not equal to 0

The MINITAB printout for fitting the reduced model

$$E(y) = \beta_0 + \beta_1 x_1$$

to the data is shown in Figure 12.24. Reading SSE_c and SSE_r from Figures 12.22 and 12.24, respectively, we obtain

Complete model: $SSE_c = 23{,}349.23$

Reduced model: $SSE_r = 34{,}056.28$

Drop in SSE: $SSE_r - SSE_c = 10{,}707.05$

The value of MSE, or s^2, for the complete model (Figure 12.22) is 1,667.80. Substituting these values, along with $k = 3$ and $g = 1$, into the formula for the F statistic yields

FIGURE 12.24
MINITAB printout for the reduced model, Example 12.7

```
The regression equation is
Y  = 1390 + 6.23 X1

Predictor         Coef       Stdev     t-ratio          p
Constant      1389.722      41.408       33.56      0.000
X1               6.233       1.332        4.68      0.000

s = 46.136      R-sq = 57.8%      R-sq(adj) = 55.2%

Analysis of Variance

SOURCE           DF           SS          MS          F          p
Regression        1     46625.33    46625.33      21.91      0.000
Error            16     34056.28     2128.52
Total            17     80681.61
```

$$F = \frac{(SSE_r - SSE_c)/(k - g)}{MSE_c} = \frac{(10{,}707.05)/2}{1{,}667.80} = 3.21$$

The numerator degrees of freedom (the number of parameters involved in H_0) is $\nu_1 = 2$ and the denominator degrees of freedom (the degrees of freedom associated with s^2 in the complete model) is $\nu_2 = 14$. If we choose $\alpha = .05$, the tabulated value of $F_{.05}$ given in Table IX of Appendix B is 3.74. Since the computed value, $F = 3.21$, is less than the tabulated value, $F_{.05} = 3.74$, there is insufficient evidence (at the $\alpha = .05$ significance level) to indicate a difference in mean worker responses to incentives between the two plants. Therefore, there is no evidence to indicate that two different lines, one for each plant, are needed to describe the relationship between mean productivity per worker $E(y)$ and the amount of incentive x_1. ◣

EXAMPLE 12.8

Refer to Example 12.7 and explain how you would determine whether the data provide sufficient evidence to indicate that the incentive x_1 affects mean productivity.

SOLUTION
If the variable incentive did not affect mean productivity, we would not need terms involving x_1 in the model. Therefore, we would test the null hypothesis

$$H_0: \beta_1 = \beta_3 = 0$$

against the alternative hypothesis

$$H_a: \text{At least one of the parameters, } \beta_1 \text{ or } \beta_3, \text{ differs from } 0$$

We would fit the reduced model

$$E(y) = \beta_0 + \beta_2 x_2$$

to the data and find SSE_r. The values of SSE_c and s^2 for the complete model would be the same as those used in Example 12.7. Finally, you would calculate the value of the F statistic and compare it with a tabulated value of F based on $\nu_1 = 2$ numerator df and $\nu_2 = 14$ denominator df. If the test leads to rejection of H_0, you have evidence to indicate that the increase in mean productivity that appears to be present in the graphs in Figure 12.23 is due to random variation in the data. ◣

![EXERCISES] **12.56–12.65**

Note: Exercises marked with 💾 *contain data for computer analysis on a 3.5" disk (file name in parentheses).*

Learning the Mechanics

12.56 Suppose you are interested in a business application with a response y, one quantitative independent variable x_1, and one qualitative variable at three levels.

a. Write a first-order model that relates the mean response $E(y)$ to the quantitative independent variable.

b. Add the main effect terms for the qualitative independent variable to the model of part a. Specify the coding scheme you use.

c. Add terms to the model of part b to allow for interaction between the quantitative and qualitative independent variables.

d. Under what circumstances will the response lines of the model in part c be parallel?

e. Under what circumstances will the model in part c have only one response line?

12.57 SAS was used to fit the following model to $n = 15$ data points:

$$y = \beta_0 + \beta_1 x_1 + \beta_2 x_2 + \beta_3 x_3 + \epsilon$$

where x_1 is a quantitative variable and x_2 and x_3 are dummy variables describing a qualitative variable at three levels using the coding scheme

$$x_2 = \begin{cases} 1 & \text{if level 2} \\ 0 & \text{otherwise} \end{cases} \qquad x_3 = \begin{cases} 1 & \text{if level 3} \\ 0 & \text{otherwise} \end{cases}$$

The resulting printout is shown below.

a. What is the response line (equation) for $E(y)$ when $x_2 = x_3 = 0$? When $x_2 = 1$ and $x_3 = 0$? When $x_2 = 0$ and $x_3 = 1$?

b. What is the general least squares prediction equation for the preceding model?

c. What is the least squares prediction equation associated with level 1? Level 2? Level 3? Plot these on the same graph.

d. Specify the null and alternative hypotheses that should be used to investigate whether a difference exists between the response lines of the qualitative variable levels 1, 2, and 3.

e. Use the printout on the next page with only the quantitative variable x_1 in the model to conduct the hypothesis test of part d. Use $\alpha = .05$.

Applying the Concepts

12.58 California State University at Long Beach researcher E. L. Hansen used multiple regression analysis to investigate the link between entrepreneurial networks and new organization growth (*Entrepreneurship Theory and Practice*, Summer 1995). The dependent variable, initial new organization growth (y), is defined as the monthly payroll of the firm at the end of its first year in business. One independent variable considered in the model (and found to be statistically significant) is entrepreneurial action set size (x_1), defined as the number of people in the entrepreneur's social network who are directly or indirectly involved with the founding of the new organization. A second independent variable considered in the study was

---

```
Dep Variable: Y

                        Analysis of Variance

                              Sum of          Mean
        Source      DF        Squares         Square     F Value    Prob>F

        Model        3      4747.70480     1582.56827     46.894     0.0001
        Error       11       371.22853       33.74805
        C Total     14      5118.93333

                Root MSE         5.80931     R-Square      0.9275
                Dep Mean        99.06667     Adj R-Sq      0.9077
                C.V.             5.86404

                        Parameter Estimates

                        Parameter      Standard     T for HO:
        Variable    DF   Estimate         Error     Parameter=0    Prob > |T|

        INTERCEP    1    44.802703     8.55817652       5.235         0.0003
        X1          1     2.172673     0.50335248       4.316         0.0012
        X2          1     9.412913     4.05315974       2.322         0.0404
        X3          1    15.631532     6.81368981       2.294         0.0425
```

```
Dep Variable: Y
                        Analysis of Variance

                             Sum of          Mean
        Source      DF       Squares        Square    F Value    Prob>F
        Model        1     4522.90741     4522.90741    98.650    0.0001
        Error       13      596.02592       45.84815
        C Total     14     5118.93333

              Root MSE       6.77113     R-Square    0.8836
              Dep Mean      99.06667     Adj R-Sq    0.8746
              C.V.           6.83492

                       Parameter Estimates

                     Parameter      Standard      T for HO:
        Variable   DF  Estimate         Error   Parameter=0   Prob > |T|
        INTERCEP    1  33.904568    6.78960378         4.994       0.0002
        X1          1   3.083380    0.31044102         9.932       0.0001
```

a dummy variable that represented the technology level of the new firm, where

$$x_2 = \begin{cases} 1 & \text{if high-tech firm} \\ 0 & \text{if low-tech firm} \end{cases}$$

a. Write a first-order model for new firm growth (y) as a function of entrepreneurial action set size (x_1) and technology level (x_2). Assume that the effect of size on new firm growth is independent of technology level.

b. In terms of the β's of the model, part **a**, give the slope of the line relating new firm growth (y) to size (x_1) for high-tech firms.

c. Repeat part **a**, but assume that the rate of change of new firm growth (y) with size (x_1) depends on technology level (x_2).

d. In terms of the β's of the model, part **c**, give the slope of the line relating new firm growth (y) to size (x_1) for high-tech firms.

12.59 The Florida Citrus Commission is interested in evaluating the performance of two orange juice extractors, brand A and brand B. It is believed that the size of the fruit used in the test may influence the juice yield (amount of juice per pound of oranges) obtained by the extractors. The commission wants to develop a regression model relating the mean juice yield $E(y)$ to the type of orange juice extractor (brand A or brand B) and the size of orange (diameter), x_1.

a. Identify the independent variables as qualitative or quantitative.

b. Write a model that describes the relationship between $E(y)$ and size of orange as two parallel lines, one for each brand of extractor.

c. Modify the model of part **b** to permit the slopes of the two lines to differ.

d. Sketch typical response lines for the model of part **b**. Do the same for the model of part **c**. Carefully label your graphs.

e. Specify the null and alternative hypotheses you would use to determine whether the model in part **c** provides more information for predicting yield than does the model in part **b**.

f. Explain how you would obtain the quantities necessary to compute the F statistic that would be used in testing the hypotheses you described in part **e**.

12.60 Numerous "sun safety" products exist on the market to prevent excessive exposure to solar radiation. But many people do not practice sun safety or fail to recognize the effectiveness of these products. A group of University of Arizona researchers examined the feasibility of educating preschool (4- to 5-year-old) children about sun safety (*American Journal of Public Health,* July 1995). A sample of 122 preschool children was divided into two groups, the control group and the intervention group. Children in the intervention group received a *Be Sun Safe* curriculum in preschool, while the control group did not. All children were tested for their knowledge, comprehension, and application of sun safety at two times: prior to the implementation of the sun safety curriculum (pretest, x_1) and seven weeks following the completion of the curriculum (posttest, y).

a. Write a first-order model for mean posttest score, $E(y)$, as a function of pretest score x_1 and group. Assume that no interaction exists between pretest score and group.

b. For the model, part **a**, show that the slope of the line relating posttest score to pretest score is the same for both groups of children.

c. Repeat part **a**, but assume that pretest score and group interact.

d. For the model, part **c**, show that the slope of the line relating posttest score to pretest score differs for the two groups of children.

e. Assuming interaction exists, give the reduced model for testing whether the mean posttest scores differ for the intervention and control groups.

f. When sun safety knowledge was used as the dependent variable, the test of part **c** resulted in a *p*-value of .03. Interpret this result.

g. When sun safety comprehension was used as the dependent variable, the test of part **e** resulted in a *p*-value of .033. Interpret this result.

h. When sun safety application was used as the dependent variable, the test of part **e** resulted in a *p*-value of .322. Interpret this result.

12.61 Researchers for a dog food company have developed a new puppy food they hope will compete with the major brands. One premarketing test involved the comparison of the new food with that of two competitors in terms of weight gain. Fifteen eight-week-old German shepherd puppies, each from a different litter, were divided into three groups of five puppies each. Each group was fed one of the three brands of food.

a. Set up a model that assumes the final weight *y* is linearly related to initial weight *x* but does not allow for differences among the three brands; that is, assume the response curve is the same for the three brands of dog food. Sketch the response curve as it might appear.

b. Set up a model that assumes the final weight is linearly related to initial weight and allows the intercepts of the lines to differ for the three brands. In other words, assume that the initial weight and brand both affect final weight, but the two variables do not interact. Sketch typical response curves.

c. Now write the main effects with interaction model. For this model we assume the final weight is linearly related to initial weight, but both the slopes and the intercepts of the lines depend on the brand. Sketch typical response curves.

12.62 **(X12.062)** In Exercise 10.38, researchers Erb, Harvey, and Viskanta considered the relationship between country credit ratings and the volatility of the countries' stock markets. In a more recent paper (*Journal of Portfolio Management,* Spring 1996), the researchers point out that this volatility can be explained by two factors: the countries' credit ratings and whether the countries in question have developed or emerging markets. The table on page 629 gives the volatility (measured as the standard deviation of stock returns), credit rating (measured as a percentage), and market type (developed or emerging) for a sample of 30 different countries.

a. Write a model that describes the relationship between volatility (*y*) and credit rating (x_1) as two nonparallel lines, one for each type of market. Specify the dummy variable coding scheme you use.

b. Plot volatility (*y*) against credit rating (x_1) for all the developed markets in the sample. On the same graph, plot *y* against x_1 for all emerging markets in the sample. Does it appear that the model specified in part **a** is appropriate? Explain.

c. Fit the model, part **a**, to the data using a statistical software package. Report the least squares prediction equation for each of the two types of markets.

d. Plot the two prediction equations of part **c** on a scattergram of the data.

e. Is there evidence to conclude that the slope of the linear relationship between volatility (*y*) and credit rating (x_1) depends on market type? Test using $\alpha = .01$.

12.63 **(X12.063)** A pharmaceutical company wishes to find a model that will predict the mean time to relief after the administration of a certain drug. Two important independent variables are considered to be good predictors of relief time. They are age of the patient and method of administration. Physicians administer a standard dose of a drug to a patient in one of three different ways: orally in liquid form (method 1), orally in pill form (method 2), and intravenously (method 3). Consequently, we might use the model

$$E(y) = \beta_0 + \beta_1 x_1 + \beta_2 x_2 + \beta_3 x_3 + \beta_4 x_1 x_2 + \beta_5 x_1 x_3$$

where

y = Time to relief (in minutes)

x_1 = Age of patient (in years)

$x_2 = \begin{cases} 1 & \text{if drug is administered orally in pill form} \\ 0 & \text{if not} \end{cases}$

$x_3 = \begin{cases} 1 & \text{if drug is administered intravenously} \\ 0 & \text{if not} \end{cases}$

The data in the following table, obtained on 12 patients, were used to fit this model.

METHOD 1		METHOD 2		METHOD 3	
Age	Time to Relief	Age	Time to Relief	Age	Time to Relief
51	22	46	28	37	19
36	25	40	24	60	17
31	20	26	23	25	21
20	25	32	25	38	20

Country	Volatility (standard deviation of return) y	Credit Rating x_1	Developed or Emerging? x_2
Afghanistan	55.7	8.3	E
Australia	23.9	71.2	D
China	27.2	57.0	E
Cuba	55.0	8.7	E
Germany	20.3	90.9	D
France	20.6	89.1	D
India	30.3	46.1	E
Belgium	22.3	79.2	D
Canada	22.1	80.3	D
Ethiopia	47.9	14.1	E
Haiti	54.9	8.8	E
Japan	20.2	91.6	D
Libya	36.7	30.0	E
Malaysia	24.3	69.1	E
Mexico	31.8	41.8	E
New Zealand	24.3	69.4	D
Nigeria	46.2	15.8	E
Oman	28.6	51.8	D
Panama	38.6	26.4	E
Spain	23.4	73.7	D
Sudan	60.5	6.0	E
Taiwan	22.2	79.9	D
Norway	21.4	84.6	D
Sweden	23.3	74.1	D
Togo	45.1	17.0	E
Ukraine	46.3	15.7	E
United Kingdom	20.8	87.8	D
United States	20.3	90.7	D
Vietnam	36.9	29.5	E
Zimbabwe	36.2	31.0	E

Source: Erb, C. B., Harvey, C. R., and Viskanta, T. E. "Expected returns and volatility in 135 countries." *Journal of Portfolio Management,* Vol. 22, No. 3, Spring 1996, pp. 54–55 (Exhibit 6). This copyrighted material is reprinted with permission from the Journal of Portfolio Management, a publication of Institutional Investor, Inc., 488 Madison Ave., New York, NY 10022.

a. A multiple regression analysis produced the results shown below. Test whether the model is useful in predicting mean time to relief. Use $\alpha = .05$.

b. What hypothesis would you use to test whether the age–drug method interaction terms contribute to the prediction of mean time to relief?

c. The reduced model

$$E(y) = \beta_0 + \beta_1 x_1 + \beta_2 x_2 + \beta_3 x_3$$

was fit to the data and produced an SSE of 38.289. Does this result provide sufficient evidence at the $\alpha = .05$ level of significance to indicate that the interaction terms should be kept in the model?

d. Use an available computer program to check the results given in parts **a** and **c**.

12.64 An economist is interested in modeling the mean monthly demand $E(y)$ (in thousands of units) for a certain product as a function of its price (in dollars) and the season of the year. The following model has been proposed:

$$E(y) = \beta_0 + \beta_1 x_1 + \beta_2 x_2 + \beta_3 x_3 + \beta_4 x_4$$

where

$$x_1 = \text{Price} \qquad x_2 = \begin{cases} 1 \text{ if spring} \\ 0 \text{ otherwise} \end{cases}$$

$$x_3 = \begin{cases} 1 \text{ if summer} \\ 0 \text{ otherwise} \end{cases} \qquad x_4 = \begin{cases} 1 \text{ if fall} \\ 0 \text{ otherwise} \end{cases}$$

SOURCE	DF	SUM OF SQUARES	MEAN SQUARE	F	PR > F
MODEL	5	87.473	17.495	4.90	0.0394
ERROR	6	21.443	3.574		
CORRECTED TOTAL	11	108.916		R-SQUARE	0.803120

A portion of the MINITAB computer printout that results from fitting this model to a sample of 16 months of sales data selected from among the last two years is shown below.

The reduced model $E(y) = \beta_0 + \beta_1 x_1$ was also fit to the same data and the resulting computer printout is partially reproduced below.

a. Do these data present sufficient evidence to conclude that mean monthly demand depends on the season of the year? Test using $\alpha = .05$.

b. Find an estimate for $E(y)$ when the price is $8 and it is summer. Interpret your result. [*Note:* We prefer to use a confidence interval for this estimate, but its calculation is beyond the scope of this text. This procedure can be found in the references.]

12.65 A company is studying three safety programs, A, B, and C, in an attempt to reduce the number of work-hours lost due to accidents. Each program is to be tried at three of the company's nine factories, and the plan is to monitor the lost work-hours, y, for one year beginning six months after the new safety program is instituted.

a. Write a main effects model relating $E(y)$ to the lost work-hours, x_1, the year before the plan is instituted and to the type of program that is instituted.

b. In terms of the model parameters from part **a**, what hypothesis would you test to determine whether the mean work-hours lost differ for the three safety programs?

c. After the three safety programs have been in effect for 18 months, the complete main effects model is fit to the $n = 9$ data points. With safety program A as the base level, the following results are obtained:

$$y = -2.1 + .88x_1 - 150x_2 + 35x_3$$

$$SSE_c = 1,527.27$$

Then the reduced model $E(y) = \beta_0 + \beta_1 x_1$ is fit, with the result

$$y = 15.3 + .84x_1 \qquad SSE_r = 3,113.14$$

Test whether the mean work-hours lost differ for the three programs. Use $\alpha = .05$.

```
Complete model

The regression equation is
Y = 12.1 - 1.11 X1 + 3.94 X2 + 7.17 X3 + 3.74 X4

Predictor        Coef      Stdev     t-ratio         p
Constant       12.067      1.473        8.19     0.000
X1             -1.113      0.187       -5.93     0.000
X2              3.942      0.858        4.59     0.001
X3              7.166      0.815        8.80     0.000
X4              3.724      0.819        4.55     0.001

s = 1.135      R-sq = 93.1%     R-sq(adj) = 90.6%

Analysis of Variance

SOURCE         DF          SS          MS          F         p
Regression      4      191.59      47.897      37.22     0.000
Error          11       14.16       1.287
Total          15      205.75
```

```
Reduced model

The regression equation is
Y = 17.4 - 1.35 X1

Predictor        Coef      Stdev     t-ratio         p
Constant       17.394      2.833        6.08     0.000
X1             -1.348      0.403       -3.34     0.006

s = 2.859      R-sq = 44.4%     R-sq(adj) = 40.4%

Analysis of Variance

SOURCE         DF          SS          MS          F         p
Regression      1       91.35       91.35      11.18     0.006
Error          14      114.40        8.17
Total          15      205.75
```

12.8 COMPARING TWO OR MORE RESPONSE CURVES

Suppose we think that the relationship between mean monthly sales $E(y)$ and advertising expenditure x_1 (Section 12.7) is second-order. We will construct, stage by stage, a model relating $E(y)$ to the quantitative variable x_1 and the qualitative variable, Type of medium. This will enable you to compare the procedure with the stage-by-stage construction of the first-order model (Section 12.7). The graphical interpretations will help you understand the contributions of the model terms.

1. The mean sales curves are identical for all three advertising media, that is, a single second-order curve will suffice to describe the relationship between $E(y)$ and x_1 for all the media (see Figure 12.25):

$$E(y) = \beta_0 + \beta_1 x_1 + \beta_2 x_1^2$$

where x_1 = Advertising expenditure

2. The response curves possess the same shapes but different y-intercepts (see Figure 12.26):

$$E(y) = \beta_0 + \beta_1 x_1 + \beta_2 x_1^2 + \beta_3 x_2 + \beta_4 x_3$$

where

$$x_1 = \text{Advertising}$$

$$x_2 = \begin{cases} 1 & \text{if radio medium} \\ 0 & \text{if not} \end{cases}$$

$$x_3 = \begin{cases} 1 & \text{if television medium} \\ 0 & \text{if not} \end{cases}$$

3. The response curves for the three advertising media are different (i.e., Advertising expenditure and Type of medium interact), as shown in Figure 12.27:

$$E(y) = \beta_0 + \beta_1 x_1 + \beta_2 x_1^2 + \beta_3 x_2 + \beta_4 x_3 + \beta_5 x_1 x_2 + \beta_6 x_1 x_3 + \beta_7 x_1^2 x_2 + \beta_8 x_1^2 x_3$$

FIGURE 12.25
The relationship between $E(y)$ and x_1 is the same for all media

FIGURE 12.26
The response curves have the same shapes but different y-intercepts

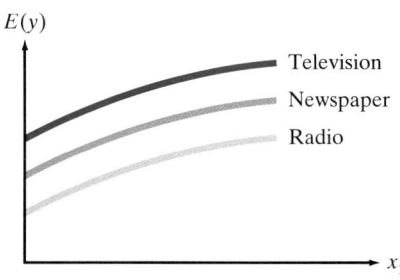

FIGURE 12.27
The response curves for
the three media differ

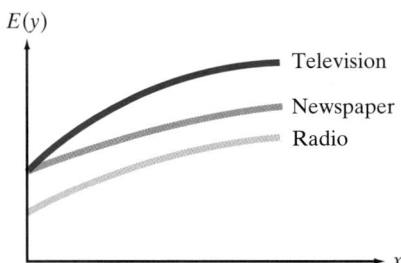

Now that you know how to write a model with two independent variables—one qualitative and one quantitative—we ask a question. Why do it? Why not write a separate second-order model for each type of medium where $E(y)$ is a function of only advertising expenditure? One reason we wrote the single model representing all three response curves is so that we can test to determine whether the curves are different. We illustrate this procedure in Examples 12.10 and 12.11. A second reason for writing a single model is that we obtain a pooled estimate of σ^2, the variance of the random error component ϵ. If the variance of ϵ is truly the same for each type of medium, the pooled estimate is superior to three separate estimates calculated by fitting a separate model for each type of medium.

EXAMPLE 12.9

Give the equation of the second-order model for the radio advertising medium.

SOLUTION

Model 3 characterizes the relationship between $E(y)$ and x_1 for the radio advertising medium (see the coding) when $x_2 = 1$ and $x_3 = 0$. Substituting these values into model 3, we obtain

$$E(y) = \beta_0 + \beta_1 x_1 + \beta_2 x_1^2 + \beta_3 x_2 + \beta_4 x_3 + \beta_5 x_1 x_2 + \beta_6 x_1 x_3 + \beta_7 x_1^2 x_2 + \beta_8 x_1^2 x_3$$
$$= \beta_0 + \beta_1 x_1 + \beta_2 x_1^2 + \beta_3(1) + \beta_4(0) + \beta_5 x_1(1) + \beta_6 x_1(0) +$$
$$\beta_7 x_1^2(0) + \beta_8 x_1^2(0)$$
$$= (\beta_0 + \beta_3) + (\beta_1 + \beta_5)x_1 + (\beta_2 + \beta_7)x_1^2$$

Note: The y-intercept of the response curve is represented by $(\beta_0 + \beta_3)$, the shift parameter by $(\beta_1 + \beta_5)$, and the rate of curvature by $(\beta_2 + \beta_7)$. ◣

EXAMPLE 12.10

What null hypothesis about the parameters of model 3 would you test if you wished to determine whether the second-order curves for the three media are identical?

SOLUTION

If the curves were identical, we would not need the independent variable Type of medium in the model; that is, we would delete all terms involving x_2 and x_3. This would produce model 1

$$E(y) = \beta_0 + \beta_1 x_1 + \beta_2 x_1^2$$

and the null hypothesis would be

$$H_0: \beta_3 = \beta_4 = \beta_5 = \beta_6 = \beta_7 = \beta_8 = 0$$ ◣

EXAMPLE 12.11

Suppose we assume that the response curves for the three media differ, but we want to know whether the second-order terms contribute information for the prediction of y. Or, equivalently, will a second-order model give better predictions than a first-order model?

SOLUTION

The only difference between model 3 and a first-order model are those terms involving x_1^2. Therefore, the null hypothesis, "the second-order terms contribute no information for the prediction of y," is equivalent to

$$H_0: \beta_2 = \beta_7 = \beta_8 = 0$$

Examples 12.10 and 12.11 identify two tests that answer practical questions concerning a collection of second-order models. Other comparisons between the curves can be made by testing appropriate sets of model parameters (see the exercises).

The models described in the preceding sections provide merely an introduction to statistical modeling. Models can be constructed to relate $E(y)$ to any number of quantitative and qualitative independent variables. You can compare response curves and surfaces for different levels of a qualitative variable or for different combinations of levels of two or more qualitative independent variables. A general explanation of how to write linear statistical models can be found in Mendenhall and Sincich (1996, Chapter 5).

STATISTICS IN ACTION

12.1 FORECASTING PEAK-HOUR TRAFFIC VOLUME*

In designing future metropolitan roadways or redesigning existing roads, highway engineers rely heavily on traffic volume forecasts. Should the road have two, three, or four lanes in each direction? How should the on- and off-ramps be configured? Should the on-ramps be metered? Should one or more lanes be reversible to accommodate rush-hour traffic? Should one or more lanes be restricted to carpools? The answers to such questions depend primarily on the traffic volumes the road must be able to handle during the peak travel times of the day—morning and evening rush hours.

Traffic forecasters at the Minnesota Department of Transportation (DOT) use regression analysis to estimate weekday peak-hour traffic volumes on existing and proposed roadways. In particular, they model the traffic volume for the hour with the highest volume (this is the *peak hour*, typically 7–8 A.M.), y, as a function of the road's total traffic volume for the day, x_1. The model is developed using traffic data from existing

roadways. Upon obtaining a forecast for the total weekday traffic volume for the road in question, the forecasters use the regression model to estimate (forecast) the mean peak-hour volume for the road.

For a recent project involving the redesign of a section of Interstate 494 in Bloomington, Minnesota, the forecasters collected data on peak-hour traffic volumes and weekday traffic volumes (using electronic sensors that count vehicles) at eight locations in the Minneapolis area believed to be similar to the one being redesigned. One of the characteristics that was common to the Interstate 494 site and the eight other locations was that the peak-hour volume at each was nearing its theoretical upper bound. A sample of $n = 72$ measurements was obtained. The data are provided in Table 12.5 and a scattergram of the data is shown in Figure 12.28.

The traffic forecasters were surprised to see the isolated group of observations at the top of the scattergram. They investigated and found that all these data points were collected on Interstate 35W at the

continued

intersection of 46th Street, on the south side of Minneapolis. (These are observations 55–72 in Table 12.5.) It turned out that, while all locations in the sample were three-lane highways (including this location), this location was unique because the highway widens to four lanes just a short distance north of the electronic sensor. Accordingly, this location was *not* similar to the section of Interstate 494 being redesigned, as was originally thought. It was decided that the 18 measurements collected at this location should be kept in the sample (in order to maintain a large sample size for the estimation of σ^2), but that a separate peak-hour-volume response curve should be estimated for this location through the use of a dummy variable in the regression model.

Knowing that peak-hour traffic volumes have a theoretical upper bound and that the locations sampled were nearing their bounds, the forecasters hypothesized that a second-order model should be used to explain the variation in peak-hour volume. Since this hypothesis was also supported by the scattergram, they fit the following model to the $n = 72$ data points:

$$E(y) = \beta_0 + \beta_1 x_1 + \beta_2 x_1^2 + \beta_3 x_2 + \beta_4 x_1 x_2$$

where

$$x_2 = \begin{cases} 1 & \text{if Interstate 35W and 46th Street} \\ 0 & \text{otherwise} \end{cases}$$

The results are shown in the MINITAB printout in Figure 12.29. In order to investigate formally whether the relationship between peak-hour volume and total traffic volume for the day at the Interstate 35W location is different from that at the other locations, they eliminated the terms $\beta_3 x_2$ and $\beta_4 x_1 x_2$ from the model and fit the resulting reduced model to the same data, with the results shown in Figure 12.30.

Focus

a. Interpret the regression results for the DOT. Specifically, is the relationship between peak-hour volume and total traffic volume different at the two locations? What are your recommendations for estimating and predicting peak-hour volumes at each site?

b. Conduct a residual analysis of the best model. Evaluate the assumptions of normality and equal variances, and determine whether any outliers exist. (The data in Table 12.5 is available in ASCII format on a 3.5-inch disk available from the publisher.)

*Personal communications from John Sem, Director; Allan E. Pint, State Traffic Forecast Engineer; and James Page Sr., Transportation Planner, Traffic and Commodities Studies Section, Minnesota Department of Transportation, St. Paul, Minnesota.

TABLE 12.5   Minnesota DOT Data (Statistics in Action 12.1)

Observation Number	Peak-Hour Volume	24-Hour Volume	Observation Number	Peak-Hour Volume	24-Hour Volume	Observation Number	Peak-Hour Volume	24-Hour Volume
1	1,990.94	20,070	25	1,923.87	18,184	49	1,978.72	24,249
2	1,989.63	21,234	26	1,922.79	16,926	50	1,975.29	23,321
3	1,986.96	20,633	27	1,917.64	19,062	51	1,973.55	22,842
4	1,986.96	20,676	28	1,916.17	18,043	52	1,973.91	20,626
5	1,983.78	19,818	29	1,916.17	18,043	53	1,972.92	26,166
6	1,983.13	19,931	30	1,916.13	16,691	54	1,966.65	21,755
7	1,982.47	19,266	31	1,912.49	17,339	55	2,120.00	20,250
8	1,981.53	19,658	32	1,912.49	17,339	56	2,140.00	20,251
9	1,979.83	19,203	33	1,909.98	17,867	57	2,160.00	21,852
10	1,979.83	19,958	34	1,907.04	17,773	58	2,186.52	23,511
11	1,978.40	19,152	35	1,907.46	17,678	59	2,180.29	22,431
12	1,978.90	21,651	36	1,905.14	18,024	60	2,174.03	23,734
13	1,977.38	20,198	37	1,902.37	17,405	61	2,174.03	23,734
14	1,972.87	20,508	38	2,017.76	23,517	62	2,167.97	23,387
15	1,964.45	19,783	39	2,009.38	23,017	63	2,160.02	24,885
16	1,962.85	20,815	40	2,007.10	22,808	64	2,160.54	23,332
17	1,964.26	20,105	41	2,007.28	23,152	65	2,159.72	23,838
18	1,961.85	20,500	42	2,004.17	24,352	66	2,155.61	23,662
19	1,961.26	19,593	43	1,997.58	20,939	67	2,147.93	22,948
20	1,958.97	20,818	44	1,994.53	21,822	68	2,147.93	22,948
21	1,943.78	17,480	45	1,984.70	22,918	69	2,147.85	23,551
22	1,927.83	17,768	46	1,984.01	21,129	70	2,144.23	21,637
23	1,928.36	17,659	47	1,983.17	21,674	71	2,142.41	23,543
24	1,925.65	18,357	48	1,982.02	26,148	72	2,137.39	22,594

FIGURE 12.28
Scattergram: Peak-hour traffic volume versus total traffic volume for the day (Statistics in Action 12.1)

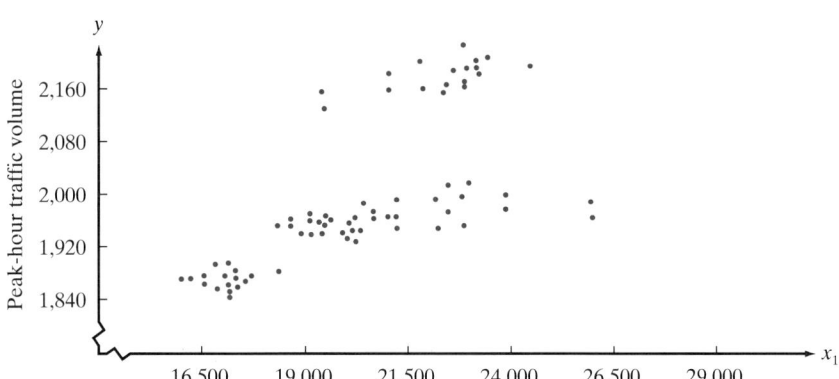

FIGURE 12.29
Peak-hour traffic volume: Complete model (Statistics in Action 12.1)

```
The regression equation is
Y = 779 + 0.104 X1 −0.000002 X1SQ + 98.0 X2 + 0.00291 X1X2

Predictor         Coef         Stdev      t-ratio          p
Constant         779.0         141.8         5.49      0.000
X1             0.10392       0.01363         7.63      0.000
X1SQ       -0.00000222    0.00000032        -6.84      0.000
X2             97.98         75.55          1.30      0.199
X1X2          0.002907      0.003320         0.88      0.384

s = 15.47         R-sq = 97.2%      R-sq(adj) = 97.0%

Analysis of Variance

SOURCE          DF            SS            MS          F          p
Regression       4        555737        138934     580.69      0.000
Error           67         16030           239
Total           71        571767
```

FIGURE 12.30
Peak-hour traffic volume: Reduced model (Statistics in Action 12.1)

```
The regression equation is
Y = 197 + 0.149 X1 −0.000003 X1SQ

Predictor         Coef         Stdev      t-ratio          p
Constant         197.5         578.9         0.34      0.734
X1             0.14921       0.05551         2.69      0.009
X1SQ       -0.00000295    0.00000132        -2.24      0.028

s = 65.45         R-sq = 48.3%      R-sq(adj) = 46.8%

Analysis of Variance

SOURCE          DF            SS            MS          F          p
Regression       2        276171        138085      32.23      0.000
Error           69        295596          4284
Total           71        571767
```

EXERCISES   12.66–12.76

Note: Exercises marked with [disk icon] contain data for computer analysis on a 3.5" disk (file name in parentheses).

Learning the Mechanics

12.66 Consider an application for which you want to relate the response variable y to one quantitative variable and one qualitative variable at three levels.

a. Write a complete second-order model that relates $E(y)$ to the quantitative variable.
b. Add the main effect terms for the qualitative variable (at three levels) to the model of part **a**.
c. Add terms to the model of part **b** to allow for interaction between the quantitative and qualitative independent variables.

12.67 Refer to Exercise 12.66, part **c.**

a. Under what circumstances will the response curves of the model have the same shape but different y-intercepts?

b. Under what circumstances will the response curves of the model be parallel lines?

c. Under what circumstances will the response curves of the model be identical?

12.68 Write a model that relates $E(y)$ to two independent variables—one quantitative and one qualitative at four levels. Construct a model that allows the associated response curves to be second-order but does not allow for interaction between the two independent variables.

12.69 MINITAB was used to fit the following model to $n = 25$ data points:

$$y = \beta_0 + \beta_1 x_1 + \beta_2 x_1^2 + \beta_3 x_2 + \beta_4 x_3 +$$
$$\beta_5 x_1 x_2 + \beta_6 x_1 x_3 + \beta_7 x_1^2 x_2 + \beta_8 x_1^2 x_3 + \epsilon$$

where x_1 is a quantitative variable and

$$x_2 = \begin{cases} 1 & \text{if level 2} \\ 0 & \text{otherwise} \end{cases} \qquad x_3 = \begin{cases} 1 & \text{if level 3} \\ 0 & \text{otherwise} \end{cases}$$

MINITAB was also used to fit the reduced model $y = \beta_0 + \beta_1 x_1 + \beta_2 x_1^2 + \epsilon$ to the same data set. Both printouts are shown below.

a. What is the general least squares prediction equation for the complete model?

b. What is the equation of the response curve for $E(y)$ when $x_2 = 0$ and $x_3 = 0$? When $x_2 = 1$ and $x_3 = 0$? When $x_2 = 0$ and $x_3 = 1$?

```
Complete model

The regression equation is
Y = 48.8 - 3.36 X1 + 0.075 X1SQ - 2.36 X2 - 7.60 X3
      + 3.71 X1X2 + 2.66 X1X3 - 0.018 X1SQX2 - 0.037 X1SQX3

Predictor      Coef      Stdev     t-ratio        p
Constant     48.784      4.186      11.65     0.000
X1           -3.362      0.471      -7.14     0.000
X1SQ          0.075      0.011       6.89     0.000
X2           -2.364      6.922      -0.34     0.779
X3           -7.595      6.102      -1.24     0.226
X1X2          3.714      0.830       4.48     0.001
X1X3          2.659      0.647       4.11     0.002
X1SQX2       -0.018      0.022      -0.84     0.455
X1SQX3       -0.037      0.015      -2.56     0.022

s = 3.190     R-sq = 98.9%      R-sq(adj) = 98.4%

Analysis of Variance

SOURCE        DF         SS         MS          F          p
Regression     8    15256.9     1907.1     186.97      0.000
Error         16      162.9       10.2
Total         24    15419.8
```

```
Reduced model

The regression equation is
Y = 33.9 + 0.86 X1 - 0.011 X1SQ

Predictor      Coef      Stdev     t-ratio        p
Constant     33.930     20.74       1.64      0.083
X1            0.862      2.218       0.39      0.705
X1SQ       -0.01102    0.05103      -0.22      0.844

s = 26.10     R-sq = 2.8%      R-sq(adj) = .0%

Analysis of Variance

SOURCE        DF         SS         MS          F          p
Regression     2      433.7      216.9       0.32      0.789
Error         22    14986.1      681.2
Total         24    15419.8
```

Complete model

SOURCE	DF	SUM OF SQUARES	MEAN SQUARE
MODEL	5	2351.70	470.34
ERROR	194	783.90	.04
TOTAL	199	3135.60	R-SQUARE
			0.750

Reduced model

SOURCE	DF	SUM OF SQUARES	MEAN SQUARE
MODEL	2	2340.37	1170.185
ERROR	197	795.23	4.04
TOTAL	199	3135.60	R-SQUARE
			0.746

c. On the same graph, plot the least squares prediction equation associated with level 1, with level 2, and with level 3.

d. Specify the null and alternative hypotheses that should be used to investigate whether the second-order response curves for the three levels differ.

e. Conduct the hypothesis test of part **d**. Use $\alpha = .05$.

Applying the Concepts

12.70 An equal rights group has charged that women are being discriminated against in terms of the salary structure in a state university system. It is thought that a complete second-order model will be adequate to describe the relationship between salary and years of experience for both men and women. A sample is to be taken from the records for faculty members (all of equal rank) within the system and the following model is fit. [*Note:* In practice, we would include other variables in the model. We include only two here to simplify the exercise.]

$$E(y) - \beta_0 + \beta_1 x_1 + \beta_2 x_1^2 + \beta_3 x_2 + \beta_4 x_1 x_2 + \beta_5 x_1^2 x_2$$

where

y = Annual salary (in thousands of dollars)

x_1 = Experience (years)

$x_2 = \begin{cases} 1 & \text{if female} \\ 0 & \text{if male} \end{cases}$

a. What hypothesis would you test to determine whether the *rate* of increase of mean salary with experience is different for males and females?

b. What hypothesis would you test to determine whether there are differences in mean salaries that are attributable to gender?

12.71 Refer to Exercise 12.70 and the model that was proposed to describe the relationship between salary and years of experience for both men and women. A portion of the computer printout that results from fitting this model to a sample of 200 faculty members in the university system is shown in the first printout above.

The reduced model $E(y) = \beta_0 + \beta_1 x_1 + \beta_2 x_1^2$ is fit to the same data, and the resulting computer printout is the second shown above.

Do the data provide sufficient evidence to support the claim that the mean salary of faculty members is dependent on gender? Use $\alpha = .05$.

12.72 Refer to the *Journal of International Business Studies* study of foreign direct investments (FDIs), Exercise 12.1. Assume that the complete second-order model below will be adequate to describe the relationship between the attractiveness of an Italian province to foreign investors (measured as the difference between the actual number and expected number of FDIs) and unemployment rate. [*Note:* In practice, we would include other variables in the model.]

$$E(y) = \beta_0 + \beta_1 x_1 + \beta_2 x_1^2 + \beta_3 x_2 + \beta_4 x_1 x_2 + \beta_5 x_1^2 x_2$$

where

y = Attractiveness of province to foreign investors

x_1 = Unemployment rate

$x_2 = \begin{cases} 1 & \text{if province borders France or Switzerland (border province)} \\ 0 & \text{if not} \end{cases}$

Analysis of Variance

Source	DF	Sum of Squares	Mean Square	F Value	Prob>F
Model	5	3.37	0.675	11.06	0.0001
Error	89	5.43	0.061		
C Total	94	8.80			

Root MSE	0.246	R-square	0.3830
Dep Mean	2.241	Adj R-sq	0.3483
C.V.	10.977		

a. What hypothesis would you test to determine whether the *rate* of change of number of FDIs with unemployment is different for border and nonborder provinces?

b. What hypothesis would you test to determine whether there are differences in mean number of FDIs for border and nonborder provinces?

c. A portion of the SAS printout that results from fitting the second-order model to a sample of 95 provinces is shown above. The reduced model $E(y) = \beta_0 + \beta_1 x_1 + \beta_2 x_1^2$ is fit to the same data, and the resulting computer printout is reproduced below. Is there sufficient evidence to support the claim that the mean attractiveness of Italian provinces to foreign investors differ for border and nonborder provinces? Use $\alpha = .05$.

12.73 Since glass is not subject to radiation damage, encapsulation of waste in glass is considered to be one of the most promising solutions to the problem of storing low-level nuclear waste. However, glass undergoes chemical changes when exposed to extreme environmental conditions, and certain of its constituents, such as silicon salts, can leach into the surroundings. In addition, these chemical reactions tend to weaken the glass. These concerns led to a study undertaken jointly by the Department of Materials Science and Engineering at the University of Florida and the U.S. Department of Energy to assess the utility of glass as a waste encapsulant. Corrosive chemical solutions (called corrosion baths) were prepared and applied directly to glass samples containing one of three types of waste (TDS-3A, FE, and AL); the chemical reactions were observed over time. A few of the key variables measured were y = Amount of silicon (in parts per million) found in solution at end of experiment. (This is both a measure of the degree of breakdown in the glass and a proxy for the amount of radioactive species released into the environment.)

x_1 = Temperature (°C) of the corrosion bath

$$x_2 = \begin{cases} 1 & \text{if waste type TDS-3A} \\ 0 & \text{if not} \end{cases}$$

$$x_3 = \begin{cases} 1 & \text{if waste type FE} \\ 0 & \text{if not} \end{cases}$$

Waste type AL is the base level. Suppose we want to model amount y of silicon as a function of temperature (x_1) and type of waste (x_2, x_3). [*Note:* The background information for this exercise was provided by Dr. David Clark, Department of Materials Science and Engineering, University of Florida.]

a. Write a model that proposes parallel straight-line relationships between amount of silicon and temperature, one line for each of the three waste types.

b. Add terms for the interaction between temperature and waste type to the model of part a.

Analysis of Variance

Source	DF	Sum of Squares	Mean Square	F Value	Prob>F
Model	2	1.29	0.645	7.86	0.0001
Error	92	7.51	0.082		
C Total	94	8.80			

Root MSE	0.286	R-square	0.1465
Dep Mean	2.241	Adj R-sq	0.1280
C.V.	12.778		

c. Refer to the model of part **b**. For each waste type, give the slope of the line relating amount of silicon to temperature.

d. Explain how you could test for the presence of temperature–waste type interaction.

12.74 **(X12.074)** Automobile accidents result in a tragic loss of life as well as a serious dollar loss to the nation's economy. The table presents data on the number of highway deaths (y) and the number of licensed vehicles on the road (x_1) for the years 1956–1994. (The years are coded 1–39 for convenience.) Traffic safety experts believe the number of deaths y may also have been affected by the existence of the national 55-mile-per-hour speed limit during the years 1974–1987 (i.e., years 19–32). Define the dummy variable:

$$x_2 = \begin{cases} 1 & \text{if 55-mile-per-hour speed limit was in effect} \\ 0 & \text{if not} \end{cases}$$

a. Write a second-order model relating the number y of highway deaths per year to the number, x_1, of licensed vehicles. Introduce the variable x_2 into the second-order model to account for the presence or absence of the 55-mile-per-hour speed limit in a given year. Include terms involving the interaction between x_2 and x_1.

b. Refer to your model for part **a**. Sketch on a single piece of graph paper your visualization of the two response curves, the second-order curves relating y to x_1 before and after the imposition of the 55-mile-per-hour speed limit.

c. Suppose that x_1 and x_2 do not interact. How would that affect the graphs of the two response curves of part **b**?

d. Refer to part **c**. Suppose that x_1 and x_2 do interact. How would this affect the graphs of the two response curves?

e. Write a second-order model for y that does not allow the relationship between number of highway deaths and number of vehicles to vary depending on speed limit.

f. The EXCEL printouts for the models proposed in parts **a** and **e** are shown on pages 640 and 641. Determine whether the data provide sufficient evidence to indicate that the qualitative variable (speed limit) contributes information for the prediction of the annual number of highway deaths. Test using $\alpha = .05$. Discuss the practical implications of your test results.

12.75 **(X12.075)** An operations manager is interested in modeling $E(y)$, the expected length of time per month (in hours) that a machine will be shut down for repairs, as a function of the type of machine (001 or 002) and the age of the machine

Year	Highway Deaths y	Licensed Vehicles x_1
1	39.6	65.2
2	38.7	67.6
3	37.0	68.8
4	37.9	72.1
5	38.1	74.5
6	38.1	76.4
7	40.8	79.7
8	43.6	83.5
9	47.7	87.3
10	49.2	91.8
11	53.0	95.9
12	52.9	98.9
13	54.9	103.1
14	55.8	107.4
15	54.6	111.2
16	54.4	116.3
17	56.3	122.3
18	55.5	129.8
19	46.4	134.9
20	45.9	137.9
21	47.0	143.5
22	49.5	148.8
23	52.4	153.6
24	53.5	159.6
25	53.1	161.6
26	51.4	164.1
27	45.8	165.2
28	44.5	169.4
29	46.2	172.0
30	45.9	177.1
31	47.9	181.4
32	48.3	183.9
33	49.1	189.0
34	47.6	191.7
35	46.8	192.9
36	43.5	192.5
37	41.0	194.4
38	42.2	198.0
39	43.0	199.4

Source: Accident Facts. National Safety Council, 1995, p. 105.

(in years). The manager has proposed the following model:

$$E(y) = \beta_0 + \beta_1 x_1 + \beta_2 x_1^2 + \beta_3 x_2$$

where

x_1 = Age of machine

$$x_2 = \begin{cases} 1 & \text{if machine type 001} \\ 0 & \text{if machine type 002} \end{cases}$$

a. Interpret the β's in the model.

b. Data obtained on $n = 20$ machine breakdowns were used to estimate the parameters of the model. The data and MINITAB printout are shown on page 642. Use the information on the printout to determine whether the curvilinear

Complete Model

SUMMARY OUTPUT

Regression Statistics	
Multiple R	0.892808667
R Square	0.797107317
Adjusted R Square	0.766366001
Standard Error	2.762373456
Observations	39

ANOVA

	df	SS	MS	F	Significance F
Regression	5	989.3025627	197.8605125	25.92951212	1.51936E-10
Residual	33	251.8133347	7.630707112		
Total	38	1241.115897			

	Coefficients	Standard Error	t Stat	P-value	Lower 95%	Upper 95%
Intercept	-24.56342516	6.531578764	-3.760717899	0.000659981	-37.85203261	-11.27481772
x1	1.198483556	0.110349017	10.86084488	1.96746E-12	0.973976614	1.42299497
x1sq	-0.004338339	0.000403859	-10.74220192	2.61573E-12	-0.005159998	-0.00351668
x2	27.98767177	79.48872484	0.352096122	0.727004831	-133.7334831	189.7088266
x1x2	-0.539747274	1.033767513	-0.522116691	0.605076471	-2.642964761	1.563470214
x1sqx2	0.002011621	0.003332555	0.603627125	0.550218636	-0.004768519	0.00879176

Reduced Model

SUMMARY OUTPUT

Regression Statistics	
Multiple R	0.79123156
R Square	0.626047381
Adjusted R Square	0.605272235
Standard Error	3.590568434
Observations	39

ANOVA

	df	SS	MS	F	Significance F
Regression	2	776.997357	388.4986785	30.13444025	2.04502E-08
Residual	36	464.1185404	12.89218168		
Total	38	1241.115897			

	Coefficients	Standard Error	t Stat	P-value	Lower 95%	Upper 95%
Intercept	-1.653899498	6.318660394	-0.261748439	0.79500724	-14.46871986	11.16092087
x1	0.798358347	0.103521479	7.712006772	3.91113E-09	0.588407333	1.008309361
x1sq	-0.002917764	0.000386932	-7.540772935	6.49476E-09	-0.003702497	-0.002133031

641

```
The regression equation is
Y = - 11.8 + 10.3 X1 - 0.418 X1SQ + 13.2 X2

Predictor        Coef        Stdev      t-ratio        p
Constant       -11.769       3.050       -3.86       0.001
X1              10.294       1.438        7.16       0.000
X1SQ           -0.4180       0.1613      -2.59       0.020
X2              13.244       1.503        8.81       0.000

s = 2.835        R-sq = 94.9%     R-sq(adj) = 94.0%

Analysis of Variance

SOURCE         DF          SS          MS          F          p
Regression      3       2396.36      798.79      99.39      0.000
Error          16        128.59        8.04
Total          19       2524.95
```

relationship between machine downtime (y) and age (x_1) differs for the two machine types.

Downtime (hours per month)	Machine Age x_1 (years)	Machine Type	x_2
10	1.0	001	1
20	2.0	001	1
30	2.7	001	1
40	4.1	001	1
9	1.2	001	1
25	2.5	001	1
19	1.9	001	1
41	5.0	001	1
22	2.1	001	1
12	1.1	001	1
10	2.0	002	0
20	4.0	002	0
30	5.0	002	0
44	8.0	002	0
9	2.4	002	0
25	5.1	002	0
20	3.5	002	0
42	7.0	002	0
20	4.0	002	0
13	2.1	002	0

c. Hypothesize a reduced model that, when compared to the complete model above, will yield results identical to those of the test, part **b**.

12.76 (X12.076) *Productivity* is typically evaluated by dividing a measure of system output by a measure of the inputs to the system. Some examples of productivity measures are Sales/Salesperson, (Yards of carpet laid)/(Number of carpet layers), Shipments/[(Direct labor) + (Indirect labor) + (Materials)]. Notice that productivity can be improved by producing greater output with the same inputs or by producing the same output with fewer inputs. In manufacturing operations, productivity ratios generally vary with the volume of output produced (Schroeder, *Operations Management,* 1993). The production data in the table below have been collected for a random sample of months at the three regional plants of a manufacturing firm. Each plant manufactures the same product.

a. Construct a scattergram for the data. Plot the data from the north plant using dots, from the south plant using small circles, and from the west plant using small triangles.

NORTH PLANT		SOUTH PLANT		WEST PLANT	
Productivity Ratio	Output	Productivity Ratio	Output	Productivity Ratio	Output
1.30	1,000	1.43	1,015	1.61	501
.90	400	1.50	925	.74	140
1.21	650	.91	150	1.19	303
.75	200	.99	222	1.88	930
1.32	850	1.33	545	1.72	776
1.29	600	1.15	402	1.39	400
1.18	756	1.51	709	1.86	810
1.10	500	1.01	176	.99	220
1.26	925	1.24	392	.79	160
.93	300	1.49	699	1.59	626
.81	258	1.37	800	1.82	640
1.12	590	1.39	660	.91	190

b. Visually fit each plant's response curve to the scattergram.

c. Based on the results of part **b**, propose a second-order regression model that could be used to estimate the relationship between productivity and volume for the three plants.

d. Fit the model you proposed in part **c** to the data.

e. Is there sufficient evidence to conclude that the productivity response curves for the three plants differ? Test using $\alpha = .05$.

f. Do the data provide sufficient evidence to conclude that the second-order model contributes more information for the prediction of productivity than a first-order model? Test using $\alpha = .05$.

g. Next month, 890 units are scheduled to be produced at the west plant. Use the model you developed in part **d** to predict next month's productivity ratio at the west plant.

12.9 STEPWISE REGRESSION

The problem of predicting executive salaries was discussed in Chapter 11. Perhaps the biggest problem in building a model to describe executive salaries is choosing the important independent variables to be included in the model. The list of potentially important independent variables is extremely long, and we need some objective method of screening out those that are not important.

The problem of deciding which of a large set of independent variables to include in a model is a common one. Trying to determine which variables influence the profit of a firm, affect blood pressure of humans, or are related to a student's performance in college are only a few examples.

A systematic approach to building a model with a large number of independent variables is difficult because the interpretation of multivariable interactions and higher-order polynomials is tedious. We therefore turn to a screening procedure known as **stepwise regression**.

The most commonly used stepwise regression procedure, available in most popular software packages, works as follows. The user first identifies the response, y, and the set of potentially important independent variables, $x_1, x_2, ..., x_k$, where k is generally large. [*Note:* This set of variables could include both first-order and higher-order terms. However, we may often include only the main effects of both quantitative variables (first-order terms) and qualitative variables (dummy variables), since the inclusion of second-order terms greatly increases the number of independent variables.] The response and independent variables are then entered into the computer software, and the stepwise procedure begins.

Step 1 The computer program fits all possible one-variable models of the form

$$E(y) = \beta_0 + \beta_1 x_i$$

to the data, where x_i is the ith independent variable, $i = 1, 2, ..., k$. For each model, the test of the null hypothesis

$$H_0: \beta_1 = 0$$

against the alternative hypothesis

$$H_a: \beta_1 \neq 0$$

is conducted using the t-test (or the equivalent F-test) for a single β parameter. The independent variable that produces the largest (absolute) t value is declared the best one-variable predictor of y.* Call this independent variable x_1.

*Note that the variable with the largest t value is also the one with the largest (absolute) Pearson product moment correlation, r (Section 10.6), with y.

Step 2 The stepwise program now begins to search through the remaining $(k - 1)$ independent variables for the best two-variable model of the form

$$E(y) = \beta_0 + \beta_1 x_1 + \beta_2 x_i$$

This is done by fitting all two-variable models containing x_1 and each of the other $(k - 1)$ options for the second variable x_i. The t values for the test H_0: $\beta_2 = 0$ are computed for each of the $(k - 1)$ models (corresponding to the remaining independent variables, $x_i, i = 2, 3, ..., k$), and the variable having the largest t is retained. Call this variable x_2.

At this point, some software packages diverge in methodology. The better packages now go back and check the t value of $\hat{\beta}_1$ after $\beta_2 x_2$ has been added to the model. If the t value has become nonsignificant at some specified α level (say $\alpha = .10$), the variable x_1 is removed and a search is made for the independent variable with a β parameter that will yield the most significant t value in the presence of $\beta_2 x_2$. Other packages do not recheck the significance of $\hat{\beta}_1$ but proceed directly to step 3.

The reason the t value for x_1 may change from Step 1 to Step 2 is that the meaning of the coefficient β_1 changes. In Step 2, we are approximating a complex response surface in two variables with a plane. The best-fitting plane may yield a different value for $\hat{\beta}_1$ than that obtained in Step 1. Thus, both the value of $\hat{\beta}_1$ and its significance usually change from Step 1 to Step 2. For this reason, the software packages that recheck the t values at each step are preferred.

Step 3 The stepwise procedure now checks for a third independent variable to include in the model with x_1 and x_2. That is, we seek the best model of the form

$$E(y) = \beta_0 + \beta_1 x_1 + \beta_2 x_2 + \beta_3 x_i$$

To do this, we fit all the $(k - 2)$ models using x_1, x_2, and each of the $(k - 2)$ remaining variables, x_i, as a possible x_3. The criterion is again to include the independent variable with the largest t value. Call this best third variable x_3.

The better programs now recheck the t values corresponding to the x_1 and x_2 coefficients, replacing the variables with t values that have become nonsignificant. This procedure is continued until no further independent variables can be found that yield significant t values (at the specified α level) in the presence of the variables already in the model.

The result of the stepwise procedure is a model containing only those terms with t values that are significant at the specified α level. Thus, in most practical situations only several of the large number of independent variables remain. However, it is very important *not* to jump to the conclusion that all the independent variables important for predicting y have been identified or that the unimportant independent variables have been eliminated. Remember, the stepwise procedure is using only *sample estimates* of the true model coefficients (β's) to select the important variables. An extremely large number of single β parameter t-tests have been conducted, and the probability is very high that one or more errors have been made in including or excluding variables. That is, we have very probably included some unimportant independent variables in the model (Type I errors) and eliminated some important ones (Type II errors).

There is a second reason why we might not have arrived at a good model. When we choose the variables to be included in the stepwise regression, we may often omit high-order terms (to keep the number of variables manageable). Consequently, we may have initially omitted several important terms from the model. Thus, we should recognize stepwise regression for what it is: an objective screening procedure.

Now, we will consider second-order terms (for quantitative variables) and other interactions among variables screened by the stepwise procedure. It would be best to develop this response surface model with a second set of data independent of that used for the screening, so the results of the stepwise procedure can be partially verified with new data. This is not always possible, however, because in many modeling situations only a small amount of data are available.

Do not be deceived by the impressive-looking t values that result from the stepwise procedure—it has retained only the independent variables with the largest t values. Also, be certain to consider second-order terms in systematically developing the prediction model. Finally, if you have used a first-order model for your stepwise procedure, remember that it may be greatly improved by the addition of higher-order terms.

> **Warning**
>
> Be cautious when using the results of stepwise regression to make inferences about the relationship between $E(y)$ and the independent variables in the resulting first-order model. First, an extremely large number of t-tests have been conducted, leading to a high probability of making either one or more Type I or Type II errors. Second, the stepwise model does not include any higher-order or interaction terms. Stepwise regression should be used only when necessary, that is, when you want to determine which of a large number of potentially important independent variables should be used in the model-building process.

EXAMPLE 12.12

In Section 11.7 we fit a multiple regression model for executive salaries as a function of experience, education, sex, etc. A preliminary step in the construction of this model was the determination of the most important independent variables. Ten independent variables (seven quantitative and three qualitative) were considered, as shown in Table 12.6. It would be very difficult to construct a complete second-order model with 10 independent variables. Therefore, use the sample of 100 executives from Section 11.7 to decide which of the 10 variables should be included in the construction of the final model for executive salaries.

TABLE 12.6   Independent Variables in the Executive Salary Example

Variable	Description	Type
x_1	Experience (years)	quantitative
x_2	Education (years)	quantitative
x_3	Sex (1 if male, 0 if female)	qualitative
x_4	Number of employees supervised	quantitative
x_5	Corporate assets (millions of dollars)	quantitative
x_6	Board member (1 if yes, 0 if no)	qualitative
x_7	Age (years)	quantitative
x_8	Company profits (past 12 mos., millions of dollars)	quantitative
x_9	Has international responsibility	qualitative
x_{10}	Company's total sales (past 12 mos., millions of dollars)	quantitative

```
STEP 1
   Variable X4 Entered        R-Square = 0.42071677     C(P) = 1274.7576

                       DF    Sum of Squares    Mean Square      F     Prob > F

   Regression           1       11.46854285     11.46854285    71.17    0.0001
   Error               98       15.79113802      0.16113696
   Total               99       27.25977087

                              B Value          Std Error        F     Prob > F

   Intercept                  10.20077500
   X4                          0.00057284       0.00006790     71.17    0.0001
----------------------------------------------------------------------------
STEP 2
   Variable X5 Entered        R-Square = 0.78299675     C(P) = 419.4947

                       DF    Sum of Squares    Mean Square      F     Prob > F

   Regression           2       21.34431198     10.67215599   175.00    0.0001
   Error               97        5.91545889      0.06098411
   Total               99       27.25977087

                              B Value          Std Error        F     Prob > F

   Intercept                   9.87702903
   X4                          0.00058353       0.00004178    195.06    0.0001
   X5                          0.00183730       0.00014438    161.94    0.0001
----------------------------------------------------------------------------
STEP 3
   Variable X1 Entered        R-Square = 0.89667614     C(P) = 152.4952

                       DF    Sum of Squares    Mean Square      F     Prob > F

   Regression           3       24.44318616      8.14772872   277.71    0.0001
   Error               96        2.81658471      0.02933942
   Total               99       27.25977087

                              B Value          Std Error        F     Prob > F

   Intercept                   9.66449288
   X4                          0.00055251       0.00002914    359.59    0.0001
   X5                          0.00191195       0.00010041    362.60    0.0001
   X1                          0.01870784       0.00182032    105.62    0.0001
----------------------------------------------------------------------------
STEP 4
   Variable X3 Entered        R-Square = 0.94815717     C(P) = 32.6757

                       DF    Sum of Squares    Mean Square      F     Prob > F

   Regression           4       25.84654710      8.46163678   434.37    0.0001
   Error               95        1.41322377      0.01487604
   Total               99       27.25977087

                              B Value          Std Error        F     Prob > F

   Intercept                   9.40077349
   X4                          0.00055288       0.00002075    710.15    0.0001
   X5                          0.00190876       0.00007150    712.74    0.0001
   X1                          0.02074868       0.00131310    249.68    0.0001
   X3                          0.30011726       0.03089939     94.34    0.0001
```

FIGURE 12.31 Stepwise regression printout for Example 12.12

SOLUTION

We will use stepwise regression with the main effects of the 10 independent variables to identify the most important variables. The dependent variable y is the natural logarithm of the executive salaries. The SAS stepwise regression printout is

```
STEP 5
   Variable X2 Entered        R-Square = 0.96039323      C(P) = 5.7215

                      DF    Sum of Squares    Mean Square      F    Prob > F

   Regression          5       26.18009940     5.23601988   455.87   0.0001
   Error              94        1.07967147     0.01148587
   Total              99       27.25977087

                            B Value         Std Error         F    Prob > F

   Intercept              8.85387930
   X4                     0.00056061        0.00001829     939.84   0.0001
   X5                     0.00193684        0.00006304     943.98   0.0001
   X1                     0.02141724        0.00116047     340.61   0.0001
   X3                     0.31927842        0.02738298     135.95   0.0001
   X2                     0.03315807        0.00615303      29.04   0.0001
-----------------------------------------------------------------------------
STEP 6
   Variable X6 Entered        R-Square = 0.96100666      C(P) = 6.2699

                      DF    Sum of Squares    Mean Square      F    Prob > F

   Regression          6       26.19682148     4.36613691   382.00   0.0001
   Error              93        1.06294939     0.01142956
   Total              99       27.25977087

                            B Value         Std Error         F    Prob > F

   Intercept              8.87509152
   X4                     0.00055820        0.00001835     925.32   0.0001
   X5                     0.00193764        0.00006289     949.31   0.0001
   X1                     0.02133460        0.00115963     338.48   0.0001
   X3                     0.31093801        0.02817264     121.81   0.0001
   X2                     0.03272195        0.00614851      28.32   0.0001
   X6                     0.03866226        0.03196369       1.46   0.2295
-----------------------------------------------------------------------------
STEP 7
   Variable X6 Removed        R-Square = 0.96039323      C(P) = 5.7215

                      DF    Sum of Squares    Mean Square      F    Prob > F

   Regression          5       26.18009940     5.23601988   455.87   0.0001
   Error              94        1.07967147     0.01148587
   Total              99       27.25977087

                            B Value         Std Error         F    Prob > F

   Intercept              8.85387930
   X4                     0.00056061        0.00001829     939.84   0.0001
   X5                     0.00193684        0.00006304     943.98   0.0001
   X1                     0.02141724        0.00116047     340.61   0.0001
   X3                     0.31927842        0.02738298     135.95   0.0001
   X2                     0.03315807        0.00615303      29.04   0.0001
```

FIGURE 12.31   Continued

shown in Figure 12.31.* Note that the first variable included in the model is x_4, the number of employees supervised by the executive. At the second step, x_5, corporate assets, enters the model. At the sixth step, x_6, a dummy variable for the qualitative variable Board member or not, is brought into the model. However,

*Note that there are several slight changes in the SAS printout labels for the stepwise procedure. For example, the $\hat{\beta}_i$ values, labeled **ESTIMATE** in the multiple regression procedure, are labeled **B VALUE** in the stepwise procedure.

because the significance (.2295) of the F statistic (SAS uses the $F = t^2$ statistic rather than the t statistic in the stepwise procedure) for x_6 is above the program default value of $\alpha = .15$, x_6 is then removed from the model. Thus, at the seventh step the procedure indicates that the five-variable model including $x_1, x_2, x_3, x_4,$ and x_5 is best. That is, none of the other independent variables can meet the $\alpha = .15$ criterion for admission to the model.

Thus, in our final modeling effort (Section 11.7) we concentrated on these five independent variables and determined that several second-order terms were important in the prediction of executive salaries.

EXERCISES 12.77–12.80

Learning the Mechanics

12.77 There are six independent variables, $x_1, x_2, x_3, x_4,$ $x_5,$ and $x_6,$ that might be useful in predicting a response y. A total of $n = 50$ observations are available, and it is decided to employ stepwise regression to help in selecting the independent variables that appear to be useful. The computer fits all possible one-variable models of the form

$$E(y) = \beta_0 + \beta_1 x_i$$

where x_i is the ith independent variable, $i = 1, 2,$ ..., 6. The information in the table is provided from the computer printout.

Independent Variable	$\hat{\beta}_i$	$s_{\hat{\beta}_i}$
x_1	1.6	.42
x_2	−.9	.01
x_3	3.4	1.14
x_4	2.5	2.06
x_5	−4.4	.73
x_6	.3	.35

a. Which independent variable is declared the best one-variable predictor of y? Explain.
b. Would this variable be included in the model at this stage? Explain.
c. Describe the next phase that a stepwise procedure would execute.

Applying the Concepts

12.78 Refer to the *Benefits Quarterly* (1995) study of entry-level job preferences, Exercise 12.5. Suppose stepwise regression is used to build a model for job preference score (y) as a function of the following independent variables:

$$x_1 = \begin{cases} 1 & \text{if flextime position} \\ 0 & \text{if not} \end{cases}$$

$$x_2 = \begin{cases} 1 & \text{if day care support required} \\ 0 & \text{if not} \end{cases}$$

$$x_3 = \begin{cases} 1 & \text{if spousal transfer support required} \\ 0 & \text{if not} \end{cases}$$

x_4 = Number of sick days allowed

$$x_5 = \begin{cases} 1 & \text{if applicant married} \\ 0 & \text{if not} \end{cases}$$

x_6 = Number of children of applicant

$$x_7 = \begin{cases} 1 & \text{if male applicant} \\ 0 & \text{if female applicant} \end{cases}$$

a. How many models are fit to the data in Step 1? Give the general form of these models.
b. How many models are fit to the data in Step 2? Give the general form of these models.
c. How many models are fit to the data in Step 3? Give the general form of these models.
d. Explain how the procedure determines when to stop adding independent variables to the model.
e. Describe two major drawbacks to using the final stepwise model as the "best" model for job preference score (y).

12.79 The *Journal of College Student Personnel* (1984) provided an analysis of data collected on 230 male and 72 female freshmen attending a midwestern university specializing in engineering and technology. Data collected on each student included a score on a self-concept of ability test (SCPT); scores on the SAT, ACT, and various other achievement tests; a standardized measure (called a T-score) of the student's rank in high school class; and the student's first-semester GPA. One aspect of the study involved fitting a stepwise regression model for GPA involving first-order terms for the test scores shown in the first column of the table on page 649. The variables are listed in the order in which they entered the model. Column 2 gives the value of R^2 at each stage of the stepwise regression; column 3 gives the simple coefficient r of correlation between each variable and GPA; column 4 gives the F value at each stage of the stepwise regression for testing the contri-

Variable	R^2	r	F
T-score	.14	.37	18.44
Mathematics test	.18	.34	10.93
SAT	.24	.18	29.57
ACT	.44	.27	14.15
Verbal test	.50	.30	3.93
SCPT	.52	.29	1.89
Trigonometry test	.52	.28	.16

Source: Robinson, D., and Cooper, S. "The influence of self-concept on academic success in technological careers." *Journal of College Student Personnel,* 1984, AACD.

bution of the last variable included in the stepwise model for the prediction of GPA.
   a. Write the models used in the first, second, third, and fourth stages of the fitting process.
   b. Does the self-concept of ability (SCPT) score come into the model?
   c. Compare the values of *r* between GPA and the individual variables. How do you explain your answer to part **b** given that the correlation coefficient for the SCPT score is larger than that for the SAT score?
   d. Use the value of R^2 given in stage 4 of the stepwise regression to calculate the value of the *F* statistic for testing the utility of the model.
   e. Calculate the approximate *p*-value for the *F* statistic in part **d** and interpret it.

12.80   Many power plants dump hot waste water into the surrounding rivers, streams, and oceans, an action that may adversely affect the marine life in the dumping areas. The Environmental Protection Agency (EPA) wants to determine whether the hot-water runoff from a particular power plant located near a large gulf is having an adverse effect on the marine life in the area. In the initial phase of the study, the biologist's goal is to acquire a prediction equation for the number of marine animals located at certain designated areas, or stations, in the gulf. Based on past experience, the EPA considered the following environmental factors as predictors for the number of animals at a particular station:

x_1 = Temperature of water (TEMP)

x_2 = Salinity of water (SAL)

x_3 = Dissolved oxygen content of water (DO)

x_4 = Turbidity index, a measure of the turbidity of the water (TI)

x_5 = Depth of the water at the station (ST_DEPTH)

x_6 = Total weight of sea grasses in sampled area (TGRSWT)

As a preliminary step in the construction of this model, the biologist used a stepwise regression procedure to identify the most important of these six variables. A total of 716 samples were taken at different stations in the gulf, producing the SAS printout shown below and on page 650. (The response measured was *y*, the logarithm of the number of marine animals found in the sampled area.)

```
STEP 1
   Variable ST_DEPTH Entered   R-Square = 0.1223

                       DF      Sum of Squares    Mean Square      F     Prob > F

   Regression           1              57.44          57.44    99.47      0.0001
   Error              714             412.33           0.58
   Total              715             469.77

                               B Value         Std Error        F     Prob > F

   Intercept                   8.38559
   ST_DEPTH                   -0.43678          0.04379       99.47      0.0001
-------------------------------------------------------------------------------
STEP 2
   Variable TGRSWT Entered     R-Square = 0.1821

                       DF      Sum of Squares    Mean Square      F     Prob > F

   Regression           2              85.55          42.78    79.38      0.0001
   Error              713             384.22           0.54
   Total              715             469.77

                               B Value         Std Error        F     Prob > F

   Intercept                   8.07682
   ST_DEPTH                   -0.35355          0.04385       65.02      0.0001
   TGRSWT                      0.00271          0.00038       52.16      0.0001
-------------------------------------------------------------------------------
```

continued

```
STEP 3
   Variable TI Entered          R-Square = 0.1870
                      DF    Sum of Squares    Mean Square       F    Prob > F

   Regression          3            87.85          29.28    54.59    0.0001
   Error             712           381.92           0.54
   Total             715           469.77

                            B Value    Std Error         F    Prob > F

   Intercept               7.38864
   TI                      0.65774      0.31783      4.28      0.0389
   ST_DEPTH               -0.31451      0.47641     43.58      0.0001
   TGRSWT                  0.00261      0.00038     47.73      0.0001
-----------------------------------------------------------------------------
STEP 4
   Variable DO Entered          R-Square = 0.1889
                      DF    Sum of Squares    Mean Square       F    Prob > F

   Regression          4            88.75          22.19    41.40    0.0001
   Error             711           381.02           0.54
   Total             715           469.77

                            B Value    Std Error         F    Prob > F

   Intercept               7.22576
   DO                      0.01769      0.01363      1.69      0.1946
   TI                      0.67347      0.31791      4.49      0.0345
   ST_DEPTH               -0.30417      0.04828     39.69      0.0001
   TRGSWT                  0.00267      0.00038     49.23      0.0001
-----------------------------------------------------------------------------
STEP 5
   Variable DO Removed          R-Square = 0.1870
                      DF    Sum of Squares    Mean Square       F    Prob > F

   Regression          3            87.85          29.28    54.59    0.0001
   Error             712           381.92           0.54
   Total             715           469.77

                            B Value    Std Error         F    Prob > F

   Intercept               7.38864
   TI                      0.65774      0.31783      4.28      0.0389
   ST_DEPTH               -0.31451      0.04764     43.58      0.0001
   TGRSWT                  0.00261      0.00038     47.73      0.0001
```

a. According to the SAS printout, which of the six independent variables should be used in the model? (Use $\alpha = .10$.)

b. Are we able to assume that the marine biologist has identified all the important independent variables for the prediction of y? Why?

c. Using the variables identified in part **a**, write the first-order model with interaction that may be used to predict y.

d. How would the marine biologist determine whether the model specified in part **c** is better than the first-order model?

e. Note the small value of R^2. What action might the biologist take to improve the model?

QUICK REVIEW

Key Terms

Base level 611	First-order model 581	Paraboloid 593	Saddle-shaped surface 593
Complete model 593	Interaction model 591	pth-order polynomial 581	Second-order model 582
Contour lines 590	Level of a variable 579	Reduced model 599	Stepwise regression 643
Dummy variables 610	Model building 578	Response surface 590	

Key Formulas

$E(y) = \beta_0 + \beta_1 x + \beta_2 x^2 + \beta_3 x^3 + \cdots + \beta_p x^p$

pth-order polynomial with one quantitative independent variable 581

$E(y) = \beta_0 + \beta_1 x_1 + \beta_2 x_2$

First-order model with two quantitative independent variables 590

$E(y) = \beta_0 + \beta_1 x_1 + \beta_2 x_2 + \beta_3 x_1 x_2$

Interaction model with two quantitative independent variables 591

$E(y) = \beta_0 + \beta_1 x_1 + \beta_2 x_2 + \beta_3 x_1 x_2 + \beta_4 x_1^2 + \beta_5 x_2^2$

Complete second-order model with two quantitative independent variables 593

$F = \dfrac{(SSE_r - SSE_c)/\text{number of } \beta\text{'s tested}}{MSE_c}$

Test statistic for comparing reduced and complete models 600

$E(y) = \beta_0 + \beta_1 x_1 + \beta_2 x_2 + \cdots + \beta_{k-1} x_{k-1}$

where $x_i = \begin{cases} 1 & \text{if level } i+1 \\ 0 & \text{if not} \end{cases}$

Model with one qualitative variable at k levels 612

LANGUAGE LAB

Symbol	Pronunciation	Description
x^p	x to the pth power	$x^p = \underbrace{(x)(x)(x)\cdots(x)}_{\text{multiply } p \text{ times}}$
SSE_r		Sum of squared errors for reduced model
SSE_c		Sum of squared errors for complete model
MSE_c		Mean square error for complete model

SUPPLEMENTARY EXERCISES 12.81–12.100

Note: Exercises marked with 💾 *contain data for computer analysis on a 3.5" disk (file name in parentheses).*

Learning the Mechanics

12.81 Why is the model-building step the key to the success or failure of a regression analysis?

12.82 Suppose you fit the regression model

$$E(y) = \beta_0 + \beta_1 x_1 + \beta_2 x_2 + \beta_3 x_2^2 + \beta_4 x_1 x_2 + \beta_5 x_1 x_2^2$$

to $n = 35$ data points and wish to test the null hypothesis

$$H_0: \beta_4 = \beta_5 = 0$$

a. State the alternative hypothesis.
b. Explain in detail how to compute the F statistic needed to test the null hypothesis.

c. What are the numerator and denominator degrees of freedom associated with the F statistic in part **b**?
d. Give the rejection region for the test if $\alpha = .05$.

12.83 Graph each of the following polynomials, and give the order of each:
a. $E(y) = 6 + 3x - 2x^2$ **b.** $E(y) = 4x$
c. $E(y) = x^2$ **d.** $E(y) = 2 - 4x$
e. $E(y) = 1 + x - x^2 + x^3$ **f.** $E(y) = 1 - 4x$

12.84 Write a model relating $E(y)$ to one qualitative independent variable that is at four levels. Define all the terms in your model.

12.85 Explain the difference between qualitative and quantitative variables.

12.86 It is desired to relate $E(y)$ to one quantitative variable x_1 and a qualitative variable at three levels.

a. Write a first-order model.

b. Write a model that will graph as three different second-order curves—one for each level of the qualitative variable.

12.87 Explain why stepwise regression is used. What is its value in the model-building process?

12.88 **a.** Write a first-order model relating $E(y)$ to two quantitative independent variables, x_1 and x_2.

b. Write a complete second-order model.

12.89 To model the relationship between y, a dependent variable, and x, an independent variable, a researcher has taken one measurement on y at each of three different x values. Drawing on his mathematical expertise, the researcher realizes that he can fit the second-order polynomial model

$$E(y) = \beta_0 + \beta_1 x + \beta_2 x^2$$

and it will pass exactly through all three points, yielding SSE = 0. The researcher, delighted with the "excellent" fit of the model, eagerly sets out to use it to make inferences. What problems will he encounter in attempting to make inferences?

Applying the Concepts

12.90 The audience for a product's advertising can be divided into four segments according to the degree of exposure received as a result of the advertising. These segments are groups of consumers who receive very high (VH), high (H), medium (M), or low (L) exposure to the advertising. A company is interested in exploring whether its advertising effort affects its product's market share. Accordingly, the company identifies 24 sample groups of consumers who have been exposed to its advertising, six groups at each exposure level. Then, the company determines its product's market share within each group.

a. Write a regression model that expresses the company's market share as a function of advertising exposure level. Define all terms in your model, and list any assumptions you make about them.

b. Did you include interaction terms in your model? Why or why not?

c. How many degrees of freedom are associated with the F-test you would use to test the overall usefulness of the model you constructed in part **a**?

12.91 **(X12.091)** Refer to Exercise 12.90, where a company was examining the relationship between its market share and its advertising effort. The data in the next table were obtained by the company.

a. Fit the model you constructed in part **a** of Exercise 12.90 to the data.

b. Is there evidence to suggest that the firm's expected market share differs for different

Market Share Within Group	Exposure Level
10.1	L
10.3	L
10.0	L
10.3	L
10.2	L
10.5	L
10.6	M
11.0	M
11.2	M
10.9	M
10.8	M
11.0	M
12.2	H
12.1	H
11.8	H
12.6	H
11.9	H
12.9	H
10.7	VH
10.8	VH
11.0	VH
10.5	VH
10.8	VH
10.6	VH

levels of advertising exposure? Test using $\alpha = .05$.

12.92 Investors are interested in knowing the relationship between the behavior of a mutual fund and the behavior of the stock market as a whole. Researchers in finance have hypothesized that the model that appropriately characterizes this relationship is

$$E(y) = \beta_0 + \beta_1 x$$

where

y = Monthly rate of return of a mutual fund

x = Monthly rate of return of the stock market as a whole as measured by the monthly rate of return to a market index such as Standard & Poor's 500 Composite Index

The value of β_1 in the model is referred to as the mutual funds' *beta coefficient*. Assuming the preceding model is true, investors can predict how the returns of an individual mutual fund will react to changes in the behavior of the market. For example, if $\beta_1 > 1$, the implication is that the return to the mutual fund will be greatly influenced by the behavior of the market and will move in the same direction as the change in the market return. If $0 \leq \beta_1 < 1$, the return to the mutual fund will be less sensitive to changes in market behavior but will also move in the same direction as the change in the market return.

In studying mutual funds, Alexander and Stover (*Journal of Economics and Business,* Spring 1980) included a dummy variable in the above model to determine whether the beta coefficient for an individual mutual fund depends on whether the market is moving generally upward (a *bull market*) or generally downward (a *bear market*).

a. Modify the regression model (as Alexander and Stover did) to reflect the possibility that $E(y)$ may depend on whether the market is bullish or bearish. Include an interaction term in your model and carefully define the dummy variable coding scheme you use.

b. Using the model you developed in part **a**, describe the differences that may exist between the response curves of $E(y)$ under bull and bear markets.

c. Specify the hypothesis you would test to determine whether a mutual fund's beta coefficient is different during bull and bear markets.

d. Specify the hypothesis you would test to determine whether $E(y)$ should be characterized as $E(y) = \beta_0 + \beta_1 x$ or as the modified model you developed in part **a**.

12.93 The *American Sociological Review* (Summer 1993) published a study of the variables that affect academic achievement in high school. Two variables hypothesized to have an impact on achievement were track (college program of courses or not) and sector (Catholic school or public school). One of the models considered in the study was:

$$E(y) = \beta_0 + \beta_1 x_1 + \beta_2 x_2 + \beta_3 x_1 x_2$$

where

y = Verbal achievement score

$x_1 = \begin{cases} 1 & \text{if college track} \\ 0 & \text{if not} \end{cases}$

$x_2 = \begin{cases} 1 & \text{if Catholic school} \\ 0 & \text{if not} \end{cases}$

How would you determine whether the impact of college track (x_1) on verbal achievement score (y) depends on sector (x_2)? Set up the null and alternative hypothesis for the test.

12.94 Refer to Exercise 12.93. The impact of interaction between two qualitative independent variables can be seen by performing the following:

a. In terms of the β's, give the mean verbal achievement score, $E(y)$, for public school students not on a college program.

b. Repeat part **a** for public school students on a college program.

c. Subtract the results, parts **a** and **b**, to obtain the difference between the means of college-track and regular-track students in public schools.

d. In terms of the β's, give the mean verbal achievement score, $E(y)$, for Catholic school students not on a college program.

e. Repeat part **a** for Catholic school students on a college program.

f. Subtract the results, parts **d** and **e**, to obtain the difference between the means of college-track and regular-track students in Catholic schools.

12.95 One factor that must be considered in developing a shipping system that is beneficial to both the customer and the seller is time of delivery. A manufacturer of farm equipment can ship its products by either rail or truck. Quadratic models are thought to be adequate in relating time of delivery to distance traveled for both modes of transportation. Consequently, it has been suggested that the model to be fit is

$$E(y) = \beta_0 + \beta_1 x_1 + \beta_2 x_1^2 + \beta_3 x_2 + \beta_4 x_1 x_2 + \beta_5 x_1^2 x_2$$

where

y = Shipping time

x_1 = Distance to be shipped $x_2 = \begin{cases} 1 & \text{if rail} \\ 0 & \text{if truck} \end{cases}$

a. What hypothesis would you test to determine whether the data indicate that the quadratic distance terms are useful in the model—i.e., whether curvature is present in the relationship between mean delivery time and distance?

b. What hypothesis would you test to determine whether there is a difference in mean delivery time by rail and by truck?

c. Suppose the model is fit to a total of 50 observations on delivery time. The sum of squared errors is SSE = 226.12. Then, the reduced model

$$E(y) = \beta_0 + \beta_1 x_1 + \beta_2 x_1^2$$

is fit to the same data, and SSE = 259.34. Test whether the data indicate that the mean delivery time differs from rail and truck deliveries. Use $\alpha = .05$.

12.96 To make a product more appealing to the consumer, an automobile manufacturer is experimenting with a new type of paint that is supposed to preserve a new-car look. The durability of this paint depends on the length of time the car body is in the oven after it has been painted. In the initial experiment, three groups of 10 car bodies each are baked for three different lengths of time—12, 24, and 36 hours—at the standard temperature setting. Then the paint finish of each of the 30 cars is analyzed to determine a durability rating, y.

a. Write a second-order model relating the mean durability $E(y)$ to the length of baking.
b. Could a third-order model be fit to the data? Explain.

12.97 Many companies must accurately estimate their costs before a job is begun in order to acquire a contract and make a profit. For example, a heating and plumbing contractor may estimate costs for new homes based on the total area of the house and whether central air conditioning is to be installed.

a. Write a main effects model relating the mean cost of material and labor, $E(y)$, to the area and central-air-conditioning variables.
b. Write a complete second-order model for the mean cost as a function of the same two variables.
c. The contractor samples 25 recent jobs and fits both the complete second-order model (part **b**) and the reduced main effects model (part **a**), so that a test can be conducted to determine whether the additional complexity of the second-order model is necessary. The resulting SSE and R^2 values are shown in the table. Is there sufficient evidence to conclude that the second-order terms are important for predicting the mean cost? Use $\alpha = .05$.

	SSE	R^2
Main effects	8.548	.950
Second-order	6.133	.964

12.98 **(X12.098)** A firm that has developed a new type of light bulb is interested in evaluating its performance in order to decide whether to market it. It is known that the light output of the bulb depends on the cleanliness of its surface area and the length of time the bulb has been in operation. Use

City	Traffic Flow (thousands of cars)	Weekly Sales y ($ thousands)
1	59.3	6.3
1	60.3	6.6
1	82.1	7.6
1	32.3	3.0
1	98.0	9.5
1	54.1	5.9
1	54.4	6.1
1	51.3	5.0
1	36.7	3.6
2	23.6	2.8
2	57.6	6.7
2	44.6	5.2
3	75.8	8.2
3	48.3	5.0
3	41.4	3.9
3	52.5	5.4
3	41.0	4.1
3	29.6	3.1
3	49.5	5.4
4	73.1	8.4
4	81.3	9.5
4	72.4	8.7
4	88.4	10.6
4	23.2	3.3

the data in the table below and the procedures you learned in this chapter to build a regression model that relates drop in light output to bulb surface cleanliness and length of operation.

12.99 **(X12.099)** A fast-food restaurant chain is interested in modeling the mean weekly sales of a restaurant, $E(y)$, as a function of the weekly traffic flow on the street where the restaurant is located and the city in which the restaurant is located. The table above contains data collected on 24 restaurants in four cities.

Drop in Light Output (% original output)	Bulb Surface (C = clean, D = dirty)	Length of Operation (hours)
0	C	0
16	C	400
22	C	800
27	C	1,200
32	C	1,600
36	C	2,000
38	C	2,400
0	D	0
4	D	400
6	D	800
8	D	1,200
9	D	1,600
11	D	2,000
12	D	2,400

```
Complete model

SOURCE              DF      SUM OF SQUARES      MEAN SQUARE

MODEL               1            111.3423          111.3423
ERROR               22             7.8073            0.3549
CORRECTED TOTAL     23           119.1496          R-SQUARE
                                                     0.934
```

The model that has been proposed is

$$E(y) = \beta_0 + \beta_1 x_1 + \beta_2 x_2 + \beta_3 x_3 + \beta_4 x_4$$

where

x_1 = Traffic flow

$x_2 = \begin{cases} 1 & \text{if city 1} \\ 0 & \text{otherwise} \end{cases}$

$x_3 = \begin{cases} 1 & \text{if city 2} \\ 0 & \text{otherwise} \end{cases}$

$x_4 = \begin{cases} 1 & \text{if city 3} \\ 0 & \text{otherwise} \end{cases}$

A portion of the computer printout that results from fitting the model to the data in the table is shown above. The reduced model, $E(y) = \beta_0 + \beta_1 x_1$, was then fit to the same data and the resulting printout is shown below.

a. Test the null hypothesis that $\beta_1 = \beta_2 = \beta_3 = \beta_4 = 0$ using $\alpha = .05$. Interpret the results of your test.

b. Is mean weekly sales, $E(y)$, dependent on the city where a restaurant is located? Test using $\alpha = .05$. Interpret the results of your test.

c. Describe the nature of the response lines that the complete model

$$E(y) = \beta_0 + \beta_1 x_1 + \beta_2 x_2 + \beta_3 x_3 + \beta_4 x_4$$

would generate. Does the model imply interaction between city and traffic flow?

d. Use the prediction equation based on the complete model to graph the response lines that relate predicted weekly sales, $\hat{y}$, to traffic flow, x_1 (for each of the four cities). Do the graphed response lines suggest an interaction between city and traffic flow?

e. Write a model that includes interaction between city and traffic flow.

f. Fit the model of part **e** to the data.

g. Do the data provide sufficient evidence to indicate that the slopes of the lines differ for at least two of the four cities? Test using $\alpha = .05$.

```
Reduced model

Dep Variable: Y

                        Analysis of Variance

                        Sum of          Mean
Source      DF          Squares         Square      F Value     Prob>F

Model       4           116.65552       29.16388    222.173     0.0001
Error       19            2.49407        0.13127
C Total     23          119.14958

            Root MSE      0.36231       R-Square     0.9791
            Dep Mean      5.99583       Adj R-Sq     0.9747
            C.V.          6.04265

                        Parameter Estimates

                        Parameter       Standard     T for H0:
Variable    DF          Estimate        Error        Parameter=0   Prob >|T|

INTERCEP    1            1.083388        0.32100795    3.375        0.0032
X1          1            0.103673        0.00409449   25.320        0.0001
X2          1           -1.215762        0.20538681   -5.919        0.0001
X3          1           -0.530757        0.28481946   -1.863        0.0779
X4          1           -1.076525        0.22650014   -4.753        0.0001
```

y = resale value in 1994

x_1 = 1991 price

x_2 = Price increase in model from 1991–1994

x_3 = *Consumer Reports* quality index

x_4 = *Consumer Reports* reliability index

x_5 = Number of model vehicles sold in 1991

$x_6 = \begin{cases} 1 & \text{if minor change made in model in 1992, 1993, or 1994} \\ 0 & \text{if not} \end{cases}$

$x_7 = \begin{cases} 1 & \text{if major change made in model in 1992, 1993, or 1994} \\ 0 & \text{if not} \end{cases}$

12.100 (X12.100) To appropriately price new car leases, car dealers need to accurately predict the value of the cars at the conclusion of the leases. These resale values are generally determined at wholesale auctions. Data collected on 54 1991 new car models are listed in the table on page 657. The variables recorded are listed above.

a. Use stepwise regression to find the best predictors of resale value, y.

b. Using the predictors, part **a**, hypothesize a complete second-order model for resale value y.

c. Fit the model, part **b**. Interpret R^2 and the test for model adequacy.

d. Fit the appropriate reduced model and conduct a test to determine if second-order terms are useful for predicting resale value y.

Model Number	Resale Value y	1991 Price x_1	Price Increase x_2	Quality x_3	Reliability x_4	1991 Sales x_5	Minor Change x_6	Major Change x_7
1	13,575	19,900	23.99	3	3	8,002	0	1
2	24,600	34,500	11.38	4	4	16,778	0	0
3	6,475	13,685	15.45	3	4	104,325	0	0
4	6,375	10,725	28.06	1	3	68,469	1	0
5	8,450	15,910	17.06	4	3	90,879	0	0
6	9,600	17,080	23.42	4	3	89,575	0	1
7	13,675	24,385	11.40	3	3	109,482	0	1
8	18,150	34,195	21.16	3	2	26,431	0	1
9	8,525	8,270	10.28	1	1	109,167	0	0
10	14,225	16,515	15.97	1	2	202,029	0	0
11	8,525	16,501	−8.36	1	3	17,752	0	0
12	5,900	10,905	14.35	3	3	97,696	0	0
13	7,350	17,045	13.52	3	3	85,532	0	1
14	5,375	8,449	28.83	1	1	212,524	0	0
15	5,525	9,095	17.10	3	3	98,537	1	0
16	6,300	13,352	21.63	4	3	235,102	1	0
17	6,875	9,680	14.36	4	5	90,679	0	1
18	8,100	10,553	11.34	4	5	119,357	0	1
19	10,650	13,225	8.36	4	5	536,477	0	1
20	26,175	39,000	29.36	5	4	15,980	1	0
21	12,525	18,300	20.08	5	5	15,529	0	0
22	32,425	38,000	34.74	5	5	37,033	1	0
23	16,325	22,050	41.50	4	5	17,257	0	1
24	16,175	27,986	24.17	4	3	124,919	0	0
25	14,625	29,422	14.71	3	3	53,109	0	0
26	7,475	9,359	−3.89	4	4	62,286	0	0
27	14,925	23,385	34.70	3	3	11,913	0	0
28	26,725	47,200	−9.96	3	4	15,909	1	0
29	19,875	28,950	3.28	3	3	13,924	0	1
30	6,400	10,605	7.69	1	1	79,091	0	0
31	7,975	15,821	12.76	4	3	77,696	1	0
32	5,625	8,969	14.28	3	3	53,235	0	0
33	8,850	18,199	11.71	3	3	79,218	0	1
34	9,175	10,999	23.65	5	5	37,577	0	0
35	14,250	19,449	15.32	5	5	102,177	0	1
36	6,950	8,900	24.15	4	4	105,366	0	0
37	6,325	12,495	28.61	2	4	92,857	0	0
38	8,200	15,059	17.72	3	3	68,385	0	0
39	9,025	17,195	22.83	4	3	49,737	0	1
40	13,425	23,695	10.45	3	3	54,905	0	0
41	5,900	10,805	15.41	3	3	113,434	0	0
42	9,575	16,834	21.33	4	3	42,797	1	0
43	7,000	10,374	21.59	1	3	82,894	0	0
44	7,750	14,294	13.71	3	3	49,163	0	0
45	5,775	8,784	12.75	1	1	45,493	0	0
46	12,050	18,815	16.87	3	3	3,965	0	1
47	14,300	22,895	25.46	4	5	7,585	0	0
48	9,275	12,599	11.11	5	4	55,421	1	0
49	7,200	8,998	34.45	4	5	43,266	0	1
50	6,400	7,898	33.68	3	5	44,784	0	0
51	9,475	11,948	39.92	4	5	230,235	0	1
52	8,750	10,385	26.38	1	2	46,167	0	1
53	12,050	15,240	51.41	2	1	13,337	0	1
54	19,350	27,885	−17.88	3	4	17,827	0	0

Sources: Consumer Reports Annual Automotive Issue, May 1991, 1992, and 1993; *Automotive News: Market Report 1991–1994; Kelly Blue Book for Used Car Pricing.*

SHOWCASE

THE CONDO SALES CASE

This case involves an investigation of the factors that affect the sale price of ocean-side condominium units. It represents an extension of an analysis of the same data by Herman Kelting (1979). Although condo sale prices have increased dramatically over the past 20 years, the relationship between these factors and sale price remain about the same. Consequently, the data provide valuable insight into today's condominium sales market.

The sales data were obtained for a new oceanside condominium complex consisting of two adjacent and connected eight-floor buildings. The complex contains 200 units of equal size (approximately 500 square feet each). The locations of the buildings relative to the ocean, the swimming pool, the parking lot, etc. are shown in the accompanying figure. There are several features of the complex that you should note:

1. The units facing south, called *ocean-view,* face the beach and ocean. In addition, units in building 1 have a good view of the pool. Units to the rear of the building, called *bay-view,* face the parking lot and an area of land that ultimately borders a bay. The view from the upper floors of these units is primarily of wooded, sandy terrain. The bay is very distant and barely visible.

2. The only elevator in the complex is located at the east end of building 1, as are the office and the game room. People moving to or from the higher floor units in building 2 would likely use the elevator and move through the passages to their units. Thus, units on the higher floors and at a greater distance from the elevator would be less convenient; they would require greater effort in moving baggage, groceries, etc., and would be farther away from the game room, the office, and the swimming pool. These units also possess an advantage: there would be the least amount of traffic through the hallways in the area and hence they are the most private.

3. Lower-floor oceanside units are most suited to active people; they open onto the beach, ocean, and pool. They are within easy reach of the game room and they are easily reached from the parking area.

4. Checking the layout of the condominium complex, you discover that some of the units in the center of the complex, units ending in numbers 11 and 14, have part of their view blocked.

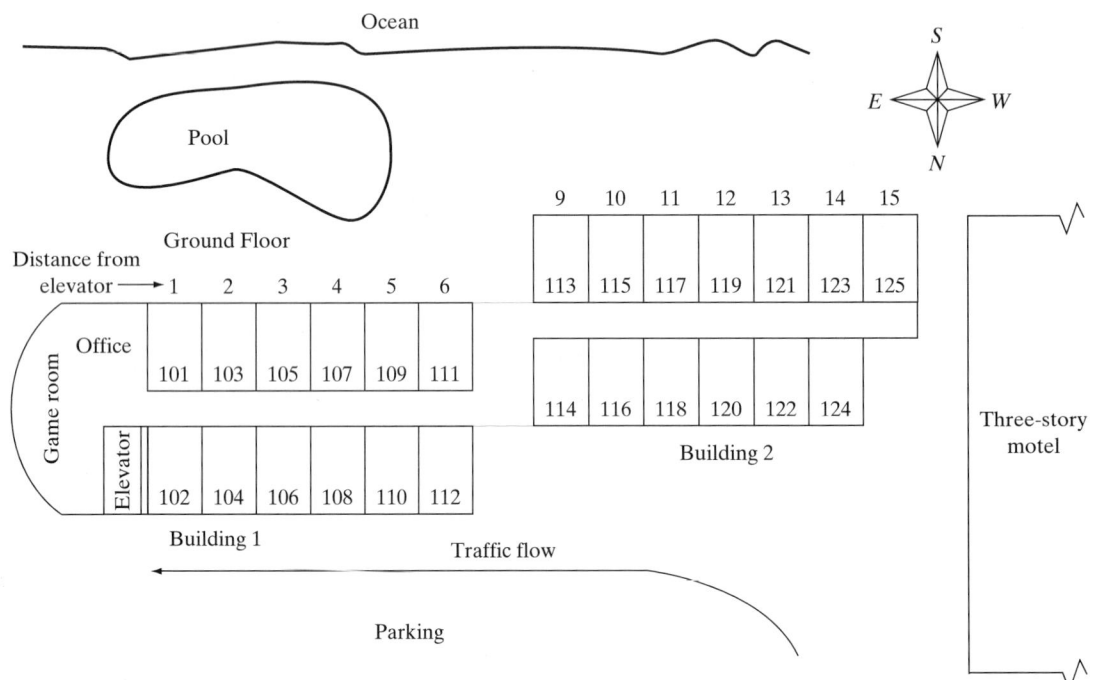

FIGURE C4.1   Layout of Condominium Complex

5. The condominium complex was completed at the time of the 1975 recession; sales were slow and the developer was forced to sell most of the units at auction approximately 18 months after opening. Consequently, the auction data are completely buyer-specified and hence consumer-oriented in contrast to most other real estate sales data which are, to a high degree, seller and broker specified.

6. Many unsold units in the complex were furnished by the developer and rented prior to the auction. Consequently, some of the units bid on and sold at auction had furniture, others did not.

This condominium complex is obviously unique. For example, the single elevator located at one end of the complex produces a remarkably high level of both inconvenience and privacy for the people occupying units on the top floors in building 2. Consequently, the developer is unsure of how the height of the unit (floor number), distance of the unit from the elevator, presence or absence of an ocean view, etc. affect the prices of the units sold at auction. To investigate these relationships, the following data were recorded for each of the 106 units sold at the auction:

1. *Sale price.* Measured in hundreds of dollars (adjusted for inflation)

2. *Floor height.* The floor location of the unit; the variable levels are 1, 2, ..., 8.

3. *Distance from elevator.* This distance, measured along the length of the complex, is expressed in number of condominium units. An additional two units of distance was added to the units in building 2 to account for the walking distance in the connecting area between the two buildings. Thus, the distance of unit 105 from the elevator would be 3, and the distance between unit 113 and the elevator would be 9. The variable levels are 1, 2, ..., 15.

4. *View of ocean.* The presence or absence of an ocean view is recorded for each unit and specified with a dummy variable (1 if the unit possessed an ocean view and 0 if not). Note that units not possessing an ocean view would face the parking lot.

5. *End unit.* We expect the partial reduction of view of end units on the ocean side (numbers ending in 11) to reduce their sale price. The ocean view of these end units is partially blocked by building 2. This qualitative variable is also specified with a dummy variable (1 if the unit has a unit number ending in 11 and 0 if not).

6. *Furniture.* The presence or absence of furniture is recorded for each unit, and represented with a single dummy variable (1 if the unit was furnished and 0 if not).

Your objective for this case is to build a regression model that accurately predicts the sale price of a condominium unit sold at auction. Prepare a professional document that presents the results of your analysis. Include graphs that demonstrate how each of the independent variables in your model affects auction price. A layout of the data file is described below.

DATA   ASCII file name: CONDO.DAT
Number of observations: 106

Variable	Column(s)	Type
PRICE	1–3	QN
FLOOR	5	QN
DISTANCE	7–8	QN
VIEW	10	QL
ENDUNIT	12	QL
FURNISH	14	QL

www.int.com
www.int.com
INTERNET LAB

USING THE CONSUMER PRICE INDEX IN BUSINESS FORECASTS OF LABOR, WAGES, AND COMPENSATION

The Consumer Price Index (CPI) is one of the most used economic indicators by business and government. It measures monthly price changes for some 300 selected consumer items, including products from the categories of food, transportation, and housing, among others. Large corporations use the CPI—or the so called cost-of-living index—in forecasting revenues and profits. Staffing decisions regarding total company employment, wages, and compensation are often directly based on the CPI.

Here we will explore using the CPI in prediction models of key labor statistics.

1. Obtain annual CPI data for the past 30 years. The site address for the Bureau of Labor Statistics: *http://stats.bls.gov:80/*

   - Here, click on: **Data**
   - Then, click on: **Most Requested Series**
   - Next, scroll down to the heading "Prices and Living Conditions"
   - Select: CPI—Urban Wage Earners and Clerical Workers

2. Download and save the data in your statistical applications software data files.

3. Go back to the Bureau of Labor Statistics site: Most Requested Series

   - Here, click on: **Overall BLS Most Requested Series**

This page from Most Requested Series allows you to select and view data for a number of key labor statistics. From the categories of Employment and Compensation, view several of these variables and select three for downloading. Include one from each of the three categories: employment level, wages, and compensation.

4. For each of the variables selected, obtain the same 30 years of data as with the CPI.

5. Download and save the data in your statistical applications software data files.

6. Analyze the data you have saved:

   a. For each of the variables selected, find the correlation of the variable with CPI. Interpret the results.

   b. Select one of the three variables as the dependent variable in a regression analysis. Assuming that CPI and the other two variables will be used to model the selected variable, assess the degree of multicollinearity in the data.

   c. Conduct a complete regression analysis on the data, including model building and an analysis of residuals. Prepare a report of your findings and present the results to your class. ○

CHAPTER 13

METHODS FOR QUALITY IMPROVEMENT

Where We've Been

In Chapters 7–9 we described methods for making inferences about populations based on sample data. In Chapters 10–12 we focused on modeling relationships between variables using regression analysis.

Where We're Going

In this chapter and the next, we turn our attention to processes. Recall from Chapter 1 that a process is a series of actions or operations that transform inputs to outputs. This chapter describes methods for improving processes and the quality of the output they produce. The next chapter is concerned with modeling and forecasting the output of processes.

Over the last two decades U.S. firms have been seriously challenged by products of superior quality from overseas, particularly from Japan. Japan currently produces 25% of the cars sold in the United States. In 1989, for the first time, the top-selling car in the United States was made in Japan: the Honda Accord. Although it's an American invention, virtually all VCRs are produced in Japan. Only one U.S. firm still manufactures televisions; the rest are made in Japan.

To meet this competitive challenge, more and more U.S. firms—both manufacturing and service firms—have begun quality-improvement initiatives of their own. Many of these firms now stress **Total Quality Management** (TQM), i.e., the management of quality in all phases and aspects of their business, from the design of their products to production, distribution, sales, and service.

Broadly speaking, TQM is concerned with (1) finding out what it is that the customer wants, (2) translating those wants into a product or service design, and (3) producing a product or service that meets or exceeds the specifications of the design. In this chapter we focus primarily on the third of these three areas and its major problem—product and service variation.

Variation is inherent in the output of all production and service processes. No two parts produced by a given machine are the same; no two transactions performed by a given bank teller are the same. Why is this a problem? With variation in output comes variation in the quality of the product or service. If this variation is unacceptable to customers, sales are lost, profits suffer, and the firm may not survive.

The existence of this ever-present variation has made statistical methods and statistical training vitally important to industry. In this chapter we present some of the tools and methods currently employed by firms worldwide to monitor and reduce product and service variation.

13.1 QUALITY, PROCESSES, AND SYSTEMS

QUALITY

Before describing various tools and methods that can be used to monitor and improve the quality of products and services, we need to consider what is meant by the term *quality*. Quality can be defined from several different perspectives. To the engineers and scientists who design products, quality typically refers to the amount of some ingredient or attribute possessed by the product. For example, high-quality ice cream contains a large amount of butterfat. High-quality rugs have a large number of knots per square inch. A high-quality shirt or blouse has 22 to 26 stitches per inch.

To managers, engineers, and workers involved in the production of a product (or the delivery of a service), quality usually means conformance to requirements, or the degree to which the product or service conforms to its design specifications. For example, in order to fit properly, the cap of a particular molded plastic bottle must be between 1.0000 inch and 1.0015 inches in diameter. Caps that do not conform to this requirement are considered to be of inferior quality. For an example in a service operation, consider the service provided to customers in a fast-food restaurant. A particular restaurant has been designed to serve customers within two minutes of the time their order is placed. If it takes more than two minutes, the service does not conform to specifications and is considered to be of inferior quality. Using this production-based interpretation of quality, well-made products are high quality; poorly made products are low quality. Thus, a well-made Rolls Royce and a well-made Chevrolet Nova are both high-quality cars.

Although quality can be defined from either the perspective of the designers or the producers of a product, in the final analysis both definitions should be derived from the needs and preferences of the *user* of the product or service. A firm that produces goods that no one wants to purchase cannot stay in business. We define quality accordingly.

DEFINITION 13.1

The **quality** of a good or service is indicated by the extent to which it satisfies the needs and preferences of its users.

Consumers' needs and wants shape their perceptions of quality. Thus, to produce a high-quality product, it is necessary to study the needs and wants of consumers. This is typically one of the major functions of a firm's marketing department. Once the necessary consumer research has been conducted, it is necessary to translate consumers' desires into a product design. This design must then be translated into a production plan and production specifications that, if properly implemented, will turn out a product with characteristics that will satisfy users' needs and wants. In short, consumer perceptions of quality play a role in all phases and aspects of a firm's operations.

But what product characteristics are consumers looking for? What is it that influences users' perceptions of quality? This is the kind of knowledge that firms need in order to develop and deliver high-quality goods and services. The basic elements of quality are summarized in the eight dimensions shown in the box.

The Eight Dimensions of Quality*

1. **Performance:** The primary operating characteristics of the product. For an automobile, these would include acceleration, handling, smoothness of ride, gas mileage, etc.

2. **Features:** The "bells and whistles" that supplement the product's basic functions. Examples include CD players and digital clocks on cars and the frequent-flyer mileage and free drinks offered by airlines.

3. **Reliability:** Reflects the probability that the product will not operate properly within a given period of time.

4. **Conformance:** The extent or degree to which a product meets preestablished standards. This is reflected in, for example, a pharmaceutical manufacturer's concern that the plastic bottles it orders for its drugs have caps that are between 1.0000 and 1.0015 inches in diameter, as specified in their order.

5. **Durability:** The life of the product. If repair is possible, durability relates to the length of time a product can be used before replacement is judged to be preferable to continued repair.

6. **Serviceability:** The ease of repair, speed of repair, and competence and courtesy of the repair staff.

7. **Aesthetics:** How a product looks, feels, sounds, smells, or tastes.

8. **Other perceptions that influence judgments of quality:** Such factors as a firm's reputation and the images of the firm and its products that are created through advertising.

In order to design and produce products of high quality, it is necessary to translate the characteristics described in the box into product attributes that can be built into the product by the manufacturer. That is, user preferences must be

* Garvin, D. *Managing Quality.* New York: Free Press/Macmillan, 1988.

interpreted in terms of product variables over which the manufacturer has control. For example, in considering the performance characteristics of a particular brand of wooden pencil, users may indicate a preference for being able to use the pencil for longer periods between sharpenings. The manufacturer may translate this performance characteristic into one or more measurable physical characteristics such as wood hardness, lead hardness, and lead composition. Besides being used to design high-quality products, such variables are used in the process of monitoring and improving quality during production.

PROCESSES

Much of this textbook focuses on methods for using sample data drawn from a population to learn about that population. In this chapter and the next, however, our attention is not on populations, but on processes—such as manufacturing processes —and the output that they generate. In general, a process is defined as follows:

> **DEFINITION 13.2**
> A **process** is a series of actions or operations that transforms inputs to outputs. A process produces output over time.

Processes can be organizational or personal in nature. Organizational processes are those associated with organizations such as businesses and governments. Perhaps the best example is a manufacturing process, which consists of a series of operations, performed by people and machines, whereby inputs such as raw materials and parts are converted into finished products (the outputs). Examples include automobile assembly lines, oil refineries, and steel mills. Personal processes are those associated with your private life. The series of steps you go through each morning to get ready for school or work can be thought of as a process. Through turning off the alarm clock, showering, dressing, eating, and opening the garage door, you transform yourself from a sleeping person to one who is ready to interact with the outside world. Figure 13.1 presents a general description of a process and its inputs.

It is useful to think of processes as *adding value* to the inputs of the process. Manufacturing processes, for example, are designed so that the value of the outputs to potential customers exceeds the value of the inputs—otherwise the firm would have no demand for its products and would not survive.

SYSTEMS

To understand what causes variation in process output and how processes and their output can be improved, we must understand the role that processes play in *systems*.

FIGURE 13.1   Graphical depiction of a process and its inputs

FIGURE 13.2   Model of a basic system

> **DEFINITION 13.3**
>
> A **system** is a collection or arrangement of interacting processes that has an ongoing purpose or mission. A system receives inputs from its environment, transforms those inputs to outputs, and delivers them to its environment. In order to survive, a system uses feedback (i.e., information) from its environment to understand and adapt to changes in its environment.

Figure 13.2 presents a model of a basic system. As an example of a system, consider a manufacturing company. It has a collection of interacting processes—marketing research, engineering, purchasing, receiving, production, sales, distribution, billing, etc. Its mission is to make money for its owners, to provide high-quality working conditions for its employees, and to stay in business. The firm receives raw materials and parts (inputs) from outside vendors which, through its production processes, it transforms to finished goods (outputs). The finished goods are distributed to its customers. Through its marketing research, the firm "listens" (receives feedback from) its customers and potential customers in order to change or adapt its processes and products to meet (or exceed) the needs, preferences, and expectations of the marketplace.

Since systems are collections of processes, the various types of system inputs are the same as those listed in Figure 13.1 for processes. System outputs are products or services. These outputs may be physical objects made, assembled, repaired, or moved by the system; or they may be symbolical, such as information, ideas, or knowledge. For example, a brokerage house supplies customers with information about stocks and bonds and the markets where they are traded.

Two important points about systems and the output of their processes are: (1) No two items produced by a process are the same; (2) Variability is an inherent characteristic of the output of all processes. This is illustrated in Figure 13.3. No two cars produced by the same assembly line are the same: No two windshields are the same; no two wheels are the same; no two tires are the same; no two hubcaps

FIGURE 13.3
Output variation

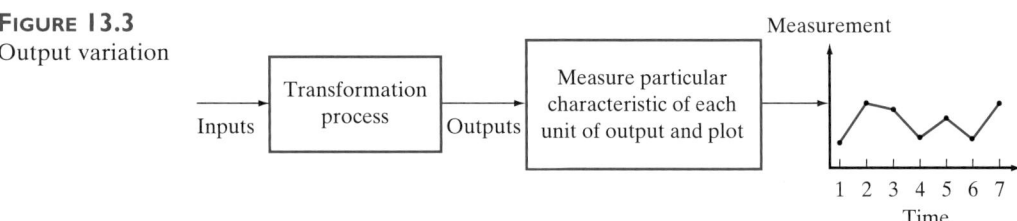

are the same. The same thing can be said for processes that deliver services. Consider the services offered at the teller windows of a bank to two customers waiting in two lines. Will they wait in line the same amount of time? Will they be serviced by tellers with the same degree of expertise and with the same personalities? Assuming the customers' transactions are the same, will they take the same amount of time to execute? The answer to all these questions is no.

In general, variation in output is caused by the six factors listed in the box.

The Six Major Sources of Process Variation

1. People
2. Machines
3. Materials
4. Methods
5. Measurement
6. Environment

Awareness of this ever-present process variation has made training in statistical thinking and statistical methods highly valued by industry. By **statistical thinking** we mean the knack of recognizing variation, and exploiting it in problem solving and decision-making. The remainder of this chapter is devoted to statistical tools for monitoring process variation.

STATISTICS IN ACTION

13.1 DEMING'S 14 POINTS

How is it that the Japanese became quality leaders? What inspired their concern for quality? In part, it was the statistical and managerial expertise exported to Japan from the United States following World War II. At the end of the war Japan faced the difficult task of rebuilding its economy. To this end, a group of engineers was assigned by the Allied command to assist the Japanese in improving the quality of their communication systems. These engineers taught the Japanese the statistical quality control methods that had been developed in the United States under the direction of Walter Shewhart of Bell Laboratories in the 1920s and 1930s. Then, in 1950, the Japanese Union of Scientists and Engineers invited W. Edwards Deming, a statistician who had studied with Shewhart, to present a series of lectures on statistical quality-improvement methods to hundreds of Japanese researchers, plant managers, and engineers. During his stay in Japan he also met with many of the top executives of Japan's largest com-

panies. At the time, Japan was notorious for the inferior quality of its products. Deming told the executives that by listening to what consumers wanted and by applying statistical methods in the production of those goods, they could export high-quality products that would find markets all over the world.

In 1951 the Japanese established the **Deming Prize** to be given annually to companies with significant accomplishments in the area of quality. In 1989, for the first time, the Deming Prize was given to a U.S. company—Florida Power and Light Company.

One of Deming's major contributions to the quality movement that is spreading across the major industrialized nations of the world was his recognition that statistical (and other) process improvement methods cannot succeed without the proper organizational climate and culture. Accordingly, he proposed 14 guidelines that, if followed, transform the organizational climate to one in which process-management efforts can flourish. These 14 points are, in essence, Deming's philosophy of management. He argues convincingly that all 14 should be implemented, not just certain subsets. We list all 14 points here, adding clarifying statements where needed. For a fuller discussion of these points, see Deming (1986), Gitlow *et al.* (1995), Walton (1986), and Joiner and Goudard (1990).

1. **Create constancy of purpose toward improvement of product and service, with the aim to become competitive and to stay in business, and to provide jobs.** The organization must have a clear goal or purpose. Everyone in the organization must be encouraged to work toward that goal day in and day out, year after year.

2. **Adopt the new philosophy.** Reject detection-rejection management in favor of a customer-oriented, preventative style of management in which never-ending quality improvement is the driving force.

3. **Cease dependence on inspection to achieve quality.** It is because of poorly designed products and excessive process variation that inspection is needed. If quality is designed into products and process management is used in their production, mass inspection of finished products will not be necessary.

4. **End the practice of awarding business on the basis of price tag.** Do not simply buy from the lowest bidder. Consider the quality of the supplier's products along with the supplier's price. Establish long-term relationships with suppliers based on loyalty and trust. Move toward using a single supplier for each item needed.

5. **Improve constantly and forever the system of production and service, to improve quality and productivity, and thus constantly decrease costs.**

6. **Institute training.** Workers are often trained by other workers who were never properly trained themselves. The result is excessive process variation and inferior products and services. This is not the workers' fault; no one has told them how to do their jobs well.

7. **Institute leadership.** Supervisors should help the workers to do a better job. Their job is to lead, not to order workers around or to punish them.

8. **Drive out fear, so that everyone may work effectively for the company.** Many workers are afraid to ask questions or to bring problems to the attention of management. Such a climate is not conducive to producing high-quality goods and services. People work best when they feel secure.

9. **Break down barriers between departments.** Everyone in the organization must work together as a team. Different areas within the firm should have complementary, not conflicting, goals. People across the organization must realize that they are all part of the same system. Pooling their resources to solve problems is better than competing against each other.

10. **Eliminate slogans, exhortations, and arbitrary numerical goals and targets for the workforce which urge the workers to achieve new levels of productivity and quality.** Simply asking the workers to improve their work is not enough; they must be shown *how* to improve it. Management must realize that significant improvements can be achieved only if management takes responsibility for quality and makes the necessary changes in the design of the system in which the workers operate.

11. **Eliminate numerical quotas.** Quotas are purely quantitative (e.g., number of pieces to produce per day); they do not take quality into consideration. When faced with quotas, people attempt to meet them at any cost, regardless of the damage to the organization.

12. **Remove barriers that rob employees of their pride of workmanship.** People must be treated as human beings, not commodities. Working conditions must be improved, including the elimination of poor supervision, poor product design, defective materials, and defective machines. These things stand in the way of workers' performing up to their capabilities and producing work they are proud of.

13. **Institute a vigorous program of education and self-improvement.** Continuous improvement requires continuous learning. Everyone in the organization must be trained in the modern methods of quality improvement, including statistical concepts and interdepartmental teamwork. Top management should be the first to be trained.

14. **Take action to accomplish the transformation.** Hire people with the knowledge to implement the 14 points. Build a critical mass of people committed to transforming the organization. Put together a top management team to lead the way. Develop a plan and an organizational structure that will facilitate the transformation.

Focus

Contact a company located near your college or university and find out how many (if any) of Deming's 14 points have been implemented at the firm. Pool your results with those of your classmates to obtain a sense of the quality movement in your area. Summarize the results.

13.2 STATISTICAL CONTROL

For the rest of this chapter we turn our attention to **control charts**—graphical devices used for monitoring process variation, for identifying when to take action to improve the process, and for assisting in diagnosing the causes of process variation. Control charts, developed by Walter Shewhart of Bell Laboratories in the mid 1920s, are the tool of choice for continuously monitoring processes. Before we go into the details of control chart construction and use, however, it is important that you have a fuller understanding of process variation. To this end, we discuss patterns of variation in this section.

As was discussed in Chapter 2, the proper graphical method for describing the variation of process output is a **time series plot**, sometimes called a **run chart**. Recall that in a time series plot the measurements of interest are plotted against time or are plotted in the order in which the measurements were made, as in Figure 13.4. Whenever you face the task of analyzing data that were generated over time, your first reaction should be to plot them. The human eye is one of our most sensitive statistical instruments. Take advantage of that sensitivity by plotting the data and allowing your eyes to seek out patterns in the data.

Let's begin thinking about process variation by examining the plot in Figure 13.4 more closely. The measurements, taken from a paint manufacturing process, are the weights of 50 one-gallon cans of paint that were consecutively filled by the same filling head (nozzle). The weights were plotted in the order of production. Do you detect any systematic, persistent patterns in the sequence of weights? For example, do the weights tend to drift steadily upward or downward over time? Do they oscillate—high, then low, then high, then low, etc.?

To assist your visual examination of this or any other time series plot, Roberts (1991) recommends enhancing the basic plot in two ways. First, compute (or simply estimate) the mean of the set of 50 weights and draw a horizontal line on the graph at the level of the mean. This **centerline** gives you a point of reference in searching for patterns in the data. Second, using straight lines, connect each of the plotted weights in the order in which they were produced. This

FIGURE 13.4

Time series plot of fill weights for 50 consecutively produced gallon cans of paint

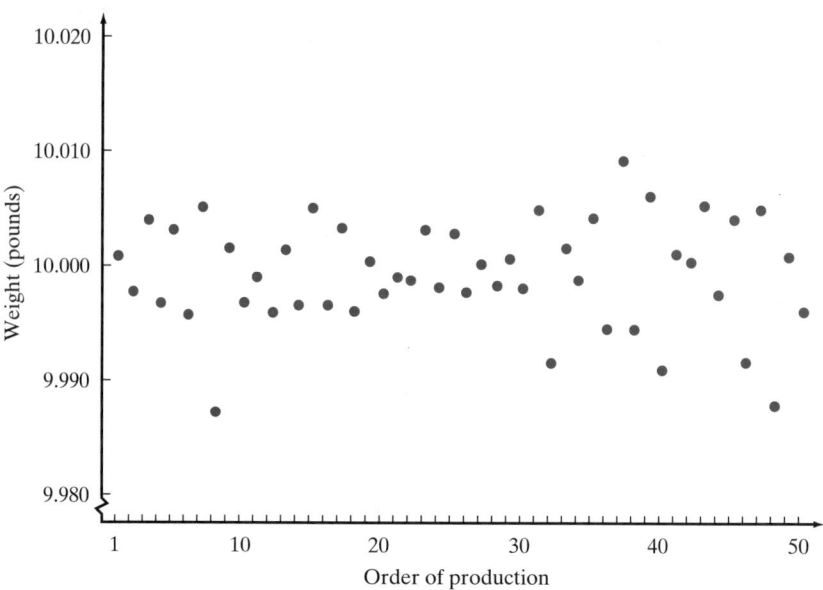

FIGURE 13.5
An enhanced version of the paint fill time series

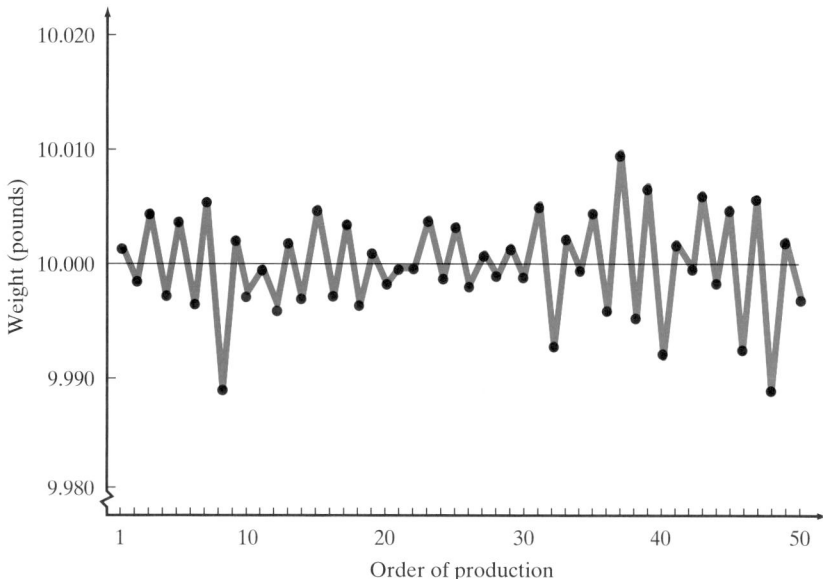

helps display the sequence of the measurements. Both enhancements are shown in Figure 13.5.

Now do you see a pattern in the data? Successive points alternate up and down, high then low, in an **oscillating sequence**. In this case, the points alternate above and below the centerline. This pattern was caused by a valve in the paint-filling machine that tended to stick in a partially closed position every other time it operated.

Other patterns of process variation are shown in Figure 13.6. We discuss several of them later.

In trying to describe process variation and diagnose its causes, it helps to think of the sequence of measurements of the output variable (e.g., weight, length, number of defects) as having been generated in the following way:

1. At any point in time, the output variable of interest can be described by a particular probability distribution (or relative frequency distribution). This distribution describes the possible values that the variable can assume and their likelihood of occurrence. Three such distributions are shown in Figure 13.7.

2. The particular value of the output variable that is realized at a given time can be thought of as being generated or produced according to the distribution described in point 1. (Alternatively, the realized value can be thought of as being generated by a random sample of size $n = 1$ from a population of values whose relative frequency distribution is that of point 1.)

3. The distribution that describes the output variable may change over time. For simplicity, we characterize the changes as being of three types: the mean (i.e., location) of the distribution may change; the variance (i.e., shape) of the distribution may change; or both. This is illustrated in Figure 13.8.

In general, when the output variable's distribution changes over time, we refer to this as a change in the *process*. Thus, if the mean shifts to a higher level, we say that the process mean has shifted. Accordingly, we sometimes refer to the distribution of the output variable as simply the **distribution of the process**, or the **output distribution of the process**.

FIGURE 13.6
Patterns of
process variation:
Some examples

a. Uptrend

b. Downtrend

c. Increasing variance

d. Cyclical

e. Meandering

f. Shock/Freak/Outlier

g. Level shift

FIGURE 13.7
Distributions
describing one
output variable at
three points in time

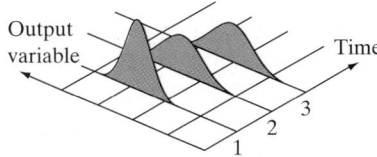

FIGURE 13.8
Types of changes in output variables

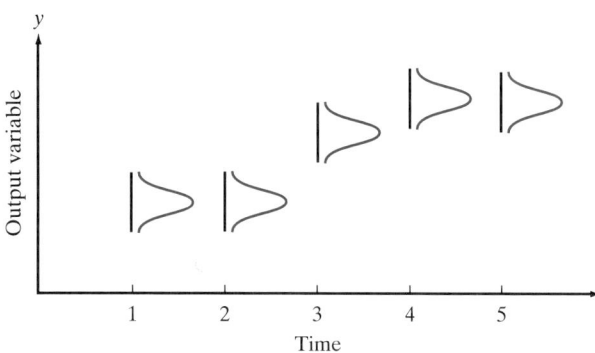

a. Change in mean (i.e., location)

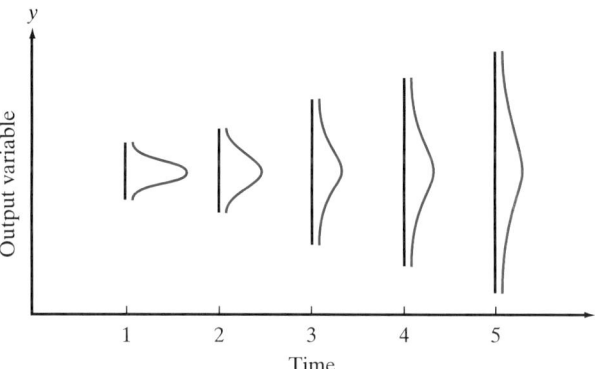

b. Change in variance (i.e., shape)

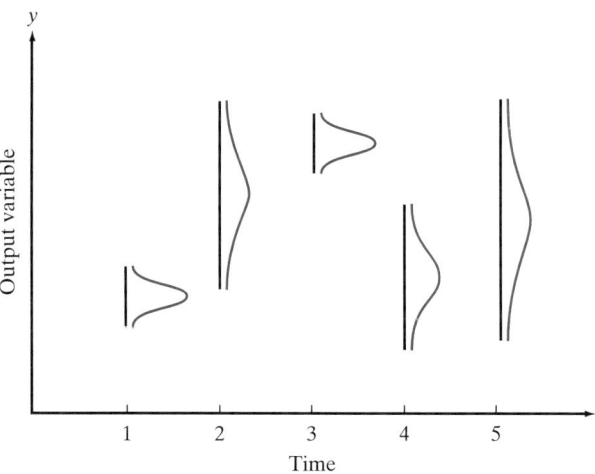

c. Change in mean and variance

Let's reconsider the patterns of variation in Figure 13.6 and model them using this conceptualization. This is done in Figure 13.9. The uptrend of Figure 13.6a can be characterized as resulting from a process whose mean is gradually shifting upward over time, as in Figure 13.9a. Gradual shifts like this are a common phenomenon in manufacturing processes. For example, as a machine wears out (e.g., cutting blades dull), certain characteristics of its output gradually change.

FIGURE 13.9
Patterns of process variation described by changing distributions

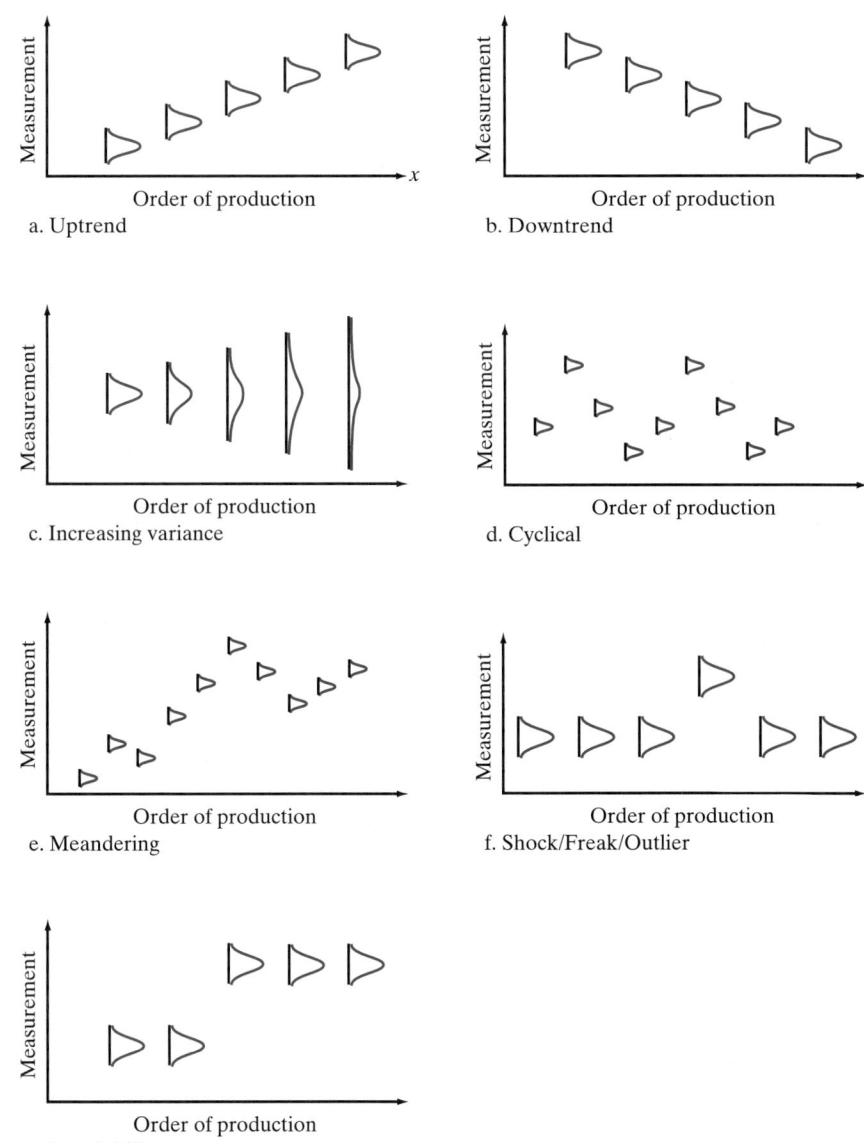

a. Uptrend

b. Downtrend

c. Increasing variance

d. Cyclical

e. Meandering

f. Shock/Freak/Outlier

g. Level shift

The pattern of increasing dispersion in Figure 13.6c can be thought of as resulting from a process whose mean remains constant but whose variance increases over time, as shown in Figure 13.9c. This type of deterioration in a process may be the result of worker fatigue. At the beginning of a shift, workers—whether they be typists, machine operators, waiters, or managers—are fresh and pay close attention to every item that they process. But as the day wears on, concentration may wane and the workers may become more and more careless or more easily distracted. As a result, some items receive more attention than other items, causing the variance of the workers' output to increase.

The sudden shift in the level of the measurements in Figure 13.6g can be thought of as resulting from a process whose mean suddenly increases but whose variance remains constant, as shown in Figure 13.9g. This type of pattern may be caused by such things as a change in the quality of raw materials used in the process or bringing a new machine or new operator into the process.

One thing that all these examples have in common is that the distribution of the output variable *changes over time.* In such cases, we say the process lacks **stability**. We formalize the notion of stability in the following definition.

> **DEFINITION 13.4**
>
> A process whose output distribution does *not* change over time is said to be in a state of **statistical control**, or simply **in control**. If it does change, it is said to be **out of statistical control**, or simply **out of control**.

Figure 13.10 illustrates a sequence of output distributions for both an in-control and an out-of-control process.

To see what the pattern of measurements looks like on a time series plot for a process that is in statistical control, consider Figure 13.11. These data are from the same paint-filling process we described earlier, but the sequence of measurements was made *after* the faulty valve was replaced. Notice that there are no discernible persistent, systematic patterns in the sequence of measurements such as those in Figures 13.5 and 13.6a–13.6e. Nor are there level shifts or transitory shocks as in Figures 13.6f–13.6g. This "patternless" behavior is called **random behavior. The output of processes that are in statistical control exhibits random behavior. Thus, even the output of stable processes exhibits variation**.

FIGURE 13.10
Comparison of in-control and out-of-control processes

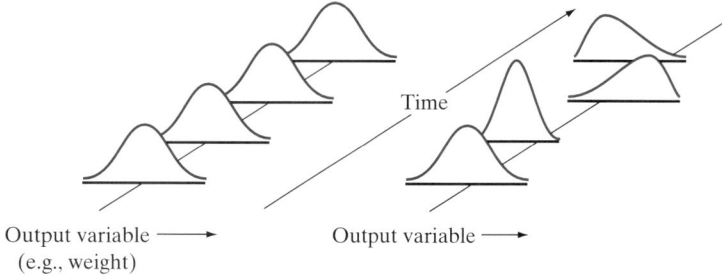

FIGURE 13.11
Time series plot of 50 consecutive paint can fills collected after replacing faulty valve

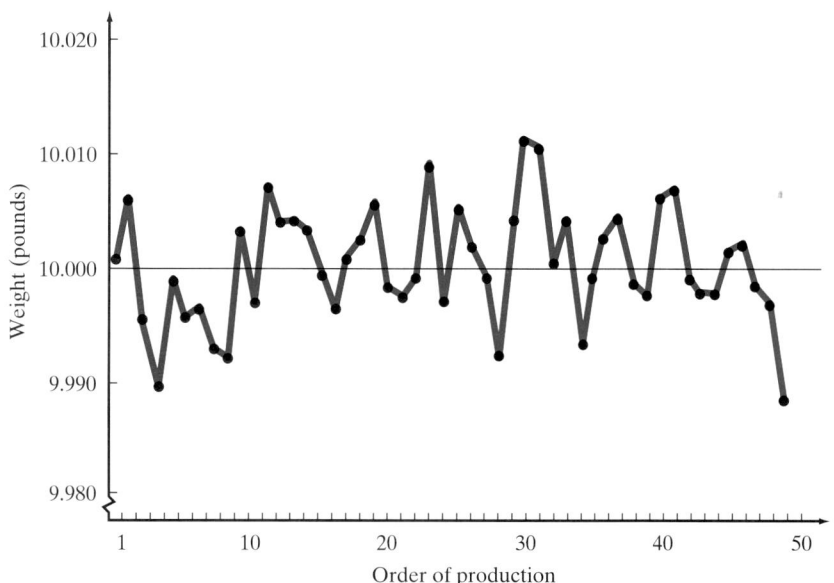

FIGURE 13.12
In-control processes
are predictable;
out-of-control
processes are not

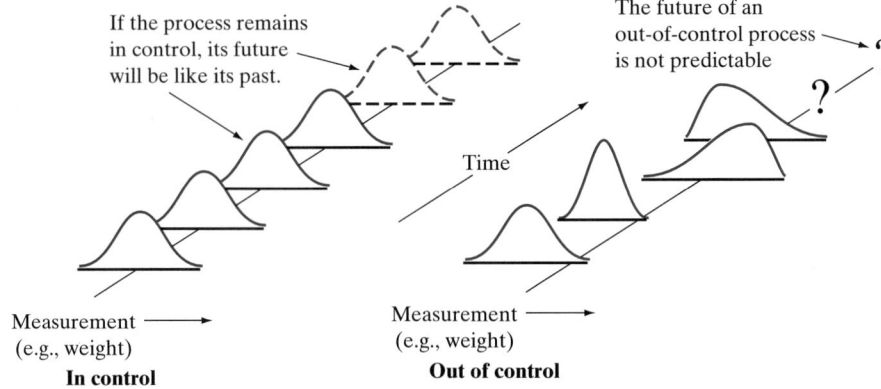

If the process remains
in control, its future
will be like its past.

The future of an
out-of-control process
is not predictable

Time

Measurement ⟶
(e.g., weight)

In control

Measurement ⟶
(e.g., weight)

Out of control

If a process is in control and remains in control, its future will be like its past. Accordingly, the process is predictable, in the sense that its output will stay within certain limits. This cannot be said about an out-of-control process. As illustrated in Figure 13.12, with most out-of-control processes you have no idea what the future pattern of output from the process may look like.* You simply do not know what to expect from the process. Consequently, a business that operates out-of-control processes runs the risk of (1) providing inferior quality products and services to its internal customers (people within the organization who use the outputs of the processes) and (2) selling inferior products and services to its external customers. In short, it risks losing its customers and threatens its own survival.

One of the fundamental goals of process management is to identify out-of-control processes, to take actions to bring them into statistical control, and to keep them in a state of statistical control. The series of activities used to attain this goal is referred to as **statistical process control**.

DEFINITION 13.5
The process of monitoring and eliminating variation in order to *keep* a process in a state of statistical control or to *bring* a process into statistical control is called **statistical process control (SPC)**.

Everything discussed in this section and the remaining sections of this chapter is concerned with statistical process control. We now continue our discussion of statistical control.

The variation that is exhibited by processes that are in control is said to be due to *common causes of variation.*

DEFINITION 13.6
Common causes of variation are the methods, materials, machines, personnel, and environment that make up a process and the inputs required by the process. Common causes are thus attributable to the design of the process. Common causes affect all output of the process and may affect everyone who participates in the process.

*The output variables of in-control processes may follow approximately normal distributions, as in Figures 13.10 and 13.12, or they may not. But any in-control process will follow the *same* distribution over time. Do not misinterpret the use of normal distributions in many figures in this chapter as indicating that all in-control processes follow normal distributions.

The total variation that is exhibited by an in-control process is due to many different common causes, most of which affect process output in very minor ways. In general, however, each common cause has the potential to affect every unit of output produced by the process. Examples of common causes include the lighting in a factory or office, the grade of raw materials required, and the extent of worker training. Each of these factors can influence the variability of the process output. Poor lighting can cause workers to overlook flaws and defects that they might otherwise catch. Inconsistencies in raw materials can cause inconsistencies in the quality of the finished product. The extent of the training provided to workers can affect their level of expertise and, as a result, the quality of the products and services for which they are responsible.

Since common causes are, in effect, designed into a process, the level of variation that results from common causes is viewed as being representative of the capability of the process. If that level is too great (i.e., if the quality of the output varies too much), the process must be redesigned (or modified) to eliminate one or more common causes of variation. Since process redesign is the responsibility of management, the *elimination of common causes of variation is typically the responsibility of management,* not of the workers.

Processes that are out of control exhibit variation that is the result of both common causes and **special causes of variation**.

DEFINITION 13.7

Special causes of variation (sometimes called **assignable causes**) are events or actions that are not part of the process design. Typically, they are transient, fleeting events that affect only local areas or operations within the process (e.g., a single worker, machine, or batch of materials) for a brief period of time. Occasionally, however, such events may have a persistent or recurrent effect on the process.

Examples of special causes of variation include a worker accidentally setting the controls of a machine improperly, a worker becoming ill on the job and continuing to work, a particular machine slipping out of adjustment, and a negligent supplier shipping a batch of inferior raw materials to the process.

In the latter case, the pattern of output variation may look like Figure 13.6f. If instead of shipping just one bad batch the supplier continued to send inferior materials, the pattern of variation might look like Figure 13.6g. The output of a machine that is gradually slipping out of adjustment might yield a pattern like Figure 13.6a, 13.6b, or 13.6c. All these patterns owe part of their variation to common causes and part to the noted special causes. In general, we treat any pattern of variation other than a random pattern as due to both common and special causes.* Since the effects of special causes are frequently localized within a process, *special causes can often be diagnosed and eliminated by workers or their immediate supervisor.* Occasionally, they must be dealt with by management, as in the case of a negligent or deceitful supplier.

It is important to recognize that **most processes are not naturally in a state of statistical control**. As Deming (1986, p. 322) observed: *"Stability [i.e., statistical*

---

*For certain processes (e.g., those affected by seasonal factors), a persistent systematic pattern—such as the cyclical pattern of Figure 13.6d—is an inherent characteristic. In these special cases, some analysts treat the cause of the systematic variation as a common cause. This type of analysis is beyond the scope of this text. We refer the interested reader to Alwan and Roberts (1988).

FIGURE 13.13
The effects of
eliminating causes
of variation

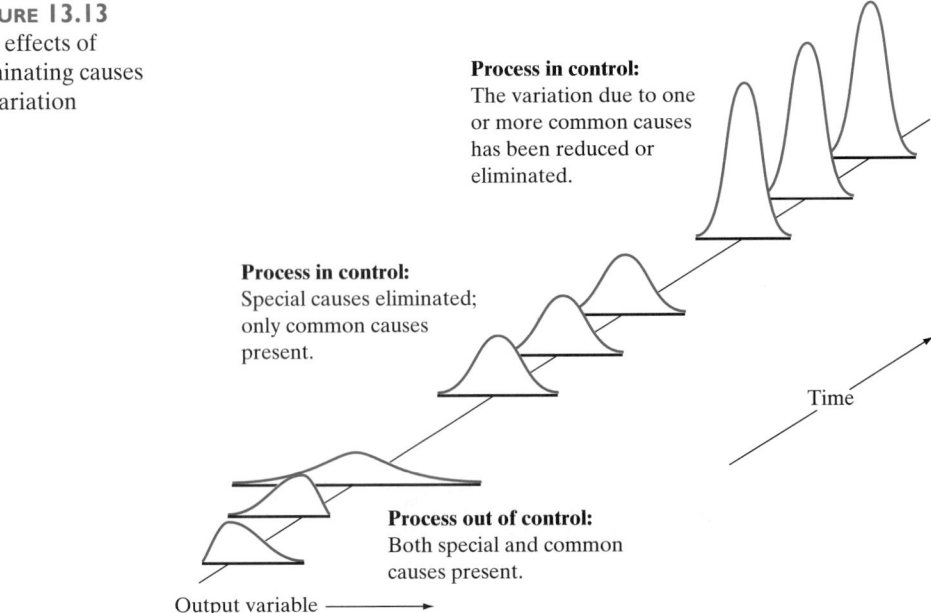

Process in control:
The variation due to one
or more common causes
has been reduced or
eliminated.

Process in control:
Special causes eliminated;
only common causes
present.

Time

Process out of control:
Both special and common
causes present.

Output variable ⟶

control] is seldom a natural state. It is an achievement, the result of eliminating special causes one by one ... leaving only the random variation of a stable process" (italics added).

Process improvement first requires the identification, diagnosis, and removal of special causes of variation. Removing all special causes puts the process in a state of statistical control. Further improvement of the process then requires the identification, diagnosis, and removal of common causes of variation. The effects on the process of the removal of special and common causes of variation are illustrated in Figure 13.13.

In the remainder of this chapter, we introduce you to some of the methods of statistical process control. In particular, we address how control charts help us determine whether a given process is in control.

13.3 THE LOGIC OF CONTROL CHARTS

We use control charts to help us differentiate between process variation due to common causes and special causes. That is, we use them to determine whether a process is under statistical control (only common causes present) or not (both common and special causes present). Being able to differentiate means knowing when to take action to find and remove special causes and when to leave the process alone. If you take actions to remove special causes that do not exist—that is called tampering with the process—you may actually end up increasing the variation of the process and, thereby, hurting the quality of the output.

In general, control charts are useful for evaluating the past performance of a process and for monitoring its current performance. We can use them to determine whether a process was in control during, say, the past two weeks or to determine whether the process is remaining under control from hour to hour or minute to minute. In the latter case, our goal is the swiftest detection and removal of any special causes of variation that might arise. Keep in mind that **the primary goal of quality-improvement activities is variance reduction**.

FIGURE 13.14
A control chart

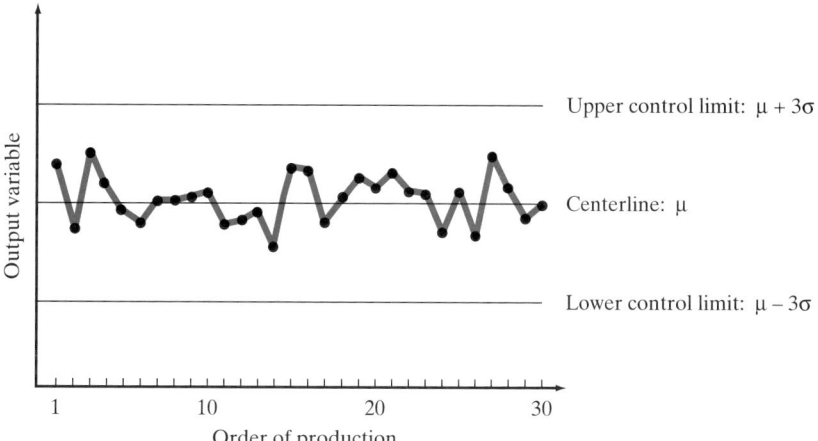

In this chapter we show you how to construct and use control charts for both quantitative and qualitative quality variables. Important quantitative variables include such things as weight, width, and time. An important qualitative variable is product status: defective or nondefective.

An example of a control chart is shown in Figure 13.14. A control chart is simply a time series plot of the individual measurements of a quality variable (i.e., an output variable), to which a centerline and two other horizontal lines called **control limits** have been added. The centerline represents the mean of the process (i.e., the mean of the quality variable) *when the process is in a state of statistical control*. The **upper control limit** and the **lower control limit** are positioned so that *when the process is in control* the probability of an individual value of the output variable falling outside the control limits is very small. Most practitioners position the control limits a distance of 3 standard deviations from the centerline (i.e., from the process mean) and refer to them as **3-sigma limits**. If the process is in control and following a normal distribution, the probability of an individual measurement falling outside the control limits is .0027 (less than 3 chances in 1,000). This is shown in Figure 13.15.

As long as the individual values stay between the control limits, the process is considered to be under control, meaning that no special causes of variation are influencing the output of the process. If one or more values fall outside the control

FIGURE 13.15
The probability of observing a measurement beyond the control limits when the process is in control

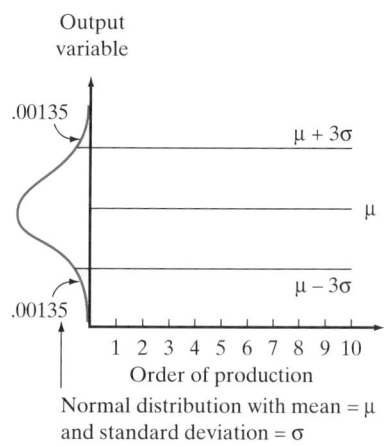

limits, either a **rare event** has occurred or the process is out of control. Following the rare-event approach to inference described earlier in the text, such a result is interpreted as evidence that the process is out of control and that actions should be taken to eliminate the special causes of variation that exist.

Other evidence to indicate that the process is out of control may be present on the control chart. For example, if we observe any of the patterns of variation shown in Figure 13.6, we can conclude the process is out of control *even if all the points fall between the control limits.* In general, any persistent, systematic variation pattern (i.e., any nonrandom pattern) is interpreted as evidence that the process is out of control. We discuss this in detail in the next section.

In Chapter 8 we described how to make inferences about populations using hypothesis-testing techniques. What we do in this section should seem quite similar. Although our focus now is on making inferences about a *process* rather than a *population,* we are again testing hypotheses. In this case, we test

$$H_0: \text{Process is under control}$$

$$H_a: \text{Process is out of control}$$

Each time we plot a new point and see whether it falls inside or outside of the control limits, we are running a two-sided hypothesis test. The control limits function as the critical values for the test.

What we learned in Chapter 8 about the types of errors that we might make in running a hypothesis test holds true in using control charts as well. Any time we reject the hypothesis that the process is under control and conclude that the process is out of control, we run the risk of making a Type I error (rejecting the null hypothesis when the null is true). Anytime we conclude (or behave as if we conclude) that the process is in control, we run the risk of a Type II error (accepting the null hypothesis when the alternative is true). There is nothing magical or mystical about control charts. Just as in any hypothesis test, the conclusion suggested by a control chart may be wrong.

One of the main reasons that 3-sigma control limits are used (rather than 2-sigma or 1-sigma limits, for example) is the small Type I error probability associated with their use. The probability we noted previously of an individual measurement falling outside the control limits—.0027—is a Type I error probability. Since we interpret a sample point that falls beyond the limits as a signal that the process is out of control, the use of 3-sigma limits yields very few signals that are "false alarms."

To make these ideas more concrete, we will construct and interpret a control chart for the paint-filling process discussed in Section 13.2. Our intention is simply to help you better understand the logic of control charts. Structured, step-by-step descriptions of how to construct control charts will be given in later sections.

TABLE 13.1   Fill Weights of 50 Consecutively Produced Cans of Paint

1. 10.0008	11. 9.9957	21. 9.9977	31. 10.0107	41. 10.0054
2. 10.0062	12. 10.0076	22. 9.9968	32. 10.0102	42. 10.0061
3. 9.9948	13. 10.0036	23. 9.9982	33. 9.9995	43. 9.9978
4. 9.9893	14. 10.0037	24. 10.0092	34. 10.0038	44. 9.9969
5. 9.9994	15. 10.0029	25. 9.9964	35. 9.9925	45. 9.9969
6. 9.9953	16. 9.9995	26. 10.0053	36. 9.9983	46. 10.0006
7. 9.9963	17. 9.9956	27. 10.0012	37. 10.0018	47. 10.0011
8. 9.9925	18. 10.0005	28. 9.9988	38. 10.0038	48. 9.9973
9. 9.9914	19. 10.0020	29. 9.9914	39. 9.9974	49. 9.9958
10. 10.0035	20. 10.0053	30. 10.0036	40. 9.9966	50. 9.9873

FIGURE 13.16
Control chart of fill weights for 50 consecutive paint can fills

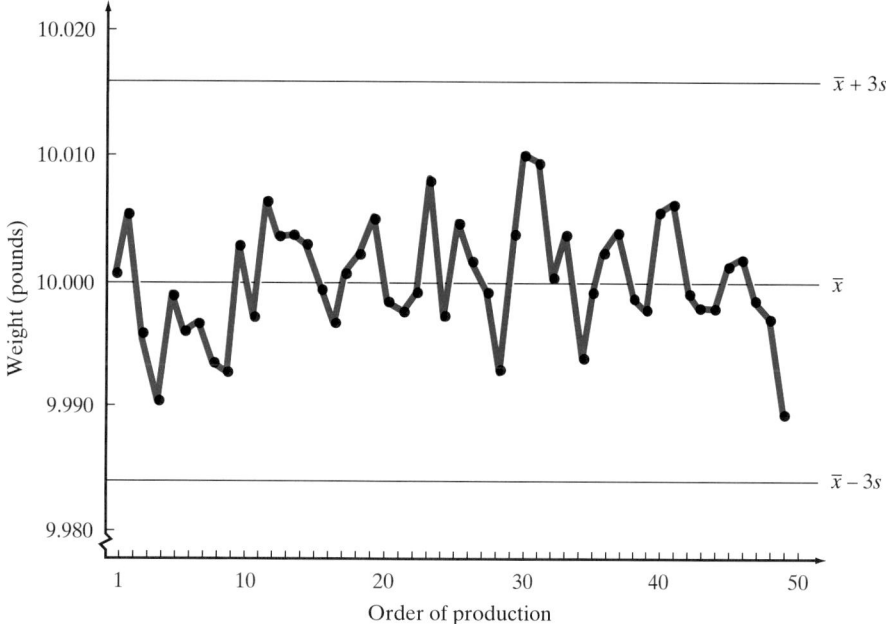

The sample measurements from the paint-filling process, presented in Table 13.1, were previously plotted in Figure 13.11. We use the mean and standard deviation of the sample, $\bar{x} = 9.9997$ and $s = .0053$, to estimate the mean and the standard deviation of the process. Although these are estimates, in using and interpreting control charts we treat them *as if* they were the actual mean μ and standard deviation σ of the process. This is standard practice in control charting.

The centerline of the control chart, representing the process mean, is drawn so that it intersects the vertical axis at 9.9997, as shown in Figure 13.16. The upper control limit is drawn at a distance of $3s = 3(.0053) = .0159$ above the centerline, and the lower control limit is $3s = .0159$ below the centerline. Then the 50 sample weights are plotted on the chart in the order that they were generated by the paint-filling process.

As can be seen in Figure 13.16, all the weight measurements fall within the control limits. Further, there do not appear to be any systematic nonrandom patterns in the data such as displayed in Figures 13.5 and 13.6. Accordingly, we are unable to conclude that the process is out of control. That is, we are unable to reject the null hypothesis that the process is in control. However, instead of using this formal hypothesis-testing language in interpreting control chart results, we prefer simply to say that the data suggest or indicate that the process is in control. We do this, however, with the full understanding that the probability of a Type II error is generally unknown in control chart applications and that we might be wrong in our conclusion. What we are really saying when we conclude that the process is in control is that *the data indicate that it is better to behave as if the process were under control than to tamper with the process.*

We have portrayed the control chart hypothesis test as testing "in control" versus "out of control." Another way to look at it is this: When we compare the weight of an *individual* can of paint to the control limits, we are conducting the following two-tailed hypothesis test:

$$H_0: \mu = 9.9997$$

$$H_a: \mu \neq 9.9997$$

where 9.9997 is the centerline of the control chart. The control limits delineate the two rejection regions for this test. Accordingly, with each weight measurement that we plot and compare to the control limits, we are testing whether the process mean (the mean fill weight) has changed. Thus, what the control chart is monitoring is the mean of the process. **The control chart leads us to accept or reject statistical control on the basis of whether the mean of the process has changed or not**. This type of process instability is illustrated in the top graph of Figure 13.8. In the paint-filling process example, the process mean apparently has remained constant over the period in which the sample weights were collected.

Other types of control charts—one of which we will describe in Section 13.5—help us determine whether the *variance* of the process has changed, as in the middle and bottom graphs of Figure 13.8.

The control chart we have just described is called an **individuals chart**, or an **x-chart**. The term *individuals* refers to the fact that the chart uses individual measurements to monitor the process—that is, measurements taken from individual units of process output. This is in contrast to plotting sample means on the control chart, for example, as we do in the next section.

Students sometimes confuse control limits with product **specification limits**. We have already explained control limits, which are a function of the natural variability of the process. Assuming we always use 3-sigma limits, the position of the control limits is a function of the size of σ, the process standard deviation.

DEFINITION 13.8

Specification limits are boundary points that define the acceptable values for an output variable (i.e., for a quality characteristic) of a particular product or service. They are determined by customers, management, and product designers. Specification limits may be two-sided, with upper and lower limits, or one-sided, with either an upper or a lower limit.

Process output that falls inside the specification limits is said to **conform to specifications**. Otherwise it is said to be **nonconforming**.

Unlike control limits, specification limits are not dependent on the process in any way. A customer of the paint-filling process may specify that all cans contain no more than 10.005 pounds of paint and no less than 9.995 pounds. These are specification limits. The customer has reasons for these specifications but may have no idea whether the supplier's process can meet them. Both the customer's specification limits and the control limits of the supplier's paint-filling process are shown in Figure 13.17. Do you think the customer will be satisfied with the quality of the product received? We don't. Although some cans are within the specification limits, most are not, as indicated by the shaded region on the figure.

13.4 A CONTROL CHART FOR MONITORING THE MEAN OF A PROCESS: THE $\bar{x}$-CHART

In the last section we introduced you to the logic of control charts by focusing on a chart that reflected the variation in individual measurements of process output. We used the chart to determine whether the process mean had shifted. The control chart we present in this section—the $\bar{x}$-chart—is also used to detect changes in the process mean, but it does so by monitoring the variation in the mean of

FIGURE 13.17

Comparison of control limits and specification limits

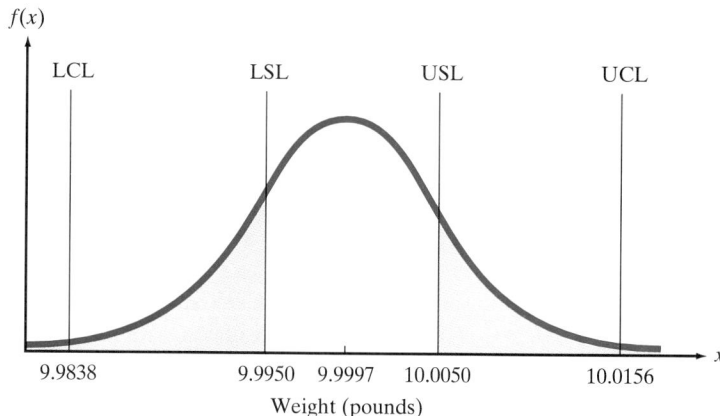

LCL = Lower control limit
UCL = Upper control limit
LSL = Lower specification limit
USL = Upper specification limit

samples that have been drawn from the process. That is, instead of plotting individual measurements on the control chart, in this case we plot sample means. Because of the additional information reflected in sample means (because each sample mean is calculated from n individual measurements), the $\bar{x}$-chart is more sensitive than the individuals chart for detecting changes in the process mean.

In practice, the $\bar{x}$-chart is rarely used alone. It is typically used in conjunction with a chart that monitors the variation of the process, usually a chart called an R-chart. The $\bar{x}$- and R-charts are the most widely used control charts in industry. Used in concert, these charts make it possible to determine whether a process has gone out of control because the variation has changed or because the mean has changed. We present the R-chart in the next section, at the end of which we discuss their simultaneous use. For now, we focus only on the $\bar{x}$-chart. **Consequently, we assume throughout this section that the process variation is stable.***

Figure 13.18 provides an example of an $\bar{x}$-chart. As with the individuals chart, the centerline represents the mean of the process and the upper and lower control limits are positioned a distance of 3 standard deviations from the mean. However, since the chart is tracking sample means rather than individual measurements, the relevant standard deviation is the standard deviation of $\bar{x}$, not σ, the standard deviation of the output variable.

FIGURE 13.18

$\bar{x}$-Chart

Upper control limit: $\mu + 3\sigma/\sqrt{n}$

Centerline: μ

Lower control limit: $\mu - 3\sigma/\sqrt{n}$

To the instructor: Technically, the R-chart should be constructed and interpreted before the $\bar{x}$-chart. However, in our experience, students more quickly grasp control chart concepts if they are familiar with the underlying theory. We begin with $\bar{x}$-charts because their underlying theory was presented in Chapters 6–8.

If the process were in statistical control, the sequence of $\bar{x}$'s plotted on the chart would exhibit random behavior between the control limits. Only if a rare event occurred or if the process went out of control would a sample mean fall beyond the control limits.

To better understand the justification for having control limits that involve $\sigma_{\bar{x}}$, consider the following. The $\bar{x}$-chart is concerned with the variation in $\bar{x}$ which, as we saw in Chapter 6, is described by $\bar{x}$'s sampling distribution. But what is the sampling distribution of $\bar{x}$? If the process is in control and its output variable x is characterized at each point in time by a normal distribution with mean μ and standard deviation σ, the distribution of $\bar{x}$ (i.e., $\bar{x}$'s sampling distribution) also follows a normal distribution with mean μ at each point in time. But, as we saw in Chapter 6, its standard deviation is $\sigma_{\bar{x}} = \sigma/\sqrt{n}$. The control limits of the $\bar{x}$-chart are determined from and interpreted with respect to the sampling distribution of $\bar{x}$, not the distribution of x. These points are illustrated in Figure 13.19.*

In order to construct an $\bar{x}$-chart, you should have at least 20 samples of n items each, where $n \geq 2$. This will provide sufficient data to obtain reasonably good estimates of the mean and variance of the process. The centerline, which represents the mean of the process, is determined as follows:

$$Centerline: \bar{\bar{x}} = \frac{\bar{x}_1 + \bar{x}_2 + \cdots + \bar{x}_k}{k}$$

FIGURE 13.19
The sampling distribution of $\bar{x}$

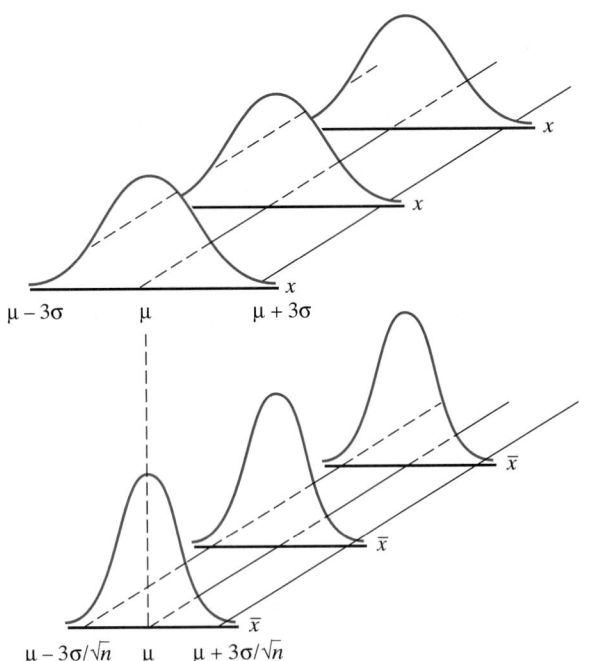

If the process is under control and follows a normal distribution with mean μ and standard deviation σ...

$\bar{x}$ also follows a normal distribution with mean μ but has standard deviation $\sigma/\sqrt{n}$.

*The sampling distribution of $\bar{x}$ can also be approximated using the Central Limit Theorem (Chapter 6). That is, when the process is under control and $\bar{x}$ is to be computed from a large sample from the process ($n \geq 30$), the sampling distribution will be approximately normally distributed with mean μ and standard deviation $\sigma/\sqrt{n}$. Even for samples as small as 4 or 5, the sampling distribution of $\bar{x}$ will be approximately normal as long as the distribution of x is reasonably symmetric and roughly bell-shaped.

where k is the number of samples of size n from which the chart is to be constructed and $\bar{x}_i$ is the sample mean of the ith sample. Thus $\bar{\bar{x}}$ is an estimator of μ.

The control limits are positioned as follows:

$$\textit{Upper control limit: } \bar{\bar{x}} + \frac{3\sigma}{\sqrt{n}}$$

$$\textit{Lower control limit: } \bar{\bar{x}} - \frac{3\sigma}{\sqrt{n}}$$

Since σ, the process standard deviation, is virtually always unknown, it must be estimated. This can be done in several ways. One approach involves calculating the standard deviations for each of the k samples and averaging them. Another involves using the sample standard deviation s from a large sample that was generated while the process was believed to be in control. We employ a third approach, however—the one favored by industry. It has been shown to be as effective as the other approaches for sample sizes of $n = 10$ or less, the sizes most often used in industry.

This approach utilizes the ranges of the k samples to estimate the process standard deviation, σ. Recall from Chapter 2 that the range, R, of a sample is the difference between the maximum and minimum measurements in the sample. It can be shown that dividing the mean of the k ranges, $\bar{R}$, by the constant d_2, obtains an unbiased estimator for σ. [For details, see Ryan (1989).] The estimator, denoted by $\hat{\sigma}$, is calculated as follows:

$$\hat{\sigma} = \frac{\bar{R}}{d_2} = \frac{R_1 + R_2 + \cdots + R_k}{k}\left(\frac{1}{d_2}\right)$$

where R_i is the range of the ith sample and d_2 is a constant that depends on the sample size. Values of d_2 for samples of size $n = 2$ to $n = 25$ can be found in Appendix B, Table XVII.

Substituting $\hat{\sigma}$ for σ in the formulas for the upper control limit (UCL) and the lower control limit (LCL), we get

$$\text{UCL:} \bar{\bar{x}} + \frac{3\left(\dfrac{\bar{R}}{d_2}\right)}{\sqrt{n}} \qquad \text{LCL:} \bar{\bar{x}} - \frac{3\left(\dfrac{\bar{R}}{d_2}\right)}{\sqrt{n}}$$

Notice that $(\bar{R}/d_2)/\sqrt{n}$ is an estimator of $\sigma_{\bar{x}}$. The calculation of these limits can be simplified by creating the constant

$$A_2 = \frac{3}{d_2\sqrt{n}}$$

Then the control limits can be expressed as

$$\text{UCL:} \bar{\bar{x}} + A_2\bar{R}$$

$$\text{LCL:} \bar{\bar{x}} - A_2\bar{R}$$

where the values for A_2 for samples of size $n = 2$ to $n = 25$ can be found in Appendix B, Table XVII.

The degree of sensitivity of the $\bar{x}$-chart to changes in the process mean depends on two decisions that must be made in constructing the chart.

The Two Most Important Decisions in Constructing an $\bar{x}$-Chart

1. The sample size, n, must be determined.

2. The frequency with which samples are to be drawn from the process must be determined (e.g., once an hour, once each shift, or once a day).

In order to quickly detect process change, we try to choose samples in such a way that the change in the process mean occurs *between* samples, not *within* samples (i.e., not during the period when a sample is being drawn). In this way, every measurement in the sample before the change will be unaffected by the change and every measurement in the sample following the change will be affected. The result is that the $\bar{x}$ computed from the latter sample should be substantially different from that of the former sample—a signal that something has happened to the process mean.

DEFINITION 13.9

Samples whose size and frequency have been designed to make it likely that process changes will occur between, rather than within, the samples are referred to as **rational subgroups**.

Rational Subgrouping Strategy

The samples (rational subgroups) should be chosen in a manner that:

1. Gives the maximum chance for the *measurements* in each sample to be similar (i.e., to be affected by the same sources of variation).

2. Gives the maximum chance for the *samples* to differ (i.e., be affected by at least one different source of variation).

The following example illustrates the concept of **rational subgrouping**. An operations manager suspects that the quality of the output in a manufacturing process may differ from shift to shift because of the preponderance of newly hired workers on the night shift. The manager wants to be able to detect such differences quickly, using an $\bar{x}$-chart. Following the rational subgrouping strategy, the control chart should be constructed with samples that are drawn *within* each shift. None of the samples should span shifts. That is, no sample should contain, say, the last three items produced by shift 1 and the first two items produced by shift 2. In this way, the measurements in each sample would be similar, but the $\bar{x}$'s would reflect differences between shifts.

The secret to designing an effective $\bar{x}$-chart is to anticipate the *types of special causes of variation* that might affect the process mean. Then purposeful rational subgrouping can be employed to construct a chart that is sensitive to the anticipated cause or causes of variation.

The preceding discussion and example focused primarily on the timing or frequency of samples. Concerning the size of the samples, practitioners typically work with samples of size $n = 4$ to $n = 10$ consecutively produced items. Using small samples of consecutively produced items helps to ensure that the measurements in each sample will be similar (i.e., affected by the same causes of variation).

Constructing an $\bar{x}$-Chart: A Summary

1. Using a rational subgrouping strategy, collect at least 20 samples (subgroups), each of size $n \geqslant 2$.

2. Calculate the mean and range for each sample.

3. Calculate the mean of the sample means, $\bar{\bar{x}}$, and the mean of the sample ranges, $\bar{R}$:

$$\bar{\bar{x}} = \frac{\bar{x}_1 + \bar{x}_2 + \cdots + \bar{x}_k}{k} \qquad \bar{R} = \frac{R_1 + R_2 + \cdots + R_k}{k}$$

where

$\quad k$ = number of samples (i.e., subgroups)

$\quad \bar{x}_i$ = sample mean for the ith sample

$\quad R_i$ = range of the ith sample

4. Plot the centerline and control limits:

$$Centerline: \bar{\bar{x}}$$

$$Upper\ control\ limit: \bar{\bar{x}} + A_2\bar{R}$$

$$Lower\ control\ limit: \bar{\bar{x}} - A_2\bar{R}$$

where A_2 is a constant that depends on n. Its values are given in Appendix B, Table XVII, for samples of size $n = 2$ to $n = 25$.

5. Plot the k sample means on the control chart in the order that the samples were produced by the process.

When interpreting a control chart, it is convenient to think of the chart as consisting of six zones, as shown in Figure 13.20. Each zone is 1 standard deviation wide. The two zones within 1 standard deviation of the centerline are called **C zones**; the regions between 1 and 2 standard deviations from the centerline are called **B zones**; and the regions between 2 and 3 standard deviations from the centerline are called **A zones**. The box describes how to construct the *zone boundaries* for an $\bar{x}$-chart.

FIGURE 13.20
The zones of a control chart

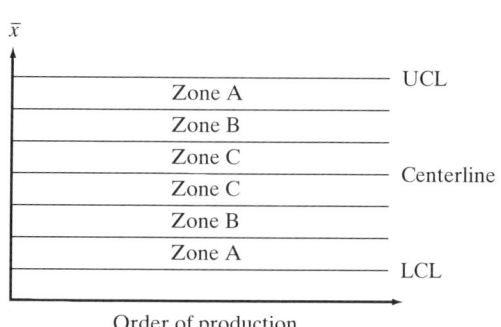

Order of production

Constructing Zone Boundaries for an $\bar{x}$-Chart

The zone boundaries can be constructed in either of the following ways:

1. Using the 3-sigma control limits:

$$\textit{Upper A–B boundary: } \bar{\bar{x}} + \frac{2}{3}(A_2\bar{R})$$

$$\textit{Lower A–B boundary: } \bar{\bar{x}} - \frac{2}{3}(A_2\bar{R})$$

$$\textit{Upper B–C boundary: } \bar{\bar{x}} + \frac{1}{3}(A_2\bar{R})$$

$$\textit{Lower B–C boundary: } \bar{\bar{x}} - \frac{1}{3}(A_2\bar{R})$$

2. Using the estimated standard deviation of $\bar{x}$, $(\bar{R}/d_2)/\sqrt{n}$:

$$\textit{Upper A–B boundary: } \bar{\bar{x}} + 2\left[\frac{\left(\frac{\bar{R}}{d_2}\right)}{\sqrt{n}}\right]$$

$$\textit{Lower A–B boundary: } \bar{\bar{x}} - 2\left[\frac{\left(\frac{\bar{R}}{d_2}\right)}{\sqrt{n}}\right]$$

$$\textit{Upper B–C boundary: } \bar{\bar{x}} + \left[\frac{\left(\frac{\bar{R}}{d_2}\right)}{\sqrt{n}}\right]$$

$$\textit{Lower B–C boundary: } \bar{\bar{x}} - \left[\frac{\left(\frac{\bar{R}}{d_2}\right)}{\sqrt{n}}\right]$$

Practitioners use six simple rules that are based on these zones to help determine when a process is out of control. The six rules are summarized in Figure 13.21. They are referred to as **pattern-analysis rules**.

Rule 1 is the familiar point-beyond-the-control-limit rule that we have mentioned several times. The other rules all help to determine when the process is out of control *even though all the plotted points fall within the control limits.* That is, the other rules help to identify nonrandom patterns of variation that have not yet broken through the control limits (or may never break through).

All the patterns shown in Figure 13.21 are **rare events** under the assumption that the process is under control. To see this, let's assume that the process is under control and follows a normal distribution. We can then easily work out the probability that an individual point will fall in any given zone. (We dealt with this type of problem in Chapters 4 and 5.) Just focusing on one side of the centerline, you can show that the probability of a point falling beyond Zone Λ is .00135, in Zone A is .02135, in Zone B is .1360, and in Zone C is .3413. Of course, the same probabilities apply to both sides of the centerline.

From these probabilities we can determine the likelihood of various patterns of points. For example, let's evaluate Rule 1. The probability of observing a point outside the control limits (i.e., above the upper control limit or below the lower control limit) is .00135 + .00135 = .0027. This is clearly a rare event.

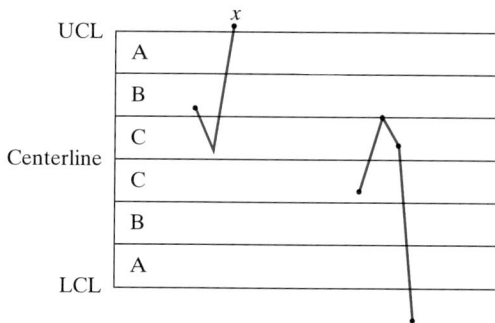

Rule 1: One point beyond Zone A

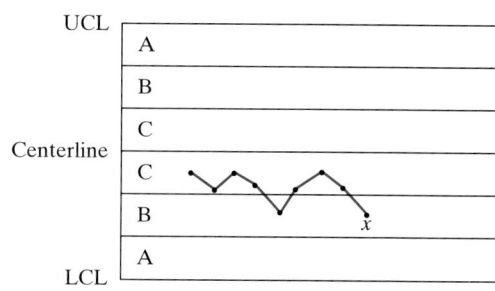

Rule 2: Nine points in a row in Zone C or beyond

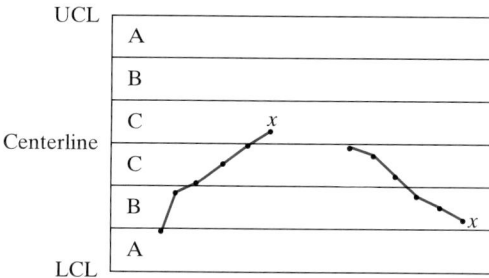

Rule 3: Six points in a row steadily increasing or decreasing

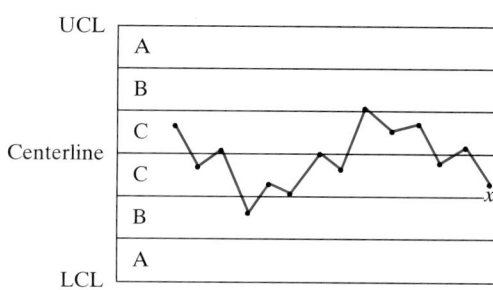

Rule 4: Fourteen points in a row alternating up and down

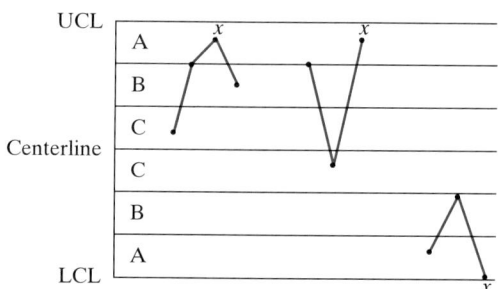

Rule 5: Two out of three points in a row in Zone A or beyond

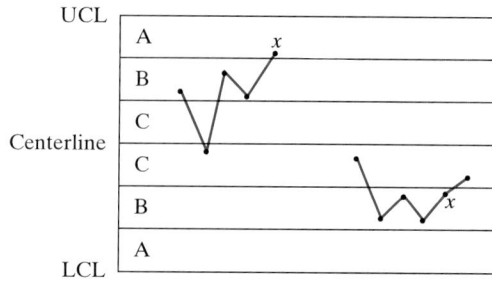

Rule 6: Four out of five points in a row in Zone B or beyond

Rules 1, 2, 5, and 6 should be applied separately to the upper and lower halves of the control chart. Rules 3 and 4 should be applied to the whole chart.

FIGURE 13.21   Pattern-analysis rules for detecting the presence of special causes of variation

As another example, Rule 5 indicates that the observation of two out of three points in a row in Zone A or beyond is a rare event. Is it? The probability of being in Zone A or beyond is $.00135 + .02135 = .0227$. We can use the binomial distribution (Chapter 5) to find the probability of observing 2 out of 3 points in or beyond Zone A. The binomial probability $P(x = 2)$ when $n = 3$ and $p = .0227$ is $.0015$. Again, this is clearly a rare event.

In general, when the process is in control and normally distributed, the probability of any one of these rules *incorrectly* signaling the presence of special causes of variation is less than .005, or 5 chances in 1,000. If all of the first four rules are applied, the overall probability of a false signal is about .01. If all six of the rules are applied, the overall probability of a false signal rises to .02, or 2 chances in 100. These three probabilities can be thought of as Type I error probabilities. Each indicates the probability of incorrectly rejecting the null hypothesis that the process is in a state of statistical control.

Explanation of the possible causes of these nonrandom patterns is beyond the scope of this text. We refer the interested reader to AT&T's *Statistical Quality Control Handbook* (1956).

We use these rules again in the next section when we interpret the *R*-chart.

Interpreting an $\bar{x}$-Chart

1. The **process is out of control** if one or more sample means fall beyond the control limits or if any of the other five patterns of variation of Figure 13.21 are observed. Such signals are an indication that one or more special causes of variation are affecting the process mean. We must identify and eliminate them to bring the process into control.

2. The **process is treated as being in control** if none of the previously noted out-of-control signals are observed. Processes that are in control should not be tampered with. However, if the level of variation is unacceptably high, common causes of variation should be identified and eliminated.

Assumption: The variation of the process is stable. (If it were not, the control limits of the $\bar{x}$-chart would be meaningless, since they are a function of the process variation. The *R*-chart, presented in the next section, is used to investigate this assumption.)

In theory, the centerline and control limits should be developed using samples that were collected during a period in which the process was in control. Otherwise, they will not be representative of the variation of the process (or, in the present case, the variation of $\bar{x}$) when the process is in control. However, we will not know whether the process is in control until after we have constructed a control chart. Consequently, when a control chart is first constructed, the centerline and control limits are treated as **trial values**. If the chart indicates that the process was in control during the period when the sample data were collected, then the centerline and control limits become "official" (i.e., no longer treated as trial values). It is then appropriate to extend the control limits and the centerline to the right and to use the chart to monitor future process output.

However, if in applying the pattern-analysis rules of Figure 13.21 it is determined that the process was out of control while the sample data were being collected, the trial values (i.e., the trial chart) should, in general, not be used to monitor the process. The points on the control chart that indicate that the process is out of control should be investigated to see if any special causes of variation can be identified. A graphical method that can be used to facilitate this investigation—a *cause-and-effect diagram*—is described in optional Section 13.7. If special causes of variation are found, (1) they should be eliminated, (2) any points on the chart determined to have been influenced by the special causes—whether inside or outside the control limits—should be discarded, and (3) *new* trial centerline and control limits should be calculated from the remaining data. However, the new trial limits may still indicate that the process is out of control. If so, repeat these three steps until all points fall within the control limits.

TABLE 13.2   Twenty-five Samples of Size 5 from the Paint-Filling Process

Sample	Measurements					Mean	Range
1	10.0042	9.9981	10.0010	9.9964	10.0001	9.99995	.0078
2	9.9950	9.9986	9.9948	10.0030	9.9938	9.99704	.0092
3	10.0028	9.9998	10.0086	9.9949	9.9980	10.00082	.0137
4	9.9952	9.9923	10.0034	9.9965	10.0026	9.99800	.0111
5	9.9997	9.9983	9.9975	10.0078	9.9891	9.99649	.0195
6	9.9987	10.0027	10.0001	10.0027	10.0029	10.00141	.0042
7	10.0004	10.0023	10.0024	9.9992	10.0135	10.00358	.0143
8	10.0013	9.9938	10.0017	10.0089	10.0001	10.00116	.0151
9	10.0103	10.0009	9.9969	10.0103	9.9986	10.00339	.0134
10	9.9980	9.9954	9.9941	9.9958	9.9963	9.99594	.0039
11	10.0013	10.0033	9.9943	9.9949	9.9999	9.99874	.0090
12	9.9986	9.9990	10.0009	9.9947	10.0008	9.99882	.0062
13	10.0089	10.0056	9.9976	9.9997	9.9922	10.00080	.0167
14	9.9971	10.0015	9.9962	10.0038	10.0022	10.00016	.0076
15	9.9949	10.0011	10.0043	9.9988	9.9919	9.99822	.0124
16	9.9951	9.9957	10.0094	10.0040	9.9974	10.00033	.0137
17	10.0015	10.0026	10.0032	9.9971	10.0019	10.00127	.0061
18	9.9983	10.0019	9.9978	9.9997	10.0029	10.00130	.0051
19	9.9977	9.9963	9.9981	9.9968	10.0009	9.99798	.0127
20	10.0078	10.0004	9.9966	10.0051	10.0007	10.00212	.0112
21	9.9963	9.9990	10.0037	9.9936	9.9962	9.99764	.0101
22	9.9999	10.0022	10.0057	10.0026	10.0032	10.00272	.0058
23	9.9998	10.0002	9.9978	9.9966	10.0060	10.00009	.0094
24	10.0031	10.0078	9.9988	10.0032	9.9944	10.00146	.0134
25	9.9993	9.9978	9.9964	10.0032	10.0041	10.00015	.0077

If special causes cannot be found and eliminated, the severity of the out-of-control indications should be evaluated and a judgment made as to whether (1) the out-of-control points should be discarded anyway and new trial limits constructed, (2) the original trial limits are good enough to be made official, or (3) new sample data should be collected to construct new trial limits.

EXAMPLE 13.1

Let's return to the paint-filling process described in Sections 13.2 and 13.3. Suppose instead of sampling 50 consecutive gallons of paint from the filling process to develop a control chart, it was decided to sample five consecutive cans once each hour for the next 25 hours. The sample data are presented in Table 13.2. This sampling strategy (rational subgrouping) was selected because several times a month the filling head in question becomes clogged. When that happens, the head dispenses less and less paint over the course of the day. However, the pattern of decrease is so irregular that minute-to-minute or even half-hour-to-half-hour changes are difficult to detect.

a. Explain the logic behind the rational subgrouping strategy that was used.

b. Construct an $\bar{x}$-chart for the process using the data in Table 13.2.

c. What does the chart suggest about the stability of the filling process (whether the process is in or out of statistical control)?

d. Should the control limits be used to monitor future process output?

SOLUTION

a. The samples are far enough apart in time to detect hour-to-hour shifts or changes in the mean amount of paint dispensed, but the individual measurements that make up each sample are close enough together in time to ensure that the process has changed little, if at all, during the time the individual measurements were made. Overall, the rational subgrouping employed affords the opportunity for process changes to occur between samples and therefore show up on the control chart as differences between the sample means.

b. Twenty-five samples ($k = 25$ subgroups), each containing $n = 5$ cans of paint, were collected from the process. The first step after collecting the data is to calculate the 25 sample means and sample ranges needed to construct the $\bar{x}$-chart. The mean and range of the first sample are

$$\bar{x} = \frac{10.0042 + 9.9981 + 10.0010 + 9.9964 + 10.0001}{5} = 9.99995$$

$$R = 10.0042 - 9.9964 = .0078$$

All 25 means and ranges are displayed in Table 13.2.

Next, we calculate the mean of the sample means and the mean of the sample ranges:

$$\bar{\bar{x}} = \frac{9.99995 + 9.99704 + \cdots + 10.00015}{25} = 9.9999$$

$$\bar{R} = \frac{.0078 + .0092 + \cdots + .0077}{25} = .01028$$

The centerline of the chart is positioned at $\bar{\bar{x}} = 9.9999$. To determine the control limits, we need the constant A_2, which can be found in Table XVII of Appendix B. For $n = 5$, $A_2 = .577$. Then,

$$\text{UCL:} \bar{\bar{x}} + A_2\bar{R} = 9.9999 + .577(.01028) = 10.0058$$

$$\text{LCL:} \bar{\bar{x}} - A_2\bar{R} = 9.9999 - .577(.01028) = 9.9940$$

After positioning the control limits on the chart, we plot the 25 sample means in the order of sampling and connect the points with straight lines. The resulting trial $\bar{x}$-chart is shown in Figure 13.22.

c. To check the stability of the process, we use the six pattern-analysis rules for detecting special causes of variation, which were presented in Figure 13.21.

FIGURE 13.22
$\bar{x}$-chart for the
paint-filling process

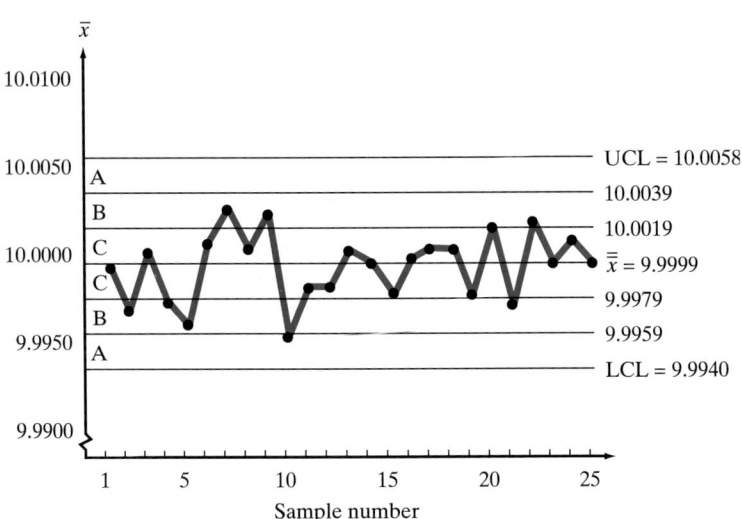

To apply most of these rules requires identifying the A, B, and C zones of the control chart. These are indicated in Figure 13.22. We describe how they were constructed below.

The boundary between the A and B zones is 2 standard deviations from the centerline, and the boundary between the B and C zones is 1 standard deviation from the centerline. Thus, using $A_2\bar{R}$ and the 3-sigma limits previously calculated, we locate the A, B, and C zones above the centerline:

A–B boundary $= \bar{\bar{x}} + \frac{2}{3}(A_2\bar{R}) = 9.9999 + \frac{2}{3}(.577)(.01028) = 10.0039$

B–C boundary $= \bar{\bar{x}} + \frac{1}{3}(A_2\bar{R}) = 9.9999 + \frac{1}{3}(.577)(.01028) = 10.0019$

Similarly, the zones below the centerline are located:

$$A\text{–}B \text{ boundary} = \bar{\bar{x}} - \frac{2}{3}(A_2\bar{R}) = 9.9959$$

$$B\text{–}C \text{ boundary} = \bar{\bar{x}} - \frac{1}{3}(A_2\bar{R}) = 9.9979$$

A careful comparison of the six pattern-analysis rules with the sequence of sample means yields no out-of-control signals. All points are inside the control limits and there appear to be no nonrandom patterns within the control limits. That is, we can find no evidence of a shift in the process mean. Accordingly, we conclude that the process is in control.

d. Since the process was found to be in control during the period in which the samples were drawn, the trial control limits constructed in part **b** can be considered official. They should be extended to the right and used to monitor future process output. ▌

EXAMPLE 13.2

Ten new samples of size $n = 5$ were drawn from the paint-filling process of the previous example. The sample data, including sample means and ranges, are shown in Table 13.3. Investigate whether the process remained in control during the period in which the new sample data were collected.

SOLUTION

We begin by simply extending the control limits, centerline, and zone boundaries of the control chart in Figure 13.22 to the right. Next, beginning with sample number 26, we plot the 10 new sample means on the control chart and connect them with straight lines. This extended version of the control chart is shown in Figure 13.23.

Now that the control chart has been prepared, we apply the six pattern-analysis rules for detecting special causes of variation (Figure 13.21) to the new

---

TABLE 13.3   Ten Additional Samples of Size 5 from the Paint-Filling Process

Sample	Measurements					Mean	Range
26	10.0019	9.9981	9.9952	9.9976	9.9999	9.99841	.0067
27	10.0041	9.9982	10.0028	10.0040	9.9971	10.00125	.0070
28	9.9999	9.9974	10.0078	9.9971	9.9923	9.99890	.0155
29	9.9982	10.0002	9.9916	10.0040	9.9916	9.99713	.0124
30	9.9933	9.9963	9.9955	9.9993	9.9905	9.99498	.0088
31	9.9915	9.9984	10.0053	9.9888	9.9876	9.99433	.0177
32	9.9912	9.9970	9.9961	9.9879	9.9970	9.99382	.0091
33	9.9942	9.9960	9.9975	10.0019	9.9912	9.99614	.0107
34	9.9949	9.9967	9.9936	9.9941	10.0071	9.99726	.0135
35	9.9943	9.9969	9.9937	9.9912	10.0053	9.99626	.0141

FIGURE 13.23
Extended $\bar{x}$-chart for paint-filling process

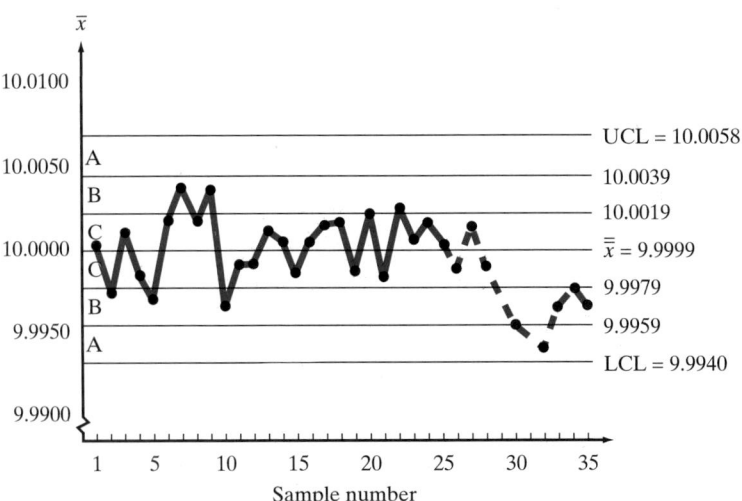

sequence of sample means. No points fall outside the control limits, but we notice six points in a row that steadily decrease (samples 27–32). Rule 3 says that if we observe six points in a row steadily increasing or decreasing, that is an indication of the presence of special causes of variation.

Notice that if you apply the rules from left to right along the sequence of sample means, the decreasing pattern also triggers signals from Rules 5 (samples 29–31) and 6 (samples 28–32).

These signals lead us to conclude that the process has gone out of control. Apparently, the filling head began to clog about the time that either sample 26 or 27 was drawn from the process. As a result, the mean of the process (the mean fill weight dispensed by the process) began to decline.

EXERCISES 13.1–13.16

Note: Exercises marked with 💾 contain data for computer analysis on a 3.5" disk (file name in parentheses).

Learning the Mechanics

13.1 What is a control chart? Describe its use.

13.2 Explain why rational subgrouping should be used in constructing control charts.

13.3 When a control chart is first constructed, why are the centerline and control limits treated as trial values?

13.4 Which process parameter is an $\bar{x}$-chart used to monitor?

13.5 Even if all the points on an $\bar{x}$-chart fall between the control limits, the process may be out of control. Explain.

13.6 What must be true about the variation of a process before an $\bar{x}$-chart is used to monitor the mean of the process? Why?

13.7 Use the six pattern-analysis rules described in Figure 13.21 to determine whether the process being monitored with the accompanying $\bar{x}$-chart is out of statistical control.

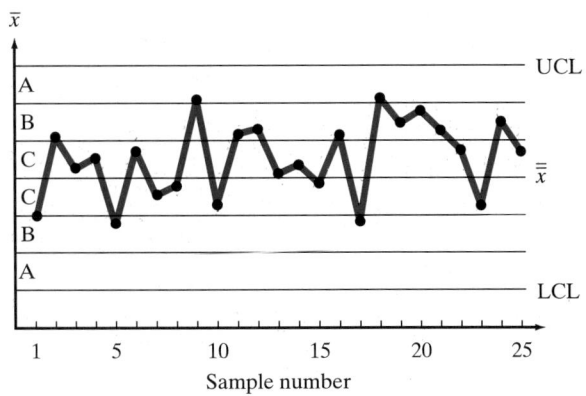

13.8   Is the process for which the accompanying $\bar{x}$-chart was constructed affected by only special causes of variation, only common causes of variation, or both? Explain.

13.9   Use Table XVII in Appendix B to find the value of A_2 for each of the following sample sizes.
   a. $n = 3$ **b.** $n = 10$ **c.** $n = 22$

13.10   **(X13.010)** Twenty-five samples of size $n = 5$ were collected to construct an $\bar{x}$-chart. The accompanying sample means and ranges were calculated for these data.

Sample	$\bar{x}$	R	Sample	$\bar{x}$	R
1	80.2	7.2	14	83.1	10.2
2	79.1	9.0	15	79.6	7.8
3	83.2	4.7	16	80.0	6.1
4	81.0	5.6	17	83.2	8.4
5	77.6	10.1	18	75.9	9.9
6	81.7	8.6	19	78.1	6.0
7	80.4	4.4	20	81.4	7.4
8	77.5	6.2	21	81.7	10.4
9	79.8	7.9	22	80.9	9.1
10	85.3	7.1	23	78.4	7.3
11	77.7	9.8	24	79.6	8.0
12	82.3	10.7	25	81.6	7.6
13	79.5	9.2			

   a. Calculate the mean of the sample means, $\bar{\bar{x}}$, and the mean of the sample ranges, $\bar{R}$.
   b. Calculate and plot the centerline and the upper and lower control limits for the $\bar{x}$-chart.
   c. Calculate and plot the A, B, and C zone boundaries of the $\bar{x}$-chart.
   d. Plot the 25 sample means on the $\bar{x}$-chart and use the six pattern-analysis rules to determine whether the process is under statistical control.

13.11   **(X13.011)** The data in the next table were collected for the purpose of constructing an $\bar{x}$-chart.
   a. Calculate $\bar{x}$ and R for each sample.

Sample	Measurements			
1	19.4	19.7	20.6	21.2
2	18.7	18.4	21.2	20.7
3	20.2	18.8	22.6	20.1
4	19.6	21.2	18.7	19.4
5	20.4	20.9	22.3	18.6
6	17.3	22.3	20.3	19.7
7	21.8	17.6	22.8	23.1
8	20.9	17.4	19.5	20.7
9	18.1	18.3	20.6	20.4
10	22.6	21.4	18.5	19.7
11	22.7	21.2	21.5	19.5
12	20.1	20.6	21.0	20.2
13	19.7	18.6	21.2	19.1
14	18.6	21.7	17.7	18.3
15	18.2	20.4	19.8	19.2
16	18.9	20.7	23.2	20.0
17	20.5	19.7	21.4	17.8
18	21.0	18.7	19.9	21.2
19	20.5	19.6	19.8	21.8
20	20.6	16.9	22.4	19.7

   b. Calculate $\bar{\bar{x}}$ and $\bar{R}$.
   c. Calculate and plot the centerline and the upper and lower control limits for the $\bar{x}$-chart.
   d. Calculate and plot the A, B, and C zone boundaries of the $\bar{x}$-chart.
   e. Plot the 20 sample means on the $\bar{x}$-chart. Is the process in control? Justify your answer.

Applying the Concepts

13.12   The central processing unit (CPU) of a microcomputer is a computer chip containing millions of transistors. Connecting the transistors are slender circuit paths only .5 to .85 micron wide. To understand how narrow these paths are, consider that a micron is a millionth of a meter, and a human hair is 70 microns wide (*Compute*, 1992). A manufacturer of CPU chips knows that if the circuit paths are not .5–.85 micron wide, a variety of problems will arise in the chips' performance. The manufacturer sampled four CPU chips six times a day (every 90 minutes from 8:00 A.M. until 4:30 P.M.) for five consecutive days and measured the circuit path widths. These data and MINITAB were used to construct the $\bar{x}$-chart shown on page 694.
   a. Assuming that $\bar{R} = .3162$, calculate the chart's upper and lower control limits, the upper and lower A–B boundaries, and the upper and lower B–C boundaries.
   b. What does the chart suggest about the stability of the process used to put circuit paths on the CPU chip? Justify your answer.
   c. Should the control limits be used to monitor future process output? Explain.

X-bar Chart for Pathwdth

13.13 **(X13.013)** A machine at K-Company fills boxes with bran flakes cereal. The target weight for the filled boxes is 24 ounces. The company would like to use an $\bar{x}$-chart to monitor the performance of the machine. To develop the control chart, the company decides to sample and weigh five consecutive boxes of cereal five times each day (at 8:00 and 11:00 A.M. and 2:00, 5:00, and 8:00 P.M.) for twenty consecutive days. The data are presented in the table, along with a SAS printout with summary statistics.

Day	Weight of Cereal Boxes (ounces)				
1	24.02	23.91	24.12	24.06	24.13
2	23.89	23.98	24.01	24.00	23.91
3	24.11	24.02	23.99	23.79	24.04
4	24.06	23.98	23.95	24.01	24.11
5	23.81	23.90	23.99	24.07	23.96
6	23.87	24.12	24.07	24.01	23.99
7	23.88	24.00	24.05	23.97	23.97
8	24.01	24.03	23.99	23.91	23.98
9	24.06	24.02	23.80	23.79	24.07
10	23.96	23.99	24.03	23.99	24.01
11	24.10	23.90	24.11	23.98	23.95
12	24.01	24.07	23.93	24.09	23.98
13	24.14	24.07	24.08	23.98	24.02
14	23.91	24.04	23.89	24.01	23.95
15	24.03	24.04	24.01	23.98	24.10
16	23.94	24.07	24.12	24.00	24.02
17	23.88	23.94	23.91	24.06	24.07
18	24.11	23.99	23.90	24.01	23.98
19	24.05	24.04	23.97	24.08	23.95
20	24.02	23.96	23.95	23.89	24.04

	WEIGHT	
DAY	MEAN	RANGE
1	24.05	0.22
2	23.96	0.12
3	23.99	0.32
4	24.02	0.16
5	23.95	0.26
6	24.01	0.25
7	23.97	0.17
8	23.98	0.12
9	23.95	0.28
10	24.00	0.07
11	24.01	0.21
12	24.02	0.16
13	24.06	0.16
14	23.96	0.15
15	24.03	0.12
16	24.03	0.18
17	23.97	0.19
18	24.00	0.21
19	24.02	0.13
20	23.97	0.15

a. Construct an $\bar{x}$-chart from the given data.

b. What does the chart suggest about the stability of the filling process (whether the process is in or out of statistical control)? Justify your answer.

c. Should the control limits be used to monitor future process output? Explain.

d. Two shifts of workers run the filling operation. Each day the second shift takes over at 3:00 P.M. Will the rational subgrouping strategy used by K-Company facilitate or hinder the identification of process variation caused by differences in the two shifts? Explain.

13.14 **(X13.014)** A precision parts manufacturer produces bolts for use in military aircraft. Ideally, the
bolts should be 37 centimeters in length. The company sampled four consecutively produced bolts
each hour on the hour for 25 consecutive hours
and measured them using a computerized precision instrument. The data are presented below. A
MINITAB printout with descriptive statistics for
each hour is shown on page 696.

Hour	Bolt Lengths (centimeters)			
1	37.03	37.08	36.90	36.88
2	36.96	37.04	36.85	36.98
3	37.16	37.11	36.99	37.01
4	37.20	37.06	37.02	36.98
5	36.81	36.97	36.91	37.10
6	37.13	36.96	37.01	36.89
7	37.07	36.94	36.99	37.00
8	37.01	36.91	36.98	37.12
9	37.17	37.03	36.90	37.01
10	36.91	36.99	36.87	37.11
11	36.88	37.10	37.07	37.03
12	37.06	36.98	36.90	36.99
13	36.91	37.22	37.12	37.03
14	37.08	37.07	37.10	37.04
15	37.03	37.04	36.89	37.01
16	36.95	36.98	36.90	36.99
17	36.97	36.94	37.14	37.10
18	37.11	37.04	36.98	36.91
19	36.88	36.99	37.01	36.94
20	36.90	37.15	37.09	37.00
21	37.01	36.96	37.05	36.96
22	37.09	36.95	36.93	37.12
23	37.00	37.02	36.95	37.04
24	36.99	37.07	36.90	37.02
25	37.10	37.03	37.01	36.90

a. What process is the manufacturer interested in
monitoring?
b. Construct an $\bar{x}$-chart from the data.
c. Does the chart suggest that special causes of
variation are present? Justify your answer.
d. Provide an example of a special cause of variation that could potentially affect this process.
Do the same for a common cause of variation.
e. Should the control limits be used to monitor
future process output? Explain.

13.15 **(X13.015)** In their text, *Quantitative Analysis of
Management* (1997), B. Render (Rollins College)
and R. M. Stair (Florida State University), present
the case of the Bayfield Mud Company. Bayfield
supplies boxcars of 50-pound bags of mud treating
agents to the Wet-Land Drilling Company. Mud
treating agents are used to control the pH and
other chemical properties of the cone during oil
drilling operations. Wet-Land has complained to
Bayfield that its most recent shipment of bags
were underweight by about 5%. (The use of
underweight bags may result in poor chemical

control during drilling, which may hurt drilling
efficiency resulting in serious economic consequences.) Afraid of losing a long-time customer,
Bayfield immediately began investigating their
production process. Management suspected that
the causes of the problem were the recently added
third shift and the fact that all three shifts were
under pressure to increase output to meet increasing demand for the product. Their quality control
staff began randomly sampling and weighing six
bags of output each hour. The average weight of
each sample over the last three days is recorded in
the table on page 697 along with the weight of the
heaviest and lightest bag in each sample.
a. Construct an $\bar{x}$-chart for these data.
b. Is the process under statistical control?
c. Does it appear that management's suspicion
about the third shift is correct? Explain?

13.16 **(X13.016)** A high-quality overnight film processing laboratory is concerned about recent processing delays that have resulted in customer complaints. The company has initiated a review of all
processing steps. One step involves the evaluation
of the quality of negatives. To determine if the
time to complete this step is in a state of statistical
control, an analyst sampled five customer orders
per day for 20 working days in August, observed
the processing, and obtained the following data:

Date	Sample Average (in minutes)	Sample Range (in minutes)
8/5	2.3	2.4
8/6	4.1	2.2
8/7	1.1	1.9
8/8	5.9	4.7
8/9	4.4	2.3
8/12	2.8	1.7
8/13	1.3	0.2
8/14	3.5	2.0
8/15	3.8	1.2
8/16	2.5	1.0
8/19	2.8	1.7
8/20	1.8	1.5
8/21	3.5	1.8
8/22	3.0	1.2
8/23	2.2	1.6
8/26	2.9	1.1
8/27	1.7	1.1
8/28	0.9	0.6
8/29	4.1	1.2
8/30	1.2	0.7

a. Construct an $\bar{x}$-chart for this process.
b. Is there evidence that special causes of variation are affecting the process? Explain.
c. Discuss the potential problems associated
with the data collection method used to study
the process.

```
Descriptive Statistics
```

Variable	HOUR	N	MEAN	MEDIAN	TR MEAN	STDEV	SE MEAN
LENGTH	1	4	36.973	36.965	36.973	0.098	0.049
	2	4	36.957	36.970	36.957	0.079	0.040
	3	4	37.067	37.060	37.067	0.081	0.040
	4	4	37.065	37.040	37.065	0.096	0.048
	5	4	36.947	36.940	36.947	0.121	0.061
	6	4	36.998	36.985	36.998	0.101	0.051
	7	4	37.000	36.995	37.000	0.054	0.027
	8	4	37.005	36.995	37.005	0.087	0.044
	9	4	37.028	37.020	37.028	0.111	0.055
	10	4	36.970	36.950	36.970	0.106	0.053
	11	4	37.020	37.050	37.020	0.098	0.049
	12	4	36.982	36.985	36.982	0.066	0.033
	13	4	37.070	37.075	37.070	0.132	0.066
	14	4	37.072	37.075	37.072	0.025	0.013
	15	4	36.993	37.020	36.993	0.069	0.035
	16	4	36.955	36.965	36.955	0.040	0.020
	17	4	37.038	37.035	37.038	0.097	0.049
	18	4	37.010	37.010	37.010	0.085	0.043
	19	4	36.955	36.965	36.955	0.058	0.029
	20	4	37.035	37.045	37.035	0.109	0.055
	21	4	36.995	36.985	36.995	0.044	0.022
	22	4	37.023	37.020	37.023	0.096	0.048
	23	4	37.003	37.010	37.003	0.039	0.019
	24	4	36.995	37.005	36.995	0.071	0.036
	25	4	37.010	37.020	37.010	0.083	0.041

Variable	HOUR	MIN	MAX	Q1	Q3
LENGTH	1	36.880	37.080	36.885	37.067
	2	36.850	37.040	36.878	37.025
	3	36.990	37.160	36.995	37.147
	4	36.980	37.200	36.990	37.165
	5	36.810	37.100	36.835	37.068
	6	36.890	37.130	36.907	37.100
	7	36.940	37.070	36.953	37.053
	8	36.910	37.120	36.927	37.092
	9	36.900	37.170	36.927	37.135
	10	36.870	37.110	36.880	37.080
	11	36.880	37.100	36.918	37.092
	12	36.900	37.060	36.920	37.043
	13	36.910	37.220	36.940	37.195
	14	37.040	37.100	37.047	37.095
	15	36.890	37.040	36.920	37.038
	16	36.900	36.990	36.913	36.987
	17	36.940	37.140	36.947	37.130
	18	36.910	37.110	36.927	37.092
	19	36.880	37.010	36.895	37.005
	20	36.900	37.150	36.925	37.135
	21	36.960	37.050	36.960	37.040
	22	36.930	37.120	36.935	37.113
	23	36.950	37.040	36.962	37.035
	24	36.900	37.070	36.922	37.058
	25	36.900	37.100	36.927	37.083

Time	Average Weight (pounds)	Lightest	Heaviest	Time	Average Weight (pounds)	Lightest	Heaviest
6:00 A.M.	49.6	48.7	50.7	6:00 P.M	46.8	41.0	51.2
7:00	50.2	49.1	51.2	7:00	50.0	46.2	51.7
8:00	50.6	49.6	51.4	8:00	47.4	44.0	48.7
9:00	50.8	50.2	51.8	9:00	47.0	44.2	48.9
10:00	49.9	49.2	52.3	10:00	47.2	46.6	50.2
11:00	50.3	48.6	51.7	11:00	48.6	47.0	50.0
12 noon	48.6	46.2	50.4	12 midnight	49.8	48.2	50.4
1:00 P.M	49.0	46.4	50.0	1:00 A.M.	49.6	48.4	51.7
2:00	49.0	46.0	50.6	2:00	50.0	49.0	52.2
3:00	49.8	48.2	50.8	3:00	50.0	49.2	50.0
4:00	50.3	49.2	52.7	4:00	47.2	46.3	50.5
5:00	51.4	50.0	55.3	5:00	47.0	44.1	49.7
6:00	51.6	49.2	54.7	6:00	48.4	45.0	49.0
7:00	51.8	50.0	55.6	7:00	48.8	44.8	49.7
8:00	51.0	48.6	53.2	8:00	49.6	48.0	51.8
9:00	50.5	49.4	52.4	9:00	50.0	48.1	52.7
10:00	49.2	46.1	50.7	10:00	51.0	48.1	55.2
11:00	49.0	46.3	50.8	11:00	50.4	49.5	54.1
12 midnight	48.4	45.4	50.2	12 noon	50.0	48.7	50.9
1:00 A.M.	47.6	44.3	49.7	1:00 P.M.	48.9	47.6	51.2
2:00	47.4	44.1	49.6	2:00	49.8	48.4	51.0
3:00	48.2	45.2	49.0	3:00	49.8	48.8	50.8
4:00	48.0	45.5	49.1	4:00	50.0	49.1	50.6
5:00	48.4	47.1	49.6	5:00	47.8	45.2	51.2
6:00	48.6	47.4	52.0	6:00	46.4	44.0	49.7
7:00	50.0	49.2	52.2	7:00	46.4	44.4	50.0
8:00	49.8	49.0	52.4	8:00	47.2	46.6	48.9
9:00	50.3	49.4	51.7	9:00	48.4	47.2	49.5
10:00	50.2	49.6	51.8	10:00	49.2	48.1	50.7
11:00	50.0	49.0	52.3	11:00	48.4	47.0	50.8
12 noon	50.0	48.8	52.4	12 midnight	47.2	46.4	49.2
1:00 P.M	50.1	49.4	53.6	1:00 A.M.	47.4	46.8	49.0
2:00	49.7	48.6	51.0	2:00	48.8	47.2	51.4
3:00	48.4	47.2	51.7	3:00	49.6	49.0	50.6
4:00	47.2	45.3	50.9	4:00	51.0	50.5	51.5
5:00	46.8	44.1	49.0	5:00	50.5	50.0	51.9

Source: Kinard, J., Western Carolina University, as reported in Render, B., and Stair, Jr., R., *Quantitative Analysis for Management,* 6th ed. Upper Saddle River, N.J.: Prentice-Hall, 1997.

13.5   A CONTROL CHART FOR MONITORING THE VARIATION OF A PROCESS: THE *R*-CHART

Recall from Section 13.2 that a process may be out of statistical control because its mean or variance or both are changing over time (see Figure 13.8). The $\bar{x}$-chart of the previous section is used to detect changes in the process mean. The control chart we present in this section—the *R*-chart—is used to detect changes in process variation.

The primary difference between the $\bar{x}$-chart and the *R*-chart is that instead of plotting *sample means* and monitoring their variation, we plot and monitor the variation of *sample ranges*. Changes in the behavior of the sample range signal changes in the variation of the process.

We could also monitor process variation by plotting *sample standard deviations*. That is, we could calculate *s* for each sample (i.e., each subgroup) and plot them

FIGURE 13.24
R-chart

on a control chart known as an **s-chart**. In this chapter, however, we focus on just the *R*-chart because (1) when using samples of size 9 or less, the *s*-chart and the *R*-chart reflect about the same information, and (2) the *R*-chart is used much more widely by practitioners than is the *s*-chart (primarily because the sample range is easier to calculate and interpret than the sample standard deviation). For more information about *s*-charts, see the references at the end of the book.

The underlying logic and basic form of the *R*-chart are similar to the $\bar{x}$-chart. In monitoring $\bar{x}$, we use the standard deviation of $\bar{x}$ to develop 3-sigma control limits. Now, since we want to be able to determine when *R* takes on unusually large or small values, we use the standard deviation of *R*, or σ_R, to construct 3-sigma control limits. The centerline of the $\bar{x}$-chart represents the process mean μ or, equivalently, the mean of the sampling distribution of $\bar{x}$, $\mu_{\bar{x}}$. Similarly, the centerline of the *R*-chart represents μ_R, the mean of the sampling distribution of *R*. These points are illustrated in the *R*-chart of Figure 13.24.

As with the $\bar{x}$-chart, you should have at least 20 samples of *n* items each ($n \geq 2$) to construct an *R*-chart. This will provide sufficient data to obtain reasonably good estimates of μ_R and σ_R. Rational subgrouping is again used for determining sample size and frequency of sampling.

The centerline of the *R*-chart is positioned as follows:

$$Centerline\!: \bar{R} = \frac{R_1 + R_2 + \cdots + R_k}{k}$$

where *k* is the number of samples of size *n* and R_i is the range of the *i*th sample. $\bar{R}$ is an estimate of μ_R.

In order to construct the control limits, we need an estimator of σ_R. The estimator recommended by Montgomery (1991) and Ryan (1989) is

$$\hat{\sigma}_R = d_3 \left(\frac{\bar{R}}{d_2} \right)$$

where d_2 and d_3 are constants whose values depend on the sample size, *n*. Values for d_2 and d_3 for samples of size $n = 2$ to $n = 25$ are given in Table XVII of Appendix B.

The control limits are positioned as follows:

$$Upper\ control\ limit\!: \bar{R} + 3\hat{\sigma}_R = \bar{R} + 3d_3 \left(\frac{\bar{R}}{d_2} \right)$$

$$Lower\ control\ limit\!: \bar{R} - 3\hat{\sigma}_R = \bar{R} + 3d_3 \left(\frac{\bar{R}}{d_2} \right)$$

Notice that $\bar{R}$ appears twice in each control limit. Accordingly, we can simplify the calculation of these limits by factoring out $\bar{R}$:

$$\text{UCL:}\ \bar{R}\left(1 + \frac{3d_3}{d_2}\right) = \bar{R}D_4 \qquad \text{LCL:}\ \bar{R}\left(1 - \frac{3d_3}{d_2}\right) = \bar{R}D_3$$

where

$$D_4 = \left(1 + \frac{3d_3}{d_2}\right) \qquad D_3 = \left(1 - \frac{3d_3}{d_2}\right)$$

The values for D_3 and D_4 have been tabulated for samples of size $n = 2$ to $n = 25$ and can be found in Appendix B, Table XVII.

For samples of size $n = 2$ through $n = 6$, D_3 is negative, and the lower control limit falls below zero. Since the sample range cannot take on negative values, such a control limit is meaningless. Thus, when $n \leqslant 6$ the *R*-chart contains only one control limit, the upper control limit.

Although D_3 is actually negative for $n \leqslant 6$, the values reported in Table XVII in Appendix B are all zeros. This has been done to discourage the inappropriate construction of negative lower control limits. If the lower control limit is calculated using $D_3 = 0$, you obtain $D_3\overline{R} = 0$. This should be interpreted as indicating that the *R*-chart has no lower 3-sigma control limit.

Constructing an *R*-Chart: A Summary

1. Using a rational subgrouping strategy, collect at least 20 samples (i.e., subgroups), each of size $n \geqslant 2$.

2. Calculate the range of each sample.

3. Calculate the mean of the sample ranges, $\overline{R}$:

$$\overline{R} = \frac{R_1 + R_2 + \cdots + R_k}{k}$$

where

k = The number of samples (i.e., subgroups)

R_i = The range of the *i*th sample

4. Plot the centerline and control limits:

Centerline: $\overline{R}$

Upper control limit: $\overline{R}D_4$

Lower control limit: $\overline{R}D_3$

where D_3 and D_4 are constants that depend on n. Their values can be found in Appendix B, Table XVII. When $n \leqslant 6$, $D_3 = 0$, indicating that the control chart does not have a lower control limit.

5. Plot the k sample ranges on the control chart in the order that the samples were produced by the process.

We interpret the completed *R*-chart in basically the same way as we did the $\bar{x}$-chart. We look for indications that the process is out of control. Those indications include points that fall outside the control limits as well as any nonrandom patterns of variation that appear between the control limits. To help spot nonrandom behavior, we include the A, B, and C zones (described in the previous section) on the *R*-chart. The next box describes how to construct the zone boundaries for the *R*-chart. It requires only Rules 1 through 4 of Figure 13.21, because Rules 5 and 6 are based on the assumption that the statistic plotted on the control chart follows a normal (or nearly normal) distribution, whereas *R*'s distribution is skewed to the right.*

---

*Some authors (e.g., Kane, 1989) apply all six pattern-analysis rules as long as $n \geqslant 4$.

Constructing Zone Boundaries for an R-Chart

The simplest method of construction uses the estimator of the standard deviation of R, which is $\hat{\sigma}_R = d_3(\bar{R}/d_2)$:

$$\text{Upper A–B boundary: } \bar{R} + 2d_3\left(\frac{\bar{R}}{d_2}\right)$$

$$\text{Lower A–B boundary: } \bar{R} - 2d_3\left(\frac{\bar{R}}{d_2}\right)$$

$$\text{Upper B–C boundary: } \bar{R} + d_3\left(\frac{\bar{R}}{d_2}\right)$$

$$\text{Lower B–C boundary: } \bar{R} - d_3\left(\frac{\bar{R}}{d_2}\right)$$

Note: Whenever $n \leq 6$ the R-chart has no lower 3-sigma control limit. However, the lower A–B, B–C boundaries can still be plotted if they are nonnegative.

Interpreting an R-Chart

1. The **process is out of control** if one or more sample ranges fall beyond the control limits (Rule 1) or if any of the three patterns of variation described by Rules 2, 3, and 4 (Figure 13.21) are observed. Such signals indicate that one or more special causes of variation are influencing the *variation* of the process. These causes should be identified and eliminated to bring the process into control.

2. The **process is treated as being in control** if none of the noted out-of-control signals are observed. Processes that are in control should not be tampered with. However, if the level of variation is unacceptably high, common causes of variation should be identified and eliminated.

As with the $\bar{x}$-chart, the centerline and control limits should be developed using samples that were collected during a period in which the process was in control. Accordingly, when an R-chart is first constructed, the centerline and the control limits are treated as **trial values** (see Section 13.4) and are modified, if necessary, before being extended to the right and used to monitor future process output.

EXAMPLE 13.3   Refer to Example 13.1.

a. Construct an R-chart for the paint-filling process.

b. What does the chart indicate about the stability of the filling process during the time when the data were collected?

c. Is it appropriate to use the control limits constructed in part **a** to monitor future process output?

SOLUTION

a. The first step after collecting the data is to calculate the range of each sample. For the first sample the range is

$$R_1 = 10.0042 - 9.9964 = .0078$$

All 25 sample ranges appear in Table 13.2.

Next, calculate the mean of the ranges:

FIGURE 13.25
R-chart for the
paint-filling process

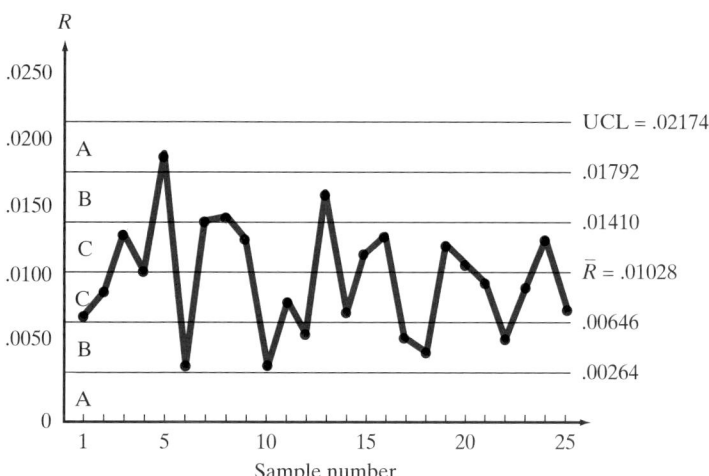

$$\overline{R} = \frac{.0078 + .0092 + \cdots + .0077}{25} + .01028$$

The centerline of the chart is positioned at $\overline{R} = .01028$. To determine the control limits, we need the constants D_3 and D_4, which can be found in Table XVII of Appendix B. For $n = 5$, $D_3 = 0$, and $D_4 = 2.115$. Since $D_3 = 0$, the lower 3-sigma control limit is negative and is not included on the chart. The upper control limit is calculated as follows:

$$\text{UCL: } \overline{R}D_4 = (.01028)(2.115) = .0217$$

After positioning the upper control limit on the chart, we plot the 25 sample ranges in the order of sampling and connect the points with straight lines. The resulting trial *R*-chart is shown in Figure 13.25.

b. To facilitate our examination of the *R*-chart, we plot the four zone boundaries. Recall that in general the A–B boundaries are positioned 2 standard deviations from the centerline and the B–C boundaries are 1 standard deviation from the centerline. In the case of the *R*-chart, we use the estimated standard deviation of *R*, $\hat{\sigma}_R = d_3(\overline{R}/d_2)$, and calculate the boundaries:

$$\textit{Upper A–B boundary: } \overline{R} + 2d_3\left(\frac{\overline{R}}{d_2}\right) = .01792$$

$$\textit{Lower A–B boundary: } \overline{R} - 2d_3\left(\frac{\overline{R}}{d_2}\right) = .00264$$

$$\textit{Upper B–C boundary: } \overline{R} + d_3\left(\frac{\overline{R}}{d_2}\right) = .01410$$

$$\textit{Lower B–C boundary: } \overline{R} - d_3\left(\frac{\overline{R}}{d_2}\right) = .00646$$

where (from Table XVII of Appendix B) for $n = 5$, $d_2 = 2.326$ and $d_3 = .864$. Notice in Figure 13.25 that the lower A zone is slightly narrower than the upper A zone. This occurs because the lower 3-sigma control limit (the usual lower boundary of the lower A zone) is negative.

All the plotted *R* values fall below the upper control limit. This is one indication that the process is under control (i.e., is stable). However, we must also look for patterns of points that would be unlikely to occur if the process were in control. To assist us with this process, we use pattern-analysis rules 1–4 (Figure 13.21). None of the rules signal the presence of special causes of variation. Accordingly, we conclude that it is reasonable to treat the process—in particular, the variation of the process—as being under control during the period in question. Apparently, no significant special causes of variation are influencing the variation of the process.

c. Yes. Since the variation of the process appears to be in control during the period when the sample data were collected, the control limits appropriately characterize the variation in R that would be expected when the process is in a state of statistical control.

In practice, the $\bar{x}$-chart and the R-chart are not used in isolation, as our presentation so far might suggest. Rather, they are used together to monitor the mean (i.e., the location) of the process and the variation of the process simultaneously. In fact, many practitioners plot them on the same piece of paper.

One important reason for dealing with them as a unit is that the control limits of the $\bar{x}$-chart are a function of R. That is, the control limits depend on the variation of the process. (Recall that the control limits are $\bar{x} \pm A_2\bar{R}$.) Thus, if the process variation is out of control the control limits of the $\bar{x}$-chart have little meaning. This is because when the process variation is changing (as in the bottom two graphs of Figure 13.8), any single estimate of the variation (such as $\bar{R}$ or s) is not representative of the process. Accordingly, **the appropriate procedure is to first construct and then interpret the R-chart. If it indicates that the process variation is in control, then it makes sense to construct and interpret the $\bar{x}$-chart**.

Figure 13.26 is reprinted from Kaoru Ishikawa's classic text on quality-improvement methods, *Guide to Quality Control* (1986). It illustrates how particular changes in a process over time may be reflected in $\bar{x}$- and R-charts. At the top of the figure, running across the page, is a series of probability distributions A, B,

FIGURE 13.26
Combined $\bar{x}$- and R-chart
Source: Reprinted from *Guide to Quality Control,* by Kaoru Ishikawa, © 1986 by Asian Productivity Organization, with permission of the publisher Asian Productivity Organization. Distributed in North America by Quality Resources, New York, NY.

and C that describe the process (i.e., the output variable) at different points in time. In practice, we never have this information. For this example, however, Ishikawa worked with a known process (i.e., with its given probabilistic characterization) to illustrate how sample data from a known process might behave.

The control limits for both charts were constructed from $k = 25$ samples of size $n = 5$. These data were generated by Distribution A. The 25 sample means and ranges were plotted on the $\bar{x}$- and R-charts, respectively. Since the distribution did not change over this period of time, it follows from the definition of statistical control that the process was under control. If you did not know this—as would be the case in practice—what would you conclude from looking at the control charts? (Remember, always interpret the R-chart before the $\bar{x}$-chart.) Both charts indicate that the process is under control. Accordingly, the control limits are made official and can be used to monitor future output, as is done next.

Toward the middle of the figure, the process changes. The mean shifts to a higher level. Now the output variable is described by Distribution B. The process is out of control. Ten new samples of size 5 are sampled from the process. Since the variation of the process has not changed, the R-chart should indicate that the variation remains stable. This is, in fact, the case. All points fall below the upper control limit. As we would hope, it is the $\bar{x}$-chart that reacts to the change in the mean of the process.

Then the process changes again (Distribution C). This time the mean shifts back to its original position, but the variation of the process increases. The process is still out of control but this time for a different reason. Checking the R-chart first, we see that it has reacted as we would hope. It has detected the increase in the variation. Given this R-chart finding, the control limits of the $\bar{x}$-chart become inappropriate (as described before) and we would not use them. Notice, however, how the sample means react to the increased variation in the process. This increased variation in $\bar{x}$ is consistent with what we know about the variance of $\bar{x}$. It is directly proportional to the variance of the process, $\sigma_{\bar{x}}^2 = \sigma^2/n$.

Keep in mind that what Ishikawa did in this example is exactly the opposite of what we do in practice. In practice we use sample data and control charts to make inferences about changes in unknown process distributions. Here, for the purpose of helping you to understand and interpret control charts, known process distributions were changed to see what would happen to the control charts.

EXERCISES 13.17–13.27

Note: Exercises marked with 💾 *contain data for computer analysis on a 3.5" disk (file name in parentheses).*

Learning the Mechanics

13.17 What characteristic of a process is an R-chart designed to monitor?

13.18 In practice, $\bar{x}$- and R-charts are used together to monitor a process. However, the R-chart should be interpreted before the $\bar{x}$-chart. Why?

13.19 Use Table XVII in Appendix B to find the values of D_3 and D_4 for each of the following sample sizes.
   a. $n = 4$ **b.** $n = 12$ **c.** $n = 24$

13.20 Construct and interpret an R-chart for the data in Exercise 13.10.

   a. Calculate and plot the upper control limit and, if appropriate, the lower control limit.

   b. Calculate and plot the A, B, and C zone boundaries on the R-chart.

   c. Plot the sample ranges on the R-chart and use pattern-analysis rules 1–4 of Figure 13.21 to determine whether the process is under statistical control.

13.21 Construct and interpret an R-chart for the data in Exercise 13.11.

   a. Calculate and plot the upper control limit and, if appropriate, the lower control limit.

   b. Calculate and plot the A, B, and C zone boundaries on the R-chart.

Sample	Measurements							$\bar{x}$	R
	1	2	3	4	5	6	7		
1	20.1	19.0	20.9	22.2	18.9	18.1	21.3	20.07	4.1
2	19.0	17.9	21.2	20.4	20.0	22.3	21.5	20.33	4.4
3	22.6	21.4	21.4	22.1	19.2	20.6	18.7	20.86	3.9
4	18.1	20.8	17.8	19.6	19.8	21.7	20.0	19.69	3.9
5	22.6	19.1	21.4	21.8	18.4	18.0	19.5	20.11	4.6
6	19.1	19.0	22.3	21.5	17.8	19.2	19.4	19.76	4.5
7	17.1	19.4	18.6	20.9	21.8	21.0	19.8	19.80	4.7
8	20.2	22.4	22.0	19.6	19.6	20.0	18.5	20.33	3.9
9	21.9	24.1	23.1	22.8	25.6	24.2	25.2	23.84	3.7
10	25.1	24.3	26.0	23.1	25.8	27.0	26.5	25.40	3.9
11	25.8	29.2	28.5	29.1	27.8	29.0	28.0	28.20	3.4
12	28.2	27.5	29.3	30.7	27.6	28.0	27.0	28.33	3.7
13	28.2	28.6	28.1	26.0	30.0	28.5	28.3	28.24	4.0
14	22.1	21.4	23.3	20.5	19.8	20.5	19.0	20.94	4.3
15	18.5	19.2	18.0	20.1	22.0	20.2	19.5	19.64	4.0
16	21.4	20.3	22.0	19.2	18.0	17.9	19.5	19.76	4.1
17	18.4	16.5	18.1	19.2	17.5	20.9	19.6	18.60	4.4
18	20.1	19.8	22.3	22.5	21.8	22.7	23.0	21.74	3.2
19	20.0	17.5	21.0	18.2	19.5	17.2	18.1	18.79	3.8
20	22.3	18.2	21.5	19.0	19.4	20.5	20.0	20.13	4.1

c. Plot the sample ranges on the R-chart and determine whether the process is in control.

13.22 (X13.022) Construct and interpret an R-chart and an $\bar{x}$-chart from the sample data shown above. Remember to interpret the R-chart *before* the $\bar{x}$-chart.

Applying the Concepts

13.23 Refer to Exercise 13.12, where the desired circuit path widths were .5 to .85 micron. The manufacturer sampled four CPU chips six times a day (every 90 minutes from 8:00 A.M. until 4:30 P.M.) for five consecutive days. The path widths were measured and used to construct the MINITAB R-chart shown.

a. Calculate the chart's upper and lower control limits.

b. What does the R-chart suggest about the presence of special causes of variation during the time when the data were collected?

c. Should the control limit(s) be used to monitor future process output? Explain.

d. How many different R values are plotted on the control chart? Notice how most of the R values fall along three horizontal lines. What could cause such a pattern?

13.24 **(X13.024)** A soft-drink bottling company is interested in monitoring the amount of cola injected into 16-ounce bottles by a particular filling head. The process is entirely automated and operates 24 hours a day. At 6 A.M. and 6 P.M. each day, a new dispenser of carbon dioxide capable of producing 20,000 gallons of cola is hooked up to the filling machine. In order to monitor the process using control charts, the company decided to sample five consecutive bottles of cola each hour beginning at 6:15 A.M. (i.e., 6:15 A.M., 7:15 A.M., 8:15 A.M., etc.). The data for the first day are given at right, followed by an SPSS descriptive statistics printout.

a. Will the rational subgrouping strategy that was used enable the company to detect variation in fill caused by differences in the carbon dioxide dispensers? Explain.

b. Construct an *R*-chart from the data.

c. What does the *R*-chart indicate about the stability of the filling process during the time when the data were collected? Justify your answer.

d. Should the control limit(s) be used to monitor future process output? Explain.

e. Given your answer to part **c**, should an $\bar{x}$-chart be constructed from the given data? Explain.

Sample	Measurements				
1	16.01	16.03	15.98	16.00	16.01
2	16.03	16.02	15.97	15.99	15.99
3	15.98	16.00	16.03	16.04	15.99
4	16.00	16.03	16.02	15.98	15.98
5	15.97	15.99	16.03	16.01	16.04
6	16.01	16.03	16.04	15.97	15.99
7	16.04	16.05	15.97	15.96	16.00
8	16.02	16.05	16.03	15.97	15.98
9	15.97	15.99	16.02	16.03	15.95
10	16.00	16.01	15.95	16.04	16.06
11	15.95	16.04	16.07	15.93	16.03
12	15.98	16.07	15.94	16.08	16.02
13	15.96	16.00	16.01	16.00	15.98
14	15.98	16.01	16.02	15.99	15.99
15	15.99	16.03	16.00	15.98	16.01
16	16.02	16.02	16.01	15.97	16.00
17	16.01	16.05	15.99	15.99	16.03
18	15.98	16.03	16.04	15.98	16.01
19	15.97	15.96	15.99	15.99	16.01
20	16.03	16.01	16.04	15.96	15.99
21	15.99	16.03	15.97	16.05	16.03
22	15.98	15.95	16.07	16.01	16.04
23	15.99	16.06	15.95	16.03	16.07
24	16.00	16.01	16.08	15.94	15.93

SAMPLE	Variable	Mean	Range	Minimum	Maximum	N
1.00	COLA	16.006	.05	15.98	16.03	5
2.00	COLA	16.000	.06	15.97	16.03	5
3.00	COLA	16.008	.06	15.98	16.04	5
4.00	COLA	16.002	.05	15.98	16.03	5
5.00	COLA	16.008	.07	15.97	16.04	5
6.00	COLA	16.008	.07	15.97	16.04	5
7.00	COLA	16.004	.09	15.96	16.05	5
8.00	COLA	16.010	.08	15.97	16.05	5
9.00	COLA	15.992	.08	15.95	16.03	5
10.00	COLA	16.012	.11	15.95	16.06	5
11.00	COLA	16.004	.14	15.93	16.07	5
12.00	COLA	16.018	.14	15.94	16.08	5
13.00	COLA	15.990	.05	15.96	16.01	5
14.00	COLA	15.998	.04	15.98	16.02	5
15.00	COLA	16.002	.05	15.98	16.03	5
16.00	COLA	16.004	.05	15.97	16.02	5
17.00	COLA	16.014	.06	15.99	16.05	5
18.00	COLA	16.008	.06	15.98	16.04	5
19.00	COLA	15.984	.05	15.96	16.01	5
20.00	COLA	16.006	.08	15.96	16.04	5
21.00	COLA	16.014	.08	15.97	16.05	5
22.00	COLA	16.010	.12	15.95	16.07	5
23.00	COLA	16.020	.12	15.95	16.07	5
24.00	COLA	15.992	.15	15.93	16.08	5

13.25 Refer to Exercise 13.15, in which the Bayfield Mud Company was concerned with discovering why their filling operation was producing under-filled bags of mud.

  a. Construct an R-chart for the filling process.

  b. According to the R-chart, is the process under statistical control? Explain.

  c. Does the R-chart provide any evidence concerning the cause of Bayfield's underfilling problem? Explain.

13.26 Refer to Exercise 13.16, in which an overnight film processing laboratory was concerned about processing delays.

  a. Construct an R-chart for the time required to complete the evaluation of negatives.

  b. Which parameter of the evaluation process does your R-chart provide information about?

  c. What does the R-chart suggest about the presence of special causes of variation during the time when the data were collected?

13.27 (X13.027) American companies have been reaping the benefits of Japanese "Just-in-Time" (JIT) production methods for more than a decade. Major benefits include shorter lead times, lower defect rates, less raw material inventory, less work-in-process inventory, less finished-goods inventory, and a more flexible workforce. One problem that production managers often face in scheduling the operations of a JIT assembly process is ensuring consistent cycle times for the subassemblies. *Cycle time* is the time it takes for a workstation to complete its set of tasks. The greater the difference in cycle times, the greater the idle time at the faster workstations. This is both inefficient and can be the cause of serious morale problems at the slower workstations (Melnyk and Denzler, *Operations Management: A Value-Driven Approach*, 1996). To evaluate the cycle time of a particular workstation in a bicycle assembly process, an operations manager measured the first five cycle times of the morning shift for five consecutive days. These measurements are given in the table.

Date	Cycle Time (in minutes)
11/12/96	45
	51
	47
	49
	53
11/13/96	44
	48
	57
	54
	43
11/14/96	54
	47
	51
	50
	46
11/15/96	50
	48
	55
	59
	42
11/16/96	46
	49
	43
	52
	58

  a. Construct an R-chart and an $\bar{x}$-chart for this workstation.

  b. Which chart should be evaluated first? Why?

  c. What do the $\bar{x}$- and R-charts suggest about the stability of the process? Explain.

  d. The bicycle company operates with two work shifts five days a week and is closed on the weekends. Will the rational subgrouping strategy that was used enable the operations manager to detect variation in cycle times due to differences in work shifts? Explain.

13.6 A CONTROL CHART FOR MONITORING THE PROPORTION OF DEFECTIVES GENERATED BY A PROCESS: THE p-CHART

Among the dozens of different control charts that have been proposed by researchers and practitioners, the $\bar{x}$- and R-charts are by far the most popular for use in monitoring **quantitative** output variables such as time, length, and weight. Among the charts developed for use with **qualitative** output variables, the chart we introduce in this section is the most popular. Called the p-**chart**, it is used when the output variable is categorical (i.e., measured on a nominal scale). With the p-chart, the proportion, p, of units produced by the process that belong to a particular category (e.g., defective or nondefective; successful or unsuccessful; early, on-time, or late) can be monitored.

The p-chart is typically used to monitor the proportion of defective units produced by a process (i.e., the proportion of units that do not conform to specification). This proportion is used to characterize a process in the same sense that the mean and variance are used to characterize a process when the output variable is quantitative. Examples of process proportions that are monitored in industry include the proportion of billing errors made by credit card companies; the proportion of nonfunctional semiconductor chips produced; and the proportion of checks that a bank's magnetic ink character-recognition system is unable to read.

As is the case for the mean and variance, the process proportion can change over time. For example, it can drift upward or downward or jump to a new level. In such cases, the process is out of control. **As long as the process proportion remains constant, the process is in a state of statistical control**.

As with the other control charts presented in this chapter, the p-chart has a centerline and control limits that are determined from sample data. After k samples of size n are drawn from the process, each unit is classified (e.g., defective or nondefective), the proportion of defective units in each sample—$\hat{p}$— is calculated, the centerline and control limits are determined using this information, and the sample proportions are plotted on the p-chart. It is the variation in the $\hat{p}$'s over time that we monitor and interpret. Changes in the behavior of the $\hat{p}$'s signal changes in the process proportion, p.

The p-chart is based on the assumption that the number of defectives observed in each sample is a binomial random variable. What we have called the process proportion is really the binomial probability, p. (We discussed binomial random variables in Chapter 4.) When the process is in a state of statistical control, p remains constant over time. Variation in $\hat{p}$—as displayed on a p-chart—is used to judge whether p is stable.

To determine the centerline and control limits for the p-chart we need to know $\hat{p}$'s sampling distribution. We described the sampling distribution of $\hat{p}$ in Section 7.4. Recall that

$$\hat{p} = \frac{\text{Number of defective items in the sample}}{\text{Number of items in the sample}} = \frac{x}{n}$$

$$\mu_{\hat{p}} = p$$

$$\sigma_{\hat{p}} = \sqrt{\frac{p(1-p)}{n}}$$

and that for large samples $\hat{p}$ is approximately normally distributed. Thus, if p were known, the centerline would be p and the 3-sigma control limits would be $s \pm 3\sqrt{p(1-p)/n}$. However, since p is unknown, it must be estimated from the sample data. The appropriate estimator is $\bar{p}$, the overall proportion of defective units in the nk units sampled:

$$\bar{p} = \frac{\text{Total number of defective units in all } k \text{ samples}}{\text{Total number of units sampled}}$$

To calculate the control limits of the p-chart, substitute $\bar{p}$ for p in the preceding expression for the control limits, as illustrated in Figure 13.27.

In constructing a p-chart it is advisable to use a much larger sample size than is typically used for $\bar{x}$- and R-charts. Most processes that are monitored in industry

FIGURE 13.27
p-chart

have relatively small process proportions, often less than .05 (i.e., less than 5% of output is nonconforming). In those cases, if a small sample size is used, say $n = 5$, samples drawn from the process would likely not contain any nonconforming output. As a result, most, if not all, $\hat{p}$'s would equal zero.

We present a rule of thumb that can be used to determine a sample size large enough to avoid this problem. This rule will also help protect against ending up with a negative lower control limit, a situation that frequently occurs when both p and n are small. See Montgomery (1991) or Duncan (1986) for further details.

Sample-Size Determination

Choose n such that $n > \dfrac{9(1 - p_0)}{p_0}$

where

n = Sample size

p_0 = An estimate (perhaps judgmental) of the process proportion p

---

For example, if p is thought to be about .05, the rule indicates that samples of at least size 171 should be used in constructing the *p*-chart:

$$n > \frac{9(1 - .05)}{.05} = 171$$

In the next three boxes we summarize how to construct a *p*-chart and its zone boundaries and how to interpret a *p*-chart.

Constructing a *p*-Chart: A Summary

1. Using a rational subgrouping strategy, collect at least 20 samples, each of size

$$n > \frac{9(1 - p_0)}{p_0}$$

where p_0 is an estimate of p, the proportion defective (i.e., nonconforming) produced by the process. p_0 can be determined from sample data (i.e., $\hat{p}$) or may be based on expert opinion.

2. For each sample, calculate $\hat{p}$, the proportion of defective units in the sample:

$$\hat{p} = \frac{\text{Number of defective items in the sample}}{\text{Number of items in the sample}}$$

3. Plot the centerline and control limits:

$$Centerline: \bar{p} = \frac{\text{Total number of defective units in all } k \text{ samples}}{\text{Total number of units in all } k \text{ samples}}$$

$$Upper \ control \ limit: \bar{p} + 3\sqrt{\frac{\bar{p}(1-\bar{p})}{n}}$$

$$Lower \ control \ limit: \bar{p} - 3\sqrt{\frac{\bar{p}(1-\bar{p})}{n}}$$

where k is the number of samples of size n and $\bar{p}$ is the overall proportion of defective units in the nk units sampled. $\bar{p}$ is an estimate of the unknown process proportion p.

4. Plot the k sample proportions on the control chart in the order that the samples were produced by the process.

Constructing Zone Boundaries for a p-Chart

$$Upper \ \text{A–B} \ boundary: \bar{p} + 2\sqrt{\frac{\bar{p}(1-\bar{p})}{n}}$$

$$Lower \ \text{A–B} \ boundary: \bar{p} - 2\sqrt{\frac{\bar{p}(1-\bar{p})}{n}}$$

$$Upper \ \text{B–C} \ boundary: \bar{p} + \sqrt{\frac{\bar{p}(1-\bar{p})}{n}}$$

$$Lower \ \text{B–C} \ boundary: \bar{p} - \sqrt{\frac{\bar{p}(1-\bar{p})}{n}}$$

Note: When the lower control limit is negative, it should not be plotted on the control chart. However, the lower zone boundaries can still be plotted if they are nonnegative.

Interpreting a p-Chart

1. The **process is out of control** if one or more sample proportions fall beyond the control limits (Rule 1) or if any of the three patterns of variation described by Rules 2, 3, and 4 (Figure 13.21) are observed. Such signals indicate that one or more special causes of variation are influencing the process proportion, p. These causes should be identified and eliminated in order to bring the process into control.

2. The **process is treated as being in control** if none of the above noted out-of-control signals are observed. Processes that are in control should not be tampered with. However, if the level of variation is unacceptably high, common causes of variation should be identified and eliminated.

As with the $\bar{x}$- and R-charts, the centerline and control limits should be developed using samples that were collected during a period in which the process was in control. Accordingly, when a p-chart is first constructed, the centerline and the control limits should be treated as *trial values* (see Section 13.4) and, if necessary, modified before being extended to the right on the control chart and used to monitor future process output.

EXAMPLE 13.4

A manufacturer of auto parts is interested in implementing statistical process control in several areas within its warehouse operation. The manufacturer wants to begin with the order assembly process. Too frequently orders received by customers contain the wrong items or too few items.

For each order received, parts are picked from storage bins in the warehouse, labeled, and placed on a conveyor belt system. Since the bins are spread over a three-acre area, items that are part of the same order may be placed on different spurs of the conveyor belt system. Near the end of the belt system all spurs converge and a worker sorts the items according to the order they belong to. That information is contained on the labels that were placed on the items by the pickers.

The workers have identified three errors that cause shipments to be improperly assembled: (1) pickers pick from the wrong bin, (2) pickers mislabel items, and (3) the sorter makes an error.

The firm's quality manager has implemented a sampling program in which 90 assembled orders are sampled each day and checked for accuracy. An assembled order is considered nonconforming (defective) if it differs in any way from the order placed by the customer. To date, 25 samples have been evaluated. The resulting data are shown in Table 13.4.

   a. Construct a p-chart for the order assembly operation.

   b. What does the chart indicate about the stability of the process?

   c. Is it appropriate to use the control limits and centerline constructed in part **a** to monitor future process output?

TABLE 13.4   **Twenty-Five Samples of Size 90 from the Warehouse Order Assembly Process**

Sample	Size	Defective Orders	Sample Proportion
1	90	12	.13333
2	90	6	.06666
3	90	11	.12222
4	90	8	.08888
5	90	13	.14444
6	90	14	.15555
7	90	12	.13333
8	90	6	.06666
9	90	10	.11111
10	90	13	.14444
11	90	12	.13333
12	90	24	.26666
13	90	23	.25555
14	90	22	.24444
15	90	8	.08888
16	90	3	.03333
17	90	11	.12222
18	90	14	.15555
19	90	5	.05555
20	90	12	.13333
21	90	18	.20000
22	90	12	.13333
23	90	13	.14444
24	90	4	.04444
25	90	6	.06666
Totals	2,250	292	

SOLUTION

a. The first step in constructing the p-chart after collecting the sample data is to calculate the sample proportion for each sample. For the first sample,

$$\hat{p} = \frac{\text{Number of defective items in the sample}}{\text{Number of items in the sample}} = \frac{12}{90} = .13333$$

All the sample proportions are displayed in Table 13.4. Next, calculate the proportion of defective items in the total number of items sampled:

$$\bar{p} = \frac{\text{Total number of defective items}}{\text{Total number of items sampled}} = \frac{292}{2250} = .12978$$

The centerline is positioned at $\bar{p}$, and $\bar{p}$ is used to calculate the control limits:

$$\bar{p} \pm 3\sqrt{\frac{\bar{p}(1-\bar{p})}{n}} = .12978 \pm 3\sqrt{\frac{.12978(1 - .12978)}{90}}$$

$$= .12978 \pm .10627$$

$$\text{UCL: } .23605$$

$$\text{LCL: } .02351$$

After plotting the centerline and the control limits, plot the 25 sample proportions in the order of sampling and connect the points with straight lines. The completed control chart is shown in Figure 13.28.

b. To assist our examination of the control chart, we add the 1- and 2-standard-deviation zone boundaries. The boundaries are located by substituting $\bar{p} = .12978$ into the following formulas:

$$\textit{Upper A–B boundary: } \bar{p} + 2\sqrt{\frac{\bar{p}(1-\bar{p})}{n}} = .20063$$

$$\textit{Upper B–C boundary: } \bar{p} + \sqrt{\frac{\bar{p}(1-\bar{p})}{n}} = .16521$$

$$\textit{Lower A–B boundary: } \bar{p} - 2\sqrt{\frac{\bar{p}(1-\bar{p})}{n}} = .05893$$

$$\textit{Lower B–C boundary: } \bar{p} - \sqrt{\frac{\bar{p}(1-\bar{p})}{n}} = .09435$$

FIGURE 13.28
p-chart for order assembly process

Because three of the sample proportions fall above the upper control limit (Rule 1), there is strong evidence that the process is out of control. None of the nonrandom patterns of Rules 2, 3, and 4 (Figure 13.21) are evident. The process proportion appears to have increased dramatically somewhere around sample 12.

c. Because the process was apparently out of control during the period in which sample data were collected to build the control chart, it is not appropriate to continue using the chart. The control limits and centerline are not representative of the process when it is in control. The chart must be revised before it is used to monitor future output.

In this case, the three out-of-control points were investigated and it was discovered that they occurred on days when a temporary sorter was working in place of the regular sorter. Actions were taken to ensure that in the future better-trained temporary sorters would be available.

Since the special cause of the observed variation was identified and eliminated, all sample data from the three days the temporary sorter was working were dropped from the data set and the centerline and control limits were recalculated:

$$Centerline: \bar{p} = \frac{223}{1980} = .11263$$

$$Control\ limits: \bar{p} \pm 3\sqrt{\frac{\bar{p}(1-\bar{p})}{n}} = .11263 \pm 3\sqrt{\frac{.11263(.88737)}{90}}$$

$$= .11263 \pm .09997$$

UCL: .21259   LCL: .01266

The revised zones are calculated by substituting $\bar{p} = .11263$ in the following formulas:

$$Upper\ A\text{–}B\ boundary: \bar{p} + 2\sqrt{\frac{\bar{p}(1-\bar{p})}{n}} = .17927$$

$$Upper\ B\text{–}C\ boundary: \bar{p} + \sqrt{\frac{\bar{p}(1-\bar{p})}{n}} = .14595$$

FIGURE 13.29
Revised *p*-chart for order assembly process

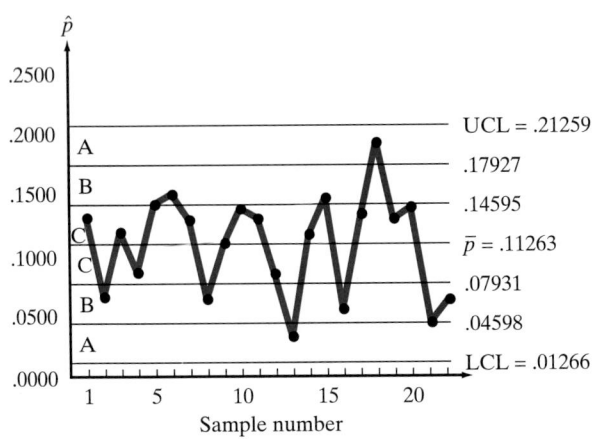

$$Lower \ A\text{–}B \ boundary: \bar{p} - 2\sqrt{\frac{\bar{p}(1-\bar{p})}{n}} = .04598$$

$$Lower \ B\text{–}C \ boundary: \bar{p} - \sqrt{\frac{\bar{p}(1-\bar{p})}{n}} = .07931$$

The revised control chart appears in Figure 13.29. Notice that now all sample proportions fall within the control limits. These limits can now be treated as official, extended to the right on the chart, and used to monitor future orders.   ▐

EXERCISES   13.28–13.36

Note: Exercises marked with 💾 *contain data for computer analysis on a 3.5" disk (file name in parentheses).*

Learning the Mechanics

13.28 What characteristic of a process is a *p*-chart designed to monitor?

13.29 The proportion of defective items generated by a manufacturing process is believed to be 8%. In constructing a *p*-chart for the process, determine how large the sample size should be to avoid ending up with a negative lower control limit.

13.30 **(X13.030)** To construct a *p*-chart for a manufacturing process, 25 samples of size 200 were drawn from the process. The number of defectives in each sample is listed here.

Sample	Sample Size	Defectives
1	200	16
2	200	14
3	200	9
4	200	11
5	200	15
6	200	8
7	200	12
8	200	16
9	200	17
10	200	13
11	200	15
12	200	10
13	200	9
14	200	12
15	200	14
16	200	11
17	200	8
18	200	7
19	200	12
20	200	15
21	200	9
22	200	16
23	200	13
24	200	11
25	200	10

a. Calculate the proportion defective in each sample.

b. Calculate and plot $\bar{p}$ and the upper and lower control limits for the *p*-chart.

c. Calculate and plot the A, B, and C zone boundaries on the *p*-chart.

d. Plot the sample proportions on the *p*-chart and connect them with straight lines.

e. Use the pattern-analysis rules 1–4 for detecting the presence of special causes of variation (Figure 13.21) to determine whether the process is out of control.

13.31 **(X13.031)** To construct a *p*-chart, 20 samples of size 150 were drawn from a process. The proportion of defective items found in each of the samples is listed in the accompanying table.

Sample	Proportion Defective	Sample	Proportion Defective
1	.03	11	.07
2	.05	12	.04
3	.10	13	.06
4	.02	14	.05
5	.08	15	.07
6	.09	16	.06
7	.08	17	.07
8	.05	18	.02
9	.07	19	.05
10	.06	20	.03

a. Calculate and plot the centerline and the upper and lower control limits for the *p*-chart.

b. Calculate and plot the A, B, and C zone boundaries on the *p*-chart.

c. Plot the sample proportions on the *p*-chart.

d. Is the process under control? Explain.

e. Should the control limits and centerline of part **a** be used to monitor future process output? Explain.

13.32 In each of the following cases, use the sample size formula to determine a sample size large enough to avoid constructing a p-chart with a negative lower control limit.

a. $p_0 = .01$ b. $p_0 = .05$ c. $p_0 = .10$ d. $p_0 = .20$

Applying the Concepts

13.33 A manufacturer produces disks for personal computers. From past experience the production manager believes that 1% of the disks are defective. The company collected a sample of the first 1,000 disks manufactured after 4:00 P.M. every other day for a month. The disks were analyzed for defects, then these data and MINITAB were used to construct the p-chart shown below.

a. From a statistical perspective, is a sample size of 1,000 adequate for constructing the p-chart? Explain.

b. Calculate the chart's upper and lower control limits.

c. What does the p-chart suggest about the presence of special causes during the time when the data were collected?

d. Critique the rational subgrouping strategy used by the disk manufacturer.

13.34 (X13.034) Goodstone Tire & Rubber Company is interested in monitoring the proportion of defective tires generated by the production process at its Akron, Ohio, production plant. The company's chief engineer believes that the proportion is about 7%. Because the tires are destroyed during the testing process, the company would like to keep the number of tires tested to a minimum. However, the engineer would also like to use a p-chart with a positive lower control limit. A positive lower control limit makes it possible to determine when the process has generated an unusually small proportion of defectives. Such an occurrence is good news and would signal the engineer to look for causes of the superior performance. That information can be used to improve the production process. Using the sample size formula, the chief engineer recommended that the company randomly sample and test 120 tires from each day's production. To date, 20 samples have been taken. The data are presented here.

Sample	Sample Size	Defectives
1	120	11
2	120	5
3	120	4
4	120	8
5	120	10
6	120	13
7	120	9
8	120	8
9	120	10
10	120	11
11	120	10
12	120	12
13	120	8
14	120	6
15	120	10
16	120	5
17	120	10
18	120	10
19	120	3
20	120	8

a. Use the sample size formula to show how the chief engineer arrived at the recommended sample size of 120.

b. Construct a p-chart for the tire production process.

c. What does the chart indicate about the stability of the process? Explain.

d. Is it appropriate to use the control limits to monitor future process output? Explain.

e. Is the *p*-chart you constructed in part **b** capable of signaling hour-to-hour changes in *p*? Explain.

13.35 **(X13.035)** Accurate typesetting is crucial to the production of high-quality newspapers. The editor of the Morristown *Daily Tribune,* a weekly publication with circulation of 27,000, has instituted a process for monitoring the performance of typesetters. Each week 100 paragraphs of the paper are randomly sampled and read for accuracy. The number of paragraphs with errors is recorded for each of the last 30 weeks in the table.

Week	Paragraph with Errors	Week	Paragraph with Errors
1	2	16	2
2	4	17	3
3	10	18	7
4	4	19	3
5	1	20	2
6	1	21	3
7	13	22	7
8	9	23	4
9	11	24	3
10	0	25	2
11	3	26	2
12	4	27	0
13	2	28	1
14	2	29	3
15	8	30	4

Primary Source: Jerry Kinard, Western Carolina University.

Secondary Source: Render, B., and Stair, Jr., R. *Quantitative Analysis for Management,* 6th ed. Upper Saddle River, N.J.: Prentice-Hall, 1997.

a. Construct a *p*-chart for the process.
b. Is the process under statistical control? Explain.
c. Should the control limits of part **a** be used to monitor future process output? Explain.
d. Suggest two methods that could be used to facilitate the diagnosis of causes of process variation.

13.36 **(X13.036)** A Japanese floppy disk manufacturer has a daily production rate of about 20,000 high density 3.5-inch diskettes. Quality is monitored by randomly sampling 200 finished disks every other hour from the production process and testing them for defects. If one or more defects are discovered, the disk is considered defective and is destroyed. The production process operates 20 hours per day, seven days a week. The table reports data for the last three days of production.

Day	Hour	Number of Defectives	Day	Hour	Number of Defectives
1	1	13		6	3
	2	5		7	1
	3	2		8	2
	4	3		9	3
	5	2		10	1
	6	3	3	1	9
	7	1		2	5
	8	2		3	2
	9	1		4	1
	10	1		5	3
2	1	11		6	2
	2	6		7	4
	3	2		8	2
	4	3		9	1
	5	1		10	1

a. Construct a *p*-chart for the diskette production process.
b. What does it indicate about the stability of the process? Explain.
c. What advice can you give the manufacturer to assist them in their search for the special cause(s) of variation that is plaguing the process?

13.7 DIAGNOSING THE CAUSES OF VARIATION (OPTIONAL)

Statistical process control (SPC) consists of three major activities or phases: (1) monitoring process variation, (2) diagnosing causes of variation, and (3) eliminating those causes. A more detailed description of SPC is shown in Figure 13.30, which depicts SPC as a quality-improvement cycle. In the monitoring phase, statistical signals from the process are evaluated in order to uncover opportunities to improve the process. This is the phase we have dealt with in Sections 13.3–13.6. We turn our attention now to the diagnosis phase.

The diagnosis phase is the critical link in the SPC improvement cycle. The monitoring phase simply identifies *whether* problems exist; the diagnosis phase identifies *what* the problems are. If the monitoring phase detected the presence of special causes of variation (i.e., an out-of-control signal was observed on a

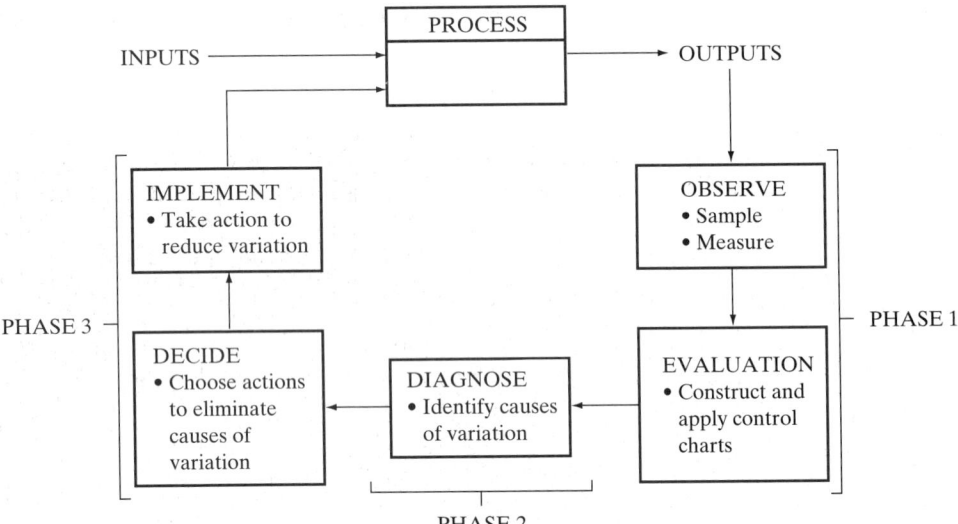

FIGURE 13.30 SPC viewed as a quality-improvement cycle

control chart), the diagnosis phase is concerned with tracking down the underlying cause or causes. If no special causes were detected in the monitoring phase (i.e., the process is under statistical control) and further improvement in the process is desired, the diagnosis phase concentrates on uncovering common causes of variation.

It is important to recognize that the achievement of process improvement requires more than the application of statistical tools such as control charts. This is particularly evident in the diagnosis phase. The diagnosis of causes of variation requires expert knowledge about the process in question. Just as you would go to a physician to diagnose a pain in your back, you would turn to people who work in the process or to engineers or analysts with process expertise to help you diagnose the causes of process variation.

Several methods have been developed for assisting process experts with process diagnosis, including *flowcharting* (see Statistics in Action 13.2) and the simple but powerful graphical tool called *Pareto analysis* (Chapter 2). Another graphical method, the **cause-and-effect diagram**, is described in this section. A fourth methodology, *experimental design*, is the topic of Chapter 15.

The cause-and-effect diagram was developed by Kaoru Ishikawa of the University of Tokyo in 1943. As a result, it is also known as an *Ishikawa diagram*. The cause-and-effect diagram facilitates the construction of causal chains that explain the occurrence of events, problems, or conditions. It is often constructed through brainstorming sessions involving a small group of process experts. It has been employed for decades by Japanese firms, but was not widely applied in the United States until the mid-1980s.

The basic framework of the cause-and-effect diagram is shown in Figure 13.31. In the right-hand box in the figure, we record the effect whose cause(s) we want to diagnose.

For instance, GOAL/QPC (a Massachusetts-based TQM consulting group) used the cause-and-effect diagram in Figure 13.32 to demonstrate why pizzas are delivered late on Fridays and Saturdays. As a second example, Figure 13.33 displays the reasons for high variation in the fill weights of 20-pound bags of dry dog food.

Examining Figure 13.31, we see the branches of the cause-and-effect diagram, which represent the major factors that influence the process and that could be

FIGURE 13.31
The basic framework for a cause-and-effect diagram

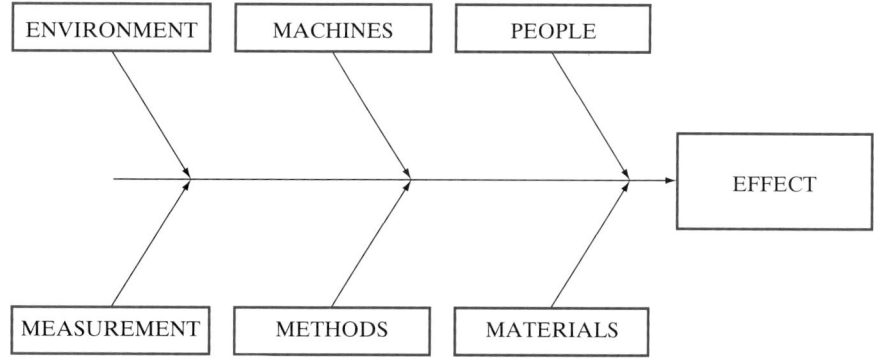

FIGURE 13.32
Cause-and-effect diagram for late pizza deliveries
Source: Reprinted with permission from *The Memory Jogger™ II*, GOAL/QPC, 13 Branch Street, Methuan, Massachusetts, 1994, p. 27.

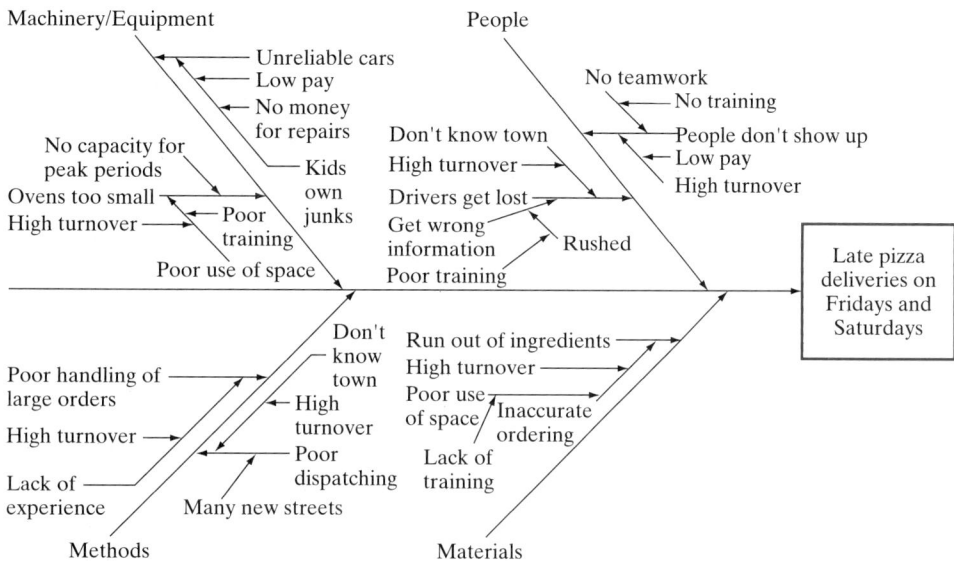

responsible for the effect. These are often taken to be the six universal sources of process variation that we described in Section 13.1: people, machines, materials, methods, measurement, and environment. Notice that in the examples of Figures 13.32 and 13.33 these categories were tailored to fit the process in question. The set of categories must be broad enough to include virtually all possible factors that could influence the process. It is less important how many categories are used or how you label the categories.

The cause-and-effect diagram is constructed using effect-to-cause reasoning. That is, you begin by specifying the effect of interest and then move backward to identify *potential* causes of the effect. After a potential cause has been identified, you treat it as an effect and try to find its cause, and so forth. The result is a **causal chain**. A completed cause-and-effect diagram typically contains many causal chains. These chains help us to track down causes whose eradication will reduce, improve, or eliminate the effect in question.

After setting up the basic framework for the cause-and-effect diagram and recording the effect of interest in the box on the right, you construct the causal chains, proceeding backward from general potential causes to increasingly specific causes. Begin by choosing one of the universal cause categories—say, people—and asking, "What factors related to people could cause the effect in question?" In the pizza delivery example of Figure 13.32, two factors were identified: (1) drivers

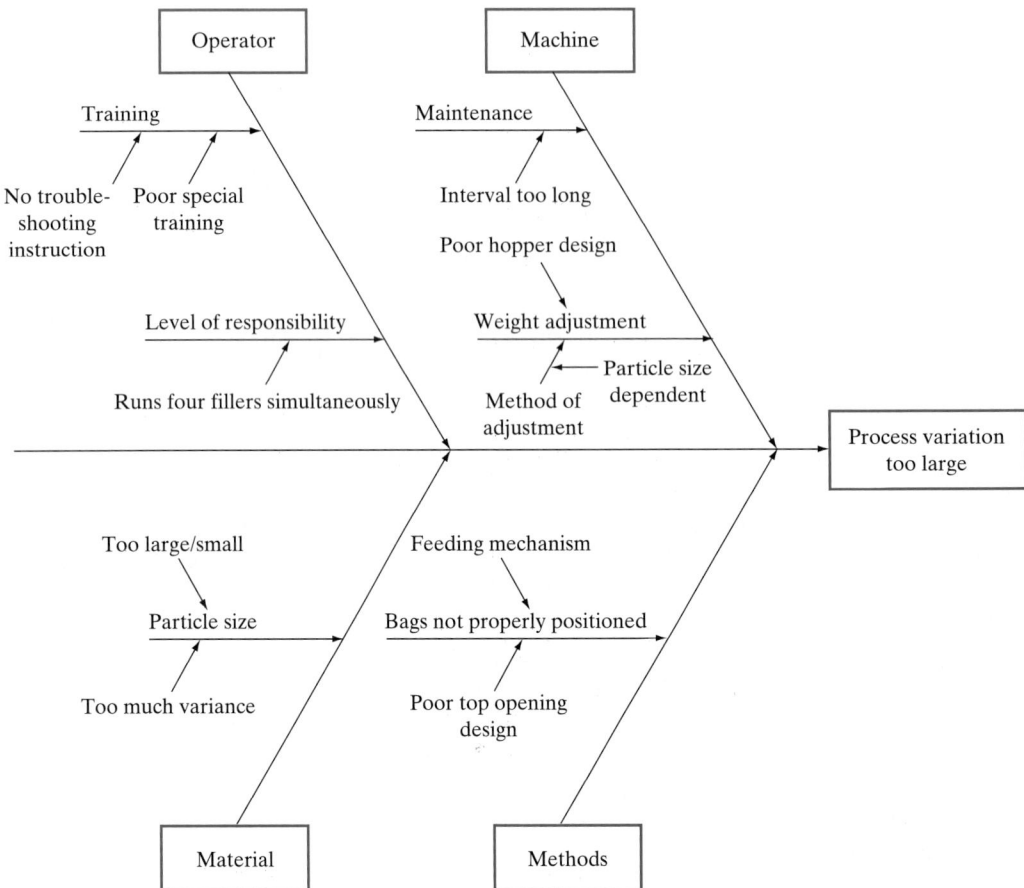

FIGURE 13.33   Cause-and-effect diagram for the filling process for 20-lb. bags of dog food
Source: R. E. DeVor, T. Chang, and J. W. Southerland, *Statistical Quality Design and Control,* New York, Macmillan, 1992. © 1992. Reprinted by permission of Prentice-Hall, Inc., Upper Saddle River, NJ.

not showing up for work and (2) drivers getting lost. Each of these causes is written on a twig of the People branch. Next, each cause is treated as an effect and an attempt is made to identify its cause. That is, we look for subcauses. For example, driver absenteeism was blamed on (1) high turnover and (2) no teamwork. The high turnover, in turn, was blamed on low pay, while lack of teamwork was blamed on insufficient training. Thus, the "No show" twig has both a "High turnover" twig and a "No teamwork" twig attached to it; and, each of these twigs has a cause twig attached. Multiple causal chains like this should be constructed for each branch of the cause-and-effect diagram.

Once completed, the various causal chains of the cause-and-effect diagram must be evaluated (often subjectively) to identify one or more factors thought most likely to be causes of the effect in question. Then actions can be chosen and implemented (see Figure 13.30) to eliminate the causes and improve the process.

Besides facilitating process diagnosis, cause-and-effect diagrams serve to document the causal factors that may potentially affect a process and to communicate that information to others in the organization. The cause-and-effect diagram is a very flexible tool that can be applied in a variety of situations. It can be used as a formal part of the SPC improvement cycle, as suggested above, or simply as a means of investigating the causes of organizational problems, events, or conditions. It can also help select the appropriate process variables to monitor with control charts.

STATISTICS IN ACTION

13.2 QUALITY CONTROL IN A SERVICE OPERATION

Many large corporations have internal service departments that are responsible for obtaining requested reports, data, and other information from sources inside the company. The **flowchart** of Figure 13.34 (page 720) provides a macro view of the report acquisition process of a U.S. automobile manufacturer. A macro flowchart ignores all the potential complexities such as what happens when an order form is incomplete or not readable. Nevertheless, such flowcharts are frequently used as the first step in understanding, monitoring, and/or reengineering a process. The process in question had never previously been studied or monitored.

A team charged with improving the report acquisition process decided that data should be collected on: (1) the time between the receipt of an order card and issuance of a report request by the service department, and (2) the time between the issuance of a report request by the service department and the receipt of the report by the service department. These two time intervals are indicated on the flowchart by Chart A and Chart B, respectively. The data were collected by randomly sampling three order cards per day from among those associated with reports that had been received that day. The time intervals in question were determined from the dates stamped on the cards. $\bar{x}$-charts and R-charts were constructed for each of the time variables and are displayed in Figure 13.35 (page 721).

Focus

a. Expand the flowchart of Figure 13.34 to include the following complexities of the process:

  1. What happens when the department receives an order card without the proper signatures?

  What happens if a report cannot be found? (While you have no way of knowing exactly how this particular department handles these situations, you can speculate.) Use the symbols in the box at right to prepare your flowchart.

b. Describe the two processes that the team decided to monitor.

c. Are the processes under statistical control? Explain.

d. Examine the measurements recorded on the control charts and answer the following questions:

  1. In the worst cases, how many five-day work weeks were required to place an order for a report?

  2. On average, about how many days are required for an order to be placed?

  3. At worst how many days were required to receive an order? At best?

e. From the customer's perspective, which time interval should the service department be monitoring?

Flowchart Symbols

▭	An operation or activity
◇	A decision, evaluation, or computation (used for branching)
▱	Input or output
⬒	Used when the input or output is a document
→	Indicates the direction of flow
⬭	Used to indicate the beginning and the end of the process
◯	Connector: used to indicate the location of the continued flowchart

---

Source: Adapted from Kane, *Defect Prevention.* New York: Marcel Dekker, Inc., 1989, pp. 77–81.

FIGURE 13.34
Flowchart for report acquisition process (Statistics in Action 13.2)

13.8 CAPABILITY ANALYSIS (OPTIONAL)

In the previous four sections, we pointed out that if a process were in statistical control, but the level of variation was unacceptably high, common causes of variation should be identified and eliminated. This was illustrated in Figure 13.13. In this optional section, we describe a methodology that can be used to help determine when such variation is unacceptably high. The methodology is called **capability analysis**. As we have seen, the achievement of process stability is vitally important to process improvement efforts. But it is not an end in itself. A process may be in control, but still not be capable of producing output that is acceptable to customers.

To see this, consider Figure 13.36. The figure displays six different in-control processes. Recall that if a process is under statistical control, its output distribution

FIGURE 13.35
Report request order
processing control
charts: (a) days to
order report; (b) days
to receive report
(Statistics in
Action 13.2)

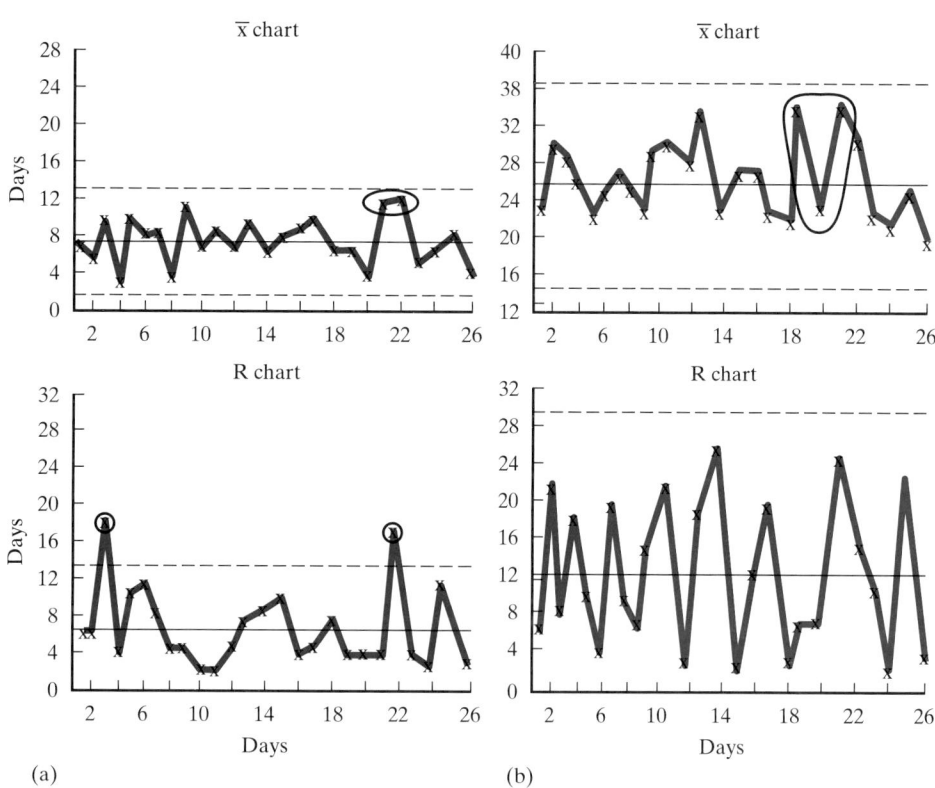

(a)   (b)

FIGURE 13.36
Output distributions of
six different in-control
processes, where LSL
= lower specification
limit and USL = upper
specification limit

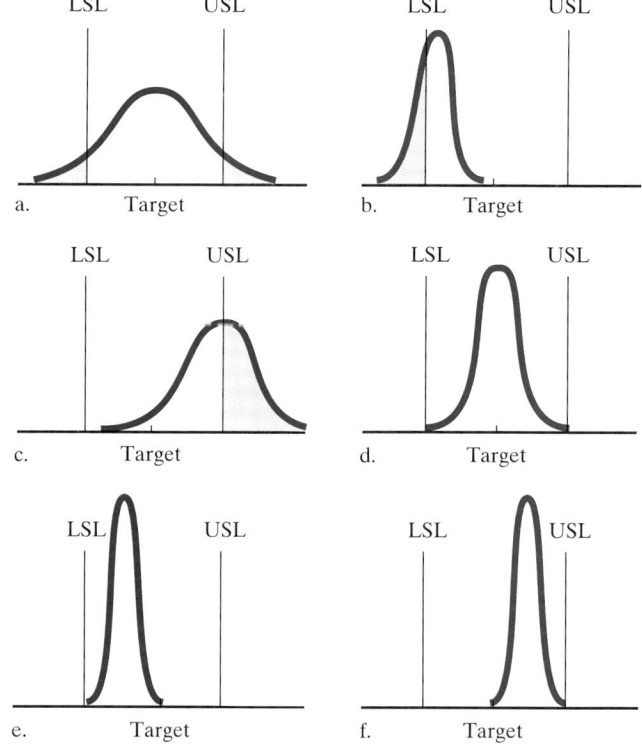

does not change over time and the process can be characterized by a single probability distribution, as in each of the panels of the figure. The upper and lower specification limits for the output of each of the six processes are also indicated on each panel, as is the target value for the output variable. Recall from Definition 13.8 that the specification limits are boundary points that define the acceptable values for an output variable.

The processes of panels **a, b,** and **c** produce a high percentage of items that are outside the specification limits. None of these processes is *capable* of satisfying its customers. In panel **a,** the process is centered on the target value, but the variation due to common causes is too high. In panel **b,** the variation is low relative to the width of the specification limits, but the process is off-center. In panel **c,** both problems exist: the variation is too high and the process is off-center. Thus, bringing a process into statistical control is not sufficient to guarantee the capability of the process.

All three processes in panels **d, e,** and **f** are capable. In each case, the process distribution fits comfortably between the specification limits. Virtually all of the individual items produced by these processes would be acceptable. However, any significant tightening of the specification limits—whether by customers or internal managers or engineers—would result in the production of unacceptable output and necessitate the initiation of process improvement activities to restore the process' capability. Further, even though a process is capable, continuous improvement of a process requires constant improvement of its capability.

When a process is known to be in control, the most direct way to assess its capability is to construct a frequency distribution or stem-and-leaf display for a large sample of individual measurements (usually 50 or more) from the process. Then, add the specification limits and the target value for the output variable on the graph. This is called a **capability analysis diagram**. It is a simple visual tool for assessing process capability.

The MINITAB dot plot (with specification limits) shown in Figure 13.37 represents a capability analysis diagram for the paint-filling process found to be under statistical control in Examples 13.1 and 13.2. You can see that the process is roughly centered on the target of 10 pounds of paint, but that a large number of paint cans fall outside the specification limits. This tells us that the process is not capable of satisfying customer requirements.

FIGURE 13.37 Capability analysis diagram for the paint-filling process

Most quality-management professionals and statisticians agree that the capability analysis diagram is the best way to describe the performance of an in-control process. However, many companies have found it useful to have a numerical measure of capability. The ability to summarize capability in a single number has the advantages of convenience, simplicity, and ease of communication. However, it also has the major disadvantage of potentially misleading those who use it. Just as when you characterize a data set by its mean and ignore its variation, the information you provide to your audience is incomplete and may adversely affect their actions and decisions. (A more thorough discussion about the dangers of numerical measures of capability are presented later in this section.)

There are several different approaches to quantifying capability. We will briefly describe two of them. The first (and most direct) consists of counting the number of items that fall outside the specification limits in the capability analysis diagram and reporting the percentage of such items in the sample. Either the original data set or a graphical technique that displays the individual measurements—such as a stem-and-leaf display or a dot plot—is used to obtain the needed count.

Figure 13.38 is a MINITAB stem-and-leaf display of the paint data with the specification limits added. You can see that 29 of the 125 paint cans fall outside the specification limits (16 below 9.995 and 13 above 10.005). Thus, 29 of the 125 cans in the sample, or 23.2%, are unacceptable.

When this percentage is used to characterize the capability of the process the implication is that over time, if this process remains in control, roughly 23% of the paint cans will be unacceptable. Remember, however, that this percentage is only an estimate, a sample statistic, not a known parameter. It is based on a sample of size 125 and is subject to both sampling error and measurement error. We discussed such percentages and proportions in detail in Chapter 7.

If it is known that the process follows approximately a normal distribution, as is often the case, a similar approach to quantifying process capability can be used. In this case, the mean and standard deviation of the sample of measurements used to construct the capability analysis diagram can be taken as estimates of the mean and standard deviation of the process. Then, the fraction of items that would fall outside the specification limits can be found by solving for the associated area

FIGURE 13.38
MINITAB stem-and-leaf display for the paint data with specification limits indicated

```
Stem-and-leaf of Weight     N  = 125
Leaf Unit = 0.0010


     2   998 89
     3   999 1
     8   999 22333
    22   999 44444444555555                              ── LSL = 9.995
    43   999 6666666666667777777777
   (22)  999 88888888889999999999
    60 1000 000000111111111
    45 1000 222222222333333333333333
    20 1000 4444445
    13 1000 666                                           ── USL = 10.005
    10 1000 8889999
     3 1001 00
     1 1001
     1 1001 4
```

FIGURE 13.39

Process spread versus specification spread

under the normal curve, as we did in Chapter 5. As we said above, if you use this percentage to characterize process capability, remember that it is only an estimate, and is subject to sampling error.

The second approach to measuring capability is to construct a **capability index**. Several such indexes have been developed. We will describe one used for stable processes that are centered on the target value. It is known as the C_p **Index**.*

When the capability analysis diagram indicates that the process is centered, capability can be measured through a comparison of the distance between the upper specification limit (USL) and the lower specification limit (LSL), called the **specification spread**, and the spread of the output distribution. The spread of the output distribution—called the **process spread**—is defined as 6σ and is estimated by $6s$, where s is the standard deviation of the sample of measurements used to construct the capability analysis diagram. These two distances are illustrated in Figure 13.39. The ratio of these distances is the capability index known as C_p.

DEFINITION 13.10

$$C_p = \frac{\text{(Specification spread)}}{\text{(Process spread)}} = \frac{(\text{USL} - \text{LSL})}{6\sigma}$$

where σ is estimated by s, the standard deviation of the sample of measurements used to construct the capability analysis diagram.

Interpretation of Capability Index, C_p

C_p summarizes the performance of a stable, centered process relative to the specification limits. It indicates the extent to which the output of the process falls within the specification limits.

1. If $C_p = 1$ (specification spread = process spread), process is capable
2. If $C_p > 1$ (specification spread > process spread), process is capable
3. If $C_p < 1$ (specification spread < process spread), process is not capable

If the process follows a normal distribution,

$C_p = 1.00$ means about 2.7 units per 1000 will be unacceptable

$C_p = 1.33$ means about 63 units per million will be unacceptable

$C_p = 1.67$ means about .6 units per million will be unacceptable

$C_p = 2.00$ means about 2 units per billion will be unacceptable

---

*For off-center processes, its sister index, C_{pk}, is used. Consult the references at the end of the book for a description of C_{pk}.

In manufacturing applications where the process follows a normal distribution (approximately), managers typically require a C_p of at least 1.33. With a C_p of 1.33 the process spread takes up only 75% of the specification spread, leaving a little wiggle room in case the process moves off center.

EXAMPLE 13.5

Let's return to the paint-filling process analyzed in Examples 13.1 and 13.3. Using 25 samples of size 5 (125 measurements), we constructed $\bar{x}$- and R-charts and concluded that the process was in a state of statistical control. The specification limits for the acceptable amount of paint fill per can are shown in the capability analysis diagram of Figure 13.37 and the stem-and-leaf display of Figure 13.38.

a. Is it appropriate to construct a capability index for this process?

b. Find C_p for this process and interpret its value.

SOLUTION

a. Since the process is stable (under control), its output distribution can be characterized by the same probability distribution at any point in time (see Figure 13.12). Accordingly, it is appropriate to assess the performance of the process using that distribution and related performance measures such as C_p.

b. From Definition 13.10,

$$C_p = \frac{(\text{USL} - \text{LSL})}{6\sigma}$$

From the capability analysis diagram of Figure 13.37, we can see that the upper and lower specification limits are 10.005 pounds and 9.995 pounds, respectively. But what is σ? Since the output distribution will never be known exactly, neither will σ, the standard deviation of the output distribution. It must be estimated with s, the standard deviation of a large sample drawn from the process. In this case, we use the standard deviation of the 125 measurements used to construct the capability analysis diagram and find that $s = .004459$. (The sample data are reported in Table 13.2.) Then,

$$C_p = \frac{(10.005 - 9.995)}{6(.004459)} = \frac{.01}{.026754} = .3738$$

Since C_p is less than 1.0, the process is not capable. The process spread is wider than the specification spread. This is consistent with the results of the capability analysis diagram.

For two reasons, great care should be exercised in using and interpreting C_p. First, like the sample standard deviation, s, used in its computation, C_p is a statistic and is subject to sampling error. That is, the value of C_p will change from sample to sample. Thus, unless you understand the magnitude of the sampling error, you should be cautious in comparing the C_p's of different processes. Second, C_p does not reflect the shape of the output distribution. Distributions with different shapes can have the same C_p value. Accordingly, C_p should not be used in isolation, but in conjunction with the capability analysis diagram.

If a capability analysis study indicates that an in-control process is not capable, as in the paint-filling example, it is usually variation, rather than off-centeredness, that is the culprit. Thus, capability is typically achieved or restored by seeking out and eliminating common causes of variation.

EXERCISES **13.37–13.48**

Note: Exercises marked with 💾 *contain data for computer analysis on a 3.5" disk (file name in parentheses).*

Learning the Mechanics

13.37 Explain why it is inappropriate to conduct a capability analysis study for a process that is not in statistical control.

13.38 Explain the difference between process spread and specification spread.

13.39 Describe two different ways to assess the capability of a process.

13.40 Why is it recommended to use and interpret C_p in conjunction with a capability analysis diagram rather than in isolation?

13.41 For a process that is in control and follows a normal distribution, interpret each of the following C_p values:
a. 1.00 b. 1.33 c. .50 d. 2.00

13.42 Find the specification spread for each of the following:
a. USL = 19.65, LSL = 12.45
b. USL = .0010, LSL = .0008
c. USL = 1.43, LSL = 1.27
d. USL = 490, LSL = 486

13.43 Find (or estimate) the process spread for each of the following.
a. $\sigma = 21$ b. $\sigma = 5.2$
c. $s = 110.06$ d. $s = .0024$

13.44 Find the value of C_p for each of the following situations:
a. USL = 1.0065, LSL = 1.0035, $s = .0005$
b. USL = 22, LSL = 21, $s = .2$
c. USL = 875, LSL = 870, $s = .75$

Applying the Concepts

13.45 An in-control, centered process that follows a normal distribution has a $C_p = 2.0$. How many standard deviations away from the process mean is the upper specification limit?

13.46 A process is in control with a normally distributed output distribution with mean 1,000 and standard deviation 100. The upper and lower specification limits for the process are 1,020 and 980, respectively.
a. Assuming no changes in the behavior of the process, what percentage of the output will be unacceptable?
b. Find and interpret the C_p value of the process.

13.47 (X13.047) The next table shows the data on weights of cereal boxes from Exercise 13.13. Assume the specification limits for the weights are USL = 24.2 ounces and LSL = 23.8 ounces.
a. Assuming the process is under control, construct a capability analysis diagram for the process.

Day	Weight of Cereal Boxes (ounces)				
1	24.02	23.91	24.12	24.06	24.13
2	23.89	23.98	24.01	24.00	23.91
3	24.11	24.02	23.99	23.79	24.04
4	24.06	23.98	23.95	24.01	24.11
5	23.81	23.90	23.99	24.07	23.96
6	23.87	24.12	24.07	24.01	23.99
7	23.88	24.00	24.05	23.97	23.97
8	24.01	24.03	23.99	23.91	23.98
9	24.06	24.02	23.80	23.79	24.07
10	23.96	23.99	24.03	23.99	24.01
11	24.10	23.90	24.11	23.98	23.95
12	24.01	24.07	23.93	24.09	23.98
13	24.14	24.07	24.08	23.98	24.02
14	23.91	24.04	23.89	24.01	23.95
15	24.03	24.04	24.01	23.98	24.10
16	23.94	24.07	24.12	24.00	24.02
17	23.88	23.94	23.91	24.06	24.07
18	24.11	23.99	23.90	24.01	23.98
19	24.05	24.04	23.97	24.08	23.95
20	24.02	23.96	23.95	23.89	24.04

b. Is the process capable? Support your answer with a numerical measure of capability.

13.48 (X13.048) Refer to Exercise 13.14. The data on lengths of bolts used in military aircraft are reproduced below.

Hour	Bolt Lengths (centimeters)			
1	37.03	37.08	36.90	36.88
2	36.96	37.04	36.85	36.98
3	37.16	37.11	36.99	37.01
4	37.20	37.06	37.02	36.98
5	36.81	36.97	36.91	37.10
6	37.13	36.96	37.01	36.89
7	37.07	36.94	36.99	37.00
8	37.01	36.91	36.98	37.12
9	37.17	37.03	36.90	37.01
10	36.91	36.99	36.87	37.11
11	36.88	37.10	37.07	37.03
12	37.06	36.98	36.90	36.99
13	36.91	37.22	37.12	37.03
14	37.08	37.07	37.10	37.04
15	37.03	37.04	36.89	37.01
16	36.95	36.98	36.90	36.99
17	36.97	36.94	37.14	37.10
18	37.11	37.04	36.98	36.91
19	36.88	36.99	37.01	36.94
20	36.90	37.15	37.09	37.00
21	37.01	36.96	37.05	36.96
22	37.09	36.95	36.93	37.12
23	37.00	37.02	36.95	37.04
24	36.99	37.07	36.90	37.02
25	37.10	37.03	37.01	36.90

Management has specified upper and lower specification limits of 37 cm and 35 cm, respectively.

a. Assuming the process is in control, construct a capability analysis diagram for the process.

b. Find the percentage of bolts that fall outside the specification limits.
c. Find the capability index, C_p.
d. Is the process capable? Explain.

QUICK REVIEW

Key Terms

Note: Starred (*) terms are from the optional sections of the chapter.

A zone   685
B zone   685
capability analysis*   720
capability analysis diagram*   722
capability index*   724
cause-and-effect diagram*   716
centerline   668
common causes of variation   674
control chart   668
control limits   677
C zone   685
flowchart   719
in control   673

individuals chart   680
lower control limit   677
oscillating sequence   669
out of control   673
output distribution   669
p-chart   706
pattern-analysis rules   686
process   664
process spread*   724
process variation   669
quality   663
R-chart   697
rational subgroups   684

run chart   668
s-chart   698
special (assignable) causes of variation   675
specification limits   680
specification spread*   724
statistical process control   674
system   665
time series plot   668
total quality management   662
upper control limit   677
x-chart   680
$\bar{x}$-chart   680

Key Formulas

Note: Starred (*) formulas are from the optional sections of the chapter.

Control Chart	Centerline	Control Limits (Lower, Upper)	A–B Boundary (Lower, Upper)	B–C Boundary (Lower, Upper)
$\bar{x}$-chart	$\bar{\bar{x}} = \dfrac{\sum_{i=1}^{k}\bar{x}_i}{k}$	$\bar{\bar{x}} \pm A_2\bar{R}$	$\bar{\bar{x}} \pm \dfrac{2}{3}(A_2\bar{R})$ or $\bar{\bar{x}} \pm 2\dfrac{(\bar{R}/d_2)}{\sqrt{n}}$	$\bar{\bar{x}} \pm \dfrac{1}{3}(A_2\bar{R})$ or $\bar{\bar{x}} \pm \dfrac{(\bar{R}/d_2)}{\sqrt{n}}$
R-chart	$\bar{R} = \dfrac{\sum_{i=1}^{k}R_i}{k}$	$(\bar{R}D_3, \bar{R}D_4)$	$\bar{R} \pm 2d_3\left(\dfrac{\bar{R}}{d_2}\right)$	$\bar{R} \pm d_3\left(\dfrac{\bar{R}}{d_2}\right)$
p-chart	$\bar{p} = \dfrac{\text{Total number defectives}}{\text{Total number units sampled}}$	$\bar{p} \pm 3\sqrt{\dfrac{\bar{p}(1-\bar{p})}{n}}$	$\bar{p} \pm 2\sqrt{\dfrac{\bar{p}(1-\bar{p})}{n}}$	$\bar{p} \pm \sqrt{\dfrac{\bar{p}(1-\bar{p})}{n}}$

$n > \dfrac{9(1-p_0)}{p_0}$ where p_0 estimates the true proportion defective   Sample size for p-chart   708

$\text{USL} - \text{LSL}$ Specification spread*   724

$6\sigma \approx 6s$ Process spread*   724

$(\text{USL} - \text{LSL})/6\sigma$ C_p Index*   724

LANGUAGE LAB

Note: Starred (*) terms are from the optional sections of the chapter.

Symbol	Pronunciation	Description
LCL	L-C-L	Lower control limit
UCL	U-C-L	Upper control limit
$\bar{\bar{x}}$	x-bar-bar	Average of the sample means
$\bar{R}$	R-bar	Average of the sample ranges
A_2	A-two	Constant obtained from Table XVII, Appendix B
D_3	D-three	Constant obtained from Table XVII, Appendix B
D_4	D-four	Constant obtained from Table XVII, Appendix B
d_2	d-two	Constant obtained from Table XVII, Appendix B
d_3	d-three	Constant obtained from Table XVII, Appendix B
$\hat{p}$	p-hat	Estimated number of defectives in sample
$\bar{p}$	p-bar	Overall proportion of defective units in all nk samples
p_0	p-naught	Estimated overall proportion of defectives for entire process
SPC	S-P-C	Statistical process control
USL*	U-S-L	Upper specification limit
LSL*	L-S-L	Lower specification limit
C_p*	C-p	Capability index

SUPPLEMENTARY EXERCISES 13.49–13.74

Note: Exercises marked with 💾 *contain data for computer analysis on a 3.5" disk (file name in parentheses). Starred (*) exercises are from the optional sections of the chapter.*

Learning the Mechanics

13.49 Define *quality* and list its important dimensions.

13.50 What is a system? Give an example of a system with which you are familiar, and describe its inputs, outputs, and transformation process.

13.51 What is a process? Give an example of an organizational process and a personal process.

13.52 Select a personal process that you would like to better understand or to improve and construct a flowchart for it.

13.53 Describe the six major sources of process variation.

13.54 Suppose all the output of a process over the last year were measured and found to be within the specification limits required by customers of the process. Should you worry about whether the process is in statistical control? Explain.

*13.55 Select a problem, event, or condition whose cause or causes you would like to diagnose. Construct a cause-and-effect diagram that would facilitate your diagnosis.

*13.56 In estimating a population mean μ using a sample mean $\bar{x}$, why is it likely that $\bar{x} \neq \mu$? Construct a cause-and-effect diagram for the effect $\bar{x} \neq \mu$.

*13.57 Construct a cause-and-effect diagram to help explain why customer waiting time at the drive-in window of a fast-food restaurant is a variable.

13.58 Processes that are in control are predictable; out-of-control processes are not. Explain.

13.59 Compare and contrast special and common causes of variation.

13.60 Explain the role of the control limits of a control chart.

13.61 Explain the difference between control limits and specification limits.

*13.62 Should control charts be used to monitor a process that is both in control and capable? Why or why not?

*13.63 Under what circumstances is it appropriate to use C_p to assess capability?

13.64 A process is under control and follows a normal distribution with mean 100 and standard deviation 10. In constructing a standard $\bar{x}$-chart for this process, the control limits are set 3 standard deviations from the mean—i.e., $100 \pm 3(10/\sqrt{n})$. The probability of observing an $\bar{x}$ outside the control limits is $.00135 + .00135 = .0027$. Suppose it is desired to construct a control chart that signals the presence of a potential special cause of variation for less extreme values of $\bar{x}$. How many standard deviations from the mean should the control limits be set such that the probability of the chart falsely indicating the presence of a special cause of variation is .10 rather than .0027?

Applying the Concepts

13.65 **(X13.065)** Consider the following time series data.

Order of Production	Weight (grams)	Order of Production	Weight (grams)
1	6.0	9	6.5
2	5.0	10	9.0
3	7.0	11	3.0
4	5.5	12	11.0
5	7.0	13	3.0
6	6.0	14	12.0
7	8.0	15	2.0
8	5.0		

a. Construct a time series plot. Be sure to connect the points and add a centerline.

b. Which type of variation pattern in Figure 13.6 best describes the pattern revealed by your plot?

13.66 **(X13.066)** The accompanying length measurements were made on 20 consecutively produced pencils.

Order of Production	Length (inches)	Order of Production	Length (inches)
1	7.47	11	7.57
2	7.48	12	7.56
3	7.51	13	7.55
4	7.49	14	7.58
5	7.50	15	7.56
6	7.51	16	7.59
7	7.48	17	7.57
8	7.49	18	7.55
9	7.48	19	7.56
10	7.50	20	7.58

a. Construct a time series plot. Be sure to connect the plotted points and add a centerline.

b. Which type of variation pattern in Figure 13.6 best describes the pattern shown in your plot?

13.67 Use the appropriate pattern-analysis rules to determine whether the process being monitored by the control chart shown below is under the influence of special causes of variation.

13.68 **(X13.068)** A company that manufactures plastic molded parts believes it is producing an unusually large number of defects. To investigate this suspicion, each shift drew seven random samples of 200 parts, visually inspected each part to determine whether it was defective, and tallied the primary type of defect present (Hart, 1992). These data are presented in the table at the top of page 730.

a. From a statistical perspective, are the number of samples and the sample size of 200 adequate for constructing a p-chart for these data? Explain.

b. Construct a p-chart for this manufacturing process.

c. Should the control limits be used to monitor future process output? Explain.

d. Suggest a strategy for identifying the special causes of variation that may be present.

13.69 **(X13.069)** A hospital has used control charts continuously since 1978 to monitor the quality of its nursing care. A set of 363 scoring criteria, or standards, are applied at critical points in the patients' stay to determine whether the patients are receiving beneficial nursing care. Auditors regularly visit each hospital unit, sample two patients, and evaluate their care. The auditors review patients' records; interview the patients, the nurse, and the head nurse; and observe the nursing care given (*International Journal of Quality and Reliability Management,* Vol. 9, 1992). The data following part **d** were collected over a three-month period for a newly opened unit of the hospital.

Sample	Shift	# of Defects	TYPE OF DEFECT				
			Crack	Burn	Dirt	Blister	Trim
1	1	4	1	1	1	0	1
2	1	6	2	1	0	2	1
3	1	11	1	2	3	3	2
4	1	12	2	2	2	3	3
5	1	5	0	1	0	2	2
6	1	10	1	3	2	2	2
7	1	8	0	3	1	1	3
8	2	16	2	0	8	2	4
9	2	17	3	2	8	2	2
10	2	20	0	3	11	3	3
11	2	28	3	2	17	2	4
12	2	20	0	0	16	4	0
13	2	20	1	1	18	0	0
14	2	17	2	2	13	0	0
15	3	13	3	2	5	1	2
16	3	10	0	3	4	2	1
17	3	11	2	2	3	2	2
18	3	7	0	3	2	2	0
19	3	6	1	2	0	1	2
20	3	8	1	1	2	3	1
21	3	9	1	2	2	2	2

a. Construct an R-chart for the nursing care process.

b. Construct an $\bar{x}$-chart for the nursing care process.

c. Should the control charts of parts **a** and **b** be used to monitor future process output? Explain.

d. The hospital would like all quality scores to exceed 335 (their specification limit). Over the three-month periods, what proportion of the sampled patients received care that did not conform to the hospital's requirements?

Sample	Scores	Sample	Scores	Sample	Scores
1	345,341	8	344,344	15	345,329
2	331,328	9	359,334	16	358,351
3	343,355	10	346,361	17	353,352
4	351,352	11	360,355	18	334,340
5	360,348	12	325,335	19	341,335
6	342,336	13	350,348	20	358,345
7	328,331	14	336,337		

13.70 **(X13.070)** AirExpress, an overnight mail service, is concerned about the operating efficiency of the package-sorting departments at its Toledo, Ohio, terminal. The company would like to monitor the time it takes for packages to be put in outgoing delivery bins from the time they are received. The sorting department operates six hours per day, from 6 P.M. to midnight. The company randomly sampled four packages during each hour of operation during four consecutive days. The time for

each package to move through the system, in minutes, is given.

Sample	Transit Time (mins.)			
1	31.9	33.4	37.8	26.2
2	29.1	24.3	33.2	36.7
3	30.3	31.1	26.3	34.1
4	39.6	29.4	31.4	37.7
5	27.4	29.7	36.5	33.3
6	32.7	32.9	40.1	29.7
7	30.7	36.9	26.8	34.0
8	28.4	24.1	29.6	30.9
9	30.5	35.5	36.1	27.4
10	27.8	29.6	29.0	34.1
11	34.0	30.1	35.9	28.8
12	25.5	26.3	34.8	30.0
13	24.6	29.9	31.8	37.9
14	30.6	36.0	40.2	30.8
15	29.7	33.2	34.9	27.6
16	24.1	26.8	32.7	29.0
17	29.4	31.6	35.2	27.6
18	31.1	33.0	29.6	35.2
19	27.0	29.0	35.1	25.1
20	36.6	32.4	28.7	27.9
21	33.0	27.1	26.2	35.1
22	33.2	41.2	30.7	31.6
23	26.7	35.2	39.7	31.5
24	30.5	36.8	27.9	28.6

a. Construct an $\bar{x}$-chart from these data. In order for this chart to be meaningful, what assumption must be made about the variation of the process? Why?

b. What does the chart suggest about the stability of the package-sorting process? Explain.

c. Should the control limits be used to monitor future process output? Explain.

13.71 **(X13.071)** Officials at Mountain Airlines are interested in monitoring the length of time customers must wait in line to check in at their airport counter in Reno, Nevada. In order to develop a control chart, five customers were sampled each day for 20 days. The data, in minutes, are presented here.

Sample	Waiting Time (mins.)				
1	3.2	6.7	1.3	8.4	2.2
2	5.0	4.1	7.9	8.1	.4
3	7.1	3.2	2.1	6.5	3.7
4	4.2	1.6	2.7	7.2	1.4
5	1.7	7.1	1.6	.9	1.8
6	4.7	5.5	1.6	3.9	4.0
7	6.2	2.0	1.2	.9	1.4
8	1.4	2.7	3.8	4.6	3.8
9	1.1	4.3	9.1	3.1	2.7
10	5.3	4.1	9.8	2.9	2.7
11	3.2	2.9	4.1	5.6	.8
12	2.4	4.3	6.7	1.9	4.8
13	8.8	5.3	6.6	1.0	4.5
14	3.7	3.6	2.0	2.7	5.9
15	1.0	1.9	6.5	3.3	4.7
16	7.0	4.0	4.9	4.4	4.7
17	5.5	7.1	2.1	.9	2.8
18	1.8	5.6	2.2	1.7	2.1
19	2.6	3.7	4.8	1.4	5.8
20	3.6	.8	5.1	4.7	6.3

a. Construct an R-chart from these data.

b. What does the R-chart suggest about the stability of the process? Explain.

c. Explain why the R-chart should be interpreted prior to the $\bar{x}$-chart.

d. Construct an $\bar{x}$-chart from these data.

e. What does the $\bar{x}$-chart suggest about the stability of the process? Explain.

f. Should the control limits for the R-chart and $\bar{x}$-chart be used to monitor future process output? Explain.

*13.72 Consider the airline check-in process described in Exercise 13.71.

a. Assume the process is under control and construct a capability analysis diagram for the process. Management has specified an upper specification limit of five minutes.

b. Is the process capable? Justify your answer.

c. If it is appropriate to estimate and interpret C_p for this process, do so. If it is not, explain why.

d. Why didn't management provide a lower specification limit?

13.73 **(X13.073)** A company called CRW runs credit checks for a large number of banks and insurance companies. Credit history information is typed into computer files by trained administrative assistants. The company is interested in monitoring the proportion of credit histories that contain one or more data entry errors. Based on her experience with the data entry operation, the director of the data processing unit believes that the proportion of histories with data entry errors is about 6%. CRW audited 150 randomly selected credit histories each day for 20 days. The sample data are presented here.

Sample	Sample Size	Histories with Errors
1	150	9
2	150	11
3	150	12
4	150	8
5	150	10
6	150	6
7	150	13
8	150	9
9	150	11
10	150	5
11	150	7
12	150	6
13	150	12
14	150	10
15	150	11
16	150	7
17	150	6
18	150	12
19	150	14
20	150	10

a. Use the sample size formula to show that a sample size of 150 is large enough to prevent the lower control limit of the p-chart they plan to construct from being negative.

b. Construct a p-chart for the data entry process.

c. What does the chart indicate about the presence of special causes of variation? Explain.

d. Provide an example of a special cause of variation that could potentially affect this process. Do the same for a common cause of variation.

e. Should the control limits be used to monitor future credit histories produced by the data entry operation? Explain.

13.74 **(X13.074)** Over the last year, a company that manufactures golf clubs has received numerous complaints about the performance of its graphite shafts and has lost several market share percentage points. In response, the company decided to monitor its shaft production process to identify new opportunities to improve its product. The process involves pultrusion. A fabric is pulled through a thermosetting polymer bath and then through a long heated steel die. As it moves through the die, the shaft is cured. Finally, it is cut to the desired length. Defects that can occur during the process are internal voids, broken strands, gaps between successive layers, and microcracks caused by improper curing. The company's newly formed quality department sampled 10 consecutive shafts every 30 minutes and non-destructive testing was used to seek out flaws in the shafts. The data from each eight-hour work shift were combined to form a shift sample of 160 shafts. Data on the proportion of defective shafts for 36 shift samples are presented in the first table. Data on the types of flaws identified are given in the second table. [*Note:* Each defective shaft may have more than one flaw.]

a. Use the appropriate control chart to determine whether the process proportion remains stable over time.
b. Does your control chart indicate that both common and special causes of variation are present? Explain.
c. To help diagnose the causes of variation in process output, construct a Pareto diagram for the types of shaft defects observed. Which are the "vital few"? The "trivial many"? (See Statistics in Action 2.1 for a description of Pareto analysis.)

Shift Number	Number of Defective Shafts	Proportion of Defective Shafts
1	9	.05625
2	6	.03750
3	8	.05000
4	14	.08750
5	7	.04375
6	5	.03125
7	7	.04375
8	9	.05625
9	5	.03125
10	9	.05625
11	1	.00625
12	7	.04375
13	9	.05625
14	14	.08750
15	7	.04375
16	8	.05000
17	4	.02500
18	10	.06250
19	6	.03750
20	12	.07500
21	8	.05000
22	5	.03125
23	9	.05625
24	15	.09375
25	6	.03750
26	8	.05000
27	4	.02500
28	7	.04375
29	2	.01250
30	6	.03750
31	9	.05625
32	11	.06875
33	8	.05000
34	9	.05625
35	7	.04375
36	8	.05000

Type of Defect	Number of Defects
Internal voids	11
Broken strands	96
Gaps between layers	72
Microcracks	150

Source: Kolarik, W. *Creating Quality: Concepts, Systems, Strategies, and Tools.* New York: McGraw-Hill, 1995.

CHAPTER 14

TIME SERIES
Descriptive Analyses, Models, and Forecasting

CONTENTS

STATISTICS IN ACTION

Where We've Been

In the last chapter we began our study of processes. We learned that variation in the output of processes is inevitable; however, we can often identify the causes of process variation. We examined both managerial and statistical methods for continuously improving processes and the quality of their output. We focused on control charts, which are statistical tools for monitoring output variation and determining when action should be taken to improve a process.

Where We're Going

In this chapter we turn from discussing methods for improving processes to methods for better understanding the output of processes. The methods of this chapter focus exclusively on the data stream generated by a process over time, i.e., on time series data. By studying the time series data generated by a process, we can learn much about both the past and future behavior of the process. We begin with index numbers, a type of time series data often used to characterize the performance of one of the most complex processes—our economy. Eventually, we discuss methods for forecasting future values of process output.

In the previous chapter we were concerned with improving processes. In this chapter, our concern is not with the improvement of the internal workings of processes but with describing and predicting the output of processes. The process outputs on which we focus are the streams of data generated by processes over time. Recall from Chapters 2 and 13 that such data streams are called **time series** or **time series data**. For example, businesses generate time series data such as weekly sales, quarterly earnings, and yearly profits that can be used to describe and evaluate the performance of the business. The U.S. economy can be thought of as a system that generates streams of data that include the Gross Domestic Product, the Consumer Price Index, and the unemployment rate.

The methods of this chapter focus exclusively on the time series data generated by a process. Properly analyzed, these data reveal much about the past and future behavior of the process. Time series data, like other types of data we have discussed in previous chapters, are subjected to two kinds of analyses: **descriptive** and **inferential**. Descriptive analyses use graphical and numerical techniques to provide a clear understanding of any patterns that are present in the time series. After graphing the data, you will often want to use it to make inferences about the future values of the time series, i.e., you will want to **forecast** future values. For example, once you understand the past and present trends of the Dow Jones Industrial Average, you would probably want to forecast its future trend before making decisions about buying and selling stocks. Since significant amounts of money may be riding on the accuracy of your forecasts, you would be interested in measures of their reliability. Forecasts and their measures of reliability are examples of **inferential techniques** in time series analysis.

14.1 DESCRIPTIVE ANALYSIS: INDEX NUMBERS

The most common technique for characterizing a business or economic time series is to compute **index numbers**. Index numbers measure how a time series changes over time. Change is measured relative to a preselected time period, called the **base period**.

DEFINITION 14.1

An **index number** is a number that measures the change in a variable over time relative to the value of the variable during a specific **base period**.

Two types of indexes dominate business and economic applications: **price** and **quantity indexes**. Price indexes measure changes in the price of a commodity or group of commodities over time. The Consumer Price Index (CPI) is a price index because it measures price changes of a group of commodities that are intended to reflect typical purchases of American consumers. On the other hand, an index constructed to measure the change in the total number of automobiles produced annually by American manufacturers would be an example of a quantity index.

Methods of calculating index numbers range from very simple to extremely complex, depending on the numbers and types of commodities represented by the index. Several important types of index numbers are described in this section.

TABLE 14.1 Silver Prices, 1975–1995

Year	Price ($/oz.)
1975	4.42
1976	4.35
1977	4.62
1978	5.40
1979	11.09
1980	20.64
1981	10.52
1982	7.95
1983	11.44
1984	8.14
1985	6.14
1986	5.47
1987	7.01
1988	6.53
1989	5.50
1990	4.82
1991	4.04
1992	3.94
1993	4.30
1994	5.30
1995	5.20

Source: U.S. Dept. of Commerce. *Survey of Current Business,* 1996.

SIMPLE INDEX NUMBERS

When an index number is based on the price or quantity of a single commodity, it is called a **simple index number**.

DEFINITION 14.2
A **simple index number** is based on the relative changes (over time) in the price or quantity of a single commodity.

For example, consider the price of silver between 1975 and 1995, shown in Table 14.1. To construct a simple index to describe the relative changes in silver prices, we must first choose a **base period**. The choice is important because the price for all other periods will be compared with the price during the base period. We select 1975 as the base period, a time just preceding the period of rapid economic inflation associated with dramatic oil price increases.

To calculate the simple index number for a particular year, we divide that year's price by the price during the base year and multiply the result by 100. Thus, for the 1980 silver price index number, we calculate

$$1980 \text{ index number} = \left(\frac{1980 \text{ silver price}}{1975 \text{ silver price}}\right)100 = \left(\frac{20.64}{4.42}\right)100 = 466.97$$

Similarly, the index number for 1995 is

$$1995 \text{ index number} = \left(\frac{1995 \text{ silver price}}{1975 \text{ silver price}}\right)100 = \left(\frac{5.20}{4.42}\right)100 = 117.65$$

The index number for the base period is always 100. In our example, we have

$$1975 \text{ index number} = \left(\frac{1975 \text{ silver price}}{1975 \text{ silver price}}\right)100 = 100$$

Thus, the silver price has risen by 366.97% (the difference between the 1980 and 1975 index numbers) between 1975 and 1980, and by only 17.65% between 1975 and 1995. The simple index numbers for silver prices between 1975 and 1995 are given in Table 14.2 and are portrayed graphically in Figure 14.1. The steps for calculating simple index numbers are summarized in the next box.

TABLE 14.2 Simple Index Numbers for Silver Prices (Base 1975)

Year	Index	Year	Index
1975	100.00	1986	123.76
1976	98.42	1987	158.60
1977	104.52	1988	147.74
1978	122.17	1989	124.43
1979	250.90	1990	109.05
1980	466.97	1991	91.40
1981	238.01	1992	89.14
1982	179.86	1993	97.28
1983	258.82	1994	119.91
1984	184.16	1995	117.65
1985	138.91		

FIGURE 14.1
Graph of silver price
index, 1975–1995

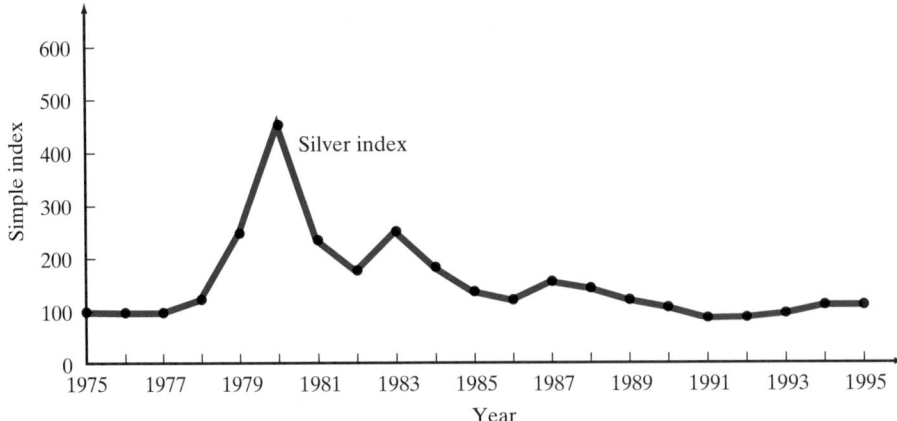

> **Steps for Calculating a Simple Index Number**
> 1. Obtain the prices or quantities for the commodity over the time period of interest.
> 2. Select a base period.
> 3. Calculate the index number for each period according to the formula
>
> $$\text{Index number at time } t = \left(\frac{\text{Time series value at time } t}{\text{Time series value at base period}} \right) 100$$
>
> Symbolically,
>
> $$I_t = \left(\frac{Y_t}{Y_0} \right) 100$$
>
> where I_t is the index number at time t, Y_t is the time series value at time t, and Y_0 is the time series value at the base period.

COMPOSITE INDEX NUMBERS

A **composite index number** represents combinations of the prices or quantities of several commodities. For example, suppose you want to construct an index for the total number of sales of the three major automobile manufacturers in the United States: General Motors, Ford, and Chrysler. The first step is to collect data on the sales of each manufacturer during the period in which you are interested, say 1980–1996. To summarize the information from all three time series in a single index, we add the sales of each manufacturer for each year. That is, we form a new time series consisting of the total number of automobiles sold by the three manufacturers. Then we construct a simple index for the *total* of the three series. The resulting index is called a **simple composite index**. We illustrate the construction of a simple composite index in Example 14.1.

> **DEFINITION 14.3**
> A **simple composite index** is a simple index for a time series consisting of the total price or total quantity of two or more commodities.

TABLE 14.3   **Monthly Closing Prices of Four High-Technology Company Stocks**

Year	Bell Industries	Xerox	Digital Equipment	IBM	Total
1995					
January	$20.625	$109.375	$33.875	$ 72.125	$236.00
February	20.875	110.875	33.625	75.25	240.625
March	21.25	117.375	37.875	82.125	258.625
April	20.125	123.375	46.125	94.625	284.25
May	19.125	113.375	44.5	93	270.00
June	21.375	117.25	40.75	96	275.375
July	23.25	119.375	38.375	108.875	289.875
August	21.125	120.875	41.75	103.375	287.125
September	21.875	134.375	45.625	94.5	296.375
October	21	129.625	54	97.25	301.875
November	22.75	137.125	58.875	96.625	315.375
December	22.5	137	64.125	91.375	315.00
1996					
January	22.25	123.625	72.625	108.5	327.00
February	21.75	130.25	72.625	122.625	347.25
March	21.375	125.5	55	111.25	313.125
April	22.125	146.5	59.875	107.75	336.25
May	22	157.375	52.125	106.75	338.25
June	16.75	160.5	45.125	99	321.375
July	16.75	151.125	35.625	107.5	311.00
August	16.75	164.625	38.625	114.375	334.375
September	15.5	160.875	35.625	124.5	336.50
October	16.75	139.125	29.5	129	314.375
November	20.25	147	36.625	159.375	363.25
December	21.375	157.875	36.25	151.5	367.00

Source: Standard & Poor's Stock Guide, 1995, 1996.

EXAMPLE 14.1

One of the primary uses of index numbers is to characterize changes in stock prices over time. Stock market indexes have been constructed for many different types of companies and industries, and several composite indexes have been developed to characterize all stocks. These indexes are reported on a daily basis in the news media (e.g., Standard and Poor's 500 Stocks Index and Dow Jones 65 Stocks Index).

Consider the monthly closing prices (i.e., closing prices on the last day of each month) given in Table 14.3 for four high-technology company stocks listed on the New York Stock Exchange between 1995 and 1996. To see how this type of stock fared, construct a simple composite index using January 1995 as the base period. Graph the index, and comment on its implications.

SOLUTION

First, we calculate the total for the four stock prices each month. These totals are shown in the last column of Table 14.3. Then the simple composite index is calculated by dividing each monthly total by the January 1995 total. The index values are given in Table 14.4, and a graph of the simple composite index is shown in Figure 14.2.

The plot of the simple composite index for these high-technology stocks shows a steadily increasing trend over the two-year period. The composite price of these high-technology stocks jumped 55.51% from January 1995 to December 1996. ◣

TABLE 14.4   Simple Composite Index of Stock Prices

1995	Index	1996	Index
Jan.	100.00	Jan.	138.56
Feb.	101.96	Feb.	147.14
Mar.	109.59	Mar.	132.68
Apr.	120.44	Apr.	142.48
May	114.41	May	143.33
June	116.68	June	136.18
July	122.83	July	131.78
Aug.	121.66	Aug.	141.68
Sept.	125.58	Sept.	142.58
Oct.	127.91	Oct.	133.21
Nov.	133.63	Nov.	153.92
Dec.	133.47	Dec.	155.51

FIGURE 14.2

Graph of simple composite index of four stocks

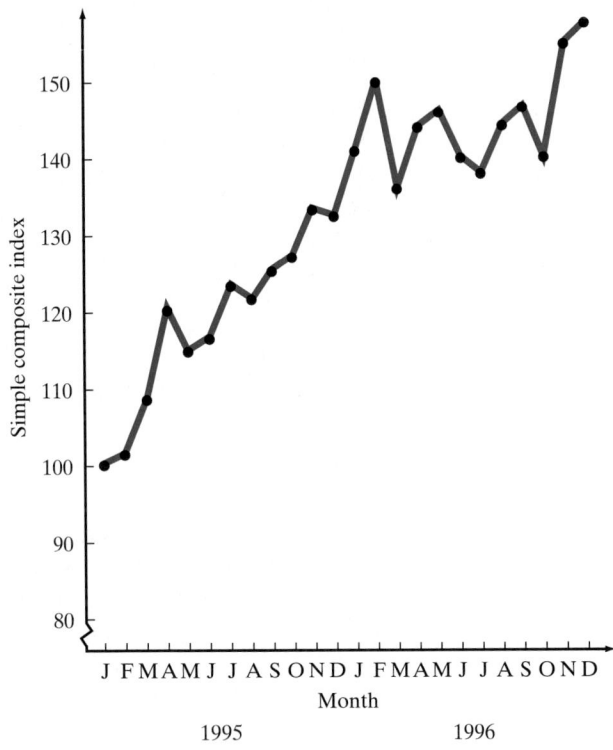

A simple composite price index has a major drawback: The quantity of the commodity that is purchased during each period is not taken into account. Only the price totals are used to calculate the index. We can remedy this situation by constructing a **weighted composite price index**.

DEFINITION 14.4

A **weighted composite price index** weights the prices by quantities purchased prior to calculating totals for each time period. The weighted totals are then used to compute the index in the same way that the unweighted totals are used for simple composite indexes.

Since the quantities purchased change from time period to time period, the choice of which time period's quantities to use as the basis for the weighted composite index is an important one. A **Laspeyres index** uses the base period quantities as weights. The rationale is that the prices at each time period should be compared as if the same quantities were purchased each period as were purchased during the base period. This method measures price inflation (or deflation) by fixing the purchase quantities at their base period values. The method for calculating a Laspeyres index is given in the box.

Steps for Calculating a Laspeyres Index

1. Collect price information for each of the k price series to be used in the composite index. Denote these series by $P_{1t}, P_{2t}, ..., P_{kt}$.

2. Select a base period. Call this time period t_0.

3. Collect purchase quantity information for the base period. Denote the k quantities by $Q_{1t_0}, Q_{2t_0}, ..., Q_{kt_0}$.

4. Calculate the weighted totals for each time period according to the formula

$$\sum_{i=1}^{k} Q_{it_0} P_{it}$$

5. Calculate the Laspeyres index, I_t, at time t by taking the ratio of the weighted total at time t to the base period weighted total and multiplying by 100. That is,

$$I_t = \frac{\sum_{i=1}^{k} Q_{it_0} P_{it}}{\sum_{i=1}^{k} Q_{it_0} P_{it_0}} \times 100$$

EXAMPLE 14.2

The January prices for the four high-technology company stocks are given in Table 14.5. Suppose that, in January 1995, an investor purchased the quantities shown in the table. [*Note:* Only January prices and quantities are used to simplify the example. The same methods can be applied to calculate the index for other months.] Calculate the Laspeyres index for the investor's portfolio of high-technology stocks using January 1995 as the base period.

SOLUTION

First, we calculate the weighted price totals for each time period, using the January 1995 quantities as weights. Thus,

---

TABLE 14.5   **January Prices of High-Technology Stocks with Quantities Purchased**

	Bell Industries	**Xerox**	**Digital Equipment**	**IBM**
Shares purchased	500	100	100	1,000
January 1995 price	20.625	109.375	33.875	72.125
January 1996 price	22.250	123.625	72.625	108.500

$$\text{January 1995 weighted total} = \sum_{i=1}^{4} Q_{i,1995} P_{i,1995}$$

$$= 500(20.625) + 100(109.375) + 100(33.875) \\ + 1,000(72.125)$$

$$= 96{,}762.5$$

$$\text{January 1996 weighted total} = \sum_{i=1}^{4} Q_{i,1995} P_{i,1996}$$

$$= 500(22.25) + 100(123.625) + 100(72.625) \\ + 1,000(108.5)$$

$$= 139{,}250.0$$

Then the Laspeyres index is calculated by multiplying the ratio of each weighted total to the base period weighted total by 100. Thus,

$$I_{1995} = \frac{\displaystyle\sum_{i=1}^{4} Q_{i,1995} P_{i,1995}}{\displaystyle\sum_{i=1}^{4} Q_{i,1995} P_{i,1995}} \times 100 = \frac{96{,}762.5}{96{,}762.5} \times 100 = 100$$

$$I_{1996} = \frac{\displaystyle\sum_{i=1}^{4} Q_{i,1995} P_{i,1996}}{\displaystyle\sum_{i=1}^{4} Q_{i,1995} P_{i,1995}} \times 100 = \frac{139{,}250.0}{96{,}762.5} \times 100 = 143.91$$

The implication is that these stocks were worth 43.91% more to the investor in January 1996 than in January 1995.

The Laspeyres index is appropriate when the base period quantities are reasonable weights to apply to all time periods. This is the case in applications such as that described in Example 14.2, where the base period quantities represent actual quantities of stock purchased and held for some period of time. Laspeyres indexes are also appropriate when the base period quantities remain reasonable approximations of purchase quantities in subsequent periods. However, it can be misleading when the relative purchase quantities change significantly from those in the base period.

Probably the best-known Laspeyres index is the all-items Consumer Price Index (CPI). This monthly composite index is made up of hundreds of item prices, and the U.S. Bureau of Labor Statistics (BLS) sampled over 30,000 families' purchases in 1982–1984 to determine the base period quantities. Thus, beginning in 1987, the all-items CPI published each month reflects quantities purchased in 1982–1984 by a sample of families across the United States. However, as prices increase for some commodities more quickly than for others, consumers tend to substitute less expensive commodities where possible. For example, as automobile and gasoline prices rapidly inflated in the mid-1970s, consumers began to purchase smaller cars. The net effect of using the base period quantities for the CPI is to overestimate the effect of inflation on consumers, because the quantities are fixed at levels that will actually change in response to price changes.

There are several solutions to the problem of purchase quantities that change relative to those of the base period. One is to change the base period regularly, so that the quantities are regularly updated. A second solution is to compute the index at each time period by using the purchase quantities of that period, rather than those of the base period. A **Paasche index** is calculated by using price totals weighted by the purchase quantities of the period the index value represents. The steps for calculating a Paasche index are given in the box.

Steps for Calculating a Paasche Index

1. Collect price information for each of the k price series to be used in the composite index. Denote these series by $P_{1t}, P_{2t}, ..., P_{kt}$.
2. Select a base period. Call this time period t_0.
3. Collect purchase quantity information for every period. Denote the k quantities for period t by $Q_{1t}, Q_{2t}, ..., Q_{kt}$.
4. Calculate the Paasche index for time t by multiplying the ratio of the weighted total at time t to the weighted total at time t_0 (base period) by 100, where the weights used are the purchase quantities for time period t. Thus,

$$I_t = \frac{\sum_{i=1}^{k} Q_{it} P_{it}}{\sum_{i=1}^{k} Q_{it} P_{it_0}} \times 100$$

EXAMPLE 14.3

The January prices and volumes (actual quantities purchased) in thousands of shares for the four high-technology company stocks are shown for 1995 and 1996 in Table 14.6. Calculate and interpret the Paasche index, using January 1995 as the base period.

SOLUTION

The key to calculating a Paasche index is to remember that the weights (purchase quantities) change for each time period. Thus,

$$I_{1995} = \frac{\sum_{i=1}^{4} Q_{i,1995} P_{i,1995}}{\sum_{i=1}^{4} Q_{i,1995} P_{i,1995}} \times 100 = 100$$

TABLE 14.6   January Prices and Volumes of High-Technology Stocks

	BELL INDUSTRIES		XEROX		DIGITAL EQUIPMENT		IBM	
	Price	Volume	Price	Volume	Price	Volume	Price	Volume
January 1995	20.625	261.9	109.375	8,723.8	33.875	24,206.0	72.125	52,484.7
January 1996	22.250	255.8	123.625	17,181.1	72.625	41,213.7	108.500	108,950.0

Source: NYSE *Daily Stock Price Record,* Jan. 1995, 1996.

$$I_{1996} = \frac{\sum_{i=1}^{4} Q_{i,1996} P_{i,1996}}{\sum_{i=1}^{4} Q_{i,1996} P_{i,1995}} \times 100$$

$$= \frac{(255.8)(22.25) + \cdots + (108{,}950.0)(108.5)}{(255.8)(20.625) + \cdots + (108{,}950.0)(72.125)}$$

$$= 152.12$$

The implication is that 1996 prices represent a 52.12% increase over 1995 prices, assuming the purchase quantities were at January 1996 levels for *both* periods.

The Paasche index is most appropriate when you want to compare current prices to base period prices at *current* purchase levels. However, there are several major problems associated with the Paasche index. First, it requires that purchase quantities be known for every time period. This rules out a Paasche index for applications such as the CPI because the time and monetary resource expenditures required to collect quantity information are considerable. (Recall that more than 30,000 families were sampled to estimate purchase quantities in 1982–1984.) A second problem is that although each period is compared to the base period, it is difficult to compare the index at two other periods because the quantities used are different for each period. Consequently, the change in the index is affected by changes in both prices *and* quantities. This fact makes it difficult to interpret the change in a Paasche index between periods when neither is the base period.

Although there are other types of indexes that use different weighting factors, the Laspeyres and Paasche indexes are the most popular composite indexes. Depending on the primary objective in constructing an index, one of them will probably be suitable for most purposes.

FIGURE 14.3

Changes in the Consumer Price Index for all urban consumers: Official (CPI-U) and experimental rental equivalence (CPI-U-X1) measures (Statistics in Action 14.1)

STATISTICS IN ACTION

14.1 THE CONSUMER PRICE INDEX: CPI-U AND CPI-W

The Consumer Price Index (CPI), first published by the U.S. Bureau of Labor Statistics (BLS) in 1919, is the country's principal measure of price changes. One major use of the CPI is as an indicator of inflation, through which the success or failure of government economic policies can be monitored. A second major use of the CPI is to escalate income payments. Millions of workers have escalator clauses in their collective bargaining contracts that call for increases in wage rates based on increases in the CPI. In addition, the incomes of Social Security beneficiaries and retired military and federal civil service employees are tied to the CPI. It has been estimated that a 1% increase in the CPI can trigger an increase of over $1 billion in income payments.

Since 1978, the BLS has published two national, all-items indexes: the new CPI-U and the traditional CPI-W. The CPI-U measures the price change of a constant market basket of goods and services that are representative of the purchases of all urban residents—approximately 80% of the U.S. population. The CPI-W measures the price change of a constant market basket of goods and services that is representative of the purchases of urban wage earners and clerical workers—approximately 50% of all urban residents. Until 1988 the base period for both indexes was 1967. Then the base period was shifted to 1982–1984 to coincide with the updating of the base period quantities. The CPI-U is the index typically reported by the press and broadcast media. The CPI-W is the index used in the escalator clauses of most labor contracts and government benefit programs. In addition to these two national indexes, the BLS publishes CPI-U and CPI-W indexes for each of 27 metropolitan areas. The national indexes and the metropolitan indexes are reported monthly in the BLS's *CPI Detailed Report.*

The market basket of goods priced by both the CPI-U and the CPI-W includes a homeownership component. Accounting for over 30% of the overall weight of the indexes, the homeownership component influences the indexes more than food, energy, or medical care. This component includes the costs associated with purchasing a home (the price of the home and mortgage interest), as well as the cost of property taxes, property insurance, and maintenance and repairs. During the 1970s and early 1980s, the use of these quantities to measure the cost of homeownership met with much criticism. Two arguments were made by critics (U.S. Department of Labor, 1980, p. 2):

1. Since the CPI is used to measure the change in purchasing power for the purpose of escalating income or determining the rate of inflation, it "should not include the impact of rising prices on the value of assets such as houses. Just as the CPI excludes changes in the value of stocks and bonds, ... the change in the asset value of the house (appreciation or depreciation) and the cost of equity in holding that asset should be distinguished from the change in the cost of the shelter provided by the house. It is the cost of consuming the shelter provided by the house—not the investment aspects of homeownership—which should be reflected in an index used to keep real income constant."

2. The CPI overstates the rate of inflation because "it uses *current* house prices and *current* mortgage interest rates.... The CPI should not measure the costs of purchasing the base period houses in today's prices and today's mortgage interest rates, but rather the CPI should measure what people are actually paying for housing."

In response to these criticisms, the BLS developed and experimented with an entirely new approach to measuring the cost of housing. As a result, instead of explicitly including in the market basket the homeownership costs described above, the BLS now recommends that a *rental equivalency* component be included. This approach assumes that a household's cost of consuming the flow of services from the housing unit can be represented by the income that the household could receive by renting the home to someone else. This rental equivalency approach to measuring homeownership costs was implemented in an experimental version of the CPI-U called the CPI-U-X1.

Figure 14.3 shows the movement that the CPI-U and CPI-U-X1 would have displayed over the period 1970–1981. [*Note:* Percentage changes are calculated using 12 months of unadjusted data. See Gillingham

continued

and Lane (1982, p. 13).] Notice that the two indexes generally move together, but that the CPI-U-X1 tends to stay below the CPI-U, particularly during the periods of high mortgage interest rates in 1970, 1974–1975, and 1978–1981. If, as some critics charge, the CPI-U overstates inflation during periods of high mortgage interest rates, it appears that the experimental CPI-U-X1 would provide a better measure of inflation. In January 1983, the BLS changed the official CPI-U to include the rental equivalency approach to measuring homeownership costs and it made a similar change in the CPI-W in 1985.

Focus

In 1996, a commission appointed by Congress to study the Consumer Price Index concluded that the CPI overstated inflation by 1.1%. Among their concerns were the following (Nease, J., "CPI fails to recognize changes in buying patterns," *Newark-Star Ledger,* Dec. 22, 1996).

- The index is slow to discover when shoppers switch from, say, beef to chicken.
- The index does not capture the sharp decreases in new product prices that often occur with the advent of increased competition and/or technological innovation. For example, VCRs cost about $1,000 when they were first introduced. But by the time this price was included in the index, actual prices had fallen to $300.
- The index does not reflect product improvement. For example, a personal computer that cost $2,000 today is significantly better than one that cost three or four times as much a decade ago.

a. In each of the above three cases, explain why the index does not capture the noted effect.

b. In each case, indicate whether the effect tends to cause the CPI to overstate or understate inflation. Justify your answers.

EXERCISES 14.1–14.14

Note: Exercises marked with 💾 contain data for computer analysis on a 3.5" disk (file name in parentheses).

Learning the Mechanics

14.1 Explain in words how to construct a simple index.

14.2 Explain in words how to calculate the following types of indexes:
a. Simple composite index
b. Weighted composite index
c. Laspeyres index
d. Paasche index

14.3 Explain in words the difference between Laspeyres and Paasche indexes.

14.4 The table below lists the U.S. median annual family income during the period 1975–1993. It also contains several values for each of two simple indexes for median family income. Calculate the missing values of each simple index.

14.5 (X14.005) The first table on page 745 describes U.S. beer production (in millions of barrels) for the period 1970–1994.
a. Use 1977 as the base period to compute the simple index for this time series.
b. Refer to part a. Is this an example of a quantity index or a price index?
c. Recompute the simple index using 1980 as the base period. Plot the two indexes on the same graph.

Year	Income ($)	Base 1975 Index	Base 1980 Index
1975	13,719	—	65.26
1976	14,958	109.03	—
1977	16,009	116.69	—
1978	17,640	—	—
1979	19,587	—	93.17
1980	21,023	153.24	—
1981	22,388	—	—
1982	23,433	—	111.46
1983	24,580	—	—
1984	26,433	192.67	—

Year	Income ($)	Base 1975 Index	Base 1980 Index
1985	27,735	202.16	—
1986	29,458	—	140.12
1987	30,970	—	147.31
1988	32,191	—	153.12
1989	34,213	249.38	—
1990	35,353	257.69	—
1991	35,939	—	—
1992	36,812	—	—
1993	36,959	—	—

Source: U.S. Bureau of the Census. Statistical Abstract of the United States, 1995.

Year	Beer	Year	Beer	Year	Beer
1970	133	1979	184	1988	197
1971	137	1980	194	1989	198
1972	141	1981	194	1990	202
1973	149	1982	196	1991	204
1974	156	1983	195	1992	202
1975	161	1984	192	1993	202
1976	164	1985	194	1994	203
1977	171	1986	194		
1978	179	1987	196		

Source: U.S. Bureau of the Census. *Statistical Abstract of the United States, 1992, 1996.*

14.6 Using 1983 as the base, compute and plot the simple composite index for the volume of futures trading (in millions of contracts) for the commodities listed in the table.

Year	Grain	Energy Products	Currencies
1983	17.8	3.2	11.4
1984	15.9	4.9	16.7
1985	10.7	7.0	16.4
1986	10.3	11.5	19.1
1987	10.9	20.3	19.9
1988	15.9	26.3	21.2
1989	15.9	31.3	25.7
1990	17.0	35.2	27.2
1991	16.6	31.8	28.8
1992	17.6	38.4	38.7
1993	16.0	42.8	28.8
1994	20.0	50.5	30.4

Source: U.S. Bureau of the Census. *Statistical Abstract of the United States, 1995.*

Applying the Concepts

14.7 (X14.007) The stock of Abbott Laboratories had the yearly closing prices shown in the table.

Year	Closing Price	Year	Closing Price
1980	$56.500	1988	$48.010
1981	27.000	1989	64.030
1982	38.750	1990	45.000
1983	45.250	1991	68.070
1984	41.750	1992	30.030
1985	68.375	1993	29.050
1986	45.625	1994	32.050
1987	48.020	1995	41.050

Sources: NYSE. *Daily Stock Price Record,* 1980–1996; Standard & Poor's. *Security Owner's Stock Guide,* Jan. 1996.

a. Using 1980 as the base period, calculate the simple index for this stock's yearly closing price between 1980 and 1995.

b. By what percentage did the stock price increase or decrease between 1980 and 1989? Between 1991 and 1995?

14.8 The table lists the price of natural gas (in dollars per 1,000 cubic feet) between 1982 and 1993.

Year	Price	Year	Price
1982	$2.46	1988	$1.69
1983	2.59	1989	1.69
1984	2.66	1990	1.71
1985	2.51	1991	1.64
1986	1.94	1992	1.74
1987	1.67	1993	1.97

Source: U.S. Bureau of the Census. *Statistical Abstract of the United States, 1994.*

a. Using 1982 as the base period, calculate and plot the simple index for the price of natural gas from 1982 through 1993.

b. Use the simple index to interpret the trend in the price of natural gas.

c. Is the index you constructed in part **a** a price or quantity index? Explain.

14.9 Civilian employment is broadly classified by the federal government into two categories—agricultural and nonagricultural. Employment figures (in thousands of workers) for farm and nonfarm categories for the years 1980–1994 are given in the table.

Year	Farm	Nonfarm	Year	Farm	Nonfarm
1980	3,364	95,938	1988	3,169	111,800
1981	3,368	97,030	1989	3,199	114,142
1982	3,401	96,125	1990	3,186	114,728
1983	3,383	97,450	1991	3,233	113,644
1984	3,321	101,685	1992	3,207	114,391
1985	3,179	103,971	1993	3,074	116,232
1986	3,163	106,434	1994	3,409	119,651
1987	3,208	109,232			

Source: U.S. Bureau of the Census. *Statistical Abstract of the United States, 1995.*

a. Compute simple indexes for each of the two time series using 1980 as the base period.

b. Which segment has shown the greater percentage change in employment over the period shown?

c. Compute a simple composite index for total employment for the years 1980–1994. Use 1980 as a base period.

d. Refer to part **c**. Interpret the composite index value for 1990.

14.10 (X14.010) The Gross Domestic Product (GDP) is the total national output of goods and services valued at market prices. As such, the GDP is a commonly used barometer of the U.S. economy. One component of the GDP is personal consumption expenditures, which is itself the sum of expenditures for durable goods, nondurable goods, and services. The GDP for these components (in billions of dollars) is shown in the table, in five-year increments from 1960 to 1980 and annually from 1980 to 1994.

Year	Durables	Nondurables	Services
1960	$ 43.5	$ 153.1	$ 135.9
1965	63.5	191.9	189.2
1970	85.3	270.4	290.8
1975	134.3	416.0	474.5
1980	212.5	682.9	852.7
1981	228.5	744.2	953.5
1982	236.5	772.3	1,050.4
1983	275.0	817.8	1,164.7
1984	317.9	873.0	1,269.4
1985	352.9	919.4	1,395.1
1986	389.6	952.2	1,508.8
1987	403.7	1,011.1	1,637.4
1988	437.1	1,073.8	1,785.2
1989	459.4	1,149.5	1,914.2
1990	468.2	1,229.2	2,063.8
1991	456.6	1,257.8	2,188.1
1992	492.7	1,295.5	2,348.7
1993	538.0	1,339.2	2,501.0
1994	591.5	1,394.3	2,642.7

Source: U.S. Bureau of the Census. *Statistical Abstract of the United States, 1995.*

a. Using these three component values, construct a simple composite index for the personal consumption component of GDP. Use 1970 as the base year.

b. Suppose we want to update the index by using 1980 as the base year. Update the index using only the index values you calculated in part a, without referring to the original data.

c. Graph the personal consumption expenditure index for the years 1960–1994 (remember that the data are in five-year increments through 1980 and annual thereafter), first using 1970 as the base year and then using 1980 as the base year. What effect does changing the base year have on the graph of this index?

14.11 Refer to Exercise 14.10. Suppose the output quantities in 1970, measured in billions of units purchased, are as follows:

Durable goods: 10.9

Nondurable goods: 14.02

Services: 42.6

a. Use the outputs to calculate the Laspeyres index from 1960 to 1994 (same increments as in Exercise 14.10) with 1970 as the base period.

b. Plot the simple composite index of Exercise 14.10 and Laspeyres index of part a on the same graph. Comment on the differences between the two indexes.

14.12 (X14.012) The level of price and production of metals in the United States is one measure of the strength of the industrial economy. The table below lists the 1994 prices (in dollars per ton) and production (in tons) for three metals important to U.S. industry.

a. Compute simple composite price and quantity indexes for the 12-month period, using January as the base period.

b. Compute the Laspeyres price index for the 12-month period, using January as the base period.

c. Plot the simple composite and Laspeyres indexes on the same graph. Comment on the differences.

d. Compute the Paasche price index for metals for the 12-month period, using January as the base period.

e. Plot the Laspeyres and Paasche indexes on the same graph. Comment on the differences.

f. Compare the Laspeyres and Paasche index values for September and December. Which index is more appropriate for describing the change in this four-month period? Explain.

	COPPER		PIG IRON		LEAD	
Month	Price	Production	Price	Production	Price	Production
Jan.	1,913.0	160.9	138.00	8,003	680.0	27.6
Feb.	1,982.6	150.0	138.00	7,598	680.0	28.8
Mar.	2,035.2	167.8	138.00	8,323	680.0	33.0
Apr.	1,997.4	157.2	138.00	8,180	680.0	31.3
May	2,246.0	165.5	123.64	8,437	680.0	32.4
June	2,411.6	160.4	110.50	7,941	714.6	29.1
July	2,473.6	148.9	117.20	7,996	754.0	29.4
Aug.	2,427.6	165.6	133.63	8,053	760.0	30.4
Sept.	2,650.6	162.1	134.50	7,993	800.0	31.2
Oct.	2,618.2	157.3	132.50	8,477	840.0	28.0
Nov.	2,838.4	153.3	137.50	8,256	874.0	31.7
Dec.	2,977.2	159.8	141.50	8,684	880.0	29.9

Source: The CRB Commodity Yearbook 1996. New York: John Wiley & Sons, Inc., 1996.

	GAS		ELECTRICITY	
Year	Price (million Btu)	Sales (trillion Btu)	Average Price (cents per kWh)	Sales (billion kWh)
1988	5.29	4,695	7.5	893
1989	5.45	4,798	7.6	906
1990	5.60	4,468	7.8	924
1991	5.66	4,550	8.0	955
1992	5.69	4,694	8.2	936
1993	5.87	5,097	8.3	999

Source: U.S. Bureau of the Census. *Statistical Abstract of the U.S., 1995,* pp. 600, 608.

14.13 The table above presents yearly price and quantity data on residential gas and electricity sales in the United States from 1988 through 1993.
  a. Compute the Laspeyres price index for these two residential energy products, using 1988 as the base year.
  b. Compute the Paasche price index for these data.
  c. Plot the Laspeyres and Paasche indexes on the same graph. Comment on the similarities and differences.
  d. Interpret the 1993 value of each index.

14.14 **(X14.014)** The table below presents the average hourly earnings and the average number of hours worked per week for each year from 1965 to 1995

	MANUFACTURING		TRANSPORTATION AND PUBLIC UTILITIES		WHOLESALE TRADE	
Year	Hourly Earnings	Weekly Hours	Hourly Earnings	Weekly Hours	Hourly Earnings	Weekly Hours
1965	2.61	41.2	3.03	41.3	2.60	40.8
1966	2.71	41.4	3.11	41.2	2.73	40.7
1967	2.82	40.6	3.23	40.5	2.87	40.3
1968	3.01	40.7	3.42	40.6	3.04	40.1
1969	3.19	40.6	3.63	40.7	3.23	40.2
1970	3.35	39.8	3.85	40.5	3.43	39.9
1971	3.57	39.9	4.21	40.1	3.64	39.4
1972	3.82	40.5	4.65	40.4	3.85	39.4
1973	4.09	40.7	5.02	40.5	4.07	39.2
1974	4.42	40.0	5.41	40.2	4.38	38.8
1975	4.83	39.5	5.88	39.7	4.72	38.6
1976	5.22	40.1	6.45	39.8	5.02	38.7
1977	5.68	40.3	6.99	39.9	5.39	38.8
1978	6.17	40.4	7.57	40.0	5.88	38.8
1979	6.70	40.2	8.16	39.9	6.39	38.8
1980	7.27	39.7	8.87	39.6	6.95	38.4
1981	7.99	39.8	9.70	39.4	7.55	38.5
1982	8.49	38.9	10.32	39.0	8.08	38.3
1983	8.83	40.1	10.79	39.0	8.54	38.5
1984	9.19	40.7	11.12	39.4	8.88	38.5
1985	9.54	40.5	11.40	39.5	9.15	38.4
1986	9.73	40.7	11.70	39.2	9.34	38.3
1987	9.91	41.0	12.03	39.2	9.59	38.1
1988	10.19	41.1	12.26	38.8	9.98	38.1
1989	10.48	41.0	12.60	38.9	10.39	38.0
1990	10.83	40.8	12.97	38.9	10.79	38.1
1991	11.18	40.7	13.22	38.7	11.15	38.1
1992	11.46	41.0	13.45	38.9	11.39	38.2
1993	11.74	41.4	13.62	39.6	11.74	38.2
1994	12.07	42.0	13.86	39.9	12.06	38.4
1995	12.37	41.6	14.23	39.5	12.43	38.3

Source: U.S. Department of Labor, Bureau of Labor Statistics. *Employment and Earnings,* Nov. 1996.

for nonsupervisory workers in three different industries.

a. Compute a simple index for average hourly earnings for manufacturing workers over the period 1965-1995. Use 1965 as the base year. Do the same for transportation and public utilities workers.

b. Plot the two simple indexes on the same graph and interpret the results.

c. Compute simple composite indexes for hourly earnings and weekly hours for the 31-year period. Use 1965 as the base year.

d. Plot the two composite indexes, part c, on the same graph and interpret the results.

14.2   DESCRIPTIVE ANALYSIS: EXPONENTIAL SMOOTHING

As you have seen in the previous section, index numbers are useful for describing trends and changes in time series. However, time series often have such irregular fluctuations that trends are difficult to describe. Index numbers can be misleading in such cases because the series is changing so rapidly. Methods for removing the rapid fluctuations in a time series so the general trend can be seen are called **smoothing** techniques.

Exponential smoothing is one type of weighted average that assigns positive weights to past and current values of the time series. A single weight, w, called the **exponential smoothing constant**, is selected so that w is between 0 and 1. Then the exponentially smoothed series, E_t, is calculated as follows:

$$E_1 = Y_1$$
$$E_2 = wY_2 + (1 - w)E_1$$
$$E_3 = wY_3 + (1 - w)E_2$$
$$\vdots$$
$$E_t = wY_t + (1 - w)E_{t-1}$$

Thus, the exponentially smoothed value at time t assigns the weight w to the current series value and the weight $(1 - w)$ to the previous smoothed value.

For example, consider the Dow Jones Industrial Average (DJIA) time series for 1970–1996 in Table 14.7.

TABLE 14.7   **Dow Jones Industrial Average (1970–1996) with Exponential Smoothing (w = .3)**

Year	DJIA	Exponentially Smoothed DJIA	Year	DJIA	Exponentially Smoothed DJIA
1970	838.92	838.92	1984	1,211.57	1,083.14
1971	884.76	852.67	1985	1,546.67	1,222.20
1972	950.71	882.08	1986	1,895.95	1,424.32
1973	923.88	894.62	1987	1,938.83	1,578.67
1974	759.37	854.05	1988	2,168.57	1,755.64
1975	802.49	838.58	1989	2,753.20	2,054.91
1976	974.92	879.48	1990	2,633.66	2,228.53
1977	835.15	866.18	1991	3,168.83	2,510.62
1978	805.01	847.83	1992	3,330.11	2,756.47
1979	838.74	845.10	1993	3,754.09	3,055.76
1980	963.99	880.77	1994	3,834.44	3,289.36
1981	875.00	879.04	1995	5,117.12	3,837.69
1982	1,046.54	929.29	1996	6,448.27	4,620.86
1983	1,258.64	1,028.09			

Sources: The Dow Jones Investor's Handbook, 1996; The Wall Street Journal, Jan. 2, 1997.

FIGURE 14.4
Exponentially
smoothed values
($w = .3$) for the DJIA

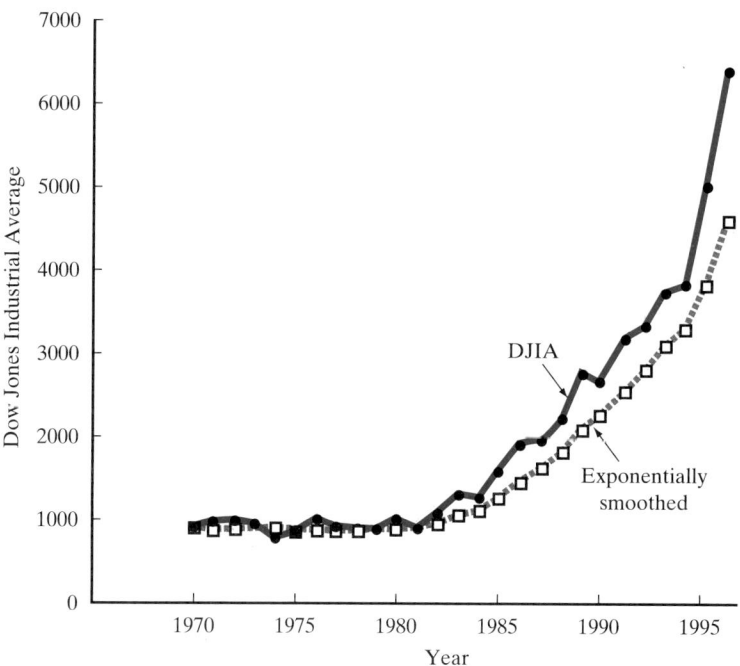

Suppose we want to calculate the exponentially smoothed series using a smoothing constant of $w = .3$. The calculations proceed as follows:

$$E_{1970} = Y_{1970} = 838.92$$

$$E_{1971} = .3Y_{1971} + (1 - .3)E_{1970} = .3(884.76) + .7(838.92) = 852.67$$

$$E_{1972} = .3Y_{1972} + (1 - .3)E_{1971} = .3(950.71) + .7(852.67) = 882.08$$
$$\vdots$$

All the exponentially smoothed values corresponding to $w = .3$ are given in Table 14.7.

The DJIA and exponentially smoothed DJIA are graphed in Figure 14.4. Like many averages, the exponentially smoothed series changes less rapidly than the time series itself. The choice of w affects the smoothness of E_t. The smaller (closer to 0) is the value of w, the smoother is E_t. Since small values of w give more weight to the past values of the time series, the smoothed series is not affected by rapid changes in the current values and, therefore, appears smoother than the original series. Conversely, choosing w near 1 yields an exponentially smoothed series that is much like the original series. That is, large values of w give more weight to the current value of the time series so the smoothed series looks like the original series. This concept is illustrated in Figure 14.5. The steps for calculating an exponentially smoothed series are given in the box.

Steps for Calculating an Exponentially Smoothed Series
1. Select an exponential smoothing constant, w, between 0 and 1. Remember that small values of w give less weight to the current value of the series and yield a smoother series. Larger choices of w assign more weight to the current value of the series and yield a more variable series.

continued

FIGURE 14.5
Exponentially smoothed values ($w = .3$ and $w = .7$) for the DJIA

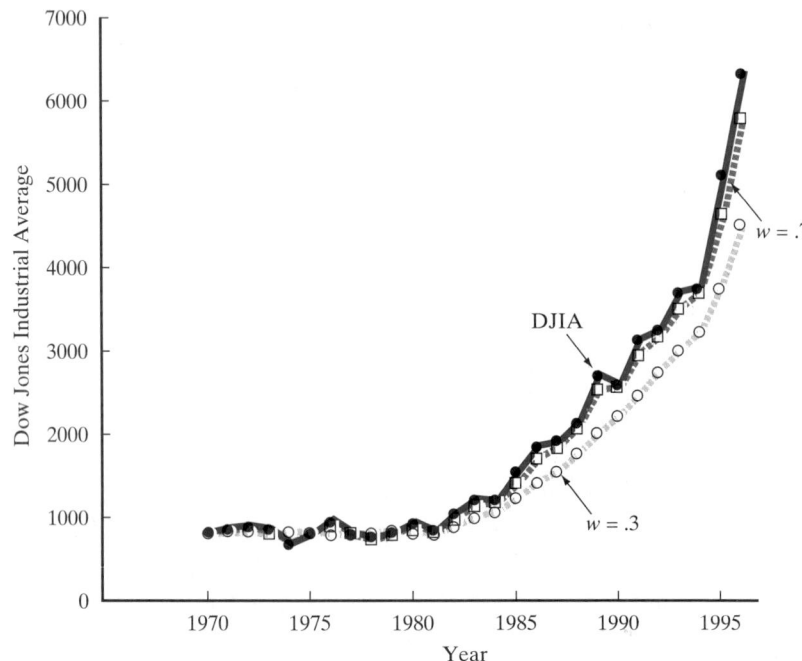

2. Calculate the exponentially smoothed series E_t from the original time series Y_t as follows:

$$E_1 = Y_1$$

$$E_2 = wY_2 + (1 - w)E_1$$

$$E_3 = wY_3 + (1 - w)E_2$$

$$\vdots$$

$$E_t = wY_t + (1 - w)E_{t-1}$$

EXAMPLE 14.4

Consider the IBM common stock price from January 1994 to December 1996, shown in Table 14.8. Create the exponentially smoothed series using $w = .5$, and plot both series.

SOLUTION

To create the exponentially smoothed series with $w = .5$, we calculate

$$E_1 = Y_1 = 56.5$$

$$E_2 = wY_2 + (1 - w)E_1 = .5(52.875) + .5(56.5) = 54.688$$

$$\vdots$$

$$E_{36} = wY_{36} + (1 - w)E_{35} = .5(151.500) + .5(141.246) = 146.373$$

The plot of the original and exponentially smoothed series is shown in Figure 14.6.

The smoothed series provides a good picture of the general trend of the original series. Note, too, that the exponentially smoothed series will be less

TABLE 14.8   IBM Stock Prices and Exponentially Smoothed Series ($w = .5$)

	IBM	Smoothed		IBM	Smoothed		IBM	Smoothed
1994			**1995**			**1996**		
January	56.500	56.500	January	72.125	72.129	January	108.500	101.394
February	52.875	54.688	February	75.250	73.690	February	122.625	112.010
March	54.625	54.656	March	82.125	77.907	March	111.250	111.630
April	57.500	56.078	April	94.625	86.266	April	107.750	109.690
May	63.000	59.539	May	93.000	89.633	May	106.750	108.220
June	58.750	59.145	June	96.000	92.817	June	99.000	103.610
July	61.875	60.510	July	108.875	100.846	July	107.500	105.555
August	68.500	64.505	August	103.375	102.110	August	114.375	109.965
September	69.625	67.065	September	94.500	98.305	September	124.500	117.232
October	74.500	70.782	October	97.250	97.778	October	129.000	123.116
November	70.750	70.766	November	96.625	97.201	November	159.375	141.246
December	73.500	72.133	December	91.375	94.288	December	151.500	146.373

Sources: Standard and Poor's Stock Guide, 1995, 1996; Dow Jones News/Retrieval Database, 1997.

sensitive to any short-term deviations of the prices from the trend as occurred in 1996.

One of the primary uses of exponential smoothing is to forecast future values of a time series. Because only current and past values of the time series are used in exponential smoothing, it is easily adapted to forecasting. We demonstrate this application of exponentially smoothed series in Section 14.4.

FIGURE 14.6
IBM stock price and exponentially smoothed price ($w = .5$)

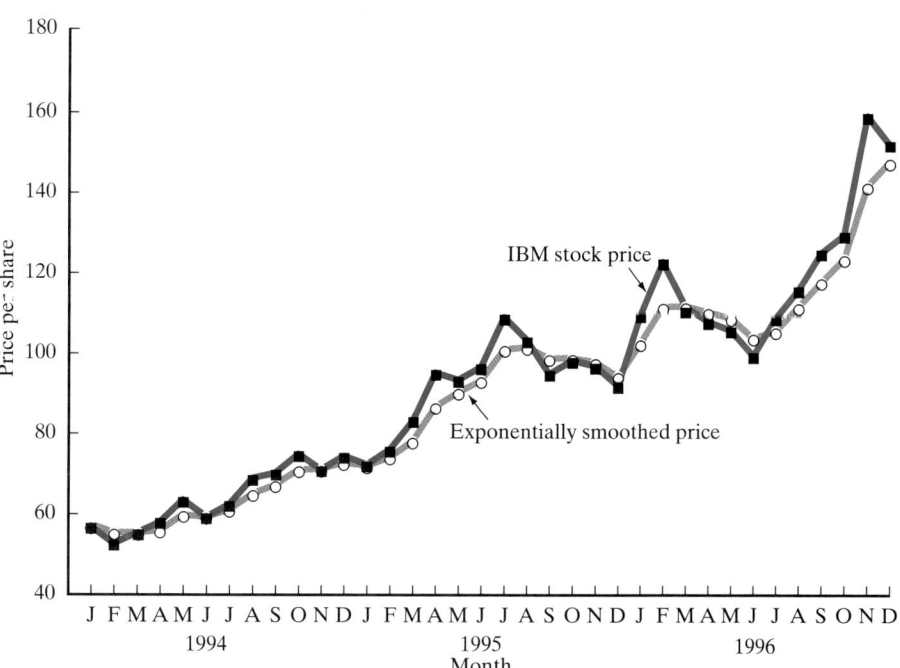

Note: Exercises marked with 💾 *contain data for computer analysis on a 3.5" disk (file name in parentheses).*

Learning the Mechanics

14.15 Describe the effect of selecting an exponential constant of $w = .2$. Of $w = .8$. Which will produce a smoother trend?

14.16 The table lists the number (in thousands) of people employed by the motor vehicle industry, one of the largest segments within the U.S. economy, for the years 1986–1996.

Year	Total Employment (thousands)	Exponentially Smoothed Series $w = .5$
1986	280.5	—
1987	281.3	—
1988	250.3	265.6
1989	246.6	256.1
1990	239.8	—
1991	218.1	—
1992	218.7	—
1993	210.0	—
1994	205.0	—
1995	206.6	—
1996	200.4	—

Source: Sawinski, D. M., ed. U.S. Industry Profiles: The Leading 100. Detroit, Mich: Gale Research Inc., 1995.

a. Calculate the missing values in the exponentially smoothed series using $w = .5$.
b. Graph the time series and the exponentially smoothed series on the same graph.

14.17 Refer to Exercise 14.5.
a. Calculate the exponentially smoothed series for U.S. beer production for the period 1970–1994 using $w = .2$.
b. Calculate the exponentially smoothed series using $w = .8$.
c. Plot the two exponentially smoothed series ($w = .2$ and $w = .8$) on the same graph.

Applying the Concepts

14.18 Overfishing and pollution of U.S. coastal waters have resulted in an increased dependence by the United States on the fishing grounds of other countries. The next table describes the annual fish catch (in thousands of metric tons) in all fishing areas of Brazil and Chile from 1983 to 1992.
a. Compute an exponentially smoothed series for both Chile and Brazil, using a smoothing coefficient of $w = .5$.
b. Plot both actual series and both smoothed series on the same graph. Describe the differences in variation of catches over time between

Year	Chile	Brazil
1983	3,977.0	880.9
1984	4,499.3	960.6
1985	4,804.4	967.6
1986	5,571.6	957.6
1987	4,814.6	948.0
1988	5,209.9	830.1
1989	6,454.2	850.0
1990	5,195.4	802.9
1991	6,002.8	800.0
1992	6,501.8	790.0

Source: Statistical Division, Department of Economics and Social Information and Policy Analysis, United Nations. Statistical Yearbook, 40th Issue, 1995.

the two countries. For example, do they move up and down together over time?

14.19 (X14.019) The price of gold is used by some financial analysts as a barometer of investors' expectations of inflation, with the price of gold tending to increase as concerns about inflation increase. The following table shows the average annual price of gold (in dollars per ounce) from 1975 through 1995.

Year	Price	Year	Price	Year	Price
1975	$161	1982	$376	1989	$383
1976	125	1983	424	1990	385
1977	148	1984	361	1991	363
1978	194	1985	318	1992	345
1979	308	1986	368	1993	361
1980	613	1987	448	1994	387
1981	460	1988	438	1995	385

Sources: U.S. Bureau of the Census. Statistical Abstract of the United States, 1995; Standard & Poor's Current Statistics, Aug. 1996.

a. Compute an exponentially smoothed series for the gold price time series for the period from 1975 to 1995, using a smoothing coefficient of $w = .8$.
b. Plot the original series and the exponentially smoothed series on the same graph.

14.20 (X14.020) There has been phenomenal growth in the transportation sector of the economy since 1970. The personal consumption expenditure figures (in billions of dollars) are given in the next table.
a. Compute exponentially smoothed values of this personal consumption time series, using the smoothing constants $w = .2$ and $w = .8$.
b. Plot the actual series and the two smoothed series on the same graph. Comment on the

Year	Expenditure on Transportation	Year	Expenditure on Transportation
1970	$ 80.6	1982	$267.3
1971	92.3	1983	291.9
1972	105.4	1984	319.5
1973	114.6	1985	359.5
1974	117.9	1986	366.3
1975	129.4	1987	377.1
1976	155.2	1988	406.4
1977	179.3	1989	425.7
1978	198.1	1990	453.7
1979	219.4	1991	438.2
1980	236.6	1992	466.3
1981	261.5	1993	504.2

Source: U.S. Bureau of the Census. *Statistical Abstract of the United States, 1995.*

Year	Imports and Exports
1984	2,212
1985	1,835
1986	2,909
1987	3,512
1988	3,348
1989	2,749
1990	3,470
1991	4,195
1992	4,860
1993	4,901

Source: Department of Economics and Social Information and Policy Analysis, United Nations. *Statistical Yearbook,* 40th issue, 1995.

trend in personal consumption expenditure on transportation in the 1980s and early 1990s as compared to the 1970s.

14.21   The total value of Peru's imports and exports each year from 1984 through 1993 are shown in the next table in millions of U.S. dollars.

a. Construct two exponentially smoothed series for this time series, using $w = .1$ and $w = .9$.

b. Plot the original series and the two smoothed series on the same graph. Which smoothed series looks more like the original series? Why?

14.3   TIME SERIES COMPONENTS

In the previous two sections we showed how to use various *descriptive* techniques to obtain a picture of the behavior of a time series. Now we want to expand our coverage to include techniques that will let us make statistical inferences about the time series. These *inferential techniques* are generally focused on the problem of *forecasting* future values of the time series.

Before forecasts of future values of a time series can be made, some type of model that can be projected into the future must be used to describe the series. Time series models range in complexity from **descriptive models**, such as the exponential smoothing models discussed in the previous section, to **inferential models**, such as the combinations of regression and specialized time series models to be discussed later in this chapter. Whether the model is simple or complex, the objective is the same: to produce accurate forecasts of future values of the time series.

Many different algebraic representations of time series models have been proposed. One of the most widely used is an **additive model*** of the form

$$Y_t = T_t + C_t + S_t + R_t$$

The **secular trend**, T_t, also known as the **long-term trend**, is a time series component that describes the long-term movements of Y_t. For example, if you want to characterize the secular trend of the production of automobiles since 1930, you would show T_t as an upward-moving time series over the period from 1930 to the present. This does not imply that the automobile production series has always moved upward from month to month and from year to year, but it does mean the long-term trend has been an increase over that period of time.

---

*Another useful form is the *multiplicative model:* $Y_t = T_t C_t S_t R_t$. This can be changed to an additive form by taking natural logarithms—i.e., $\ln Y_t = \ln T_t + \ln C_t + \ln S_t + \ln R_t$. See Section 14.8.

The **cyclical effect**, C_t, generally describes fluctuations of the time series about the secular trend that are attributable to business and economic conditions. For example, refer back to the Dow Jones Industrial Average (DJIA) time series for the years 1970–1996, Table 14.7. Recall that a plot of the time series (Figure 14.4) showed a generally increasing secular trend. However, during periods of recession, the DJIA tends to lie below the secular trend, while in times of general economic expansion, it lies above the long-term trend line.

The **seasonal effect**, S_t, describes the fluctuations in the time series that recur during specific time periods. For example, quarterly power loads for a utility company tend to be highest in the summer months (quarter III), with another smaller peak in the winter months (quarter I). The spring and fall (quarters II and IV) seasonal effects are negative, meaning that the series tends to lie below the long-term trend line during those quarters.

The **residual effect**, R_t, is what remains of Y_t after the secular, cyclical, and seasonal components have been removed. Part of the residual effect may be attributable to unpredictable rare events (earthquake, presidential assassination, etc.) and part to the randomness of human actions. In any case, the presence of the residual component makes it impossible to forecast the future values of a time series without error. Thus, the presence of the residual effect emphasizes a point we first made in Chapter 10 in connection with regression models: No business phenomena should be described by deterministic models. All realistic business models, time series or otherwise, should include a residual component.

Each of the four components contributes to the determination of the value of Y_t at each time period. Although it will not always be possible to characterize each component separately, the component model provides a useful theoretical formulation that helps the time series analyst achieve a better understanding of the phenomena affecting the path followed by the time series.

14.4 FORECASTING: EXPONENTIAL SMOOTHING

In Section 14.2, we discussed exponential smoothing as a method for describing a time series that involved removing the irregular fluctuations. In terms of the time series components discussed in the previous section, exponential smoothing tends to de-emphasize (or "smooth") most of the residual effects. This, coupled with the fact that exponential smoothing uses only past and current values of the series, makes it a useful tool for forecasting time series.

Recall that the formula for exponential smoothing is

$$E_t = wY_t + (1 - w)E_{t-1}$$

where w, the **exponential smoothing constant**, is a number between 0 and 1. We learned that the selection of w controls the smoothness of E_t. A choice near 0 places more emphasis (weight) on *past* values of the time series, and therefore yields a smoother series; a choice near 1 gives more weight to *current* values of the series.

Suppose the objective is to forecast the next value of the time series, Y_{t+1}. The **exponentially smoothed forecast** for Y_{t+1} is simply the smoothed value at time t:

$$F_{t+1} = E_t$$

where F_{t+1} is the **forecast** of Y_{t+1}. To help interpret this forecast formula, substitute the smoothing formula for E_t:

$$F_{t+1} = E_t = wY_t + (1 - w)E_{t-1}$$
$$= wY_t + (1 - w)F_t$$
$$= F_t + w(Y_t - F_t)$$

Note that we have substituted F_t for E_{t-1}, since the forecast for time t is the smoothed value for time $(t - 1)$. The final equation provides insight into the exponential smoothing forecast: The forecast for time $(t + 1)$ is equal to the forecast for time t, F_t, plus a correction for the error in the forecast for time t, $(Y_t - F_t)$. This is why the exponentially smoothed forecast is called an **adaptive forecast**—the forecast for time $(t + 1)$ is explicitly adapted for the error in the forecast for time t.

Because exponential smoothing consists of averaging past and present values, the smoothed values will tend to lag behind the series when a long-term trend exists. In addition, the averaging tends to smooth any seasonal component. Therefore, exponentially smoothed forecasts are appropriate only when the trend and seasonal components are relatively insignificant. Since the exponential smoothing model assumes that the time series has little or no trend or seasonal component, the forecast F_{t+1} is used to forecast not only Y_{t+1} but also all future values of Y_t. That is, the forecast for two time periods ahead is

$$F_{t+2} = F_{t+1}$$

and for three time periods ahead is

$$F_{t+3} = F_{t+2} = F_{t+1}$$

The exponential smoothing forecasting technique is summarized in the box.

Calculation of Exponentially Smoothed Forecasts

1. Given the observed time series $Y_1, Y_2, ..., Y_t$, first calculate the exponentially smoothed values $E_1, E_2, ..., E_t$, using

$$E_1 = Y_1$$
$$E_2 = wY_2 + (1 - w)E_1$$
$$\vdots$$
$$E_t = wY_t + (1 - w)E_{t-1}$$

2. Use the last smoothed value to forecast the next time series value:

$$F_{t+1} = E_t$$

3. Assuming that Y_t is relatively free of trend and seasonal components, use the same forecast for all future values of Y_t:

$$F_{t+2} = F_{t+1}$$
$$F_{t+3} = F_{t+1}$$
$$\vdots$$

Two important points must be made about exponentially smoothed forecasts:

1. The choice of w is crucial. If you decide that w will be small (near 0), you will obtain a smooth, slowly changing series of forecasts. On the other hand, the

selection of a large value of w (near 1) will yield more rapidly changing forecasts that depend mostly on the current values of the series. In general, several values of w should be tried to determine how sensitive the forecast series is to the choice of w. Forecasting experience will provide the best basis for the choice of w for a particular application.

2. The further into the future you forecast, the less certain you can be of accuracy. Since the exponentially smoothed forecast is constant for all future values, any changes in trend or seasonality are not taken into account. However, the uncertainty associated with future forecasts applies not only to exponentially smoothed forecasts, but also to all methods of forecasting. In general, time series forecasting should be confined to the short term.

EXAMPLE 14.5

The annual Dow Jones Industrial Averages from 1970 to 1996 are repeated in Table 14.9, along with the exponentially smoothed values using $w = .3$ and $w = .7$. Use the exponential smoothing technique to forecast the values from 1994 to 1996 using both $w = .3$ and $w = .7$.

SOLUTION

First, we calculate the exponentially smoothed forecasts using $w = .3$. Following the steps outlined in the box, we find

$$F_{1994} = E_{1994} = 3{,}289.36$$

$$F_{1995} = F_{1994} = 3{,}289.36$$

$$F_{1996} = F_{1995} = F_{1994} = 3{,}289.36$$

The same steps are repeated using $w = .7$, and both sets of forecasts are shown in Table 14.10. Also shown are the actual Dow Jones Industrial Averages from

TABLE 14.9 Dow Jones Industrial Average (1970–1996) with Exponentially Smoothed Values

Year	DJIA	EXPONENTIALLY SMOOTHED DJIA		Year	DJIA	EXPONENTIALLY SMOOTHED DJIA	
		$w = .3$	$w = .7$			$w = .3$	$w = .7$
1970	838.92	838.92	838.92	1984	1,211.57	1,083.14	1,202.37
1971	884.76	852.67	871.01	1985	1,546.67	1,222.20	1,443.38
1972	950.71	882.08	926.80	1986	1,895.95	1,424.32	1,760.18
1973	923.88	894.62	924.75	1987	1,938.83	1,578.67	1,885.23
1974	759.37	854.05	808.98	1988	2,168.57	1,755.64	2,083.57
1975	802.49	838.58	804.44	1989	2,753.20	2,054.91	2,552.31
1976	974.92	879.48	923.77	1990	2,633.66	2,228.53	2,609.26
1977	835.15	866.18	861.74	1991	3,168.83	2,510.62	3,000.96
1978	805.01	847.83	822.03	1992	3,330.11	2,756.47	3,231.36
1979	838.74	845.10	833.73	1993	3,754.09	3,055.76	3,547.27
1980	963.99	880.77	924.91	1994	3,834.44	3,289.36	3,763.29
1981	875.00	879.04	889.97	1995	5,117.12	3,837.69	4,710.97
1982	1,046.54	929.29	999.57	1996	6,448.27	4,620.86	5,927.08
1983	1,258.64	1,028.09	1,180.92				

Sources: The Dow Jones Investor's Handbook, 1996; The Wall Street Journal, Jan. 2, 1997.

TABLE 14.10   Dow Jones Industrial Average (1994–1996): Actual versus Forecast Values

Year	Actual	Forecast ($w = .3$)	Forecast Error	Forecast ($w = .7$)	Forecast Error
1994	3,834.44	3,289.36	545.08	3,763.29	71.15
1995	5,117.12	3,289.36	1,827.76	3,763.29	1,353.83
1996	6,448.27	3,289.36	3,158.91	3,763.29	2,684.98

1994 to 1996. The **forecast error**, defined as the actual value minus the forecast value, is given for each exponentially smoothed forecast.

Notice that the one-step-ahead forecasts for 1994 have considerably smaller forecast errors than the two- and three-steps-ahead forecasts for 1995 and 1996. Neither the $w = .3$ nor the $w = .7$ forecast projects the unusual upturn in the DJIA in 1995 and 1996, because exponentially smoothed forecasts implicitly assume no trend exists in the time series. This example dramatically illustrates the risk associated with anything other than very short-term forecasting.

Many time series have long-term, or secular, trends. For such series the exponentially smoothed forecast is inappropriate for all but the very short term. In the next section we present an extension of the exponentially smoothed forecast—the *Holt-Winters forecast*—that allows for secular trend in the forecasts.

14.5   FORECASTING TRENDS: THE HOLT-WINTERS FORECASTING MODEL (OPTIONAL)

The exponentially smoothed forecasts for the Dow Jones Industrial Average in the previous section have large forecast errors, in part because they do not recognize the trend in the time series. In this section we present an extension of the exponential smoothing method of forecasting that explicitly recognizes the trend in a time series. The **Holt-Winters forecasting model** consists of both an exponentially smoothed component (E_t) and a trend component (T_t). The trend component is used in the calculation of the exponentially smoothed value. The following equations show that both E_t and T_t are weighted averages:

$$E_t = wY_t + (1 - w)(E_{t-1} + T_{t-1})$$

$$T_t = v(E_t - E_{t-1}) + (1 - v)T_{t-1}$$

Note that the equations require *two* smoothing constants, w and v, each of which is between 0 and 1. As before, w controls the smoothness of E_t; a choice near 0 places more emphasis on past values of the time series, while a value of w near 1 gives more weight to current values of the series, and de-emphasizes the past.

The trend component of the series is estimated **adaptively**, using a weighted average of the most recent change in the level, represented by ($E_t - E_{t-1}$), and the trend estimate, represented by T_{t-1}, from the previous period. A choice of the weight v near 0 places more emphasis on the past estimates of trend, while a choice of v near 1 gives more weight to the current change in level.

The calculation of the Holt-Winters components, which proceeds much like the exponential smoothing calculations, is summarized in the box.

Steps for Calculating Components of the Holt-Winters Model

1. Select an exponential smoothing constant w between 0 and 1. Small values of w give less weight to the current values of the time series, and more weight to the past. Larger choices assign more weight to the current value of the series.

2. Select a trend smoothing constant v between 0 and 1. Small values of v give less weight to the current changes in the level of the series, and more weight to the past trend. Larger values assign more weight to the most recent trend of the series and less to past trends.

3. Calculate the two components, E_t and T_t, from the time series Y_t beginning at time $t = 2$ as follows:*

$$E_2 = Y_2$$

$$T_2 = Y_2 - Y_1$$

$$E_3 = wY_3 + (1 - w)(E_2 + T_2)$$

$$T_3 = v(E_3 - E_2) + (1 - v)T_2$$

$$\vdots$$

$$E_t = wY_t + (1 - w)(E_{t-1} + T_{t-1})$$

$$T_t = v(E_t - E_{t-1}) + (1 - v)T_{t-1}$$

[*Note:* E_1 and T_1 are not defined.]

EXAMPLE 14.6

The yearly sales data for a firm's first 35 years of operation are given in Table 14.11. Calculate the Holt-Winters exponential smoothing and trend components for this time series using $w = .7$ and $v = .5$. Show the data and the exponential smoothing component E_t on the same graph.

SOLUTION

Following the formulas for the Holt-Winters components given in the box, we calculate

TABLE 14.11   A Firm's Yearly Sales Revenue (thousands of dollars)

t	Y_t	t	Y_t	t	Y_t
1	4.8	13	48.4	25	100.3
2	4.0	14	61.6	26	111.7
3	5.5	15	65.6	27	108.2
4	15.6	16	71.4	28	115.5
5	23.1	17	83.4	29	119.2
6	23.3	18	93.6	30	125.2
7	31.4	19	94.2	31	136.3
8	46.0	20	85.4	32	146.8
9	46.1	21	86.2	33	146.1
10	41.9	22	89.9	34	151.4
11	45.5	23	89.2	35	150.9
12	53.5	24	99.1		

*The calculation begins at time $t = 2$ rather than at $t = 1$ because the first two observations are needed to obtain the first estimate of trend, T_2.

TABLE 14.12   **Holt-Winters Components for Sales Data**

Year	Sales Y_t	E_t ($w = .7$)	T_t ($v = .5$)	Year	Sales Y_t	E_t ($w = .7$)	T_t ($v = .5$)	Year	Sales Y_t	E_t ($w = .7$)	T_t ($v = .5$)
1	4.8	—	—	13	48.4	50.5	1.1	25	100.3	100.1	3.8
2	4.0	4.0	−.8	14	61.6	58.6	4.6	26	111.7	109.4	6.5
3	5.5	4.8	.0	15	65.6	64.9	5.4	27	108.2	110.5	3.8
4	15.6	12.4	3.8	16	71.4	71.1	5.8	28	115.5	115.1	4.2
5	23.1	21.0	6.2	17	83.4	81.5	8.1	29	119.2	119.3	4.2
6	23.3	24.5	4.8	18	93.6	92.4	9.5	30	125.2	124.7	4.8
7	31.4	30.8	5.6	19	94.2	96.5	6.8	31	136.3	134.2	7.2
8	46.0	43.1	8.9	20	85.4	90.8	.5	32	146.8	145.2	9.1
9	46.1	47.9	6.9	21	86.2	87.7	−1.2	33	146.1	148.5	6.2
10	41.9	45.8	2.4	22	89.9	88.9	−.1	34	151.4	152.4	5.0
11	45.5	46.3	1.4	23	89.2	89.1	.1	35	150.9	152.9	2.7
12	53.5	51.8	3.5	24	99.1	96.1	3.6				

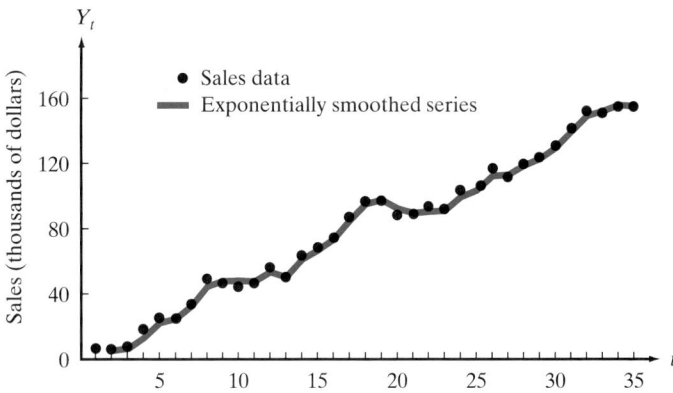

FIGURE 14.7
Sales data and Holt-Winters exponentially smoothed series

$$E_2 = Y_2 = 4.0$$

$$T_2 = Y_2 - Y_1 = 4.0 - 4.8 = -.8$$

$$E_3 = .7Y_3 + (1 - .7)(E_2 + T_2) = .7(5.5) + .3(4.0 - .8) = 4.8$$

$$T_3 = .5(E_3 - E_2) + (1 - .5)T_2 = .5(4.8 - 4.0) + .5(-.8) = 0$$

$$\vdots$$

All the E_t and T_t values are given in Table 14.12, and a graph of Y_t and E_t is shown in Figure 14.7. Note that the trend component T_t measures the general upward trend in Y_t. The choice of $v = .5$ gives equal weight to the most recent trend and to past trends in the sales of the firm. The result is that the exponential smoothing component E_t provides a smooth, upward-trending description of the firm's sales. �!

Our objective is to use the Holt-Winters exponentially smoothed series to forecast the future values of the time series. For the one-step-ahead forecast, this is accomplished by adding the most recent exponentially smoothed component to the most recent trend component. That is, the forecast at time $(t + 1)$, given observed values up to time t, is

$$F_{t+1} = E_t + T_t$$

The idea is that we are constructing the forecast by combining the most recent smoothed estimate, E_t, with the estimate of the expected increase (or decrease) attributable to trend, T_t.

The forecast for two steps ahead is similar, except that we add estimated trend for *two* periods:

$$F_{t+2} = E_t + 2T_t$$

Similarly, for the k-step-ahead forecast, we add the estimated increase (or decrease) in trend over k periods:

$$F_{t+k} = E_t + kT_t$$

The Holt-Winters forecasting methodology is summarized in the box.

Holt-Winters Forecasting

1. Calculate the exponentially smoothed and trend components, E_t and T_t, for each observed value of Y_t $(t \geq 2)$ using the formulas given in the previous box.

2. Calculate the one-step-ahead forecast using

$$F_{t+1} = E_t + T_t$$

3. Calculate the k-step-ahead forecast using

$$F_{t+k} = E_t + kT_t$$

EXAMPLE 14.7

Refer to Example 14.6 and Table 14.12, where we listed the firm's 35 yearly sales figures, along with the Holt-Winters components using $w = .7$ and $v = .5$. Use the Holt-Winters forecasting technique to forecast the firm's annual sales in years 36–40.

SOLUTION

For year 36 we calculate

$$F_{36} = E_{35} + T_{35} = 152.9 + 2.7 = 155.6$$

The forecast two years ahead is

$$F_{37} = E_{35} + 2T_{35} = 152.9 + 2(2.7) = 158.3$$

For years 38–40 we find

$$F_{38} = 152.9 + 3(2.7) = 161.0$$
$$F_{39} = 152.9 + 4(2.7) = 163.7$$
$$F_{40} = 152.9 + 5(2.7) = 166.4$$

These forecasts are displayed in Figure 14.8. Note that the upward trend in the forecast is a result of the Holt-Winters estimated trend component. ◣

The selection of $w = .7$ and $v = .5$ as the smoothing and trend weights for the sales forecasts in Example 14.7 was based on the objectives of assigning more weight to recent series values in the exponentially smoothed component, and of assigning equal weights to the recent and past trend estimates. However, you may want to try several different combinations of weights when using the Holt-Winters forecasting model so that you can assess the sensitivity of the forecasts to the choice of weights. Experience with the particular time series and Holt-Winters forecasts will help in the selection of w and v in a practical application.

FIGURE 14.8
Holt-Winters trend
and sales forecasts,
years 36–40

![Holt-Winters trend and sales forecasts chart with Y_t axis showing Sales (thousands of dollars) from 100 to 160, and t axis from 25 to 40]

EXERCISES   14.22–14.29

Note: Exercises marked with 💾 *contain data for computer analysis on a 3.5" disk (file name in parentheses).*

Learning the Mechanics

14.22 State two criteria for evaluating the accuracy of an exponentially smoothed forecast.

14.23 The table lists the number (in thousands) of new privately owned housing units started each year during the period 1975–1995. Some exponentially smoothed values ($w = .6$) are also shown.

Year	Starts	Smoothed	Year	Starts	Smoothed
1975	1,160		1986	1,805	1,763.59
1976	1,538		1987	1,620	1,677.44
1977	1,987	1,746.92	1988	1,488	
1978	2,020	1,910.77	1989	1,376	1,451.11
1979	1,745		1990	1,193	
1980	1,292		1991	1,014	
1981	1,084		1992	1,200	
1982	1,062	1,137.32	1993	1,288	
1983	1,703	1,476.73	1994	1,457	
1984	1,750		1995	1,354	
1985	1,742				

Source: U.S. Bureau of the Census. Statistical Abstract of the United States, 1995.

a. Calculate the missing values of the exponentially smoothed housing-starts series.

b. Plot the housing-starts series and the exponentially smoothed series on the same graph.

c. Use the exponentially smoothed data from 1975–1994 to forecast the number of housing starts in 1995.

14.24 **(X14.005)** Refer to Exercise 14.5. The U.S. beer production (in millions of barrels) for the years 1970–1994 is reproduced in the table.

Year	Beer	Year	Beer	Year	Beer
1970	133	1979	184	1987	196
1971	137	1980	194	1988	197
1972	141	1981	194	1989	198
1973	149	1982	196	1990	202
1974	156	1983	195	1991	204
1975	161	1984	192	1992	202
1976	164	1985	194	1993	202
1977	171	1986	194	1994	203
1978	179				

Source: U.S. Bureau of the Census. Statistical Abstract of the United States, 1992, 1996.

a. Use the 1970–1991 values to forecast the 1992–1994 production, using simple exponential smoothing with $w = .3$. With $w = .7$.

b. Use the Holt-Winters model with $w = .7$ and $v = .3$ to forecast the 1992–1994 production. Repeat with $w = .3$ and $v = .7$.

14.25 Refer to part **a** of Exercise 14.24. Use the 1970–1991 values to forecast the 1995 production, using exponential smoothing with $w = .3$ and then with $w = .7$.

Applying the Concepts

14.26 **(X14.026)** Standard & Poor's 500 Stock Composite Average (S&P 500) is a stock market index. Like the Dow Jones Industrial Average, it is an indicator of stock market activity. The table at the top of page 762 contains end-of-quarter values of the S&P 500 for the years 1980–1996.

a. Use $w = .7$ to smooth the series from 1980 through 1995. Then forecast the four quarterly

Year	Quarter	S&P 500	Year	Quarter	S&P 500	Year	Quarter	S&P 500
1980	I	104.7	1986	I	232.3	1992	I	407.3
	II	114.6		II	245.3		II	408.27
	III	126.5		III	238.3		III	418.48
	IV	133.5		IV	248.6		IV	435.64
1981	I	133.2	1987	I	292.5	1993	I	450.2
	II	132.3		II	301.4		II	448.1
	III	118.3		III	318.7		III	459.2
	IV	123.8		IV	241.0		IV	466.0
1982	I	110.8	1988	I	265.7	1994	I	463.8
	II	109.7		II	270.7		II	454.8
	III	122.4		III	268.0		III	467.0
	IV	139.4		IV	276.5		IV	455.2
1983	I	151.9	1989	I	292.7	1995	I	493.2
	II	166.4		II	323.7		II	539.4
	III	167.2		III	347.3		III	578.8
	IV	164.4		IV	348.6		IV	614.6
1984	I	157.4	1990	I	338.5	1996	I	645.5
	II	153.1		II	360.4		II	670.63
	III	166.1		III	315.4		III	687.31
	IV	164.5		IV	328.8		IV	740.74
1985	I	179.4	1991	I	372.3			
	II	188.9		II	378.3			
	III	184.1		III	387.2			
	IV	207.3		IV	388.5			

Sources: Standard & Poor's Statistical Service. *Security Price Index Record,* 1996; *Standard & Poor's Current Statistics,* Jan. 1997.

values in 1996 using *only* the information through the fourth quarter of 1995.

b. Repeat part **a** using $w = .3$.

14.27 Refer to Exercise 14.26. Suppose you want to use only the 1990–1994 S&P values to forecast the quarterly 1996 values. Calculate the forecasts using the Holt-Winters model with $w = .3$ and $v = .5$. Repeat with $w = .7$ and $v = .5$.

14.28 (X14.028) The fluctuation of gold and other precious metal prices in the mid-1980s and early 1990s was a reflection of the strength or weakness

of the U.S. dollar and subsequent turmoil among European currencies. The table at the bottom of the page shows monthly gold prices from January 1990 to November 1996.

a. Use exponential smoothing with $w = .5$ to calculate monthly smoothed values from January 1990 to November 1995. Then forecast the monthly gold prices for December 1995 to November 1996.

b. Calculate 12 one-step-ahead forecasts for December 1995 to November 1996 by updat-

	GOLD PRICES						
Month	**1990**	**1991**	**1992**	**1993**	**1994**	**1995**	**1996**
Jan.	411.5	384.9	355.7	330.2	408.3	379.8	400.9
Feb.	418.5	365.1	355.2	330.9	383.3	377.8	406.1
Mar.	394.4	347.2	346.0	331.3	385.4	383.4	397.5
Apr.	375.5	359.6	339.8	343.2	378.4	391.3	394.3
May	370.4	358.1	338.5	368.0	382.5	386.6	393.3
June	353.6	368.0	342.0	373.2	387.0	388.9	386.6
July	382.0	369.7	338.9	391.6	386.7	387.7	384.9
Aug.	396.5	341.9	344.2	379.7	381.7	384.9	388.7
Sept.	390.8	368.4	346.7	356.1	393.1	384.5	384.3
Oct.	382.0	360.1	345.6	365.4	391.1	384.4	382.4
Nov.	383.0	344.2	336.3	374.9	385.7	381.0	379.5
Dec.	379.3	380.3	335.5	385.3	386.7	388.7	—

Source: Standard & Poor's Current Statistics, 1996.

ing the exponentially smoothed values with each month's actual value, and then forecasting the next month's value.

   c. Repeat parts **a–b** using the Holt-Winters technique with $w = .5$ and $v = .5$.

14.29 **(X14.029)** The table at right reports the monthly production of passenger car tires (in billions) for U.S. manufacturers for the period January 1994 through February 1996.

   a. Create an exponentially smoothed time series using $w = .5$.

   b. Using exponential smoothing with $w = .5$, forecast passenger car tire production for March, April, May, and June of 1996.

   c. Under what circumstances would you expect this approach to forecasting to yield relatively accurate forecasts of tire production?

Month	1994	1995	1996
Jan.	16.94	17.50	18.56
Feb.	16.70	17.52	17.73
Mar.	18.75	19.34	
Apr.	17.23	17.89	
May	17.81	18.16	
June	17.39	17.91	
July	14.72	15.58	
Aug.	16.53	19.25	
Sept.	15.83	17.60	
Oct.	17.77	18.66	
Nov.	16.45	16.88	
Dec.	15.00	13.83	

Source: Standard and Poor's Current Statistics, 1996.

14.6   MEASURING FORECAST ACCURACY: MAD AND RMSE

As demonstrated in Example 14.5, forecast error (i.e., the difference between the actual time series value and its forecast) can be used to evaluate the accuracy of the forecast. Knowledge of a forecast's accuracy aids in the selection of both the forecasting methodology to be utilized and the parameters of the forecast formula (e.g., the weights in the exponentially smoothed or Holt-Winters forecasts). Two popular measures of forecast accuracy, both based on forecast errors, are the **mean absolute deviation (MAD)** and the **root mean squared error (RMSE)** of the forecasts. Their formulas are given in the box.

Measures of Forecast Accuracy

1. The **mean absolute deviation (MAD)** is defined as the mean absolute difference between the forecast and actual values of the time series:

$$MAD = \frac{\sum_{t=1}^{N} |F_t - Y_t|}{N}$$

where N is the number of forecasts used for evaluation.

2. The **root mean squared error (RMSE)** is defined as the square root of the mean squared difference between the forecast and actual values of the time series:

$$RMSE = \sqrt{\frac{\sum_{t=1}^{N} (F_t - Y_t)^2}{N}}$$

Note that both measures require one or more actual values of the time series against which to compare the forecasts. Thus, we can either wait several time periods until the observed values are available, or we can hold out several of the values at the end of the time series, not using them to model the time series, but saving them for evaluating the forecasts obtained from the model.

TABLE 14.13 Dow Jones Industrial Average (1970–1993) with Two Holt-Winters Forecasting Models

| | | HOLT-WINTERS MODEL 1 | | HOLT-WINTERS MODEL 2 | |
Year	DJIA	$E(w = .5)$	$T(v = .2)$	$E(w = .5)$	$T(v = .8)$
1970	838.92	—	—	—	—
1971	884.76	844.76	45.84	844.76	45.84
1972	950.71	940.66	47.85	940.66	53.88
1973	923.88	956.19	41.39	959.21	25.62
1974	759.37	878.48	17.57	872.10	−64.56
1975	802.49	849.27	8.21	805.01	−66.58
1976	974.92	916.20	19.96	856.68	28.01
1977	835.15	885.65	9.86	859.92	8.20
1978	805.01	850.26	0.81	836.56	−17.05
1979	838.74	844.90	−0.43	829.13	−9.36
1980	963.99	904.23	11.52	891.88	48.33
1981	875.00	895.38	7.45	907.61	22.25
1982	1,046.54	974.68	21.82	988.20	68.92
1983	1,258.64	1,127.57	48.03	1,157.88	149.53
1984	1,211.57	1,193.59	51.63	1,259.49	111.20
1985	1,546.67	1,395.94	81.73	1,458.68	181.59
1986	1,895.95	1,686.83	123.60	1,768.11	283.86
1987	1,938.83	1,874.63	136.44	1,995.40	238.61
1988	2,168.57	2,089.82	152.19	2,201.29	212.43
1989	2,753.20	2,497.60	203.31	2,583.46	348.22
1990	2,633.66	2,667.29	196.58	2,782.67	229.01
1991	3,168.83	3,016.35	227.08	3,090.26	291.87
1992	3,330.11	3,286.77	235.75	3,356.12	271.06
1993	3,754.09	3,638.30	258.90	3,690.64	321.83

EXAMPLE 14.8

In Section 14.4 we found that the exponentially smoothed forecasts of the 1994–1996 Dow Jones Industrial Average were generally unsatisfactory, because they did not recognize trend in the time series. We now try the Holt-Winters model of Section 14.5 to account for trend. Table 14.13 shows the original series through 1993, with two Holt-Winters models: one with a trend weight $v = .2$, and the other with a trend weight $v = .8$. Both have smoothing weight $w = .5$. Use the time period 1994–1996 and apply the MAD and RMSE criteria to evaluate the two forecasting models.

SOLUTION

The first step is to calculate the Holt-Winters forecasts for 1994–1996 corresponding to the two models. The formula

$$F_{t+k} = E_t + kT_t$$

is used to obtain the forecasts given in Table 14.14, which also presents the actual DJIA values and the forecast errors. To compare the two models, we first calculate the mean absolute deviations:

$$\text{MAD (Model 1)} = \frac{|-62.76| + |961.02| + |2,033.27|}{3} = 1,019.2$$

$$\text{MAD (Model 2)} = \frac{|-178.03| + |782.82| + |1,792.14|}{3} = 917.7$$

Next, we calculate the root mean squared errors:

TABLE 14.14 **Forecasts and Forecast Errors for Two Holt-Winters Models: Dow Jones Industrial Average (1994–1996)**

Year	DJIA Actual	MODEL 1 Forecast	Error	MODEL 2 Forecast	Error
1994	3,834.44	3,897.20	−62.76	4,012.47	−178.03
1995	5,117.12	4,156.10	961.02	4,334.30	782.82
1996	6,448.27	4,415.00	2,033.27	4,656.13	1,792.14

$$\text{RMSE (Model 1)} = \sqrt{\frac{(-62.76)^2 + (961.02)^2 + (2{,}033.27)^2}{3}} = 1{,}298.9$$

$$\text{RMSE (Model 2)} = \sqrt{\frac{(-178.03)^2 + (782.82)^2 + (1{,}792.14)^2}{3}} = 1{,}133.8$$

Note that both criteria lead to the same conclusion: Model 2 provides more accurate predictions of the Dow Jones Industrial Average for the period 1994–1996 than does Model 1. Note that the only difference between the two Holt-Winters models is the value in Model 2 gives more weight to the short-term trend than to the long-term trend. For the three years in question the model sensitive to the short-term trend better forecasts the market's rally in the late 1980s and early 1990s than does the model that is more sensitive to the long-term trend of the market. Both models, however, fail to accurately forecast the dramatic increase in the DJIA in 1995 and 1996. Note the large forecast errors for these two years. Although the Holt-Winters forecasting method explicitly accounts for trend, the accuracy of the forecasts will decrease the further we forecast into the future.

Criteria such as MAD and RMSE for assessing forecast accuracy require special care in interpretation. The number of time periods included in the evaluation is critical to the decision about which model is preferred. The choice also depends on how many time periods ahead the analyst plans to forecast. Once these decisions are made, the criteria can be used to measure forecast accuracy. Nevertheless, only *inferential* models, such as regression models, that have explicit random error components can be used to estimate the reliability of a forecast *before* the actual value of the time series is observed. We discuss an inferential model in the next section.

EXERCISES 14.30–14.37

Note: Exercises marked with ▢ contain data for computer analysis on a 3.5" disk (file name in parentheses).

Learning the Mechanics

14.30 Refer to Exercise 14.23, part **c**. Calculate the error associated with the forecast of the number of housing starts in 1995.

14.31 Refer to the beer production time series, Exercise 14.24. In part **a** you obtained forecasts of 1992–1994 beer production using exponential smoothing with $w = .3$ and $w = .7$.

a. Calculate the forecast errors for the $w = .3$ exponentially smoothed forecasts.
b. Calculate the forecast errors for the $w = .7$ exponentially smoothed forecasts.
c. Calculate MAD for the exponential smoothing forecasts using $w = .3$.
d. Calculate MAD for the exponential smoothing forecasts using $w = .7$.
e. Calculate RMSE for the exponential smoothing forecasts using $w = .3$.
f. Calculate RMSE for the exponential smoothing forecasts using $w = .7$.

14.32 Refer to the beer production time series, Exercise 14.24. In part **b** you obtained forecasts of 1992–1994 beer production using the Holt-Winters model with $(w = .3, v = .7)$ and $(w = .7, v = .3)$.
   a. Calculate the forecast errors for the $w = .3$, $v = .7$ Holt-Winters forecasts.
   b. Calculate the forecast errors for the $w = .7$, $v = .3$ Holt-Winters forecasts.
   c. Calculate MAD for the $w = .3, v = .7$ Holt-Winters forecasts.
   d. Calculate MAD for the $w = .7, v = .3$ Holt-Winters forecasts.
   e. Calculate RMSE for the $w = .3, v = .7$ Holt-Winters forecasts.
   f. Calculate RMSE for the $w = .7, v = .3$ Holt-Winters forecasts.

Applying the Concepts

14.33 **(X14.033)** The table reports yearly tourist arrivals in France (in thousands) during the period 1980–1995.

Year	Tourists	Year	Tourists
1980	30,100	1988	38,288
1981	31,340	1989	45,100
1982	33,467	1990	52,497
1983	34,018	1991	55,041
1984	35,429	1992	59,590
1985	36,748	1993	61,300
1986	36,080	1994	61,314
1987	36,974	1995	60,000

Source: European Marketing Data and Statistics, 1988, 1991, 1997.

   a. Use the 1980 to 1992 tourist counts and simple exponential smoothing to forecast the 1993 to 1995 tourist counts. Use $w = .8$.
   b. Use the Holt-Winters model with $w = .8$ and $v = .7$ to forecast the 1993 to 1995 tourist counts.

   c. Apply the MAD and RMSE criteria to evaluate the two forecasting models of parts **a** and **b**. Which model is better? Why?

14.34 Refer to your exponential smoothing forecasts of the quarterly S&P 500 for 1996, Exercise 14.26.
   a. Calculate MAD and RMSE for the forecasts with $w = .7$.
   b. Calculate MAD and RMSE for the forecasts with $w = .3$.
   c. Compare MAD and RMSE for the two simple exponential smoothing forecast models. Which model leads to more accurate forecasts?

14.35 Refer to your Holt-Winters forecasts of the quarterly S&P 500 for 1996, Exercise 14.27.
   a. Calculate MAD and RMSE for the forecasts with $w = .3$ and $v = .5$.
   b. Calculate MAD and RMSE for the forecasts with $w = .7$ and $v = .5$.
   c. Compare MAD and RMSE for the two Holt-Winters forecasts models. Which model leads to more accurate forecasts?

14.36 Refer to Exercise 14.28. Two models were used to forecast the December 1995 to November 1996 gold prices: an exponential smoothing model with $w = .5$ and a Holt-Winters model with $w = .5$ and $v = .5$.
   a. Use MAD and RMSE criteria to evaluate the two models' accuracy for forecasting the December 1995 to November 1996 values using only the January 1994–November 1995 data.
   b. Use the MAD and RMSE criteria to evaluate the two models' accuracy when making the 12 one-step-ahead forecasts, updating the models with each month's actual value before forecasting the next month's value.

14.37 Refer to your forecasts of monthly tire production, Exercise 14.29. Look up the actual tire production for the four months in question and measure the accuracy of your forecasts using MAD and RMSE.

14.7 FORECASTING TRENDS: SIMPLE LINEAR REGRESSION

Perhaps the simplest **inferential** forecasting model is one with which you are familiar: the simple linear regression model. A straight-line model is used to relate the time series, Y_t, to time, t, and the least squares line is used to forecast future values of Y_t.

Suppose a firm is interested in forecasting its sales revenues for each of the next five years. To make such forecasts and assess their reliability, a time series model must be constructed. Refer again to the yearly sales data for a firm's 35

FIGURE 14.9
Plot of sales data

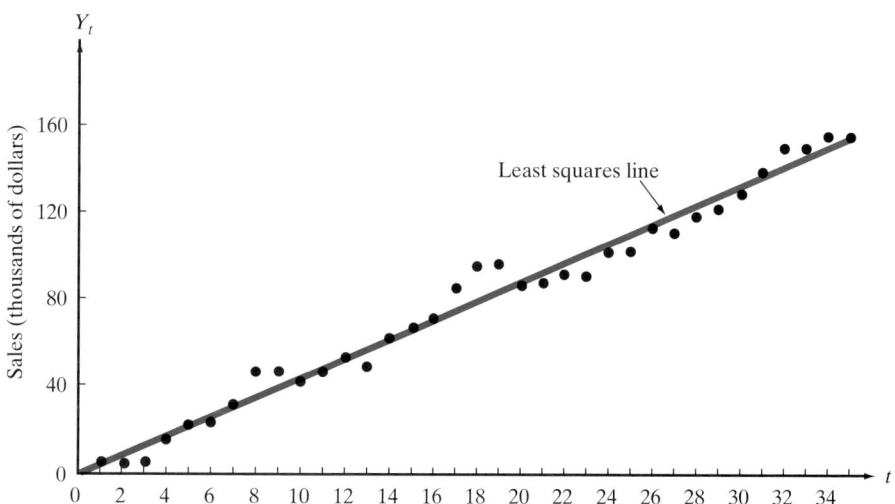

years of operation given in Table 14.11. A plot of the data (Figure 14.9) reveals a linearly increasing trend, so the model

$$E(Y_t) = \beta_0 + \beta_1 t$$

seems plausible for the secular trend. Fitting the model using the method of least squares (see Section 10.2), we obtain the least squares model

$$\hat{Y}_t = \hat{\beta}_0 + \hat{\beta}_1 t = .4015 + 4.2956t \quad \text{with} \quad \text{SSE} = 1,345.45$$

This least squares line is shown in Figure 14.9, and the SAS printout is given in Figure 14.10.

We can now forecast sales for years 36–40. The forecasts of sales and the corresponding 95% prediction intervals are shown (highlighted) in the printout. For example, for $t = 36$, we have

$$\hat{Y}_{36} = 155.0$$

with the 95% prediction interval (141.3, 168.8). Similarly, we can obtain the forecasts and prediction intervals for years 37–40. The observed sales, forecast sales, and prediction intervals are shown in Figure 14.11. Although it is not easily perceptible in the figure, the prediction intervals widen as we attempt to forecast further into the future (see the printout in Figure 14.10). This agrees with the intuitive notion that short-term forecasts should be more reliable than long-term forecasts.

There are two problems associated with forecasting time series using a least squares model.

Problem 1   We are using the least squares model to forecast values outside the region of observation of the independent variable, t. That is, we are forecasting for values of t between 36 and 40, but the observed sales are for t values between 1 and 35. As we noted in Chapters 10–12, it is extremely risky to use a least squares regression model for prediction outside the experimental region.

Problem 1 obviously cannot be avoided. Since forecasting always involves predictions about the future values of a time series, some or all of the independent variables will probably be outside the

Analysis of Variance

Source	DF	Sum of Squares	Mean Square	F Value	Prob>F
Model	1	65875.20817	65875.20817	1615.724	0.0001
Error	33	1345.45355	40.77132		
C Total	34	67220.66171			

Root MSE	6.38524	R-square	0.9800
Dep Mean	77.72286	Adj R-sq	0.9794
C.V.	8.21540		

Parameter Estimates

Variable	DF	Parameter Estimate	Standard Error	T for H0: Parameter=0	Prob > |T|
INTERCEP	1	0.401513	2.20570829	0.182	0.8567
T	1	4.295630	0.10686692	40.196	0.0001

T	Dep Var Y	Predict Value	Std Err Predict	Lower95% Predict	Upper95% Predict	Residual
1	4.8000	4.6971	2.113	-8.9866	18.3809	0.1029
2	4.0000	8.9928	2.022	-4.6338	22.6194	-4.9928
3	5.5000	13.2884	1.932	-0.2843	26.8611	-7.7884
4	15.6000	17.5840	1.845	4.0619	31.1061	-1.9840
5	23.1000	21.8797	1.759	8.4048	35.3545	1.2203
6	23.3000	26.1753	1.676	12.7444	39.6062	-2.8753
7	31.4000	30.4709	1.596	17.0805	43.8613	0.9291
8	46.0000	34.7666	1.519	21.4133	48.1198	11.2334
9	46.1000	39.0622	1.446	25.7426	52.3818	7.0378
10	41.9000	43.3578	1.377	30.0684	56.6472	-1.4578
11	45.5000	47.6534	1.313	34.3908	60.9161	-2.1534
12	53.5000	51.9491	1.255	38.7096	65.1886	1.5509
13	48.4000	56.2447	1.204	43.0249	69.4645	-7.8447
14	61.6000	60.5403	1.161	47.3366	73.7441	1.0597
15	65.6000	64.8360	1.126	51.6448	78.0272	0.7640
16	71.4000	69.1316	1.100	55.9494	82.3138	2.2684
17	83.4000	73.4272	1.085	60.2504	86.6041	9.9728
18	93.6000	77.7229	1.079	64.5478	90.8979	15.8771
19	94.2000	82.0185	1.085	68.8416	95.2	12.1815
20	85.4000	86.3141	1.100	73.1319	99.5	-0.9141
21	86.2000	90.6097	1.126	77.4185	103.8	-4.4097
22	89.9000	94.9	1.161	81.7016	108.1	-5.0054
23	89.2000	99.2	1.204	85.9812	112.4	-10.0010
24	99.1	103.5	1.255	90.2571	116.7	-4.3966
25	100.3	107.8	1.313	94.5	121.1	-7.4923
26	111.7	112.1	1.377	98.8	125.4	-0.3879
27	108.2	116.4	1.446	103.1	129.7	-8.1835
28	115.5	120.7	1.519	107.3	134.0	-5.1792
29	119.2	125.0	1.596	111.6	138.4	-5.7748
30	125.2	129.3	1.676	115.8	142.7	-4.0704
31	136.3	133.6	1.759	120.1	147.0	2.7339
32	146.8	137.9	1.845	124.3	151.4	8.9383
33	146.1	142.2	1.932	128.6	155.7	3.9427
34	151.4	146.5	2.022	132.8	160.1	4.9471
35	150.9	150.7	2.113	137.1	164.4	0.1514
36	.	155.0	2.206	141.3	168.8	.
37	.	159.3	2.300	145.5	173.1	.
38	.	163.6	2.394	149.8	177.5	.
39	.	167.9	2.490	154.0	181.9	.
40	.	172.2	2.587	158.2	186.2	.

FIGURE 14.10 SAS printout for least squares fit (straight line) to Y_t = Sales

FIGURE 14.11
Observed (years 25–35) and forecast (years 36–40) sales using the straight-line model

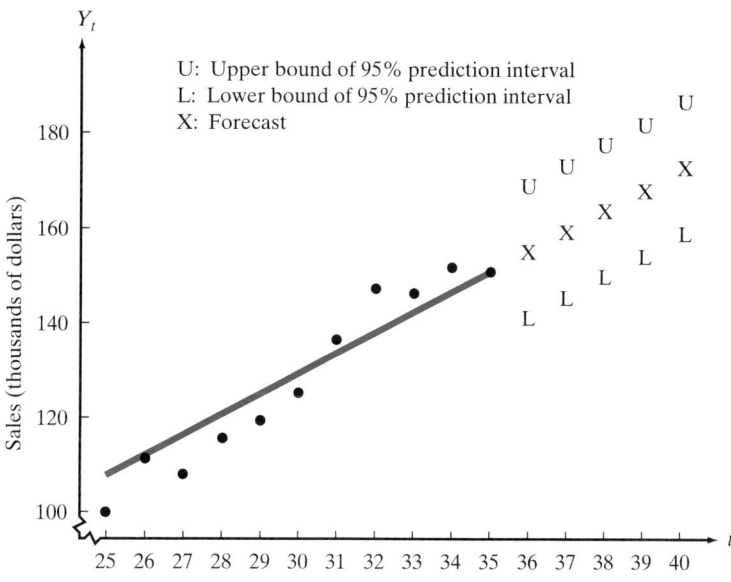

region of observation on which the model was developed. It is important that the forecaster recognize the dangers of this type of prediction. If underlying conditions change drastically after the model is estimated (e.g., if federal price controls are imposed on the firm's products during the 36th year of operation), the forecasts and their confidence intervals are probably useless.

Problem 2   Although the straight-line model may adequately describe the secular trend of the sales, we have not attempted to build any cyclical effects into the model. Thus, the effect of inflationary and recessionary periods will be to increase the error of the forecasts because the model does not anticipate such periods.

Fortunately, the forecaster often has some degree of control over problem 2, as we demonstrate in the remainder of the chapter.

In forming the prediction intervals for the forecasts, we made the standard regression assumptions (Chapters 10 and 12) about the random error component of the model. We assumed the errors have mean 0, constant variance, and normal probability distributions, and are **independent**. The latter assumption is dubious in time series models, especially in the presence of short-term trends. Often, if a year's value lies above the secular trend line, the next year's value has a tendency to be above the line also. That is, the errors tend to be correlated (see Figure 14.9).

We discuss how to deal with correlated errors in Section 14.9. For now, we can characterize the simple linear regression forecasting method as useful for discerning secular trends, but probably too simplistic for most time series. And, as with all forecasting methods, the simple linear regression forecasts should be applied only over the short term.

STATISTICS IN ACTION

14.2 FORECASTING THE DEMAND FOR EMERGENCY ROOM SERVICES

With the advent of managed care, U.S. hospitals have begun to operate like businesses. More than ever before, hospital administrators need to know and apply the theories and methods taught in business schools. For example, hospitals apply the methods of this chapter to forecast demand for their services. More specifically, hospitals like Richmond Memorial in Richmond, Virginia, and Abbott-Northwestern in Minneapolis, Minnesota, have used regression analysis to forecast the demand for emergency room services.

Richmond Memorial uses data on patient visits to the emergency room during each of the past 10 Augusts to forecast next August's demand. Data for a recent 10-year period are shown in Table 14.15 below.

A straight-line regression model is used to model the trend in Y_t, the average number of visits per day during August. With time t (measured in years) as the independent variable, the following least squares model was obtained: $\hat{Y}_t = 38.171 + 7.319t$. This least squares line is plotted on a scattergram of the data in

Figure 14.12. The plot reveals an upward trend in emergency room visits. Based on this analysis, it was determined that the increase in the demand for emergency room services was greater than the growth in the Richmond area population. This finding substantiated management's belief that the emergency room was increasingly serving as a replacement for the family physician.

Focus

1. Using the least squares model, construct a point forecast for emergency room demand for each of the next three Augusts.

2. Explain why such point forecasts should be accompanied by prediction intervals.

3. Describe the potential dangers associated with using simple linear regression to forecast demand for emergency room services.

4. Which other method described in this chapter would be appropriate for forecasting patient visits to the emergency room?

14.8   SEASONAL REGRESSION MODELS

Many time series have distinct seasonal patterns. Retail sales are usually highest around Christmas, spring, and fall, with lulls in the winter and summer periods. Energy usage is highest in summer and winter, and lowest in spring and fall. Teenage unemployment rises in summer months when schools are not in session and falls near Christmas when many businesses hire part-time help.

Multiple regression models can be used to forecast future values of a time series with strong seasonal components. To accomplish this, the mean value of the time series, $E(Y_t)$, is given a mathematical form that describes both the secular

---

TABLE 14.15   **Emergency Room Data for the Month of August: Past 10 Years (Statistics in Action 14.2)**

Year t	Visits	Daily Average Y_t	Year t	Visits	Daily Average Y_t
1	1,367	44.09	6	3,019	97.38
2	1,642	52.96	7	2,794	90.12
3	1,780	57.41	8	2,846	91.80
4	2,060	66.45	9	3,001	96.80
5	2,257	72.80	10	3,548	114.45

Source: Adapted from Bolling, W. B. "Queuing model of a hospital emergency room," *Industrial Engineering,* Sept. 1972.

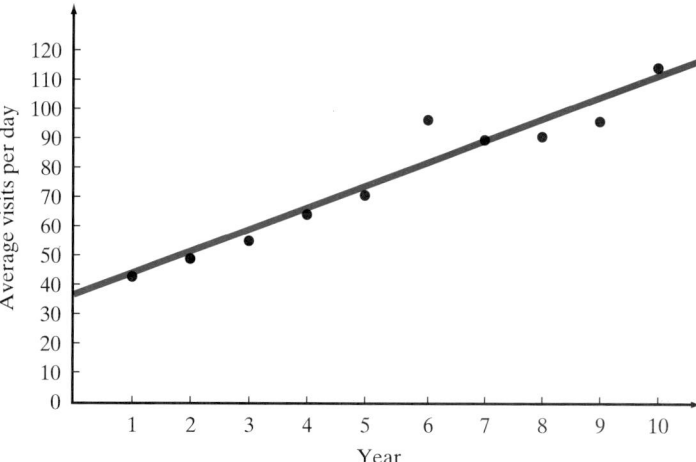

FIGURE 14.12
Trend in emergency room data (Statistics in Action 14.2)

trend and seasonal components of the time series. Although the seasonal model can assume a wide variety of mathematical forms, the use of dummy variables to describe seasonal differences is common.

For example, consider the power load data for a southern utility company shown in Table 14.16. Data were obtained for each quarter from 1985 through 1996. A model that combines the expected growth in usage and the seasonal component is

$$E(Y_t) = \beta_0 + \beta_1 t + \beta_2 Q_1 + \beta_3 Q_2 + \beta_4 Q_3$$

TABLE 14.16   Quarterly Power Loads (megawatts) for a Southern Utility Company, 1985–1996

Year	Quarter	Power Load	Year	Quarter	Power Load
1985	1	68.8	1991	1	130.6
	2	65.0		2	116.8
	3	88.4		3	144.2
	4	69.0		4	123.3
1986	1	83.6	1992	1	142.3
	2	69.7		2	124.0
	3	90.2		3	146.1
	4	72.5		4	135.5
1987	1	106.8	1993	1	147.1
	2	89.2		2	119.3
	3	110.7		3	138.2
	4	91.7		4	127.6
1988	1	108.6	1994	1	143.4
	2	98.9		2	134.0
	3	120.1		3	159.6
	4	102.1		4	135.1
1989	1	113.1	1995	1	149.5
	2	94.2		2	123.3
	3	120.5		3	154.4
	4	107.4		4	139.4
1990	1	116.2	1996	1	151.6
	2	104.4		2	133.7
	3	131.7		3	154.5
	4	117.9		4	135.1

```
Dependent Variable: LOAD
                          Analysis of Variance

                          Sum of          Mean
      Source        DF    Squares        Square    F Value      Prob>F
      Model          4   28374.9925    7093.7481    114.88      0.0001
      Error         43    2655.1356      61.7473
      C Total       47   31030.1281

            Root MSE      7.85795     R-square      0.9144
            Dep Mean    117.69375     Adj R-sq      0.9065
            C.V.          6.67662

                          Parameter Estimates
                       Parameter     Standard    T for H0:
      Variable    DF   Estimate         Error   Parameter=0   Prob > |T|
      INTERCEP    1    70.508523    3.11552479      22.63      0.0001
      T           1     1.636211    0.08213932      19.92      0.0001
      Q1          1    13.658632    3.21744388       4.25      0.0001
      Q2          1    -3.735912    3.21219719      -1.16      0.2512
      Q3          1    18.469544    3.20904506       5.76      0.0001
```

FIGURE 14.13 SAS printout of least squares fit to power load time series

where

t = Time period, ranging from $t = 1$ for quarter 1 of 1985 to $t = 48$ for quarter 4 of 1996

$$Q_1 = \begin{cases} 1 & \text{if quarter 1} \\ 0 & \text{if quarter 2, 3, or 4} \end{cases}$$

$$Q_2 = \begin{cases} 1 & \text{if quarter 2} \\ 0 & \text{if quarter 1, 3, or 4} \end{cases}$$

$$Q_3 = \begin{cases} 1 & \text{if quarter 3} \\ 0 & \text{if quarter 1, 2, or 4} \end{cases}$$

The SAS printout in Figure 14.13 shows the least squares fit of this model to the data in Table 14.16.

Note that the model appears to fit well, with $R^2 = .91$, indicating that the model accounts for 91% of the sample variability in power loads over the 12-year period. The global $F = 114.88$ strongly supports the hypothesis that the model has predictive utility. The standard deviation (**Root MSE**) of 7.86 indicates that the model predictions will usually be accurate to within approximately $\pm 2(7.86)$, or about ± 16 megawatts. Furthermore, $\hat{\beta}_1 = 1.64$ indicates an estimated average growth in load of 1.64 megawatts per quarter. Finally, the seasonal dummy variables have the following interpretations (refer to Chapter 12):*

$\hat{\beta}_2 = 13.66$ Quarter 1 loads average 13.66 megawatts more than quarter 4 loads.

*These interpretations assume a fixed value of t. In practical terms this is unrealistic, since each quarter is associated with a different value of t. Nevertheless, the coefficients of the seasonal dummy variables provide insight into the seasonality of these time series data.

TABLE 14.17   Predicted Power Loads, Confidence Intervals, and Actual Power Loads (megawatts) for 1997

Quarter	Predicted Load	Lower 95% Confidence Limit	Upper 95% Confidence Limit	Actual Load
1	164.3	147.3	181.4	151.3
2	148.6	131.5	165.6	132.9
3	172.4	155.4	189.5	160.5
4	155.6	138.5	172.6	161.0

FIGURE 14.14
Regression forecasting model for a southern utility company

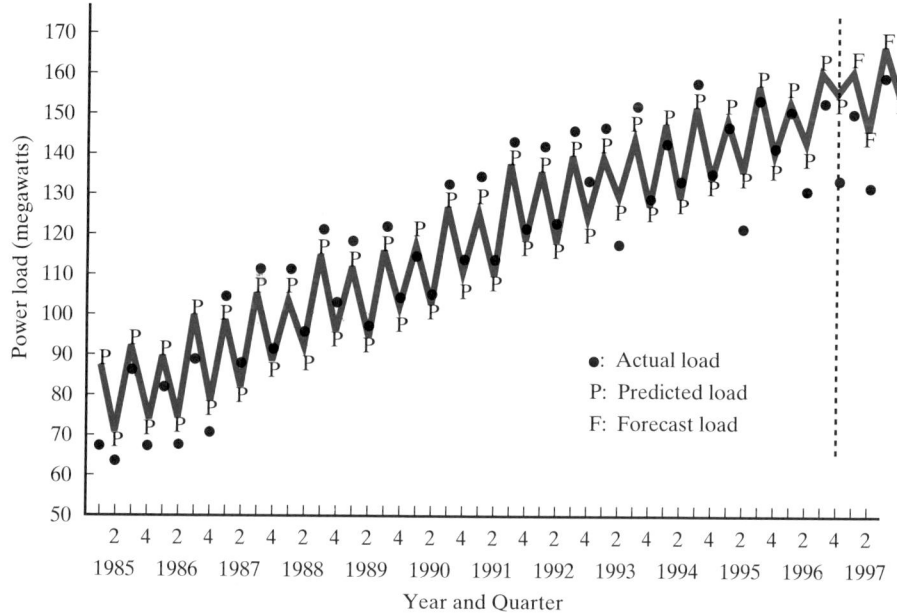

$$\hat{\beta}_3 = -3.74 \qquad \text{Quarter 2 loads average 3.74 megawatts less than quarter 4 loads.}$$

$$\hat{\beta}_4 = 18.47 \qquad \text{Quarter 3 loads average 18.47 megawatts more than quarter 4 loads.}$$

Thus, as expected, winter and summer loads exceed spring and fall loads, with the peak occurring during the summer months.

In order to forecast the 1997 power loads, we calculate the predicted value $\hat{Y}$ for $k = 49, 50, 51$, and 52, at the same time substituting the dummy variable appropriate for each quarter. Thus, for 1997,

$$\hat{Y}_{\text{Quarter 1}} = \hat{\beta}_0 + \hat{\beta}_1(49) + \hat{\beta}_2 = 70.51 + 1.636(49) + 13.66 = 164.3$$

$$\hat{Y}_{\text{Quarter 2}} = \hat{\beta}_0 + \hat{\beta}_1(50) + \hat{\beta}_3 = 148.6$$

$$\hat{Y}_{\text{Quarter 3}} = \hat{\beta}_0 + \hat{\beta}_1(51) + \hat{\beta}_4 = 172.4$$

$$\hat{Y}_{\text{Quarter 4}} = \hat{\beta}_0 + \hat{\beta}_1(52) = 155.6$$

The predicted values and 95% prediction intervals are given in Table 14.17; the data and least squares predicted values are graphed in Figure 14.14. The color line on the graph connects the predicted values. Also shown in Table 14.17 and Figure 14.14 are the actual 1997 quarterly power loads. Notice that all 1997 power loads fall inside the forecast intervals.

The seasonal model used to forecast the power loads is an **additive model** because the secular trend component ($\beta_1 t$) is added to the seasonal component ($\beta_2 Q_1 + \beta_3 Q_2 + \beta_4 Q_3$) to form the model. A **multiplicative model** would have the same form, except that the dependent variable would be the natural logarithm of power load; i.e.,

$$\ln Y_t = \beta_0 + \beta_1 t + \beta_2 Q_1 + \beta_3 Q_2 + \beta_4 Q_3 + \epsilon$$

To see the multiplicative nature of this model, we take the antilogarithm of both sides of the equation to get

$$Y_t = \exp\{\beta_0 + \beta_1 t + \beta_2 Q_1 + \beta_3 Q_2 + \beta_4 Q_3 + \epsilon\}$$
$$= \exp\{\beta_0\} \exp\{\beta_1 t\} \exp\{\beta_2 Q_1 + \beta_3 Q_2 + \beta_4 Q_3\} \exp\{\epsilon\}$$

| Constant | Secular trend | Seasonal component | Residual component |

The multiplicative model often provides a better forecasting model when the time series is changing at an increasing rate over time.

When time series data are observed monthly, a regression forecasting model needs 11 dummy variables to describe monthly seasonality; three dummy variables can be used (as in the previous models) if the seasonal changes are hypothesized to occur quarterly. In general, this approach to seasonal modeling requires one dummy variable fewer than the number of seasonal changes expected to occur.

There are approaches besides the regression dummy variable method for forecasting seasonal time series. Trigonometric (sine and cosine) terms can be used in regression models to model periodicity. Other time series models (the Holt-Winters exponential smoothing model, for example) do not use the regression approach at all, and there are various methods for adding seasonal components to these models. We have chosen to discuss the regression approach because it makes use of the important modeling concepts covered in Chapters 11 and 12, and because the regression forecasts are accompanied by prediction intervals that provide some measure of the forecast reliability. While most other methods do not have explicit measures of reliability, many have proved their merit by providing good forecasts for particular applications. Consult the references at the end of the book for details of other seasonal models.

EXERCISES 14.38–14.45

Note: Exercises marked with a disk contain data for computer analysis on a 3.5" disk (file name in parentheses).

Learning the Mechanics

14.38 What advantage do regression forecasts have over exponentially smoothed forecasts? Does this advantage ensure that regression forecasts will prove to be more accurate? Explain.

14.39 The annual price of finished steel (in cents per pound) from 1980 to 1995 is given in the table, followed by a SAS printout (on page 775) for the simple linear regression model fit to these data.

The time variable t begins with $t = 1$ in 1980 and is incremented by 1 for each additional year.

Year	t	Price	Year	t	Price
1980	1	21.73	1988	9	24.42
1981	2	24.32	1989	10	25.49
1982	3	25.31	1990	11	26.19
1983	4	26.36	1991	12	27.31
1984	5	27.31	1992	13	24.40
1985	6	27.58	1993	14	24.24
1986	7	24.79	1994	15	25.87
1987	8	25.36	1995	16	26.86

Source: Standard & Poor's. Current Statistics, Dec. 1996.

Dependent Variable: PRICE

Analysis of Variance

Source	DF	Sum of Squares	Mean Square	F Value	Prob>F
Model	1	2.81736	2.81736	1.257	0.2811
Error	14	31.37941	2.24139		
C Total	15	34.19678			

Root MSE	1.49713	R-square	0.0824	
Dep Mean	25.47125	Adj R-sq	0.0168	
C.V.	5.87771			

Parameter Estimates

Variable	DF	Parameter Estimate	Standard Error	T for H0: Parameter=0	Prob > |T|
INTERCEP	1	24.697500	0.78509959	31.458	0.0001
T	1	0.091029	0.08119307	1.121	0.2811

Obs	YEAR	Dep Var PRICE	Predict Value	Std Err Predict	Lower95% Predict	Upper95% Predict	Residual
1	1980	21.7300	24.7885	0.715	21.2303	28.3467	-3.0585
2	1981	24.3200	24.8796	0.647	21.3815	28.3776	-0.5596
3	1982	25.3100	24.9706	0.583	21.5250	28.4162	0.3394
4	1983	26.3600	25.0616	0.523	21.6603	28.4630	1.2984
5	1984	27.3100	25.1526	0.470	21.7872	28.5181	2.1574
6	1985	27.5800	25.2437	0.426	21.9053	28.5820	2.3363
7	1986	24.7900	25.3347	0.394	22.0146	28.6548	-0.5447
8	1987	25.3600	25.4257	0.376	22.1148	28.7367	-0.0657
9	1988	24.4200	25.5168	0.376	22.2058	28.8277	-1.0968
10	1989	25.4900	25.6078	0.394	22.2877	28.9279	-0.1178
11	1990	26.1900	25.6988	0.426	22.3605	29.0372	0.4912
12	1991	27.3100	25.7899	0.470	22.4244	29.1553	1.5201
13	1992	24.4000	25.8809	0.523	22.4795	29.2822	-1.4809
14	1993	24.2400	25.9719	0.583	22.5263	29.4175	-1.7319
15	1994	25.8700	26.0629	0.647	22.5649	29.5610	-0.1929
16	1995	26.8600	26.1540	0.715	22.5958	29.7122	0.7060
17	1996	.	26.2450	0.785	22.6193	29.8707	.
18	1997	.	26.3360	0.857	22.6358	30.0363	.

a. Find the least squares estimates of the β's on the printout.

b. Use the least squares prediction equation to obtain the forecasts for 1996 and 1997. Do your results agree with those shown on the SAS printout?

c. Locate the 95% forecast intervals for 1996 and 1997 on the printout. Interpret the results.

14.40 **(X14.040)** Retail sales in quarters 1–4 over a 10-year period for a department store are shown (in hundreds of thousands of dollars) in the table.

a. Write a regression model that contains trend and seasonal components to describe the sales data.

	QUARTER			
Year	1	2	3	4
1	8.3	10.3	8.7	13.5
2	9.8	12.1	10.1	15.4
3	12.1	14.5	12.7	17.1
4	13.7	16.0	14.2	19.2
5	17.4	19.7	18.0	23.1
6	18.2	20.5	18.6	24.0
7	20.0	22.2	20.5	25.1
8	22.3	25.1	22.9	27.7
9	24.7	26.9	25.1	29.8
10	25.8	28.7	26.0	32.2

b. Use a least squares regression program to fit the model. Evaluate the fit of the model.
c. Use the regression model to forecast the quarterly sales during year 11. Give 95% confidence intervals for the forecasts.

Applying the Concepts

14.41 The table reports the total personal annual income (in billions of dollars) of people in the state of California over the period 1980 to 1995. A simple linear regression model, $E(Y_t) = \beta_0 + \beta_1 t$, is fit to the 1980–1993 income data, where t is the number of years since 1979. A MINITAB printout is shown at the bottom of the page.

Year	Personal Income	Year	Personal Income
1980	$281	1988	$547
1981	314	1989	588
1982	335	1990	637
1983	361	1991	651
1984	402	1992	683
1985	437	1993	698
1986	468	1994	716
1987	505	1995	760

Source: U.S. Dept. of Commerce. *Survey of Current Business*, 1996.

a. Find the least squares estimates of the β's and interpret their values.
b. Evaluate the model's fit.
c. The 95% prediction intervals for the years 1994–1995 are shown at the bottom of the MINITAB printout. Do these intervals contain the actual income values?

d. Describe the problems associated with using a simple linear regression model to predict time series data.

14.42 (X14.042) There was phenomenal growth in the transportation sector of the U.S. economy during the 1960s and 1970s. The personal consumption expenditure figures (in billions of dollars) for this sector are given in the table.

Year	Expenditure	Year	Expenditure
1970	80.6	1983	291.9
1971	92.3	1984	319.5
1972	105.4	1985	359.5
1973	114.6	1986	366.3
1974	117.9	1987	377.1
1975	129.4	1988	406.4
1976	155.2	1989	425.7
1977	179.3	1990	453.7
1978	198.1	1991	438.2
1979	219.4	1992	466.3
1980	236.6	1993	504.2
1981	261.5	1994	536.6
1982	267.3		

Source: U.S. Bureau of the Census. *Statistical Abstract of the United States*, 1995.

a. Fit the simple regression model

$$E(Y_t) = \beta_0 + \beta_1 t$$

where t is the number of years since 1970 (i.e., $t = 0, 1, ..., 24$).
b. Forecast the personal consumption expenditure from 1995 to 1997. Calculate 95% confidence intervals for these forecasts.

```
The regression equation is
INCOME = 237 + 34.2 T

Predictor        Coef       Stdev      t-ratio          p
Constant       236.989      6.319        37.50      0.000
T              34.1824     0.7421        46.06      0.000

s = 11.19       R-sq = 99.4%    R-sq(adj) = 99.4%

Analysis of Variance

SOURCE         DF          SS          MS          F          p
Regression      1      265820      265820    2121.40      0.000
Error          12        1504         125
Total          13      267323

    Fit   Stdev.Fit          95% C.I.            95% P.I.
 749.73        6.32   ( 735.95, 763.50)   ( 721.71, 777.74)

 783.91        6.98   ( 768.69, 799.12)   ( 755.16, 812.66)
```

14.43   **(X14.043)** The table reports the total weight of shipments of Portland cement (in thousands of tons) from plants in the United States and Puerto Rico during 1990 and 1991.

	Jan	Feb	Mar	Apr	May	June
1990	5,571	5,105	6,667	7,343	8,447	8,748
1991	3,999	4,390	5,163	6,678	7,500	7,499

	Jul	Aug	Sep	Oct	Nov	Dec
1990	8,205	9,206	7,904	8,676	7,184	4,780
1991	8,029	8,150	7,575	9,957	4,222	4,896

Source: Construction Review, Nov.–Dec., 1991.

a. Write a regression model that describes the variation in the cement shipments. Include both trend and seasonal components in the model.

b. Use the method of least squares to fit your model to the data.

c. Use the results of part **b** to forecast cement shipments in January, February, and March of 1992.

d. The actual shipment weights (thousands of tons) for January, February, and March of 1992 were 4,566, 4,614, and 5,774, respectively. Use these data and the MAD to evaluate your forecasting model.

14.44   The next table presents the quarterly sales index for one brand of calculator at a campus bookstore. The quarters are based on an academic year, so the first quarter represents fall; the second, winter; the third, spring; and the fourth, summer.

Year	First Quarter	Second Quarter	Third Quarter	Fourth Quarter
1992	438	398	252	160
1993	464	429	376	216
1994	523	496	425	318
1995	593	576	456	398
1996	636	640	526	498

We defined the time variable as $t = 1$ for the first quarter of 1992, $t = 2$ for the second quarter of 1992, etc. The seasonal dummy variables are as follows:

$$Q_1 = \begin{cases} 1 & \text{if quarter 1} \\ 0 & \text{otherwise} \end{cases}$$

$$Q_2 = \begin{cases} 1 & \text{if quarter 2} \\ 0 & \text{otherwise} \end{cases}$$

$$Q_3 = \begin{cases} 1 & \text{if quarter 3} \\ 0 & \text{otherwise} \end{cases}$$

The SAS printout for the model

$$E(Y_t) = \beta_0 + \beta_1 t + \beta_2 Q_1 + \beta_3 Q_2 + \beta_4 Q_3$$

is reproduced on page 778.

a. Interpret the least squares estimates, and evaluate the usefulness of the model.

b. Which of the assumptions about the random error component is in doubt when a regression model is fit to time series data?

c. Find the forecasts and the 95% prediction intervals for the 1997 quarterly sales. Interpret the result.

14.45   **(X14.045)** The table below represents all life insurance policies (in millions) in force on the lives of U.S. residents for the years 1970 through 1993:

Year	No. of Policies (in millions)	Year	No. of Policies (in millions)
1970	355	1982	390
1971	357	1983	387
1972	365	1984	385
1973	369	1985	386
1974	380	1986	391
1975	380	1987	395
1976	382	1988	391
1977	390	1989	394
1978	401	1990	389
1979	407	1991	375
1980	402	1992	366
1981	400	1993	363

Source: U.S. Bureau of the Census. *Statistical Abstract of the United States, 1995.*

a. Use the method of least squares to fit a simple regression model to the data.

b. Forecast the number of life insurance policies in force for 1994 and 1995.

c. Construct 95% confidence intervals for the forecasts of part **b**.

d. Check the accuracy of your forecasts by looking up the actual number of life insurance policies in force for 1994 and 1995 in the *Statistical Abstract of the United States.*

```
Dep Variable: Y
                       Analysis of Variance
                       Sum of          Mean
      Source    DF     Squares        Square      F Value    Prob>F

      Model      4  318560.30000    79640.07500   117.817    0.0001
      Error     15   10139.50000      675.96667
      C Total   19  328699.80000

          Root MSE      25.99936    R-Square     0.9692
          Dep Mean     440.90000    Adj R-Sq     0.9609
          C.V.          5.89688

                       Parameter Estimates

                     Parameter      Standard    T for H0:
      Variable   DF   Estimate        Error    Parameter=0    Prob > |T|

      INTERCEP    1   119.850000   16.94950835     7.071        0.0001
      T           1    16.512500    1.02771490    16.067        0.0001
      Q1          1   262.337500   16.72998649    15.681        0.0001
      Q2          1   222.825000   16.57140484    13.446        0.0001
      Q3          1   105.512500   16.47552320     6.404        0.0001

                          Predict              Lower95%   Upper95%
        Obs      Y         Value    Residual    Predict    Predict

         1     438.0      398.7     39.3000      335.5      461.9
         2     398.0      375.7     22.3000      312.5      438.9
         3     252.0      274.9    -22.9000      211.7      338.1
         4     160.0      185.9    -25.9000      122.7      249.1
         5     464.0      464.7     -0.7500      403.4      526.1
         6     429.0      441.7    -12.7500      380.4      503.1
         7     376.0      340.9     35.0500      279.6      402.3
         8     216.0      251.9    -35.9500      190.6      313.3
         9     523.0      530.8     -7.8000      470.1      591.5
        10     496.0      507.8    -11.8000      447.1      568.5
        11     425.0      407.0     18.0000      346.3      467.7
        12     318.0      318.0          0       257.3      378.7
        13     593.0      596.9     -3.8500      535.5      658.2
        14     576.0      573.9      2.1500      512.5      635.2
        15     456.0      473.1    -17.0500      411.7      534.4
        16     398.0      384.0     13.9500      322.7      445.4
        17     636.0      662.9    -26.9000      599.7      726.1
        18     640.0      639.9      0.1000      576.7      703.1
        19     526.0      539.1    -13.1000      475.9      602.3
        20     498.0      450.1     47.9000      386.9      513.3
        21       .        729.0        .         662.8      795.1
        22       .        706.0        .         639.8      772.1
        23       .        605.1        .         539.0      671.3
        24       .        516.1        .         450.0      582.3
```

14.9 AUTOCORRELATION AND THE DURBIN-WATSON TEST

Recall that one of the assumptions we make when using a regression model for predictions is that the errors are independent. However, with time series data, this assumption is questionable. The cyclical component of a time series may result in

FIGURE 14.15
Illustration of cyclical
errors

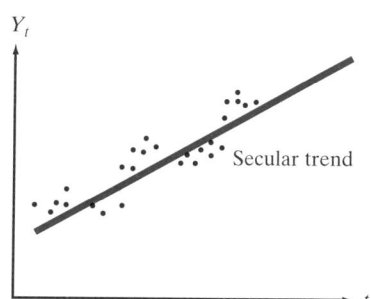

deviations from the secular trend that tend to cluster alternately on the positive and negative sides of the trend, as shown in Figure 14.15.

The observed errors between the time series and the regression model for the secular trend (and seasonal component, if present) are called **time series residuals**. Thus, if the time series Y_t has an estimated trend of $\hat{Y}_t$, then the time series residual* is

$$\hat{R}_t = Y_t - \hat{Y}_t$$

Note that time series residuals are defined just as the residuals for any regression model. However, we will usually plot time series residuals versus time to determine whether a cyclical component is apparent.

For example, consider the sales forecasting data in Table 14.11, to which we fit a simple straight-line regression model. The plot of the data and model is repeated in Figure 14.16, and a plot of the time series residuals is shown in Figure 14.17.

Notice the tendency of the residuals to group alternately into positive and negative clusters. That is, if the residual for year t is positive, there is a tendency for the residual for year $(t + 1)$ to be positive. These cycles are indicative of possible positive correlation between neighboring residuals. The correlation between time series residuals at different points in time is called **autocorrelation**, and the autocorrelation of neighboring residuals (time periods t and $t + 1$) is called **first-order autocorrelation**.

FIGURE 14.16
Plot of sales data

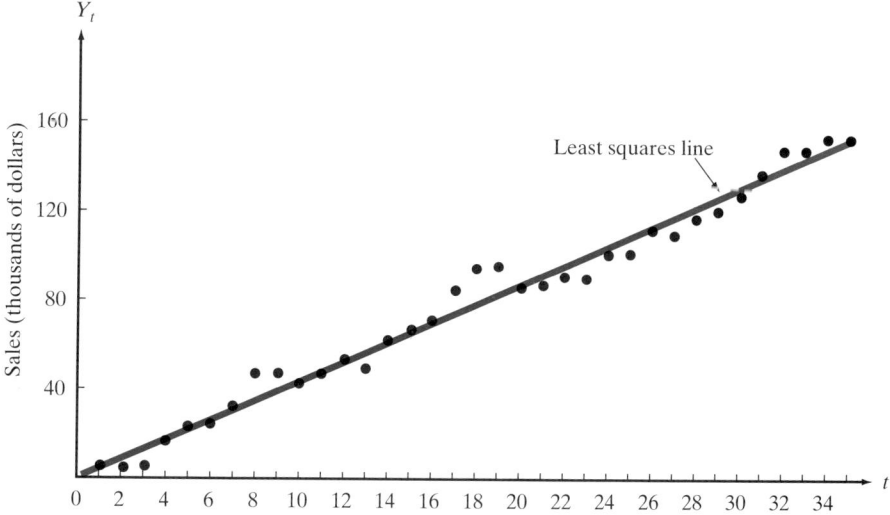

*We use $\hat{R}_t$ rather than $\hat{\epsilon}$ to denote a time series residual because, as we shall see, time series residuals often do not satisfy the regression assumptions associated with the random component ϵ.

FIGURE 14.17

Plot of residuals versus
time for the sales data:
Least squares model

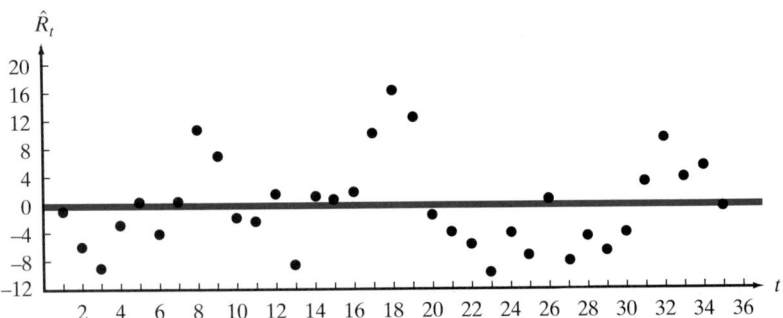

DEFINITION 14.5

The correlation between time series residuals at different points in time is called
autocorrelation. Correlation between neighboring residuals (at times t and $t + 1$) is
called **first-order autocorrelation**. In general, correlation between residuals at times
t and $t + d$ is called dth-order autocorrelation.

　　Rather than speculate about the presence of autocorrelation among time series
residuals, we prefer to test for it. For most business and economic time series, the
relevant test is for first-order autocorrelation. Other higher-order autocorrelations
may indicate seasonality, e.g., fourth-order autocorrelation in a quarterly time
series. However, when we use the term *autocorrelation* in this text we are referring
to first-order autocorrelation unless otherwise specified. So, we test

　　H_0: No first-order autocorrelation of residuals

　　H_a: Positive first-order autocorrelation of residuals

　　The **Durbin-Watson d statistic** is used to test for the presence of first-order
autocorrelation. The statistic is given by the formula

$$d = \frac{\sum_{t=2}^{n}(\hat{R}_t - \hat{R}_{t-1})^2}{\sum_{t=1}^{n}\hat{R}_t^2}$$

where n is the number of observations (time periods) and $(\hat{R}_t - \hat{R}_{t-1})$ represents
the difference between a pair of successive time series residuals. The value of d
always falls in the interval from 0 to 4. The interpretations of the values of d are
given in the box. Most statistical software packages include a routine that calculates d for time series residuals.

Interpretation of Durbin-Watson d Statistic

$$d = \frac{\sum_{t=2}^{n}(\hat{R}_t - \hat{R}_{t-1})^2}{\sum_{t=1}^{n}\hat{R}_t^2} \qquad \text{Range of } d: 0 \leqslant d \leqslant 4$$

1. If the residuals are uncorrelated, then $d \approx 2$.

2. If the residuals are positively autocorrelated, then $d < 2$, and if the autocorrelation is very strong, $d \approx 0$.

3. If the residuals are negatively autocorrelated, then $d > 2$, and if the autocorrelation is very strong, $d \approx 4$.

Durbin and Watson (1951) give tables for the lower-tail values of the d statistic, which are shown in Tables XIV ($\alpha = .05$) and XV ($\alpha = .01$) of Appendix B. Part of Table XIV is reproduced in Table 14.18. For the sales example, we have $k = 1$ independent variable and $n = 35$ observations. Using $\alpha = .05$ for the one-tailed test for positive autocorrelation, we obtain the tabled values $d_L = 1.40$ and $d_U = 1.52$. The meaning of these values is illustrated in Figure 14.18. Because of the complexity of the sampling distribution of d, it is not possible to specify a single point that acts as a boundary between the rejection and nonrejection regions, as we did for the z, t, F, and other test statistics. Instead, an upper (d_U) and lower (d_L) bound are specified. Thus a d value less than d_L *does* provide strong evidence of positive autocorrelation at $\alpha = .05$ (recall that small d values indicate positive autocorrelation); a d value greater than d_U does *not* provide evidence of positive autocorrelation at $\alpha = .05$; and a value of d between d_L and d_U might or might not be significant at the $\alpha = .05$ level. If $d_L < d < d_U$, more information is needed before we can reach any conclusion about the presence of autocorrelation.

TABLE 14.18   Reproduction of Part of Table XIV of Appendix B: Critical Values for the Durbin-Watson d Statistic, $\alpha = .05$

	$k = 1$		$k = 2$		$k = 3$		$k = 4$		$k = 5$	
n	d_L	d_U	d_L	d_U	d_L	d_U	d_L	d_U	d_L	d_U
31	1.36	1.50	1.30	1.57	1.23	1.65	1.16	1.74	1.09	1.83
32	1.37	1.50	1.31	1.57	1.24	1.65	1.18	1.73	1.11	1.82
33	1.38	1.51	1.32	1.58	1.26	1.65	1.19	1.73	1.13	1.81
34	1.39	1.51	1.33	1.58	1.27	1.65	1.21	1.73	1.15	1.81
35	1.40	1.52	1.34	1.58	1.28	1.65	1.22	1.73	1.16	1.80
36	1.41	1.52	1.35	1.59	1.29	1.65	1.24	1.73	1.18	1.80
37	1.42	1.53	1.36	1.59	1.31	1.66	1.25	1.72	1.19	1.80
38	1.43	1.54	1.37	1.59	1.32	1.66	1.26	1.72	1.21	1.79
39	1.43	1.54	1.38	1.60	1.33	1.66	1.27	1.72	1.22	1.79
40	1.44	1.54	1.39	1.60	1.34	1.66	1.29	1.72	1.23	1.79

FIGURE 14.18
Rejection region for the Durbin-Watson d test: Sales example

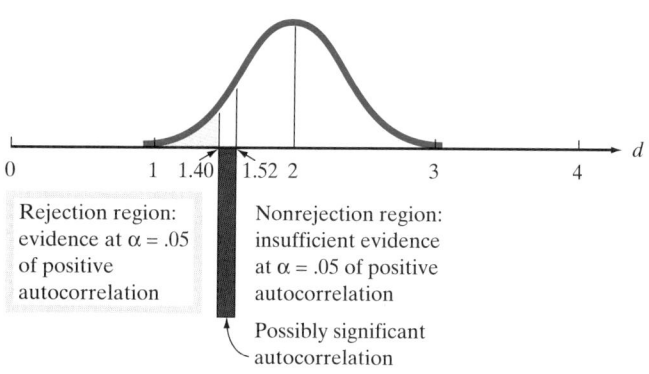

Rejection region: evidence at $\alpha = .05$ of positive autocorrelation

Nonrejection region: insufficient evidence at $\alpha = .05$ of positive autocorrelation

Possibly significant autocorrelation

Tests for negative autocorrelation and two-tailed tests can be conducted by making use of the symmetry of the sampling distribution of the d statistic about its mean, 2 (see Figure 14.18). The test procedure is summarized in the next box.

Durbin-Watson d Test

One-Tailed Test

H_0: No first-order autocorrelation

H_a: Positive first-order autocorrelation (or H_a: Negative first-order autocorrelation)

Test statistic:

$$d = \frac{\sum_{t=2}^{n}(\hat{R}_t - \hat{R}_{t-1})^2}{\sum_{t=1}^{n}\hat{R}_t^2}$$

Rejection region: $d < d_{L,\alpha}$
[or $(4 - d) < d_{L,\alpha}$ if H_a: Negative first-order autocorrelation]

where $d_{L,\alpha}$ is the lower tabled value corresponding to k independent variables and n observations. The corresponding upper value $d_{U,\alpha}$ defines a "possibly significant" region between $d_{L,\alpha}$ and $d_{U,\alpha}$ (see Figure 14.18).

Two-Tailed Test

H_0: No first-order autocorrelation

H_a: Positive or negative first-order autocorrelation

Test statistic:

$$d = \frac{\sum_{t=2}^{n}(\hat{R}_t - \hat{R}_{t-1})^2}{\sum_{t=1}^{n}\hat{R}_t^2}$$

Rejection region: $d < d_{L,\alpha/2}$
or $(4 - d) < d_{L,\alpha/2}$

where $d_{L,\alpha/2}$ is the lower tabled value corresponding to k independent variables and n observations. The corresponding upper value $d_{U,\alpha/2}$ defines a "possibly significant" region between $d_{L,\alpha/2}$ and $d_{U,\alpha/2}$ (see Figure 14.18).

Assumption: The residuals are normally distributed.

The SAS regression printout for the sales example is presented in Figure 14.19. It shows that the computed value of d is .82 (highlighted), which is less than the tabulated value of $d_L = 1.40$ for $\alpha = .05$. Thus, we conclude that the residuals of the straight-line model for sales are positively autocorrelated.

Once strong evidence of first-order autocorrelation has been established, as in the case of the sales example, doubt is cast on the least squares results and any inferences drawn from them. Under these circumstances, a time series model that accounts for the autocorrelation of the random errors is needed. A useful model is the first-order autoregressive model. Consult the references at the end of the book.

EXERCISES 14.46–14.51

Note: Exercises marked with 💾 *contain data for computer analysis on a 3.5" disk (file name in parentheses).*

Learning the Mechanics

14.46 Define autocorrelation. Explain why it is important in time series modeling and forecasting.

14.47 What do the following Durbin-Watson statistics suggest about the autocorrelation of the time series residuals from which each was calculated?
a. $d = 3.9$ b. $d = .2$ c. $d = 1.99$

14.48 For each case, indicate the decision regarding the test of the null hypothesis of no first-order auto-

Dependent Variable: Y

Analysis of Variance

Source	DF	Sum of Squares	Mean Square	F Value	Prob>F
Model	1	65875.20817	65875.20817	1615.724	0.0001
Error	33	1345.45355	40.77132		
C Total	34	67220.66171			

Root MSE	6.38524	R-Square	0.9800
Dep Mean	77.72286	Adj R-Sq	0.9794
C.V.	8.21540		

Parameter Estimates

Variable	DF	Parameter Estimate	Standard Error	T for H0: Parameter=0	Prob > |T|
INTERCEP	1	0.401513	2.20570829	0.182	0.8567
T	1	4.295630	0.10686692	40.196	0.0001

Durbin-Watson D   0.821
(For Number of Obs.)   35
1st Order Autocorrelation   0.590

FIGURE 14.19 SAS printout for the regression analysis: Annual sales data

correlation against the alternative hypothesis of positive first-order autocorrelation.
a. $k = 2, n = 20, \alpha = .05, d = 1.1$
b. $k = 2, n = 20, \alpha = .01, d = 1.1$
c. $k = 5, n = 65, \alpha = .05, d = .95$
d. $k = 1, n = 31, \alpha = .01, d = 1.35$

Applying the Concepts

14.49 (X14.049) The decrease in the value of the dollar, Y_t, from 1960 to 1991 is illustrated by the data in the table at right. The buying power of the dollar (compared with 1982) is listed for each year. The first-order model

$$Y_t = \beta_0 + \beta_1 t + \epsilon$$

was fit to the data using the method of least squares. The SAS printout, with regression residuals, is shown on page 784.
a. Plot the regression residuals against t. Is there a tendency for the residuals to have long positive and negative runs? To what do you attribute this phenomenon?
b. Locate the Durbin-Watson d statistic on the printout and test the null hypothesis that the time series residuals are uncorrelated. Use $\alpha = .10$.
c. What assumption(s) must be satisfied in order for the test of part **b** to be valid?

14.50 (X14.050) In December 1988, a pharmaceutical company based in New Jersey introduced a new cold medicine called Coldex (for proprietary rea-

t	Y_t	t	Y_t	t	Y_t
1960	2.994	1971	2.469	1982	1.000
1961	2.994	1972	2.392	1983	0.984
1962	2.985	1973	2.193	1984	0.964
1963	2.994	1974	1.901	1985	0.955
1964	2.985	1975	1.718	1986	0.969
1965	2.933	1976	1.645	1987	0.949
1966	2.841	1977	1.546	1988	0.926
1967	2.809	1978	1.433	1989	0.880
1968	2.732	1979	1.289	1990	0.839
1969	2.632	1980	1.136	1991	0.822
1970	2.545	1981	1.041		

Source: U.S. Bureau of the Census. *Statistical Abstract of the United States, 1992.*

sons, the actual name of the product is withheld) It is sold in drugstores and supermarkets across the United States. Monthly sales data for December 1988 through December 1990 are reported in the first table on page 785.
a. Construct a time series plot for these data.
b. Fit a simple linear regression model to the data.
c. Calculate and plot the regression residuals against time. Does the plot suggest the presence of autocorrelation? Explain.
d. Use the Durbin-Watson statistic to formally test for the presence of autocorrelation.
e. Based on the results of parts **a**, **b**, **c**, and **d** suggest a model other than the simple linear

Dependent Variable: Y

Analysis of Variance

Source	DF	Sum of Squares	Mean Square	F Value	Prob>F
Model	1	21.31446	21.31446	509.692	0.0001
Error	30	1.25455	0.04182		
C Total	31	22.56901			

Root MSE	0.20450	R-Square	0.9444
Dep Mean	1.85922	Adj R-Sq	0.9426
C.V.	10.99899		

Parameter Estimates

Variable	DF	Parameter Estimate	Standard Error	T for H0: Parameter=0	Prob > |T|
INTERCEP	1	176.478429	7.73468888	22.816	0.0001
T	1	-0.088392	0.00391526	-22.576	0.0001

Durbin-Watson D	0.122
(For Number of Obs.)	32
1st Order Autocorrelation	0.873

Obs	T	Dep Var Y	Predict Value	Residual
1	1960	2.9940	3.2293	-0.2353
2	1961	2.9940	3.1409	-0.1469
3	1962	2.9850	3.0525	-0.0675
4	1963	2.9940	2.9641	0.0299
5	1964	2.9850	2.8757	0.1093
6	1965	2.9330	2.7873	0.1457
7	1966	2.8410	2.6989	0.1421
8	1967	2.8090	2.6106	0.1984
9	1968	2.7320	2.5222	0.2098
10	1969	2.6320	2.4338	0.1982
11	1970	2.5450	2.3454	0.1996
12	1971	2.4690	2.2570	0.2120
13	1972	2.3920	2.1686	0.2234
14	1973	2.1930	2.0802	0.1128
15	1974	1.9010	1.9918	-0.0908
16	1975	1.7180	1.9034	-0.1854
17	1976	1.6450	1.8150	-0.1700
18	1977	1.5460	1.7266	-0.1806
19	1978	1.4330	1.6382	-0.2052
20	1979	1.2890	1.5498	-0.2608
21	1980	1.1360	1.4615	-0.3255
22	1981	1.0410	1.3731	-0.3321
23	1982	1.0000	1.2847	-0.2847
24	1983	0.9840	1.1963	-0.2123
25	1984	0.9640	1.1079	-0.1439
26	1985	0.9550	1.0195	-0.0645
27	1986	0.9690	0.9311	0.0379
28	1987	0.9490	0.8427	0.1063
29	1988	0.9260	0.7543	0.1717
30	1989	0.8800	0.6659	0.2141
31	1990	0.8390	0.5775	0.2615
32	1991	0.8220	0.4891	0.3329

COLDEX SALES (THOUSANDS OF $)					
	Jan	Feb	Mar	Apr	May	June
1988						
1989	3,394	4,010	924	205	293	1,130
1990	4,568	3,710	1,675	999	986	1,786

	Jul	Aug	Sep	Oct	Nov	Dec
1988						1,993
1989	1,116	4,009	5,692	3,458	2,849	3,470
1990	2,253	5,237	6,679	4,116	4,109	5,124

Source: Personal communication from Carol Cowley, Carla Marchesini, and Ginny Wilson, Rutgers University, Graduate School of Management.

Month	Time t	1994 Sales Y_t	Time t	1995 Sales Y_t
Jan.	1	35.17	13	37.05
Feb.	2	37.87	14	40.53
Mar.	3	47.34	15	50.69
Apr.	4	46.21	16	47.09
May	5	45.80	17	51.96
June	6	48.08	18	54.16
July	7	44.49	19	49.20
Aug.	8	46.91	20	49.29
Sept.	9	45.23	21	45.10
Oct.	10	45.08	22	44.46
Nov.	11	42.59	23	41.90
Dec.	12	41.55	24	40.25

Source: Standard & Poor's Current Statistics, 1996.

regression model of part **b** that could be used to forecast future sales of Coldex.

14.51 The table at upper right gives the volume of retail sales (in millions of dollars) of passenger cars in the United States by motor vehicle dealers for the years 1994 and 1995. The first-order time series model

$$Y_t = \beta_0 + \beta_1 t + \epsilon$$

was fit to the data using SAS; the printout is shown below.

a. Interpret the least squares estimates.

b. With what approximate precision do you expect this model to predict annual sales (assuming the necessary assumptions about the random component ϵ are satisfied)?

c. Is there evidence at the $\alpha = .10$ level of significance that the residuals are autocorrelated?

```
Dependent Variable: SALES

                          Analysis of Variance

                              Sum of          Mean
        Source       DF      Squares         Square      F Value      Prob>F

        Model         1      30.89761       30.89761        1.428      0.2448
        Error        22     475.93872       21.63358
        C Total      23     506.83633

            Root MSE         4.65119      R-Square      0.0610
            Dep Mean        44.91667      Adj R-Sq      0.0183
            C.V.            10.35516

                          Parameter Estimates

                      Parameter     Standard     T for H0:
        Variable  DF   Estimate       Error     Parameter=0     Prob > |T|

        INTERCEP   1   42.867754    1.95978162     21.874        0.0001
        T          1    0.163913    0.13715614      1.195        0.2448

Durbin-Watson D                 0.757
(For Number of Obs.)               24
1st Order Autocorrelation       0.511
```

QUICK REVIEW

Key Terms

Adaptive forecast   755
Additive model   753
Autocorrelation   780
Base period   734
Composite index number   736
Cyclical effect   754
Durbin-Watson test   782
Exponential smoothing   748
Exponential smoothing constant   754

First-order autocorrelation   780
Forecast error   757
Holt-Winters forecasting model   757
Index number   734
Inferential forecasting model   753
Laspeyres index   739
Long-term trend   753
Mean absolute deviation   763
Paasche index   741

Residual effect   754
Root mean squared error   763
Seasonal model   754
Secular trend   753
Simple composite index number   736
Simple index number   735
Time series   734
Weighted composite price index   738

Key Formulas

$$I_t = \left(\frac{Y_t}{Y_0}\right)100$$

Simple index   736

$$I_t = \left(\frac{\text{Total of all } Y\text{-values at time } t}{\text{Total of all } Y\text{-values at time } t_0}\right)100$$

Simple composite index   736

Weighted composite price indexes:

$$I_t = \left(\frac{\sum_{i=1}^{k} Q_{it_0} P_{it}}{\sum_{i=1}^{k} Q_{it_0} P_{it_0}}\right)100$$

Laspeyres   739

$$I_t = \left(\frac{\sum_{i=1}^{k} Q_{it} P_{it}}{\sum_{i=1}^{k} Q_{it} P_{it_0}}\right)100$$

Paasche   741

Exponential smoothing:
$$E_t = wY_t + (1-w)E_{t-1} \quad \text{Note: } E_1 = Y_1$$
750
$$\text{Forecast:} F_{t+k} = E_t$$
755

Holt-Winters model:
$$E_t = wY_t + (1-w)(E_{t-1} + T_{t-1}) \quad \text{Note: } E_2 = Y_2, T_2 = Y_2 - Y_1$$
758
$$T_t = v(E_t - E_{t-1}) + (1-v)T_{t-1}$$
$$\text{Forecast: } F_{t+k} = E_t + kT_t$$
760

$$\text{MAD} = \frac{\sum_{t=1}^{N}|F_t - Y_t|}{N}$$

Mean absolute deviation   763

$$\text{RMSE} = \sqrt{\frac{\sum_{t=1}^{N}(F_t - Y_t)^2}{N}}$$

Root mean square error   763

$$d = \frac{\sum_{t=2}^{n}(\hat{R}_t - \hat{R}_{t-1})^2}{\sum_{t=1}^{n}\hat{R}_t^2}$$

Durbin-Watson test statistic   780

LANGUAGE LAB

Symbol	Pronunciation	Description
Y_t	Y sub t	Time series value at time t
I_t	I sub t	Index at time t
P_t	P sub t	Price series at time t
Q_t	Q sub t	Quantity series at time t
E_t	E sub t	Exponentially smoothed value at time t
T_t	T sub t	Smoothed trend at time t
F_{t+k}	F sub t-plus-k	k-step-ahead forecast value
MAD	Mad	Mean absolute deviation
RMSE	R-M-S-E	Root mean squared error
$\hat{R}_t$	R-hat sub t	Residual at time t
d	d	Value of Durbin-Watson test statistic
d_L	d sub L	Lower critical value of d
d_U	d sub U	Upper critical value of d

SUPPLEMENTARY EXERCISES 14.52–14.67

Note: Exercises marked with *contain data for computer analysis on a 3.5" disk (file name in parentheses).*

14.52 **(X14.052)** The U.S. steel industry was the object of much economic attention in the 1980s due to the increasing market share of imported steel, the effects of several recessions, and other economic woes. Prices (in cents per pound) of three varieties of U.S. steel are given in the table for the period 1980–1994.

Year	Cold Rolled	Hot Rolled	Galvanized
1980	21.91	18.46	23.88
1981	23.90	20.15	26.88
1982	24.65	20.80	26.75
1983	26.36	22.23	28.43
1984	28.15	23.75	30.30
1985	28.15	23.75	30.30
1986	25.65	21.15	30.30
1987	27.38	21.64	30.49
1988	28.15	21.50	31.05
1989	28.15	21.50	32.48
1990	25.37	22.25	33.55
1991	25.75	22.88	35.35
1992	24.03	19.13	30.88
1993	23.83	17.25	30.90
1994	25.70	17.25	32.24

Sources: Standard & Poor's Statistics: Metals, 1995; The CRB Community Yearbook, 1996.

a. Compute the exponentially smoothed series corresponding to each of the price series using the smoothing constant $w = .5$.

b. Plot the prices and their exponentially smoothed series on the same graph.

c. Find the exponential smoothing forecasts of 1997 prices of the three varieties of steel. What are the drawbacks to these forecasts?

14.53 Refer to Exercise 14.52.

a. Calculate a simple composite index for the three steel price series using 1980 as the base period.

b. Is the index a price index or a quantity index?

c. What information would you need in order to calculate a Laspeyres index with a base period of 1980? A Paasche index with a base period of 1980?

14.54 **(X14.054)** In the mid-1990s, the U.S. Congress began focusing on ways to rein in the ballooning federal budget. The table on page 788 reports total federal spending from 1973 through 1996, in billions of actual dollars—referred to as *current dollars*—and in billions of 1996 dollars. When current dollars are reexpressed as 1996 dollars, the resulting figure is the number of dollars that would have to have been spent in 1996 to equal the purchasing power of the current dollars.

a. Plot the two original federal spending time series on the same graph and describe in words the movement of the two series over time.

b. Explain why the current-dollars series remains below the 1996-dollar series for all but the last observation.

c. Using 1973 as the base period, calculate a simple index for both time series over the period 1973-1996.

TOTAL FEDERAL SPENDING (IN BILLIONS)

	In Current Dollars	In 1996 Dollars
1973	4.6	16.2
1974	5.8	18.4
1975	6.8	19.8
1976	8.6	23.7
1977	9.9	25.6
1978	10.7	25.7
1979	12.4	26.7
1980	14.0	26.6
1981	16.8	28.9
1982	17.4	28.2
1983	19.0	29.9
1984	20.1	30.3
1985	22.7	33.0
1986	25.0	35.7
1987	27.4	37.8
1988	30.5	40.4
1989	34.6	43.7
1990	41.1	49.2
1991	52.5	60.4
1992	67.8	75.7
1993	75.8	82.1
1994	82.0	86.6
1995	89.1	91.6
1996	92.0	92.0

Source: The New York Times, Jan. 14, 1997.

d. Plot the two indexes on the same graph.

e. Using the results of parts **c** and **d**, determine the percentage increase in federal spending from 1973 to 1996 in current dollars and in 1996 dollars. Which of these two figures is more appropriate for describing federal spending? Justify your answer.

14.55 In 1990, the average weekly food cost for a suburban family of four was estimated to be $154.40. In 1994, it had grown to $167.50, a modest increase in comparison to the inflationary days of the late 1970s and early 1980s. From 1978 through 1980, food prices rose over 30%. The following table presents the retail prices of selected food items.

Year	Bread ($/lb.)	Sirloin Steak ($/lb.)	Eggs ($/doz.)	Potatoes ($/lb.)
1990	.70	5.45	1.00	.32
1991	.72	5.21	1.01	.28
1992	.74	5.39	.93	.31
1993	.76	5.77	.87	.36
1994	.75	5.86	.87	.34

Source: U.S. Bureau of the Census. *Statistical Abstract of the United States,* 1995.

Assume a typical suburban family of four purchased the following quantities of food, on average, each week during 1990:

Bread	Sirloin Steak	Eggs	Potatoes
2 lbs.	4 lbs.	1 doz.	10 lbs.

a. Calculate a Laspeyres price index for 1990 to 1994, using 1990 as the base year.

b. According to your index, how much did the above "basket" of foods increase or decrease in price from 1990 to 1994?

14.56 Refer to the annual personal consumption time series, Exercise 14.42. Use $w = .3$ and $v = .7$ to compute the Holt-Winters forecasts for 1995–1997. Compare these to the linear regression forecasts obtained in Exercise 14.42 using MAD and RMSE. [*Note:* You will need to obtain the actual values of the time series for 1995–1997 to complete this exercise.]

14.57 **(X14.057)** The stock of Abbott Laboratories has had the yearly closing prices shown in the table.

Year	Closing Price	Year	Closing Price
1980	56.50	1988	48.01
1981	27.00	1989	64.03
1982	38.75	1990	45.00
1983	45.25	1991	68.07
1984	41.75	1992	30.03
1985	68.37	1993	29.05
1986	45.62	1994	32.05
1987	48.02	1995	41.05

Sources: NYSE. *Daily Stock Price Record,* 1980–1996; Standard & Poor's. *Security Owners' Stock Guide,* Jan. 1996.

a. Use exponential smoothing with $w = .8$ to forecast the 1996 and 1997 closing prices. If you buy at the end of 1995 and sell at the end of 1997, what is your expected gain (loss)?

b. Repeat part **a** using the Holt-Winters model with $w = .8$ and $v = .5$.

c. In which forecast do you have more confidence? Explain.

14.58 Refer to Exercise 14.57.

a. Fit a simple linear regression model to the stock price data.

b. Plot the fitted regression line on a scattergram of the data.

c. Forecast the 1996 and 1997 closing prices using the regression model.

d. Construct 95% prediction intervals for the forecasts of part **c**. Interpret the intervals in the context of the problem.

e. Obtain the time series residuals for the simple linear model, and use the Durbin-Watson d statistic to test for the presence of autocorrelation.

14.59 The yearly production of cereals (in thousands of metric tons) in Canada and Mexico for the period 1984 to 1993 are displayed in the next table.

Year	Canada	Mexico
1984	42,800	23,707
1985	48,239	27,403
1986	56,965	23,553
1987	51,682	23,636
1988	35,788	21,067
1989	48,402	21,429
1990	56,797	25,570
1991	53,850	23,616
1992	49,500	26,976
1993	52,241	25,825

Source: Department of Economic and Social Information and Policy Analysis, United Nations. *Statistical Yearbook,* 40th Issue, 1995.

a. Compute simple indexes for each of the two time series using 1986 as the base period.

b. Construct a time series plot that displays both indexes.

c. Using the results of parts **a** and **b**, compare and contrast cereal production in Canada and Mexico for the period 1984–1988.

14.60 **(X14.060)** The Gross Domestic Product (GDP) is the total U.S. output of goods and services valued at market prices. The quarterly GDP values (in billions of dollars) for the period 1980–1995 are given in the accompanying table.

	QUARTERS			
Year	1	2	3	4
1980	2,650.1	2,643.9	2,705.3	2,832.9
1981	2,953.5	2,993.0	3,079.6	3,096.3
1982	3,092.9	3,146.2	3,164.2	3,195.1
1983	3,254.9	3,367.1	3,450.9	3,547.3
1984	3,666.9	3,754.6	3,818.2	3,869.1
1985	3,940.0	3,997.5	4,076.9	4,140.5
1986	4,215.7	4,232.0	4,290.2	4,336.6
1987	4,408.3	4,494.9	4,573.5	4,683.0
1988	4,752.4	4,857.2	4,947.3	5,044.6
1989	5,139.9	5,218.5	5,277.3	5,340.4
1990	5,422.4	5,504.7	5,570.5	5,557.5
1991	5,589.0	5,652.6	5,709.2	5,739.7
1992	5,896.8	5,971.3	6,043.6	6,169.3
1993	6,235.9	6,299.9	6,359.2	6,478.1
1994	6,772.8	6,885.0	6,987.6	7,080.0
1995	7,147.8	7,196.5	7,298.5	7,348.1

Source: U.S. Bureau of Economic Analysis. *Business Statistics,* 1996.

Using only the data for 1993–1995 and weights $w = .5$ and $v = .5$, calculate Holt-Winters forecasts for the four quarters of 1996. Then complete as many entries as possible in the following table.

14.61 Refer to Exercise 14.60.

a. Use the simple linear regression model fit to the 1980–1995 data to forecast the 1996 quar-

Quarter	Actual 1996 GDP	Forecast	Forecast Error
1	7,421.4	—	—
2	7,545.1	—	—
3	7,611.8	—	—
4	—	—	—

terly GDP. Place 95% confidence limits on the forecasts.

b. The GDP values given are **seasonally adjusted**, which means that an attempt to remove seasonality has been made prior to reporting the figures. Add quarterly dummy variables to the model. Use the partial F-test (discussed in Section 12.4) to determine whether the data indicate the significance of the seasonal component. Does the test support the assertion that the GDP figures are seasonally adjusted?

c. Use the seasonal model to forecast the 1996 quarterly GDP values.

d. Calculate the time series residuals for the seasonal model, and use the Durbin-Watson test to determine whether the residuals are autocorrelated. Use $\alpha = .05$.

14.62 Refer to Exercises 14.60 and 14.61. For each of the forecasting models apply the MAD and RMSE criteria to evaluate the forecasts for the first three quarters of 1996. Which of the forecasting models performs best according to each criterion?

14.63 **(X14.063)** Three of the many indicators used for measuring the level of economic activity are the index of net business formation, the index of industrial production, and the index of new private housing units. End-of-year values of these indicators for the period 1980–1994 are given in the table.

Year	Index of Net Business Formation	Index of Industrial Production	Index of New Private Housing Units
1980	130	84	98
1981	125	85	102
1982	116	82	105
1983	118	85	108
1984	121	93	111
1985	121	94	115
1986	120	95	119
1987	121	102	123
1988	124	105	125
1989	125	108	128
1990	121	106	131
1991	115	106	133
1992	116	104	136
1993	121	108	140
1994	126	112	144

Source: U.S. Bureau of the Census. *Statistical Abstract of the United States, 1995.*

a. Calculate a simple composite index for the three indicator series, using 1980 as the base period.

b. Compute the simple index for each of the three indicator series, using a base period of 1980 for each. Plot the three simple indexes and the simple composite index on the same graph.

14.64 Refer to Exercise 14.63.

a. Calculate an exponentially smoothed series corresponding to the business formation index using $w = .2$. Using $w = .8$.

b. Plot on a graph both the business formation index and the two exponentially smoothed series from part **a**. Which exponential smoothing constant yields a smoother series? Explain.

14.65 **(X14.065)** A major portion of total consumer credit is extended in the categories of automobile loans, revolving credit loans, and other credit. Amounts outstanding (in billions of dollars) for the period 1980–1994 are given in the table.

Year	Automobile	Other	Revolving
1980	112.0	131.0	55.1
1981	119.0	131.2	61.1
1982	125.9	133.4	66.5
1983	143.6	146.4	79.1
1984	173.6	168.8	100.3
1985	210.2	185.7	121.8
1986	247.8	188.4	135.8
1987	266.3	189.3	153.1
1988	285.5	203.2	174.3
1989	292.5	233.3	198.5
1990	283.1	228.3	223.5
1991	259.6	223.5	245.3
1992	257.7	216.1	257.3
1993	282.0	224.4	287.9
1994	324.5	249.1	337.7

Source: U.S. Bureau of the Census. *Statistical Abstract of the United States, 1995.*

a. Use simple linear regression models for each credit category to forecast the 1995 and 1996 values. Place 95% confidence bounds on each forecast.

b. Calculate the Holt-Winters forecasts for 1995 and 1996 using $w = .7$ and $v = .7$. Compare the results with the simple linear regression forecasts of part **a**.

14.66 **(X14.066)** The number of dollars a person receives in a year is referred to as his or her **monetary** (or **money**) **income**. This figure can be adjusted to reflect the purchasing power of the dollars received relative to the purchasing power of dollars in some base period. The result is called a person's **real income**. Monetary income and real income can be compared to determine, for example, whether an increase in a person's monetary income truly reflects an increase in his or her purchasing power. The Consumer Price Index (CPI) can be used to adjust monetary income to obtain real income (in terms of 1982–1984 dollars). To compute your real income for a specific year, simply divide your monetary income for that year by that year's CPI and multiply by 100. The table lists the CPI for each year during the period 1970–1994.

Year	CPI	Year	CPI	Year	CPI
1970	38.8	1979	72.6	1987	113.6
1971	40.5	1980	82.4	1988	118.3
1972	41.8	1981	90.9	1989	124.0
1973	44.4	1982	96.5	1990	130.7
1974	49.3	1983	99.6	1991	136.2
1975	53.8	1984	103.9	1992	140.3
1976	56.9	1985	107.6	1993	144.5
1977	60.6	1986	109.6	1994	148.2
1978	65.2				

Source: U.S. Bureau of the Census. *Statistical Abstract of the United States, 1995.*

a. Suppose your monetary income increased from $20,000 in 1970 to $60,000 in 1994. What were your real incomes in 1970 and 1994? Were you able to buy more goods and services in 1970 or 1994? Explain.

b. What monetary income would have been required in 1994 to provide equivalent purchasing power to a 1970 monetary income of $20,000?

1994	IBM	Smoothed	1995	IBM	Smoothed	1996	IBM	Smoothed
January	56.500	56.500	January	72.125	72.129	January	108.500	101.394
February	52.875	54.688	February	75.250	73.690	February	122.625	112.010
March	54.625	54.656	March	82.125	77.907	March	111.250	111.630
April	57.500	56.078	April	94.625	86.266	April	107.750	109.690
May	63.000	59.539	May	93.000	89.633	May	106.750	108.220
June	58.750	59.145	June	96.000	92.817	June	99.000	103.610
July	61.875	60.510	July	108.875	100.846	July	107.500	105.555
August	68.500	64.505	August	103.375	102.110	August	114.375	109.965
September	69.625	67.065	September	94.500	98.305	September	124.500	117.232
October	74.500	70.782	October	97.250	97.778	October	129.000	123.116
November	70.750	70.766	November	96.625	97.201	November	159.375	141.246
December	73.500	72.133	December	91.375	94.288	December	151.500	146.373

Sources: Standard and Poor's Stock Guide, 1995, 1996; Dow Jones News/Retrieval Database, 1997.

14.67 **(X14.067)** In Example 14.4 we considered the monthly IBM stock prices from January 1994 to December 1996. The original data, as well as the exponentially smoothed values for $w = .5$, are repeated above.

a. Use the exponentially smoothed series calculated from January 1994 to September 1996 to forecast the monthly values of the IBM stock price from October to December 1996. Calculate the forecast errors.

b. The SAS printout for a simple linear regression model fit to the IBM stock prices from January 1994 to September 1996 is shown on the next page. The time t ranges from 1 to 33, representing the 33 months in the sample. Interpret the least squares estimates.

c. With what approximate precision do you expect to be able to predict the IBM stock price using the regression model?

d. Give the simple linear regression forecasts and the 95% forecast intervals for the October–December 1996 prices. How does the precision of these forecasts agree with the approximation obtained in part **c**?

e. Compare the exponential smoothing forecasts, part **a**, to the regression forecasts, part **d**, using MAD and RMSE.

f. What assumptions does the random error component of the regression model have to satisfy in order to make the model inferences (such as the forecast intervals in part **c**) valid?

g. Test to determine whether there is evidence of first-order autocorrelation in the random error component of the regression model. Use $\alpha = .05$. What can you infer about the validity of the model inferences?

Dependent Variable: IBM

Analysis of Variance

Source	DF	Sum of Squares	Mean Square	F Value	Prob>F
Model	1	13126.76771	13126.76771	258.156	0.0001
Error	31	1576.29289	50.84816		
C Total	32	14703.06061			

Root MSE	7.13079	R-Square	0.8928
Dep Mean	86.95076	Adj R-Sq	0.8893
C.V.	8.20095		

Parameter Estimates

Variable	DF	Parameter Estimate	Standard Error	T for H0: Parameter=0	Prob > |T|
INTERCEP	1	51.342803	2.54014233	20.213	0.0001
T	1	2.094586	0.13036374	16.067	0.0001

Durbin-Watson D	0.941
(For Number of Obs.)	33
1st Order Autocorrelation	0.521

Obs	Dep Var IBM	Predict Value	Std Err Predict	Lower95% Predict	Upper95% Predict	Residual
1	56.5000	53.4374	2.427	38.0747	68.8001	3.0626
2	52.8750	55.5320	2.316	40.2408	70.8232	-2.6570
3	54.6250	57.6266	2.207	42.4026	72.8506	-3.0016
4	57.5000	59.7211	2.101	44.5600	74.8823	-2.2211
5	63.0000	61.8157	1.997	46.7129	76.9185	1.1843
6	58.7500	63.9103	1.897	48.8614	78.9592	-5.1603
7	61.8750	66.0049	1.800	51.0054	81.0044	-4.1299
8	68.5000	68.0995	1.708	53.1449	83.0541	0.4005
9	69.6250	70.1941	1.621	55.2797	85.1085	-0.5691
10	74.5000	72.2887	1.541	57.4099	87.1675	2.2113
11	70.7500	74.3832	1.467	59.5354	89.2311	-3.6332
12	73.5000	76.4778	1.402	61.6561	91.2995	-2.9778
13	72.1250	78.5724	1.346	63.7722	93.3726	-6.4474
14	75.2500	80.6670	1.301	65.8835	95.5	-5.4170
15	82.1250	82.7616	1.268	67.9901	97.5	-0.6366
16	94.6	84.8562	1.248	70.0918	99.6	9.7688
17	93.0000	86.9508	1.241	72.1888	101.7	6.0492
18	96.0	89.0453	1.248	74.2810	103.8	6.9547
19	108.9	91.1399	1.268	76.3684	105.9	17.7351
20	103.4	93.2345	1.301	78.4510	108.0	10.1405
21	94.5	95.3	1.346	80.5289	110.1	-0.8291
22	97.2	97.4	1.402	82.6020	112.2	-0.1737
23	96.6	99.5	1.467	84.6704	114.4	-2.8933
24	91.3750	101.6	1.541	86.7340	116.5	-10.2379
25	108.5	103.7	1.621	88.7930	118.6	4.7926
26	122.6	105.8	1.708	90.8474	120.8	16.8230
27	111.2	107.9	1.800	92.8971	122.9	3.3534
28	107.7	110.0	1.897	94.9	125.0	-2.2412
29	106.7	112.1	1.997	97.0	127.2	-5.3358
30	99.0	114.2	2.101	99.0	129.3	-15.1804
31	107.5	116.3	2.207	101.1	131.5	-8.7750
32	114.4	118.4	2.316	103.1	133.7	-3.9945
33	124.5	120.5	2.427	105.1	135.8	4.0359
34	.	122.6	2.540	107.1	138.0	.
35	.	124.7	2.655	109.1	140.2	.
36	.	126.7	2.771	111.1	142.4	.

SHOWCASE THE GASKET MANUFACTURING CASE

The Problem. A Midwestern manufacturer of gaskets for automotive and off-road vehicle applications was suddenly and unexpectedly notified by a major customer—a U.S. auto manufacturer—that they had significantly tightened the specification limits on the overall thickness of a hard gasket used in their automotive engines. Although the current specification limits were by and large being met by the gasket manufacturer, their product did not come close to meeting the new specification.

The gasket manufacturer's first reaction was to negotiate with the customer to obtain a relaxation of the new specification. When these efforts failed, the customer-supplier relationship became somewhat strained. The gasket manufacturer's next thought was that if they waited long enough, the automotive company would eventually be forced to loosen the requirements and purchase the existing product. However, as time went on it became clear that this was not going to happen and that some positive steps would have to be taken to improve the quality of their gaskets. But what should be done? And by whom?

The Product. Figure C5.1 shows the product in question, a hard gasket. A hard gasket is comprised of two outer layers of soft gasket material and an inner layer consisting of a perforated piece of sheet metal. These three pieces are assembled, and some blanking and punching operations follow, after which metal rings are installed around the inside of the cylinder bore clearance holes and the entire outside periphery of the gasket. The quality characteristic of interest in this case is the assembly thickness.

The Process. An initial study by the staff engineers revealed that the variation in the thickness of soft gasket material—the two outer layers of the hard gasket—was large and undoubtedly responsible for much of the total variability in the final product. Figure C5.2 shows the roll mill process that fabricates the sheets of soft gasket material from which the two outer layers of the hard gasket are made. To manufacture a sheet of soft gasket material, an operator adds raw material, in a soft pelletlike form, to the gap—called the knip—between the two rolls. The larger roll rotates about its axis with no lateral movement; the smaller roll rotates and moves back and forth laterally to change the size of the knip. As the operator adds more and more material to the knip, the sheet is formed around the larger roll. When the smaller roll reaches a preset destination (i.e., final gap/sheet thickness), a bell rings and a red light goes on telling the operator to stop adding raw material. The operator stops the rolls and cuts the sheet horizontally along the larger roll so that it may be pulled off the roll. The finished sheet, called a pull, is pulled onto a table where the operator checks its thickness with a micrometer. The operator can adjust the final gap if he or she believes that the sheets are coming out too thick or too thin relative to the prescribed nominal value (i.e., the target thickness).

Process Operation. Investigation revealed that the operator runs the process in the following way. After each sheet is made, the operator measures the thickness with a micrometer. The thickness values for three consecutive sheets are averaged and the average is plotted on a piece of graph paper that, at the start of the shift, has only a solid horizontal line drawn on it to indicate the target thickness value for the particular soft gasket sheet the operator is making. Periodically, the operator reviews these evolving data and makes a decision as to whether or not the process mean—the sheet thickness—needs to be adjusted. This can be accomplished by stopping the machine, loosening some clamps on the small roll, and jogging the small roll laterally in or out by a few thousandths of an inch—whatever the operator feels is needed. The clamps are tightened, the gap is checked with a taper gage, and if adjusted properly, the operator begins to make sheets again. Typically, this adjustment process takes 10 to 15 minutes. The questions of when to make such adjustments and how much to change the roll gap for each adjustment are completely at the operator's discretion, based on the evolving plot of thickness averages.

FIGURE C5.1
A hard gasket for automotive applications

FIGURE C5.2   Roll mill for the manufacture of soft gasket material

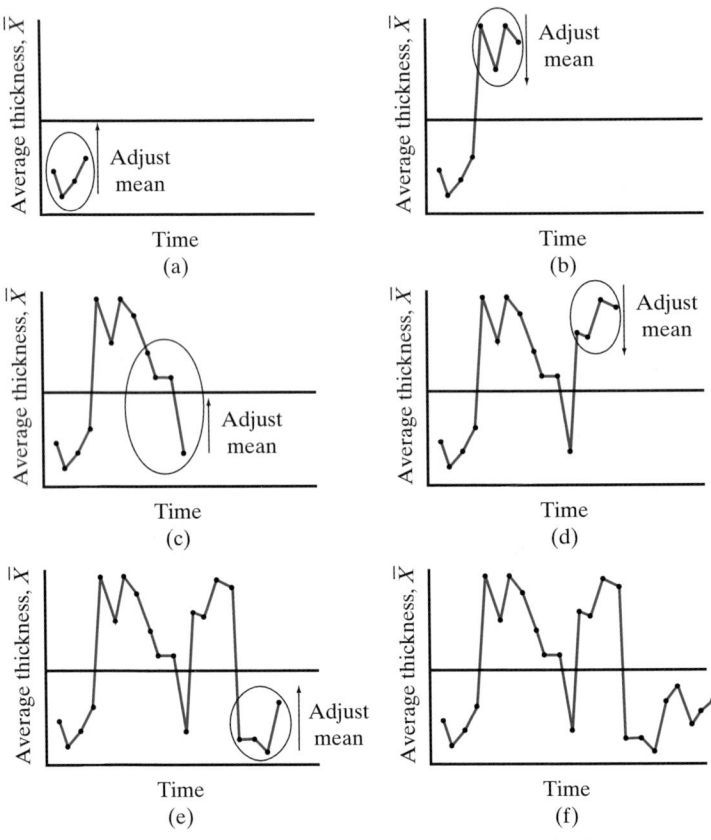

FIGURE C5.3 Process adjustment history over one shift

Figure C5.3 shows a series of plots that detail the history of one particular work shift over which the operator made several process adjustments. (These data come from the same shift that the staff engineers used to collect data for a process capability study that is described later.) Figure C5.3(a) shows the process data after the first 12 sheets have been made—four averages of three successive sheet thicknesses. At this point the operator judged that the data were telling her that the process was running below the target, so she stopped the process and made an adjustment to slightly increase the final roll gap. She then proceeded to make more sheets. Figure C5.3(b) shows the state of the process somewhat later. Now it appeared to the operator that the sheets were coming out too thick, so she stopped and made another adjustment. As shown in Figure C5.3(c), the process seemed to run well for a while, but then an average somewhat below the target led the operator to believe that another adjustment was necessary. Figures C5.3(d) and C5.3(e) show points in time where other adjustments were made.

Figure C5.3(f) shows the complete history of the shift. A total of 24 × 3, or 72, sheets were made during this shift. When asked, the operator indicated that the history of this shift was quite typical of what happens on a day-to-day basis.

The Company's Stop-Gap Solution. While the staff engineers were studying the problem to formulate an appropriate action plan, something had to be done to make it possible to deliver hard gaskets within the new specification limits. Management decided to increase product inspection and, in particular, to grade each piece of material according to thickness so that the wide variation in thickness could be balanced out at the assembly process. Extra inspectors were used to grade each piece of soft gasket material. Sheets of the same thickness were shipped in separate bundles on pallets to a sister plant for assembly. Thick and thin sheets were selected as needed to make a hard gasket that met the specification. The process worked pretty well and there was some discussion about making it permanent. However, some felt it was too costly and did not get at the root cause of the problem.

The Engineering Department's Analysis. Meanwhile, the staff engineers in the company were continuing to study the problem and came to the conclusion that the existing roll mill process equipment for making the soft gasket

TABLE C5.1   **Measurements of Sheet Thickness**

Sheet	Thickness (in.)	Sheet	Thickness (in.)	Sheet	Thickness (in.)
1	0.0440	25	0.0464	49	0.0427
2	0.0446	26	0.0457	50	0.0437
3	0.0437	27	0.0447	51	0.0445
4	0.0438	28	0.0451	52	0.0431
5	0.0425	29	0.0447	53	0.0448
6	0.0443	30	0.0457	54	0.0429
7	0.0453	31	0.0456	55	0.0425
8	0.0428	32	0.0455	56	0.0442
9	0.0433	33	0.0445	57	0.0432
10	0.0451	34	0.0448	58	0.0429
11	0.0441	35	0.0423	59	0.0447
12	0.0434	36	0.0442	60	0.0450
13	0.0459	37	0.0459	61	0.0443
14	0.0466	38	0.0468	62	0.0441
15	0.0476	39	0.0452	63	0.0450
16	0.0449	40	0.0456	64	0.0443
17	0.0471	41	0.0471	65	0.0423
18	0.0451	42	0.0450	66	0.0447
19	0.0472	43	0.0472	67	0.0429
20	0.0477	44	0.0465	68	0.0427
21	0.0452	45	0.0461	69	0.0464
22	0.0457	46	0.0462	70	0.0448
23	0.0459	47	0.0463	71	0.0451
24	0.0472	48	0.0471	72	0.0428

sheets simply was not capable of meeting the new specifications. This conclusion was reached as a result of the examination of production data and scrap logs over the past several months. They had researched some new equipment that had a track record for very good sheet-to-sheet consistency and had decided to write a proposal to replace the existing roll mills with this new equipment.

To strengthen the proposal, their boss asked them to include data that demonstrated the poor capability of the existing equipment. The engineers, confident that the equipment was not capable, selected what they thought was the best operator and the best roll mill (the plant has several roll mill lines) and took careful measurements of the thickness of each sheet made on an eight-hour shift. During that shift, a total of 72 sheets/pulls were made. This was considered quite acceptable since the work standard for the process is 70 sheets per shift. The measurements of the sheet thickness (in the order of manufacture) for the 72 sheets are given in Table C5.1. The engineers set out to use these data to conduct a process capability study.

Relying on a statistical methods course that one of the engineers had in college 10 years ago, the group decided to construct a frequency distribution from the data and use it to estimate the percentage of the measurements that fell within the specification limits. Their histogram is shown in Figure C5.4. Also shown in the figure are the upper and lower specification values. The dark shaded part of the histogram represents the amount of the product that lies outside of the specification limits. It is immediately apparent from the histogram that a large proportion of the output does not meet the customer's needs. Eight of the 72 sheets fall outside the specification limits. Therefore, in terms of percent conforming to specifications, the engineers estimated the process capability to be 88.8%. This was clearly unacceptable. This analysis confirmed the engineer's low opinion of the roll mill process equipment. They included it in their proposal and sent

FIGURE C5.4   Histogram of data from process capability study

TABLE C5.2   **Measurements of Sheet Thickness for a Shift Run with No Operator Adjustment**

Sheet	Thickness (in.)	Sheet	Thickness (in.)	Sheet	Thickness (in.)
1	.0445	25	.0443	49	.0445
2	.0455	26	.0450	50	.0471
3	.0457	27	.0441	51	.0465
4	.0435	28	.0449	52	.0438
5	.0453	29	.0448	53	.0445
6	.0450	30	.0467	54	.0472
7	.0438	31	.0465	55	.0453
8	.0459	32	.0449	56	.0444
9	.0428	33	.0448	57	.0451
10	.0449	34	.0461	58	.0455
11	.0449	35	.0439	59	.0435
12	.0467	36	.0452	60	.0443
13	.0433	37	.0443	61	.0440
14	.0461	38	.0434	62	.0438
15	.0451	39	.0454	63	.0444
16	.0455	40	.0456	64	.0444
17	.0454	41	.0459	65	.0450
18	.0461	42	.0452	66	.0467
19	.0455	43	.0447	67	.0445
20	.0458	44	.0442	68	.0447
21	.0445	45	.0457	69	.0461
22	.0445	46	.0454	70	.0450
23	.0451	47	.0445	71	.0463
24	.0436	48	.0451	72	.0456

their recommendation to replace the equipment to the president's office.

Your Assignment. You have been hired as an external consultant by the company's president, Marilyn Carlson. She would like you to critique the engineers' analysis, conclusion, and recommendations.

Suspecting that the engineers' work may be flawed, President Carlson would also like you to conduct your own study and make your own recommendations concerning how to resolve the company's problem. She would like you to use the data reported in Table C5.1 along with the data of Table C5.2, which she ordered be collected for you. These data were collected in the same manner as the data in Table C5.1. However, they were collected during a period of time when the roll mill operator was instructed *not* to adjust the sheet thickness. In your analysis, if you choose to construct control charts, use the same three-measurement subgrouping that the operators use.

Prepare an in-depth, written report for the president that responds to her requests. It should begin with an executive summary and include whatever tables and figures are needed to support your analysis and recommendations. (A layout of the data file available for this case is described below.)

DATA   ASCII file name: GASKET.DAT
Number of observations: 144

Variable	Column(s)	Type	
SHEET	1–2	QN	
THICKNSS	7–11	QN	
ADJUST	13	QL	(A=operator adjustments, N=no adjustments)

This case is based on the experiences of an actual company whose identity is disguised for confidentiality reasons. The case was originally written by DeVor, Chang, and Sutherland (*Statistical Quality Design and Control* [New York: Macmillan Publishing Co., 1992] pp. 298–329) and has been adapted to focus on the material presented in Chapter 13.

www.int.com
www.int.com
INTERNET LAB
www.int.com

QUALITY MANAGEMENT OUTSIDE OF MANUFACTURING OPERATION

Statistical quality control methods originated in manufacturing and today are being widely applied beyond it. Service operations such as marketing, sales, and customer service are benefiting from process management concepts. As you might expect, both the choice of which quality characteristic to measure and how to measure it are topics receiving much attention in these newer settings.

Here we will visit the American Productivity & Quality Center (APQC), a member-based organization that provides educational and standardization services to industry in support of quality improvement efforts.

1. The site address for the APQC is: *http://www.apqc.org/*

2. At the APQC home page, please note the variety of quality improvement applications for which the organization maintains information.

   - Click on the icon: **Measurement**
   - Next, scroll down to the heading "Publications" and click on **Measurement in Practice**, a new case study series devoted to measuring.

This case study series offers you a selection of articles that are updated biweekly. You are encouraged to review the full variety of information available here.

3. Selecte an article and read it on the screen or download it to your notepad or other word-processing software.

4. After reading the article, answer the following questions:

   a. What functional areas of the company are measuring the quality of their work?

   b. What company goals are being advanced by the measurement activity?

   c. Identify specific measures being used and the related data collection processes.

   d. Comment on how clearly the specific measures are related to the goals identified in part **b**.

   e. How did the company arrive at the adopted quality measures? What were the criteria for choosing them? Who is responsible for the quality monitoring process?

   f. What goals has the company met so far? What does it expect to achieve in the future?

   g. Does the company plan to revise any of its quality measurements or its monitoring processes? If so, for what reasons? ○

CHAPTER 15

DESIGN OF EXPERIMENTS AND ANALYSIS OF VARIANCE

CONTENTS

STATISTICS IN ACTION

Where We've Been

As we've seen in preceding chapters, the solutions of many practical problems are based on inferences about population means. Methods for estimating and testing hypotheses about a single mean and the comparison of two means were presented in Chapters 7–9, and Chapters 10–12 dealt with methods for estimating the mean value of a response using regression models. Methods for monitoring the mean of a process were presented in Chapter 13.

Where We're Going

In this chapter we extend the methodology of Chapters 7–13 in two important ways. First, we discuss the critical elements in the *design* of a sampling experiment. Then we show how to *analyze* the experiment in order to compare more than two populations. We'll look at two of the more popular experimental designs, and we'll show how to use the computer to analyze designed experiments, using both analysis of variance and regression programs.

Most of the data analyzed in previous chapters were collected in *observational* sampling experiments rather than *designed* sampling experiments. In *observational experiments* the analyst has little or no control over the variables under study and merely observes their values. In contrast, *designed experiments* are those in which the analyst attempts to control the levels of one or more variables to determine their effect on a variable of interest. Although many practical business situations do not present the opportunity for such control, it is instructive, even for observational experiments, to have a working knowledge of the analysis and interpretation of data that result from designed experiments and to know the basics of how to design experiments when the opportunity arises.

We first present the basic elements of an experimental design in Section 15.1. We then discuss two of the simpler, and more popular, experimental designs in Sections 15.2 and 15.4. In optional Section 15.5 we show how the statistical analysis of designed experiments can be accomplished using the regression methodology of Chapters 10–12.

15.1 ELEMENTS OF A DESIGNED EXPERIMENT

Certain elements are common to almost all designed experiments, regardless of the specific area of application. For example, the *response* is the variable of interest in the experiment. The response might be the SAT scores of a high school senior, the total sales of a firm last year, or the total income of a particular household this year. In regression analysis we referred to the response as the *dependent variable, y.* We use these terms interchangeably in this chapter.

DEFINITION 15.1

The **response variable** is the variable of interest to be measured in the experiment. We also refer to the response as the **dependent variable**.

The intent of most statistical experiments is to determine the effect of one or more variables on the response. These variables, which we called the *independent variables* in regression analysis, are often referred to as the *factors* in a designed experiment. Like independent variables, factors are either *quantitative* or *qualitative,* depending on whether the variable is measured on a numerical scale or not. For example, we might want to explore the effect of the qualitative factor Gender on the response SAT score. In other words, we want to compare the SAT scores of male and female high school seniors. Or, we might wish to determine the effect of the quantitative factor Number of salespeople on the response Total sales for retail firms. Often two or more factors are of interest. For example, we might want to determine the effect of the quantitative factor Number of wage earners and the qualitative factor Location on the response Household income.

DEFINITION 15.2

Factors are those variables whose effect on the response is of interest to the experimenter. **Quantitative factors** are measured on a numerical scale, whereas **qualitative factors** are those that are not (naturally) measured on a numerical scale. We referred to factors as **independent variables** in regression analysis, and we use the terms synonymously.

Levels are the values of the factors that are utilized in the experiment. The levels of qualitative factors are usually nonnumerical. For example, the levels of Gender are Male and Female, and the levels of Location might be North, East, South, and West.* The levels of quantitative factors are numerical values. For example, the Number of salespeople may have levels 1, 3, 5, 7, and 9. The factor Years of education may have levels 8, 12, 16, and 20.

DEFINITION 15.3
Factor levels are the values of the factor utilized in the experiment.

When a *single factor* is employed in an experiment, the *treatments* of the experiment are the levels of the factor. For example, if the effect of the factor Gender on the response SAT score is being investigated, the treatments of the experiment are the two levels of Gender—Female and Male. Or, if the effect of the Number of wage earners on Household income is the subject of the experiment, the numerical values assumed by the quantitative factor Number of wage earners are the treatments. If *two or more factors* are utilized in an experiment, the treatments are the factor-level combinations used. For example, if the effects of the factors Gender and GPA on the response SAT score are being investigated, the treatments are the combinations of the levels of Gender and GPA used; thus (Female, 2.61), (Male, 3.43), and (Female, 3.82) would all be treatments.

DEFINITION 15.4
The **treatments** of an experiment are the factor-level combinations utilized.

The objects on which the response variable and factors are observed are the *experimental units.* For example, SAT score, High school GPA, and Gender are all variables that can be observed on the same experimental unit—a high school senior. Or, the Total sales, the Earnings per share, and the Number of salespeople can be measured on a particular firm in a particular year, and the firm-year combination is the experimental unit. The Total income, the Number of female wage earners, and the Location can be observed for a household at a particular point in time, and the household-time combination is the experimental unit. Every experiment, whether observational or designed, has experimental units on which the variables are observed. However, the identification of the experimental units is more important in designed experiments, when the experimenter must actually sample the experimental units and measure the variables.

DEFINITION 15.5
An **experimental unit** is the object on which the response and factors are observed or measured.†

---

*The levels of a qualitative variable may bear numerical labels. For example, the Locations could be numbered 1, 2, 3, and 4. However, in such cases the numerical labels for a qualitative variable will usually be codes representing nonnumerical levels.
†Recall (Chapter 1) that the set of all experimental units is the population.

When the specification of the treatments and the method of assigning the experimental units to each of the treatments are controlled by the analyst, the experiment is said to be *designed*. In contrast, if the analyst is just an observer of the treatments on a sample of experimental units, the experiment is *observational*. For example, if you give one randomly selected group of employees a training program and withhold it from another randomly selected group in order to evaluate the effect of the training on worker productivity, then you are designing an experiment. If, on the other hand, you compare the productivity of employees with college degrees with the productivity of employees without college degrees, the experiment is observational.

> **DEFINITION 15.6**
> A **designed experiment** is one for which the analyst controls the specification of the treatments and the method of assigning the experimental units to each treatment. An **observational experiment** is one for which the analyst simply observes the treatments and the response on a sample of experimental units.

The diagram in Figure 15.1 provides an overview of the experimental process and a summary of the terminology introduced in this section. Note that the experimental unit is at the core of the process. The method by which the sample of experimental units is selected from the population determines the type of exper-

FIGURE 15.1
Sampling experiment: Process and terminology

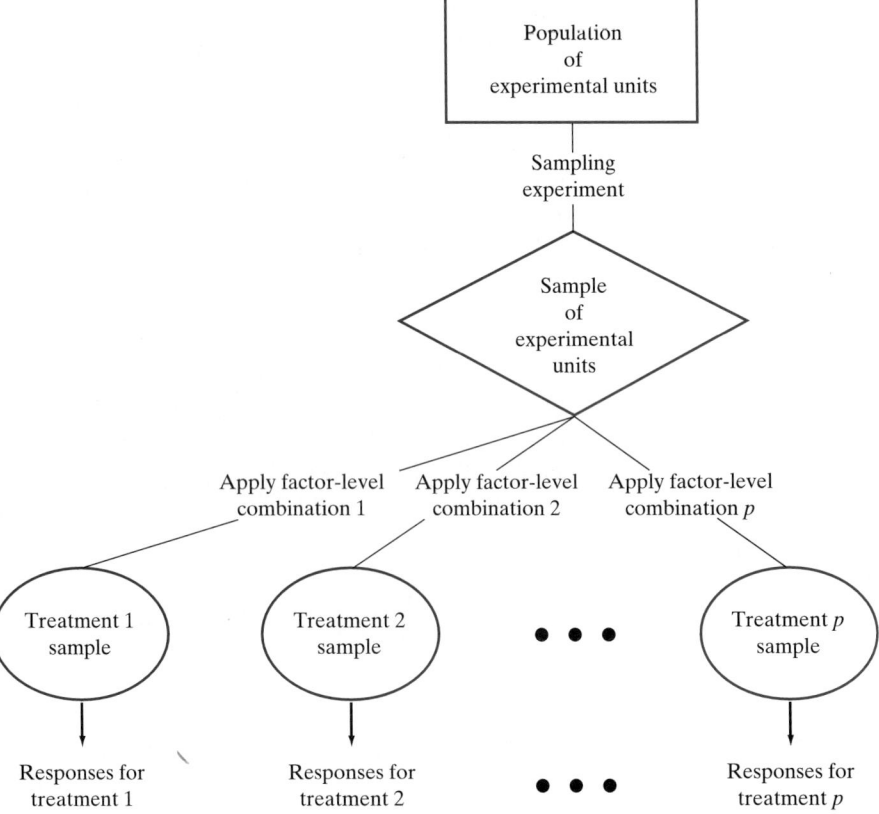

iment. The level of every factor (the treatment) and the response are all variables that are observed or measured on each experimental unit.

EXAMPLE 15.1

The USGA (United States Golf Association) regularly tests golf equipment to ensure that it conforms to USGA standards. Suppose it wishes to compare the mean distance traveled by four different brands of golf balls when struck by a driver (the club used to maximize distance). The following experiment is conducted: 10 balls of each brand are randomly selected. Each is struck by "Iron Byron" (the USGA's golf robot named for the famous golfer, Byron Nelson) using a driver, and the distance traveled is recorded. Identify each of the following elements in this experiment: response, factors, factor types, levels, treatments, and experimental units.

SOLUTION

The response is the variable of interest, Distance traveled. The only factor being investigated is Brand of golf ball, and it is nonnumerical and therefore qualitative. The four brands (say A, B, C, and D) represent the levels of this factor. Since only one factor is utilized, the treatments are the four levels of this factor—that is, the four brands. The experimental unit is a golf ball; more specifically, it is a golf ball at a particular position in the striking sequence, since the distance traveled can be recorded only when the ball is struck, and we would expect the distance to be different (due to random factors such as wind resistance, landing place, and so forth) if the same ball is struck a second time. Note that 10 experimental units are sampled for each treatment, generating a total of 40 observations.

This experiment, like many real applications, is a blend of designed and observational: The analyst cannot control the assignment of the brand to each golf ball (observational), but he or she can control the assignment of each ball to the position in the striking sequence (designed).

EXAMPLE 15.2

Suppose the USGA is also interested in comparing the mean distances the four brands of golf balls travel when struck by a five-iron and by a driver. Ten balls of each brand are randomly selected, five to be struck by the driver, and five by the five-iron. Identify the elements of the experiment, and construct a schematic diagram similar to Figure 15.1 to provide an overview of this experiment.

SOLUTION

The response is the same as in Example 15.1—Distance traveled. The experiment now has two factors, Brand of golf ball and Club utilized. There are four levels of Brand (A, B, C, and D) and two of Club (driver and five-iron, or 1 and 5). Treatments are factor-level combinations of golf ball and hitting position. Note that five experimental units are sampled per treatment, generating 40 observations. The experiment is summarized in Figure 15.2.

Our objective in designing an experiment is usually to maximize the amount of information obtained about the relationship between the treatments and the response. Of course, we are almost always subject to constraints on budget, time, and even the availability of experimental units. Nevertheless, designed experiments are generally preferred to observational experiments. Not only do we have better control of the amount and quality of the information collected, but we also avoid the biases inherent in observational experiments in the selection of the

FIGURE 15.2
Two-factor golf
experiment summary:
Example 15.2

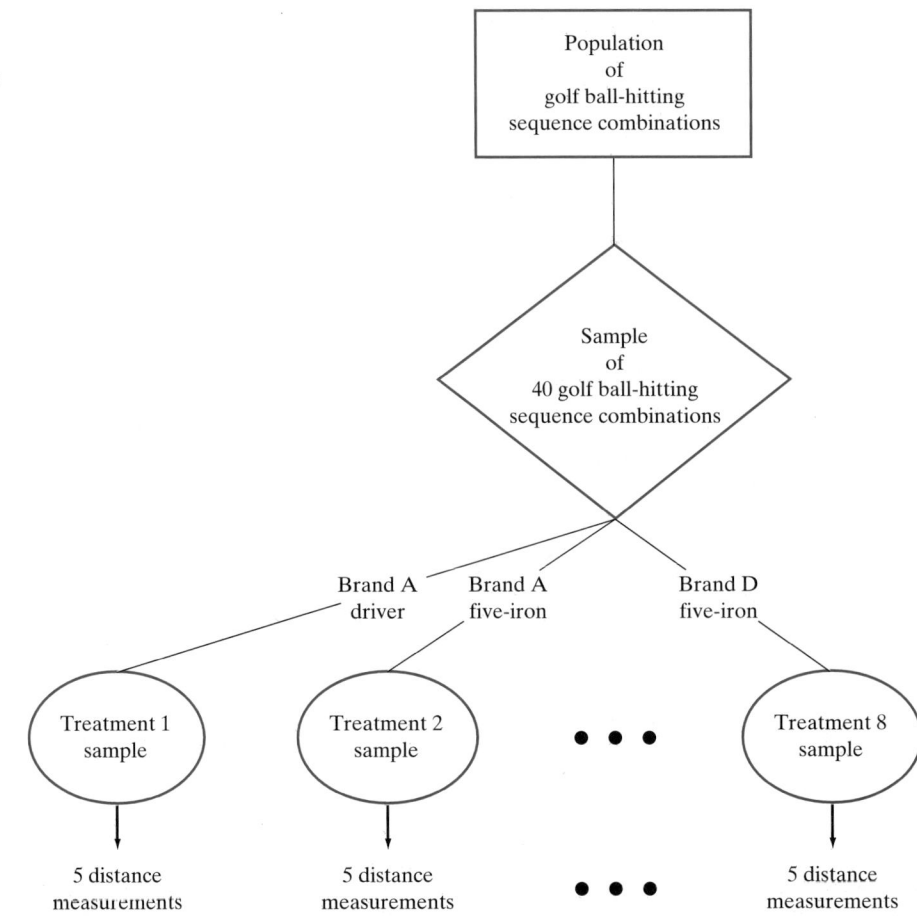

experimental units representing each treatment. Inferences based on observational experiments always carry the implicit assumption that the sample has no hidden bias that was not considered in the statistical analysis. Better understanding of the potential problems with observational experiments is a by-product of our study of experimental design in the remainder of this chapter.

EXERCISES 15.1–15.8

Learning the Mechanics

15.1 What are the treatments for a designed experiment that utilizes one qualitative factor with four levels—A, B, C, and D?

15.2 What are the treatments for a designed experiment with two factors, one qualitative with two levels (A and B) and one quantitative with five levels (50, 60, 70, 80, and 90)?

15.3 What are the experimental units on which each of the following responses are observed?
a. College GPA

b. Household income

c. Gasoline mileage rating for an automobile model

d. Number of defective sectors on a computer diskette

e. December unemployment rate for a state

15.4 What is the difference between an observational and a designed experiment?

Applying the Concepts

15.5 Marketers use wording such as "was $25, now $20" to indicate a price promotion. The promotion price is typically compared to the retailer's previous price or to a competitor's price. Research has shown that between-store comparisons result in greater perceptions of value by consumers than within-store comparisons. But is this effect dependent on whether the consumer receives the price information at home in an advertisement or in a store while shopping? Marketing professors D. Grewal, H. Marmorstein, and A. Sharma of the University of Miami conducted an experiment to answer this question (*Journal of Consumer Research,* Sept. 1996). They used two situations (advertisements read at home versus in-store ad) and two types of discount comparisons (to previous price at same store versus competitor's price). For each of the four treatments, a different sample of undergraduate students were asked to give their opinions of the value of the discount offer. Identify each of the following elements of their experiment:

a. Response **b.** Factor(s) and factor type(s)
c. Treatments **d.** Experimental units

15.6 A quality control supervisor measures the quality of a steel ingot on a scale of 0 to 10. He designs an experiment in which three different temperatures (ranging from 1,100 to 1,200°F) and five different pressures (ranging from 500 to 600 psi) are utilized, with 20 ingots produced at each Temperature-Pressure combination. Identify the following elements of the experiment:

a. Response **b.** Factor(s) and factor type(s)
c. Treatments **d.** Experimental units

15.7 Brief descriptions of a number of experiments are given next. Determine whether each is observational or designed, and explain your reasoning.

a. An economist obtains the unemployment rate and gross state product for a sample of states over the past 10 years, with the objective of examining the relationship between the unemployment rate and the gross state product by census region.

b. A manager in a paper production facility installs one of three incentive programs in each of nine plants to determine the effect of each program on productivity.

c. A marketer of personal computers runs ads in each of four national publications for one quarter, and keeps track of the number of sales that are attributable to each publication's ad.

d. An electric utility engages a consultant to monitor the discharge from its smokestack on a monthly basis over a one-year period in order to relate the level of sulfur dioxide in the discharge to the load on the facility's generators.

e. Intrastate trucking rates are compared before and after governmental deregulation of prices charged, with the comparison also taking into account distance of haul, goods hauled, and the price of diesel fuel.

15.8 Within marketing, the area of personal sales has long suffered from a poor ethical image, particularly in the eyes of college students. An article in *Journal of Business Ethics* (Vol. 15, 1996) investigated whether such opinions by college students are a function of the type of sales job (high tech versus low tech) and/or the sales task (new account development versus account maintenance). Four different samples of college students were confronted with the four different situations (new account development in a high-tech sales task; new account development in a low-tech sales task; account maintenance in a high-tech sales task; and account maintenance in a low-tech sales task), and were asked to evaluate the ethical behavior of the salesperson on a seven-point scale ranging from 1 (not a serious ethical violation) to 7 (a very serious ethical violation). Identify each of the following elements of the experiment:

a. Response **b.** Factor(s) and factor level(s)
c. Treatments **d.** Experimental units

15.2 THE COMPLETELY RANDOMIZED DESIGN: SINGLE FACTOR

The simplest experimental design, a *completely randomized design,* consists of the *independent random selection* of experimental units representing each treatment. For example, we could independently select random samples of 20 female and 15 male high school seniors to compare their mean SAT scores. Or, we could independently select random samples of 30 households from each of four census districts to compare the mean income per household among the districts. In both examples our objective is to compare treatment means by selecting random, independent samples for each treatment.

DEFINITION 15.7

A **completely randomized design** is a design for which independent random samples of experimental units are selected for each treatment.*

The objective of a completely randomized design is usually to compare the treatment means. If we denote the true, or population, means of the p treatments as $\mu_1, \mu_2, \ldots, \mu_p$, then we will test the null hypothesis that the treatment means are all equal against the alternative that at least two of the treatment means differ:

$$H_0: \mu_1 = \mu_2 = \cdots = \mu_p$$

H_a: At least two of the p treatment means differ

The μ's might represent the means of *all* female and male high school seniors' SAT scores or the means of *all* households' income in each of four census regions.

To conduct a statistical test of these hypotheses, we will use the means of the independent random samples selected from the treatment populations using the completely randomized design. That is, we compare the p sample means, $\bar{x}_1$, $\bar{x}_2, \ldots, \bar{x}_p$.

For example, suppose you select independent random samples of five female and five male high school seniors and obtain sample mean SAT scores of 550 and 590, respectively. Can we conclude that males score 40 points higher, on average, than females? To answer this question, we must consider the amount of sampling variability among the experimental units (students). If the scores are as depicted in the dot plot shown in Figure 15.3, then the difference between the means is small relative to the sampling variability of the scores within the treatments, Female and Male. We would be inclined not to reject the null hypothesis of equal population means in this case.

In contrast, if the data are as depicted in the dot plot of Figure 15.4, then the sampling variability is small relative to the difference between the two means. We

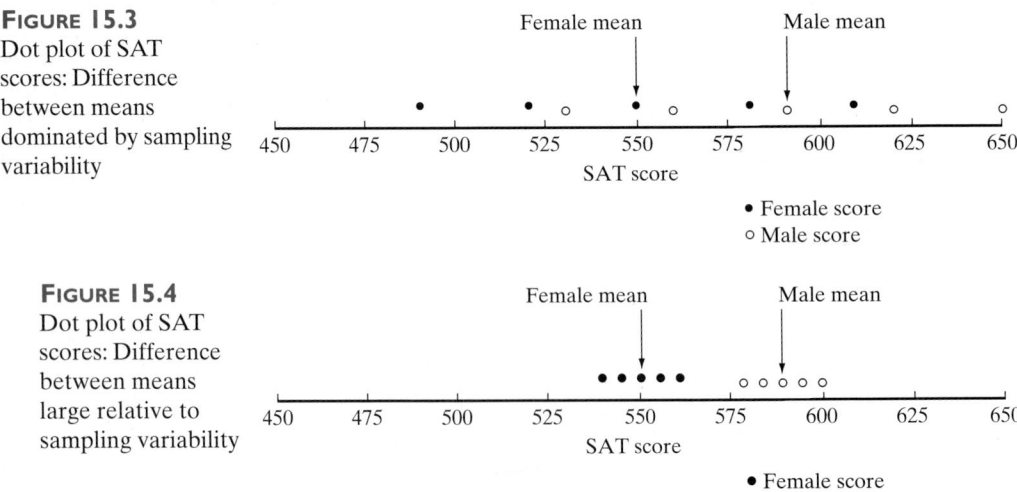

FIGURE 15.3
Dot plot of SAT scores: Difference between means dominated by sampling variability

FIGURE 15.4
Dot plot of SAT scores: Difference between means large relative to sampling variability

*We use *completely randomized design* to refer to both designed and observational experiments. Thus, the only requirement is that the experimental units to which treatments are applied (designed) or on which treatments are observed (observational) are independently selected for each treatment.

would be inclined to favor the alternative hypothesis that the population means differ in this case.

You can see that the key is to compare the difference between the treatment means to the amount of sampling variability. To conduct a formal statistical test of the hypotheses requires numerical measures of the difference between the treatment means and the sampling variability within each treatment. The variation between the treatment means is measured by the **Sum of Squares for Treatments** (SST), which is calculated by squaring the distance between each treatment mean and the overall mean of *all* sample measurements, multiplying each squared distance by the number of sample measurements for the treatment, and adding the results over all treatments:

$$SST = \sum_{i=1}^{p} n_i(\bar{x}_i - \bar{x})^2 = 5(550 - 570)^2 + 5(590 - 570)^2 = 4{,}000$$

where we use $\bar{x}$ to represent the overall mean response of all sample measurements, that is, the mean of the combined samples. The symbol n_i is used to denote the sample size for the ith treatment. You can see that the value of SST is 4,000 for the two samples of five female and five male SAT scores depicted in Figures 15.3 and 15.4.

Next, we must measure the sampling variability within the treatments. We call this the **Sum of Squares for Error** (SSE) because it measures the variability around the treatment means that is attributed to sampling error. Suppose the 10 measurements in the first dot plot (Figure 15.3) are 490, 520, 550, 580, and 610 for females, and 530, 560, 590, 620, and 650 for males. Then the value of SSE is computed by summing the squared distance between each response measurement and the corresponding treatment mean, and then adding the squared differences over all measurements in the entire sample:

$$SSE = \sum_{j=1}^{n_1}(x_{1j} - \bar{x}_1)^2 + \sum_{j=1}^{n_2}(x_{2j} - \bar{x}_2)^2 + \cdots + \sum_{j=1}^{n_p}(x_{pj} - \bar{x}_p)^2$$

where the symbol x_{1j} is the jth measurement in sample 1, x_{2j} is the jth measurement in sample 2, and so on. This rather complex-looking formula can be simplified by recalling the formula for the sample variance, s^2, given in Chapter 3:

$$s^2 = \sum_{i=1}^{n} \frac{(x_i - \bar{x})^2}{n - 1}$$

Note that each sum in SSE is simply the numerator of s^2 for that particular treatment. Consequently, we can rewrite SSE as

$$SSE = (n_1 - 1)s_1^2 + (n_2 - 1)s_2^2 + \cdots + (n_p - 1)s_p^2$$

where $s_1^2, s_2^2, \ldots, s_p^2$ are the sample variances for the p treatments. For our samples of SAT scores, we find $s_1^2 = 2{,}250$ (for females) and $s_2^2 = 2{,}250$ (for males); then we have

$$SSE = (5 - 1)(2{,}250) + (5 - 1)(2{,}250) = 18{,}000$$

To make the two measurements of variability comparable, we divide each by the degrees of freedom to convert the sums of squares to mean squares. First, the **Mean Square for Treatments** (MST), which measures the variability *among* the treatment means, is equal to

$$MST = \frac{SST}{p - 1} = \frac{4{,}000}{2 - 1} = 4{,}000$$

where the number of degrees of freedom for the p treatments is $(p - 1)$. Next, the **Mean Square for Error** (MSE), which measures the sampling variability *within* the treatments, is

$$\text{MSE} = \frac{\text{SSE}}{n - p} = \frac{18{,}000}{10 - 2} = 2{,}250$$

Finally, we calculate the ratio of MST to MSE—an *F* **statistic**:

$$F = \frac{\text{MST}}{\text{MSE}} = \frac{4{,}000}{2{,}250} = 1.78$$

Values of the F statistic near 1 indicate that the two sources of variation, between treatment means and within treatments, are approximately equal. In this case, the difference between the treatment means may well be attributable to sampling error, which provides little support for the alternative hypothesis that the population treatment means differ. Values of F well in excess of 1 indicate that the variation among treatment means well exceeds that within means and therefore support the alternative hypothesis that the population treatment means differ.

When does F exceed 1 by enough to reject the null hypothesis that the means are equal? This depends on the degrees of freedom for treatments and for error, and on the value of α selected for the test. We compare the calculated F value to a table F value (Tables VII–X of Appendix B) with $v_1 = (p - 1)$ degrees of freedom in the numerator and $v_2 = (n - p)$ degrees of freedom in the denominator and corresponding to a Type I error probability of α. For the SAT score example, the F statistic has $v_1 = (2 - 1) = 1$ numerator degree of freedom and $v_2 = (10 - 2) = 8$ denominator degrees of freedom. Thus, for $\alpha = .05$ we find (Table VIII of Appendix B)

$$F_{.05} = 5.32$$

The implication is that MST would have to be 5.32 times greater than MSE before we could conclude at the .05 level of significance that the two population treatment means differ. Since the data yielded $F = 1.78$, our initial impressions for the dot plot in Figure 15.3 are confirmed—there is insufficient information to conclude that the mean SAT scores differ for the populations of female and male high school seniors. The rejection region and the calculated F value are shown in Figure 15.5.

In contrast, consider the dot plot in Figure 15.4. Since the means are the same as in the first example, 550 and 590, respectively, the variation between the means is the same, MST = 4,000. But the variation within the two treatments appears to be considerably smaller. The observed SAT scores are 540, 545, 550, 555, and 560 for females, and 580, 585, 590, 595, and 600 for males. These values yield $s_1^2 = 62.5$ and $s_2^2 = 62.5$. Thus, the variation within the treatments is measured by

FIGURE 15.5
Rejection region and calculated F values for SAT score samples

$$\text{SSE} = (5 - 1)(62.5) + (5 - 1)(62.5)$$
$$= 500$$

$$\text{MSE} = \frac{\text{SSE}}{n - p} = \frac{500}{8} = 62.5$$

Then the F-ratio is

$$F = \frac{\text{MST}}{\text{MSE}} = \frac{4,000}{62.5} = 64.0$$

Again, our visual analysis of the dot plot is confirmed statistically: $F = 64.0$ well exceeds the tabled F value, 5.32, corresponding to the .05 level of significance. We would therefore reject the null hypothesis at that level and conclude that the SAT mean score of males differs from that of females.

Recall that we performed a hypothesis test for the difference between two means in Section 9.1, using a two-sample t statistic for two independent samples. When two independent samples are being compared, the t- and F-tests are equivalent. To see this, recall the formula

$$t = \frac{\bar{x}_1 - \bar{x}_2}{\sqrt{s_p^2\left(\frac{1}{n_1} + \frac{1}{n_2}\right)}} = \frac{590 - 550}{\sqrt{(62.5)\left(\frac{1}{5} + \frac{1}{5}\right)}} = \frac{40}{5} = 8$$

where we used the fact that $s_p^2 = \text{MSE}$, which you can verify by comparing the formulas. Note that the calculated F for these samples ($F = 64$) equals the square of the calculated t for the same samples ($t = 8$). Likewise, the tabled F value (5.32) equals the square of the tabled t value at the two-sided .05 level of significance ($t_{.025} = 2.306$ with 8 df). Since both the rejection region and the calculated values are related in the same way, the tests are equivalent. Moreover, the assumptions that must be met to ensure the validity of the t- and F-tests are the same:

1. The probability distributions of the populations of responses associated with each treatment must all be normal.
2. The probability distributions of the populations of responses associated with each treatment must have equal variances.
3. The samples of experimental units selected for the treatments must be random and independent.

In fact, the only real difference between the tests is that the F-test can be used to compare *more than two* treatment means, whereas the t-test is applicable to two samples only. The **F-test** is summarized in the accompanying box.

Test to Compare p Treatment Means for a Completely Randomized Design

$$H_0: \mu_1 = \mu_2 = \cdots = \mu_p$$

H_a: At least two treatment means differ

Test statistic: $F = \dfrac{\text{MST}}{\text{MSE}}$

continued

> *Assumptions*: **1.** Samples are selected randomly and independently from the respective populations.
> **2.** All p population probability distributions are normal.
> **3.** The p population variances are equal.
>
> *Rejection region:* $F > F_\alpha$, where F_α is based on $(p - 1)$ numerator degrees of freedom (associated with MST) and $(n - p)$ denominator degrees of freedom (associated with MSE).

Computational formulas for MST and MSE are given in Appendix C. We will rely on some of the many statistical software packages available to compute the F statistic, concentrating on the interpretation of the results rather than their calculations.

EXAMPLE 15.3

Suppose the USGA wants to compare the mean distances associated with four different brands of golf balls when struck with a driver. A completely randomized design is employed, with Iron Byron, the USGA's robotic golfer, using a driver to hit a random sample of 10 balls of each brand in a random sequence. The distance is recorded for each hit, and the results are shown in Table 15.1, organized by brand.

a. Set up the test to compare the mean distances for the four brands. Use $\alpha = .10$.

b. Use the SAS Analysis of Variance program to obtain the test statistic and p-value. Interpret the results.

SOLUTION

a. To compare the mean distances of the four brands, we first specify the hypotheses to be tested. Denoting the population mean of the ith brand by μ_i, we test

$$H_0: \mu_1 = \mu_2 = \mu_3 = \mu_4$$

H_a: The mean distances differ for at least two of the brands

The test statistic compares the variation among the four treatment (Brand) means to the sampling variability within each of the treatments.

TABLE 15.1   **Results of Completely Randomized Design: Iron Byron Driver**

	Brand A	Brand B	Brand C	Brand D
	251.2	263.2	269.7	251.6
	245.1	262.9	263.2	248.6
	248.0	265.0	277.5	249.4
	251.1	254.5	267.4	242.0
	260.5	264.3	270.5	246.5
	250.0	257.0	265.5	251.3
	253.9	262.8	270.7	261.8
	244.6	264.4	272.9	249.0
	254.6	260.6	275.6	247.1
	248.8	255.9	266.5	245.9
Sample Means	250.8	261.1	270.0	249.3

FIGURE 15.6
F-Test for completely randomized design: Golf ball experiment

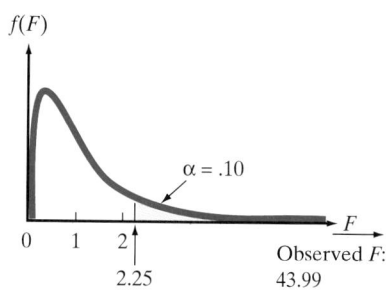

Test statistic: $F = \dfrac{\text{MST}}{\text{MSE}}$

Rejection region: $F > F_{\alpha} = F_{.10}$
    with $v_1 = (p - 1) = 3$ df and $v_2 = (n - p) = 36$ df

From Table VII of Appendix B, we find $F_{.10} \approx 2.25$ for 3 and 36 df. Thus, we will reject H_0 if $F > 2.25$. (See Figure 15.6.)

The assumptions necessary to ensure the validity of the test are as follows:

1. The samples of 10 golf balls for each brand are selected randomly and independently.

2. The probability distributions of the distances for each brand are normal.

3. The variances of the distance probability distributions for each brand are equal.

b. The SAS printout for the data in Table 15.1 resulting from this completely randomized design is given in Figure 15.7. Note that the top part of the printout is identical to that in a regression analysis. The Total Sum of Squares is designated the **Corrected Total**, and it is partitioned into the **Model** and **Error Sums of Squares**. The bottom part of the printout further partitions the **Model** component into the factors that comprise the model. In this single-factor experiment, the Model and Brand sums of squares are the same. The **Sum of Squares** column is headed **Anova SS**.

The values of the mean squares, MST and MSE (highlighted on the printout), are 931.46 and 21.18, respectively. The *F*-ratio, 43.99, also highlighted on the printout, exceeds the tabled value of 2.25. We therefore reject the

```
                        Analysis of Variance Procedure
Dependent Variable: DISTANCE

                                  Sum of              Mean
Source                   DF       Squares            Square    F Value    Pr > F

Model                     3    2794.388750       931.462917     43.99     0.0001
Error                    36     762.301000        21.175028
Corrected Total          39    3556.689750

                     R-Square            C.V.       Root MSE       DISTANCE Mean
                     0.785671        1.785118       4.601633          257.777500

Source                   DF      Anova SS    Mean Square    F Value    Pr > F

BRAND                     3    2794.388750     931.462917     43.99     0.0001
```

FIGURE 15.7   SAS analysis of variance printout for golf ball distance data: Completely randomized design

TABLE 15.2 **General ANOVA Summary Table for a Completely Randomized Design**

Source	df	SS	MS	F
Treatments	$p - 1$	SST	$MST = \dfrac{SST}{p - 1}$	$\dfrac{MST}{MSE}$
Error	$n - p$	SSE	$MSE = \dfrac{SSE}{n - p}$	
Total	$n - 1$	SS(Total)		

null hypothesis at the .10 level of significance, concluding that at least two of the brands differ with respect to mean distance traveled when struck by the driver.

The observed significance level of the F-test is also highlighted on the print-out: .0001. This is the area to the right of the calculated F value and it implies that we would reject the null hypothesis that the means are equal at any α level greater than .0001.

The results of an **analysis of variance** (ANOVA) can be summarized in a simple tabular format similar to that obtained from the SAS program in Example 15.3. The general form of the table is shown in Table 15.2, where the symbols df, SS, and MS stand for degrees of freedom, Sum of Squares, and Mean Square, respectively. Note that the two sources of variation, Treatments and Error, add to the Total Sum of Squares, SS(Total). The ANOVA summary table for Example 15.3 is given in Table 15.3, and the partitioning of the Total Sum of Squares into its two components is illustrated in Figure 15.8.

Suppose the F-test results in a rejection of the null hypothesis that the treatment means are equal. Is the analysis complete? Usually, the conclusion that at least two of the treatment means differ leads to other questions. Which of the

TABLE 15.3 **ANOVA Summary Table for Example 15.3**

Source	df	SS	MS	F	p-Value
Brands	3	2,794.39	931.46	43.99	.0001
Error	36	762.30	21.18		
Total	39	3,556.69			

FIGURE 15.8

Partitioning of the Total Sum of Squares for the completely randomized design

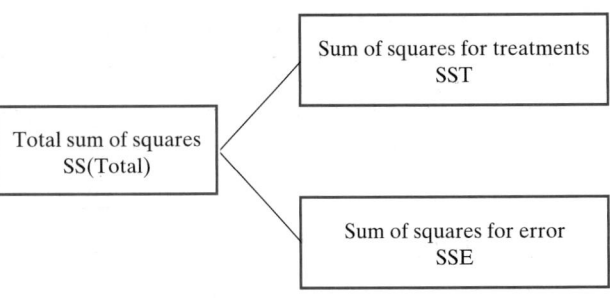

means differ, and by how much? For example, the *F*-test in Example 15.3 leads to the conclusion that at least two of the brands of golf balls have different mean distances traveled when struck with a driver. Now the question is, which of the brands differ? How are the brands ranked with respect to mean distance?

One way to obtain this information is to construct a confidence interval for the difference between the means of any pair of treatments using the method of Section 9.1. For example, if a 95% confidence interval for $\mu_A - \mu_C$ in Example 15.3 is found to be $(-24, -13)$, we are confident that the mean distance for Brand C exceeds the mean for Brand A (since all differences in the interval are negative). Constructing these confidence intervals for all possible brand pairs will allow you to rank the brand means. A method for conducting these *multiple comparisons*—one that controls for Type I errors—is presented in Section 15.3.

EXAMPLE 15.4   Refer to the completely randomized design ANOVA conducted in Example 15.3. Are the assumptions required for the test approximately satisfied?

SOLUTION
The assumptions for the test are repeated below.

1. The samples of golf balls for each brand are selected randomly and independently.
2. The probability distributions of the distances for each brand are normal.
3. The variances of the distance probability distributions for each brand are equal.

Since the sample consisted of 10 randomly selected balls of each brand and the robotic golfer Iron Byron was used to drive all the balls, the first assumption of independent random samples is satisfied. To check the next two assumptions, we will employ two graphical methods presented in Chapter 2: stem-and-leaf displays and dot plots. A MINITAB stem-and-leaf display for the sample distances of each brand of golf ball is shown in Figure 15.9, followed by a MINITAB dot plot in Figure 15.10.

The normality assumption can be checked by examining the stem-and-leaf displays in Figure 15.9. With only 10 sample measurements for each brand, however, the displays are not very informative. More data would need to be collected for each brand before we could assess whether the distances come from normal distributions. Fortunately, analysis of variance has been shown to be a very **robust method** when the assumption of normality is not satisfied exactly: That is, moderate departures from normality do not have much effect on the significance level of the ANOVA *F*-test or on confidence coefficients. Rather than spend the time, energy, or money to collect additional data for this experiment in order to verify the normality assumption, we will rely on the robustness of the ANOVA methodology.

Dot plots are a convenient way to obtain a rough check on the assumption of equal variances. With the exception of a possible outlier for Brand D, the dot plots in Figure 15.10 show that the spread of the distance measurements is about the same for each brand. Since the sample variances appear to be the same, the assumption of equal population variances for the brands is probably satisfied. Although robust with respect to the normality assumption, ANOVA is *not robust* with respect to the equal variances assumption. Departures from the assumption

FIGURE 15.9
MINITAB stem-and-leaf displays for distance data: Completely randomized design

```
Stem-and-leaf of BrandA   N = 10
Leaf Unit = 1.0

    2     24 45
    2     24
    4     24 88
   (3)    25 011
    3     25 3
    2     25 4
    1     25
    1     25
    1     26 0

Stem-and-leaf of BrandB   N = 10
Leaf Unit = 1.0

    2     25 45
    3     25 7
    3     25
    4     26 0
   (3)    26 223
    3     26 445

Stem-and-leaf of BrandC   N = 10
Leaf Unit = 1.0

    1     26 3
    2     26 5
    4     26 67
    5     26 9
    5     27 00
    3     27 2
    2     27 5
    1     27 7

Stem-and-leaf of BrandD N = 10
Leaf Unit = 1.0

    1     24 2
    2     24 5
    4     24 67
   (3)    24 899
    3     25 11
    1     25
    1     25
    1     25
    1     25
    1     26 1
```

of equal population variances can affect the associated measures of reliability (e.g., *p*-values and confidence levels). Fortunately, the effect is slight when the sample sizes are equal, as in this experiment.

Although graphs can be used to check the ANOVA assumptions, as in Example 15.4, no measures of reliability can be attached to these graphs. When you have a plot that is unclear as to whether or not an assumption is satisfied, you can use formal statistical tests, which are beyond the scope of this text. (Consult the references for information on these tests.) When the validity of the ANOVA assumptions is in doubt, nonparametric statistical methods are useful.

FIGURE 15.10   MINITAB dot plots for distance data: Completely randomized design

> **What Do You Do When the Assumptions Are Not Satisfied for the Analysis of Variance for a Completely Randomized Design?**
> *Answer:* Use a nonparametric statistical method such as the Kruskal-Wallis H-Test of Section 16.4.

The procedure for conducting an analysis of variance for a completely randomized design is summarized in the following box. Remember that the hallmark of this design is independent random samples of experimental units associated with each treatment. However, designs with dependent samples may be more appropriate in certain situations. Consult the references for information on the use of these designs.

> **Steps for Conducting an ANOVA for a Completely Randomized Design**
> 1. Be sure the design is truly completely randomized, with independent random samples for each treatment.
> 2. Check the assumptions of normality and equal variances.
> 3. Create an ANOVA summary table that specifies the variability attributable to treatments and error, making sure that it leads to the calculation of the F statistic for testing the null hypothesis that the treatment means are equal in the population. Use a statistical software program to obtain the numerical results. If no such package is available, use the calculation formulas in Appendix C.
> 4. If the F-test leads to the conclusion that the means differ:
>   a. Conduct a multiple comparisons procedure for as many of the pairs of means as you wish to compare (see Section 15.3). Use the results to summarize the statistically significant differences among the treatment means.
>   b. If desired, form confidence intervals for one or more individual treatment means.
> 5. If the F-test leads to the nonrejection of the null hypothesis that the treatment means are equal, consider the following possibilities:
>   a. The treatment means are equal—that is, the null hypothesis is true.
>   b. The treatment means really differ, but other important factors affecting the response are not accounted for by the completely randomized design. These factors inflate the sampling variability, as measured by MSE, resulting in smaller values of the F statistic. Either increase the sample size for each treatment, or use a different experimental design (as in Section 15.4) that accounts for the other factors affecting the response.

continued

[*Note:* Be careful not to automatically conclude that the treatment means are equal since the possibility of a Type II error must be considered if you accept H_0.]

EXERCISES 15.9–15.26

Note: Exercises marked with 💾 *contain data for computer analysis on a 3.5" disk (file name in parentheses).*

Learning the Mechanics

15.9 Use Tables VII–X of Appendix B to find each of the following F values:
a. $F_{.05}, v_1 = 4, v_2 = 4$ **b.** $F_{.01}, v_1 = 4, v_2 = 4$
c. $F_{.10}, v_1 = 30, v_2 = 40$ **d.** $F_{.025}, v_1 = 15, v_2 = 12$

15.10 Find the following probabilities:
a. $P(F \le 3.48)$ for $v_1 = 5, v_2 = 9$
b. $P(F > 3.09)$ for $v_1 = 15, v_2 = 20$
c. $P(F > 2.40)$ for $v_1 = 15, v_2 = 15$
d. $P(F \le 1.83)$ for $v_1 = 8, v_2 = 40$

15.11 Consider dot plots **a** and **b** shown below. In which plot is the difference between the sample means small relative to the variability within the sample observations? Justify your answer.

15.12 Refer to Exercise 15.11. Assume that the two samples represent independent, random samples corresponding to two treatments in a completely randomized design.
a. Calculate the treatment means, i.e., the means of samples 1 and 2, for both dot plots.
b. Use the means to calculate the Sum of Squares for Treatments (SST) for each dot plot.
c. Calculate the sample variance for each sample and use these values to obtain the Sum of Squares for Error (SSE) for each dot plot.
d. Calculate the Total Sum of Squares [SS(Total)] for the two dot plots by adding the Sums of Squares for Treatment and Error. What percentage of SS(Total) is accounted for by the treatments—that is, what percentage of the Total Sum of Squares is the Sum of Squares for Treatment—in each case?

e. Convert the Sum of Squares for Treatment and Error to mean squares by dividing each by the appropriate number of degrees of freedom. Calculate the F-ratio of the Mean Square for Treatment (MST) to the Mean Square for Error (MSE) for each dot plot.
f. Use the F-ratios to test the null hypothesis that the two samples are drawn from populations with equal means. Use $\alpha = .05$.
g. What assumptions must be made about the probability distributions corresponding to the responses for each treatment in order to ensure the validity of the F-tests conducted in part **f**?

15.13 Refer to Exercises 15.11 and 15.12. Conduct a two-sample t-test (Section 9.1) of the null hypothesis that the two treatment means are equal for each dot plot. Use $\alpha = .05$ and two-tailed tests. In the course of the test, compare each of the following with the F-tests in Exercise 15.12:
a. The pooled variances and the MSEs
b. The t- and F-test statistics
c. The tabled values of t and F that determine the rejection regions
d. The conclusions of the t- and F-tests
e. The assumptions that must be made in order to ensure the validity of the t- and F-tests

15.14 Refer to Exercises 15.11 and 15.12. Complete the following ANOVA table for each of the two dot plots:

Source	df	SS	MS	F
Treatments				
Error				
Total				

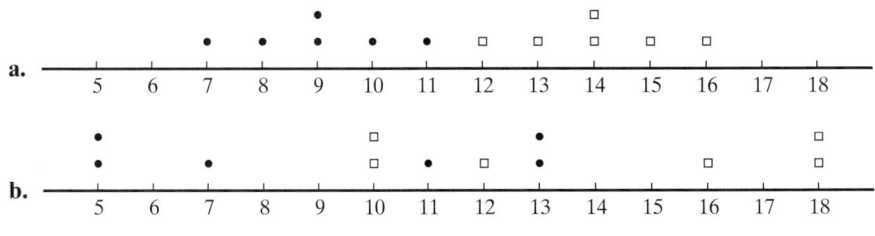

• Sample 1
□ Sample 2

15.15 Suppose the Total Sum of Squares for a completely randomized design with $p = 6$ treatments and $n = 36$ total measurements (six per treatment) is equal to 500. In each of the following cases, conduct an F-test of the null hypothesis that the mean responses for the five treatments are the same. Use $\alpha = .10$.

  a. Sum of Squares for Treatment (SST) is 20% of SS(Total)
  b. SST is 50% of SS(Total)
  c. SST is 80% of SS(Total)
  d. What happens to the F-ratio as the percentage of the Total Sum of Squares attributable to treatments is increased?

15.16 A partially completed ANOVA table for a completely randomized design is shown here:

Source	df	SS	MS	F
Treatments	6	17.5	___	___
Error	___	___	___	
Total	41	46.5		

  a. Complete the ANOVA table.
  b. How many treatments are involved in the experiment?
  c. Do the data provide sufficient evidence to indicate a difference among the population means? Test using $\alpha = .10$.
  d. Find the approximate observed significance level for the test in part **c**, and interpret it.
  e. Suppose that $\bar{x}_1 = 3.7$ and $\bar{x}_2 = 4.1$. Do the data provide sufficient evidence to indicate a difference between μ_1 and μ_2? Assume that there are six observations for each treatment. Test using $\alpha = .10$.
  f. Refer to part **e**. Find a 90% confidence interval for $(\mu_1 - \mu_2)$.
  g. Refer to part **e**. Find a 90% confidence interval for μ_1.

15.17 See the accompanying MINITAB printout for an experiment utilizing a completely randomized design. [*Note:* MINITAB uses "FACTOR" instead of "Treatments" in this printout.]

  a. How many treatments are involved in the experiment? What is the total sample size?
  b. Conduct a test of the null hypothesis that the treatment means are equal. Use $\alpha = .10$.

  c. What additional information is needed in order to be able to compare specific pairs of treatment means?

15.18 The data in the accompanying table resulted from an experiment that utilized a completely randomized design.

Treatment 1	Treatment 2	Treatment 3
3.8	5.4	1.3
1.2	2.0	.7
4.1	4.8	2.2
5.5	3.8	
2.3		

  a. Use the appropriate calculation formulas in Appendix C to complete the following ANOVA table:

Source	df	SS	MS	F
Treatments	___	___	___	___
Error	___	___	___	
Total	___	___		

  b. Test the null hypothesis that $\mu_1 = \mu_2 = \mu_3$, where μ_i represents the true mean for treatment i, against the alternative that at least two of the means differ. Use $\alpha = .01$.

Applying the Concepts

15.19 Speech recognition technology has advanced to the point that it is now possible to communicate with a computer through verbal commands. A study was conducted to evaluate the value of speech recognition in human interactions with computer systems (*Special Interest Group on Computer-Human Interaction Bulletin*, July 1993.) A sample of 45 subjects was randomly divided into three groups (15 subjects per group), and each subject was asked to perform tasks on a basic voice-mail system. A different interface was employed in each group: (1) touch-tone, (2) human operator, or (3) simulated speech recognition. One of the variables measured was overall time (in seconds) to perform the assigned tasks. An analysis was conducted to compare the mean overall performance times of the three groups.

```
ANALYSIS OF VARIANCE ON Y
SOURCE    DF      SS       MS       F       p
FACTOR     3    57258    19086    14.80   0.002
ERROR     34    43836     1289
TOTAL     37   101094
```

a. Identify the experimental design employed in this study.

b. The sample mean performance times for the three groups are given below. Although the sample means are different, the null hypothesis of the ANOVA could not be rejected at $\alpha = .05$. Explain how this is possible.

Group	Mean Performance Time (seconds)
Touchtone	1,400
Human operator	1,030
Speech recognition	1,040

15.20 (X15.020) An accounting firm that specializes in auditing the financial records of large corporations is interested in evaluating the appropriateness of the fees it charges for its services. As part of its evaluation, it wants to compare the costs it incurs in auditing corporations of different sizes. The accounting firm decided to measure the size of its client corporations in terms of their yearly sales. Accordingly, its population of client corporations was divided into three subpopulations:

A: Those with sales over $250 million

B: Those with sales between $100 million and $250 million

C: Those with sales under $100 million

The firm chose random samples of 10 corporations from each of the subpopulations and determined the costs (in thousands of dollars), given in the next table, from its records.

a. Construct a dot plot (refer to Figures 15.3 and 15.4) for the sample data, using different types of dots for each of the three samples. Indicate the location of each of the sample means. Based on the information reflected in your dot plot, do you believe that a significant difference exists among the subpopulation means? Explain.

A	B	C
250	100	80
150	150	125
275	75	20
100	200	186
475	55	52
600	80	92
150	110	88
800	160	141
325	132	76
230	233	200

b. SAS was used to conduct the analysis of variance calculations, resulting in the printout shown below. Conduct a test to determine whether the three classes of firms have different mean costs incurred in audits. Use $\alpha = .05$.

c. What is the observed significance level for the test in part **b**? Interpret it.

d. What assumptions must be met in order to ensure the validity of the inferences you made in parts **b** and **c**?

15.21 The Minnesota Multiphasic Personality Inventory (MMPI) is a questionnaire used to gauge personality type. Several scales are built into the MMPI to assess response distortion; these include the Infrequency (I), Obvious (O), Subtle (S), Obvious-subtle (O-S), and Dissimulation (D) scales. *Psychological Assessment* (Mar. 1995) published a study that investigated the effectiveness of these MMPI scales in detecting deliberately distorted responses. A completely randomized design with four treatments was employed. The treatments consisted of independent random samples of females in the following four groups: nonforensic psychiatric patients ($n_1 = 65$), forensic psychiatric patients ($n_2 = 28$), college students who were requested to respond honestly ($n_3 = 140$), and college students who were instructed to provide

```
                  General Linear Models Procedure

Dependent Variable: COST

                                   Sum of          Mean
Source                   DF       Squares        Square     F Value    Pr > F
Model                     2    318861.667    159430.833       8.44     0.0014
Error                    27    510163.000     18894.926
Corrected Total          29    829024.667

                  R-Square         C.V.      Root MSE               COST Mean
                  0.384623    72.220043       137.459              190.333333

Source                   DF    Type 1 SS  Mean Square    F Value    Pr > F
TREATMNT                  2    318861.67    159430.83       8.44     0.0014
```

"fake bad" responses ($n_4 = 45$). All 278 participants were given the MMPI and the I, O, S, O-S, and D scores were recorded for each. Each scale was treated as a response variable and an analysis of variance conducted. The ANOVA *F*-values are reported in the table.

Response Variable	ANOVA *F*-Value
Infrequency (I)	155.8
Obvious (O)	49.7
Subtle (S)	10.3
Obvious-subtle (O-S)	45.4
Dissimulation (D)	39.1

a. For each response variable, determine whether the mean scores of the four groups completing the MMPI differ significantly. Use $\alpha = .05$ for each test.

b. If the MMPI is effective in detecting distorted responses, then the mean score for the "fake bad" treatment group will be largest. Based on the information provided, can the researchers make an inference about the effectiveness of the MMPI? Explain.

15.22 (X15.022) Organic chemical solvents are used for cleaning fabricated metal parts in industries such as aerospace, electronics, and automobiles. These solvents, when disposed of, have the potential to become hazardous waste. The *Journal of Hazardous Materials* (July 1995) published the results of a study of the chemical properties of three different types of hazardous organic solvents used to clean metal parts: aromatics, chloroalkanes, and esters. One variable studied was sorption rate, measured as mole percentage. Independent samples of solvents from each type were tested and their sorption rates were recorded, as shown in the next table. A MINITAB analysis of variance of the data is shown in the printout below.

a. Construct an ANOVA table from the MINITAB printout.

b. Is there evidence of differences among the mean sorption rates of the three organic solvent types? Test using $\alpha = .10$.

15.23 Industrial sales professionals have long debated the effectiveness of various sales closing techniques. University of Akron researchers S. Hawes,

Aromatics		Chloroalkanes		Esters		
1.06	.95	1.58	1.12	.29	.43	.06
.79	.65	1.45	.91	.06	.51	.09
.82	1.15	.57	.83	.44	.10	.17
.89	1.12	1.16	.43	.61	.34	.60
1.05				.55	.53	.17

Source: Reprinted from *Journal of Hazardous Materials*, Vol. 42, No. 2, J. D. Ortego *et al.*, "A review of polymeric geosynthetics used in hazardous waste facilities," p. 142 (Table 9), July 1995, with kind permission of Elsevier Science-NL, Sara Burgerhartstraat 25, 1055 KV Amsterdam, The Netherlands.

J. Strong, and B. Winick investigated the impact of five different closing techniques and a no-close condition on the level of a sales prospect's trust in the salesperson (*Industrial Marketing Management*, Sept. 1996). Two of the five closing techniques were the *assumed close* and the *impending event technique*. In the former, the salesperson simply writes up the order or behaves as if the sale has been made. In the latter, the salesperson encourages the buyer to buy now before some future event occurs that makes the terms of the sale less favorable for the buyer. Sales scenarios were presented to a sample of 238 purchasing executives. Each subject received one of the five closing techniques or a scenario in which no close was achieved. After reading the sales scenario, each executive was asked to rate their level of trust in the salesperson on a 7-point scale. The table reports the six treatments employed in the study and the number of subjects receiving each treatment.

Treatments: Closing Techniques	Sample Size
1. No close	38
2. Impending event	36
3. Social validation	29
4. If-then	42
5. Assumed close	36
6. Either-or	56

a. The investigator's hypotheses were

H_0: The salesperson's level of prospect trust *is not* influenced by the choice of closing method

H_a: The salesperson's level of prospect trust *is* influenced by the choice of closing method

```
Analysis of Variance for SORPRATE

Source    DF     SS       MS      F      p

SOLVENT    2    3.3054   1.6527  24.51  0.000
Error     29    1.9553   0.0674
Total     31    5.2607
```

Rewrite these hypotheses in the form required for an analysis of variance.

b. The researchers reported the ANOVA F statistic as $F = 2.21$. Is there sufficient evidence to reject H_0 at $\alpha = .05$?

c. What assumptions must be met in order for the test of part **a** to be valid?

d. Would you classify this experiment as observational or designed? Explain.

15.24 On average, over a million new businesses are started in the United States every year. An article in the *Journal of Business Venturing* (Vol. 11, 1996) reported on the activities of entrepreneurs during the organization creation process. Among the questions investigated were what activities and how many activities do entrepreneurs initiate in attempting to establish a new business? A total of 71 entrepreneurs were interviewed and divided into three groups: those that were successful in founding a new firm (34), those still actively trying to establish a firm (21), and those who tried to start a new firm, but eventually gave up (16). The total number of activities undertaken (i.e., developed a business plan, sought funding, looked for facilities, etc.) by each group over a specified time period during organization creation was measured and the following incomplete ANOVA table produced:

Source	df	SS	MS	F
Groups	2	128.70	___	___
Error	68	27,124.52	___	

Source: Carter, N., Garner, W., and Reynolds, P. "Exploring start-up event sequences." *Journal of Business Venturing,* Vol. 11, 1996, p. 159.

a. Complete the ANOVA table.

b. Do the data provide sufficient evidence to indicate that the total number of activities undertaken differed among the three groups of entrepreneurs? Test using $\alpha = .05$.

c. What is the p-value of the test you conducted in part **b**?

d. One of the conclusions of the study was that the behaviors of entrepreneurs who have successfully started a new company can be differentiated from the behaviors of entrepreneurs that failed. Do you agree? Justify your answer.

e. Classify this study as observational or experimental. Justify your answer.

15.25 Auditors may be called upon to perform compilations, reviews, or audits for their nonpublic clients. To do compilations and reviews of financial statements requires auditors an average of 25% and 50% fewer hours, respectively, than to perform an annual audit. Both auditors and clients fear that users of compilations and reviews might not rec-

ognize the limited nature of these reports and might assume that the auditor accepts the same degree of responsibility for them as for audited annual financial statements. To investigate these fears, an experiment designed to measure bankers' reactions to these three alternative forms of auditors' reports was conducted (*Auditing: A Journal of Practice and Theory,* Spring 1983). Ninety-eight loan officers responded to a questionnaire in which they were asked to review a financial statement and background information for a commercial loan applicant. Thirty-one of the officers received a compilation, 25 received a review, 27 an audit, and 15 received a financial statement with no auditor association. One of the questions dealt with the loan officers' level of confidence in the financial statement's conformance to generally accepted accounting principles. They were asked to indicate their level of confidence on a scale of 0 to 10 (no confidence to extreme confidence). The researchers hypothesized that the mean level of confidence would not be the same for all four types of financial statements. Further, they hypothesized that the mean level of confidence associated with the audit would be greater than with the next highest form of auditor association, the review. Some of the data obtained from their experiment are summarized in the tables.

Source	df	SS
Type of report	3	273
Error	94	494
Total	97	767

Source: Johnson, D. A., Pany, K., and White, R. "Audit reports and the loan decision: Actions and perceptions." *Auditing: A Journal of Practice and Theory,* Vol. 2, Spring 1983, pp. 38–51.

	Treatment Means
No auditor association	3.9
Compilation	5.5
Review	6.1
Audit	8.8

a. Do the data provide sufficient evidence to conclude that the mean level of confidence differs among the four forms of auditor association?

b. Report the approximate p-value of your test.

c. Do the data provide sufficient evidence to conclude that the mean level of confidence associated with the audit is significantly higher than the mean for the review? Test using $\alpha = .05$.

d. Relate your findings for parts **a** and **c** to the expressed fear that users of financial reports might assume auditors were accepting the same degree of responsibility for each form of financial report.

15.26 A recent study in the *Journal of Psychology and Marketing* (Jan. 1992) investigates consumer attitudes toward product tampering. One variable considered was the education level of the consumer. Consumers were divided into five educational classifications and asked to rate their concern about product tampering on a scale of 1 (little or no concern) to 9 (very concerned). The education levels and the means are shown in the table.

  a. Identify the type of ANOVA design used in this experiment. Identify the treatments in this experiment.

Education Level	Mean	Sample Size
Non–high school graduate	3.731	26
High school graduate	3.224	49
Some college completed	3.330	94
College graduate	3.167	60
Some postgraduate work	4.341	86

  b. The article compared the mean concern ratings for the five education levels. The F statistic for this test was reported to be 3.298. Conduct a test of hypothesis to determine whether the mean concern ratings differ for at least two of the education levels. [*Hint:* Calculate the degrees of freedom for Treatment and Error from the information given.]

15.3 MULTIPLE COMPARISONS OF MEANS

Consider a completely randomized design with three treatments, A, B, and C. Suppose we determine that the treatment means are statistically different via the ANOVA F-test of Section 15.2. To complete the analysis, we want to rank the three treatment means. As mentioned in Section 15.2, we start by placing confidence intervals on the difference between various pairs of treatment means in the experiment. In the three-treatment experiment, for example, we would construct confidence intervals for the following differences: $\mu_A - \mu_B, \mu_A - \mu_C$, and $\mu_B - \mu_C$.

In general, if there are p treatment means, there are

$$c = \frac{p(p-1)}{2}$$

pairs of means that can be compared. If we want to have $100(1-\alpha)\%$ confidence that each of the c confidence intervals contains the true difference it is intended to estimate, we must use a smaller value of α for each individual confidence interval than we would use for a single interval. For example, suppose we want to rank the means of the three treatments, A, B, and C, with 95% confidence that all three confidence intervals comparing the means contain the true differences between the treatment means. Then each individual confidence interval will need to be constructed using a level of significance smaller than $\alpha = .05$ in order to have 95% confidence that the three intervals collectively include the true differences.*

To make **multiple comparisons** of a set of treatment means we can use a number of procedures that, under various assumptions, ensure that the overall

---

*The reason each interval must be formed at a higher confidence level than that specified for the collection of intervals can be demonstrated as follows:

$P\{$At least one of c intervals fails to contain the true difference$\}$

$= 1 - P\{$All c intervals contain the true differences$\}$

$= 1 - (1-\alpha)^c \geq \alpha$

Thus, to make this probability of at least one failure equal to α, we must specify the individual levels of significance to be less than α.

confidence level associated with all the comparisons remains at or above the specified $100(1 - \alpha)\%$ level. Three widely used techniques are the Bonferroni, Scheffé, and Tukey methods. For each of these procedures, the risk of making a Type I error applies to the comparisons of the treatment means in the experiment; thus, the value of α selected is called an **experimentwise error rate** (in contrast to a **comparisonwise error rate**).

The choice of a multiple comparisons method in ANOVA will depend on the type of experimental design used and the comparisons of interest to the analyst. For example, Tukey (1949) developed his procedure specifically for pairwise comparisons when the sample sizes of the treatments are equal. The Bonferroni method (see Miller, 1981), like the Tukey procedure, can be applied when pairwise comparisons are of interest; however, Bonferroni's method does not require equal sample sizes. Scheffé (1953) developed a more general procedure for comparing all possible linear combinations of treatment means (called *contrasts*). Consequently, when making pairwise comparisons, the confidence intervals produced by Scheffé's method will generally be wider than the Tukey or Bonferroni confidence intervals.

The formulas for constructing confidence intervals for differences between treatment means using the Tukey, Bonferroni, or Scheffé method are beyond the scope of this text. However, these procedures (and many others) are available in the ANOVA programs of most statistical software packages. The programs generate a confidence interval for the difference between two treatment means for all possible pairs of treatments, based on the experimentwise error rate (α) selected by the analyst.

EXAMPLE 15.5

Refer to the completely randomized design of Example 15.3, in which we concluded that at least two of the four brands of golf balls are associated with different mean distances traveled when struck with a driver.

a. Use Tukey's multiple comparisons procedure to rank the treatment means with an overall confidence level of 95%.

b. Estimate the mean distance traveled for balls manufactured by the brand with the highest rank.

SOLUTION

a. To rank the treatment means with an overall confidence level of .95, we require the experimentwise error rate of $\alpha = .05$. The confidence intervals generated by Tukey's method appear at the bottom of the SAS ANOVA printout, Figure 15.11.

Note that for any pair of means, μ_i and μ_j, SAS computes two confidence intervals—one for $(\mu_i - \mu_j)$ and one for $(\mu_j - \mu_i)$. Only one of these intervals is necessary to decide whether the means differ significantly.

In this example, we have $p = 4$ brand means to compare. Consequently, the number of relevant pairwise comparisons—that is, the number of nonredundant confidence intervals is $c = 4(3)/2 = 6$. These six intervals, highlighted in Figure 15.11, are given in Table 15.4.

We are 95% confident that the intervals *collectively* contain all the differences between the true brand mean distances. Note that intervals that contain 0, such as the (Brand A–Brand D) interval from -4.082 to 7.002, do not support a conclusion that the true brand mean distances differ. If both endpoints of the interval are positive, as with the (Brand B–Brand D) interval

```
                    Analysis of Variance Procedure
Dependent Variable: DISTANCE
                              Sum of         Mean
Source                 DF     Squares        Square     F Value   Pr > F
Model                   3   2794.388750    931.462917    43.99    0.0001
Error                  36    762.301000     21.175028
Corrected Total        39   3556.689750

              R-Square          C.V.      Root MSE     DISTANCE Mean
              0.785671       1.785118     4.601633       257.777500

Source                 DF    Anova SS   Mean Square   F Value   Pr > F
BRAND                   3   2794.388750  931.462917    43.99    0.0001
```

```
     Tukey's Studentized Range (HSD) Test for variable: DISTANCE
   NOTE: This test controls the type I experimentwise error rate.
        Alpha= 0.05   Confidence= 0.95   df= 36   MSE= 21.17503
            Critical Value of Studentized Range= 3.809
              Minimum Significant Difference= 5.5424

  Comparisons significant at the 0.05 level are indicated by '***'.

                        Simultaneous          Simultaneous
                           Lower    Difference   Upper
                BRAND    Confidence  Between    Confidence
             Comparison    Limit      Means       Limit

       C    - B           3.348       8.890      14.432      ***
       C    - A          13.628      19.170      24.712      ***
       C    - D          15.088      20.630      26.172      ***

       B    - C         -14.432      -8.890      -3.348      ***
       B    - A           4.738      10.280      15.822      ***
       B    - D           6.198      11.740      17.282      ***

       A    - C         -24.712     -19.170     -13.628      ***
       A    - B         -15.822     -10.280      -4.738      ***
       A    - D          -4.082       1.460       7.002

       D    - C         -26.172     -20.630     -15.088      ***
       D    - B         -17.282     -11.740      -6.198      ***
       D    - A          -7.002      -1.460       4.082
```

FIGURE 15.11 SAS printout for Example 15.5

TABLE 15.4 Pairwise Comparisons for Example 15.5

Brand Comparison	Confidence Interval
$(\mu_A - \mu_B)$	$(-15.822, -4.738)$
$(\mu_A - \mu_C)$	$(-24.712, -13.628)$
$(\mu_A - \mu_D)$	$(-4.082, 7.002)$
$(\mu_B - \mu_C)$	$(-14.432, -3.348)$
$(\mu_B - \mu_D)$	$(6.198, 17.282)$
$(\mu_C - \mu_D)$	$(15.088, 26.172)$

from 6.198 to 17.282, the implication is that the first brand (B) mean distance exceeds the second (D). Conversely, if both endpoints of the interval are negative, as with the (Brand A–Brand C) interval from −24.712 to

Brand	Mean
C	270.0
B	261.1
A	250.8
D	249.3

FIGURE 15.12
Summary of Tukey
multiple comparisons

-13.628, the implication is that the second brand (C) mean distance exceeds the first brand (A) mean distance.

A convenient summary of the results of the Tukey multiple comparisons is a listing of the brand means from highest to lowest, with a solid line connecting those that are *not* significantly different. This summary is shown in Figure 15.12. The interpretation is that brand C's mean distance exceeds all others; brand B's mean exceeds that of brands A and D; and the means of brands A and D do not differ significantly. All these inferences are made simultaneously with 95% confidence, the overall confidence level of the Tukey multiple comparisons.

b. Brand C is ranked highest; thus, we want a confidence interval for μ_C. Since the samples were selected independently in a completely randomized design, a confidence interval for an individual treatment mean is obtained with the one-sample t confidence interval of Section 7.2, using the standard deviation, $s = \sqrt{\text{MSE}}$, as the measure of sampling variability for the experiment. A 95% confidence interval on the mean distance traveled by brand C (apparently the "longest ball" of those tested), is

$$\bar{x}_C \pm t_{.025}s\sqrt{1/n}$$

where $n = 10$, $t_{.025} \approx 2$ (based on 36 degrees of freedom), and $s = 4.601633$ (obtained from the SAS printout, Figure 15.11). Substituting, we obtain

$$270.0 \pm (2)(4.60)(\sqrt{.1})$$

$$270.0 \pm 2.9 \text{ or } (267.1, 272.9)$$

Thus, we are 95% confident that the true mean distance traveled for brand C is between 267.1 and 272.9 yards, when hit with a driver by Iron Byron. ▐

Many of the available statistical software packages that have multiple comparisons routines will also produce the rankings shown in Figure 15.12. For example, the SAS printout in Figure 15.13 displays the ranking of the mean distances for the four golf ball brands using Bonferroni's method.

The experimentwise error rate (.05), MSE value (21.175), and critical t value (2.79) used in the analysis are highlighted on the printout. The Bonferroni rankings

```
                  Analysis of Variance Procedure
              Bonferroni (Dunn) T tests for variable: DISTANCE
   NOTE: This test controls the type I experimentwise error rate, but
        generally has a higher type II error rate than REGWQ.
              Alpha= 0.05 df= 36 MSE= 21.17503
                 Critical Value of T= 2.79
              Minimum Significant Difference= 5.7456

     Means with the same letter are not significantly different.

          Bon Grouping          Mean        N   BRAND
                      A        269.950      10   C
                      B        261.060      10   B
                      C        250.780      10   A
                      C
                      C        249.320      10   D
```

FIGURE 15.13   SAS Bonferroni analysis for four golf ball brands of the means are displayed at the bottom of Figure 15.13. Instead of a solid line, note that SAS uses a **Bon Grouping** letter to connect means that are not significantly different. You can see that the mean for Brand C is ranked highest, followed by the mean for Brand B. These two brand means are significantly different since they are associated with a different Bon Grouping letter. Brands A and D are ranked lowest and their means are not significantly different (since they have the same Bon Grouping letter).

Remember that the Tukey and Bonferroni methods are just two of numerous multiple comparisons procedures available. Another technique may be more appropriate for the experimental design you employ. Consult the references for details on these other methods and when they should be applied.

STATISTICS IN ACTION

15.1 IS THERAPY THE NEW "DIET PILL" FOR BINGE EATERS?

In the United States, dieting to combat obesity is big business. New diet aid products, if successfully marketed, can be worth millions of dollars to the manufacturer. However, most physicians believe that these products are not long-term solutions to the problem of being overweight. Rather, a change in eating habits coupled with an exercise program may be more effective in treating weight problems.

Obesity can often be linked to a mental or physical disorder. For instance, a person with binge eating disorder (BED) experiences episodes of excessive eating accompanied by being overweight. Clinical psychologists estimate that between 25% and 35% of overweight patients are binge eaters. Cognitive-behavioral therapy (CBT), in which patients are taught how to make changes in specific behavior patterns, can be effective in treating BED. For example, CBT is used to teach binge eaters to weigh themselves each week, adopt an exercise program, eat only low-fat foods, and monitor their thoughts and moods before binge eating. However, only about half of BED patients treated with CBT actually stop binge eating. Consequently, binge eaters who do not respond to CBT need a second level of treatment.

A group of Stanford University researchers investigated the effectiveness of interpersonal therapy (IPT) as a second level of treatment for binge eaters. In IPT, patients meet in a group format to discuss the source of their binge eating (e.g., depression, personal problems) and how to deal with the problem. The 24-week study, published in the *Journal of Consulting and*

Clinical Psychology (June 1995), used as subjects 41 overweight individuals diagnosed with BED.

The subjects were selected from a pool of 260 individuals who either were referred to the researchers or responded to advertisements placed in the local media. Some were excluded from the study because they lacked interest or time, others were excluded because they did not meet the criteria for being both overweight and a binge eater. Sixty-four subjects were deemed eligible for the study, and all agreed to participate; however, 14 did not complete a baseline assessment and nine dropped out in the middle of the study, leaving a final sample size of $n = 41$.

The researchers employed a design that randomly assigned subjects to either a treatment group (30 subjects) or a control group (11 subjects). Subjects in the treatment group received 12 weeks of cognitive-behavioral therapy. At the end of the 12 weeks, the 30 subjects who underwent CBT were subdivided into two groups. Those who responded successfully to CBT by losing weight, limiting binge eating, and establishing a minimum exercise program (17 subjects) were assigned to a weight loss therapy (WLT) program for the next 12 weeks. Those CBT subjects who did not respond to treatment (13 subjects), received 12 weeks of IPT. The 11 subjects in the control group received no therapy of any type, but were assessed at the end of the 12-week and 24-week periods. Thus, the study ultimately consisted of three groups of overweight, BED subjects: the CBT-WLT group, the CBT-IPT group, and the control group.

continued

The researchers measured several outcome (response) variables for each subject, including the number of binge eating episodes per week and weight (in kilograms). Summary statistics for each of the three groups at the end of the 24-week period are shown in Table 15.5.

One way to analyze the data is to treat the design as completely randomized with three treatments (CBT-WLT, CBT-IPT, and Control), then conduct an analysis of variance for each response variable. Although the ANOVA tables were not provided in the article, sufficient information is provided in Table 15.5 to reconstruct them.

Focus

a. Consider number of binges per week as the response variable, x. Compute SST for the ANOVA on number of binges per week using the following formula:

$$SST = \sum_{i=1}^{3} n_i (\bar{x}_i - \bar{x})^2$$

where $\bar{x}$ is the overall mean number of binges per week of 41 subjects. [*Hint:* $\bar{x} = \left(\sum_{i=1}^{3} n_i \bar{x}_i \right) / 41$.]

b. Again, consider the number of binges per week as the response variable. Recall that the SSE for the ANOVA can be written as

$$SSE = (n_1 - 1)s_1^2 + (n_2 - 1)s_2^2 + (n_3 - 1)s_3^2$$

where s_1^2, s_2^2, and s_3^2 are the sample variances associated with the three treatments. Compute SSE for the ANOVA.

c. Refer to parts **a** and **b**. Complete the ANOVA table in the next column.

Source	df	SS	MS	F
Treatments	___	___	___	__
Error	___	___	___	
Total	___	___	___	__

d. Is there sufficient evidence (at $\alpha = .01$) of differences among the mean number of binges experienced per week by the subjects in the three groups?

e. Refer to part **d**. If appropriate, conduct a Bonferroni analysis to rank the three treatment means. Use an experimentwise error rate of $\alpha = .03$. Interpret the results for the researchers. [*Hint:* The Bonferroni formula for a confidence interval for the difference $(\mu_i - \mu_j)$ is:

$$(\bar{x}_i - \bar{x}_j) \pm t_{a^*/2}(s) \sqrt{\left(\frac{1}{n_i}\right) + \left(\frac{1}{n_j}\right)}$$

where $\alpha^* = 2\alpha/[(p)(p - 1)]$, α is the experimentwise error rate, and p is the total number of treatment means compared.]

f. Repeat parts **a–e** for the response variable, weight.

g. Comment on the validity of the ANOVA assumptions. How might this affect the results of the study?

h. Comment on the use of a completely randomized design for this study. Have subjects been randomly and independently assigned to each group? How might this impact the results of the study?

i. Comment on the manner in which subjects were selected for the study. Will the sample of 41 subjects adequately represent the target population? Explain the impact of this on the inferences derived from the study.

TABLE 15.5 **Summary Data Table for Three Groups of Binge Eaters (Statistics in Action 15.1)**

	CBT-WLT	CBT-IPT	Control
Sample size	17	13	11
Mean number of binges per week	0.2	1.9	2.9
(Standard deviation)	(0.4)	(1.7)	(2.0)
Mean weight	98.8	119.2	110.2
(Standard deviation)	(22.3)	(32.1)	(22.8)

Source: Agras, W. S., *et al.* "Does interpersonal therapy help patients with binge eating disorder who fail to respond to cognitive-behavioral therapy?" *Journal of Consulting and Clinical Psychology,* Vol. 63, No. 3, June 1995, p. 358 (Tables 1 and 2).

EXERCISES 15.27–15.37

Learning the Mechanics

15.27 Consider a completely randomized design with p treatments. Assume all pairwise comparisons of treatment means are to be made using a multiple comparisons procedure. Determine the total number of treatment means to be compared for the following values of p.
  a. $p = 3$ **b.** $p = 5$ **c.** $p = 4$ **d.** $p = 10$

15.28 Define an experimentwise error rate.

15.29 Define a comparisonwise error rate.

15.30 Consider a completely randomized design with five treatments, A, B, C, D, and E. The ANOVA F-test revealed significant differences among the means. A multiple comparisons procedure was used to compare all possible pairs of treatment means at $\alpha = .05$. The ranking of the five treatment means is summarized below. Identify which pairs of means are significantly different.

  a. $\overline{A \quad C} \quad \overline{E \quad B} \quad D$

  b. $\overline{A \quad C \quad E} \quad B \quad D$

  c. $\overline{A} \quad \overline{C \quad E \quad B \quad D}$

  d. $\overline{A \quad C} \quad \overline{E \quad B} \quad D$

Applying the Concepts

15.31 Refer to the study of an accounting firm's client corporations, Exercise 15.20. In Exercise 15.20 you found significant differences in mean costs among the three subpopulations of client corporations using an ANOVA F-test. In order to rank the three subpopulation means, a multiple comparisons of means will be performed.
  a. How many pairwise comparisons are required to achieve your objective?

b. Suppose you use an experimentwise error rate of $\alpha = .05$. Interpret this value.
c. Is Tukey's multiple comparisons method appropriate for this study? Explain.
d. A SAS printout of Tukey's analysis is provided below. Fully interpret the results.

15.32 Refer to the *Psychological Assessment* (Mar. 1995) study of the effectiveness of the Minnesota Multiphasic Personality Inventory (MMPI) in detecting distorted responses, Exercise 15.21. You conducted an ANOVA on each of five MMPI scales and determined that the mean scores of four groups of females differed significantly for each scale. Recall that the four groups were nonforensic psychiatric patients (NFP), forensic psychiatric patients (FP), college students who responded honestly (CSH), and college students who "faked bad" (CSFB) responses. The Bonferroni method was used to rank the means of the four groups using an experimentwise error rate of $\alpha = .05$. The results for each response variable are shown in the table at the top of page 828. [*Note:* Overbars connect means that are not significantly different.] Interpret the results for each response variable. Recall that the MMPI will be deemed effective in detecting distorted responses if the mean score of the "fake bad" group is largest.

15.33 Refer to the *Journal of Hazardous Materials* (July 1995) study of mean sorption rates for three types of organic solvents, Exercise 15.22. SAS was used to produce Bonferroni confidence intervals for all pairs of treatment means. The SAS printout is shown on page 828.
  a. Find and interpret the experimentwise error rate shown on the printout.

```
            Analysis of Variance Procedure
    Tukey's Studentized Range (HSD) Test for variable: COST

 NOTE: This test controls the type I experimentwise error rate, but
       generally has a higher type II error rate than REGWQ.

          Alpha= 0.05 df= 27 MSE= 18894.93
          Critical Value of Studentized Range= 3.506
           Minimum Significant Difference= 152.41

     Means with the same letter are not significantly different.

        Tukey Grouping          Mean      N  CLIENT
                     A         335.50     10  A
                     B         129.50     10  B
                     B
                     B         106.00     10  C
```

Response Variable

Infrequency (F)	Mean	7.1	11.3	14.6	33.6
	Group	CSH	NFP	FP	CSFB
Obvious (O)	Mean	240.9	270.7	287.5	341.9
	Group	CSH	FP	NFP	CSFB
Subtle (S)	Mean	231.4	244.1	244.5	259.7
	Group	CSFB	CSH	FP	NFP
Obvious-subtle (O-S)	Mean	51.3	88.2	93.4	198.8
	Group	CSH	NFP	FP	CSFB
Dissimulation (D)	Mean	12.0	12.1	20.8	21.0
	Group	FP	NFP	CSH	CSFB

Source: Bagby, R. M., Burs, T., and Nicholson, R. A. "Relative effectiveness of the standard validity scales in detecting fake-bad and fake-good responding: Replication and extension." *Psychological Assessment,* Vol. 7, No. 1, Mar. 1995, p. 86 (Table 1).

```
            Analysis of Variance Procedure

     Bonferroni (Dunn) T tests for variable: SORPRATE

NOTE: This test controls the type I experimentwise error rate but
      generally has a higher type II error rate than Tukey's for all
      pairwise comparisons.

        Alpha= 0.05  Confidence= 0.95  df= 29  MSE= 0.067426
                  Critical Value of T= 2.54091
     Comparisons significant at the 0.05 level are indicated by '***'.

                        Simultaneous              Simultaneous
                          Lower      Difference     Upper
              SOLVENT   Confidence    Between    Confidence
            Comparison    Limit        Means        Limit

          CHLOR - AROMA   -0.2566      0.0640       0.3846
          CHLOR - ESTER    0.3874      0.6763       0.9651     ***
          AROMA - CHLOR   -0.3846     -0.0640       0.2566
          AROMA - ESTER    0.3340      0.6122       0.8904     ***
          ESTER - CHLOR   -0.9651     -0.6763      -0.3874     ***
          ESTER - AROMA   -0.8904     -0.6122      -0.3340     ***
```

b. Locate and interpret the confidence interval for the difference between the mean sorption rates of aromatics and esters.

c. Use the confidence intervals to determine which pairs of treatment means are significantly different.

15.34 Refer to the *Industrial Marketing Management* (Sept. 1996) comparison of six sales closing techniques, Exercise 15.23. The "level of trust" means for prospects of salespeople using each of the six closing techniques are listed at right. A multiple comparisons of means analysis was conducted (at $\alpha = .05$), with the results shown in the third column of the table. Fully interpret the results.

15.35 Refer to the *Journal of Business Venturing* (Vol. 11, 1996) study of entrepreneurs, Exercise 15.24.

Treatments: Closing Technique	Mean Level of Trust	Differing Treatments
1 No close	4.67	1 from 5 and 6
2. Impending event	4.48	2 from 6
3. Social validation	4.40	No differences
4. If-then	4.33	No differences
5. Assumed close	4.04	5 from 1
6. Either-or	3.98	6 from 1 and 2

Source: Hawes, S. M., Strong, J. T., and Winick, B. S. "Do closing techniques diminish prospect trust?" *Industrial Marketing Management,* Vol. 25, No. 5, Sept. 1996, p. 355.

Pairwise comparisons of the three entrepreneur groups in the study were conducted using the Bonferroni method at $\alpha = .05$. The comparisons

Mean number of activities	8.00	6.56	5.05
Entrepreneur group	Successful firm	Gave up	Still trying

of the means of the number of activities undertaken are summarized above. Interpret the results.

15.36 Refer to the *Auditing* study of confidence in
financial statements, Exercise 15.25. The treatment means and sample sizes for the experiment
are reproduced below.

Treatment	Mean Level of Confidence	Sample Size
No auditor association	3.9	15
Compilation	5.5	31
Review	6.1	25
Audit	8.8	27

a. Determine the number of pairwise comparisons of treatment means that can be made in
this experiment.

b. Using an experimentwise error rate of $\alpha = .04$,
determine the Bonferroni adjusted α-value, α^*,
used in constructing confidence intervals for
the difference between treatment means. (See
part **e** of Statistics in Action 15.1.)

c. Construct Bonferroni confidence intervals for
the differences between all possible pairs of
treatment means using the formula in part **e** of
Statistics in Action 15.1. [*Note:* $s = \sqrt{MSE}$.]

d. Use the results, part **c**, to rank the four treatments of the experiment.

15.37 Refer to the *Journal of Psychology and Marketing*
study, Exercise 15.26. Using $\alpha = .05$, a Bonferroni
analysis yielded the result shown below. Interpret
the result.

Mean Education Level	3.167	3.224	3.330	3.731	4.3441
	College graduate	High school graduate	Some college	Non–high school graduate	Postgraduate

15.4 FACTORIAL EXPERIMENTS

All the experiments discussed in Sections 15.2 and 15.3 were **single-factor experiments**. The treatments were levels of a single factor, with the sampling of experimental units performed using a completely randomized design. However, most
responses are affected by more than one factor, and we will therefore often wish
to design experiments involving more than one factor.

Consider an experiment in which the effects of two factors on the response are
being investigated. Assume that factor A is to be investigated at a levels, and
factor B at b levels. Recalling that treatments are factor-level combinations, you
can see that the experiment has, potentially, ab treatments that could be included
in the experiment. A *complete factorial experiment* is one in which all possible ab
treatments are utilized.

> **DEFINITION 15.8**
>
> A **complete factorial experiment** is one in which every factor-level combination is uti-
> lized. That is, the number of treatments in the experiment equals the total number of
> factor-level combinations.

For example, suppose the USGA wants to determine not only the relationship
between distance and brand of golf ball, but also between distance and the club
used to hit the ball. If they decide to use four brands and two clubs (say, driver and
five-iron) in the experiment, then a complete factorial would call for utilizing all
$4 \times 2 = 8$ Brand-Club combinations. This experiment is referred to more specifically as a **complete 4×2 factorial**. A layout for a two-factor factorial experiment

TABLE 15.6 Schematic Layout of Two-Factor Factorial Experiment

		FACTOR B AT b LEVELS				
	Level	**1**	**2**	**3**	**...**	**b**
	1	Trt. 1	Trt. 2	Trt. 3	...	Trt. b
	2	Trt. $b+1$	Trt. $b+2$	Trt. $b+3$	...	Trt. $2b$
FACTOR A	3	Trt. $2b+1$	Trt. $2b+2$	Trt. $2b+3$	...	Trt. $3b$
AT a LEVELS	⋮	⋮	⋮	⋮	...	⋮
	a	Trt. $(a-1)b+1$	Trt. $(a-1)b+2$	Trt. $(a-1)b+3$	...	Trt. ab

(we are henceforth referring to a *complete factorial* when we use the term *factorial*) is given in Table 15.6. The factorial experiment is also referred to as a **two-way classification** because it can be arranged in the row-column format exhibited in Table 15.6.

In order to complete the specification of the experimental design, the treatments must be assigned to the experimental units. If the assignment of the ab treatments in the factorial experiment is random and independent, the design is completely randomized. For example, if the machine Iron Byron is used to hit 80 golf balls, 10 for each of the eight Brand-Club combinations, in a random sequence, the design would be completely randomized. In the remainder of this section, we confine our attention to factorial experiments utilizing completely randomized designs.

If we utilize a completely randomized design to conduct a factorial experiment with ab treatments, we can proceed with the analysis in exactly the same way as we did in Section 15.2. That is, we calculate (or let the computer calculate) the measure of treatment mean variability (MST) and the measure of sampling variability (MSE) and use the F-ratio of these two quantities to test the null hypothesis that the treatment means are equal. However, if this hypothesis is rejected, so that we conclude some differences exist among the treatment means, important questions remain. Are both factors affecting the response, or only one? If both, do they affect the response independently, or do they interact to affect the response?

For example, suppose the distance data indicate that at least two of the eight treatment (Brand-Club combinations) means differ in the golf experiment. Does the brand of ball (factor A) or the club utilized (factor B) affect mean distance, or do both affect it? Several possibilities are shown in Figure 15.14. In Figure 15.14a, the brand means are equal (only three are shown for the purpose of illustration), but the distances differ for the two levels of factor B (Club). Thus, there is no effect of Brand on distance, but a Club main effect is present. In Figure 15.14b, the Brand means differ, but the Club means are equal for each Brand. Here a Brand main effect is present, but no effect of Club is present.

Figures 15.14c and 15.14d illustrate cases in which both factors affect the response. In Figure 15.14c, the mean distances between clubs does not change for the three Brands, so that the effect of Brand on distance is independent of Club. That is, the two factors Brand and Club *do not interact*. In contrast, Figure 15.14d shows that the difference between mean distances between Clubs varies with Brand. Thus, the effect of Brand on distance depends on Club, and therefore the two factors *do interact*.

In order to determine the nature of the treatment effect, if any, on the response in a factorial experiment, we need to break the treatment variability into three components: Interaction Between Factors A and B, Main Effect of Factor A, and Main Effect of Factor B. The **factor Interaction** component is used to test whether

FIGURE 15.14
Illustration of possible
treatment effects:
Factorial experiment

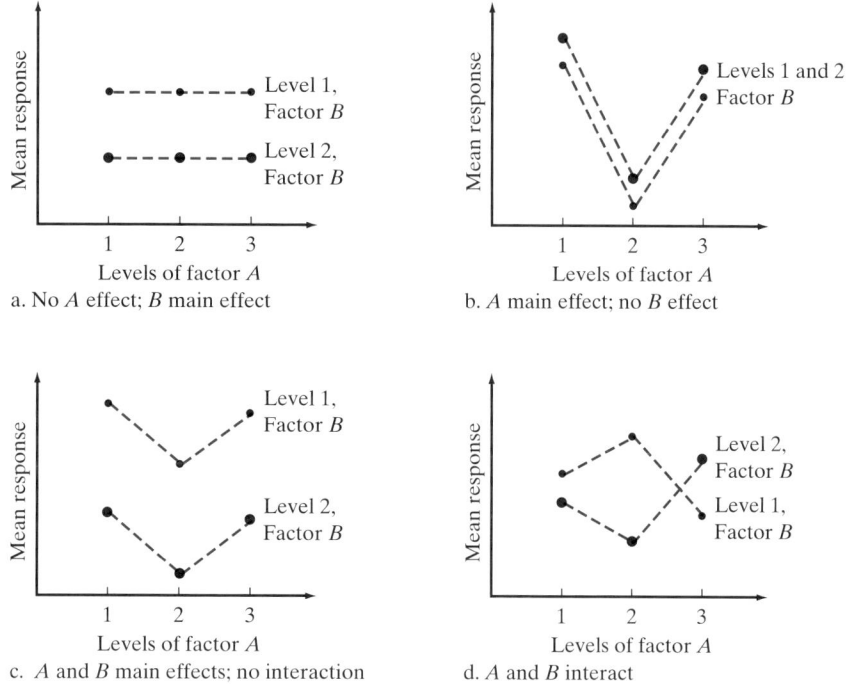

a. No A effect; B main effect

b. A main effect; no B effect

c. A and B main effects; no interaction

d. A and B interact

FIGURE 15.15
Partitioning the Total
Sum of Squares for a
two-factor factorial

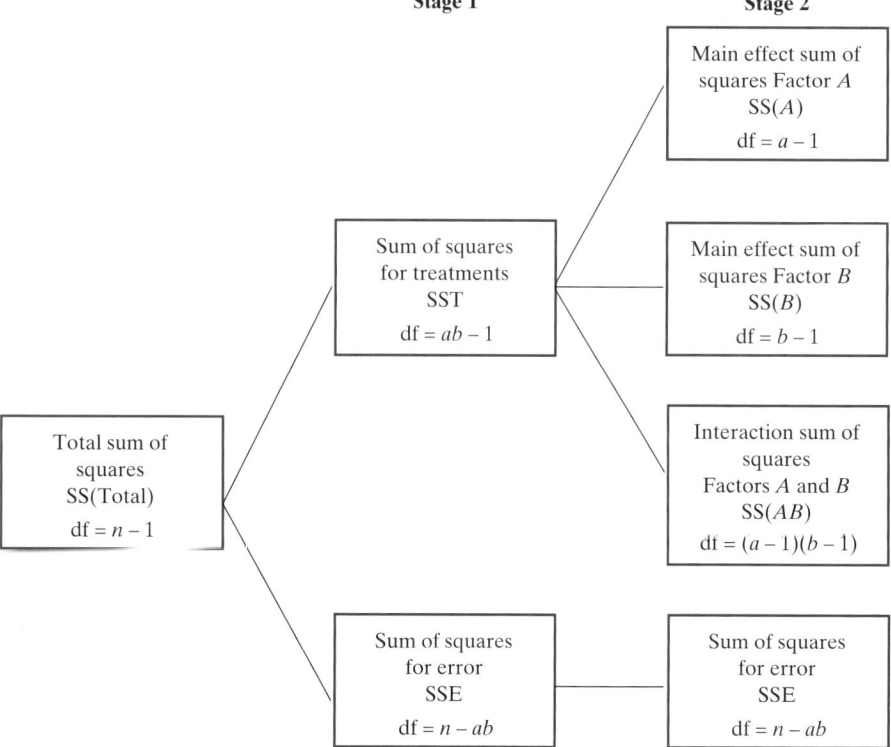

the factors combine to affect the response, while the **factor Main Effect** components are used to determine whether the factors separately affect the response.

The partitioning of the Total Sum of Squares into its various components is
illustrated in Figure 15.15. Notice that at stage 1 the components are identical to

those in the one-factor, completely randomized designs of Section 15.2; the Sums of Squares for Treatment and Error sum to the Total Sum of Squares. The degrees of freedom for treatments is equal to $(ab - 1)$, one less than the number of treatments. The degrees of freedom for error is equal to $(n - ab)$, the total sample size minus the number of treatments. Only at stage 2 of the partitioning does the factorial experiment differ from those previously discussed. Here we divide the Treatment Sum of Squares into its three components: Interaction and the two Main Effects. These components can then be used to test the nature of the differences, if any, among the treatment means.

There are a number of ways to proceed in the testing and estimation of factors in a factorial experiment. We present one approach in the next box.

Procedure for Analysis of Two-Factor Factorial Experiment

1. Partition the Total Sum of Squares into the Treatment and Error components (stage 1 of Figure 15.15). Use either a statistical software package or the calculation formulas in Appendix C to accomplish the partitioning.

2. Use the F-ratio of Mean Square for Treatments to Mean Square for Error to test the null hypothesis that the treatment means are equal.*

   a. If the test results in nonrejection of the null hypothesis, consider refining the experiment by increasing the number of replications or introducing other factors. Also consider the possibility that the response is unrelated to the two factors.

   b. If the test results in rejection of the null hypothesis, then proceed to step 3.

3. Partition the Treatment Sum of Squares into the Main Effect and Interaction Sum of Squares (stage 2 of Figure 15.15). Use either a statistical software package or the calculation formulas in Appendix C to accomplish the partitioning.

4. Test the null hypothesis that factors A and B do not interact to affect the response by computing the F-ratio of the Mean Square for Interaction to the Mean Square for Error.

   a. If the test results in nonrejection of the null hypothesis, proceed to step 5.

   b. If the test results in rejection of the null hypothesis, conclude that the two factors interact to affect the mean response. Then proceed to step 6a.

5. Conduct tests of two null hypotheses that the mean response is the same at each level of factor A and factor B. Compute two F-ratios by comparing the Mean Square for each Factor Main Effect to the Mean Square for Error.

   a. If one or both tests result in rejection of the null hypothesis, conclude that the factor affects the mean response. Proceed to step 6b.

   b. If both tests result in nonrejection, an apparent contradiction has occurred. Although the treatment means apparently differ (step 2 test), the interaction (step 4) and main effect (step 5) tests have not supported that result. Further experimentation is advised.

6. Compare the means:

   a. If the test for interaction (step 4) is significant, use a multiple comparisons procedure to compare any or all pairs of the treatment means.

   b. If the test for one or both main effects (step 5) is significant, use a multiple comparisons procedure to compare the pairs of means corresponding to the levels of the significant factor(s).

---

*Some analysts prefer to proceed directly to test the interaction and main effect components, skipping the test of treatment means. We begin with this test to be consistent with our approach in the one-factor completely randomized design.

Tests Conducted in Analyses of Factorial Experiments: Completely Randomized Design, r Replicates per Treatment

Test for Treatments Means

H_0: No difference among the ab treatment means

H_a: At least two treatment means differ

Test statistic: $F = \dfrac{\text{MST}}{\text{MSE}}$

Rejection region: $F \geq F_{\alpha}$, based on $(ab - 1)$ numerator and $(n - ab)$ denominator degrees of freedom [*Note:* $n = abr$.]

Test for Factor Interaction

H_0: Factors A and B do not interact to affect the response mean

H_a: Factors A and B do interact to affect the response mean

Test statistic: $F = \dfrac{\text{MS}(AB)}{\text{MSE}}$

Rejection region: $F \geq F_{\alpha}$, based on $(a - 1)(b - 1)$ numerator and $(n - ab)$ denominator degrees of freedom

Test for Main Effect of Factor A

H_0: No difference among the a mean levels of factor A

H_a: At least two factor A mean levels differ

Test statistic: $F = \dfrac{\text{MS}(A)}{\text{MSE}}$

Rejection region: $F \geq F_{\alpha}$, based on $(a - 1)$ numerator and $(n - ab)$ denominator degrees of freedom

Test for Main Effect of Factor B

H_0: No difference among the b mean levels of factor B

H_a: At least two factor B mean levels differ

Test statistic: $F = \dfrac{\text{MS}(B)}{\text{MSE}}$

Rejection region: $F \geq F_{\alpha}$, based on $(b - 1)$ numerator and $(n - ab)$ denominator degrees of freedom

Assumptions for All Tests

1. The response distribution for each factor-level combination (treatment) is normal.
2. The response variance is constant for all treatments.
3. Random and independent samples of experimental units are associated with each treatment.

We assume the completely randomized design is a **balanced design**, meaning that the same number of observations are made for each treatment. That is, we assume that r experimental units are randomly and independently selected for each treatment. The numerical value of r must exceed 1 in order to have any degrees of freedom with which to measure the sampling variability. [Note that if $r = 1$, then $n = ab$, and the degrees of freedom associated with Error (Figure 15.15) is $df = n - ab = 0$.] The value of r is often referred to as the number of **replicates** of the factorial experiment since we assume that all ab treatments are repeated, or replicated, r times. Whatever approach is adopted in the analysis of a factorial experiment, several tests of hypotheses are usually conducted. The tests are summarized in the preceding box.

EXAMPLE 15.6

Suppose the USGA tests four different brands (A, B, C, D) of golf balls and two different clubs (driver, five-iron) in a completely randomized design. Each of the eight Brand-Club combinations (treatments) is randomly and independently assigned to four experimental units, each experimental unit consisting of a specific position in the sequence of hits by Iron Byron. The distance response is recorded for each of the 32 hits, and the results are shown in Table 15.7.

a. Use a statistical software package to partition the Total Sum of Squares into the components necessary to analyze this 4×2 factorial experiment.

b. Follow the steps for analyzing a two-factor factorial experiment and interpret the results of your analysis. Use $\alpha = .10$ for the tests you conduct.

SOLUTION

a. The SAS printout that partitions the Total Sum of Squares for this factorial experiment is given in Figure 15.16. The partitioning takes place in two stages: First, the Total Sum of Squares is partitioned into the Model (Treatment) and Error Sums of Squares at the top of the printout. Note that SST is 33,659.8 with 7 degrees of freedom, and SSE is 822.2 with 24 degrees of freedom, adding to 34,482.0 and 31 degrees of freedom. In the second stage of partitioning, the Treatment Sum of Squares is further divided into the Main Effect and Interaction Sums of Squares. At the bottom of the printout we see that SS(Club) is 32,093.1 with 1 degree of freedom, SS(Brand) is 800.7 with 3 degrees of freedom, and SS(Club $\times$ Brand) is 766.0 with 3 degrees of freedom, adding to 33,659.8 and 7 degrees of freedom.

b. Once partitioning is accomplished, our first test is:

H_0: The eight treatment means are equal

H_a: At least two of the eight means differ

TABLE 15.7   Distance Data for 4 × 2 Factorial Golf Experiment

		BRAND			
		A	**B**	**C**	**D**
CLUB	**Driver**	226.4	238.3	240.5	219.8
		232.6	231.7	246.9	228.7
		234.0	227.7	240.3	232.9
		220.7	237.2	244.7	237.6
	Five-Iron	163.8	184.4	179.0	157.8
		179.4	180.6	168.0	161.8
		168.6	179.5	165.2	162.1
		173.4	186.2	156.5	160.3

```
                        Analysis of Variance Procedure
Dependent Variable: DISTANCE

                                Sum of           Mean
Source                  DF      Squares          Square    F Value   Pr > F

Model                    7    33659.8087       4808.5441    140.35   0.0001
Error                   24      822.2400         34.2600
Corrected Total         31    34482.0487

                R-Square          C.V.       Root MSE      DISTANCE Mean
                0.976155     2.8964608         5.85320        202.081250

Source                  DF     Anova SS   Mean Square    F Value   Pr > F

CLUB                     1     32093.11      32093.11     936.75    0.0001
BRAND                    3       800.74        266.91       7.79    0.0008
CLUB*BRAND               3       765.96        255.32       7.45    0.0011
```

FIGURE 15.16 SAS printout for factorial golf experiment

Test statistic: $F = \dfrac{\text{MST}}{\text{MSE}} = 140.35$ (top of printout)

Observed significance level: $p = .0001$ (top of printout)

Since $\alpha = .10$ exceeds p, we reject this null hypothesis and conclude that at least two of the Brand-Club combinations differ in mean distance.

After accepting the hypothesis that the treatment means differ, and therefore that the factors Brand and/or Club somehow affect the mean distance, we want to determine how the factors affect the mean response. We begin with a test of interaction between Brand and Club:

H_0: The factors Brand and Club do not interact to affect the mean response

H_a: Brand and Club interact to affect mean response

$$\textit{Test statistic}: F = \frac{\text{MS}(AB)}{\text{MSE}} = \frac{\text{MS(Brand} \times \text{Club)}}{\text{MSE}}$$

$$= \frac{255.32}{34.26} = 7.45 \quad \text{(bottom of printout)}$$

Observed significance level: $p = .0011$ (bottom of printout)

Since $\alpha = .10$ exceeds the p-value, we conclude that the factors Brand and Club interact to affect mean distance.

Because the factors interact, we do not test the main effects for Brand and Club. Instead, we compare the treatment means in an attempt to learn the nature of the interaction. Rather than compare all $8(7)/2 = 28$ pairs of treatment means, we test for differences only between pairs of brands within each club. That differences exist *between* clubs can be assumed. Therefore, only $4(3)/2 = 6$ pairs of means need to be compared for each club, or a total of 12 comparisons for the two clubs. The results of these comparisons using Tukey's method with an experimentwise error rate of $\alpha = .10$ for each club are displayed in the SAS printout, Figure 15.17. For each club, the brand means are listed in descending order in Figure 15.17, and those not

```
--------------------------CLUB=5IRON--------------------------
                  Analysis of Variance Procedure

       Tukey's Studentized Range (HSD) Test for variable: DISTANCE

   Note: This test controls the type I experimentwise error rate, but
         generally has a higher type II error rate than REGWQ.

              Alpha= 0.1  df= 12  MSE= 36.10792
              Critical Value of Studentized Range= 3.621
              Minimum Significant Difference= 10.878

     Means with the same letter are not significantly different.

          Tukey Grouping        Mean        N  BRAND

                 A            182.675        4  B
                 B            171.300        4  A
                 B
                 B            167.175        4  C
                 B
                 B            160.500        4  D

--------------------------CLUB=DRIVER--------------------------
                  Analysis of Variance Procedure

       Tukey's Studentized Range (HSD) Test for variable: DISTANCE

   Note: This test controls the type I experimentwise error rate, but
         generally has a higher type II error rate than REGWQ.

              Alpha= 0.1  df= 12  MSE= 32.41208
              Critical Value of Studentized Range= 3.621
              Minimum Significant Difference= 10.306

     Means with the same letter are not signifcantly different.

          Tukey Grouping        Mean        N  BRAND

                 A            243.100        4  C
                 A
             B   A            233.725        4  B
             B
             B            229.750        4  D
             B
             B            228.425        4  A
```

FIGURE 15.17 SAS ranking of treatment means for factorial golf experiment

significantly different are connected by the same letter in the **Tukey Grouping** column.

As shown in Figure 15.17, the picture is unclear with respect to Brand means. For the five-iron (top of Figure 15.17), the brand B mean significantly exceeds all other brands. However, when hit with a driver (bottom of Figure 15.17), brand B's mean is not significantly different from any of the other brands. Note the nontransitive nature of the multiple comparisons. For example, for the driver the Brand C mean can be "the same" as the brand B mean, and the brand B mean can be "the same" as the brand D mean, and yet the brand C mean can significantly exceed the brand D mean. The reason lies in the definition of "the same"—we must be careful not to conclude two means are equal simply because they are connected by a vertical

FIGURE 15.18
Sample mean plot for factorial golf experiment

line. The line indicates only that *the connected means are not significantly different.* You should conclude (at the overall α level of significance) only that means *not* connected are different, while withholding judgment on those that are connected. The picture of which means differ and by how much will become clearer as we increase the number of replicates of the factorial experiment.

The Club $\times$ Brand interaction can be seen in the plot of means in Figure 15.18. Note that the difference between the mean distances of the two clubs (driver and five-iron) varies depending on brand. The biggest difference appears for Brand C while the smallest difference is for Brand B. ∎

EXAMPLE 15.7

Refer to Example 15.6. Suppose the same factorial experiment is performed on four other brands (E, F, G, and H), and the results are as shown in Table 15.8. Repeat the factorial analysis and interpret the results.

SOLUTION

The printout for the second factorial experiment is shown in Figure 15.19. The F-ratio for Treatments is $F = 290.1$, which exceeds the tabled value of $F_{.10} = 1.98$ for 7 numerator and 24 denominator degrees of freedom. (Note that the same rejection regions will apply in this example as in Example 15.6 since the factors, treatments, and replicates are the same.) We conclude that at least two of the Brand-Club combinations have different mean distances.

We next test for interaction between Brand and Club:

$$F = \frac{\text{MS}(\text{Brand} \times \text{Club})}{\text{MSE}} = 1.42$$

TABLE 15.8 Distance Data for Second Factorial Golf Experiment

		BRAND			
		E	**F**	**G**	**H**
CLUB	**Driver**	238.6	261.4	264.7	235.4
		241.9	261.3	262.9	239.8
		236.6	254.0	253.5	236.2
		244.9	259.9	255.6	237.5
	Five-Iron	165.2	179.2	189.0	171.4
		156.9	171.0	191.2	159.3
		172.2	178.0	191.3	156.6
		163.2	182.7	180.5	157.4

```
                   Analysis of Variance Procedure
Dependent Variable: DISTANCE
                            Sum of          Mean
Source                 DF   Squares        Square   F Value  Pr > F
Model                   7  49959.3747    7137.0535   290.12  0.0001
Error                  24    590.4075      24.6003
Corrected Total        31  50549.7822

              R-Square        C.V.    Root MSE        DISTANCE Mean
              0.988320   2.3515897     4.95987           210.915625

Source                 DF   Anova SS  Mean Square  F Value  Pr > F
CLUB                    1   46443.90     46443.90  1887.94  0.0001
BRAND                   3    3410.32      1136.77    46.21  0.0001
CLUB*BRAND              3     105.16        35.05     1.42  0.2600
```

FIGURE 15.19   SAS printout for second factorial golf experiment

Since this F-ratio does *not* exceed the tabled value of $F_{.10} = 2.33$ with 3 and 24 df, we cannot conclude at the .10 level of significance that the factors interact. In fact, note that the observed significance level (on the SAS printout) for the test of interaction is .26. Thus, at any level of significance lower than $\alpha = .26$, we could not conclude that the factors interact. We therefore test the main effects for Brand and Club.

We first test the Brand main effect:

H_0: No difference exists among the true Brand mean distances

H_a: At least two Brand mean distances differ

Test statistic: $F = \dfrac{\text{MS(Brand)}}{\text{MSE}} = \dfrac{1{,}136.77}{24.60} = 46.21$ (bottom of printout)

Observed significance level: $p = .0001$ (bottom of printout)

Since $\alpha = .10$ exceeds the p-value, we conclude that at least two of the brand means differ. We will subsequently determine which brand means differ using Tukey's multiple comparisons procedure. But first, we want to test the Club main effect:

H_0: No differences exist between the Club mean distances

H_a: The Club mean distances differ

Test statistic: $F = \dfrac{\text{MS(Club)}}{\text{MSE}} = \dfrac{46{,}443.9}{24.60} = 1{,}887.94$ (bottom of printout)

Observed significance level: $p = .0001$ (bottom of printout)

Since $\alpha = .10$ exceeds the p-value, we conclude that the two clubs are associated with different mean distances. Since only two levels of Club were utilized in the experiment, this F-test leads to the inference that the mean distance differs for the two clubs. It is no surprise (to golfers) that the mean distance for balls hit with the driver is significantly greater than the mean distance for those hit with the five-iron.

```
                  Analysis of Variance Procedure
       Tukey's Studentized Range (HSD) Test for variable: DISTANCE
   Note: This test controls the type I experimentwise error rate, but
       generally has a higher type II error rate than REGWQ.

              Alpha= 0.1   df= 12   MSE= 24.60031
           Critical Value of Studentized Range= 3.423
              Minimum Significant Difference= 6.003

      Means with the same letter are not significantly different.
           Tukey Grouping          Mean        N   BRAND
                        A        223.587        8   G
                        A
                        A        218.437        8   F

                        B        202.438        8   E
                        B
                        B        199.200        8   H
```

FIGURE 15.20 SAS comparison of mean distances by brand: Tukey's method

To determine which of the Brands' mean distances differ, we wish to compare the four Brand means using Tukey's method at $\alpha = .10$. The results of these multiple comparisons are displayed in the SAS printout, Figure 15.20. Again, the Brand means are shown in descending order in Figure 15.20, with a **Tukey Grouping** letter connecting the means that are not significantly different. Brands G and F are apparently associated with significantly greater mean distances than brands E and H, but we cannot distinguish between brands G and F or between brands E and H using these data. Since the interaction between Brand and Club was not significant, we conclude that this difference among brands applies to both clubs. The sample means for all Club-Brand combinations are shown in Figure 15.21 and appear to support the conclusions of the tests and comparisons. Note that the Brand means maintain their relative positions for each Club—brands F and G dominate brands E and H for both the driver and five-iron. ⌐╵

The analysis of factorial experiments can become complex if the number of factors is increased. Even the two-factor experiment becomes more difficult to analyze if some factor combinations have different numbers of observations than others. We have provided an introduction to these important experiments using two-factor factorials with equal numbers of observations for each treatment. Although similar principles apply to most factorial experiments, you should consult the references for this chapter at the end of the book if you need to design and analyze more complex factorials.

FIGURE 15.21
Sample mean plot for second factorial golf experiment

STATISTICS IN ACTION

15.2 IMPROVING A GROUND MEAT CANNING PROCESS THROUGH EXPERIMENTAL DESIGN

Griffith, Westman, and Lloyd (1990) describe an experiment that was conducted by a dog food manufacturer to improve a filling process in which ground meat is packed into cans. The process uses a rotary filling machine with six cylinders, each of which dispenses ground meat.

The company was experiencing significant variation in the weight of filled cans. It was decided to study the effects of differences in batches of meat and differences in cylinders on the weight of the final product. Batches of meat vary because of differences in the fat-lean ratio, air content, and moisture content. A significant batch effect would indicate the need for closer monitoring and control of meat density further upstream in the production process. Differences in cylinder performance are typically mechanical in nature and due primarily to differences in the piston stroke. A significant cylinder effect would call for mechanical adjustment of the filling machine.

Five batches of meat were used in the experiment. Three filled cans were randomly selected from each cylinder while each batch was being run. The cans were weighed and the weights were recorded. To simplify the analysis, the weights were coded by subtracting 12 ounces from each weight. The coded data appear in Table 15.9.

Focus

a. What type of experimental design was used by the dog food manufacturer?

b. Identify the factors used in the study and their levels.

c. How many different treatments were used in the experiment?

d. Analyze the data with an analysis of variance. Summarize the results in an ANOVA table.

e. In the context of the problem, explain what it means to say that batch and cylinder interact. Speculate on what could cause such an interaction.

f. Test for an interaction between batches and cylinders. Use $\alpha = .05$.

g. If appropriate, test for main effects using $\alpha = .05$.

h. Using your results from parts **f** and **g**, make recommendations for ways to improve the dog food filling process.

EXERCISES 15.38–15.50

Note: Exercises marked with 💾 *contain data for computer analysis on a 3.5″ disk (file name in parentheses).*

Learning the Mechanics

15.38 Suppose you conduct a 4 × 3 factorial experiment.
  a. How many factors are used in the experiment?
  b. Can you determine the factor type(s)—qualitative or quantitative—from the information given? Explain.
  c. Can you determine the number of levels used for each factor? Explain.
  d. Describe a treatment for this experiment, and determine the number of treatments used.
  e. What problem is caused by using a single replicate of this experiment? How is the problem solved?

15.39 The partially completed ANOVA for a 3 × 4 factorial experiment with two replications is shown here.

Source	df	SS	MS	F
A	—	.8	—	—
B	—	5.3	—	—
AB	—	9.6	—	—
Error	—	—	—	—
Total	—	17.0		

  a. Complete the ANOVA table.
  b. Which sums of squares are combined to find the Sum of Squares for Treatment? Do the data provide sufficient evidence to indicate that the treatment means differ? Use $\alpha = .05$.

TABLE 15.9 Coded Weight Data for Dog Food Cans (Statistics in Action 15.2)

CYLINDER		BATCH 1	2	3	4	5
	1	1	4	6	3	1
		1	3	3	1	3
		2	5	7	3	3
	2	−1	−2	3	2	1
		3	1	1	0	0
		−1	0	5	1	1
	3	1	2	2	1	3
		1	0	4	3	3
		1	1	3	3	3
	4	−2	−2	3	0	0
		3	0	3	0	1
		0	1	4	2	1
	5	1	2	0	1	−2
		1	1	1	0	3
		−1	5	2	−1	1
	6	0	0	3	3	3
		1	0	3	0	1
		1	3	4	2	2

Source: Griffith, B. A., Westman, A. E. R., and Lloyd, B. H. "Analysis of Variance." *Quality Engineering*, Vol. 2, No. 2, 1990, pp. 195–226.

c. Does the result of the test in part **b** warrant further testing? Explain.

d. What is meant by factor interaction, and what is the practical implication if it exists?

e. Test to determine whether these factors interact to affect the response mean. Use $\alpha = .05$, and interpret the result.

f. Does the result of the interaction test warrant further testing? Explain.

15.40 The partially complete ANOVA table given here is for a two-factor factorial experiment.

Source	df	SS	MS	F
A	3	—	.75	—
B	1	.95	—	—
AB	—	—	.50	—
Error	—	—	—	
Total	23	6.5		

a. Give the number of levels for each factor.

b. How many observations were collected for each factor-level combination?

c. Complete the ANOVA table.

d. Test to determine whether the treatment means differ. Use $\alpha = .10$.

e. Conduct the tests of factor interaction and main effects, each at the $\alpha = .10$ level of significance. Which of the tests are warranted as part of the factorial analysis? Explain.

15.41 The following two-way table gives data for a 2×3 factorial experiment with two observations for each factor-level combination.

		FACTOR B		
	Level	1	2	3
FACTOR A	1	3.1, 4.0	4.6, 4.2	6.4, 7.1
	2	5.9, 5.3	2.9, 2.2	3.3, 2.5

a. Identify the treatments for this experiment. Calculate and plot the treatment means, using the response variable as the y-axis and the levels of factor B as the x-axis. Use the levels of factor A as plotting symbols. Do the treatment means appear to differ? Do the factors appear to interact?

b. The MINITAB ANOVA printout for this experiment is shown on page 842. Test to determine whether the treatment means differ at the $\alpha = .05$ level of significance. Does the test support your visual interpretation from part **a**?

c. Does the result of the test in part **b** warrant a test for interaction between the two factors? If so, perform it using $\alpha = .05$.

d. Do the results of the previous tests warrant tests of the two factor main effects? If so, perform them using $\alpha = .05$.

e. Interpret the results of the tests. Do they support your visual interpretation from part **a**?

```
ANALYSIS OF VARIANCE ON RESPONSE

SOURCE              DF          SS          MS

A                    1       4.441       4.441
B                    2       4.127       2.063
INTERACTION          2      18.007       9.003
ERROR                6       1.475       0.246
TOTAL               11      28.049
```

15.42 The accompanying two-way table gives data for a 2×2 factorial experiment with two observations per factor-level combination.

		FACTOR B	
	Level	**1**	**2**
FACTOR A	**1**	29.6, 35.2	47.3, 42.1
	2	12.9, 17.6	28.4, 22.7

a. Identify the treatments for this experiment. Calculate and plot the treatment means, using the response variable as the y-axis and the levels of factor B as the x-axis. Use the levels of factor A as plotting symbols. Do the treatment means appear to differ? Do the factors appear to interact?

b. Use the computational formulas in Appendix C to create an ANOVA table for this experiment.

c. Test to determine whether the treatment means differ at the $\alpha = .05$ level of significance. Does the test support your visual interpretation from part **a**?

d. Does the result of the test in part **b** warrant a test for interaction between the two factors? If so, perform it using $\alpha = .05$.

e. Do the results of the previous tests warrant tests of the two factor main effects? If so, perform them using $\alpha = .05$.

f. Interpret the results of the tests. Do they support your visual interpretation from part **a**?

g. Given the results of your tests, which pairs of means, if any, should be compared?

15.43 Suppose a 3×3 factorial experiment is conducted with three replications. Assume that SS(Total) $=$ 1,000. For each of the following scenarios, form an ANOVA table, conduct the appropriate tests, and interpret the results.

a. The Sum of Squares of factor A main effect [SS(A)] is 20% of SS(Total), the Sum of Squares for factor B main effect [SS(B)] is 10% of SS(Total), and the Sum of Squares for interaction [SS(AB)] is 10% of SS(Total).

b. SS(A) is 10%, SS(B) is 10%, and SS(AB) is 50% of SS(Total).

c. SS(A) is 40%, SS(B) is 10%, and SS(AB) is 20% of SS(Total).

d. SS(A) is 40%, SS(B) is 40%, and SS(AB) is 10% of SS(Total).

Applying the Concepts

15.44 Are resource allocation decisions in organizations influenced by managers' and other professionals' attitudes toward risk-taking? Louisiana State University professor D. C. Kim investigated the effects of accountants' attitudes toward risk and recent budget-setting performance (relative to their colleagues) on their current budgetary decisions (*Accounting Review*, Apr. 1992). Eighty-one undergraduate students were used as subjects in the study. Using standard risk measurement methods, 40 subjects were found to be risk-seeking and 41 were risk-averse. Subjects were asked to play the role of an entry-level accountant in a public accounting firm. Each was asked to read a hypothetical audit engagement case. Each subject had either a case in which his or her recent performance at budgeting audit costs (billable hours) was either favorable or unfavorable relative to colleagues. After reading the case, each subject was asked to establish either a tight (risky) budget or a safe (riskless) budget and to indicate the strength of his or her preference for the budget. Subjects responded on an 11-point scale that varied from -5 (strong preference for a risky choice) to $+5$ (strong preference for a riskless choice). From these data, Kim generated the following partial ANOVA table:

Source	df	SS	MS	F
Recent performance (A)	1	243.2	——	——
Risk assessment (B)	1	57.8	——	——
AB	1	——	——	——
Error	77	670.8	——	
Total	80	976.3		

Source: Kim, D. C. "Risk preferences in participative budgeting." *Accounting Review,* Vol. 67, No. 2, Apr. 1992, pp. 303–318.

a. Complete the ANOVA table.

b. Do the data indicate that factors A and B interact? Test using $\alpha = .05$.

c. Does an individual's risk attitude affect his or her budgetary decisions? Test using $\alpha = .05$.

d. Does recent budgeting performance affect current budgeting decisions? Test using $\alpha = .01$.

15.45 The cattle raised on the Biological Reserve of Doñana (Spain) live under free-range conditions, with virtually no human interference. The cattle population is organized into four herds (LGN, MTZ, PLC, and QMD). The *Journal of Zoology* (July 1995) investigated the ranging behavior of the four herds across the four seasons. Thus, a 4×4 factorial experiment was employed, with Herd and Season representing the two factors. Three animals from each herd during each season were sampled and the home range of each individual was measured (in square kilometers). The data were subjected to an ANOVA, with the results shown in the table below.

Source	df	F	p-Value
Herd (H)	3	17.2	$p < .001$
Season (S)	3	3.0	$p < .05$
$H \times S$	9	1.2	$p > .05$
Error	32		
Total	47		

a. Conduct the appropriate ANOVA F-tests and interpret the results.
b. The researcher ranked the four herd means independently of season. Do you agree with this strategy? Explain.
c. Refer to part **b**. The Bonferroni rankings of the four herd means (at $\alpha = .05$) are shown at upper right. Interpret the results.

Mean home range (km^2)	.75	1.0	2.7	3.8
Herd	PLC	LGN	QMD	MTZ

15.46 (X15.046) Most short-run supermarket strategies such as price reductions, media advertising, and in-store displays are designed to increase unit sales of particular products temporarily. Factorial designs have been employed in the *Journal of Marketing Research* (Feb. 1982) to evaluate the effectiveness of such strategies. Two of the factors were Price level (regular, reduced price, cost to supermarket) and Display level (normal display space, normal display space plus end-of-aisle display, twice the normal display space). A complete factorial design based on these two factors involves nine treatments. Suppose each treatment was applied three times to a particular product at a particular supermarket. Each application lasted a full week and the dependent variable of interest was unit sales for the week. To minimize treatment carryover effects, each treatment was preceded and followed by a week in which the product was priced at its regular price and was displayed in its normal manner. The table below reports the data collected. A SAS printout for this experiment also follows.

a. Use the printout to complete the diagram on page 844 partitioning the Total Sum of Squares.
b. Do the data indicate that the mean sales differ among the nine treatments? Test using $\alpha = .10$.

	PRICE		
Display	**Regular**	**Reduced**	**Cost to Supermarket**
Normal	989, 1,025, 1,030	1,211, 1,215, 1,182	1,577, 1,559, 1,598
Normal Plus	1,191, 1,233, 1,221	1,860, 1,910, 1,926	2,492, 2,527, 2,511
Twice Normal	1,226, 1,202, 1,180	1,516, 1,501, 1,498	1,801, 1,833, 1,852

```
                    Analysis of Variance Procedure
Dependent Variable: SALES

                                  Sum of          Mean
Source                  DF        Squares         Square   F Value   Pr > F

Model                    8      5291151.19      661393.90  1336.85   0.0001
Error                   18         8905.33         494.74
Corrected Total         26      5300056.52

                R-Square           C.V.        Root MSE           SALES Mean

                0.998320      1.4344689         22.2428           1550.59259

Source                  DF      Anova SS   Mean Square   F Value   Pr > F

DISPLAY                  2     1691392.5       845696.3   1709.37   0.0001
PRICE                    2     3089053.9      1544526.9   3121.89   0.0001
DISPLAY*PRICE            4      510704.8       127676.2    258.07   0.0001
```

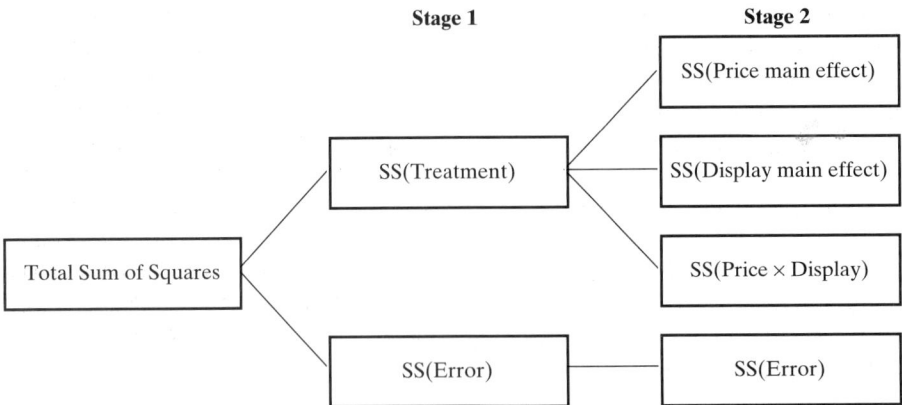

c. Is the test of interaction between the factors Price and Display warranted as a result of the test in part **b**? If so, conduct the test using $\alpha = .10$.

d. Are the tests of the main effects for Price and Display warranted as a result of the previous tests? If so, conduct them using $\alpha = .10$.

e. Which pairs of treatment means should be compared as a result of the tests in parts **b–d**?

f. The treatment means are graphically portrayed in the SAS graph printout below. Use the graph to interpret the results of your tests.

15.47 Traditionally, people protect themselves from mosquito bites by applying insect repellent to their skin and clothing. Recent research suggests that permethrin, an insecticide with low toxicity to humans, can provide protection from mosquitoes. A study in the *Journal of the American Mosquito Control Association* (Mar. 1995) investigated whether a tent sprayed with a commercially available 1% permethrin formulation would protect people, both inside and outside the tent, against biting mosquitoes. Two canvas tents—one treated with permethrin, the other untreated—

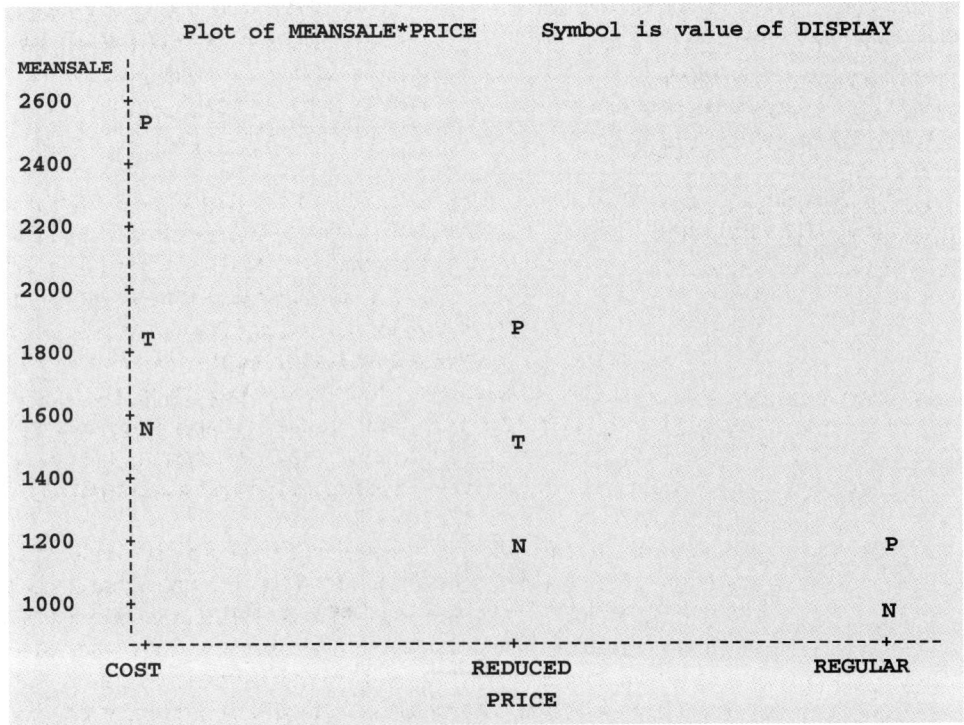

[*Note:* The means for the Normal plus (P) and Twice normal (T) displays are nearly equal for Regular price. Both are represented by the symbol P at this level of price.]

were positioned 25 meters apart on flat dry ground in an area infested with mosquitoes. Eight people participated in the experiment, with four randomly assigned to each tent. Of the four stationed at each tent, two were randomly assigned to stay inside the tent (at opposite corners) and two to stay outside the tent (at opposite corners). During a specified 20-minute period during the night, each person kept count of the number of mosquito bites received. The goal of the study was to determine the effect of both Tent type (treated or untreated) and Location (inside or outside the tent) on the mean mosquito bite count.

a. What type of design was employed in the study?
b. Identify the factors and treatments.
c. Identify the response variable.
d. The study found statistical evidence of interaction between Tent type and Location. Give a practical interpretation of this result.

15.48 It has been argued that trust between members of an organization enhances the performance of the organization. Research published in *Accounting, Organizations and Society* (Vol. 19, 1994) investigated whether the effects of different performance evaluation styles (PES) on the level of job-related tension is affected by trust. Three performance evaluation styles were considered. Each is related to the way in which accounting information is used for the purpose of evaluation. The three styles are budget-constrained (BC), profit-conscious (PC), and the nonaccounting style (NA), which focuses on factors such as quality of output and attitude toward the job. A questionnaire was administered to 215 managers working in 18 Australian organizations. It measured the performance evaluation style of each manager's superior, the manager's job-related tension, and the manager's level of trust (low, medium, and high) in his or her superior. These data were used to produce the next partial ANOVA table and table of treatment means.

a. Describe the treatments of this study.
b. Complete the ANOVA table.
c. Investigate the presence of an interaction effect by conducting the appropriate hypothesis test using $\alpha = .05$.
d. Use a plot of treatment means to investigate the interaction effect. Interpret your results. Are your results of parts **c** and **d** consistent?
e. Explain why the *F*-tests for the two main effects are irrelevant given your answers to parts **c** and **d**.

15.49 How do women compare with men in their ability to perform laborious tasks that require strength? Some information on this question is provided in a study of the firefighting ability of men and women (*Human Factors*, 1982). The researchers

Source	df	SS	MS	F
PES	2	2.1774	———	———
Trust	——	7.6367	———	———
PES × Trust	4	1.7380	———	———
Error	206	———		
Total	214	161.1162		

	PERFORMANCE EVALUATION STYLE		
Trust	**BC**	**PC**	**NA**
Low	3.2350 n=32	3.1111 n=24	3.2290 n=16
Medium	2.7601 n=26	2.8530 n=31	2.6373 n=14
High	2.3067 n=30	2.4436 n=26	3.1810 n=16

Source: Ross, A. "Trust as a moderator of the effect of performance evaluation style on job-related tension: A research note." *Accounting, Organizations and Society,* Vol. 19, No. 7, 1994, pp. 633 (Tables 3 and 4).

conducted a 2 × 2 factorial experiment to investigate the effect of the factor Sex (male or female) and the factor Weight (light or heavy) on the length of time required for a person to perform a particular firefighting task. Eight persons were selected for each of the 2 × 2 = 4 Sex-Weight categories of the 2 × 2 factorial experiment, and the length of time needed to complete the task was recorded for each of the 32 persons. The means and standard deviations of the four samples are shown in the table.

	LIGHT		HEAVY	
	Mean	**Standard Deviation**	**Mean**	**Standard Deviation**
Female	18.30	6.81	14.50	2.93
Male	13.00	5.04	12.25	5.70

Source: Phillips, M. D. and Pepper, R. L. "Shipboard firefighting performance of females and males." Reprinted with permission from *Human Factors,* Vol. 24, No. 3, 1982.

a. Calculate the total of the $n = 8$ time measurements for each of the four categories of the 2 × 2 factorial experiment.
b. Calculate the correction for mean, CM. (See Appendix C for computational formulas.)
c. Use the results of parts **a** and **b** to calculate the sums of squares for Sex, Weight, and for the Sex × Weight interaction.
d. Calculate each sample variance. Then calculate the sum of squares of deviations *within* each sample for each of the four samples.
e. Calculate SSE. [*Hint:* SSE is the pooled sum of squares for the deviations calculated in part **d**.]

```
* * * A N A L Y S I S   O F   V A R I A N C E * * *

        SALES
    BY  AGENCY
        MEDIUM

                          Sum of              Mean            Signif
Source of Variation       Squares    DF      Square      F     of F

Main Effects              238.299     3      79.433   13.934   .004
   AGENCY                  39.967     1      39.967    7.011   .038
   MEDIUM                 198.332     2      99.166   17.395   .003

2-way Interactions         77.345     2      38.672    6.784   .029
   AGENCY    MEDIUM        77.345     2      38.672    6.784   .029

Explained                 315.644     5      63.129   11.074   .005

Residual                   34.205     6       5.701

Total                     349.849    11      31.804
```

f. Now that you know SS(Sex), SS(Weight), SS(Sex × Weight), and SSE, find SS(Total).

g. Summarize the calculations in an ANOVA table.

h. Conduct a complete analysis of these data. Use $\alpha = .05$ for any inferential techniques you employ. Interpret your conclusions graphically.

i. What assumptions are necessary to ensure the validity of the inferential techniques you utilized? State them in terms of this experiment.

15.50 **(X15.050)** A beverage distributor wanted to determine the combination of advertising agency (two levels) and advertising medium (three levels) that would produce the largest increase in sales per advertising dollar. Each of the advertising agencies prepared copy or film, as required for each of the media—newspaper, radio, and television. Twelve small towns of roughly the same size were selected for the experiment and two each were assigned to receive an advertisement prepared and transmitted by each of the six agency-medium combinations. The dollar increases in sales per advertising dollar, based on a one-month sales period, are shown in the accompanying table.

a. Describe the experiment. Include the identification of the response variable, factors, factor types, factor levels, treatments, and experimen-

| | | ADVERTISING MEDIUM | | |
		Newspaper	Radio	Television
AGENCY	1	15.3	20.1	12.7
		12.7	17.4	16.2
	2	18.9	24.3	12.5
		22.4	28.8	9.4

tal units. What is the experiment called? What type of design was employed?

b. The SPSS ANOVA printout for this experiment is reproduced above. Use it to perform a complete analysis of the experiment. Be sure to conduct relevant tests, and use the Bonferroni technique (outlined in Statistics in Action 15.1) to compare relevant pairs of means. Use $\alpha = .10$ throughout. [*Note:* SPSS uses **Explained** instead of "Treatment" and **Residual** instead of "Error."]

c. Graph the treatment means, placing advertising medium on the horizontal axis, and using agency as a plotting symbol. Do the results of your analysis in part **b** appear reasonable? Use the graph to interpret the results of your analysis.

15.5 **USING REGRESSION ANALYSIS FOR ANOVA (OPTIONAL)**

We have seen in previous sections that analysis of variance involves the statistical analysis of the relationship between a response and one or more factors. In Chapters 10–12 we performed very similar analyses using regression techniques, so it is not surprising that the two methodologies are closely related. In fact, each of the ANOVAs performed in this chapter can be formulated as a regression model, and the same analysis can be performed in a regression context. We will illustrate the ANOVA–regression correspondence in this section.

A one-factor experiment utilizing a completely randomized design provides the simplest example of this correspondence. Suppose the factor has p levels—that is, there are p treatments in the experiment. Assuming the factor is qualitative, the corresponding regression model is

$$y = \beta_0 + \beta_1 x_1 + \beta_2 x_2 + \cdots + \beta_{p-1} x_{p-1} + \epsilon$$

where $x_1, x_2, \ldots, x_{p-1}$ are $(p-1)$ dummy variables describing the p levels of the factor. If the factor is quantitative, then the x's become powers of the variable, i.e., $x_i = x^i$. In either case, to test the null hypothesis of interest in the ANOVA, we test

$$H_0: \mu_1 = \mu_2 = \cdots = \mu_p$$

using the F-ratio between mean square for treatments and mean square for error. This is precisely the same test as the global model test in the corresponding regression example:

$$H_0: \beta_1 = \beta_2 = \cdots = \beta_{p-1} = 0$$

which we test using the F-ratio of the mean square for (regression) model to the mean square for error. Both tests result in the same F-ratio and have the same numerator and denominator degrees of freedom, $(p-1)$ and $(n-p)$, respectively.

To better understand the equivalence of these two procedures, note that if all the β's are equal to 0 in the regression model, the mean response is equal to β_0 *no matter which level of the qualitative factor is utilized as the base level.* That is, the mean response is equal for all p treatments, which is exactly the ANOVA null hypothesis. For example, in Section 15.2 we used ANOVA to test the null hypothesis that four brands of golf balls travel the same distance, on average, when hit by Iron Byron with a driver. We tested

$$H_0: \mu_A = \mu_B = \mu_C = \mu_D$$

where μ_i is the mean distance for brand i. Equivalently, we could have defined the regression model

$$E(y) = \beta_0 + \beta_1 x_1 + \beta_2 x_2 + \beta_3 x_3$$

with

$$x_1 = \begin{cases} 1 & \text{if brand A} \\ 0 & \text{otherwise} \end{cases}$$

$$x_2 = \begin{cases} 1 & \text{if brand B} \\ 0 & \text{otherwise} \end{cases}$$

$$x_3 = \begin{cases} 1 & \text{if brand C} \\ 0 & \text{otherwise} \end{cases}$$

Then β_0 represents the mean distance for brand D, β_1 the difference between the mean distances of brand A and brand D, etc. The null hypothesis

$$H_0: \beta_1 = \beta_2 = \beta_3 = 0$$

is equivalent to the ANOVA null hypothesis that the Brand means are equal.

TABLE 15.10   **Distance Data for Golf Experiment: Completely Randomized Design**

	Brand A	Brand B	Brand C	Brand D
	251.2	263.2	269.7	251.6
	245.1	262.9	263.2	248.6
	248.0	265.0	277.5	249.4
	251.1	254.5	267.4	242.0
	260.5	264.3	270.5	246.5
	250.0	257.0	265.5	251.3
	253.9	262.8	270.7	261.8
	244.6	264.4	272.9	249.0
	254.6	260.6	275.6	247.1
	248.8	255.9	266.5	245.9
Means	250.78	261.06	269.95	249.32

EXAMPLE 15.8

Refer to Example 15.3, in which we used ANOVA for a completely randomized design to test the hypothesis that the mean distances associated with four brands of golf balls were the same. Ten experimental units were randomly and independently assigned to each brand, and the distance was recorded. The data are repeated in Table 15.10. Use a regression program to fit the equivalent regression model, and conduct the global F-test for the model's usefulness in predicting the response y. Compare the test to that conducted in Example 15.3, and interpret the results. Use $\alpha = .10$.

SOLUTION

The MINITAB printout for the regression model using three dummy variables to describe Brand is given in Figure 15.22. To test the model's usefulness, we test the null hypothesis

$$H_0: \beta_1 = \beta_2 = \beta_3 = 0$$

The test statistic, highlighted on the printout, is $F = 43.99$. Its associated p-value (also highlighted) is approximately 0. We therefore reject the null hypothesis that the model is not useful and conclude at the .10 level of significance that brand is related to mean distance.

FIGURE 15.22
MINITAB printout
for regression model
of Example 15.8

```
The regression equation is
DISTANCE = 249 + 1.46 X1 + 11.7 X2 + 20.6 X3

Predictor        Coef        Stdev      t-ratio          p
Constant      249.320        1.455       171.33      0.000
X1              1.460        2.058         0.71      0.483
X2             11.740        2.058         5.70      0.000
X3             20.630        2.058        10.02      0.000

s = 4.602      R-sq = 78.6%      R-sq(adj) = 76.8%

Analysis of Variance

SOURCE         DF           SS           MS          F         p
Regression      3      2794.39       931.46      43.99     0.000
Error          36       762.30        21.18
Total          39      3556.69
```

The regression F-value is identical to that obtained in Example 15.3 using ANOVA. The conclusion may sound somewhat different, but on closer inspection they are also identical. In the ANOVA we concluded that the mean distances differ for at least two of the four brands, while here we conclude that the model is useful for predicting distance. But for the model to be useful, the factor Brand must have some association with mean distance, since Brand is the only factor in the regression model. That is, the mean distance must vary with Brand, which implies that at least two of the brands have different mean distances.

It is instructive to interpret the least squares estimates of the β parameters in Figure 15.22. The value of $\hat{\beta}_0 = 249.32$ is the sample mean distance for brand D (Table 15.10), since brand D is the base level at which all three dummy variables are equal to 0. The value of $\hat{\beta}_1 = 1.46$ is the difference between the sample mean distances of brand A and brand D $(250.78 - 249.32 = 1.46)$. Similarly, you can see that $\hat{\beta}_2$ and $\hat{\beta}_3$ are the sample mean differences between brand B and brand D and between brand C and brand D, respectively. Finally, note that the standard deviation of the regression model, $s = 4.602$, is the same as $\sqrt{\text{MSE}}$ in the ANOVA, and that both measure the variation in distance within a brand. In fact, we would expect to be able to predict the distance Iron Byron will hit a specified brand to within about ± 10 yards using this model. Or, to put it another way, we expect the actual distances for a specific brand to vary within a range of about 10 yards around the mean. Of course, this variability might be partially attributable to other factors that could be included in an expanded regression model. **L**

The assumptions necessary to ensure the validity of an ANOVA and a regression analysis are also identical, although usually phrased differently. Using the golf experiment as an example, we assumed that the distance probability distributions are normal with equal variances for each brand when we conducted the ANOVA. The regression assumption that the error component is normally distributed with constant variance for all settings of the independent variables is seen to be equivalent when we recognize that the error component of this particular model describes the random variability of distance within a particular brand. Thus, we are assuming that the distance measurements within each brand are normally distributed with the same variance for each brand. Similarly, the ANOVA assumption that the samples are random and independent is matched by the regression assumption that the error components are independent with mean 0.

The use of a regression model for a completely randomized design with a single factor can be extended to one with more than one factor.

EXAMPLE 15.9

Refer to Example 15.6, in which we employed a factorial experiment in a completely randomized design to evaluate the effects of two factors, Brand of golf ball and Club utilized, on mean distance. Four brands and two clubs were utilized, and the 4×2 factorial was replicated four times. The data are repeated in Table 15.11.

a. Write a regression model to represent the factorial experiment.

b. Use a computer program to fit the regression model. Conduct an analysis similar to that employed in the ANOVA of Example 15.6.

SOLUTION

a. The two factors Brand and Club are qualitative, so we employ dummy variables to describe them. Also, in contrast to the randomized block experiment, we are very interested in knowing whether the factors interact—that

TABLE 15.11   Data for 4 x 2 Factorial Golf Experiment

		BRAND			
		A	**B**	**C**	**D**
CLUB	**Driver**	226.4	238.3	240.5	219.8
		232.6	231.7	246.9	228.7
		234.0	227.7	240.3	232.9
		220.7	237.2	244.7	237.6
	Five-Iron	163.8	184.4	179.0	157.8
		179.4	180.6	168.0	161.8
		168.6	179.5	165.2	162.1
		173.4	186.2	156.5	160.3

is, whether the difference in the Brand mean distances depends on the Club. Therefore, the model is

$$y = \beta_0 + \overbrace{\beta_1 x_1 + \beta_2 x_2 + \beta_3 x_3}^{\text{Brand main effect}} + \overbrace{\beta_4 x_4}^{\text{Club main effect}} + \overbrace{\beta_5 x_1 x_4 + \beta_6 x_2 x_4 + \beta_7 x_3 x_4}^{\text{Brand} \times \text{Club interaction}} + \epsilon$$

where x_1 to x_3 are dummy variables representing the three brands (using brand D as the base level at which all three dummy variables are equal to 0), and x_4 is the dummy variable representing the two clubs (using five-iron as the base level at which the dummy variable is equal to 0). Note that the interaction terms are just the cross-products of the Brand dummy variables with the Club dummy variable.

b. The SAS printout for the regression model is shown in Figure 15.23. The global F-test for the model tests the null hypothesis

```
Model: MODEL1
Dep Variable: DISTANCE
                        Analysis of Variance

                      Sum of          Mean
  Source      DF      Squares        Square      F Value      Prob>F

  Model        7    33659.80875    4808.54411    140.354      0.0001
  Error       24      822.24000      34.26000
  C Total     31    34482.04875

        Root MSE        5.85320      R-Square      0.9762
        Dep Mean      202.08125      Adj R-Sq      0.9692
        C.V.            2.89646

                        Parameter Estimates

                    Parameter      Standard    T for H0:
  Variable   DF      Estimate         Error    Parameter=0   Prob > |T|

  INTERCEP    1     167.175000    2.92660213      57.123       0.0001
  X1          1       4.125000    4.13884042       0.997       0.3289
  X2          1      15.500000    4.13884042       3.745       0.0010
  X3          1      -6.675000    4.13884042      -1.613       0.1199
  X4          1      75.925000    4.13884042      18.345       0.0001
  X1X4        1     -18.800000    5.85320425      -3.212       0.0037
  X2X4        1     -24.875000    5.85320425      -4.250       0.0003
  X3X4        1      -6.675000    5.85320425      -1.140       0.2654
```

FIGURE 15.23   SAS printout for factorial golf experiment: Complete model including interaction

$$H_0: \beta_1 = \beta_2 = \cdots = \beta_7 = 0$$

In general, this hypothesis implies that the model has no predictive value. In this example, it implies that the mean distance is unrelated to Brand and Club; that is, the mean distance is the same for all brand-club combinations. This should be the same test as the ANOVA test that the $4 \times 2 = 8$ treatment means are all equal.

We see that the value $F = 140.35$ for the SAS printout (Figure 15.23) is the same value we calculated using the ANOVA $F = $ MST/MSE in Example 15.6. The SAS printout gives the observed significance level of the test statistic as .0001 based on 7 numerator and 24 denominator df, implying that the null hypothesis is rejected at any level of significance greater than .0001. Therefore, using $\alpha = .10$ (as in Example 15.6), we reach the same conclusion as in the ANOVA analysis: There is sufficient evidence that the mean distance varies among two or more brand-club combinations.

The next test in a two-factor factorial experiment involves the interaction between the factors. In regression context the null hypothesis that the factors Brand and Club do not interact is

$$H_0: \beta_5 = \beta_6 = \beta_7 = 0$$

This test requires a comparison of the complete model in Figure 15.23 with the reduced model *without* the interaction terms. The SAS printout for the reduced model is shown in Figure 15.24. We then calculate

$$F = \frac{[\text{SSE(Reduced model)} - \text{SSE(Complete model)}]/3}{\text{MSE(Complete model)}}$$

$$= \frac{(1{,}588.201 - 822.240)/3}{34.260} = 7.45$$

```
Model: MODEL2
Dep Variable: DISTANCE

                    Analysis of Variance

                    Sum of          Mean
Source      DF      Squares         Square      F Value      Prob>F

Model        4    32893.84750    8223.46187    139.802       0.0001
Error       27     1588.20125      58.82227
C Total     31    34482.04875

      Root MSE        7.66957    R-Square        0.9539
      Dep Mean      202.08125    Adj R-Sq        0.9471
      C.V.            3.79529

                    Parameter Estimates

                    Parameter      Standard    T for H0:
Variable    DF      Estimate          Error    Parameter=0    Prob > |T|

INTERCEP     1    173.468750     3.03166282       57.219        0.0001
X1           1     -5.275000     3.83478384       -1.376        0.1803
X2           1      3.062500     3.83478384        0.799        0.4315
X3           1    -10.012500     3.83478384       -2.611        0.0146
X4           1     63.337500     2.71160166       23.358        0.0001
```

FIGURE 15.24   SAS printout for factorial golf experiment: Reduced model without interaction

This F-ratio is identical to that obtained in the ANOVA in Example 15.6 and again results in rejection of the null hypothesis at the $\alpha = .10$ level of significance, since $F_{.10} = 2.33$ with 3 numerator and 24 denominator df. We therefore conclude that both Brand and Club affect the mean distance and that the differences among the Brand mean distances depend on the Club (i.e., the factors interact). The presence of interaction makes the tests of the factor main effects unnecessary.

We can use the least squares estimates of the β parameters in the complete model to estimate particular treatment means and differences between particular pairs of means. However, it is probably easier to use the Bonferroni procedure or some other multiple comparisons procedure, as we did in Example 15.6.

Note that the variability of the random error component is measured by the standard deviation of the regression model, $s = 5.85$. This measure is identical to that we obtained in the ANOVA, $\sqrt{\text{MSE}} = \sqrt{34.260} = 5.85$. The implication is that the model can be used to predict the distance Iron Byron will hit the ball to within approximately $\pm 2s = \pm 11.7$ yards if we specify the brand and club. Furthermore, the model accounts for $R^2 = .976$, or 97.6%, of the total sample variation in distance. ◣

Most designed experiments can be analyzed using either ANOVA or regression techniques with identical results. The recommended method of analysis depends on a number of factors, including the ultimate objectives of the analysis (e.g., prediction of response or estimation of differences among treatment means), the type of computer software available, and—perhaps most important—the methodology with which the analyst is more familiar. Whichever analytical tools are employed, it is important to recognize that both ANOVA and regression relate the response mean to one or more factors and that both provide an estimate of sampling variability with which to make inferences.

EXERCISES 15.51–15.55

Note: Exercises marked with 💾 *contain data for computer analysis on a 3.5" disk (file name in parentheses).*

Learning the Mechanics

15.51 Suppose you conduct an experiment with one factor at five levels, utilizing a completely randomized design. Each level of the factor is randomly assigned three experimental units.

   a. Write a regression model for this experiment. Interpret the β parameters of the model.

   b. How many degrees of freedom will be available for estimating the standard deviation σ of the error component?

   c. Write the null hypothesis that the treatment means are equal in terms of the β parameters of the model.

   d. What is the rejection region for the test in part **c** using an $\alpha = .10$ level of significance?

15.52 The following regression model was proposed to describe a designed experiment:

$$y = \beta_0 + \beta_1 x_1 + \beta_2 x_2 + \beta_3 x_3 + \beta_4 x_1 x_3 + \beta_5 x_2 x_3 + \epsilon$$

where

$$x_1 = \begin{cases} 1 & \text{if factor } A, \text{ level 1} \\ 0 & \text{otherwise} \end{cases}$$

$$x_2 = \begin{cases} 1 & \text{if factor } A, \text{ level 2} \\ 0 & \text{otherwise} \end{cases}$$

$$x_3 = \begin{cases} 1 & \text{if factor } B, \text{ level 1} \\ 0 & \text{if factor } B, \text{ level 2} \end{cases}$$

a. What type of experiment does the model describe?

b. Describe how you would test the null hypothesis that the treatment means are equal. Include the hypotheses, test statistic, and rejection region. (Assume that three experimental units are randomly and independently assigned to each factor-level combination.)

c. Describe how you would test for interaction.

Applying the Concepts

15.53 **(X15.020)** Refer to Exercise 15.20, which used a completely randomized design to compare the mean costs associated with the audits of firms in three size groups. The data are repeated in the accompanying table.

COSTS INCURRED IN AUDITS		
A	**B**	**C**
250	100	80
150	150	125
275	75	20
100	200	186
475	55	52
600	80	92
150	110	88
800	160	141
325	132	76
230	233	200

The model

$$E(y) = \beta_0 + \beta_1 x_1 + \beta_2 x_2$$

where

$$x_1 = \begin{cases} 1 & \text{if group A} \\ 0 & \text{otherwise} \end{cases} \quad x_2 = \begin{cases} 1 & \text{if group B} \\ 0 & \text{otherwise} \end{cases}$$

was fit using the SAS regression program. The result is shown in the printout below.

a. Use the regression printout to conduct the test of the null hypothesis that the mean costs are the same for the three groups, and compare the result to that you obtained in Exercise 15.20.

b. Compare the observed significance levels of the tests.

c. Use the regression printout to partition the total sum of squares into the sums of squares for treatments and error. Compare them with those in Exercise 15.20.

d. Interpret the value of R^2 and the least squares estimates of the β parameters.

15.54 **(X15.054)** Studies have indicated that the intensity of employees' negative reactions to unfavorable managerial decisions can be influenced by their perception of the fairness of the decision process. For example, employees who receive unfavorable budgets should have milder negative reactions when they participate in the budgetary process than when they have not participated. This latter situation was examined in *Accounting, Organizations and Society* (Vol. 20, 1995). Thirty-six managers from Europe, Africa, Asia, and South America served as subjects in a 2×2 factorial experiment with factors Budgetary Participation (yes or no) and Budget Favorability

```
Model: MODEL1
Dep Variable: COST

                        Analysis of Variance

                         Sum of          Mean
    Source      DF       Squares         Square      F Value     Prob>F

    Model        2   318861.66667   159430.83333       8.438     0.0014
    Error       27   510163.00000    18894.92593
    C Total     29   829024.66667

           Root MSE       137.45882      R-Square      0.3846
           Dep Mean       190.33333      Adj R-Sq      0.3390
           C.V.            72.22004

                        Parameter Estimates

                      Parameter      Standard     T for H0:
    Variable   DF     Estimate        Error     Parameter=0    Prob > |T|

    INTERCEP    1    106.000000    43.46829411       2.439        0.0216
    X1          1    229.500000    61.47345106       3.733        0.0009
    X2          1     23.500000    61.47345106       0.382        0.7052
```

(favorable or unfavorable). Six managers fell in each of 4 cells of the design. Each manager was asked to evaluate the trustworthiness of the superior who was responsible for setting the budget. A well-established interpersonal trust scale was used. The scale ranges from 4 (low trust) to 28 (high trust). The following data resulted:

		BUDGETARY PARTICIPATION			
		Yes		No	
BUDGET FAVORABILITY	Favorable	19	22	17	16
		25	18	20	24
		25	23	23	21
	Unfavorable	23	28	16	12
		20	26	15	18
		18	23	15	14

Source: Data adapted from Magner, N., Welker, R., and Campbell, T. "The interactive effect of budgetary participation and budget favorability on attitudes toward budgetary decision makers: A research note." *Accounting, Organizations and Society,* Vol. 20, No. 7/8, 1995, pp. 611–618.

a. Are the factors quantitative or qualitative? Explain.

b. Write a regression model that describes the variation in y, interpersonal trust.

c. Fit the regression model and evaluate the model's usefulness using the global F-test. Interpret your results.

d. The researchers hypothesized that an interaction exists between Budgetary Participation and Budget Favorability such that employees who receive unfavorable budgets will have less negative attitudes toward their superior when they have participated in the budgetary process than when they have not. Do the data support their hypothesis? Test using $\alpha = .05$.

e. Examine the hypothesis of part **d** in more detail by constructing and interpreting the appropriate treatment means plot.

15.55 **(X15.055)** Refer to Exercise 15.46, which used a 3×3 factorial experiment to examine the effects

of the factors Price and Display on the unit sales of a product. The data are repeated in the table below. The following regression model is proposed for the analysis of this experiment:

$$y = \beta_0 + \beta_1 x_1 + \beta_2 x_2 + \beta_3 x_3 + \beta_4 x_4 + \beta_5 x_1 x_3 + \beta_6 x_1 x_4 + \beta_7 x_2 x_3 + \beta_8 x_2 x_4 + \epsilon$$

where

$$x_1 = \begin{cases} 1 & \text{if Price = Regular} \\ 0 & \text{otherwise} \end{cases}$$

$$x_2 = \begin{cases} 1 & \text{if Price = Reduced} \\ 0 & \text{otherwise} \end{cases}$$

$$x_3 = \begin{cases} 1 & \text{if Display = Normal} \\ 0 & \text{otherwise} \end{cases}$$

$$x_4 = \begin{cases} 1 & \text{if Display = Normal Plus} \\ 0 & \text{otherwise} \end{cases}$$

The EXCEL printout for this model is shown on page 855.

a. Interpret the least squares estimates by using them to estimate the mean response for each of the $3 \times 3 = 9$ treatments.

b. Interpret the standard deviation and R^2 for the model.

c. Is there evidence that the mean unit sales differ for the nine treatments? Specify the null hypothesis in terms of the regression model and test it using $\alpha = .10$. Compare the result with that obtained in Exercise 15.46.

d. What is the appropriate null hypothesis to test for interaction between the factors, Price and Display? What are the test statistic and rejection region for this test at $\alpha = .10$?

e. An EXCEL printout for the reduced model without interaction is shown on page 856. Conduct the test you set up in part **d**. Compare the result with that obtained for the interaction test in Exercise 15.46.

f. Do you recommend any further testing of the parameters in the model? Explain.

		PRICE		
		Regular	Reduced	Cost to Supermarket
DISPLAY	Normal	989	1,211	1,577
		1,025	1,215	1,559
		1,030	1,182	1,598
	Normal Plus	1,191	1,860	2,492
		1,233	1,910	2,527
		1,221	1,926	2,511
	Twice Normal	1,226	1,516	1,801
		1,202	1,501	1,833
		1,180	1,498	1,852

Interaction model

SUMMARY OUTPUT

Regression Statistics

Multiple R	0.99915953
R Square	0.998319766
Adjusted R Square	0.997572996
Standard Error	22.24276828
Observations	27

ANOVA

	df	SS	MS	F	Significance F
Regression	8	5291151.185	661393.8981	1336.849472	2.33764E-23
Residual	18	8905.333333	494.7407407		
Total	26	5300056.519			

	Coefficients	Standard Error	t Stat	P-value	Lower 95%	Upper 95%
Intercept	1828.666667	12.84186825	142.3988029	6.29968E-29	1801.686882	1855.646452
x1	-626	18.16114425	-34.46919376	6.85697E-18	-664.1551778	-587.8448222
x2	-323.6666667	18.16114425	-17.82193138	6.97959E-13	-361.8218444	-285.5114889
x3	-250.6666667	18.16114425	-13.80236086	5.1434E-11	-288.8218444	-212.5114889
x4	681.3333333	18.16114425	37.5159915	1.5228E-18	643.1781556	719.4885111
x1x3	62.66666667	25.68373651	2.439935741	0.025262966	8.707096803	116.6262365
x1x4	-669	25.68373651	-26.04761187	9.65321E-16	-722.9595699	-615.0404301
x2x3	-51.66666667	25.68373651	-2.011649148	0.059472777	-105.6262365	2.292903197
x2x4	-287.6666667	25.68373651	-11.20034332	1.51892E-09	-341.6262365	-233.7070968

855

Reduced model

SUMMARY OUTPUT

Regression Statistics	
Multiple R	0.949716481
R Square	0.901961395
Adjusted R Square	0.884136194
Standard Error	153.6835811
Observations	27

ANOVA

	df	SS	MS	F	Significance F
Regression	4	4780446.37	1195111.593	50.60034938	8.78322E-11
Residual	22	519610.1481	23618.6431		
Total	26	5300056.519			

	Coefficients	Standard Error	t Stat	P-value	Lower 95%	Upper 95%
Intercept	1933.740741	66.13488335	29.23934606	4.21534E-19	1796.58524	2070.896241
x1	-828.1111111	72.4471349	-11.43055709	1.00539E-10	-978.3574343	-677.8647879
x2	-436.7777778	72.4471349	-6.028917201	4.55577E-06	-587.0241009	-286.5314546
x3	-247	72.4471349	-3.409382584	0.002514362	-397.2463232	-96.75367683
x4	362.4444444	72.4471349	5.002881687	5.23178E-05	212.1981213	512.6907676

QUICK REVIEW

Key Terms

Analysis of variance (ANOVA)   812
Balanced design   833
Bonferroni multiple comparisons procedure   822
Comparisonwise error rate   822
Complete factorial experiment   829
Completely randomized design   806
Dependent variable   800
Designed experiment   802
Experimental unit   801
Experimentwise error rate   822

F-test   809
Factorial experiments   829
Factor interaction   830
Factor levels   801
Factor main effect   831
Factors   800
Multiple comparisons of means   821
Observational experiment   802
Qualitative factors   800
Quantitative factors   800
Replicates of the experiment   834

Response variable   800
Robust method   813
Scheffé multiple comparisons procedure   822
Single-factor experiment   829
Treatments   801
Tukey multiple comparisons procedure   822
Two-factor experiment   832

Key Formulas

Note: Computing formulas for sums of squares (SS) and mean squares (MS) in ANOVA are provided in Appendix C.

Completely randomized design:

$$F = \frac{MST}{MSE}$$ Testing treatments   809

Factorial design with 2 factors:

$$F = \frac{MS(A)}{MSE}$$ Testing main effect A 833

$$F = \frac{MS(B)}{MSE}$$ Testing main effect B 833

$$F = \frac{MS(AB)}{MSE}$$ Testing $A \times B$ interaction   833

$$c = \frac{p(p-1)}{2}$$ Number of pairwise comparisons for p treatment means   821

LANGUAGE LAB

Symbol	Description
ANOVA	Analysis of variance
SST	Sum of Squares for Treatments (i.e., the variation among treatment means)
SSE	Sum of Squares for Error (i.e., the variability around the treatment means due to sampling error)
MST	Mean Square for Treatments
MSE	Mean Square for Error (an estimate of σ^2)
$a \times b$ factorial	Two-factor factorial experiment with one factor at a levels and the other at b levels (thus, there are $a \times b$ treatments in the experiment)
SS(A)	Sum of Square for Factor A
MS(A)	Mean Square for Factor A
SS(B)	Sum of Square for Factor B
MS(B)	Mean Square for Factor B
SS(AB)	Sum of Squares for $A \times B$ interaction
MS(AB)	Mean Square for $A \times B$ interaction

SUPPLEMENTARY EXERCISES 15.56–15.76

Note: List the assumptions necessary to ensure the validity of the procedure you use to solve these problems. Exercises marked with 💾 *contain data for computer analysis on a 3.5" disk (file name in parentheses). Starred (*) exercises are from the optional section.*

Learning the Mechanics

15.56 Explain the difference between an experiment that utilizes a completely randomized design and one that utilizes a factorial design.

15.57 What are the treatments in a two-factor experiment, with factor *A* at three levels and factor *B* at two levels?

15.58 Why does the experimentwise error rate of a multiple comparisons procedure differ from the significance level for each comparison (assuming the experiment has more than two treatments)?

15.59 **(X15.059)** A completely randomized design is utilized to compare four treatment means. The data are shown in the table below.

Treatment 1	Treatment 2	Treatment 3	Treatment 4
8	6	9	12
10	9	10	13
9	8	8	10
10	8	11	11
11	7	12	11

   a. Given that SST = 36.95 and SS(Total) = 62.55, complete an ANOVA table for this experiment.

   b. Is there evidence that the treatment means differ? Use $\alpha = .10$.

   c. Place a 90% confidence interval on the mean response for treatment 4.

15.60 The table shows a partially completed ANOVA table for a two-factor factorial experiment.

Source	df	SS	MS	F
A	3	2.6		
B	5	9.2		
A × B			3.1	
Error		18.7		
Total	47			

   a. Complete the ANOVA table.

   b. How many levels were used for each factor? How many treatments were used? How many replications were performed?

   c. Find the value of the Sum of Squares for Treatments. Test to determine whether the data provide evidence that the treatment means differ. Use $\alpha = .05$.

   d. Is further testing of the nature of factor effects warranted? If so, test to determine whether the factors interact. Use $\alpha = .05$. Interpret the result.

Applying the Concepts

15.61 The *Journal of Testing and Evaluation* (July 1992) published an investigation of the mean compression strength of corrugated fiberboard shipping containers. Comparisons were made for boxes of five different sizes: A, B, C, D, and E. Twenty identical boxes of each size were tested and the peak compression strength (pounds) recorded for each box. The accompanying figure shows the sample means for the five box types as well as the variation around each sample mean.

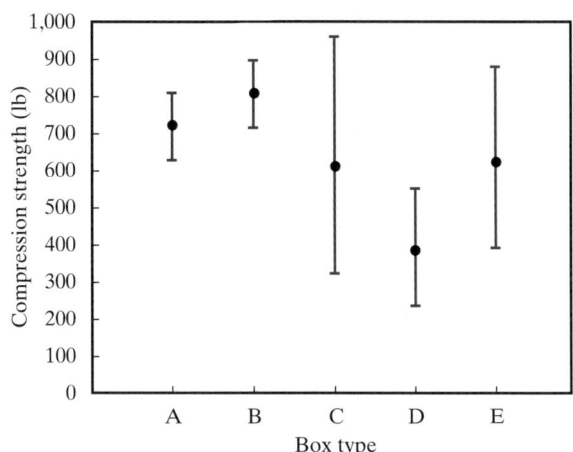

Source: Singh, S. P., *et. al.* "Compression of single-wall corrugated shipping containers using fixed and floating test platens." *Journal of Testing and Evaluation,* Vol. 20, No. 4, July 1992, p. 319 (Figure 3). Copyright American Society for Testing and Materials. Reprinted with permission.

   a. Explain why the data is collected as a completely randomized design.

   b. Refer to box types B and D. Based on the graph, does it appear that the mean compressive strengths of these two box types are significantly different? Explain.

   c. Based on the graph, does it appear that the mean compressive strengths of all five box types are significantly different? Explain.

15.62 Marketing researchers generally agree that *how* you ask a question of consumers is as important as *what* you ask. An article in the *Journal of the Market Research Society* (July 1996) investigated the effects of positively versus negatively worded questions on consumer responses. At issue was whether the use of positive versus negative statements enhances or lessens the validity of the results especially when the individual's level of involvement in the topic varies. The following is an example of alternative wordings: Health and safety warnings on alcoholic products are adequate (are inadequate) to inform the consumer of possible dangers. Consumers were asked to express their level of agreement with positively worded statements on a scale of 1 (strongly disagree) to 5 (strongly agree). The scale values were reversed for negatively worded questions. A total of 154 subjects from the Midwest were randomly assigned to four treatment conditions defined by the two levels of the variables Involvement in Topic (high and low) and Question Wording (positive/negative). Each subject was asked to respond to 11 questions (positively worded for one group and negatively worded for the other group). The 5-point scales described above were used. Those in the high-involvement condition received questions about the Gulf War (the experiment was conducted in 1991 during the war); those in the low-involvement condition received general questions about shopping and products. Each subject's 11 answers were averaged and the resulting data were analyzed using ANOVA and a multiple comparisons procedure.

a. What type of experimental design was used by the researcher?

b. Identify the factors used in the experiment. Are they quantitative or qualitative?

c. Describe the levels of each factor.

d. Describe the experiment's treatments.

e. What is the experiment's dependent variable?

15.63 Leadership acts occur when one person tries to influence the behavior of others toward the attainment of some goal. The effects of leadership style on the behavior of subordinates were investigated in *Accounting, Organizations and Society* (Vol. 20, 1995). Four types of leadership style were

defined based on two variables: the degree of control applied (high or low) and the level of consideration shown for subordinates (high or low). A sample of 257 senior auditors in Big-Six accounting firms yielded the following distribution of leadership styles for the auditors' leaders:

Leadership Style	*n*
A. High control, Low consideration	51
B. Low control, Low consideration	63
C. High control, High consideration	79
D. Low control, High consideration	64
Total	257

All subjects were asked to indicate (confidentially) how frequently their auditing fieldwork had been intentionally substandard in a particular way. They were asked to respond using a scale that ranged from 1 (never) to 5 (always). These data are summarized in the table at the bottom of the page. An ANOVA was conducted to test for differences in the four treatment means. It yielded $F = 30.4$.

a. Do the data indicate that leadership style affects the behavior of subordinates? Test using $\alpha = .05$.

b. The Bonferroni multiple comparisons procedure was used to rank the four treatment means at an experimentwise error rate of $\alpha = .05$. Carefully interpret the results shown in the table.

c. What assumptions must hold to ensure the validity of the Bonferroni procedure?

15.64 **(X15.064)** A direct-mail company assembles and stores paper products (envelopes, letters, brochures, order cards, etc.) for its customers. The company estimates the total number of pieces received in a shipment by estimating the weight per piece and then weighing the entire shipment. The company is unsure whether the sample of pieces used to

Leadership Style	Mean	Standard Deviation	Bonferroni Analysis: Significantly Smaller Means
A	4.27	1.13	B, C, D
B	2.83	1.18	D
C	2.54	1.24	None
D	2.87	1.31	None
Overall	2.87	1.42	

Source: Otley, D. T., and Pierce, B. J. "The control problem in public accounting firms: An empirical study of the impact of leadership style." *Accounting, Organizations and Society,*" Vol. 20, No. 5, 1995, pp. 405–420.

estimate the mean weight per piece should be drawn from a single carton, or whether it is worth the extra time required to pull a few pieces from several cartons. To aid management in making a decision, eight brochures were pulled from each of five cartons of a typical shipment and weighed. The weights (in pounds) are shown in the table.

Carton 1	Carton 2	Carton 3	Carton 4	Carton 5
.01851	.01872	.01869	.01899	.01882
.01829	.01861	.01853	.01917	.01895
.01844	.01876	.01876	.01852	.01884
.01859	.01886	.01880	.01904	.01835
.01854	.01896	.01880	.01923	.01889
.01853	.01879	.01882	.01905	.01876
.01844	.01879	.01862	.01924	.01891
.01833	.01879	.01860	.01893	.01879

a. Identify the response, factor(s), treatments, and experimental units.
b. Do these data provide sufficient evidence to indicate differences in the mean weight per brochure among the five cartons?
c. What assumptions must be satisfied in order for the test of part **b** to be valid?
d. Use Bonferroni multiple comparisons to compare all pairs of means, with $\alpha = .05$ as the overall level of significance.
e. Given the results, make a recommendation to management about whether to sample from one carton or from many cartons.

15.65 Mowen *et al.* (1985) hypothesized that in evaluating salespeople, sales managers underutilize data on the salesperson's territory and instead rely on data associated with how much effort the salesperson expended. To investigate their hypothesis, they developed four scenarios based on the four factor-level combinations associated with the factors Salesperson's effort (high, low) and Sales territory difficulty (high, low). A random sample of 120 sales managers were selected, and 30 were randomly assigned to each of the four factor-level combinations. Each group was presented with the scenario corresponding to the appropriate factor-level combination, and then each sales manager was asked to evaluate the performance of a salesperson using a 7-point scale (1 = high, 7 = low). The authors summarized their results in the accompanying partial ANOVA table.

a. What type of experimental design was used in this study?
b. How many degrees of freedom are associated with SSE?
c. Do the data suggest that a sales manager's perceptions of sales performance are subject to an interaction effect between the difficulty of the

Source	df	F
Sales territory difficulty	1	.39
Effort	1	53.27
Interaction	1	1.95

Source: Mowen, J. C., *et. al.* "Utilizing effort and task difficulty information in evaluating salespeople." *Journal of Marketing Research,* Vol. 22, May 1985, pp. 185–191.

territory and the level of effort? Test using $\alpha = .05$.
d. Do the data indicate that sales managers' performance ratings are influenced by sales territory data? Test using $\alpha = .05$.
e. Do the data indicate that the level of effort expended by a salesperson influences perceived performance? Test using $\alpha = .05$.
f. Do the results of parts **d** and **e** tend to confirm or to refute the hypothesis of Mowen *et al.*? Explain.
g. What assumptions must hold in order for the tests you conducted in parts **c**, **d**, and **e** to be valid?

15.66 A large citrus products company is interested in purchasing several new orange juice extractors. To help them with their purchase decision, six different manufacturers of juice extractors have agreed to let the company conduct an experiment to compare the yields of juices for the six different brands of extractors. Because of the possibility of a variation in the amount of juice per orange from one truckload of oranges to another, equal weights of oranges from a single truckload were assigned to each extractor, and this process was repeated for 15 loads. The amount of juice recorded for each extractor for each truckload produced the sums of squares shown in the accompanying table.

Source	df	SS	MS	F
Extractors		84.71		
Truckloads		159.29		
Error		95.33		
Total		339.33		

a. Complete the ANOVA table.
b. Do the data provide sufficient evidence to indicate a difference among the mean amounts of juice extracted by the six extractors? Use $\alpha = .05$.

15.67 **(X15.067)** *Quality Engineering* (Vol. 6, 1994) reported the results of an experiment that was designed to find ways to improve the output of an industrial lathe. The lathe is controlled by a computer that automatically feeds bar stock, cuts the stock, machines the surface finish, and releases the part. As it is machined, the bar stock spins and is held in place by a collet. The lathe operator sets the feed (the rate at which bars are machined) and the speed (spin rate). The product characteristic of interest is surface finish. It is measured on a gauge that records the vertical distance a probe travels as it moves along a given horizontal distance on the bar. The rougher the surface, the higher the gauge measurement. The factors that were manipulated in the experiment were speed, feed, collet tightness, and tool wear. The following table reports the factor-level settings and the resulting surface-finish measurements (H=High; L=Low):

Speed	Feed	Collet Tightness	Tool Wear	Surface Finish
H	H	H	H	216
L	H	H	H	212
H	L	H	H	48
L	L	H	H	40
H	H	L	H	232
L	H	L	H	248
H	L	L	H	514
L	L	L	H	298
H	H	H	L	238
L	H	H	L	219
H	L	H	L	40
L	L	H	L	33
H	H	L	L	230
L	H	L	L	253
H	L	L	L	273
L	L	L	L	101
H	H	H	H	217
L	H	H	H	221
H	L	H	H	39
L	L	H	H	31
H	H	L	H	235
L	H	L	H	238
H	L	L	H	437
L	L	L	H	87
H	H	H	L	245
L	H	H	L	226
H	L	H	L	51
L	L	H	L	33
H	H	L	L	226
L	H	L	L	214
H	L	L	L	691
L	L	L	L	130

Source: Collins, W. H., and Collins, C. B. "Including residual analysis in designed experiments: Case studies." *Quality Engineering,* Vol. 6, No. 4, 1994, pp. 547–565.

a. What type of experimental design was used?
b. How many different treatments were applied?
c. Perform an analysis of variance for these data.
d. Do significant interaction effects exist? Test using $\alpha = .05$ Interpret your results.
e. Is it necessary to perform main effect tests? Why or why not? If so, perform the tests using $\alpha = .05$.

f. What assumptions must hold to ensure the validity of your results in parts **c**, **d**, and **e**?

15.68 **(X15.068)** It has been hypothesized that treatment, after casting, of a plastic used in optic lenses will improve wear. Four treatments (A–D) are to be tested. To determine whether any differences in mean wear exist among treatments, 28 castings from a single formulation of the plastic were made, and seven castings were randomly assigned to each of the treatments. Wear was determined by measuring the increase in "haze" after 200 cycles of abrasion (better wear indicated by smaller increases). The results are given in the table.

A	B	C	D
9.16	11.95	11.47	11.35
13.29	15.15	9.54	8.73
12.07	14.75	11.26	10.00
11.97	14.79	13.66	9.75
13.31	15.48	11.18	11.71
12.32	13.47	15.03	12.45
11.78	13.06	14.86	12.38

a. What type of experiment was utilized? Identify the response, factor(s), factor type(s), treatments, and experimental units.
b. Use a computer program (or the computational formulas in Appendix C) to analyze the data. Is there evidence of a difference in mean wear among the treatments? Use $\alpha = .05$.
c. What is the observed significance level of the test? Interpret it.
d. Use the Tukey technique to compare all the pairs of treatment means with an overall significance level of $\alpha = .10$.
e. Use a 90% confidence interval to estimate the mean wear for lenses receiving treatment A.

15.69 Several companies are experimenting with the concept of paying production workers (generally paid by the hour) on a salary basis. It is believed that absenteeism and tardiness will increase under this plan, yet some companies feel that the working environment and overall productivity will improve. Fifty production workers under the salary plan are monitored at company A, and 50 under the hourly plan are monitored at company B. The number of work-hours missed due to tardiness or absenteeism over a one-year period is recorded for each worker. The results are partially summarized in the table.

Source	df	SS	MS	F
Companies		3,237.2		
Error		16,167.7		
Total	99			

a. Fill in the information missing from the table.

b. Is there evidence at $\alpha = .05$ that the mean number of hours missed differs for employees of the two companies?

c. Is there sufficient information given to form a confidence interval for the difference between the mean number of hours missed at the two companies?

15.70 (X15.070) A composite of a metal powder mixed with a plastic resin was invented to stop a radiation beam used for skin or oral cancer therapy. A 2×2 factorial experiment with two replications was conducted in a dental research lab to measure the degree of radiation traveling through the composite when the density of the metal powder was either a heavy alloy or a light alloy and when a second layer of plastic under the composite was present or absent. The accompanying table shows the data collected. Use the techniques presented in this chapter to analyze these data, and make a recommendation regarding the preferred method of protecting patients from overexposure to potentially harmful radiation.

		ALLOY DENSITY	
		Heavy	**Light**
SECOND PLASTIC	**Present**	0.04, 0.02	0.46, 0.40
	Absent	0.38, 0.13	1.84, 2.29

Source: Personal communication from F. Eichmiller, Paffenbarger Research Center, Gaithersburg, Md., 1991.

15.71 (X15.071) Sixteen workers were randomly selected to participate in an experiment to determine the effects of work scheduling and method of payment on attitude toward the job. Two schedules were employed, the standard 8–5 workday and a modification whereby the worker could decide each day whether to start at 7 or 8 A.M.; in addition, the worker could choose between a half-hour or one-hour lunch period each day. The two methods of payment were a standard hourly rate and a reduced hourly rate with an added piece rate based on the worker's production. Four workers were randomly assigned to each of the four scheduling-payment combinations, and each completed an attitude test after one month on the job. The test scores are shown in the table.

	PAYMENT	
Scheduling	**Hourly Rate**	**Hourly and Piece Rate**
8–5	54, 68, 55, 63	89, 75, 71, 83
Worker-Modified Schedule	79, 65, 62, 74	83, 94, 91, 86

a. What type of experiment was performed? Identify the response, factor(s), factor type(s), treatments, and experimental units.

b. The SAS printout for this experiment is shown below. Is there evidence that the treatment means differ? Use $\alpha = .05$.

c. If the test in part **b** warrants further analysis, conduct the appropriate tests of interaction and main effects. Interpret your results.

d. What assumptions are necessary to ensure the validity of the inferences? State the assumptions in terms of this experiment.

15.72 A researcher at St. Louis University conducted a study to determine whether entrepreneurs, newly hired managers, and newly promoted managers differ in their risk-taking propensities. For the purpose of this study, entrepreneurs were defined as individuals who, within three months prior to the study, had ceased working for their employers in

```
                  Analysis of Variance Procedure
Dependent Variable: SCORE

                              Sum of          Mean
Source              DF        Squares        Square     F Value   Pr > F
Model                3     1806.00000     602.00000      12.29    0.0006
Error               12      588.00000      49.00000
Corrected Total     15     2394.00000

               R-Square          C.V.      Root MSE       SCORE Mean
               0.754386     9.3959732       7.00000       74.5000000

Source              DF      Anova SS    Mean Square     F Value   Pr > F
SCHEDULE             1      361.0000       361.0000       7.37    0.0188
PAYMENT              1     1444.0000      1444.0000      29.47    0.0002
SCHEDULE*PAYMENT     1        1.0000         1.0000       0.02     0.888
```

Group	Sample Size	Sample Mean	Standard Deviation	Group Totals
Entrepreneurs	31	71.00	11.94	2,201
Newly hired managers	31	72.52	12.19	2,248
Promoted managers	31	66.97	10.84	2,076
	93			6,525

Source: Brockhaus, R. H. "Risk-taking propensity of entrepreneurs," *Academy of Management Journal,* Vol. 23, Sept. 1980, pp. 509–520.

order to manage their own business ventures. Thirty-one individuals of each type were selected to participate in the study. Each was asked to complete a questionnaire that required the respondent to choose between a safe alternative and a more attractive but risky one. Test scores were designed to measure risk-taking propensity. (Lower scores are associated with greater conservatism in risk-taking situations.) Summary statistics for the test scores are given in the table above.

Source	df	SS	MS	F
Treatments		509.87		
Error		12,259.96		
Total				

a. The partial ANOVA table above is calculated from the data. Complete the table.

b. Do the data provide sufficient evidence to indicate differences in the mean risk-taking propensities among the three groups? Test using $\alpha = .05$.

c. What assumptions must be satisfied in order for the test of part **b** to be valid?

d. Would you advise conducting tests to compare the individual pairs of means? Explain.

e. Would you classify this experiment as observational or designed? Explain.

15.73 **(X15.073)** Independent random samples of size 36 were drawn from stocks listed on the New York Stock Exchange (NYSE), the American Stock Exchange (ASE), and NASDAQ National Market, respectively. The closing prices of all 108 stocks on March 3, 1997, are listed in the table in the next column.

a. Is this experiment designed or observational? What type of experiment is it?

b. The data are analyzed using SAS. According to the printout at the top of page 864, is there evidence that the mean closing price differed among the three markets? Test using $\alpha = .10$.

c. The SAS printout shows the Tukey rankings of the means for the three markets. Interpret the

NYSE		ASE		NASDAQ	
$31\frac{3}{4}$	$27\frac{1}{2}$	$5\frac{3}{4}$	$5\frac{1}{2}$	$8\frac{1}{2}$	$6\frac{3}{4}$
$22\frac{1}{4}$	$36\frac{3}{4}$	$23\frac{1}{8}$	$123\frac{1}{2}$	$5\frac{1}{8}$	$21\frac{1}{2}$
$18\frac{3}{4}$	$20\frac{1}{4}$	2	23	$10\frac{1}{4}$	12
$11\frac{1}{4}$	$78\frac{3}{4}$	$11\frac{1}{4}$	$15\frac{3}{4}$	$4\frac{1}{8}$	$4\frac{3}{4}$
43	$13\frac{5}{8}$	$11\frac{3}{4}$	$5\frac{1}{4}$	$7\frac{3}{4}$	$27\frac{3}{4}$
$32\frac{7}{8}$	$12\frac{3}{4}$	$10\frac{1}{4}$	$11\frac{3}{4}$	$22\frac{3}{4}$	16
$20\frac{1}{2}$	$19\frac{3}{4}$	$15\frac{5}{8}$	$15\frac{1}{8}$	$8\frac{1}{2}$	$5\frac{7}{8}$
$3\frac{7}{8}$	$25\frac{1}{4}$	$7\frac{1}{8}$	$2\frac{1}{4}$	$18\frac{7}{8}$	$25\frac{1}{4}$
$9\frac{1}{4}$	$27\frac{1}{2}$	$5\frac{1}{2}$	$19\frac{7}{8}$	$14\frac{5}{8}$	$17\frac{1}{8}$
$11\frac{1}{8}$	$58\frac{1}{2}$	$15\frac{3}{4}$	16	10	$27\frac{3}{4}$
$25\frac{7}{8}$	$18\frac{3}{4}$	1	$7\frac{1}{8}$	$2\frac{1}{4}$	$5\frac{5}{8}$
$16\frac{3}{8}$	$13\frac{1}{8}$	5	$26\frac{1}{4}$	$55\frac{3}{4}$	$2\frac{3}{4}$
$20\frac{7}{8}$	$57\frac{5}{8}$	$30\frac{7}{8}$	$10\frac{3}{8}$	$79\frac{1}{2}$	$26\frac{3}{4}$
8	$40\frac{3}{8}$	$23\frac{3}{4}$	$9\frac{1}{4}$	$5\frac{7}{8}$	$15\frac{7}{8}$
$9\frac{5}{8}$	$21\frac{3}{4}$	$4\frac{3}{8}$	14	53	17
22	$13\frac{1}{4}$	$8\frac{1}{8}$	19	$17\frac{1}{2}$	$14\frac{1}{2}$
$37\frac{3}{4}$	32	$30\frac{3}{8}$	$5\frac{1}{4}$	$4\frac{3}{8}$	$1\frac{7}{8}$
$9\frac{3}{4}$	$38\frac{3}{8}$	$1\frac{7}{8}$	$\frac{5}{8}$	25	$18\frac{1}{4}$

Source: The New York Times, Mar. 4, 1997.

results. What is the experimentwise error rate for the analysis?

*15.74 Refer to Exercise 15.73.

a. Write a regression model to describe this experiment. Define all the variables you use.

b. The SAS regression printout for this experiment is shown at the bottom of page 864. Interpret the least squares estimates. Deduce the coding that was utilized for the dummy variables.

c. Use the regression printout to test the null hypothesis that the three markets had the same mean closing prices on March 3, 1997. Use $\alpha = .10$. What is the observed significance level of the test?

15.75 **(X15.075)** In hope of attracting more riders, a city transit company plans to have express bus service from a suburban terminal to the downtown business district. These buses will travel along a major city street where there are numerous traffic lights that affect travel time. The city decides to perform a study of the effect of four different plans (a special bus lane, traffic signal progression, etc.) on the travel times for the buses. Travel times (in minutes)

Analysis of Variance Procedure

Dependent Variable: PRICE

Source	DF	Sum of Squares	Mean Square	F Value	Pr > F
Model	2	2082.334201	1041.167101	3.34	0.0394
Error	105	32767.348090	312.069982		
Corrected Total	107	34849.682292			

R-Square	C.V.	Root MSE	PRICE Mean
0.059752	91.93467	17.66550	19.2152778

Source	DF	Anova SS	Mean Square	F Value	Pr > F
STOCK	2	2082.334201	1041.167101	3.34	0.0394

Tukey's Studentized Range (HSD) Test for variable: PRICE

NOTE: This test controls the type I experimentwise error rate, but generally has a higher type II error rate than REGWQ.

Alpha= 0.05   df= 105   MSE= 312.07
Critical Value of Studentized Range= 3.362
Minimum Significant Difference= 9.8991

Means with the same letter are not significantly different.

Tukey Grouping		Mean	N	STOCK
	A	25.299	36	NYSE
	A			
B	A	17.253	36	NASDAQ
B				
B		15.094	36	ASE

Dependent Variable: PRICE

Analysis of Variance

Source	DF	Sum of Squares	Mean Square	F Value	Prob>F
Model	2	2082.33420	1041.16710	3.336	0.0394
Error	105	32767.34809	312.06998		
C Total	107	34849.68229			

Root MSE	17.66550	R-Square	0.0598
Dep Mean	19.21528	Adj R-sq	0.0418
C.V.	91.93467		

Parameter Estimates

Variable	DF	Parameter Estimate	Standard Error	T for H0: Parameter=0	Prob > |T|
INTERCEP	1	17.253472	2.94425043	5.860	0.0001
X1	1	8.045139	4.16379889	1.932	0.0560
X2	1	-2.159722	4.16379889	-0.519	0.6051

are measured for several weekdays during a morning rush-hour trip while each plan is in effect. The results are recorded in the following table.

PLAN			
1	**2**	**3**	**4**
27	25	34	30
25	28	29	33
29	30	32	31
26	27	31	
	24	36	

a. What experimental design was used?
b. Use the appropriate formulas in Appendix D or a computer program to construct an ANOVA summary table for this experiment.
c. Is there evidence of a difference between the mean travel times for the four plans? Use $\alpha = .01$.
d. If warranted, use a multiple comparisons procedure to compare the pairs of mean travel times corresponding to the four plans. Use $\alpha = .05$.

*15.76 (X15.076) To be able to provide her clients with comparative information on two large suburban residential communities, a realtor wants to know the average home value in each community. Eight homes are selected at random within each community and are appraised by the realtor. The appraisals are given in the table (in thousands of dollars). Can you conclude that the average home value is different in the two communities?

Suburb A		Suburb B	
43.5	57.5	73.5	44.5
49.5	32.0	62.0	56.0
38.0	67.5	47.5	68.0
66.5	71.5	36.5	63.5

a. Use the two-sample t statistic (Section 9.1) to test $H_0: \mu_A = \mu_B$.
b. Consider the regression model $y = \beta_0 + \beta_1 x + \epsilon$, where

$$x = \begin{cases} 1 & \text{if community B} \\ 0 & \text{if community A} \end{cases} \qquad y = \text{Appraised price}$$

Since $\beta_1 = \mu_B - \mu_A$, testing $H_0: \beta_1 = 0$ is equivalent to testing $H_0: \mu_A = \mu_B$. Use the partial reproduction of the SAS printout shown here to test $H_0: \beta_1 = 0$. Use $\alpha = .05$.

Dependent Variable: Y

Analysis of Variance

Source	DF	Sum of Squares	Mean Square	F Value	Prob>F
Model	1	40.64063	40.64063	0.215	0.6501
Error	14	2648.71875	189.19420		
C Total	15	2689.35937			

Root MSE	13.75479	R-Square	0.0151	
Dep Mean	54.84375	Adj R-sq	-0.0552	
C.V.	25.07996			

Parameter Estimates

Variable	DF	Parameter Estimate	Standard Error	T for H0: Parameter=0	Prob > |T|
INTERCEP	1	53.250000	4.86305198	10.950	0.0001
X	1	3.187500	6.87739406	0.463	0.6501

```
                    General Linear Models Procedure
Dependent Variable: PRICE

                             Sum of          Mean
Source               DF     Squares         Square     F Value    Pr > F

Model                 1   40.6406250    40.6406250        0.21    0.6501

Error                14  2648.718750   189.1941964

Corrected Total      15  2689.359375

             R-Square           C.V.      Root MSE            PRICE Mean

             0.015112      25.079956       13.7548            54.8437500

Source               DF   Type I SS  Mean Square     F Value    Pr > F

COMMUNTY              1     40.6406      40.6406          0.21    0.6501
```

c. The SAS ANOVA printout for this experiment is given above. Is there evidence that the treatment means differ? Use $\alpha = .05$.

d. Using the results of the three tests in parts **a–c**, verify that the tests are equivalent (for this special case, $p = 2$) of the completely randomized design in terms of the test statistic value and rejection region.

CHAPTER 16

NONPARAMETRIC STATISTICS

Where We've Been

In Chapters 7–9 and 15, we explored techniques for making inferences about the mean of a single population and for comparing the means of two or more populations. Most of the techniques discussed in those chapters are based on the assumption that the sampled populations have probability distributions that are approximately normal with equal variances. But how can you analyze data from populations that do not satisfy these assumptions?

Where We're Going

In this chapter, we present inferential techniques that are based on an ordering of the sample measurements according to their relative magnitudes. These techniques, which require fewer or less stringent assumptions concerning the nature of the probability distributions of the populations, are called *nonparametric statistical methods*.

16.1 INTRODUCTION

The *t*- and *F*-tests for making inferences about means presented in Chapters 7–9 and 15 are unsuitable for analyzing some types of data. These data fall into two categories. The first includes data from populations that do not satisfy the assumptions upon which the *t*- and *F*-tests are based. Both tests require that the random variables being measured have normal probability distributions with equal variances. In practice, however, the observations from one population may exhibit much greater variability than those from another, or the probability distributions may be decidedly nonnormal. For example, the distribution might be very flat, peaked, or strongly skewed to the right or left. When any of the assumptions required for the *t*- and *F*-tests are seriously violated, the computed *t* and *F* statistics may not follow the standard *t*- and *F*-distributions. In this case, the tabulated values of *t* and *F* (Tables VI–X in Appendix B) are not applicable, the correct value of α for the test is unknown, and the *t*- and *F*-tests are of dubious value.

The second type of data for which *t*- and *F*-tests are inappropriate are responses that are not susceptible to numerical measurement but can be *ranked in order of magnitude*.* For example, if we want to compare the teaching ability of two college MBA instructors based on subjective evaluations of students, we cannot assign a number that exactly measures the teaching ability of a single instructor. But we can compare two instructors by ranking them according to a subjective evaluation of their teaching abilities. If instructors A and B are evaluated by each of 10 students, we have the standard problem of comparing the probability distributions for two populations of ratings—one for instructor A and one for B. But the *t*-test of Chapter 9 would be inappropriate because the only data that can be recorded are preference statements of 10 students—that is, each student decides that either A is better than B or vice versa.

Nonparametric tests—the counterparts of the *t*- and *F*-tests—compare the probability distributions of the sampled populations rather than specific parameters of these populations (such as the means or variances). For example, nonparametric tests can be used to compare the probability distribution of the strengths of preferences for a new product to the probability distributions of the strengths of preferences for the currently popular brands. If it can be inferred that the distribution for the new product is *shifted* above (to the right of) the others (see Figure 16.1), the implication is that the new product tends to be more preferred than the currently popular products. Such an inference might lead to a decision to market the product nationally.

Most nonparametric methods use the **relative ranks** of the sample observations, rather than their actual numerical values. These tests are particularly valuable when we are unable to obtain numerical measurements of some phenomena but are able to rank them in comparison to each other. Statistics based on ranks of

FIGURE 16.1
Probability distributions of strengths of preference measurements: New product is preferred

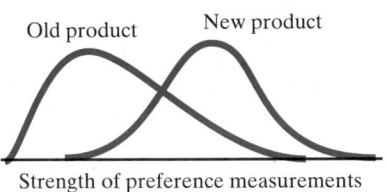

*Qualitative data that can be ranked in order of magnitude are called **ordinal** data.

measurements are called **rank statistics**. In Section 16.2, we develop a test to make inferences about the central tendency of a single population. In Sections 16.3 and 16.5, we present rank statistics for comparing two or more probability distributions using independent samples. In Section 16.4, the matched-pairs design is used to make nonparametric comparisons of populations. Finally, in Section 16.6, we present a nonparametric measure of correlation between two variables—*Spearman's rank correlation coefficient*.

16.2   SINGLE POPULATION INFERENCES: THE SIGN TEST

In Chapter 8 we utilized the z and t statistics for testing hypotheses about a population mean. The z statistic is appropriate for large random samples selected from "general" populations—that is, with few limitations on the probability distribution of the underlying population. The t statistic was developed for small-sample tests in which the sample is selected at random from a *normal* distribution. The question is: How can we conduct a test of hypothesis when we have a small sample from a *nonnormal* distribution?

The **sign test** is a relatively simple nonparametric procedure for testing hypotheses about the central tendency of a nonnormal probability distribution. Note that we used the phrase *central tendency* rather than *population mean*. This is because the sign test, like many nonparametric procedures, provides inferences about the population *median* rather than the population mean μ. Denoting the population median by the Greek letter, η, we know (Chapter 2) that η is the 50th percentile of the distribution (Figure 16.2) and as such is less affected by the skewness of the distribution and the presence of outliers (extreme observations). Since the nonparametric test must be suitable for all distributions, not just the normal, it is reasonable for nonparametric tests to focus on the more robust (less sensitive to extreme values) measure of central tendency, the median.

For example, increasing numbers of both private and public agencies are requiring their employees to submit to tests for substance abuse. One laboratory that conducts such testing has developed a system with a normalized measurement scale, in which values less than 1.00 indicate "normal" ranges and values equal to or greater than 1.00 are indicative of potential substance abuse. The lab reports a normal result as long as the median level for an individual is less than 1.00. Eight independent measurements of each individual's sample are made. Suppose, then, that one individual's results were as follows:

.78   .51   3.79   .23   .77   .98   .96   .89

If the objective is to determine whether the *population* median (that is, the true median level if an indefinitely large number of measurements were made on the same individual sample) is less than 1.00, we establish that as our alternative hypothesis and test

FIGURE 16.2
Location of the population median, η

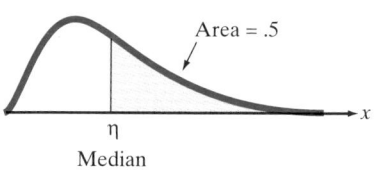

$$H_0: \eta = 1.00$$

$$H_a: \eta < 1.00$$

The one-tailed sign test is conducted by counting the number of sample measurements that "favor" the alternative hypothesis—in this case, the number that are less than 1.00. If the null hypothesis is true, we expect approximately half of the measurements to fall on each side of the hypothesized median and if the alternative is true, we expect significantly more than half to favor the alternative—that is, to be less than 1.00. Thus,

Test statistic: S = Number of measurements less than 1.00,
the null hypothesized median

If we wish to conduct the test at the $\alpha = .05$ level of significance, the rejection region can be expressed in terms of the observed significance level, or p-value of the test:

Rejection region: p-value $\leq .05$

In this example, $S = 7$ of the 8 measurements are less than 1.00. To determine the observed significance level associated with this outcome, we note that the number of measurements less than 1.00 is a binomial random variable (check the binomial characteristics presented in Chapter 4), and *if* H_0 *is true,* the binomial probability p that a measurement lies below (or above) the median 1.00 is equal to .5 (Figure 16.2). What is the probability that a result is *as contrary to or more contrary to* H_0 than the one observed? That is, what is the probability that 7 *or more* of 8 binomial measurements will result in Success (be less than 1.00) if the probability of Success is .5? Binomial Table II in Appendix B (using $n = 8$ and $p = .5$) indicates that

$$P(x \geq 7) = 1 - P(x \leq 6) = 1 - .965 = .035$$

Thus, the probability that at least 7 of 8 measurements would be less than 1.00 *if the true median were* 1.00 is only .035. The p-value of the test is therefore .035.

This p-value can also be obtained using a statistical software package. The MINITAB printout of the analysis is shown in Figure 16.3, with the p-value highlighted on the printout. Since $p = .035$ is less than $\alpha = .05$, we conclude that this sample provides sufficient evidence to reject the null hypothesis. The implication of this rejection is that the laboratory can conclude at the $\alpha = .05$ level of significance that the true median level for the tested individual is less than 1.00. However, we note that one of the measurements greatly exceeds the others, with a value of 3.79, and deserves special attention. Note that this large measurement is an outlier that would make the use of a t-test and its concomitant assumption of normality dubious. The only assumption necessary to ensure the validity of the sign test is that the probability distribution of measurements is continuous.

The use of the sign test for testing hypotheses about population medians is summarized in the box.

FIGURE 16.3
MINITAB printout of sign test

```
SIGN TEST OF MEDIAN = 1.000 VERSUS L.T.   1.000

             N  BELOW  EQUAL  ABOVE  P-VALUE   MEDIAN
READING      8    7      0      1    0.0352    0.8350
```

Sign Test for a Population Median η

One-Tailed Test

$H_0: \eta = \eta_0$

$H_a: \eta > \eta_0$ [or $H_a: \eta < \eta_0$]

Test statistic:

S = Number of sample measurements greater than η_0 [or S = number of measurements less than η_0]

Observed significance level:

p-value = $P(x \geq S)$

Two-Tailed Test

$H_0: \eta = \eta_0$

$H_a: \eta \neq \eta_0$

S = Larger of S_1 and S_2, where S_1 is the number of measurements less than η_0 and S_2 is the number of measurements greater than η_0

p-value = $2P(x \geq S)$

where x has a binomial distribution with parameters n and $p = .5$. (Use Table II, Appendix B.)

Rejection region: Reject H_0 if p-value $\leq .05$.

Assumption: The sample is selected randomly from a continuous probability distribution. [*Note*: No assumptions need to be made about the shape of the probability distribution.]

Recall that the normal probability distribution provides a good approximation for the binomial distribution when the sample size is large. For tests about the median of a distribution, the null hypothesis implies that $p = .5$, and the normal distribution provides a good approximation if $n \geq 10$. (Samples with $n \geq 10$ satisfy the condition that $np \pm 3\sqrt{npq}$ is contained in the interval 0 to n.) Thus, we can use the standard normal z-distribution to conduct the sign test for large samples. The large-sample sign test is summarized in the next box.

Large-Sample Sign Test for a Population Median η

One-Tailed Test

$H_0: \eta = \eta_0$

$H_a: \eta > \eta_0$
  [or $H_a: \eta < \eta_0$]

Two-Tailed Test

$H_0: \eta = \eta_0$

$H_a: \eta \neq \eta_0$

Test statistic: $z = \dfrac{(S - .5) - .5n}{.5\sqrt{n}}$

[*Note*: S is calculated as shown in the previous box. We subtract .5 from S as the "correction for continuity." The null hypothesized mean value is $np = .5n$, and the standard deviation is

$$\sqrt{npq} = \sqrt{n(.5)(.5)} = .5\sqrt{n}$$

See Chapter 5 for details on the normal approximation to the binomial distribution.]

Rejection region: $z > z_\alpha$ *Rejection region*: $z > z_{\alpha/2}$

where tabulated z values can be found inside the front cover.

EXAMPLE 16.1

A manufacturer of compact disk (CD) players has established that the median time to failure for its players is 5,250 hours of utilization. A sample of 20 CDs from a competitor is obtained, and they are continuously tested until each fails. The 20 failure times range from five hours (a "defective" player) to 6,575 hours, and 14 of the 20 exceed 5,250 hours. Is there evidence that the median failure time of the competitor differs from 5,250 hours? Use $\alpha = .10$.

SOLUTION

The null and alternative hypotheses of interest are

$$H_0: \eta = 5{,}250 \text{ hours}$$

$$H_a: \eta \neq 5{,}250 \text{ hours}$$

Test statistic: Since $n \geq 10$, we use the standard normal z statistic:

$$z = \frac{(S - .5) - .5n}{.5\sqrt{n}}$$

where S is the maximum of S_1, the number of measurements greater than 5,250, and S_2, the number of measurements less than 5,250.

Rejection region: $z > 1.645$ where $z_{\alpha/2} = z_{.05} = 1.645$

Assumptions: The distribution of the failure times is continuous (time is a continuous variable), but nothing is assumed about the shape of its probability distribution.

Since the number of measurements exceeding 5,250 is $S_2 = 14$ and thus the number of measurements less than 5,250 is $S_1 = 6$, then $S = 14$, the greater of S_1 and S_2. The calculated z statistic is therefore

$$z = \frac{(S - .5) - .5n}{.5\sqrt{n}} = \frac{13.5 - 10}{.5\sqrt{20}} = \frac{3.5}{2.236} = 1.565$$

The value of z is not in the rejection region, so we cannot reject the null hypothesis at the $\alpha = .10$ level of significance. Thus, the CD manufacturer should not conclude, on the basis of this sample, that its competitor's CDs have a median failure time that differs from 5,250 hours. ◼

The one-sample nonparametric sign test for a median provides an alternative to the *t*-test for small samples from nonnormal distributions. However, if the distribution is approximately normal, the *t*-test provides a more powerful test about the central tendency of the distribution.

EXERCISES   16.1–16.10

Note: Exercises marked with 💾 *contain data for computer analysis on a 3.5" disk (file name in parentheses).*

Learning the Mechanics

16.1   Under what circumstances is the sign test preferred to the *t*-test for making inferences about the central tendency of a population?

16.2   What is the probability that a randomly selected observation exceeds the
a. Mean of a normal distribution?
b. Median of a normal distribution?
c. Mean of a nonnormal distribution?
d. Median of a nonnormal distribution?

16.3   Use Table II of Appendix B to calculate the following binomial probabilities:
a. $P(x \geq 7)$ when $n = 8$ and $p = .5$
b. $P(x \geq 5)$ when $n = 8$ and $p = .5$
c. $P(x \geq 8)$ when $n = 8$ and $p = .5$
d. $P(x \geq 10)$ when $n = 15$ and $p = .5$. Also use the normal approximation to calculate this

probability, then compare the approximation with the exact value.

e. $P(x \geq 15)$ when $n = 25$ and $p = .5$. Also use the normal approximation to calculate this probability, then compare the approximation with the exact value.

16.4 Consider the following sample of 10 measurements:

8.4   16.9   15.8   12.5   10.3   4.9   12.9   9.8   23.7   7.3

Use these data to conduct each of the following sign tests using the binomial tables (Table II, Appendix B) and $\alpha = .05$:

a. H_0: $\eta = 9$ versus H_a: $\eta > 9$
b. H_0: $\eta = 9$ versus H_a: $\eta \neq 9$
c. H_0: $\eta = 20$ versus H_a: $\eta < 20$
d. H_0: $\eta = 20$ versus H_a: $\eta \neq 20$
e. Repeat each of the preceding tests using the normal approximation to the binomial probabilities. Compare the results.
f. What assumptions are necessary to ensure the validity of each of the preceding tests?

16.5 Suppose you wish to conduct a test of the research hypothesis that the median of a population is greater than 75. You randomly sample 25 measurements from the population and determine that 17 of them exceed 75. Set up and conduct the appropriate test of hypothesis at the .10 level of significance. Be sure to specify all necessary assumptions.

Applying the Concepts

16.6 According to the National Restaurant Association, hamburgers were the number one selling fast-food item in the United States in 1996. The $39 billion market was dominated by McDonald's (42%), Burger King (19%), and Wendy's (11%) (*Newark Star-Ledger*, Mar. 17, 1997). An economist studying the fast-food buying habits of Americans paid graduate students to stand outside two suburban McDonald's restaurants near Boston and ask departing customers whether they spent more or less than $2.25 on hamburger products for their lunch. Twenty answered "less than"; 50 said "more than"; and 10 refused to answer the question.

a. Is there sufficient evidence to conclude that the median amount spent for hamburgers at lunch at McDonald's is less than $2.25?
b. Does your conclusion apply to all Americans who eat lunch at McDonald's? Justify your answer.

c. What assumptions must hold to ensure the validity of your test in part **a**?

16.7 The biting rate of a particular species of fly was investigated in a study reported in the *Journal of the American Mosquito Control Association* (Mar. 1995). Biting rate was defined as the number of flies biting a volunteer during 15 minutes of exposure. This species of fly is known to have a median biting rate of 5 bites per 15 minutes on Stanbury Island, Utah. However, it is theorized that the median biting rate is higher in bright, sunny weather. (This information is of interest to marketers of pesticides.) To test this theory, 122 volunteers were exposed to the flies during a sunny day on Stanbury Island. Of these volunteers, 95 experienced biting rates greater than 5.

a. Set up the null and alternative hypotheses for the test.
b. Calculate the approximate p-value of the test. [*Hint:* Use the normal approximation for a binomial probability.]
c. Make the appropriate conclusion at $\alpha = .01$.

16.8 (**X16.008**) Since the early 1990s many firms have found it necessary to reduce the size of their workforces in order to reduce costs. These reductions are referred to as *corporate downsizing* and *reductions in force* (RIF) by the business community and media (*Business Week*, Feb. 24, 1997). Following RIFs, companies are often sued by former employees who allege that the RIFs were discriminatory with regard to age. Federal law protects employees over 40 years of age against such discrimination. Suppose one large company's employees have a median age of 37. Its RIF plan is to fire 15 employees aged 43, 32, 39, 28, 54, 41, 50, 62, 22, 45, 47, 54, 43, 33, and 59 years.

a. Calculate the median age of the employees who are being terminated.
b. What are the appropriate null and alternative hypotheses to test whether the population from which the terminated employees were selected has a median age that exceeds the entire company's median age?
c. The test of part **b** was conducted using MINITAB. Find the significance level of the test on the accompanying MINITAB printout and interpret its value.
d. Assuming that courts generally require statistical evidence at the .10 level of significance before ruling that age discrimination laws were

```
SIGN TEST OF MEDIAN = 37.00 VERSUS  G.T.   37.00

            N   BELOW   EQUAL   ABOVE   P-VALUE    MEDIAN
AGE        15      4       0      11     0.0592     43.00
```

violated, what do you advise the company about its planned RIF? Explain.

16.9 Airline industry analysts expect that the Federal Aviation Administration (FAA) will increase the frequency and thoroughness of its review of aircraft maintenance procedures in response to the admission by ValuJet Airlines in the summer of 1996 that it had not met some maintenance requirements. Suppose that the FAA samples the records of six aircraft currently utilized by one airline and determines the number of flights between the last two complete engine maintenances for each, with the following results: 24, 27, 25, 94, 29, 28. The FAA requires that this maintenance be performed at least every 30 flights. Although it is obvious that not all aircraft are meeting the requirement, the FAA wishes to test whether the airline is meeting this particular maintenance requirement "on average."

a. Would you suggest the *t*-test or sign test to conduct the test? Why?

b. Set up the null and alternative hypotheses such that the burden of proof is on the airline to show it is meeting the "on-average" requirement.

c. What are the test statistic and rejection region for this test if the level of significance is $\alpha = .01$? Why would the level of significance be set at such a low value?

d. Conduct the test, and state the conclusion in terms of this application.

16.10 In Exercise 7.27 the average cost of a major kitchen remodeling job in each of a sample of 11 U.S. cities was investigated. The data are reproduced below.

City	Average Cost
Atlanta	$20,427
Boston	27,255
Des Moines	22,115
Kansas City, Mo.	23,256
Louisville	21,887
Portland, Ore.	24,255
Raleigh-Durham	19,852
Reno, Nev.	23,624
Ridgewood, N.J.	25,885
San Francisco	28,999
Tulsa	20,836

Source: Auerbach, J. "A guide to what's cooking in kitchens." *The Wall Street Journal,* Nov. 17, 1995, p. B10.

a. Under what circumstances could a *t*-test be used to determine whether the mean cost of remodeling a kitchen in the United States is greater than $25,000?

b. What is the name of an alternative nonparametric test? Specify the null and alternative hypotheses of the test.

c. Conduct the test of part **b** using $\alpha = .05$. Interpret your results in the context of the problem.

16.5 COMPARING TWO POPULATIONS: THE WILCOXON RANK SUM TEST FOR INDEPENDENT SAMPLES

Suppose two independent random samples are to be used to compare two populations and the *t*-test of Chapter 9 is inappropriate for making the comparison. We may be unwilling to make assumptions about the form of the underlying population probability distributions or we may be unable to obtain exact values of the sample measurements. If the data can be ranked in order of magnitude for either of these situations, the **Wilcoxon rank sum test** (developed by Frank Wilcoxon) can be used to test the hypothesis that the probability distributions associated with the two populations are equivalent.

For example, suppose six economists who work for the federal government and seven university economists are randomly selected, and each is asked to predict next year's percentage change in cost of living as compared with this year's figure. The objective of the study is to compare the government economists' predictions to those of the university economists. The data are shown in Table 16.1.

The two populations of predictions are those that would be obtained from *all* government and *all* university economists if they could all be questioned. To compare their probability distributions, we first *rank the sample observations as though they were all drawn from the same population.* That is, we pool the measurements

TABLE 16.1   Percentage Cost of Living Change, as Predicted by Government and University Economists

GOVERNMENT ECONOMIST		UNIVERSITY ECONOMIST	
Prediction	Rank	Prediction	Rank
3.1	4	4.4	6
4.8	7	5.8	9
2.3	2	3.9	5
5.6	8	8.7	11
0.0	1	6.3	10
2.9	3	10.5	12
		10.8	13

from both samples and then rank the measurements from the smallest (a rank of 1) to the largest (a rank of 13). The ranks of the 13 economists' predictions are indicated in Table 16.1.

The test statistic for the Wilcoxon test is based on the totals of the ranks for each of the two samples—that is, on the **rank sums**. If the two rank sums are nearly equal, the implication is that there is no evidence that the probability distributions from which the samples were drawn are different. On the other hand, if the two rank sums are very different, the implication is that the two samples may have come from different populations.

For the economists' predictions, we arbitrarily denote the rank sum for government economists by T_A and that for university economists by T_B. Then

$$T_A = 4 + 7 + 2 + 8 + 1 + 3 = 25$$

$$T_B = 6 + 9 + 5 + 11 + 10 + 12 + 13 = 66$$

The sum of T_A and T_B will always equal $n(n+1)/2$, where $n = n_1 + n_2$. So, for this example, $n_1 = 6$, $n_2 = 7$, and

$$T_A + T_B = \frac{13(13+1)}{2} = 91$$

Since $T_A + T_B$ is fixed, a small value for T_A implies a large value for T_B (and vice versa) and a large difference between T_A and T_B. Therefore, the smaller the value of one of the rank sums, the greater the evidence to indicate that the samples were selected from different populations.

The test statistic for this test is the rank sum for the smaller sample; or, in the case where $n_1 = n_2$, either rank sum can be used. Values that locate the rejection region for this rank sum are given in Table XI of Appendix B. A partial reproduction of this table is shown in Table 16.2. The columns of the table represent n_1, the first sample size, and the rows represent n_2, the second sample size. *The* T_L *and* T_U *entries in the table are the boundaries of the lower and upper regions, respectively, for the rank sum associated with the sample that has fewer measurements.* If the sample sizes n_1 and n_2 are the same, either rank sum may be used as the test statistic. To illustrate, suppose $n_1 = 8$ and $n_2 = 10$. For a two-tailed test with $\alpha = .05$, we consult part **a** of the table and find that the null hypothesis will be rejected if the rank sum of sample 1 (the sample with fewer measurements), T, is less than or equal to $T_L = 54$ or greater than or equal to $T_U = 98$. The Wilcoxon rank sum test is summarized in the next box.

TABLE 16.2 **Reproduction of Part of Table XI in Appendix B: Critical Values for the Wilcoxon Rank Sum Test**

$\alpha = .025$ one-tailed; $\alpha = .05$ two-tailed

n_2 \ n_1	3		4		5		6		7		8		9		10	
	T_L	T_U	T_L	T_U	T_L	T_U	T_L	T_U	T_L	T_U	T_L	T_U	T_L	T_U	T_L	T_U
3	5	16	6	18	6	21	7	23	7	26	8	28	8	31	9	33
4	6	18	11	25	12	28	12	32	13	35	14	38	15	41	16	44
5	6	21	12	28	18	37	19	41	20	45	21	49	22	53	24	56
6	7	23	12	32	19	41	26	52	28	56	29	61	31	65	32	70
7	7	26	13	35	20	45	28	56	37	68	39	73	41	78	43	83
8	8	28	14	38	21	49	29	61	39	73	49	87	51	93	54	98
9	8	31	15	41	22	53	31	65	41	78	51	93	63	108	66	114
10	9	33	16	44	24	56	32	70	43	83	54	98	66	114	79	131

Wilcoxon Rank Sum Test: Independent Samples*

One-Tailed Test

H_0: Two sampled populations have identical probability distributions

H_a: The probability distribution for population A is shifted to the right of that for B

Test statistic: The rank sum T associated with the sample with fewer measurements (if sample sizes are equal, either rank sum can be used)

Rejection region: Assuming the smaller sample size is associated with distribution A (if sample sizes are equal, we use the rank sum T_A), we reject the null hypothesis if

$$T_A \geq T_U$$

where T_U is the upper value given by Table XI in Appendix B for the chosen *one-tailed* α value.

Two-Tailed Test

H_0: Two sampled populations have identical probability distributions

H_a: The probability distribution for population A is shifted to the left *or* to the right of that for B

Test statistic: The rank sum T associated with the sample with fewer measurements (if sample sizes are equal, either rank sum can be used)

Rejection region: $T \leq T_L$
  or $T \geq T_U$

where T_L is the lower value given by Table XI in Appendix B for the chosen *two-tailed* α value and T_U is the upper value from Table XI.

[*Note:* If the one-sided alternative is that the probability distribution for A is shifted to the *left* of B (and T_A is the test statistic), we reject the null hypothesis if $T_A \leq T_L$.]

Assumptions: **1.** The two samples are random and independent.

2. The two probability distributions from which the samples are drawn are continuous.

Ties: Assign tied measurements the average of the ranks they would receive if they were unequal but occurred in successive order. For example, if the third-ranked and fourth-ranked measurements are tied, assign each a rank of $(3 + 4)/2 = 3.5$.

---

*Another statistic used for comparing two populations based on independent random samples is the **Mann-Whitney U statistic**. The U statistic is a simple function of the rank sums. It can be shown that the Wilcoxon rank sum test and the Mann-Whitney U-test are equivalent.

Note that the assumptions necessary for the validity of the Wilcoxon rank sum test do not specify the shape or type of probability distribution. However, the distributions are assumed to be continuous so that the probability of tied measurements is 0 (see Chapter 5), and each measurement can be assigned a unique rank. In practice, however, rounding of continuous measurements will sometimes produce ties. As long as the number of ties is small relative to the sample sizes, the Wilcoxon test procedure will still have an approximate significance level of α. The test is not recommended to compare discrete distributions for which many ties are expected.

EXAMPLE 16.2

Test the hypothesis that the university economists' predictions of next year's percentage change in cost of living tend to be higher than the government economists'. Conduct the test using the data in Table 16.1 and $\alpha = .05$.

SOLUTION

H_0: The probability distributions corresponding to the government and university economists' predictions of inflation rate are identical

H_a: The probability distribution for the university economists' predictions lies above (to the right of) the probability distribution for the government economists' predictions*

Test statistic: Since fewer government economists ($n_1 = 6$) than university economists ($n_2 = 7$) were sampled, the test statistic is T_A, the rank sum of the government economists' predictions.

Rejection region: Since the test is one-sided, we consult part **b** of Table XI for the rejection region corresponding to $\alpha = .05$. We reject H_0 only for $T_A \leq T_L$, the lower value from Table XI, since we are specifically testing that the distribution of the government economists' predictions lies *below* the distribution of university economists' predictions, as shown in Figure 16.4. Thus, we reject H_0 if $T_A \leq 30$.

Since T_A, the rank sum of the government economists' predictions in Table 16.1, is 25, it is in the rejection region (see Figure 16.4). Therefore, we can conclude

FIGURE 16.4
Alternative hypothesis and rejection region for Example 16.2

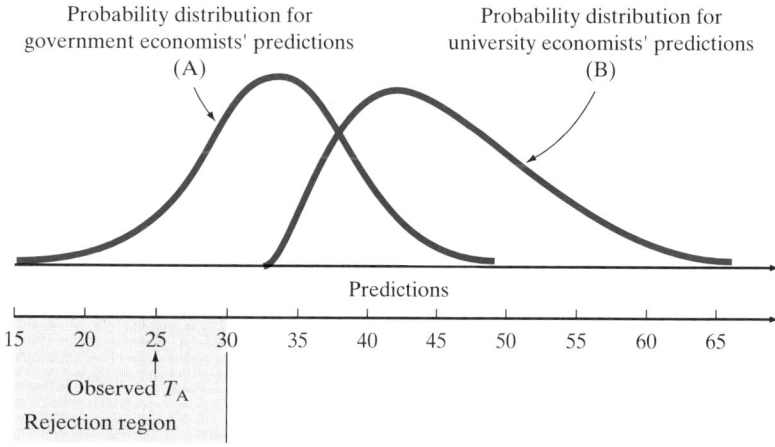

*The alternative hypotheses in this chapter will be stated in terms of a difference in the *location* of the distributions. However, since the shapes of the distributions may also differ under H_a, some of the figures (e.g., Figure 16.4) depicting the alternative hypothesis will show probability distributions with different shapes.

```
              N P A R 1 W A Y   P R O C E D U R E
         Wilcoxon Scores (Rank Sums) for Variable PCTCHNG
                 Classified by Variable ECONOMST

                    Sum of      Expected      Std Dev         Mean
ECONOMST     N      Scores      Under H0      Under H0       Score
A            6       25.0         42.0          7.0       4.16666667
B            7       66.0         49.0          7.0       9.42857143

    Wilcoxon 2-Sample Test (Normal Approximation)
    (with Continuity Correction of .5)

    S=  25.0000      Z= -2.35714     Prob > |Z| = 0.0184

    T-Test approx. Significance =      0.0362

    Kruskal-Wallis Test (Chi-Square Approximation)
      CHISQ=  5.8980     DF= 1     Prob > CHISQ=     0.0152
```

FIGURE 16.5 SAS printout for Example 16.2

that the university economists' predictions tend, in general, to exceed the government economists' predictions. This same conclusion can be reached using a statistical software package. The SAS printout of the analysis is shown in Figure 16.5. Both the test statistic ($T_A = 25$) and two-tailed p-value ($p = .0184$) are highlighted on the printout. The one-tailed p-value, $p = .0184/2 = .0092$, is less than $\alpha = .05$, leading us to reject H_0.

Table XI in Appendix B gives values of T_L and T_U for values of n_1 and n_2 less than or equal to 10. When both sample sizes n_1 and n_2 are 10 or larger, the sampling distribution of T_A can be approximated by a normal distribution with mean and variance

$$E(T_A) = \frac{n_1(n_1 + n_2 + 1)}{2} \quad \text{and} \quad \sigma^2_{T_A} = \frac{n_1 n_2(n_1 + n_2 + 1)}{12}$$

Therefore, for $n_1 \geq 10$ and $n_2 \geq 10$ we can conduct the Wilcoxon rank sum test using the familiar z-test of Chapters 8 and 9. The test is summarized in the next box.

Wilcoxon Rank Sum Test: Large Independent Samples

One-Tailed Test

H_0: Two sampled populations have identical probability distributions

H_a: The probability distribution for population A is shifted to the right of that for B

Two-Tailed Test

H_0: Two sampled populations have identical probability distributions

H_a: The probability distribution for population A is shifted to the left *or* to the right of that for B

$$\text{Test statistic: } z = \frac{T_A - \dfrac{n_1(n_1 + n_2 + 1)}{2}}{\sqrt{\dfrac{n_1 n_2(n_1 + n_2 + 1)}{12}}}$$

Rejection region: $z > z_\alpha$

Rejection region: $|z| > z_{\alpha/2}$

Assumptions: $n_1 \geq 10$ and $n_2 \geq 10$

Assumptions: $n_1 \geq 10$ and $n_2 \geq 10$

EXERCISES 16.11–16.21

Note: Exercises marked with 💾 *contain data for computer analysis on a 3.5" disk (file name in parentheses).*

Learning the Mechanics

16.11 Specify the test statistic and the rejection region for the Wilcoxon rank sum test for independent samples in each of the following situations:

    a. $n_A = 10, n_B = 6, \alpha = .10$

H_0: Two probability distributions, A and B, are identical

H_a: Probability distribution for population A is shifted to the right or left of the probability distribution for population B

    b. $n_A = 5, n_B = 7, \alpha = .05$

H_0: Two probability distributions, A and B, are identical

H_a: Probability distribution for population A is shifted to the right of the probability distribution for population B

    c. $n_A = 9, n_B = 8, \alpha = .025$

H_0: Two probability distributions, A and B, are identical

H_a: Probability distribution for population A is shifted to the left of the probability distribution for population B

    d. $n_A = 15, n_B = 15, \alpha = .05$

H_0: Two probability distributions, A and B, are identical

H_a: Probability distribution for population A is shifted to the right or left of the probability distribution for population B

16.12 Suppose you want to compare two treatments, A and B. In particular, you wish to determine whether the distribution for population B is shifted to the right of the distribution for population A. You plan to use the Wilcoxon rank sum test.

    a. Specify the null and alternative hypotheses you would test.

    b. Suppose you obtained the following independent random samples of observations on experimental units subjected to the two treatments:

Sample A: 37, 40, 33, 29, 42, 33, 35, 28, 34

Sample B: 65, 35, 47, 52

    Conduct a test of the hypotheses described in part **a**. Test using $\alpha = .05$.

16.13 Explain the difference between the one-tailed and two-tailed versions of the Wilcoxon rank sum test for independent random samples.

16.14 Independent random samples are selected from two populations. The data are shown in the table.

    a. Use the Wilcoxon rank sum test to determine whether the data provide sufficient evidence to indicate a shift in the locations of the probability distributions of the sampled populations. Test using $\alpha = .05$.

Population 1		Population 2		
15	16	5	9	5
10	13	12	8	10
12	8	9	4	

    b. Do the data provide sufficient evidence to indicate that the probability distribution for population 1 is shifted to the right of the probability distribution for population 2? Use the Wilcoxon rank sum test with $\alpha = .05$.

Applying the Concepts

16.15 💾 (X16.015) University of Queensland researchers J. Hann and R. Weber sampled private sector and public sector organizations in Australia to study the planning undertaken by their information systems departments (*Management Science*, July 1996). As part of that process they asked each sample organization how much it had spent on information systems and technology in the previous fiscal year as a percentage of the organization's total revenues. The results are reported in the table.

Private Sector	Public Sector
2.58%	5.40%
5.05	2.55
.05	9.00
2.10	10.55
4.30	1.02
2.25	5.11
2.50	12.42
1.94	1.67
2.33	3.33

Source: Adapted from Hann, J., and Weber, R. "Information systems planning: A model and empirical tests." *Management Science*, Vol. 42, No. 2, July, 1996, pp. 1043–1064.

    a. Do the two sampled populations have identical probability distributions or is the distribution for public sector organizations in Australia located to the right of Australia's private sector firms? Test using $\alpha = .05$.

    b. Is the *p*-value for the test less than or greater than .05? Justify your answer.

    c. What assumptions must be met to ensure the validity of the test you conducted in part **a**?

16.16 💾 (X16.016) In Exercise 9.18, the solid waste generation rates for cities in industrialized countries and cities in middle-income countries were investigated. In this exercise, the focus is on middle-income countries versus low-income countries. The table, extracted from the *International Journal* *of Environmental Health Research* (1994), reports waste generation values (kg per capita per day) for two independent samples. Do the rates differ for the two categories of countries?

Cities of Low-Income Countries		Cities of Middle-Income Countries	
Jakarta	.60	Singapore	.87
Surabaya	.52	Hong Kong	.85
Bandung	.55	Medellin	.54
Lahore	.60	Kano	.46
Karachi	.50	Manila	.50
Calcutta	.51	Cairo	.50
Kanpur	.50	Tunis	.56

Source: Al-Momani, A. H. "Solid-waste management: Sampling, analysis and assessment of household waste in the city of Amman." *International Journal of Environmental Health Research,* 1994, pp. 208–222.

a. Which nonparametric hypothesis-testing procedures could be used to answer the question?
b. Specify the null and alternative hypotheses of the test.
c. Conduct the test using $\alpha = .01$. Interpret the results in the context of the problem.

16.17 (X16.017) Are tax assessments fair? One measure of "fairness" is the ratio of a property's assessed value to its market value—or a proxy for market value such as a recent sale price (*Journal of Business and Economic Statistics,* Jan. 1985). The accompanying table lists assessment ratios for random samples of 10 properties in neighborhood A and eight properties in neighborhood B.

Neighborhood A		Neighborhood B	
.850	.880	.911	.835
1.060	.895	.770	.800
.910	.844	.815	.793
.813	.965	.748	.796
.737	.875		

a. Use the Wilcoxon rank sum test to investigate the fairness of the assessments between the two neighborhoods. Use $\alpha = .05$ and interpret your findings in the context of the problem.
b. Under what circumstances could the two-sample *t*-test of Chapter 9 be used to investigate the fairness issue of part **a**?
c. What assumptions are necessary to ensure the validity of the test you conducted in part **a**?

16.18 (X16.018) The data in the table, extracted from *Technometrics* (Feb. 1986), represent daily accumulated stream flow and precipitation (in inches) for two U.S. Geological Survey stations in Colorado. Conduct a test to determine whether the distributions of daily accumulated stream flow and precipitation for the two stations differ in location. Use $\alpha = .10$. Why is a nonparametric test appropriate for this data?

Station 1			Station 2		
127.96	108.91	100.85	114.79	85.54	280.55
210.07	178.21	85.89	109.11	117.64	145.11
203.24	285.37		330.33	302.74	95.36

Source: Gastwirth, J. L., and Mahmoud, H. "An efficient robust nonparametric test for scale change for data from a gamma distribution." *Technometrics,* Vol. 28, No. 1, Feb. 1986, p. 83 (Table 2).

16.19 (X16.019) Recall that the variance of a binomial sample proportion, $\hat{p}$, depends on the value of the population parameter, p. As a consequence, the variance of a sample percentage, $(100\hat{p})\%$, also depends on p. Thus if you conduct an unpaired *t*-test (Section 9.1) to compare the means of two populations of percentages, you may be violating the assumption that $\sigma_1^2 = \sigma_2^2$, upon which the *t*-test is based. If the disparity in the variances is large, you will obtain more reliable test results using the Wilcoxon rank sum test for independent samples. In Exercise 9.21, we used a Student's *t*-test to compare the mean annual percentages of labor turnover between U.S. and Japanese manufacturers of air conditioners. The annual percentage turnover rates for five U.S. and five Japanese plants are shown in the table. Do the data provide sufficient evidence to indicate that the mean annual percentage turnover for American plants exceeds the corresponding mean for Japanese plants? Test using the Wilcoxon rank sum test with $\alpha = .05$. Do your test conclusions agree with those of the *t*-test in Exercise 9.21?

U.S. Plants	Japanese Plants
7.11%	3.52%
6.06	2.02
8.00	4.91
6.87	3.22
4.77	1.92

16.20 (X16.020) A major razor blade manufacturer advertises that its twin-blade disposable razor "gets you lots more shaves" than any single-blade disposable razor on the market. A rival company that has been very successful in selling single-blade razors plans to test this claim. Independent random samples of eight single-blade users and eight twin-blade users are taken, and the number of shaves that each gets before indicating a preference to change blades is recorded. The results are shown in the table.

Twin Blades		Single Blades	
8	15	10	13
17	10	6	14
9	6	3	5
11	12	7	7

```
               N P A R 1 W A Y   P R O C E D U R E
        Wilcoxon Scores (Rank Sums) for Variable QUALITY
               Classified by Variable FIRM

                     Sum of      Expected       Std Dev        Mean
      FIRM      N     Scores     Under H0       Under H0       Score

      GOOD      16  290.500000     248.0       23.9858196   18.1562500
      POOR      14  174.500000     217.0       23.9858196   12.4642857
                Average Scores were used for Ties
        Wilcoxon 2-Sample Test (Normal Approximation)
        (with Continuity Correction of .5)

        S=  174.500     Z= -1.75103     Prob > |Z| = 0.0799

        T-Test approx. Significance =    0.0905

        Kruskal-Wallis Test (Chi-Square Approximation)
        CHISQ=  3.1396     DF= 1     Prob > CHISQ=    0.0764
```

a. Do the data support the twin-blade manufacturer's claim? Use $\alpha = .05$.

b. Do you think this experiment was designed in the best possible way? If not, what design might have been better?

c. What assumptions are necessary for the validity of the test you performed in part **a**? Do the assumptions seem reasonable for this application?

16.21 **(X16.021)** A *management information system* (MIS) is a computer-based information-processing system designed to support the operations, management, and decision functions of an organization. The development of an MIS involves three stages: definition, physical design, and implementation of the system (Davis and Hamilton, 1993). The successful implementation of an MIS is related to the quality of the entire development process. It could fail due to inadequate planning by and negotiating between the designers and the future users of the system prior to construction, or simply because the users were improperly trained. Thirty firms that recently implemented an MIS were surveyed: 16 were satisfied with the implementation results, 14 were not. Each firm was asked to rate the quality of the planning and negotiation stages of the development process,

using a scale of 0 to 100, with higher numbers indicating better quality. (A score of 100 indicates that all the problems that occurred in the planning and negotiation stages were successfully resolved, while 0 indicates that none were resolved.) The results obtained are shown in the table.

Firms with a Good MIS			Firms with a Poor MIS		
52	59	95	60	40	90
70	60	90	50	55	85
40	90	86	55	65	80
80	75	95	70	55	90
82	80	93	41	70	
65					

a. The Wilcoxon rank sum test was used to compare the quality of the development processes of successfully and unsuccessfully implemented MISs. The results are shown in the SAS printout above. Determine whether the distribution of quality scores for successfully implemented systems lies above the distribution of scores for unsuccessfully implemented systems. Test using $\alpha = .05$.

b. Under what circumstances could you use the two-sample *t*-test of Chapter 9 to conduct the same test?

16.4   COMPARING TWO POPULATIONS: THE WILCOXON SIGNED RANK TEST FOR THE PAIRED DIFFERENCE EXPERIMENT

Nonparametric techniques can also be employed to compare two probability distributions when a paired difference design is used. For example, consumer preferences for two competing products are often compared by having each of a

TABLE 16.3 **Softness Ratings of Paper**

Judge	PRODUCT A	PRODUCT B	DIFFERENCE (A − B)	Absolute Value of Difference	Rank of Absolute Value
1	6	4	2	2	5
2	8	5	3	3	7.5
3	4	5	−1	1	2
4	9	8	1	1	2
5	4	1	3	3	7.5
6	7	9	−2	2	5
7	6	2	4	4	9
8	5	3	2	2	5
9	6	7	−1	1	2
10	8	2	6	6	10

$$T_+ = \text{Sum of positive ranks} = 46$$
$$T_- = \text{Sum of negative ranks} = 9$$

sample of consumers rate both products. Thus, the ratings have been paired on each consumer. Here is an example of this type of experiment.

For some paper products, softness is an important consideration in determining consumer acceptance. One method of determining softness is to have judges give a sample of the products a softness rating. Suppose each of ten judges is given a sample of two products that a company wants to compare. Each judge rates the softness of each product on a scale from 1 to 10, with higher ratings implying a softer product. The results of the experiment are shown in Table 16.3.

Since this is a paired difference experiment, we analyze the differences between the measurements (see Section 9.2). However, the nonparametric approach—called the **Wilcoxon signed rank test**—requires that we calculate the ranks of the absolute values of the differences between the measurements, that is, the ranks of the differences after removing any minus signs. *Note that tied absolute differences are assigned the average of the ranks they would receive if they were unequal but successive measurements.* After the absolute differences are ranked, the sum of the ranks of the positive differences of the original measurements, T_+, and the sum of the ranks of the negative differences of the original measurements, T_-, are computed.

We are now prepared to test the nonparametric hypotheses:

H_0: The probability distributions of the ratings for products A and B are identical

H_a: The probability distributions of the ratings differ (in location) for the two products (Note that this is a two-sided alternative and that it implies a two-tailed test.)

Test statistic: $T = $ Smaller of the positive and negative rank sums T_+ and T_-

The smaller the value of T, the greater the evidence to indicate that the two probability distributions differ in location. The rejection region for T can be determined by consulting Table XII in Appendix B (part of the table is shown in Table 16.4).

This table gives a value T_0 for both one-tailed and two-tailed tests for each value of n, the number of matched pairs. For a two-tailed test with $\alpha = .05$, we will

TABLE 16.4   Reproduction of Part of Table XII of Appendix B: Critical Values for the Wilcoxon Paired Difference Signed Rank Test

One-Tailed	Two-Tailed	$n = 5$	$n = 6$	$n = 7$	$n = 8$	$n = 9$	$n = 10$
$\alpha = .05$	$\alpha = .10$	1	2	4	6	8	11
$\alpha = .025$	$\alpha = .05$		1	2	4	6	8
$\alpha = .01$	$\alpha = .02$			0	2	3	5
$\alpha = .005$	$\alpha = .01$				0	2	3
		$n = 11$	$n = 12$	$n = 13$	$n = 14$	$n = 15$	$n = 16$
$\alpha = .05$	$\alpha = .10$	14	17	21	26	30	36
$\alpha = .025$	$\alpha = .05$	11	14	17	21	25	30
$\alpha = .01$	$\alpha = .02$	7	10	13	16	20	24
$\alpha = .005$	$\alpha = .01$	5	7	10	13	16	19
		$n = 17$	$n = 18$	$n = 19$	$n = 20$	$n = 21$	$n = 22$
$\alpha = .05$	$\alpha = .10$	41	47	54	60	68	75
$\alpha = .025$	$\alpha = .05$	35	40	46	52	59	66
$\alpha = .01$	$\alpha = .02$	28	33	38	43	49	56
$\alpha = .005$	$\alpha = .01$	23	28	32	37	43	49
		$n = 23$	$n = 24$	$n = 25$	$n = 26$	$n = 27$	$n = 28$
$\alpha = .05$	$\alpha = .10$	83	92	101	110	120	130
$\alpha = .025$	$\alpha = .05$	73	81	90	98	107	117
$\alpha = .01$	$\alpha = .02$	62	69	77	85	93	102
$\alpha = .005$	$\alpha = .01$	55	61	68	76	84	92

reject H_0 if $T \leq T_0$. You can see in Table 16.4 that the value of T_0 that locates the boundary of the rejection region for the judges' ratings for $\alpha = .05$ and $n = 10$ pairs of observations is 8. Thus, the rejection region for the test (see Figure 16.6) is

Rejection region: $T \leq 8$ for $\alpha = .05$

Since the smaller rank sum for the paper data, $T_- = 9$, does not fall within the rejection region, the experiment has not provided sufficient evidence to indicate that the two paper products differ with respect to their softness ratings at the $\alpha = .05$ level.

Note that if a significance level of $\alpha = .10$ had been used, the rejection region would have been $T \leq 11$ and we would have rejected H_0. In other words, the samples do provide evidence that the probability distributions of the softness ratings differ at the $\alpha = .10$ significance level.

The Wilcoxon signed rank test is summarized in the following box. Note that the difference measurements are assumed to have a continuous probability distribution so that the absolute differences will have unique ranks. Although tied (absolute) differences can be assigned ranks by averaging, the number of ties should be small relative to the number of observations to ensure the validity of the test.

FIGURE 16.6

Rejection region for paired difference experiment

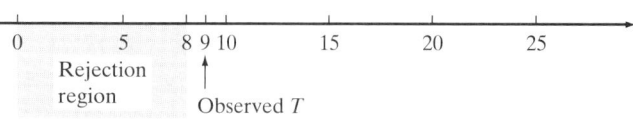

Wilcoxon Signed Rank Test for a Paired Difference Experiment

One-Tailed Test	**Two-Tailed Test**
H_0: Two sampled populations have identical probability distributions	H_0: Two sampled populations have identical probability distributions
H_a: The probability distribution for population A is shifted to the right of that for population B	H_a: The probability distribution for population A is shifted to the right *or* to the left of that for population B
Test statistic: T_-, the negative rank sum (we assume the differences are computed by subtracting each paired B measurement from the corresponding A measurement)	*Test statistic*: T, the smaller of the positive and negative rank sums, T_+ and T_-
Rejection region: $T_- \leq T_0$, where T_0 is found in Table XII (in Appendix B) for the one-tailed significance level α and the number of untied pairs, n.	*Rejection region*: $T \leq T_0$, where T_0 is found in Table XII (in Appendix B) for the two-tailed significance level α and the number of untied pairs, n.

[*Note:* If the alternative hypothesis is that the probability distribution for A is shifted to the left of B, we use T_+ as the test statistic and reject H_0 if $T_+ \leq T_0$.]

Assumptions: 1. The sample of differences is randomly selected from the population of differences.

2. The probability distribution from which the sample of paired differences is drawn is continuous.

Ties: Assign tied absolute differences the average of the ranks they would receive if they were unequal but occurred in successive order. For example, if the third-ranked and fourth-ranked differences are tied, assign both a rank of $(3 + 4)/2 = 3.5$.

EXAMPLE 16.3

Suppose the U.S. Consumer Product Safety Commission (CPSC) wants to test the hypothesis that New York City electrical contractors are more likely to install unsafe electrical outlets in urban homes than in suburban homes. A pair of homes, one urban and one suburban and both serviced by the same electrical contractor, is chosen for each of ten randomly selected electrical contractors. A CPSC inspector assigns each of the 20 homes a safety rating between 1 and 10, with higher

---

TABLE 16.5 Electrical Safety Ratings for 10 Pairs of New York City Homes

	LOCATION		**DIFFERENCE**	
Contractor	**Urban A**	**Suburban B**	**(A − B)**	**Rank of Absolute Difference**
1	7	9	−2	4.5
2	4	5	−1	2
3	8	8	0	(Eliminated)
4	9	8	1	2
5	3	6	−3	6
6	6	10	−4	7.5
7	8	9	−1	2
8	10	8	2	4.5
9	9	4	5	9
10	5	9	−4	7.5

Positive rank sum = $T_+ = 15.5$

FIGURE 16.7
The alternative
hypothesis for
Example 16.3:
We expect T_+ to
be small

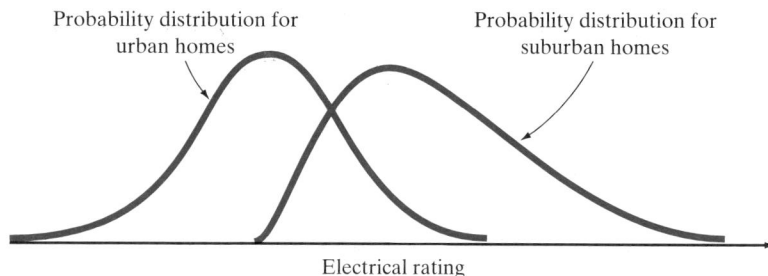

numbers implying safer electrical conditions. The results are shown in Table 16.5. Use the Wilcoxon signed rank test to determine whether the CPSC hypothesis is supported at the $\alpha = .05$ level.

SOLUTION

The null and alternative hypotheses are

H_0: The probability distributions of home electrical ratings are identical for urban and suburban homes

H_a: The electrical ratings for suburban homes tend to exceed the electrical ratings for urban homes

Since a paired difference design was used (the homes were selected in urban-suburban pairs so that the electrical contractor was the same for both), we first calculate the difference between the ratings for each pair of homes, and then rank the absolute values of the differences (see Table 16.5). Note that one pair of ratings was the same (both 8), and the resulting 0 difference contributes to neither the positive nor the negative rank sum. Thus, we eliminate this pair from the calculation of the test statistic.

Test statistic: T_+, the positive rank sum

In Table 16.5, we compute the urban minus suburban rating differences, and if the alternative hypothesis is true, we would expect most of these differences to be negative. Or, in other words, we would expect the *positive* rank sum T_+ to be small if the alternative hypothesis is true (see Figure 16.7).

Rejection region: For $\alpha = .05$, from Table XII of Appendix B, we use $n = 9$ (remember, one pair of observations was eliminated) to find the rejection region for this one-tailed test: $T_+ \leq 8$

Since the computed value $T_+ = 15.5$ exceeds the critical value of 8, we conclude that this sample provides insufficient evidence at $\alpha = .05$ to support the alternative hypothesis. We *cannot* conclude on the basis of this sample information that suburban homes have safer electrical outlets than urban homes. A MINITAB printout of the analysis, shown in Figure 16.8, confirms this conclusion. The *p*-value of the test (highlighted) is .221, which exceeds $\alpha = .05$.

FIGURE 16.8
MINITAB printout for
Example 16.3

```
TEST OF MEDIAN = 0.000000 VERSUS MEDIAN L.T. 0.000000

                  N FOR    WILCOXON                ESTIMATED
           N     TEST    STATISTIC   P-VALUE        MEDIAN
AminusB    10       9        15.5     0.221        -1.000
```

STATISTICS IN ACTION

16.1 REANALYZING THE SCALLOP WEIGHT DATA

In Statistics in Action 7.1: Scallops, Sampling, and the Law, you were presented with the problem of determining whether a fishing vessel was in violation of the minimum weight restriction on scallops established by the U.S. Fisheries and Wildlife Service. Recall that the government requires that "the average meat per scallop weigh at least $1/36$ of a pound" in order to prevent the harvesting of baby scallops.

The vessel in question arrived at a New England port with 11,000 bags of scallops. To check if the vessel was in compliance with the weight standard, the harbormaster randomly selected 18 bags for weighing. The data, reproduced in Table 16.6, are the scallop weight measurements (expressed as a multiple of $1/36$ of a pound) for the 18 sampled bags.

Focus

a. In Statistics in Action 7.1, you analyzed the data using a parametric method. Explain why the method may not yield valid inferences.

b. Use an appropriate nonparametric method to analyze the data of Table 16.6. Make an inference about whether or not the fishing vessel was in violation of the minimum weight restriction. (The data is available on disk under the file name TAB07.005.)

TABLE 16.6 Scallop Weight Measurements for 18 Bags Sampled (Statistics in Action 16.1)

.93	.88	.85	.91	.91	.84	.90	.98	.88
.89	.98	.87	.91	.92	.99	1.14	1.06	.93

Source: Bennett, A. "Misapplications review: Jail terms." *Interfaces,* Vol. 25, No. 2, Mar.–Apr. 1995, p. 20.

As is the case for the rank sum test for independent samples, the sampling distribution of the signed rank statistic can be approximated by a normal distribution when the number n of paired observations is large (say, $n \geq 25$). The large-sample z-test is summarized in the next box.

Wilcoxon Signed Rank Test for a Paired Difference Experiment: Large Sample

One-Tailed Test

H_0: Two sampled populations have identical probability distributions

H_a: The probability distribution for population A is shifted to the right of that for population B

Two-Tailed Test

H_0: Two sampled populations have identical probability distributions

H_a: The probability distribution for population A is shifted to the right *or* to the left of that for population B

Test statistic: $z = \dfrac{T_+ - \dfrac{n(n+1)}{4}}{\sqrt{\dfrac{n(n+1)(2n+1)}{24}}}$

Rejection region: $z > z_\alpha$

Assumptions: $n \geq 25$

Rejection region: $|z| > z_{\alpha/2}$

Assumptions: $n \geq 25$

EXERCISES   16.22–16.33

Note: Exercises marked with 💾 contain data for computer analysis on a 3.5" disk (file name in parentheses).

Learning the Mechanics

16.22 Specify the test statistic and the rejection region for the Wilcoxon signed rank test for the paired difference design in each of the following situations:

  a. $n = 30, \alpha = .10$

  H_0: Two probability distributions, A and B, are identical

  H_a: Probability distribution for population A is shifted to the right or left of probability distribution for population B

  b. $n = 20, \alpha = .05$

  H_0: Two probability distributions, A and B, are identical

  H_a: Probability distribution for population A is shifted to the right of the probability distribution for population B

  c. $n = 8, \alpha = .005$

  H_0: Two probability distributions, A and B, are identical

  H_a: Probability distribution for population A is shifted to the left of the probability distribution for population B

16.23 **(X16.023)** Suppose you want to test a hypothesis that two treatments, A and B, are equivalent against the alternative hypothesis that the responses for A tend to be larger than those for B. You plan to use a paired difference experiment and to analyze the resulting data using the Wilcoxon signed rank test.

  a. Specify the null and alternative hypotheses you would test.

  b. Suppose the paired difference experiment yielded the data in the following table. Conduct the test of part **a**. Test using $\alpha = .025$.

	TREATMENT				TREATMENT	
Pair	**A**	**B**		**Pair**	**A**	**B**
1	54	45		6	77	75
2	60	45		7	74	63
3	98	87		8	29	30
4	43	31		9	63	59
5	82	71		10	80	82

16.24 Explain the difference between the one- and two-tailed versions of the Wilcoxon signed rank test for the paired difference experiment.

16.25 In order to conduct the Wilcoxon signed rank test, why do we need to assume the probability distribution of differences is continuous?

16.26 Suppose you wish to test a hypothesis that two treatments, A and B, are equivalent against the alternative that the responses for A tend to be larger than those for B.

  a. If the number of pairs equals 25, give the rejection region for the large-sample Wilcoxon signed rank test for $\alpha = .05$.

  b. Suppose that $T_+ = 273$. State your test conclusions.

  c. Find the p-value for the test and interpret it.

16.27 A paired difference experiment with $n = 30$ pairs yielded $T_+ = 354$.

  a. Specify the null and alternative hypotheses that should be used in conducting a hypothesis test to determine whether the probability distribution for population A is located to the right of that for population B.

  b. Conduct the test of part **a** using $\alpha = .05$.

  c. What is the approximate p-value of the test of part **b**?

  d. What assumptions are necessary to ensure the validity of the test you performed in part **b**?

Applying the Concepts

16.28 **(X16.028)** An atlas is a compendium of geographic, economic, and social information that describes one or more geographic regions. Atlases are used by the sales and marketing functions of businesses, local chambers of commerce, and educators. One of the most critical aspects of a new atlas design is its thematic content. In a survey of atlas users (*Journal of Geography*, May/June 1995), a large sample of high school teachers in British Columbia ranked 12 thematic atlas topics for usefulness. The consensus rankings of the teachers (based on the percentage of teachers who responded they "would definitely use" the topic) are given in the table.

	RANKINGS	
Theme	**High School Teachers**	**Geography Alumni**
Tourism	10	2
Physical	2	1
Transportation	7	3
People	1	6
History	2	5
Climate	6	4
Forestry	5	8
Agriculture	7	10
Fishing	9	7
Energy	2	8
Mining	10	11
Manufacturing	12	12

Source: Keller, C. P., *et al.* "Planning the next generation of regional atlases: Input from educators." *Journal of Geography*, Vol. 94, No. 3, May/June 1995, p. 413 (Table 1).

These teacher rankings were compared to the rankings of a group of university geography alumni made three years earlier. Compare the distributions of theme rankings for the two groups with an appropriate nonparametric test. Use $\alpha = .05$. Interpret the results practically.

16.29 A study published in the *Journal of Business Communications* (Fall 1985) considered the question: "Which is the more effective means of dealing with complex group problem-solving tasks—face-to-face meetings or video teleconferencing?" Using an experiment similar to the one described below, two Stetson University researchers concluded that video teleconferencing may be the more effective method. Ten groups of four people each were randomly assigned both to a specific communication setting (face-to-face or video teleconferencing) and to one of two specific complex problems. On completion of the problem-solving task, the same groups were placed in the alternative communication setting and asked to complete the second problem-solving task. The percentage of each problem task correctly completed was recorded for each group, with the results given in the accompanying table.

Group	Face-to-Face	Video Teleconferencing
1	65%	75%
2	82	80
3	54	60
4	69	65
5	40	55
6	85	90
7	98	98
8	35	40
9	85	89
10	70	80

a. What type of experimental design was used in this study?
b. Specify the null and alternative hypotheses that should be used in determining whether the data provide sufficient evidence to conclude that the problem-solving performance of video teleconferencing groups is superior to that of groups that interact face-to-face.
c. Conduct the hypothesis test of part **b**. Use $\alpha = .05$. Interpret the results of your test in the context of the problem.
d. What is the *p*-value of the test in part **c**?

16.30 In Exercise 9.37 inflation forecasts of nine economists that were made in June 1995 and in January 1996 were reported. These forecasts are reproduced here. To determine whether the economists were more optimistic about the prospects for low inflation in late 1996 than they were for late 1995, the Wilcoxon signed rank test will be applied.

	INFLATION FORECASTS (%)	
Economist	June 1995 Forecast for 11/95	January 1996 Forecast for 11/96
Maureen Allyn	3.1	2.4
Wayne Angell	3.4	3.1
David Blitzer	3.0	3.1
Michael Cosgrove	4.0	3.5
Gail Fosler	3.7	3.8
Irwin Kellner	3.3	2.3
Donald Ratajczak	3.5	2.9
Thomas Synott	3.5	3.2
John Williams	3.3	2.6

Source: The Wall Street Journal, Jan. 2, 1996.

a. Specify the null and alternative hypotheses you would employ.
b. Conduct the test using $\alpha = .05$. Interpret your results in the context of the problem.
c. Explain the difference between a Type I and a Type II error in the context of the problem.

16.31 Traditionally, workers in the United States have had a fixed eight-hour workday. A job-scheduling innovation that has helped managers overcome motivation and absenteeism problems associated with the fixed workday is a concept called *flextime*. This flexible working hours program permits employees to design their own 40-hour work week to meet their personal needs (*New York Times,* Mar. 31, 1996). The management of a large manufacturing firm may adopt a flextime program for its administrators and professional employees, depending on the success or failure of a pilot program. Ten employees were randomly selected and given a questionnaire designed to measure their attitude toward their job. Each was then permitted to design and follow a flextime workday. After six months, attitudes toward their jobs were again measured. The resulting attitude scores are displayed in the table. The higher the score, the more favorable the employee's attitude toward his or her work. Use a nonparametric test procedure to evaluate the success of the pilot flextime program. Test using $\alpha = .05$.

Employee	Before	After	Employee	Before	After
1	54	68	6	82	88
2	25	42	7	94	90
3	80	80	8	72	81
4	76	91	9	33	39
5	63	70	10	90	93

16.32 The stocks that comprise Standard and Poor's 500 Index account for 69% of the market capitalization of all U.S. stocks. The index is a benchmark against which investors compare the performance of individual stocks. A sample of eight of the man-

```
- - - - - Wilcoxon Matched-pairs Signed-ranks Test

        PCHD
with EERF

     Mean Rank    Cases
         8.40       10    - Ranks (EERF Lt PCHD)
         7.20        5    + Ranks (EERF Gt PCHD)
                     0      Ties (EERF Eq PCHD)
                    --
                    15 Total

        Z = -1.3631              2-tailed P = .1728
```

ufacturing companies included in the index were evaluated for profitability in 1995 and 1996. The profitability measure used was net margin. *Net margin* is defined as net income from continuing operations before extraordinary items as a percentage of sales.

Firm	1996 Net Margin (%)	1995 Net Margin (%)
Tyco International	6.1	5.6
Applied Materials	11.6	15.6
Caterpillar	8.2	7.1
Ingersoll-Rand	5.3	4.7
Johnson Controls	2.3	2.4
3M	10.6	9.7
Black & Decker	3.2	4.5
Rubbermaid	6.5	2.6

Source: Business Week, Mar. 24, 1997, pp. 119–149.

a. Is there sufficient evidence to conclude that U.S. manufacturing firms were more profitable in 1996 than 1995? Test using $\alpha = .05$.

b. What assumptions must be met to ensure the validity of the test in part **a**?

16.33 In Exercise 9.92, you compared matched pairs of measurements on the radon exhalation rate (a measure of radiation) of 15 soil samples from waste gypsum and phosphate mounds in Polk County, Florida. Each soil sample was measured for exhalation rate by the Polk County Health Department (PCHD) and the Eastern Environmental Radiation Facility (EERF). The data are reproduced below. Do the data provide sufficient evidence (at $\alpha = .05$) to indicate that one of the measuring facilities, PCHD or EERF, tends to read higher or lower than the other? Use the SPSS Wilcoxon signed rank printout above to make your conclusions.

Charcoal Canister No.	PCHD	EERF
71	1,709.79	1,479.0
58	357.17	257.8
84	1,150.94	1,287.0
91	1,572.69	1,395.0
44	558.33	416.5
43	4,132.28	3,993.0
79	1,489.86	1,351.0
61	3,017.48	1,813.0
85	393.55	187.7
46	880.84	630.4
4	2,996.49	3,707.0
20	2,367.40	2,791.0
36	599.84	706.8
42	538.37	618.5
55	2,770.23	2,639.0

Source: Horton, T. R. "Preliminary radiological assessment of radon exhalation from phosphate gypsum piles and inactive uranium mill tailings piles." EPA-520/5-79-004. Washington, D.C.: Environmental Protection Agency, 1979.

16.5 THE KRUSKAL-WALLIS *H*-TEST FOR A COMPLETELY RANDOMIZED DESIGN

In Chapter 15 we used an analysis of variance and the *F*-test to compare the means of p populations (treatments) based on random sampling from populations that were normally distributed with a common variance σ^2. We now present a nonparametric technique—**Kruskal-Wallis *H*-test**—for comparing the populations that requires no assumptions concerning the population probability distributions.

A health administrator wants to compare the unoccupied bed space for three hospitals in the same city. She randomly selects 10 different days from the records of each hospital and lists the number of unoccupied beds for each day

TABLE 16.7   **Number of Available Beds**

HOSPITAL 1		HOSPITAL 2		HOSPITAL 3	
Beds	**Rank**	**Beds**	**Rank**	**Beds**	**Rank**
6	5	34	25	13	9.5
38	27	28	19	35	26
3	2	42	30	19	15
17	13	13	9.5	4	3
11	8	40	29	29	20
30	21	31	22	0	1
15	11	9	7	7	6
16	12	32	23	33	24
25	17	39	28	18	14
5	4	27	18	24	16
$R_1 = 120$		$R_2 = 210.5$		$R_3 = 134.5$	

(see Table 16.7). Because the number of unoccupied beds per day may occasionally be quite large, it is conceivable that the population distributions of data may be skewed to the right and that this type of data may not satisfy the assumptions necessary for a parametric comparison of the population means. We therefore use a nonparametric analysis and base our comparison on the rank sums for the three sets of sample data. Just as with two independent samples (Section 16.3), the ranks are computed for each observation according to the relative magnitude of the measurements *when the data for all the samples are combined* (see Table 16.7). Ties are treated as they were for the Wilcoxon rank sum and signed rank tests by assigning the average value of the ranks to each of the tied observations.

We test

H_0: The probability distributions of the number of unoccupied beds are the same for all three hospitals

H_a: At least two of the three hospitals have probability distributions of the number of unoccupied beds that differ in location

If we denote the three sample rank sums by R_1, R_2, and R_3, the test statistic is given by

$$H = \frac{12}{n(n+1)}\sum\frac{R_j^2}{n_j} - 3(n+1)$$

where n_j is the number of measurements in the jth sample and n is the total sample size ($n = n_1 + n_2 + \cdots + n_p$). For the data in Table 16.7, we have $n_1 = n_2 = n_3 = 10$ and $n = 30$. The rank sums are $R_1 = 120$, $R_2 = 210.5$, and $R_3 = 134.5$. Thus,

$$H = \frac{12}{30(31)}\left[\frac{(120)^2}{10} + \frac{(210.5)^2}{10} + \frac{(134.5)^2}{10}\right] - 3(31)$$

$$= 99.097 - 93 = 6.097$$

The H statistic measures the extent to which the p samples differ with respect to their relative ranks. This is more easily seen by writing H in an alternative but equivalent form:

$$H = \frac{12}{n(n+1)}\sum n_j(\overline{R}_j - \overline{R})^2$$

FIGURE 16.9
Several χ^2 probability distributions

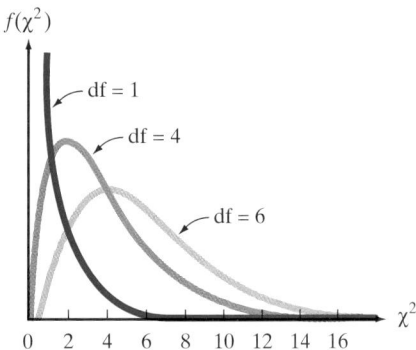

where $\overline{R}_j$ is the mean rank corresponding to sample *j*, and $\overline{R}$ is the mean of all the ranks [that is, $\overline{R} = \frac{1}{2}(n + 1)$]. Thus, the *H* statistic is 0 if all samples have the same mean rank, and becomes increasingly large as the distance between the sample mean rank grows.

If the null hypothesis is true, the distribution of *H* in repeated sampling is approximately a χ^2 **(chi-square) distribution**. This approximation for the sampling distribution of *H* is adequate as long as one of the *p* sample sizes exceeds 5. (See the references for more detail.) The χ^2 probability distribution is characterized by a single parameter, called the **degrees of freedom associated with the distribution**. The shapes of several χ^2 probability distributions with different degrees of freedom are shown in Figure 16.9.

The degrees of freedom corresponding to the approximate sampling distribution of *H* will always be $(p - 1)$—one less than the number of probability distributions being compared. Because large values of *H* support the alternative hypothesis that the populations have different probability distributions, the rejection region for the test is located in the upper tail of the χ^2 distribution.

For the data of Table 16.7, the test statistic *H* has a χ^2 distribution with $(p - 1)$ = 2 df. To determine how large *H* must be before we will reject the null hypothesis, we consult Table XIII in Appendix B; part of this table is reproduced in Table 16.8. Entries in the table give an upper-tail value of χ^2, call it χ^2_α, such that $P(\chi^2 > \chi^2_\alpha) = \alpha$. The columns of the table identify the value of α associated with the tabulated value of χ^2_α, and the rows correspond to the degrees of freedom. Thus, for $\alpha = .05$ and df = 2, we can reject the null hypothesis that the three probability distributions are the same if $H > \chi^2_{.05}$ where $\chi^2_{.05} = 5.99147$.

The rejection region is pictured in Figure 16.10. Since the calculated $H = 6.097$ exceeds the critical value of 5.99147, we conclude that at least one of the three hospitals tends to have a larger number of unoccupied beds than the others.

The same conclusion can be reached from a computer printout of the analysis. The rank sums, test statistic, and *p*-value of the nonparametric test are highlighted on the SAS printout in Figure 16.11. Since $\alpha = .05$ exceeds *p*-value $= .0474$, there is sufficient evidence to reject H_0.

The **Kruskal-Wallis *H*-test** for comparing more than two probability distributions is summarized in the box. Note that we can use the Wilcoxon rank sum test of Section 16.3 to compare the separate pairs of populations if the Kruskal-Wallis *H*-test supports the alternative hypothesis that at least two of the probability distributions differ.*

---

*The multiple comparisons procedure of Chapter 15 can be used to determine the appropriate significance level of each test such that the overall level of significance is less than or equal to a prespecified α. If *c* Wilcoxon rank sum tests are to be performed with an overall level of significance α, then conduct each test at $\alpha^* = \alpha/c$.

TABLE 16.8 **Reproduction of Part of Table XIII of Appendix B: Critical Values of χ^2**

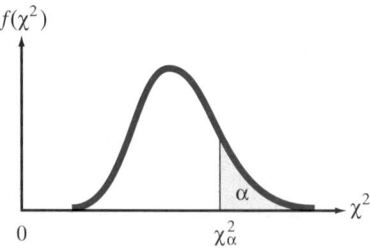

Degrees of Freedom	$\chi^2_{.100}$	$\chi^2_{.050}$	$\chi^2_{.025}$	$\chi^2_{.010}$	$\chi^2_{.005}$
1	2.70554	3.84146	5.02389	6.63490	7.87944
2	4.60517	5.99147	7.37776	9.21034	10.5966
3	6.25139	7.81473	9.34840	11.3449	12.8381
4	7.77944	9.48773	11.1433	13.2767	14.8602
5	9.23635	11.0705	12.8325	15.0863	16.7496
6	10.6446	12.5916	14.4494	16.8119	18.5476
7	12.0170	14.0671	16.0128	18.4753	20.2777
8	13.3616	15.5073	17.5346	20.0902	21.9550
9	14.6837	16.9190	19.0228	21.6660	23.5893
10	15.9871	18.3070	20.4831	23.2093	25.1882
11	17.2750	19.6751	21.9200	24.7250	26.7569

Kruskal-Wallis H-Test for Comparing p Probability Distributions

H_0: The p probability distributions are identical

H_a: At least two of the p probability distributions differ in location

Test statistic: $H = \dfrac{12}{n(n+1)}\sum \dfrac{R_j^2}{n_j} - 3(n+1)$

where

n_j = Number of measurements in sample j

R_j = Rank sum for sample j, where the rank of each measurement is computed according to its relative magnitude in the totality of data for the p samples

n = Total sample size = $n_1 + n_2 + \cdots + n_p$

Rejection region: $H > \chi^2_\alpha$ with $(p-1)$ degrees of freedom

Assumptions: **1.** The p samples are random and independent.

2. There are 5 or more measurements in each sample.

3. The p probability distributions from which the samples are drawn are continuous.

Ties: Assign tied measurements the average of the ranks they would receive if they were unequal but occurred in successive order. For example, if the third-ranked and fourth-ranked measurements are tied, assign both a rank of $(3 + 4)/2 = 3.5$. The number of ties should be small relative to the total number of observations.

FIGURE 16.10
Rejection region for the comparison of three probability distributions

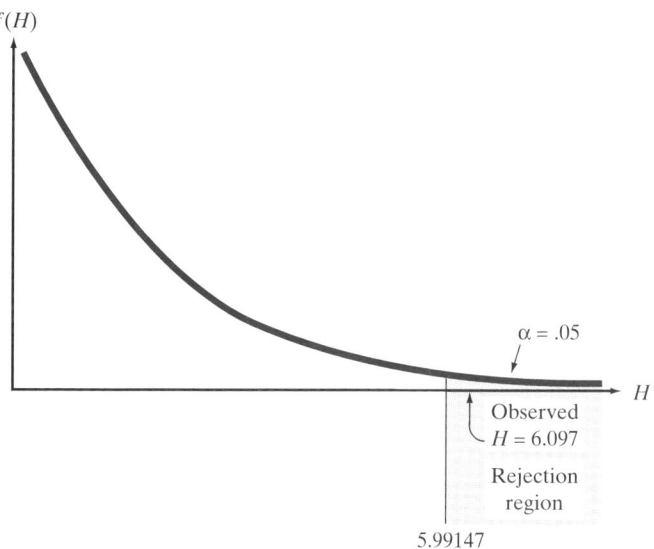

N P A R 1 W A Y   P R O C E D U R E

Wilcoxon Scores (Rank Sums) for Variable BEDS
Classified by Variable HOSPITAL

HOSPITAL	N	Sum of Scores	Expected Under H0	Std Dev Under H0	Mean Score
1	10	120.000000	155.0	22.7277743	12.0000000
2	10	210.500000	155.0	22.7277743	21.0500000
3	10	134.500000	155.0	22.7277743	13.4500000

Average Scores were used for Ties

Kruskal-Wallis Test (Chi-Square Approximation)
CHISQ= 6.0988   DF= 2   Prob > CHISQ=   0.0474

FIGURE 16.11   SAS Kruskal-Wallis printout

𝒮𝒯𝒜𝒯𝐼𝒮𝒯𝐼𝒞𝒮 𝐼𝒩 𝒜𝒞𝒯𝐼𝒪𝒩

16.2 TAXPAYERS VERSUS THE IRS: SELECTING THE TRIAL COURT

The Internal Revenue Service (IRS) is empowered by the U.S. Treasury to administer the tax laws. Because taxpayers are responsible for determining and paying their taxes, the IRS periodically audits tax returns to ensure that taxpayers are in compliance with the tax laws. The audit typically requires that the taxpayer provide detailed records and explanations to support the tax return.

Most audits result in a mutual agreement between the IRS and taxpayer, usually requiring the taxpayer to pay additional taxes. If the disagreement cannot be resolved, the IRS may decide to litigate the tax dispute, that is, take the taxpayer to court.

Did you know that in litigating tax disputes with the IRS, taxpayers are permitted to choose the court forum? Three mutually exclusive trial courts are available: (1) U.S. Tax Court, (2) Federal District Court, and

continued

(3) U.S. Claims Court. Each court possesses different requirements and restrictions that make the choice an important one for the taxpayer.

For example, the U.S. Tax Court does not require prepayment of the disputed amount owed. On the other hand, District Court offers the taxpayer a trial by jury, while the Claims Court tends to favor the taxpayer when the amount disputed is high. Of course, the probability of the taxpayer winning the case in the selected court will also influence the decision.

Accounting professors B. A. Billings (Wayne State University) and B. P. Green (University of Michigan—Dearborn), and business law professor W. H. Volz (Wayne State University) conducted a study of taxpayers' choice of forum in litigating tax issues (*Journal of Applied Business Research*, Fall 1996). The researchers collected data on litigated tax disputes that were decided in 1987, available from *The American Federal Tax Reports* (Prentice-Hall) and *United States Tax Court Reports* (U.S. Government Printing Office). A random sample of 161 court decisions were obtained for analysis. Two of the many variables measured for each case were taxpayer's choice of forum (Tax, District, or Claims Court) and tax deficiency (i.e., the disputed amount, in dollars).

One of the objectives of the study was to determine those factors that taxpayers consider important in their choice of forum. Consider the variable tax deficiency—called DEF by Billings, Green, and Volz. If DEF is an important factor, then the mean DEF values for the three tax courts should be significantly different.

Focus

a. The researchers applied a nonparametric test rather than a parametric test to compare the DEF distributions of the three tax litigation forums. Give a plausible reason for their choice.

b. What nonparametric test is appropriate for this analysis? Explain.

c. Table 16.9 summarizes the data analyzed by the researchers. Use the information in the table to compute the appropriate test statistic.

d. The observed significance level (*p*-value) of the test was reported as $p = .0037$. Fully interpret this result.

e. Conduct nonparametric tests that compare the DEF distributions for each pair of court forums. Use the Bonferroni approach of Chapter 15 to control the experimentwise error rate.

TABLE 16.9 Summary of DEF Data (Statistics in Action 16.2)

Court Selected by Taxpayer	Sample Size	Sample Mean DEF	Rank Sum of DEF Values
Tax	67	$ 80,357	5,335
District	57	74,213	3,937
Claims	37	185,648	3,769

Source: Billings, B. A., Green, B. P., and Volz, W. H. "Selection of forum for litigated tax issues." *Journal of Applied Business Research*, Vol. 12, Fall 1996, p. 38 (Table 2).

EXERCISES 16.34–16.43

Note: Exercises marked with 💾 *contain data for computer analysis on a 3.5" disk (file name in parentheses).*

Learning the Mechanics

16.34 Use Table XIII in Appendix B to find each of the following χ^2 values.
  a. $\chi^2_{.05}$, df = 22 b. $\chi^2_{.025}$, df = 17 c. $\chi^2_{.01}$, df = 31
  d. $\chi^2_{.10}$, df = 80 e. $\chi^2_{.05}$, df = 3 f. $\chi^2_{.005}$, df = 10

16.35 Use Table XIII in Appendix B to find each of the following probabilities.
  a. $P(\chi^2 \geq 3.07382)$ where df = 12
  b. $P(\chi^2 \leq 24.4331)$ where df = 40
  c. $P(\chi^2 \geq 14.6837)$ where df = 9

  d. $P(\chi^2 < 34.1696)$ where df = 20
  e. $P(\chi^2 < 6.26214)$ where df = 15
  f. $P(\chi^2 \leq .584375)$ where df = 3

16.36 Data were collected from three populations, A, B, and C, using a completely randomized design. The following describes the sample data:

$$n_A = n_B = n_C = 15$$

$$R_A = 230 \qquad R_B = 440 \qquad R_C = 365$$

  a. Specify the null and alternative hypotheses that should be used in conducting a test of hypothesis to determine whether the probability distributions of populations A, B, and C differ in location.

b. Conduct the test of part **a**. Use $\alpha = .05$.

c. What is the approximate *p*-value of the test of part **b**?

d. Calculate the mean rank for each sample, and compute *H* according to the formula that utilizes these means. Verify that this formula yields the same value of *H* that you obtained in part **b**.

16.37 (**X16.037**) Suppose you want to use the Kruskal-Wallis *H*-test to compare the probability distributions of three populations. The following are independent random samples selected from the three populations:

I: 66, 23, 55, 88, 58, 62, 79, 49

II: 19, 31, 16, 29, 30, 33, 40

III: 75, 96, 102, 75, 98, 78

a. What type of experimental design was used?

b. Specify the null and alternative hypotheses you would test.

c. Specify the rejection region you would use for your hypothesis test, at $\alpha = .01$.

d. Conduct the test at $\alpha = .01$.

16.38 Under what circumstances does the χ^2 distribution provide an appropriate characterization of the sampling distribution of the Kruskal-Wallis *H* statistic?

Applying the Concepts

16.39 Refer to the *Journal of the American Mosquito Control Association* study of biting flies, Exercise 16.7. The effect of wind speeds in kilometers per hour (kph) on the biting rate of the fly on Stanbury Island, Utah, was investigated by exposing samples of volunteers to one of six wind speed conditions. The distributions of the biting rates for the six wind speeds were compared using the Kruskal-Wallis test. The rank sums of the biting rates for the six conditions are shown in the accompanying table.

Wind Speed (kph)	Number of Volunteers (n_j)	Rank Sum of Biting Rates (R_j)
< 1	11	1,804
1–2.9	49	6,398
3–4.9	62	7,328
5–6.9	39	4,075
7–8.9	35	2,660
9–20	21	1,388
Totals	217	23,653

Source: Strickman, D., *et al.* "Meteorological effects on the biting activity of *Leptoconops americanus* (Diptera: Ceratopogonidae)." *Journal of the American Mosquito Control Association*, Vol. II, No. 1, Mar. 1995, p. 17 (Table 1).

a. The researchers reported the test statistic as $H = 35.2$. Verify this value.

b. Find the rejection region for the test using $\alpha = .01$.

c. Make the proper conclusions.

d. The researchers reported the *p*-value of the test as $p < .01$. Does this value support your inference in part **c**? Explain.

16.40 (**X16.040**) Random samples of seven lawyers employed as public defenders were selected from each of three major cities. Their salaries were determined and are recorded in the table. You have been hired to determine whether differences exist among the salary distributions for public defenders in the three cities.

Atlanta	Los Angeles	Washington, D.C.
$34,600	$ 42,400	$38,000
84,900	135,000	76,900
61,700	63,000	48,000
38,900	43,700	72,600
77,200	69,400	73,200
83,600	97,000	51,800
59,800	49,500	55,000

Source: Adapted from *American Almanac of Jobs and Salaries, 1997–1998 Edition,* New York: Avon Books, 1996, pp. 246–260.

a. Under what circumstances would it be appropriate to use the *F*-test for a completely randomized design to perform the required analysis?

b. Which assumptions required by the *F*-test are likely to be violated in this problem? Explain.

c. Use the Kruskal-Wallis *H*-test to determine whether the salary distributions differ among the three cities. Specify your null and alternative hypotheses, and state your conclusions in the context of the problem. Use $\alpha = .05$.

d. What assumptions are necessary to ensure the validity of the nonparametric test in part **c**?

16.41 (**X16.041**) Investors handed over some $223 billion to equity-fund managers in 1996. The average investor owned three mutual funds. Three of the categories *Business Week* uses to classify mutual funds are growth, blend, and value. Those with significantly lower-than-average price-earnings ratios (p-e) and price-to-book ratios (p-b) are *value funds;* those with higher than average p-e's and p-b's are called *growth funds;* those in the middle are called *blend funds.* The first table on page 896 lists the after tax rate of return to investors for samples of seven mutual funds in each of these three categories.

a. Do the data provide sufficient evidence to conclude that the rate-of-return distributions

Growth

Citizens Index	22.7%
Fidelity Advisor Growth	15.1
Gabelli Growth	16.5
Northern Growth Equity	16.1
Preferred Growth	14.0
Seligman Growth	18.6
RYDEX OTC	43.1
Blend	
American National	14.9
Columbia Common Stock	16.0
Federated American Leaders	16.8
Gateway Index Plus	10.2
Janus	15.8
Lexington Growth & Income	24.1
Oppenheimer	16.6
Value	
American Mutual	13.2
Composite Growth & Income	19.7
IDS Equity Value	17.2
Marshal Equity Income	18.3
New England Value	21.8
Pioneer Equity Income	12.8
Putnam Equity Income	20.4

Source: "Mutual fund scoreboard." *Business Week,* Feb. 3, 1997, pp. 82–109.

differ among the three types of mutual funds? Test using $\alpha = .05$.

b. What assumptions must hold for your test of part **a** to be valid?

c. Describe the Type I and II errors associated with the test of part **a** in the context of the problem.

d. Under what circumstances could the ANOVA *F*-test of Chapter 15 help answer part **a**?

16.42 **(X15.022)** Refer to the *Journal of Hazardous Materials* (July 1995) study of the chemical properties of three different types of hazardous solvents used to clean metal parts, Exercise 15.22.

Aromatics		Chloralkanes		Esters		
1.06	.95	1.58	1.12	.29	.43	.06
.79	.65	1.45	.91	.06	.51	.09
.82	1.15	.57	.83	.44	.10	.17
.89	1.12	1.16	.43	.61	.34	.60
1.05				.55	.53	.17

Source: Ortego, J. D., *et al.* "A review of polymeric geosynthetics used in hazardous waste facilities." *Journal of Hazardous Materials,* Vol. 42, No. 2, July 1995, p. 142 (Table 9).

Independent samples of solvents from each of the three types—aromatics, chloralkanes, and esters—were collected. The data on sorption rates for the three solvents are reproduced in the table above. Use the information provided in the SAS printout below to compare the sorption rate distributions.

16.43 **(X16.043)** In Exercise 12.50, regression analysis was applied to investigate whether the mean debt/capital ratio varies among four industries. The data are repeated in the table on page 897.

a. Compare the assumptions required by the regression analysis and the Kruskal-Wallis *H*-test for comparing the mean debt/capital ratios among the four industries.

b. Use the Kruskal-Wallis *H*-test to investigate whether debt/capital ratios differ among the four industries. Be sure to specify your null and alternative hypotheses and to state your conclusion in the context of the problem. Use $\alpha = .05$.

c. Assuming the Kruskal-Wallis *H*-test indicates that differences exist among the four industries, which nonparametric procedure could be employed to compare the distribution of debt/capital ratios for the retailing and chemical industries?

```
                          SAS

              N P A R 1 W A Y  P R O C E D U R E

      Wilcoxon Scores (Rank Sums) for Variable SORPRATE
             Classified by Variable SOLVENT

                   Sum of      Expected      Std Dev        Mean
   SOLVENT    N    Scores      Under H0      Under H0       Score

   AROMA      9   210.500000  148.500000    23.8502130    23.3888889
   CHLOR      8   189.000000  132.000000    22.9698259    23.6250000
   ESTER     15   128.500000  247.500000    26.4714164     8.5666667
           Average Scores were used for Ties

      Kruskal-Wallis Test (Chi-Square Approximation)
        CHISQ=  20.211    DF= 2    Prob > CHISQ=     0.0001
```

Field	Firm	Debt/capital (%)
Aerospace and Defense	Raytheon	26.1
	Boeing	19.7
	Textron	76.8
	Thiokol	0.6
	Lockheed Martin	31.5
	Rohr	75.4
Electric Utilities	Pacific G & E	37.3
	Houston Ind.	37.4
	Florida Progress	34.5
	Duke Power	31.2
	North States Power	32.1
	Ohio Edison	37.7
	Hawaiian Electric	38.5

Field	Firm	Debt/capital (%)
Retailing	Rite Aid	46.3
	Kmart	38.6
	Bradlees	59.8
	Spiegel	65.5
	Fay's	43.7
Chemical	Olin	32.7
	Valspar	44.9
	Dow Chemical	32.5
	FMC	59.7
	Union Carbide	41.5

Source: "Annual Report on American Industry." *Forbes,* Jan. 1, 1996.

16.6 SPEARMAN'S RANK CORRELATION COEFFICIENT

Suppose 10 new car models are evaluated by two consumer magazines and each magazine ranks the braking systems of the cars from 1 (best) to 10 (worst). We want to determine whether the magazines' ranks are related. Does a correspondence exist between their ratings? If a car is ranked high by magazine 1, is it likely to be ranked high by magazine 2? Or do high rankings by one magazine correspond to low rankings by the other? That is, are the rankings of the magazines **correlated**?

If the rankings are as shown in the "Perfect Agreement" columns of Table 16.10, we immediately notice that the magazines agree on the rank of every car. High ranks correspond to high ranks and low ranks to low ranks. This is an example of **perfect positive correlation** between the ranks. In contrast, if the rankings appear as shown in the "Perfect Disagreement" columns of Table 16.10, high ranks for one magazine correspond to low ranks for the other. This is an example of **perfect negative correlation**.

In practice, you will rarely see perfect positive or negative correlation between the ranks. In fact, it is quite possible for the magazines' ranks to appear as shown

TABLE 16.10 Brake Rankings of 10 New Car Models by Two Consumer Magazines

Car Model	PERFECT AGREEMENT		PERFECT DISAGREEMENT	
	Magazine 1	Magazine 2	Magazine 1	Magazine 2
1	4	4	9	2
2	1	1	3	8
3	7	7	5	6
4	5	5	1	10
5	2	2	2	9
6	6	6	10	1
7	8	8	6	5
8	3	3	4	7
9	10	10	8	3
10	9	9	7	4

TABLE 16.11   Brake Rankings of New Car Models: Less Than Perfect Agreement

Car Model	MAGAZINE 1	MAGAZINE 2	DIFFERENCE BETWEEN RANK 1 AND RANK 2 d	d^2
1	4	5	−1	1
2	1	2	−1	1
3	9	10	−1	1
4	5	6	−1	1
5	2	1	1	1
6	10	9	1	1
7	7	7	0	0
8	3	3	0	0
9	6	4	2	4
10	8	8	0	0
				$\Sigma d^2 = 10$

in Table 16.11. You will note that these rankings indicate some agreement between the consumer magazines, but not perfect agreement, thus indicating a need for a measure of rank correlation.

Spearman's rank correlation coefficient, r_s, provides a measure of correlation between ranks. The formula for this measure of correlation is given in the next box. We also give a formula that is identical to r_s when there are no ties in rankings; this provides a good approximation to r_s when the number of ties is small relative to the number of pairs.

Note that if the ranks for the two magazines are identical, as in the second and third columns of Table 16.10, the differences between the ranks, d, will all be 0. Thus,

$$r_s = 1 - \frac{6\sum d^2}{n(n^2 - 1)} = 1 - \frac{6(0)}{10(99)} = 1$$

That is, *perfect positive correlation* between the pairs of ranks is characterized by a Spearman correlation coefficient of $r_s = 1$. When the ranks indicate perfect disagreement, as in the fourth and fifth columns of Table 16.10, $\Sigma d_i^2 = 330$ and

$$r_s = 1 - \frac{6(330)}{10(99)} = -1$$

Thus, *perfect negative correlation* is indicated by $r_s = -1$.

Spearman's Rank Correlation Coefficient

$$r_s = \frac{SS_{uv}}{\sqrt{SS_{uu}SS_{vv}}}$$

where

$$SS_{uv} = \sum(u_i - \bar{u})(v_i - \bar{v}) = \sum u_i v_i - \frac{\left(\sum u_i\right)\left(\sum v_i\right)}{n}$$

$$SS_{uu} = \sum(u_i - \bar{u})^2 = \sum u_i^2 - \frac{\left(\sum u_i\right)^2}{n}$$

$$SS_{vv} = \sum (v_i - \bar{v})^2 = \sum v_i^2 - \frac{\left(\sum v_i\right)^2}{n}$$

u_i = Rank of the ith observation in sample 1

v_i = Rank of the ith observation in sample 2

n = Number of pairs of observations (number of observations in each sample)

Shortcut Formula for r_s*

$$r_s = 1 - \frac{6\sum d_i^2}{n(n^2 - 1)}$$

where

$d_i = u_i - v_i$ (difference in the ranks of the ith observations for samples 1 and 2)

For the data of Table 16.11,

$$r_s = 1 - \frac{6\sum d^2}{n(n^2 - 1)} = 1 - \frac{6(10)}{10(99)} = 1 - \frac{6}{99} = .94$$

The fact that r_s is close to 1 indicates that the magazines tend to agree, but the agreement is not perfect.

The value of r_s *always falls between* −1 *and* +1, *with* +1 *indicating perfect positive correlation and* −1 *indicating perfect negative correlation.* The closer r_s falls to +1 or −1, the greater the correlation between the ranks. Conversely, the nearer r_s is to 0, the less the correlation.

Note that the concept of correlation implies that two responses are obtained for each experimental unit. In the consumer magazine example, each new car model received two ranks (one for each magazine) and the objective of the study was to determine the degree of positive correlation between the two rankings. Rank correlation methods can be used to measure the correlation between any pair of variables. If two variables are measured on each of n experimental units, we rank the measurements associated with each variable separately. Ties receive the average of the ranks of the tied observations. Then we calculate the value of r_s for the two rankings. This value measures the rank correlation between the two variables. We illustrate the procedure in Example 16.4.

EXAMPLE 16.4

Manufacturers of perishable foods often use preservatives to retard spoilage. One concern is that too much preservative will change the flavor of the food. Suppose an experiment is conducted using samples of a food product with varying amounts of preservative added. Both length of time until the food shows signs of spoiling and a taste rating are recorded for each sample. The taste rating is the average rating for three tasters, each of whom rates each sample on a scale from 1 (good) to 5 (bad). Twelve sample measurements are shown in Table 16.12.

    a. Calculate Spearman's rank correlation coefficient between spoiling time and taste rating.

---

*The shortcut formula is not exact when there are tied measurements, but it is a good approximation when the total number of ties is not large relative to n.

TABLE 16.12 Data and Correlations for Example 16.4

Sample	Days Until Spoilage	Rank	Taste Rating	Rank	d	d^2
1	30	2	4.3	11	-9	81
2	47	5	3.6	7.5	-2.5	6.25
3	26	1	4.5	12	-11	121
4	94	11	2.8	3	8	64
5	67	7	3.3	6	1	1
6	83	10	2.7	2	8	64
7	36	3	4.2	10	-7	49
8	77	9	3.9	9	0	0
9	43	4	3.6	7.5	-3.5	12.25
10	109	12	2.2	1	11	121
11	56	6	3.1	5	1	1
12	70	8	2.9	4	4	16

Total = 536.5

Note: Tied measurements are assigned the average of the ranks they would be given if they were different but consecutive.

b. Use a nonparametric test to find out whether the spoilage times and taste ratings are negatively correlated. Use $\alpha = .05$.

SOLUTION

a. We first rank the days until spoilage, assigning a 1 to the smallest number (26) and a 12 to the largest (109). Similarly, we assign ranks to the 12 taste ratings. [*Note:* The tied taste ratings receive the average of their respective ranks.] Since the number of ties is relatively small, we will use the shortcut formula to calculate r_s. The differences d between the ranks of days until spoilage and the ranks of taste rating are shown in Table 16.12. The squares of the differences, d^2, are also given. Thus,

$$r_s = 1 - \frac{6\sum d_i^2}{n(n^2 - 1)} = 1 - \frac{6(536.5)}{12(12^2 - 1)} = 1 - 1.876 = -.876$$

The value of r_s can also be obtained using a computer. An EXCEL printout of the analysis is shown in Figure 16.12. The value of r_s, highlighted on the printout, is $-.879$ and agrees (except for rounding) with our hand-calculated value. This negative correlation coefficient indicates that in this sample an

FIGURE 16.12
EXCEL printout for
Example 16.4

Sample		Days	Taste
	1	30	4.3
	2	47	3.6
	3	26	4.5
	4	94	2.8
	5	67	3.3
	6	83	2.7
	7	36	4.2
	8	77	3.9
	9	43	3.6
	10	109	2.2
	11	56	3.1
	12	70	2.9
Spearman r(s)		-0.879160718	0.000165104

TABLE 16.13   Reproduction of Part of Table XVI in Appendix B: Critical Values of Spearman's Rank Correlation Coefficient

n	$\alpha = .05$	$\alpha = .025$	$\alpha = .01$	$\alpha = .005$
5	.900	—	—	—
6	.829	.886	.943	—
7	.714	.786	.893	—
8	.643	.738	.833	.881
9	.600	.683	.783	.833
10	.564	.648	.745	.794
11	.523	.623	.736	.818
12	.497	.591	.703	.780
13	.475	.566	.673	.745
14	.457	.545	.646	.716
15	.441	.525	.623	.689
16	.425	.507	.601	.666
17	.412	.490	.582	.645
18	.399	.476	.564	.625
19	.388	.462	.549	.608
20	.377	.450	.534	.591

increase in the number of days until spoilage is *associated with* (but is not necessarily the *cause of*) a decrease in the taste rating.

b. If we define ρ as the **population rank correlation coefficient** [i.e., the rank correlation coefficient that could be calculated from all (x, y) values in the population], this question can be answered by conducting the test

H_0: $\rho = 0$ (no population correlation between ranks)

H_a: $\rho < 0$ (negative population correlation between ranks)

Test statistic: r_s (the *sample* Spearman rank correlation coefficient)

To determine a rejection region, we consult Table XVI in Appendix B, which is partially reproduced in Table 16.13. Note that the left-hand column gives values of n, the number of pairs of observations. The entries in the table are values for an upper-tail rejection region, since only positive values are given. Thus, for $n = 12$ and $\alpha = .05$, the value .497 is the boundary of the upper-tailed rejection region, so that $P(r_s > .497) = .05$ if H_0: $\rho = 0$ is true. Similarly, for negative values of r_s, we have $P(r_s < -.497) = .05$ if $\rho = 0$. That is, we expect to see $r_s < -.497$ only 5% of the time if there is really no relationship between the ranks of the variables. The lower-tailed rejection region is therefore

Rejection region $(\alpha = .05)$: $r_s < -.497$

Since the calculated $r_s = -.876$ is less than $-.497$, we reject H_0 at the $\alpha = .05$ level of significance. That is, this sample provides sufficient evidence to conclude that a negative correlation exists between number of days until spoilage and taste rating of the food product. It appears that the preservative does affect the taste of this food adversely. [*Note:* The two-tailed p-value of the test is highlighted on the EXCEL printout next to the value of r_s in Figure 16.12. Since the lower-tailed p-value, $p = .00016/2 = .00008$, is less than $\alpha = .05$, our conclusion is the same: reject H_0.] ◣

A summary of Spearman's nonparametric test for correlation is given in the next box.

Spearman's Nonparametric Test for Rank Correlation

One-Tailed Test

H_0: $\rho = 0$

H_a: $\rho > 0$ (or H_a: $\rho < 0$)

Two-Tailed Test

H_0: $\rho = 0$

H_a: $\rho \neq 0$

Test statistic: r_s, the sample rank correlation (see the formulas for calculating r_s)

Rejection region: $r_s > r_{s,\alpha}$
    (or $r_s < -r_{s,\alpha}$ when H_a: $\rho_s < 0$)

where $r_{s,\alpha}$ is the value from Table XVI corresponding to the upper-tail area α and n pairs of observations

Rejection region: $|r_s| > r_{s,\alpha/2}$

where $r_{s,\alpha/2}$ is the value from Table XVI corresponding to the upper-tail area $\alpha/2$ and n pairs of observations

Assumptions: **1.** The sample of experimental units on which the two variables are measured is randomly selected.

2. The probability distributions of the two variables are continuous.

Ties: Assign tied measurements the average of the ranks they would receive if they were unequal but occurred in successive order. For example, if the third-ranked and fourth-ranked measurements are tied, assign each a rank of $(3 + 4)/2 = 3.5$. The number of ties should be small relative to the total number of observations.

EXERCISES 16.44–16.54

Note: Exercises marked with 💾 *contain data for computer analysis on a 3.5" disk (file name in parentheses).*

Learning the Mechanics

16.44 Use Table XVI of Appendix B to find each of the following probabilities:
  a. $P(r_s > .508)$ when $n = 22$
  b. $P(r_s > .448)$ when $n = 28$
  c. $P(r_s \leq .648)$ when $n = 10$
  d. $P(r_s < -.738$ or $r_s > .738)$ when $n = 8$

16.45 Specify the rejection region for Spearman's nonparametric test for rank correlation in each of the following situations:
  a. H_0: $\rho = 0$; H_a: $\rho \neq 0$, $n = 10$, $\alpha = .05$
  b. H_0: $\rho = 0$; H_a: $\rho > 0$, $n = 20$, $\alpha = .025$
  c. H_0: $\rho = 0$; H_a: $\rho < 0$, $n = 30$, $\alpha = .01$

16.46 Compute Spearman's rank correlation coefficient for each of the following pairs of sample observations:

  a.

x	33	61	20	19	40
y	26	36	65	25	35

  b.

x	89	102	120	137	41
y	81	94	75	52	136

  c.

x	2	15	4	10
y	11	2	15	21

  d.

x	5	20	15	10	3
y	80	83	91	82	87

16.47 The following sample data were collected on variables x and y:

x	0	3	0	-4	3	0	4
y	0	2	2	0	3	1	2

  a. Specify the null and alternative hypotheses that should be used in conducting a hypothesis test to determine whether the variables x and y are correlated.
  b. Conduct the test of part **a** using $\alpha = .05$.
  c. What is the approximate p-value of the test of part **b**?
  d. What assumptions are necessary to ensure the validity of the test of part **b**?

Applying the Concepts

16.48 **(X16.048)** There has been growing recognition of 💾 and appreciation for the role that corporations play in the vitality of metropolitan economies. For example, metropolitan areas with many corporate headquarters are finding it easier to transition from a manufacturing economy to a service economy through job growth in small companies and subsidiaries that service the corporate parent. James O. Wheeler of the University of Georgia studied the relationship between the number of corporate headquarters in eleven metropolitan areas and the number of subsidiaries located there (*Growth and Change,* Spring 1988). He hypothesized that there would be a positive relationship between the variables.

Metropolitan Area	No. of Parent Companies	No. of Subsidiaries
New York	643	2,617
Chicago	381	1,724
Los Angeles	342	1,867
Dallas–Ft. Worth	251	1,238
Detroit	216	890
Boston	208	681
Houston	192	1,534
San Francisco	141	899
Minneapolis	131	492
Cleveland	128	579
Denver	124	672

Source: Wheeler, J. O. "The corporate role of large metropolitan areas in the United States." *Growth and Change,* Spring 1988, pp. 75–88.

a. Calculate Spearman's rank correlation coefficient for these data. What does it indicate about Wheeler's hypothesis?
b. To conduct a formal test of Wheeler's hypothesis using Spearman's rank correlation coefficient, certain assumptions must hold. What are they? Do they appear to hold? Explain.

16.49 Universities receive gifts and donations from corporations, foundations, friends, and alumni. It has long been argued that universities rise or fall depending on the level of support of their alumni. The table below reports the total dollars raised during 1994–1995 by a sample of major U.S. universities. In addition, it reports the percentage of that total donated by alumni:

University	Total Funds Raised	Alumni Contribution
Harvard	$323,406,242	47.5%
Yale	199,646,606	54.6
Cornell	198,736,229	56.2
Wisconsin	164,349,458	17.4
Michigan	145,757,642	45.4
Pennsylvania	135,324,761	34.3
Illinois	116,578,975	36.6
Princeton	103,826,392	53.2
Brown	102,513,437	34.7
Northwestern	101,041,213	27.3

Source: The Chronicle of Higher Education, Sept. 2, 1996, p. 27.

a. Do these data indicate that total fundraising and alumni contributions are correlated? Test using $\alpha = .05$.
b. What assumptions must hold to ensure the validity of your test?

16.50 Two expert wine tasters were asked to rank six brands of wine. Their rankings are shown in the table. Do the data present sufficient evidence to indicate a positive correlation in the rankings of the two experts?

Brand	Expert 1	Expert 2
A	6	5
B	5	6
C	1	2
D	3	1
E	2	4
F	4	3

16.51 (X16.051) An *employee suggestion system* is a formal process for capturing, analyzing, implementing, and recognizing employee-proposed organizational improvements. (The first known system was implemented by the Yale and Towne Manufacturing Company of Stamford, Connecticut, in 1880). Using data from the National Association of Suggestion Systems, D. Carnevale and B. Sharp examined the strengths of the relationships between the extent of employee participation in suggestion plans and cost savings realized by employers (*Review of Public Personnel Administration,* Spring 1993). The data in the table are representative of the data they analyzed for 1991 for a sample of federal, state, and local government agencies. Savings are calculated from the first year measurable benefits were observed.

Employee Involvement (% of all employees submitting suggestions)	Savings Rate (% of total budget)
10.1%	8.5%
6.2	6.0
16.3	9.0
1.2	0.0
4.8	5.1
11.5	6.1
.6	1.2
2.8	4.5
8.9	5.4
20.2	15.3
2.7	3.8

Source: Data adapted from Carnevale, D. G., and Sharp, B. S. "The old employee suggestion box." *Review of Public Personnel Administration,* Spring 1993, pp. 82–92.

a. Explain why the savings data used in this study may understate the total benefits derived from the implemented suggestions.

b. Carnevale and Sharp concluded that a significant moderate positive relationship exists between participation rates and cost savings rates in public sector suggestion systems. Do you agree? Test using $\alpha = .01$.

c. Justify the statistical methodology you used in part **b**.

16.52 (X16.052) A *negotiable certificate of deposit* is a marketable receipt for funds deposited in a bank for a specified period of time at a specified rate of interest (Lee, Finnerty, and Norton, 1997). The accompanying table lists the end-of-quarter interest rate for three-month certificates of deposit from January 1982 through December 1995 with the concurrent end-of-quarter values of Standard & Poor's 500 Stock Composite Average (an indicator of stock market activity).

a. Locate Spearman's rank correlation coefficient on the SAS printout below. [*Note:* To compute Spearman's rank correlation coefficient, SAS first ranks the values of the two variables, then calculates Pearson's correlation coefficient for the ranked values.] Interpret the result.

b. Test the null hypothesis that the interest rate on certificates of deposit and the S&P 500 are not correlated against the alternative hypothesis that these variables are correlated. Use $\alpha = .10$.

Year	Quarter	Interest Rate, x	S&P 500, y	Year	Quarter	Interest Rate, x	S&P 500, y
1982	I	14.21	111.96	1989	I	10.09	294.87
	II	14.46	109.61		II	9.20	317.98
	III	10.66	120.42		III	8.78	349.15
	IV	8.66	135.28		IV	8.32	353.40
1983	I	8.69	152.96	1990	I	8.27	339.94
	II	9.20	168.11		II	8.33	358.02
	III	9.39	166.07		III	8.08	306.05
	IV	9.69	164.93		IV	7.96	330.22
1984	I	10.08	159.18	1991	I	6.71	375.22
	II	11.34	153.18		II	6.01	371.16
	III	11.29	166.10		III	5.70	387.86
	IV	8.60	167.24		IV	4.91	417.09
1985	I	9.02	180.66	1992	I	4.25	403.69
	II	7.44	191.85		II	3.86	408.14
	III	7.93	182.08		III	3.13	417.80
	IV	7.80	211.28		IV	3.48	435.71
1986	I	7.24	238.90	1993	I	3.11	451.67
	II	6.73	250.84		II	3.21	450.53
	III	5.71	231.32		III	3.12	458.93
	IV	6.04	242.17		IV	3.17	466.45
1987	I	6.17	291.70	1994	I	3.77	445.77
	II	6.94	304.00		II	4.52	444.27
	III	7.37	321.83		III	5.03	462.69
	IV	7.66	247.08		IV	6.29	459.27
1988	I	6.63	258.89	1995	I	6.15	500.71
	II	7.51	273.50		II	5.90	544.75
	III	8.23	271.91		III	5.73	584.41
	IV	9.25	277.72		IV	5.62	615.93

Source: Standard & Poor's Current Statistics. Standard & Poor's Corporation, 1992, 1996.

```
                        CORRELATION ANALYSIS

        Pearson Correlation Coefficients / Prob > |R| under Ho: Rho=0 / N = 56

                                    INTRANK           SP5RANK

            INTRANK                 1.00000          -0.79215
            RANK FOR VARIABLE INTRATE   0.0             0.0001

            SP5RANK                -0.79215           1.00000
            RANK FOR VARIABLE SP500     0.0001          0.0
```

Location Factor	Firms Choosing Arkansas: Rank	Firms Rejecting Arkansas: Rank
Labor	1	1
Taxes	2	2
Industrial site	3	4
Information sources, special inducements	4	5
Legislative laws and structure	5	3
Utilities and resources	6	7
Transportation facilities	7	8
Raw material supplies	8	10
Community	9	6
Industrial financing	10	9
Markets	11	12
Business services	12	11
Personal preferences	13	13

c. Repeat parts **a** and **b** using data from 1996 through the present, which can be obtained at your library in *Standard & Poor's Current Statistics*. Compare your results for the newer data with your results for the earlier period.

16.53 (X16.053) The decision to build a new plant or to move an existing plant to a new location involves long-term commitment of both human and monetary resources. Accordingly, such decisions should be made only after carefully considering the relevant factors at alternative sites. G. Michael Epping examined the relationship between the location factors deemed important by businesses that located in Arkansas and those that considered Arkansas but located elsewhere (*Growth and Change,* Apr. 1982). A questionnaire that asked manufacturers to rate the importance of 13 general location factors on a 9-point scale was completed by 118 firms that had moved a plant to Arkansas in the period 1955–1977 and by 73 firms that had considered Arkansas but went elsewhere. Epping averaged the importance ratings and arrived at the rankings shown in the table above. Calculate Spearman's rank correlation coefficient

and carefully interpret its value in the context of the problem.

16.54 Health maintenance organizations (HMOs) provide and monitor a variety of short-term outpatient services, including crisis intervention mental health services. To investigate the standards used by HMOs in interpreting crisis intervention, two researchers (Cheifetz and Salloway, 1985) conducted a comprehensive questionnaire survey of 145 national HMOs. Each HMO was asked to "write a brief, descriptive definition of situations or states you would include as qualifying for 'crisis intervention.'" The researchers sorted these situations into 10 categories and then asked three experienced clinicians to rate each category for two criteria: validity of crisis intervention (i.e., is the situation defined really a "crisis") and clarity of guidelines for offering service. A 4-point rating scale was provided for both criteria. The mean ratings for the 10 categories on both the crisis intervention and clarity scales are given in the table below. Is there evidence of a positive relationship between the mean crisis intervention and mean clarity ratings? Test using $\alpha = .05$.

Category (Situation)	Crisis Intervention Rating (1 = definitely a crisis, 4 = definitely not a crisis)	Clarity Rating (1 = very clear guideline, 4 = very unclear guideline)
Psychosis	1.31	1.33
Drug/alcohol abuse	1.33	1.29
Depression/anxiety	1.48	1.59
Emphasis on acuteness	1.76	2.50
Insistence on "short-term" response	2.48	3.22
Suicide	1.13	1.32
Family problems	2.59	2.30
Violence/harm	1.06	1.86
Miscellaneous	2.60	2.33
Nondefinition	3.57	3.57

Source: Cheifetz, D. I., and Salloway, J. C. "Crisis intervention: Interpretation and practice by HMO." *Medical Care,* Vol. 23, No. 1, Jan. 1985, pp. 89–93.

QUICK REVIEW

Key Terms

Correlation 897
Kruskal-Wallis *H*-test 889
Nonparametric tests 868
Population correlation
  coefficient 901
Rank statistics 869

Rank sum 875
Relative ranks 868
Shift in probability distributions 868
Sign test 869
Spearman's nonparametric test for
  rank correlation 902

Spearman's rank correlation
  coefficient 898
Wilcoxon rank sum test 874
Wilcoxon signed rank test 882

Key Formulas

Test	Test Statistic	Large Sample Approximation	
Sign	S = number of sample measurements greater than (or less than) hypothesized mean, η_0	$z = \dfrac{(S - .5) - .5n}{.5\sqrt{n}}$	871
Wilcoxon rank sum	T_A = rank sum of sample A or 876 T_B = rank sum of sample B	$z = \dfrac{T_A - \dfrac{n_1(n_1 + n_2 + 1)}{2}}{\sqrt{\dfrac{n_1 n_2(n_1 + n_2 + 1)}{12}}}$	878
Wilcoxon signed ranks	T_- = negative rank sum or 884 T_+ = positive rank sum	$z = \dfrac{T_+ - \dfrac{n(n + 1)}{4}}{\sqrt{\dfrac{n(n + 1)(2n + 1)}{24}}}$	886
Kruskal-Wallis	$H = \dfrac{12}{n(n + 1)}\sum\dfrac{R_j^2}{n_j} - 3(n + 1)$		892
Spearman rank correlation (shortcut formula)	$r_s = 1 - \dfrac{6\sum d_i^2}{n(n^2 - 1)}$ where d_i = difference in ranks of *i*th observations for samples 1 and 2		899

LANGUAGE LAB

Symbol	Pronunciation	Description
η	eta	Population median
S		Test statistic for sign test (see Key Formulas)
T_A		Sum of ranks of observations in sample A
T_B		Sum of ranks of observations in sample B
T_L		Critical lower Wilcoxon rank sum value
T_U		Critical upper Wilcoxon rank sum value
T_+		Sum of ranks of positive differences of paired observations
T_-		Sum of ranks of negative differences of paired observations
T_0		Critical value of Wilcoxon signed ranks test
R_j		Rank sum of observations in sample *j*
H		Test statistic for Kruskal-Wallis test (see Key Formulas)
r_s		Spearman's rank correlation coefficient (see Key Formulas)
ρ	rho	Population correlation coefficient

SUPPLEMENTARY EXERCISES 16.55–16.77

Note: Exercises marked with contain data for computer analysis on a 3.5" disk (file name in parentheses).

Learning the Mechanics

16.55 When is it appropriate to use the *t*- and *F*-tests of Chapters 9 and 10 for comparing two or more population means?

16.56 The data for three independent random samples are shown in the table below. It is known that the sampled populations are not normally distributed. Use an appropriate test to determine whether the data provide sufficient evidence to indicate that at least two of the populations differ in location. Test using $\alpha = .05$.

Sample from Population 1		Sample from Population 2		Sample from Population 3	
18	15	12	34	87	50
32	63	33	18	53	64
43		10		65	77

16.57 A random sample of nine pairs of observations are recorded on two variables, *x* and *y*. The data are shown in the following table.

Pair	*x*	*y*	Pair	*x*	*y*
1	19	12	6	29	10
2	27	19	7	16	16
3	15	7	8	22	10
4	35	25	9	16	18
5	13	11			

a. Do the data provide sufficient evidence to indicate that ρ, the rank correlation between *x* and *y*, differs from 0? Test using $\alpha = .05$.

b. Do the data provide sufficient evidence to indicate that the probability distribution for *x* is shifted to the right of that for *y*? Test using $\alpha = .05$.

16.58 Two independent random samples produced the measurements listed in the table (see next column). Do the data provide sufficient evidence to conclude that there is a difference between the locations of the probability distributions for the sampled populations? Test using $\alpha = .05$.

Sample from Population 1		Sample from Population 2	
1.2	1.0	1.5	1.9
1.9	1.8	1.3	2.7
.7	1.1	2.9	3.5
2.5			

Applying the Concepts

16.59 **(X16.059)** An economist is interested in knowing whether property tax rates differ among three types of school districts—urban, suburban, and rural. A random sample of several districts of each type produced the data in the table (rate is in mills, where 1 mill = $1/1,000). Do the data indicate a difference in the level of property taxes among the three types of school districts? Use $\alpha = .05$.

Urban	Suburban	Rural
4.3	5.9	5.1
5.2	6.7	4.8
6.2	7.6	3.9
5.6	4.9	6.2
3.8	5.2	4.2
5.8	6.8	4.3
4.7		

16.60 **(X16.060)** Dividends are cash payments made to stockholders by the corporation. A stock's *dividend yield* is the total amount of cash paid on a single share of stock over the period of a year expressed as a percentage of the current market price of the stock (Alexander, Sharpe, and Bailey, 1993). The table below reports the dividend yields for samples of corporations in three different industries.

a. Under what circumstances would it be appropriate to use an *F*-test to determine whether the mean dividend yield differs among the three industries?

Consumer Products		Telecommunications		Utilities	
Nike	.54	Bellsouth	3.09	Williams	2.50
Coca-Cola	.81	Sprint	2.26	Oneok	4.12
Clorox	1.92	Ameritech	3.50	Nicor	3.84
Russell	1.38	NYNEX	4.52	Unicom	7.11
Maytag	3.03	Frontier	3.86	Entergy	6.76
Tandy	1.63	AT&T	3.31	Enserch	.95
Seagram	1.64	Bell Atlantic	4.11	Peco Energy	8.23
Stride Rite	1.67	Scientific-Atlanta	0.34	PG&E	5.33

Source: Business Week, Mar. 24, 1997.

b. Assume the circumstances of part **a** do not hold. What nonparametric test could be performed to shed light on the issue of differences in the dividend yields across the three industries?

c. Conduct the test. Use $\alpha = .05$. Interpret your results in the context of the problem.

16.61 The length of time required for a human subject to respond to a new painkiller was tested in the following manner. Seven randomly selected subjects were assigned to receive both aspirin and the new drug. The two treatments were spaced in time and assigned in random order. The length of time (in minutes) required for a subject to indicate that he or she could feel pain relief was recorded for both the aspirin and the drug. The data are shown in the next table. Do the data provide sufficient evidence to indicate that the probability distribution of the times required to obtain relief with aspirin is shifted to the right of the probability distribution of the times required to obtain relief with the new drug?

Subject	Aspirin	New Drug
1	15	7
2	20	14
3	12	13
4	20	11
5	17	10
6	14	16
7	17	11

16.62 A state highway patrol was interested in knowing whether frequent patrolling of highways substantially reduces the number of speeders. Two similar interstate highways were selected for the study—one heavily patrolled and the other only occasionally patrolled. After 1 month, random samples of 100 cars were chosen on each highway, and the number of cars exceeding the speed limit was recorded. This process was repeated on five randomly selected days. The data are shown in the following table.

	HIGHWAY 1	HIGHWAY 2
Day	**Heavily Patrolled**	**Occasionally Patrolled**
1	35	60
2	40	36
3	25	48
4	38	54
5	47	63

a. Do the data provide evidence to indicate that the heavily patrolled highway tends to have

fewer speeders per 100 cars than the occasionally patrolled highway? Test using $\alpha = .05$.

b. Use the paired t-test with $\alpha = .05$ to compare the population mean number of speeders per 100 cars for the two highways. What assumptions are necessary for this procedure to be valid?

16.63 The Wilcoxon signed rank test was used to compare the performance of organizations using an innovative decentralized organization structure, the M-form, and their principal competitors. D. S. Teece identified the first firm in each of 20 industries that adopted the M-form structure (*Journal of Industrial Economics*, Dec. 1981). The principal competitor of each of these firms was identified, and if it also had adopted the M-form structure, but at a later date, it qualified for the sample. The difference in performance within the 14 qualifying pairs of firms was measured over two three-year time periods: "before," when only the M-form originator in each pair used the M-form, and "after," when both had M-form structures. Differential performance in each time period was measured as the average difference in yearly return on stockholders' equity, where the differences were formed by subtracting the competitor's return on equity from the M-form originator's. The performance data appear in the accompanying table.

	AVERAGE DIFFERENCE IN YEARLY RETURN ON EQUITY	
Industry	**Before**	**After**
Grocery	25.70%	10.78%
Chemicals	6.26	−.39
Textiles	5.84	1.94
Aluminum	4.16	.56
Meat packing	−2.43	−5.80
Packaged foods	.77	−1.18
Can manufacturing	3.79	2.49
Grain milling	3.86	4.81
Petroleum	3.29	2.38
Tires	−3.36	−2.46
Autos	13.48	14.38
Electrical equipment	−10.85	−10.40
Tobacco	1.50	1.90
Retail department stores	12.32	12.37

a. Teece concluded that "the M-form innovation has been shown to display a statistically significant impact on firm performance." Do you agree? Test using $\alpha = .05$.

b. What is the approximate p-value of the test of part **a**?

c. What assumptions are necessary to ensure the validity of the test procedure you used in part **a**?

Truck	Static Weight x	Weigh-in-Motion Reading Prior to Calibration Adjustment y_1	Weigh-in-Motion Reading After Calibration Adjustment y_2
1	27.9	26.0	27.8
2	29.1	29.9	29.1
3	38.0	39.5	37.8
4	27.0	25.1	27.1
5	30.3	31.6	30.6
6	34.5	36.2	34.3
7	27.8	25.1	26.9
8	29.6	31.0	29.6
9	33.1	35.6	33.0
10	35.5	40.2	35.0

16.64 Exercise 10.55 described a calibration study (Wright, Owen, and Pena, 1983) undertaken by the Minnesota Department of Transportation to evaluate a new weigh-in-motion scale. Pearson's product moment correlation coefficient was used to measure the strength of the relationship between the static weight of a truck and the truck's weight as measured by the weigh-in-motion equipment. The data (in thousands of pounds) are repeated in the table above.

   a. Calculate Spearman's rank correlation coefficient for x and y_1 and for x and y_2. Interpret, in the context of the problem, the values you obtain. Compare your results with those of Exercise 10.55, part **c**.

   b. In the context of this problem, what circumstances would result in Spearman's rank correlation coefficient being exactly 1? Being exactly 0?

16.65 An experiment was conducted to compare two print types, A and B, to determine whether type A is easier to read. Ten subjects were randomly divided into two groups of five. Each subject was given the same material to read, one group receiving the material printed with type A, the other group receiving print type B. The times necessary for each subject to read the material (in seconds) were

Type A: 95, 122, 101, 99, 108

Type B: 110, 102, 115, 112, 120

   Do the data provide sufficient evidence to indicate that print type A is easier to read? Test using $\alpha = .05$.

16.66 Refer to Exercise 16.65. Test the research hypothesis that the median of the type A probability distribution exceeds 100 seconds. Repeat the test for the type B probability distribution. Use $\alpha = .05$ for both tests.

16.67 (X16.067) Suppose a company wants to study how personality relates to leadership. Four supervisors (1–4) with different types of personalities are selected. Several employees are then selected from the group supervised by each and asked to rate the leader of their group on a scale from 1 to 20 (20 signifies highly favorable). The resulting data are shown in the table.

1	2	3	4
20	17	16	8
19	11	15	12
20	13	13	10
18	15	18	14
17	14	11	9
	16		10

   a. What type of experimental design was employed? Identify the key elements of the experiment: response, factor(s), factor type(s), treatments, and experimental units.

   b. Test to determine whether evidence exists that the probability distributions of ratings differ for at least two of the four supervisors. Use $\alpha = .05$.

   c. What assumptions are necessary to ensure the validity of the test?

   d. Do the results of the test warrant further comparisons of the pairs of supervisors? If so, compare all pairs of probability distributions using $\alpha = .05$ for each comparison. Does one supervisor appear to be most popular?

16.68 A drug company has synthesized two new compounds to be used in sleeping pills. The data in the table at the top of page 910 represent the additional hours of sleep gained by ten patients through the use of the two drugs. Do the data present sufficient evidence to indicate that the probability distributions of additional hours of sleep differ for the two drugs? Test using $\alpha = .10$.

Patient	Drug A	Drug B	Patient	Drug A	Drug B	Patient	Drug A	Drug B
1	.4	.7	5	−1.6	−.2	9	3.1	.0
2	−.7	−1.6	6	2.9	3.4	10	1.9	2.0
3	−.4	−.2	7	4.0	3.7			
4	−1.4	−1.4	8	.1	.8			

16.69 (X16.069) Weevils cause millions of dollars worth of damage each year to cotton crops. Three chemicals (A, B, and C) designed to control weevil populations were applied, one to each of three fields of cotton. After three months, 10 plots of equal size were randomly selected within each field and the percentage of cotton plants with weevil damage was recorded for each. Do the data in the accompanying table provide sufficient evidence to indicate a difference in location among the distributions of damage rates corresponding to the three treatments? Use $\alpha = .05$.

A		B		C	
10.8	9.8	22.3	20.4	9.8	10.8
15.6	16.7	19.5	23.6	12.3	12.2
19.2	19.0	18.6	21.2	16.2	17.3
17.9	20.3	24.3	19.8	14.1	15.1
18.3	19.4	19.9	22.6	15.3	11.3

16.70 Many water treatment facilities supplement the natural fluoride concentration with hydrofluosilicic acid in order to reach a target concentration of fluoride in drinking water. Certain levels are thought to enhance dental health, but very high concentrations can be dangerous. Suppose that one such treatment plant targets .75 milligrams per liter (mg/L) for their water. The plant tests 25 samples each day to determine whether the median level differs from the target.
  a. Set up the null and alternative hypotheses.
  b. Set up the test statistic and rejection region using $\alpha = .10$.
  c. Explain the implication of a Type I error in the context of this application. A Type II error.
  d. Suppose that one day's samples result in 18 values that exceed .75 mg/L. Conduct the test and state the appropriate conclusion in the context of this application.
  e. When it was suggested to the plant's supervisor that a t-test should be used to conduct the daily test, she replied that the probability distribution of the fluoride concentrations was "heavily skewed to the right." Show graphically what she meant by this, and explain why this is a reason to prefer the sign test to the t-test.

16.71 A hotel had a problem with people reserving rooms for a weekend and then not honoring their reservations (no-shows). As a result, the hotel developed a new reservation and deposit plan that it hoped would reduce the number of no-shows. One year after the policy was initiated, management evaluated its effect in comparison with the old policy. Compare the records given in the table on the number of no-shows for the 10 nonholiday weekends preceding the institution of the new policy and the 10 nonholiday weekends preceding the evaluation time. Has the situation improved under the new policy? Test at $\alpha = .05$.

Before		After	
10	11	4	4
5	8	3	2
3	9	8	5
6	6	5	7
7	5	6	1

16.72 A manufacturer wants to determine whether the number of defectives produced by its employees tends to increase as the day progresses. Unknown to the employees, a complete inspection is made of every item that was produced on one day, and the hourly fraction defective is recorded. The resulting data are given in the accompanying table. Do they provide evidence that the fraction defective increases as the day progresses? Test at the $\alpha = .05$ level.

Hour	Fraction Defective
1	.02
2	.05
3	.03
4	.08
5	.06
6	.09
7	.11
8	.10

16.73 Refer to Exercise 16.72. Assume that the eight measurements of the fraction defective constitute a random sample from the probability distribution of all fraction defective measurements. The manufacturer wants to determine whether the median hourly fraction defective exceeds .05.

a. Conduct the appropriate test to make this determination at the .10 level of significance.

b. Why might the manufacturer wish to conduct the test with this relatively high level of significance?

c. What assumptions are necessary to ensure the validity of this test? How do they differ from the assumptions that would be necessary to conduct a *t*-test about the mean fraction defective?

16.74 **(X16.074)** A savings and loan association is considering three locations in a large city as potential office sites. The company has hired a marketing firm to compare the incomes of people living in the area surrounding each site. The market researchers interview 10 households chosen at random in each area to determine the type of job, length of employment, etc., of those in the households who work. This information enables them to estimate the annual income of each household, as shown in the table (in thousands of dollars).

Site 1		Site 2		Site 3	
34.3	36.2	39.3	42.2	34.5	38.3
35.5	43.5	45.5	103.5	29.3	43.3
32.1	34.7	50.2	47.9	37.2	36.7
28.3	38.0	72.1	41.2	33.2	40.0
40.5	35.1	48.6	44.0	32.6	35.2

a. What type of design was utilized for this experiment?

b. Use the appropriate nonparametric test to compare the treatments. Specify the hypotheses and interpret the results in terms of this experiment. Use $\alpha = .05$.

c. Does the result of your test warrant further comparison of the pairs of treatments? If so, compare the pairs using the appropriate nonparametric technique and $\alpha = .05$ for each comparison. Interpret the results in terms of this experiment.

d. What assumptions are necessary to ensure the validity of the nonparametric procedures you employed? How do they compare with the assumptions that would have to be satisfied in order to use the appropriate parametric technique to analyze this experiment?

16.75 The personnel director of a company interviewed six potential job applicants without knowing anything about their backgrounds and then rated them on a scale of 1 to 10. Independently, the director's supervisor made an evaluation of the background qualifications of each candidate on the same scale. The results are shown in the table. Is there evidence that candidates' qualification scores are related to their interview performance? Use $\alpha = .10$.

Candidate	Qualifications	Interview Performance
1	10	8
2	8	9
3	9	10
4	4	5
5	5	3
6	6	6

16.76 **(X16.076)** D. Campbell, J. Gaertner, and R. Vecchio investigated the perceptions of accounting professors with respect to the present and desired importance of various factors considered in promotion and tenure decisions at major universities (*Journal of Education*, Spring 1983). One hundred fifteen professors at universities with accredited doctoral programs responded to a mailed questionnaire. The questionnaire asked the professors to rate (1) the actual importance placed on 20 factors in the promotion and tenure decisions at their universities and (2) how they believe the factors *should* be weighted. Responses were obtained on a 5-point scale ranging from "no importance" to "extreme importance." The resulting ratings were averaged and converted to the rankings shown in the table. Calculate Spearman's rank correlation coefficient for the data and carefully interpret its value in the context of the problem.

Factor	Actual	Ideal
I. Teaching (and related items):		
Teaching performance	6	1
Advising and counseling students	19	15
Students' complaints/praise	14	17
II. Research:		
Number of journal articles	1	6.5
Quality of journal articles	4	2
Refereed publications:		
a. Applied studies	5	4
b. Theoretical empirical studies	2	3
c. Educationally oriented	11	8
Papers at professional meetings	10	12
Journal editor or reviewer	9	10
Other (textbooks, etc.)	7.5	11
III. Service and professional interaction:		
Service to profession	15	9
Professional/academic awards	7.5	6.5
Community service	18	19
University service	16	16
Collegiality/cooperativeness	12	13
IV. Other:		
Academic degrees attained	3	5
Professional certification	17	14
Consulting activities	20	20
Grantsmanship	13	18

Source: Campbell, D. K., Gaertner, J., and Vecchio, R. P. "Perceptions of promotion and tenure criteria: A survey of accounting educators." *Journal of Accounting Education,* Vol. 1, Spring 1983, pp. 83–92.

16.77 **(X16.077)** It has been conjectured that income is a primary determinant of job satisfaction. To investigate this theory, 15 employees of a particular firm are chosen at random and their gross salaries are noted. Each employee is then asked to complete a questionnaire designed to measure job satisfaction. The resulting scores (higher scores mean greater satisfaction) and gross incomes (in thousands of dollars) are given in the table.

a. Compute Spearman's rank correlation coefficient for these data.

b. Is there evidence that job satisfaction and income are positively correlated? Use $\alpha = .05$.

c. Is there evidence that the median job score of all employees of the firm exceeds 75? Use $\alpha = .05$.

Employee	Job Score	Income
1	92	29.9
2	51	18.7
3	88	32.0
4	65	15.0
5	80	26.0
6	31	9.0
7	38	11.3
8	75	22.1
9	45	16.0
10	72	25.0
11	53	17.2
12	43	9.7
13	87	20.1
14	30	15.5
15	74	16.5

THE CHI-SQUARE TEST AND THE ANALYSIS OF CONTINGENCY TABLES

CONTENTS

Where We've Been

In the preceding chapters we examined several statistical methods for analyzing many types of data. Except for those that pertain to binomial proportions, most of the techniques presented in Chapters 7–9 and 15 are appropriate for populations of data on quantitative random variables. Regression models were presented in Chapters 10–12 for the purpose of predicting a quantitative dependent variable from the values of both quantitative and qualitative independent variables. Nonparametric statistics were presented in Chapter 16.

Where We're Going

The methods we discuss in this chapter are appropriate for *count*, or *enumerative, data,* a type exemplified by the binomial data of Chapters 7–9. Recall that the binomial experiment (Chapter 4) consists of n trials, each of which results in *two* outcomes. Thus, we have two classifications into which all the data fall. In this chapter, we consider the analysis of data that fall into *two or more* categories.

Many business analyses consist of *enumerating* the number of occurrences of some event. For example, we may *count* the number of defectives during one shift at a manufacturing plant, or the number of consumers who choose each of three brands of coffee, or the number of sales made by each of five automobile salespeople during the month of June. In some instances, the objective of collecting the **count data** is to analyze the distribution of the counts in the various **classes**, or **cells**. For example, we may want to estimate the proportion of smokers who prefer each of three different brands of cigarettes by counting the number in a sample of smokers who buy each brand. We say that count data classified on a single scale have a **one-dimensional classification**. The analysis of one-dimensional count data is discussed in Section 17.1.

In other instances, the objective of collecting the count data is to study the relationship between two different categorical factors. For example, we may be interested in investigating whether the color of automobile purchased is related to the sex of the buyer. Or the relationship between shift and number of defectives produced in a manufacturing plant could be of interest. When count data are classified in a *two-dimensional table,* we call the result a *contingency table.* The analysis of contingency tables is discussed in Section 17.2.

17.1 ONE-DIMENSIONAL COUNT DATA: THE MULTINOMIAL DISTRIBUTION

Consumer preference surveys can be valuable aids in making marketing decisions. Suppose a large supermarket chain conducts a consumer preference survey by recording the brand of bread purchased by customers in its stores. Assume the chain carries three brands of bread—two major brands (A and B) and its own store brand. The brand preferences of a random sample of 150 consumers are observed, and the resulting count data appear in Table 17.1. Do these data indicate that a preference exists for any of the brands?

To answer this question, we have to know the underlying probability distribution of these count data. This distribution, called the **multinomial probability distribution**, is an extension of the binomial distribution (Section 4.4). The properties of the multinomial distribution are shown in the box.

Properties of the Multinomial Probability Distribution
1. The experiment consists of n identical trials.
2. There are k possible outcomes to each trial.
3. The probabilities of the k outcomes, denoted by $p_1, p_2, \ldots, p_k$, remain the same from trial to trial, where $p_1 + p_2 + \cdots + p_k = 1$.
4. The trials are independent.
5. The random variables of interest are the counts $n_1, n_2, \ldots, n_k$ in each of the k cells.

TABLE 17.1 Consumer Preference Survey

A	B	Store Brand
61	53	36

Note that our consumer-preference survey satisfies the properties of a **multinomial experiment**. The experiment consists of randomly sampling $n = 150$ buyers from a large population of consumers containing an unknown proportion p_1 who prefer brand A, a proportion p_2 who prefer brand B, and a proportion p_3 who prefer the store brand. Each buyer represents a single trial that can result in one of three outcomes: The consumer prefers brand A, B, or the store brand with probabilities p_1, p_2, and p_3, respectively. (Assume that all consumers will have a preference.) The buyer preference of any single consumer in the sample does not affect the preference of another; consequently, the trials are independent. And, finally, you can see that the recorded data are the number of buyers in each of three consumer-preference categories. Thus, the consumer-preference survey satisfies the five properties of a multinomial experiment. You can see that the properties of the multinomial experiment closely resemble those of the binomial experiment and that, in fact, a binomial experiment is a multinomial experiment for the special case where $k = 2$.

In the consumer-preference survey, and in most practical applications of the multinomial experiment, the k outcomes probabilities $p_1, p_2, ..., p_k$ are unknown and we want to use the survey data to make inferences about their values. The unknown probabilities in the consumer-preference survey are

$$p_1 = \text{Proportion of all buyers who prefer brand A}$$

$$p_2 = \text{Proportion of all buyers who prefer brand B}$$

$$p_3 = \text{Proportion of all buyers who prefer the store brand}$$

To decide whether the consumers have a preference for any of the brands, we will want to test the null hypothesis that the brands of bread are equally preferred (that is, $p_1 = p_2 = p_3 = \frac{1}{3}$) against the alternative hypothesis that one brand is preferred (that is, at least one of the probabilities p_1, p_2, and p_3 exceeds $\frac{1}{3}$). Thus, we want to test

$H_0: p_1 = p_2 = p_3 = \frac{1}{3}$ (no preference)

$H_a:$ At least one of the proportions exceeds $\frac{1}{3}$ (a preference exists)

If the null hypothesis is true and $p_1 = p_2 = p_3 = \frac{1}{3}$, the expected value (mean value) of the number of customers who prefer brand A is given by

$$E(n_1) = np_1 = (n)\frac{1}{3} = (150)\frac{1}{3} = 50$$

Similarly, $E(n_2) = E(n_3) = 50$ if the null hypothesis is true and no preference exists.

The following test statistic—the **chi-square test**—measures the degree of disagreement between the data and the null hypothesis:

$$\chi^2 = \frac{[n_1 - E(n_1)]^2}{E(n_1)} + \frac{[n_2 - E(n_2)]^2}{E(n_2)} + \frac{[n_3 - E(n_3)]^2}{E(n_3)}$$

$$= \frac{(n_1 - 50)^2}{50} + \frac{(n_2 - 50)^2}{50} + \frac{(n_3 - 50)^2}{50}$$

Note that the farther the observed numbers n_1, n_2, and n_3 are from their expected value (50), the larger χ^2 will become. That is, large values of χ^2 imply that the null hypothesis is false.

We have to know the distribution of χ^2 in repeated sampling before we can decide whether the data indicate that a preference exists. When H_0 is true, χ^2 can be shown to have (approximately) the familiar chi-square distribution of Section 15.5. For this one-way classification, the χ^2 distribution has $(k - 1)$ degrees of freedom.* The rejection region for the consumer-preference survey for $\alpha = .05$ and $k - 1 = 3 - 1 = 2$ df is

---

*The derivation of the degrees of freedom for χ^2 involves the number of linear restrictions imposed on the count data. In the present case, the only constraint is that $\Sigma n_i = n$, where n (the sample size) is fixed in advance. Therefore, df $= k - 1$. For other cases, we will give the degrees of freedom for each usage of χ^2 and refer the interested reader to the references for more detail.

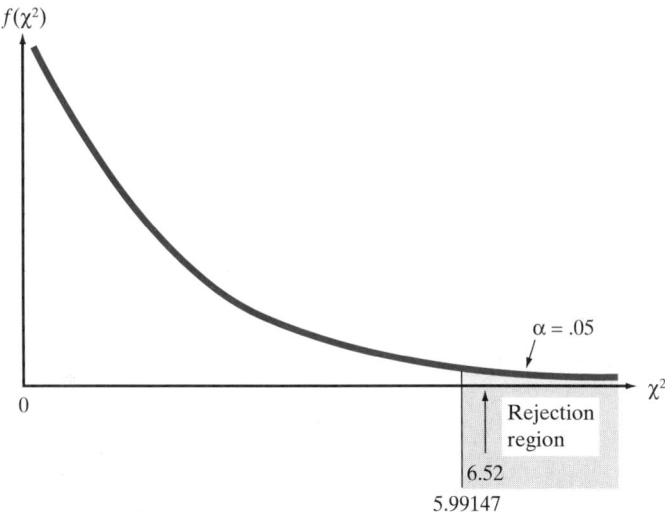

FIGURE 17.1
Rejection region for consumer-preference survey

$$\text{Rejection region: } \chi^2 > \chi^2_{.05}$$

The value of $\chi^2_{.05}$ (found in Table XIII of Appendix B) is 5.99147. (See Figure 17.1.) The computed value of the test statistic is

$$\chi^2 = \frac{(n_1 - 50)^2}{50} + \frac{(n_2 - 50)^2}{50} + \frac{(n_3 - 50)^2}{50}$$

$$= \frac{(61 - 50)^2}{50} + \frac{(53 - 50)^2}{50} + \frac{(36 - 50)^2}{50} = 6.52$$

Since the computed $\chi^2 = 6.52$ exceeds the critical value of 5.99147, we conclude at the $\alpha = .05$ level of significance that there does exist a consumer preference for one or more of the brands of bread.

Now that we have evidence to indicate that the proportions $p_1, p_2,$ and p_3 are unequal, we can make inferences concerning their individual values using the methods of Section 7.3. [*Note:* We cannot use the methods of Section 9.3 to compare two proportions because the cell counts are dependent random variables.] The general form for a test of a hypothesis concerning multinomial probabilities is shown in the next box.

A Test of a Hypothesis About Multinomial Probabilities: One-Way Table

$$H_0: p_1 = p_{1,0}, p_2 = p_{2,0}, ..., p_k = p_{k,0}$$

where $p_{1,0}, p_{2,0}, ..., p_{k,0}$ represent the hypothesized values of the multinomial probabilities

H_a: At least one of the multinomial probabilities
does not equal its hypothesized value

Test statistic: $\chi^2 = \sum \dfrac{[n_i - E(n_i)]^2}{E(n_i)}$

where $E(n_i) = np_{i,0}$ is the **expected cell count**, that is, the expected number of outcomes of type i assuming that H_0 is true. The total sample size is n.

Rejection region: $\chi^2 > \chi^2_\alpha$,

where χ^2_α has $(k - 1)$ df.

Assumptions: **1.** A multinomial experiment has been conducted. This is generally satisfied by taking a random sample from the population of interest.

2. The sample size n will be large enough so that for every cell, the expected cell count $E(n_i)$ will be equal to 5 or more.*

EXAMPLE 17.1

A large firm has established what it hopes is an objective system of deciding on annual pay increases for its employees. The system is based on a series of evaluation scores determined by the supervisors of each employee. Employees with scores above 80 receive a merit pay increase, those with scores between 50 and 80 receive the standard increase, and those below 50 receive no increase. The firm designed the plan with the objective that, on the average, 25% of its employees would receive merit increases, 65% would receive standard increases, and 10% would receive no increase. After one year of operation using the new plan, the distribution of pay increases for the 600 company employees was as shown in Table 17.2. Test at the $\alpha = .01$ level to determine whether these data indicate that the distribution of pay increases differs significantly from the proportions established by the firm.

SOLUTION

Define

$$p_1 = \text{Proportion of employees who receive no pay increase}$$

$$p_2 = \text{Proportion of employees who receive a standard increase}$$

$$p_3 = \text{Proportion of employees who receive a merit increase}$$

Then the null and alternative hypotheses are:

$H_0: p_1 = .10, p_2 = .65, p_3 = .25$

$H_a:$ At least two of the proportions differ from the firm's proposed plan

Test statistic: $\chi^2 = \sum \dfrac{[n_i - E(n_i)]^2}{E(n_i)}$

where

$E(n_1) = np_{1,0} = 600(.10) = 60$
$E(n_2) = np_{2,0} = 600(.65) = 390$
$E(n_3) = np_{3,0} = 600(.25) = 150$

Rejection region: For $\alpha = .01$ and df $= k - 1 = 2$, reject H_0 if $\chi^2 > \chi^2_{.01}$, where (from Table XIII of Appendix B) $\chi^2_{.01} = 9.21034$.

We now calculate the test statistic:

$$\chi^2 = \frac{(42 - 60)^2}{60} + \frac{(365 - 390)^2}{390} + \frac{(193 - 150)^2}{150} = 19.33$$

Since this value exceeds the table value of χ^2 (9.21034), the data provide strong evidence ($\alpha = .01$) that the company's pay plan is not working as planned.

TABLE 17.2
Distribution of Pay Increases

None	Standard	Merit
42	365	193

*The assumption that all expected cell counts are at least 5 is necessary in order to ensure that the χ^2 approximation is appropriate. Exact methods for conducting the test of a hypothesis exist and may be used for small expected cell counts, but these methods are beyond the scope of this text.

FIGURE 17.2
EXCEL analysis of
data in Table 17.2

CHI-SQUARE	P-VALUE
19.33	6.34664E-05

The χ^2 test can also be conducted using an available statistical software package. Figure 17.2 is a portion of an EXCEL printout of the analysis of the data in Table 17.2; note that the p-value of the test is .0000634664. Since $\alpha = .01$ exceeds this p-value, there is sufficient evidence to reject H_0. **▎**

If we focus on one particular outcome of a multinomial experiment, we can use the methods developed in Section 7.4 for a binomial proportion to establish a confidence interval for any one of the multinomial probabilities.* For example, if we want a 95% confidence interval for the proportion of the company's employees who will receive merit increases under the new system, we calculate

$$\hat{p}_3 \pm 1.96\sigma_{\hat{p}_3} \approx \hat{p}_3 \pm 1.96\sqrt{\frac{\hat{p}_3(1 - \hat{p}_3)}{n}} \qquad \text{where } \hat{p}_3 = \frac{n_3}{n} = \frac{193}{600} = .32$$

$$= .32 \pm 1.96\sqrt{\frac{(.32)(1 - .32)}{600}} = .32 \pm .04$$

Thus, we estimate that between 28% and 36% of the firm's employees will qualify for merit increases under the new plan. It appears that the firm will have to raise the requirements for merit increases in order to achieve the stated goal of a 25% employee qualification rate.

*Note that focusing on one outcome has the effect of lumping the other $(k - 1)$ outcomes into a single group. Thus, we obtain, in effect, two outcomes—or a binomial experiment.

EXERCISES 17.1–17.17

Learning the Mechanics

17.1 Use Table XIII of Appendix B to find each of the following χ^2 values:
a. $\chi^2_{.05}$ for df = 17   b. $\chi^2_{.990}$ for df = 100
c. $\chi^2_{.10}$ for df = 15   d. $\chi^2_{.005}$ for df = 3

17.2 Use Table XIII of Appendix B to find the following probabilities:
a. $P(\chi^2 \le 1.063623)$ for df = 4
b. $P(\chi^2 > 30.5779)$ for df = 15
c. $P(\chi^2 \ge 82.3581)$ for df = 100
d. $P(\chi^2 < 18.4926)$ for df = 30

17.3 Find the rejection region for a one-dimensional χ^2-test of a null hypothesis concerning $p_1, p_2, ..., p_k$ if
a. $k = 3; \alpha = .05$
b. $k = 5; \alpha = .10$
c. $k = 4; \alpha = .01$

17.4 What are the characteristics of a multinomial experiment? Compare the characteristics to those of a binomial experiment.

17.5 What conditions must n satisfy to make the χ^2-test valid?

17.6 A multinomial experiment with $k = 3$ cells and $n = 320$ produced the data shown in the following table. Do these data provide sufficient evidence to contradict the null hypothesis that $p_1 = .25$, $p_2 = .25$, and $p_3 = .50$? Test using $\alpha = .05$.

	CELL		
	1	2	3
n_i	78	60	182

17.7 A multinomial experiment with $k = 4$ cells and $n = 205$ produced the data shown in the table.
a. Do these data provide sufficient evidence to conclude that the multinomial probabilities differ? Test using $\alpha = .05$.
b. What are the Type I and Type II errors associated with the test of part **a**?

	CELL			
	1	2	3	4
n_i	43	56	59	47

17.8   Refer to Exercise 17.7. Construct a 95% confidence interval for the multinomial probability associated with cell 3.

Applying the Concepts

17.9   *Inc. Technology* (Mar. 18, 1997) reported the results of the 1996 Equifax/Harris Consumer Privacy Survey in which 328 Internet users indicated their level of agreement with the following statement: "The government needs to be able to scan Internet messages and user communications to prevent fraud and other crimes." The number of users in each response category is summarized below.

Agree Strongly	Agree Somewhat	Disagree Somewhat	Disagree Strongly
59	108	82	79

a. Specify the null and alternative hypotheses you would use to determine if the opinions of Internet users are evenly divided among the four categories.
b. Conduct the test of part **a** using $\alpha = .05$.
c. In the context of this exercise, what is a Type I error? A Type II error?
d. What assumptions must hold in order to ensure the validity of the test you conducted in part **b**?

17.10   Data from supermarket scanners are used by researchers to understand the purchasing patterns and preferences of consumers. Researchers frequently study the purchases of a sample of households, called a *scanner panel*. When shopping, these households present a magnetic identification card that permits their purchase data to be identified and aggregated. Marketing researchers recently studied the extent to which panel households' purchase behavior is representative of the population of households shopping at the same stores (*Marketing Research*, Nov. 1996). The next table reports the peanut butter purchase data collected by A. C. Nielsen Company for a panel of 2,500 households in Sioux Falls, South Dakota, over a 102-week period. The market share percentages in the righthand column are derived from all peanut butter purchases at the same 15 stores at which the panel shopped during the same 102-week period.
a. Do the data provide sufficient evidence to conclude that the purchases of the household

Brand	Size	Number of Purchases by Household Panel	Market Shares
Jif	18 oz.	3,165	20.10%
Jif	28	1,892	10.10
Jif	40	726	5.42
Peter Pan	10	4,079	16.01
Skippy	18	6,206	28.65
Skippy	28	1,627	12.38
Skippy	40	1,420	7.32
Total		19,115	

Source: Gupta, S., *et al.* "Do household scanner data provide representative inferences from brand choices? A comparison with store data." *Journal of Marketing Research,* Vol. 33, Nov. 1996, pp. 393 (Table 6).

panel are representative of the population of households? Test using $\alpha = .05$.
b. What assumptions must hold to ensure the validity of the testing procedure you used in part **a**?
c. Find the approximate *p*-value for the test of part **a** and interpret it in the context of the problem.

17.11   Each year, approximately 1.3 million Americans suffer adverse drug effects (ADEs), that is, unintended injuries caused by prescribed medication. A study in the *Journal of the American Medical Association* (July 5, 1995) identified the cause of 247 ADEs that occurred at two Boston hospitals. The researchers found that dosing errors (that is, wrong dosage prescribed and/or dispensed) were the most common. The table summarizes the proximate cause of 95 ADEs that resulted from a dosing error. Conduct a test (at $\alpha = .10$) to determine whether the true percentages of ADEs in the five "cause" categories are different. Use the accompanying EXCEL printout to arrive at your decision.

Wrong Dosage Cause	Number of ADEs
(1) Lack of knowledge of drug	29
(2) Rule violation	17
(3) Faulty dose checking	13
(4) Slips	9
(5) Other	27

CAUSE	ADEs
NO KNOWLEDGE	29
RULE VIOLATE	17
FAULTY DOSE	13
SLIPS	9
OTHER	27
CHI-SQUARE	16
P-VALUE	0.003019

17.12 In education, the term *instructional technology* refers to products such as computers, spreadsheets, CD-ROMs, videos, and presentation software. How frequently do professors use instructional technology in the classroom? To answer this question, researchers at Western Michigan University surveyed 306 of their fellow faculty (*Educational Technology,* Mar.–Apr. 1995). Responses to the frequency-of-technology use in teaching were recorded as "weekly to every class," "once a semester to monthly," or "never." The faculty responses (number in each response category) for the three technologies are summarized in the table.

Technology	Weekly	Once a Semester/ Monthly	Never
Computer spreadsheets	58	67	181
Word processing	168	61	77
Statistical software	37	82	187

a. Determine whether the percentages in the three frequency-of-use response categories differ for computer spreadsheets. Use $\alpha = .01$.
b. Repeat part **a** for word processing.
c. Repeat part **a** for statistical software.
d. Construct a 99% confidence interval for the true percentage of faculty who never use computer spreadsheets in the classroom. Interpret the interval.

17.13 A Gallup survey portrays U.S. entrepreneurs as "the mavericks, dreamers, and loners whose rough edges and uncompromising need to do it their own way set them in sharp contrast to senior executives in major American corporations" (*The Wall Street Journal,* May 1985). One of the many questions put to a sample of $n = 100$ entrepreneurs about their job characteristics, work habits, social activities, etc., concerned the origin of the car they personally drive most frequently. The responses given in the table were obtained.

United States	Europe	Japan
45	46	9

a. Do these data provide evidence of a difference in the preference of entrepreneurs for the cars made in the United States, Europe, and Japan? Test using $\alpha = .05$.
b. Do these data provide evidence of a difference in the preference of entrepreneurs for domestic versus foreign cars? Test using $\alpha = .05$.
c. What assumptions must you make in order to ensure that your inferences of parts **a** and **b** are valid?

17.14 Refer to Exercise 17.13. Use a 90% confidence interval to estimate the proportion of U.S. entrepreneurs who drive foreign cars.

17.15 Overweight trucks are responsible for much of the damage sustained by our local, state, and federal highway systems. Although illegal, overloading is common. Truckers may avoid weigh stations run by enforcement officers by taking back roads or by traveling when weigh stations are likely to be closed. A state highway planning agency (Minnesota Department of Transportation) monitored the movements of overweight trucks on an interstate highway using an unmanned, computerized scale that is built into the highway. Unknown to the truckers, the scale weighed their vehicles as they passed over it. Each day's proportion of one week's total truck traffic (five-axle tractor truck semitrailers) is shown in the first table below. During the same week, the number of overweight trucks per day is given in the second table.
a. The planning agency would like to know whether the number of overweight trucks per week is distributed over the seven days of the week in direct proportion to the volume of truck traffic. Test using $\alpha = .05$.
b. Find the approximate p-value for the test of part **a**.

17.16 The threat of earthquakes is a part of life in California, where scientists have warned about "the big one" for decades. An article in the *Annals of the Association of American Geographers* (June 1992) investigated what influences homeowners in purchasing earthquake insurance. One factor investigated was the proximity to a major fault. The researchers hypothesized that the nearer a county is to a major fault, the more likely residents are to own earthquake insurance. Suppose that a random sample of 700 earthquake-insured residents from four California counties is selected,

Monday	Tuesday	Wednesday	Thursday	Friday	Saturday	Sunday
.191	.198	.187	.180	.155	.043	.046

Monday	Tuesday	Wednesday	Thursday	Friday	Saturday	Sunday
90	82	72	70	51	18	31

and the number in each county is counted and recorded in the table:

	Contra Costa	Santa Clara	Los Angeles	San Bernardino
Number Insured	103	213	241	143

a. What are the appropriate null and alternative hypotheses to test whether the proportions of all earthquake-insured residents in the four counties differ?

b. Do the data provide sufficient evidence that the proportions of all earthquake-insured residents differ among the four counties? Test using $\alpha = .05$.

c. Los Angeles County is closest to a major earthquake fault. Construct a 95% confidence interval for the proportion of all earthquake-

insured residents in the four counties that reside in Los Angeles County.

d. Does the confidence interval you formed in part **c** support the conclusion of the test conducted in part **b**? Explain.

17.17 A company that manufactures dice for gambling casinos regularly inspects its product to be sure that only "fair" (balanced) dice are supplied to the casinos. One die was randomly chosen from a production lot and rolled 120 times. Counts of the numbers showing face up are recorded in the table. Do the data provide sufficient evidence to indicate that the die is unbalanced? Test using $\alpha = .10$.

Numbers Face Up	1	2	3	4	5	6
Frequency	28	27	20	18	15	12

17.2   CONTINGENCY TABLES

In Section 17.1, we introduced the multinomial probability distribution and considered data classified according to a single criterion. We now consider multinomial experiments in which the data are classified according to two criteria, that is, *classification with respect to two factors.*

For example, high gasoline prices have made many consumers more aware of the size of the automobiles they purchase. Suppose an automobile manufacturer is interested in determining the relationship between the size and manufacturer of newly purchased automobiles. One thousand recent buyers of cars made in the United States are randomly sampled, and each purchase is classified with respect to the size and manufacturer of the automobile. The data are summarized in the **two-way table** shown in Table 17.3. This table is called a **contingency table**; it presents multinomial count data classified on two scales, or **dimensions**, of classification—namely, automobile size and manufacturer.

The symbols representing the cell counts for the multinomial experiment in Table 17.3 are shown in Table 17.4a; and the corresponding cell, row, and column probabilities are shown in Table 17.4b. Thus, n_{11} represents the number of buyers who purchase a small car of manufacturer A and p_{11} represents the corresponding cell probability. Note the symbols for the row and column totals and also the symbols for the probability totals. The latter are called **marginal probabilities** for each row and column. The marginal probability p_{r1} is the probability that a small car is purchased; the marginal probability p_{c1} is the probability that a car by manufacturer A is purchased. Thus,

TABLE 17.3   Contingency Table for Automobile Size Example

		MANUFACTURER				
		A	**B**	**C**	**D**	**Totals**
AUTO SIZE	**Small**	157	65	181	10	413
	Intermediate	126	82	142	46	396
	Large	58	45	60	28	191
	Totals	341	192	383	84	1,000

TABLE 17.4A   Observed Counts for Contingency Table 17.3

		MANUFACTURER				
		A	B	C	D	Totals
AUTO SIZE	Small	n_{11}	n_{12}	n_{13}	n_{14}	r_1
	Intermediate	n_{21}	n_{22}	n_{23}	n_{24}	r_2
	Large	n_{31}	n_{32}	n_{33}	n_{34}	r_3
	Totals	c_1	c_2	c_3	c_4	n

TABLE 17.4B   Probabilities for Contingency Table 17.3

		MANUFACTURER				
		A	B	C	D	Totals
AUTO SIZE	Small	p_{11}	p_{12}	p_{13}	p_{14}	p_{r1}
	Intermediate	p_{21}	p_{22}	p_{23}	p_{24}	p_{r2}
	Large	p_{31}	p_{32}	p_{33}	p_{34}	p_{r3}
	Totals	p_{c1}	p_{c2}	p_{c3}	p_{c4}	1

$$p_{r1} = p_{11} + p_{12} + p_{13} + p_{14} \quad \text{and} \quad p_{c1} = p_{11} + p_{21} + p_{31}$$

Thus, we can see that this really is a multinomial experiment with a total of 1,000 trials, (3)(4) = 12 cells or possible outcomes, and probabilities for each cell as shown in Table 17.4B. If the 1,000 recent buyers are randomly chosen, the trials are considered independent and the probabilities are viewed as remaining constant from trial to trial.

Suppose we want to know whether the two classifications, manufacturer and size, are dependent. That is, if we know which size car a buyer will choose, does that information give us a clue about the manufacturer of the car the buyer will choose? In a probabilistic sense we know (Chapter 3) that independence of events A and B implies $P(AB) = P(A)P(B)$. Similarly, in the contingency table analysis, if the **two classifications are independent**, the probability that an item is classified in any particular cell of the table is the product of the corresponding marginal probabilities. Thus, under the hypothesis of independence, in Table 17.4B, we must have

$$p_{11} = p_{r1}p_{c1}$$

$$p_{12} = p_{r1}p_{c2}$$

and so forth.

To test the hypothesis of independence, we use the same reasoning employed in the one-dimensional tests of Section 17.1. First, we calculate the *expected*, or *mean, count in each cell* assuming that the null hypothesis of independence is true. We do this by noting that the expected count in a cell of the table is just the total number of multinomial trials, *n*, times the cell probability. Recall that n_{ij} represents the **observed count** in the cell located in the *i*th row and *j*th column. Then the expected cell count for the upper lefthand cell (first row, first column) is

$$E(n_{11}) = np_{11}$$

or, when the null hypothesis (the classifications are independent) is true,

$$E(n_{11}) = np_{r1}p_{c1}$$

Since these true probabilities are not known, we estimate p_{r1} and p_{c1} by the same proportions $\hat{p}r_1 = r_1/n$ and $\hat{p}_{c1} = c_1/n$. Thus, the estimate of the expected value $E(n_{11})$ is

$$\hat{E}(n_{11}) = n\left(\frac{r_1}{n}\right)\left(\frac{c_1}{n}\right) = \frac{r_1 c_1}{n}$$

Similarly, for each i, j,

$$\hat{E}(n_{ij}) = \frac{(\text{Row total})(\text{Column total})}{\text{Total sample size}}$$

Thus,

$$\hat{E}(n_{12}) = \frac{r_1 c_2}{n}$$
$$\vdots \qquad \vdots$$
$$\hat{E}(n_{34}) = \frac{r_3 c_4}{n}$$

Using the data in Table 17.3, we find

$$\hat{E}(n_{11}) = \frac{r_1 c_1}{n} = \frac{(413)(341)}{1,000} = 140.833$$

$$\hat{E}(n_{12}) = \frac{r_1 c_2}{n} = \frac{(413)(192)}{1,000} = 79.296$$
$$\vdots \qquad \vdots \qquad \vdots \qquad \vdots$$
$$\hat{E}(n_{34}) = \frac{r_3 c_4}{n} = \frac{(191)(84)}{1,000} = 16.044$$

The observed data and the estimated expected values (in parentheses) are shown in Table 17.5.

We now use the χ^2 statistic to compare the observed and expected (estimated) counts in each cell of the contingency table:

$$\chi^2 = \frac{[n_{11} - \hat{E}(n_{11})]^2}{\hat{E}(n_{11})} + \frac{[n_{12} - \hat{E}(n_{12})]^2}{\hat{E}(n_{12})} + \cdots + \frac{[n_{34} - \hat{E}(n_{34})]^2}{\hat{E}(n_{34})}$$

$$= \sum \frac{[n_{ij} - \hat{E}(n_{ij})]^2}{\hat{E}(n_{ij})}$$

TABLE 17.5   Observed and Estimated Expected (in Parentheses) Counts

		MANUFACTURER				
		A	**B**	**C**	**D**	**Totals**
	Small	157	65	181	10	
		(140.833)	(79.296)	(158.179)	(34.692)	413
AUTO	**Intermediate**	126	82	142	46	
SIZE		(135.036)	(76.032)	(151.668)	(33.264)	396
	Large	58	45	60	28	
		(65.131)	(36.672)	(73.153)	(16.044)	191
	Totals	341	192	383	84	1,000

Note: The use of Σ in the context of a contingency table analysis refers to a sum over all cells in the table.

Substituting the data of Table 17.5 into this expression, we get

$$\chi^2 = \frac{(157 - 140.833)^2}{140.833} + \frac{(65 - 79.296)^2}{79.296} + \cdots + \frac{(28 - 16.044)^2}{16.044} = 45.81$$

Large values of χ^2 imply that the observed counts do not closely agree and hence that the hypothesis of independence is false. To determine how large χ^2 must be before it is too large to be attributed to chance, we make use of the fact that the sampling distribution of χ^2 is approximately a χ^2 probability distribution when the classifications are independent.

When testing the null hypothesis of independence in a two-way contingency table, the appropriate degrees of freedom will be $(r - 1)(c - 1)$, where r is the number of rows and c is the number of columns in the table.

For the size and make of automobiles example, the degrees of freedom for χ^2 is $(r - 1)(c - 1) = (3 - 1)(4 - 1) = 6$. Then, for $\alpha = .05$, we reject the hypothesis of independence when

$$\chi^2 > \chi^2_{.05} = 12.5916$$

Since the computed $\chi^2 = 45.81$ exceeds the value 12.5916, we conclude that the size and manufacturer of a car selected by a purchaser are dependent events.

The pattern of **dependence** can be seen more clearly by expressing the data as percentages. We first select one of the two classifications to be used as the base variable. In the automobile size preference example, suppose we select manufacturer as the classificatory variable to be the base. Next, we represent the responses for each level of the second categorical variable (size of automobile in our example) as a percentage of the subtotal for the base variable. For example, from Table 17.5 we convert the response for small car sales for manufacturer A (157) to a percentage of the total sales for manufacturer A (341). That is,

$$\left(\frac{157}{341}\right)100\% = 46\%$$

The conversions of all Table 17.5 entries are similarly computed, and the values are shown in Table 17.6. The value shown at the right of each row is the row's total expressed as a percentage of the total number of responses in the entire table. Thus, the small car percentage is $413/1,000(100\%) = 41\%$ (rounded to the nearest percent).

If the size and manufacturer variables are independent, then the percentages in the cells of the table are expected to be approximately equal to the corresponding row percentages. Thus, we would expect the small car percentages for each of the four manufacturers to be approximately 41% if size and manufacturer are inde-

---

TABLE 17.6   Percentage of Car Sizes by Manufacturer

		MANUFACTURER				
		A	B	C	D	All
AUTO SIZE	Small	46	34	47	12	41
	Intermediate	37	43	37	55	40
	Large	17	23	16	33	19
	Totals	100	100	100	100	100

FIGURE 17.3
Size as a percentage of
manufacturer subtotals

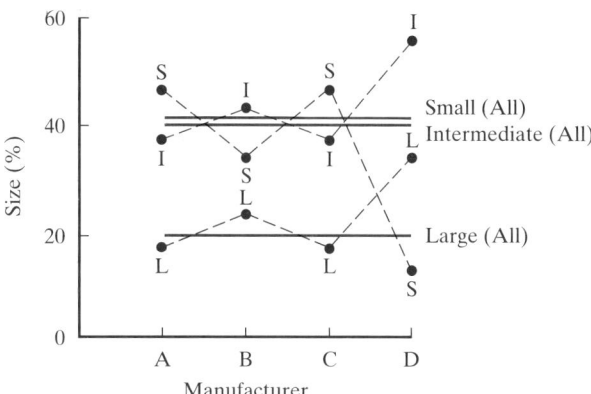

pendent. The extent to which each manufacturer's percentage departs from this value determines the dependence of the two classifications, with greater variability of the row percentages meaning a greater degree of dependence. A plot of the percentages helps summarize the observed pattern. In Figure 17.3 we show the manufacturer (the base variable) on the horizontal axis, and the size percentages on the vertical axis. The "expected" percentages under the assumption of independence are shown as horizontal lines, and each observed value is represented by a symbol indicating the size category.

Figure 17.3 clearly indicates the reason that the test resulted in the conclusion that the two classifications in the contingency table are dependent. Note that the sales of manufacturers A, B, and C fall relatively close to the expected percentages under the assumption of independence. However, the sales of manufacturer D deviate significantly from the expected values, with much higher percentages for large and intermediate cars and a much smaller percentage for small cars than expected under independence. Also, manufacturer B deviates slightly from the expected pattern, with a greater percentage of intermediate than small car sales. Statistical measures of the degree of dependence and procedures for making comparisons of pairs of levels for classifications are available. They are beyond the scope of this text, but can be found in the references. We will, however, utilize descriptive summaries such as Figure 17.3 to examine the degree of dependence exhibited by the sample data.

The general form of a two-way contingency table containing r rows and c columns (called an $r \times c$ contingency table) is shown in Table 17.7. Note that the observed count in the (ij) cell is denoted by n_{ij}, the ith row total is r_i, the jth column total is c_j, and the total sample size is n. Using this notation, we give the general form of the contingency table test for independent classifications in the next box.

TABLE 17.7   General $r \times c$ Contingency Table

		COLUMN			
		1	**2**	**...**	**c**	**Row Totals**
ROW	**1**	n_{11}	n_{12}	$\cdots$	n_{1c}	r_1
	2	n_{21}	n_{22}	$\cdots$	n_{2c}	r_2
	$\vdots$	$\vdots$	$\vdots$		$\vdots$	$\vdots$
	r	n_{r1}	n_{r2}	$\cdots$	n_{rc}	r_r
Column Totals		c_1	c_2	$\cdots$	c_c	n

General Form of a Contingency Table Analysis: A Test for Independence

H_0: The two classifications are independent

H_a: The two classifications are dependent

Test statistic: $\chi^2 = \sum \dfrac{[n_{ij} - \hat{E}(n_{ij})]^2}{\hat{E}(n_{ij})}$

where $\hat{E}(n_{ij}) = \dfrac{r_i c_j}{n}$.

Rejection region: $\chi^2 > \chi_\alpha^2$, where χ_α^2 has $(r - 1)(c - 1)$ df.

Assumptions: **1.** The n observed counts are a random sample from the population of interest. We may then consider this to be a multinomial experiment with $r \times c$ possible outcomes.

2. The sample size, n, will be large enough so that, for every cell, the expected count, $E(n_{ij})$, will be equal to 5 or more.

EXAMPLE 17.2

A large brokerage firm wants to determine whether the service it provides to affluent clients differs from the service it provides to lower-income clients. A sample of 500 clients are selected, and each client is asked to rate his or her broker. The results are shown in Table 17.8.

a. Test to determine whether there is evidence that broker rating and customer income are independent. Use $\alpha = .10$.

b. Plot the data and describe the patterns revealed. Is the result of the test supported by the plot?

SOLUTION

a. The first step is to calculate estimated expected cell frequencies under the assumption that the classifications are independent. Rather than compute these values by hand, we resort to a computer. The SAS printout of the analysis of Table 17.8 is displayed in Figure 17.4. Each cell in Figure 17.4 contains the observed (top) and expected (bottom) frequency in that cell. Note that $\hat{E}(n_{11})$, the estimated expected count for the Outstanding, Under $30,000 cell is 53.856. Similarly, the estimated expected count for the Outstanding, $30,000–$60,000 cell is $\hat{E}(n_{12}) = 66.402$. Since all the estimated expected cell frequencies are greater than 5, the χ^2 approximation for the test statistic is appropriate. Assuming the clients chosen were randomly selected from all clients of the brokerage firm, the characteristics of the

TABLE 17.8   Survey Results (Observed Clients), Example 17.2

		CLIENT'S INCOME			
		Under $30,000	$30,000–$60,000	Over $60,000	Totals
BROKER RATING	Outstanding	48	64	41	153
	Average	98	120	50	268
	Poor	30	33	16	79
Totals		176	217	107	500

FIGURE 17.4
SAS contingency table printout

```
                    TABLE OF RATING BY INCOME

    RATING          INCOME

    Frequency|
    Expected |UNDER30K |30K-60K | OVER60K|     Total
    ---------+---------+--------+--------+
    OUTSTAND |     48  |    64  |    41  |      153
             | 53.856  | 66.402 | 32.742 |
    ---------+---------+--------+--------+
    AVERAGE  |     98  |   120  |    50  |      268
             | 94.336  | 116.31 | 57.352 |
    ---------+---------+--------+--------+
    POOR     |     30  |    33  |    16  |       79
             | 27.808  | 34.286 | 16.906 |
    ---------+---------+--------+--------+
    Total          176      217      107        500

         STATISTICS FOR TABLE OF RATING BY INCOME

    Statistic                      DF     Value    Prob
    ------------------------------------------------------
    Chi-Square                      4     4.278    0.370
    Likelihood Ratio Chi-Square     4     4.184    0.382
    Mantel-Haenszel Chi-Square      1     2.445    0.118
    Phi Coefficient                       0.092
    Contingency Coefficient               0.092
    Cramer's V                            0.065

    Sample Size = 500
```

multinomial probability distribution are satisfied. The null and alternative hypotheses we want to test are:

H_0: The rating a client gives his or her broker is independent of client's income

H_a: Broker rating and client income are dependent

The test statistic, $\chi^2 = 4.278$, is highlighted at the bottom of the printout as is the observed significance level (*p*-value) of the test. Since $\alpha = .10$ is less than $p = .370$, we fail to reject H_0. This survey does not support the firm's alternative hypothesis that affluent clients receive different broker service than lower-income clients.

b. The broker rating frequencies are expressed as percentages of income category frequencies in Table 17.9. The expected percentages under the assumption of independence are shown at the right of each row. The plot of the percentage data is shown in Figure 17.5, where the horizontal lines represent the

TABLE 17.9 Broker Ratings as Percentage of Income Class

		CLIENT'S INCOME			
		Under $30,000	$30,000–$60,000	Over $60,000	Totals
BROKER RATING	Outstanding	27	29	38	31
	Average	56	55	47	54
	Poor	17	15	15	16
Totals		100	99*	100	101*

*Percentages do not add up to 100 because of rounding.

FIGURE 17.5
Plot of broker rating–customer income contingency table

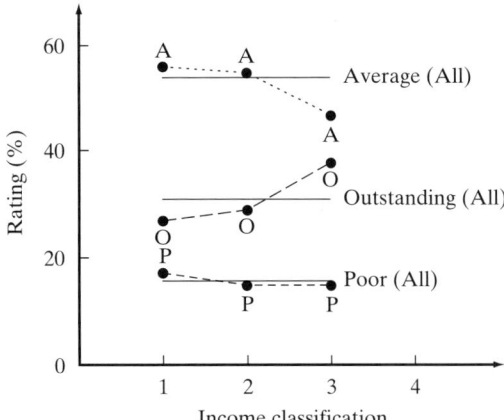

expected percentages assuming independence. Note that the response percentages deviate only slightly from those expected under the assumption of independence, supporting the result of the test in part **a**. That is, neither the descriptive plot nor the statistical test provides evidence that the rating given the broker services depends on (varies with) the customer's income.

STATISTICS IN ACTION

17.1 ETHICS IN COMPUTER TECHNOLOGY AND USE

Ethics refers to a set of rules or principles used for moral decision-making. Employees in the computer industry face ethical problems every day in the workplace. Illegal and improper actions are practiced knowingly and unknowingly by computer technology users. Some recent examples of unethical practices include Robert Morris's introduction of a "worm" into the Internet and software copyright infringements by several reputable colleges and universities.

Professors Margaret A. Pierce and John W. Henry of Georgia Southern University explored the ethical decision-making behavior of users of computers and computer technology and published their results in the *Journal of Business Ethics* (Vol. 15, 1996). Three primary influencing factors were considered by Pierce and Henry: (1) the individual's own personal code of ethics; (2) any informal code of ethical behavior that is operative in the workplace; and (3) the company's formal code of computer ethics (i.e., policies regarding computer technology).

The researchers mailed a computer ethics questionnaire to a random sample of 2,551 information systems (IS) professionals selected from members of the Data Processing Management Association (DPMA). The issues and questions addressed in the survey are given in Figure 17.6. Approximately 14% of the questionnaires were returned, yielding a total of 356 usable responses. Table 17.10 (page 930) gives a breakdown of the respondents by industry type. Tables 17.11 and 17.12 summarize the responses to two questions on the survey and their relationship to the three influencing factors identified by the researchers. (The tables show the number of responses in each category. Due to nonresponse for some questions, the sample size is less than 356.)

Focus

a. Does the existence of a company code of ethics influence computer users' perceptions of the importance of formal, informal, and personal ethics codes? If so, investigate the pattern of dependence by plotting the appropriate percentages on a graph.

b. Does the position of the computer user (professional or employee) influence the use of formal, informal, and personal ethics codes? If so, investigate the pattern of dependence by plotting the appropriate percentages on a graph.

c. With respect to industry type, is the sample of returned questionnaires representative of the 2,551 IS professionals who were mailed the survey? Explain.

Part I.   Please answer the following statements/questions regarding ethics. In all parts of this survey "ethics" is defined as ethics related to computer technology/computer use. "Your company" refers to the organization or educational institution where you work.

1. Gender: Female _____   male _____
2. Your age on your last birthday. _____
3. Education   (1) high school   (2) 2-yr college   (3) 4-yr college
   (Please circle the highest level attained.)   (4) master's   (5) doctorate
4. Circle the category which best describes   (1) CS/MIS educator   (2) other educator   (3) programmer
   your position.   (4) DP manager   (5) system supervisor   (6) other _____
5. Do you hold any professional certification or license?   (1) no   (2) yes, please specify _____
6. Number of years: (1) in profession _____   (2) with present employer_____
7. Type of company you work for: (1) Manufacture   (2) Government   (3) Education   (4) Finance
   (Please circle one or specify.)   (5) Utilities   (6) Service   (7) Consulting   (8) Wholesale/retail
   (9) Other (specify) _____
8. Size of company (Number of employees) _____
9. Do you think of yourself as (Please circle one.)   (1) DP/computer professional   (2) an employee of the company
10. Circle the professional organizations listed to which you belong.   (1) DPMA   (2) ACM   (3) IEEE-CS
11. (a) Are you familiar with any of the codes of ethics of the above professional organizations?   (1) yes   (2) no
    (b) If yes which one(s)?   (1) DPMA   (2) ACM   (3) IEEE-CS
    (c) If yes do you use the code(s) to guide your own behavior?   (1) yes   (2) no
12. Have you had any formal study concerning theories of ethics or ethical behavior?   (1) yes   (2) no

---

Part II.   Please respond to the following statements/questions about a formal company code of ethics (stated in writing or orally, representing the official position of the company), an informal code of ethics (ethical behavior actually practiced in the workplace), and a personal code of ethics (your own principles) related to computer use/computer technology.

1. Does your company have a formal company code of ethics?   (1) yes   (2) no
   (If there is a written code, please include a copy of the code.)
2. Which code of ethics is most important in guiding   (1) formal code   (2) informal code   (3) personal code
   the behavior of employees where you work?   (if there is one)
3. Which code of ethics do *you* use most   (1) formal code   (2) informal code   (3) personal code
   frequently to guide ethical decisions?   (if there is one)
4. These codes of ethics are deterrents to unethical behavior.
   a. formal company code of ethics   strongly agree   1 2 3 4 5   strongly disagree
   b. informal code of ethics   strongly agree   1 2 3 4 5   strongly disagree
   c. personal code of ethics   strongly agree   1 2 3 4 5   strongly disagree
5. There are opportunities in my company   strongly agree   1 2 3 4 5   strongly disagree
   to engage in unethical behavior.
6. Many people in my company engage in what   strongly agree   1 2 3 4 5   strongly disagree
   I consider unethical behavior.
7. I am aware of the specifics of the   strongly agree   1 2 3 4 5   strongly disagree
   informal company code of ethics.
8. I have a well-formulated personal code of ethics   strongly agree   1 2 3 4 5   strongly disagree
   related to computer use/computer technology

FIGURE 17.6   Computer ethics questionnaire
Source: Margaret A. Pierce and John W. Henry, "Computer Ethics: the Role of Personal, Informal, and Formal Codes," *Journal of Business Ethics,* Vol. 15/4, 1996, pp. 425–437. Reprinted with kind permission of Kluwer Academic Publishers.

TABLE 17.10 Number of Questionnaires Returned, by Industry (Statistics in Action 17.1)

Industry Type	Number Returned	Percent in Original Sample of 2,551
Manufacturing	67	19
DP Service/Consult	57	16
Utilities	20	5.5
Wholesale/Retail	18	5
Financial/Real Estate	42	12
Education/Medical/Legal	80	22
Government	21	6
Other	51	14.5
Total	356	100.0

Source: Pierce, M. A., and Henry, J. W. "Computer ethics: The role of personal, informal, and formal codes." *Journal of Business Ethics,* Vol. 15, 1996, p. 429 (Table I).

TABLE 17.11 What Type of Code Is Important in Making Ethical Decisions? (Statistics in Action 17.1)

	COMPANY CODE	
Code	Yes	No
Formal	51	6
Informal	47	69
Personal	70	100

Source: Pierce, M. A., and Henry, J. W. "Computer ethics: The role of personal, informal, and formal codes." *Journal of Business Ethics,* Vol. 15, 1996, p. 431 (Table II).

TABLE 17.12 Which Code Do You Use? (Statistics in Action 17.1)

	POSITION	
Ethics Code	CS Professional	Employee
Formal	27	2
Informal	34	5
Personal	208	63

Source: Pierce, M. A., and Henry, J. W. "Computer ethics: The role of personal, informal, and formal codes." *Journal of Business Ethics,* Vol. 15, 1996, p. 432 (Table IV).

EXERCISES 17.18–17.31

Learning the Mechanics

17.18 Find the rejection region for a test of independence of two classifications where the contingency table contains r rows and c columns.

  a. $r = 5, c = 5, \alpha = .05$
  b. $r = 3, c = 6, \alpha = .10$
  c. $r = 2, c = 3, \alpha = .01$

17.19 Consider the accompanying 2×3 (i.e., $r = 2$ and $c = 3$) contingency table.

  a. Specify the null and alternative hypotheses that should be used in testing the independence of the row and column classifications.
  b. Specify the test statistic and the rejection region that should be used in conducting the hypothesis test of part **a**. Use $\alpha = .01$.

	COLUMN		
	1	**2**	**3**
ROW **1**	9	34	53
2	16	30	25

c. Assuming the row classification and the column classification are independent, find estimates for the expected cell counts.

d. Conduct the hypothesis test of part **a**. Interpret your result.

17.20 Refer to Exercise 17.19.

a. Convert the frequency responses to percentages by calculating the percentage of each column total falling in each row. Also convert the row totals to percentages of the total number of responses. Display the percentages in a table.

b. Create a graph with percentage on the vertical axis and column number on the horizontal axis. Showing the row total percentages as horizontal lines on the graph, plot the cell percentages from part **a** using the row number as a plotting symbol.

c. What pattern do you expect to see if the rows and columns are independent? Does the plot support the result of the test of independence in Exercise 17.19?

17.21 Test the null hypothesis of independence of the two classifications, A and B, of the 3 × 3 contingency table shown here. Test using $\alpha = .05$.

	B		
	B₁	**B₂**	**B₃**
A₁	40	72	42
A A₂	63	53	70
A₃	31	38	30

17.22 Refer to Exercise 17.21. Convert the responses to percentages by calculating the percentage of each B class total falling into each A classification. Also, calculate the percentage of the total number of responses that constitute each of the A classification totals. Create a graph with percentage on

the vertical axis and B classification on the horizontal axis. Show the percentages corresponding to the A classification totals as horizontal lines on the graph, and plot the individual cell percentages using the A class number as a plotting symbol. Does the graph support the result of the test of hypothesis in Exercise 17.21? Explain.

Applying the Concepts

17.23 The *American Journal of Public Health* (July 1995) reported on a population-based study of trauma in Hispanic children. One of the objectives of the study was to compare the use of protective devices in motor vehicles used to transport Hispanic and non-Hispanic white children. On the basis of data collected from the San Diego County Regionalized Trauma System, 792 children treated for injuries sustained in vehicular accidents were classified according to ethnic status (Hispanic or non-Hispanic white) and seatbelt usage (worn or not worn) during the accident. The data are summarized in the table below.

a. Calculate the sample proportion of injured Hispanic children who were not wearing seatbelts during the accident.

b. Calculate the sample proportion of injured non-Hispanic white children who were not wearing seatbelts during the accident.

c. Compare the two sample proportions, parts **a** and **b**. Do you think the true population proportions differ?

d. Conduct a test to determine whether seatbelt usage in motor vehicle accidents depends on ethnic status in the San Diego County Regionalized Trauma System. Use $\alpha = .01$.

e. Construct a 99% confidence interval for the difference between the proportions, parts **a** and **b**. Interpret the interval.

17.24 To better understand whether and how Total Quality Management (TQM) is practiced in U.S. companies, University of Scranton researchers N. Tamimi and R. Sebastianelli interviewed one manager in each of a sample of 86 companies in Pennsylvania, New York, and New Jersey (*Production and Inventory Management Journal*, 1996). Concerning whether or not the firms were

	Hispanic	Non-Hispanic White	Totals
Seatbelts worn	31	148	179
Seatbelts not worn	283	330	613
Totals	314	478	792

Source: Matteneci, R. M. *et al.* "Trauma among Hispanic children: A population-based study in a regionalized system of trauma care." *American Journal of Public Health*, Vol. 85, No. 7, July 1995, p. 1007 (Table 2).

involved with TQM, the following data were obtained:

	Service Firms	Manufacturing Firms
Number practicing TQM	34	23
Number not practicing TQM	18	11
Total	52	34

Source: Adapted from Tamimi, N., and Sebastianelli, R. "How firms define and measure quality." *Production and Inventory Management Journal*, Third Quarter, 1996, p. 35.

  a. The researchers concluded that "manufacturing firms were not significantly more likely to be involved with TQM than service firms." Do you agree? Test using $\alpha = .05$.

  b. Find and interpret the approximate *p*-value for the test you conducted in part **a**.

  c. What assumptions must hold in order for your test of part **a** and your *p*-value of part **b** to be valid?

17.25 Are all employees equally likely to have accidents? Are certain employee groups—say, younger employees—more prone to particular kinds of accidents? The effective implementation of hiring policies, training programs, and safety programs requires such knowledge. A study conducted to address these questions for a particular manufacturing company was published in *Professional Safety* (Oct. 1985). A portion of the research results is summarized in the accompanying contingency table.

		KIND OF ACCIDENT		
		Sprain	Burn	Cut
AGE	Under 25	9	17	5
	25 and Over	61	13	12

Source: Parry, A. E. "Changing assumptions about loss frequency." *Professional Safety*, Oct. 1985, pp. 39–43.

  a. From the contingency table, the researcher concluded that there is a relationship between an employee's age and the kind of accident that the employee may have. Do you agree? Test using $\alpha = .05$.

  b. According to the frequencies of the contingency table, which is the most frequent type of accident? Are younger or older employees more likely to have sprains? Burns? Justify your answers.

  c. What assumptions must hold in order for your test of part **a** to be valid?

  d. Plot the percentage of employees under 25 who are injured based on the total injuries for each kind of accident. Compare this to the percentage of the total number of employees under 25

who are injured based on the total of all kinds of accidents. What does the plot indicate about the pattern of dependence in the data?

17.26 In recent years, the accounting profession has become increasingly concerned with ethics. University of Louisville professor Julia Karcher conducted an experiment to investigate the ethical behavior of accountants (*Journal of Business Ethics*, Vol. 15, 1996). She focused on auditor abilities to detect ethical problems that may not be obvious. Seventy auditors from Big-Six accounting firms were given a detailed case study that contained several problems including tax evasion by the client. In 35 of the cases the tax evasion issue was severe; in the other 35 cases it was moderate. The auditors were asked to identify any problems they detected in the case. The table summarizes the results for the ethical issue.

	SEVERITY OF ETHICAL ISSUE	
	Moderate	Severe
Ethical Issue Identified	27	26
Ethical Issue Not Identified	8	9

Source: Karcher, J. "Auditors' ability to discern the presence of ethical problems." *Journal of Business Ethics*, Vol. 15, 1996, p. 1041 (Table V).

  a. Did the severity of the ethical issue influence whether the issue was identified or not by the auditors? Test using $\alpha = .05$.

  b. Suppose the lefthand column of the table contained the counts 35 and 0 instead of 27 and 8. Should the test of part **a** still be conducted? Explain.

  c. Keeping the sample size the same, change the numbers in the contingency table so that the answer you would get for the question posed in part **a** changes.

17.27 Many companies use well-known celebrities in their ads, while other companies create their own spokesperson (such as the Maytag repairman). A study in the *Journal of Marketing* (Fall 1992) investigated the relationship between the gender of the spokesperson and the gender of the viewer in order to see how this relationship affected brand awareness. Three hundred television viewers were asked to identify the products advertised by celebrity spokespersons. See the next two tables at the top of page 933.

  a. For the products advertised by male spokespersons, conduct a test to determine whether audience gender and product identification are dependent factors. Test using $\alpha = .05$.

  b. Repeat part **a** for the products advertised by female spokespersons.

  c. How would you interpret these results?

Male Spokesperson

	AUDIENCE GENDER		
	Male	Female	Total
Identified Product	95	41	136
Could Not Identify Product	55	109	164
Total	150	150	300

Female Spokesperson

	AUDIENCE GENDER		
	Male	Female	Total
Identified Product	47	61	108
Could Not Identify Product	103	89	192
Total	150	150	300

17.28 In recent years, corporate boards of directors have been pressed to improve their monitoring of corporate economic performance and to become more careful overseers of the activities of management. In addition, boards are being asked to guide the long-term responsiveness of their respective organizations to the economic and social climate. These pressures have forced many boards of directors to better articulate the mission and strategies of their firms. To study the extent and nature of strategic planning being undertaken by boards of directors, A. Tashakori and W. Boulton questioned a sample of 119 chief executive officers of major U.S. corporations (*Journal of Business Strategy,* Winter 1983). One objective was to determine if a relationship exists between the composition of a board—i.e., a majority of outside directors versus a majority of in-house directors—and its level of participation in the strategic planning process. To this end, the questionnaire data were used to classify the responding corporations according to the level of their board's participation in the strategic planning process:

Level 1: Board participates in formulation or implementation or evaluation of strategy

Level 2: Board participates in formulation and implementation, formulation and evaluation, or implementation and evaluation of strategy

Level 3: Board participates in formulation, implementation, and evaluation of strategy

The results obtained are shown in the next table. Of these 119 firms, 100 had boards where outside directors constituted a majority. Their levels of participation in strategic planning are shown in the second table.

a. The researchers concluded that a relationship exists between a board's level of participation

ALL FIRMS			
Level	1	2	3
Number of firms	22	37	60

OUTSIDE DIRECTED			
Level	1	2	3
Number of firms	20	27	53

in the strategic planning process and the composition of the board. Do you agree? Construct the appropriate contingency table, and test using $\alpha = .10$.

b. In the context of this problem, specify the Type I and Type II errors associated with the test of part **a**.

c. Find the *p*-value for the test in the SAS printout on page 934. Based on the *p*-value, would the null hypothesis have been rejected at $\alpha = .05$? Explain.

d. Construct a graph that helps to interpret the result of the test in part **a**.

17.29 Research has indicated that the stress produced by today's lifestyles results in health problems for a large proportion of society. An article in the *International Journal of Sports Psychology* (July–Sept. 1990) evaluated the relationship between physical fitness and stress. Five hundred forty-nine employees of companies that participate in the Health Examination Program offered by Health Advancement Services (HAS) were classified into three groups of fitness levels: good, average, and poor. Each person was tested for signs of stress. The table reports the results for the three groups. [*Note:* The proportions given are the proportions of the entire group that show signs of stress and fall into each particular fitness level.] Do the data provide evidence to indicate that the likelihood for stress is dependent on an employee's fitness level?

Fitness Level	Sample Size	Proportions with Signs of Stress
Poor	242	.155
Average	212	.133
Good	95	.108

17.30 In the United States, people over age 50 represent 25% of the population, yet they control 70% of the wealth. Research indicates that the highest priority of retirees is travel. A study in the *Annals of Tourism Research* (Vol. 19, 1992) investigates the relationship of retirement status (pre- and postretirement) to various items related to the travel industry. One part of the study investigated

```
               TABLE OF LEVEL BY COMPOSIT

         LEVEL       COMPOSIT

         Frequency|
         Expected |INSIDE | OUTSIDE |   Total
         ---------+-------+---------+
                1 |     2 |     20  |    22
                  |3.5126 | 18.487  |
         ---------+-------+---------+
                2 |    10 |     27  |    37
                  |5.9076 | 31.092  |
         ---------+-------+---------+
                3 |     7 |     53  |    60
                  |9.5798 |  50.42  |
         ---------+-------+---------+
         Total         19      100       119

         STATISTICS FOR TABLE OF LEVEL BY COMPOSIT

         Statistic                  DF    Value    Prob
         --------------------------------------------------
         Chi-Square                  2    4.976    0.083
         Likelihood Ratio Chi-Square 2    4.696    0.096
         Mantel-Haenszel Chi-Square  1    0.120    0.729
         Phi Coefficient                  0.204
         Contingency Coefficient          0.200
         Cramer's V                       0.204

         Sample Size = 119
```

the differences in the length of stay of a trip for pre- and postretirees. A sample of 703 travelers were asked how long they stayed on a typical trip. The results are shown in the table. Use the information in the table to determine whether the retirement status of a traveler and the duration of a typical trip are dependent. Test using $\alpha = .05$.

Number of Nights	Preretirement	Postretirement
4–7	247	172
8–13	82	67
14–21	35	52
22 or more	16	32
Total	**380**	**323**

17.31 According to research reported in the *Journal of the National Cancer Institute* (Apr. 1991), eating foods high in fiber may help protect against breast cancer. The researchers randomly divided 120 laboratory rats into four groups of 30 each. All rats were injected with a drug that causes breast cancer, then each rat was fed a diet of fat and fiber for 15 weeks. However, the levels of fat and fiber varied from group to group. At the end of the feeding period, the number of rats with cancer tumors was determined for each group. The data is summarized in the accompanying contingency table.

a. Does the sampling appear to satisfy the assumptions for a multinomial experiment (see Section 17.1)? Explain.

b. Calculate the expected cell counts for the contingency table.

c. Calculate the χ^2 statistic.

d. Is there evidence to indicate that diet and presence/absence of cancer are independent? Test using $\alpha = .05$.

e. Compare the percentage of rats on a high-fat/no-fiber diet with cancer to the percentage of rats on a high-fat/fiber diet with cancer using a 95% confidence interval. Interpret the result.

		DIET				
		High-Fat/No-Fiber	High-Fat/Fiber	Low-Fat/No-Fiber	Low-Fat/Fiber	Totals
CANCER TUMORS	Yes	27	20	19	14	80
	No	3	10	11	16	40
	Totals	30	30	30	30	120

Source: Tampa Tribune, Apr. 3, 1991.

17.5 A WORD OF CAUTION ABOUT CHI-SQUARE TESTS

Because the χ^2 statistic for testing hypotheses about multinomial probabilities is one of the most widely applied statistical tools, it is also one of the most abused statistical procedures. Consequently, the user should always be certain that the experiment satisfies the assumptions given with each procedure. Furthermore, the user should be certain that the sample is drawn from the correct population—that is, from the population about which the inference is to be made.

The use of the χ^2 probability distribution as an approximation to the sampling distribution for χ^2 should be avoided when the expected counts are very small. The approximation can become very poor when these expected counts are small, and thus the true α level may be quite different from the tabled value. As a rule of thumb, an expected cell count of at least 5 means that the χ^2 probability distribution can be used to determine an approximate critical value.

If the χ^2 value does not exceed the established critical value of χ^2, *do not accept the hypothesis of independence.* You would be risking a Type II error (accepting H_0 if it is false), and the probability β of committing such an error is unknown. The usual alternative hypothesis is that the classifications are dependent. Because the number of ways in which two classifications can be dependent is virtually infinite, it is difficult to calculate one or even several values of β to represent such a broad alternative hypothesis. Therefore, we avoid concluding that two classifications are independent, even when χ^2 is small.

Finally, if a contingency table χ^2 value does exceed the critical value, we must be careful to avoid inferring that a *causal* relationship exists between the classifications. Our alternative hypothesis states that the two classifications are statistically dependent—and a statistical dependence does not imply causality. Therefore, *the existence of a causal relationship cannot be established by a contingency table analysis.*

QUICK REVIEW

Key Terms

Key Formulas

$$\chi^2 = \sum \frac{[n_i - E(n_i)]^2}{E(n_i)}$$

where n_i = count for cell i

    $E(n_i) = np_{i,0}$

        $p_{i,0}$ = hypothesized value of p_i in H_0

$$\chi^2 = \sum \frac{[n_{ij} - \hat{E}(n_{ij})]^2}{\hat{E}(n_{ij})}$$

Two-way table   926

where n_{ij} = count for cell in row i, column j

$\hat{E}(n_{ij}) = r_i c_j / n$

r_i = total for row i
c_j = total for column j
n = total sample size

LANGUAGE LAB

Symbol	Pronunciation	Description
$p_{i,0}$	p-i-zero	Value of multinomial probability p_i hypothesized in H_0
χ^2	Chi-square	Test statistic used in analysis of count data
n_i	n-i	Number of observed outcomes in cell i of one-way table
$E(n_i)$	Expected value of n-i	Expected number of outcomes in cell i of one-way table when H_0 is true
p_{ij}	p-i-j	Probability of an outcome in row i and column j of a two-way contingency table
n_{ij}	n-i-j	Number of observed outcomes in row i and column j of a two-way contingency table
$\hat{E}(n_{ij})$	Estimated expected value of n-i-j	Estimated expected number of outcomes in row i and column j of a two-way contingency table
r_i	r-i	Total number of outcomes in row i of a contingency table
c_j	c-j	Total number of outcomes in column j of a contingency table

SUPPLEMENTARY EXERCISES   17.32–17.49

Note: Exercises marked with 💾 contain data for computer analysis on a 3.5" disk (file name in parentheses).

Learning the Mechanics

17.32 A random sample of 250 observations was classified according to the row and column categories shown in the table.

		COLUMN		
		1	2	3
	1	20	20	10
ROW	2	10	20	70
	3	20	50	30

a. Do the data provide sufficient evidence to conclude that the rows and columns are dependent? Test using $\alpha = .05$.

b. Would the analysis change if the row totals were fixed before the data were collected?

c. Do the assumptions required for the analysis to be valid differ according to whether the row (or column) totals are fixed? Explain.

d. Convert the table entries to percentages by using each column total as a base and calcu-lating each row response as a percentage of the corresponding column total. In addition, calculate the row totals and convert them to percentages of all 250 observations.

e. Plot the row percentages on the vertical axis against the column number on the horizontal axis. Draw horizontal lines corresponding to the row total percentages. Does the deviation (or lack thereof) of the individual row percentages from the row total percentages support the result of the test conducted in part **a**?

17.33 A random sample of 150 observations was classified into the categories shown in the table below.

	CATEGORY				
	1	2	3	4	5
n_i	28	35	33	25	29

a. Do the data provide sufficient evidence that the categories are not equally likely? Use $\alpha = .10$.

b. Form a 90% confidence interval for p_2, the probability that an observation will fall in category 2.

Applying the Concepts

17.34 Because shareholders control the firm, they can transfer wealth from the firm's bondholders to themselves through several different dividend strategies. This potential conflict of interest between shareholders and bondholders can be reduced through the use of debt covenants. Accountants E. Griner and H. Huss of Georgia State University investigated the effects of insider ownership and the size of the firm on the types of debt covenants required by a firm's bondholders (*Journal of Applied Business Research*, Vol. 11, 1995). As part of the study, they examined a sample of 31 companies whose bondholders required covenants based on tangible assets rather than on liquidity or net assets or retained earnings. Characteristics of those 31 firms are summarized below. The objective of the study is to determine if there is a relationship between the extent of insider ownership and the size of the firm for firms with tangible asset covenants.

		SIZE	
		Small	**Large**
INSIDE OWNERSHIP	Low	3	17
	High	8	3

Source: Griner, E., and Huss, H. "Firm size, insider ownership, and accounting-based debt covenants." *Journal of Applied Business Research,* Vol. 11, No. 4, 1995, p. 7 (Table 4).

a. Assuming the null hypothesis of independence is true, how many firms are expected to fall in each cell of the table?

b. The researchers were unable to use the chi-square test to analyze the data. Show why.

c. A test of the null hypothesis can be conducted using a small-sample method known as Fisher's exact test. This method calculates the exact probability (*p*-value) of observing sample results at least as contradictory to the null hypothesis as those observed for the researchers' data. The researchers reported the *p*-value for this test as .0043. Interpret this result.

d. Investigate the nature of the dependence exhibited by the contingency table by plotting the appropriate contingency table percentages. Describe what you find.

17.35 Over the years, pollsters have found that the public's confidence in big business is closely tied to the economic climate. When businesses are growing and employment is increasing, public confidence is high. When the opposite occurs, public confidence is low. Harvey Kahalas hypothesized that there is a relationship between the level of confidence in business and job satisfaction, and that this is true for both union and nonunion workers (*Baylor Business Studies*, Feb.–Apr. 1981). He analyzed sample data collected by the National Opinion Research Center and shown in the tables below.

Kahalas concluded that his hypothesis was not supported by the data. Do you agree? Use the SPSS printouts on page 938 to conduct the appropriate tests using $\alpha = .05$. Be sure to specify your null and alternative hypotheses.

17.36 Despite a good winning percentage, a certain major league baseball team has not drawn as many fans as expected. In hopes of finding ways to increase attendance, the management plans to interview fans who come to the games to find out why they attend. One thing that the management might want to know is whether there are differences in support for the team among various age groups. Suppose the information in the table on page 938 was collected during interviews with

		JOB SATISFACTION			
		Very Satisfied	**Moderately Satisfied**	**A Little Dissatisfied**	**Very Dissatisfied**
UNION MEMBER CONFIDENCE IN MAJOR CORPORATIONS	**A Great Deal**	26	15	2	1
	Only Some	95	73	16	5
	Hardly Any	34	28	10	9

		JOB SATISFACTION			
		Very Satisfied	**Moderately Satisfied**	**A Little Dissatisfied**	**Very Dissatisfied**
NONUNION CONFIDENCE IN MAJOR CORPORATIONS	**A Great Deal**	111	52	12	4
	Only Some	246	142	37	18
	Hardly Any	73	51	19	9

UNIONCON by JOBSAT

```
                JOBSAT
        Count
        Exp Val
                                                        Row
                Little   Moderate  None    Very         Total
UNIONCON
        GreatDeal    2       15       1       26          44
                    3.9     16.3     2.1     21.7        14.0%

        HardlyAny   10       28       9       34          81
                    7.2     29.9     3.9     40.0        25.8%

        OnlySome    16       73       5       95         189
                   16.9     69.8     9.0     93.3        60.2%

        Column      28      116      15      155         314
        Total      8.9%    36.9%    4.8%    49.4%       100.0%
```

Chi-Square	Value	DF	Significance
Pearson	13.36744	6	.03756
Likelihood Ratio	12.08304	6	.06014

Minimum Expected Frequency -   2.102
Cells with Expected Frequency < 5 -   3 OF   12 (25.0%)

NOUNCON by JOBSAT

```
                JOBSAT
        Count
        Exp Val
                                                        Row
                Little   Moderate  None    Very         Total
NOUNCON
        GreatDeal   12       52       4      111         179
                   15.7     56.7     7.2     99.4        23.1%

        HardlyAny   19       51       9       73         152
                   13.4     48.1     6.1     84.4        19.6%

        OnlySome    37      142      18      246         443
                   38.9    140.2    17.7    246.1        57.2%

        Column      68      245      31      430         774
        Total      8.8%    31.7%    4.0%    55.6%       100.0%
```

Chi-Square	Value	DF	Significance
Pearson	9.63514	6	.14088
Likelihood Ratio	9.55907	6	.14449

Minimum Expected Frequency -   6.088

		NUMBER OF GAMES ATTENDED PER YEAR		
		1 or 2	3–5	Over 5
	Under 20	78	107	17
	21–30	147	87	13
AGE OF FAN	31–40	129	86	19
	41–55	55	103	40
	Over 55	23	74	22

fans selected at random. Can you conclude that there is a relationship between age and number of games attended per year? Use $\alpha = .05$.

17.37 Many investors believe that the stock market's directional change in January signals the market's direction for the remainder of the year. This so-called January indicator is frequently cited in the popular press. But is this indicator valid? If so, the well-known *random walk and efficient markets* theories (basically postulating that market movements are unpredictable) of stock-price behavior would be called into question. The accompanying table summarizes the relevant changes in the Dow Jones Industrial Average for the period December 31, 1927, through January 31, 1981. J. Martinich applied the chi-square test of independence to these data to investigate the January indicator (*Mid-South Business Journal,* Vol. 4, 1984).

		NEXT 11-MONTH CHANGE	
		Up	Down
JANUARY CHANGE	Up	25	10
	Down	9	9

a. Examine the contingency table. Based solely on your visual inspection, do the data appear to confirm the validity of the January indicator? Explain.

b. Construct a plot of the percentage of years for which the 11-month movement is up based on the January change. Compare these two percentages to the percentage of times the market moved up during the last 11 months over all years in the sample. What do you think of the January indicator now?

c. If a chi-square test of independence is to be used to investigate the January indicator, what are the appropriate null and alternative hypotheses?

d. Conduct the test of part **c**. Use $\alpha = .05$. Interpret your results in the context of the problem.

e. Would you get the same result in part **d** if $\alpha = .10$ were used? Explain.

17.38 If a company can identify times of day when accidents are most likely to occur, extra precautions can be instituted during those times. A random sampling of the accident reports over the last year at a plant gives the frequency of occurrence of accidents during the different hours of the workday. Can it be concluded from the data in the table that the proportions of accidents are different for at least two of the four time periods?

Hours	1–2	3–4	5–6	7–8
Number of Accidents	31	28	45	47

17.39 The classification of solder joints as acceptable or rejectable is a particularly difficult inspection task owing to its subjective nature. Westinghouse Electric Company has experimented with different means of evaluating the performance of solder inspectors. One approach involves comparing an individual inspector's classifications with those of the group of experts that comprise Westinghouse's Work Standards Committee. In an experiment reported by J. Meagher and J. Scazzero (1985) of Westinghouse, 153 solder connections were evaluated by the committee and 111 were classified as acceptable. An inspector evaluated the same 153 connections and classified 124 as acceptable. Of the items rejected by the inspector, the committee agreed with 19.

a. Construct a contingency table that summarizes the classifications of the committee and the inspector.

b. Based on a visual examination of the table you constructed in part **a**, does it appear that there is a relationship between the inspector's classifications and the committee's? Explain. (A plot of the percentage rejected by committee and inspector will aid your examination.)

c. Conduct a chi-square test of independence for these data. Use $\alpha = .05$. Carefully interpret the results of your test in the context of the problem.

17.40 (X17.040) An economist was interested in knowing whether sons have a tendency to choose the same occupation as their fathers. To investigate this question, 500 males were polled and questioned concerning their occupation and the occupation of their father. A summary of the numbers of father-son pairs falling in each occupational category is shown in the table below. Do the data provide sufficient evidence at $\alpha = .05$ to indicate

		SON			
		Professional or Business	Skilled	Unskilled	Farmer
FATHER	Professional or Business	55	38	7	0
	Skilled	79	71	25	0
	Unskilled	22	75	38	10
	Farmer	15	23	10	32

```
                  TABLE OF FATHER BY SON

FATHER       SON
Frequency
Expected  Farmer   Prof/Bus  Skill   Unskill    Total
Farmer     32       15       23       10         80
           6.72     27.36    33.12    12.8

Prof/Bus    0       55       38        7        100
           8.4      34.2     41.4     16

Skill       0       79       71       25        175
           14.7     59.85    72.45    28

Unskill    10       22       75       38        145
           12.18    49.59    60.03    23.2

Total      42      171      207       80        500

          STATISTICS FOR TABLE OF FATHER BY SON

Statistic                         DF    Value    Prob

Chi-Square                         9   180.874   0.000
Likelihood Ratio Chi-Square        9   160.832   0.000
Mantel-Haenszel Chi-Square         1    52.040   0.000
Phi Coefficient                        0.601
Contingency Coefficient                0.515
Cramer's V                             0.347

Sample Size = 500
```

a dependence between a son's choice of occupation and his father's occupation? Use the SAS printout above to conduct the analysis.

17.41 A study was done on the accuracy of newspaper advertisements by the five types of food stores in a southeastern city. On each of four days, items were randomly selected from the advertisements for each type of store and the actual price was compared to the advertised price. Each of the stores in the city was classified as one of the following types: national, regional chain A, regional chain B, regional chain C, or independent. Values in the table represent the number of items that were correctly and incorrectly priced.

Type of Store	Number Correctly Priced	Number Incorrectly Priced
National chain	89	10
Regional chain A	53	14
Regional chain B	43	12
Regional chain C	32	13
Independent	41	7

a. Determine whether these data provide sufficient evidence to conclude that the proportion of correctly priced items differs for at least two types of stores. Use $\alpha = .10$.

b. Use a 95% confidence interval to estimate the proportion of correctly priced items in the stores in the national chain category.

17.42 According to the Magnuson-Moss Warranty Act (enacted by Congress in 1977 to reform consumer product warranty practices), all warranties must be designated as "full" or "limited" and must be clearly written in readily understood language. A study was undertaken to investigate consumer satisfaction with warranty practices since the advent of the Magnuson-Moss Warranty Act (*Baylor Business Studies,* Nov.–Dec. 1983). Using a mailed questionnaire, 237 midwestern consumers who had purchased a major appliance within the past 6 to 18 months were sampled. One of the questions asked of the consumers was, "Do most retailers and dealers make a conscientious effort to satisfy their customers' warranty claims?" One hundred fifty-six answered yes, 61 were uncertain, and 20 said no. The population of consumers from which this sample was drawn had also been investigated two years prior to the passage of the Magnuson-Moss Warranty Act. At that time, 37.0% of the population answered yes to the same question, 53.3% were uncertain, and 9.7% said no.

a. As reflected in the answers to the above question, have consumer attitudes toward warranties changed since the pre-Magnuson-Moss Act study? Test using $\alpha = .05$.

b. Compare the pre- and post-Magnuson-Moss Warranty Act responses, and describe the changes that have occurred.

17.43 A computer used by a 24-hour banking service is supposed to assign each transaction to one of five memory locations at random. A check at the end of a day's transactions gives the following counts to each of the five memory locations:

1	2	3	4	5
90	78	100	72	85

Is there evidence to indicate a difference among the proportions of transactions assigned to the five memory locations? Test using $\alpha = .025$.

17.44 A statistical analysis is to be done on a set of data consisting of 1,000 monthly salaries. The analysis requires the assumption that the sample was drawn from a normal distribution. A preliminary test, called the χ^2 *goodness-of-fit test,* can be used to help determine whether it is reasonable to assume that the sample is from a normal distribution. Suppose the mean and standard deviation of the 1,000 salaries are hypothesized to be $1,200 and $200, respectively. Using the standard normal table, we can approximate the probability of a salary being in the intervals listed in the table below. The third column represents the expected number of the 1,000 salaries to be found in each interval if the sample was drawn from a normal distribution with $\mu = \$1,200$ and $\sigma = \$200$. Suppose the last column contains the actual observed frequencies in the sample. Large differences between the observed and expected frequencies cast doubt on the normality assumption.

Interval	Probability	Expected Frequency	Observed Frequency
Less than $800	.023	23	26
$800 < $1,000	.136	136	146
$1,000 < $1,200	.341	341	361
$1,200 < $1,400	.341	341	311
$1,400 < $1,600	.136	136	143
$1,600 or above	.023	23	13

a. Compute the χ^2 statistic based on the observed and expected frequencies—just as you did in Section 17.1.

b. Find the tabulated χ^2 value when $\alpha = .05$ and there are 5 degrees of freedom. (There are $k - 1 = 5$ df associated with this χ^2 statistic.)

c. Based on the χ^2 statistic and the tabulated χ^2 value, is there evidence that the salary distribution is nonnormal?

d. Find an approximate observed significance level for the test in part **c**.

17.45 When a buyer charges a purchase, the seller records the sale in his or her record books under a category called *accounts receivable.* Some retailers monitor the status of their accounts receivable by regularly classifying each in one of the following categories: current, 1–30 days late, 31–60 days late, more than 60 days late, or uncollectable. Historical data indicate that the status of a particular retailer's accounts receivable can be described as follows:

Current	65%
1–30 days late	15%
31–60 days late	10%
Over 60 days late	7%
Uncollectable	3%

Six months after the interest rate charged to late accounts was increased, the status of the retailer's 200 accounts receivable was as follows:

Current	78%
1–30 days late	12%
31–60 days late	5%
Over 60 days late	2%
Uncollectable	3%

a. Is there evidence to indicate that the increase in interest rates affected the timing of buyers' payments? Test using $\alpha = .10$.

b. Find the approximate observed significance level for the test.

17.46 It is commonly assumed that the more experience a job applicant has, the better that person will perform the necessary duties. Other factors, such as whether the person has a college degree or is male or female, may also be indicative of future performance. H. M. Greenberg and J. Greenberg argue that for sales jobs, the most important factor is matching the job requirement with an applicant's personal characteristics (*Harvard Business Review,* Sept.–Oct. 1980). This, they claim, will result in better retention rates and higher levels of job performance. To validate this claim they studied two groups of recently hired sales personnel. In the first group, which numbered 1,980, all were job-matched; the 3,961 members of the second group were not. After six months they were evaluated, and the aggregate data are shown in the table on page 942 (1, highest performance; 4, lowest). The tabulated values are the percentages of total sales personnel contained in the respective samples.

a. Use both the percentages given in the table and the sample sizes to construct a contingency

		PERFORMANCE				
	1	2	3	4	Quit or Fired	Totals
Job-Matched	9%	40%	32%	14%	5%	100%
Not Job-Matched	2%	17%	25%	31%	25%	100%

table that shows the numbers of sales personnel falling in each category of the table.

b. Do the data provide sufficient evidence to indicate that the proportions of sales personnel falling in the performance categories depend on whether the people are job-matched? Test using $\alpha = .05$.

c. Do the data provide sufficient evidence to indicate the proportion of sales personnel receiving the highest rating (1) is larger if job-matched than if not? Test using $\alpha = .05$. [*Note:* This will require a one-sided test.]

17.47 Product or service quality is often defined as *fitness for use*. This means the product or service meets the customer's needs. Generally speaking, fitness for use is based on five quality characteristics: technological (e.g., strength, hardness), psychological (taste, beauty), time-oriented (reliability), contractual (guarantee provisions), and ethical (courtesy, honesty). The quality of a service may involve all these characteristics, while the quality of a manufactured product generally depends on technological and time-oriented characteristics (Schroeder, *Operations Management*, 1993). After a barrage of customer complaints about poor quality, a manufacturer of gasoline filters for cars had its quality inspectors sample 600 filters—200 per work shift—and check for defects. The data in the table resulted.

Shift	Defectives Produced
First	25
Second	35
Third	80

a. Do the data indicate that the quality of the filters being produced may be related to the shift producing the filter? Test using $\alpha = .05$.

b. Estimate the proportion of defective filters produced by the first shift. Use a 95% confidence interval.

17.48 An industrial security firm wants to conduct a study of criminal cases involving stolen company money in which employees were found guilty. Among the data recorded are the employee's salary (wages) and the amount of money stolen from the company for 400 recent cases. The results are given below.

a. Does this information provide evidence of a relationship between employee income and amount stolen? Use $\alpha = .05$.

b. Convert the responses to percentages by calculating the percentage in each income category based on the total number of cases in each amount stolen category. Also calculate the percentage of all 400 cases in each income category. Plot percentage on the vertical axis and amount stolen on the horizontal axis, showing the overall income category percentages as horizontal lines on the plot. Plot the income percentages for each cell using 1, 2, and 3 as the plotting symbols for the three categories. Does the plot support the result of the test in part **a**?

17.49 A corporation owns several convenience stores that are open 24 hours a day. It is interested in knowing whether there is a relationship between time of day and size of purchase. One of its stores is selected at random to be involved in a study.

		AMOUNT STOLEN ($)			
		Under 5,000	5,000–9,999	10,000–19,999	20,000 or More
INCOME OF EMPLOYEE ($1,000s)	Under 15	46	39	17	5
	15–25	78	79	61	19
	Over 25	5	14	25	12

		SIZE OF PURCHASE		
		$2 or Less	$2.01–$7	Over $7
TIME OF PURCHASE	8 A.M.–3:59 P.M.	65	38	14
	4 P.M.–11:59 P.M.	61	49	10
	12 Midnight–7:59 A.M.	29	27	7

Store records are collected over a period of several weeks and then 300 purchases are randomly selected. Since the register also prints the time of the purchase, this random selection procedure yields both amount and time of purchase. The information is summarized in the table.

a. Is there a relationship between time and size of purchase? Use $\alpha = .05$.

b. Use a 90% confidence interval to estimate the difference between the proportions of customers who spend $2 or less for the periods 8 A.M.–3:59 P.M. and 12 midnight–7:59 A.M.

DISCRIMINATION IN THE WORKPLACE

SHOWCASE

Title VII of the Civil Rights Act of 1964 prohibits discrimination in the workplace on the basis of race, color, religion, gender, or national origin. The Age Discrimination in Employment Act of 1967 (ADEA) protects workers age 40 to 70 against discrimination based on age. The potential for discrimination exists in such processes as hiring, promotion, compensation, and termination.

In 1971 the U.S. Supreme Court established that employment discrimination cases fall into two categories: **disparate treatment** and **disparate impact**. In the former, the issue is whether the employer intentionally discriminated against a worker. For example, if the employer considered an individual's race in deciding whether to terminate him, the case is one of disparate treatment. In a disparate impact case, the issue is whether employment practices have an adverse impact on a protected group or class of people, even when the employer does not intend to discriminate.

PART I: DOWNSIZING AT A COMPUTER FIRM

Disparate impact cases almost always involve the use of statistical evidence and expert testimony by professional statisticians. Attorneys for the plaintiffs frequently use hypothesis test results in the form of *p*-values in arguing the case for their clients.

Table C6.1 was recently introduced as evidence in a race case that resulted from a round of layoffs during the downsizing of a division of a computer manufacturer. The company had selected 51 of the division's 1,215 employees to lay off. The plaintiff's—in this case 15 of the 20 African Americans who were laid off—were suing the company for $20 million in damages.

The company's lawyers argued that the selections followed from a performance-based ranking of all employees. The plaintiffs legal team and their expert witnesses,

citing the results of a statistical test of hypothesis, argued that layoffs were a function of race.

The validity of the plaintiff's interpretation of the data is dependent on whether the assumptions of the test are met in this situation. In particular, like all hypothesis tests presented in this text, the assumption of random sampling must hold. If it does not, the results of the test may be due to the violation of this assumption rather than to discrimination. In general, the appropriateness of the testing procedure is dependent on the test's ability to capture the relevant aspects of the employment process in question (DeGroot, Fienberg, and Kadane, *Statistics and the Law,* 1986).

Prepare a document to be submitted as evidence in the case (i.e., an exhibit), in which you evaluate the validity of the plaintiff's interpretation of the data. Your evaluation should be based in part on your knowledge of the processes companies use to lay off employees and how well those processes are reflected in the hypothesis-testing procedure employed by the plaintiffs.

PART II: AGE DISCRIMINATION— YOU BE THE JUDGE

In 1996, as part of a significant restructuring of product lines, AJAX Pharmaceuticals (a fictitious name for a real company) laid off 24 of 55 assembly-line workers in its Pittsburgh manufacturing plant. Citing the ADEA, 11 of the laid-off workers claimed they were discriminated against on the basis of age and sued AJAX for $5,000,000. Management disputed the claim, saying that since the workers were essentially interchangeable, they had used random sampling to choose the 24 workers to be terminated.

Table C6.2 lists the 55 assembly-line workers and identifies which were terminated and which remained active. Plaintiffs are denoted by an asterisk. These data were used by both the plaintiffs and the defendants to determine whether the layoffs had an adverse impact on workers

TABLE C6.1 **Summary of Downsizing Data for Race Case**

		DECISION	
		Retained	Laid off
RACE	White	1,051	31
	Black	113	20

Source: Confidential personal communication with P. George Benson, 1997.

TABLE C6.2   Data for Age Discrimination Case

Employee	Yearly Wages	Age	Employment Status	Employee	Yearly Wages	Age	Employment Status
* Adler, C.J.	$41,200	45	Terminated	* Huang, T.J.	42,995	48	Terminated
Alario, B.N.	39,565	43	Active	Jatho, J.A.	31,755	40	Active
Anders, J.M.	30,980	41	Active	Johnson, C.H.	29,540	32	Active
Bajwa, K.K.	23,225	27	Active	Jurasik, T.B.	34,300	41	Active
Barny, M.L.	21,250	26	Active	Klein, K.L.	43,700	51	Terminated
* Berger, R.W.	41,875	45	Terminated	Lang, T.F.	19,435	22	Active
Brenn, L.O.	31,225	41	Active	Liao, P.C.	28,750	32	Active
Cain, E.J.	30,135	36	Terminated	* Lostan, W.J.	44,675	52	Terminated
Carle, W.J.	29,850	32	Active	Mak, G.L.	35,505	38	Terminated
Castle, A.L.	21,850	22	Active	Maloff, V.R.	33,425	38	Terminated
Chan, S.D.	43,005	48	Terminated	McCall, R.M.	31,300	36	Terminated
Cho, J.Y.	34,785	41	Active	* Nadeau, S.R.	42,300	46	Terminated
Cohen, S.D.	25,350	27	Active	* Nguyen, O.L.	43,625	50	Terminated
Darel, F.E.	36,300	42	Active	Oas, R.C.	37,650	42	Active
* Davis, D.E.	40,425	46	Terminated	* Patel, M.J.	38,400	43	Terminated
* Dawson, P.K.	39,150	42	Terminated	Porter, K.D.	32,195	35	Terminated
Denker, U.H.	19,435	19	Active	Rosa, L.M.	19,435	21	Active
Dorando, T.R.	24,125	28	Active	Roth, J.H.	32,785	39	Terminated
Dubois, A.G.	30,450	40	Active	Savino, G.L.	37,900	42	Active
England, N.	24,750	25	Active	Scott, I.W.	29,150	30	Terminated
Estis, K.B.	22,755	23	Active	Smith, E.E.	35,125	41	Active
Fenton, C.K.	23,000	24	Active	Teel, Q.V.	27,655	33	Active
Finer, H.R.	42,000	46	Terminated	* Walker, F.O.	42,545	47	Terminated
* Frees, O.C.	44,100	52	Terminated	Wang, T.G.	22,200	32	Active
Gary, J.G.	44,975	55	Terminated	Yen, D.O.	40,350	44	Terminated
Gillen, D.J.	25,900	27	Active	Young, N.L.	28,305	34	Active
Harvey, D.A.	40,875	46	Terminated	Zeitels, P.W.	36,500	42	Active
Higgins, N.M.	38,595	41	Active				

*Denotes plaintiffs

age 40 and over and to establish the credibility of management's random sampling claim.

Using whatever statistical methods you think are appropriate, build a case that supports the plaintiff's position. (Call documents related to this issue Exhibit A.) Similarly, build a case that supports the defendant's position. (Call these documents Exhibit B.) Then discuss which of the two cases is more convincing and why. [*Note:* The data for this case are available in ASCII format in the file described at right.] ▲

DATA   ASCII file name: DISCRIM.DAT
Number of observations: 55

Variable	Column(s)	Type
LASTNAME	1–10	QL
WAGES	15–19	QN
AGE	35–36	QN
STATUS	47	QL (A=active, T=terminated)

www.int.com
www.int.com
INTERNET LAB
www.int.com

SAMPLING AND ANALYZING NYSE STOCK QUOTES

The success of any investment in common stock depends, to a certain extent, on timing, particularly as it relates to movement and changes in the stock market and the economy. Stock market indexes, such as the Dow Jones Industrial Average, act both as indicators of stock market activity and as economic indicators. Other information on stock market behavior is available, including the Composite daily summaries of all stocks traded on the New York Stock Exchange (NYSE).

In this lab exercise we will experiment with sampling and analyzing current NYSE data. Following are relevant NYSE site addresses:

NYSE Home Page: *http://www.nyse.com/*
(Select *Data* icon)

Data Page: *http://www.nyse.com/public/data.html*
(Select *NYSE Historical Statistics Archive*)

NYSE Historical Statistics:
http://www.nyse.com/public/data/stathtoc.html

1. Obtain the daily closing prices for a random sample of 30 stocks on the last business day of 1995. Repeat for the last days of 1996 and for 1997. (Be sure that your three samples of stocks are independent.)

2. Download and save the data in your statistical applications software data files.

3. Use available statistical software to compare the closing prices for 1995, 1996, and 1997. Use both parametric and nonparametric statistical tests and compare the results. ○

CHAPTER 18

DECISION ANALYSIS

Where We've Been

In previous chapters we used a decision procedure to test hypotheses about population parameters. Using sample information, we decided to reject or accept the null hypothesis based on the calculated probabilities of making incorrect decisions—namely, the probability (α) of rejecting the null hypothesis if it was in fact true, and the probability (β) of accepting the null hypothesis if it was actually false.

Where We're Going

In this chapter, we present the basic concepts of a general theory for making decisions that explicitly accounts for the gains or losses associated with alternative decisions and the probabilities of the occurrence of these gains or losses. First, we describe how to handle decision problems using only information that is currently available about the problem. Then we extend the analysis to include the case in which additional information can be obtained by sampling.

18.1 INTRODUCTION

Suppose you have been given the responsibility of determining whether your firm should expand its sales region to include the southwestern part of the United States. Before making your decision, you would probably want answers to many questions. How large would the yearly demand for the product be? How many salespeople would be assigned to the new territory? How much and what types of advertising would be used? Are adequate warehousing facilities available? Who would the company's principal competitors be, and how would they react to new competition? Even if it were possible to obtain accurate answers *(perfect information)* to these and other pertinent questions, your decision problem would be extremely complex. Realistically, however, you cannot expect to receive perfect information. Thus, in making your decision, you will face the more complex problem of having to deal with answers about which you are uncertain.

How would you tackle such a decision problem? The most natural first step—and one that is used by most decision analysts—is to reduce the problem to a manageable size by considering only questions that bear significantly on the objective of your decision. In this case, your objective may be to increase corporate profit. It may turn out that the profitability of the decision to expand the sales region depends primarily on the extent of the demand for the product in the new territory during the first year after it has been introduced. However, since this demand is unknown, even with this simplified decision problem you still must make your decision in the face of uncertainty. Given your uncertainty about the demand, how much information about demand in the new region would you want prior to making your decision, and how would you process such information? Answers to these questions are provided by the methodology referred to as *decision analysis,* which is the subject of this chapter.

Decision analysis is a systematic approach to solving decision problems under conditions of uncertainty. It does not *describe* how or why an individual makes a decision; rather, it *prescribes* a decision for the individual that is consistent with his or her *preferences and attitudes toward risk.* You might be asking yourself: "Why do I need to study decision-making as though it were a science, when I know most decisions (business or otherwise) are made on an intuitive level?" The answer is fourfold:

1. Yes, the vast majority of decisions made in business do not require, and are made without, formal analysis. But for that one crucial decision upon which "everything depends," it is important to have a systematic, logical decision procedure to follow.

2. Most of us have had little experience intuitively processing the probabilistic and sample information that may confront us in a complex decision-making problem. Consequently, it is frequently better to rely on the systematically generated information of decision analysis to guide decision-making than on the less reliable information-processing capabilities of our intuition.

3. Decision analysis forces us to consider carefully and logically all possible courses of action and the outcomes that could result from each. By so doing, we may disclose a new aspect of the problem or even find we have been addressing the wrong problem. Thus, the information obtained from decision analysis may more than compensate for the effort expended.

4. Another reason business and economics majors should study decision analysis is that many firms and government agencies use it regularly. Consequently,

you may very well be required to use decision analysis in your future employment.

One of the alternatives we face in making a decision is whether the decision should be made *now*—utilizing information we currently possess about the problem (we will refer to this as **prior information**)—or *postponed* until we have gathered additional information. We first study decision-making under uncertainty and assume that only prior information is available. Next, we expand our study of decision-making to include situations in which additional information is available. We discuss how to determine the value of additional information as well as when and how to use additional information in decision-making.

18.2   THREE TYPES OF DECISION PROBLEMS

Although all decision problems involve the selection of a course of action from among two or more alternatives, we can classify them into one of three categories:

1. Decision-making under certainty
2. Decision-making under uncertainty
3. Decision-making under conflict

Decision-making under certainty entails the selection of a course of action when we *know* the result that each alternative action will yield. If the number of alternatives being considered is small, such decisions may be easy to make. However, if the number of alternatives is large, the optimal decision may be difficult—if not impossible—to obtain. It may take too long or cost too much to evaluate so many alternatives individually and select the one with the most favorable results. Decision problems of this type are not addressed in this text, but here is a simple example of this type of problem:

> A furniture company constructs and finishes tables and chairs. Each table produced by the company nets a profit of $100 and each chair a profit of $60. During one week the company has 305 work-hours available for assembly operations and 355 work-hours available for finishing. From past experience it is known that each chair requires 3 hours to be assembled and $1\frac{1}{2}$ hours of finishing, while each table requires 4 hours for assembly and 2 hours for finishing. How many tables and how many chairs should the company produce over the week in order to maximize profits?

Note that a unique solution to this problem exists that will maximize the firm's profit. Many problems involving decision-making under certainty, including this one, are solved using a technique known as **linear programming**.

Decision-making under uncertainty entails the selection of a course of action when we *do not* know with certainty the results that each alternative action will yield.* Furthermore, we assume that the outcome of whatever course of action we select is affected only by chance and not by an opponent or competitor. We discuss decision-making under uncertainty in detail in this chapter. Our introductory example concerning the decision of whether to expand the sales region to the southwestern United States demonstrates decision-making under uncertainty.

Decision-making under conflict is similar to decision-making under uncertainty in that we do not know with certainty the result that each available alternative

---

*Some texts further distinguish "decision-making under risk" if probabilities are available to describe the degree of uncertainty. Since probabilities can always be obtained through judgment and reasoning (subjective probabilities; Section 18.5), we make no such distinction.

course of action will yield. However, the reason for this uncertainty is different in the case of decision-making under conflict. In such cases, we are in effect "playing against" one or more opponents or competitors. The outcome of our chosen course of action depends on decisions made by our competitors. Decision problems of this type require the approach known as **game theory**. Game theory is not discussed in this text; however, an example of this type of decision problem follows:

> An entrepreneur is interested in purchasing real estate near Dallas for the purpose of building a fast-food restaurant. He has narrowed his alternatives to five suburban neighborhoods. He is certain his venture will be profitable as long as no major fast-food chain decides to locate nearby. Thus, the decision problem involves choosing a parcel of land while knowing that the results of this decision depend on the expansion plans of potential competitors. Furthermore, the location decision facing other fast-food chains interested in the area depends to some extent on the decision of the Dallas entrepreneur. They, too, would prefer not to locate near another restaurant of the same type.

Since our objective throughout this text has been to make inferences when we have only partial (or *imperfect*) information, we concentrate on decision-making under uncertainty in the remaining sections.

EXERCISES 18.1–18.5

Learning the Mechanics

18.1 Compare and contrast decision-making under certainty, uncertainty, and conflict.

18.2 Describe two decision problems that you face every day. Categorize each as being a problem requiring a decision made under certainty, uncertainty, or conflict. Justify your categorization.

Applying the Concepts

18.3 Categorize the following decision problems as decision-making under certainty, uncertainty, or conflict. Justify your categorization.
  a. A bank manager is considering an application for a commercial loan. If she decides to make the loan but the customer defaults, the bank will lose the amount of the loan plus the lost profits. On the other hand, if the bank fails to grant the loan and the customer would have repaid it, the bank will lose the interest on the loan.
  b. A manufacturer must decide about the price of an electric lawn mower it makes. If the company sets the price too high, potential customers will purchase competitors' mowers. If, on the other hand, the price is set too low, the competitors will also drop their prices, thereby reducing everyone's profits.
  c. A computer hardware company has two contracts for producing electronic components for the space program. Since the contracts are for a fixed number of components at a fixed price,

the decision problem involves how to allocate fixed production resources to maximize profit.

18.4 Categorize the following decision problems as decision-making under certainty, uncertainty, or conflict. Justify your categorization.
  a. A plant manager wants to replace an obsolete piece of machinery with a new model. The two brands on the market from which to choose are of equal quality, have the same guarantee, and give the same yield per hour. However, brand B is $500 cheaper than brand A.
  b. A company is faced with the decision of whether or not to increase its production capacity by adding a new building to the existing facilities. If the company decides not to expand, it expects to make a profit of $550,000 for each of the next three years regardless of the state of the economy. If it builds the addition and the economy continues to expand, the addition is expected to increase company profits to at least $650,000 a year for the next three years. If it builds the addition and the economy remains stable or experiences a downward trend over the next three years, the company would incur a reduction in profits to $475,000 or less per year for the next three years.

18.5 Categorize the following decision problem. Justify your answer. In 1984 the federal government broke up the Bell System, making the regional Bell operating companies independent of their parent, AT&T. Over the next eight years, the earnings of the regional operating companies (e.g., Bell Atlantic, U.S. West, NYNEX, etc.) remained relatively flat while their stock prices soared. Wilde, Tunstall, and Smist (*Interfaces,* July–Aug. 1992) argued that for the regional operating companies to succeed in the face of this investor optimism, they needed to solve the following decision problem: either invest heavily in emerging competitive markets (cellular telephones, broadband video, business and residency gateway services, etc.) or do not invest and simply harvest profits from existing products and services. If successful, the former choice could lead to a 120% increase in the base value of the firm. If unsuccessful, the firm could decrease in value by 40% and be chronically unprofitable. The decision to not invest could result in a 55% increase to the base value of the firm or in a 10% loss in value.

18.3   DECISION-MAKING UNDER UNCERTAINTY: BASIC CONCEPTS

We will use the following example to introduce some basic concepts: A profit-motivated entrepreneur is committed to producing a concert that will feature a major rock star sometime in late June of next year. The promoter has been unable to finalize plans, however, due to indecision over whether to take a chance on rain and hold the concert in Memorial Stadium (40,000 seats outdoors) or play it safe and hold the concert in the Civic Center (15,000 seats indoors). A sellout is expected at least a month in advance, whichever facility is chosen. If the stadium is chosen and the weather cooperates, the promoter will make a net profit of about $350,000 (ticket proceeds less costs, taxes, and other expenses). If it is raining at concert time, the rock star may choose not to perform (according to the contract) and the promoter will lose about $40,000 (stadium rental, commitment to the rock star, administrative costs, salaries of security personnel, advertising). However, if the Civic Center is chosen, the entrepreneur would make a net profit of about $150,000 regardless of the weather. Which option would you choose? We will use decision analysis to make our selection later in the chapter.

We can identify three specific elements of this decision problem: First, a choice must be made between two possible courses of action—rent the stadium or rent the Civic Center. We refer to these alternatives as **actions**. Second, it is uncertain which event will occur—rain or no rain. We refer to these events as **states of nature**. Third, depending on which action is chosen and which state of nature occurs on the evening of the concert, the decision-maker* will receive either a financial reward or a penalty for the chosen action. The consequences of the decision problem are referred to as *outcomes;* they may be either positive or negative. For example, if the action chosen by the promoter is Rent the stadium and the state of nature that occurs is Rain, the outcome that results is −$40,000. That is, the action/state of nature combination Rent the stadium/Rain will *cost* the promoter $40,000. The combination Rent the stadium/No rain will yield a *profit* of $350,000. The reward (or penalty) corresponding to each action/state of nature combination is called the **outcome**, or **payoff**.

We can conveniently summarize all three elements of a decision problem in a **payoff table** (Table 18.1). Each of the set of possible actions the decision-maker has chosen to consider is associated with a *row* of the payoff table. Each state of nature is associated with a *column*. The numbers in the table are the outcomes of the decision problem. For example, $350,000 is the outcome that would result from the implementation of the action associated with the top row of the table

---

*The term *decision-maker* is used to refer not only to an individual but also to a corporation, a community, or, in general, any entity faced with a decision problem.

TABLE 18.1 Payoff Table for the Rock Concert Decision Problem

		STATE OF NATURE	
		Rain	**No Rain**
ACTION	**Rent Stadium**	−$40,000	$350,000
	Rent Civic Center	$150,000	$150,000

(Rent stadium) and the occurrence of the state of nature associated with the right-hand column of the table (No rain).

A decision problem can also be illustrated by a **decision tree**. A payoff table and a decision tree may display the same information, but as we will see, it is sometimes more convenient to use a decision tree. The decision tree in Figure 18.1 corresponds to Table 18.1. Conceptually, the promoter's movement through time toward the outcome of the decision problem is represented by movement from left to right through the decision tree. The ■ denotes a **decision fork** and signals that a decision must be made. At this position on the tree, the decision-maker must choose between the two actions, Rent stadium and Rent Civic Center. If Rent stadium is chosen, then from the decision fork we move along the upper branch of the tree. The ● denotes a **chance fork** and signals that the next branch of the tree the promoter will follow will be determined by the chance occurrence of a state of nature. If the decision-maker is positioned at the upper chance fork of Figure 18.1 and it rains on the day of the concert, then the upper branch of the chance fork (labeled Rain) will lead the promoter to the consequence (−$40,000) of the action/state combination Rent stadium/Rain.

Both the selection of actions to be considered in a decision problem and the choice of an action to implement are under the control of the decision-maker, but the state of nature is not. The decision-maker must choose a course of action *prior* to knowing which state of nature will occur and *without* being able to influence the random process generating the states of nature. *Note also that the states of nature considered in any decision problem must be mutually exclusive and collectively exhaustive.* That is, the state of nature that occurs must be clearly identifiable as one and only one of the listed states, and the list of states considered must include all possible states that can occur. The former constraint precludes any overlapping of, or vagueness in, state definitions; the latter precludes the possibility of any state occurrence not anticipated by the decision-maker. For practical purposes, the states of nature in the above example are mutually exclusive and collectively exhaustive. They are mutually exclusive because the weather on a June evening can be classified as either rainy or not rainy, but not both. They are

FIGURE 18.1
Decision tree for the rock concert decision problem

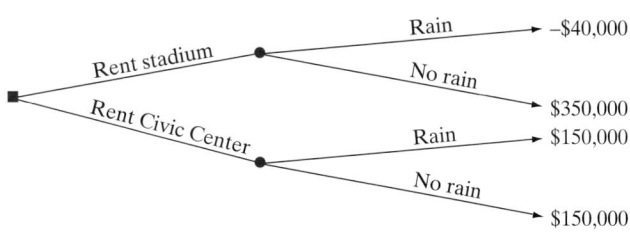

collectively exhaustive because the list of possible weather patterns can be narrowed to include only rainy or not rainy.

All outcomes in a decision problem should be stated in terms of the same numerical quantity, and that quantity should be chosen to rank the outcomes relative to the decision-maker's overall objective. We refer to this measure of the outcomes of a decision problem as the **objective variable**. In the preceding example, the promoter's motive—or objective—for producing the rock concert was net profit. Accordingly, the decision outcomes are expressed in terms of net profit (dollars). If the objective were to give as many people as possible an opportunity to see a live performance by the rock star, we would measure the outcomes of potential actions in terms of the number of people attending the concert.

We conclude by summarizing the concept of decision-making under uncertainty, the four elements common to this type of decision problem, and the methods for displaying these elements.

Decision-Making Under Uncertainty

If a decision-maker is faced with choosing one action from among two or more alternative actions, and at least one of these actions has possible outcomes that depend on the chance occurrence of one of a set of mutually exclusive and collectively exhaustive states of nature, the decision-maker is said to be faced with **decision-making under uncertainty**.

Four Elements Common to Decision Problems Involving Uncertainty

1. *Actions:* The set of two or more alternatives the decision-maker has chosen to consider. The decision-maker's problem is to choose one action from this set.

2. *States of nature:* The set of two or more mutually exclusive and collectively exhaustive chance events upon which the outcome of the decision-maker's chosen action depends.

3. *Outcomes:* The set of consequences resulting from all possible action/state of nature combinations.

4. *Objective variable:* The quantity used to measure and express the outcomes of a decision problem.

Table 18.2 and Figure 18.2 depict the general format for the payoff table and the decision tree, respectively. If the ith action is denoted by a_i and the jth state of nature by S_j, then the outcome resulting from the combination of the ith action with the jth state of nature is O_{ij}.

TABLE 18.2 General Form of a Payoff Table

		STATE OF NATURE			
		S_1	S_2	$\cdots$	S_m
	a_1	O_{11}	O_{12}	$\cdots$	O_{1m}
	a_2	O_{21}	O_{22}	$\cdots$	O_{2m}
ACTION	$\vdots$	$\vdots$	$\vdots$		$\vdots$
	a_n	O_{n1}	O_{n2}	$\cdots$	O_{nm}

FIGURE 18.2
General form of
a decision tree

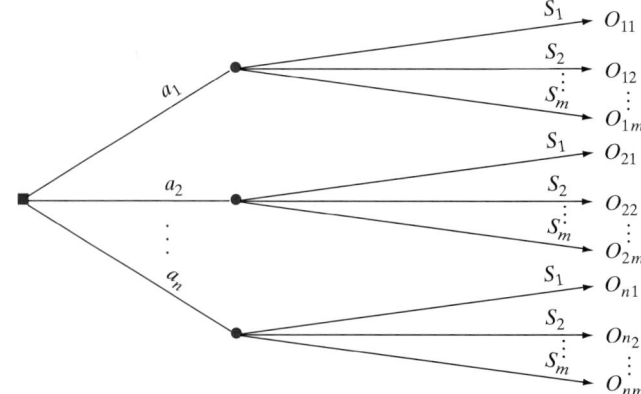

EXERCISES 18.6–18.12

Learning the Mechanics

18.6 List and define the four primary elements of a decision problem under uncertainty.

18.7 The states of nature that are defined in a decision problem must be mutually exclusive and collectively exhaustive. In this context, what is meant by the phrase *mutually exclusive and collectively exhaustive*?

18.8 Describe a decision you make every day that is done in the face of uncertainty. Identify the actions and states of nature of your decision problem. Construct a decision tree to illustrate your decision problem.

Applying the Concepts

18.9 For each of these decision problems, identify the actions, states of nature, outcomes, and objective variable:

a. A winery is considering introducing an inexpensive dinner wine. The introduction of the wine will cost $3 million in promotional and fixed costs per year. Each bottle sold will contribute $.30 to profits. The management

believes that sales could range from 5 to 25 million bottles per year.

b. An administrator in the Environmental Protection Agency (EPA) must determine how much to fine companies that discharge a certain effluent into U.S. waterways. If the fine is set too low, all companies will simply pay the fine because it will be less costly than installing pollution-control equipment. On the other hand, if the fine is set too high, small companies may be driven out of business because they cannot afford the capital expenditures necessary to meet the new EPA standard. Thus, the problem is to set the fine to minimize the total social cost—that is, the cost to society of (1) firms being driven out of business and (2) waterways being polluted.

18.10 *Interfaces* (Nov.–Dec. 1992) describes a decision problem faced by a large U.S. bank: whether or not to purchase and install an emergency generator to protect its data-processing operations. Consider the decision tree shown here. Outcomes are expressed as the impact on annualized earnings. Identify the four primary elements of this decision problem.

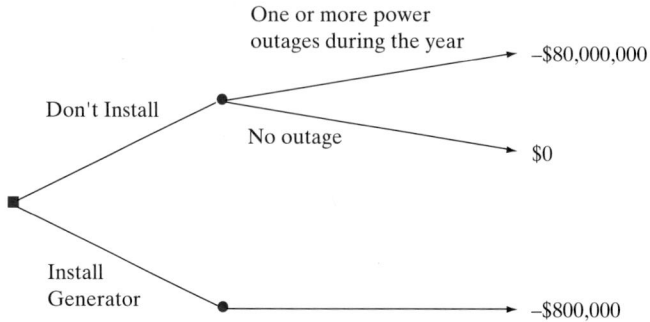

Source: Adapted from K. J. Engemann and H. E. Miller. "Operations risk management at a major bank." *Interfaces,* Vol. 22, No. 6 (Nov.–Dec. 1992), pp. 140–149.

18.11   Refer to Exercise 18.5, in which an investment decision facing the regional telephone companies was considered. Identify the actions, states of nature, outcomes, and the objective variable. If any of these elements are not described in Exercise 18.5, speculate as to what they could be. That is, provide your own definitions of the missing elements.

18.12   A company that manufactures a well-known line of designer jeans is contemplating whether to increase its advertising budget by $1 million for next year. If the expanded advertising campaign is successful, the company expects sales to increase by $1.6 million next year. If the advertising campaign fails, the company expects sales to increase by only $400,000 next year. If the company decides not to increase its advertising expenditures, it expects sales to increase by $200,000 next year.

   a. Identify the actions, states of nature, outcomes, and objective variable for this decision problem.

   b. Construct a decision tree that illustrates the jeans manufacturer's decision problem.

18.4   TWO WAYS OF EXPRESSING OUTCOMES: PAYOFFS AND OPPORTUNITY LOSSES

The outcomes of the rock concert example discussed in the previous section were in terms of the net profit that would be realized by the promoter depending on the decision (action) concerning the location of the concert and on the weather (state of nature) on the day of the concert. That is, net profit was the objective variable. Recall that the objective variable can assume both positive and negative values. In general, we refer to outcomes that reflect the *actual* reward to the decision-maker in terms of the objective variable as **payoffs**.

Alternatively, outcomes can be expressed in terms of *opportunities* for higher profits that the decision-maker has *lost* as a result of the action selected. For example, in the rock concert example, if the weather is not rainy, a decision to hold the concert in the Civic Center will bring in a profit of $150,000 and a decision to use the stadium will bring in a profit of $350,000. If, in fact, the Civic Center was chosen, then by not choosing to rent the stadium, the promoter will have *lost the opportunity* to net an additional $200,000. We refer to this $200,000 as the *opportunity loss* (or *regret*) associated with the action/state combination Rent Civic Center/No rain. An opportunity loss may be determined in a similar fashion for each action/state combination of a decision problem, and an **opportunity loss table** may be constructed as in Table 18.3. Notice that none of the opportunity losses of Table 18.3 is less than 0. A little thought should convince you that this is true in general for any opportunity loss. In Section 18.6, we show that decision problems may be solved using outcomes expressed either as payoffs or as opportunity losses.

DEFINITION 18.1

The **opportunity loss** is the difference between the payoff a decision-maker receives for a chosen action and the maximum that the decision-maker could have received for choosing the action yielding the highest payoff for the state of nature that occurred.

TABLE 18.3   Opportunity Loss Table for the Rock Concert Decision Problem

		STATE OF NATURE	
		Rain	No Rain
ACTION	Rent Stadium	$190,000	0
	Rent Civic Center	0	$200,000

Opportunity Loss Determination

Repeat the following procedure for each state of nature in a decision problem—i.e., each column of a payoff table:

1. Find the maximum payoff in a column. The opportunity loss associated with this payoff is 0.

2. The opportunity loss associated with any other payoff in this column is found by subtracting that payoff from the maximum payoff in the column.

EXAMPLE 18.1

A beer producer with breweries located in the western part of the United States and a distribution network that extends only as far east as the Mississippi River is considering expanding its sales region to include the northeastern part of the country. The producer would need to build a new brewery in the Northeast to overcome refrigeration problems in transporting its beer. The problem is to determine how large a brewery to construct.

It has been decided that the size should be based on the projected gross profits (profit before taxes) for the fifth year of operation for each of the four sizes of breweries under consideration. The firm's marketing department recognizes that the company cannot possibly obtain more than a 15% market share during the fifth year of operation and has put together a payoff table for the firm's planning committee (Table 18.4). Construct the corresponding opportunity loss table.

SOLUTION

For each column of the payoff table (Table 18.4) find the maximum payoff:

	Column 1	Column 2	Column 3
Maximum payoff:	$300,000	$700,000	$1,000,000

The opportunity loss associated with each column maximum is 0. The opportunity associated with, for example, any other payoff in column 1 is found by subtracting that payoff from the column's maximum payoff, $300,000, as shown in Table 18.5. The resulting opportunity loss table is shown in Table 18.6.

After formulating and displaying a decision problem as just described, we may notice that an action has been included that should never be selected *no matter which state of nature occurs*. In Example 18.1, a_4 is such an action. Inspection of the payoff table (Table 18.4) or the opportunity loss table (Table

TABLE 18.4   Payoff Table for the Brewer's Decision Problem

		STATE OF NATURE: MARKET SHARE IN YEAR 5		
		S_1: 0% < 5%	S_2: 5% < 10%	S_3: 10%–15%
ACTION: BREWERY SIZE	a_1: Small	$300,000	$350,000	$450,000
	a_2: Medium	$250,000	$700,000	$800,000
	a_3: Large	$200,000	$600,000	$1,000,000
	a_4: Very Large	−$100,000	$100,000	$500,000

TABLE 18.5   Calculation of Opportunity Losses for the Brewer's Decision Problem

		STATE OF NATURE: MARKET SHARE IN YEAR 5		
		$S_1: 0\% < 5\%$	$S_2: 5\% < 10\%$	$S_3: 10\% - 15\%$
	a_1: Small	0	$700,000 - $350,000 = $350,000	$1,000,000 - $450,000 = $550,000
	a_2: Medium	$300,000 - $250,000 = $50,000	0	$1,000,000 - $800,000 = $200,000
ACTION: BREWERY SIZE	a_3: Large	$300,000 - $200,000 = $100,000	$700,000 - $600,000 = $100,000	0
	a_4: Very Large	$300,000 - (-$100,000) = $400,000	$700,000 - $100,000 = $600,000	$1,000,000 - $500,000 = $500,000

TABLE 18.6   Opportunity Loss Table for the Brewer's Decision Problem

		STATE OF NATURE: MARKET SHARE IN YEAR 5		
		$S_1: 0\% < 5\%$	$S_2: 5\% < 10\%$	$S_3: 10\% - 15\%$
ACTION: BREWERY SIZE	a_1: Small	$0	$350,000	$550,000
	a_2: Medium	$50,000	0	$200,000
	a_3: Large	$100,000	$100,000	0
	a_4: Very Large	$400,000	$600,000	$500,000

18.6) reveals that both actions a_2 and a_3 result in higher payoffs (and lower opportunity losses) than a_4 for each possible state of nature. Thus, a_4 is said to be *dominated* by both actions a_2 and a_3 and should never be chosen by the decision-maker. Accordingly, dominated actions are dropped from consideration. Because dominated actions should not be admitted for consideration by the decision-maker, they are sometimes referred to as being *inadmissible actions*. We will see later that eliminating inadmissible actions eases the computation burdens in solving a decision problem.

DEFINITION 18.2

Action a_i is said to **dominate** action a_j, thereby making a_j **inadmissible**, if each of the following is true:

1. For each state of nature, the payoff for action a_i is greater than or equal to the payoff for a_j.

2. For at least one state of nature, the payoff for action a_i is greater than the payoff for a_j.

The decision-maker should eliminate any dominated actions (inadmissible actions) from all decision problems.

To use decision analysis to prescribe a decision in the face of uncertainty, we must characterize our uncertainty concerning the states of nature of the problem with a probability distribution. We discuss the determination of such distributions in the next section.

EXERCISES 18.13–18.24

Learning the Mechanics

18.13 Explain the difference between payoffs and opportunity losses.

18.14 Why should a dominated action be eliminated from a decision problem?

18.15 Refer to the following table. Eliminate any inadmissible actions from the payoff table and convert it to an opportunity loss table.

		STATE OF NATURE			
		S_1	S_2	S_3	S_4
ACTION	a_1	−58	−2	0	50
	a_2	−69	−10	40	71
	a_3	−70	−15	40	70
	a_4	−100	−40	−10	80

18.16 Identify any inadmissible actions in the decision tree shown here, and redraw the tree without the inadmissible actions. The objective variable is total sales (in thousands of dollars).

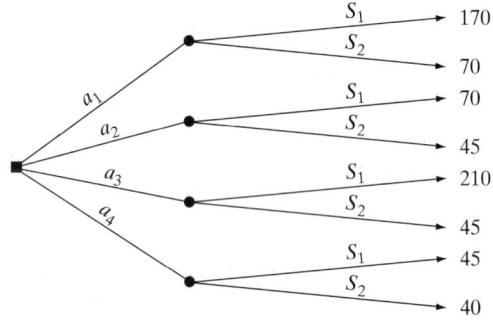

18.17 An opportunity loss table that has been derived from a payoff table is shown.

	S_1	S_2	S_3
a_1	15	40	0
a_2	0	10	8
a_3	43	0	15
a_4	20	20	10

  a. Which action(s) in the table is (are) inadmissible? Justify your answer.
  b. Why is it not possible to convert this opportunity loss table to the original payoff table?

18.18 The outcomes displayed on the decision tree (top right) are in terms of payoffs. Convert the outcomes to opportunity losses.

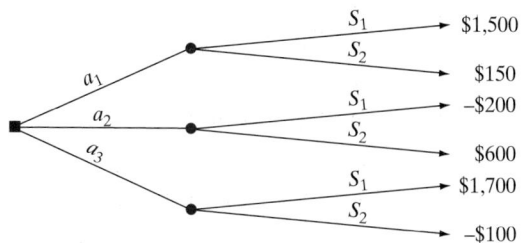

Applying the Concepts

18.19 Balson, Welsh, and Wilson (*Interfaces*, Nov.–Dec. 1992) describe a simplified version of a decision problem faced by an electric utility company. The company must decide whether to replace a PCB transformer in a generating station. The total cost of the replacement has a present value of $75,000. If the company does not replace the transformer and a major fire occurs, the present value of the cost of cleaning up the PCB pollution after the fire is $30 million. If a major fire occurs in the new transformer, the associated cost of PCB cleanup has a present value of $20 million.
  a. Construct a payoff table for this decision problem.
  b. Convert the table in part **a** to an opportunity loss table.
  c. Construct a decision tree for this problem.

18.20 In Exercise 18.10, a large U.S. bank was confronted with the decision problem illustrated on page 959:
  a. Convert the decision tree to a payoff table.
  b. Convert the payoff table to an opportunity loss table.

18.21 A U.S. manufacturer of laptop computers is considering marketing its product in Europe. If it does so, the company expects to attain a European market share of no more than 3% and no less than 1% over the next three years. The company's accounting department has determined that the payoff for this expansion should be an increase in total company profits for the next three years of $3 million if the product is able to attain a 3% market share, an increase of $1 million for a 2% market share, and a decrease of $1 million for a 1% market share. Total domestic profits for the next three years are expected to be $15 million regardless of whether or not the laptop computer is marketed in Europe.
  a. Formulate the payoff table for this decision problem.
  b. Convert the payoff table to an opportunity loss table.

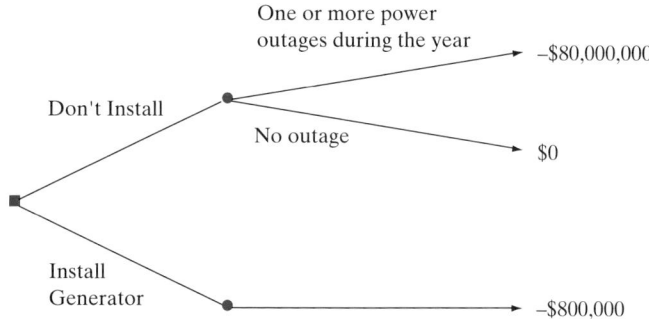

Source: Adapted from K. J. Engemann and H. E. Miller. "Operations risk management at a major bank." *Interfaces,* Vol. 22, No. 6 (Nov.–Dec. 1992), pp. 140–149.

18.22 A common problem in business is the management of perishable inventories—items that lose most of their economic value after a given date due to obsolescence or spoilage. For example, if a corner newsstand orders too many papers and cannot sell them all, the excess papers have little value. Hence, these types of problems are called *newsboy problems.* Newsboy problems are common in retailing situations such as the following: A buyer for a large department store must decide how many of a new style of dress to order. Because of rapid changes in fashion, she does not want to order too many dresses, but if she orders too few she will lose profits for her department. Each dress purchased costs the store $30 and sells for $50. Any dresses not sold at the end of the season are sold at the annual half-price sale. The buyer believes the department will sell three, four, five, six, seven, or eight dozen dresses. Dresses must be purchased by the department store in lots of one dozen.

  a. Formulate the payoff table for this decision problem.

  b. Convert the payoff table to an opportunity loss table.

18.23 The purchasing agent for an automobile manufacturer is concluding a purchase agreement with a supplier of preformed body pieces. The pieces will be purchased in lots of 500, and the cost of a lot is $15,000. The body stamping has a frequent defect called a *burr,* which can be filed off by the automobile manufacturer at a cost of $10 per piece. Past experience with this supplier has shown that the proportion of defects tends to be 5%, 10%, or 50%. The supplier now offers a guarantee that it will assume the costs for all defective body moldings greater than 50 in a production lot of 500. This guarantee may be purchased for a cost of $1,000 before the lot begins production. The purchasing agent is interested in determining whether the guarantee should be purchased.

  a. Formulate the payoff table for this problem.

  b. Draw the decision tree that corresponds to your payoff table.

18.24 Computer products company A has sued computer products company B for patent infringements. The management of B is deciding whether to settle the suit out of court. If they do so, the accounting and marketing departments calculate that company B would lose $50 million over the next five years in royalty payments. If they go to court and win, they will have $1 million in court costs. However, if they lose they will owe company A $100 million in royalties.

  a. Formulate the payoff table for this decision problem.

  b. Draw the decision tree that corresponds to your payoff table.

18.5 CHARACTERIZING THE UNCERTAINTY IN DECISION PROBLEMS

In Chapter 3 we explained that probability distributions are used to characterize an individual's uncertainty about the outcomes of an experiment. In a decision problem, the observation of a state of nature associated with the problem may be regarded as an experiment and the various states of nature as experimental outcomes. Thus, it follows that a decision-maker can use a probability distribution to characterize the uncertainties associated with the states of nature in a decision problem. These probabilities indicate the likelihood of the occurrence of the various states of nature and may be unknown. Consequently, we assess these values using one of the following:

1. Information about the relative frequencies of the states
2. Judgmental (subjective) information about the states
3. A combination of relative frequency information and subjective information

In other words, we use any type of information that is available to assign probabilities to the states of nature.

For example, in the rock concert example of Section 18.3, the concert promoter could use historical weather data (relative frequency data) along with personal knowledge of the rock star's tendency to declare a day too rainy to perform (subjective information) to assess judgmentally the probabilities of states for the decision problem. Or, if you wanted to decide whether to open your own business next year, you would be interested in knowing whether the economy will move at a healthy pace for the next three years or whether it will fall into a recession. Since the observation of this experiment—observing the health of the economy over the next three years—can never be repeated, you must rely on your own experience or the advice of economic experts to assess the probabilities associated with these states of nature. *Caution:* Great care must be taken in determining probabilities for the states of nature. Decision analyses based on poorly chosen probabilities may lead to inappropriate actions.

18.6 SOLVING THE DECISION PROBLEM USING THE EXPECTED PAYOFF CRITERION

Now that we have shown you how to structure a decision problem by constructing a payoff table or an opportunity loss table and how to characterize the uncertainty associated with the states of nature in a decision problem, we have to choose a rule for reaching a decision. Numerous rules have been proposed, but the one most commonly used in decision analyses uses a payoff table and chooses the action that produces the **maximum expected payoff**. This is called the **expected payoff criterion**. Equivalently, you could use an opportunity loss table and choose the action that produces the **minimum expected opportunity loss**. This is called the **expected opportunity loss criterion**. It can be shown that both criteria lead to the same solution.

To understand how the expected payoff criterion is used to reach a decision, recall the definition of the expected value of a discrete random variable (Chapter 4). If x is a discrete random variable with probability distribution $p(x)$, then the expected (or mean) value of x is

$$E(x) = \sum_{\text{All } x} x p(x)$$

As we will illustrate, the random variable x in a decision problem is the payoff, and the probabilities associated with x are the same as those that describe the likelihood of occurrence of states of nature.

For example, consider the brewery decision problem in Example 18.1. The payoff table is reproduced in Table 18.7. Note that we have eliminated the inadmissible action, a_4: Very large brewery.

STATISTICS IN ACTION

18.1 EVALUATING UNCERTAINTY IN RESEARCH AND DEVELOPMENT

A subjective probability is a numerical expression of an individual's degree of belief in the outcome of an event (Browne, Curley, and Benson, *Management Science,* Jan. 1997). Sandoz, a Swiss pharmaceutical company, uses subjective probabilities as a basis for its research and development (R&D) planning and decisions:

> Although all management functions must cope with uncertainty, R&D is generally agreed to be the function involving the largest number and the widest range of uncertainties. Thus, the R&D manager faces huge problems not only in selecting the most promising avenues for R&D effort and expenditures but also in attempting to ensure a steady flow of technically successful projects (Balthasar, Boschi, and Menke, *Harvard Business Review,* May–June 1978).

Twice a year a small group of experts is asked to assess the probability of technical success for each of Sandoz's R&D projects. The group of experts includes R&D line managers and other technical experts familiar with particular requirements for a project's success. When the program was begun, these probability assessments were obtained through interviews. Two basic methods of eliciting subjective probabilities were used—direct and indirect. A *direct method* is one that requires the expert to state the probability, or odds, of a project's success explicitly in numerical terms. An *indirect method* is one in which the expert's responses are not probabilities but are capable of being converted to probabilities.

One indirect method used by Sandoz in the early stages of the program is the *probability wheel,* a disk divided into a blue section and an orange one. The relative size of each section is adjustable. In the center is a pointer to spin that will stop in one of the two sections. The expert is asked which event is more likely: (1) the spinner will stop in the orange section, or (2) project A will succeed. If the answer is (1), the wheel is adjusted to reduce the orange section. If the answer is (2), the wheel is adjusted to enlarge the orange section. This procedure is repeated until the expert says the two events are equally likely. The relative size of the orange section is the expert's subjective probability of the success of project A.

Initially, all probabilities were elicited indirectly. As individual forecasters became more familiar with the process, probabilities were assigned directly to each project. When all the experts were sufficiently familiar with the technique, Sandoz replaced interviews by questionnaires. After individual probability assessments have been obtained from each expert, the entire group meets to discuss their assessments and arrive at one consensus probability for each R&D project. The advantage of the group assessment is that it brings together the opinions of individuals with different experience and information.

The consensus probabilities are then used in making decisions concerning R&D projects. There are many models and techniques for planning and controlling R&D that require input regarding the probability of a project's success. Obtaining subjective probability assessments allows management to use these models as an aid in decision-making.

Sandoz is pleased with the results of using subjective probabilities in managing R&D. By comparing the experts' consensus success probabilities with the actual relative frequency of project successes over time, Balthasar, Boschi, and Menke (1978) found that the probabilistic predictions are reliable indicators of future results. In line with its goal of "a steady flow of technically successful projects," Sandoz has found that decision-making based on subjective probabilities has reduced the variability in its expected success rate for projects in the early stage of development. The R&D managers at Sandoz consider subjective probabilities a useful input to assist in management planning and control in a highly uncertain environment.

Focus

a. What is a subjective probability?

b. Differentiate between direct and indirect probability assessment techniques.

c. In the indirect probability assessment method described above, what types of responses are elicited from the experts?

d. What is a consensus probability? Why are consensus probabilities frequently superior to the assessments of individual forecasters?

e. What general factors may cause an individual's assessed subjective event probability to not be representative of his or her underlying data, information, and beliefs?

Table 18.7   **Payoff Table for the Brewery Example**

		STATE OF NATURE: MARKET SHARE IN YEAR 5		
		S_1: 0% < 5%	S_2: 5% < 10%	S_3: 10%–15%
ACTION:	a_1: Small	$300,000	$350,000	$450,000
BREWERY	a_2: Medium	$250,000	$700,000	$800,000
SIZE	a_3: Large	$200,000	$600,000	$1,000,000

Suppose the brewery has assessed the following probability distribution for the states of nature:

State	0% < 5%	5% < 10%	10%–15%
P(State will occur)	.4	.5	.1

Then if you choose action a_1 (see row 1 of Table 18.7), the payoffs can be $300,000, $350,000, or $450,000, with probabilities .4, .5, and .1, respectively. Thus, the probability distribution for the payoff x if you choose action a_1 is

Payoff x	$300,000	$350,000	$450,000
$p(x)$	.4	.5	.1

The expected payoff of action a_1, denoted by the symbol $EP(a_1)$, is

$$EP(a_1) = \sum xp(x)$$
$$= (\$300,000)(.4) + (\$350,000)(.5) + (\$450,000)(.1) = \$340,000$$

This tells us that, if we were faced with this decision problem a very large number of times and chose action a_1 each time, the mean or expected payoff would be $340,000—assuming that the probabilities accurately reflect the likelihood of occurrence for the states of nature.

Similarly, we can write the probability distributions and expected payoffs for actions a_2 and a_3. For action a_2:

Payoff x	$250,000	$700,000	$800,000
$p(x)$	.4	.5	.1

$$EP(a_2) = \sum xp(x)$$
$$= (\$250,000)(.4) + (\$700,000)(.5) + (\$800,000)(.1) = \$530,000$$

For action a_3:

Payoff x	$200,000	$600,000	$1,000,000
$p(x)$	.4	.5	.1

$$EP(a_3) = \sum xp(x)$$
$$= (\$200,000)(.4) + (\$600,000)(.5) + (\$1,000,000)(.1) = \$480,000$$

Now examine the expected (mean) payoffs for each action, as summarized in Table 18.8. Which action would you choose? We think you would choose action a_2;

TABLE 18.8   Expected Payoff Table for the Brewer's Decision Problem

Action	Expected Payoff for Action a_i
a_i	$EP(a_i)$
a_1	\$340,000
a_2	\$530,000
a_3	\$480,000

i.e., you would recommend that the brewer construct a medium-sized brewery because this strategy will produce the largest expected payoff—namely, \$530,000.

The Expected Payoff Criterion
Choose the action that produces the largest expected payoff.

As noted at the beginning of this section, we arrive at the same solution to the brewer's decision problem if we use an opportunity loss table, find the expected opportunity loss for each action, and then choose the action that produces the *minimum* expected opportunity loss. The solution is again action a_2.

The Expected Opportunity Loss Criterion
Choose the action that produces the smallest expected opportunity loss. (This always leads to the same decision as the expected payoff criterion.)

EXERCISES   18.25–18.35

Learning the Mechanics

18.25 Consider the payoff table shown here. Find the action that would be prescribed by the expected payoff criterion. Probabilities are in parentheses in the table.

		STATE OF NATURE			
		$S_1(.1)$	$S_2(.3)$	$S_3(.4)$	$S_4(.2)$
	a_1	-150	-500	10	300
ACTION	a_2	-200	-100	300	100
	a_3	-150	-40	-10	85

18.26 In the decision tree shown here, state of nature probabilities are displayed in parentheses to the right of the state of nature symbols, S_1 and S_2.
   a. Identify any inadmissible actions, and explain why they are inadmissible.
   b. The expected payoff for each action has been computed and appears to the left of the chance

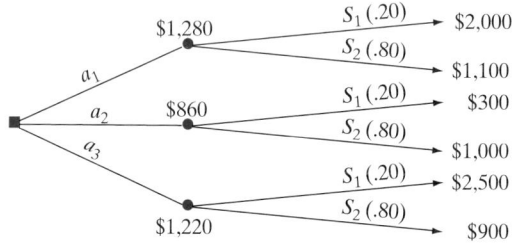

fork associated with each action in the decision tree. Verify that these expected payoffs are correct.
   c. Identify the action that is prescribed by the expected payoff criterion.

18.27 Construct the decision tree for the decision problem described in Exercise 18.25. Include on your decision tree the state probabilities and the expected payoffs associated with each action. (For an example of such a tree, see Exercise 18.26.)

18.28 Consider the accompanying payoff table (probabilities are in parentheses).

		STATE OF NATURE		
		$S_1(.20)$	$S_2(.30)$	$S_3(.50)$
ACTION	a_1	150	55	130
	a_2	−35	0	210

a. Use the expected payoff criterion to select the better action.

b. Convert the payoff table to an opportunity loss table and use the expected opportunity loss criterion to select the better action.

18.29 In the decision tree shown below, state of nature probabilities are displayed in parentheses to the right of the state of nature symbols, S_1 and S_2. The outcomes on the decision tree are expressed in terms of opportunity losses. According to the expected opportunity loss criterion, which action should be selected?

Applying the Concepts

18.30 *Materials requirements planning* (MRP) systems are computerized planning and control systems for manufacturing operations. Since their introduction in the mid-1960s, MRP systems have made it possible to simultaneously reduce inventories and improve customer service (Starr, *Operations Management,* 1996). The operations manager for a company that produces a defense product wants an MRP system. He has narrowed his choices to three vendors, X, Y, and Z, whose systems cost $5,000, $4,000, and $3,000, respectively. In addition, each vendor charges a fee for implementing the system (e.g., adapting the system to fit the purchaser's need, installing the system, and debugging the system); the size of the fee depends primarily on the extent to which the system must be modified to meet the purchaser's needs. Systems X, Y, and Z are similar and would require basically the same modifications, but the implementation fees charged by the vendors vary widely. These fees are described in the next table. The manager, in consultation with the vendors, has determined that the probability of a major modification being required is .3, the probability

of a moderate modification is .5, and the probability of a minor modification is .2. This uncertainty concerning the extent of the modification required exists because the operations manager has not finalized the specifications of the system he desires so the vendors are not yet sure how much modification will be required.

Modification	X	Y	Z
Major	$3,000	$4,000	$6,000
Moderate	1,000	1,400	2,000
Minor	200	400	500

a. The objective variable for this decision problem is the initial cost plus the implementation fee for a system. Since we want to minimize (rather than maximize) the value of this objective variable, we need to convert our problem to one of maximization. This can be done by multiplying each value of system cost (initial cost plus implementation fee) by −1. The action that maximizes the value of this new objective variable will be the one that minimizes the system cost. Eliminate any inadmissible actions, and formulate the payoff table for this decision problem.

b. According to the expected payoff criterion, which MRP system should the manager purchase? Explain.

18.31 Refer to the *Interfaces* (Nov.–Dec. 1992) decision problem of Exercise 18.19, in which an electric utility company must decide whether to replace a PCB transformer in a generating station. The probability of a major fire occurring in the remaining life of the existing transformer has been assessed at .0025. The probability of a major fire in the new transformer over its lifetime is .0005.

a. Use the expected payoff criterion to determine whether the transformer should be replaced.

b. Interpret the value of the expected payoff in the context of the problem.

c. Find the expected opportunity loss for each action. Interpret each in the context of the problem.

d. According to the expected opportunity loss criterion, what should the company do?

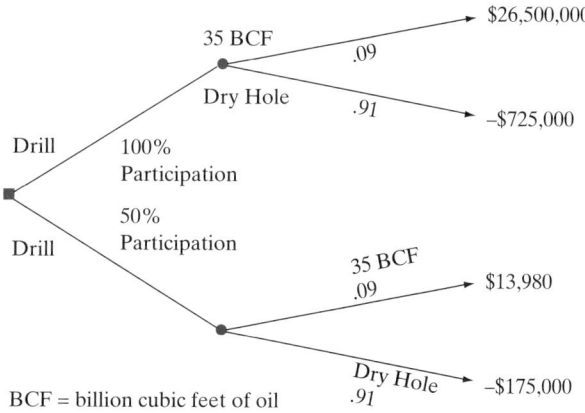

BCF = billion cubic feet of oil

Source: Adapted from M. R. Walls, G. T. Morahan, and J. S. Dyer. "Decision analysis of exploration opportunities in the onshore U.S. at Phillips Petroleum." *Interfaces,* Vol. 25, No. 6, (Nov.–Dec. 1995), pp. 39–56.

18.32 In Exercises 18.10 and 18.20, a large bank was confronted with deciding whether to install a power generator to protect its data processing operation against power outages. The probability of one or more power outages a year was assessed by the local electric utility company to be .10.

a. According to the expected payoff criterion, what should the bank do?

b. Convert the decision tree to an opportunity loss table.

c. According to the expected opportunity loss criterion, what should the bank do?

18.33 Petroleum companies regularly face difficult risk management decisions associated with oil exploration projects. Managers often spread the risk among one or more partner firms. The decision tree above was adapted from a problem faced by Phillips Petroleum Company. The tree was used to help decide whether to take on the drilling project alone (100% participation) or with a partner (50% participation).

a. Is either action inadmissible? Explain.

b. According to the expected payoff criterion, which level of participation in the drilling venture should Phillips Petroleum Company choose?

c. Convert the decision tree to an opportunity loss table.

d. According to the opportunity loss criterion, which level of participation should be chosen?

18.34 Refer to the payoff table for the decision problem in Exercise 18.22. The dress buyer has assessed the probability distribution given in the table for the number of dresses (in dozens) she can sell. How many dozen dresses should the buyer order according to the expected payoff criterion?

Sales	3	4	5	6	7	8
Probability	.15	.25	.30	.15	.10	.05

18.35 Reconsider Exercise 18.23, which concerned the purchase of body pieces by an automobile manufacturer. A lot of 500 pieces is purchased for $15,000, and the proportion of defects in each lot is .05, .10, or .50. The supplier offers a guarantee that it will assume the costs for all defective body moldings greater than 50 in a production lot of 500. This guarantee may be purchased for a cost of $1,000 before the lot begins production. The data in the table have been gathered on 100 past production lots of preformed body pieces. Given only this information, should the guarantee be purchased? Explain. [*Hint:* Use the sample of 100 lots to assess the probabilities of the states of nature.]

Proportion of Defects	.05	.10	.50
Times Observed	55	24	21

18.7   THE EXPECTED UTILITY CRITERION

The expected payoff (or opportunity loss) criterion sometimes fails to provide decisions that are consistent with the decision-maker's attitude toward risk. For example, suppose you were required to choose one of these two actions:

a_1: Deposit your $100,000 inheritance in the bank for one year at 7% interest

a_2: Invest your $100,000 inheritance for one year with a .5 probability of having a total of $250,000 at the end of the year and a .5 probability of losing all your inheritance

Which would you choose? Why? Most of us would probably choose action a_1, basing our decision on a "safety first" strategy. The usual argument goes, "Why pass up a chance for a sure $107,000 at the end of the year for a 50-50 chance to end up with nothing?" Notice that if you choose a_1, your decision is not in accord with the action prescribed by the expected payoff criterion, because

$$EP(a_1) = \$107,000(1) = \$107,000$$

$$EP(a_2) = \$250,000(.5) + 0(.5) = \$125,000$$

Thus, if we use the expected payoff criterion, we would select action a_2.

The expected payoff criterion can be adapted to reflect our attitude toward risk if we can express the outcomes of the decision problem in terms of an objective variable that better reflects the true relative values of outcomes. An objective variable that reflects the decision-maker's attitude toward risk is called a **utility function**, and the values assigned to the outcomes are referred to as **utility values**, or **utilities** (or sometimes **utiles**).

Definition 18.3

A **utility function** is a rule that assigns numerical values to the potential outcomes of a decision problem in such a way that

1. The values rank the outcomes in accordance with the decision-maker's preferences.
2. The function itself describes the decision-maker's attitude toward risk.

We now illustrate how to assign utility values to the monetary outcomes of the inheritance example. The payoff table for this example is shown in Table 18.9. As noted previously, many of us would be reluctant to gamble on the outcome of the investment if the chance of success were only .5, even though the expected payoff is higher for action a_2 ($125,000) than for action a_1 ($107,000). *The key to assigning utility values to the action/state of nature combinations is to answer the following question: What would the probability of success for the investment have to be for you to value actions* a_1 *and* a_2 *equally?* The answer to this question is a probability, p, such that if the probability of the investment's success exceeds p, you would prefer to invest the money (a_2), but if the success probability is less than p, you would prefer to deposit the money in the bank and take the safe return. The probability p is called the **utility of the outcome** $107,000, and we write $U(107,000) = p$. The minimum payoff ($0) and the maximum payoff ($250,000) are assigned utility values of 0 and 1, respectively, so that $U(0) = 0$, and $U(250,000) = 1$.

Table 18.9 Payoff Table for the Inheritance Example

		STATE OF NATURE	
		S_1: Investment Fails	S_2: Investment Succeeds
ACTION	a_1: Deposit $100,000	$107,000	$107,000
	a_2: Invest $100,000	0	$250,000

TABLE 18.10	**Payoff Table for the Inheritance Example with Utility Values as Payoffs**		
		STATE OF NATURE (PROBABILITIES IN PARENTHESES)	
		S_1: Investment Fails (.5)	S_2: Investment Succeeds (.5)
ACTION	a_1: Deposit $100,000	.7	.7
	a_2: Invest $100,000	0	1

Suppose you decide that the probability of the investment's success would have to be .7 before the two actions were equally appealing. Then the utility value assigned to $107,000 is .7, and the payoff table with the utility values as outcomes is shown in Table 18.10.

The general rule for assigning utility values to monetary outcomes* is given in the box.

> **Assigning Utility Values to Monetary Outcomes†**
> 1. Identify the maximum and minimum payoffs in the decision table. Call them O_M and O_L, respectively.
> 2. Set $U(O_M) = 1$ and $U(O_L) = 0$, where $U(O)$ represents the utility value of outcome O.
> 3. To determine the utility value for any other outcome O_{ij} in the payoff table, determine the value of p that makes you indifferent between the following:
>   a. Receiving O_{ij} with certainty
>   b. Participating in a gamble in which you can win O_M with probability p or O_L with probability $(1 - p)$
>
> Then, $U(O_{ij}) = p$.

We are now prepared to make a decision based on the **expected utility criterion**. We first find the expected utility for each action using the formula

$$EU(a_i) = \sum_{\substack{\text{All states} \\ \text{of nature}}} \left(\begin{array}{c} \text{Utility of the} \\ \text{action } a_i/\text{state of nature} \\ \text{combination} \end{array} \right) \left(\begin{array}{c} \text{Probability} \\ \text{of the} \\ \text{state of nature} \end{array} \right)$$

Thus, for the inheritance example,

$$EU(a_1) = .7(.5) + .7(.5) = .7$$

$$EU(a_2) = 0(.5) + 1(.5) = .5$$

We now choose the action with the higher expected utility, which is action a_1. You can see that this decision differs from that yielded by the expected payoff criterion and that it more accurately reflects a safety-first attitude toward risk.

*Utility functions may be assessed for the outcomes corresponding to any objective variable, but because the objective variable in business decision-making is typically monetary (or can be converted to a monetary equivalent), we have restricted our discussion to utility functions for money.

†The choice of 0 and 1 as the minimum and maximum utility values is arbitrary. The same result is obtained if the utility values are all multiplied by the same constant or if a constant is added to each value—but then the utility values lose their probabilistic interpretation. For more detail on the choice of scale, its implications for interpersonal and intrapersonal comparisons of utility values, and other methods for assessing utility functions, consult the references for this chapter.

> **Expected Utility Criterion**
> Choose the action that has the greatest expected utility, where the expected utility of action a_i is given by
>
> $$EU(a_i) = \sum_{\substack{\text{All states} \\ \text{of nature}}} \left(\begin{array}{c} \text{Utility of the} \\ \text{action } a_i/\text{state of nature} \\ \text{combination} \end{array} \right) \left(\begin{array}{c} \text{Probability} \\ \text{of the} \\ \text{state of nature} \end{array} \right)$$

The assignment of utility values is personal and subjective. If careful thought is given to this task, the result will be a utility function that reflects your preferences for outcomes and your attitude toward risk. Applying the expected utility criterion will then yield a decision consistent with your preferences and risk attitude.

EXERCISES 18.36–18.43

Learning the Mechanics

18.36 Suppose you are indifferent (have no preference) between receiving $150 with certainty and participating in a gamble that offers you a probability of .3 of receiving $1,000 and a probability of .7 of receiving nothing. You are also indifferent between receiving $400 with certainty and participating in a gamble that offers you a probability of .6 of receiving $1,000 and a probability of .4 of receiving nothing. Finally, you are also indifferent between receiving $800 with certainty and participating in a gamble that offers you a probability of .95 of receiving $1,000 and a probability of .05 of receiving nothing.

  a. Let $U(\$1,000) = 1$ and $U(\$0) = 0$. Find $U(\$150)$, $U(\$400)$, and $U(\$800)$.

  b. Use these utility values to plot your utility function for money over the range from $0 to $1,000.

18.37 Consider the utility function for money,

$$U(x) = x^2 \qquad 0 \leqslant x \leqslant 100$$

and the payoff table shown here (probabilities in parentheses).

		STATE OF NATURE		
		$S_1(.25)$	$S_2(.30)$	$S_3(.45)$
ACTION	a_1	$100	$75	$25
	a_2	$70	$95	0

[*Note:* Notice that the minimum and maximum values of this utility function are not 0 and 1, respectively. Refer to the second footnote on page 967.]

  a. Use the utility function to convert the outcomes in the payoff table from monetary values to utility values (utiles).

  b. Which action would be prescribed by the expected utility criterion?

18.38 Consider the utility function for money,

$$U(x) = \frac{\ln(x + 51)}{5.525} \qquad -50 < x < 200$$

and the given payoff table (probabilities in parentheses).

		STATE OF NATURE		
		$S_1(.50)$	$S_2(.40)$	$S_3(.10)$
ACTION	a_1	$-$10	$50	$90
	a_2	0	$20	$20
	a_3	$-$10	$60	$50
	a_4	$-$10	$-$50	$200

  a. Eliminate any inadmissible actions.

  b. Use the utility function to convert the outcomes in the payoff table from monetary values to utility values (utiles).

  c. Which action is prescribed by the expected utility criterion?

  d. Does this decision differ from the decision prescribed by the expected payoff criterion?

18.39 Consider the utility function for money,

$$U(x) = -1 + .01x \qquad 100 \leqslant x \leqslant 200$$

and the payoff table shown (probabilities in parentheses).

		STATE OF NATURE			
		$S_1(.30)$	$S_2(.05)$	$S_3(.45)$	$S_4(.20)$
ACTION	a_1	$150	$180	$100	$80
	a_2	$130	$165	$190	$140
	a_3	$115	$120	$160	$210

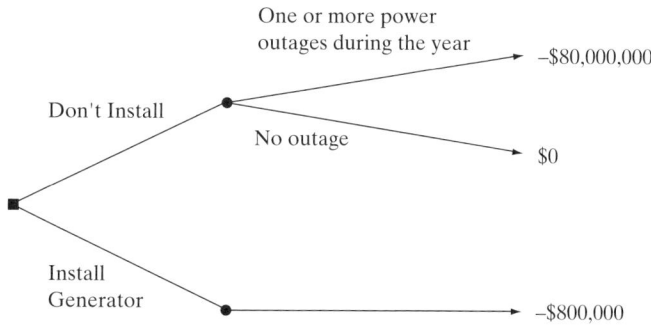

Source: Adapted from K. J. Engemann and H. E. Miller. "Operations risk management at a major bank." *Interfaces,* Vol. 22, No. 6 (Nov.–Dec. 1992), pp. 140–149.

a. Use the utility function to convert the outcomes in the payoff table from monetary values to utility values (utiles).

b. Which action is prescribed by the expected utility criterion?

Applying the Concepts

18.40 In Exercises 18.10 and 18.32, a large U.S. bank was confronted with the problem concerning whether to purchase and install an emergency generator to protect its data-processing operation, indicated in the decision tree above:

a. The bank's president assessed the following utilities: $U(\$0) = 1$, $U(\$-800,000) = .95$, and $U(-\$80 \text{ million}) = 0$. According to the expected utility criterion, should the bank install the generator?

b. In this case, do the expected utility criterion and the expected payoff criterion prescribe the same action? Justify your answer.

18.41 An investor is trying to decide whether to invest in a wildcat oil well. If the well is drilled and it is dry, she will lose $500,000. On the other hand, if the well is a gusher, she will make $1.5 million. It is also possible for the well to yield less oil than a gusher, in which case she will make $600,000.

a. A decision analyst asks her the following questions.

1. At what value of p would you be indifferent between the two situations: receive $600,000 with certainty, and receive $1.5 million with probability p or lose $500,000 with probability $(1 - p)$? She replies, at $p = .90$. What is the investor's utility value for $600,000?

2. At what value of p would you be indifferent between receiving $0 with certainty, and receiving $1.5 million with probability p or losing $500,000 with probability $(1 - p)$? She replies, at $p = .8$. Find her utility value for $0.

b. Graph the utility function for this investor for dollar values between $-\$500,000$ and $\$1,500,000$.

18.42 Refer to Exercise 18.41. The investor now must decide whether to keep the $500,000 or invest it in the oil well. She assesses the probabilities of the states as

$$P(\text{Dry well}) = .5$$
$$P(\text{Moderate success}) = .3$$
$$P(\text{Gusher}) = .2$$

a. Set up the payoff table for this decision problem.

b. Use the expected payoff criterion to determine which action the investor should select.

c. Substitute the utility values for the monetary outcomes in the payoff table of part **a** and use the expected utility criterion to select the action.

18.43 Refer to Exercise 18.34, in which you selected an action for the dress purchaser using the expected payoff criterion. Now suppose the buyer's utility function for money is

$$U(x) = \frac{\sqrt{x + 2,000}}{110} \qquad -2,000 \leq x \leq 10,000$$

How many dresses should she order? Should she be using her own utility function to make this decision? Why or why not?

18.8 CLASSIFYING DECISION-MAKERS BY THEIR UTILITY FUNCTIONS

The attitude of a decision-maker toward risk is revealed by the shape of his or her utility function. Recall the inheritance decision problem of Section 18.7, with the payoff table given in Table 18.9 and a table of utility values given in Table 18.10. These tables are repeated for convenience as Tables 18.11 and 18.12.

TABLE 18.11 **Payoff Table for the Inheritance Example**

		STATE OF NATURE (PROBABILITIES IN PARENTHESES)	
		Investment Fails (.5)	Investment Succeeds (.5)
ACTION	a_1: Deposit $100,000	$107,000	$107,000
	a_2: Invest $100,000	0	250,000

TABLE 18.12 **Utility Value Table for the Inheritance Example**

		STATE OF NATURE (PROBABILITIES IN PARENTHESES)	
		Investment Fails (.5)	Investment Succeeds (.5)
ACTION	a_1: Deposit $100,000	.7	.7
	a_2: Invest $100,000	0	1

We know that these utility values reflect a conservative attitude toward risk, since the expected payoff of the investment must exceed $0(.3) + 250,000(.7) = \$175,000$ before the decision-maker prefers this gamble to the fixed $107,000 return. This attitude may be graphically portrayed by plotting the utility values on a vertical axis against the payoffs on a horizontal axis, as shown in Figure 18.3. The points are connected with a smooth curve. Utility functions with this shape are called **concave utility functions**. This shape is characteristic of a conservative attitude toward risk, and decision-makers whose utility functions are concave are called **risk-avoiders**.

Now, suppose we decided to assign a utility value of .2 to the $107,000 payoff in Table 18.11. This value reflects a liberal, or gambling, attitude toward risk, since the interpretation is that we have no preference between a sure $107,000 and a .2 probability of receiving $250,000 (with a .8 probability of nothing). The expected payoff of the gamble is $0(.8) + \$250,000(.2) = \$50,000$, which is less than the fixed payoff if we deposit the money in the bank. The graph of this utility function is shown in Figure 18.4. Utility functions with this shape are called **convex utility functions**. This shape is characteristic of an aggressive attitude toward risk, and decision-makers who have convex utility functions are called **risk-takers**.

FIGURE 18.3
Utility function for the inheritance example: A risk-avoiding attitude

FIGURE 18.4
Utility function for the
inheritance example:
A risk-taking attitude

FIGURE 18.5
Utility function for the
inheritance example:
A risk-neutral attitude

If the utility value of .428 is assigned to the $107,000 outcome, the implication is that we would have no preference between accepting $107,000 and gambling on receiving $250,000 with probability .428, a gamble that has an expected payoff of 0(.572) + 250,000(.428) = $107,000. The fact that both courses of action have the same expected payoff reflects a neutral attitude toward risk. The graph of the utility function in this case and, for **risk-neutral** decision-makers in general, is a straight line, as shown in Figure 18.5. Since the expected utility of action a_i is equal to the utility of the expected payoff for action a_i for **straight-line utility functions**, *the expected payoff criterion and the expected utility criterion are equivalent for risk-neutral decision-makers.*

The three types of utility functions and the risk attitudes they characterize are summarized in the box.

Three Types of Utility Functions*
1. The concave utility function indicates that the decision-maker is a risk-avoider.

continued

*Other types of utility functions may be obtained by combining these. For example, a decision-maker may be risk-neutral for relatively small monetary outcomes and a risk-avoider for relatively large monetary outcomes. Thus, the utility function might appear S-shaped.

2. The straight-line utility function indicates that the decision-maker is risk-neutral.

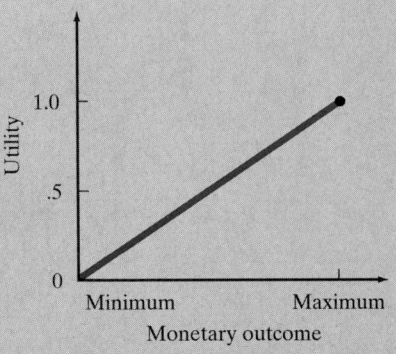

3. The convex utility function indicates that the decision-maker is a risk-taker.

EXERCISES 18.44–18.50

Learning the Mechanics

18.44 Graph each of the following utility functions for money and classify each as the utility function of a risk-avoiding, risk-taking, or risk-neutral decision-maker. [*Note:* Notice that the minimum and maximum values of these utility functions are not 0 and 1, respectively. Refer to the second footnote on page 967.]
a. $U(x) = 2x^3$ $0 \le x \le 100$
b. $U(x) = (1/100)x$ $0 \le x \le 100$
c. $U(x) = \log(x + 100)$ $10 \le x \le 100$
d. $U(x) = -1 + .01x$ $100 \le x \le 200$

18.45 Consider the following utility function for money:

$$U(x) = (x + 1{,}000)^{\frac{1}{2}} \quad -1{,}000 \le x \le 1{,}000$$

a. Plot the function.
b. Is this the utility function of a risk-avoiding, risk-taking, or risk-neutral decision-maker?
c. Use this utility function and the expected utility criterion to identify the optimal action for

the decision problem characterized by the payoff table shown here (probabilities in parentheses).

| | | STATE OF NATURE | | |
		$S_1(.1)$	$S_2(.5)$	$S_3(.4)$
ACTION	a_1	-\$600	\$1,000	\$300
	a_2	-\$800	0	\$750
	a_3	\$60	-\$175	\$610

18.46 Consider the utility function for money,

$$U(x) = .001x \quad 0 \le x \le 1{,}000$$

and the payoff table shown on page 973 (probabilities in parentheses).
a. What does this utility function indicate about the decision-maker's attitude toward risk?
b. Which action is prescribed by the expected utility criterion? Should it differ from the

		STATE OF NATURE			
		$S_1(.05)$	$S_2(.30)$	$S_3(.45)$	$S_4(.20)$
ACTION	a_1	0	$50	$310	$900
	a_2	$1,000	$400	$200	$80
	a_3	$100	$500	$1,000	$100

action prescribed by the expected payoff criterion? Explain.

Applying the Concepts

18.47 In Exercise 18.19 an electric utility company faced the problem concerning whether to replace a PCB transformer in a generating station, as shown in the decision tree below.

a. The company's risk manager assessed the following utility function for use in addressing this decision problem:

$$U(x) = 1 + (1/30,000,000)x$$

Plot this utility function.

b. Describe the manager's attitude towards risk.

c. According to the expected utility criterion, should the company replace the transformer? Justify your answer.

18.48 Refer to Exercise 18.41, in which an investor considers whether to invest in a wildcat oil well.

a. Plot the utility function you constructed for the investor.

b. Categorize her as a risk-avoider, a risk-taker, or risk-neutral.

18.49 Refer to Exercise 18.43, in which the dress purchaser used the utility function

$$U(x) = \frac{\sqrt{x + 2,000}}{110} \qquad -2,000 \leqslant x \leqslant 10,000$$

a. Plot the purchaser's utility function.

b. Is she a risk-taker, a risk-avoider, or risk-neutral?

18.50 In the early 1970s the Mexican government was faced with two conflicting recommendations regarding airport expansion in Mexico City. One step in the decision analysis was to evaluate the utility function for the average access time (in minutes) to the airport. A survey of air travelers determined that the bounds on average access time over all strategies were 12 minutes and 90 minutes. The best possible time, 12 minutes, was assigned a utility of 1; the worst possible time, 90 minutes, was assigned a utility of 0. The travelers were then presented with a series of choices of the following type: 62 minutes access time for certain, or a lottery with p chance at 12 minutes and $(1 - p)$ chance at 90 minutes. The size of p was varied until the traveler indicated indifference between these two choices. In the case of 62 minutes, the traveler was indifferent for $p = .5$. Thus, $U(62 \text{ minutes}) = .5$. This process was repeated for several other access times, and the results were plotted as shown in the figure. Classify the air travelers' attitude toward risk.

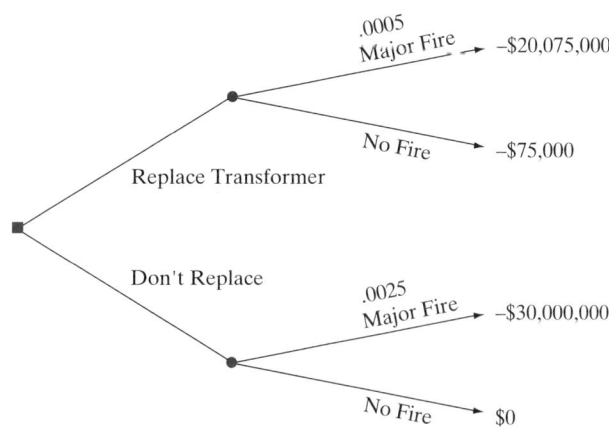

Source: Adapted from W. E. Balson, J. L. Welsh, and D. S. Wilson. "Using decision analysis and risk analysis to manage utility environmental risk." *Interfaces,* Vol. 22, No. 6 (Nov.–Dec. 1992), pp. 126–139.

18.9 REVISING STATE OF NATURE PROBABILITIES: BAYES' RULE

Up until now in this chapter, we have presented solutions to decision problems using only currently available information. Now, we incorporate **sample information** into the decision process.

Suppose you are trying to decide whether to purchase 100 shares of common stock in a company. You have decided that you want to make the purchase only if the probability is at least .75 that the stock's price will be higher a month from now. Based on your *prior information* about the company and stock market conditions, you assign a *prior probability* of only .6 to this event. Therefore, if you base your decision on your prior information, you will not buy the stock.

However, you may want to obtain sample information about the stock before making your decision. Your sample information might be an opinion from a reputable stock analyst whose predictions have the following reliability. Among the stocks that increase in price over a one-month period, the analyst is able to predict the increase in 80% of the cases. But for stocks that will be stable or decrease in price, she predicts an increase in 40% of the cases. The analyst advises you that, in her opinion, the price of the stock in which you are interested will be higher one month from now. How should you revise your prior probability to incorporate this sample information?

Define the events

S_1: {Stock price will be higher one month from now}

S_2: {Stock price will be the same or lower one month from now}

I: {Analyst predicts the price will be higher one month from now}

We are interested in the conditional probability that the stock price will increase *given that* the analyst says it will increase—i.e., $P(S_1|I)$. Recall that the definition of conditional probability stipulates

$$P(S_1|I) = \frac{P(I \cap S_1)}{P(I)}$$

where $P(I \cap S_1)$ is the probability that the analyst says it will increase *and* it does in fact increase. We will find $P(S_1|I)$ in two steps.

Step 1 Find $P(I \cap S_1)$. Recall that $P(I \cap S_1) = P(I|S_1)P(S_1)$. We know that $P(I|S_1)$—the probability that the analyst predicts a stock price will be higher in a month given that it will in fact be higher—is .8. Furthermore, $P(S_1)$ is the probability that the price will be higher a month from now, given no sample information; i.e., this is the prior probability of S_1, which we have assessed to be .6. Then,

$$P(I \cap S_1) = P(I|S_1)P(S_1) = (.8)(.6) = .48$$

Step 2 Find $P(I)$. Note that $P(I)$ is the probability that the analyst predicts an increase in the stock's price. This will occur simultaneously with one of the two mutually exclusive, collectively exhaustive (i.e., no other states can occur) states of nature, S_1 and S_2. That is, either the stock will in fact cost more one month from now, or its price will be the same or lower. Thus,

$$P(I) = P(I \cap S_1) + P(I \cap S_2)$$

We have already found that $P(I \cap S_1) = .48$. In the same way,

$$P(I \cap S_2) = P(I|S_2)P(S_2)$$

We know that $P(I|S_2)$—the probability that the analyst predicts a stock will increase in price when in fact it will not—is .4. Also,

$$P(S_2) = 1 - P(S_1) = 1 - .6 = .4$$

Then

$$P(I \cap S_2) = P(I|S_2)P(S_2) = (.4)(.4) = .16$$

and

$$P(I) = P(I \cap S_1) + P(I \cap S_2) = .48 + .16 = .64$$

Finally, we combine steps 1 and 2 to find

$$P(S_1|I) = \frac{P(I \cap S_1)}{P(I)} = \frac{.48}{.64} = .75$$

Thus, the probability that the stock will increase in price, given the sample information that the analyst predicts its rise, is .75. We refer to probabilities revised on the basis of sample information as *posterior probabilities*.* Since this posterior probability meets our previously established criterion that the probability of increase be at least .75, we now decide to purchase the stock.

DEFINITION 18.4

A probability $P(S_i)$ of the state of nature S_i that does not incorporate sample information is called a **prior probability** of S_i.

A probability $P(S_i|I)$ of the state of nature S_i, given the sample information I, is called a **posterior probability** of S_i.

The process of revising prior probabilities to incorporate sample information is known as **Bayes' rule**. It is named for Thomas Bayes, an English Presbyterian minister and mathematician who lived from 1702 to 1761. He was one of the first to develop methods of calculating posterior probabilities. Bayes' rule for two states of nature and for k states of nature is given in the accompanying box. The states of nature are assumed to be mutually exclusive, collectively exhaustive events.

Bayes' Rule for Calculating Posterior Probabilities

Two states of nature: S_1 and S_2

$$P(S_1|I) = \frac{P(I \cap S_1)}{P(I)}$$

$$= \frac{P(I|S_1)P(S_1)}{P(I|S_1)P(S_1) + P(I|S_2)P(S_2)}$$

where I is the sample information.

continued

*We use the term *posterior* because the probabilities are determined *after* the sample information has been obtained, whereas *prior* probabilities are determined *before* sample information is obtained.

$$k \text{ states of nature: } S_1, S_2, \dots, S_k$$

$$P(S_i|I) = \frac{P(I \cap S_i)}{P(I)} = \frac{P(I|S_i)P(S_i)}{\sum\limits_{j=1}^{k} P(I|S_j)P(S_j)}$$

A **probability revision table** organizes the calculation of posterior probabilities. In Table 18.13 we show the probability revision table for the stock price example, and the general form of the table is given in Table 18.14.

In Example 18.2, we show how to apply Bayes' rule to a decision problem with monetary outcomes.

EXAMPLE 18.2

A company has developed a home smoke detector that is considerably more reliable than those currently on the market, but it is also more expensive to produce. To market the detector competitively, the company will have to price it so low that the profit margin per unit will be quite small. Accordingly, the sales volume, and therefore the market share, will have to be high for the product to be worth marketing.

The company's accounting and marketing departments prepared Table 18.15 using the objective variable Net contribution to profit by the detector during its first 2 years on the market. The marketing department assessed the prior state probabilities (shown in parentheses in the table) using industry sales data for other detectors.

Now suppose the company wants to incorporate *sample information* into the decision analysis. Twenty prospective purchasers are randomly sampled and asked their opinion of the new detector. Two of the 20 say they will purchase the detector if it is marketed. Use this sample information to *revise* the prior state probabilities by calculating the *posterior probabilities* associated with the states of nature.

TABLE 18.13   Probability Revision Table for the Stock Price Example

(1)	(2)	(3)	(4)	(5)
State of Nature	Prior Probability	Conditional Probability of Sample Information	Probability of Intersection of State and Sample Information (2) × (3)	Posterior Probability (4) ÷ Total of (4)
S_1	.6	.8	.48	.75
S_2	.4	.4	.16	.25
	Total 1.0		.64	1.00

TABLE 18.14   Probability Revision Table (General)

(1)	(2)	(3)	(4)	(5)
State of Nature	Prior Probability	Conditional Probability of Sample Information	Probability of Intersection of State and Sample Information (2) × (3)	Posterior Probability (4) ÷ Total of (4)
S_1	$P(S_1)$	$P(I|S_1)$	$P(I \cap S_1)$	$P(S_1|I)$
S_2	$P(S_2)$	$P(I|S_2)$	$P(I \cap S_2)$	$P(S_2|I)$
$\vdots$	$\vdots$	$\vdots$	$\vdots$	$\vdots$
S_k	$P(S_k)$	$P(I|S_k)$	$P(I \cap S_k)$	$P(S_k|I)$
	Total 1		$P(I)$	1

TABLE 18.15 **Payoff Table for Example 18.2**

		STATE OF NATURE: MARKET SHARE BY YEAR 3 (PRIOR PROBABILITIES IN PARENTHESES)			
		S_1: .01 (.10)	S_2: .05 (.40)	S_3: .10 (.40)	S_4: .15 (.10)
ACTION	a_1: Market Detector	$-\$1,500,000$	$-\$200,000$	$\$300,000$	$\$1,000,000$
	a_2: Do Not Market Detector	0	0	0	0

SOLUTION

This decision problem has four states of nature, and the prior probabilities are known (see Table 18.15). The next step is to calculate the probability of the sample information given each state of nature (column 3 of the probability revision table). Note that the sample consists of a consumer preference survey and that we can regard its outcome as a binomial random variable (see Section 4.4). The number of trials is $n = 20$, and the probability, p, represents the true market share the company will obtain upon marketing the detector. Thus, each state of nature represents a different value of p. The binomial random variable, x, is the number of the sampled consumers who will purchase the new smoke detector, and the survey result is $x = 2$. We now calculate the conditional probabilities of this sample result (using Table II in Appendix B):

$$P(I|S_1) = P(x = 2|p = .01) = \binom{20}{2}(.01)^2(.99)^{18} = .016$$

$$P(I|S_2) = P(x = 2|p = .05) = \binom{20}{2}(.05)^2(.95)^{18} = .189$$

$$P(I|S_3) = P(x = 2|p = .10) = \binom{20}{2}(.10)^2(.90)^{18} = .285$$

$$P(I|S_4) = P(x = 2|p = .15) = \binom{20}{2}(.15)^2(.85)^{18} = .229$$

We are now prepared to use the probability revision table to calculate the posterior probabilities for the states of nature. The calculations are shown in Table 18.16. Note that the sample information revised the probabilities of states S_3 and S_4 *upward* and the probabilities of states S_1 and S_2 *downward*. The posterior probabilities indicate that the company can be more optimistic about the market share of the smoke detector than it was prior to obtaining the sampled information. �◣

TABLE 18.16 **Probability Revision Table for Example 18.2**

(1)	(2)	(3)	(4)	(5)
State of Nature	Prior Probability	Conditional Probability of Sample Information	Probability of Intersection of State and Sample Information (2) × (3)	Posterior Probability (4) ÷ Total of (4)
S_1: $p = .01$	.10	.016	.0016	.0075
S_2: $p = .05$	.40	.189	.0756	.3531
S_3: $p = .10$	.40	.285	.1140	.5325
S_4: $p = .15$	.10	.229	.0229	.1070
Total	**1.00**		.2141	1.0001[a]

[a]Rounding error

TABLE 18.17 **Prior and Posterior Probabilities for the Smoke Detector Example: Two Different Sample Sizes**

		POSTERIOR PROBABILITY	
State	Prior Probability	$n = 20$ $(x = 2)$	$n = 100$ $(x = 10)$
$S_1: p = .01$	.10	.008	.000
$S_2: p = .05$	.40	.353	.104
$S_3: p = .10$	.40	.532	.826
$S_4: p = .15$	.10	.107	.069

The extent to which the prior probabilities are revised depends on the amount of information contained in the sample. For example, if 100 consumers had been surveyed in Example 18.2 and if the same *proportion* had responded favorably to the new smoke detector (i.e., $x = 10$), the four posterior state probabilities would be 0, .104, .826, and .069, respectively. Thus, the prior probability of state $S_3: p = .10$ is revised from .4 to .826. These probabilities are shown in Table 18.17 along with the posterior probabilities for a survey of $n = 20$ consumers (Example 18.2). As the sample size is increased, the weight given to the prior probabilities is diminished and more importance is attached to the sample information.

EXERCISES 18.51–18.60

Learning the Mechanics

18.51 Give Bayes' rule for the case in which there are three states of nature, S_1, S_2, and S_3, and information I has been received by sampling.

18.52 Use the formula from Exercise 18.51 to complete the first probability revision table below.

18.53 Complete the second probability revision table.

18.54 What role does sampling play in decision analysis?

(1)	(2)	(3)	(4)	(5)
State of Nature	Prior Probability	Conditional Probability of Sample Information	(2) × (3)	Posterior Probability (4) ÷ Total of (4)
S_1	.30	.60		
S_2	.50	.80		
S_3	.20	.10		
Total	1.00			

(1)	(2)	(3)	(4)	(5)
State of Nature	Prior Probability	Conditional Probability of Sample Information	(2) × (3)	Posterior Probability (4) ÷ Total of (4)
S_1	.10	.90		
S_2	.25	.10		
S_3	.45	.65		
S_4	.20	.30		
Total	1.00			

18.55 Compare and contrast prior and posterior information.

Applying the Concepts

18.56 A systems analyst is concerned about the proportion, p, of records that are in error in the inventory control system he designed. The probability distribution shown characterizes his beliefs regarding p.

Proportion of Errors	Prior Probability
.09	.40
.10	.25
.11	.15
.12	.10
.13	.10

a. Find the mean and variance of the analyst's prior probability distribution for p.

b. A random sample of 25 records yielded three incorrect records. Find the analyst's posterior probability distribution for p.

c. Find the mean and variance of the analyst's posterior probability distribution for p.

d. The posterior probability distribution you computed in part **b** combines the analyst's beliefs about p and the information about p contained in the sample. Using your results from parts **a** and **c** and graphs of the prior and posterior probability distributions, describe how the posterior distribution differs from the prior distribution. In so doing, you are explaining what the analyst learned about p by sampling.

18.57 A press produces masks used in the manufacture of television tubes. If the press is correctly adjusted, it produces masks with a scrap rate of 5%. If it is not adjusted correctly, it produces scrap at a 50% rate. From past company records, the machine is known to be correctly adjusted 90% of the time. A quality control inspector randomly selects one mask from those recently produced by the press and discovers it is defective. What is the probability that the machine is incorrectly adjusted?

18.58 Refer to Exercise 18.57. The quality control inspector observes a second mask and finds that it is also defective. Using the posterior probabilities from Exercise 18.56 as prior probabilities, calculate the posterior probability that the machine is incorrectly adjusted. What assumptions are required to make this calculation?

18.59 Suppose the proportion of defectives produced by a certain production process is .01, .05, or .10. The prior probability that it is .05 is twice the probability that it is .10. The prior probability that it is .01 is equal to the probability that it is .10.

a. Determine the prior probabilities associated with the proportion of defectives produced by the production process.

b. A sample of five units drawn at random yields three defectives. Revise the prior distribution you obtained in part **a**.

18.60 [*Note: This exercise refers to optional Section 4.5.*] A replacement parts inventory manager for a computer manufacturer believes the demand of a certain component is distributed as a Poisson random variable with a mean monthly demand of two, three, or four units. Experience suggests that a mean monthly demand of three units is twice as likely as a mean monthly demand of two units, and that a mean monthly demand of two units is as likely as a mean monthly demand of four units.

a. If the demand for this component last month was four units, find the posterior distribution for the mean monthly demand for next month.

b. If the demand in the following month was two units, find the posterior distribution for the mean monthly demand.

c. Comment on the ability of Bayes' rule to help a decision-maker "learn" about the shifting values of a parameter over time.

18.10 SOLVING DECISION PROBLEMS USING POSTERIOR PROBABILITIES

Recall that the expected payoff criterion (Section 18.6) selects the action with the highest expected payoff. The expected payoff for each action is computed using either the *prior probabilities* or the *posterior probabilities* of the states of nature, depending on whether sample information is available. For example, for the smoke detector decision problem (Example 18.2), the payoff table prior to obtaining sample information is given in Table 18.18.

TABLE 18.18   Payoff Table for the Smoke Detector Decision Problem

		STATE OF NATURE (PRIOR PROBABILITIES IN PARENTHESES)			
		S_1: $p = .01$ (.10)	S_2: $p = .05$ (.40)	S_3: $p = .10$ (.40)	S_4: $p = .15$ (.10)
ACTION	a_1: **Market Detector**	$-\$1,500,000$	$-\$200,000$	$\$300,000$	$\$1,000,000$
	a_2: **Do Not Market Detector**	0	0	0	0

The expected payoffs for the two actions are

$$EP(a_1) = \sum_{\text{All states}} (\text{Payoff})(\text{Prior probability of state})$$

$$= (-1,500,000)(.10) + (-200,000)(.40)$$
$$+ (300,000)(.40) + (1,000,000)(.10)$$

$$= -\$10,000$$

$$EP(a_2) = 0(.10) + 0(.40) + 0(.40) + 0(.10) = 0$$

Thus, the expected payoff criterion, using prior probabilities, selects action a_2 and indicates that the firm should not market the new smoke detector.

In Example 18.2 we revised these prior probabilities based on the sample information that 2 out of 20 randomly sampled consumers would purchase the new detector if it were marketed. The payoff table with the posterior state probabilities is shown in Table 18.19.

The expected payoffs for the actions using the posterior probabilities are

$$EP(a_1) = \sum_{\text{All states}} (\text{Payoff})(\text{Posterior probability of state})$$

$$= (-1,500,000)(.008) + (-200,000)(.353)$$
$$+ (300,000)(.532) + (1,000,000)(.107)$$

$$= +\$184,000$$

$$EP(a_2) = 0$$

Thus, the expected payoff criterion using posterior probabilities selects action a_1, indicating that the company should market the new detector. The sample information has altered the selection of the expected payoff criterion, changing it from a_2: Do not market, to a_1: Market. Since the **posterior decision analysis** incorporates both prior and sample information, whereas the **prior decision analysis** incorporates only prior information, we *prefer the posterior decision to the prior decision*.

The expected payoff criterion using posterior probabilities is summarized in the next box.

TABLE 18.19   Payoff Table for the Smoke Detector Decision Problem

		STATE OF NATURE (POSTERIOR PROBABILITIES IN PARENTHESES)			
		S_1: $p = .01$ (.008)	S_2: $p = .05$ (.353)	S_3: $p = .10$ (.532)	S_4: $p = .15$ (.107)
ACTION	a_1: **Market Detector**	$-\$1,500,000$	$-\$200,000$	$\$300,000$	$\$1,000,000$
	a_2: **Do Not Market Detector**	0	0	0	0

> **Expected Payoff Criterion Using Posterior Probabilities**
> Choose the action with the maximum expected payoff, where the expected payoffs are calculated using the posterior state probabilities.
>
> $$EP(a_i) = \sum_{\text{All states}} \left(\begin{array}{c} \text{Payoff for} \\ \text{action } a_i/\text{state} \\ \text{combination} \end{array} \right) \left(\begin{array}{c} \text{Posterior} \\ \text{probability} \\ \text{of state} \end{array} \right)$$

EXAMPLE 18.3

Suppose the company that is considering marketing the new smoke detector randomly samples 100 consumers and finds that 10 would purchase the new detector if it were marketed. The payoff table with the posterior probabilities is shown in Table 18.20. Which action should the company take if the expected payoff criterion is used?

SOLUTION
We calculate the expected payoffs using the posterior probabilities. Thus,

$$EP(a_1) = \sum_{\text{All states}} \left(\begin{array}{c} \text{Payoff for} \\ \text{action } a_i/\text{state} \\ \text{combination} \end{array} \right) \left(\begin{array}{c} \text{Posterior} \\ \text{probability} \\ \text{of state} \end{array} \right)$$

$$= (-1,500,000)(.000) + (-200,000)(.104)$$
$$+ (300,000)(.826) + (1,000,000)(.069)$$

$$= \$296,000$$

$$EP(a_2) = 0(.000) + 0(.104) + 0(.826) + 0(.069) = 0$$

The expected payoff criterion selects action a_1. This selection criterion incorporates both prior information and the information contained in the sample of 100 consumers.

The expected utility criterion presented in Section 18.7 may also be extended to incorporate sample information. Simply replace the prior probabilities by the posterior probabilities. This criterion will then prescribe an action that is consistent with the decision-maker's preferences for outcomes and risk attitude, as well as with the sample information. Thus, no matter which probabilistic criterion you use—expected payoff or expected utility—the incorporation of sample information requires only the substitution of posterior probabilities for prior probabilities.

TABLE 18.20   Payoff Table for the Smoke Detector Example

		STATE OF NATURE (POSTERIOR PROBABILITIES IN PARENTHESES)			
		S_1: $p = .01$ (.000)	S_2: $p = .05$ (.104)	S_3: $p = .10$ (.826)	S_4: $p = .15$ (.069)
ACTION	a_1: Market Detector	−$1,500,000	−$200,000	$300,000	$1,000,000
	a_2: Do Not Market Detector	0	0	0	0

EXERCISES 18.61–18.65

Learning the Mechanics

18.61 Use the posterior probabilities of Exercise 18.51 to select the action with the highest expected payoff in the following payoff table (outcomes are in thousands of dollars).

		STATE OF NATURE			
		S_1	S_2	S_3	S_4
	a_1	30	20	0	15
ACTION	a_2	40	20	5	0
	a_3	9	15	−21	25

18.62 Consider the payoff table given here (with prior probabilities in parentheses).

		STATE OF NATURE		
		S_1 (.4)	S_2 (.1)	S_3 (.5)
	a_1	9	25	−14
ACTION	a_2	−16	18	15
	a_3	25	12	9
	a_4	6	30	−20

a. Use the expected payoff criterion to choose an action.

b. Sampling information I has been obtained that suggests that S_1 is the true state of nature. The reliability of this information is reflected in the following probabilities:

$$P(I|S_1) = .80 \qquad P(I|S_2) = .30 \qquad P(I|S_3) = .10$$

Find the posterior state probabilities.

c. Compute the expected payoff for each action using the posterior probabilities.

d. Use your results of part **c** to determine which action is prescribed by the expected payoff criterion. Compare this action with the action selected in part **a** using prior probabilities.

18.63 Consider the accompanying payoff table.

		STATE OF NATURE		
		S_1 (.5)	S_2 (.3)	S_3 (.2)
	a_1	−150	225	120
ACTION	a_2	200	−172	100
	a_3	300	80	−100

a. Use the expected payoff criterion to choose an action.

b. Sampling information I has been obtained that suggests that S_2 is the true state of nature. The reliability of this information is reflected by the following probabilities:

$$P(I|S_1) = .20 \qquad P(I|S_2) = .60 \qquad P(I|S_3) = .20$$

Find the posterior state probabilities.

c. Given the sample information I in part **b**, which action does the expected payoff criterion imply?

Applying the Concepts

18.64 A large hospital is considering purchasing 100 new color television sets under one of two different purchase agreements. Under one agreement the TV sets would cost $460 each and all sets that are seriously defective would be replaced at no cost. Under the other agreement, the TV sets would cost $400 each and any seriously defective sets would have to be replaced by the hospital at $400 each. (Assume all replacement sets are nondefective.) The hospital's purchasing agent believes the probabilities shown in the table appropriately characterize the proportion of seriously defective sets in a shipment of 100 sets from the manufacturer.

Proportion Defective	.00	.05	.10	.15	.20
Probability	.4	.3	.1	.1	.1

a. Construct the payoff table for this decision problem. [*Note:* Costs represent negative payoffs.]

b. By the expected payoff criterion, which purchase agreement should the hospital choose?

c. Suppose the hospital was able to randomly sample one TV set from the incoming shipment of 100 sets before deciding which purchase agreement to choose. According to the expected payoff criterion, which agreement should it select if the sampled set was defective? Nondefective?

18.65 A small company that produces auto parts for American-made cars expects to lose $1.5 million next year unless Congress passes a bill to limit the number of foreign-made cars that can be imported into the United States. If the bill passes, the company expects to make a profit of $2.5 million next year. The company's lobbyists in Washington have reported that the probability of the bill passing this year is .6. The auto parts company must decide whether to stay in business and risk a huge loss next year or to lease its facility for a year to a Japanese firm for $500,000. The company has just received new information from "a source close to the White House" that indicates Congress will pass the bill. The company assesses the reliability of the source as follows:

$P(\text{Source says bill will pass} \mid \text{Bill will pass}) = .8$

$P(\text{Source says bill will pass} \mid \text{Bill will not pass}) = .1$

a. Construct the payoff table for the company's decision problem. Include the company's prior state probabilities.

b. Compute the posterior state probabilities.

c. Describe the effect of the sample information on the company's prior beliefs regarding the passage of the bill by comparing the company's prior and posterior state probabilities.

d. Given the sample information, which action is prescribed by the expected payoff criterion?

18.11   THE EXPECTED VALUE OF SAMPLE INFORMATION: PREPOSTERIOR ANALYSIS (OPTIONAL)

We now want to make a realistic assessment of the expected worth of sample information. Of course, for the information to be of any use to us in deciding whether to obtain sample information, we must make the assessment *before* the sample is taken. Accordingly, the analysis is referred to as **preposterior analysis**.

For example, consider the smoke detector example of the previous sections. We repeat the payoff table with the prior state probabilities in Table 18.21. The expected payoff criterion using the prior probabilities yields $EP(a_1) = \$10,000$ and $EP(a_2) = 0$, so we would not market the detector (action a_2) based on the prior information.

Now suppose the company is considering taking a sample of two consumers to obtain their opinions about the detector. (We choose a small sample size to reduce the computational difficulty.) The value of x, the number of the sampled consumers who state they will purchase the detector, will be either 0, 1, or 2. *Preposterior analysis involves examining the decision problem for each possible sample outcome.* Thus, in Table 18.22 we use a probability revision table to derive the posterior probabilities for each of the three possible sample outcomes. The first two columns show the states and prior probabilities, respectively. Column 3 presents the conditional probability of observing the sample outcome given a particular state of nature. For the smoke detector example, these are binomial probabilities with $n = 2$ and a value of p corresponding to the market share of each state. Thus, for the first two entries in column 3 under the heading $x = 0$, we find

$$P(x = 0 \mid p = .01) = \binom{2}{x}p^x(1-p)^{2-x} = \binom{2}{0}(.01)^0(.99)^2 = (.99)^2 = .9801$$

$$P(x = 0 \mid p = .05) = \binom{2}{0}(.05)^0(.95)^2 = (.95)^2 = .9025$$

TABLE 18.21   Payoff Table for the Smoke Detector Example

		STATE OF NATURE (PRIOR PROBABILITIES IN PARENTHESES)			
		$S_1: p = .01$ (.10)	$S_2: p = .05$ (.40)	$S_3: p = .10$ (.40)	$S_4: p = .15$ (.10)
ACTION	a_1: Market Detector	−$1,500,000	−$200,000	$300,000	$1,000,000
	a_2: Do Not Market Detector	0	0	0	0

TABLE 18.22 **Probability Revision Table for Each Sample Outcome in the Smoke Detector Example**

		(1)	(2)	(3)	(4)	(5)
		State	Prior Probability	Conditional Probability of Sample Outcome Given State	Intersection of States and Sample Outcome (2) × (3)	Posterior Probability (4) ÷ Total of (4)
$x = 0$	S_1: $p = .01$		.10	.9801	.0980	.1146
	S_2: $p = .05$		.40	.9025	.3610	.4221
	S_3: $p = .10$		.40	.8100	.3240	.3789
	S_4: $p = .15$		.10	.7225	.0722	.0844
	Total 1.00				.8552	1.0000
$x = 1$	S_1: $p = .01$		.10	.0198	.0020	.0145
	S_2: $p = .05$		.40	.0950	.0380	.2764
	S_3: $p = .10$		.40	.1800	.0720	.5236
	S_4: $p = .15$		.10	.2550	.0255	.1855
	Total 1.00				.1375	1.0000
$x = 2$	S_1: $p = .01$		.10	.0001	.0000	.0000
	S_2: $p = .05$		.40	.0025	.0010	.1389
	S_3: $p = .10$		.40	.0100	.0040	.5556
	S_4: $p = .15$		.10	.0225	.0022	.3056
	Total 1.00				.0072	1.0001[a]

[a]Rounding error

and so on. In column 4 we find the probability of the intersection of the states and the sample outcome using the formula

$$P(x \cap S_i) = P(S_i)P(x|S_i)$$

which is the product of the respective entries in columns 2 and 3. Finally, we find the revised state probabilities—the posterior probabilities—in column 5 by applying Bayes' rule:

$$P(S_i|x) = \frac{P(x \cap S_i)}{\displaystyle\sum_{\substack{\text{All states} \\ j}} P(x \cap S_j)} = \frac{P(S_i)P(x|S_i)}{\displaystyle\sum_{\substack{\text{All states} \\ j}} P(S_j)P(x|S_j)}$$

Then each element in column 5 is equal to the corresponding element in column 4 divided by the column 4 total.

We now determine which action is dictated by each posterior distribution. That is, if none of the two sampled consumers will buy the detector (i.e., $x = 0$), which action should be selected? We use the expected payoff criterion with the posterior probabilities corresponding to $x = 0$:

$$EP(a_1|x = 0) = \sum_{\text{All states}} (\text{Payoff})(\text{Posterior probability of state for } x = 0)$$

$$= (-1,500,000)(.1146) + (-200,000)(.4221)$$
$$+ (300,000)(.3789) + (1,000,000)(.0844)$$
$$= -\$58,250$$

$$EP(a_2|x = 0) = 0(.1146) + 0(.4221) + 0(.3789) + 0(.0844) = 0$$

Thus, the expected payoff criterion selects action a_2: Do not market the detector when $x = 0$ is the sample outcome.

TABLE 18.23   Actions Selected and Expected Payoffs for the Smoke Detector Example

Sample Outcome	Action Selected	Expected Payoff	Marginal Probability of Sample Outcome
$x = 0$	a_2	0	.8552
$x = 1$	a_1	$265,550	.1375
$x = 2$	a_1	$444,500	.0072
			$.9999^a \approx 1.0$

[a]Rounding error

Now suppose we observe $x = 1$ when the sample information is collected:

$$EP(a_1|x = 1) = \sum_{\text{All states}} (\text{Payoff})(\text{Posterior probability of state for } x = 1)$$

$$= (-1,500,000)(.0145) + (-200,000)(.2764)$$
$$+ (300,000)(.5556) + (1,000,000)(.3056)$$

$$= \$265,550$$

$$EP(a_2|x = 1) = 0$$

So we choose a_1: Market the detector if $x = 1$.
   Finally.

$$EP(a_1|x = 2) = (-1,500,000)(.0000) + (-200,000)(.1389)$$
$$+ (300,000)(.5556) + (1,000,000)(.3056)$$

$$= \$444,500$$

$$EP(a_2|x = 2) = 0$$

Therefore, the expected payoff criterion selects action a_1: Market the detector when $x = 2$.
   Table 18.23 summarizes our work to this point. Note that we included the probability of observing each of the sample outcomes in the last column of Table 18.23. These probabilities are the sums of the column 4 entries for each sample outcome in the probability revision table (Table 18.22). Thus,

$$P(x = 0) = \sum_{\text{All states}} P[(x = 0) \cap S_i]$$

$$= .0980 + .3610 + .3240 + .0722 = .8552$$

$P(x = 1)$ and $P(x = 2)$ can be computed in a similar manner. They form the **marginal** (or **predictive**) **probability distribution** for the random variable x. Note that the marginal probabilities are not dependent on the state, and they will sum to 1 if no rounding errors are present.
   Now recall our ultimate objective. We are trying to determine how much is to be gained from sampling. Since we now know the expected payoff and the marginal probability of each sample outcome (Table 18.23), we can calculate the **expected payoff of sampling** (EPS):

$$EPS = \sum_x (EP|x)p(x) = \sum_{\substack{\text{All sample} \\ \text{outcomes}}} \begin{pmatrix} \text{Maximum expected} \\ \text{payoff for} \\ \text{sample outcome} \end{pmatrix} \begin{pmatrix} \text{Marginal} \\ \text{probability of} \\ \text{sample outcome} \end{pmatrix}$$

$$= (0)(.8552) + (265,550)(.1375) + (444,500)(.0072) = \$39,713.53$$

or $39,700, rounding to the nearest hundred dollars. Thus, the mean payoff is $39,700 when $n = 2$ consumers are sampled.

To determine the expected gain attributed to sampling, we compare the EPS to the *expected payoff for no sampling* (EPNS). But EPNS is the expected payoff of the action selected by the expected payoff criterion using prior probabilities. We showed in previous sections that action a_2 is chosen using prior decision analysis, so that

$$\text{EPNS} = EP(a_2) = 0$$

Finally, the *expected value of sample information* (EVSI) is the expected payoff of sampling less the expected payoff with no sampling; i.e.,

$$\text{EVSI} = \text{EPS} - \text{EPNS} = \$39,700 - \$0 = \$39,700$$

This figure represents the mean dollar amount the company will gain from sampling and therefore provides a figure it will be reluctant to exceed in the cost of obtaining the sample information.

The steps for computing the expected value of sample information are summarized in the box. The calculation of EVSI becomes very tedious when the number of possible sample outcomes is large. However, because the method is the same no matter how many possible outcomes exist, computers can be useful aids in determining EVSI.

Computing the Expected Value of Sample Information (EVSI)

Step 1 Obtain the posterior state probabilities for each possible sample outcome using a probability revision table.

Step 2 Use the expected payoff criterion with the posterior probabilities to determine the action with the maximum expected payoff *for each sample outcome*.

Step 3 Find the marginal probability distribution for the sample outcomes by using

$$P(x) = \sum_{\text{All states}} P(x \cap S_i)$$

For each sample outcome, the marginal probability will be the sum of column 4 in the probability revision table (step 1).

Step 4 Find the expected payoff of sampling (EPS) by combining the results of steps 2 and 3:

$$\text{EPS} = \sum_{\substack{\text{All sample} \\ \text{outcomes}}} \left(\begin{array}{c} \text{Maximum} \\ \text{expected payoff} \\ \text{for sample outcome} \end{array} \right) \left(\begin{array}{c} \text{Marginal} \\ \text{probability of} \\ \text{sample outcome} \end{array} \right)$$

Step 5 Calculate the EVSI by

$$\text{EVSI} = \text{EPS} - \text{EPNS}$$

where EPNS is the expected payoff of no sampling, computed using the prior probabilities.

After the EVSI has been determined, it should be compared with the *cost of sampling* (CS) by computing the **expected net gain for sampling** (ENGS). For example, if the smoke detector company determines that a total cost of $500 will be incurred during the sampling of two consumers, the expected net gain of sampling is

$$\text{ENGS} = \text{EVSI} - \text{CS} = \$39{,}700 - \$500 = \$39{,}200$$

As long as the net gain is positive, the company can expect to gain by obtaining the sample information. We thus have the preposterior expected gain decision rule given in the next box.

Preposterior Expected Gain Decision Rule

If the expected net gain of sampling (ENGS) is greater than 0, the decision analyst should obtain the sample information before making a decision.

The ENGS calculation formula is ENGS = EVSI − CS, where CS is the cost of sampling.

Decision trees (Section 18.3) are often used to conduct a preposterior analysis or to summarize the results of a preposterior analysis. The decision tree for the smoke detector example is shown in Figure 18.6. The first decision fork (always reading from left to right) represents the decision of whether to sample. Along the upper branch (Do not sample) we place a decision fork representing the two possible actions of the decision problem. Beside this fork we write the expected payoff of no sampling (EPNS), which is 0 for this example. At the ends of the action branches, we place chance forks and branch into the four states of nature. Beside each chance fork we write the expected payoff for the associated action, where the expected payoffs are computed using the prior probabilities. The expected payoff is −$10,000 for action a_1 and $0 for action a_2 in our example. On the state branches, we write the prior probabilities, and at the ends of the branches are the outcomes corresponding to the action/state combinations.

The lower branch of the decision tree in Figure 18.6, the Sample branch, has an extra chance fork corresponding to the possible sample outcomes. The expected payoff of sampling (EPS), which is $39,700 for this example, is written beside the sampling chance fork. The marginal probability for each sample outcome is written on the appropriate sample outcome branch, and the expected payoff for the optimal action corresponding to each sample outcome is recorded beside the decision fork at the end of each sample outcome branch. The remainder of the branching is into actions and then into states, just as for the Do not sample branch. The only difference is that posterior rather than prior probabilities are recorded on each state of nature branch. Note that two vertical lines are used to block the branches corresponding to actions with expected payoffs that are not maximum. This reminds us which action should be chosen at each decision fork.*

In the context of decision analysis, the term *sampling* means any procedure or process for gathering information. This includes statistical sampling, such as random sampling, as well as less technical methods, such as obtaining an expert opinion, as in the preceding example. If we are interested in random sampling, the *optimal sample size* can be determined by conducting a preposterior analysis for each potential sample size and choosing the sample size with the maximum ENGS. If this optimal sample size is 0 (or negative), the decision should be based on presently available information. In the former case, the decision-maker should select a sample of the optimal size and then repeat the analysis to determine whether further sampling is expected to yield a positive net gain.

---

*The computations for EVSI are often performed directly from a decision tree such as Figure 18.6. Both EPNS and EPS can be determined by starting at the far right-hand side of the tree and taking expectations backward through the tree.

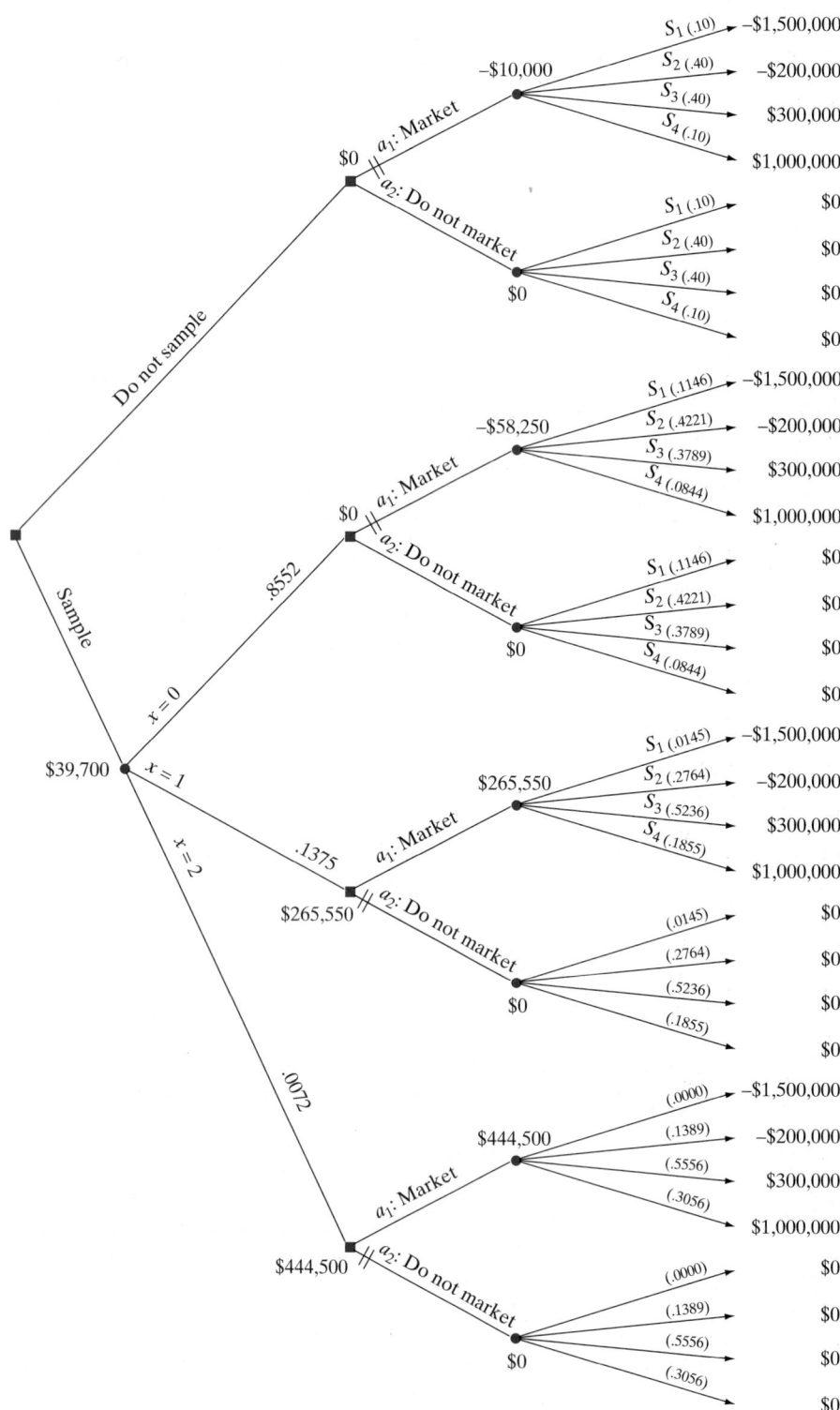

Figure 18.6 Decision tree for the smoke detector example

Considerable effort is required to conduct a preposterior analysis when the sample size is moderate or large. Because the methodology remains the same for any sample size, computers are typically used to conduct preposterior analyses.

STATISTICS IN ACTION

18.2 HURRICANES: TO SEED OR NOT TO SEED?

The seeding of hurricanes as a means of lessening their destructive power was suggested by R. H. Simpson in the early 1960s. Even though the results of experimental hurricane seeding were encouraging, government policy through the early 1970s prohibited the seeding of hurricanes that threatened coastal areas. Howard, Matheson, and North (*Science,* June 1971) used decision analysis to determine (1) whether existing government policy should be modified and (2) whether further experiments on hurricane seeding should be carried out.

To answer the first question, Howard, Matheson, and North had to define the states of nature, assign probabilities to each of the possible states, and assess the consequences of each action/state combination. The actions specified were Seed a threatening hurricane and Do not seed a threatening hurricane. The states of nature were defined in terms of the percentage change in maximum wind speed over a 12-hour period. This measure was chosen because it is related to the primary cause of the destruction inflicted by most hurricanes, and it is this characteristic that seeding is expected to influence. Based on historical data, a probability distribution was assessed for changes in wind speed for a "representative hurricane" over a 12-hour period. Using Simpson's theoretical work on hurricane seeding and early experimental work on seeding, Howard, Matheson, and North also assessed a probability distribution for changes in wind speed of a seeded hurricane. These probability distributions are given in Table 18.24 (page 990).

The consequences of the action/state combinations considered were property damage resulting from the hurricane and government liability in the case of seeded hurricanes. Using a least squares regression analysis (see Chapter 10) and past records of hurricane damage, the authors modeled the relationship between changes in wind speed and property damage

(in millions of dollars) for a "representative hurricane." Results of their analysis appear in Table 18.25 (page 991).

It was assumed that if a hurricane did not slow after seeding, the government would bear increased legal and social costs. A percentage of the property damage resulting from the states S_1, S_2, and S_3 was used to estimate these costs. The total costs associated with a particular state were found by adding these government responsibility costs to the predicted property damages. Estimates were 50% for S_1, 30% for S_2, and 5% for S_3. Thus, the outcomes for each state under the decision to seed would be (including the \$.25 million cost of seeding) as shown in Table 18.26 (page 992). These quantities are expressed (in millions of dollars) in terms of negative gains—i.e., losses.

Focus I

a. Find EL(No seeding), where EL stands for Expected Loss.

b. Find EL(Seeding).

c. According to the expected loss criterion, should the government change its policy and allow seeding of hurricanes that threaten coastal areas? Explain.

In addition to studying whether hurricanes should be seeded, Howard, Matheson, and North addressed the question of whether more evidence on the effects of hurricane seeding should be gathered before the government reverses it policy against seeding. Would the expected loss from a representative hurricane be reduced by carrying out an additional seeding experiment?

First, the authors looked at the cost and possible outcomes of a seeding experiment. The cost to seed a hurricane and observe the results is $250,000. The possible outcomes are the same as those given above for a seeded hurricane; the prior probabilities for

continued

these outcomes are also given. Using the probabilities of each experimental outcome conditioned on each of the states of nature, the prior probabilities of the outcomes of seeding can be revised using Bayes' rule. The resulting posterior probabilities can then be used to evaluate the expected loss for seeding and not seeding. The decision to experiment or not can be made by comparing the expected loss associated with experimenting to the expected loss of not experimenting. A condensed decision tree is shown in Figure 18.7 below.

Focus 2

d. What is the expected loss of experimenting? How is this value determined?

e. What is the expected loss of not experimenting?

f. Based on the expected loss criterion, would you recommend that further experiments with hurricane seeding be conducted before the government policy against seeding is changed? Justify your answer.

FIGURE 18.7
Decision tree for expected loss from seeding (Statistics in Action 18.2)

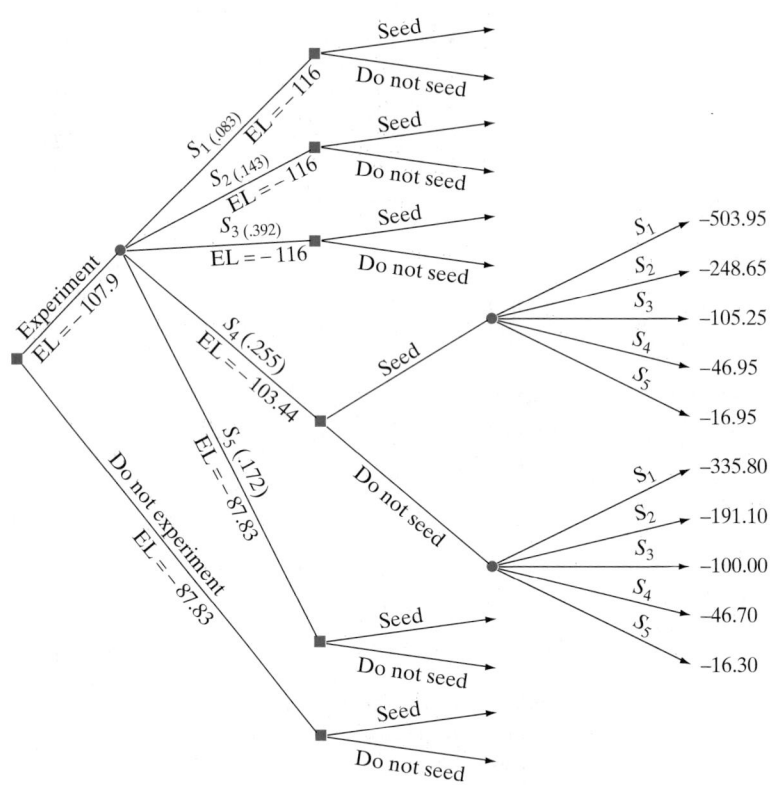

TABLE 18.24   Probability Distributions for States of Nature (Statistics in Action 18.2)

State	State Probability	State Probability
Change in Wind Speed	**Unseeded Hurricanes**	**Seeded Hurricanes**
S_1: +25% or more	.054	.038
S_2: +10% to +25%	.206	.143
S_3: −10% to +10%	.480	.392
S_4: −25% to −10%	.206	.255
S_5: −25% or more	.054	.172

TABLE 18.25   Predicted Property Damage for Hurricane (Statistics in Action 18.2)

Change in Wind Speed	Predicted Damage
+25% or more	335.8
+10% to +25%	191.1
−10% to +10%	100.0
−25% to −10%	46.7
−25% or more	16.3

TABLE 18.26   Outcomes Associated with States of Nature (Statistics in Action 18.2)

State	Outcome
S_1: +25% or more	−503.95
S_2: +10% to +25%	−248.65
S_3: −10% to +10%	−105.25
S_4: −25% to −10%	−46.95
S_5: −25% or more	−16.55

EXERCISES   18.66–18.71

Learning the Mechanics

18.66 Consider the following payoff table (prior probabilities are shown in parentheses).

		STATE OF NATURE	
		S_1 (.40)	S_2 (.60)
ACTION	a_1	$600	−$100
	a_2	−$200	$300

The decision-maker must decide whether to purchase sample information about the true state of nature prior to choosing an action. The sample information would cost $100. The reliability of the sample information is described by the following conditional probabilities:

P(Sample information indicates S_1 true $|$ S_1 is true) = .8

P(Sample information indicates S_2 true $|$ S_1 is true) = .2

P(Sample information indicates S_1 true $|$ S_2 is true) = .1

P(Sample information indicates S_2 true $|$ S_2 is true) = .9

 a. Find the expected payoff of sampling (EPS) and the expected payoff of no sampling (EPNS).
 b. Use the results of part **a** to find the expected value of sample information (EVSI).
 c. Find the expected net gain of sampling (ENGS).

 d. According to the ENGS, should the decision-maker purchase the sample information prior to making a decision? Explain.

18.67 Refer to Exercise 18.66. A second source of sample information is also available to the decision-maker. This information costs only $10, but it is much less reliable than the first source, as indicated by the following conditional probabilities:

P(Sample information indicates S_1 true $|$ S_1 is true) = .4

P(Sample information indicates S_2 true $|$ S_1 is true) = .6

P(Sample information indicates S_1 true $|$ S_2 is true) = .3

P(Sample information indicates S_2 true $|$ S_2 is true) = .7

 a. Find the expected net gain of sampling (ENGS) for the second source of sample information.
 b. From which source should the decision-maker purchase sample information? Explain.

18.68 Consider the decision tree shown at the top of page 992, with outcomes expressed as payoffs and prior probabilities shown in parentheses.

The decision-maker is considering purchasing sample information about the true state of nature prior to choosing an action. The sample information costs $250. The reliability of the sample information is described by the following conditional probabilities:

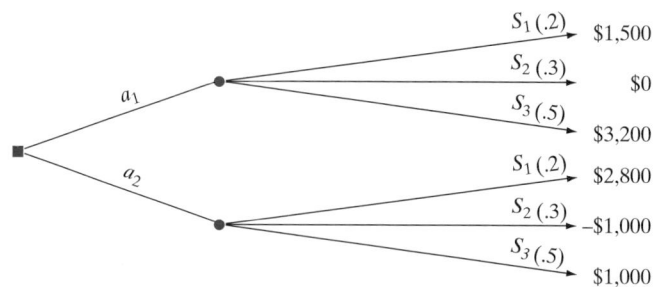

P(Sample information indicates S_1 true$|S_1$ true) = .7

P(Sample information indicates S_2 true$|S_1$ true) = .2

P(Sample information indicates S_3 true $|S_1$ true) = .1

P(Sample information indicates S_1 true $|S_2$ true) = .05

P(Sample information indicates S_2 true $|S_2$ true) = .9

P(Sample information indicates S_3 true $|S_2$ true) = .05

P(Sample information indicates S_1 true $|S_3$ true) = .1

P(Sample information indicates S_2 true $|S_3$ true) = .1

P(Sample information indicates S_3 true $|S_3$ true) = .8

a. What are the prior probabilities for $S_1, S_2,$ and S_3?
b. Find the posterior probabilities for $S_1, S_2,$ and S_3 when the sample information indicates S_1 is true.
c. Repeat part **b** for the case when the sample information indicates S_2 is true.
d. Repeat part **b** for the case when the sample information indicates S_3 is true.
e. Find the predictive (marginal) probabilities for the three sample results.
f. Expand the decision tree to include the decision-maker's sampling decision. Enter the payoffs on the tree along with all the probabilities you found in parts **a–e**.
g. Find EPNS and EPS, and enter them on your tree.
h. Find EVSI.
i. Use the preposterior expected gain decision rule to determine whether the decision-maker should purchase the sample information.

Applying the Concepts

18.69 The decision problem for a company that may market a new product is characterized in the payoff table at the bottom of the page (prior probabilities are in parentheses).

The company is considering whether to conduct a $30,000 market survey to gain information concerning the product's potential for success. One of four different conclusions would be yielded by the survey: "Product will be very successful," "Product will be successful," "Product will be a failure," or "Product's status after 1 year is uncertain." The reliability of the conclusions yielded by the survey can be described by the conditional probabilities shown at the top of page 993.
a. Find the expected value of sample information (EVSI), and interpret your result in the context of the problem.
b. Find the expected net gain of sampling (ENGS), and use it to determine whether the company should undertake the proposed market survey.

18.70 Reconsider Exercises 18.22 and 18.34. The dress buyer expects to sell between three and eight dozen dresses with the prior probabilities shown in the table.

Sales	Probability
3	.15
4	.25
5	.30
6	.15
7	.10
8	.05

	PRODUCT'S STATUS AFTER 1 YEAR ON THE MARKET		
	Failure (.6)	Successful (.3)	Very Successful (.1)
Market	−$200,000	$300,000	$600,000
Do Not Market	0	0	0

$$P(\text{Survey concludes "very successful"} \mid \text{Product is very successful}) = .6$$

$$P(\text{Survey concludes "successful"} \mid \text{Product is very successful}) = .2$$

$$P(\text{Survey concludes "failure"} \mid \text{Product is very successful}) = .1$$

$$P(\text{Survey concludes "uncertain"} \mid \text{Product is very successful}) = .1$$

$$P(\text{Survey concludes "very successful"} \mid \text{Product is successful}) = .2$$

$$P(\text{Survey concludes "successful"} \mid \text{Product is successful}) = .4$$

$$P(\text{Survey concludes "failure"} \mid \text{Product is successful}) = .2$$

$$P(\text{Survey concludes "uncertain"} \mid \text{Product is successful}) = .2$$

$$P(\text{Survey concludes "very successful"} \mid \text{Product is a failure}) = .1$$

$$P(\text{Survey concludes "successful"} \mid \text{Product is a failure}) = .1$$

$$P(\text{Survey concludes "failure"} \mid \text{Product is a failure}) = .5$$

$$P(\text{Survey concludes "uncertain"} \mid \text{Product is a failure}) = .3$$

A market research firm can be hired to forecast the demand for the new style of dress. Past records indicate that the research firm's conditional probabilities of forecasts, given the various states of nature (sales), are as shown in the table at right (sales numbers are in dozens). Perform a preposterior analysis and indicate how much the buyer should be willing to spend for the sample information.

18.71 Refer to Exercise 18.64, in which a hospital was considering purchasing 100 color television sets. On the basis of its prior information, what is it worth to the hospital to be able to test one of the 100 television sets before selecting a purchase agreement?

		ACTUAL SALES					
		3	**4**	**5**	**6**	**7**	**8**
	3	.70	.10	.06	.04	0	0
	4	.20	.50	.10	.05	.05	0
FORECAST	**5**	.10	.20	.50	.11	.05	.05
SALES	**6**	0	.10	.20	.40	.20	.10
	7	0	.10	.04	.30	.60	.15
	8	0	0	.10	.10	.10	.70

QUICK REVIEW

Key Terms

Note: Starred (*) terms are from the optional section in this chapter.

Key Formulas

Note: Starred (*) formulas are from the optional section.

$OL = (\text{Payoff}) - (\text{Maximum payoff of state of nature})$ Opportunity loss 955

$EP(a_i) = \Sigma xp(x) = \Sigma(\text{Payoff for action})(\text{Probability of state of nature})$ Expected payoff 962

$EOL(a_i) = \Sigma(\text{Opportunity loss for action})(\text{Probability of state of nature})$ Expected opportunity loss 960

$EU(a_i) = \Sigma(\text{Utility for action})(\text{Probability of state of nature})$ Expected utility 968

$$P(S_i|I) = \frac{P(I \cap S_i)}{P(I)} = \frac{P(I|S_i)P(S_i)}{\sum_{j=1}^{k} P(I|S_j)P(S_j)}$$ Bayes' rule 975

$$EPS = \Sigma \left(\begin{array}{c} \text{Maximum} \\ \text{expected payoff} \\ \text{for sample outcome} \end{array} \right) \left(\begin{array}{c} \text{Marginal} \\ \text{probability of} \\ \text{sample outcome} \end{array} \right)$$ Expected payoff of sampling* 985

$EPNS = EP(a_i)$ using prior probabilities   Expected payoff for no sampling* 986

$EVSI = EPS - EPNS$ Expected value of sample information* 986

$ENGS = EVSI - CS$, where CS = cost of sampling   Expected net gain of sampling* 987

LANGUAGE LAB

Note: Starred (*) terms are from the optional section.

Symbol	Description
a_i	The ith action
S_j	The jth state of nature
O_{ij}	The outcome (i.e., payoff or opportunity loss) associated with action i and state of nature j
$EP(a_i)$	Expected payoff for action i
O_M	The maximum outcome (e.g., payoff) in the decision table
O_L	The minimum outcome (e.g., payoff) in the decision table
$U(O_{ij})$	The utility of outcome O_{ij}
$EU(a_i)$	The expected utility of action i
I	Sample information
EPS*	Expected payoff of sampling
EPNS*	Expected payoff for no sampling
EVSI*	Expected value of sample information
CS*	Cost of sampling
ENGS*	Expected net gain of sampling

SUPPLEMENTARY EXERCISES 18.72–18.89

Note: Starred (*) exercises refer to the optional section in this chapter.

Learning the Mechanics

18.72 Consider the payoff table at right, with state probabilities shown in parentheses:
  a. Eliminate any inadmissible actions.
  b. Construct an opportunity loss table for this decision problem.
  c. Calculate both the expected payoffs and the expected opportunity losses for the actions, and verify that both criteria select the same action.

  d. Construct a decision tree for this problem that includes both state probabilities and expected payoffs.

	S_1 (.5)	S_2 (.3)	S_3 (.2)
a_1	12	77	−27
a_2	24	2	12
a_3	−20	41	80
a_4	25	5	70
a_5	40	50	10

18.73 Graph each of the following utility functions and classify the decision-maker's attitude toward risk.

a. $U(x) = \dfrac{100 + .5x}{250}$ $-200 \leqslant x \leqslant 300$

b. $U(x) = \dfrac{\sqrt{x + 100}}{20}$ $-100 \leqslant x \leqslant 300$

c. $U(x) = \dfrac{x^3 - 2x^2 - x + 10}{800}$ $0 \leqslant x \leqslant 10$

d. $U(x) = \dfrac{.1x^2 + 10x}{110}$ $0 \leqslant x \leqslant 10$

18.74 Consider the payoff table shown. The decision-maker is indifferent to the following pairs of events: (1) Receive $0 with certainty, and win $80 with probability .15 or lose $20 with probability .85; (2) Receive $20 with certainty, and win $80 with probability .3 or lose $20 with probability .7; (3) Receive $40 with certainty, and win $80 with probability .55 or lose $20 with probability .45; and (4) Receive $60 with certainty, and win $80 with probability .8 or lose $20 with probability .2.

	S_1	S_2	S_3
a_1	12	77	-10
a_2	-20	41	80
a_3	25	5	70
a_4	40	50	10

a. Plot the utility values versus monetary values between $-$20 and $80 (assign these endpoints utility values of 0 and 1, respectively).

b. Draw a smooth curve through the points in part **a**, and use this curve to assign utility values to all the payoffs in the table.

c. If the state probabilities are $P(S_1) = .4$, $P(S_2) = .35$, and $P(S_3) = .25$, which action should be selected according to the expected utility criterion? How does this compare with the action selected by the expected payoff criterion?

Applying the Concepts

18.75 Managers who are responsible for maintaining fleets of motor vehicles must decide whether or not to implement oil analysis programs. Oil analysis involves the periodic sampling of the lubricating oil from the vehicles and subjecting it to chemical analyses to determine whether it contains metals or contaminants. Such findings are predictive of certain kinds of engine failures that can often be avoided with preventative maintenance. Failure to detect such problems may lead to expensive emergency maintenance and equipment downtime. The Southern Company was faced with choosing among three maintenance strategies for its fleet of automobiles and light trucks: No preventative maintenance; oil analysis; or change oil in all vehicles. The following decision tree characterizes the problem for a particular type of vehicle. The oil analysis cost is $100 per vehicle; an oil change costs $200 per vehicle. Both costs are included in the total costs shown on the right-hand side of the tree.

a. Find the expected cost for each of the three strategies.

b. According to the expected payoff criterion, which strategy should be adopted?

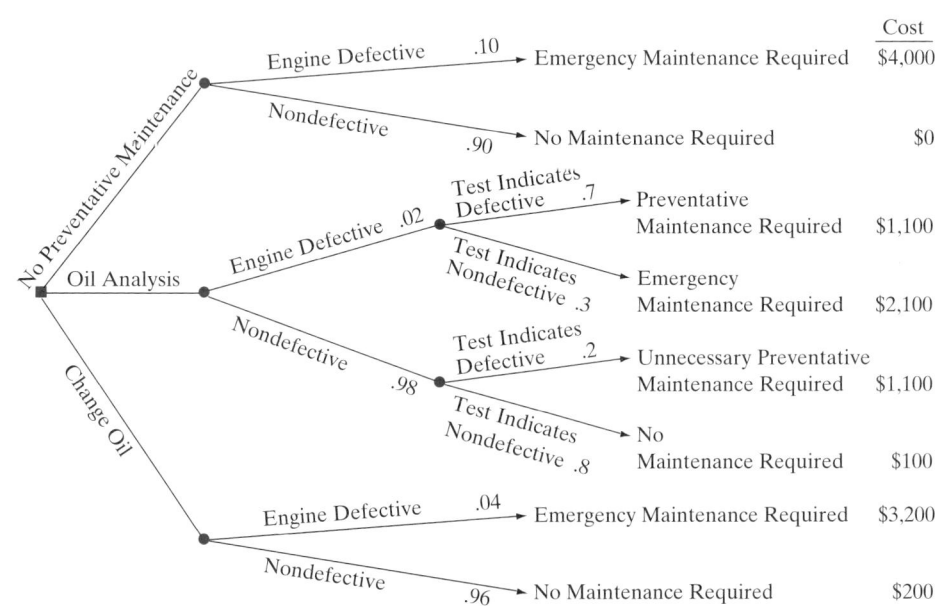

c. If the oil analysis test were 90% effective in identifying defective engines and 95% effective in identifying nondefective engines, would your answer to part **b** change? Explain.

18.76 Refer to Exercise 18.65. Assume that the auto parts manufacturer's utility function for money is

$$U(x) = .5 + .20x \qquad -2.5 \text{ million} \leqslant x \leqslant 2.5 \text{ million}$$

a. Plot the utility function.

b. Is the utility function that of a risk-avoiding, risk-taking, or risk-neutral decision-maker?

c. According to the expected utility criterion, which action should the parts manufacturer select?

18.77 Indicate what type of information (subjective, relative frequency, or both) you would use to assign probabilities to the events described here. Explain the reasoning behind your choice. How would you obtain the necessary information to assign the probabilities?

a. Your firm is in the automobile insurance business, and you want to assess a probability distribution to characterize the total dollar value of damage to a certain model car when an 18- to 21-year-old driver is in an accident.

b. Your company is introducing a new product, and you are assigned the task of assessing a probability distribution for the market share the product will obtain.

c. A drug company is attempting to develop a new type of antihistamine. The research is still in the early stages, and you want to assess the probability that the research will be successful.

d. You are a banker and are considering giving a 30-year mortgage of $75,000 to a family with a yearly income of $25,000. You want to assess the probability of a default on the loan.

18.78 A bank is trying to decide whether to make a 1-year commercial loan of $75,000 to an automobile repair shop. Past experience has shown that one of three outcomes will result if the loan is made:

Outcome 1: The customer repays the loan plus the 10% interest with no complications.

Outcome 2: The customer has difficulty repaying the loan. It is eventually repaid with the 10% interest, but a $1,000 collection cost is incurred by the bank.

Outcome 3: The customer declares bankruptcy, and the bank recovers only 60% of the loan.

If the bank decides not to make the loan, the money will earn 8% for the year.

a. Construct the payoff table for this decision problem.

b. Convert the payoff table to an opportunity loss table.

c. Draw a decision tree for this problem.

18.79 Refer to Exercise 18.78. Suppose past records yield the frequency distribution for commercial loans shown in the table.

Outcome	Frequency
1. Repaid	1,104
2. Repaid with difficulty	120
3. Defaulted	56

a. Use this information to assess the probabilities of the three outcomes.

b. Using the assessed probabilities and the expected payoff criterion, decide whether the bank should make the loan.

18.80 Refer to Exercises 18.78 and 18.79. Suppose the bank uses the following utility function for money:

$$U(x) = \frac{\sqrt{x + 100,000}}{1,000} \qquad -100,000 \leqslant x \leqslant 900,000$$

a. Graph this function over the given range of x, and classify the bank as risk-avoiding, risk-neutral, or risk-taking.

b. Use this function to assign utility values to the monetary payoffs in the decision table of Exercise 18.78. Based on the expected utility criterion, should the loan be made?

18.81 A hosiery company must make a pricing decision regarding its new line of stockings. Two economists have been hired to develop forecasting equations that relate the quantity demanded to the price of the stockings. The forecasting equations the economists derive are

Economist 1: $q = 10 - 2p$

Economist 2: $q = 16 - 4p$

where q is the quantity demanded in units of 100,000 and p is the price in dollars. Four prices are being considered: $.99, $1.98, $2.75, and $3.50. Assume that one of the economists' forecasting equations will be correct, but you do not know which one.

a. Construct the payoff table for this problem.

b. Construct the opportunity loss table for this problem.

c. If the company believes the forecasting equations have an equal probability of being correct, which price should be charged according to the expected payoff criterion?

18.82 A common problem with management information systems (MIS) is that managers fail to use them, even when they are technically sound. A large computer firm is considering an MIS that will cost $1,000,000 to build and operate over a five-year period. If the company's managers use the system, a savings of $750,000 per year will be realized.

a. Construct the payoff table for this decision problem.

b. Convert the payoff table to an opportunity loss table.

c. Suppose the probability that the MIS will be used is assessed to be only .05. Use the expected opportunity loss criterion to decide whether to install the MIS.

18.83 The management of a bank must decide whether to install a commercial loan decision-support system (an on-line management information system) to aid its analysts. Experience suggests that each correct loan decision (accepting good loan applications and rejecting those that will eventually be defaulted) adds, on the average, approximately $25,000 per decision to the bank's profit. Further, it is estimated that the additional number, x, of correct loan decisions (per year) that could be attributed to the decision-support system has the probability distribution given in the table.

x	0	10	20	30	40	50	60	70	80	90
$p(x)$	.01	.04	.10	.15	.20	.15	.10	.10	.10	.05

a. If the decision-support system is estimated to have a useful life of five years, what would be the expected increase in profits that could be attributed to it?

b. The increase in profits will accrue only if the system is used by the analysts. Past experience has shown that for various behavioral and political reasons the system was not used by analysts in 80% of the installations. Given this information and that the system costs $1,500,000 to purchase, install, and maintain over a five-year period, should the bank purchase the system?

*c. The bank could hire a consulting firm for $50,000 to interview its loan analysts and then predict whether this group of analysts will use the decision-support system. The reliability of the firm's predictions is measured by the probabilities given in the table below. Should the bank purchase the survey? Explain.

18.84 *Acceptance sampling* is commonly used by manufacturers to screen incoming lots of material for an excessive number of defective units. A sample is selected from each incoming lot of units, the number of defective units is counted, and the lot

is either rejected or accepted depending on whether the number of defectives, x, exceeds a predetermined acceptance number (Montgomery, *Introduction to Statistical Quality Control*, 1991). As an example of the decision analysis approach to acceptance sampling, assume the proportion of the number of defectives in an incoming lot is either 5% or 10%. The prior probability that the proportion of defectives will be 5% is .80. Suppose the cost of accepting a lot with 10% defectives is $4,100, and the cost of rejecting a lot with 5% defectives is $1,000. There are no costs for making a correct decision (i.e., accepting a lot with 5% defectives or rejecting a lot with 10% defectives).

a. Formulate the payoff table for this problem.

b. If no sample is drawn, should the lot be accepted or rejected?

c. Assume a unit is drawn at random from the lot and is found to be defective. Should the lot be accepted or rejected?

d. If the unit drawn in part **d** is not defective, should the lot be accepted or rejected?

*e. Calculate the EVSI when the sample size is 1. Draw the corresponding decision tree.

*f. It will cost management $10 in fixed costs plus $10 for every item inspected. Should management use a sample size equal to 1?

*18.85 Assume the same basic facts given in Exercise 18.84, but now consider a sample size of 3.

a. Draw a decision tree for a preposterior analysis and calculate EVSI.

b. What is the ENGS?

*18.86 Repeat Exercise 18.84 with a sample size of 5. Then, using these results and the results of Exercises 18.84 and 18.85, plot ENGS versus sample size.

18.87 The chief forester of a large midwestern city must plan for the identification and removal next year of trees infected with Dutch elm disease. State law requires that all diseased elms must be removed and disposed of by October 30. For each diseased tree left standing after October 30, the city loses $300 in state funds budgeted for reforestation. Since the forester's staff can cut only 15,000 trees per season, private contractors must be hired to cut the trees in excess of 15,000. Unfortunately, the private contractors must be hired at the beginning of the disease season (May) before the spread of the epidemic is known. There is a fixed

		ACTUAL OUTCOME	
		Used System	Did Not Use System
FORECAST	**Will Use System**	.7	.1
	Will Not Use System	.3	.9

cost of $2,000 per contract signed, and each contractor is paid $250 for each tree removed. Assume each contractor can perform 6,000 removals per season. The forester has hired a consultant to help determine how many contractors to hire. The first action taken by the consultant is to assess a probability distribution that characterizes local experts' prior opinions regarding the number of elms that will be infected in the coming season. This distribution is given in the table.

Number of Trees	Probability
0– 5,000	.05
5,001–10,000	.20
10,001–20,000	.30
20,001–30,000	.20
30,001–40,000	.10
40,001–50,000	.08
50,001–60,000	.07

a. Using the midpoints of the intervals in the probability distribution as the states of nature, formulate the payoff table for this decision problem.

b. From your payoff table, construct a decision tree for the forester's decision problem.

c. Based on the prior probabilities, how many contractors should be hired to maximize the expected payoff?

*18.88 Refer to Exercise 18.87. The consultant reports to the forester that a statistical model can be developed to predict the number of trees that will be infected. The conditional probabilities of the forecasts given the various states of nature are shown in the accompanying table. It will cost $5 million to develop the model. Conduct a preposterior analysis to determine whether the model should be developed.

18.89 Certified Public Accounting (CPA) firms are hired by private corporations to audit or certify their accounting records. The auditors check two main problem areas—possible fraud by company employees and acceptability of record-keeping practices. Upon completing its audit, the CPA firm either will certify that the client firm's records and financial statements are in order or will fail to certify them and will report on existing irregularities. If the auditor certifies the records when in fact errors or irregularities exist, the CPA firm may be sued by the client firm's stockholders for malpractice. If the CPA firm refuses to certify the records when in fact the records contain no errors or irregularities, it may be sued by the client.

Suppose you have audited a company's financial records and now face a certification decision. In your judgment, you have assessed the following costs. If you report incorrectly that the books are not certifiable when in fact they are, then you will lose the account and be sued by the client; you estimate the total cost for this error to be $2 million. If, on the other hand, you certify the accounts when irregularities exist, you will be sued for $10 million by the stockholders.

a. Formulate the payoff table for this problem.

b. Describe how you would assess the state probabilities for this decision problem.

c. Assume you have assessed that the probability that the records are in order is .9. Which action would decision analysis prescribe?

d. What should you be willing to pay for perfect information about the records?

		ACTUAL NUMBER OF TREES INFECTED						
		0–5,000	5,001–10,000	10,001–20,000	20,001–30,000	30,001–40,000	40,001–50,000	50,001–60,000
	0– 5,000	.5	.3	.1	0	0	0	0
	5,001–10,000	.35	.4	.2	.1	0	0	0
	10,001–20,000	.15	.2	.5	.2	.1	0	0
FORECAST	20,001–30,000	0	.1	.2	.5	.2	0	0
	30,001–40,000	0	0	0	.2	.5	.1	.1
	40,001–50,000	0	0	0	0	.2	.5	.4
	50,001–60,000	0	0	0	0	0	.4	.5

APPENDIX A
BASIC COUNTING RULES

Sample points associated with many experiments have identical characteristics. If you can develop a counting rule to count the number of sample points, it can be used to aid in the solution of many probability problems. For example, many experiments involve sampling n elements from a population of N. Then, as explained in Section 3.1, we can use the formula

$$\binom{N}{n} = \frac{N!}{n!(N - n)!}$$

to find the number of different samples of n elements that could be selected from the total of N elements. This gives the number of sample points for the experiment.

Here, we give you a few useful counting rules. You should learn the characteristics of the situation to which each rule applies. Then, when working a probability problem, carefully examine the experiment to see whether you can use one of the rules.

Learning how to decide whether a particular counting rule applies to an experiment takes patience and practice. If you want to develop this skill, try to use the rules to solve some of the exercises in Chapter 3. Proofs of the rules below can be found in the text by W. Feller listed in the references to Chapter 3.

Multiplicative Rule

You have k sets of different elements, n_1 in the first set, n_2 in the second set, …, and n_k in the kth set. Suppose you want to form a sample of k elements *by taking one element from each of the* k *sets*. The number of different samples that can be formed is the product

$$n_1 \cdot n_2 \cdot n_3 \cdots \cdot n_k$$

EXAMPLE **A.1**

A product can be shipped by four airlines and each airline can ship via three different routes. How many distinct ways exist to ship the product?

SOLUTION

A method of shipment corresponds to a pairing of one airline and one route. Therefore, $k = 2$, the number of airlines is $n_1 = 4$, the number of routes is $n_2 = 3$, and the number of ways to ship the product is

$$n_1 \cdot n_2 = (4)(3) = 12$$

How the multiplicative rule works can be seen by using a tree diagram, introduced in Section 3.6. The airline choice is shown by three branching lines in Figure A.1.

FIGURE A.1
Tree diagram for
airline example

EXAMPLE A.2   You have twenty candidates for three different executive positions, E_1, E_2, and E_3. How many different ways could you fill the positions?

SOLUTION
For this example, there are $k = 3$ sets of elements:

Set 1: The candidates available to fill position E_1

Set 2: The candidates remaining (after filling E_1) that are available to fill E_2

Set 3: The candidates remaining (after filling E_1 and E_2) that are available to fill E_3

The numbers of elements in the sets are $n_1 = 20$, $n_2 = 19$, and $n_3 = 18$. Thus, the number of different ways to fill the three positions is

$$n_1 \cdot n_2 \cdot n_3 = (20)(19)(18) = 6,480$$

Partitions Rule
You have a *single* set of N distinctly different elements, and you want to partition it into k sets, the first set containing n_1 elements, the second containing n_2 elements, …, and the kth containing n_k elements. The number of different partitions is

$$\frac{N!}{n_1! n_2! \cdots n_k!} \qquad \text{where } n_1 + n_2 + n_3 + \cdots + n_k = N$$

EXAMPLE A.3   You have twelve construction workers available for three job sites. Suppose you want to assign three workers to job 1, four to job 2, and five to job 3. How many different ways could you make this assignment?

SOLUTION
For this example, $k = 3$ (corresponding to the $k = 3$ job sites), $N = 12$, and $n_1 = 3$, $n_2 = 4$, $n_3 = 5$. Then, the number of different ways to assign the workers to the job sites is

$$\frac{N!}{n_1! n_2! n_3!} = \frac{12!}{3!4!5!} = \frac{12 \cdot 11 \cdot 10 \cdot \cdots \cdot 3 \cdot 2 \cdot 1}{(3 \cdot 2 \cdot 1)(4 \cdot 3 \cdot 2 \cdot 1)(5 \cdot 4 \cdot 3 \cdot 2 \cdot 1)} = 27,720$$

Combinations Rule

The combinations rule given in Chapter 3 is a special case ($k = 2$) of the partitions rule. That is, sampling is equivalent to partitioning a set of N elements into $k = 2$ groups: elements that appear in the sample and those that do not. Let $n_1 = n$, the number of elements in the sample, and $n_2 = N - n$, the number of elements remaining. Then the number of different samples of n elements that can be selected from N is

$$\frac{N!}{n_1! n_2!} = \frac{N!}{n!(N - n)!} = \binom{N}{n}$$

This formula was given in Section 3.1.

EXAMPLE A.4   How many samples of four fire fighters can be selected from a group of 10?

SOLUTION

We have $N = 10$ and $n = 4$; then,

$$\binom{N}{n} = \binom{10}{4} = \frac{10!}{4!6!} = \frac{10 \cdot 9 \cdot 8 \cdots 3 \cdot 2 \cdot 1}{(4 \cdot 3 \cdot 2 \cdot 1)(6 \cdot 5 \cdots 2 \cdot 1)} = 210$$

APPENDIX B
TABLES

Contents

TABLE I Random Numbers

Row	1	2	3	4	5	6	7	8	9	10	11	12	13	14
1	10480	15011	01536	02011	81647	91646	69179	14194	62590	36207	20969	99570	91291	90700
2	22368	46573	25595	85393	30995	89198	27982	53402	93965	34095	52666	19174	39615	99505
3	24130	48360	22527	97265	76393	64809	15179	24830	49340	32081	30680	19655	63348	58629
4	42167	93093	06243	61680	07856	16376	39440	53537	71341	57004	00849	74917	97758	16379
5	37570	39975	81837	16656	06121	91782	60468	81305	49684	60672	14110	06927	01263	54613
6	77921	06907	11008	42751	27756	53498	18602	70659	90655	15053	21916	81825	44394	42880
7	99562	72905	56420	69994	98872	31016	71194	18738	44013	48840	63213	21069	10634	12952
8	96301	91977	05463	07972	18876	20922	94595	56869	69014	60045	18425	84903	42508	32307
9	89579	14342	63661	10281	17453	18103	57740	84378	25331	12566	58678	44947	05585	56941
10	85475	36857	53342	53988	53060	59533	38867	62300	08158	17983	16439	11458	18593	64952
11	28918	69578	88231	33276	70997	79936	56865	05859	90106	31595	01547	85590	91610	78188
12	63553	40961	48235	03427	49626	69445	18663	72695	52180	20847	12234	90511	33703	90322
13	09429	93969	52636	92737	88974	33488	36320	17617	30015	08272	84115	27156	30613	74952
14	10365	61129	87529	85689	48237	52267	67689	93394	01511	26358	85104	20285	29975	89868
15	07119	97336	71048	08178	77233	13916	47564	81056	97735	85977	29372	74461	28551	90707
16	51085	12765	51821	51259	77452	16308	60756	92144	49442	53900	70960	63990	75601	40719
17	02368	21382	52404	60268	89368	19885	55322	44819	01188	65255	64835	44919	05944	55157
18	01011	54092	33362	94904	31273	04146	18594	29852	71585	85030	51132	01915	92747	64951
19	52162	53916	46369	58586	23216	14513	83149	98736	23495	64350	94738	17752	35156	35749
20	07056	97628	33787	09998	42698	06691	76988	13602	51851	46104	88916	19509	25625	58104
21	48663	91245	85828	14346	09172	30168	90229	04734	59193	22178	30421	61666	99904	32812
22	54164	58492	22421	74103	47070	25306	76468	26384	58151	06646	21524	15227	96909	44592
23	32639	32363	05597	24200	13363	38005	94342	28728	35806	06912	17012	64161	18296	22851
24	29334	27001	87637	87308	58731	00256	45834	15398	46557	41135	10367	07684	36188	18510
25	02488	33062	28834	07351	19731	92420	60952	61280	50001	67658	32586	86679	50720	94953
26	81525	72295	04839	96423	24878	82651	66566	14778	76797	14780	13300	87074	79666	95725
27	29676	20591	68086	26432	46901	20849	89768	81536	86645	12659	92259	57102	80428	25280
28	00742	57392	39064	66432	84673	40027	32832	61362	98947	96067	64760	64584	96096	98253
29	05366	04213	25669	26422	44407	44048	37937	63904	45766	66134	75470	66520	34693	90449
30	91921	26418	64117	94305	26766	25940	39972	22209	71500	64568	91402	42416	07844	69618
31	00582	04711	87917	77341	42206	35126	74087	99547	81817	42607	43808	76655	62028	76630
32	00725	69884	62797	56170	86324	88072	76222	36086	84637	93161	76038	65855	77919	88006
33	69011	65795	95876	55293	18988	27354	26575	08625	40801	59920	29841	80150	12777	48501
34	25976	57948	29888	88604	67917	48708	18912	82271	65424	69774	33611	54262	85963	03547
35	09763	83473	73577	12908	30883	18317	28290	35797	05998	41688	34952	37888	38917	88050

continued

TABLE I Continued

Row	1	2	3	4	5	6	7	8	9	10	11	12	13	14
36	91576	42595	27958	30134	04024	86385	29880	99730	55536	84855	29080	09250	79656	73211
37	17955	56349	90999	49127	20044	59931	06115	20542	18059	02008	73708	83517	36103	42791
38	46503	18584	18845	49618	02304	51038	20655	58727	28168	15475	56942	53389	20562	87338
39	92157	89634	94824	78171	84610	82834	09922	25417	44137	48413	25555	21246	35509	20468
40	14577	62765	35605	81263	39667	47358	56873	56307	61607	49518	89656	20103	77490	18062
41	98427	07523	33362	64270	01638	92477	66969	98420	04880	45585	46565	04102	46880	45709
42	34914	63976	88720	82765	34476	17032	87589	40836	32427	70002	70663	88863	77775	69348
43	70060	28277	39475	46473	23219	53416	94970	25832	69975	94884	19661	72828	00102	66794
44	53976	54914	06990	67245	68350	82948	11398	42878	80287	88267	47363	46634	06541	97809
45	76072	29515	40980	07391	58745	25774	22987	80059	39911	96189	41151	14222	60697	59583
46	90725	52210	83974	29992	65831	38857	50490	83765	55657	14361	31720	57375	56228	41546
47	64364	67412	33339	31926	14883	24413	59744	92351	97473	89286	35931	04110	23726	51900
48	08962	00358	31662	25388	61642	34072	81249	35648	56891	69352	48373	45578	78547	81788
49	95012	68379	93526	70765	10592	04542	76463	54328	02349	17247	28865	14777	62730	92277
50	15664	10493	20492	38391	91132	21999	59516	81652	27195	48223	46751	22923	32261	85653
51	16408	81899	04153	53381	79401	21438	83035	92350	36693	31238	59649	91754	72772	02338
52	18629	81953	05520	91962	04739	13092	97662	24822	94730	06496	35090	04822	86774	98289
53	73115	35101	47498	87637	99016	71060	88824	71013	18735	20286	23153	72924	35165	43040
54	57491	16703	23167	49323	45021	33132	12544	41035	80780	45393	44812	12512	98931	91202
55	30405	83946	23792	14422	15059	45799	22716	19792	09983	74353	68668	30429	70735	25499
56	16631	35006	85900	98275	32388	52390	16815	69290	82732	38480	73817	32523	41961	44437
57	96773	20206	42559	78985	05300	22164	24369	54224	35083	19687	11052	91491	60383	19746
58	38935	64202	14349	82674	66523	44133	00697	35552	35970	19124	63318	29686	03387	59846
59	31624	76384	17403	53363	44167	64486	64758	75366	76554	31601	12614	33072	60332	92325
60	78919	19474	23632	27889	47914	02584	37680	20801	72152	39339	34806	08930	85001	87820
61	03931	33309	57047	74211	63445	17361	62825	39908	05607	91284	68833	25570	38818	46920
62	74426	33278	43972	10110	89917	15665	52872	73823	73144	88662	88970	74492	51805	99378
63	09066	00903	20795	95452	92648	45454	09552	88815	16553	51125	79375	97596	16296	66092
64	42238	12426	87025	14267	20979	04508	64535	31355	86064	29472	47689	05974	52468	16834
65	16153	08002	26504	41744	81959	65642	74240	56302	00033	67107	77510	70625	28725	34191
66	21457	40742	29820	96783	29400	21840	15035	34537	33310	06116	95240	15957	16572	06004
67	21581	57802	02050	89728	17937	37621	47075	42080	97403	48626	68995	43805	33386	21597
68	55612	78095	83197	33732	05810	24813	86902	60397	16489	03264	88525	42786	05269	92532
69	44657	66999	99324	51281	84463	60563	79312	93454	68876	25471	93911	25650	12682	73572
70	91340	84979	46949	81973	37949	61023	43997	15263	80644	43942	89203	71795	99533	50501

TABLE I Continued

Row	1	2	3	4	5	6	7	8	9	10	11	12	13	14
71	91227	21199	31935	27022	84067	05462	35216	14486	29891	68607	41867	14951	91696	85065
72	50001	38140	66321	19924	72163	09538	12151	06878	91903	18749	34405	56087	82790	70925
73	65390	05224	72958	28609	81406	39147	25549	48542	42627	45233	57202	94617	23772	07896
74	27504	96131	83944	41575	10573	08619	64482	73923	36152	05184	94142	25299	84387	34925
75	37169	94851	39117	89632	00959	16487	65536	49071	39782	17095	02330	74301	00275	48280
76	11508	70225	51111	38351	19444	66499	71945	05422	13442	78675	84081	66938	93654	59894
77	37449	30362	06694	54690	04052	53115	62757	95348	78662	11163	81651	50245	34971	52924
78	46515	70331	85922	38329	57015	15765	97161	17869	45349	61796	66345	81073	49106	79860
79	30986	81223	42416	58353	21532	30502	32305	86482	05174	07901	54339	58861	74818	46942
80	63798	64995	46583	09785	44160	78128	83991	42865	92520	83531	80377	35909	81250	54238
81	82486	84846	99254	67632	43218	50076	21361	64816	51202	88124	41870	52689	51275	83556
82	21885	32906	92431	09060	64297	51674	64126	62570	26123	05155	59194	52799	28225	85762
83	60336	98782	07408	53458	13564	59089	26445	29789	85205	41001	12535	12133	14645	23541
84	43937	46891	24010	25560	86355	33941	25786	54990	71899	15475	95434	98227	21824	19585
85	97656	63175	89303	16275	07100	92063	21942	18611	47348	20203	18534	03862	78095	50136
86	03299	01221	05418	38982	55758	92237	26759	86367	21216	98442	08303	56613	91511	75928
87	79626	06486	03574	17668	07785	76020	79924	25651	83325	88428	85076	72811	22717	50585
88	85636	68335	47539	03129	65651	11977	02510	26113	99447	68645	34327	15152	55230	93448
89	18039	14367	64337	06177	12143	46609	32989	74014	64708	00533	35398	58408	13261	47908
90	08362	15656	60627	36478	65648	16764	53412	09013	07832	41574	17639	82163	60859	75567
91	79556	29068	04142	16268	15387	12856	66227	38358	22478	73373	88732	09443	82558	05250
92	92608	82674	27072	32534	17075	27698	98204	63863	11951	34648	88022	56148	34925	57031
93	23982	25835	40055	67006	12293	02753	14827	23235	35071	99704	37543	11601	35503	85171
94	09915	96306	05908	97901	28395	14186	00821	80703	70426	75647	76310	88717	37890	40129
95	59037	33300	26695	62247	69927	76123	50842	43834	86654	70959	79725	93872	28117	19233
96	42488	78077	69882	61657	34136	79180	97526	43092	04098	73571	80799	76536	71255	64239
97	46764	86273	63003	93017	31204	36692	40202	35275	57306	55543	53203	18098	47625	88684
98	03237	45430	55417	63282	90816	17349	88298	90183	36600	78406	06216	95787	42579	90730
99	86591	81482	52667	61582	14972	90053	89534	76036	49199	43716	97548	04379	46370	28672
100	38534	01715	94964	87288	65680	43772	39560	12918	86537	62738	19636	51132	25739	56947

Source: Abridged from W. H. Beyer (ed.). *CRC Standard Mathematical Tables*, 24th edition. (Cleveland: The Chemical Rubber Company), 1976. Reproduced by permission of the publisher.

TABLE II Binomial Probabilities

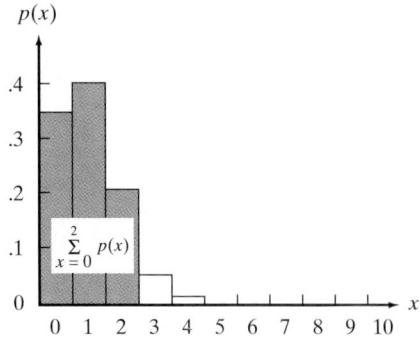

Tabulated values are $\sum_{x=0}^{k} p(x)$. (Computations are rounded at the third decimal place.)

a. $n = 5$

k	.01	.05	.10	.20	.30	.40	.50	.60	.70	.80	.90	.95	.99
0	.951	.774	.590	.328	.168	.078	.031	.010	.002	.000	.000	.000	.000
1	.999	.977	.919	.737	.528	.337	.188	.087	.031	.007	.000	.000	.000
2	1.000	.999	.991	.942	.837	.683	.500	.317	.163	.058	.009	.001	.000
3	1.000	1.000	1.000	.993	.969	.913	.812	.663	.472	.263	.081	.023	.001
4	1.000	1.000	1.000	1.000	.998	.990	.969	.922	.832	.672	.410	.226	.049

b. $n = 6$

k	.01	.05	.10	.20	.30	.40	.50	.60	.70	.80	.90	.95	.99
0	.941	.735	.531	.262	.118	.047	.016	.004	.001	.000	.000	.000	.000
1	.999	.967	.886	.655	.420	.233	.109	.041	.011	.002	.000	.000	.000
2	1.000	.998	.984	.901	.744	.544	.344	.179	.070	.017	.001	.000	.000
3	1.000	1.000	.999	.983	.930	.821	.656	.456	.256	.099	.016	.002	.000
4	1.000	1.000	1.000	.998	.989	.959	.891	.767	.580	.345	.114	.033	.001
5	1.000	1.000	1.000	1.000	.999	.996	.984	.953	.882	.738	.469	.265	.059

c. $n = 7$

k	.01	.05	.10	.20	.30	.40	.50	.60	.70	.80	.90	.95	.99
0	.932	.698	.478	.210	.082	.028	.008	.002	.000	.000	.000	.000	.000
1	.998	.956	.850	.577	.329	.159	.063	.019	.004	.000	.000	.000	.000
2	1.000	.996	.974	.852	.647	.420	.227	.096	.029	.005	.000	.000	.000
3	1.000	1.000	.997	.967	.874	.710	.500	.290	.126	.033	.003	.000	.000
4	1.000	1.000	1.000	.995	.971	.904	.773	.580	.353	.148	.026	.004	.000
5	1.000	1.000	1.000	1.000	.996	.981	.937	.841	.671	.423	.150	.044	.002
6	1.000	1.000	1.000	1.000	1.000	.998	.992	.972	.918	.790	.522	.302	.068

TABLE II   Continued

d. *n* = 8

k \ p	.01	.05	.10	.20	.30	.40	.50	.60	.70	.80	.90	.95	.99
0	.923	.663	.430	.168	.058	.017	.004	.001	.000	.000	.000	.000	.000
1	.997	.943	.813	.503	.255	.106	.035	.009	.001	.000	.000	.000	.000
2	1.000	.994	.962	.797	.552	.315	.145	.050	.011	.001	.000	.000	.000
3	1.000	1.000	.995	.944	.806	.594	.363	.174	.058	.010	.000	.000	.000
4	1.000	1.000	1.000	.990	.942	.826	.637	.406	.194	.056	.005	.000	.000
5	1.000	1.000	1.000	.999	.989	.950	.855	.685	.448	.203	.038	.006	.000
6	1.000	1.000	1.000	1.000	.999	.991	.965	.894	.745	.497	.187	.057	.003
7	1.000	1.000	1.000	1.000	1.000	.999	.996	.983	.942	.832	.570	.337	.077

e. *n* = 9

k \ p	.01	.05	.10	.20	.30	.40	.50	.60	.70	.80	.90	.95	.99
0	.914	.630	.387	.134	.040	.010	.002	.000	.000	.000	.000	.000	.000
1	.997	.929	.775	.436	.196	.071	.020	.004	.000	.000	.000	.000	.000
2	1.000	.992	.947	.738	.463	.232	.090	.025	.004	.000	.000	.000	.000
3	1.000	.999	.992	.914	.730	.483	.254	.099	.025	.003	.000	.000	.000
4	1.000	1.000	.999	.980	.901	.733	.500	.267	.099	.020	.001	.000	.000
5	1.000	1.000	1.000	.997	.975	.901	.746	.517	.270	.086	.008	.001	.000
6	1.000	1.000	1.000	1.000	.996	.975	.910	.768	.537	.262	.053	.008	.000
7	1.000	1.000	1.000	1.000	1.000	.996	.980	.929	.804	.564	.225	.071	.003
8	1.000	1.000	1.000	1.000	1.000	1.000	.998	.990	.960	.866	.613	.370	.086

f. *n* = 10

k \ p	.01	.05	.10	.20	.30	.40	.50	.60	.70	.80	.90	.95	.99
0	.904	.599	.349	.107	.028	.006	.001	.000	.000	.000	.000	.000	.000
1	.996	.914	.376	.376	.149	.046	.011	.002	.000	.000	.000	.000	.000
2	1.000	.988	.930	.678	.383	.167	.055	.012	.002	.000	.000	.000	.000
3	1.000	.999	.987	.879	.650	.382	.172	.055	.011	.001	.000	.000	.000
4	1.000	1.000	.998	.967	.850	.633	.377	.166	.047	.006	.000	.000	.000
5	1.000	1.000	1.000	.999	.953	.834	.623	.367	.150	.033	.002	.000	.000
6	1.000	1.000	1.000	.999	.989	.945	.828	.618	.350	.121	.013	.001	.000
7	1.000	1.000	1.000	1.000	.998	.988	.945	.833	.617	.322	.070	.012	.000
8	1.000	1.000	1.000	1.000	1.000	.998	.989	.954	.851	.624	.264	.086	.004
9	1.000	1.000	1.000	1.000	1.000	1.000	.999	.994	.972	.893	.651	.401	.096

continued

TABLE II Continued

g. $n = 15$

k	.01	.05	.10	.20	.30	.40	.50	.60	.70	.80	.90	.95	.99
0	.860	.463	.206	.035	.005	.000	.000	.000	.000	.000	.000	.000	.000
1	.990	.829	.549	.167	.035	.005	.000	.000	.000	.000	.000	.000	.000
2	1.000	.964	.816	.398	.127	.027	.004	.000	.000	.000	.000	.000	.000
3	1.000	.995	.944	.648	.297	.091	.018	.002	.000	.000	.000	.000	.000
4	1.000	.999	.987	.838	.515	.217	.059	.009	.001	.000	.000	.000	.000
5	1.000	1.000	.998	.939	.722	.403	.151	.034	.004	.000	.000	.000	.000
6	1.000	1.000	1.000	.982	.869	.610	.304	.095	.015	.001	.000	.000	.000
7	1.000	1.000	1.000	.996	.950	.787	.500	.213	.050	.004	.000	.000	.000
8	1.000	1.000	1.000	.999	.985	.905	.696	.390	.131	.018	.000	.000	.000
9	1.000	1.000	1.000	1.000	.996	.966	.849	.597	.278	.061	.002	.000	.000
10	1.000	1.000	1.000	1.000	.999	.991	.941	.783	.485	.164	.013	.001	.000
11	1.000	1.000	1.000	1.000	1.000	.998	.982	.909	.703	.352	.056	.005	.000
12	1.000	1.000	1.000	1.000	1.000	1.000	.996	.973	.873	.602	.184	.036	.000
13	1.000	1.000	1.000	1.000	1.000	1.000	1.000	.995	.965	.833	.451	.171	.010
14	1.000	1.000	1.000	1.000	1.000	1.000	1.000	1.000	.995	.965	.794	.537	.140

h. $n = 20$

k	.01	.05	.10	.20	.30	.40	.50	.60	.70	.80	.90	.95	.99
0	.818	.358	.122	.012	.001	.000	.000	.000	.000	.000	.000	.000	.000
1	.983	.736	.392	.069	.008	.001	.000	.000	.000	.000	.000	.000	.000
2	.999	.925	.677	.206	.035	.004	.000	.000	.000	.000	.000	.000	.000
3	1.000	.984	.867	.411	.107	.016	.001	.000	.000	.000	.000	.000	.000
4	1.000	.997	.957	.630	.238	.051	.006	.000	.000	.000	.000	.000	.000
5	1.000	1.000	.989	.804	.416	.126	.021	.002	.000	.000	.000	.000	.000
6	1.000	1.000	.998	.913	.608	.250	.058	.006	.000	.000	.000	.000	.000
7	1.000	1.000	1.000	.968	.772	.416	.132	.021	.001	.000	.000	.000	.000
8	1.000	1.000	1.000	.990	.887	.596	.252	.057	.005	.000	.000	.000	.000
9	1.000	1.000	1.000	.997	.952	.755	.412	.128	.017	.001	.000	.000	.000
10	1.000	1.000	1.000	.999	.983	.872	.588	.245	.048	.003	.000	.000	.000
11	1.000	1.000	1.000	1.000	.995	.943	.748	.404	.113	.010	.000	.000	.000
12	1.000	1.000	1.000	1.000	.999	.979	.868	.584	.228	.032	.000	.000	.000
13	1.000	1.000	1.000	1.000	1.000	.994	.942	.750	.392	.087	.002	.000	.000
14	1.000	1.000	1.000	1.000	1.000	.998	.979	.874	.584	.196	.011	.000	.000
15	1.000	1.000	1.000	1.000	1.000	1.000	.994	.949	.762	.370	.043	.003	.000
16	1.000	1.000	1.000	1.000	1.000	1.000	.999	.984	.893	.589	.133	.016	.000
17	1.000	1.000	1.000	1.000	1.000	1.000	1.000	.996	.965	.794	.323	.075	.001
18	1.000	1.000	1.000	1.000	1.000	1.000	1.000	.999	.992	.931	.608	.264	.017
19	1.000	1.000	1.000	1.000	1.000	1.000	1.000	1.000	.999	.988	.878	.642	.182

TABLE II Continued

i. $n = 25$

k	.01	.05	.10	.20	.30	.40	.50	.60	.70	.80	.90	.95	.99
0	.778	.277	.072	.004	.000	.000	.000	.000	.000	.000	.000	.000	.000
1	.974	.642	.271	.027	.002	.000	.000	.000	.000	.000	.000	.000	.000
2	.998	.873	.537	.098	.009	.000	.000	.000	.000	.000	.000	.000	.000
3	1.000	.966	.764	.234	.033	.002	.000	.000	.000	.000	.000	.000	.000
4	1.000	.993	.902	.421	.090	.009	.000	.000	.000	.000	.000	.000	.000
5	1.000	.999	.967	.617	.193	.029	.002	.000	.000	.000	.000	.000	.000
6	1.000	1.000	.991	.780	.341	.074	.007	.000	.000	.000	.000	.000	.000
7	1.000	1.000	.998	.891	.512	.154	.022	.001	.000	.000	.000	.000	.000
8	1.000	1.000	1.000	.953	.677	.274	.054	.004	.000	.000	.000	.000	.000
9	1.000	1.000	1.000	.983	.811	.425	.115	.013	.000	.000	.000	.000	.000
10	1.000	1.000	1.000	.994	.902	.586	.212	.034	.002	.000	.000	.000	.000
11	1.000	1.000	1.000	.998	.956	.732	.345	.078	.006	.000	.000	.000	.000
12	1.000	1.000	1.000	1.000	.983	.846	.500	.154	.017	.000	.000	.000	.000
13	1.000	1.000	1.000	1.000	.994	.922	.655	.268	.044	.002	.000	.000	.000
14	1.000	1.000	1.000	1.000	.998	.966	.788	.414	.098	.006	.000	.000	.000
15	1.000	1.000	1.000	1.000	1.000	.987	.885	.575	.189	.017	.000	.000	.000
16	1.000	1.000	1.000	1.000	1.000	.996	.946	.726	.323	.047	.000	.000	.000
17	1.000	1.000	1.000	1.000	1.000	.999	.978	.846	.488	.109	.002	.000	.000
18	1.000	1.000	1.000	1.000	1.000	1.000	.993	.926	.659	.220	.009	.000	.000
19	1.000	1.000	1.000	1.000	1.000	1.000	.998	.971	.807	.383	.033	.001	.000
20	1.000	1.000	1.000	1.000	1.000	1.000	1.000	.991	.910	.579	.098	.007	.000
21	1.000	1.000	1.000	1.000	1.000	1.000	1.000	.998	.967	.766	.236	.034	.000
22	1.000	1.000	1.000	1.000	1.000	1.000	1.000	1.000	.991	.902	.463	.127	.002
23	1.000	1.000	1.000	1.000	1.000	1.000	1.000	1.000	.998	.973	.729	.358	.026
24	1.000	1.000	1.000	1.000	1.000	1.000	1.000	1.000	1.000	.996	.928	.723	.222

Table III   Poisson Probabilities

Tabulated values are $\sum_{x=0}^{k} p(x)$. (Computations are rounded at the third decimal place.)

λ \ x	0	1	2	3	4	5	6	7	8	9
.02	.980	1.000								
.04	.961	.999	1.000							
.06	.942	.998	1.000							
.08	.923	.997	1.000							
.10	.905	.995	1.000							
.15	.861	.990	.999	1.000						
.20	.819	.982	.999	1.000						
.25	.779	.974	.998	1.000						
.30	.741	.963	.996	1.000						
.35	.705	.951	.994	1.000						
.40	.670	.938	.992	.999	1.000					
.45	.638	.925	.989	.999	1.000					
.50	.607	.910	.986	.998	1.000					
.55	.577	.894	.982	.998	1.000					
.60	.549	.878	.977	.997	1.000					
.65	.522	.861	.972	.996	.999	1.000				
.70	.497	.844	.966	.994	.999	1.000				
.75	.472	.827	.959	.993	.999	1.000				
.80	.449	.809	.953	.991	.999	1.000				
.85	.427	.791	.945	.989	.998	1.000				
.90	.407	.772	.937	.987	.998	1.000				
.95	.387	.754	.929	.981	.997	1.000				
1.00	.368	.736	.920	.981	.996	.999	1.000			
1.1	.333	.699	.900	.974	.995	.999	1.000			
1.2	.301	.663	.879	.966	.992	.998	1.000			
1.3	.273	.627	.857	.957	.989	.998	1.000			
1.4	.247	.592	.833	.946	.986	.997	.999	1.000		
1.5	.223	.558	.809	.934	.981	.996	.999	1.000		

TABLE III   **Continued**

λ \ x	0	1	2	3	4	5	6	7	8	9
1.6	.202	.525	.783	.921	.976	.994	.999	1.000		
1.7	.183	.493	.757	.907	.970	.992	.998	1.000		
1.8	.165	.463	.731	.891	.964	.990	.997	.999	1.000	
1.9	.150	.434	.704	.875	.956	.987	.997	.999	1.000	
2.0	.135	.406	.677	.857	.947	.983	.995	.999	1.000	
2.2	.111	.355	.623	.819	.928	.975	.993	.998	1.000	
2.4	.091	.308	.570	.779	.904	.964	.988	.997	.999	1.000
2.6	.074	.267	.518	.736	.877	.951	.983	.995	.999	1.000
2.8	.061	.231	.469	.692	.848	.935	.976	.992	.998	.999
3.0	.050	.199	.423	.647	.815	.916	.966	.988	.996	.999
3.2	.041	.171	.380	.603	.781	.895	.955	.983	.994	.998
3.4	.033	.147	.340	.558	.744	.871	.942	.977	.992	.997
3.6	.027	.126	.303	.515	.706	.844	.927	.969	.988	.996
3.8	.022	.107	.269	.473	.668	.816	.909	.960	.984	.994
4.0	.018	.092	.238	.433	.629	.785	.889	.949	.979	.992
4.2	.015	.078	.210	.395	.590	.753	.867	.936	.972	.989
4.4	.012	.066	.185	.359	.551	.720	.844	.921	.964	.985
4.6	.010	.056	.163	.326	.513	.686	.818	.905	.955	.980
4.8	.008	.048	.143	.294	.476	.651	.791	.887	.944	.975
5.0	.007	.040	.125	.265	.440	.616	.762	.867	.932	.968
5.2	.006	.034	.109	.238	.406	.581	.732	.845	.918	.960
5.4	.005	.029	.095	.213	.373	.546	.702	.822	.903	.951
5.6	.004	.024	.082	.191	.342	.512	.670	.797	.886	.941
5.8	.003	.021	.072	.170	.313	.478	.638	.771	.867	.929
6.0	.002	.017	.062	.151	.285	.446	.606	.744	.847	.916

λ	10	11	12	13	14	15	16
2.8	1.000						
3.0	1.000						
3.2	1.000						
3.4	.999	1.000					
3.6	.999	1.000					
3.8	.998	.999	1.000				
4.0	.997	.999	1.000				
4.2	.996	.999	1.000				
4.4	.994	.998	.999	1.000			
4.6	.992	.997	.999	1.000			
4.8	.990	.996	.999	1.000			
5.0	.986	.995	.998	.999	1.000		
5.2	.982	.993	.997	.999	1.000		
5.4	.977	.990	.996	.999	1.000		
5.6	.972	.988	.995	.998	.999	1.000	
5.8	.965	.984	.993	.997	.999	1.000	
6.0	.957	.980	.991	.996	.999	.999	1.000

continued

Table III   Continued

λ \ x	0	1	2	3	4	5	6	7	8	9
6.2	.002	.015	.054	.134	.259	.414	.574	.716	.826	.902
6.4	.002	.012	.046	.119	.235	.384	.542	.687	.803	.886
6.6	.001	.010	.040	.105	.213	.355	.511	.658	.780	.869
6.8	.001	.009	.034	.093	.192	.327	.480	.628	.755	.850
7.0	.001	.007	.030	.082	.173	.301	.450	.599	.729	.830
7.2	.001	.006	.025	.072	.156	.276	.420	.569	.703	.810
7.4	.001	.005	.022	.063	.140	.253	.392	.539	.676	.788
7.6	.001	.004	.019	.055	.125	.231	.365	.510	.648	.765
7.8	.000	.004	.016	.048	.112	.210	.338	.481	.620	.741
8.0	.000	.003	.014	.042	.100	.191	.313	.453	.593	.717
8.5	.000	.002	.009	.030	.074	.150	.256	.386	.523	.653
9.0	.000	.001	.006	.021	.055	.116	.207	.324	.456	.587
9.5	.000	.001	.004	.015	.040	.089	.165	.269	.392	.522
10.0	.000	.000	.003	.010	.029	.067	.130	.220	.333	.458

	10	11	12	13	14	15	16	17	18	19
6.2	.949	.975	.989	.995	.998	.999	1.000			
6.4	.939	.969	.986	.994	.997	.999	1.000			
6.6	.927	.963	.982	.992	.997	.999	.999	1.000		
6.8	.915	.955	.978	.990	.996	.998	.999	1.000		
7.0	.901	.947	.973	.987	.994	.998	.999	1.000		
7.2	.887	.937	.967	.984	.993	.997	.999	.999	1.000	
7.4	.871	.926	.961	.980	.991	.996	.998	.999	1.000	
7.6	.854	.915	.954	.976	.989	.995	.998	.999	1.000	
7.8	.835	.902	.945	.971	.986	.993	.997	.999	1.000	
8.0	.816	.888	.936	.966	.983	.992	.996	.998	.999	1.000
8.5	.763	.849	.909	.949	.973	.986	.993	.997	.999	.999
9.0	.706	.803	.876	.926	.959	.978	.989	.995	.998	.999
9.5	.645	.752	.836	.898	.940	.967	.982	.991	.996	.998
10.0	.583	.697	.792	.864	.917	.951	.973	.986	.993	.997

	20	21	22
8.5	1.000		
9.0	1.000		
9.5	.999	1.000	
10.0	.998	.999	1.000

TABLE III   Continued

λ \ x	0	1	2	3	4	5	6	7	8	9
10.5	.000	.000	.002	.007	.021	.050	.102	.179	.279	.397
11.0	.000	.000	.001	.005	.015	.038	.079	.143	.232	.341
11.5	.000	.000	.001	.003	.011	.028	.060	.114	.191	.289
12.0	.000	.000	.001	.002	.008	.020	.046	.090	.155	.242
12.5	.000	.000	.000	.002	.005	.015	.035	.070	.125	.201
13.0	.000	.000	.000	.001	.004	.011	.026	.054	.100	.166
13.5	.000	.000	.000	.001	.003	.008	.019	.041	.079	.135
14.0	.000	.000	.000	.000	.002	.006	.014	.032	.062	.109
14.5	.000	.000	.000	.000	.001	.004	.010	.024	.048	.088
15.0	.000	.000	.000	.000	.001	.003	.008	.018	.037	.070

	10	11	12	13	14	15	16	17	18	19
10.5	.521	.639	.742	.825	.888	.932	.960	.978	.988	.994
11.0	.460	.579	.689	.781	.854	.907	.944	.968	.982	.991
11.5	.402	.520	.633	.733	.815	.878	.924	.954	.974	.986
12.0	.347	.462	.576	.682	.772	.844	.899	.937	.963	.979
12.5	.297	.406	.519	.628	.725	.806	.869	.916	.948	.969
13.0	.252	.353	.463	.573	.675	.764	.835	.890	.930	.957
13.5	.211	.304	.409	.518	.623	.718	.798	.861	.908	.942
14.0	.176	.260	.358	.464	.570	.669	.756	.827	.883	.923
14.5	.145	.220	.311	.413	.518	.619	.711	.790	.853	.901
15.0	.118	.185	.268	.363	.466	.568	.664	.749	.819	.875

	20	21	22	23	24	25	26	27	28	29
10.5	.997	.999	.999	1.000						
11.0	.995	.998	.999	1.000						
11.5	.992	.996	.998	.999	1.000					
12.0	.988	.994	.987	.999	.999	1.000				
12.5	.983	.991	.995	.998	.999	.999	1.000			
13.0	.975	.986	.992	.996	.998	.999	1.000			
13.5	.965	.980	.989	.994	.997	.998	.999	1.000		
14.0	.952	.971	.983	.991	.995	.997	.999	.999	1.000	
14.5	.936	.960	.976	.986	.992	.996	.998	.999	.999	1.000
15.0	.917	.947	.967	.981	.989	.994	.997	.998	.999	1.000

continued

TABLE III Continued

λ \ x	4	5	6	7	8	9	10	11	12	13
16	.000	.001	.004	.010	.022	.043	.077	.127	.193	.275
17	.000	.001	.002	.005	.013	.026	.049	.085	.135	.201
18	.000	.000	.001	.003	.007	.015	.030	.055	.092	.143
19	.000	.000	.001	.002	.004	.009	.018	.035	.061	.098
20	.000	.000	.000	.001	.002	.005	.011	.021	.039	.066
21	.000	.000	.000	.000	.001	.003	.006	.013	.025	.043
22	.000	.000	.000	.000	.001	.002	.004	.008	.015	.028
23	.000	.000	.000	.000	.000	.001	.002	.004	.009	.017
24	.000	.000	.000	.000	.000	.000	.001	.003	.005	.011
25	.000	.000	.000	.000	.000	.000	.001	.001	.003	.006

	14	15	16	17	18	19	20	21	22	23
16	.368	.467	.566	.659	.742	.812	.868	.911	.942	.963
17	.281	.371	.468	.564	.655	.736	.805	.861	.905	.937
18	.208	.287	.375	.469	.562	.651	.731	.799	.855	.899
19	.150	.215	.292	.378	.469	.561	.647	.725	.793	.849
20	.105	.157	.221	.297	.381	.470	.559	.644	.721	.787
21	.072	.111	.163	.227	.302	.384	.471	.558	.640	.716
22	.048	.077	.117	.169	.232	.306	.387	.472	.556	.637
23	.031	.052	.082	.123	.175	.238	.310	.389	.472	.555
24	.020	.034	.056	.087	.128	.180	.243	.314	.392	.473
25	.012	.022	.038	.060	.092	.134	.185	.247	.318	.394

	24	25	26	27	28	29	30	31	32	33
16	.978	.987	.993	.996	.998	.999	.999	1.000		
17	.959	.975	.985	.991	.995	.997	.999	.999	1.000	
18	.932	.955	.972	.983	.990	.994	.997	.998	.999	1.000
19	.893	.927	.951	.969	.980	.988	.993	.996	.998	.999
20	.843	.888	.922	.948	.966	.978	.987	.992	.995	.997
21	.782	.838	.883	.917	.944	.963	.976	.985	.991	.994
22	.712	.777	.832	.877	.913	.940	.959	.973	.983	.989
23	.635	.708	.772	.827	.873	.908	.936	.956	.971	.981
24	.554	.632	.704	.768	.823	.868	.904	.932	.953	.969
25	.473	.553	.629	.700	.763	.818	.863	.900	.929	.950

	34	35	36	37	38	39	40	41	42	43
19	.999	1.000								
20	.999	.999	1.000							
21	.997	.998	.999	.999	1.000					
22	.994	.996	.998	.999	.999	1.000				
23	.988	.993	.996	.997	.999	.999	1.000			
24	.979	.987	.992	.995	.997	.998	.999	.999	1.000	
25	.966	.978	.985	.991	.991	.997	.998	.999	.999	1.000

TABLE IV   Normal Curve Areas

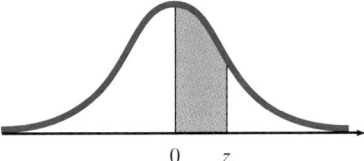

z	.00	.01	.02	.03	.04	.05	.06	.07	.08	.09
.0	.0000	.0040	.0080	.0120	.0160	.0199	.0239	.0279	.0319	.0359
.1	.0398	.0438	.0478	.0517	.0557	.0596	.0636	.0675	.0714	.0753
.2	.0793	.0832	.0871	.0910	.0948	.0987	.1026	.1064	.1103	.1141
.3	.1179	.1217	.1255	.1293	.1331	.1368	.1406	.1443	.1480	.1517
.4	.1554	.1591	.1628	.1664	.1700	.1736	.1772	.1808	.1844	.1879
.5	.1915	.1950	.1985	.2019	.2054	.2088	.2123	.2157	.2190	.2224
.6	.2257	.2291	.2324	.2357	.2389	.2422	.2454	.2486	.2517	.2549
.7	.2580	.2611	.2642	.2673	.2704	.2734	.2764	.2794	.2823	.2852
.8	.2881	.2910	.2939	.2967	.2995	.3023	.3051	.3078	.3106	.3133
.9	.3159	.3186	.3212	.3238	.3264	.3289	.3315	.3340	.3365	.3389
1.0	.3413	.3438	.3461	.3485	.3508	.3531	.3554	.3577	.3599	.3621
1.1	.3643	.3665	.3686	.3708	.3729	.3749	.3770	.3790	.3810	.3830
1.2	.3849	.3869	.3888	.3907	.3925	.3944	.3962	.3980	.3997	.4015
1.3	.4032	.4049	.4066	.4082	.4099	.4115	.4131	.4147	.4162	.4177
1.4	.4192	.4207	.4222	.4236	.4251	.4265	.4279	.4292	.4306	.4319
1.5	.4332	.4345	.4357	.4370	.4382	.4394	.4406	.4418	.4429	.4441
1.6	.4452	.4463	.4474	.4484	.4495	.4505	.4515	.4525	.4535	.4545
1.7	.4554	.4564	.4573	.4582	.4591	.4599	.4608	.4616	.4625	.4633
1.8	.4641	.4649	.4656	.4664	.4671	.4678	.4686	.4693	.4699	.4706
1.9	.4713	.4719	.4726	.4732	.4738	.4744	.4750	.4756	.4761	.4767
2.0	.4772	.4778	.4783	.4788	.4793	.4798	.4803	.4808	.4812	.4817
2.1	.4821	.4826	.4830	.4834	.4838	.4842	.4846	.4850	.4854	.4857
2.2	.4861	.4864	.4868	.4871	.4875	.4878	.4881	.4884	.4887	.4890
2.3	.4893	.4896	.4898	.4901	.4904	.4906	.4909	.4911	.4913	.4916
2.4	.4918	.4920	.4922	.4925	.4927	.4929	.4931	.4932	.4934	.4936
2.5	.4938	.4940	.4941	.4943	.4945	.4946	.4948	.4949	.4951	.4952
2.6	.4953	.4955	.4956	.4957	.4959	.4960	.4961	.4962	.4963	.4964
2.7	.4965	.4966	.4967	.4968	.4969	.4970	.4971	.4972	.4973	.4974
2.8	.4974	.4975	.4976	.4977	.4977	.4978	.4979	.4979	.4980	.4981
2.9	.4981	.4982	.4982	.4983	.4984	.4984	.4985	.4985	.4986	.4986
3.0	.4987	.4987	.4987	.4988	.4988	.4989	.4989	.4989	.4990	.4990

Source: Abridged from Table I of A. Hald, *Statistical Tables and Formulas* (New York: Wiley), 1952. Reproduced by permission of A. Hald.

TABLE V   Exponentials

λ	$e^{-\lambda}$	λ	$e^{-\lambda}$	λ	$e^{-\lambda}$	λ	$e^{-\lambda}$	λ	$e^{-\lambda}$
.00	1.000000	2.05	.128735	4.05	.017422	6.05	.002358	8.05	.000319
.05	.951229	2.10	.122456	4.10	.016573	6.10	.002243	8.10	.000304
.10	.904837	2.15	.116484	4.15	.015764	6.15	.002133	8.15	.000289
.15	.860708	2.20	.110803	4.20	.014996	6.20	.002029	8.20	.000275
.20	.818731	2.25	.105399	4.25	.014264	6.25	.001930	8.25	.000261
.25	.778801	2.30	.100259	4.30	.013569	6.30	.001836	8.30	.000249
.30	.740818	2.35	.095369	4.35	.012907	6.35	.001747	8.35	.000236
.35	.704688	2.40	.090718	4.40	.012277	6.40	.001661	8.40	.000225
.40	.670320	2.45	.086294	4.45	.011679	6.45	.001581	8.45	.000214
.45	.637628	2.50	.082085	4.50	.011109	6.50	.001503	8.50	.000204
.50	.606531	2.55	.078082	4.55	.010567	6.55	.001430	8.55	.000194
.55	.576950	2.60	.074274	4.60	.010052	6.60	.001360	8.60	.000184
.60	.548812	2.65	.070651	4.65	.009562	6.65	.001294	8.65	.000175
.65	.522046	2.70	.067206	4.70	.009095	6.70	.001231	8.70	.000167
.70	.496585	2.75	.063928	4.75	.008652	6.75	.001171	8.75	.000158
.75	.472367	2.80	.060810	4.80	.008230	6.80	.001114	8.80	.000151
.80	.449329	2.85	.057844	4.85	.007828	6.85	.001059	8.85	.000143
.85	.427415	2.90	.055023	4.90	.007447	6.90	.001008	8.90	.000136
.90	.406570	2.95	.052340	4.95	.007083	6.95	.000959	8.95	.000130
.95	.386741	3.00	.049787	5.00	.006738	7.00	.000912	9.00	.000123
1.00	.367879	3.05	.047359	5.05	.006409	7.05	.000867	9.05	.000117
1.05	.349938	3.10	.045049	5.10	.006097	7.10	.000825	9.10	.000112
1.10	.332871	3.15	.042852	5.15	.005799	7.15	.000785	9.15	.000106
1.15	.316637	3.20	.040762	5.20	.005517	7.20	.000747	9.20	.000101
1.20	.301194	3.25	.038774	5.25	.005248	7.25	.000710	9.25	.000096
1.25	.286505	3.30	.036883	5.30	.004992	7.30	.000676	9.30	.000091
1.30	.272532	3.35	.035084	5.35	.004748	7.35	.000643	9.35	.000087
1.35	.259240	3.40	.033373	5.40	.004517	7.40	.000611	9.40	.000083
1.40	.246597	3.45	.031746	5.45	.004296	7.45	.000581	9.45	.000079
1.45	.234570	3.50	.030197	5.50	.004087	7.50	.000553	9.50	.000075
1.50	.223130	3.55	.028725	5.55	.003887	7.55	.000526	9.55	.000071
1.55	.212248	3.60	.027324	5.60	.003698	7.60	.000501	9.60	.000068
1.60	.201897	3.65	.025991	5.65	.003518	7.65	.000476	9.65	.000064
1.65	.192050	3.70	.024724	5.70	.003346	7.70	.000453	9.70	.000061
1.70	.182684	3.75	.023518	5.75	.003183	7.75	.000431	9.75	.000058
1.75	.173774	3.80	.022371	5.80	.003028	7.80	.000410	9.80	.000056
1.80	.165299	3.85	.021280	5.85	.002880	7.85	.000390	9.85	.000053
1.85	.157237	3.90	.020242	5.90	.002739	7.90	.000371	9.90	.000050
1.90	.149569	3.95	.019255	5.95	.002606	7.95	.000353	9.95	.000048
1.95	.142274	4.00	.018316	6.00	.002479	8.00	.000336	10.00	.000045
2.00	.135335								

Table VI   Critical Values of t

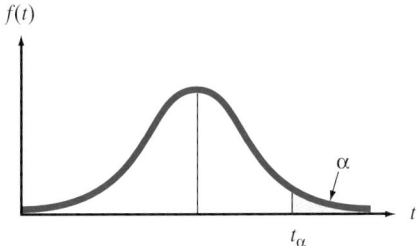

ν	$t_{.100}$	$t_{.050}$	$t_{.025}$	$t_{.010}$	$t_{.005}$	$t_{.001}$	$t_{.0005}$
1	3.078	6.314	12.706	31.821	63.657	318.31	636.62
2	1.886	2.920	4.303	6.965	9.925	22.326	31.598
3	1.638	2.353	3.182	4.541	5.841	10.213	12.924
4	1.533	2.132	2.776	3.747	4.604	7.173	8.610
5	1.476	2.015	2.571	3.365	4.032	5.893	6.869
6	1.440	1.943	2.447	3.143	3.707	5.208	5.959
7	1.415	1.895	2.365	2.998	3.499	4.785	5.408
8	1.397	1.860	2.306	2.896	3.355	4.501	5.041
9	1.383	1.833	2.262	2.821	3.250	4.297	4.781
10	1.372	1.812	2.228	2.764	3.169	4.144	4.587
11	1.363	1.796	2.201	2.718	3.106	4.025	4.437
12	1.356	1.782	2.179	2.681	3.055	3.930	4.318
13	1.350	1.771	2.160	2.650	3.012	3.852	4.221
14	1.345	1.761	2.145	2.624	2.977	3.787	4.140
15	1.341	1.753	2.131	2.602	2.947	3.733	4.073
16	1.337	1.746	2.120	2.583	2.921	3.686	4.015
17	1.333	1.740	2.110	2.567	2.898	3.646	3.965
18	1.330	1.734	2.101	2.552	2.878	3.610	3.922
19	1.328	1.729	2.093	2.539	2.861	3.579	3.883
20	1.325	1.725	2.086	2.528	2.845	3.552	3.850
21	1.323	1.721	2.080	2.518	2.831	3.527	3.819
22	1.321	1.717	2.074	2.508	2.819	3.505	3.792
23	1.319	1.714	2.069	2.500	2.807	3.485	3.767
24	1.318	1.711	2.064	2.492	2.797	3.467	3.745
25	1.316	1.708	2.060	2.485	2.787	3.450	3.725
26	1.315	1.706	2.056	2.479	2.779	3.435	3.707
27	1.314	1.703	2.052	2.473	2.771	3.421	3.690
28	1.313	1.701	2.048	2.467	2.763	3.408	3.674
29	1.311	1.699	2.045	2.462	2.756	3.396	3.659
30	1.310	1.697	2.042	2.457	2.750	3.385	3.646
40	1.303	1.684	2.021	2.423	2.704	3.307	3.551
60	1.296	1.671	2.000	2.390	2.660	3.232	3.460
120	1.289	1.658	1.980	2.358	2.617	3.160	3.373
∞	1.282	1.645	1.960	2.326	2.576	3.090	3.291

Source: This table is reproduced with the kind permission of the Trustees of Biometrika from E. S. Pearson and H. O. Hartley (eds.), *The Biometrika Tables for Statisticians*, Vol. 1, 3d ed., Biometrika, 1966.

TABLE VII   Percentage Points of the F-distribution, $\alpha = .10$

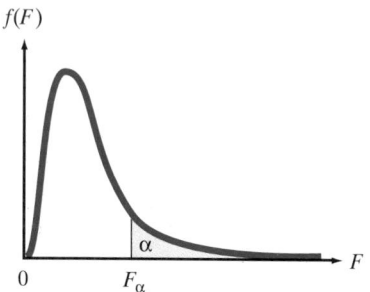

ν_1	NUMERATOR DEGREES OF FREEDOM								
ν_2	1	2	3	4	5	6	7	8	9
1	39.86	49.50	53.59	55.83	57.24	58.20	58.91	59.44	59.86
2	8.53	9.00	9.16	9.24	9.29	9.33	9.35	9.37	9.38
3	5.54	5.46	5.39	5.34	5.31	5.28	5.27	5.25	5.24
4	4.54	4.32	4.19	4.11	4.05	4.01	3.98	3.95	3.94
5	4.06	3.78	3.62	3.52	3.45	3.40	3.37	3.34	3.32
6	3.78	3.46	3.29	3.18	3.11	3.05	3.01	2.98	2.96
7	3.59	3.26	3.07	2.96	2.88	2.83	2.78	2.75	2.72
8	3.46	3.11	2.92	2.81	2.73	2.67	2.62	2.59	2.56
9	3.36	3.01	2.81	2.69	2.61	2.55	2.51	2.47	2.44
10	3.29	2.92	2.73	2.61	2.52	2.46	2.41	2.38	2.35
11	3.23	2.86	2.66	2.54	2.45	2.39	2.34	2.30	2.27
12	3.18	2.81	2.61	2.48	2.39	2.33	2.28	2.24	2.21
13	3.14	2.76	2.56	2.43	2.35	2.28	2.23	2.20	2.16
14	3.10	2.73	2.52	2.39	2.31	2.24	2.19	2.15	2.12
15	3.07	2.70	2.49	2.36	2.27	2.21	2.16	2.12	2.09
16	3.05	2.67	2.46	2.33	2.24	2.18	2.13	2.09	2.06
17	3.03	2.64	2.44	2.31	2.22	2.15	2.10	2.06	2.03
18	3.01	2.62	2.42	2.29	2.20	2.13	2.08	2.04	2.00
19	2.99	2.61	2.40	2.27	2.18	2.11	2.06	2.02	1.98
20	2.97	2.59	2.38	2.25	2.16	2.09	2.04	2.00	1.96
21	2.96	2.57	2.36	2.23	2.14	2.08	2.02	1.98	1.95
22	2.95	2.56	2.35	2.22	2.13	2.06	2.01	1.97	1.93
23	2.94	2.55	2.34	2.21	2.11	2.05	1.99	1.95	1.92
24	2.93	2.54	2.33	2.19	2.10	2.04	1.98	1.94	1.91
25	2.92	2.53	2.32	2.18	2.09	2.02	1.97	1.93	1.89
26	2.91	2.52	2.31	2.17	2.08	2.01	1.96	1.92	1.88
27	2.90	2.51	2.30	2.17	2.07	2.00	1.95	1.91	1.87
28	2.89	2.50	2.29	2.16	2.06	2.00	1.94	1.90	1.87
29	2.89	2.50	2.28	2.15	2.06	1.99	1.93	1.89	1.86
30	2.88	2.49	2.28	2.14	2.05	1.98	1.93	1.88	1.85
40	2.84	2.44	2.23	2.09	2.00	1.93	1.87	1.83	1.79
60	2.79	2.39	2.18	2.04	1.95	1.87	1.82	1.77	1.74
120	2.75	2.35	2.13	1.99	1.90	1.82	1.77	1.72	1.68
∞	2.71	2.30	2.08	1.94	1.85	1.77	1.72	1.67	1.63

Source: From M. Merrington and C. M. Thompson, "Tables of Percentage Points of the Inverted Beta (*F*)-Distribution," *Biometrika*, 1943, 33, 73–88. Reproduced by permission of the *Biometrika* Trustees.

TABLE VII   Continued

ν_2 \ ν_1	NUMERATOR DEGREES OF FREEDOM									
	10	12	15	20	24	30	40	60	120	∞
1	60.19	60.71	61.22	61.74	62.00	62.26	62.53	62.79	63.06	63.33
2	9.39	9.41	9.42	9.44	9.45	9.46	9.47	9.47	9.48	9.49
3	5.23	5.22	5.20	5.18	5.18	5.17	5.16	5.15	5.14	5.13
4	3.92	3.90	3.87	3.84	3.83	3.82	3.80	3.79	3.78	3.76
5	3.30	3.27	3.24	3.21	3.19	3.17	3.16	3.14	3.12	3.10
6	2.94	2.90	2.87	2.84	2.82	2.80	2.78	2.76	2.74	2.72
7	2.70	2.67	2.63	2.59	2.58	2.56	2.54	2.51	2.49	2.47
8	2.54	2.50	2.46	2.42	2.40	2.38	2.36	2.34	2.32	2.29
9	2.42	2.38	2.34	2.30	2.28	2.25	2.23	2.21	2.18	2.16
10	2.32	2.28	2.24	2.20	2.18	2.16	2.13	2.11	2.08	2.06
11	2.25	2.21	2.17	2.12	2.10	2.08	2.05	2.03	2.00	1.97
12	2.19	2.15	2.10	2.06	2.04	2.01	1.99	1.96	1.93	1.90
13	2.14	2.10	2.05	2.01	1.98	1.96	1.93	1.90	1.88	1.85
14	2.10	2.05	2.01	1.96	1.94	1.91	1.89	1.86	1.83	1.80
15	2.06	2.02	1.97	1.92	1.90	1.87	1.85	1.82	1.79	1.76
16	2.03	1.99	1.94	1.89	1.87	1.84	1.81	1.78	1.75	1.72
17	2.00	1.96	1.91	1.86	1.84	1.81	1.78	1.75	1.72	1.69
18	1.98	1.93	1.89	1.84	1.81	1.78	1.75	1.72	1.69	1.66
19	1.96	1.91	1.86	1.81	1.79	1.76	1.73	1.70	1.67	1.63
20	1.94	1.89	1.84	1.79	1.77	1.74	1.71	1.68	1.64	1.61
21	1.92	1.87	1.83	1.78	1.75	1.72	1.69	1.66	1.62	1.59
22	1.90	1.86	1.81	1.76	1.73	1.70	1.67	1.64	1.60	1.57
23	1.89	1.84	1.80	1.74	1.72	1.69	1.66	1.62	1.59	1.55
24	1.88	1.83	1.78	1.73	1.70	1.67	1.64	1.61	1.57	1.53
25	1.87	1.82	1.77	1.72	1.69	1.66	1.63	1.59	1.56	1.52
26	1.86	1.81	1.76	1.71	1.68	1.65	1.61	1.58	1.54	1.50
27	1.85	1.80	1.75	1.70	1.67	1.64	1.60	1.57	1.53	1.49
28	1.84	1.79	1.74	1.69	1.66	1.63	1.59	1.56	1.52	1.48
29	1.83	1.78	1.73	1.68	1.65	1.62	1.58	1.55	1.51	1.47
30	1.82	1.77	1.72	1.67	1.64	1.61	1.57	1.54	1.50	1.46
40	1.76	1.71	1.66	1.61	1.57	1.54	1.51	1.47	1.42	1.38
60	1.71	1.66	1.60	1.54	1.51	1.48	1.44	1.40	1.35	1.29
120	1.65	1.60	1.55	1.48	1.45	1.41	1.37	1.32	1.26	1.19
∞	1.60	1.55	1.49	1.42	1.38	1.34	1.30	1.24	1.17	1.00

DENOMINATOR DEGREES OF FREEDOM

TABLE VIII   Percentage Points of the *F*-distribution, $\alpha = .05$

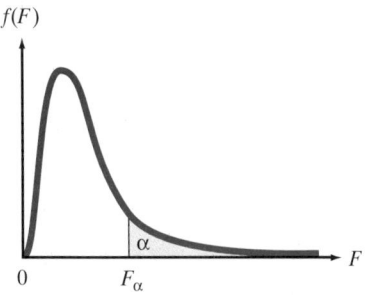

v_1				NUMERATOR DEGREES OF FREEDOM					
v_2	**1**	**2**	**3**	**4**	**5**	**6**	**7**	**8**	**9**
1	161.4	199.5	215.7	224.6	230.2	234.0	236.8	238.9	240.5
2	18.51	19.00	19.16	19.25	19.30	19.33	19.35	19.37	19.38
3	10.13	9.55	9.28	9.12	9.01	8.94	8.89	8.85	8.81
4	7.71	6.94	6.59	6.39	6.26	6.16	6.09	6.04	6.00
5	6.61	5.79	5.41	5.19	5.05	4.95	4.88	4.82	4.77
6	5.99	5.14	4.76	4.53	4.39	4.28	4.21	4.15	4.10
7	5.59	4.74	4.35	4.12	3.97	3.87	3.79	3.73	3.68
8	5.32	4.46	4.07	3.84	3.69	3.58	3.50	3.44	3.39
9	5.12	4.26	3.86	3.63	3.48	3.37	3.29	3.23	3.18
10	4.96	4.10	3.71	3.48	3.33	3.22	3.14	3.07	3.02
11	4.84	3.98	3.59	3.36	3.20	3.09	3.01	2.95	2.90
12	4.75	3.89	3.49	3.26	3.11	3.00	2.91	2.85	2.80
13	4.67	3.81	3.41	3.18	3.03	2.92	2.83	2.77	2.71
14	4.60	3.74	3.34	3.11	2.96	2.85	2.76	2.70	2.65
15	4.54	3.68	3.29	3.06	2.90	2.79	2.71	2.64	2.59
16	4.49	3.63	3.24	3.01	2.85	2.74	2.66	2.59	2.54
17	4.45	3.59	3.20	2.96	2.81	2.70	2.61	2.55	2.49
18	4.41	3.55	3.16	2.93	2.77	2.66	2.58	2.51	2.46
19	4.38	3.52	3.13	2.90	2.74	2.63	2.54	2.48	2.42
20	4.35	3.49	3.10	2.87	2.71	2.60	2.51	2.45	2.39
21	4.32	3.47	3.07	2.84	2.68	2.57	2.49	2.42	2.37
22	4.30	3.44	3.05	2.82	2.66	2.55	2.46	2.40	2.34
23	4.28	3.42	3.03	2.80	2.64	2.53	2.44	2.37	2.32
24	4.26	3.40	3.01	2.78	2.62	2.51	2.42	2.36	2.30
25	4.24	3.39	2.99	2.76	2.60	2.49	2.40	2.34	2.28
26	4.23	3.37	2.98	2.74	2.59	2.47	2.39	2.32	2.77
27	4.21	3.35	2.96	2.73	2.57	2.46	2.37	2.31	2.25
28	4.20	3.34	2.95	2.71	2.56	2.45	2.36	2.29	2.24
29	4.18	3.33	2.93	2.70	2.55	2.43	2.35	2.28	2.22
30	4.17	3.32	2.92	2.69	2.53	2.42	2.33	2.27	2.21
40	4.08	3.23	2.84	2.61	2.45	2.34	2.25	2.18	2.12
60	4.00	3.15	2.76	2.53	2.37	2.25	2.17	2.10	2.04
120	3.92	3.07	2.68	2.45	2.29	2.17	2.09	2.02	1.96
∞	3.84	3.00	2.60	2.37	2.21	2.10	2.01	1.94	1.88

Left axis: DENOMINATOR DEGREES OF FREEDOM

Source: From M. Merrington and C. M. Thompson, "Tables of Percentage Points of the Inverted Beta (*F*)-Distribution." *Biometrika*, 1943, 33, 73–88. Reproduced by permission of the *Biometrika* Trustees.

TABLE **VIII**   **Continued**

v_1 / v_2	\multicolumn{10}{c}{NUMERATOR DEGREES OF FREEDOM}

v_2	10	12	15	20	24	30	40	60	120	∞
1	241.9	243.9	245.9	248.0	249.1	250.1	251.1	252.2	253.3	254.3
2	19.40	19.41	19.43	19.45	19.45	19.46	19.47	19.48	19.49	19.50
3	8.79	8.74	8.70	8.66	8.64	8.62	8.59	8.57	8.55	8.53
4	5.96	5.91	5.86	5.80	5.77	5.75	5.72	5.69	5.66	5.63
5	4.74	4.68	4.62	4.56	4.53	4.50	4.46	4.43	4.40	4.36
6	4.06	4.00	3.94	3.87	3.84	3.81	3.77	3.74	3.70	3.67
7	3.64	3.57	3.51	3.44	3.41	3.38	3.34	3.30	3.27	3.23
8	3.35	3.28	3.22	3.15	3.12	3.08	3.04	3.01	2.97	2.93
9	3.14	3.07	3.01	2.94	2.90	2.86	2.83	2.79	2.75	2.71
10	2.98	2.91	2.85	2.77	2.74	2.70	2.66	2.62	2.58	2.54
11	2.85	2.79	2.72	2.65	2.61	2.57	2.53	2.49	2.45	2.40
12	2.75	2.69	2.62	2.54	2.51	2.47	2.43	2.38	2.34	2.30
13	2.67	2.60	2.53	2.46	2.42	2.38	2.34	2.30	2.25	2.21
14	2.60	2.53	2.46	2.39	2.35	2.31	2.27	2.22	2.18	2.13
15	2.54	2.48	2.40	2.33	2.29	2.25	2.20	2.16	2.11	2.07
16	2.49	2.42	2.35	2.28	2.24	2.19	2.15	2.11	2.06	2.01
17	2.45	2.38	2.31	2.23	2.19	2.15	2.10	2.06	2.01	1.96
18	2.41	2.34	2.27	2.19	2.15	2.11	2.06	2.02	1.97	1.92
19	2.38	2.31	2.23	2.16	2.11	2.07	2.03	1.98	1.93	1.88
20	2.35	2.28	2.20	2.12	2.08	2.04	1.99	1.95	1.90	1.84
21	2.32	2.25	2.18	2.10	2.05	2.01	1.96	1.92	1.87	1.81
22	2.30	2.23	2.15	2.07	2.03	1.98	1.94	1.89	1.84	1.78
23	2.27	2.20	2.13	2.05	2.01	1.96	1.91	1.86	1.81	1.76
24	2.25	2.18	2.11	2.03	1.98	1.94	1.89	1.84	1.79	1.73
25	2.24	2.16	2.09	2.01	1.96	1.92	1.87	1.82	1.77	1.71
26	2.22	2.15	2.07	1.99	1.95	1.90	1.85	1.80	1.75	1.69
27	2.20	2.13	2.06	1.97	1.93	1.88	1.84	1.79	1.73	1.67
28	2.19	2.12	2.04	1.96	1.91	1.87	1.82	1.77	1.71	1.65
29	2.18	2.10	2.03	1.94	1.90	1.85	1.81	1.75	1.70	1.64
30	2.16	2.09	2.01	1.93	1.89	1.84	1.79	1.74	1.68	1.62
40	2.08	2.00	1.92	1.84	1.79	1.74	1.69	1.64	1.58	1.51
60	1.99	1.92	1.84	1.75	1.70	1.65	1.59	1.53	1.47	1.39
120	1.91	1.83	1.75	1.66	1.61	1.55	1.50	1.43	1.35	1.25
∞	1.83	1.75	1.67	1.57	1.52	1.46	1.39	1.32	1.22	1.00

DENOMINATOR DEGREES OF FREEDOM

TABLE IX Percentage Points of the *F*-distribution, $\alpha = .025$

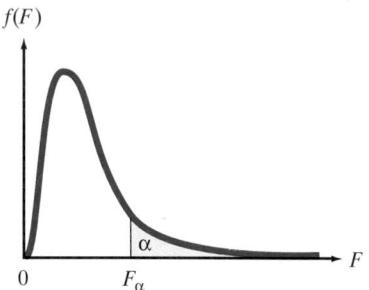

ν_1	NUMERATOR DEGREES OF FREEDOM								
ν_2	1	2	3	4	5	6	7	8	9
1	647.8	799.5	864.2	899.6	921.8	937.1	948.2	956.7	963.3
2	38.51	39.00	39.17	39.25	39.30	39.33	39.36	39.37	39.39
3	17.44	16.04	15.44	15.10	14.88	14.73	14.62	14.54	14.47
4	12.22	10.65	9.98	9.60	9.36	9.20	9.07	8.98	8.90
5	10.01	8.43	7.76	7.39	7.15	6.98	6.85	6.76	6.68
6	8.81	7.26	6.60	6.23	5.99	5.82	5.70	5.60	5.52
7	8.07	6.54	5.89	5.52	5.29	5.12	4.99	4.90	4.82
8	7.57	6.06	5.42	5.05	4.82	4.65	4.53	4.43	4.36
9	7.21	5.71	5.08	4.72	4.48	4.32	4.20	4.10	4.03
10	6.94	5.46	4.83	4.47	4.24	4.07	3.95	3.85	3.78
11	6.72	5.26	4.63	4.28	4.04	3.88	3.76	3.66	3.59
12	6.55	5.10	4.47	4.12	3.89	3.73	3.61	3.51	3.44
13	6.41	4.97	4.35	4.00	3.77	3.60	3.48	3.39	3.31
14	6.30	4.86	4.24	3.89	3.66	3.50	3.38	3.29	3.21
15	6.20	4.77	4.15	3.80	3.58	3.41	3.29	3.20	3.12
16	6.12	4.69	4.08	3.73	3.50	3.34	3.22	3.12	3.05
17	6.04	4.62	4.01	3.66	3.44	3.28	3.16	3.06	2.98
18	5.98	4.56	3.95	3.61	3.38	3.22	3.10	3.01	2.93
19	5.92	4.51	3.90	3.56	3.33	3.17	3.05	2.96	2.88
20	5.87	4.46	3.86	3.51	3.29	3.13	3.01	2.91	2.84
21	5.83	4.42	3.82	3.48	3.25	3.09	2.97	2.87	2.80
22	5.79	4.38	3.78	3.44	3.22	3.05	2.93	2.84	2.76
23	5.75	4.35	3.75	3.41	3.18	3.02	2.90	2.81	2.73
24	5.72	4.32	3.72	3.38	3.15	2.99	2.87	2.78	2.70
25	5.69	4.29	3.69	3.35	3.13	2.97	2.85	2.75	2.68
26	5.66	4.27	3.67	3.33	3.10	2.94	2.82	2.73	2.65
27	5.63	4.24	3.65	3.31	3.08	2.92	2.80	2.71	2.63
28	5.61	4.22	3.63	3.29	3.06	2.90	2.78	2.69	2.61
29	5.59	4.20	3.61	3.27	3.04	2.88	2.76	2.67	2.59
30	5.57	4.18	3.59	3.25	3.03	2.87	2.75	2.65	2.57
40	5.42	4.05	3.46	3.13	2.90	2.74	2.62	2.53	2.45
60	5.29	3.93	3.34	3.01	2.79	2.63	2.51	2.41	2.33
120	5.15	3.80	3.23	2.89	2.67	2.52	2.39	2.30	2.22
∞	5.02	3.69	3.12	2.79	2.57	2.41	2.29	2.19	2.11

DENOMINATOR DEGREES OF FREEDOM

Source: From M. Merrington and C. M. Thompson, "Tables of Percentage Points of the Inverted Beta (*F*)-Distribution," *Biometrika*, 1943, 33, 73–88. Reproduced by permission of the *Biometrika* Trustees.

TABLE **IX**   **Continued**

v_2	NUMERATOR DEGREES OF FREEDOM v_1									
	10	12	15	20	24	30	40	60	120	∞
1	968.6	976.7	984.9	993.1	997.2	1,001	1,006	1,010	1,014	1,018
2	39.40	39.41	39.43	39.45	39.46	39.46	39.47	39.48	39.49	39.50
3	14.42	14.34	14.25	14.17	14.12	14.08	14.04	13.99	13.95	13.90
4	8.84	8.75	8.66	8.56	8.51	8.46	8.41	8.36	8.31	8.26
5	6.62	6.52	6.43	6.33	6.28	6.23	6.18	6.12	6.07	6.02
6	5.46	5.37	5.27	5.17	5.12	5.07	5.01	4.96	4.90	4.85
7	4.76	4.67	4.57	4.47	4.42	4.36	4.31	4.25	4.20	4.14
8	4.30	4.20	4.10	4.00	3.95	3.89	3.84	3.78	3.73	3.67
9	3.96	3.87	3.77	3.67	3.61	3.56	3.51	3.45	3.39	3.33
10	3.72	3.62	3.52	3.42	3.37	3.31	3.26	3.20	3.14	3.08
11	3.53	3.43	3.33	3.23	3.17	3.12	3.06	3.00	2.94	2.88
12	3.37	3.28	3.18	3.07	3.02	2.96	2.91	2.85	2.79	2.72
13	3.25	3.15	3.05	2.95	2.89	2.84	2.78	2.72	2.66	2.60
14	3.15	3.05	2.95	2.84	2.79	2.73	2.67	2.61	2.55	2.49
15	3.06	2.96	2.86	2.76	2.70	2.64	2.59	2.52	2.46	2.40
16	2.99	2.89	2.79	2.68	2.63	2.57	2.51	2.45	2.38	2.32
17	2.92	2.82	2.72	2.62	2.56	2.50	2.44	2.38	2.32	2.25
18	2.87	2.77	2.67	2.56	2.50	2.44	2.38	2.32	2.26	2.19
19	2.82	2.72	2.62	2.51	2.45	2.39	2.33	2.27	2.20	2.13
20	2.77	2.68	2.57	2.46	2.41	2.35	2.29	2.22	2.16	2.09
21	2.73	2.64	2.53	2.42	2.37	2.31	2.25	2.18	2.11	2.04
22	2.70	2.60	2.50	2.39	2.33	2.27	2.21	2.14	2.08	2.00
23	2.67	2.57	2.47	2.36	2.30	2.24	2.18	2.11	2.04	1.97
24	2.64	2.54	2.44	2.33	2.27	2.21	2.15	2.08	2.01	1.94
25	2.61	2.51	2.41	2.30	2.24	2.18	2.12	2.05	1.98	1.91
26	2.59	2.49	2.39	2.28	2.22	2.16	2.09	2.03	1.95	1.88
27	2.57	2.47	2.36	2.25	2.19	2.13	2.07	2.00	1.93	1.85
28	2.55	2.45	2.34	2.23	2.17	2.11	2.05	1.98	1.91	1.83
29	2.53	2.43	2.32	2.21	2.15	2.09	2.03	1.96	1.89	1.81
30	2.51	2.41	2.31	2.20	2.14	2.07	2.01	1.94	1.87	1.79
40	2.39	2.29	2.18	2.07	2.01	1.94	1.88	1.80	1.72	1.64
60	2.27	2.17	2.06	1.94	1.88	1.82	1.74	1.67	1.58	1.48
120	2.16	2.05	1.94	1.82	1.76	1.69	1.61	1.53	1.43	1.31
∞	2.05	1.94	1.83	1.71	1.64	1.57	1.48	1.39	1.27	1.00

DENOMINATOR DEGREES OF FREEDOM

TABLE X Percentage Points of the *F*-distribution, $\alpha = .01$

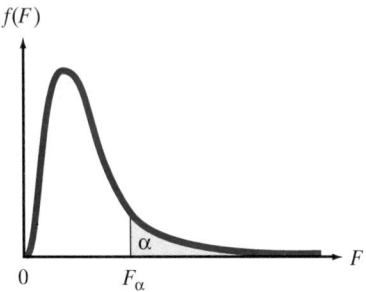

v_2 \ v_1	NUMERATOR DEGREES OF FREEDOM								
	1	**2**	**3**	**4**	**5**	**6**	**7**	**8**	**9**
1	4,052	4,999.5	5,403	5,625	5,764	5,859	5,928	5,982	6,022
2	98.50	99.00	99.17	99.25	99.30	99.33	99.36	99.37	99.39
3	34.12	30.82	29.46	28.71	28.24	27.91	27.67	27.49	27.35
4	21.20	18.00	16.69	15.98	15.52	15.21	14.98	14.80	14.66
5	16.26	13.27	12.06	11.39	10.97	10.67	10.46	10.29	10.16
6	13.75	10.92	9.78	9.15	8.75	8.47	8.26	8.10	7.98
7	12.25	9.55	8.45	7.85	7.46	7.19	6.99	6.84	6.72
8	11.26	8.65	7.59	7.01	6.63	6.37	6.18	6.03	5.91
9	10.56	8.02	6.99	6.42	6.06	5.80	5.61	5.47	5.35
10	10.04	7.56	6.55	5.99	5.64	5.39	5.20	5.06	4.94
11	9.65	7.21	6.22	5.67	5.32	5.07	4.89	4.74	4.63
12	9.33	6.93	5.95	5.41	5.06	4.82	4.64	4.50	4.39
13	9.07	6.70	5.74	5.21	4.86	4.62	4.44	4.30	4.19
14	8.86	6.51	5.56	5.04	4.69	4.46	4.28	4.14	4.03
15	8.68	6.36	5.42	4.89	4.56	4.32	4.14	4.00	3.89
16	8.53	6.23	5.29	4.77	4.44	4.20	4.03	3.89	3.78
17	8.40	6.11	5.18	4.67	4.34	4.10	3.93	3.79	3.68
18	8.29	6.01	5.09	4.58	4.25	4.01	3.84	3.71	3.60
19	8.18	5.93	5.01	4.50	4.17	3.94	3.77	3.63	3.52
20	8.10	5.85	4.94	4.43	4.10	3.87	3.70	3.56	3.46
21	8.02	5.78	4.87	4.37	4.04	3.81	3.64	3.51	3.40
22	7.95	5.72	4.82	4.31	3.99	3.76	3.59	3.45	3.35
23	7.88	5.66	4.76	4.26	3.94	3.71	3.54	3.41	3.30
24	7.82	5.61	4.72	4.22	3.90	3.67	3.50	3.36	3.26
25	7.77	5.57	4.68	4.18	3.85	3.63	3.46	3.32	3.22
26	7.72	5.53	4.64	4.14	3.82	3.59	3.42	3.29	3.18
27	7.68	5.49	4.60	4.11	3.78	3.56	3.39	3.26	3.15
28	7.64	5.45	4.57	4.07	3.75	3.53	3.36	3.23	3.12
29	7.60	5.42	4.54	4.04	3.73	3.50	3.33	3.20	3.09
30	7.56	5.39	4.51	4.02	3.70	3.47	3.30	3.17	3.07
40	7.31	5.18	4.31	3.83	3.51	3.29	3.12	2.99	2.89
60	7.08	4.98	4.13	3.65	3.34	3.12	2.95	2.82	2.72
120	6.85	4.79	3.95	3.48	3.17	2.96	2.79	2.66	2.56
∞	6.63	4.61	3.78	3.32	3.02	2.80	2.64	2.51	2.41

(column labeled "DENOMINATOR DEGREES OF FREEDOM" along left side)

TABLE X   Continued

ν_2 \ ν_1	NUMERATOR DEGREES OF FREEDOM									
	10	12	15	20	24	30	40	60	120	∞
1	6,056	6,106	6,157	6,209	6,235	6,261	6,287	6,313	6,339	6,366
2	99.40	99.42	99.43	99.45	99.46	99.47	99.47	99.48	99.49	99.50
3	27.23	27.05	26.87	26.69	26.60	26.50	26.41	26.32	26.22	26.13
4	14.55	14.37	14.20	14.02	13.93	13.84	13.75	13.65	13.56	13.46
5	10.05	9.89	9.72	9.55	9.47	9.38	9.29	9.20	9.11	9.02
6	7.87	7.72	7.56	7.40	7.31	7.23	7.14	7.06	6.97	6.88
7	6.62	6.47	6.31	6.16	6.07	5.99	5.91	5.82	5.74	5.65
8	5.81	5.67	5.52	5.36	5.28	5.20	5.12	5.03	4.95	4.86
9	5.26	5.11	4.96	4.81	4.73	4.65	4.57	4.48	4.40	4.31
10	4.85	4.71	4.56	4.41	4.33	4.25	4.17	4.08	4.00	3.91
11	4.54	4.40	4.25	4.10	4.02	3.94	3.86	3.78	3.69	3.60
12	4.30	4.16	4.01	3.86	3.78	3.70	3.62	3.54	3.45	3.36
13	4.10	3.96	3.82	3.66	3.59	3.51	3.43	3.34	3.25	3.17
14	3.94	3.80	3.66	3.51	3.43	3.35	3.27	3.18	3.09	3.00
15	3.80	3.67	3.52	3.37	3.29	3.21	3.13	3.05	2.96	2.87
16	3.69	3.55	3.41	3.26	3.18	3.10	3.02	2.93	2.84	2.75
17	3.59	3.46	3.31	3.16	3.08	3.00	2.92	2.83	2.75	2.65
18	3.51	3.37	3.23	3.08	3.00	2.92	2.84	2.75	2.66	2.57
19	3.43	3.30	3.15	3.00	2.92	2.84	2.76	2.67	2.58	2.49
20	3.37	3.23	3.09	2.94	2.86	2.78	2.69	2.61	2.52	2.42
21	3.31	3.17	3.03	2.88	2.80	2.72	2.64	2.55	2.46	2.36
22	3.26	3.12	2.98	2.83	2.75	2.67	2.58	2.50	2.40	2.31
23	3.21	3.07	2.93	2.78	2.70	2.62	2.54	2.45	2.35	2.26
24	3.17	3.03	2.89	2.74	2.66	2.58	2.49	2.40	2.31	2.21
25	3.13	2.99	2.85	2.70	2.62	2.54	2.45	2.36	2.27	2.17
26	3.09	2.96	2.81	2.66	2.58	2.50	2.42	2.33	2.23	2.13
27	3.06	2.93	2.78	2.63	2.55	2.47	2.38	2.29	2.20	2.10
28	3.03	2.90	2.75	2.60	2.52	2.44	2.35	2.26	2.17	2.06
29	3.00	2.87	2.73	2.57	2.49	2.41	2.33	2.23	2.14	2.03
30	2.98	2.84	2.70	2.55	2.47	2.39	2.30	2.21	2.11	2.01
40	2.80	2.66	2.52	2.37	2.29	2.20	2.11	2.02	1.92	1.80
60	2.63	2.50	2.35	2.20	2.12	2.03	1.94	1.84	1.73	1.60
120	2.47	2.34	2.19	2.03	1.95	1.86	1.76	1.66	1.53	1.38
∞	2.32	2.18	2.04	1.88	1.79	1.70	1.59	1.47	1.32	1.00

DENOMINATOR DEGREES OF FREEDOM

TABLE XI   Critical Values of T_L and T_U for the Wilcoxon Rank Sum Test: Independent Samples

Test statistic is the rank sum associated with the smaller sample (if equal sample sizes, either rank sum can be used).

a. $\alpha = .025$ one-tailed; $\alpha = .05$ two-tailed

n_2 \\ n_1	3		4		5		6		7		8		9		10	
	T_L	T_U	T_L	T_U	T_L	T_U	T_L	T_U	T_L	T_U	T_L	T_U	T_L	T_U	T_L	T_U
3	5	16	6	18	6	21	7	23	7	26	8	28	8	31	9	33
4	6	18	11	25	12	28	12	32	13	35	14	38	15	41	16	44
5	6	21	12	28	18	37	19	41	20	45	21	49	22	53	24	56
6	7	23	12	32	19	41	26	52	28	56	29	61	31	65	32	70
7	7	26	13	35	20	45	28	56	37	68	39	73	41	78	43	83
8	8	28	14	38	21	49	29	61	39	73	49	87	51	93	54	98
9	8	31	15	41	22	53	31	65	41	78	51	93	63	108	66	114
10	9	33	16	44	24	56	32	70	43	83	54	98	66	114	79	131

b. $\alpha = .05$ one-tailed; $\alpha = .10$ two-tailed

n_2 \\ n_1	3		4		5		6		7		8		9		10	
	T_L	T_U	T_L	T_U	T_L	T_U	T_L	T_U	T_L	T_U	T_L	T_U	T_L	T_U	T_L	T_U
3	6	15	7	17	7	20	8	22	9	24	9	27	10	29	11	31
4	7	17	12	24	13	27	14	30	15	33	16	36	17	39	18	42
5	7	20	13	27	19	36	20	40	22	43	24	46	25	50	26	54
6	8	22	14	30	20	40	28	50	30	54	32	58	33	63	35	67
7	9	24	15	33	22	43	30	54	39	66	41	71	43	76	46	80
8	9	27	16	36	24	46	32	58	41	71	52	84	54	90	57	95
9	10	29	17	39	25	50	33	63	43	76	54	90	66	105	69	111
10	11	31	18	42	26	54	35	67	46	80	57	95	69	111	83	127

Source: From F. Wilcoxon and R. A. Wilcox, "Some Rapid Approximate Statistical Procedures," 1964, 20–23. Courtesy of Lederle Laboratories Division of American Cyanamid Company, Madison, NJ.

TABLE XII **Critical Values of T_0 in the Wilcoxon Paired Difference Signed Rank Test**

One-Tailed	Two-Tailed	n = 5	n = 6	n = 7	n = 8	n = 9	n = 10
$\alpha = .05$	$\alpha = .10$	1	2	4	6	8	11
$\alpha = .025$	$\alpha = .05$		1	2	4	6	8
$\alpha = .01$	$\alpha = .02$			0	2	3	5
$\alpha = .005$	$\alpha = .01$				0	2	3
		n = 11	n = 12	n = 13	n = 14	n = 15	n = 16
$\alpha = .05$	$\alpha = .10$	14	17	21	26	30	36
$\alpha = .025$	$\alpha = .05$	11	14	17	21	25	30
$\alpha = .01$	$\alpha = .02$	7	10	13	16	20	24
$\alpha = .005$	$\alpha = .01$	5	7	10	13	16	19
		n = 17	n = 18	n = 19	n = 20	n = 21	n = 22
$\alpha = .05$	$\alpha = .10$	41	47	54	60	68	75
$\alpha = .025$	$\alpha = .05$	35	40	46	52	59	66
$\alpha = .01$	$\alpha = .02$	28	33	38	43	49	56
$\alpha = .005$	$\alpha = .01$	23	28	32	37	43	49
		n = 23	n = 24	n = 25	n = 26	n = 27	n = 28
$\alpha = .05$	$\alpha = .10$	83	92	101	110	120	130
$\alpha = .025$	$\alpha = .05$	73	81	90	98	107	117
$\alpha = .01$	$\alpha = .02$	62	69	77	85	93	102
$\alpha = .005$	$\alpha = .01$	55	61	68	76	84	92
		n = 29	n = 30	n = 31	n = 32	n = 33	n = 34
$\alpha = .05$	$\alpha = .10$	141	152	163	175	188	201
$\alpha = .025$	$\alpha = .05$	127	137	148	159	171	183
$\alpha = .01$	$\alpha = .02$	111	120	130	141	151	162
$\alpha = .005$	$\alpha = .01$	100	109	118	128	138	149
		n = 35	n = 36	n = 37	n = 38	n = 39	
$\alpha = .05$	$\alpha = .10$	214	228	242	256	271	
$\alpha = .025$	$\alpha = .05$	195	208	222	235	250	
$\alpha = .01$	$\alpha = .02$	174	186	198	211	224	
$\alpha = .005$	$\alpha = .01$	160	171	183	195	208	
		n = 40	n = 41	n = 42	n = 43	n = 44	n = 45
$\alpha = .05$	$\alpha = .10$	287	303	319	336	353	371
$\alpha = .025$	$\alpha = .05$	264	279	295	311	327	344
$\alpha = .01$	$\alpha = .02$	238	252	267	281	297	313
$\alpha = .005$	$\alpha = .01$	221	234	248	262	277	292
		n = 46	n = 47	n = 48	n = 49	n = 50	
$\alpha = .05$	$\alpha = .10$	389	408	427	446	466	
$\alpha = .025$	$\alpha = .05$	361	379	397	415	434	
$\alpha = .01$	$\alpha = .02$	329	345	362	380	398	
$\alpha = .005$	$\alpha = .01$	307	323	339	356	373	

Source: From F. Wilcoxon and R. A. Wilcox, "Some Rapid Approximate Statistical Procedures," 1964, p. 28. Courtesy of Lederle Laboratories Division of American Cyanamid Company, Madison, NJ.

TABLE XIII   Critical Values of χ^2

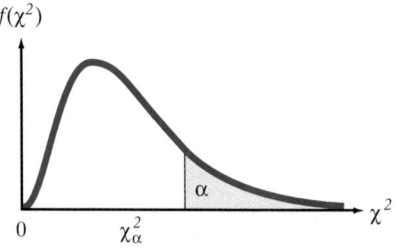

Degrees of Freedom	$\chi^2_{.995}$	$\chi^2_{.990}$	$\chi^2_{.975}$	$\chi^2_{.950}$	$\chi^2_{.900}$
1	.0000393	.0001571	.0009821	.0039321	.0157908
2	.0100251	.0201007	.0506356	.102587	.210720
3	.0717212	.114832	.215795	.351846	.584375
4	.206990	.297110	.484419	.710721	1.063623
5	.411740	.554300	.831211	1.145476	1.61031
6	.675727	.872085	1.237347	1.63539	2.20413
7	.989265	1.239043	1.68987	2.16735	2.83311
8	1.344419	1.646482	2.17973	2.73264	3.48954
9	1.734926	2.087912	2.70039	3.32511	4.16816
10	2.15585	2.55821	3.24697	3.94030	4.86518
11	2.60321	3.05347	3.81575	4.57481	5.57779
12	3.07382	3.57056	4.40379	5.22603	6.30380
13	3.56503	4.10691	5.00874	5.89186	7.04150
14	4.07468	4.66043	5.62872	6.57063	7.78953
15	4.60094	5.22935	6.26214	7.26094	8.54675
16	5.14224	5.81221	6.90766	7.96164	9.31223
17	5.69724	6.40776	7.56418	8.67176	10.0852
18	6.26481	7.01491	8.23075	9.39046	10.8649
19	6.84398	7.63273	8.90655	10.1170	11.6509
20	7.43386	8.26040	9.59083	10.8508	12.4426
21	8.03366	8.89720	10.28293	11.5913	13.2396
22	8.64272	9.54249	10.9823	12.3380	14.0415
23	9.26042	10.19567	11.6885	13.0905	14.8479
24	9.88623	10.8564	12.4011	13.8484	15.6587
25	10.5197	11.5240	13.1197	14.6114	16.4734
26	11.1603	12.1981	13.8439	15.3791	17.2919
27	11.8076	12.8786	14.5733	16.1513	18.1138
28	12.4613	13.5648	15.3079	16.9279	18.9392
29	13.1211	14.2565	16.0471	17.7083	19.7677
30	13.7867	14.9535	16.7908	18.4926	20.5992
40	20.7065	22.1643	24.4331	26.5093	29.0505
50	27.9907	29.7067	32.3574	34.7642	37.6886
60	35.5346	37.4848	40.4817	43.1879	46.4589
70	43.2752	45.4418	48.7576	51.7393	55.3290
80	51.1720	53.5400	57.1532	60.3915	64.2778
90	59.1963	61.7541	65.6466	69.1260	73.2912
100	67.3276	70.0648	74.2219	77.9295	82.3581

TABLE XIII Continued

Degrees of Freedom	$\chi^2_{.100}$	$\chi^2_{.050}$	$\chi^2_{.025}$	$\chi^2_{.010}$	$\chi^2_{.005}$
1	2.70554	3.84146	5.02389	6.63490	7.87944
2	4.60517	5.99147	7.37776	9.21034	10.5966
3	6.25139	7.81473	9.34840	11.3449	12.8381
4	7.77944	9.48773	11.1433	13.2767	14.8602
5	9.23635	11.0705	12.8325	15.0863	16.7496
6	10.6446	12.5916	14.4494	16.8119	18.5476
7	12.0170	14.0671	16.0128	18.4753	20.2777
8	13.3616	15.5073	17.5346	20.0902	21.9550
9	14.6837	16.9190	19.0228	21.6660	23.5893
10	15.9871	18.3070	20.4831	23.2093	25.1882
11	17.2750	19.6751	21.9200	24.7250	26.7569
12	18.5494	21.0261	23.3367	26.2170	28.2995
13	19.8119	22.3621	24.7356	27.6883	29.8194
14	21.0642	23.6848	26.1190	29.1413	31.3193
15	22.3072	24.9958	27.4884	30.5779	32.8013
16	23.5418	26.2962	28.8454	31.9999	34.2672
17	24.7690	27.5871	30.1910	33.4087	35.7185
18	25.9894	28.8693	31.5264	34.8053	37.1564
19	27.2036	30.1435	32.8523	36.1908	38.5822
20	28.4120	31.4104	34.1696	37.5662	39.9968
21	29.6151	32.6705	35.4789	38.9321	41.4010
22	30.8133	33.9244	36.7807	40.2894	42.7956
23	32.0069	35.1725	38.0757	41.6384	44.1813
24	33.1963	36.4151	39.3641	42.9798	45.5585
25	34.3816	37.6525	40.6465	44.3141	46.9278
26	35.5631	38.8852	41.9232	45.6417	48.2899
27	36.7412	40.1133	43.1944	46.9630	49.6449
28	37.9159	41.3372	44.4607	48.2782	50.9933
29	39.0875	42.5569	45.7222	49.5879	52.3356
30	40.2560	43.7729	46.9792	50.8922	53.6720
40	51.8050	55.7585	59.3417	63.6907	66.7659
50	63.1671	67.5048	71.4202	76.1539	79.4900
60	74.3970	79.0819	83.2976	88.3794	91.9517
70	85.5271	90.5312	95.0231	100.425	104.215
80	96.5782	101.879	106.629	112.329	116.321
90	107.565	113.145	118.136	124.116	128.299
100	118.498	124.342	129.561	135.807	140.169

TABLE XIV Critical Values for the Durbin-Watson d Statistic, $\alpha = .05$

n	$k = 1$		$k = 2$		$k = 3$		$k = 4$		$k = 5$	
	d_L	d_U	d_L	d_U	d_L	d_U	d_L	d_U	d_L	d_U
15	1.08	1.36	.95	1.54	.82	1.75	.69	1.97	.56	2.21
16	1.10	1.37	.98	1.54	.86	1.73	.74	1.93	.62	2.15
17	1.13	1.38	1.02	1.54	.90	1.71	.78	1.90	.67	2.10
18	1.16	1.39	1.05	1.53	.93	1.69	.92	1.87	.71	2.06
19	1.18	1.40	1.08	1.53	.97	1.68	.86	1.85	.75	2.02
20	1.20	1.41	1.10	1.54	1.00	1.68	.90	1.83	.79	1.99
21	1.22	1.42	1.13	1.54	1.03	1.67	.93	1.81	.83	1.96
22	1.24	1.43	1.15	1.54	1.05	1.66	.96	1.80	.96	1.94
23	1.26	1.44	1.17	1.54	1.08	1.66	.99	1.79	.90	1.92
24	1.27	1.45	1.19	1.55	1.10	1.66	1.01	1.78	.93	1.90
25	1.29	1.45	1.21	1.55	1.12	1.66	1.04	1.77	.95	1.89
26	1.30	1.46	1.22	1.55	1.14	1.65	1.06	1.76	.98	1.88
27	1.32	1.47	1.24	1.56	1.16	1.65	1.08	1.76	1.01	1.86
28	1.33	1.48	1.26	1.56	1.18	1.65	1.10	1.75	1.03	1.85
29	1.34	1.48	1.27	1.56	1.20	1.65	1.12	1.74	1.05	1.84
30	1.35	1.49	1.28	1.57	1.21	1.65	1.14	1.74	1.07	1.83
31	1.36	1.50	1.30	1.57	1.23	1.65	1.16	1.74	1.09	1.83
32	1.37	1.50	1.31	1.57	1.24	1.65	1.18	1.73	1.11	1.82
33	1.38	1.51	1.32	1.58	1.26	1.65	1.19	1.73	1.13	1.81
34	1.39	1.51	1.33	1.58	1.27	1.65	1.21	1.73	1.15	1.81
35	1.40	1.52	1.34	1.58	1.28	1.65	1.22	1.73	1.16	1.80
36	1.41	1.52	1.35	1.59	1.29	1.65	1.24	1.73	1.18	1.80
37	1.42	1.53	1.36	1.59	1.31	1.66	1.25	1.72	1.19	1.80
38	1.43	1.54	1.37	1.59	1.32	1.66	1.26	1.72	1.21	1.79
39	1.43	1.54	1.38	1.60	1.33	1.66	1.27	1.72	1.22	1.79
40	1.44	1.54	1.39	1.60	1.34	1.66	1.29	1.72	1.23	1.79
45	1.48	1.57	1.43	1.62	1.38	1.67	1.34	1.72	1.29	1.78
50	1.50	1.59	1.46	1.63	1.42	1.67	1.38	1.72	1.34	1.77
55	1.53	1.60	1.49	1.64	1.45	1.68	1.41	1.72	1.38	1.77
60	1.55	1.62	1.51	1.65	1.48	1.69	1.44	1.73	1.41	1.77
65	1.57	1.63	1.54	1.66	1.50	1.70	1.47	1.73	1.44	1.77
70	1.58	1.64	1.55	1.67	1.52	1.70	1.49	1.74	1.46	1.77
75	1.60	1.65	1.57	1.68	1.54	1.71	1.51	1.74	1.49	1.77
80	1.61	1.66	1.59	1.69	1.56	1.72	1.53	1.74	1.51	1.77
85	1.62	1.67	1.60	1.70	1.57	1.72	1.55	1.75	1.52	1.77
90	1.63	1.68	1.61	1.70	1.59	1.73	1.57	1.75	1.54	1.78
95	1.64	1.69	1.62	1.71	1.60	1.73	1.58	1.75	1.56	1.78
100	1.65	1.69	1.63	1.72	1.61	1.74	1.59	1.76	1.57	1.78

Source: From J. Durbin and G. S. Watson, "Testing for Serial Correlation in Least Squares Regression, II," *Biometrika*, 1951, 30, 159–178. Reproduced by permission of the *Biometrika* Trustees.

TABLE **XV** **Critical Values for the Durbin-Watson d Statistic, $\alpha = .01$**

	$k = 1$		$k = 2$		$k = 3$		$k = 4$		$k = 5$	
n	d_L	d_U	d_L	d_U	d_L	d_U	d_L	d_U	d_L	d_U
15	.81	1.07	.70	1.25	.59	1.46	.49	1.70	.39	1.96
16	.84	1.09	.74	1.25	.63	1.44	.53	1.66	.44	1.90
17	.87	1.10	.77	1.25	.67	1.43	.57	1.3	.48	1.85
18	.90	1.12	.80	1.26	.71	1.42	.61	1.60	.52	1.80
19	.93	1.13	.83	1.26	.74	1.41	.65	1.58	.56	1.77
20	.95	1.15	.86	1.27	.77	1.41	.68	1.57	.60	1.74
21	.97	1.16	.89	1.27	.80	1.41	.72	1.55	.63	1.71
22	1.00	1.17	.91	1.28	.83	1.40	.75	1.54	.66	1.69
23	1.02	1.19	.94	1.29	.86	1.40	.77	1.53	.70	1.67
24	1.04	1.20	.96	1.30	.88	1.41	.80	1.53	.72	1.66
25	1.05	1.21	.98	1.30	.90	1.41	.83	1.52	.75	1.65
26	1.07	1.22	1.00	1.31	.93	1.41	.85	1.52	.78	1.64
27	1.09	1.23	1.02	1.32	.95	1.41	.88	1.51	.81	1.63
28	1.10	1.24	1.04	1.32	.97	1.41	.90	1.51	.83	1.62
29	1.12	1.25	1.05	1.33	.99	1.42	.92	1.51	.85	1.61
30	1.13	1.26	1.07	1.34	1.01	1.42	.94	1.51	.88	1.61
31	1.15	1.27	1.08	1.34	1.02	1.42	.96	1.51	.90	1.60
32	1.16	1.28	1.10	1.35	1.04	1.43	.98	1.51	.92	1.60
33	1.17	1.29	1.11	1.36	1.05	1.43	1.00	1.51	.94	1.59
34	1.18	1.30	1.13	1.36	1.07	1.43	1.01	1.51	.95	1.59
35	1.19	1.31	1.14	1.27	1.08	1.44	1.03	1.51	.97	1.59
36	1.21	1.32	1.15	1.38	1.10	1.44	1.04	1.51	.99	1.59
37	1.22	1.32	1.16	1.38	1.11	1.45	1.06	1.51	1.00	1.59
38	1.23	1.33	1.18	1.39	1.12	1.45	1.07	1.52	1.02	1.58
39	1.24	1.34	1.19	1.39	1.14	1.45	1.09	1.52	1.03	1.58
40	1.25	1.34	1.20	1.40	1.15	1.46	1.10	1.52	1.05	1.58
45	1.29	1.38	1.24	1.42	1.20	1.48	1.16	1.53	1.11	1.58
50	1.32	1.40	1.28	1.45	1.24	1.49	1.20	1.54	1.16	1.59
55	1.36	1.43	1.32	1.47	1.28	1.51	1.25	1.55	1.21	1.59
60	1.38	1.45	1.35	1.48	1.32	1.52	1.28	1.56	1.25	1.60
65	1.41	1.47	1.38	1.50	1.35	1.53	1.31	1.57	1.28	1.61
70	1.43	1.49	1.40	1.52	1.37	1.55	1.34	1.58	1.31	1.61
75	1.45	1.50	1.42	1.53	1.39	1.56	1.37	1.59	1.34	1.62
80	1.47	1.52	1.44	1.54	1.42	1.57	1.39	1.60	1.36	1.62
85	1.48	1.53	1.46	1.55	1.43	1.58	1.41	1.60	1.39	1.63
90	1.50	1.54	1.47	1.56	1.45	1.59	1.43	1.61	1.41	1.64
95	1.51	1.55	1.49	1.57	1.47	1.60	1.45	1.62	1.42	1.64
100	1.52	1.56	1.50	1.58	1.48	1.60	1.46	1.63	1.44	1.65

TABLE XVI **Critical Values of Spearman's Rank Correlation Coefficient**

The α values correspond to a one-tailed test of H_0: $\rho = 0$. The value should be doubled for two-tailed tests.

n	$\alpha = .05$	$\alpha = .025$	$\alpha = .01$	$\alpha = .005$	n	$\alpha = .05$	$\alpha = .025$	$\alpha = .01$	$\alpha = .005$
5	.900	—	—	—	18	.399	.476	.564	.625
6	.829	.886	.943	—	19	.388	.462	.549	.608
7	.714	.786	.893	—	20	.377	.450	.534	.591
8	.643	.738	.833	.881	21	.368	.438	.521	.576
9	.600	.683	.783	.833	22	.359	.428	.508	.562
10	.564	.648	.745	.794	23	.351	.418	.496	.549
11	.523	.623	.736	.818	24	.343	.409	.485	.537
12	.497	.591	.703	.780	25	.336	.400	.475	.526
13	.475	.566	.673	.745	26	.329	.392	.465	.515
14	.457	.545	.646	.716	27	.323	.385	.456	.505
15	.441	.525	.623	.689	28	.317	.377	.448	.496
16	.425	.507	.601	.666	29	.311	.370	.440	.487
17	.412	.490	.582	.645	30	.305	.364	.432	.478

Source: From E. G. Olds, "Distribution of Sums of Squares of Rank Differences for Small Samples," *Annals of Mathematical Statistics*, 1938, 9. Reproduced with the permission of the Editor, *Annals of Mathematical Statistics*.

TABLE **XVII** **Control Chart Constants**

Number of Observations in Subgroup, n	A_2	d_2	d_3	D_3	D_4
2	1.880	1.128	.853	.000	3.267
3	1.023	1.693	.888	.000	2.574
4	.729	2.059	.880	.000	2.282
5	.577	2.326	.864	.000	2.114
6	.483	2.534	.848	.000	2.004
7	.419	2.704	.833	.076	1.924
8	.373	2.847	.820	.136	1.864
9	.337	2.970	.808	.184	1.816
10	.308	3.078	.797	.223	1.777
11	.285	3.173	.787	.256	1.744
12	.266	3.258	.778	.283	1.717
13	.249	3.336	.770	.307	1.693
14	.235	3.407	.762	.328	1.672
15	.223	3.472	.755	.347	1.653
16	.212	3.532	.749	.363	1.637
17	.203	3.588	.743	.378	1.622
18	.194	3.640	.738	.391	1.608
19	.187	3.689	.733	.403	1.597
20	.180	3.735	.729	.415	1.585
21	.173	3.778	.724	.425	1.575
22	.167	3.819	.720	.434	1.566
23	.162	3.858	.716	.443	1.557
24	.157	3.895	.712	.451	1.548
25	.153	3.931	.709	.459	1.541
More than 25	$3/\sqrt{n}$				

Source: ASTM Manual on the Presentation of Data and Control Chart Analysis, Philadelphia, PA: American Society for Testing Materials, pp. 134–136, 1976.

APPENDIX C
CALCULATION FORMULAS FOR
ANALYSIS OF VARIANCE

C.1 Formulas for the Calculations in the Completely Randomized Design

CM = Correction for mean

$$= \frac{(\text{Total of all observations})^2}{\text{Total number of observations}} = \frac{\left(\sum_{i=1}^{n} y_i\right)^2}{n}$$

$SS(\text{Total})$ = Total sum of squares

$$= (\text{Sum of squares of all observations}) - CM = \sum_{i=1}^{n} y_i^2 - CM$$

SST = Sum of squares for treatments

$$= \left(\begin{array}{c} \text{Sum of squares of treatment totals with} \\ \text{each square divided by the number of} \\ \text{observations for that treatment} \end{array}\right) - CM$$

$$= \frac{T_1^2}{n_1} + \frac{T_2^2}{n_2} + \cdots + \frac{T_p^2}{n_p} - CM$$

SSE = Sum of squares for error = $SS(\text{Total}) - SST$

MST = Mean square for treatments = $\dfrac{SST}{p-1}$

MSE = Mean square for error = $\dfrac{SSE}{n-p}$

$$F = \text{Test statistic} = \frac{MST}{MSE}$$

where

n = Total number of observations

p = Number of treatments

T_i = Total for treatment i $(i = 1, 2, ..., p)$

C.2   Formulas for the Calculations for a Two-factor Factorial Experiment

$\text{CM} =$ Correction for mean

$$= \frac{(\text{Total of all } n \text{ measurements})^2}{n} = \frac{\left(\sum_{i=1}^{n} y_i\right)^2}{n}$$

$\text{SS(Total)} =$ Total sum of squares

$$= (\text{Sum of squares of all } n \text{ measurements}) - \text{CM} = \sum_{i=1}^{n} y_i^2 - \text{CM}$$

$\text{SS}(A) =$ Sum of squares for main effects, factor A

$$= \left(\begin{array}{c} \text{Sum of squares of the totals } A_1, A_2, \dots, A_a \\ \text{divided by the number of measurements} \\ \text{in a single total, namely } br \end{array} \right) - \text{CM}$$

$$= \frac{\sum_{i=1}^{a} A_i^2}{br} - \text{CM}$$

$\text{SS}(B) =$ Sum of squares for main effects, factor B

$$= \left(\begin{array}{c} \text{Sum of squares of the totals } B_1, B_2, \dots, B_b \\ \text{divided by the number of measurements} \\ \text{in a single total, namely } ar \end{array} \right) - \text{CM}$$

$$= \frac{\sum_{i=1}^{b} B_i^2}{ar} - \text{CM}$$

$\text{SS}(AB) =$ Sum of squares for AB interaction

$$= \left(\begin{array}{c} \text{Sum of squares of the cell totals} \\ AB_{11}, AB_{12}, \dots, AB_{ab} \text{ divided by} \\ \text{the number of measurements} \\ \text{in a single total, namely } r \end{array} \right) - \text{SS}(A) - \text{SS}(B) - \text{CM}$$

$$= \frac{\sum_{j=1}^{b}\sum_{i=1}^{a} AB_{ij}^2}{r} - \text{SS}(A) - \text{SS}(B) - \text{CM}$$

where

$a =$ Number of levels of factor A

$b =$ Number of levels of factor B

$r =$ Number of replicates (observations per treatment)

$A_i =$ Total for level i of factor A ($i = 1, 2, \dots, a$)

$B_i =$ Total for level i of factor B ($i = 1, 2, \dots, b$)

$AB_{ij} =$ Total for treatment (i, j) i.e. for ith level of factor A and jth level of factor B

CHAPTER 1

1.13 Qualitative, qualitative   **1.15a.** Citizens of U.S.   **b.** President's performance, qualitative   **c.** 2,000 individuals   **d.** 0   **e.** Survey   **f.** Not likely
1.17a. Quantitative   **b.** Qualitative   **c.** Qualitative   **d.** Quantitative
1.19a. Quantitative   **b.** Quantitative   **c.** Qualitative   **d.** Quantitative
e. Qualitative   **f.** Quantitative   **g.** Qualitative   **1.21a.** All department store executives   **b.** Job satisfaction and Machiavellian rating   **c.** 218 executives
d. Survey   **1.23b.** All bank presidents in U.S.   **1.25a.** All major U.S. firms
b. Job-sharing availability   **c.** 1,035 firms   **1.27I.** Qualitative
II. Quantitative   **III.** Quantitative   **IV.** Qualitative   **V.** Qualitative
VI. Quantitative   **1.29b.** Speed, accuracy, and packaging   **c.** Total number of questionnaires received

CHAPTER 2

2.3a. .642, .204, .083, .071   **2.5a.** Length of time   **c.** 3,570   **d.** No
2.7a. Length of time   **c.** .08   **2.9a.** 195   **b.** 90   **c.** .016, .024, .355, .327, .187, .091   **2.11b.** Inflation rate   **c.** Yes   **2.13** (See figure below)
2.15a. Frequency histogram   **b.** 14   **c.** 49   **2.17b.** .733   **2.21b.** Yes
2.23a. Stem: 1000's, Leaf 100's; Largest: 11,968.23 represented by 12.0
2.25b. P/E ratios in manufacturing exceed P/E ratios in holding   **2.27a.** 33
b. 175   **c.** 20   **d.** 71   **e.** 1,089   **2.29a.** 6   **b.** 50   **c.** 42.8   **2.31** Mean = 2.717, median = 2.65   **2.35a.** 2.5, 3, 3   **b.** 3.08, 3, 3   **c.** 49.6, 49, 50
2.37a. Health care: mean = 38,956.9, median = 33,254.5; Banks: mean = 18,481.1, median = 16,065   **b.** Both skewed right   **c.** No   **2.43a.** Joint: mean = 2.6545, median = 1.5; No: mean = 4.2364, median = 3.2; Prepack: mean = 1.8185, median = 1.4   **2.45a.** Mean = 91.99, median = 90.5, mode = all values
b. Mean = 90.57, median = 90, mode = all values   **c.** 80% trimmed mean = 91.175   **2.47c.** No   **2.49a.** 4, 2.3, 1.52   **b.** 6, 3.619, 1.90   **c.** 10, 7.111, 2.67
d. 5, 1.624, 1.274   **2.51a.** 5.6, 17.3, 4.1593   **b.** 13.75 feet, 152.25 square feet, 12.339 feet   **c.** .33 ounce, .0587 square ounces, .2422 ounce   **2.53** (See figure below)   **2.55a.** U.S. Index: $\bar{x}$ = 150.3042; Chicago Index: $\bar{x}$ = 150.9542

Exercise 2.13

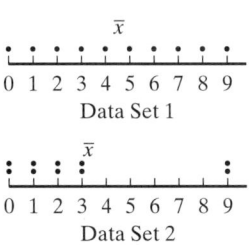

Exercise 2.53

b. U.S. Index: Range = 7.5; Chicago Index: Range = 7.8 **c.** U.S. Index: s = 2.4108; Chicago Index: s = 2.6572 **d.** Chicago Index **2.57a.** Range = 455.2, s^2 = 25,367.88238, s = 159.2730 **b.** Million dollars, million dollars squared, million dollars **c.** Increase, increase **2.59** Any data, mound-shaped and symmetric **2.61a.** Nothing **b.** At least $\frac{3}{4}$ **c.** At least $\frac{8}{9}$ **2.63a.** 8.24, 3.357, 1.83 **b.** 72%, 96%, 100% **c.** $s \approx 1.75$ **2.65b.** $(-100.266, 219.906)$ **2.67a.** Not appropriate **b.** $(-1.107, 6.205)$ **c.** 95.9% **2.69b.** No **2.71** Do not buy the land. **2.73a.** $-1.83, 11.2942$ **c.** No **2.75a.** 2 **b.** .5 **c.** 0 **d.** -2.5 **e.** Sample, population, population, sample **f.** Above, above, at, below **2.77** Median **2.79a.** 3.7, 2.2, 2.95, 1.45 **b.** 1.9 **c.** $z = 1, 2$; GPA = 3.2, 3.7; Assume mound-shaped **2.81** No **2.83b.** Japan: $z = 2.57$; Egypt: $z = .61$ **2.85a.** 0 **b.** 21 **c.** 5.90 **d.** Yes **2.89a.** 39 **b.** 31.5, 45 **c.** ≈ 13.5 **d.** Skewed left **e.** 50%, 75% **2.93c.** No **d.** Yes **2.95b.** 238, 268, 269, 264 **c.** 1.92, 2.06, 2.13, 3.14 **2.99a.** $-1, 1, 2$ **b.** $-2, 2, 4$ **c.** 1, 3, 4 **d.** .1, .3, .4 **2.101a.** $\bar{x} = 6, s^2 = 27, s = 5.20$ **b.** $\bar{x} = 6.25, s^2 = 28.25, s = 5.32$ **c.** $\bar{x} = 7$, $s^2 = 37.67, s = 6.14$ **d.** $\bar{x} = 3, s^2 = 0, s = 0$ **2.107b.** 6.5 days, 7.0 days, 8.5 days **2.111a.** Skewed right **b.** Chebyshev's Rule appropriate **c.** ≈ 38 homes **d.** $z = 3.333$, no **2.115a.** Frequency bar chart **c.** 70% successful **2.119a.** High GNP: $\bar{x} = 4.4125, s = 1.965$; Low GNP: Median = 23.15, $s = 127.54$ **c.** No

CHAPTER 3

3.1a. .5 **b.** .3 **c.** .6 **3.3** $P(A) = .55, P(B) = .50, P(C) = .70$ **3.5** $P(A) = \frac{1}{10}$, $P(B) = \frac{2}{5}, P(C) = \frac{3}{10}$ **3.7a.** Strongly agree, agree, neither, disagree, strongly disagree **b.** .189, .403, .258, .113, .038 **c.** .592 **d.** .812 **3.9** $\frac{1}{20}$ **3.11c.** .556, .444 **3.13a.** 1 to 2 **b.** $\frac{1}{2}$ **c.** $\frac{2}{5}$ **3.15b.** $\frac{1}{16}$ **c.** $\frac{5}{16}$ **3.17** (See figure at left) **3.19a.** $\frac{3}{4}$ **b.** $\frac{13}{20}$ **c.** 1 **d.** $\frac{2}{5}$ **e.** $\frac{1}{4}$ **f.** $\frac{7}{20}$ **g.** 1 **h.** $\frac{1}{4}$ **3.21a.** .5 **b.** .31875 **c.** .125 **d.** .75 **e.** .75 **f.** .3125 **g.** $(A, B), (A, C), (B, C), (D, E),$ $(D, F), (E, F)$ are mutually exclusive. **3.23a.** $B \cap C$ **b.** A^c **c.** $C \cup B$ **d.** $A \cap C^c$ **3.25d.** $\frac{5}{6}, \frac{1}{2}, \frac{1}{3}, 1, \frac{1}{6}$ **e.** 1, no **3.27b** Sample space **c.** .24 **d.** .10 **e.** .47 **f.** .62 **g.** .28 **3.29a.** .06 **b.** .27 **c.** .17 **d.** .70 **3.31a.** Yes **b.** .26, .35, .72, .28, .05 **c.** .56, .05, .77 **d.** .74 **e.** $C \cap D$ and $D \cap E$ contains no events **3.33a.** .8, .7, .6 **b.** .25, .375, .375 **c.** .75, .75 **d.** No **3.35a.** .37 **b.** .68 **c.** .15 **d.** .2206 **e.** 0 **f.** 0 **g.** None **3.37a.** $A \cap C$ and $B \cap C$ **b.** None **c.** $P(A \cup B) = .65, P(A \cap C) = .90$ **3.39a.** .08, .4, .52 **b.** .12, .30 **3.41a.** .550 **b.** .450 **c.** .272 **d.** .040 **e.** .182 **f.** .857 **g.** .182 **3.43a.** .543 **b.** .221 **c.** .052 **d.** .914 **3.45** .005 **3.47a.** .02 **b.** .08 **3.49a.** .116 **b.** .728 **3.51a.** .3, .6 **b.** Dependent **c.** Independent **3.53a.** 35,820,200 **b.** $\frac{1}{35,820,200}$ **3.55a.** .000186 **c.** No **3.61** .5 **3.63a.** 0, .2, .9, 1, .7, .3, .4, 0 **b.** No, yes **c.** No, no **3.65a.** 720 **b.** 10 **c.** 10 **d.** 20 **e.** 1 **3.67a.** .75 **b.** .2875 **c.** .6 **d.** .06 **e.** No **g.** Yes **3.69a.** $P(A) = \frac{1}{10}, P(B) = \frac{1}{10}$ **b.** .641, .359 **c.** Upper bounds **3.71a.** .00000625 **b.** .0135 **c.** Doubt claim; $p = .000475$ **d.** Not positive, but $p = .00000625$ **3.73** .801 **3.75a.** (See figure at left) **b.** .95 **c.** .25 **d.** .5 **3.77a.** .24 **b.** .1 **c.** .14 **3.79** .79 **3.81a.** .7127 **b.** .2873 **3.83b.** $\frac{1}{10}$ **c.** $\frac{1}{10}, \frac{3}{10}$ **3.85a.** 6 **b.** $\frac{1}{3}$ **3.87a.** 142,506 **b.** .2361 **c.** .6711

Exercise 3.17

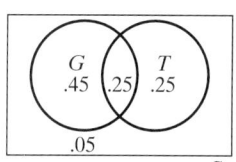

Exercise 3.75a

CHAPTER 4

4.3a. Discrete **b.** Discrete **c.** Discrete **d.** Continuous **e.** Discrete **f.** Continuous **4.11a.** .25 **b.** .40 **c.** .75 **4.13a.** $x = 0, 1, 2, 3$ **b.** $p(3) = \frac{1}{8}$, $p(2) = \frac{3}{8}, p(1) = \frac{3}{8}, p(0) = \frac{1}{8}$ **d.** $\frac{1}{2}$ **4.17b.** $p(x > 200,000) = .011$, $p(x > 100,000) = .052, p(x < 100,000) = .948$ **d.** $p(6) = .138, p(1$ or $9) = .196$

Cost	p
$1,000	.25
$2,000	.25
$3,000	.50

Exercise 4.33a

4.19b. .85 **c.** a_2: .6, a_3: 0, a_4: 0, a_5: 0, a_6: .7 **d.** .51 **4.23a.** $\mu = 34.5, \sigma^2 = 174.75$, $\sigma = 13.219$ **c.** 1.00 **4.25a.** $\mu = 1$ **b.** Distribution of x **c.** For x: $\mu = 1$, $\sigma^2 = .6$; for y: $\mu = 1, \sigma^2 = .2$ **4.27** $E(x) = \$.25$ **4.29a.** $\mu = 2.9$, median $= 3$ **b.** 3, 4 **c.** 3, 3 **4.31** $\mu_{a_1} = 2.4, \mu_{a_2} = 1.5, \mu_{a_3} = .90, \mu_{a_4} = .90, \mu_{a_5} = .90$, $\mu_{a_6} = 1.65$ **4.33a.** (See table at left) **b.** .25 **c.** $\mu = \$2,250$ **d.** $\mu = \$2,250$ **4.35a.** 15 **b.** 10 **c.** 1 **d.** 1 **e.** 4 **4.37a.** .4096 **b.** .3456 **c.** .027 **d.** .0081 **e.** .3456 **f.** .027 **4.39a.** $\mu = 12.5, \sigma^2 = 6.25, \sigma = 2.5$ **b.** $\mu = 16$, $\sigma^2 = 12.8, \sigma = 3.578$ **c.** $\mu = 60, \sigma^2 = 24, \sigma = 4.899$ **d.** $\mu = 63, \sigma^2 = 6.3$, $\sigma = 2.510$ **e.** $\mu = 48, \sigma^2 = 9.6, \sigma = 3.098$ **f.** $\mu = 40, \sigma^2 = 38.4, \sigma = 6.197$ **4.41a.** $p = .5$ **b.** $p < .5$ **c.** $p > .5$ **e.** $p = .5$ symmetric; $p < .5$ skewed right; $p > .5$ skewed left **4.43a.** .006, .01, .049 **b.** .0293, .0003 **c.** .0480, .0010 **d.** .8936 **4.45b.** $\mu = 2.4, \sigma = 1.47$ **c.** $p = .90, q = .10, n = 24; \mu = 21.60$, $\sigma = 1.47$ **4.47** No, $z = 4.95$ **4.49a.** $\mu = 520, \sigma = 13.491$ **b.** No, $z = -8.895$ **4.51a.** 1 **b.** .998 **c.** .537 **d.** .009 **e.** ≈ 0 **f.** ≈ 0 **g.** ≈ 0 **h.** $= 0$ **4.53a.** Discrete **b.** Poisson **d.** $\mu = 3, \sigma = 1.7321$ **e.** $\mu = 3, \sigma = 1.7321$ **4.55a.** .934 **b.** .191 **c.** .125 **d.** .223 **e.** .777 **f.** .001 **4.57a.** $\mu = 128.6$, $\sigma = 11.340$ **b.** $z = -7.72$ **4.59a.** $\sigma = 2$ **b.** No, $P(x > 10) = .003$ **4.61** $P(x > 4) = .1088$ **4.63a.** .193 **b.** .660 **4.65** $P(3) = .224, P(0) = .050$, $.05^8$ **4.67a.** .2734 **b.** .4096 **c.** .3432 **4.69a.** .192 **b.** .228 **c.** .772 **d.** .987 **e.** .960 **f.** $\mu = 14, \sigma^2 = 4.2, \sigma = 2.049$ **g.** .975 **4.71a.** Discrete **b.** Continuous **c.** Continuous **d.** Continuous **4.73a.** 497,000 **b.** 6.6055975×10^{11} **4.75** .009 **4.77a.** True **b.** .017 **4.79b.** $E(x) = 14$, $\sigma = 3.742$ **c.** Yes **d.** .002 **4.81a.** $\mu = 1.25, \sigma = 1.09$, no **b.** .007 **c.** $p > 5\%$ **4.83a.** .006 **b.** $p < .80$ **4.85a.** .0314 **b.** .0166

CHAPTER 5

5.1b. $\mu = 32.5, \sigma = 7.2169$ **5.3b.** $\mu = 5, \sigma = 1.155$ **c.** .5775 **5.5a.** 0 **b.** 1 **c.** 1 **5.7a.** Continuous **c.** $\mu = 7, \sigma = .2887$ **d.** .5 **e.** 0 **f.** .75 **g.** .0002 **5.11** .4444 **5.13a.** .4772 **b.** .4987 **c.** .4332 **d.** .2881 **5.15a.** .0721 **b.** .0594 **c.** .2434 **d.** .3457 **e.** .5 **f.** .9233 **5.17a.** .6826 **b.** .9500 **c.** .90 **d.** .9544 **5.19a.** $-.81$ **b.** .55 **c.** 1.43 **d.** .21 **e.** -2.05 **f.** .50 **5.21a.** -2.5 **b.** 0 **c.** $-.625$ **d.** -3.75 **e.** 1.25 **f.** -1.25 **5.23a.** .3830 **b.** .3023 **c.** .1525 **d.** .7333 **e.** .1314 **f.** .9545 **5.25a.** .9544 **b.** .0918 **c.** .0228 **d.** .8607 **e.** .0927 **f.** .7049 **5.27a.** .3050, .1020 **b.** .6879, .8925 **c.** .0032 **5.29a.** .5124 **b.** Yes, $p = .2912$ **c.** No, $p = .0027$ **5.31a.** .68% **5.33** $\mu = 5.068$ **5.35a.** XYZ **b.** ABC: $E(x) = \$105$; XYZ: $E(y) = \$107$ **c.** ABC **5.37a.** $z_L = -.67; z_U = .67$ **b.** $-2.68, 2.68$ **c.** $-4.69, 4.69$ **d.** .0074, 0 **5.41a.** Yes **b.** $\mu = 17.5, \sigma^2 = 5.25$ **c.** .902 **d.** .9049 **5.43a.** .488 **b.** .2334 **c.** 0 **5.45** ≈ 0 **5.47a.** No **b.** .6026 **c.** No, yes, yes **d.** .7190 **5.49a.** .0559 **c.** No **5.51b.** ≈ 0 **c.** No, $p \approx 0$ **d.** Yes **5.53a.** .367879 **b.** .082085 **c.** .000553 **d.** .223130 **5.55a.** .999447 **b.** .999955 **c.** .981684 **d.** .632121 **5.57a.** .018316 **b.** .950213 **c.** .383401 **5.59a.** .279543 **b.** .1123887 **5.61a.** $R(x) = e^{-.5x}$ **b.** .13535 **c.** .367879 **d.** No **e.** 820.85, 3,934.69 **f.** 36.5 days **5.63a.** .550671 **b.** .263597 **5.65a.** $\mu = 250$ **b.** .135335 **c.** .135335 **5.67b.** $\mu = 50, \sigma = 23.094011$ **d.** .625 **e.** 0 **f.** .875 **g.** .577 **h.** .1875 **5.69a.** .02 **b.** $-.13$ **c.** 1.04 **d.** $-.69$ **5.71a.** .3821 **b.** .5398 **c.** 0 **d.** .1395 **e.** .0045 **f.** .4602 **5.73** $E(\text{Profit}) = \$9.6582$ **5.75a.** .0918 **b.** 0 **c.** $\mu = 95.13$ lower 4.87 decibels **5.77a.** .221199 **b.** .002394 **c.** .082085 **5.79a.** .8264 **b.** 17.36 times **c.** .6217 **d.** $\mu = 0$, $\mu = -157$ **5.81a.** .0548 **b.** .6006 **c.** .3446 **d.** $\mu = \$6503.80$ **5.83a.** i. .384;

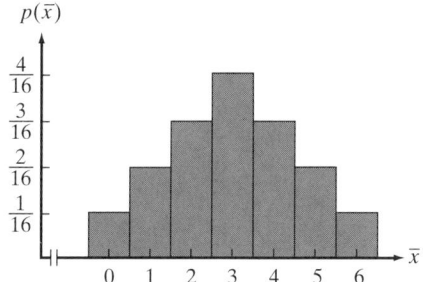

Exercise 6.1e

ii. .49; iii. .212; iv. .84   **b.** i. .3849; ii. .4938; iii. .2119; iv. .8413   **c.** i. .0009; ii. .0038; iii. .0001; iv. .0013   **5.87a.** .135335   **b.** .594

CHAPTER 6

6.1c. $\frac{1}{16}$ **e.** (See figure above)   **6.3c.** .05   **d.** No   **6.9a.** $\mu = 5$ **d.** Sample mean   **6.13b.** $\sigma^2 = 1.61$ **c.** $E(s^2) = 1.61$ **e.** $E(s) = 1.00394 \neq 1.269 = \sigma$ **6.15a.** 100, 5   **b.** 100, 2   **c.** 100, 1   **d.** 100, 1.414   **e.** 100, .447   **f.** 100, .316   **6.17a.** $\mu = 2.9, \sigma^2 = 3.29, \sigma = 1.814$ **c.** $\mu_{\bar{x}} = 2.9, \sigma_{\bar{x}} = 1.283$ **6.19a.** $\mu_{\bar{x}} = 20$, $\sigma_{\bar{x}} = 2$ **b.** Approximately normal   **c.** $z = -2.25$ **d.** $z = 1.50$ **6.21a.** .8944   **b.** .0228   **c.** .1292   **d.** .9699   **6.25a.** $\mu_{\bar{x}} = 406, \sigma_{\bar{x}} = 1.6833$, approximately normal   **b.** .0010   **c.** The first   **6.27a.** $\mu_{\bar{x}} = 89.34, \sigma_{\bar{x}} = 1.3083$ **c.** .8461   **d.** .0367   **6.29a.** .0031, claim is too high   **b.** .2643, 0   **c.** 0, .0853   **6.33a.** .5   **b.** .0606   **c.** .0985   **d.** .8436   **6.39a.** $\mu_x = 26, \sigma_x = \sigma$ **b.** $\mu_{\bar{x}} = 26, \mu_{\bar{x}} = \sigma/\sqrt{n}$, approximately normal   **c.** .2843   **d.** .1292   **6.41a.** Approximately normal with $\mu_{\bar{x}} = 10$ and $\sigma_{\bar{x}} = 2.0486$ **b.** .0446, no   **6.43a.** .9525 or 95.25%   **b.** 100%   **6.45a.** .4514   **b.** Not at all   **6.47a.** 1.5% above and below μ **b.** .0026   **c.** .1587   **6.49a.** .05   **b.** 1   **c.** .000625   **6.51a.** $E(\bar{x}) = 60, \sigma_{\bar{x}}^2 = 36$ **b.** Normal distribution   **c.** ≈ 0

CHAPTER 7

7.1a. 1.645   **b.** 2.58   **c.** 1.96   **d.** 1.28   **7.3a.** $28 \pm .784$ **b.** $102 \pm .65$ **c.** $15 \pm .0588$ **d.** $4.05 \pm .163$ **e.** No   **7.5a.** $26.2 \pm .96$ **c.** 26.2 ± 1.26 **d.** Increases   **e.** Yes   **7.9** Yes, if $n \geqslant 30$ **7.11a.** 33.583 ± 5.751 **7.13c.** 1 ± 48.84 **e.** Not very accurate   **7.15a.** 23.43 ± 1.817 **d.** Yes   **7.17a.** Younger: $4.17 \pm .095$; middle-age: $4.04 \pm .057$; older: $4.31 \pm .062$ **b.** More likely   **7.19a.** $z = 1.28, t = 1.533$ **b.** $z = 1.645, t = 2.132$ **c.** $z = 1.96, t = 2.776$ **d.** $z = 2.33, t = 3.747$ **e.** $z = 2.575, t = 4.604$ **7.21a.** 2.228   **b.** 2.228   **c.** -1.812 **d.** 2.086   **e.** 4.032   **7.23a.** 97.94 ± 4.240 **b.** 97.94 ± 6.737 **7.25a.** 49.3 ± 8.60 **c.** Normal population   **7.27b.** $23,490.09 \pm 1,958.97$ **7.29** 184.99 ± 133.94 **7.31a.** 22.455 ± 11.177 **c.** Normal population   **d.** Assumption is suspect   **7.33** $E(\hat{p}) = p$ **7.35a.** $.10 \pm .045$ **b.** $.10 \pm .127$ **c.** $.5 \pm .335$ **d.** $.3 \pm .307$ **7.37a.** Yes   **b.** $.46 \pm .065$ **7.39a.** $.694 \pm .106$ **b.** Randomly sample   **7.41a.** All are large   **b.** Poor: $.155 \pm .046$; average: $.133 \pm .046$; good: $.108 \pm .062$ **7.43** $.85 \pm .002$ **7.45a.** $\hat{p} = .24$ **b.** $.24 \pm .118$ **7.47** $n = 308$ **7.49a.** $n = 68$ **b.** $n = 31$ **7.51** $n = 34$ **7.53a.** $n = 16$: .98; $n = 25$: .784; $n = 49$: .56; $n = 100$: .392; $n = 400$: .196   **7.55a.** $.226 \pm .007$ **b.** .014   **c.** $n = 1,680$ **7.57** $s = 10$: $n = 43$; $s = 20$: $n = 171$; $s = 30$: $n = 385$

7.59 $n = 1,351$ **7.61** $n = 271$ **7.63** $n = 3,701$ **7.65a.** 4.90 **b.** 5.66 **c.** 6.00 **d.** 6.293 **7.67a.** 1.00 **b.** .6124 **c.** 0 **d.** $\sigma_{\bar{x}}$ decreases **7.69** $.42 \pm .021$ **7.71a.** $\bar{x} = 156.46$ **b.** $\hat{\sigma}_{\bar{x}} = 20.6998$ **c.** 156.46 ± 41.40 **d.** Probably wrong **7.73** 1 ± 41.43 **7.75** $.694 \pm .092$ **7.77a.** -1.725 **b.** 3.250 **c.** 1.860 **d.** 2.898 **7.79a.** 32.5 ± 5.16 **b.** $n = 23,964$ **7.81a.** .9874 **b.** .8944 **c.** .8944 **7.83a.** (298.6, 582.3) **7.85a.** $.876 \pm .003$ **7.87a.** Men: $7.4 \pm .979$; women: $4.5 \pm .755$ **b.** Men: 9.3 ± 1.185; women: 6.6 ± 1.138 **7.89a.** 12.2 ± 1.645 **b.** $n = 167$ **7.91a.** No **b.** $n = 1,337$ **7.93a.** $n = 191$ **7.95a.** Random sample **b.** $3.256 \pm .348$ **7.99a.** 985.6 ± 25.61 **b.** Not "out of control" **c.** 985.6 ± 14.198; process is out of control **d.** 99% **e.** Normal population **7.101** $n = 818$

CHAPTER 8

8.1 Null; alternative **8.3** α **8.11a.** $\alpha = .025$ **b.** $\alpha = .05$ **c.** $\alpha = .005$ **d.** $\alpha = .1003$ **e.** $\alpha = .10$ **f.** $\alpha = .01$ **8.13a.** $z = 1.67$, reject H_0 **b.** $z = 1.67$, fail to reject H_0 **8.15a.** $H_0: \mu = 16$; $H_a: \mu < 16$ **b.** $z = -4.31$, reject H_0 **8.17a.** $z = 7.02$, reject H_0 **8.19** $z = 1.58$, reject H_0 **8.21a.** $H_0: \mu = 1,502.5$; $H_a: \mu > 1,502.5$ **b.** $z = 3.74$, reject H_0 **c.** No **d.** Yes **8.23** $z = -4.34$, reject H_0 **8.25a.** Fail to reject H_0 **b.** Reject H_0 **c.** Reject H_0 **d.** Fail to reject H_0 **e.** Fail to reject H_0 **8.27** $p = .0150$ **8.29** $p = .9279$, fail to reject H_0 **8.31a.** Fail to reject H_0 **b.** Fail to reject H_0 **c.** Reject H_0 **d.** Fail to reject H_0 **8.33a.** $H_0: \mu = 30\%$; $H_a: \mu > 30\%$ **b.** $p = .1271$ **c.** Fail to reject H_0 **8.35a.** $H_0: \mu = 2.5$; $H_a: \mu > 2.5$ **b.** $p \approx 0$ **c.** Reject H_0 **8.37a.** $H_0: \mu = 16.5$; $H_a: \mu > 16.5$ **b.** $p = .0681$ **8.43a.** $t < -2.160$ or $t > 2.160$ **b.** $t > 2.500$ **c.** $t > 1.397$ **d.** $t < -2.718$ **e.** $t < -1.729$ or $t > 1.729$ **f.** $t < -2.353$ **8.45b.** $p = .0382$, reject H_0 at $\alpha > .0382$ **c.** $p = .0764$, fail to reject H_0 at $\alpha = .05$ **8.47** $t = 8.75$, reject H_0 **8.49a.** $H_0: \mu = 15$; $H_a: \mu < 15$ **b.** $p = .0556$ **c.** At $\alpha = .05$, fail to reject H_0 **8.51** $t = 2.97$, fail to reject H_0 **8.53a.** Yes **b.** No **c.** Yes **d.** No **e.** No **8.55a.** $z = -2.33$ **c.** Reject H_0 **d.** $p = .0099$, reject H_0 **8.57a.** $z = 1.13$, fail to reject H_0 **b.** $p = .1292$ **8.59a.** $H_0: p = .4$; $H_a: p < .4$ **b.** $z = -.19$, fail to reject H_0 **c.** $p = .4247$, fail to reject H_0 **8.61** $z = 33.47$, reject H_0 **8.63a.** $z = 15.61$, reject H_0 **b.** $p \approx 0$, reject H_0 **8.67b.** $\bar{x}_0 = 532.9$ **d.** $\beta = .1949$ **e.** Power $= .8051$ **8.69c.** $\beta = .1469$ **d.** Power $= .8531$ **8.71c.** $\beta = .5359$ **d.** $\beta = .0409$ **8.73a.** $z = 2.43$, reject H_0 **b.** Power $= .9850$ **8.75** $\beta = .1075$ **8.77** Alternative **8.79** Big **8.81a.** $t = -7.51$, reject H_0 **b.** $t = -7.51$, reject H_0 **8.83a.** $z = -1.67$, fail to reject H_0 **b.** $z = -3.35$, reject H_0 **8.85c.** Type II **8.87a.** $z = -1.93$, reject H_0 **8.89a.** $.025 < p < .05$ **b.** $p = .0362$, reject H_0 at $\alpha = .0362$ **c.** Type I **8.91a.** $z = 12.97$, reject H_0 **b.** $p \approx 0$, reject H_0 **c.** $\beta = .6844$ **8.93a.** $z = 1.41$, fail to reject H_0 **b.** Small **c.** $p = .0793$, fail to reject H_0 **8.95a.** No **b.** $\beta = .5910$, power $= .4090$ **c.** Increases **8.97b.** $\beta = .8264$ **c.** Decreases **8.99a.** $H_0: \mu = 12,432$; $H_a: \mu > 12,432$ **b.** $z = 1.86$, $p = .0314$; at $\alpha = .05$, reject H_0 **8.101a.** $p = .0304$, reject H_0 at $\alpha = .10$ **b.** $p = .0152$ **8.103** $\beta = .7389$; power $= .2611$

CHAPTER 9

9.1a. 150 ± 6 **b.** 150 ± 8 **c.** $\mu_{\bar{x}_1 - \bar{x}_2} = 0$; $\sigma_{\bar{x}_1 - \bar{x}_2} = 5$ **d.** 0 ± 10 **9.3a.** 35 ± 24.5 **b.** $p = .0052$, reject H_0 at $\alpha = .05$ **c.** $p = .0026$ **d.** $p = .4238$, fail to reject H_0 **9.5a.** No **b.** No **c.** No **d.** Yes **e.** No **9.7a.** $s_p^2 = 110$ **b.** $s_p^2 = 14.5714$ **c.** $s_p^2 = .1821$ **d.** $s_p^2 = 2,741.9355$ **9.9a.** $\sigma_{\bar{x}_1 - \bar{x}_2} = .5$ **d.** $z > 1.96$ or $z < -1.96$ **e.** $z = -42.2$, reject H_0 **9.11a.** $z = -1.576$, $p = .1150$

b. $p = .0575$ **9.13a.** $t = -1.646, p = .1114$, fail to reject H_0 at $\alpha = .10$
b. -2.50 ± 3.12 **9.15a.** $t = 1.9557$, reject H_0 **c.** $p = .0579$, reject H_0
d. -7.4 ± 6.382 **9.17a.** $z = -2.76$, reject H_0 **b.** $p = .0029$ **c.** No
9.19b. $H_0: \mu_1 - \mu_2 = 0; H_a: \mu_1 - \mu_2 < 0$ **c.** Fail to reject H_0 **9.21a.** $t = 4.46$,
reject H_0 **b.** $p = .00155$, reject H_0 **9.23a.** Beginning: 6.09 ± 41.835; first:
-52.24 ± 40.842; second: -48.41 ± 40.643; third: -37.68 ± 39.784; fourth:
-38.54 ± 42.958 **9.25a.** $H_0: \mu_1 - \mu_2 = 0; H_a: \mu_1 - \mu_2 > 0$ **b.** $t = 2.616$,
$.01 < p < .025$, reject H_0 at $\alpha = .05$ **9.29a.** $H_0: \mu_D = 0; H_a: \mu_D < 0$
b. $t = -5.29; p = .0002$ **c.** $(-5.284, -2.116)$ **9.31a.** $t = .81$, fail to reject H_0
b. $p > .20$, fail to reject H_0 **9.33a.** -174.625 ± 67.666 **c.** Yes **9.35a.** $t = .40$,
fail to reject H_0 **b.** $.4167 \pm 2.2963$ **c.** Part **b** is wider **d.** No
9.37a. $H_0: \mu_D = 0; H_a: \mu_D > 0$ **b.** $t = 3.506$, reject H_0 **9.39** $t = .46, p = .65$, fail
to reject H_0 **9.43a.** $z < -2.33$ **b.** $z < -1.96$ **c.** $z < -1.645$ **d.** $z < -1.28$
9.45a. $.07 \pm .067$ **b.** $.06 \pm .086$ **c.** $-.15 \pm .131$ **9.47** $z = 1.14$, fail to reject
H_0 **9.49a.** Yes **b.** $-.0568 \pm .0270$ **9.51** $z = -2.25$, reject H_0
9.53a. $H_0: p_1 - p_2 = 0; H_a: p_1 - p_2 \neq 0$ **b.** Yes **c.** $z = -4.30$, reject H_0
9.55a. $H_0: p_1 - p_2 = 0; H_a: p_1 - p_2 > 0$ **b.** $z = .664$, fail to reject H_0
c. $H_0: p_1 - p_3 = 0; H_a: p_1 - p_3 > 0$ **d.** $z = 1.11, p = .1335$, fail to reject H_0
9.57 $n_1 = n_2 = 34$ **9.59a.** $n_1 = n_2 = 29,954$ **b.** $n_1 = n_2 = 2,165$ **c.** $n_1 = n_2 = 1,113$ **9.61** $n_1 = n_2 = 3,383$ **9.63** $n_1 = n_2 = 542$ **9.65** $n_1 = n_2 = 4,802$
9.67a. $n_1 = n_2 = 546$ **b.** $p = .0107$, reject H_0 for any $\alpha > .0107$ **9.69a.** 4.10
b. 3.57 **c.** 8.805 **d.** 3.21 **9.71a.** $F > 1.74$ **b.** $F > 2.04$ **c.** $F > 2.35$
d. $F > 2.78$ **9.73a.** $F > 2.11$ **b.** $F > 3.01$ **c.** $F > 2.04$ **d.** $F > 2.30$
e. $F > 5.27$ **9.75a.** $F = 4.29$, fail to reject H_0 **b.** $.05 < p < .10$
9.77a. $F = 2.26$, fail to reject H_0 **b.** $.05 < p < .10$ **9.79a.** $F = 8.29, p = .007$,
reject H_0 **b.** No **9.85a.** $t = 5.73$, reject H_0 **b.** 3.8 ± 1.84 **9.87a.** Reject H_0
b. Do not reject H_0 **c.** Reject H_0 **d.** Reject H_0 **e.** Do not reject H_0 **f.** Do
not reject H_0 **9.89** 205.243 ± 182.454 **9.91** $n_1 = n_2 = 542$ **9.93b.** $t = .80$, fail
to reject H_0 **c.** 84.17 ± 226.47 **9.100a.** $H_0: \mu_1 - \mu_2 = 0, H_a: \mu_1 - \mu_2 \neq 0$
b. Hours: $p = .813$, fail to reject H_0; free: $p = .047$, reject H_0 at $\alpha = .047$; breaks:
$p = .0073$, reject H_0 at $\alpha = .0073$ **9.104** $n_1 = n_2 = 1,905$ **9.106a.** Age: yes;
education: yes; employment: yes **b.** $z = -5.22$; reject H_0 **c.** $\pm.215 \pm .109$
d. Confidence intervals

CHAPTER 10

10.3a. $y = \frac{14}{3} + \frac{1}{3}x$ **10.9** No **10.13c.** $\hat{\beta}_1 = -.9939, \hat{\beta}_0 = 8.543$ **d.** $\hat{y} = 8.543$
$- .994x$ **10.15a.** Decreases **b.** $\hat{y} = 569.58 - .00192x$ **10.17a.** Positive
c. $\hat{y} = -131.185 + 765.101x$ **10.19a.** $y = \beta_0 + \beta_1 x + \epsilon$ **b.** $\hat{y} = 141.347 - .208x$ **10.21b.** $\hat{\beta}_0 = -51.3616, \hat{\beta}_1 = 17.7545$ **10.23a.** $s^2 = .3475$ **b.** 1.179
10.27a. SSE $= 623.857; s^2 = 51.988; s = 7.210$ **10.29a.** $\hat{y} = 3.068 - .015x$
c. $\hat{y}_{10} = 2.918, \hat{y}_{16} = 2.828$ **d.** SSE $= .01926; s = .0801$ **e.** $.1602$
10.31a. $31 \pm 1.13; 31 \pm .92$ **b.** $64 \pm 4.28; 64 \pm 3.53$ **c.** $-8.4 \pm .67; -8.4 \pm .55$
10.33 80%: $.8214 \pm .3325$; 98%: $.8214 \pm .7581$ **10.35a.** $p < .001$, reject H_0
10.37a. $t = 4.98, p = .001$, reject H_0 **b.** $\hat{y} = .607$ **10.39a.** $t = 3.384; p = .0035$,
reject H_0 **b.** 17.754 ± 16.627 **10.41a.** $\hat{y} = 12.71 + 1.50x$ **b.** $t = 18.258$,
reject H_0 **c.** Independent errors **10.43** $t = -.96$, fail to reject H_0
10.45a. Positive **b.** Negative **c.** 0 **d.** Positive or negative **10.47a.** $r^2 = .9438$
b. $r^2 = .8020$ **10.51a.** $r = .9844$ **10.53** $r^2 = .57873$ **10.55c.** $r_1 = .9653$;
$r_2 = .9960$ **d.** Yes **10.57b.** $\hat{y} = 1.5 + .946x$ **c.** $s^2 = 2.221$ **d.** 4.338 ± 1.170
e. 4.338 ± 3.223 **f.** Prediction interval **10.59a.** 2.2 ± 1.382 **c.** Yes
d. $t = 6.10$, reject H_0 **10.61b.** $\hat{y} = 5341.9 - 192.58x$ **c.** $t = -7.09$, reject H_0

d. $r^2 = .820$ **e.** (3,269.9, 3,562.4) **f.** (2,893.7, 3,938.6) **10.63a.** $t = 15.35$, reject H_0 **b.** 28.183 ± 4.629 **10.65a.** Indirect manufacturing cost
c. $\hat{y} = 300.976 + 10.312x$ **d.** $t = 3.301$, reject H_0 **e.** $r^2 = .5214$ **f.** 816.596 ± 187.420 **10.67a.** $\hat{y} = 37.08 - 1.6x$ **c.** SSE $= 57.2$ **d.** $s^2 = 4.4$ **e.** $-1.6 \pm .501$ **f.** 13.08 ± 6.929 **g.** 13.08 ± 7.862 **10.69b.** $r = -.1245, r^2 = .0155$
c. $t = -.35$, fail to reject H_0 **10.71b.** $\hat{y} = 12.594 + .10936x$ **c.** $t = 3.50$, reject H_0 **d.** 28.988 ± 12.500 **10.73** $t = -1.926$, fail to reject $H_0; r^2 = .3073$
10.75b. $\hat{y} = -39,001.1 + 84.987x$ **c.** $r^2 = .8983$ **d.** $t = 13.942$, reject H_0
e. 84.987 ± 12.642 **f.** $p = .0001$, reject H_0 **g.** (205,524, 226,396)
10.77a. $\hat{\beta}_0 = -99045, \hat{\beta}_1 = 102.814$, **b.** $t = 6.483$, reject H_0 **c.** $p < .00005$
d. $r^2 = .6776$ **e.** $(-631,806, 2,078,740)$ **10.79b.** $\hat{y} = 12,024 + 3.582x$
c. $r^2 = .7972$ **d.** $t = 8.641; p = .0001$, reject H_0 **e.** ($12,862.60, $16,915.30)

CHAPTER 11

11.1a. $\hat{\beta}_0 = 506.346, \hat{\beta}_1 = -941.900, \hat{\beta}_2 = -429.060$ **b.** $\hat{y} = 506.346 - 941.900x_1 - 429.060x_2$ **c.** SSE $= 151,015$, MSE $= 8,883.3, s = 94.25$
d. $t = -3.424$, reject H_0 **e.** -429.060 ± 801.432 **11.3a.** $t = 3.133$, reject H_0
b. $t = 3.133$, reject H_0 **c.** $F = 9.816$ **d.** No **11.5a.** SSE $= .0438; s^2 = .0110$
b. $t = -13.97$, reject H_0 **c.** $\hat{y} = 1.095 + 1.636x_1 - .1595x_1^2$ **11.7** $\hat{\beta}_0 = 39.05$,
$\hat{\beta}_1 = -5.41, \hat{\beta}_2 = 5.86, \hat{\beta}_3 = -3.09, \hat{\beta}_4 = 1.75$ **11.9a.** $\hat{y} = 20.0911 - .6705x + .0095x^2$ **c.** $t = 1.51$, fail to reject H_0 **d.** $\hat{y} = 19.279 - .445x$ **e.** $-.445 \pm .0727$
11.11a. $\hat{y} = -72.558 - .058x_1 + 84.925x_2 - .022x_3$ **b.** $s = 8.563$ **c.** $t = -.293$,
fail to reject H_0 **11.13a.** Yes **b.** $F = 32.12$, reject H_0 **11.15a.** $R^2 = .4792$
b. $F = 7.82$, reject H_0 **11.17a.** $\hat{y} = -4.30 - .002x_1 + .336x_2 + .384x_3 + .067x_4 - .143x_5 + .081x_6 + .134x_7$ **b.** $F = 111.1$, reject H_0 **c.** $\hat{\beta}_3 = .384$ **d.** $t = 1.76$,
fail to reject H_0 **e.** $t = -.049$, fail to reject H_0 **11.19a.** $R^2 = .51$ **b.** $F = 13.53$,
reject H_0 **11.21a.** $E(y) = \beta_0 + \beta_1x_1 + \beta_2x_2 + \beta_3x_1x_2$ **b.** $p = .02$, reject H_0
11.23a. $\hat{y} = 295.33 - 480.84x_1 - 829.46x_2 + .0079x_3 + 2.3608x_4$ **b.** $s = 46.767$
c. $F = 28.18$, reject H_0 **d.** $t = -3.197$, reject H_0 **11.25b.** $F = 58.56$, reject H_0
c. $t = -50$, reject H_0 **d.** (See figure on page 1045) **11.27a.** $E(y) = \beta_0 + \beta_1x_1 + \beta_2x_2 + \beta_3x_3 + \beta_4x_4 + \beta_5x_5$ **b.** $\hat{y} = 15.491 + 12.774x_1 + .713x_2 + 1.519x_3 + .32x_4 + .205x_5$ **c.** $R^2 = .240, F = 11.68$, reject H_0 **d.** $p = .025$, reject H_0
11.29 Confidence interval **11.31** Quadratics needed **11.33a.** $\hat{y} = -754.711 + 217.493x_1 + .713x_2$ **b.** $(-1,991.8, 1,630.5)$ **c.** No **d.** $r = .36332$
11.35b. $s_1 = .35014; s_2 = .62859$ **c.** $F_1 = 52.138$, reject $H_0; F_2 = 22.523$, reject
H_0 **d.** Model 1: $.354 \pm .0730$; Model 2: $.394 \pm .1291$ **f.** Large amount
11.37 26th observation skews the distribution to the right **11.39** Observation
#25 is a possible outlier **11.41a.** "Year GRE taken" and "years in graduate
program"; "race" and "foreign status" **11.43a.** $F = 24.41$, reject H_0
b. $t = -2.01$, reject H_0 **c.** $t = .31$, fail to reject H_0 **d.** $t = 2.38$, reject H_0
11.47a. $\hat{y} = -50.489 + 7.3694x_1 + 2.2324x_2$ **b.** $\hat{y} = -22.505 + 2.0352x_1 - 2.8072x_2 + 1.0296x_1x_2$ **c.** Interaction model **11.49a.** $E(y) = \beta_0 + \beta_1x_1 + \beta_2x_2 + \beta_3x_3 + \beta_4x_4 + \beta_5x_5$ **b.** $p < .001$, reject H_0 **c.** $E(y) = \beta_0 + \beta_1x_1 + \beta_2x_2 + \beta_3x_3 + \beta_4x_4 + \beta_5x_5 + \beta_6x_6 + \beta_7x_7$ **e.** Both are useful predictors of GSI **11.51** No
11.53 $t = -1.10$, fail to reject H_0 **11.55b.** Reject H_0 when testing β_3, β_5, and β_6
c. $.007 \pm .0033$ **11.57a.** $E(y) = \beta_0 + \beta_1x_1 + \beta_2x_2 + \beta_3x_3 + \beta_4x_4 + \beta_5x_5 + \beta_6x_6 + \beta_7x_7$ **b.** $\hat{y} = .998 - .022x_1 + .156x_2 - .017x_3 - .010x_4 + .421x_5 + .417x_6 - .155x_7$ **c.** $F = 5.292$, reject H_0 **d.** $\hat{y} = -.60075$ **f.** Model has higher R^2 and
lower s **h.** For obs. #14: $(-1.282, 1.218)$ **11.59b.** $t = 5$, reject H_0 **c.** $\hat{y} = 825$
11.61 Add x_1^2 to the model **11.63** Second-order model is better

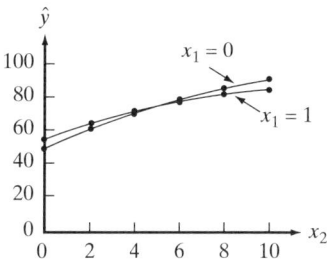

Exercise 11.25d

CHAPTER 12

12.1a. Quantitative **b.** Quantitative **c.** Quantitative **d.** Qualitative **e.** Quantitative **f.** Quantitative **g.** Qualitative **12.3a.** All quantitative **b.** Student cohort—negative; all other variables—positive **12.5a.** Qualitative **b.** Qualitative **c.** Qualitative **d.** Quantitative **e.** Qualitative **f.** Quantitative **g.** Qualitative **12.7a.** First-order, $\beta_0 = 10, \beta_1 = .5$ **b.** First-order, $\beta_0 = 80; \beta_1 = -.5$ **12.9a.** First **b.** Second **c.** Third **d.** Third **e.** Second **f.** First **12.11a.** $\hat{y} = 63.1 + 1.17x - .0374x^2$ **c.** $H_0: \beta_2 = 0,$ $H_a: \beta_2 < 0$ **d.** $t = -3.03,$ reject H_0 **12.13a.** $E(y) = \beta_0 + \beta_1x + \beta_2x^2$ **b.** $\beta_0 > 0,$ $\beta_2 > 0$ **12.15** $E(y) = \beta_0 + \beta_1x + \beta_2x^2$ **12.17a.** $E(y) = \beta_0 + \beta_1x + \beta_2x^2$ **12.19** $t = -6.60,$ reject H_0 **12.21a.** $E(y) = \beta_0 + \beta_1x_1 + \beta_2x_2$ **b.** $E(y) = \beta_0 + \beta_1x_1 + \beta_2x_2 + \beta_3x_1x_2$ **c.** $E(y) = \beta_0 + \beta_1x_1 + \beta_2x_2 + \beta_3x_1x_2 + \beta_4x_1^2 + \beta_5x_2^2$ **12.23a.** A twisted plane **e.** By -4 units **12.25a.** $\hat{y} = -2.55 + 3.82x_1 + 2.63x_2 - 1.29x_1x_2$ **b.** Twisted plane **e.** $H_0: \beta_3 = 0; H_a: \beta_3 \neq 0$ **f.** $t = -8.06,$ reject H_0 **12.27a.** $E(y) = \beta_0 + \beta_1x_1 + \beta_2x_2 + \beta_3x_1x_2 + \beta_4x_1^2 + \beta_5x_2^2$ **b.** $\beta_4x_1^2 + \beta_5x_2^2$ **12.31a.** $\hat{y} = 149.5 + .472x_1 - .099x_2 - .00054x_1^2 + .000015x_2^2$ **b.** Saddle-shaped **c.** $F = 31.66,$ reject H_0 **d.** Yes **12.33a.** $H_a:$ At least one $\beta_i \neq 0$ **c.** $3, 24$ **12.37a.** $H_0: \beta_1 = \beta_2 = \beta_3 = \beta_4 = \beta_5 = 0, H_a:$ At least one $\beta_i \neq 0$ **b.** $F = 18.24,$ reject H_0 **c.** $H_0: \beta_3 = \beta_4 = \beta_5 = 0, H_a:$ At least one $\beta_i \neq 0$ **d.** $F = 8.46,$ reject H_0 **e.** Second-order model **12.39a.** $\hat{y} = 172{,}788 - 10{,}739x_1 - 499x_2 - 20.2x_1x_2 + 197.57x_1^2 + 14.678x_2^2$ **b.** $F = 38.24,$ reject H_0 **c.** No **12.41a.** $\hat{y} = -214.5 - .91x_1 + 78.68x_2 + .14x_1x_2 - .0001x_1^2 - 5.99x_2^2$ **b.** $F = 289.89,$ reject H_0 **c.** $\hat{y} = \$167{,}073$ **12.43a.** $E(y) = \beta_0 + \beta_1x_1 + \beta_2x_2 + \beta_3x_3 + \beta_4x_1x_2 + \beta_5x_1x_3 + \beta_6x_2x_3 + \beta_7x_1^2 + \beta_8x_2^2 + \beta_9x_3^2$ **b.** $E(y) = \beta_0 + \beta_1x_1 + \beta_2x_2 + \beta_3x_3$ **d.** $F = 2.25,$ fail to reject H_0 **12.45** $E(y) = \beta_0 + \beta_1x_1 + \beta_2x_2$ **12.47a.** $\hat{y} = 80 + 16.8x_1 + 40.4x_2$ **d.** $F = 24.72,$ reject H_0 **12.49a.** $E(y) = \beta_0 + \beta_1x_1 + \beta_2x_2$ **b.** $H_0: \beta_1 = \beta_2 = 0$ **12.51a.** $E(y) = \beta_0 + \beta_1x_1 + \beta_2x_2 + \beta_3x_3 + \beta_4x_4$ **b.** $\hat{y} = 20.35 + 4.75x_1 + 8.6x_2 + 11.3x_3 + 2.1x_4$ **c.** $H_0: \beta_1 = \beta_2 = \beta_3 = \beta_4 = 0, H_a:$ At least one $\beta_i \neq 0$ **d.** $F = 23.966,$ reject H_0 **e.** 2.1 ± 2.846 **12.53a.** Qualitative **b.** $E(y) = \beta_0 + \beta_1x_1 + \beta_2x_2$ **c.** $\beta_2 + \beta_0$ **12.55a.** $F = 4.80,$ reject H_0 **b.** $\$11{,}400$ **c.** $\$20{,}000$ **12.57a.** $E(y) = \beta_0 + \beta_1x_1, E(y) = \beta_0 + \beta_1x_1 + \beta_2, E(y) = \beta_0 + \beta_1x_1 + \beta_3$ **b.** $\hat{y} = 44.803 + 2.173x_1 + 9.413x_2 + 15.632x_3$ **c.** $\hat{y} = 44.803 + 2.173x_1, \hat{y} = 54.216 + 2.173x_1, \hat{y} = 60.435 + 2.173x_1$ **d.** $H_0: \beta_2 = \beta_3 = 0, H_a:$ At least one $\beta_i \neq 0$ **e.** $F = 3.33,$ fail to reject H_0 **12.59a.** Juice extracter is qualitative, size is quantitative **b.** $E(y) = \beta_0 + \beta_1x_1 + \beta_2x_2$ **c.** $E(y) = \beta_0 + \beta_1x_1 + \beta_2x_2 + \beta_3x_1x_2$ **e.** $H_0: \beta_3 = 0, H_a: \beta_3 \neq 0$ **12.61a.** $E(y) = \beta_0 + \beta_1x_1$ **b.** $E(y) = \beta_0 + \beta_1x_1 + \beta_2x_2 + \beta_3x_3$ **c.** $E(y) = \beta_0 + \beta_1x_1 + \beta_2x_2 + \beta_3x_3 + \beta_4x_1x_2 + \beta_5x_1x_3$ **12.63a.** $F = 4.90,$ reject H_0 **b.** $H_0: \beta_4 = \beta_5 = 0, H_a:$ At least one $\beta_i \neq 0$ **c.** $F = 2.36,$ fail to reject H_0 **12.65a.** $E(y) = \beta_0 + \beta_1x_1 + \beta_2x_2 + \beta_3x_3$ **b.** $H_0: \beta_2 = \beta_3 = 0, H_a:$ At least one $\beta_i \neq 0$ **c.** $F = 2.60,$ fail to reject H_0 **12.67a.** If $\beta_5 = \beta_6 = \beta_7 = \beta_8 = 0$ **b.** If $\beta_2 = \beta_5 = \beta_6 = \beta_7 = \beta_8 = 0$

Exercise 13.47a

Exercise 12.69c

c. If $\beta_3 = \beta_4 = \beta_5 = \beta_6 = \beta_7 = \beta_8 = 0$ **12.69a.** $\hat{y} = 48.8 - 3.36x_1 + .075x_1^2 - 2.36x_2 - 7.60x_3 + 3.71x_1x_2 + 2.66x_1x_3 - .0181x_1^2x_2 - .037x_1^2x_3$ **b.** $\hat{y} = 48.8 - 3.36x_1 + .075x_1^2, \hat{y} = 46.44 + .35x_1 + .057x_1^2, \hat{y} = 41.2 - .7x_1 + .038x_1^2$ **c.** (See figure at left) **d.** $H_0: \beta_3 = \beta_4 = \beta_5 = \beta_6 = \beta_7 = \beta_8 = 0$ vs. H_a: At least one $\beta_i \neq 0$ **e.** $F = 242.65$, reject H_0 **12.71** $F = .93$, fail to reject H_0 **12.73a.** $E(y) = \beta_0 + \beta_1x_1 + \beta_2x_2 + \beta_3x_3$ **b.** $E(y) = \beta_0 + \beta_1x_1 + \beta_2x_2 + \beta_3x_3 + \beta_4x_1x_2 + \beta_5x_1x_3$ **c.** For AL, slope $= \beta_1$; for TDS-3A, slope $= \beta_1 + \beta_4$; for FE, slope $= \beta_1 + \beta_5$ **d.** Test $H_0: \beta_4 = \beta_5 = 0, H_a$: at least one $\beta_i \neq 0$ **12.75b.** $t = 8.81$, reject H_0 **c.** $E(y) = \beta_0 + \beta_1x_1 + \beta_2x_1^2$ **12.77a.** x_2 **b.** Yes **12.79b.** No **d.** $F = 58.34$ **e.** $p < .01$ **12.83a.** Second **b.** First **c.** Second **d.** First **e.** Third **f.** First **12.89** Degrees of freedom = 0 **12.91a.** $\hat{y} = 10.2 + .5x_1 + 2.02x_2 + .683x_3$ **b.** $F = 63.09$, reject H_0 **12.93** Test $H_0: \beta_3 = 0$; $H_a: \beta_3 \neq 0$ **12.95a.** $H_0: \beta_2 = \beta_5 = 0, H_a$: At least one $\beta_i \neq 0$ **b.** $H_0: \beta_3 = \beta_4 = \beta_5 = 0; H_a$: At least one $\beta_i \neq 0$ **c.** $F = 2.15$, fail to reject H_0 **12.97a.** $E(y) = \beta_0 + \beta_1x_1 + \beta_2x_2$ **b.** $E(y) = \beta_0 + \beta_1x_1 + \beta_2x_2 + \beta_3x_1^2 + \beta_4x_1x_2 + \beta_5x_1^2x_2$ **c.** $F = 2.49$, fail to reject H_0 **12.99a.** $F = 222.173$, reject H_0 **b.** $F = 13.49$, reject H_0 **e.** $E(y) = \beta_0 + \beta_1x_1 + \beta_2x_2 + \beta_3x_3 + \beta_4x_4 + \beta_5x_1x_2 + \beta_6x_1x_3 + \beta_7x_1x_4$ **g.** $F = 1.78$, fail to reject H_0

CHAPTER 13

13.7 Out of control **13.9a.** 1.023 **b.** .308 **c.** .167 **13.11b.** $\bar{\bar{x}} = 20.11625$, $\bar{R} = 3.31$ **c.** UCL $= 22.529$, LCL $= 17.703$ **e.** In control **13.13b.** In control **c.** Yes **13.15b.** Out of control **c.** No **13.17** Variation **13.19a.** $D_3 = .000$, $D_4 = 2.282$ **b.** $D_3 = .283, D_4 = 1.717$ **c.** $D_3 = .451, D_4 = 1.548$ **13.21a.** UCL $= 7.553$ **c.** In control **13.23a.** UCL $= .7216$ **b.** In control **c.** Yes **13.25b.** Out of control **c.** Yes **13.27b.** $\bar{R}$ chart **c.** Both suggest it is in control **d.** No **13.29** $n \approx 104$ **13.31a.** $\bar{p} = .0575$, UCL $= .1145$, LCL $= .0005$ **d.** No, out of control **e.** No **13.33a.** Yes **b.** UCL $= .02013$, LCL $= .00081$ **c.** In control **13.35a.** $\bar{p} = .04$, UCL $= .099$, LCL $= -.019$ **b.** No **c.** No **13.43a.** 126 **b.** 31.2 **c.** 660.36 **d.** .0144 **13.45** 6σ **13.47a.** (See figure above) **b.** No, $C_p = .866$ **13.65a.** $\bar{x} = 6.4$ **b.** Increasing variance **13.67** Process is out of control **13.69a.** UCL $= 24.18$ **b.** UCL $= 358.06$, LCL $= 330.24$ **c.** No **d.** .25 **13.71a.** UCL $= 11.532$ **b.** In control **d.** UCL $= 7.015$, LCL $= .719$ **e.** In control **f.** Yes **13.73a.** $n > 141$ **b.** UCL $= .123$, LCL $= .003$ **c.** They are present **e.** No

CHAPTER 14

14.5b. Quantity index **14.7b.** 13.33%, 47.83% **14.9b.** Nonfarm segment **14.13a.** (See the table at the top of page 1047) **b.** (See the table at the top of page 1047) **c.** (See figure on page 1047) **14.15** $w = .2$ **14.23c.** $F_{1995} = 1,370.64$ **14.27** 459.85, 458.06, 456.27, 454.48; 447.37, 445.17, 442.97, 440.77

Year	Total	Laspeyres Index
1988	31,534.05	100.00
1989	32,374.55	102.67
1990	33,257.40	105.47
1991	33,717.70	106.92
1992	34,037.15	107.94
1993	34,971.55	110.90

Exercise 14.13a

Year	Paasche Numerator	Paasche Denominator	Paasche Index
1988	31,534.05	32,534.05	100.00
1989	33,034.70	32,176.42	102.67
1990	32,228.00	30,565.72	105.44
1991	33,393.00	31,232.00	106.92
1992	34,384.06	31,851.26	107.95
1993	38,211.09	34,455.63	110.90

Exercise 14.13b

14.29b. $F_{Mar} = 17.43, F_{Apr} = 17.43, F_{May} = 17.43, F_{Jun} = 17.43$ **14.31a.** 2.61, 2.61, 3.61   **b.** $-1, -1, 0$ **c.** 2.943   **d.** .667   **e.** 2.981   **f.** .816
14.33a. 58,507.89   **b.** 64,101.48, 68,416.36, 72,731.24   **c.** Exponentially smoothed is better   **14.35a.** MAD $= 228.88$, RMSE $= 231.828$ **b.** MAD $= 241.975$; RMSE $= 244.832$ **c.** $w = .3, v = .5$, better   **14.39a.** $\hat{\beta}_0 = 24.6975$, $\hat{\beta}_1 = .091029$ **b.** 1996: 26.245, 1997: 26.336   **c.** 1996: (22.6193, 29.8707), 1997: (22.6358, 30.0363)   **14.41a.** $\hat{\beta}_0 = 236.989, \hat{\beta}_1 = 23.1824$ **b.** $t = 46.06$, reject H_0
c. 1994: no, 1995: yes   **14.43a.** $y_t = \beta_0 + \beta_1 + \beta_2 x_1 + \beta_3 x_2 + \cdots + \beta_{12} x_{11}$
c. Jan: $\hat{y} = 3,562.8$, Feb: $\hat{y} = 3,525.3$, Mar: $\hat{y} = 4,692.8$ **d.** 1,057.7
14.45a. $\hat{y} = 377.149 + .4948t$ **b.** 1994: $\hat{y} = 389.52$, 1995: $\hat{y} = 390.01$
c. 1994: (357.06, 421.97), 1995: (357.25, 422.78)   **14.47a.** Strong negative correlation   **b.** Strong positive correlation   **c.** Very little correlation
14.49b. $d = .122$; reject H_0 **14.51b.** To within 9.30238   **c.** $d = .757$, reject H_0
14.53b. Price index   **14.55b.** 6.61%   **14.57a.** -1.86 **b.** .72   **14.61b.** $F = .040$, fail to reject H_0 **c.** I: 7,213.7, II: 7,281.0, III: 7,352.0, IV: 7,421.2   **d.** $d = .128$, reject H_0 **14.65a.** Automobile: 1995: (268.7, 417.8), 1996: (281.7, 434.2); other: 1995: (228.1, 289.1), 1996: (236.0, 298.4); revolve: 1995: (288.7, 359.6), 1996: (307.6, 380.2)   **b.** Automobile: $F_{1995} = 339.42, F_{1996} = 368.95$; other: $F_{1995} = 253.38, F_{1996} = 266.36$; revolve: $F_{1995} = 365.76, F_{1996} = 402.88$
14.67a. $F_{Oct} = \$117.232, F_{Nov} = \$117.232, F_{Dec}\ \$117.232$; errors $= \$11.768$, $\$42.143, \$34.268$ **c.** To within $14.26   **d.** Oct: (107.1, 138.0), Nov: (109.1, 140.2), Dec: (111.1, 142.4)   **e.** $MAD_1 = 29.393$, $RMSE_1 = 32.087$; $MAD_2 = 21.958$, $RMSE_2 = 24.889$ **g.** $d = .941$, reject H_0

CHAPTER 15

15.3a. College student   **b.** Household   **c.** Automobile model   **d.** Diskette
e. State   **15.5c.** 4 treatments   **d.** College students   **15.7a.** Observational
b. Designed   **c.** Observational   **d.** Observational   **e.** Observational

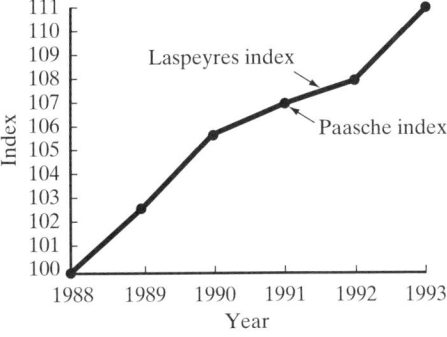

Exercise 14.13c

15.9a. 6.39 **b.** 15.98 **c.** 1.54 **d.** 3.18 **15.11** Diagram b **15.13c.** Plot **a**: $t = -6.12$, reject H_0; plot **b**: $t = -2.28$, reject H_0 **15.15a.** $F = 1.5$, fail to reject H_0 **b.** $F = 6$, reject H_0 **c.** $F = 24$, reject H_0 **d.** Increases **15.17a.** $4, n = 38$ **b.** $F = 14.80$, reject H_0 **15.19a.** Completely randomized design **15.21a.** Infrequency: $F = 155.8$, reject H_0; obvious: $F = 49.7$, reject H_0; subtle: $F = 10.3$, reject H_0; obvious-subtle: $F = 45.4$, reject H_0; dissimulation: $F = 39.1$, reject H_0 **b.** No **15.23a.** H_0: $\mu_1 = \mu_2 = \mu_3 = \mu_4 = \mu_5 = \mu_6$; H_a: At least two means differ **b.** Fail to reject H_0 **d.** Designed **15.25a.** $F = 17.32$, reject H_0 **b.** $p < .01$ **c.** $t = 4.24$, reject H_0 **15.27a.** 3 **b.** 10 **c.** 6 **d.** 45 **15.31a.** 3 **c.** Yes **d.** $\mu_A > \mu_B, \mu_C$ **15.33c.** $\mu_C > \mu_E, \mu_A > \mu_E$ **15.35** $\mu_S > \mu_G, \mu_{ST}$ **15.39b.** $F = 13.18$, reject H_0 **c.** Yes **e.** $F = 14.77$, reject H_0 **f.** No **15.41b.** $F = 21.62$, reject H_0 **c.** Yes, $F = 36.6$, reject H_0 **d.** No **15.43a.** $F = 1.50$, fail to reject H_0 **b.** $F = 5.25$, reject H_0; interaction: $F = 7.50$, reject H_0 **c.** $F = 5.25$, reject H_0; interaction: $F = 3.00$, reject H_0 **d.** $F = 20.25$, reject H_0; interaction: $F = 4.50$, reject H_0 **15.45a.** Interaction: $F = 1.2$, fail to reject H_0; four herds: $F = 17.2$, reject H_0; four seasons: $F = 3.0$, fail to reject H_0 **b.** Yes **c.** $\mu_{PLC}, \mu_{LGN} < \mu_{QMD}, \mu_{MTZ}$ **15.47a.** 2×2 factorial design **c.** Number of bites **15.49a.** 262.4, 202.0 **b.** 6,739.605 **c.** 114.005, 41.405, 18.605 **e.** 789.9682 **f.** 963.9832 **h.** $F = 2.06$, fail to reject H_0 **15.51a.** $E(y) = \beta_0 + \beta_1 x_1 + \beta_2 x_2 + \beta_3 x_3 + \beta_4 x_4$ **b.** 10 **c.** 0 **d.** $F > 2.61$ **15.53a.** $F = 8.438$, reject H_0 **b.** $p = .0014$ **c.** Same **d.** $R^2 = .3846$ **15.55b.** $s = 22.25; R^2 = .999$ **c.** $F = 1,336.85$, reject H_0 **d.** H_0: $\beta_5 = \beta_6 = \beta_7 = \beta_8 = 0$ **e.** $F = 258.07$, reject H_0 **f.** No **15.57** 6 treatments **15.59b.** $F = 7.70$, reject H_0 **c.** $11.4 \pm .99$ **15.63a.** $F = 30.4$, reject H_0 **b.** $\mu_A > \mu_B, \mu_C, \mu_D$; $\mu_B > \mu_D$ **15.65a.** 2×2 factorial **b.** 116 **c.** $F = 1.95$, fail to reject H_0 **d.** $F = .39$, fail to reject H_0 **e.** $F = 53.27$, reject H_0 **f.** Confirm **15.67a.** $2 \times 2 \times 2 \times 2$ factorial **b.** 16 **d.** $F = 3.87$, reject H_0 **e.** Yes (wear main effect): $t = .05$, fail to reject H_0 **15.69b.** $F = 19.62$, reject H_0 **c.** No **15.71b.** $F = 12.29$, reject H_0 **c.** Interaction: $F = .02$, fail to reject H_0; scheduling: $F = 7.37$, reject H_0; payments: $F = 29.47$, reject H_0 **15.73a.** Observational, completely randomized **b.** $F = 3.34$, reject H_0 **c.** $\mu_{NYSE} > \mu_{ASE}, \alpha = .05$

CHAPTER 16

16.3a. .035 **b.** .363 **c.** .004 **d.** .151, .1515 **e.** .212, .2119 **16.5** $p = .054$, reject H_0 **16.7a.** H_0: $\eta = 5$; H_a: $\eta > 5$ **b.** $p \approx 0$ **c.** Reject H_0 **16.9a.** Sign test **b.** H_0: $\eta = 30$; H_a: $\eta < 30$ **c.** $s = 5$ **d.** $p = .109$, fail to reject H_0 **16.11a.** T_B; $T_B \leq 35$ or $T_B \geq 67$ **b.** T_A; $T_A \geq 43$ **c.** T_B; $T_B \geq 93$ **d.** z; $z < -z_{\alpha/2}$ or $z > z_{\alpha/2}$ **16.15a.** $T_2 = 105$, fail to reject H_0 **b.** $p < .05$ **16.17a.** $T_B = 53$, reject H_0 **16.19** $T_A = 39$, reject H_0 **16.21a.** $z = -1.75$, reject H_0 **16.23b.** $T_- = 3.5$, reject H_0 **16.27b.** $z = 2.499$, reject H_0 **c.** $p = .0062$ **16.29a.** Paired difference design **c.** $T_+ = 3.5$, reject H_0 **d.** $.01 < p < .025$ **16.31** $T_+ = 2$, reject H_0 **16.33** $z = -1.3631, p = .1728$, fail to reject H_0 **16.35a.** .995 **b.** .025 **c.** .10 **d.** .975 **e.** .025 **f.** .10 **16.37a.** Completely randomized design **c.** $H > 9.21034$ **d.** Reject H_0 **16.39a.** $H = 35.23$ **b.** $H > 15.0863$ **c.** Reject H_0 **d.** $p < .01$ **16.41a.** $H = .9425$, fail to reject H_0 **16.43b.** $H = 5.8617$, fail to reject H_0 **c.** Wilcoxon rank sum test **16.45a.** $r_s > .648$ or $r_s < -.648$ **b.** $r_s > .450$ **c.** $r_s < -.432$ **16.47a.** H_0: $\rho_s = 0$; H_a: $\rho_s \neq 0$ **b.** $r_s = .745$, fail to reject H_0 **c.** $.05 < p < .10$ **16.49a.** $r_s = .491$,

Exercise 17.37b

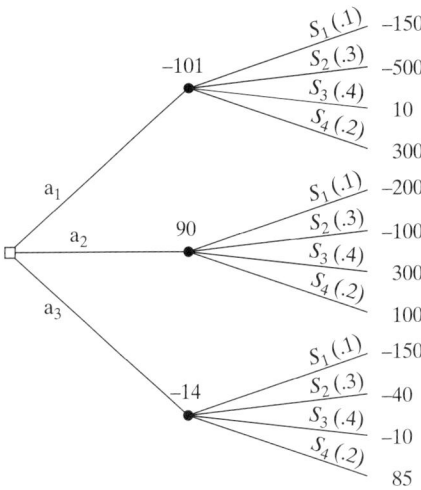

Exercise 18.27

fail to reject H_0 **16.51b.** $r_s = .972$, reject H_0 **16.53** $r_s = .9341$ **16.57a.** $r_s = .40$, fail to reject H_0 **b.** $T_- = 1.5$, reject H_0 **16.59** $H = 5.8498$, fail to reject H_0 **16.61** $T_- = 3$, reject H_0 **16.63a.** $T_- = 22$, reject H_0 **b.** $.025 < p < .05$ **16.65** $T_A = 21$, fail to reject H_0 **16.67b.** $H = 14.6101$, reject H_0 **d.** 1 is most popular **16.69** $H = 19.466$, reject H_0 **16.71** $T_{Before} = 132.5$, reject H_0 **16.73a.** $s = 5, p = .363$, fail to reject H_0 **16.75** $r_s = .7714$, fail to reject H_0 **16.77a.** $r_s = .861$ **b.** Reject H_0 **c.** $s = 4, p = .982$, fail to reject H_0

CHAPTER 17

17.1a. 27.5871 **b.** 70.0648 **c.** 22.3072 **d.** 12.8381 **17.3a.** $\chi^2 > 5.99147$ **b.** $\chi^2 > 7.77944$ **c.** $\chi^2 > 11.3449$ **17.7a.** $\chi^2 = 3.293$, fail to reject H_0 **17.9a.** $H_0: p_1 = p_2 = p_3 = p_4 = .25$; H_a: At least one $p \neq .25$ **b.** $\chi^2 = 14.805$, reject H_0 **17.11** $\chi^2 = 16, p = .003019$, reject H_0 **17.13a.** $\chi^2 = 26.66$, reject H_0 **b.** $\chi^2 = 1$, fail to reject H_0 **17.15a.** $\chi^2 = 12.374$, fail to reject H_0 **b.** $p < .10$ **17.17** $\chi^2 = 10.3$, reject H_0 **17.19b.** $\chi^2 > 9.21034$ **d.** $\chi^2 = 8.71$, fail to reject H_0 **17.21** $\chi^2 = 12.36$, reject H_0 **17.23a.** $\hat{p} = .901$ **b.** $\hat{p} = .690$ **d.** $\chi^2 = 48.191$, reject H_0 **e.** $.211 \pm .070$ **17.25a.** $\chi^2 = 20.78$, reject H_0 **b.** Older, younger **17.27a.** $\chi^2 = 39.22$, reject H_0 **b.** $\chi^2 = 2.84$, fail to reject H_0 **17.29** $\chi^2 = 24.524$, reject H_0 **17.31a.** No **c.** $\chi^2 = 12.9$ **d.** Reject H_0 **e.** $.233 \pm .200$ **17.33a.** $\chi^2 = 2.133$, fail to reject H_0 **b.** $.233 \pm .057$ **17.35** Union: $\chi^2 = 13.36744$, reject H_0; nonunion: $\chi^2 = 9.63514$, fail to reject H_0 **17.37a.** No **b.** (See figure above) **d.** $\chi^2 = 2.373$, fail to reject H_0 **e.** Yes **17.39b.** Yes **c.** $\chi^2 = 26.034$, reject H_0 **17.41a.** $\chi^2 = 9.16$, reject H_0 **b.** $.90 \pm .06$ **17.43** $\chi^2 = 5.506$, fail to reject H_0 **17.45a.** $\chi^2 = 18.54$, reject H_0 **b.** $p < .005$ **17.47a.** $\chi^2 = 47.98$, reject H_0 **b.** $.125 \pm .046$ **17.49a.** $\chi^2 = 3.13$, fail to reject H_0 **b.** $.095 \pm .128$

CHAPTER 18

18.3a. Uncertainty **b.** Conflict **c.** Certainty **18.5** Uncertainty **18.17a.** a_4 is inadmissible **18.25** a_2 **18.27** (See figure above) **18.29** a_2 **18.31a.** Do not replace **b.** $E(a_2) = -\$75,000$ **c.** Do not replace

Exercise 18.41b

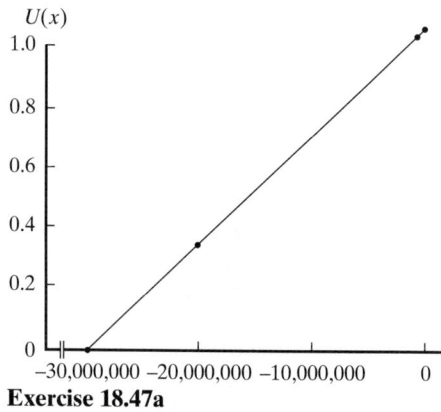

Exercise 18.47a

18.33a. No   **b.** 100%   **d.** 100%   **18.35** No   **18.37b.** a_1 **18.39b.** a_2
18.41a. $p = .9, p = .8$ **b.** (See figure above)   **18.43** 6 dozen   **18.45b.** Risk-
avoider   **c.** a_1 **18.47a.** (See figure above)   **b.** Risk-neutral   **c.** No
18.49b. Risk-avoider   **18.57** .526   **18.61** a_2 **18.63a.** a_3 **c.** a_3 **18.65d.** Stay
in business   **18.67a.** ENGS = -10.014 **b.** First source   **18.69b.** Undertake
the survey   **18.71** \$2.68   **18.75a.** \$400, \$322, \$320   **b.** Change oil   **c.** Do oil
analysis   **18.79b.** Do not make loan   **18.81c.** \$1.98   **18.83a.** \$5,987,500
b. No   **c.** Yes   **18.85a.** EVSI = \$88.16   **b.** ENGS = \$48.16   **18.87c.** 7
18.89c. Certify the account   **d.** \$1,000,000

REFERENCES

CHAPTER 1

Careers in Statistics. American Statistical Association, Biometric Society, Institute of Mathematical Statistics and Statistical Society of Canada, 1995.

Chervany, N. L., Benson, P. G., and Iyer, R. K. "The planning stage in statistical reasoning." *American Statistician,* Nov. 1980, pp. 222–239.

Ethical Guidelines for Statistical Practice. American Statistical Association, 1995.

Tanur, J. M., Mosteller, F., Kruskal, W. H., Link, R. F., Pieters, R. S., and Rising, G. R. *Statistics: A Guide to the Unknown.* (E. L. Lehmann, special editor.) San Francisco: Holden-Day, 1989.

U.S. Bureau of the Census. *Statistical Abstract of the United States: 1995.* Washington, D.C.: U.S. Government Printing Office, 1995.

What Is a Survey? Section on Survey Research Methods, American Statistical Association, 1995.

CHAPTER 2

Adler, P. S., and Clark, K. B. "Behind the learning curve: A sketch of the learning process." *Management Science,* March 1991, p. 267.

Alexander, G. J., Sharpe, W. F., and Bailey, J. V. *Fundamentals of Investments,* 2nd ed. Englewood Cliffs, N.J.: Prentice-Hall, 1993.

Deming, W. E. *Out of the Crisis.* Cambridge, Mass: M.I.T. Center for Advanced Engineering Study, 1986.

Fogarty, D. W., Blackstone, J. H., Jr., and Hoffman, T. R. *Production and Inventory Management.* Cincinnati, Ohio: South-Western, 1991.

Gaither, N. *Production and Operations Management,* 7th ed. Belmont, Calif: Duxbury Press, 1996.

Gitlow, H., Oppenheim, A., and Oppenheim, R. *Quality Mangement: Methods for Improvement,* 2nd ed., Burr Ridge, Ill.: Irwin, 1995.

Huff, D. *How to Lie with Statistics.* New York: Norton, 1954.

Ishikawa, K. *Guide to Quality Control,* 2nd ed. White Plains, N.Y.: Kraus International Publications, 1982.

Juran, J. M. *Juran on Planning for Quality.* New York: The Free Press, 1988.

Mendenhall, W. *Introduction to Probability and Statistics,* 9th ed. North Scituate, Mass.: Duxbury, 1994.

Schroeder, R. G. *Operations Management,* 4th ed. New York: McGraw-Hill, 1993.

Wasserman, P., and Bernero, J. *Statistics Sources,* 5th ed. Detroit: Gale Research Company, 1978.

Zabel, S. L. "Statistical proof of employment discrimination." *Statistics: A Guide to the Unknown,* 3rd ed. Pacific Grove, Calif. Wadsworth, 1989.

CHAPTER 3

Benson, G. "Process thinking: The quality catalyst." *Minnesota Management Review,* University of Minnesota, Minneapolis, Fall 1992.

Feller, W. *An Introduction to Probability Theory and Its Applications,* 3rd ed., Vol. 1. New York: Wiley, 1968.

Kotler, Philip. *Marketing Management,* 8th ed. Englewood Cliffs, N.J.: Prentice-Hall, 1994.

Lindley, D. V. *Making Decisions,* 2nd ed. London: Wiley, 1985.

Parzen, E. *Modern Probability Theory and Its Applications.* New York: Wiley, 1960.

Radcliffe, R. C. *Investment: Concepts, Analysis, Strategy,* 4th ed. New York: HarperCollins College Publishers, 1994.

Scheaffer, R. L., and Mendenhall, W. *Introduction to Probability: Theory and Applications.* North Scituate, Mass.: Duxbury, 1975.

Stickney, C. P. and Weil, R. L. *Financial Accounting: An Introduction to Concepts, Methods, and Uses,* 7th ed. Fort Worth: The Dryden Press, 1994.

Williams, B. *A Sampler on Sampling.* New York: Wiley, 1978.

Winkler, R. L. *An Introduction to Bayesian Inference and Decision.* New York: Holt, Rinehart and Winston, 1972.

CHAPTER 4

Alexander, G. J., and Francis, J. C. *Portfolio Analysis.* Englewood Cliffs, N.J.: Prentice-Hall, 1996.

Alexander, G. J., Sharpe, W. F., and Bailey, J. V. *Fundamentals of Investments,* 2nd ed., Englewood Cliffs, N.J.: Prentice-Hall, 1993.

Cowling, A. and James, P. *The Essence of Personnel Management and Industrial Relations.* New York: Prentice-Hall, 1994.

Doswell, C., and Brooks, H. *Probabilistic Forecasting: A Primer.* http://www.hssl.voknor.edu/~brooks/prob/probability.html

Elton, E. J., and Gruber, M. J. *Modern Portfolio Theory and Investment Analysis.* New York: Wiley, 1981.

Hogg, R. V., and Craig, A. T. *Introduction to Mathematical Statistics,* 4th ed. New York: Macmillan, 1978.

Markowitz, H. M. "Portfolio Selection." *Journal of Finance,* Vol. 6, Mar. 1992.

Mendenhall, W. *Introduction to Mathematical Statistics,* 8th ed. Boston: Duxbury, 1991.

Mendenhall, W., Wackerly, D., and Scheaffer, R. L. *Mathematical Statistics with Applications,* 4th ed. Boston: PWS-Kent, 1990.

Parzen, E. *Modern Probability Theory and Its Applications.* New York: Wiley, 1960.

Radcliffe, R. C. *Investments: Concepts, Analysis, Strategy,* 4th ed. New York: HarperCollins, 1994.

Willis, R. E., and Chervany, N. L. *Statistical Analysis and Modeling for Management Decision-Making.* Belmont, Calif.: Wadsworth, 1974.

Wright, G., and Ayton, P., eds. *Subjective Probability.* New York: John Wiley and Sons, 1994.

Chapter 5

Agnihothri, S. R., and Taylor, D. F. "Staffing a centralized appointment scheduling department in Lourdes Hospital." *Interfaces,* Vol. 21, No. 5, Sept.–Oct. 1991.

Camm, J. D., and Evans, J. R. *Management Science: Modeling, Analysis, and Interpretation.* Cincinnati, Ohio: South-Western, 1996.

Cowling, A., and James, P. *The Essence of Personnel Management and Industrial Relations.* New York: Prentice-Hall, 1994.

Devlin, B., Fienberg, S. E., Resnick, D. P., and Roeder, K. "Wringing *The Bell Curve:* A cautionary tale about relationships among race, genes, and IQ," *Chance,* Vol. 8, No. 3, Summer 1995.

Edwards, J. P., Jr., ed. *Transportation Planning Handbook.* Englewood Cliffs, N.J.: Prentice-Hall, 1992.

Fama, E. F. *Foundations of Finance.* New York: Basic Books, 1976.

Herrnstein, R. J., and Murray, C. *The Bell Curve.* New York: The Free Press, 1994.

Hogg, R. V., and Craig, A. T. *Introduction to Mathematical Statistics,* 4th ed. New York: Macmillan, 1978.

Lindgren, B. W. *Statistical Theory,* 3rd ed. New York: Macmillan, 1976.

Mendenhall, W., Wackerly, D., and Scheaffer, R. *Mathematical Statistics with Applications,* 4th ed. Boston: PWS-Kent, 1990.

Montgomery, D. C. *Introduction to Statistical Quality Control,* 2nd ed. New York: Wiley, 1991.

Mood, A. M., Graybill, F. A., and Boes, D. C. *Introduction to the Theory of Statistics,* 3rd ed. New York: McGraw-Hill, 1974.

Moss, M. A. *Applying TQM to Product Design and Development.* New York: Marcel Dekker, 1996.

Neter, J., Wasserman, W., and Whitmore, G. A. *Applied Statistics,* 4th ed. Boston: Allyn and Bacon, 1993.

Render, B., and Heizer, J. *Principles of Operations Management.* Englewood Cliffs, N.J.: Prentice-Hall, 1995.

Ross, S. M. *Stochastic Processes,* 2nd ed. New York: Wiley, 1996.

Winkler, R. L., and Hays, W. *Statistics: Probability, Inference, and Decision,* 2nd ed. New York: Holt, Rinehart and Winston, 1975.

Wright, G., and Ayton, P., eds. *Subjective Probability.* New York: Wiley, 1994.

Chapter 6

Alexander, G. J., Sharpe, W. F., and Bailey, J. *Fundamentals of Investments,* 2nd ed. Englewood Cliffs, N.J.: Prentice-Hall, 1993.

Blume, M. "On the assessment of risk." *Journal of Finance,* Mar. 1971, 26, pp. 1–10.

Clauss, F. J. *Applied Management Science and Spreadsheet Modeling.* Belmont, Calif.: Duxbury Press, 1996.

Deming, W. E. *Out of the Crisis.* Cambridge, Mass.: MIT Center for Advanced Engineering Study, 1986.

Deming, W. E. *Quality, Productivity, and Competitive Position.* Cambridge, Mass.: MIT Center for Advanced Engineering Study, 1982.

DeVor, R. E., Chang, T., and Sutherland, J. W. *Statistical Quality Control: Contemporary Concepts and Methods.* New York: Macmillan, 1992.

Hartley, S. W. "Judgmental Sales Forecasting: An Experimental Investigation of Task Structure and Environmental Complexity." Unpublished Ph.D. dissertation, University of Minnesota, 1983.

Hogg, R. V., and Craig, A. T. *Introduction to Mathematical Statistics,* 4th ed. New York: Macmillan, 1978.

Lindgren, B. W. *Statistical Theory,* 3rd ed. New York: Macmillan, 1976.

Mendenhall, W., Wackerly, D., and Scheaffer, R. L. *Mathematical Statistics with Applications,* 4th ed. Boston: PWS-Kent, 1990.

Montgomery, D. C. *Introduction to Statistical Quality Control,* 2nd ed. New York: Wiley, 1991.

Radcliffe, R. C. *Investment: Concepts, Analysis, Strategy,* 4th ed. New York: HarperCollins College Publishers, 1994.

Stevenson, W. J. *Production/Operations Management,* 5th ed. Chicago: Irwin, 1996.

Chapter 7

Arkin, H. *Sampling Methods for the Auditor.* New York: McGraw-Hill, 1982.

Bryson, M. C. "The *Literary Digest* poll: Making of a statistical myth." *American Statistician,* Nov. 1976.

Cochran, W. G. *Sampling Techniques,* 3rd ed. New York: Wiley, 1977.

Deming, W. E. *Out of the Crisis.* Cambridge, Mass.: M.I.T. Center for Advanced Study of Engineering, 1986.

Freedman, D., Pisani, R., and Purves, R. *Statistics.* New York: Norton, 1978.

Horngren, C. T., Foster, G., and Datar, S. M. *Cost Accounting: A Managerial Emphasis,* 8th ed. Englewood Cliffs, NJ: Prentice-Hall, 1994.

Kish, L. *Survey Sampling.* New York: Wiley, 1965.

Mendenhall, W., and Beaver, B. *Introduction to Probability and Statistics,* 8th ed. Boston: PWS-Kent, 1991.

CHAPTER 8

Alexander, G. J., Sharpe, William F., and Bailey, J. *Fundamentals of Investments,* 2nd ed. Englewood Cliffs, N.J.: Prentice-Hall, 1993.

Duncan, A. J. *Quality Control and Industrial Statistics,* 5th ed. Homewood, Ill.: Richard D. Irwin, 1986.

Montgomery, D. C. *Introduction to Statistical Quality Control,* 2nd ed. New York: Wiley, 1991.

Schonberger, R. J., and Knod E. M., Jr. *Operations Management,* 5th ed. Burr Ridge, Ill.: Irwin, 1994.

Snedecor, G. W., and Cochran, W. G. *Statistical Methods,* 7th ed. Ames: Iowa State University Press, 1980.

Stevenson, W. J. *Production/Operations Management,* 5th ed. Chicago: Irwin, 1996.

CHAPTER 9

Freedman, D., Pisani, R., and Purves, R. *Statistics.* New York: W. W. Norton and Co., 1978.

Gibbons, J. D. *Nonparametric Statistical Inference,* 2nd ed. New York: McGraw-Hill, 1985.

Hollander, M., and Wolfe, D. A. *Nonparametric Statistical Methods.* New York: Wiley, 1973.

Lee, C. F., Finnerty, J. E., and Norton, E. A. *Foundations of Financial Management.* Minneapolis–St. Paul: West Publishing Co., 1997.

McLaren, J. W., Fjerstad, W. H., and Brubaker, R. R. "New video pupillometer." *Optical Engineering,* Vol. 34, No. 3, Mar. 1, 1995.

Mendenhall, W. *Introduction to Probability and Statistics,* 8th ed. Boston: PWS-Kent, 1991.

Satterthwaite, F. W. "An approximate distribution of estimates of variance components." *Biometrics Bulletin,* Vol. 2, 1946, pp. 110–114.

Snedecor, G. W., and Cochran, W. *Statistical Methods,* 7th ed. Ames: Iowa State University Press, 1980.

Steel, R. G. D., and Torrie, J. H. *Principles and Procedures of Statistics,* 2nd ed. New York: McGraw-Hill, 1980.

Stevenson, William J. *Production/Operations Management,* 5th ed. Chicago: Irwin, 1996.

Twomey, D. P. *Labor and Employment Law,* 9th ed. Cincinnati: South-Western Publishing Co., 1994.

CHAPTER 10

Gitlow, H., Oppenheim, A., and Oppenheim, R. *Quality Management: Tools and Methods for Improvement,* 2nd ed. Burr Ridge, Ill.: Irwin, 1995.

Graybill, F. *Theory and Application of the Linear Model.* North Scituate, Mass.: Duxbury, 1976.

Horngren, C. T., Foster, G., and Datar, S. M. *Cost Accounting,* 8th ed. Englewood Cliffs, N.J.: Prentice-Hall, 1994.

Mendenhall, W. *Introduction to Linear Models and the Design and Analysis of Experiments.* Belmont, Calif.: Wadsworth, 1968.

Mintzberg, H. *The Nature of Managerial Work.* New York: Harper and Row, 1973.

Younger, M. S. *A First Course in Linear Regression,* 2nd ed. Boston, Mass.: Duxbury, 1985.

CHAPTER 11

Benston, G. J. "Multiple regression analysis of cost behavior." *Accounting Review,* Vol. 41, Oct. 1966, pp. 657-672.

Chase, R. B., and Aquilano, N. J. *Production and Operations Management,* 6th ed. Homewood, Ill.: Richard D. Irwin, 1992.

Chatterjee, S., and Price, B. *Regression Analysis by Example,* 2nd ed. New York: Wiley, 1991.

Draper, N. R., and Smith, H. *Applied Regression Analysis,* 2nd ed. New York: Wiley, 1981.

Graybill, F. *Theory and Application of the Linear Model.* North Scituate, Mass.: Duxbury, 1976.

Horngren, Charles T., Foster, G., and Datar, S. M. *Cost Accounting,* 8th ed. Englewood Cliffs, N.J.: Prentice-Hall, 1994.

Kleinbaum, D., and Kupper, L. *Applied Regression Analysis and Other Multivariable Methods.* North Scituate, Mass.: Duxbury, 1978.

Mansfield, E. *Applied Microeconomics.* New York: Norton, 1994.

Mendenhall, W. *Introduction to Linear Models and the Design and Analysis of Experiments.* Belmont, Calif.: Wadsworth, 1968.

Mendenhall, W., and Sincich, T. *A Second Course in Statistics: Regression Analysis,* 5th ed. Saddle Lake, N.J.: Prentice-Hall, 1996.

Neter, J., Wasserman, W., and Kutner, M. *Applied Linear Statistical Models,* 3rd ed. Homewood, Ill.: Richard D. Irwin, 1992.

Weisberg, S. *Applied Linear Regression,* 2nd ed. New York: Wiley, 1985.

Wonnacott, R. J., and Wonnacott, T. H. *Econometrics,* 2nd ed. New York: Wiley, 1979.

Younger, M. S. *A First Course in Linear Regression,* 2nd ed. Boston: Duxbury, 1985.

CHAPTER 12

Chatterjee, S., and Price, B. *Regression Analysis by Example,* 2nd ed. New York: Wiley, 1991.

Diamond, M. *Financial Accounting,* 4th ed. Cincinnati, Ohio: South-Western, 1996.

Draper, N., and Smith, H. *Applied Regression Analysis,* 2nd ed. New York: Wiley, 1981.

Graybill, F. *Theory and Application of the Linear Model.* North Scituate, Mass.: Duxbury, 1976.

Kelting, H. "Investigation of condominium sale prices in three market scenarios: Utility of stepwise, interactive, multiple regression analysis and implications for design and appraisal methodology." Unpublished paper, University of Florida, Gainesville, 1979.

Lee, C., Finnerty, J., and Norton, E. *Foundations of Financial Management.* Minneapolis, Minn.: West Publishing Co., 1997.

Mendenhall, W. *Introduction to Linear Models and the Design and Analysis of Experiments.* Belmont, Calif.: Wadsworth, 1968.

Mendenhall, W., and Sincich, T. *A Second Course in Statistics: Regression Analysis,* 5th ed. Upper Saddle River, N.J.: Prentice-Hall, 1996.

Miller, R., and Wichern, D. *Intermediate Business Statistics: Analysis of Variance, Regression, and Time Series.* New York: Holt, Rinehart and Winston, 1977.

Myers, R. *Classical Modern Regression Analysis with Applications.* Boston: PWS-Kent, 1990.

Neter, J., Wasserman, W., and Kutner, M. *Applied Linear Regression Models,* 4th ed. Homewood, Ill.: Richard D. Irwin, 1996.

Schroeder, R. *Operations Management: Decision Making in the Operations Function,* 4th ed. New York: McGraw-Hill, 1993.

Starr, M. *Operations Management: A Systems Approach.* Danvers, Mass.: Boyd and Fraser, 1996.

Weisberg, S. *Applied Linear Regression,* 2nd ed. New York: Wiley, 1985.

Wittink, D. *The Application of Regression Analysis.* Boston: Allyn and Bacon, 1988.

Younger, M. *A First Course in Linear Regression,* 2nd ed. Boston: Duxbury, 1985.

CHAPTER 13

Alwan, L., and Roberts, H. "Time-series modeling for statistical process control." *Journal of Business and Economic Statistics,* Vol. 6, 1988, pp. 87–95.

Banks, J. *Principles of Quality Control.* New York: Wiley, 1989.

Checkland, P. *Systems Thinking, Systems Practice.* New York: Wiley, 1981.

Deming, W. *Out of the Crisis.* Cambridge, Mass.: MIT Center for Advanced Engineering Study, 1986.

DeVor, R., Chang, T., and Southerland, J. *Statistical Quality Design and Control.* New York: Macmillan, 1992.

Duncan, A. *Quality Control and Industrial Statistics.* Homewood, Ill.: Irwin, 1986.

Feigenbaum, A. *Total Quality Control,* 3rd ed. New York: McGraw-Hill, 1983.

Garvin, D. *Managing Quality.* New York: Free Press/Macmillan, 1988.

Gitlow, H., et al. *Quality Management: Tools and Methods for Improvement,* 2nd ed. Burr Ridge, Ill.: Irwin, 1995.

Grant, E., and Leavenworth, R. *Statistical Quality Control,* 6th ed. New York: McGraw-Hill, 1988.

Hart, M. "Quality tools for improvement." *Production and Inventory Management Journal,* Vol. 33, No. 1, First Quarter 1992, p. 59.

Ishikawa, K. *Guide to Quality Control,* 2nd ed. White Plains, N.Y.: Kraus International Publications, 1986.

Joiner, B., and Goudard, M. "Variation, management, and W. Edwards Deming." *Quality Process,* Dec. 1990, pp. 29–37.

Juran, J. *Juran of Planning for Quality.* New York: Free Press/Macmillan, 1988.

Juran, J., and Gryna, Jr., F. *Quality Planning Analysis,* 2nd ed. New York: McGraw-Hill, 1980.

Kane, V. *Defect Prevention.* New York: Marcel Dekker, 1989.

Latzko, W. *Quality and Productivity for Bankers and Financial Managers.* New York: Marcel Dekker, 1986.

Melynk, S., and Denzler, D. *Operations Management: A Value-Driven Approach.* Chicago: Irwin, 1996.

Moen, R., Nolan, T., and Provost, L. *Improving Quality Through Planned Experimentation.* New York: McGraw-Hill, 1991.

Montgomery, D. *Introduction to Statistical Quality Control,* 2nd ed. New York: Wiley, 1991.

Nelson, L. "The Shewhart control chart—Tests for special causes." *Journal of Quality Technology,* Vol. 16, No. 4, Oct. 1984, pp. 237–239.

Roberts, H. *Data Analysis for Managers,* 2nd ed. Redwood City, Calif.: Scientific Press, 1991.

Rosander, A. *Applications of Quality Control in the Service Industries.* New York: Marcel Dekker, 1985.

Rummler, G., and Brache, A. *Improving Performance: How to Manage the White Space on the Organization Chart.* San Francisco: Jossey-Bass, 1991.

Ryan, T. *Statistical Methods for Quality Improvement.* New York: Wiley, 1989.

Statistical Quality Control Handbook. Indianapolis, Ind.: AT&T Technologies, Select Code 700-444 (inquiries: 800-432-6600); originally published by Western Electric Company, 1956.

The Ernst and Young Quality Improvement Consulting Group. *Total Quality: An Executive's Guide for the 1990s.* Homewood, Ill.: Dow-Jones Irwin, 1990.

Wadsworth, H., Stephens, K., and Godfrey, A. *Modern Methods for Quality Control and Improvement.* New York: Wiley, 1986.

Walton, M. *The Deming Management Method.* New York: Dodd, Mead, and Company, 1986.

Wheeler, D., and Chambers, D. *Understanding Statistical Process Control.* Knoxville, Tenn.: Statistical Process Controls, Inc., 1986.

CHAPTER 14

Abraham, B., and Ledholter, J. *Statistical Methods for Forecasting.* New York: Wiley, 1983.

Anderson, T. W. *The Statistical Analysis of Time Series.* New York: Wiley, 1971.

Box, G. E. P., and Jenkins, G. M. *Time Series Analysis: Forecasting and Control,* 2nd ed. San Francisco: Holden-Day, 1977.

Durbin, J., and Watson, G. S. "Testing for serial correlation in least squares regression, I." *Biometrika,* Vol. 37, 1950, pp. 409–428.

Durbin, J., and Watson, G. S. "Testing for serial correlation in least squares regression, II." *Biometrika,* Vol. 38, 1951, pp. 159–178.

Durbin, J., and Watson, G. S. "Testing for serial correlation in least squares regression, III." *Biometrika,* Vol. 58, 1971, pp. 1–19.

Fuller, W. A. *Introduction to Statistical Time Series.* New York: Wiley, 1976.

Gillingham, R., and Lane, W. "Changing the treatment of shelter costs for homeowners in the CPI." *The Monthly Labor Review,* June, 1982, pp. 9–14.

Granger, C. W. J., and Newbold, P. *Forecasting Economic Time Series.* New York: Academic Press, 1977.

Gross, C. W., and Patterson, R. J. *Business Forecasting,* 2nd ed. Boston: Houghton Mifflin, 1983.

Nelson, C. R. *Applied Time Series Analysis for Managerial Forecasting.* San Francisco: Holden-Day, 1983.

Willis, R. E. *A Guide to Forecasting for Planners.* Englewood Cliffs, N.J.: Prentice-Hall, 1987.

CHAPTER 15

Mendenhall, W. *Introduction to Linear Models and the Design and Analysis of Experiments.* Belmont, Calif.: Wadsworth, 1968.

Miller, R. G., Jr. *Simultaneous Statistical Inference.* New York: Springer-Verlag, 1981.

Neter, J., Wasserman, W., and Kutner, M. *Applied Linear Statistical Models,* 3rd ed. Homewood, Ill.: Richard D. Irwin, 1990.

Snedecor, G. W., and Cochran, W. G. *Statistical Methods,* 7th ed. Ames: Iowa State University Press, 1980.

Steele, R. G. D., and Torrie, J. H. *Principles and Procedures of Statistics: A Biometrical Approach,* 2nd ed. New York: McGraw-Hill, 1980.

Winer, B. J. *Statistical Principles in Experimental Design,* 2nd ed. New York: McGraw-Hill, 1971.

CHAPTER 16

Agresti, A., and Agresti, B. F. *Statistical Methods for the Social Sciences,* 2nd ed. San Francisco: Dellen, 1986.

Alexander, G. J., Sharpe, W. F., and Bailey, J. V. *Fundamentals of Investment,* 2nd ed. Englewood Cliffs, N.J.: Prentice-Hall, 1993.

Conover, W. J. *Practical Nonparametric Statistics,* 2nd ed. New York: Wiley, 1980.

Davis, G. B., and Hamilton, S. *Managing Information.* Homewood, Ill.: Richard D. Irwin, Inc., 1993.

Freedman, D. A. "The mean versus the median: A case study in 4-R Act litigation." *Journal of Business and Economic Statistics,* Vol. 3, Jan. 1985, pp. 1–13.

Gibbons, J. D. *Nonparametric Statistical Inference,* 2nd ed. New York: McGraw-Hill, 1985.

Hollander, M., and Wolfe, D. A. *Nonparametric Statistical Methods.* New York: Wiley, 1973.

Lehmann, E. L. *Nonparametrics: Statistical Methods Based on Ranks.* San Francisco: Holden-Day, 1975.

Noether, G. E. *Elements of Nonparametric Statistics.* New York: Wiley, 1967.

Rosenthal, R., and Rosnow, R. L. *The Volunteer Subject.* New York: Wiley, 1975.

Siegel, S. *Nonparametric Statistics for the Behavioral Sciences.* New York: McGraw-Hill, 1956.

Winkler, R. L., and Hays, W. L. *Statistics: Probability, Inference, and Decision,* 2nd ed. New York: Holt, Rinehart and Winston, 1975.

CHAPTER 17

Agresti, A., and Agresti, B. F. *Statistical Methods for the Social Sciences,* 2nd ed. San Francisco: Dellen, 1986.

Cochran, W. G. "The χ^2 test of goodness of fit." *Annals of Mathematical Statistics,* Vol. 23, 1952.

Conover, W. J. *Practical Nonparametric Statistics,* 2nd ed. New York: Wiley, 1980.

DeGroot, M. H., Fienberg, S. E., and Kane, J. B. (ed.) *Statistics and the Law.* New York: John Wiley and Sons, 1986.

Hollander, M., and Wolfe, D. A. *Nonparametric Statistical Methods.* New York: Wiley, 1973.

Savage, I. R. "Bibliography of nonparametric statistics and related topics." *Journal of the American Statistical Association,* Vol. 48, 1953.

Schroeder, R. G. *Operations Management,* 4th ed. New York: McGraw-Hill, 1993.

Siegel, S. *Nonparametric Statistics for the Behavioral Sciences.* New York: McGraw-Hill, 1956.

Winkler, R. L., and Hays, W. L. *Statistics: Probability, Inference and Decision,* 2nd ed. New York: Holt, Rinehart and Winston, 1975.

CHAPTER 18

Baird, B. F. *Introduction to Decision Analysis.* North Scituate, Mass.: Duxbury, 1978.

Balthasar, H. U., Boschi, R. A. A., and Menke, M. M. "Calling the shots in R&D." *Harvard Business Review,* Vol. 56, (May–June 1978), pp. 151–160.

Brown, R. V., Kahr, A. S., and Peterson, C. *Decision Analysis for the Manager.* New York: Holt, Rinehart and Winston, 1974.

Browne, G. J., Curley, S. P., and Benson, P. G. "Evoking information in probability assessment: Knowledge maps and reasoning-based directed questions." *Management Science,* Vol. 43, No. 1 (Jan. 1997).

Bunn, D. *Applied Decision Analysis.* New York: McGraw-Hill, 1984.

Clemen, R. *Making Hard Decisions.* Boston: PWS-Kent, 1991.

Dawes, R. M. *Rational Choice in an Uncertain World.* San Diego: Harcourt Brace Jovanovich, 1988.

Keeney, R. L., and Raiffa, H. *Decisions with Multiple Objectives: Preferences and Value Trade-offs.* New York: Wiley, 1976.

LaValle, I. *Fundamentals of Decision Analysis.* New York: Holt, Rinehart and Winston, 1978.

Lindley, D. V. *Making Decisions,* 2nd ed. London: Wiley, 1985.

Luce, R. D., and Raiffa, H. *Games and Decisions.* New York: Wiley, 1957.

Montgomery, D. C. *Introduction to Statistical Quality Control,* 2nd ed. New York: Wiley, 1991.

Raiffa, H. *Decision Analysis. Introductory Lectures on Choices Under Uncertainty.* Reading, Mass.: Addison-Wesley, 1968.

Raiffa, H., and Schlaifer, R. *Applied Statistical Decision Theory.* Cambridge, Mass.: MIT Press, 1961.

Samson, D. *Managerial Decision Analysis.* Homewood, Ill.: Irwin, 1988.

Smith, J. Q. *Decision Analysis: A Bayesian Approach.* London: Chapman and Hull, 1988.

Starr, M. K. *Operations Management: A Systems Approach.* Danvers, Mass.: Boyd & Fraser, 1996.

von Winterfeldt, D., and Edwards, W. *Decision Analysis and Behavioral Research.* Cambridge: Cambridge University Press, 1986.

Watson, S. R., and Buede, D. M. *Decision Synthesis.* Cambridge: Cambridge University Press, 1987.

Winkler, R. L. *An Introduction to Bayesian Inference and Decision.* New York: Holt, Rinehart and Winston, 1972.

Winkler, R. L., and Hays, W. L. *Statistics: Probability, Inference, and Decision,* 2nd ed. New York: Holt, Rinehart and Winston, 1975.

INDEX